ENCYCLOPEDIA OF AESTHETICS

ENCYCLOPEDIA OF

AESTHETICS

MICHAEL KELLY

Editor in Chief

Volume 1

OXFORD UNIVERSITY PRESS

New York   1998   Oxford

The encyclopedia is dedicated to Annabel Manning, my wife of fourteen years,
for reasons I trust she understands and readers can likely imagine,
if they have been as fortunate as I.

OXFORD UNIVERSITY PRESS

Oxford   New York
Athens   Auckland   Bangkok   Bogotá
Buenos Aires   Calcutta   Cape Town   Chennai
Dar es Salaam   Delhi   Florence   Hong Kong   Istanbul
Karachi   Kuala Lumpur   Madrid   Melbourne   Mexico City
Mumbai   Nairobi   Paris   São Paulo   Singapore
Taipei   Tokyo   Toronto   Warsaw

and associated companies in
Berlin   Ibadan

Copyright © 1998 by Oxford University Press, Inc.

Published by Oxford University Press, Inc.,
198 Madison Avenue, New York, New York 10016
http://www.oup-usa.org

Library of Congress Cataloging-in-Publication Data
Encyclopedia of aesthetics / editor in chief, Michael Kelly.
p.   cm.
Includes bibliographical references and index.
1. Aesthetics—Encyclopedias.   I. Kelly, Michael, 1953–.
BH56.E53   1998   111′.85′03—dc21   98-18741 CIP
ISBN 0-19-511307-1 (set)
ISBN 0-19-512645-9 (vol. 1)

Printing (last digit): 9 8 7 6 5 4 3 2 1

Printed in the United States of America
on acid-free paper

CONTENTS

EDITORIAL BOARD

PREFACE

AESTHETICS IS UNIQUELY SITUATED TO SERVE AS A MEETING PLACE FOR NUMEROUS academic disciplines and cultural traditions. While it is a single branch of philosophy concerned with art, aesthetics is also a part of other disciplines—such as art history, literary theory, law, sociology—that reflect equally, if differently, about art in its natural and cultural contexts. At the same time, aesthetics is an eighteenth-century European development that has not been duplicated anywhere else. Of course, all other cultures around the world have their own "art," and most also have traditions of reflecting philosophically about it. To the extent that they have developed such reflection, whatever they have chosen to call it, these cultures are engaged in a practice related to Western aesthetics. So aesthetics is, in academic terms, both singular and general, and, in cultural terms, both local and global. To capture these multiple dimensions, the *Encyclopedia of Aesthetics* has been created using a definition of aesthetics as "critical reflection on art, culture, and nature."

The purpose of this encyclopedia is to contribute to a discursive public sphere in which people representing the disciplines and traditions engaged in aesthetics will be able to articulate their perspectives on the field, thereby fostering dialogue and, where possible, constructing common ground without imposing consensus. To this end, the encyclopedia, which is the first English-language reference work on this scale devoted to aesthetics, offers a combination of historical reference material and critical discussions of contemporary aesthetics intended for general readers and experts alike.

HISTORY OF AESTHETICS

The term *aesthetics* is derived from the ancient Greek word *aisthesis* (also spelled *aesthesis*), which means perception or sensation. In its original usage, the word was related to perceptual or sensory knowledge, usually in contrast to conceptual or rational knowledge, but had little or no specific relevance to art. The initial lack of connection between aesthetics and art reflects the fact that, at the time, there was no word for what Westerners now regard as art; the Greek word for art, *techne*, is closer to the English word *craft*. Of course, the philosophy of art existed in Plato and Aristotle's age, just as there was Greek "art." Nevertheless, aesthetics did not become connected to art until the eighteenth century. Developments within art and philosophy—as well as within other disciplines concerned with art—account for the eventual link between aesthetics and art that is the historical subject of this encyclopedia.

From the classical era to the Middle Ages, reflection on art developed through the work of philosophers such as Augustine, Plotinus, Aquinas, and others. During the Renaissance, when art flourished in unparalleled ways, such reflection also experienced a revival as many classical aesthetic ideas were rediscovered and developed in new directions. What was most common during these periods, however, were treatises about individual arts, such as painting, music, or poetry, rather than any theory about art in general. There was also considerable discussion about whether it was possible to distinguish art from craft. Finally, when people wrote about the arts, they typically did so without philosophically analyzing the principles of criticism they were implicitly invoking. In short, aesthetics proper had not yet emerged.

All of this changed in the eighteenth century, mostly in France, Germany, and Great Britain. There was a historical coincidence between a new-found tendency on the part of writers to generalize about the arts and a heightened concern in philosophy for sensory knowledge independent of logical knowledge. The distinction of types of knowledge, inspired in part by the birth of modern science based on empiricism, introduced aesthetics into philosophy; but, following the lead of Alexander Baumgarten, aesthetics still had little to do with art. This was a strange development indeed in the inaugural century of aesthetics: those beginning to generalize about art did not use the term *aesthetics,* while those practicing aesthetics were not principally interested in art. It was not until Immanuel Kant's *Critique of Judgment* (1790) that these two tendencies were systematically united, setting the agenda for aesthetics ever since.

Although this union was unquestionably an important step in the early and subsequent history of aesthetics, overemphasis on it tends to obscure an equally important dimension of this history, which is central to the rationale for the encyclopedia. Although it is true that aesthetics emerged in the eighteenth century within philosophy, this would not have been possible without developments in art and cultural criticism that had been evolving since at least the Renaissance. Critics—whether philosophers, poets, or writers—began writing about art in general rather than just about the individual arts. Some compared the different arts, as was the case in the "Ut pictura poesis" ("as a painting, so a poem") tradition, whereas others argued that each art form could be properly understood only on individual terms: painting is independent of poetry, which is independent of music, and so on. In its first century, aesthetics was thus marked by a fundamental philosophical disagreement about whether generalizing about art was an advancement in the understanding of the arts. It is this disagreement, rather than just the tendency toward generalizations, that separated Western aesthetics in the eighteenth century from its prior history as well as from other cultural traditions.

In that same period, the individual arts in Europe were becoming more accessible to the public than they had ever been before, for they were no longer so closely tied to religion and politics once the church and monarchy ceased being the exclusive patrons of the arts. There was, in short, a secularization and democratization of the arts and culture in the eighteenth century that contributed to the formation of a cultural public sphere. *Criticism* was the term most widely used to characterize discussions about the arts and culture; in fact, the term *critique,* which Kant transformed in his *Critique of Pure Reason,* began in part as the German translation of the English word *criticism.* This transformation marks the birth of aesthetics as a part of philosophy, but it also highlights the fact that philosophical aesthetics emerged out of a broader cultural context.

From its inception until the present, aesthetics has continued to be distinguished by both its philosophical and cultural roles, even though some theorists have at times attempted to restrict aesthetics to just one of its roles. Moreover, the fact that aesthetics has always had these dual roles has made the present encyclopedia both possible and necessary: possible, because the entries here could not have been written unless there were people in various disciplines outside of philosophy writing philosophically about art, culture, and nature; and necessary, because aesthetics remains incomplete if its cultural role is not developed. The goal of the *Encyclopedia of Aesthetics* is to trace the genealogy of aesthetics in such a way as to integrate these two roles.

MISCONCEPTIONS ABOUT AESTHETICS AND ENCYCLOPEDIAS

The *Encyclopedia of Aesthetics* has been created, and may now be received, in a skeptical environment. It is important to address this skepticism here because it is based on a misconception of aesthetics that the encyclopedia aims to correct in an effort to revitalize the field.

Many people concerned with art and culture today seem to want to distance themselves from aesthetics. Ask students or general readers what aesthetics is, and most will say that it has something to do with beauty (an impression reinforced by the colloquial use of *aesthetic* to mean "beautiful") and that it is a thing of the past. Artists, as a group, rarely express any more interest in aesthetics than Barnett Newman did when he remarked that aesthetics is for artists what ornithology is for birds. Art historians and anthropologists typically do not identify with aesthetics either, unless their research involves art created in periods when aesthetics was still considered relevant. Finally, others involved with contemporary art—critics, legal theorists, sociologists—also do not generally see themselves as concerned with aesthetics, since they regard it as part of philosophy rather than of their own fields.

Why do these diverse groups of people distance themselves from aesthetics, even though they all are involved with art and culture? What they typically object to is the idea that art can be understood according to a set of universal principles about its immutable properties; the term *aesthetics* suggests this idea to them. It is seen as a branch of philosophy that effectively died once modern art began to challenge the classical view of art as the imitation, often in the guise of beauty, of the universal qualities of nature or reality. So aesthetics is thereby relegated to the history of art and philosophy prior to modernism.

Ask contemporary aestheticians what they do, however, and they are likely to respond that aesthetics is the philosophical analysis of the beliefs, concepts, and theories implicit in the creation, experience, interpretation, or critique of art. It would be unusual for them to include beauty as one of their major research topics; they talk more often about the problems of meaning or representation in connection with works of art. Moreover, most aestheticians—both analytic (Anglo-American) and continental (European, exclusive of Great Britain) alike—would agree that there are no universal properties of art and that *art* can be defined, if at all, only in historical (if still philosophical) terms. In fact, both analytic and continental aesthetics in the last fifty years have been dominated by anti-essentialism: the view either that art has no essence or that it is impossible for us to ascertain what its essence is. This means that nearly all contemporary aestheticians are equally critical of the idea of aesthetics that is rejected by nonphilosophers.

Moreover, not only is it a misconception to identify contemporary aesthetics with the universalist idea of aesthetics, the history of aesthetics is replete with critiques of that same idea and alternatives to it. These critiques were evident even in the eighteenth century. For example, although there was considerable discussion of beauty at that time, aesthetics emerged only once beauty lost its status as an objective or transcendental property, which it virtually had since Plato. Modern philosophers argued that beauty is not a property of objects (e.g., works of art) experienced or judged as beautiful; rather, it is a relational property between subjects and objects. So aesthetics began, in part, with the following problem: How is it possible to speak with any objectivity about matters of taste if beauty is subjective? The question of the universality of taste arose in this same context. Whereas some philosophers argued that taste is universal despite being subjective, others were doubtful that universality was possible again after the subjective turn in our understanding of beauty. This debate was not resolved at the time, nor has it been since. This means, however, that the conventional view of aesthetics held by its critics (and some of its supporters) is as imprecise relative to the history of aesthetics as it is to its present state. So the skepticism about aesthetics is best addressed by reevaluating the meaning and history of aesthetics; such reevaluation is what this encyclopedia offers.

There is also a prevailing skepticism today about encyclopedias that should be discussed here as well. One of the marks of our present age, which is typically characterized as postmodern, is a skepticism toward any claims about philosophical systems or historical grand narratives (i.e., ones that emphasize the unity and ultimate goal of historical development). Many people today believe that, in principle, such systems are incomplete and all historical narratives impose a false unity while they exclude certain cultures' perspectives. In the interest of pluralism, we are encouraged to abandon any and all systems and narratives. The publication of an encyclopedia, especially one that gives philosophy a central role, may seem to violate these postmodern injunctions, though only if it is thought to venture a narrative or system of aesthetics. Because of this attitude, it was even suggested that we exclude the word *encyclopedia* from the title of this work.

Our response to this skepticism was to incorporate the contemporary doubts about the encyclopedia into its very structure. This has been achieved in various ways, principally by including the following among the entries themselves: (1) critiques of aesthetics; (2) discussions of postmodernism; (3) composite (multi-article) entries so topics could be analyzed from several perspectives; and (4) representations of virtually all the disciplines involved with art and culture, even though people in these fields may not see themselves as being engaged in aesthetics. In none of these cases was any effort made to shape a system or a grand narrative of aesthetics. Efforts were made to be comprehensive, however, though here *comprehensive* means as complete a representation as possible of all the competing ideas about aesthetics.

GENERAL STRUCTURE OF THE ENCYCLOPEDIA

The encyclopedia includes more than six hundred essays, alphabetically arranged, on approximately four hundred individuals, concepts, periods, theories, issues, and movements in the history of aesthetics. The entries range from the most ancient aesthetic traditions around the world to the Greco-Roman era, the Middle Ages, the Renaissance, the Enlightenment, Romanticism, Modernism, and Postmodernism, up to the present. The central historical focus, however, is the genealogy of Western aesthetics from its inception in the early eighteenth century in Europe to the present. How was the Western understanding of art and culture transformed during that period? How has it developed since then? What is its present status? Specifically, how have key aesthetic concepts and issues—such as appropriation, autonomy, beauty, genius, iconology, ideology, metaphor, originality, semiotics, sexuality, taste, and truth—evolved?

The entries in the encyclopedia have been written by more than five hundred philosophers, art historians, literary theorists, psychologists, feminist theorists, legal theorists, sociologists, anthropologists, and others who reflect critically on art, culture, and nature. The range of contributors is important because of the interdisciplinary nature of aesthetics, both now and throughout its history. For example, one cannot understand Romanticism and appreciate its aesthetic significance without studying what it means in philosophical and literary terms as well as how it manifested itself differently in the visual arts and in music. There are numerous topics of such conceptual or historical complexity in the encyclopedia that can be fully understood only if they are approached through multiple disciplines.

The goal, however, is not to impose or legitimate any single discipline's way of understanding aesthetics. Philosophy, for example, certainly occupies a central position in the encyclopedia; its important task is to clarify the terms, principles, concepts, and theories employed by the disciplines (including philosophy) engaged in aesthetics. But philosophy is also just one of many disciplines, evidenced by the fact that a majority of the encyclopedia entries were written by nonphilosophers. Moreover, the purpose of the work is not to resolve the differences among the various disciplines; rather, it is to provide, as a good encyclopedia should, a comprehensive catalog of what these differences are, how they originated, what the disciplines may have in common, and what is at stake in the conflicting views contributors espouse. Our aim has been to provide as much reliable information as we could assemble so that readers can make informed decisions about how best to understand "Beauty," the "Origins of Aesthetics," "Popular Culture," the "Comparative Aesthetics" of the African and Western traditions, "Kant," or any of the other topics included in the encyclopedia.

At every moment of its history, aesthetics has been related in complementary and critical ways to the art of its time. So there is considerable discussion in the encyclopedia of major art periods (e.g., the Renaissance), movements (Modernism), and issues (perspective) in the history of art. Such discussions range from Greco-Roman, Baroque, or Impressionist art to the most contemporary art forms, such as conceptual, installation, or performance art. The focus in these entries is both historical and theoretical so readers will understand what is unique about each art-historical issue and how it has influenced aesthetic theory.

While the aesthetic history and art periodization utilized here are largely Western, comparisons are made throughout the encyclopedia with non-Western art forms and their distinct aesthetic traditions. Such comparisons are made in two ways: (1) by having overview essays on each of these traditions (e.g., Chinese, Indian, Islamic, Latin American) and, where possible, (2) by integrating non-Western perspectives into discussions of central aesthetic concepts, principles, and issues (e.g., Japanese appreciation of nature). The first measure helps readers to understand these other traditions, which in some cases have greatly influenced their Western counterparts or have been shaped by them. The second measure is important so that non-Western ideas of aesthetics are not isolated from their Western counterparts. The two practices combined serve, in effect, to historicize the tradition of Western aesthetics by demonstrating that it is, after all, just one of many traditions.

The emphasis in the entries on key figures (e.g., Plato, Kant, Heidegger) is theoretical rather than biographical. The contributors explain the subjects' ideas about aesthetics, while clarifying the historical and conceptual contexts for these ideas. References to clarify these contexts are provided in the bibliographies, along with biographical titles, where possible. In addition to the lengthy entries on major thinkers, there are short (five-hundred-word) entries on some significant but lesser-known figures (e.g., Charles Batteux and Moses Mendelssohn). The aim here is to paint a comprehensive picture of the historical background of modern and contemporary aesthetics.

Coverage of many central individuals and concepts in aesthetics and most major art forms (e.g., architecture, dance, photography) has been arranged in composite entries, that is, several separate articles arranged under one headword. The rationale for this type of entry is to give voice to: (1) extensive histories of a specific topic (e.g., beauty or landscape) too broad to be handled by one contributor; (2) independent philosophical views of a single central issue (e.g., metaphor or autonomy); (3) individual perspectives on a topic (e.g., historicism) that is important in each of several disciplines (e.g., aesthetics, art history, literary theory); (4) several accounts of an activity (e.g., criticism) that is practiced differently in the particular arts (e.g., music, art, dance); (5) individuals (e.g., Kant) who are central in the history of aesthetics because of their influential accounts of key aesthetic concepts; and (6) other cases where there are significantly diverse aspects or accounts of a single aesthetic issue.

Each composite entry combines conceptual and historical overviews with in-depth analyses of particular issues or ideas. For example, the entry on Immanuel Kant begins with an overview essay explaining who Kant was, what he wrote, and what he wrote particularly on aesthetics. This is followed by essays on Kant's concepts of beauty, the sublime, and nature; a brief history of Kantian aesthetics; essays on Kant's reception in art history, on the hermeneutic reading of Kant, and on the feminist critique of Kant; and, finally, an essay on the connection between Kant and Marcel Duchamp in terms of the concept of judgment. The combined essays offer a wide range of interpretations to the general reader and allow those possessing more advanced understanding to pursue the finer points of aesthetics. The contributors of articles in these entries were not asked to discuss each others' work directly; rather, they were invited to articulate their own positions on the selected issues as clearly and forcefully as possible, knowing that other points of view would be similarly represented in the same entry. (Such representation of diverse perspectives on key issues in aesthetics is what I have referred to as a discursive public sphere.)

CRITERIA FOR THE INCLUSION OF ENTRIES

Topics were chosen according to the following general criteria: (1) philosophical or critical significance in the histories of aesthetics, art, or fields related to aesthetics or art; (2) relevance to contemporary aesthetics; and (3) historical or contemporary importance in non-Western cultures. In the entries devoted to particular cultural traditions (e.g., Islamic, Latin American), the contributors were asked to address the following questions: What difference do their sovereign cultural histories make to their conceptions of aesthetics in comparison to their Western counterparts? Do they have unique ways of thinking about aesthetics as well as original art? Does their critical reflection on art and culture provide evidence of a universal aesthetic or, on the contrary, does it confirm the radical historicist's claim that aesthetics, like art, is fundamentally different in each culture?

The topics of the composite entries were selected (1) because of their significance in the history of aesthetics, or (2) because of ongoing debates among experts in the relevant specialties who represent diverse disciplinary, philosophical, or cultural perspectives. The aim of this structure is to achieve with these entries the comprehensiveness one expects from encyclopedia entries, but also to make the rich variety of ideas about individual aesthetic topics more accessible to one another.

With these criteria in mind, the encyclopedia has aimed to have historical depth and representative breadth to encompass (1) the key centuries (eighteenth to twentieth) and countries (Germany, France, Great Britain, United States) in the history of Western aesthetics; (2) the different disciplinary perspectives (e.g., philosophy, art history, law, sociology) on the key topics; (3) the various cultures (e.g., African, Indian, Latin American) that have a history of thinking critically on their "art" and culture without necessarily calling such thinking "aesthetics"; (4) many of the arts, traditional and new, that have had a defining impact on aesthetics; (5) various historical and contemporary critiques of aesthetics (e.g., Romanticism, hermeneutics, anti-essentialism, feminism); and (6) the few disciplines that have emerged, in part, as the result of critiques of aesthetics (e.g., cultural studies).

There are undoubtedly some missing topics, and there are several reasons for this. In some instances we planned an entry but either could not find a suitable contributor or the contributor was not able to respond in a timely fashion; we considered some additional entries but decided in the end that they were not appropriate, given the overall goals of the encyclopedia; finally, despite all our efforts to be inclusive and thorough, we regrettably have overlooked certain possible entries. Every encyclopedia has its limitations when it comes to the list of entries; for, as critics are likely to point out, the categorization of entries in an encyclopedia is arbitrary. But the choices and ordering of categories can be intelligible and reasonable nonetheless. We have tried to be comprehensive without being systematic, and we have stated the criteria for the selection of entries as clearly as possible so that readers will know how and why we have made the choices embodied in the encyclopedia. Readers are asked to remember that the encyclopedia is intended as the beginning rather than the end of critical discussion about the genealogy and contemporary practice of aesthetics within philosophy and related disciplines.

EDITORIAL PRACTICES

Entries are alphabetically arranged, strictly letter by letter. In order to explain the structure and content of the composite entries, each of them begins with an editorial headnote. Brief headnotes are also occasionally present in cases where the entry comprises a single essay (e.g., "Gaze," "Theory, History of") to clarify the topic or offer a rationale for its inclusion for the general reader.

In order to maximize the interconnections among the entries and to guide the reader to related discussion, numerous cross-references have been included throughout the work. These are located within individual articles (mostly at the end of the discussion) as well as in the headnotes to the composite entries. In addition, within the alphabetical order of headwords, there are numerous "blind entries" that provide cross-references to the articles where the subject is discussed. Blind entries are used for alternate spellings and synonyms (e.g., "Ekphrasis. *See* Ecphrasis"; "Cinema. *See* Film") as well as in cases where instead of an independent entry devoted to a subject, there is a significant discussion within another article ("Boas, Franz. *See* Anthropology and Aesthetics") or, for broad topics (e.g., painting), spread among several articles. The comprehensive index at the end of volume 4 provides additional connections among the topics and disciplines for readers interested in further research.

The illustration program is modest if it is compared to art reference works, but generous if compared to reference works in philosophy, which typically have few or no images. We have tried to strike a balance between these extremes. While we could not possibly offer a complete representation of the history of art because this is an encyclopedia of aesthetics, we wanted to make it clear that aesthetics is intimately related to the history of art. At the same time, it is important that we have some imagery so that it does not seem that words are taking the place of art. The relationship between aesthetics and art is a very sensitive issue within aesthetics, as it assuredly is for those who criticize aesthetics for being iconoclastic. The presence of some images here makes it clear that this relationship is open-ended: aesthetic theory is always responding to art rather than supplanting it. The illustrations are also intended to reflect a wide spectrum of different art traditions and cultures (e.g., African, Pre-Columbian, Indian), as well as the historical depth (e.g., Greek, Modern), stylistic breadth (e.g., Gothic, Surrealist), and diversity of art mediums (e.g., sculpture, film) within art.

ACKNOWLEDGMENTS

The encyclopedia's passage from concept to reality over the last six years was guided by the intellectual devotion of many people. I cannot thank them all enough, but I will try.

The encyclopedia was initiated in 1992 by Christopher Collins, now a senior editor at Oxford University Press, when he was at Garland Publishing. Once the encyclopedia evolved from one to four volumes, it joined Chris at Oxford in 1996. His editorial insight, commitment, and humor have been invaluable throughout. Claude Conyers, editorial director of the Scholarly and Professional Reference Department, secured the encyclopedia's move to Oxford and ensured that it was produced in the most professional manner possible. Jeffrey Edelstein, managing editor, carried the work through the often prosaic stages of production, contributing his editorial expertise and, as situations demanded it, his wit. The copy editors at Clarinda Publication Services did an excellent job while being respectful of the contributors. I would especially like to thank Emily Autumn, Clarinda project manager, with whom I worked almost daily for the last nine months. I would also like to thank the indexer, Cynthia Crippen, who has created a detailed index that is vital to the encyclopedia, as it aids readers in their efforts to discover implicit links among the diverse topics.

Without the dedication and knowledge of all the editorial advisers, who are distinguished in their respective fields, producing the encyclopedia would have been inconceivable. In particular, I would like to thank Arthur C. Danto, first for recommending me when he was approached by Christopher Collins with the idea for this encyclopedia, and then for providing personal and philosophical support along the way. Daniel Shapiro donated his legal advice to the project as it moved to Oxford; without him, the encyclopedia would not have moved and, had it not done so, it may never have been completed. Richard Kuhns came by my office on a regular basis to share his erudition and offer his assistance. Mary Mothersill was also a constant source of encouragement, especially as the encyclopedia was changing publishers. Mark Tansey, an artist, was singularly helpful in thinking about how to make the encyclopedia useful to practicing artists. Paul Guyer recommended a host of contributors and wrote seven essays himself, adding greatly to the historical depth of the encyclopedia. Norton Batkin, David Carrier, Susan L. Feagin, Kenneth Frampton, Alexander Nehamas, and Anita Silvers likewise contributed much more than I could have expected of the editorial advisers. Marx Wartofsky, who introduced me to aesthetics in graduate school, was a generous friend and resource before his sudden death in March 1997.

On the suggestion of Oxford, four particular editorial advisers—Ted Cohen, Daniel Herwitz, Salim Kemal, and Stephen Melville—each reviewed more than one hundred essays after they had been read by other advisers or reviewers. The duty of these editors, to whom I am truly indebted, was to help us develop a coherent picture of the encyclopedia while it was taking shape. This additional editorial process was essential in making sure that the overall goals of the encyclopedia were clarified and, as much as possible, realized.

The sine qua non of the encyclopedia, of course, are the contributors who graciously agreed to write articles, knowing that there is often not enough academic recognition for such work. I would like to thank every single one of them, especially those who wrote several articles or who offered their assistance in other ways: Frederick Beiser, Whitney Davis, Ed Dimendberg, Gregg Horowitz, and Christopher Wood. Each contributor will receive a copy of the encyclopedia as a gesture of our gratitude.

In the last several years, I worked on the encyclopedia mostly in my office at the *Journal of Philosophy* at Columbia University. I would like to thank the trustees and editors of the journal—particularly Arthur C. Danto, president of the trustees—for giving the encyclopedia a home. John Smylie, my editorial assistant at the journal, was also my assistant on the encyclopedia. His specific responsibility in the last two years was to verify all the bibliographies, a formidable task that he accomplished with great accuracy. Several people helped me to keep pace with the encyclopedia while they were work-study students or interns at Columbia: Elizabeth Cornwell, Shauna Grob, Alla Rachkov, Jo Kim, and Kathleya Chotiros—thank you.

Finally, I would like to thank my parents, John and Anita Kelly, for their confidence in me since the project began six years ago, especially during the moments that the encyclopedia's future seemed in question. Even as my father lay dying (March 1997), just as the manuscript deadline with Oxford approached, he continued to inquire about the progress of the encyclopedia. His concern was a true inspiration.

The efforts of all these people have culminated in an encyclopedia that I believe will enable readers to appreciate and develop further the philosophical and cultural conceptions of aesthetics that inspired it.

—MICHAEL KELLY
New York & Montauk
April 1998

ENCYCLOPEDIA OF AESTHETICS

A

ABHINAVAGUPTA (tenth to eleventh century), medieval Indian philosopher. Besides being an aesthete and a Tantric mystic, Abhinavagupta was a prolific writer and polymath. His fame rests chiefly on his philosophical works on Kashmir Śaivism (which is part metaphysics and part theology) and on "Abhinavabhāratī" and "Locana," his commentaries on the two seminal texts of Sanskrit literary theory, namely, Bharata's *Nāṭyaśāstra* and Ānandavardhana's *Dhvanyāloka,* respectively. Both as a philosopher and as an aesthetician, Abhinavagupta belonged to the ancient tradition of commentators whose object was to explicate the standard texts, often adding their own refinement according to their individual standpoints. In his commentaries on Bharata and Ānandavardhana, Abhinavagupta not only exhibits an acute understanding of semantic and aesthetic issues, but also adds such a transcendental dimension to his theorizing, following his Śaivite metaphysical stance, that one can discern a certain continuity between his metaphysics and his aesthetics. Abhinavagupta's aesthetics is not a general philosophy of art or beauty, but primarily a theory of art as emotional expression, based on Bharata's doctrine of *rasa* and confined to poetry and the performing arts. The application of *rasa* to portrait painting and sculpture was worked out in the Purāṇa, Āgama, and Vāstu texts.

Kashmir Śaivism (also called Tantric Śaivism), which provided the conceptual frame as well as the vocabulary for Abhinavagupta's aesthetic theory, is a major philosophical system with its own ontology and epistemology. It may be viewed primarily as a theory of consciousness that states that the objective universe is an emission of the self or "I-consciousness" (personified as Śiva), born, not out of any dialectical necessity, but out of the self's free will or simply as an exertion of its sportive nature. In epistemological terms, it argues that nothing that is opposed or alien to the subject can be appropriated by it as the object of its knowledge. Kashmir Śaivism also holds, however, that the objective universe is real because it is given in perception, but that it exists only as a reflection (*ābhāsa*) or mirror image of the self-luminous consciousness. Following as a corollary to this theory of reality is the concept of recognition. All cognition is recognition—strictly, self-recognition or recognition of the object as being of the nature of the self itself. The goal of spiritual life is to assimilate the object back into consciousness through identification with it (*tādātmya*). The re-

ward of that effort is a transcendental bliss (*ānanda*) that is freed from all determinations of place, time, and individuality.

Abhinavagupta's views on art and aesthetic experience touch at several points, or even derive from, the metaphysical postulates just outlined. First, he conceives of art creation as a spontaneous, noncompulsive activity that has no end beyond the expression of the artist's own innate impulse. In Abhinavagupta's cosmic analogy, art is like the cosmic dance of Śiva, which emanated out of his overflowing bliss, devoid of any pragmatic aim. Such a theory accords more with the conception of art as a Dionysian play than with theories that assign to it a serious heuristic, utilitarian, or cognitive function. The cosmic analogy also supports a second point of Abhinavagupta's aesthetics, namely, that the experience of art is primarily an emotive experience or *rasa* that is realized as a thrill (*camatkāra*) or pulsation (*spanda*) rather than as a purely cognitive perception. The emphasis of Tantric Śaivism on the blissful aspect of self-consciousness and its belief that sensuous joy (*bhoga*) is essentially spiritual and a form of release may have attracted Abhinavagupta to Bharata's doctrine of dramatic emotions and of emotionality (*rasa*) as the quintessence of dramatic experience. The theory of *spanda* (vibration), which holds that in acute emotional states the self is, so to say, vibrated back to itself, might similarly have lent support to Bharata's emotive doctrine. Therefore Abhinavagupta builds his entire aesthetic on the principle of *rasa*.

A third point of his theory concerns the ontological status of the aesthetic object—the play or poem. Abhinavagupta's position is that, as a configuration of certain elements of consciousness—specifically, the emotions—the art object is not, in the ultimate analysis or at the highest stage of contemplation, something objective or other than the self. Instead, latent traces of the object are already embedded in the psyche, ready to be quickened into action at the least spark. What one apprehends is no doubt a perceptual object, but the mind appropriates it, not as an other but as an external reality of one's own self, which one comes to "recognize" as one's own. Thus, the object serves merely as a stimulus or medium. The *rasa* perception, then, is a form of recognition of what one already knows. No new knowledge is added. At the initial stage of perception, of course, one has a sense of encounter with the object. But what began as

1

an object-directed attention quickly turns into subjective consciousness and pure gustation. [See Rasa.] Thus, true to his Śaivite premises, Abhinavagupta seeks to preserve both the subjective and the objective poles of the aesthetic situation. He argues that the *rasa* experience is, in the final analysis, a tasting of one's own consciousness. At the same time, it is also a surrendering of oneself to the object of contemplation, to live its life with complete attunement and identification *(tanmayībhāva, tādātmya),* although the final outcome is the awakening of one's own latent emotional dispositions.

Abhinavagupta's theory that all is consciousness and that it is one and universal also leads him to the assumption that aesthetic experience, at its most basic level, must be the same for all people. An implication of the *rasa* doctrine is that although a poem or play must necessarily be about what a particular person (say, Alcibiades) has undergone, its import is generalized in the audience's consciousness owing to this ability of the emotions to be shared. This process of generalization is called *sādhāraṇīkaraṇa*—a concept that had already been adumbrated by Bharata but was fully expounded by Abhinavagupta and by his predecessor Bhaṭṭanāyaka. Abhinavagupta explains further that the generalization of the deictics of the poem is aided by the very semantics of the poetic situation—the otherness and pastness of the events presented and consequently their remoteness from any personal concerns of the reader, which will prompt the reader to contemplate the general human significance of the poem.

Another important element of Abhinavagupta's theory is the claim (also made by his predecessors Śaṅkuka and Bhaṭṭanāyaka, albeit from different angles) that *rasa*, in the sense of gustation, although still a mode of awareness, is unique and supramundane *(alaukika, lokottara),* transcending the empirical modes of cognition such as sense perception, inference, and recollection. Here Abhinavagupta isolates the state of savoring the art object *(rasanā)* from all other preceding cognitive stages, such as the initial sense contact with the perceptual object, verbal comprehension, associational thinking, deduction, and the like, which are necessarily involved in apprehending the meanings of a poem or stage drama. He argues that this state of pure awareness is an unmediated inner perception in which the mind, undivided by analytic distinctions, reposes in the cognizing subjectivity—hence its supernormal character. This state is also supernormal in that it is neither entirely self-directed *(svagata)* nor other-directed *(paragata)*—it completely negates all distinctions of person, place, and time, which obstruct our enjoyment of emotions in real life. Abhinavagupta's theory turns upon the distinction between life emotions *(bhāvas)* and the *rasas*, which are emotions in their aesthetically enjoyed form. He states emphatically that there can be no *rasas* in actual life. They are possible only in the context of an artistic presentation where one can contemplate the emotive situation at a distance and in a disinterested, tranquil frame of mind. Abhinavagupta further insists that because consciousness (of the sort he describes) is essentially of the nature of bliss, all aesthetic emotions *(rasas)*, including the painful and disagreeable varieties, are delectable. They are all transformed into pure delight. Hence he likens aesthetic pleasure to the bliss of tasting the highest reality *(brahman).*

Abhinavagupta's point that there must be some difference between art experience and life experience may be allowed under the conditions he specifies, namely, aesthetic distance and generalization. But these features of aesthetic experience can be explained even at the phenomenological/empirical level without the aid of the metaphysical scaffolding. The very artifactuality of the art object will eliminate the need for any responsive action and ensure the kind of intransitive attention that Abhinavagupta is speaking of. Moreover, Abhinavagupta's view of *rasa* perception as a cognitively privileged position may be questioned on psychological grounds inasmuch as all the cognitive functions—perception, inference, association, and memory—may be involved in aesthetic appreciation. His attempt to focus on the pure moment of the ecstasy of relish to the exclusion of all other accompanying mental processes can be of interest only to the mystic, not to the aesthetician. Nor does it help us to distinguish the distinctive properties of the art object that produced that relish. Besides, the rhapsodic description of aesthetic delight that he gives can apply equally to any sensual ecstasy, as was pointed out by some later critics (Rāmacandra and Guṇacandra in *Nāṭyadarpaṇa* and Siddacandragaṇi in *Kāvyaprakāśakhaṇḍana).* Further, his insistence that the reader's *rasa* experience is radically different from the emotion presented in the work cannot be accepted because there can be no qualitative difference between the sorrow that a character—Rāma or Lear—feels and the sorrow felt by the reader. The only difference is that the emotions produced by a poem are directed not toward a real object or person, but toward an imaginary object and are enjoyed in a generalized way. In addition, his claim that all *rasas*, including the tragic emotion, are pleasant cannot be sustained because neither artistic treatment nor transformation through the process of apprehension, in terms of fictionality, emotional distance, and generalization, can turn unpleasant emotions into pleasant emotions. It is possible, as the authors of *Nāṭyadarpaṇa* suggest, that unpleasant emotions are still enjoyed for their artistry—for the mimetic fidelity with which they are portrayed (as Aristotle thought).

In spite of the rather excessive emphasis that Abhinavagupta places on the transcendental character of the *rasa* experience, inspired no doubt by his metaphysical beliefs, he nevertheless derives that experience from the phenomenally objective properties of the work of art or from the perceptual situation in which the work is realized. He admits quite clearly that the *rasa* experience is triggered by the objective presentation of the emotions and that it endures only as long as the stimulus lasts. Thus, the experience is anchored in the object and controlled by it. The yogic contemplation, he points out, has altogether no use for objects: it is turned away from them, whereas in the *rasa* experience one is entranced by the object. In this respect, then, Abhinavagupta is faithful to the objective, analytic emphasis of Bharata and Ānandavardhana, whose primary concern was with the technical aspects of the dramatic/poetic art rather than with the psychology of response.

In other ways, too, Abhinavagupta never fails to furnish empirical validation for his theories. For instance, he adduces powerful reasons for repudiating the imitation/illusion theory of his predecessors. He rejects imitation in the narrow sense of reproduction or likeness making on the ground that neither the verbal description nor the nonverbal (gestural) enactment of the objective signs of an emotional state can rightly be called a likeness of that state because these depicted externals are the criteria of its identification, not a formal likeness of it. Moreover, by requiring faithfulness to an external model, the mimetic theory fails to account for the subjectivity involved in dramatic experience. It cannot be denied that the poet, the actor, and the audience experience a direct infusion of feeling. All three live the given situation as if it were their own. They do not perceive that they are dealing with a simulation of some real thing. In reinterpreting Bharata's term *anukaraṇa* ("reproduction"), however, Abhinavagupta does accept imitation in drama and poetry in the wider representational sense of "following the ways and actions of the world," which was the sense intended by Bharata. In his extensive comments on dance and music, Abhinavagupta defends Bharata's position that these art forms have no expressible content and do not imitate anything in nature. Their value in the theater is simply evocative: they heighten the emotional impact of the stage presentation. On the question of poetic truth, Abhinavagupta recognizes that the poetic world is fictitious in the sense that it is an imaginative construction and that the particulars referred to in the work may have no existence in the real world. But the poetic world is not unreal or illusory either because as a formula for an emotional experience it draws upon recognizable human models. It is therefore not autonomous or autoreferential, but fully referential, and it fulfills the criteria for truth, namely, correspondence or consistency with common human experience (what Aristotle called the laws of probability). Again, because evocation, not historical veracity, is the aim of poetry, the truthfulness or otherwise of the presented situation will not make the slightest difference to its evocative force. Abhinavagupta admits the existence of stage illusion, but holds that there is nothing illusory about the content of the dramatic experience itself, namely, the emotions, which are apprehended in their generalized form. In any case, according to him, an inquiry into the truth or falsity of poetic propositions is irrelevant to aesthetic appreciation—a position also maintained by Ānandavardhana.

In arguing for the essentiality of the emotions in poetry, again, Abhinavagupta does not rest his case on the reader's reaction alone. Instead, he shows that poetry is evocative, not only in the perlocutionary or affective sense of arousing emotions, but also in the sense that the formal presentation of an emotional situation has the efficacy or the illocutionary force (*bhāvanā*—a hermeneutic principle that he borrows from the Vedic exegetes) to prompt the reader to contemplate the described situation for its emotive significance, not merely as a piece of information. *Rasa* (evocation) is thus the illocutionary object *(artha)* of the poetic utterance and hence is not dependent on a special "aesthetic attitude" for its communication.

The most signal contribution that Abhinavagupta, as an exponent of *rasa* theory, made to Indian poetics is his attempt to integrate all of the semantic and formal elements of poetic language, such as figures, style, and deviant expression, into the aesthetics of *rasa*. Whereas his predecessors had advanced each element as a rival doctrine, Abhinavagupta, following the lead of Bharata and Ānandavardhana, shows that they were all subservient to the one overarching principle of *rasa*. As *rasa* is the end of poetry, all of these other elements can function only as reinforcing or evocative devices in their proper emotive contexts and should be judged by the sole criterion of their appropriateness to the *rasa* on hand (*rasaucitya*—a principle emphasized by both Bharata and Ānandavardhana). Ānandavardhana propounds the theory of *dhvani* or suggestion, which argues that indirection or implication is a distinct semantic power in addition to the well-known literal and metaphoric modes and that it is the essence of poetic speech. But he is equally committed to *rasa* and seeks to bring that principle under the rubric of *dhvani*. He tries to show that in poetry emotions are expressed, not directly by naming them, but indirectly through the description of their objects and other circumstances. He also recognizes *rasa* as the ultimate end of poetry, however, and thus implies that *dhvani* is the means to that end. Abhinavagupta clarifies this ambiguity in Ānandavardhana's position and affirms categorically the primacy of the *rasa* principle. Abhinavagupta still retains the concept of *dhvani*, but conflates it with *rasa* as *rasa-dhvani* (suggestion of *rasa* or emotive meaning).

But neither Abhinavagupta's nor Ānandavardhana's arguments succeed in countering the criticism of the *dhvani* theory by the language philosophers—the logicians and the Vedic exegetes. Abhinavagupta and Ānandavardhana fail to show how *rasa* or emotive meaning, which is taken to be the purport of the sentence describing the objective conditions of an emotion, can be called another meaning of that sentence, or a meaning derived through indirection, and how it can be considered a distinct semantic operation or even an exclusive feature of poetic speech. Whether the *rasa*s (poetic emotions) are suggested or directly expressed in literal language, however, Ānandavardhana and Abhinavagupta must be given credit for advancing a consistent general theory of literature centered on the concept of *rasa* and for giving that concept a firm semantic basis. As *rasa* is the purport (or import, if you like) of the poetic sentence, it is the referential meaning of that sentence, not the affective response to it alone.

Although Abhinavagupta's theory of aesthetics was largely built upon earlier views and upon the texts on which he was commenting, his own contributions are not inconsiderable. He clarified and elaborated many of the implications in the texts. As a practical critic, he displayed great analytical skill and imagination. In short, he discharged his task as a commentator with unique distinction, so much so that the poetic theory he offered in an enriched and consolidated form, as well as his expositions of the principles of music and dance, became canonical for subsequent critics and commentators.

[*See also* Indian Aesthetics, *overview article; and* Poetics.]

BIBLIOGRAPHY

Chari, V. K. *Sanskrit Criticism.* Honolulu, 1990.
Dyczkowski, Mark S. G. *The Doctrine of Vibration: An Analysis of the Doctrines and Practices of Kashmir Shaivism.* Albany, N.Y., 1987.
Gnoli, Raniero, ed. *The Aesthetic Experience according to Abhinavagupta.* 2d ed., rev. and enl. Varanasi, 1968.
Masson, J. L., and M. V. Patwardhan. *Aesthetic Rapture: The Rasādhyāya of the Nāṭyaśāstra,* vol. 1, *Text.* Poona, 1970.
Pandey, K. C. *Comparative Aesthetics,* vol. 1, *Indian Aesthetics.* 2d ed. Varanasi, 1959.
Pandey, K. C. *Abhinavagupta: An Historical and Philosophical Study.* 2d ed., rev. and enl. Varanasi, 1963.

V. K. CHARI

ABSTRACT EXPRESSIONISM. The art movement known as Abstract Expressionism was characterized by gestural and/or nonobjective paintings and direct-welded metal sculptures. Also known as "action painting" or the "New York school," the movement was centered in New York City between approximately 1940 and 1955.

Jackson Pollock gave a pithy summary of Abstract Expressionist aesthetics years before he would produce his characteristic nonobjective canvases of dripped oil enamel. Pressed by German modernist Hans Hofmann in 1942 to paint from nature, Pollock famously retorted, "I *am* Nature." His phrase reflects the complex admixture of discourses in which abstract expressionism participated: Jungian psychoanalysis, primitivism, existentialism, nationalism, and the romantic sublime.

Alfred Barr Jr. coined the term *Abstract Expressionism* in 1929 to describe the early improvisations of Wassily Kandinsky; it was applied to the artists with whom it is now associated by the art critic Robert Coates, writing in the *New Yorker* magazine in 1946. Like most art movements, it had no hard historical or stylistic boundaries. Its existence became obvious only after World War II, when a small group of impoverished middle-aged artists were propelled into prominence on the international stage. At the time, their visibility was taken as proof of the formal and psychological superiority of their art; recent revisionist histories have instead touted the economic and geopolitical achievements of a victorious United States as the motive force behind the movement's ascendency. In either account, the best-known American artists prior to Abstract Expressionism are understood to have occupied opposing sides of the political spectrum—Social Realists on the left, identified with communism, and regionalists on the right, associated with the nationalist and isolationist sentiments of the "America First" group. Both approaches demanded a traditional representational style only slightly inflected by European modernist abstraction; both became highly politicized in the tumultuous years leading up to American involvement in World War II. The dominance of Abstract Expressionism after the war was achieved in part by avoiding such overt political references, as formerly left-wing artists sought to chart a noncommittal course free from the increasingly rigid demands of communism on the left and nascent McCarthyists on the right.

These artists eliminated recognizable ("objective") subject matter from their work in favor of individual symbolic systems and abstract ("nonobjective") form. Nonetheless, the artists held that their individual systems were universally accessible through a variety of means. Accessibility could be achieved through the mediation of a "collective unconsciousness" (the concept of a universal and innate system of symbolic forms promulgated by Swiss analyst Carl Gustav Jung), through the achievement of a form vocabulary that was sufficiently "primitive" to be intuitively comprehensible to all, or through the communication of emotion through sheer color or painterly gesture. Each of these modes had precedents in earlier modern art, but their confluence in Abstract Expressionism resulted in a style of painting that seemed so unprecedented that few critics were initially able to tease out its connections to previous artistic movements. A certain anxiety of influence may have been in play as the movement's New York supporters downplayed linkages with German Expressionism (with its search for the "primitive" roots of expression), on the one hand, and the utopian geometric abstraction of Russian Suprematists and de Stijl painters (both groups had pertinent theories about the intrinsic expressivity of color and form), on the other.

Certainly, the dislocations and disasters of the first half of the century played a major role in both the appearance of Abstract Expressionism and its cluster of unarticulated aesthetic philosophies. Crucial to the formation of the tenuous collective identity only later identified as "Abstract Expressionism" was the U.S. government's Federal Art Project. Established as part of the Works Progress Administration (WPA) in 1935, its first administrators openly espoused the ideas of John Dewey, whose *Art as Experience* had been published the year before. The project acknowledged that "artist" was a profession worth supporting (a development unprecedented in American culture), and it gave employment to immigrant artists (Arshile Gorky, Willem de Kooning), as well as American-born painters (Lee Krasner, Pollock, and Philip Guston), all of whom would contribute to Abstract Expressionism's genesis. Although most of the WPA murals followed the prevailing representational styles (featuring heroic workers, churning assembly lines, and rolling farmland), the program had room for artists interested in adopting the "foreign" abstract modes then current in Paris (the undisputed capital of modern art until the Vichy regime). Some of the WPA painters, such as de Kooning and Gorky, had come from Europe in the 1920s; their U.S. government–funded art already revealed a sophisticated grasp of European modernism, particularly the Cubists' achievement of a shallow, minimally illusionist space and the Surrealists' innovative biomorphic abstract forms. The living presence of many Surrealists in New York during the late 1930s and 1940s (driven from European capitals by the rise of fascism) provided another impetus for the New York painters' developing interests in nonobjective painting. Through the Surrealists, psychoanalysis received further reinforcement as a compelling source of artistic invention and interpretation.

Among the many concepts supported by the Surrealists were the importance of the unconscious to creativity and the use of a new technique called "automatism," which proved to be the most essential components of Abstract Expressionism's first phase. The French painter André Masson (who was working in New York in the early 1940s) had been making automatist drawings as early as 1924. In this technique (also employed in Surrealist poetry), the artist tried to dissociate the drawing (or writing) hand from the mind's conscious control, supposedly thereby tapping forms and motives directly from the unconscious. The Surrealists had used automatism as a form of suggestion to initiate the more conscious process of making poetry or drawings. The Abstract Expressionists, however, valued automatism as an end in itself, a primary means of revealing the artist's unmediated emotional state. As Adolph Gottlieb commented, ". . . I prefer the no-content of purism to the shoddy content of social realism. . . . I love all paintings that look the way I feel" (as quoted in Tuchman, 1977, p. 71). This is one sense of Pollock's assertion that he *was* Nature—from the vantage point of the unstructured id and its instincts, human beings and human nature were but part of a vast continuum of organic life and its expressions. Claims to work from the unconscious were predicated on such a continuum, and Pollock's first poured paintings

(which began in 1947) proclaimed both their natural and automatist origins with titles such as *Galaxy, Phosphorescence,* and *Vortex.* Not even the eerie tableaux of the Surrealists' dreamscapes survived Pollock's radically automatist process. In the photographs by Hans Namuth that made Pollock's working method famous, he was shown moving his whole body around a horizontal, unprimed canvas, flinging paint in loops and trails, and pursuing spontaneously generated order in a rhythmic, repetitive, trancelike dance.

The Abstract Expressionist subject was thus constructed as a visionary, a solitary and possessed individual in a world of mass formations. The much-vaunted alienation and anguish of the artist were held to resist everything from fascist totalitarianism to an emerging consumer culture. The isolated gestural painter was figured as male, white, and, above all, free—a subject position that proved problematic for nonmales such as Krasner and nonwhites such as Norman Lewis. Predicated on spontaneity, the "action" painter's volcanic productions were taken as both proof and guarantor of democratic liberalism and free speech. As scholars of Abstract Expressionism have determined, this heightened indi-

ABSTRACT EXPRESSIONISM. Hans Namuth, *Jackson Pollock* (1950), black and white photograph; collection of the Center for Creative Photography, University of Arizona, Tucson. (Copyright 1991 by the Hans Namuth Estate; used by permission.)

vidualism meshed with free market ideologies of global capital, serving the very mass formations it imagined it was inoculating itself against. Increasingly throughout the immediate postwar period, exhibitions of the "New American Painting" were sent overseas as vivid emissaries of democracy in the cultural cold war.

The artists working in cultivated bohemian alienation during the war anticipated none of this, however. The interior world revealed by automatism was deeply private, and the artists resisted collective identity through their statements and through the very disjunctions of their jealously protected "signature styles." The optimism of the WPA's vision of an art linked to its public (the Dewey legacy) had not entirely dissipated, however. Both artists and critics forged connections between the private id and a wider system of signification, predicated on Jungian concepts of shared archetypes and a faith in the "primitivist" themes and images that were emerging from the popular anthropologies of scholars such as Franz Boas, Ruth Benedict, and Sir James Frazer. The romantic sublime would be key to these connections as well, but primitivism came first.

Throughout the 1940s, Abstract Expressionists emphasized their works' continuities with both archaic Greek myth and Native American belief systems (continuities clearly charted by Freud's metaphors of the Oedipal narrative or *Totem and Taboo*). There is a long tradition of modern artists appropriating African or "Oriental" art (e.g., Pablo Picasso's 1907 *Demoiselles d'Avignon* and Paul Gauguin's interest in Tahiti) as antidotes to supposedly hypercivilized bourgeois European life. But New York painters felt themselves to be dwelling in a barbarous age and experienced their thinking as continuous with the supposedly "primitive" mind. Theirs was a positive identification, but it found reinforcement in anthropological theories (most of them deeply racist) that articulated a supposedly subconscious process of assimilation of others' ethnic traits (as in Jung's 1930 essay "Your Negroid and Indian Behavior: The Primitive Elements in the American Mind" [see Leja, 1993, p. 104]). The Abstract Expressionists thus simultaneously claimed a link with the source of Western European culture (Greek myth) and asserted their unique access to Native American art as *national* myth structures. In doing so, they made a virtue of the kind of aspersions cast routinely on American culture by Europeans (e.g., Jung). Although inheritors of the same magisterial colonial gaze that animated Gauguin, Picasso, and countless other Western artists before them, the Abstract Expressionists' tropism toward the "primitive" was experienced as a deep identification rather than appropriation. Sharing the avant-garde's long-standing ambivalence toward Enlightenment ideals of the progress of civilization, the Abstract Expressionists were also part of a different geohistorical moment that gave such critiques a more desperate relevance. Given the *second* world war, the binary between what French anthropologist Lucien Lévy-Bruhl had called the

"pre-logical" mind of *les sociétés inférieures* and the supposedly more evolutionarily advanced western mental apparatus seemed untenable to the Abstract Expressionists. As Mark Rothko and Adolph Gottlieb stated in a 1943 radio broadcast: "Those who think the world of today is more gentle and graceful than the primeval and predatory passions from which these myths spring, are either not aware of reality or do not wish to see it in art. The myth holds us . . . because it expresses to us something real and existing in ourselves" (as quoted in Leja, 1993, p. 68). Barnett Newman, defending forms of Northwest Coast tribes such as the Kwakiutl with similar passion in 1947, wrote: "To [the Kwakiutl artist] a shape was a living thing, a vehicle for an abstract thought-complex, a carrier of the awesome feelings he felt before the terror of the unknowable. [Now] a new force in American painting . . . is the modern counterpart of the primitive art impulse." Insisting that their nonobjective paintings offered the accessible equivalent of these highly complex ideographic signifiers, Newman continued, "For here is a group of artists who are not abstract painters, although working in what is known as the abstract style" (as quoted in Newman, 1992, pp. 107–108).

Critics were able to distinguish two broad modes within the new abstract painting during the 1950s. Pollock and de Kooning most centrally, but also James Brooks, Guston, Franz Kline, Krasner, Robert Motherwell, and Bradley Walker Tomlin were all identified with a gestural, calligraphic brush stroke or line; these were the "action" or "gesture" painters. Newman, Rothko, and Ad Reinhardt produced "field" pictures, in which large areas of pigment were soaked, scrubbed, or brushed into canvas in such a way that the individual mark merged into areas of saturated hue. The artists were at great pains to distinguish their work from what they described as the "meaningless" geometric abstraction of northern European modernists such as Piet Mondrian and Wassily Kandinsky. They insisted that their works had subject matter beyond that of pure form and color.

Both modes of what Newman had called "non-abstract painting in the abstract style" were thus believed to have a broad yet specific cultural meaning. Depending on the moment and the interpreter, such meanings shifted over the course of the movement. In the "mythmaking" discourse of Abstract Expressionism's primitivizing first phase, a painting's meaning was taken to lie in its totemic value as a graphic, nonverbal signifier for terror and the destructive, primeval forces of human nature. Congruent with this early emphasis on what has been called the "Modern Man" discourse of the primitive during the immediate postwar period, the artists developed an interest in the more sophisticated tenets of Continental philosophy. The ideas of Friedrich Nietzsche and Martin Heidegger were discussed in artist-run periodicals through essays by and about existentialist philosophers such as Jean-Paul Sartre and less well known phenomenologists such as Emmanuel Lévinas. The existentialist struggle to *act* after being "thrown into being" was further popularized by film noir and the hardboiled detective novel, where meaningful subjectivity is carved out of modern barbarism by sheer force of will. Where mythmaking had still assumed a terrified collectivity (vaguely congruent with prewar political activism), the emerging emphasis on existentialism (in its American interpretations after the war) signaled a shift toward alienated individualism. As in the earlier mythmaking phase, the existentialist tenor of postwar Abstract Expressionism found a route to shared meaning, this time through Sartre's emphasis on the "situation" in which man finds himself. In this potentially common "situation," the individual act or choice became (if only symbolically) a choice for all men. The echo of the Nietzschean superman was emphasized in Abstract Expressionist periodicals such as *Possibilities* and *Tiger's Eye*. One interpreter wrote in the latter: "It is because individualism is grounded in self-confidence that the individual who has extreme self-confidence and great will power can rise above others and become a hero" (as quoted in Ashton, 1973, p. 188). Newman, in particular, emphasized Nietzsche, choosing the Dionysian mode from Nietzsche's *Birth of Tragedy* to describe the small Abstract Expressionist community: "The artist in America is . . . like a barbarian. . . . This is, then, our opportunity, free of the ancient paraphernalia, to come closer to the sources of the tragic emotion. Shall we not, as artists, search out the new objects for its image?" (as quoted in Newman, 1992, p. 170).

Newman, who had been responsible for the scornful witticism that aesthetics is to artists as ornithology is to birds, nonetheless emerged (with Motherwell) as one of the most powerful philosophical thinkers in the Abstract Expressionist circle. In the artist-run periodical *Tiger's Eye*, he provided the most sustained analysis of a theme that would come to dominate the painting and interpretation of Abstract Expressionism: the sublime. The little magazine was reflecting a discourse already in progress when it solicited "Six Opinions on What Is Sublime in Art" in 1948; in addition to Newman, the artist contributors included Motherwell and Clyfford Still. Newman worked explicitly with Edmund Burke's concepts of sublimity, seeing those quintessentially eighteenth-century meditations as "a surrealist manual" that had helped him develop a crucial contrast between the specious (European) search for beauty and the noble (American) quest for the sublime. Having lost ready access to God, as Newman saw it, modern Abstract Expressionists were still seeking to create a sublime art. The answer lay specifically within the artist *as an individual* (as existentialism had already confirmed). Acting only from internal emotions, the artist would create objects that produced in the viewer (as in the artist) the sublime trajectory of terror and ego dissolution, followed by those forms of aesthetic representation that would produce the coherent ego once again.

ABSTRACT EXPRESSIONISM. Joan Mitchell, *Hemlock* (1956), oil on canvas, 91 × 80 inches (231.1 × 203.2 cm); collection of the Whitney Museum of American Art, New York (Purchase, with funds from the Friends of the Whitney Museum of American Art [58.20.]). (Photograph by Geoffrey Clements. Copyright by the Estate of Joan Mitchell, courtesy of Robert Miller Gallery, New York; used by permission.)

Obviously, this sublime trajectory was predicated on the same processes of mythologization, individuation, and personal expression that had animated earlier phases of the movement. As Newman summarized it: "Instead of making *cathedrals* out of Christ, man, or 'life,' we are making it [*sic*] out of ourselves, out of our own feelings" (Newman, 1992, p. 173). [*See* Sublime.]

The constant reference to "man" in Abstract Expressionist statements was not merely a false generic (although it clearly participated in the blithe masculinism of the time). Manhood was a gendered requirement for the achievement of sublimity, following Kant's declaration, in his *Observations on the Feeling of the Beautiful and Sublime* (1764), that "the fair sex has . . . a *beautiful understanding*, whereas ours should be a *deep understanding*, an expression that signifies identity with the sublime." Just as he had been careful to separate his Kwakiutl artist from "the women basket weavers" who merely decorated objects with "the pleasant play of non-objective pattern . . .," Newman (who quoted Kant on the subject) saw the sublime as an exclusively masculine (or masculinizing) pursuit defined in opposition to the "feminine" search for beauty. Newman's thinking culminated in the first of his large-scale works, the eight-by-eighteen-foot "field" painting *Vir Heroicus Sublimis* from 1950. A taut horizontal canvas with a smoothly brushed surface of saturated red, *Vir* is punctuated by verticals of brushier pinks and browns and one narrow strip of unpainted canvas. Newman called these verticals "zips," and scholars have connected them with Swiss sculptor Alberto Giacometti's spindly and cadaverous figures of the postwar period, lone men standing isolated in the existential void. Like so many other Abstract Expressionists (whether biologically male or female), Newman painted as "sublime heroic man," seeking to enact—rather than depict—(his) contemporary existence. "The self, terrible and constant, is for me the subject matter of painting and sculpture" (as quoted in Newman, 1992, p. 187). The sublime *terribilita* came from the ongoing encounter between the self and the void.

Abstract Expressionist canvases did not invoke the discourse of sublimity merely through their titles or their evocation of figures devoured by space (for example). This discourse was produced for the most part by the artists' intense involvement with the processes by which their paintings were produced and received. In this as in so many other areas, Pollock "broke the ice" (as de Kooning had remarked), establishing through his infrequent statements and even less frequent interviews that "on the floor . . . I feel nearer, more a part of the painting, since this way I can . . . literally be *in* the painting" or "when I am *in* my painting, I'm not aware of what I'm doing" (as quoted in Jones, 1996, p. 47). Being lost in the act of painting was analogous to being lost in the act of *viewing* the painting. Pollock's dense skeins of enamel, intermittently soaking into the canvas or standing slightly off the surface in taut whipcords of paint, produced such shimmering absorptive fields for vision. De Kooning's more aggressive slashes and licks of pigment achieved their effects of sublimation through more visceral means, taking the viewer through the tangled and exhilarating jungle of his active strokes. The field painters chose a still different route to sublimity. Rothko explained that he painted large canvases so that "you are in it. It isn't something you command" (in Jones, 1996, p. 50). He requested that his canvases be grouped together in separate galleries, where they would surround the viewer with their characteristic somber, soft-edged rectangles of hovering color. Newman also enforced postures of viewing that would maximize the desired state of absorption; visitors to his 1951 exhibition were asked to stand so close to his enormous canvases that their entire field of vision would be saturated by intense chroma. Viewers would thus be visually dissolved in an oceanic experience of sublimity, their identity reconstituted only later in a process of reflection on that overwhelming aesthetic encounter.

Sculpture fared badly within the evolving discourse of Abstract Expressionism, as artists such as Theodore Roszak and Seymour Lipton attempted to find "direct metal" equivalents to Action Painting. Their sculp-metal and cast works seemed frozen in the mythologizing phase of the movement and never achieved the magisterial sublimity of the canvases of their painter colleagues in the postwar period. Only the direct-welded assemblages of David Smith rose above the dominance of painting in the movement, and even he described himself as a "pictorial thinker" and was praised by critics in similar terms.

From the welter of critical approaches to Abstract Expressionism during its peak, two divergent interpretations came to dominate; both emerged from the Marxist culture of New York in the 1930s, but with markedly different slants. The first was codified by Harold Rosenberg, who coined the rubric "action painting" to describe the risky, spontaneous, volcanic process seemingly recorded in Namuth's photographs of Pollock painting. Describing the canvas as "an arena in which to act" in 1952, Rosenberg concluded: "What was to go on the canvas was not a picture but an event" (Rosenberg, 1959, p. 25). Lost in the scorn subsequently heaped on this existential position was its deep effect on younger artists. Allan Kaprow, for example, under the influence of both Pollock and the aleatory composer John Cage, was introducing an action-oriented art form that would begin as "Happenings" in 1958 and continue into "performance art," still vital in the 1990s. An unanticipated offspring of existentialist "action painting," Kaprow's new genre emphasized what he articulated as "The Legacy of Jackson Pollock": "Not satisfied with the *suggestion* through paint of our other senses, we shall utilize the specific substances of sight, sound, movements, people, odors, touch" (Kaprow, 1958, p. 56).

It was precisely against this promiscuous mingling of varieties of sensuous experience (and specifically against the intermingling of different art forms) that Clement Greenberg had earlier articulated the grounds for what would be the second formulation of Abstract Expressionism's meaning. As early as 1940, Greenberg revisited Gotthold Lessing's 1766 essay, *Laocoön: An Essay on the Limits of Painting and Poetry,* against the confusion of the arts epitomized by the Hellenistic sculpture of Laocoön. Greenberg's "Towards a Newer Laocoön" was the first of many influential polemics in which he argued that modernism, constituted as it was by a progressive, even teleological, purification of the arts, was also opposed to this confusion. Before ever seeing a Pollock drip painting, Greenberg pursued a Marxist theory of the artist's alienation from his bourgeois patrons to argue that each of the avant-garde arts sought to define itself "solely in the terms of the sense or faculty which perceived its effect" (Greenberg, 1986, p. 31). In Greenberg's formalist view, painting was both historically and philosophically constituted by its uniquely visual nature. When he did come to claim Pollock, Greenberg described the drip paintings not as "events," but as shallow optical fields available to cognition through eyesight alone. For Greenberg, Pollock's importance lay solely within the history of modernist painting, where his skeins were seen as working to push Cubism's achievements further toward "flatness," which emerged as the teleological goal for modernism in Greenberg's account.

American postmodernism revisited these debates over Abstract Expressionism and its interpreters in the 1980s; Greenberg, in particular, emerged as the postmodernists' bête noire. Abstract Expressionism, no longer available as a method inhabited from within, became a manner or style for postmodern pastiche, while its heroic stance was subjected to withering critique. The effort to guarantee readings of deep humanistic meaning in canvases employing largely nonobjective visual forms appeared naive in a poststructuralist, postmodern frame. At the same time, even for postmodernists, Abstract Expressionism remains a strong example of art that believed itself to function philosophically, whether prompting reflections on the nature of man or on modernist aesthetics. Although clearly naive from the perspective of both revisionist historians and poststructuralist, postmodern artists, such a condition of philosophical conviction is one to which postmodernists still aspire, as their fascination with Greenberg and the heroic first generation of Abstract Expressionists attests.

[*See also* Abstraction; Expression Theory of Art; Greenberg; *and* Primitivism.]

BIBLIOGRAPHY

Ashton, Dore. *The New York School: A Cultural Reckoning.* New York, 1973.

Auping, Michael, ed. *Abstract Expressionism: The Critical Developments.* New York, 1987.

Gibson, Ann Eden. *Issues in Abstract Expressionism: The Artist-Run Periodicals.* Ann Arbor, 1990.

Gibson, Ann Eden. *Abstract Expressionism: Other Politics.* New Haven, 1997.

Greenberg, Clement. *The Collected Essays and Criticism,* vol. 1, *Perceptions and Judgments, 1939–1944.* Edited by John O'Brian. Chicago, 1986.

Guilbaut, Serge. *How New York Stole the Idea of Modern Art: Abstract Expressionism, Freedom, and the Cold War.* Translated by Arthur Goldhammer. Chicago, 1983.

Jones, Caroline A. "The Romance of the Studio and the Abstract Expressionist Sublime." In *Machine in the Studio: Constructing the Postwar American Artist,* pp. 1–59. Chicago, 1996.

Kaprow, Allan. "The Legacy of Jackson Pollock." *Art News* 57 (October 1958): 24–26, 55–57.

Leja, Michael. *Reframing Abstract Expressionism: Subjectivity and Painting in the 1940s.* New Haven, 1993.

Newman, Barnett. *Selected Writings and Interviews.* Edited by John P. O'Neill. New York, 1990; reprint, Berkeley, 1992.

Polcari, Stephen. *Abstract Expressionism and the Modern Experience.* Cambridge and New York, 1991.

Rosenberg, Harold. "The American Action Painters." *Art News* 51 (December 1952). Anthologized in *The Tradition of the New,* pp. 23–39. Chicago, 1959.

Sandler, Irving. *The Triumph of American Painting: A History of Abstract Expressionism.* New York, 1970.

Tuchman, Maurice. *New York School: The First Generation: Paintings of the 1940s and 1950s.* Reprint, New York, 1977.

CAROLINE A. JONES

ABSTRACTION. In its aesthetic use, the term *abstraction* refers to a historical style, primarily in the visual arts, in which representational or mimetic subject matter is replaced by other concerns. The development of these concerns, which comprises a central aspect of modern art, can be divided into two phases: an early European phase, about 1907–1938, and a later postwar phase in the United States, about 1945–1960. Actually, this division somewhat compresses

ABSTRACTION. Georgia O'Keeffe, *Black and White* (1930), oil on canvas, 36 × 24 inches (91.4 × 61 cm); collection of the Whitney Museum of American Art, New York (50th Anniversary Gift of Mr. and Mrs. R. Crosby Kemper [81.9]). (Copyright 1998 by the Georgia O'Keeffe Foundation/Artists Rights Society, New York; used by permission.)

the historical sequence of events, for abstract works were being created in the United States as early as 1930 and continue to be produced today as one of the multiple styles of postmodernism. Additionally, the construal of art as a medium of information and cultural exchange has extended the interest in abstract art into non-Western cultures. Nevertheless, this division offers a way of identifying the periods of major innovation in abstract art through a delimitation of their historical positions.

In its European phase, abstract art developed in a context of theoretical and social concerns where artworks were given prophetic or pedagogical roles in the task of creating an ideal society. These roles were often articulated both in manifestos associated with various movements, such as Constructivism, Suprematism, and the Bauhaus, and in the copious writings of individual artists such as Piet Mondrian and Wassily Kandinsky. Indeed, the intimacy between practice and ideology is a major characteristic of this phase—the artwork assuming meaning through its exemplification of theory. A central theme of European abstraction is "progress," and its theoretical source is the doctrine of Georg Wilhelm Friedrich Hegel that artworks exemplify advanced developmental stages within their cultures and that the history of art demonstrates the principle of cultural (spiritual) progress. [*See* Hegel.] The tendency in much European abstraction to use geometric form and to achieve compositional unity through the reduction of naturalistic forms brings to mind Hegel's thesis that progress is a process of dematerialization, the triumph of spirit (rationality) over matter. In this context, aesthetic value is found primarily in the role of artworks as precocious exemplars of the future, and only secondarily in their purely aesthetic qualities. Major artists of this European phase include Kazimir Malevich, Wassily Kandinsky, Piet Mondrian, Joan Miró, Naum Gabo, Constantin Brancusi, and Jean Arp.

The American phase of abstract art came to prominence shortly after the end of World War II, and its stylistic dominance continued until the advent of "Pop art" in the 1960s. Although this new abstract art had European ideological and stylistic roots, it was soon regarded, with considerable domestic satisfaction, as distinctly American. This art, identified by the term *Abstract Expressionism*, exhibits singular characteristics of extended scale, energy, and immediacy. Although the Hegelian theme of artistic progress remains influential, other themes, such as Immanuel Kant's emphasis on formal values and Arthur Schopenhauer's notion of the expressive will, gain importance. In the main, however, the ideologies of abstract expressionism are neither speculative nor utopian; rather, they are psychological, personal, and largely apolitical. As the name implies, the relevant aesthetic virtue is self-expression, and its pictorial exposition functions to make public the realm of primal, nonconventional meanings hidden within the artistic psyche. Although artistic value is first located in the uniqueness of the individ-

ual psyche, it gains scope through the presumption of a common source of psychic reality for which the artwork is a conduit. Two theoretical models for this context are Sigmund Freud's posit of a layered consciousness, to which access is both problematic and rewarding, and the existential doctrines of Jean-Paul Sartre and Søren Kierkegaard, which stress the primacy of individual experience over the institutional rubric. Somewhat paradoxically, the large scale and pictorial richness of the art through which such experience is projected give it an architectural dimension that facilitates its acquisition by corporate institutions and its incorporation into public settings. The critical justifications for American abstraction, unlike its European counterpart, were articulated less by artists than by influential critics such as Clement Greenberg, Harold Rosenberg, and Thomas Hess. Major artists of this period include Jackson Pollock, Mark Rothko, Willem de Kooning, Ad Reinhardt, Barnett Newman, Helen Frankenthaler, and David Smith. Some later artists of the 1960s, who stress the formal concreteness of the abstract work rather than the factors of its creation, include Frank Stella, Donald Judd, and Kenneth Noland.

Although this brief account has focused on the different ideologies and procedures that mark the two historical phases of abstract art, the style has an evident unifying characteristic in the move toward eliminating representational subject matter from an artwork's formal concerns. In some cases, however, the pictorial strategies adopted have retained variants or vestiges of recognizable imagery, while in others the aim has been to achieve a purely nonmimetic pictorial "language." These strategies can usefully be contrasted with each other although they cannot be associated with either the European or the American phase, but rather move across the phases and thus occur throughout the entire category of abstract art.

In one variation, specifically representational imagery is abandoned gradually, in the sense of a reductive working through the varieties of representational sources in order to find the basic formal components they all share and to discard the components that seem less central to the elucidation of form. In this process, resemblance to particulars is shed but some reference, however attenuated, to their natural origins is maintained. In this usage, the name *abstraction* indicates a stylistic continuity with representational art by treating "abstracted" forms as generalizations or essences of a pictorial content that is common to both. Accordingly, the term *image* comes to refer not only to distinctly mimetic forms, but to the range of forms that exemplify every degree and variant of the abstracting process.

In this historical development, the art of Paul Cézanne and its later adumbration through analytic Cubism are of particular importance. Cézanne's dictum that nature can best be represented through a reduction to the geometric solids common to all particular forms moved artistic attention away from the differences between subjects, such as

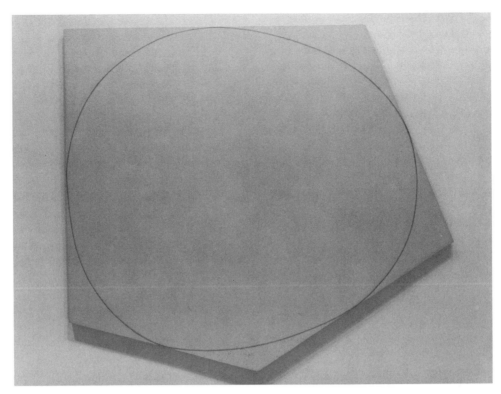

ABSTRACTION.   Robert Mangold, *Distorted Circle within a Polygon, I* (1972), synthetic polymer paint on canvas, 6′8″ × 7′5″ (202.8 × 225.6 cm); Museum of Modern Art, New York; Riklis Collection of the McCrory Corporation (fractional gift). (Photograph copyright 1998 by the Museum of Modern Art; used by permission.)

figures, landscapes, and still lifes, to the continuity between them. This move identifies the picture plane as an arena of continuous rather than hierarchic value. In the Cubist works of Pablo Picasso and Georges Braque, a further generalization of pictorial sources is achieved through techniques of faceting and transparency. This emphasizes the autonomy of the painting relative to its sources and suggests pictorial self-reference as a stylistic value for abstract art. A similar development can be found in the sculptural works of Constantin Brancusi and Jean Arp. In the oeuvre of Piet Mondrian, a Cubist phase is followed by works in which the formal elements are reduced to primary colors in vertical-horizontal opposition. In his theoretical writings, Mondrian speaks of these later works as constituting a historical reification of the abstracting process, a culmination of the history of painting such that further progress is to be made through application of these principles to social and environmental needs, not through further stylistic development. [*See* Mondrian.]

The influence of Cubism on American abstract art was tempered by the emphasis on gesture and immediacy. In the paintings of Willem de Kooning, the two come together in novel and cohesive ways. De Kooning's works move between a range of subject matters and varying degrees of abstractness. Some works, such as *Montauk Highway,* may evoke particular landscapes but are not specifically referential; other works, such as the *Woman* series, contain direct and intense psychological and visual reference to the named subject.

In another variation within the general category of abstract art, the rejection of representational sources and imagery occurs at a more abrupt point in the artistic oeuvre and thus announces a programmatic disjunction between past and present. This strategy calls for the replacement of natural objects with a new realm for artistic interest and the identification of a new subject matter with its own unique imagery and formal strategies. In this ideological climate, the sense of opposition between old and new gives rise to the stylistic designator *nonobjective art,* whose images are presented as autonomous, quasi-linguistic inventions or are derived from such sources as mathematics or the structures of other arts. These images and sources can be theoretically distinguished from those of the first variant discussed here—images abstracted from the realm of natural appearances.

In nonobjective works, music often serves as a model for the symbolic function of visual art, perhaps as a way of appropriating and defusing Hegel's placement of music above the visual arts in his account of style and history. The artworks and writings of the Russian painter Wassily Kandinsky are a case in point: he gives his paintings such musical titles as *Fugue* and *Improvisation,* and he uses the concept of musical harmony, the arrangement of discrete notational elements into harmonic clusters and progressions, as an analogue to the distribution of visual elements—"point, line, and plane"—into extended compositions. [*See* Kandinsky.] The Swiss painter Paul Klee, whose working friendship with Kandinsky mirrors the one between Picasso and Braque, is an important figure in this development as is the Russian painter Kazimir Malevich, whose Suprematist paintings—notably *White on White*—present austere examples of this ideology.

In the postwar period of American abstraction, a number of artists avoided the analytic procedures of Cubism in their development. Barnett Newman's conjunction of minimal vertical stripes with large scale is given an ideological context through such titles as *Vir Heroicus Sublimus* with its invocation of a realm of ideals and universals. The painter Mark Rothko objected to the application of the term *abstract* to his works because the "distancing" implied is inappropriate to the intimacy he wanted and the subjective immediacy of his content. The painter Jackson Pollock was influenced by the experiments in automatic writing and chance-directed composition that are found in Surrealism and Dadaism.

Although the terms *abstract* and *nonobjective* are often used as synonyms, such usage glosses over a useful referential distinction. In the development of abstract art, where the move from representing to abstracting is identified as seeking the common basis of pictorial imagery, the emphasis is on a process of analysis. Here, "abstract" is understood as an "abstracting from" the diverse particulars of natural appearances, through procedures of reduction, simplification, and generalization, in order to find the form, the "abstraction," which shows the underlying pictorial, if not historical, commonality of the artistic subject.

In contrast, the development of a nonobjective style can be understood as the disengagement from both mimetic and analytic responses to natural objects in favor of inventions in which the visual elements are conceived on linguistic or notational models. In many instances, these nonobjective elements are seen as exemplifying a realm of psychic-spiritual subjectivity, a realm that purports to replace nature as a pictorial source and competes with nature for ideological significance. Historically, nonobjective art can be considered a subcategory of the abstract movement in twentieth-century art.

[*See also* Abstract Expressionism; Formalism, *overview article; and* Modernism.]

BIBLIOGRAPHY

American Abstract Artists. *The World of Abstract Art.* New York, 1958.
Bois, Yve-Alain. *Painting as Model.* Cambridge, Mass., 1990.
Gabo, Naum. *Of Divers Arts.* New York, 1962.
Greenberg, Clement. *Art and Culture: Critical Essays.* Boston, 1961.
Hess, Thomas B. *Abstract Painting: Background and American Phase.* New York, 1951.
Holtzman, Harry, and Martin S. James, eds. *The New Art, the New Life: Collected Writings of Piet Mondrian.* Boston, 1986.
Kandinsky, Wassily. *Complete Writings on Art.* Edited by Kenneth C. Lindsay and Peter Vergo. Boston, 1982; reprint, New York, 1994.
Klee, Paul. *Pedagogical Sketchbook.* Translated by Sybil Moholy-Nagy. New York, 1953.
Krukowski, Lucian. *Art and Concept.* Amherst, Mass., 1987.
Krukowski, Lucian. *Aesthetic Legacies.* Philadelphia, 1992.
Motherwell, Robert, and Ad Reinhardt, eds. *Modern Artists in America.* New York, 1952.
Poggioli, Renato. *The Theory of the Avant-Garde.* Translated by Gerald Fitzgerald. Cambridge, Mass., 1968.
Popper, Karl. *The Poverty of Historicism.* Boston, 1957.
Rosenberg, Harold. *The Tradition of the New.* New York, 1959.
Roskill, Mark. *Klee, Kandinsky, and the Thought of Their Time.* Urbana, Ill., 1992.
Rotzler, Willy. *Constructive Concepts: A History of Constructive Art from Cubism to the Present.* Translated by Stanley Mason. New York, 1977.
Sandler, Irving. *The Triumph of American Painting: A History of Abstract Expressionism.* New York, 1970.
Weinberg, Julius R. *Abstraction, Relation, and Induction.* Madison, Wis., 1965.
Zhadova, Larisa A. *Malevich: Suprematism and Revolution in Russian Art, 1910–1930.* New York, 1982.

LUCIAN KRUKOWSKI

ADDISON, JOSEPH (1672–1719), English poet, playwright, and politician. Addison's most important contributions to aesthetics were published as essays in *The Spectator,* a daily newspaper that he edited with Richard Steele. Addison's most sustained consideration of aesthetics in *The Spectator* comes in the eleven essays on "the Pleasures of the Imagination" published as a continual series from 21 June to 3 July, 1712 (essays 411–421). For Samuel H. Monk, these essays constitute "the first sustained piece of writing on aesthetics in eighteenth-century England" (1960, p. 57).

Addison's prefatory essay on taste (no. 409) became a kind of blueprint for numerous essays on taste in the eighteenth century. For Addison, taste is primarily concerned with a reader's affective, psychological response to literature: it is "that Faculty of the Soul, which discerns the Beauties of an Author with Pleasure, and the Imperfections with Dislike." Whether "a Man . . . is possessed of this Faculty" or not can be discovered by empirical experiment: a reader need only read the celebrated works of antiquity or the modern period and observe his own reactions. If he finds himself "delighted in an extraordinary manner," he has taste; if he "finds a Coldness or Indifference in his Thoughts," then he "wants the Faculty." In other words, although taste is a faculty of the soul, not everyone has such a faculty. Yet even though the faculty of taste "must in some degree be born with us," it also needs to be cultivated through what amounts to a polite, literary education, which should include reading "the Writings of the most Polite Authors," conversing "with Men of a Polite Genius," and becoming "well versed in the Works of the best *Criticks* both Ancient and Modern."

By criticism, Addison means more than the application of "Mechanical Rules which a Man of very little Taste may discourse upon." Although it is necessary to explain and understand the rules of poetry—such as the unities of time, place, and action—Addison wishes for critics who "would enter into the very Spirit and Soul of fine Writing, and show us the several Sources of that Pleasure which rises in the Mind upon the Perusal of a noble Work." Addison is thus proposing an affective criticism that would attend to that mysterious something in poetry that "elevates and astonishes the Fancy, and gives a Greatness of Mind to the Reader, which few of the Criticks besides *Longinus* have consider'd." The reference to Longinus's discussion of how poetry may arouse "greatness of mind" in the reader is crucial, because Addison's own aesthetic theory centers on a category he calls "greatness."

In the first of the essays on the pleasures of the imagination (no. 411), Addison grounds his aesthetic theory in John Locke's empirical epistemology—which he neatly summarizes:

We cannot indeed have a single Image in the Fancy that did not make its first Entrance through the Sight; but we have the Power of retaining, altering and compounding those Images, which we have once received, into all the varieties of Picture and Vision that are most agreeable to the Imagination.

This allows Addison to distinguish two kinds of imaginative material and experience:

I divide these Pleasures into two kinds: My Design being first of all to Discourse of those Primary Pleasures of the Imagination, which entirely proceed from such Objects as are before our Eyes; and in the next place to speak of those Secondary Pleasures of the Imagination which flow from the Ideas of visible Objects, when the Objects are not actually before the Eye, but are called up into our Memories, or form'd into agreeable Visions of Things that are either Absent or Fictitious.

In this preromantic conception of the imagination, aesthetic pleasure is produced simply through the mind's contemplation of the ideas—or *images*—it receives from looking at external objects. The material of the secondary pleasures of the imagination can be supplied by various kinds of mimetic art, such as "Paintings, Statues, Descriptions, or any the like Occasion." We will see that the terms *primary* and *secondary* do not necessarily mean that Addison elevates the aesthetic effects of nature over those of art (as Monk claims).

Addison begins by comparing the pleasures of the imagination with those of the senses and the understanding, sug-

gesting that they are less gross than sensual pleasure but "as great and as transporting" as cognitive pleasure. The advantage of aesthetic over cognitive pleasure is that the former is "more easie to be acquired":

It is but opening the Eye, and the Scene enters. The Colours paint themselves on the Fancy, with very little Attention of Thought or Application of Mind in the Beholder. We are struck, we know not how, with the Symmetry of any thing we see, and immediately assent to the beauty of an Object, without enquiring into the particular Causes and Occasions of it.

Yet if aesthetic pleasure can be had with as little effort as the opening of an eye, this is not to suggest that such pleasure will be experienced by anyone who has eyes to see. If this were the case, there would be no need for the aesthetic education on offer in *The Spectator* and no way of disputing about tastes. Thus, Addison claims:

A Man of a Polite Imagination, is let into a great many Pleasures that the Vulgar are not capable of receiving. He can converse with a Picture, and find an agreeable Companion in a Statue. He meets with a secret Refreshment in a Description, and often feels a greater Satisfaction in the Prospect of Fields and Meadows, than another does in the Possession. It gives him, indeed, a kind of Property in every thing he sees, and makes the most rude uncultivated Parts of Nature administer to his Pleasures.

These extra pleasures experienced by the man of taste are not only those "secondary pleasures" made available through a cultural education (the companionable or "secret" interactions with works of art such as pictures, statues, or descriptions). He also derives pleasures from nature that are apparently unavailable to "the Vulgar" (he has "a kind of Property in every thing he sees" that "makes the most rude uncultivated Parts of Nature administer to his Pleasures"). This aesthetic proprietorship over the visual field also allows the polite spectator to possess a "Prospect of Fields and Meadows" in a more profound way than the actual landowner. In this way, Addison's aesthetics paves the way for the complex politics of the picturesque.

Addison's man of taste, then, is not a landowner but one who knows how to respond aesthetically to the landscape. Addison is addressing not the leisured, propertied class, but men of middle-class professions in need of guidance about how to use their hard-won moments of leisure. Thus, Addison is responding to one of the early symptoms of modernity—the spread of leisure beyond the propertied classes into the rising bourgeoisie. This question is of moment for Addison because, he warns, the "very first Step out of Business" for most people is "into Vice or Folly." The pleasures of the imagination, by contrast, occupy an innocent and beneficial middle ground between work and sensual pleasure:

> [They] do not require such a Bent of Thought as is necessary to our more serious Employments, nor, at the same time, suffer the mind to sink into that Negligence and Remissness, which are apt to accompany our more sensual Delights, but, like a gentle Exercise to the Faculties, awaken them from Sloth and Idleness, without putting them upon any Labour or Difficulty.

Addison prescribes the "gentle Exercise" of aesthetic experience for its cathartic, therapeutic effects on mind and body alike:

> The Pleasures of the Fancy are more conducive to Health, than those of the Understanding, which are worked out by Dint of Thinking, and attended with too violent a Labour of the Brain. Delightful Scenes, whether in Nature, Painting, or Poetry, have a kindly Influence on the Body, as well as the Mind, and not only serve to clear and brighten the Imagination, but are able to disperse Grief and Melancholy, and to set the Animal Spirits in pleasing and agreeable Motions.

Having distinguished between the primary and secondary pleasures of the imagination and described the general effects of both, Addison begins in the next paper (no. 412) to concentrate on the primary pleasures derived from "outward Objects." He divides such objects into "what is *Great, Uncommon,* or *Beautiful*" and discusses the origins and effects of each. Addison's initial examples of greatness are drawn solely from natural phenomena:

> The Prospects of an open Champian [i.e., flat] Country, a vast uncultivated Desart, of huge Heaps of Mountains, high Rocks and Precipices, or a wide Expanse of Waters, where we are not struck with the Novelty or Beauty of the Sight, but with that rude kind of Magnificence which appears in many of these stupendous Works of Nature.

Addison's attempt to account for the aesthetic effects of viewing such scenes in psychological terms contains the germs of ideas that would be elaborated on later in more extended accounts of the sublime (such as those by Edmund Burke and Immanuel Kant):

> Our Imagination loves to be filled with an Object, or to graspe at any thing that is too big for its Capacity. We are flung into a pleasing Astonishment at such unbounded Views, and feel a delightful Stillness and Amazement in the Soul at the Apprehension of them. The Mind of Man naturally hates every thing that looks like a Restraint upon it, and is apt to fancy it self under a sort of Confinement, when the Sight is pent up in a narrow Compass, and shortened on every side by the Neighbourhood of Walls or Mountains. On the contrary, a spacious Horison is an Image of Liberty, where the Eye has Room to range abroad, to expiate at large on the Immensity of its Views, and to lose it self amidst the Variety of Objects that offer themselves to its Observation.

In this passage, the relationship between subject and object is shifting, complex, and dynamic. In the first sentence, the imagination is both a passive container (it "loves to be filled with an Object") and an active agent that grapples with the outside world (it "loves . . . to graspe at any thing that is too big for its Capacity"). And if we are "flung into a pleasing Astonishment" and reduced to "a delightful Stillness" by "unbounded Views," the eye also loves "to range abroad, to expiate at large on the Immensity of its Views."

In essay 413, Addison considers how the great, the new, and the beautiful cause aesthetic pleasure. He rules out the possibility of assigning necessary or efficient causes "because we know neither the Nature of an Idea, nor the Substance of a Human Soul." He is more willing to speculate about final causes, or divine purposes, for our aesthetic reactions. This allows him to propose an extraordinary fusion of Lockean epistemology and Christian piety. God has made the world and all its objects appear beautiful to us "So that it is impossible for us to behold his Works with Coldness or Indifference." God has done this by so configuring our minds that objects convey ideas or sense impressions to us (such as colors) that are quite different from the objects in themselves. Thus, Addison assigns a divine purpose to Locke's argument in book 2, chapter 8 of *An Essay Concerning Human Understanding* that, in Addison's words, "Light and Colours, as apprehended by the Imagination, are only Ideas in the Mind, and not Qualities that have any Existence in Matter."

Addison completes his consideration of the primary pleasures of the imagination with some reflections on gardening and landscaping (no. 414) and on architecture (no. 415). He discusses architecture entirely in terms of its ability to generate the effects of greatness. Such effects are not produced merely through "the Bulk and Body of the Structure," since "Greatness of Manner" is equally requisite. Greatness of manner is epitomized in the simplicity of classical arches, pillars, and domes and contrasts with the mean effects achieved by the excessively intricate ornamentation of Gothic architecture. As always with Addison, this can be verified not according to the rules and authority of architectural theory but by the individual using his own responses as experimental evidence:

> Let any one reflect on the Disposition of Mind he finds in himself, at his first Entrance into the *Pantheon* at *Rome,* and how his Imagination is filled with something Great and Amazing; and, at the same time, consider how little, in proportion, he is affected with the Inside of a *Gothick* Cathedral, tho' it be five times larger than the other; which can arise from nothing else, but the Greatness of the Manner in the one, and the Meanness in the other.

Addison is here using his own experience, recorded in his *Remarks on Italy* (1705), to make a general claim about what anyone will experience under the same conditions. In this, he is assuming, with Locke, that everyone has the same perceptual and mental system. Yet we have also seen that, like Locke, Addison believes that such common physiological responses need to be guided by a taste that is not common to everyone and that needs to be properly cultivated. These assumptions are implicit within what Addison presents as an experiment that "any one" can try. Addison is addressing a privileged readership for whom a trip to Rome was considered, precisely, part of an education in taste. The bulk of the population—"the Vulgar," together with most of Addison's women readers—would not have been able to carry out this aesthetic experiment.

Addison moves on, in essay 416, to consider the secondary pleasures of the imagination—that is, those generated by mimetic art forms such as statues, paintings, and descriptions. (Music is virtually excluded from Addison's aesthetics because its sounds "have no Ideas annexed to them" and so cannot "represent visible Objects.") The aesthetic pleasure we derive from such mimetic media "proceeds from that Action of the Mind, which compares the Ideas arising from the Original Objects, with the Ideas we receive from the Statue, Picture, Description, or Sound that represents them." He says that it is impossible for us to know the necessary reason why such mental operations are pleasurable, though he once again speculates that God has a final cause or purpose for a Lockean description of mental activity:

The *final Cause*, probably, of annexing Pleasure to this Operation of the Mind, was to quicken and encourage us in our Searches after Truth, since the distinguishing one thing from another, and the right discerning betwixt our Ideas, depends wholly upon our comparing them together, and observing the Congruity or Disagreement that appears among the several Works of Nature.

This gives a new twist to Locke's epistemology: whereas Locke had argued that the aesthetic effects of figurative language (or wit) are deceptive and facile, Addison is claiming that they are the basis of discriminative judgment and play a major role in "our searches after truth."

Addison confines his discussion of the secondary pleasures of the imagination to those that "proceed from Ideas raised by *Words*." Far from shifting aesthetic discussion from art onto nature, Addison claims:

Words, when well chosen, have so great a Force in them, that a Description often gives us more lively Ideas than the Sight of things themselves. The Reader finds a Scene drawn in stronger Colours, and painted more to the Life in his Imagination, by the help of Words, than by an actual Survey of the Scene which they describe. In this Case the Poet seems to get the better of Nature.

But such effects depend not only on the skill of the writer but on the responsive capacity of the reader. Because reading involves the mind's comparing the ideas it has received from outward things with the ideas raised by the words, a reader's capacity to respond to descriptions depends on the combination of a good imagination (the capacity to retain vivid ideas of outward objects) and an educated knowledge

of the ideas annexed to words: "The Fancy must be warm, to retain the Print of those Images it hath received from outward Objects; and the Judgment discerning, to know what Expressions are most proper to cloath and adorn them to the best Advantage." Thus, for Addison, there are not different tastes but different degrees of taste, ranging from readers with the most acute taste to those who have no taste at all. And there is no antipathy between fancy and judgment, as there is in Locke, because both are requisite for responsive and tasteful reading.

In the final five papers of the series (nos. 417–421), Addison concentrates on the aesthetic pleasures of literature. In essay 417, he suggests that the secondary pleasures of reading have still more advantages over those of sight. We are able to derive pleasure from reading descriptions of disagreeable things that would be simply unpleasant to see in reality. Descriptions are also able to "raise a secret Ferment in the Mind of the Reader, and to Work, with Violence, upon his Passions." This leads Addison to question an Aristotelian commonplace:

The two leading Passions which the more serious Parts of Poetry endeavour to stir up in us, are Terror and Pity. And here, by the way, one would wonder how it comes to pass, that such Passions as are very unpleasant at all other times, are very agreeable when excited by proper Descriptions.

Addison's answer to this anticipates later accounts of the sublime (such as Burke's):

If we consider . . . the Nature of this Pleasure, we shall find that it does not arise so properly from the Description of what is Terrible, as from the Reflection we make on our selves at the time of reading it. When we look on such hideous Objects, we are not a little pleased to think we are in no Danger of them. We consider them at the same time, as Dreadful and Harmless; so that the more frightful Appearance they make, the greater is the Pleasure we receive from the Sense of our own Safety. In short, we look upon the Terrors of a Description, with the same Curiosity and Satisfaction that we survey a dead Monster.

Thus, we derive pleasure from reading about dangerous things because we know that we are really safe. On the same principle, we experience aesthetic pleasure in contemplating "dangers that are past, or in looking on a precipice at a distance." Likewise, in the case of pity, our pleasure in reading of the torments of others is made possible "from the secret Comparison which we make between our selves and the Person who suffers." In the actual presence of suffering, however, we derive no aesthetic pleasure because "the Object presses too close upon our Senses" and our thoughts "are so intent upon the Miseries of the sufferer, that we cannot turn them on our own Happiness."

Addison closes his account of the pleasures of the imagination by arguing that such pleasures are not wholly confined to literary or fictitious writing. In essay 420 he suggests that the writings of "the Authors of the new

Philosophy" (i.e., the science or natural philosophy of figures such as Isaac Newton) "gratifie and enlarge the Imagination" at least as much as any other set of writers. Such scientific writings have opened up new prospects for the human mind that threaten to exercise and extend the imagination beyond its capacities:

> when we survey the whole Earth at once, and the several Planets that lie within its Neighbourhood, we are filled with a pleasing Astonishment. . . . If, after this, we contemplate those wide Fields of *Ether*, that reach in height *as far as from Saturn* to the fixt Stars, and run abroad almost to an Infinitude, our Imagination finds its Capacity filled with so immense a Prospect, and puts it self upon the Stretch to comprehend it. But if we yet rise higher, and consider the fixt Stars as so many vast Oceans of Flame, that are each of them attended with a different Sett of Planets, and still discover new Firmaments, and new Lights, that are sunk farther in those unfathomable Depths of *Ether*, so as not to be seen by the strongest of our Telescopes, we are lost in such a Labyrinth of Suns and Worlds, and confounded with the Immensity and Magnificence of Nature.

[*See also* Expression Theory of Art; Imagination; Pleasure; Poetics; *and* Taste, *article on* Early History.]

BIBLIOGRAPHY

Work by Addison

With Richard Steele. *The Spectator.* 5 vols. Edited by Donald F. Bond. Oxford, 1965. See Bond's introduction, vol. 1, pp. xiii–cix, for information on *The Spectator*'s relation to its historical context.

Other Sources

Fabricant, Carole. "The Aesthetics and Politics of Landscape in the Eighteenth Century." In *Studies in Eighteenth-Century British Art and Aesthetics,* edited by Ralph Cohen, pp. 49–81. Berkeley, 1985.
Ketcham, Michael G. *Transparent Designs: Reading, Performance, and Form in the "Spectator" Papers.* Athens, Ga., 1985.
Monk, Samuel H. *The Sublime: A Study of Critical Theories in Eighteenth-Century England* (1935). Ann Arbor, 1960.
Saccamano, Neil. "The Sublime Force of Words in Addison's 'Pleasures.'" *English Literary History* 58.1 (Spring 1991): 83–106.
Sitter, John. "About Wit: Locke, Addison, Prior, and the Order of Things." In *Rhetorics of Order/Ordering Rhetorics in English Neoclassical Literature,* edited by J. Douglas Canfield and J. Paul Hunter, pp. 137–157. Newark, Del., 1989.
Thorpe, Clarence D. "Addison and Hutcheson on the Imagination." *English Literary History* 2 (November 1935): 215–234.
Thorpe, Clarence D. "Addison's Theory of the Imagination as Perceptive Response." *Papers of the Michigan Academy of Science, Arts, and Letters* 21 (1936): 509–530.
Thorpe, Clarence D. "Addison's Contribution to Criticism." In *The Seventeenth Century: Studies in the History of English Thought and Literature from Bacon to Pope,* by Richard Foster Jones and others writing in his honor, pp. 316–329. Stanford, Calif., 1951.
Youngren, William H. "Addison and the Birth of Eighteenth-Century Aesthetics." *Modern Philology* 79.3 (1982): 267–283.

THOMAS FURNISS

ADORNO, THEODOR WIESENGRUND. [*This entry comprises five separate essays that clarify and contextualize Adorno's aesthetic theory:*

> Survey of Thought
> Adorno's Dialectic of Appearance
> Adorno and Mimesis
> Adorno's Philosophy of Music
> Adorno and Kant

The first essay is a survey of Adorno's philosophy in general and the Frankfurt school (Germany) of critical theory that he helped to establish in the 1930s. The other essays treat "appearance" and "mimesis," key concepts of Adorno's aesthetics; music, the art form he discusses most often; and Kant, one of the main philosophers in dialogue with whom he developed his aesthetic theory. For related discussions, see Marxism, *article on* Marxism and Materialism; *and* Sublime, *article on* The Sublime from Burke to the Present.]

Survey of Thought

Theodor W. Adorno (1903–1969) was a German philosopher, aesthetic theorist, and social theorist in the Western Marxist tradition, as well as a leading member of the first generation of critical theory. It is the combination of a modernist aesthetic sensibility with rigorous philosophical theory and biting social criticism that make *Aesthetic Theory,* his uncompleted *summa aesthetica,* as provocative and significant as it has proved to be.

Adorno grew up in Frankfurt am Main, where he attended the university and entered the professoriate prior to being expelled along with other Jewish scholars. During the Nazi era he resided in Oxford, New York City, and southern California, writing in exile several of the articles and books for which he would later become famous, including *Dialectic of Enlightenment* (with Max Horkheimer), *Philosophy of Modern Music, The Authoritarian Personality* (a collaborative project), and *Minima Moralia.* From these years come Adorno's landmark critiques of popular culture and the culture industry.

Returning to Frankfurt in the early 1950s, Adorno quickly established himself as a leading theorist and critic of high culture as well as a central figure in the Institute of Social Research. Founded in 1923, led by Max Horkheimer since 1930, and reopened in 1951, the institute was the hub for what has become known as the Frankfurt School. Adorno became the institute's director in 1958 and in that capacity supervised a number of pathbreaking interdisciplinary studies of contemporary social issues. During the 1950s he published *In Search of Wagner,* an ideology-critique of the Nazis' favorite composer; *Prisms,* a collection of social and cultural studies and the first of his books to be translated into English; *Against Epistemology,* an antifoundationalist critique of Husserlian phenomenology; and the first volume of *Notes to Literature,* a collection of essays in literary criticism.

The last decade of Adorno's life was marked by conflict and consolidation. A leading figure in the "positivism dispute" in German sociology, Adorno was also a key player in debates about restructuring German universities. He continued to publish at an astounding rate, including numerous volumes of music criticism, monographs on the composers Gustav Mahler and Alban Berg, two more volumes of *Notes to Literature,* books on Hegel and on existentialism, and collected essays in sociology and in aesthetics. *Negative Dialectics,* Adorno's magnum opus on epistemology and metaphysics, appeared in 1966. *Aesthetic Theory,* on which he had been working for most of the 1960s, appeared posthumously in 1970.

Although a torso, *Aesthetic Theory* marks the culmination of Adorno's multifaceted scholarship. In it are found all the conflicting impulses said by Martin Jay to make up the historical "force field" of Adorno's writings: "Western Marxism, aesthetic modernism, mandarin cultural despair, and Jewish self-identification, as well as the more anticipatory pull of deconstructionism" (1984, p. 22). Adorno's links to Marxism and his sophisticated dialectical critique of twentieth-century culture make him, in the words of Fredric Jameson, a "philosopher for the nineties," a crucial figure for these postmodern, post–cold war, postcolonial, poststructural, postanalytical, and, some would say, postaesthetic times.

Four topics in Adorno's writings are of particular relevance to contemporary aesthetics and cultural theory: (1) his critique of the culture industry, (2) autonomy in the arts, (3) the aesthetics of nature, and (4) the status of philosophical aesthetics.

The Culture Industry. Adorno's critique of the culture industry arose in part from his debate with Walter Benjamin in the 1930s over the implications of film and radio for the democratization of culture. Whereas Benjamin had suggested that film has a progressive impact on ordinary experience and can serve to politicize the masses, Adorno's 1938 essay "On the Fetish-Character in Music and the Regression of Listening" argues that the broadcast and recording industries resist musical innovation, make a fetish of commercial success, and promote the regression of both musical and political consciousness.

Adorno expanded his argument to include all the mass media in "The Culture Industry," a chapter in *Dialectic of Enlightenment* (1944). Under capitalist conditions, he says, artworks and other cultural artifacts are produced as commodities. According to Marx, commodities are products whose use value (their ability to satisfy human wants) is dominated by their exchange value (their ability to command other products in exchange). Capitalist commodity production also obscures the facts that human labor power is the source of value and that laborers must be exploited to

generate the surplus value from which capitalists make their profit.

Building on this Marxian analysis and on György Lukács's theory of "reification," Adorno argues that a new level of sophistication and obfuscation characterizes commodity production in advanced capitalism and both directs and hides within the culture industry. Under such conditions, cultural artifacts are mass-produced without regard for their use value, and their exchange value is presented *as* use value, as something to be enjoyed for its own sake. The culture industry pushes people to consume films, recordings, broadcast concerts, and the like, not so their filmic or musical qualities can be appreciated, but so they can become a commercial success—a "hit" or a "star." In this process, the consumer is a willing contributor. Twentieth-century capitalism has become, as it were, a self-celebrating system in which the cultural industry proves indispensable. Consequently, concerns about artistic quality become harder to raise, and the "masses," whose exploited labor keeps the system going, become less conscious of their genuine and unfulfilled needs. Both of these consequences, together with the "standardization" of culture in the service of economic and political power, are the target of Adorno's critique of the culture industry.

Critics of Adorno frequently describe his approach as elitist and monolithic, and not without reason. His published essays on jazz, for example, betray a failure to comprehend the ways in which African-American music has arisen from conditions of oppression and served emancipatory purposes. Yet the central theoretical claims in his critique remain relevant at a time when new mergers and globalization have swept the entertainment, telecommunications, and information industries. Without a theory of their economic underpinnings and cultural impact, such trends cannot be properly understood or evaluated.

Autonomy. According to Adorno, the emergence of advanced capitalism, with its ever-tighter fusion of state and economic power, does not leave the arts unaffected. Where these do not provide fodder for the culture industry apparatus, they become all the more alienated from mainstream society. Increased alienation does not lessen their social significance, however, for it gives them the distance needed for social critique and utopian projection. Moreover, the alienation of the arts from society is itself socially produced. Arts that resist the culture industry are, in a phrase from *Aesthetic Theory,* "the social antithesis of society" (1984, p. 11).

Adorno's account of artistic autonomy is highly complex. On the one hand, the independence of the arts from religious, political, and other social structures, as institutionalized and theorized in Western societies, creates a space where societal wounds can be exposed and alternative arrangements imagined. On the other hand, because such independence itself depends on the division of labor, class conflict, and the dominance in society of the capitalist "exchange principle," the space of exposure and imagination serves to shore up the societal system even as that space becomes internally problematic and externally irrelevant. As Adorno puts it at the beginning of *Aesthetic Theory*, referring to the modern art movements, absolute freedom in art stands in a contradiction with the abiding unfreedom of society as a whole. Yet it is only because of autonomy that certain works of art can achieve a critical and utopian "truth content" *(Wahrheitsgehalt)*, in the absence of which a fundamental transformation of society would be even more difficult to envision.

This complex position puts Adorno at odds not only with formalist approaches, which either assume or ignore art's social significance, but also with the socialist realism of Marxism-Leninism and the political commitment *(engagement)* promoted by Bertolt Brecht, Jean-Paul Sartre, and much of the New Left. The controversial claim in his 1962 essay "Commitment" must be situated in that polemical field: "This is not the time for political works of art," he writes; "rather, politics has migrated into the autonomous work of art, and it has penetrated most deeply into works that present themselves as politically dead . . ." (*Notes to Literature*, vol. 2, pp. 93–94).

Both societal structures and cultural contexts have shifted in the intervening years. The rise of new social movements such as feminism, ecology, and gay and lesbian liberation has helped turn the focus of cultural theory from autonomous works to emancipatory practices; postmodernism has challenged the normative assumptions built into modernist legitimations of high art; and the institutions of the art world—museums, publishers, symphony orchestras, and the like—have increasingly acknowledged and exploited their symbiotic relations with corporations, foundations, and the culture industry. Such developments cast doubt on the validity of Adorno's dialectical autonomism.

At the same time, however, concerns about the need for artistic autonomy have arisen within the new social movements, particularly in response to moralistic and antimodern pressures from a revitalized right. The increasing dependence of arts organizations on business strategies and corporate generosity has also raised questions about the future of alternative modes of artistic expression. Although Adorno's approach needs to be rethought in this environment, it nevertheless provides a crucial counterweight to prevailing assumptions about the social significance of the arts and their institutional frames.

Natural Beauty. Adorno himself was a master "rethinker." Much of the *Aesthetic Theory* can be read as a modernist reconceptualizing of philosophical aesthetics, especially the writings of Immanuel Kant and Georg Wilhelm Friedrich Hegel. Nowhere is this project more provocative than in Adorno's return to an aesthetics of nature. On the one hand, Adorno rejects Hegel's dismissal of natural beauty as inferior to the humanly produced beauty of art.

On the other hand, he also rejects Kant's reduction of natural beauty to an indefinite object of taste. Yet he also refuses either to celebrate natural beauty as such or to define its independent nature. Rather, he sketches a genealogy of the modern discourse of "natural beauty," and from this he identifies the referent in question as the trace of the nonidentical, which the arts seek to rescue, with unavoidably mixed results.

Initially, such an approach does not seem promising for the recently developed field of environmental aesthetics. Adorno does not so much theorize the aesthetic dimension of nature and daily life as challenge the assumption that these "have" an "aesthetic dimension." What is important about Adorno's approach, however, is his insistence that such matters are socially constructed within a political and economic system, and that any discourse of "natural beauty" must be linked to contemporary artistic practices.

More specifically, Adorno describes natural beauty as the trace of the nonidentical in things under the spell of universal identity. Amid its social construction as a category of alterity, that which is experienced as natural beauty reminds us that not everything is exchange value, not everything submits to the control of instrumental reason, not everything fits the grid of our definitions and categories. Contrary to Hegel, natural beauty is not deficient because it is indeterminate, but rather natural beauty is indeterminate because discursive thought is deficient. Among the various ways in which Western societies "relate" to "nature," only art has the capacity to preserve this trace of indeterminacy while giving it definite contours. In that capacity art not only challenges the dominance of exchange value and instrumental rationality but also raises the trace of the nonidentical into a hint of reconciliation between nature and culture, a reconciliation that would presuppose an end to class domination in society.

Closely related to this figure of art's "rescuing" natural beauty from sheer indeterminacy are Adorno's notions of "mimesis" and "expression" in art, which he usually pairs with "rationality" and "semblance" (Schein) as their dialectical opposites. Mimesis, a truly protean concept, refers to an archaic openness to the other, to the disparate, diffuse, and contrary. Such openness lives on in artworks whose form accommodates the conflicting impulses of their content. Successful artworks embody a mimetic rationality and thereby provide a crucial alternative to the control and reduction characterizing the instrumental rationality that prevails under capitalist conditions. Similarly, expression refers to a capacity to register that which impresses itself upon human experience despite the various control mechanisms set up by society and the psyche. In artworks such a capacity is mediated by the mimetic behavior that goes into artists' productive activity. The more expressive artworks become, the more their semblance of self-sufficiency is shaken, even though this semblance is required if artworks are to be expressions of something more than what society and the individual psyche permit.

Playing throughout such polarities is a continual reversal of the subject-object relation, such that the supposedly rational and controlling subject becomes an accomplice of the object, and the supposedly controlled and meaningless object begins to speak for itself. For Adorno, such a reversal—common in modern art—holds open the possibility that the alienation of subject and object, a central fissure within the dialectic of enlightenment, can itself be alienated, not only in art but also in other modes of social labor. In other words, a reconciliation between culture and nature, together with the lessening of social domination, is not out of the question. This is the underlying issue that an Adornoesque "environmental aesthetic" would have to address.

Aesthetic Theory. In some respects the reception of Adorno's aesthetics in Anglo-American philosophy has yet to begin, despite the many translations of his writings and the abundance of secondary literature from scholars in literature, music, cultural theory, religion, and the social sciences. In philosophy, and especially among Anglo-American philosophers, there has not been a serious engagement with Adorno's aesthetics on the scale of, say, the reception of Hans-Georg Gadamer's *Truth and Method*.

Many factors might account for this, not the least of which is the Habermasian turn in critical theory away from Adorno's traditional, albeit explosive, subject-object paradigm toward a theory of communicative and intersubjective rationality. The rise of poststructuralism and postmodernism have also made Adorno's dialectical method and paradoxical modernism seem outmoded. Then, too, the theme of a possible "end" of philosophy does not bode well for an author who unrelentingly rewrites the philosophical tradition. Add to this some unreliable translations, analytical philosophy's avoidance of difficult German thinkers, and the long ascendancy of Martin Heidegger among so-called continental philosophers, and the relative neglect of Adorno becomes understandable.

Yet few philosophers have been as well versed in contemporary art forms as he, and even fewer aestheticians have written so much of interest to the social sciences. Perhaps as aesthetics itself becomes ever more interdisciplinary and shades into cultural theory, Adorno's multifaceted aesthetics will receive the attention it so manifestly deserves.

An unavoidable topic in this connection is the status of what Adorno called, ambiguously enough, an aesthetic theory. Clearly, he does not intend to give a theory of the aesthetic. If anything, his book by that title provides what has been described as "a paratactical and dialectical phenomenology of (modern) art" (Zuidervaart, 1991, p. 45), where "phenomenology" is understood in a modified Hegelian and not Husserlian sense, and where the parentheses indicate that Adorno tries to derive insights into the entire field from the peculiarities and dilemmas of modern art.

Adorno refuses to posit an essence to the arts or to treat normative notions such as beauty or meaning as timeless universals. Yet he retains the assumption, derived from Hegel, that philosophical reflection is crucial for the proper reception of art. To do justice to the artistic phenomena, such reflection must itself be aesthetic, in the sense of incorporating that openness to the other that successful artworks embody. Hence the theory in question cannot take the form of straightforward analysis or deduction, but must construct constellations of concepts, hoping that their continually shifting light will illuminate the subject matter and do justice to its alterity. For this sort of writing, there is hardly any precedent, nor can there be an imitation. *Aesthetic Theory* is a singular achievement, which, although cut short by Adorno's untimely death in 1969, will continue to challenge well into the twenty-first century.

[*See also* Autonomy, *article on* Critique of Autonomy; Benjamin, *survey article;* Hegel; *and* Truth.]

BIBLIOGRAPHY

Works by Adorno

Aesthetic Theory. Edited by Gretel Adorno and Rolf Tiedemann, translated by C. Lenhardt. London and Boston, 1984. New translation by Robert Hullot-Kentor (Minneapolis, 1997).

Gesammelte Schriften. 20 vols. Edited by Gretel Adorno and Rolf Tiedemann. Frankfurt am Main, 1970–. Since 1993, the posthumous writings have followed in six subdivisions, edited by the T. W. Adorno Archives.

Notes to Literature. Edited by Rolf Tiedemann, translated by Shierry Weber Nicholsen. 2 vols. New York, 1991–1992.

Philosophy of Modern Music. Translated by Anne G. Mitchell and Wesley V. Blomster. New York, 1973.

Other Sources

Bernstein, J. M. *The Fate of Art: Aesthetic Alienation from Kant to Derrida and Adorno.* University Park, Pa., 1992.

Buck Morss, Susan. *The Origin of Negative Dialectics: Theodor W. Adorno, Walter Benjamin, and the Frankfurt Institute.* Hassocks, 1977.

Dews, Peter. *Logics of Disintegration: Post-structuralist Thought and the Claims of Critical Theory.* London and New York, 1987.

Habermas, Jürgen. *The Theory of Communicative Action.* Translated by Thomas McCarthy. 2 vols. Boston, 1984.

Huhn, Tom, and Lambert Zuidervaart, eds. *The Semblance of Subjectivity: Essays in Adorno's Aesthetic Theory.* Cambridge, Mass., 1997.

Jameson, Fredric. *Late Marxism: Adorno, or, the Persistence of the Dialectic.* London and New York, 1990.

Jay, Martin. *The Dialectical Imagination: A History of the Frankfurt School and the Institute of Social Research, 1923–1950.* Boston, 1973; reprint, Berkeley, 1996.

Jay, Martin. *Adorno.* Cambridge, Mass., 1984.

Lunn, Eugene. *Marxism and Modernism: An Historical Study of Lukács, Brecht, Benjamin, and Adorno.* Berkeley, 1982.

Roberts, David. *Art and Enlightenment: Aesthetic Theory after Adorno.* Lincoln, Nebr., 1991.

Roblin, Ronald, ed. *The Aesthetics of the Critical Theorists: Studies on Benjamin, Adorno, Marcuse, and Habermas.* Lewiston, N.Y., 1990.

Rose, Gillian. *The Melancholy Science: An Introduction to the Thought of Theodor W. Adorno.* London, 1978.

van Reijen, Willem, et al. *Adorno: An Introduction.* Translated by Dieter Engelbrecht. Philadelphia, 1992.

Wellmer, Albrecht. *The Persistence of Modernity: Essays on Aesthetics, Ethics, and Postmodernism.* Translated by David Midgley. Cambridge, Mass., 1991.

Wiggershaus, Rolf. *The Frankfurt School: Its History, Theory, and Political Significance.* Translated by Michael Robertson. Cambridge, Mass., 1994.

Wolin, Richard. *Walter Benjamin: An Aesthetic of Redemption.* 2d ed. Berkeley, 1994.

Zuidervaart, Lambert. *Adorno's Aesthetic Theory: The Redemption of Illusion.* Cambridge, Mass., 1991.

LAMBERT ZUIDERVAART

Adorno's Dialectic of Appearance

Adorno's aesthetic thinking, from his early music criticism in the 1920s to his late *Aesthetic Theory* of 1970, covers a wide range of aesthetic topics and literary and musical objects. His thinking is also articulated in a variety of forms: in criticism written for newspapers and journals; in essays, themselves aesthetically composed; in scholarly monographs, which treat the work of composers as well as the technical problems of musical education and composition; and in philosophical reflections on the central problems of aesthetics and art theory. Nevertheless, one philosophical motif lies at the very heart of Adorno's aesthetic thinking in all of its forms and stages. This is the moment of a "dialectic of (aesthetic) appearance" *(Dialektik des Scheins)* that Adorno tried to formulate in ever new ways from *Kierkegaard,* his first book, to *Aesthetic Theory,* his last.

The "Right" of Aesthetic Appearance: Kierkegaard. The first formulation of the idea of a "dialectic of aesthetic appearance" can be found in the richly anticipatory final chapter of Adorno's *Habilitationsschrift,* published in 1933 as *Kierkegaard: Construction of the Aesthetic* (*Gesammelte Schriften* [hereafter *GS*], vol. 2). In a review of this work, Walter Benjamin suggested "that the later [books] of the author would arise from this one," a comment that proved to be prescient. According to Adorno, appearance is the definition of aesthetics as the domain of the unreal, of "images." Its "dialectic" consists in that aesthetic *appearance* is also the place of *truth.*

Herein lie both Adorno's nearness to and distance from Søren Kierkegaard. With Kierkegaard, Adorno distances himself from the "neutrality," with which aesthetics usually "looks at" art "without ever seriously asking about its fundamental right" *(Recht).* Kierkegaard had criticized the aesthetic as a domain of *mere* appearance. Aesthetic theory cannot escape this criticism, for it must confront the question of the *right* of aesthetic appearance.

Unlike Kierkegaard, however, Adorno answers this question in the affirmative. According to Adorno, Kierkegaard's critique of aesthetic appearance depends on a false concept of the latter. It is false because it overlooks the "dialectical course" of aesthetic appearance. This dialectic consists in the self-questioning of appearance. More precisely, it is the ("dialectical") achievement of *art* to question aesthetic appearance. Appearance is a closed, unitary, meaningful counter-reality. Art allows this appearance to "disintegrate": it is "fragment," "riddle," "ruin," "caesura," "error"—that is, the *dissolution* of aesthetic and apparent unity and closure.

In Adorno's concept of a "dialectic of appearance," dissolution is bound up with two aspects. The *internal* aspect is the questioning of aesthetic appearance in art: the dissolution of the appearance of unity, closure, and meaning in each individual work of art. The *external* aspect is the overstepping of aesthetic appearance into truth, which *thereby* takes place in art. It is Adorno's fundamental conviction that the "disintegration" of aesthetic appearance is the "trace" of truth. Furthermore, we know truth not as "devoid of appearance," but only *through* the dialectic of aesthetic appearance. Therein lies what Adorno calls the "redemption" of the "aesthetic in its downfall."

Critique of the Culture Industry: On Jazz and Dialectic of Enlightenment. The concept of a "dialectic of (aesthetic) appearance" forms the backdrop to Adorno's aesthetic works (devoted above all to music) of the 1930s and 1940s. At the center of his interest, however, is not the successful fulfillment of the dialectic of appearance, but rather its *breaking off* in the aesthetic phenomena of mass culture. "Music in the managed world"—the subtitle of the volume entitled *Dissonances* (1956; *GS,* vol. 14)—is a music that is *only* appearance, without "dialectical" conversion into truth. It is a music that conforms in undifferentiated and "dreamless" fashion to existing society. Here aesthetic appearance is "mere" appearance, and that means ideological appearance.

Adorno describes this first in two essays published in the *Zeitschrift für Sozialforschung (Journal for Social Research):* "On Jazz" (1937; *GS,* vol. 17) and "On the Fetish-Character in Music and the Regression of Hearing" (1938; *GS,* vol. 14). Both essays are directed against the interpretation of mass culture that Benjamin had undertaken for film. Benjamin had described the manner of film's reception as one of "distraction" and seen therein a positive potential of disintegrating traditional aesthetic "aura." Adorno, in contrast, judges this change in aesthetic reception to be a "regression," a loss of those capacities without which there can be no art at all.

In addition to judging the aesthetic phenomena of mass culture differently than Benjamin, Adorno describes them differently. Adorno finds the same "distraction" that Benjamin had emphasized in film in the "atomistic" listening to jazz, which is directed to single, unintegrated moments of stimulus. But the "breakout" of these moments, experienced in sensual pleasure, is illusionary; in jazz, it remains bound by an "iron discipline." Jazz "accomplishes normalization and individualization at the same time."

In the chapter entitled "Culture Industry: Enlightenment as Mass Deception" in the *Dialectic of Enlightenment,* written with Max Horkheimer (1947; *GS*, vol. 3), Adorno sets these analyses into a larger theoretical framework. Following and radicalizing Karl Marx and György Lukács as well as Arthur Schopenhauer and Friedrich Nietzsche, this framework consists of a historico-philosophical description of contemporary society as a state of total reification: a state in which the principle of compulsive, external unity ("identity") rules over the moments of qualitative specificity (as Adorno would later say, "the non-identical"). This state governs all levels, both of society and of the individual, of knowledge and morality.

Against this background of a philosophy of history and a critique of society, Adorno formulates his thesis of a loss of aesthetic "truth" taking place in the culture industry. The art forms of the culture industry are "untrue" for Adorno, because they merely "repeat" existing societal relations; they "absolutize imitation." For Adorno, art is "true" if it knows social relations as "negative," as alienated and reified. Art can do this only where it "goes beyond" existing social reality—where it anticipates that which is not possible in alienated society. Thus, art is "true" for Adorno, not where it imitates reality, but only where it is other than the real: "Useless and fragile beauty . . . means a protest against a hardened, reified society." Art has lost this force of protest in the culture industry.

Aesthetic Subjectivity: In Search of Wagner and Philosophy of Modern Music. Adorno's critique of the culture industry is, as many critics have objected, not free from elitist presumptions regarding popular art. It follows, however, the much more general program of confronting aesthetic phenomena with the question of their "right," their "truth," that Adorno had set out in *Kierkegaard.* Adorno understands this question to be critical of society, and he asks it not only of the culture industry and mass culture, but also of so-called serious art: in *In Search of Wagner* (1939/52; *GS*, vol. 13) and the *Philosophy of Modern Music* (1940/48; *GS*, vol. 12).

In both books, Adorno is concerned with indicating a change in musical "technique," which either anticipates the aesthetic regression of the culture industry (Richard Wagner) or accompanies it (Igor Stravinsky). The normative model on which this critique is based is the "construction of complete musical unity in multiplicity"; Adorno takes this idea from Viennese classicism and, above all, from Ludwig van Beethoven. This model breaks apart in Wagner and Stravinsky, where the individual moment becomes independent at the cost of the constructive, synthetic tendency of music. As he had done earlier with jazz, Adorno described this in the case of Wagner and Stravinsky as "regression." At the same time, however, Adorno points to the consistency, even legitimacy, of this independence of the particular from unity: for it means also a release from false, "repressive" unity.

Above all, *In Search of Wagner* and the *Philosophy of Modern Music* mark a new step in Adorno's aesthetics, in that

both make fruitful use of the fundamental category of the *Dialectic of Enlightenment* in a context of (music) aesthetics: namely, the concept of subjectivity. For Horkheimer and Adorno, "dialectic of enlightenment" means that social reification is the result of the tendencies of enlightenment toward the emancipation of the subject: that is, tendencies that had originally gone in the opposite direction from that reification. Enlightenment can only realize this emancipatory goal as domination, as control of outer and inner nature. In this, a reversion of the emancipation of the subject into reification takes place.

Adorno also now defines the connection of art and society in terms of "subjectivity." This connection is not a matter of the "content" of artworks, but rather of their "technique." Thus, the technical structure of a work of art is defined by the form of the "aesthetic subject" that produces it. Thus, Adorno describes the aesthetic subject in Wagner's music as the bourgeois subject, which has "shrunk" to a private individual, and which "renounces sovereignty, lets itself fall into the archaic, onto the ground of drives" *(Triebgrund).* In this the aesthetic subject is socially determined: the "regression" of the aesthetic subject into a mere state of nature, without the force to produce valid form, corresponds to the fate of the "social subject" and to the latter's loss of autonomy.

Similar in content, but using a much clearer method, the *Philosophy of Modern Music* describes Stravinsky's music as a "virtuoso act of regression," which ratifies the "social liquidation of the subject." At the same time, the *Philosophy of Modern Music* repeats the critique of aesthetic "depersonalization," and not only in the section devoted to Stravinsky. In its first large section, devoted to Arnold Schoenberg and twelve-tone music, Adorno describes a form of aesthetic subjectivity that is both contrary to Stravinsky's and yet precisely complementary to it. The aesthetic subject of twelve-tone music is not the late bourgeois subject that has regressed to mere individuality, as it is in Wagner and Stravinsky. Instead, it is the attempt to realize yet again via technical means the "primordially bourgeois longing" to realize "the control of nature in music." This program of the "technical work of art," which seeks to attain "total organization" through "total rationality," must "fail," however, for "the integral work of art is an absolutely senseless one."

Thus, in the *Philosophy of Modern Music,* aesthetic subjectivity splits into two extremes: natural-amorphous expression, on the one hand, and rational control, on the other. For Adorno, both extremes, and their division from each other, are socially determined, as an expression of the fatal "dialectic," which allows the emancipation of the subject to end in the "managed world." Further, both forms of aesthetic subjectivity are incapable of producing an art that can still claim "truth," that is, a critical difference from society. The sentence in "Culture Criticism and Society" in which Adorno summed up this pessimistic diagnosis reads: "Cultural criticism finds itself faced with the last stage of the dialectic of culture and barbarism: to write a poem after Auschwitz is barbarous" (1949; *GS*, vol. 10).

The Disintegration of Aesthetic Appearance: *Notes to Literature*. When Adorno returned to Frankfurt after the war, he continued his studies on music theory and music criticism, along with his investigations of epistemology, social philosophy, and the critique of culture. In addition, during this period his concern with literature gained increasing meaning. The texts that he produced were collected in three volumes with the title *Notes to Literature* (1958–1965; *GS*, vol. 11). The first text in the first volume has the programmatic title "The Essay as a Form." Here Adorno stresses the "anti-systematic impulsion" of the essay. The essay follows no method and applies no rules and boundaries, but is rather the expression of an open spiritual experience, which is realized in reading.

Thus, it is impossible to subsume the wealth of insights and considerations that are collected in Adorno's literary-critical essays under any one common factor. At the center of Adorno's interest, however, is again and again the experience of the questioning and dissolution of aesthetic meaning that modern literature opens up. The aesthetic experience of the dissolution of meaning is the content, at once divergent and common, of the authors Adorno interprets—from Friedrich Hölderlin's paratactical breaks and Joseph von Eichendorff's linguistic rustling to the becoming independent of language in the poetry of Stefan George, Rudolf Borchardt, and Paul Valéry, the allegorical prose of Franz Kafka, and the splintered dramas of Samuel Beckett.

What is new in Adorno's literary-critical description of aesthetic dissolution of meaning is not the phenomenon itself, but its interpretation. Continuing the programmatic openness of the essay, Adorno's *Notes to Literature* leads beyond the system of the *Dialectic of Enlightenment,* on which the analysis of aesthetic subjectivity in the *Philosophy of Modern Music* was based. Adorno does relate the aesthetic dissolution of meaningful unity back to the social dialectic that lets subjectivity be converted to reification. But Adorno now insists more decisively than previously on two things. First, he no longer understands the aesthetic dissolution of meaning as a consequence or expression of the social fate of the subject. Now—and most exemplarily in the essay on Beckett—he understands art in such a way that it *reflects* the social situation; that is, art represents *and* criticizes the "omnipresent regression," so that it makes a "protocol" out of it and thereby "protests" against it.

The second new aspect of Adorno's literary-critical essays is that they no longer judge the dissolution of aesthetic meaning from the perspective of a normative concept of the "integral" work of art, which was derived from classical bourgeois art. Adorno now describes the aesthetic dissolution of meaning positively, above all in his interpretations of poetry from Eichendorff to George and Borchardt. Two

motives are combined in this: first, language's becoming independent in a sonorous "rustling," in which language, free from intentional meaning and the intention of speakers, speaks "itself," so that, second, there arises *through this* the bursting of the unity of the I in a nonregressive experience of its "self-extinction." The "fragmentation" and "depersonalization," which Adorno had until now described predominantly negatively, now appear as a positive aesthetic achievement. Adorno recognizes its ground in the immanent logic of the work of art, which is a "logic of disintegration" of closed meaning and (self-) ruling subject.

Through two aspects, Adorno's aesthetic thought frees itself from the compulsions of the systematism it had followed since the early 1950s (thereby returning to motifs from *Kierkegaard*). Aesthetic dissolution of sense is no mere symptom, but rather the medium of a critical reflection of the social crisis of sense and subjectivity. The aesthetic dissolution of meaning does not signify mere decadence, but rather the stringent and pleasurable dissolution of aesthetic meaning and subject.

The "Breakthrough" of Musical Unity: *Mahler* and *Berg*. Parallel to his literary criticism in the 1950s and 1960s, Adorno also wrote a myriad of music-critical and music-theoretical texts, which describe the two aspects of aesthetic dissolution of meaning. This is shown in exemplary fashion in *Mahler: A Musical Physiognomy* (1960; *GS*, vol. 13), at the center of which stands the "critique of the appearance" of a successful musical unity. Musical stringency consists not in a "disempowering of the multiple" through its integration in unity, but in the refusal of this unity in the stress on the traits of the musical material that are irreducibly strange and not fully assimilable. For Adorno, the central achievement of Mahler's music lies in its making the "breakthrough" of the moments through the aesthetic unity, and that of the material through aesthetic meaning, into its artistic principle of organization.

Adorno assigns a double social significance to this characteristic of Mahler's music: critique and redemption. The questioning of aesthetic unity and meaning is *critical* because it refuses to produce an illusion of reconciliation and reflects the social "split between subject and object." Above all, however, through the questioning of aesthetic unity and meaning, a *redemption* of the incommensurable and plural is effected, of what cannot be integrated without violence. In this "gesture" consists music's "promise."

Adorno's other musical works from this period, such as *Berg: The Master of the Smallest Transition* (1968; *GS*, vol. 13), make clear the degree to which his normative ideas have changed since the *Philosophy of Modern Music*. Adorno now defines the success of aesthetic unity *as* its failure (as the failure of aesthetic unity in the traditional sense): that is, as a questioning and self-surrender of aesthetic unity that is not immediate and naive, but strict and formed. With this aesthetic transvaluation, the social significance of art is transformed: art no longer points to the social split between subject and object, but develops a concept of success beyond the utopia of a seamless identity of subject and object.

A Summation: *Aesthetic Theory*. *Aesthetic Theory* (*GS*, vol. 7), which was published posthumously in 1970, is the sum of Adorno's aesthetic thought. In this work, Adorno once again develops all the important themes of his theory of art. Until now, following the example of authors like Friedrich Schlegel, Nietzsche, and Benjamin, Adorno had written about art virtually exclusively via interpretation and criticism of specific artistic phenomena. General aesthetic insights were meant to result from this specific criticism, but could not be separated out from it. In *Aesthetic Theory,* this relationship is inverted: the reference to individual phenomena remains evident, but the goal is the development of a general *theory.*

At the center of *Aesthetic Theory* are still the two aspects of a "dialectic of appearance" that Adorno had sketched out in *Kierkegaard:* the dissolution of appearance in art and the conversion of appearance into truth that results from this.

Thus, *Aesthetic Theory* seeks to systematically reconstruct the dissolution of aesthetic appearance that is *internal to art* and had been announced in the literary and musical criticism of the postwar period. In doing so, it becomes clear that aesthetic appearance takes two opposing forms: the appearance of an integral unity of the work and the appearance of the immediacy of its individual moments. Against the appearance of integral unity, Adorno mobilizes the modernist experience of the constitutive fragility of every aesthetic coherence. The moments make themselves independent relative to their unity. This does not, however, mean that they "literally" have significance in their immediacy, for they are irrevocably mediated through their unity. The "dialectical" movement between the two poles— independence and the mediation of the moments—defines the specific "processuality" of the artwork.

Aesthetic Theory offers a whole series of conceptual pairs to describe the poles of this movement from ever new perspectives: totality and moment, construction and mimesis, meaning and letter, spirit and material, processuality and objectivity. For Adorno, only tension-laden *pairs* of concepts can do justice to the "dialectical" constitution of the artwork. Moreover no *one* pair of concepts alone is adequate; instead, a "constellation" of various pairs of concepts is needed.

The second large theme that *Aesthetic Theory* takes up again is the "external" aspect of the dialectic of aesthetic appearance: its conversion into "truth." Adorno speaks of the "truth" of art in its relation to existing and reified society. Art is a *fait social,* but is only "true" where it is simultaneously more than this, as the "other" of society. Art gains this otherness relative to social reification through the dissolution of aesthetic appearance. Thus, art succeeds in exploding the "false," socially pre-given forms of unity—meaning and subjectivity. In doing this it opens an experience of the individual moments as both mediated and independent at the same time: as particular and "non-identical."

As much as *Aesthetic Theory* owes to this impulse to think of art as the medium of truth, it also reflects clearly on the difficulties of formulating this in an aesthetically consistent manner. For Adorno, to speak of the truth of art should not (and cannot) mean the reduction of art to a comprehensible and statable "truth content." Rather, art is true precisely in its refusal of any comprehensible and statable content, in its "enigmatic character." One may then ask how it is possible to speak of "truth" at all with regard to this rupture with all comprehension and statement in art. *Aesthetic Theory* in no way overlooked this difficulty; it circles around it in paradoxes, which seem insoluble to it: "The truth of discursive knowledge is unveiled, but knowledge thus does not possess it; the knowledge which art is, has this truth, but only as something incommensurate to it."

BIBLIOGRAPHY

Works by Adorno

Gesammelte Schriften. 20 vols. Edited by Gretel Adorno and Rolf Tiedemann. Frankfurt am Main, 1970–.
Kompositionen. 2 vols. Edited by Heinz-Klaus Metzger and Rainer Riehn. Munich, 1980.

Other Sources

Brunkhorst, Hauke. *Theodor W. Adorno: Dialektik der Moderne.* Munich, 1990.
Friedeberg, Ludwig von, and Jürgen Habermas, eds. *Adorno-Konferenz, 1983.* Frankfurt am Main, 1983.
Lindner, Burkhardt, and W. Martin Ludke, eds. *Materialien zur ästhetischen Theorie T. W. Adornos Konstruktion der Moderne.* Frankfurt am Main, 1980.
Reijen, Willem van. *Adorno zur Einführung.* 4th ed. Hanover, 1990.
Scheible, Hartmut. *Theodor W. Adorno: mit Selbstzeugnissen und Bilddokumenten.* Reinbek, 1989.
Wiggershaus, Rolf. *Theodor W. Adorno.* Munich, 1987.

CHRISTOPH MENKE

Adorno and Mimesis

Theodor W. Adorno claimed that his philosophy, by virtue of its essence, would resist all summarization. He countered the requirements of the Cartesian method with a conception of form based on the essay style and the play of shifting constellations. In keeping with this view, he never explicated the concept of mimesis in any single, comprehensive treatment. The significance of the concept can only be gathered by exploring the individual constellations in which it appears. This structuralist procedure yields a series of concepts—imitation, mimicry, sympathy, inner nature, expression, identification, idiosyncrasy, affinity, elective affinity, similarity, and differentiation—that are centered on three loci: anthropology, a theory of drives, and epistemology. The concept of mimesis, therefore, has primary significance for these (three) discourses (anthropology, drive theory, epistemology). The basic figure of mimesis is that of a sensitive faculty—to be understood as ontogenetic and phylogenetic—that holds the dual function of assuring the self-preservation of the naturally and socially weak subject and serving to cultivate humanity.

Characteristically, when Adorno defines the concept of mimesis, he does not refer to the philosophical tradition of aesthetics that commences with Plato, but rather cites two contemporary authors: Sigmund Freud and Roger Caillois. In the *Dialectic of Enlightenment,* which introduced the concept of mimesis into critical theory in systematic fashion, he defines it as "the tendency, which resides deep in the living to lose oneself in the environment . . . the inclination to let oneself go and sink back into nature. Freud called it the death instinct, Caillois 'le mimétisme.'" Thus, from the outset Adorno situates the aesthetic significance of the concept within an extensive context: the philosophy of history and the critique of civilization predicated upon cultural anthropology and psychoanalysis. Accordingly, in the *Dialectic of Enlightenment,* "imitation" *(Nachahmung)* is the central concept in the history of civilization from prehistoric times to the present. Primordially, and in one essential aspect, the history of the human species is no different from that of other natural species: imitation of nature in the sign of terror *(im Zeichen des Schreckens).* This remains true even when the civilization makes increasing attempts to override the mimetic, context-sensitive behavior that continually confronts the individual with the threat of a loss of identity. As this overriding of the mimetic impulse proves, in psychoanalytic terms, to be a repression, that which is repressed returns. The return of the repressed forms a part of the unholy dialectic of a one-sided enlightenment.

At this point, one must be clear about the dual meaning of the concept of nature in Adorno. On the one hand, it represents the inorganic, the lifeless, the dead, the spatially external relation that gains primacy via instrumental rationality. On the other hand, the concept of nature represents the temporally antecedent and the historically prior *(historische Zurückliegende),* which is subjected to the repressions of the civilizing process and which various forms of regression seek to reestablish. In this second sense, the concept of nature refers primarily to the history of the individual, to the structure of the drives and affects of the human being, and therefore refers specifically to "inner nature."

This twofold meaning corresponds to a twofold evaluation. It applies to both the concept of nature and the concept of mimesis. First, in reference to the relation to inner nature, mimesis destabilizes the subject—reduces it to a mere sequence of isolated moments of presence and resembles the mimicry performed by small animals. Adorno qualifies this mimesis as "false mimesis." At the same time, mimesis eludes the dominance of the ego in the same act. Because it counteracts the identity (of the ego), something

remains impervious to domination; to this extent, mimesis is "the representative of the undamaged life right in the middle of the damaged one." Second, in reference to the relation to outer nature, mimesis facilitates domination because it, too, if only minimally, distances and alienates nature. At the same time, however, it does not yet presuppose that unity of nature that provides the substratum of domination for the concept and instrumental rationality; thus, in magic, the rites of the shaman are not addressed to substances or specimens, but to the wind, the rain, the snake, or the demon in those who are ill.

Analogous to mimesis, nature reveals itself in two moments: as inner and outer nature. As a spatially external relation, it supplies the substratum not only of domination, but also of emancipation, which is to say, the substratum for the self-assertion of the human species. As the temporally primary, as something amorphous, as the undifferentiated state in which subject and outside world are not yet separated and which psychoanalysis calls "primary narcissism," nature reminds us of the absence of domination and at the same time of unfreedom, for Adorno sets the emergence from nature as a condition of freedom; in the tradition stretching from Thomas Hobbes through Immanuel Kant and Friedrich Schiller to Georg Wilhelm Friedrich Hegel and Karl Marx—the partial validity of which is thus recognized by Adorno in this respect—nature is not ascribed any normative status. By and large, however, the double character of nature in Adorno brings him closest to Friedrich Nietzsche. The fear of death accompanies the longing for reconciliation, because nature—its telos as supplied by memory—is highly ambivalent.

The equivocal and ambivalent concept of nature, as well as that of mimesis, is more narrowly defined by Adorno with the aid of two psychological concepts, each bearing the same epistemological relevance: projection and identification. These also have a twofold sense and are subject to twofold evaluation. In the *Dialectic of Enlightenment* Adorno notes three phases in the history of mimesis: the archaic-biological, the magical, and the historical-bourgeois phases. In the final phase, beginning already with Homer's Odysseus, the dialectic of (instrumental) rationality and mimesis present in the first phase is realized: "The ratio which supplants mimesis is not simply its counterpart. It is itself mimesis: mimesis unto death." Nature is the object of imitation not as a changeable, animated nature, but as a unified and, in this sense, dead nature. Thus, it is nothing but a "false projection." Rationalistic mimesis, which is practiced at the level of the established ego, is the projection of the fixed, persistent identity onto what was once alive. Since the reflection of reason comes about as "conscious projection," however, true mimesis must be understood as a projection that is both unconscious and correct. If psychoanalysis defines (false) projection as the transference of the subject's tabooed impulses onto the object, then (correct) projection in Adorno should be defined as the transference of unrepressed impulses. Outer nature is thus the projection of inner nature, or to express it epistemologically, the object is the subject's constitutum. This again, however, should be taken in a twofold sense: As controllable and repressed, nature forms the projection of the fixed, the persistent, the identical—an achievement paradigmatic of instrumental rationality. As uncontrollable and unrepressed, nature forms the projection of the yielding, the changeable, and the nonidentical—an achievement paradigmatic of mimesis.

The concept of identification confirms this. Adorno distinguishes between reflective-psychological and transitive-logical definitions of it. In the first case, it is a question of the identification of an object, in the second of the identification with human beings and things. Under the "reflective-psychological" sense, Adorno further differentiates between alter-centric and ego-centric identification. In the first case, the subject identifies itself with another subject or object and makes an intentional movement toward the other. In the second case, the subject identifies another subject or object with itself and can thus only understand the other to the extent that this other resembles (the subject) itself. Ultimately, the "transitive-logical" identification presupposes the "reflective psychological" in Adorno: to identify an object correctly, one must identify *with* it correctly, that is to say, alter-centrically.

The constant ambivalence that runs through Adorno's work and its endeavor to historicize the concept of mimesis should make clear—and this may not be overlooked—that Adorno does not adopt the anthropological (that is, antihistorical and antisociological) implications of Freud's hypothesis concerning the death drive or Caillois's biologization of social relations.

Ultimately, Adorno sees art or the "aesthetic mode of conduct" as heir to the biological-archaic and magical-cultic mimesis. He grounds this thesis by reference to historical materialism and psychoanalysis. In the preface to *A Critique of Political Economy,* Marx indicates that the superstructure does not necessarily change at the same pace as the economic foundations, but rather proceeds more quickly or more slowly. In the case of the artistic superstructure, the change can be so slow as to be mistaken for stagnation. The "cultural lag," to use the parlance of modern sociology, is most pronounced in the case of art. For this reason, it is able to retain "remnants" of biological and magical mimesis. A second reason for this is predicated upon psychoanalytic theory. For psychoanalysis, mimetic remnants are "regressive": culture depends upon the suppression of drives, and suppressed drives find expression in various forms of regression. Therefore a cultural medium that preserves access to the regressive can become a reservoir of critique. In Adorno's view, this medium is art because it alone can block the repressive authority—instrumental rationality (perfected under capitalism). Art represents "full"

rationality, not a one-sided and repressive rationality, and, as Adorno positively intimates, its standard lies in the "potential" of human beings and even of nature.

[*See also* Mimesis.]

BIBLIOGRAPHY

Works by Adorno

Ästhetische Theorie. In *Gesammelte Schriften,* vol. 7, edited by Gretel Adorno and Rolf Tiedemann. Frankfurt am Main, 1970.
Dialectic of Enlightenment. Co-written by Max Horkheimer, translated by John Cumming. New York, 1972.
Minima Moralia: Reflections from Damaged Life. Translated by E. F. N. Jephcott. London, 1974.

Other Sources

Früchtl, Josef. *Mimesis: Konstellation eines Zentralbegriffs bei Adorno.* Würzburg, 1986.
Jay, Martin. "Mimesis und Mimetologie: Adorno und Lacoue-Labarthe." In *Auge und Affekt: Wahrnehmung und Interaktion,* edited by Gertrud Koch, pp. 175–201. Frankfurt am Main, 1995.
Kager, Reinhard. *Herrschaft und Versöhnung: Einführung in das Denken Theodor W. Adornos.* Frankfurt am Main and New York, 1988.
Schultz, Karla L. *Mimesis on the Move: Theodor W. Adorno's Concept of Imitation.* Bern and New York, 1990.

JOSEF FRÜCHTL

Adorno's Philosophy of Music

Alban Berg, with whom Adorno studied composition in 1925, believed his pupil would have to decide "in favor of Kant *or* Beethoven." Berg had become "thoroughly convinced" that Adorno had "a calling to achieve the highest in the realm of deepest insight into music (in all its hitherto unexamined aspects, whether philosophical, art-historical, theoretical, social, historical, etc.) and to fulfill that calling in the form of great philosophical works" (Adorno, *Gesammelte Schriften* [hereafter *GS*], vol. 19, p. 635). Two decades later Thomas Mann would appreciate these talents, now fully developed, and freely draw on them when enlisting Adorno's advice, both philosophical and technical, on the musical aspects of his magnum opus, *Doktor Faustus* (1947). As Mann wrote in *Die Entstehung des Doktor Faustus: Roman eines Romans* (1949), his account of the novel's genesis (an account whose published form downplays the extent of the adviser's substantial contribution): "All his life this remarkable intellect refused to choose between a career in philosophy and one in music. He was too convinced that in the two divergent realms he was really pursuing the same thing" (as quoted in Richard Winston and Clara Winston [translators], *The Story of a Novel: The Genesis of Doctor Faustus,* 1961). Mann's description of Adorno's professional profile points to an inevitable preoccupation with aesthetics that Berg had rightly perceived as Adorno's calling. Yet although he was no Beethoven, or even a Berg, Adorno never gave up composition. Over a career of uncommon productivity lasting forty-nine years (the first of his numerous publications dates from 1920), he successfully combined his diverse interests and skills—in philosophy, sociology, belles-lettres, and musical composition—to produce a body of work matched in substance and influence by few other twentieth-century thinkers. (His compositional oeuvre comprising some thirty works has received a certain amount of critical attention, though it is generally unknown.)

Despite and also because of Adorno's huge influence, the significance of his musical aesthetics is equivocal. Depending on the perspective from which they are viewed, his writings can be characterized by either the breadth or the narrowness of their focus, by either their radical modernity or their conservative subservience to tradition. Either way, they declare an unswerving commitment to an intellectual elitism that has engaged even Adorno's detractors, who have variously criticized his work as arrogantly out of touch and rebarbatively snobbish. Of his lifework, assembled in the twenty volumes of the *Collected Works* and nearly as many supplementary volumes (most of the latter yet to be published), about a third is devoted expressly to music. His musicological chef d'oeuvre, now available as one of those supplementary volumes, was to be a study of Ludwig van Beethoven, which occupied him sporadically for thirty-six years. Ironically and perhaps also fittingly, it remained a fragment.

Adorno's nearest predecessor was Friedrich Nietzsche, an abundantly literate philosopher who not only wrote extensively about music but, like Adorno, also composed. The parallel extends beyond the evident centrality of music in their lives—in both their philosophical thought and their technical expertise and connoisseurship—to the terse, aphoristic style that each cultivated as a reaction against the system philosophy of German idealism. If Adorno also eschewed professorial pedantry as fervently as Nietzsche did, he was seemingly immune to the latter's caustically ironic tone, as a comparison of their writings on Richard Wagner reveals. Nor was there much room in his work for the kind of sarcastic humor that Nietzsche reveled in. The topics Adorno addressed and the way he addressed them were strictly serious. Whether in large books or short reviews, he mastered a form of higher criticism to which many have aspired but only a few have achieved. His gnomic, lofty style, as unmistakable as it is inimitable, insinuated itself into the minds of two generations of postwar German intellectuals. Coming from the pens of lesser minds, Adorno-isms turn all too easily into irritatingly empty mannerisms. The language and content of his prose are one, as the mixed success of numerous translations demonstrates.

For all of his fundamental critique, most explicit in the *Negative Dialectics,* Adorno's debt to Georg Wilhelm Friedrich Hegel was enormous, itself a demonstration of a dialectical relationship. Emblematic of this relationship are the three quotations from Hegel that head the introduction and two halves of Adorno's best-known and most frequently cited work on music, the *Philosophy of Modern Music* (1949). The first quotation, in particular, from Hegel's *Aesthetics,* can stand as a motto for Adorno's entire approach to aesthetics: "In art we are dealing not with a merely pleasurable or useful plaything, but with . . . an unfolding of truth."

The spirit of Hegel is never more palpable than in the concept of "musical material," which informs Adorno's musical thinking from early on. It surfaces as early as 1928 in a notice of Kurt Weill's *Three Penny Opera.* The enormous commercial success of this work along with the means employed to achieve it posed a critical dilemma for "progressive intellectuals," as Adorno described them, and by implication for himself. Igor Stravinsky had made comparable use of "dead music," and although Adorno acknowledged the parallel, he was rarely so charitable about the Russian master:

> How distant I at first feel from music that does not draw any consequences from the current state of musical material, but rather seeks its effect by transforming old, atrophied material: Weill achieves this effect with such force and originality that, faced with the fact, the objection pales. In Weill there is regression, one which exposes the demonic traits of dead music and uses them.   (*GS,* vol. 19, p. 137)

In his subsequent writings, Adorno's concept of "musical material" would gradually become a *terminus technicus.* Crudely put, in a way that might make Adorno balk, "material" is the musical manifestation or (to use Adorno's own expression) "sedimentation" of "objective spirit" *(objektiver Geist),* which in Hegel's philosophy of history pertains to legal and moral aspects of the world spirit. Material, then, is not the stuff of descriptive music theory but of prescriptive and proscriptive aesthetics. It is not the raw material of music given by nature, something essentially pre-musical and available to composers at any time, but, as Adorno would say, is "historical through and through." In the *Philosophy of Modern Music,* he writes not just of a "state" of musical material but also of a "tendency," a historical dictate that composers ignore at the price of consigning themselves to the forces of reaction and regression. Hence the headings for the book's two halves: "Schoenberg and Progress" and "Stravinsky and Restauration."

For the postwar musical avant-garde in Germany and beyond, the *Philosophy of Modern Music* became a canonical text, not only informing critical sensibilities but guiding the very history of musical composition. As the doyen of postwar German music critics Joachim Kaiser put it, his generation received from Adorno's tract "the analytical utensils . . . for diagnosing that which was inadequate or neoclassical or . . . no longer permitted by the world spirit." Yet in the same tract, which Adorno wanted to be understood as an "extended excursus to *Dialectic of Enlightenment*," he had also drawn attention to the "fetishism of the tone-row," as he described Anton von Webern's precompositional rationalization of material. Born of subjective freedom, rationalization may turn (and for Adorno did turn) into its opposite, unfreedom: a fetish in the strict Marxist sense. And it was from Webern's approach to twelve-tone composition that the postwar generation took its cue. For Adorno, Arnold Schoenberg was never "dead," as he was for Pierre Boulez and his contemporaries.

The aesthetic yardstick of the *Philosophy of Modern Music* was supplied not by Schoenberg's twelve-tone compositions, still less Webern's, as much as they may have embodied the current state of musical material, but by the earlier, pre–World War I works, especially the monodrama *Erwartung*, which linked the composer of so-called free atonality so compellingly with the Expressionist movement. "Expressionist music," Adorno writes, "took quite literally the principle of expression from the traditional romantic principle so as to assume the character of a protocol." (Adorno saw expressionism in music as a kind of psychoanalysis, as the word *protocol* suggests, taken as it is from the Freudian term used to describe the clinical documentation of dreams. A decade earlier, in a review of Ernst Krenek's 1937 book *Über neue Musik* (On Modern Music), Adorno had asserted: "It is questionable whether the aspect of expressionist expression can even be reduced to romantic expression; whether between the two there is not the difference between the proclamation of a protocol and fiction; whether Schoenberg's battle against musical ornament, the innermost motive of atonality, did not derive from the principally changed content of his music, which stands in the same relation to romantic content as Freud does to the psychological novel of the nineteenth century." The four-page review is remarkable for the clarity with which it presents the central ideas of the *Philosophy;* see *GS,* vol. 20.2, p. 805.) With the analogy to Sigmund Freud's clinical protocol of dreams, Adorno argues that music can transcend the merely subjective realm. It records, so to speak objectively, the malaise of the socially alienated subject. Although the notion of the individual, isolated and anxious, may become precariously fragile in Adorno's sociological view, it still serves a critical purpose in the modern music that he defined in a celebrated phrase in the *Philosophy* as "the true message in a bottle" *(die wahre Flaschenpost)*. Such is Adorno's expressionist "dialectics of loneliness": "lonely speech expresses" for him "more about the social tendency than communicative speech does."

The same yardstick obtains in the essay "Vers une musique informelle" (1961), a riposte to those younger composers at Darmstadt who misread Adorno's earlier work as legitimizing total serialism (that is, the precompositional manipulation not just of pitch but also of the musical parameters of rhythm, attack, and dynamics). Ever circumspect but resolute, he sketches a musical ideal charting "a third way between the jungle of *Erwartung,* on the one hand, and the tectonics of *Die glückliche Hand,* on the other"— both works from Schoenberg's atonal period. While delineating a program yet to be realized, Adorno invokes earlier achievements, particularly the organic coherence of tonal compositions, now undermined by the historical tendencies of musical material:

> A composition as a whole creates tension and resolution, just as used to happen in the tonal idiom with its primal model, the cadence. This shift to the totality, however, has stripped the parts of their power. In order to become equal to the task, then, which at present remains hidden, it would be necessary to construct down to the last detail the entire texture of the composition, as Schoenberg did in his day with larger forms, like the sonata and the variation, trusting that construction at the level of detail would be carried out by the twelve-tone technique. Relationships have to be established between events which succeed each other directly and indirectly—and this applies to events within simultaneous complexes—relationships which themselves provide the necessary stringency.

This description elaborates the technical aspect of the "expressive-dynamic principle" with which, in the *Philosophy,* Adorno associates "the essence of all great music since Bach" and with which he contrasts the "rhythmic-spatial" principle of Stravinsky's music. Negating that essence, he believed, represented not only a "death of subjective time," but a regression into irresponsible primitivism. The 1962 essay "Stravinsky: Ein dialektisches Bild" (A Dialectical Portrait), while qualifying and tempering his earlier polemic, nonetheless serves to confirm Adorno's essentialization of the "expressive-dynamic principle." He thus asserts:

> What we may conceive of as musical transcendence, namely the fact that at any given moment it has become something and something other than what it was, that points beyond itself—all that is no mere metaphysical imperative dictated by some external authority. It lies in the nature of music and will not be denied. Ever since music has existed, it has always been a protest, however ineffectual, against myth, against a fate which was always the same, and even against death.

The shift of focus from the alienated individual to the cause of alienation, the "administered" capitalist world, and back again is precisely reflected in the mix of Freudian and Marxist terminology employed throughout Adorno's writings. In an essay published shortly after his immigration to the United States in 1938, the mix is nicely contained in the very title: "On the Fetish-Character in Music and the Regression of Listening" ("Über den Fetischcharakter der Musik und die Regression des Hörens"). The essay has attracted notoriety as one of several critiques from his pen directed at his then host country's national music: jazz. (In 1937, before leaving England for the United States, he had viciously lambasted Jean Sibelius, whom British critics and concert audiences had accorded something approaching cult status.) As the title suggests, Adorno's jazz essays focus less on the aesthetic object than on audience attitudes—a diagnosis that derives from his belief in jazz's complicity with the ubiquitous "culture industry," the latter itself a function of the "administered world." Regressive listening habits, Adorno argued, amount to an essentially "pathological" approach to music, leaving consumers at the mercy of social manipulation and exploitation. But it is not just jazz that falls victim to the charge of such complicity—most composers outside the second Viennese school of Schoenberg, Webern, and Berg do so as well. Even many of the critics who are sympathetic toward Adorno's sociological perspicuity are unhappy about his musical judgment. In the case of jazz, it has been shown that his understanding of the phenomenon derived mainly from the commercial dance music he knew from Weimar Germany, not from American jazz music. To avoid terminological confusion, he directed his critique in the *Introduction to the Sociology of Music* at "light music," which is principally what he had meant all along.

His deciphering of music, whether jazz or Stravinsky, as sadomasochistic or even Fascist has been frequently dismissed as absurd. The negative sociological criteria, it is argued, fit too snugly with his negative aesthetic values. In a society deemed fundamentally "false," his attribution of positive aesthetic values, like the prospect of truth, must be severely limited. Of the handful of German or Austrian composers who represent "progress," none of them wholly complies with his rigorously demanding standards, even Schoenberg and Berg. But it is with society that Adorno principally finds fault. Like Nietzsche, he mistrusts the masses, all those listeners not in possession of his level of musical sophistication who must inevitably succumb to music's ideological influence.

For Adorno, the critical theorist, ideology in the Marxist sense of "false consciousness" lies at the core of aesthetic theory. His elaboration of musical "false consciousness," however, betrays an aesthetic understanding rooted in German romanticism. At issue is music's transcendental quality. Of all the arts, music most effectively supports the fiction that, to quote *Aesthetic Theory,* "by its mere existence, the limit [of our existence] had already been overcome." Thus, in a passage from the unfinished Beethoven monograph, Adorno can unequivocally state that music's ideological nature resides in its mere commencing: "Its language is, of itself, magic, and the transition to its isolated sphere has, a priori, something transfiguring about it. Suspending empirical reality and constituting a secondary one *sui generis* proclaims, as it were in advance: it is good." All music is thus "caught under the spell of appearance." The only escape from such appearance is for music permanently to revoke

its premise. This it does, according to Adorno, by remaining in a state of becoming, rather than by positing closed, self-contained aesthetic totalities. Compositionally speaking, this amounts to an apology for the technique of developing variation, which Schoenberg inherited from Beethoven and Johannes Brahms, and by means of which music can articulate a continuously unfolding thematic process (in the *Philosophy* Adorno boldly claims that "in Brahms there is no longer anything unthematic").

Philosophically, Adorno draws an exact parallel between Beethoven's music and Hegel's *Logik,* between the "becoming" of developing variation and the "becoming" of spirit in the *Phenomenology of Spirit.* But just as in the *Negative Dialectics,* where Adorno had branded the closed system of Hegel's philosophy as an untruth, he criticizes the Beethoven of the heroic middle period for the "affirmative gesture of recapitulation." Such a literal restatement of thematic material, introduced so triumphantly in the middle-period works, is "Beethoven's forced tribute to the ideological essence whose spell is cast by even the highest music that ever connoted freedom in the midst of enduring unfreedom." Only in Beethoven's late style, then, did Adorno sense a satisfactory, because dynamically dialectical, formal balance between part and whole—or, put sociologically, between individual and society.

Despite the unyielding criticisms of middle-period Beethoven, whom Adorno fondly apostrophizes as the "prototype of the revolutionary bourgeoisie," the posthumously published fragments of *Beethoven: Philosophy of Music* also reveal that Adorno's critique of modern society is derived from a nostalgic belief that things were once better. Like Hegel and earlier romantics, he looks back more than forward to a Golden Age, remaining tied to his roots as representative of the nineteenth-century *Bildungsbürger.* Translated into musical terms, his nostalgia manifests itself unabashedly in the fragment in which he bemoans the inevitable loss of nuance enjoyed by the supposedly stable language of the Viennese classics: "With us language itself is increasingly the problem, not the idiom. As a result we have, in a sense, become coarser and ourselves poorer. . . . Romanticism is the history of musical language being subverted and replaced by 'material.'"

It was that historical process of subversion, less than its outcome, that so fascinated Adorno as a philosopher of music. All three of his completed composer monographs were on prime representatives of that romantic heritage: Wagner, Gustav Mahler, and Berg, with each illuminating a different phase (the Berg monograph is subtitled "The Master of the Smallest Transition," alluding to Wagner's description of his own music as "the art of transition"). Whereas Adorno was unable to finish the Beethoven monograph, he wrote almost nothing on Wolfgang Amadeus Mozart. A short review from 1932 puts it bluntly: "The mastery is beyond discussion" (*GS*, vol. 19, p. 326).

The narrowly defined limits of Adorno's musical tastes were amply compensated for by the breadth of his methodological context and by his frequent flashes of brilliance as an insightful, eloquent critic. His legacy will endure in the continuing attempts to find fresh answers to the numerous questions he formulated and addressed, above all to the vexed problem he set himself of mediating between philosophy, sociology, and music analysis. Although a passionate advocate of absolute music and "aesthetic" (as opposed to "pathological") listening in the tradition of Eduard Hanslick, he refused to accept any clear demarcation between autonomy and heteronomy. Perhaps that is why his dialectical defense of the former may ultimately fail to convince. And even though his cultural diagnoses often seem misplaced in their specifics, the commercial and ideological abuses of music that he identified have in no way diminished. If the overall tone of this assessment is reminiscent of an obituary, it is because the value Adorno attached to the cultivated bourgeois musical experience in the modern industrial age has lost much of the vitality that is possessed—in no small measure thanks to him—until quite recently.

[*See also* Music, *historical overview article.*]

BIBLIOGRAPHY

Works by Adorno

Beethoven: Philosophie der Musik. Edited by Rolf Tiedemann. Frankfurt am Main, 1993.
Gesammelte Schriften. 20 vols. Edited by Rolf Tiedemann. Frankfurt am Main, 1970–.

Other Sources

Arnold, Heinz Ludwig, ed. *Theodor W. Adorno.* 2d ed. Munich, 1983.
Dahlhaus, Carl, Ludwig Finscher, and Joachim Kaiser. "Was haben wir von Adorno gehabt?" *Musica* 24 (1970): 435–439.
Dahlhaus, Carl. "Adornos Begriff des musikalischen Materials." In *Schönberg und andere: Gesammelte Aufsätze zur Neuen Musik,* pp. 336–342. Mainz, 1978.
Dahlhaus, Carl. "Das Problem der 'höheren Kritik': Adornos Polemik gegen Strawinsky." *Neue Zeitschrift für Musik* 148 (1987): 9–15.
Gabbard, Krin, ed. *Representing Jazz.* Durham, N.C., 1995.
Hinton, Stephen. "Adorno's Unfinished Beethoven." *Beethoven Forum* 5 (1996): 139–153.
Kolleritsch, Otto, ed. *Adorno und die Musik.* Graz, 1979.
Metzger, Heinz-Klaus, and Rainer Riehn. *Theodor W. Adorno: Komponist.* Musik-Konzepte 63/64. Munich, 1989.
Paddison, Max. *Adorno's Aesthetics of Music.* Cambridge and New York, 1993.
Roberts, David. *Art and Enlightenment: Aesthetic Theory after Adorno.* Lincoln, Nebr., 1991.
Robinson, J. Bradford. "The Jazz Essays of Theodor Adorno: Some Thoughts on Jazz Reception in Weimar Germany." *Popular Music* (1994): 1–25.
Schubert, Giselher. "Adornos Auseinandersetzung mit der Zwölftontechnik Schönbergs." *Archiv für Musikwissenschaft* 46 (1989): 235–254.
Steinert, Heinz. *Die Entdeckung der Kulturindustrie oder: Warum Professor Adorno Jazz-Musik nicht ausstehen konnte.* Vienna, 1992.

STEPHEN HINTON

Adorno and Kant

Theodor Adorno owes an immense debt to Immanuel Kant's *Critique of Judgment.* The major terms and categories of Adorno's aesthetics are informed by a thoroughly sympathetic understanding of what Kant posits as the centrality of aesthetic judgment and experience to the shape and formation, as well as experience, of subjective life. Yet despite the continuity between Kant and Adorno's aesthetic theories, Adorno finds Kant's aesthetics unfinished. Adorno begins to draw the trajectory of his own aesthetic theorizing in the Kantian passages that are incomplete or unreconciled—in particular, those dealing with beauty and the sublime and with the opposition between the beauty of nature and that of art.

Adorno is a faithful Kantian both in his elaboration of the *subject* of aesthetics and in the *subjectivity* he imagines is constituted by aesthetic judgment. Adorno's insights regarding the nature of aesthetic appearance are modeled on Kant's descriptions of the form of beauty and the character of the sublime. Just as Kant finds the legible image of subjective constitution in aesthetic judgment, Adorno theorizes that the artwork is its reverse image. Adorno, like Kant, attempts to see by means of this image, as well as through it. For Adorno, perhaps the only substantive difference between his aesthetics and Kant's is two hundred years of history. For him, that history consists of a transfiguration of what was once embodied by aesthetic judgment into what now occurs as the history and process of art.

The most profound intimacy between Kant and Adorno's texts lies precisely in the inextinguishability of the aesthetic hope for reconciliation within human life. Yet Adorno reads the *Critique of Judgment* as the richest, most nuanced treatise on aesthetics and, simultaneously, as a site of immense repression. Rather than fault Kant's text for the latter, Adorno instead reads that repression as integral to the aesthetic. Specifically, what is being repressed is the subject in whose name aesthetic taste occurs, only on the basis of a thorough disinterest and a pervasive disavowal of sensuousness. Adorno does not attempt a liberation of sensuousness or of subjective interests, but instead examines the specific sites of repression within the judgments of beauty and the experiences of the sublime, as well as in their relation to one another. Whereas the hope for reconciliation registers itself in Kant as a refusal to forsake nature as the realm in which human freedom comes to fruition, Adorno proceeds instead to recount the historical migration of this hope from the Kantian site of natural beauty to that of the sublime and finally (or at least up until the present) from there to art-beauty, and a subsequent self-evisceration.

It is as though Kant and Adorno peer at the same phenomenon from opposite points of view. Kant glimpses a view of the constitution of subjectivity, and intersubjectivity as well, by suppressing the view of the object, which, ironically, is the occasion for the judgment of beauty. The Kantian aesthetic subject congeals in the evacuated space of the object. For Adorno, Kant's aesthetic theory—especially in its overdetermined rigidification and suppression of the object—is thus a mimetic recapitulation of the very dynamic by which judgment functions. Indeed, we might well say that for Adorno the ontogeny of each Kantian aesthetic judgment recapitulates the phylogeny not only of judgment in general, but also of subjectivity. Adorno's own aesthetic theory, rather than attempting, like Kant's, to look past the object of judgment in order to discern its subject, draws a precise focus on the object as the best way to illuminate both object and subject. The object of aesthetic judgment is thereby to reveal itself as subjectivity in its otherness. Thus, it is the artwork, and no longer Kant's (nonetheless correct critique of) aesthetic judgment, that becomes the richest and most privileged site of alienation for Adorno.

Adorno's critique of the third *Critique* is that it attempts to hold at a standstill what Adorno sees as an unceasing dialectical momentum within aesthetic judgment between an expanding and a contracting subjectivity. Kant's inclination is to keep natural beauty separate from art-beauty and, further, to keep both these instances of taste separate from the judgment of the sublime that occurs within—though seemingly above—the all-too-civilized heads of men. Adorno's immanent critique of Kant's account of the sublime contains the insight that the very *movement* of Kant's sublime—encompassing the *move* from beauty to the sublime, from the mathematical to the dynamical sublime, as well as the *move* within the sublime from pain to pleasure—is already a symptom of the seeming success of taste's judgments of beauty. Thus, for Adorno the symptomatic expression of what ails the success of taste is found in the account of the sublime.

Adorno's aesthetics persists with the theme that nature might indeed "free itself from . . . imperious subjectivity" by way of an art aligned in opposition to us. Although Adorno suggests that art's opposition to us might also be taken as the return of repressed nature, this return is motivated by something more than revenge for what we have technologically inflicted on nature. This revenge is also prompted by our having ceased to hold regard for nature in any of its guises; that is, since art's ascendancy necessitated a continuing disregard for nature, the return of repressed nature in art (i.e., the sublime) produces an *appearance* of nature as exaggeratedly oppositional. Art's contrariness, then, is a historical product of the sublime that has migrated, following Kant, from nature into art. For Adorno, the third *Critique* is the avant-garde of this migration.

The historical era of the sublime appearing *in* nature, say, the second half of the eighteenth century, Adorno describes as coincident with a development in which "the unleashing of elemental forces was one with the emancipation of the subject and hence with the self-consciousness of spirit."

The subject did indeed come into its own (Kant's account of aesthetic judgment records this), even though it (mis)recognized itself as sublime nature. This misrecognition and arrival, this hope and reflection, could not persist, however, if only because of the subjective failure to realize itself as indeed something more than mere life. In this regard it is helpful to recall Friedrich Schiller's *Letters on the Aesthetic Education of Man* as the failed but valiant attempt to realize and sustain the achievement of the Kantian sublime.

For Adorno, it is Kant's account of taste—the experience of beauty in contrast to that of the sublime—that might best be described as a diagnosis of subjectivity's somewhat blinding attempt to universalize itself. For Adorno's Kant, subjectivity succeeds as a universal project in the moment of aesthetic (tasteful) pleasure. But that same moment must also be judged—by Kant's own account—a failure, insofar as it is precisely the universality of that moment that remains unrecognized by subjectivity. Indeed, for Adorno, it is just this inability and opacity, the persistent failure of aesthetically realized subjectivity to recognize itself as such, and therefore as an agent, that calls forth the need for a continuing critique of aesthetic judgment.

Subjectivity, pace Kant, realizes itself in taste, but fails to recognize itself therein and thereby likewise fails to reproduce itself as explicitly social. Although the singular success of taste lies, according to Kant, in the achievement of positing and "feeling" intersubjectivity, its failure nonetheless is twofold: taste fails either to transform its achieved universal intersubjectivity into something objective (for example, a political state) or, what seems the very least, to apprehend its achievement—hence its continuing opacity. This particular failure of taste—again, in the very moment of its success—sets in motion, according to Adorno's reading of Kant, the project of the sublime.

The first task of the sublime is to remove from taste the presentation that allows it to misrecognize itself as objective. For Adorno, the migration of the sublime from nature to art is not the product of nature's revenge alone: it is also a symptom of the reciprocally increasing reification of the social and the subjective. If the sublime begins as the withdrawal of the purportedly objective, it continues more purely as the force of the negative. As reification increases, so too does the urgency for a dynamism that cuts across it. The migration of the sublime into art might then well be construed not merely as the product of a disregard of nature, but also as the signal of an increased reification within the confines of art itself. For Adorno, if art was ever a realm of free play, the arrival of the sublime indicates that it exists as such no longer. Since art, for Adorno, now requires the sublime, art is no longer the realm of mere appearance but, beyond that, the realm of false appearance, which is to say, of appearances that demand to be disavowed. If aesthetic appearance once served, pace Friedrich Nietzsche, as a goad to reflection and life, it must have since hardened into an impediment, especially to itself.

Adorno finds in Kant's aesthetics a symptomatic readiness to posit, in the object of beauty, too smooth and seamless a relation between particularity and universality. Hence, despite his aesthetic theory's having originated in critique, Kant nonetheless helps keep invisible the technological machinery of transition from particular to universal. Since the object of beauty—whether artistic or natural—therefore occurs for Kant as a wholly harmonious identity between particular and universal, it thereby fails to serve as a dynamic site of promise or reconciliation. In Kantian beauty, for Adorno, there is no productive tension, slippage, or dialectic. These qualities instead reside in Kant's *theory* of beauty. It is as if Kantian natural beauty too readily avoids what Adorno considers art's inescapable telos: "Since time immemorial art has sought to rescue the particular; advancing particularity was immanent to it."

So too, for Adorno, the Kantian redemption and promotion of the particular object (but so too surreptitiously of the subject) come at too high a cost: at the price of the complete obliteration of what, for Adorno, ought to be the persistent tension between particular and universal in a still unreconciled world. In the end, the Kantian aesthetic elevation of the particular becomes the total effacement of the object of beauty itself. For Adorno, Kantian beauty severs forever—in order to gain the universality of subjectivity—whatever remaining ties bound it to the particularity of the object. With this effacement of the object for the sake of beauty, or with what Adorno will formulate as the later evisceration of art, art's immemorial project of redeeming and promoting the particular now becomes the problem of the sublime. More simply put, Kant's formulation of beauty resolves, but all too quickly and completely, the immemorial tension between particular and universal. Adorno suggests that this immemorial tension migrates into the domain of the sublime, where the fault line within subjectivity becomes all the more precipitous.

Yet Adorno finds in Kant's favoring of natural over artistic beauty an implicit recognition of the importance of some resistance to an all-pervasive and seamless identity of particular and universal. For Adorno, Kant's natural beauty is also a precise cipher of that which resists identity: "The beauty of nature is the residue of nonidentity in things spellbound by universal identity. As long as this spell rules, nothing nonidentical is positively there." Natural beauty is not itself the nonidentical but the cipher or promise that nonidentity might be possible. "Natural beauty partakes of the weakness of all promisings: they are inextinguishable." This inextinguishable promise is also fragile: "The reason one shies away from natural beauty is that one might wound the not-yet-existing by grasping it in what exists." The sublime, in its attempt to extinguish the promise once borne by natural beauty, bears no regard for this fragility. At the same time, however, the sublime is also the attempt to allow the not-yet-existing to come into being.

Adorno reads the historical genealogy of art-beauty as the dialectical response to the implicit failure of Kantian natural beauty: the beauty of art now carries the burden of what was once promised of nature in the guise of natural beauty. Natural beauty might then be understood as a dynamic, indeed a dialectical one: it begins as the hope for identity and comes near to achieving it, but in the proximity of this near-identity, it "conceals itself anew," which is to say, it retreats finally from positing identity. It is as if the sublime arrived in the eighteenth century as the most advanced dialectical technique for producing human freedom, and so too reconciliation. Adorno describes the traditional concept of the sublime as an "infinite presence . . . animated by the belief that negation could bring about positivity." In having sacrificed empirical existence so completely and readily, the sublime thereby also discarded nature, the realm that until then was requisite for the prolongation of hope provided by natural beauty. With the sublation of human existence in the sublime's hope for transcendence, the place where, as well as the means by which, reconciliation might occur is disregarded. If this sweeping, purposive disavowal is already a feature of natural beauty, then the negation of empirical existence effected by the sublime is but a more thorough version of the effacement of nature achieved in Kant's account of taste. The salient difference, then, between Kant's theory of taste and his account of the sublime is that in the former beauty still required nature (whatever that might have been or comes to be) as an *occasion* for an aesthetic experience—for the harmonization of the particular and universal—even though Kant explains the functional importance of that occasion as merely as opportunity for subjectivity to misrecognize itself.

What Adorno means by the autonomy of art may well be a result of the historical piling up of functions onto art and art-beauty such that art, merely by the accumulation and variety of tasks and expectations that fall to it, comes to be autonomous. Art thus functions as the default sphere into which migrate the historic frustrations of the failed dreams and projects of human emancipation. Yet insofar as this sphere not only serves as a reservoir of these frustrations, but also maintains them, the aesthetic sphere of art thereby becomes—for Adorno—an active, independent agency. This, of course, is not to suggest that all art is autonomous, or that all or any art making occurs in autonomy, but rather that some art *achieves*—like Kant's aesthetic judgment—autonomy. Put differently, the autonomy of art signals the transfer of human autonomy (that is, freedom) from the human subject to the aesthetic artifact. When we speak of the spirit of art, we do not just infer our own alienation but posit *the* privileged site of alienation.

Like natural beauty, the sublime is hope. It is also a good deal more, and less. It is more than hope insofar as it attempts to make actual the hoped-for identity between particular and universal. The sublime, in this regard, is the refusal of the solace of hope evoked by and sustained in natural beauty. We might well recall here Adorno's statement explaining how the sublime and taste come into conflict in the late eighteenth century as a result of the "unleashing of elemental forces" that were "one with the emancipation of the subject." The subject, however, was not emancipated, and to paraphrase a well-known passage from *Negative Dialectics,* we might say that the moment when the subject was to realize itself has passed. The residue of this passed moment, of a subject stillborn, is not the hope for some future birth but the refusal of nature as the locus of generation and regeneration. The sublime, after Kant, thus migrates to art, to the realm of artifice par excellence. The fact of this migration means that hope has been transferred, not extinguished. The question is how this migration affects the hope, and whether there is more to hope for from art and art-beauty than once was allowed by nature and natural beauty. This, for Adorno, is the task of aesthetic theory.

[*See also* Kant.]

BIBLIOGRAPHY

Work by Adorno

Aesthetic Theory. Edited by Gretel Adorno and Rolf Tiedemann, translated by Robert Hullot-Kentor. Minneapolis, 1997.

Other Sources

Bernstein, J. M. *The Fate of Art: Aesthetic Alienation from Kant to Derrida and Adorno,* University Park, Pa., 1992.

Bürger, Peter. *Theory of the Avant-Garde.* Translated by Michael Shaw. Minneapolis, 1984.

Cooper, Harry. "On *Über Jazz:* Replaying Adorno with the Grain." *October* 75 (Winter 1996): 99–133.

Hansen, Miriam. "Of Mice and Ducks: Benjamin and Adorno on Disney." *South Atlantic Quarterly* 92 (Winter 1993): 27–61.

Hohendahl, Peter Uwe. *Prismatic Thought: Theodor W. Adorno.* Lincoln, Nebr., 1995.

Hullot-Kentor, Robert. "Back to Adorno." *Telos* 81 (Fall 1989): 5–29.

Jameson, Fredric. *Late Marxism: Adorno, or, The Persistence of the Dialectic.* London and New York, 1990.

Jay, Martin. *The Dialectical Imagination: A History of the Frankfurt School and the Institute of Social Research, 1923–1950.* Reprint, Berkeley, 1996.

Kaufman, Robert. "Legislators of the Post-Everything World: Shelley's *Defence* of Adorno." *English Literary History* 63 (1996): 707–733.

Koch, Gertrude. "Mimesis and *Bilderverbot*." *Screen* 34 (Autumn 1993): 211–222.

Levin, Thomas Y. "For the Record: Adorno on Music in the Age of its Technological Reproducibility." *October* 55 (Winter 1990): 23–47.

Menke, Christoph. *Die Souveränität der Kunst: Ästhetische Erfahrung nach Adorno und Derrida.* Frankfurt am Main, 1988.

Wellmer, Albrecht. *The Persistence of Modernity: Essays on Aesthetics, Ethics, and Postmodernism.* Translated by David Midgley. Cambridge, Mass., 1991.

Whitebook, Joel. *Perversion and Utopia: A Study in Psychoanalysis and Critical Theory.* Cambridge, Mass., 1995.

Zuidervaart, Lambert. *Adorno's Aesthetic Theory: The Redemption of Illusion.* Cambridge, Mass., 1991.

TOM HUHN

AESTHESIS. *See* Definition of Art; Origins of Aesthetics, *article on* History of Aisthesis.

AESTHETIC ATTITUDE. *See* Attitude, *article on* Aesthetic Attitude.

AESTHETIC EDUCATION. *See* Education, Aesthetic.

AESTHETICISM. A complex movement of artistic reform within later Victorian culture, culminating around 1875–1885, Aestheticism began by emphasizing the power of visual art and beauty to regenerate social life, and ended by insisting on the complete independence of art from life and on the alienation of the artist from society. The movement was widely influential in its impact on the visual environment of late-nineteenth-century Britain and the United States—especially on architecture, interior design, furnishings, advertising, apparel, and children's books. It also served as the ideological camouflage through which an otherwise "dangerous" rationalism and agnosticism were able to enter the mainstream of Victorian thought.

Although Aestheticism would be substantially discredited as a cultural posture by the brilliant ridicule of George Du Maurier in *Punch* and William Schwenck Gilbert in *Patience* (1881), certain characteristic Aestheticist emphases—beauty and simplicity in design, sincerity in materials, craftsmanship in execution, beauty and functionality in use—would continue through the Arts and Crafts movement and Art Nouveau to influence Anglo-American and European taste well into the twentieth century. In aesthetics and literary criticism, Aestheticist theories of the artist's freedom from moral or didactic claims and of art as constituting a separate ontological realm would powerfully influence such twentieth-century developments as literary modernism (see Donoghue, 1995), New Criticism (see Wimsatt and Brooks, 1957), and Anglo-American deconstructionism (see Loesberg, 1991).

Aestheticism arose in England out of the revolutionary energies released by the Pre-Raphaelite Brotherhood, which had been founded amid the insurrectionary idealism of the Continental political revolutions of 1848. The Pre-Raphaelite Brotherhood, a group of young artists including William Holman Hunt, John Everett Millais, and Dante Gabriel Rossetti, renounced the pictorial conventionalism and "Grand Style" orthodoxy of the Royal Academy in favor of the simplicity and fidelity to nature that they discovered in the work of the then disregarded Italian medieval painters. "Frank expression and unaffected grace were what had made Italian art so essentially vigorous and progressive," declared Hunt, "until the showy followers of Michael

Angelo had grafted their Dead Sea fruit on to the vital tree" (Warner and Hough, 1983, vol. 1, p. 117).

Although the Pre-Raphaelites drew on earlier Romantic traditions of medievalism (e.g., Walter Scott's *Waverly* novels, John Keats's *Eve of St. Agnes*, Augustus Welby Northmore Pugin's *Contrasts*, Thomas Carlyle's *Past and Present*, their appeal to the medieval past differed significantly from earlier neo-Gothic revivals in being "progressive" or consciously utopian. The very name of their association was meant to suggest a medieval "brotherhood" of artists revived in the modern age. Like the earlier German "Nazarene" painters who influenced them, the Pre-Raphaelites meant to take from medieval society the materials for contemporary experiments in artistic life and work. Thus, in the immediate background of the Pre-Raphaelite project may be glimpsed something like Auguste Comte's celebrated doctrine that the Positivist society of the future would take its pattern from the Middle Ages, renewing medieval art and completing the medieval social structure on a more authentic intellectual basis.

This utopian dimension gave to Pre-Raphaelitism its unexpectedly broad appeal among Victorian liberals, and in turn prepared the way for popular acceptance of Aestheticism. Under the influence of John Stuart Mill's *On Liberty* (1859), the mid-Victorian generation of liberal reformers would come to perceive in the Pre-Raphaelites' artistic dissent the resistance to stultifying authority by gifted individuals—"variety not uniformity," in Mill's phrase—that Mill declared to be necessary if England were to escape the social regimentation and intellectual torpor that seemed an otherwise inevitable consequence of modern mass democracy. The argument of *On Liberty,* moreover, drew on Johann Wolfgang von Goethe and Friedrich Schiller's powerful post-Kantian analysis of the maiming effects of industrial modernity on human personality. This is the sense in which Mill himself may be heard as a proponent of something very like Schiller's "aesthetic education of man," making him, along with Samuel Taylor Coleridge, Carlyle, and Matthew Arnold, an eloquent spokesman in England for the German notions of *Kultur* and *Bildung*—human development in its richest diversity—that would become a central ideal of Victorian liberalism.

The greatest influence on aesthetic education among the Victorians, however, was John Ruskin. An early champion of the Pre-Raphaelites, Ruskin, in a famous chapter in volume 2 of *Stones of Venice* (1853), "The Nature of Gothic," provided an enduring utopian vision of the medieval craftsman, united with his fellows through work at once individually satisfying and socially beneficent, that would inspire two generations of European artists. Ruskin was able to captivate theologically orthodox Victorian readers with his incomparable, biblically cadenced prose style, while at the same time his portrayal of the socially transformative powers of art won the assent of such agnostic and intellectually advanced Victorians as George Eliot, George Henry Lewes, Frederic Harrison, John Morley, and Walter Pater. So remarkable was Ruskin's influence in every area, social and aesthetic, that one Victorian declared it "the greatest event in our literary history since *Lyrical Ballads* and *Waverly*." [*See* Ruskin.]

The single most crucial element in Ruskin's teaching was perhaps his portrayal of the medieval world of the Gothic artisan as a harmonious totality in which art and life had become interpenetrating realities. In Ruskin's Gothic cathedral, feudal distinctions of rank and ability dwindled to insignificance, individual expressiveness found its fullest scope, and even the imperfect work of the least talented artisan could play a legitimate part in adorning the glorious communal whole. Especially stirring was Ruskin's demand that his nineteenth-century reader "look round this English room of yours" and recognize not only the unredeemed conventionality of middle-class taste but evidence of "a slavery in our England"—that is, the dehumanization of the industrial worker (Warner and Hough, 1983, vol. 1, p. 55). Ruskin's insistence on the social consequences of aesthetic preferences, and specifically on the power of consumers to determine the quality of the social environment through their choices, has influenced purchasers to the present day.

The medieval utopianism of Ruskin and the Pre-Raphaelites inspired the careers of the two greatest artists of the English Aesthetic movement, William Morris and Edward Burne-Jones. Together with such older painters as Rossetti and Ford Madox Brown, these two men formed a decorative arts firm in 1861 to produce, under conditions of cooperative labor, aesthetically satisfying interior designs and furnishings that were otherwise completely unobtainable in the conventional market. So garish and uncomfortable had Victorian middle-class interiors become by the 1860s under the influence of French Second Empire plutocratic taste—lavish gilding, ponderous mahogany, glaring aniline dyes—that Morris soon became convinced that only a complete transformation of Victorian interior space, by means of the revived methods of an older craftsmanship, could begin to realize Ruskin's Gothic ideal of a harmonious totality of art and life.

The beginning of the high Aesthetic period is marked by Morris's reorganization of the design partnership into his own hands as Morris & Co. in 1875. The exclusive medievalism of Ruskin and the Pre-Raphaelites gave way at this point to an eclecticism that moved freely through geography and history in its search for authentic beauty. Along with medieval, Elizabethan, and "Queen Anne" design elements, the Aesthetic style now incorporated Moorish, Arabian, and Indian motifs as well as, more famously, a great deal of japonaiserie. Although the flood of Aestheticist exotica was no doubt made possible in purely material terms by the expansion and consolidation of the British Empire (see Stein, 1986), its stylistic eclecticism demands at a deeper level to be understood ideologically, as the visual expression of the cardinal values of Victorian liberalism: tolerance, "receptivity," liberty, and sympathy. This is the level at which Algernon Charles Swinburne, the chief transmitter of French *l'art pour l'art* (art for art's sake) theories to the English during the 1860s and 1870s, and Walter Pater, whose "Conclusion" to *Studies in the History of the Renaissance* (1873) became the bible of English Aestheticism, would ceaselessly stress that, to the aesthetic observer, all periods and places of art, all types and schools of taste, were in themselves equal. In the same way, a leading Aestheticist designer like Christopher Dresser declared that his own artistic success depended entirely on "the extent to which I become, in feeling, for the time a Chinaman, or Arabian," in a sense, "a citizen of the country whose ornament I wish to simulate" (Dresser, 1876, p. 3).

In this wider vision of sympathy and tolerance, the ultimate Aesthetic ideal becomes Walter Pater's "House Beautiful," that purely imaginary or metaphysical domicile of the spirit that "the creative minds of all generations—the artists and those who have treated life in the spirit of art—are always building together, for the refreshment of the human spirit" (Warner and Hough, 1983, vol. 2, p. 39). This is the moment as well that Aestheticist social utopianism, as though repenting the naïveté of its own earlier hopes for a widespread aesthetic democracy, begins to dwell on the importance of a gifted and guiding elite. Undaunted by the tyranny of public opinion, daring to make what Mill had called "different experiments of living," artists and those living their lives in the spirit of art begin to be portrayed in the later 1870s as a potential new aristocracy, an "optimacy" of passion and genius that might replace the older hierarchies of birth and wealth (Myers, 1883, p. 558). It was a powerful vision. As peers' daughters did their best to resemble Pre-Raphaelite models, and peeresses competed to follow the directives of Morris & Co. in their interior decoration, high Victorian Aestheticism seemed poised to inaugurate a moment when the English aristocracy of birth would yield its cultural precedence to "advanced" members of an artistic and intellectual elite.

The patronage so eagerly bestowed on the Aesthetic movement by the English royalty and aristocracy not only added enormously to its social acceptance but permitted Aestheticist style to serve as a socially presentable camouflage for "advanced" and socially radical sympathies. When Morris's firm was commissioned to redecorate rooms in St. James's Palace (completed 1869), or when the Grosvenor Gallery was opened by a Scots baronet, Sir Coutts Lindsay, as a progressive alternative to the Royal Academy exhibition (1877), the impression grew that "Aesthetes are supposed to belong to the 'Upper Crust'" (Hamilton, 1882, p. 83). During the late 1870s, amid the aura of fashionability and social prestige surrounding Aestheticism, children dressed by their parents in Kate Greenaway smocks were able to be

deployed as the unrecognized shock troops of an otherwise scandalous Positivism. By the 1880s, Walter Crane was similarly able to insinuate his socialist principles into thousands of philistine nurseries through children's books that enchanted both his young readers and their unsuspecting parents. With the Grosvenor Gallery boldly opening on Sundays, and "Show Sundays" (the new custom of inviting members of the middle-class public to visit artists' studios instead of attending afternoon church services), the Aestheticist "Religion of Beauty" became the tolerable "human face" of a Victorian rationalism and agnosticism that otherwise alarmed and outraged orthodox religious sensibilities.

The impingement of the Aesthetic movement on a broader public consciousness may be traced to the moment the Aestheticist ideal of the House Beautiful began to be realized in the actual bricks and mortar of Victorian England, as in the celebrated London real-estate development of Bedford Park, begun in 1875. Widespread journalistic coverage made it inevitable that the captivating architectural eclecticism of Bedford Park—Richard Norman Shaw's combination of seventeenth-century Dutch and English design elements, soon termed by common agreement the "Queen Anne" style—would become generally imitated. Inside, Bedford Park houses were filled with heterogeneous yet harmonious arrangements of Morris wallpapers, Persian rugs, rush-bottomed chairs, and Indian matting. Outside, the groups of detached and semidetached houses were so "exceedingly varied in *matters of detail*," as one journalist observed, that "no two houses are exactly alike" (Hamilton, 1882, p. 117). Nothing, he marveled, could be further removed from the "conventionality" and "the usual dull monotony" produced by the typical speculative builder (118). As though fulfilling Comte's dictum that "what Philosophy elaborates, Art will propagate" Bedford Park incarnated in red brick and white sash windows the Victorian liberal ideal of "variety not uniformity." Visiting the garden suburb in 1880, Ernest Renan declared it "une véritable utopie!"

In the event, Aestheticism was undone by its own success. Its social prestige attracted intense popular interest, popularity brought vulgarization, and vulgarization—the spectacle of thousands of ordinary souls attempting to be "aesthetic"—drew satiric attacks in *Punch* and *Patience* that drove away its elite adherents. Thus did the grand utopian project of "aesthetic education," still recognizable as late as Pater's *Renaissance*, dwindle into decorating tips in how-to books. Such guides as Charles Locke Eastlake's *Hints on Household Taste* (1868), Clarence Cook's *House Beautiful* (1878), and Eliza Haweis's *Beautiful Houses* (1881) would convert the exquisite aesthetic intuitions of artists and designers into simple, reproducible, and soon predictable formulas for the philistine masses. Morris's very creativity in an extraordinary range of media—stained glass, furniture design, wallpapers, rug making, tilework, tapestry weaving—would similarly ensure that plagiarized versions of his designs, reproduced in cheaper materials, would come eventually within the economic reach of everyone who aspired to be thought "aesthetic." Not even Morris's influential ideas about art and craftsmanship would ultimately be exempt; they were plagiarized and popularized among the American millions by Oscar Wilde during his celebrated 1882 U.S. and Canadian lecture tour.

No one did more to popularize the Aesthetic movement than Wilde, partly in a spirit of self-parody, but partly too as the living symbol of a serious commitment to Aestheticist values. The ambivalence of his role was reflected in the fact that, universally understood to be a target of Gilbert and Sullivan's anti-Aesthete comic opera *Patience,* he could nonetheless agree to serve, for handsome remuneration, as its publicist in the United States. A disciple of Ruskin and Pater while a student at Oxford, and later part of the circle surrounding Morris and Burne-Jones, Wilde boldly announced to all who would listen that the "English Renaissance of Art" had begun. No less boldly, he dressed the part of the Apostle of Beauty in velvet knee breeches and silken hose. Wilde's genius for self-advertisement was amplified by the power and profitability of the new Victorian communications industry, whose vast machinery had been mobilized in the years following the Education Act of 1870 to supply entertainment to millions of newly literate readers. Chromolithographs, steam-driven printing presses, penny newspapers—all the newer technologies of print combined to spread Wilde's flamboyantly Aestheticist gospel throughout two continents. It soon became difficult, remarked Max Beerbohm, to remember that beauty had even existed before 1880: surely "it was Mr. Oscar Wilde who first trotted her round" (Beerbohm, 1895, 278). [*See* Wilde.]

The vulgarization of the Aesthetic movement eventually provoked many late-Victorian artists and writers, ultimately including Wilde himself, to turn away from the utopian impulse in which Aestheticism had its earliest beginnings. In one of the lucid intervals of his recurrent bouts of mental disease, Ruskin denounced the Aesthetic movement in 1881, finally spurning even the word *aesthetic,* which had first been introduced into English from the German by his beloved mentor, Carlyle. Walter Pater, charged with dangerously misleading young men with his injunction to "burn always" with the "hard, gem-like flame" of aesthetic experience (Pater, 1980, p. 189), would drop from the next edition of *The Renaissance* the "Conclusion" in which the famous words appeared and retreat to London to write his apologia in the form of a novel, *Marius the Epicurean* (1885). Morris, sickened and furious at the effete and supercilious caricatures that "art" and "culture" seemed to have produced, declared himself in 1883 to be a socialist and threw himself into revolutionary activities.

At this point, the French doctrine of *l'art pour l'art* moved to the center of Victorian thought as the theoretical stronghold of those who wanted to renounce all indiscriminately democratic projects of "aesthetic education." First among these was the expatriate American painter James Abbott McNeill Whistler. When Algernon Swinburne introduced the notions of Théophile Gautier and Charles Baudelaire into England during the 1860s, *l'art pour l'art* had been taken to signal primarily a dedication to perfect craftsmanship. [*See* Art for Art's Sake.] The only absolute duty of art, Swinburne said then, was the duty art owed to itself. This craftsmanly ideal was in itself taken to be a neutral imperative, able to guide work of the socially detached Rossetti quite as much as the socially engaged Morris.

Whistler, by contrast, would dwell with a certain ferocity on the purely negative dimensions of *l'art pour l'art:* its absolute opposition between art and nature, its hostility to any instrumentalization of art, its ressentiment toward artistic amateurs, its contempt for the unseeing public. These doctrines, molded by the extreme pressures of French political life in the years following the July Revolution of 1830, Louis Napoleon's coup d'état of 1851 and the disastrous Franco-Prussian War of 1870–1871, constituted a separate line of development from the otherwise dominant German post-Kantian and English "moral-aesthetic sense" traditions nourishing the French Eclectic school of Victor Cousin and Théodore Jouffroy. With the collapse of democratic legitimacy in France, a bitter reaction arose against Anglo-German claims for the universality of the aesthetic sense and the civic role of art. In giving expression to their own disillusionment, Gautier, Baudelaire, Gustave Flaubert, and Jules and Edmond de Goncourt in turn made available an incomparably witty and compelling vocabulary to English and American artists disillusioned by the betrayal of Aestheticist hopes for art.

Whistler, embittered and bankrupted by the court costs from his victorious but ruinous libel case against Ruskin (1878), sought in the 1880s to avenge himself on an English public that had, as he knew, been taught by Ruskin to prefer a "moral" art to a purely artistic one, and beyond that to prefer nature to either. In his famous "Ten O'Clock Lecture" of 1885, Whistler arraigned all the various "preachers" of art—art lecturers, newspaper critics, dilettantes—who had reduced painting to a province of literature, rejecting not only their hopes for art as a socially transformative power but their fantasy of an earlier age in which art and life had been parts of an inseparable whole: "Listen! There never was an artistic period. There never was an Art-loving nation" (Warner and Hough, 1983, p. 78). Having learned to despise the aesthetic capacities of the British populace from his experience of the obtuse jury in *Whistler v. Ruskin* and the spectacle of Sunday picnickers in the National Gallery, Whistler was moved ultimately to declare that art was "selfishly occupied with her own perfection only" and sought no other audience than "the Artist alone" (pp. 76, 88).

Whistler's deliberate affront to his listeners' feelings in the "Ten O'Clock" enacted in dramatic fashion a disdain for the obtuseness of the general public, commonplace enough among French artists but unpleasantly new to the English. Accustomed by the long tradition of Whig aesthetics to regard art in its moral and social relations (see Dowling, 1996), the English had normally been willing to consider art "selfish" or asocial only if it happened to be "foreign." Yet, as Whistler's unrepentant disdain helped to make clear, within British Aestheticism a largely suppressed tendency to self-absorption and escapism had lurked all along. Rossetti's refusal to exhibit his paintings in public and his contempt for all public issues, Burne-Jones's retreat into a Helleno-medieval world of unearthly beauty, and Albert Moore's repetitive, richly patterned canvases of drowsy damsels could now be taken to suggest that a desire for release from all socially utopian agendas had been present in Aestheticism from the first.

In the same way, Whistler's celebrated prose picture in the "Ten O'Clock" of London as it revealed itself to the artist's gaze alone (that fleeting moment "when the evening mist clothes the riverside with poetry") suggested that the transformation of industrial ugliness might be pursued in art rather than in actuality. His sumptuously gilded and enameled Peacock Room (1876–1877) was now able to persuade many "advanced" Victorians that the unified Aestheticist interior might better serve as a refuge from urban modernity and altruistic social duties than as a model for any harmoniously integrated society of the future. Darkened and cocoon-like, the "exotic" interiors of late Aestheticist taste became a stage setting for such inward liberations of the sensuous self as the drug and sexual experimentation found first among "decadent" avant-gardists of the 1890s and later among the neo-Aesthetes of the 1960s (see Stokes, 1990).

Although Oscar Wilde accepted Whistler's vision of a wholly autonomous art and increasingly shared Whistler's disdain for the public, he mounted a complex and powerful counterargument to the third of Whistler's major claims: the natural superiority of the artist over the critic. In *The Decay of Lying* and *The Critic as Artist,* the two great critical dialogues collected in *Intentions* (1891), Wilde brought his powerful intellect and wide reading in Georg Wilhelm Friedrich Hegel and Greek philosophy to bear on questions of mimesis and aesthetic autonomy. There was nothing that Plato ever said about metaphysics, he later remarked to a friend, that could not be applied to questions of art as such. Clearly moving in *The Decay of Lying* toward a theory of the artwork as constituting a separate ontological sphere, Wilde outlined four doctrines of the "new aesthetics": (1) that Art "has an independent life, just as Thought has, and develops purely on its own lines"; (2) that "All bad Art comes from returning to Life and Nature, and elevating them into ideals"; (3) that "Life imitates Art far more than Art imitates Life"; and (4) that "Lying, the telling of beautiful untrue things, is the proper aim of Art" (Wilde, 1969, pp. 319–320).

An equally important axiom of late Aestheticism emerged from the way Wilde chose to counter Whistler's denigration of critics, which was to describe criticism, envisioned by him as an ordered and intense mode of aesthetic response, as itself belonging to the realm of autonomous art. Whistler had, for instance, dismissed Ruskin and Pater as "littérateurs," parasitical upon the creative art of Joseph Mallord William Turner and Leonardo da Vinci. Yet, countered Wilde, we can very easily imagine Ruskin's magnificent prose descriptions of Turner's paintings outliving the "corrupted canvases" (p. 366) that had been their occasion. Nor did the superiority of Ruskin's prose lie merely in its belonging to language, a medium more permanent than paint and canvas. Ruskin's commentary would outlast Turner's painting, Wilde argued, because criticism bore the least reference "to any standard external to itself." It was therefore "its own reason for existing, and, as the Greeks would put it, in itself, and to itself, an end" (p. 365). The translation of Platonic metaphysics into this last version of *l'art pour l'art* doctrine could scarcely be more explicit.

The Aestheticist conception of a unified and autonomous art would remain as the great obstacle encountered by twentieth-century artists determined to reestablish a vital relation between art and life. For such avant-gardist movements as Vorticism and Surrealism, Aestheticist art became an escapist, "affirmative" realm that needed to be smashed before it could be reintegrated into the life-world of praxis and sociopolitical effect. For the Imagists and modernists, Aestheticist art was taken as the very embodiment of a specious "literariness," "beauty mongering," and impressionist "muzziness," symptomatic of Victorian repressions and hypocrisy, and destructive of the clear outline and psychic power of the symbol. Even the direct heirs of the Aesthetes—Henry James, James Joyce, and the Anglo-American modernist poets, William Butler Yeats, Ezra Pound, Thomas Stearns Eliot, and Wallace Stevens—would seek to minimize or obscure or deny their debt, so compromised had the Aestheticist inheritance become by the late extreme mode of Aestheticism known as fin de siècle decadence, notoriously symbolized by the homosexual practices for which Wilde was tried and imprisoned in 1895.

The larger artistic influence of the Victorian Aestheticist movement, though visible enough in the contemporary world, has remained largely unacknowledged. The Aestheticist reforms of color, space, form, and materials have simply been too massively and successfully absorbed into twentieth-century architecture and design for them to be readily distinguishable *as* Aestheticist. After the Aestheticist revolution, what Henry James with irony termed certain consecrated forms of Victorian ugliness—wax fruit under glass, layer upon layer of flea-infested wallpaper, literally poisonous hues such as iodine green, magenta, and coralline (the latter two dyes contained arsenic)—became unthinkable. The deeper cultural transformations of Aestheticism would remain similarly invisible: regard for the importance of beautiful physical surroundings to human health and development; a conviction that artistic labor remains the standard for all meaningful work; a disposition to see in the freedom of the artwork a model for potential human freedom. This silent transformation in attitudes constituted one of the genuine improvements of modernity. It is to such attitudes, as much as to any revolution in upholstery or interior design, that one Victorian observer was referring when he asked rhetorically, "To whom are we indebted for these advantages? Why, to the Aesthetes" (Hamilton, 1882, p. 127).

[*See also* Autonomy; Bloomsbury Group; Lesbian Aesthetics; Pater; Politics and Aesthetics, *article on* AIDS and Aesthetics; *and* Romanticism.]

BIBLIOGRAPHY

Aslin, Elizabeth. *The Aesthetic Movement: Prelude to Art Nouveau.* New York, 1969.
Beerbohm, Max. "1880." *Yellow Book* 4 (January 1895): 275–283.
Chai, Leon. *Aestheticism: The Religion of Art in Post-Romantic Literature.* New York, 1990.
Donoghue, Denis. *Walter Pater: Lover of Strange Souls.* New York, 1995.
Dowling, Linda C. *Aestheticism and Decadence: A Selective Annotated Bibliography.* New York, 1977.
Dowling, Linda. *The Vulgarization of Art: The Victorians and Aesthetic Democracy.* Charlottesville, Va., 1996.
Dresser, Christopher. *Studies in Design.* London, 1876. Reprinted as *The Language of Ornament: Style in the Decorative Arts* (New York, 1988).
Fletcher, Ian. "Some Aspects of Aestheticism." In *Twilight of Dawn: Studies in English Literature in Transition,* edited by O. M. Brack, Jr., pp. 1–31. Tucson, Ariz., 1987.
Fraser, Hilary. *Beauty and Belief: Aesthetics and Religion in Victorian Literature.* Cambridge and New York, 1986.
Gagnier, Regina. *Idylls of the Marketplace: Oscar Wilde and the Victorian Public.* Stanford, Calif., 1986.
Hamilton, Walter. *The Aesthetic Movement in England.* London, 1882; reprint, New York, 1971.
Harris, Wendell V. "An Anatomy of Aestheticism." In *Victorian Literature and Society: Essays Presented to Richard D. Altick,* edited by James R. Kincaid and Albert J. Kuhn, pp. 831–847. Columbus, Ohio, 1984.
Lambourne, Lionel. *The Aesthetic Movement.* London, 1996.
Loesberg, Jonathan. *Aestheticism and Deconstruction: Pater, Derrida and de Man.* Princeton, N.J., 1991.
Myers, Frederick. "Rossetti and the Religion of Beauty." In *Essays: Classical and Modern,* pp. 538–560. London, 1883.
Pater, Walter. *The Renaissance: Studies in Art and Poetry: The 1983 Text.* Edited by Donald L. Hill. Berkeley, 1980.
Stein, Roger B. "Artifact as Ideology: The Aesthetic Movement in Its American Cultural Context." In *In Pursuit of Beauty: Americans and the Aesthetic Movement,* pp. 23–51. New York, 1986.
Stokes, John. "Aestheticism." In *Encyclopedia of Literature and Criticism,* edited by Martin Coyle, pp. 1055–1067. London, 1990.
Warner, Eric, and Graham Hough. *Strangeness and Beauty: An Anthology of Aesthetic Criticism, 1840–1910.* 2 vols. Cambridge and New York, 1983.
Wilde, Oscar. *The Artist as Critic: Critical Writings of Oscar Wilde.* Edited by Richard Ellmann. New York, 1969.
Wimsatt, William K., Jr., and Cleanth Brooks. "Art for Art's Sake." In *Literary Criticism: A Short History,* pp. 475–498. New York, 1957.

LINDA DOWLING

AESTHETIC QUALITIES. *See* Qualities, Aesthetic.

AFRICAN AESTHETICS. In academic (Western) scholarship, the systematic study of indigenous African aesthetic criteria really just began during the last decades of the twentieth century. Prior to then, the kinds of objects that are coveted by Western museums and collectors as "African art" had to undergo a convoluted process of intercultural aesthetic integration. In the West they have evolved from being exotic curiosities picked up by merchant sailors and explorers in remote places (fifteenth to eighteenth century) to being cultural artifacts produced by primitive craftsmen (nineteenth century), and finally artistic masterpieces that transcend their cultural origins and are of universal aesthetic distinction (twentieth century). This latest phase has coincided with a rekindled interest in the aesthetic priorities of the cultures in which they were originally created, and it is this research that has finally given birth to a discipline of truly African aesthetics.

Connoisseurship. The notion of the connoisseur appears to be peculiarly Western in origin. The word connotes a variety of attributes having to do with the highest sensitivity in matters of aesthetic taste and judgment. More ordinary humans are meant to defer to connoisseurs with regard to such matters. How the Western connoisseur came to be involved with the art of Africa is an interesting story (Price, 1989). But to be clear about its significance it must first be acknowledged that the aesthetic standards used to evaluate "African art" by connoisseurs for and in Western culture were not of African origin.

The objects found in museum and private collections (primarily sculpture—masks and figurative carvings) were created by Africans for more than decorative purposes; they served instrumental ends, for example, worship, perpetuation of the memory of an ancestor, and as one component of a masquerade. Only when they are severed from their African background and context and hung on a museum or gallery wall are they transformed into exclusively artistic works for Western(ized) eyes.

It is difficult to be precise about when the arts of Africa were first accorded a significant aesthetic status by Western connoisseurs. One noteworthy venue that is mentioned regularly in the literature is the old Trocadéro Ethnographic Museum in Paris. Reference is made to the encounters Pablo Picasso and other early modern artists (Georges Braque, André Derain, André Lhote, Henri Matisse, Valminck) had with its collection of African artifacts during the first decade of the twentieth century.

Picasso's observations on this experience thirty years later, as paraphrased by André Malraux, are noteworthy:

"I stayed. I stayed." He felt that "something was happening [to him] . . . that it was very important." He suddenly realized "why he was a painter." For unlike Derain, Matisse, and Braque, for whom "fetishes," *"les nègres,"* were simply "good sculptures . . . like any other," he had discovered that these masks were first of all "magical things," "mediators," "intercessors" between man and the obscure forces of evil, just as potent as the "threatening spirits" present throughout the world, and "tools" and "weapons" with which to free oneself from the dangers and anxieties that burden humanity.

(Malraux, 1974, pp. 17ff.; quoted in [and apparently translated into English by] Paudrat, 1984, p. 141)

Picasso was not an ethnographer and never demonstrated interest in obtaining detailed information about African cultures. Art historians therefore tend to depict his relationship with African objects on a purely formal level (W. Rubin, 1984, p. 20). "For Picasso, who usually did not even distinguish between African and Oceanic art, tribal sculpture represented primarily an elective affinity and secondarily a substance to be cannibalized" (ibid., p. 14). What is remarkable about the quoted passage is the insight it provides into how this apparently significant aesthetic experience influenced Picasso to associate African forms with the spiritual, and that at this point he too saw this as a dimension to his own work.

Viewings of the Trocadéro's permanent ethnographic collection are said to have provided an opportunity for an influential number of Western artists, critics, and connoisseurs to begin to accord genuine aesthetic merit to African sculptures as "works of art" (Leiris and Delange, 1968, p. 8). Yet, to demonstrate how extended and how recent the process of Western aesthetic integration has been, the second-most frequently mentioned exhibition of what came to be called "African Primitive Art" took place in 1984 at the Museum of Modern Art in New York City (W. Rubin, 1984). It was only in the latter that displayed pieces were unabashedly accorded the title "masterpiece."

For the Western connoisseur, "masterpiece" signifies a work whose aesthetic distinction transcends its cultural origins and acquires universal appeal. Yet one paradox concerning the relationship between African aesthetic masterpieces and Western connoisseurs was (and in many cases still is) that this work was said to have been created by primitive tribesmen who were incapable of aesthetic sensitivity.

Characterized as irrational, emotive, instinctual, preliterate, and childlike, the inhabitants of African cultures were rated relatively low on the cross-cultural index of aesthetic sensitivity. They were said to be at too elementary a stage of development to have produced art, much less fine art, in the sense that has become conventional in modern societies. How inarticulate and instinctual primitive tribes were able to create sculpted pieces that could be "discovered" and christened artistic and aesthetic masterpieces by Western connoisseurs is a problem that was never satisfactorily resolved. And although many Western connoisseurs claim that their aesthetic sensitivities are culturally transcendent and

in principle universal in scope, it is difficult to reconcile this with the fact that they did not award masterpiece status to such objects from the very beginning.

Although the status of the connoisseur remains relatively secure at the apex of the Western aesthetic establishment, such problems have inspired a growing number of critics to challenge the notion of an aesthetic overlord. Connoisseurs are said to be a product of Western cultures, and as such their aesthetic sensitivities must also be products of Western acculturation (Clifford, 1988). If artistic tastes and fashions have changed over the course of Western history, so too have the aesthetic sensitivities that govern the discriminating taste of that culture's connoisseurs. It was such underlying processes of cultural change that made it historically appropriate for Western connoisseurs to confer artistic and masterpiece status on a selection of African artifacts at a certain point in time. But it may well be that the objects selected for "masterpiece" status evidence formal properties, conjoined with features associated with titillating Western images of "savagery," that members of that culture have been conditioned to find appealing and intriguing.

African Aesthetics in Western Scholarship. The history of Western scholarship detailing how Africans themselves regard the objects the West has transformed into "African art" is considerably more complex than this brief discussion of connoisseurship might imply. Yet one assumption underlying Western theoretical approaches to the arts of alien cultures, which is now said to be a distinguishing characteristic of "modern" Western culture itself (Rorty, 1980), is that properly trained researchers can transcend their Western cultural background and identify the aesthetic priorities of alien cultures in an objective manner.

Two approaches on indigenous African aesthetic sensitivities that originated early in the twentieth century are still of consequence today. One is a more expansive version of that already mentioned—inarticulate primitive tribesmen carving artifacts to serve a variety of traditional functions for communities whose members were unable to distinguish between myth and fact, magic and science, reason and emotion, art and craft. In Western intellectual history, this viewpoint is perhaps most closely identified with the work of the French philosopher Lucien Lévy-Bruhl (1928).

As a philosopher, Lévy-Bruhl was primarily concerned with the cognitive character of primitive cultures. Nevertheless, his signal influence at a certain point in time had important consequences for the collection and exegesis of "African Primitive Art." For example, his analyses persuaded many scholars that African cultures could only be considered authentically primitive—autocthonous and pristine—prior to the onset of European imperialism and colonialism. The forceful intervention of European powers into African societies inevitably resulted in cultural disruption and contamination. This opinion was later reinforced by the work of the French anthropologist Claude Lévi-Strauss

(1966). As a result, museums and private collectors (as well as connoisseurs) have come to place a distinctly higher value on the authenticity and integrity of "Primitive African Art" that was produced prior to colonialism.

A second consequence for African aesthetics that may be linked to the influence of Lévy-Bruhl was the relative de-emphasis that came to be placed on the study of indigenous African aesthetic criteria or discourse. Primitive craftsmen (rather than artists) were seen as fashioning a wide variety of artifacts (rather than works of art) that served a variety of sacred and profane instrumental (rather than decorative) ends in their cultures. Whether the objects involved were royal regalia, masquerade costumes, figurative carvings in a shrine, textiles, pots, or even baskets, the motives for their creation were not decorative. The forms or styles of such pieces and the decorations with which they appeared to be embellished were in fact the products of traditional tribal heritages that made them fundamentally emotive, symbolic, and ritualistic in character. The meanings of these preliterate forms and design motifs, if they could be decoded and expressed in discursive writing, would "say" something about such peoples' feelings for and beliefs about the world. But for anthropologists to express emotive forms of expression by means of discursive texts could not help but fail to distort their true meanings. As a result, Western aestheticians, anthropologists, and philosophers were discouraged from studying African cultures with a view to systematizing in analytic form their aesthetic priorities and sensitivities.

An alternative approach to the study of African aesthetic sensitivities derives from the work of the anthropologist Franz Boas (1927). He rejected cultural evolutionism and argued for cultural relativism—that all cultures should be regarded in principle as equal and comparable intellectually, artistically, and aesthetically. Evaluative judgments made by the members of one culture about the level of development or sophistication of another, therefore, inevitably become ethnocentric in nature.

Boas stressed the importance of empirical fieldwork, of learning about an alien culture by living in it and becoming fluent in the language. Overreliance on any form of scientific or transcendent anthropological theory as a basis on which to compose a definitive study of alien cultures (rather than empirical fieldwork) would be a sure source of factual error. Although this approach has often been overshadowed by the disproportionate media and popular attention attracted by exotic notions of primitive peoples with radically different forms of cognition, its proponents and modern descendants have stubbornly persevered over the years, and it is today in a position to become more influential than ever before.

The importance that came to be assigned to fieldwork as a sine qua non of anthropological research resulted in dedicated professionals, such as Bronislaw Malinowski and A. R. Radcliffe-Brown, spending lengthy periods of time living in non-Western societies. In Anglophone countries during this period, roughly corresponding to the midpoint of the twentieth century, the anthropological approach that reigned supreme was what has come to be known as functionalism. With its stress on analyzing a culture on the basis of the social institutions that compose it, functionalism laid greater emphasis on kinship and economic relations than on topics like art and aesthetics. If and when "art" objects were discussed, it was in terms of their symbolic functions in (social) rituals.

Nevertheless, a methodological seed had been sown. At the least, these objects were being reintegrated with their native cultural contexts rather than treated only as museum artifacts attributed to amorphous primitive peoples. Indeed, the next major step in the history of "African art" was for objects to be grouped formally and stylistically according to their tribal affiliations—Dogon "art," Yoruba "art," Kuba "art," and so on (Fagg, 1968).

This notion of "context" grew more expansive with the passage of time (Biebuyck, 1985–1986). African ideas and sentiments about beauty—in effect, aesthetics—that were involved in the creation, fashioning, and evaluation of "African art" objects in indigenous African cultures, as well as their use, became topics for research. In addition, arguments began to be advanced that "African art" objects were in fact also regarded as art in the societies in which they were created (A. Rubin, 1974; Brain, 1980).

The Yoruba of southwestern Nigeria have one of the most widely studied cultures in sub-Saharan Africa. Among Africanists, it is a commonplace generalization that more material has been published on Yoruba art and aesthetics than that of any other African people. Yet the limited intercultural understanding these publications have yielded is an indication of how much remains to be done before a substantive appreciation of African aesthetic sensitivities is achieved.

In ordinary, everyday Yoruba discourse, the term most frequently mentioned that is of fundamental relevance to aesthetic concerns is *ewa*, normally translated into English as "beauty." Rather than being primarily associated with the arts or crafts, however, its most common usage, as might be expected, is with reference to human beings. In this regard, the Yoruba make an explicit distinction between outer (or physical) beauty and inner (or moral) beauty. The former is considered comparatively superficial and therefore unimportant. The latter serves as a measure of a person's moral character *(iwa)* and is said to involve one of the most important observations that can be made about human being.

The qualities that are associated with a beautiful, and therefore good, moral character are what one might expect in a culture that is still predominantly oral; for in such a culture, all information must come out of people's mouths. Persons who cannot be relied upon to speak the truth—to not be candid about what they do and do not know—earn a

AFRICAN AESTHETICS. *Figure of Ogboni or Osugbo Chief, Ijebu,* Nigeria, Yoruba culture (date unknown), terra-cotta, 30 1/2 inches high; Walt Disney-Tishman African Art Collection, Glendale, California. (Photograph by Jerry L. Thompson, courtesy of Museum for African Art, New York; used by permission.)

reputation for being irresponsible and hence for having a bad or unattractive moral character. This means that a person of remarkable physical beauty may become notorious for not possessing "true" (inner, moral) beauty. On the other hand, a person who is physically ugly may be praised for being truly (morally) beautiful.

Other behavioral but also aesthetic criteria associated with having a good/beautiful character have epistemic overtones. Good/beautiful moral character tends to be associated with persons who generally appear composed, self-controlled, patient, and alert. Such individuals are thought more likely to understand what is going on around them

and therefore to be in a better position to provide accurate information and to give useful advice.

When beauty *(ewa)* is attributed to natural or human-made objects (arts and crafts included), the criteria change. The explanation given for this is that such things are not persons and therefore their character *(iwa)* cannot be judged by the same moral/aesthetic standards. A tree or a chicken may be appreciated purely for its physical beauty, though again it is to be regarded as something comparatively superficial. But if the tree produces succulent fruit or the chicken is a plentiful source of eggs, both could be said to have good character and therefore to be exceptionally attractive because of their *usefulness* to the human community.

With regard to the human-made—anything that is the product of labor—the usefulness of the finished product is still the ultimate criterion. The farm that provides ample produce as well as looking well maintained, the armchair that proves to be sturdy and comfortable as well as new, the textile, pot, or basket that is found to be durable as well as inexpensive—all of these would be regarded as having character and therefore being truly beautiful.

The Yoruba attitude to the figurative carvings that Western collectors have found so aesthetically powerful also is essentially utilitarian. A carving is made to serve a practical purpose—to serve as a repository for offerings to a distinguished ancestor, or to comfort a mother or child when a sibling has died. If it is judged to serve that purpose in an effective manner, it is regarded as having character. The types of "formal" qualities preferred in the sculptural representation of a human being would depend on the person being portrayed. In the case of an adult male, certain figurative qualities have come to be associated with the representation of good character. Generally, one would expect a figure to be standing upright, to appear both composed and alert, to appear healthy, and to be properly attired.

The scholarly impetus generated by sustained interest in indigenous African notions of beauty was to have several noteworthy consequences. It resulted in the establishment of a specialized discipline that has come to be known as African art history. African art historians seek to distance themselves from anthropology and its narrow functionalism by embracing at least the following disciplinary priorities: (1) to concentrate on "art" objects and underlying standards of beauty in African cultures; fieldwork, which remains as much a priority here as it does for anthropology, is undertaken with the aim of shedding further light on the aesthetic and artistic standards of the culture involved; (2) to detail and analyze the aesthetic vocabularies and semantic networks internal to African languages; (3) to expand the boundaries of "African art" so that it includes elements of material culture heretofore ignored by Western museums and private collections (bodily adornment, architecture, crafts—baskets and pots, tourist art, modern African art—oil and watercolor painting, etc.); (4) to enable the inhabitants of Western cultures to better appreciate that their artistic and aesthetic preferences are a product of Western acculturation and may be fundamentally different from those taken for granted in an African culture; (5) to improve the cross-cultural appreciation of African ideals of artistic and aesthetic beauty so that the African arts may assume a status comparable to that of other art historical traditions—Islamic art, Oriental art, Western art, and so on.

The importance attached to identifying indigenous standards of beauty and the substantial fieldwork resources that have been committed to achieving this aim are what is providing the data for a subdiscipline devoted exclusively to African aesthetics. No consensus exists about whether certain aesthetic standards are common to African cultures, although there is a consensus among African art historians that the safest way to proceed is to study a wide variety of language cultures individually and then determine whether an inductive basis exists for secure generalizations (Van Damme, 1987). One art historian who pioneered this type of research is Robert Farris Thompson (1973). His articles on Yoruba aesthetic criteria generated widespread interest in identifying comparable criteria in other African cultures (Vogel, 1980; Boone, 1986).

One reservation that has been expressed about some of these studies is the degree to which they represent what Africans themselves actually think and feel about aesthetic matters. A predisposition to treat Africans as being less concerned to articulate their sentiments and thoughts about beauty in a precise manner may tempt field-workers into intuiting, articulating, and systematizing them on Africans' behalf. The danger with this approach is that the criteria "discovered" by art historians might be more a product of their own imagined interpretations of African sentiments than an accurate rendering of indigenous African meanings.

The discovery that Africans have indigenous aesthetic standards has encouraged African art historians to advocate a much more diverse program of intercultural comparisons between Africa and the West. They are now experimenting with intercultural perspectives derived from (Western) disciplines such as history, literary criticism, performance studies, philosophy, and psychology with a view to better integrating the aesthetic values and practices that Africans may or may not have in common with their wider cultural contexts (Blier, 1990).

African Aesthetics in African Scholarship. Throughout the history of African studies in Western academia a number of African scholars have expressed dissatisfaction with the ways in which their cultures were portrayed, and consequently formulated their own alternative theoretical interpretations. The best known of these is negritude, but today it too has been supplanted by the work of university-trained African researchers who believe they are in a better position to analyze the aesthetic nuances of their native cultures than many alien field-workers.

The most prominent advocate of negritude was the scholar, poet, and onetime president of Senegal, Léopold Sédar Senghor (1971). Offended by the unflattering terms with which the African intellect was characterized by early Western anthropologists, Senghor sought to defend the continent's integrity by proposing an alternative African worldview and system of values that were fundamentally aesthetic in character.

Senghor adapted several of the unflattering characteristics previously attributed to the African consciousness and incorporated them into a lyrical, positive theory (some say ideology) of an alternative form of cognition. Africans did view and interpret their experience in an emotive manner. But this was no different from the artist whose views of reality are mediated and formed on the basis of intuition, imagination, and the act of creation. For Africans, feelings rather than abstraction and analysis were the keys to understanding, and this is why the aesthetic (myths, rhythm, the arts, and crafts) was assigned so prominent a role in their cultures.

It was African scholars too who expressed reservations about negritude as an alternative, and as an accurate rendering of the African consciousness (Soyinka, 1997). Apart from its gross generalizations about a mentality supposedly common to all African societies, they argued that it granted too much credence to the advocates of a primitive mentality.

These critics argued that the African mind was not qualitatively different from that of other races. The types of metaphors and other forms of expression characteristic of African cultures might prove to be distinctive, but this was insufficient reason to attribute their creation to a deviant form of cognition. If anything, the tendency of foreign scholars to do so reflected an insufficient fluency in the languages of the cultures they were studying. This was now said to be the most probable cause of exotic and bizarre renderings of African meanings (artistic and nonartistic) and of the consciousness from which they were said to arise.

Of course, contemporary non-African anthropologists and art historians also strongly endorse the indispensability of fluency in the language of whatever culture they are researching. This is what one would expect, especially at a time when field-workers are targeting the semantic networks underlying African aesthetic discourse. Nonetheless, there are clear signs of a coincidence of findings and conclusions common to African and non-African researchers who have become concerned with the aesthetics of the same culture. With reference to Yoruba aesthetics, for example, the work of Rowland Abiodun (1990) and Babatunde Lawal (1996), both native Yoruba art historians, builds on the pioneering efforts of scholars such as Robert Farris Thompson and Henry and Margaret Drewal (1983).

With regard to the substance of Yoruba aesthetics, as more comes to be known about the semantic networks underlying a variety of fields of discourse in that language, it appears that the values that underlie epistemological, moral, and aesthetic priorities are systematically interrelated. This means that the criteria enunciated as ensuring reliable perception and cognition become essential prerequisites to having a good moral character, while the latter (as mentioned earlier) is regarded as a paradigm case of the beautiful (Hallen, 1996).

The study of African aesthetics today constitutes one of the most exciting and dynamic subdisciplines in African and intercultural studies. Yet, because it is also a discipline in which African meanings must of necessity be translated into and expressed by one of the few "world" languages (English, French), it is in the interests of all concerned—Africans and non-Africans—to work together to ensure that the highest possible professional standards are maintained; for it is intercultural dialogue based on reciprocal language fluency that will best enable researchers to see where Western and African values and beliefs overlap and where they diverge.

[*See also* Black Aesthetic; Caribbean Aesthetics; Comparative Aesthetics; Locke; Postcolonialism; *and* Tribal Art.]

BIBLIOGRAPHY

Abiodun, Rowland. "The Future of African Art Studies: An African Perspective." In *African Art Studies: The State of the Discipline*, pp. 63–89. Washington, D.C., 1990.

Appiah, Kwane Anthony. "Is the Post- in Postmodern the Post- in Postcolonial?" *Critical Inquiry* 17.2 (winter 1991): 336–357.

Biebuyck, Daniel. *The Arts of Zaire*. 2 vols. Berkeley, 1985–1986.

Blier, Suzanne Preston. "African Art Studies at the Crossroads: An American Perspective." In *African Art Studies: The State of the Discipline*, pp. 91–107. Washington, D.C., 1990.

Boas, Franz. *Primitive Art*. Cambridge, Mass., 1927.

Boone, Sylvia Ardyn. *Radiance from the Waters: Ideals of Feminine Beauty in Mende Art*. New Haven, 1986.

Brain, Robert. *Art and Society in Africa*. London and New York, 1980.

Clifford, James. *The Predicament of Culture: Twentieth-Century Ethnography, Literature, and Art*. Cambridge, Mass., 1988.

Drewal, Henry John, and Margaret Thompson Drewal. *Gelede: Art and Female Power among the Yoruba*. Bloomington, Ind., 1983.

Fagg, William. *African Tribal Images*. Cleveland, Ohio, 1968.

Hallen, Barry. "The Good, the Bad, and the Beautiful: Discourse about Values in Yoruba Culture." *SAPINA* (a bulletin of the Society for African Philosophy in North America) 9.3 (July–December 1996): 41–175.

Lawal, Babatunde. *The Gelede Spectacle: Art, Gender, and Social Harmony in an African Culture*. Seattle, 1996.

Leiris, Michel, and Jacqueline Delange. *African Art*. Translated by Michael Ross. New York, 1968.

Lévi-Strauss, Claude. *The Savage Mind*. Chicago, 1966.

Lévy-Bruhl, Lucien. *The "Soul" of the Primitive*. Translated by Lilian A. Clare. New York, 1928.

Malraux, André. *La tête d'obsidienne*. Paris, 1974.

Meyer, Laure. *Art and Craft in Africa: Everyday Life, Ritual, Court Art*. Edited by Jean-Claude Dubost and Jean-François Gonthier, English adaptation by Jean-Marie Clarke. Paris, 1995.

Paudrat, Jean-Louis. "The Arrival of Tribal Objects in the West: From Africa." In *"Primitivism" in 20th Century Art: Affinity of the Tribal and the Modern*, edited by William Rubin, vol. I, pp. 125–175. New York, 1984.

Price, Sally. *Primitive Art in Civilized Places*. Chicago, 1989.

Rorty, Richard. *Philosophy and the Mirror of Nature*. Corr. ed. Princeton, N.J., 1980.

Rubin, Arnold. *African Accumulative Sculpture: Power and Display*. New York, 1974.

Rubin, William. "Modernist Primitivism." In *"Primitivism" in 20th Century Art: Affinity of the Tribal and the Modern*, edited by William Rubin, vol. I, pp. 1–81. New York, 1984.

Senghor, Léopold Sédar. *The Foundations of "Africanite" or "Negritude" and "Arabite."* Translated by Mercer Cook. Paris, 1971.

Soyinka, Wole. *The Burden of Memory and the Muse of Remission*. Oxford, 1997.

Thompson, Robert Farris. "Yoruba Artistic Criticism." In *The Traditional Artist in African Societies*, edited by Warren L. d'Azevedo, pp. 19–61. Bloomington, Ind., 1973.

Van Damme, Wilfried. *A Comparative Analysis concerning Beauty and Ugliness in Sub-Saharan Africa*. Ghent, 1987.

Vogel, Susan Mullin. *Beauty in the Eyes of the Baule: Aesthetics and Cultural Values*. Working Papers in the Traditional Arts 6. Philadelphia, 1980.

BARRY HALLEN

AFRICAN-AMERICAN AESTHETICS. *See* Black Aesthetic; Harlem Renaissance; Locke.

AISTHESIS. *See* Definition of Art; Origins of Aesthetics, *article on* History of Aisthesis; *and* Rhetoric.

AL-FARABI, MUHAMMAD. *See* Farabi, Muhammad al-.

ALBERTI, LEON BATTISTA (1404–1472), humanist of the fifteenth century. Alberti wrote on a wide variety of subjects and in different genres including dialogues, plays, tales, and treatises. He took an active interest in the arts, knew many of the leading painters and architects of the time, such as Fra Angelico and Filippo Brunelleschi, and was on familiar terms with many important patronal families, such as the Rucellai in Florence, the Este in Ferrara, the Gonzaga in Mantua, and the Montefeltros in Urbino. His artistic interests were more than merely academic. By the time of his death he had received some of the most important architectural commissions of the day: the completion of Santa Maria Novella, the facade of the Palazzo Rucellai, and the chapel of San Pancrazio, all in Florence, San Andrea and San Sebastiano in Mantua, and the Tempio Maletestiano in Rimini. It is possible that he also tried his hand at painting. The *Birth of the Virgin,* now in the National Gallery in Washington, D.C., is thought by some scholars to be a work by his hand. No other humanist or artist accomplished as much, and with such a wide degree of success, as Alberti, and it is thus for good reason that many consider him to embody the highest aspirations of the Renaissance.

Alberti was born in Genoa to a family of powerful merchants and bankers who had been exiled from their native Florence in 1393. In the 1420s he began his legal studies at the University of Bologna in preparation for a high clerical career. He became interested in mathematics, which would later manifest itself in his *Ludi Matematici* (1450), but it was to being a writer that he thought he would actually dedicate his life. He published his first play, *Philodoxeos,* a comedy written in a pseudoantique manner, in 1424. This was followed by the treatise *De commodus litterarum atque incommodus* (1429) on the vicissitudes of pursuing a literary career. During this time he also began an intense investigation into the arts, prompted by his return to Florence in 1428 when the ban against his family was at last lifted. There he came into contact for the first time with the work of Masaccio, Donatello, and Filippo Brunelleschi. By 1432, he had moved to Rome and was employed in the papal curia preparing documents for publication. He may even have been ordained as a priest.

Alberti soon became an important figure in the papal retinue, serving as an adviser and consultant on matters in the arts, and even possibly in politics. Nicholas V (1447–1455), who knew Alberti as a student in Bologna, had become a close friend, and it was to Nicholas that Alberti presented a manuscript version of his treatise on architecture in 1452. A later pope, Pius II (1458–1464), was also a friend and shared Alberti's humanistic perspective. Pius's rebuilding of his home village, Corsigniano, just east of Siena, into a spectacular papal residence renamed Pienza is considered by many to have been conducted under Alberti's influence. It still exists and is heralded as one of the most important urban designs of the fifteenth century. Pius's successor, Paul II, however, had little sympathy for humanism and forced many humanists, including Alberti, to quit the curia. Alberti was sufficiently well-off by this time to support himself on his own. He lived the rest of his life as a much-respected luminary of Italian learning, traveling the circuit of humanist courts. He spent autumns at the court of the renowned Count Federico da Montefeltro in Urbino.

From the point of view of his aesthetic theories, it is useful to divide Alberti's writings into two groups: (1) his treatises on painting, sculpture, and architecture; and (2) his numerous other works, which, though not directly relating to the topic of art, nonetheless contain important clues to his cultural theories. Had Alberti written only the treatises,

they alone would have guaranteed his name for posterity: *De pictura* (1435), of which Alberti wrote an Italian version (*Della pittura* [1436]) dedicated to Brunelleschi, *De statua* (1435?), and *De re aedificatoria* (manuscript, c.1452; first printed edition, 1485) fundamentally transformed attitudes on the arts, largely because they were the first attempts in the Renaissance to address questions of theory at a level understandable to practitioners and patrons alike. This is not to say that his treatises lacked a philosophical basis but that they attempted to make theoretical and philosophical views directly meaningful in art production. In a sense, these works ushered in a modern attitude toward theory in that art was linked to explicitly articulated codes of intention. The treatises thus set the stage for rigorous disciplinary distinctions between painting, sculpture, and architecture, with each having its own theoretical-historical discourse. Alberti's writings are also modern in that they recognize the need for artists to explain their work to the lay public.

De pictura is divided into three parts, a division rooted in medieval academic practices: theoretical, practical, and pedagogical. It is a truly extraordinary text. Nothing like it had been attempted in the Middle Ages, and possibly even in antiquity. *De pictura* covers a range of issues such as color theory, composition, content, and pedagogy, and is sprinkled with knowledge and opinions gleaned from classical texts.

Book 1, in which Alberti presented the mathematics of perspective, was to become the most famous part of the treatise. Although painters had used something akin to perspective for decades, they relied on intuition and appearances. With Alberti's introduction of concepts like the "vanishing point" and the "horizon line" and a system by which spatial depth could be constructed easily and precisely on the canvas or on a wall, perspective quickly became one of the preeminent tools of painters and architects alike. It remains an essential aspect of art and architectural training to this day. Alberti described perspective not only mathematically, but also metaphorically, explaining it as a window with a screen in it through which the painter reconstructs reality.

In Book 2, Alberti introduces the important term *istoria,* the first modern articulation of the theory of composition. It was not enough, he argued, simply to represent the actions and movements of the individual bodies in a correct way; everything had to be related by a unified action and positioned in an ordered space. Instead of dividing a painting up between different times and different spatial zones, as was common in the Middle Ages, *istoria,* though limiting in its temporal restrictions, made it possible to portray events with deeper social and psychological content.

Alberti's contribution to the arts also took the form of practical devices. In *De statua,* he introduced the *orizzonte,* a cylindrical disk with a rotating dial that was to be placed on top of the head of a body in order both to better record antique statues and to let sculptors become better informed about the dimension and proportion of the human body. Alberti used something akin to an *orizzonte,* but on a larger scale, to construct one of the first modern maps of Rome. Unlike earlier maps, which were drawn by intuition, Alberti used measurements taken from a single vantage point in the middle of the city.

With such extraordinary imagination and energy, it was only a matter of time before Alberti began to interest himself in architecture. He pursued it with such diligence that still today, his principal fame stems from *De re aedificatoria* (On the art of building in ten books, 1450). This text was so valued that when it was printed in 1486, fourteen years after Alberti's death, the first copy went to none other than Lorenzo de Medici, the ruler of Florence, who zealously guarded it and even had the great scholar-poet Angelo Poliziano write an introduction.

The model that Alberti used for his treatise was a newly uncovered complete manuscript of Vitruvius's *De architectura,* written in 42 BCE for Emperor Augustus. Alberti's work was, however, no mere copy, but a full reevaluation of Vitruvius and of classical and medieval building practices. A testament to his vast erudition and his familiarity with Roman ruins, the book discussed everything from the nature of building materials to the final details of the ornament, and from choosing a site for a building to the layout of cities. It also provided one of the first descriptions in the Renaissance of the role of the architect in making a design. Particularly important was the architect's ability to envision the project in his mind before beginning to set it down on paper. Alberti also addresses the role of the patron, exhorting him to see the architect as an important contributor not only to the patron's good name but to the splendor of the whole city. Alberti's treatise was so complete that it continued to have importance throughout subsequent centuries. Even today it has its admirers.

Given that there was no other contemporaneous book of comparable scale and erudition, *De re aedificatoria* is an invaluable source of information about fifteenth-century knowledge. Significant is the emphasis on proportion and number harmony, a detailed account of which is given in book 9, chapters 5 and 6. In synthesizing classical and medieval theories, Alberti argued that the proportion of a building should conform to the harmonies one finds in the ratios of music and in the human body. "All must harmonize in order to appear as a single, well-articulated body, not a jumble of unrelated fragments" (book 1, chap. 9). He also states that "I shall define beauty as a unity to which nothing can be added, diminished, or altered but for the worse" (book 6, chap. 2). Beauty is the agreement and harmony of the parts in relation to the whole. Alberti points out, however, that there are different types of bodies, big and small and short and fat. Proportion was, therefore, not a set of

rules stemming from a single, ideal body, but rules that emerged from nature in conjunction with study and experience.

This argument is different from the earlier definition of beauty presented in *De pictura.* There Alberti suggested that because no one person's features are all equally beautiful, the painter needs to construct a beautiful body out of elements that come from various people. Beauty is a composite outside of and above the realm of nature. In *De re aedificatoria,* Alberti's concept of beauty is more dynamic. Beauty is linked not only to the appearance of things, but to the process of making it real. Buildings should, for example, be designed with functional criteria in mind. Furthermore, the architect has to differentiate public from private, representative from nonrepresentative, hot environments from moist ones, and so on. The word Alberti used to tie all this together was *concinnitas:* the harmonization of all considerations into an acceptable design. *Concinnitas* was also something that linked humans and nature, for "nature seeks nothing greater than to make all her works perfect, which they could never be unless they had *concinnitas*" (book 9, chap. 5).

Despite Alberti's admiration of classical authors, he emphasized early on the need to be independent of the ancients. This flexibility, similar to his intentions of synthesizing reason and experience, is evident not only in his criticism of Vitruvius, but also in his built architecture. San Andrea in Mantua and the Tempio Maletestiano in Rimini are, for example, important landmarks in the return to an *all'antica* mode of design. But to label them neoclassical would be too extreme for they portray an eclectic and inventive sense of detailing. They demonstrate not only a desire for experimentation, but also an awareness of medieval prototypes. This is true of Alberti's writings as well. In fact, in one of his literary sketches he pokes fun at those who try too hard to imitate Cicero at the expense of all else. Perhaps the most ingenious example of his synthetic approach is his completion of the medieval facade of the Florentine church Santa Maria Novella, which was only built up to one story. Alberti designed the upper part in a style that strikes such a good balance with the preexisting medieval structure that the untrained eye views them as one and same.

Alberti's contributions to aesthetics outlined thus far can be grouped into at least four different categories: (1) his mathematics of perspective; (2) the introduction of a theoretical terminology like *istoria* in painting and *concinnitas* in architecture; (3) the organizing of the various aesthetic fields into disciplines; and (4) his art and architectural production. Each introduces a different set of scholarly and hermeneutical problems.

From a more philosophical perspective, one cannot ignore a fifth category: Alberti's interest in the moral problems associated with aesthetics. This is a question that has to do with Alberti's lifelong interest in masking and deception, which he developed in his writings. Until recently, however, most of Alberti's numerous plays, dialogues, and comic tales have been considered to have little direct significance for his aesthetic theories. *De commodus litterarum atque incommodus* (1429), *Intercoenales* (c.1439), *Theogenius* (1439), *Della Famiglia* (1443), and *Momus* (c.1450), among others, are usually described and discussed as "literary" works. Nonetheless, many of them deal with ethical issues relating to art. *Momus,* for example, describing the life of the Greek god of ridicule, is a comic/tragic exploration of how mankind is driven to art not because of an urge to make beautiful things but because of the need to conceal one's true identity. Although heavily indebted to the Hellenistic author Lucian, this work is, as with the writing of *De re aedificatoria,* no mere copy of classical material. It is a type of history of—as Alberti put it—"mankind's disease-ridden life."

The story begins with the gods giving gifts to Jove to celebrate the creation of the earth. Minerva gives the house, to which Momus responds by giving the cockroach. Nothing is what it seems anymore. Momus also teaches women how to apply makeup. The story line thickens into a complex plot of humans and gods engaged in a farce of masking and countermasking in which Momus, outdoing Fraud, becomes the true master of deception. A genius of "many-tonguedness," he can easily simulate even "those who are believed to be beautiful and wise." Jove is concerned that the level of deception has become so great that it has infected even the gods and orders the destruction of the earth. Momus, now turning serious, prepares a treatise on how the new world should be governed, but his credibility has been so eroded that Jove throws his book onto the heap of rotting books in his library. Uncertain, however, as to how to design the new world, Jove disguises his identity and attends a conference of philosophers, hoping that they will provide answers; in all their debating, they fail to discover the deity in their midst. In the end, the destruction of the world begins more by accident than through planning.

Many of the themes of *Momus* are foreshadowed in *Intercoenales* (Table talks), a collection of more than forty short dialogues and monologues that portray a world in which the forces of goodness struggle against mankind's inherent aesthetic capacities. The work is constructed around a host of characters with names like Libripeta (bookworm), Scriptor (writer), and Neofronus (newfound wisdom), all of whom are part of a network of interrelated dramatis personae, many with autobiographical overtones. *Somnium* (Dream) and *Defunctus* (Death) are two pieces that portray particularly dark images of an inverted world in which the difference between good and evil is no longer absolutely clear. In *Somnium,* a cynical writer named Libripeta travels through the sewer pipes of a city in a horrific journey that forces him to reevaluate whatever lingering hope he had in the future of humanity. He sees a volcano that spews out material goods to a crowd of greedy people, as well as an abyss

where everything that is good has been discarded, including part of his own brain. The wisdom learned from the sewer, the *cloacarium prudentiam,* leaves Libripeta with permanent scars. In *Defunctus,* a humanist writer dies, becomes a ghost, and views the unraveling of his widow's virtue, the destruction of his literary works, and the demise of the family in the matter of a few days. Unable to communicate with society and warn them of mankind's foul nature, he lives an anguished afterlife in the gloom of Hades. On the optimistic side is the dialogue *Anuli* (Little rings), the hero of which is Philoponius (lover of hard work). The story begins with his struggles against Envy, Calumny, and Poverty. Despite their efforts, he remained dedicated to goodness. The gods are impressed and convene to judge on his beatification. With Hope and Minerva presiding over the ceremony, they confirm that he "will make the lives of princes, as well as of private citizens, happy and blessed." Yet, here too the "happy omens" will end with "a sad prediction." It is the prediction of cynicism and disappointment.

All in all, Alberti's thinking lacks an identifiable philosophical niche, which is why some historians of philosophy have relegated him to the position of "a man of letters" below the great philosophical giants of the age, such as Nicholas of Cusa. And, it is true, Alberti was neither a strict Neoplatonist nor a convinced neo-Aristotelian. But this is to measure him with the wrong model in mind, especially since Alberti expressed considerable distaste for what he suggested were the empty speculations of the *literati, philosophi,* and *eruditi.* Instead, he saw himself as something of a cultural critic hoping to rekindle a purer way of life that had been forgotten in a world of *varietà e varietà.*

At first glance, it might seem difficult to reconcile the humor, skepticism, and even cynicism that punctuate Alberti's dialogues with the optimism toward art that seems to be the project of his well-known treatises and architecture. The rift between them can be explained partially by the fact that his "humanistic" writings were written for a much smaller audience of intellectuals and friends than his treatises. It can also be argued that his intention was, on the one hand, to ground the arts in a theoretical autonomy that would bind the artist, patron, and even the critic in a shared social vision around a single, useful text, and, on the other hand, to make sure that one did not lose sight of the basic moral problems associated with mankind's aesthetic nature.

[*See also* Architecture, *article on* Italian Renaissance Aesthetics; Formalism, *article on* Formalism in Analytic Aesthetics; Perspective; *and* Renaissance Italian Aesthetics.]

BIBLIOGRAPHY

Works by Alberti

Dinner Pieces. Translated by David Marsh. Binghamton, N.Y., 1987.
Momo o del principe. Edited by Nanni Balestrini. Genoa, 1986.
On Painting and On Sculpture. Edited and translated by Cecil Grayson. London, 1972.

On the Art of Building in Ten Books. Translated by Joseph Rykwert, Neil Leach, and Robert Tavernor. Cambridge, Mass., 1988.

Other Sources

Behn, Irene. *Leone Battista Alberti als Kunstphilosoph.* Strasbourg, 1911.

Borsi, Franco. *Leon Battista Alberti: The Complete Works.* Translated by Rudolf G. Carpanini. New York, 1977.

Carpo, Mario. *Alberti, Raffaello, Serlio, e Camillo: Metodo ed ordini nella teoria architettonica dei primi moderni.* Geneva, 1993.

Choay, Françoise. *La règle et le modèle: sur la théorie de l'architecture et de l'urbanisme.* Paris, 1980. Translated as *The Rule and the Model: On the Theory of Architecture and Urbanism,* edited by Denise Bratton (Cambridge, Mass., 1997).

Damisch, Hubert. *L'origine de la perspective.* Paris, 1987. Translated by John Goodman as *The Origin of Perspective* (Cambridge, Mass., 1994).

Jarzombek, Mark. *On Leon Battista Alberti: His Literary and Aesthetic Theories.* Cambridge, Mass., 1989.

Johnson, Eugene J. *S. Andrea in Mantua: The Building History.* University Park, Pa., 1975.

Kelly, Joan. *Leon Battista Alberti: Universal Man of the Early Renaissance.* Chicago, 1969.

Mühlmann, Heiner. *Ästhetische Theorie der Renaissance: Leon Battista Alberti.* Bonn, 1981.

Parronchi, Alessandro. *Studi su la dolce prospettiva.* Milan, 1964.

Rykwert, Joseph, and Anne Engel, eds. *Leon Battista Alberti.* Milan, 1994.

Salmi, Mario, and Eugenio Garin, eds. *Rinascimento,* vol. 12. Florence, 1972.

Smith, Christine. *Architecture in the Culture of Early Humanism: Ethics, Aesthetics, and Eloquence, 1400–1470.* New York and Oxford, 1992.

Vignetti, Luigi, ed. *Omaggio ad Alberti.* Studi e Documenti di Architettura Nr. 1. Florence, 1972.

Westfall, Carroll William. *In This Most Perfect Paradise: Alberti, Nicholas V, and the Invention of Conscious Urban Planning in Rome, 1447–1455.* University Park, Pa., 1974.

MARK JARZOMBEK

ALEATORIC PROCESSES. The Latin root for *alea* is a dice game: it represents an act of introducing elements of uncertainty in outcome with a predefined set of conditions. Chance, indeterminacy, and randomness may be defined as specific attributes of an aleatoric process. With respect to aesthetic appreciation, it is important to distinguish between chance as a generating mechanism for aleatoric processes, indeterminacy as uncertainty in outcome resulting from them, and randomness as a type and a measure of uncertainty. In application, aleatoric processes manifest in the way(s) in which an artist or composer (1) incorporates chance techniques in the generation of a composition, and (2) introduces levels of indeterminacy in the performance or presentation of an artwork. The concept of *alea* raises the fundamental question: what are the aesthetic motivations for incorporating chance and indeterminacy in art? What aesthetic values does it hold for the viewer? The justification of chance, as a compositional principle, has given rise to intriguing musical aesthetic debates in the second half of the twentieth century.

Harriett Watts, in *Chance: A Perspective on Dada* (1980), discusses how random or accidental relationships are manifested in Western art long before Dada, but emphasizes that chance emerged as a distinctive aesthetic and compositional principle only in the twentieth century. The twentieth-century preoccupation with chance emanates from the confluence of cultural, scientific, philosophical, and psychological trends that emerged at the turn of the century. Dadaists, in their rebellion against establishment, initiated radical experimentation with chance in the domains of visual art, music, and poetry. In the scientific world, Niels Bohr and Werner Heisenberg's interpretation of quantum physics replaced Newtonian principles, emphasizing the dynamic and relativistic models of subatomic particles: atomic particles are not small, hard objects but their conditions are indeterminate—they change according to the observer. This trend was paralleled by an increasing awareness of Eastern philosophies and myths, for example, Daoism (Taoism), the oracles of *Yi jing (I Ching),* that emphasize the mutual interrelation of all things and events that are in ceaseless transformation. This perspective also resonates with the Jungian theory of synchronicity that upholds the importance of coincidences in the realm of psychology. This essay traces the application of aleatoric processes in the representative artistic and musical trends that emerged in the course of the twentieth century.

Dadaism. Dadaism emerged in the first decade of the twentieth century as a social and artistic revolt against traditional forms of art. The movement originated in Zurich around 1917, in New York between 1915 and 1916, and then spread to Berlin, Cologne, Hanover, Paris, the Netherlands, and Italy into the early 1920s. In the face of social upheavals and the catastrophes of war, Dadaist aesthetics embraced antilogic or negation of casuality, absurdity, ambiguity, pun, and irony. Dadaism emerged as the most important movement that impacted the arts (i.e., visual, literary, musical) in legitimizing chance procedures as a modus operandi for artistic creation in the course of the twentieth century. Chance techniques were used mainly as a weapon against logical control of materials. Dadaist doctrine also fostered a reconciliation of art and people through direct audience participation.

The beginning of Dadaism is commonly attributed to the creative activities that unfolded at the Cabaret Voltaire in Zurich around 1917. Hugo Ball and other proponents (e.g., Emmy Hennings, Jean Arp, Tristan Tzara, Richard Huelsenbeck) organized nightly shows featuring the recitation of conventional and experimental poetry, simultaneous readings, songs, dances, and orchestral compositions. They welcomed chance combinations of verbal or visual materials as part of their creative process, and they used these to place their art in a state of indeterminacy aimed at thwarting all reasonable expectations. Provocation was the main goal in Dada exhibits, evenings, and presentations: to influence people in the audience to rethink their own positions on public issues.

Of the Zurich Dadaists, Jean Arp's works exhibit a lifelong preoccupation with chance. *Collages Arranged According to the Laws of Chance* (1916–1919) features chance-based arrangements of nonoverlapping geometric shapes. Arp took the idea of chance further in 1930, creating *Papiers déchirés* by tearing, rearranging, and pasting his own earlier drawings and prints. In 1932, he also began to use uniform black paper for torn collage elements and, in the 1940s, added to his repertoire the effects of stained and wrinkled paper—*Papiers froissés*. In his article "Die Musen und der Zufall," Arp declared chance occurrences to be a form of providential guidance. He allowed random intrusions to offer him new points of departure, which he then controlled in their development. No formal decisions guided the process as he used chance as a dynamic means to stimulate further variations in the process of construction.

Dadaism in New York (1915–1920) emerged independently of its counterpart in Zurich. Its chief proponents included Alfred Stieglitz, Marcel Duchamp, Man Ray, and Francis Picabia. Photographer Stieglitz provided a center for exhibiting American and European works at his gallery known as 291. Man Ray worked with collages between 1916 and 1917, one such work being *Revolving Doors,* which consisted of ten graphic plates mounted on a revolving stand so the spectator might see its successive views. Futurism, in its glorification of modern technology and impersonality, occupied the works of Francis Picabia.

Duchamp offered the most radical aesthetic doctrines of his time by emphasizing the intellectual conception of art over sensual experience. His aesthetic aim is captured in his manifesto to reconcile art and the people by "bringing art down from its pedestal." In his "ready-mades"—for example, *Fountain* (1917)—he took an ordinary object such as a urinal and displaced it from its utilitarian context. This set up a contradiction in the minds of the viewer: the object's functional reference collides with the new aesthetic context in which to define the object, producing a visual pun. The artist's choice creates an indeterminate "ruler" for redefining the meaning of everyday objects.

It is important to note that Duchamp's method for incorporating chance, unlike Arp's intuitive one, was rigorously systematic; for example, he insisted that there is no need to repeat a procedure more than three times to gain a fruitful impression of the results. Duchamp's experimentation with chance is best exemplified in the series titled *Three Standard Stoppages* (1913–1914) in which the artist records the ways in which a one-meter string falls. The variety of shapes and forms the strings took were recorded in threes, then transferred onto wood and cut into undulating rulers to be used in constructing the *Grand Verre* (Large Glass). These

"canned" chance works were often preserved in glass, an environment that is liable to change without the artist's intervention.

With poetry, Tristan Tzara emerged as the first Dadaist to manipulate language through chance by cutting up words from a text page and drawing out the pieces of paper at random to compose a new poem. Dadaist poetry was influenced by Surrealists and Symbolists in its exploration of the subconscious impulses in relation to chance. Duchamp's use of pun in every literary pronouncement he made symbolizes the underlying ambiguity in all experience that belies the pretensions of any one system to contain it. Duchamp's inclinations were inspired by Symbolist poets such as Stéphane Mallarmé, who in his most radical poem, "Un coup de dés jamais n'abolira le hasard" (1897), inaugurates a poetic form that contains a plurality of readings. Duchamp also experimented with various ways of reordering and reconstructing language in order to break away from preestablished syntax and styles. Jean Arp combines the techniques of interpolation, expansion of some element within the text, mixing semantic fragments with sound units to create "sound" poems.

Beyond Dada. Dada aesthetics, in particular Duchamp's, had a wide-reaching influence on the succeeding generation of painters. Ambiguity and impersonality are recurring themes found in paintings by Jasper Johns, Robert Rauschenberg, and others. In Johns's *Painting with Ruler and "Gray"* (1960), a ruler was dragged through paint to create a chance pattern. Chance also played an integral part in the works of Abstract Expressionist painters, as in Jackson Pollack's series of "drip" or action paintings, Richard Sella's "Belt Pieces," and so forth.

A clear revival of Dadaism can be seen in the Fluxus movement that emerged in the early 1960s in New York. John Cage initiated a movement called a "happening," the first postwar mixed-media event, in the spirit of Dada. It involved lecture, poetry reading, dance, slide projections, and paintings that yielded a complex of differently timed, autonomous activities, unfolding in its own time-space. Fluxus is another trend that followed in the early 1960s and fused Dadaist aesthetics with a reductionist aim. Theatrical expression of boredom, violence, destruction, meaninglessness, as well as various social situations, formed an integral part of the performances. Its chief protagonist, George Maciunas, described Fluxus as "the fusion of Spike Jones, vaudeville, gag, children's games, and Duchamp." George Brecht's "Drip Event" (1959–1962), for instance, contains a simple instruction to drip water into an empty vessel. Other notable proponents of the Fluxus movement include Dick Higgins, LaMonte Young, Cornelius Cardew, Nam June Paik, and Jackson MacLow.

Post-1945 Musical Trends. Composers prior to the twentieth century (e.g., Guillaume de Machaut, Johann

Sebastian Bach, Wolfgang Amadeus Mozart) used various permutational systems for composing music. The most wide-ranging application of aleatoric processes, however, can be witnessed in the avant-garde musical trends that evolved after World War II. Interest in chance and indeterminacy evolved in the early 1950s in part as a reaction against the serialism that pervaded the musical climate in the preceding decades. Dadaist aesthetics formed a close link with the experimental trends led by John Cage, Morton Feldman, and others. The advent of computer technology paved the path toward the algorithmic musical compositions of Lejarin Hiller, Iannis Xenakis, and others. In "automated" musical compositions, aleatoric processes provide systematic ways of regulating the statistical distribution of musical elements within a continuum of order and randomness.

The experimental school around John Cage went so far as to redefine the nature of the roles of listening, performing, and composing, as well as to suggest new sociological functions for music. In such landmark works as *4'33"* (1952), Cage openly challenged the traditional relationships among the acts of composition, performance, and audition by demonstrating that they may function independently of one another. In addition, he sought to eliminate the boundary between what is traditionally considered to be music and "noise," or ordinary environmental sounds.

Central to Cage's ideology is the elimination of conscious "will" or intention in the act of composing and listening to sounds. He also eliminates the need to structure sounds or interpret their meaning. Chance operations are used to bring about "acts the outcome of which are unknown" in the compositional process in order to allow sounds to exist for themselves. Cage's interest in the principles of indeterminacy was inspired by his acquaintance with Zen and Daoist philosophy; he strove to dispense with individual taste and allegiance to the past through the chance operations suggested by the principles of the *Yi jing,* a collection of ancient Chinese oracles indexed by sixty-four hexagrams. His first works written systematically using the *Yi jing* are the *Music of Changes* and *Imaginary Landscape No. 4* (1951).

The function of the *Yi jing,* nonetheless, exceeded that of a simple random-number generator—a mechanical process that selects the sound material arbitrarily. In Cage's use of the *Yi jing,* the operation allowed the user to change and renew the content of predefined charts. In addition, although the succession and combination of musical gestures were dictated by the hexagrams obtained through tossing coins, Cage allowed for various concessions in the realization of the score to facilitate the performance. The compositional outcome, therefore, was constantly mediated by Cage's subjective choice.

During the same period, American composers in Cage's circle resorted to other compositional means to induce various degrees of indeterminacy in the quest toward "liberat-ing" sounds from prescribed systems and structures. Morton Feldman was the first to introduce graphic notation; in *Projections* (1950–1951) and *Intersections* (1951–1953), dynamics and/or articulation are specified graphically within time squares, while the dimension of pitch remains indeterminate so that the performer is left alone to project sounds based on his or her skill and intuition; similarly, events are given in "time slots" rather than in traditional, determinate rhythmic notation. Inspired by contemporaneous works in the visual art by Alexander Calder and Jackson Pollock, Earle Brown experimented with the concepts of formal mobility, where the content of the music is roughly notated but the temporal ordering of musical events is indeterminate. In the collection of works titled *Folio* (1952–1953), Brown steered toward a highly ambiguous graphic notation and pushed the level of indeterminacy to an extreme, with respect to both form and content. Christian Wolff's contribution from this period includes pieces using a very restricted number of pitches; for instance, the *Trio for Flute, Cello and Viola* utilizes only three pitches that are shuffled around apparently without any system.

The influence of Dadaists on Cage can be seen in his adaptation of "ready-mades": he used a point-drawing system that follows the imperfections on paper to derive sounds in the *Music for Piano Series* 1–84 (1953–1956). Star charts were used to derive compositional materials for *Atlas Eclipticalis* (1960–1961), *Études Australes* (1974–1975), and other works. During these years, Cage also experimented with extreme forms of graphic notation and indeterminacy, exemplified in *Concert for Piano and Orchestra* (1957–1958). In his monumental theater piece, *Europera* (1988), he photocopied individual parts of standard operas at random and distributed the instruments to those other than the ones for which they were intended.

Cage's arrival in Europe in 1954 had a significant impact on the young generation of composers thirsting for new directions in the avant-garde. Composers Karlheinz Stockhausen, Luciano Berio, and others were quick to adopt various means of indeterminacy found in earlier works by Cage, Brown, and Feldman; Stockhausen's *Klavierstücke VI* (1954–1955; revised 1961) and *Klavierstücke XI* (1956), *Zyklus* and *Refrain* (1959), and Berio's *Epiphany* (1959–1961) and *Circles* (1960) show efforts to accommodate indeterminate procedures within determined, structural musical frameworks. In an article titled "Alea," Pierre Boulez chided his colleagues who had latched on to chance operations indiscriminately; he, in turn, proposed a reconciliation through integrating indeterminacy within a controlled, serial framework, as demonstrated in his *Third Piano Sonata* (1956–1957). Konrad Boehmer also delivered a scathing criticism of Cage's use of chance and indeterminacy in his book on the theories of "open" form.

Additionally, techniques derived from electronic music and acoustical studies pointed Stockhausen to new ways of organizing and unifying the musical relationships. The indeterminate distribution of frequencies within a formant spectrum led him to employ statistical processes to control surface musical events in works such as *Zeitmasse* for woodwind quintet (1955–1956).

By the end of the 1950s, interests in serialism and indeterminacy were superseded by other concerns. In *Formalized Music,* Iannis Xenakis delivers a critical attack on European serial music from the 1950s. He observes how linear relationships are dissolved in works such as Boulez's *Structures Ia* where the twelve-tone rows are dispersed and combined without registral or contrapuntal differentiations. In short, the end does not justify the means—the statistical distribution of musical elements does not bear any relationship to the underlying serial method. Similarly, Xenakis denounces the musical practice of indeterminacy that had also emerged as a distinct trend in the 1950s; he speaks of chance as a phenomenon that cannot be casually improvised or "intellectually imitated," but that can only be modeled by complex reasoning based on mathematical analysis.

Xenakis's critique of serialism and indeterminacy served as a springboard for development of a new, alternative compositional theory based on "stochastic laws." Instead of constructing musical structures systematically from the "atomistic" elements onward, he set out to transform sonic elements at the global level of structure based on various laws of probability found in nature, for example, the use of the Boltzmann Maxwell law of thermodynamics to regulate the distribution of glissandi notes in *Pithoprakta* (1959). In less systematic ways, György Ligeti renounced individually perceptible sounds and rhythms and concentrated instead on vast textures and density of sounds to organize musical events by adopting a partially indeterminate style of graphic notation (*Volumina* [1961]) or through smaller pitch differentiation (*Atmospheres* [1961])—a technique that became identified as *mikropolyphonie*. Textured music of a similar nature can be found in the works of Kryzstof Penderecki and Witold Lutoslawski.

The developments in computer music technology since the 1950s have led to a surge of algorithmic musical compositions that incorporate various aleatoric processes at the computer. Prominent composers in this field include Lejarin Hiller, James Tenney, Herbert Brün, Gottfried Michael Koenig, and Charles Ames. In algorithmic compositions, chance is no longer an ad hoc system; rather, it is systematically defined in terms of mathematical functions that generate specific types of randomness in time. Hiller and L. M. Isaacson's *Illiac Suite* (1956) is the first to employ Markov chains to control the probability of occurrence of a musical event. More recently, Charles Dodge and Thomas Jerse have formalized specific random processes based on conditional probabilities to generate aleatoric compositions. David Little and others have experimented with musical composition based on chaos theory (principles that control natural phenomena such as weather and population cycles). Centers for acoustical and computer music studies, notably IRCAM and CeMAMu in France, ZKM in Germany, and CCRMA at Stanford University, have provided courses for studying and composing algorithmic compositions in various operational environments since the 1980s.

Conclusion. The aesthetic motivations for incorporating aleatoric processes in twentieth-century art and music range from negation of causality, liberation from the conscious will, to the emulation of natural phenomena through mathematical modeling. The Dadaists' aesthetics, in particular, had pervasive influence across the arts as it forged a close link between the visual/literary arts and music. Chance takes on an elusive, paradoxical nature as its mode of generation ranges from ad hoc, intuitive (e.g., Arp) to systematic, controlled application (e.g., Duchamp, Cage), and its outcome is always mediated, to a lesser or greater degree, by the conditions defined by the artist. The aesthetic appreciation of an aleatoric art, therefore, needs to take into account the interplays among the artist's intention, method, and outcome.

[*See also* Cage; Dadaism; Daoist Aesthetics; Music; *and* Stein.]

BIBLIOGRAPHY

Ames, Charles. "Statistics and Compositional Balance." *Perspectives of New Music* 28.1 (Winter 1990): 80–111.

Boehmer, Konrad. *Zur Theorie der offenen Form in der neuen Musik.* Darmstadt, 1967.

Boulez, Pierre. "Alea" (1964). In *Perspectives on Contemporary Music Theory,* edited by Benjamin Boretz and Edward T. Cone, pp. 45–56. New York, 1972.

D'Harnoncourt, Anne, and Kynaston McShine. *Marcel Duchamp.* New York, 1973.

Dodge, Charles, and Thomas A. Jerse. *Computer Music: Synthesis, Composition, and Performance.* New York, 1985.

Erickson, John D. *Dada: Performance, Poetry, and Art.* Boston, 1984.

Foster, Stephen C., ed. *Dada/Dimensions.* Ann Arbor, 1985.

Leach, Jeremy, and John Fitch. "Nature, Music, and Algorithmic Composition." *Computer Music Journal* 19.2 (1995): 23–33.

Little, David. "Composing with Chaos: Applications of a New Science for Music." *Interface* 22 (1993): 23–51.

Nyman, Michael. *Experimental Music: Cage and Beyond.* New York, 1974.

Pritchett, James. "The Development of Chance Techniques in the Music of John Cage, 1950–1956." Ph.D. diss., New York University, 1988.

Young, LaMonte, ed. *An Anthology of Chance Operations . . . by George Brecht and Others.* Bronx, N.Y., 1963.

Uno, Yayoi. "The Roles of Compositional Aim, Syntax, and Design in the Assessment of Musical Styles: Analyses of Piano Music by Pierre Boulez, John Cage, Milton Babbitt, and Iannis Xenakis circa 1950." Ph.D. diss., University of Rochester, 1994.

Watts, Harriett Ann. *Chance: A Perspective on Dada.* Ann Arbor, 1980.

Xenakis, Iannis. *Formalized Music: Thought and Mathematics in Music.* Rev. ed. Edited by Sharon Kanach. Harmonologia Series, No. 6. Stuyvesant, N.Y., 1992.

YAYOI UNO

ALEMBERT, JEAN LE ROND D' (1717–1783), French philosopher, mathematician, art theorist, and encyclopediaist. D'Alembert was named after the Paris church of Saint-Jean-le-Rond on whose steps he was abandoned shortly after his birth.

He studied at the Collège des Quatre Nations, founded by Jules Mazarin. A precocious and original mind, he soon evidenced a special gift for mathematics and physics, and at the age of twenty-two presented his first paper at the Academy of Sciences, to whose membership he was soon elected (1741). In 1743, at the age of twenty-six, he published his *Treatise on Dynamics*, a landmark in Newtonian mechanics, to be followed by other significant works in mathematics, dynamics, and astronomy. In 1755, he became a member of the French Academy; in 1772, he was appointed its secretary, and in this capacity wrote a number of *Éloges* (Eulogies) of notable personalities in the sciences and letters and a history of the members of the Academy. In 1751, he assumed with Denis Diderot the co-editorship of the *Encyclopédie,* for which he wrote the influential *Preliminary Discourse,* as well as numerous articles on mainly scientific but also literary topics. But in 1758 he somewhat unexpectedly resigned, in the midst of the storm of controversy raging over the unorthodox views expressed in a number of articles, including his own article "Geneva."

D'Alembert's important works on mathematics, especially dynamics and mechanics, together with his other writings, notably on belles-lettres and music, which brilliantly testified to his intellectual versatility and wide-ranging interests, earned him an international reputation, membership in a number of the most distinguished academies and societies of Europe, the warm friendship of François Marie Arouet de Voltaire, as well as the supportive interest of Frederic II and Catherine the Great, and the respect of the most eminent scientists of his time, with whom he regularly corresponded. Despite his defection from the *Encyclopédie* at a critical juncture of the history of its publication, and his tendency to adopt the stance of the ivory-tower scientist and philosopher, he retained a lifelong special place as a leading exponent of the Enlightenment movement and continued to be held in high regard in French intellectual circles, although his cautious, somewhat retiring nature made him a more shadowy, secretive presence on the tumultuous French cultural scene than Voltaire, Diderot, or Jean Jacques Rousseau. In spite of his unworldliness and solitary habits, he frequented the influential salons of Madame du Deffand and Madame Geoffrin, and he could be generous in his friendships, especially with the ailing and impecunious Julie de Lespinasse and with such struggling young scientists and philosophers as Joseph Luis de Lagrange, Pierre Simon Laplace, and Marie Jean Antoine Nicolas Caritat Condorcet.

D'Alembert's contributions as a mathematician are unquestionably of the first magnitude, and his writings on aesthetics, although not on a par with his scientific contributions, and lacking in the striking originality and boldness of insight of a Diderot or Rousseau or the wit and stylistic elegance of a Voltaire, are nevertheless fully deserving of our interest, precisely because they are generally so eminently representative of the major universalist, rationalistic trends of his time and because they are revealing of the way in which an exceptionally gifted scientific mind endeavored to deal both empirically and analytically with the vexing problems of artistic creativity and originality.

D'Alembert's 1751 *Preliminary Discourse* to the *Encyclopédie,* which sets out to explain the arrangement of the material in the dictionary and which propelled him into the limelight, is strongly reminiscent of John Locke in the way it endeavors to examine the origin and order of knowledge and the problem of linguistic communication. All our knowledge, even our most apparently abstract concepts, has a sensory origin. As for language, it fulfills the primary human needs, which are preeminently social in nature. Words emerge as arbitrary signs referring to simple notions that primitive humans felt an overwhelming need to communicate. D'Alembert, like many of his contemporaries (especially Étienne Bonnot de Condillac), owed a great deal to both Isaac Newton and Locke, and the latter's influence is particularly evident in the "Preliminary Discourse." D'Alembert distinguishes three faculties of the mind: memory, reason, and imagination. Memory is the faculty that passively recalls the sensory perceptions; reason involves the combining, comparing, and judging of these sensations; and imagination involves the creation of new ideas based on the perceptions accumulated by memory and the comparisons and judgments provided by reason. In the course of human history, these faculties have evolved into certain disciplines, which are categorized in a manner that justifies the arrangement adopted in the *Encyclopédie.* All the disciplines that deal with memory fall under the heading of history; all those that deal with reason under the heading of philosophy; and the arts under the heading of imagination, although it is acknowledged that there is some interaction in the various disciplines with the three faculties; hence, a certain ambiguity in this analytical systematization, which d'Alembert himself is the first to acknowledge and even welcome in the name of empiricism. The "Preliminary Discourse" contains as well the elements of a philosophy of history, which emphasizes gradual intellectual progress, the study of the relationship of ideas to society, as well as what would later be called cultural history. It is also a ringing proclamation of the eventual triumph of secularism over Christian dogma and fanaticism, of the inherent equality of humankind, and of the advent of universal enlightenment through freedom of thought and action. The success that greeted this first publication outside his field of mathematics prompted d'Alembert to pursue his philosophical, literary, and aesthetic ventures as a popularizer, educator, and propagandist for a noble cause.

In *Essaie sur les éléments de philosophie* (Elements of philosophy), published in 1759, d'Alembert emphasizes grammar and logic in formulating universally applicable principles. He subscribes to a theory of universal grammar, based on reason, which promptly shapes language after need has brought it into existence. The philosopher-grammarian's goal is to seek out a primeval rationalist structure and uniform order in the bewildering diversity, indeed chaos, of modern languages. Despite a proclaimed allegiance to Baconian and Lockean empiricism and experimentalism, d'Alembert retained a strong Cartesian predilection for rationalistic principles of clarity and order, which is particularly reflected in his theories of language, grammar, and rhetoric.

In his works more closely bearing on aesthetics, d'Alembert consistently strove for the kind of clarity, simplicity, and universality he found so rewarding in his scientific research. In his 1753 *Essai sur la société des gens de lettres et des grands, sur la réputation, sur les mécènes, et sur les récompenses littéraires* (Essay on the society of men of letters and the powerful and famous, on repute, on art patrons, and on literary rewards), he deals with the vexing problem of the creative artist's relation to society, and especially to the rich and powerful. In his 1757 *Réflexions sur l'usage et sur l'abus de la philosophie dans les matières de goût* (Reflections on the use and abuse of philosophy in matters of taste), he acknowledges the role of cultural conditioning in the formation of "good taste." He subscribes to the notion of the enthusiastic élan in the initial inspirational stage of the creative genius, necessarily corrected and refined in the course of the technical process of execution.

In his essays on poetry, notably his 1753 *Dialogue entre la poésie et la philosophie* (Dialogue between poetry and philosophy), his 1760 *Réflexions sur la poésie* (Reflections on poetry), and his 1762 *Réflexions sur l'ode* (Reflections on the ode), he acknowledges, as others had done before him, that such serious poetic genres as the sonnet, the elegy, the eclogue, and even the ode were failing, while lightly entertaining verse, such as the fables, madrigals, epigrams, and all manner of *pièces fugitives* continued to flourish. Once more, d'Alembert endeavors to take the rational, middle-of-the-road approach by extolling the noble, didactic genres, which commingle philosophical truths and moral ideas with elevated language, but also by recognizing the value of a lyrical poetry of *pur agrément* (mere pleasure), providing it reveals in its images something at once new and sui generis.

D'Alembert had a special interest in music, which he believed expresses the thoughts and emotions that resonate the most compellingly in the human mind and heart. But if he held that music possesses a unique ability to depict the deepest sentiments and the most violent passions, for him, as for practically all his contemporaries (even including Diderot), the notion of imitation of nature, or more precisely *vraisemblance* (verisimilitude), was paramount; hence,

his reservations with regard to the opera, as expressed in his 1754 work on the theoretical and practical elements of music, *Réflexions sur la musique en général, et sur la musique française en particulier* (Reflections on music in general, and on French music in particular). It is also worth noting that in the "Querelle des Bouffons" (Quarrel of the Buffoons), which bitterly pitted the partisans of Italian music versus those of French music, d'Alembert, although partial to French opera and an admirer of the French composer Jean Philippe Rameau, whose theories he expounded in his 1752 *Éléments de musique théorique et pratique suivant les principes de M. Rameau* (Elements of theoretical and practical music in accordance with the principles of M. Rameau), out of loyalty to his friends, notably Diderot and Rousseau, felt compelled to side with the Encyclopedists in their strident advocacy of Italian music and opera. This prompted Rameau, once on friendly terms with the Encyclopedists, to criticize publicly Rousseau's *Encyclopédie* articles on music (articles he himself had been invited to write but had declined to do so). All this may help to explain d'Alembert's ambivalence with regard to Rameau's musical theory, even though he probably felt a personal kinship with its rationalistic, mathematical line of reasoning. Always the good-willed mediator, he endeavored to reconcile the two sides in this notorious "Querelle" by suggesting, in his 1759 *De la liberté de la musique* (On the freedom of music), that French music could be made to lose some of its cold rationalism and formalism by incorporating the rich, emotional, and expressive features characteristic of Italian music.

D'Alembert's aesthetics is unique, not by virtue of its prescient originality, but precisely because, with all its ambivalences, compromises, and attempts to reconcile staid, orderly, neoclassical rules with new, more disruptive notions of artistic originality and individuality, it evidences a special sensitivity to the complex and at times contradictory trends and currents of a turbulent time of change and transition.

[*See also* Diderot; French Aesthetics, *article on* Eighteenth-Century French Aesthetics; *and* Poetics.]

BIBLIOGRAPHY

Works by d'Alembert

Discours préliminaire de l'Encyclopédie (1751). Paris, 1965.
Éléments de musique théorique et pratique suivant les principes de M. Rameau. Paris, 1752; facs. ed., New York, 1966.
Éloges lus dans les séances publiques de l'Académie Française. Paris, 1779.
Esprit, maximes et principes de d'Alembert. Paris, 1789.
Essai sur les éléments de philosophie. Paris, 1767; reprint, Paris, 1986.
Histoire des membres de l'Académie Française morts depuis 1700 jusqu'à 1771. 5 vols. Paris, 1787.
Mélanges de littérature, d'histoire, et de philosophie. 4th ed. 5 vols. Amsterdam, 1767. Republished in 1770 and 1773.
Œuvres. 5 vols. Paris, 1821–1822.
Œuvres de d'Alembert. 5 vols. Geneva, 1967.
Œuvres et correspondances inédites de d'Alembert. Edited by Charles Henry. Paris, 1887; reprint, Geneva, 1967.
Œuvres philosophiques, historiques et littéraires. 18 vols. Paris, 1805.

Translations

Encyclopedia: Selections: Diderot, d'Alembert and a Society of Men of Letters. Translated by Nelly S. Hoyt and Thomas Cassirer. Indianapolis, 1963.

Preliminary Discourse to the Encyclopedia of Diderot. Translated by Richard N. Schwab and Walter E. Rex. Indianapolis, 1963.

Critical Studies

Chouillet, Jacques. *L'esthétique des lumières.* Paris, 1974.

Essar, Dennis F. *The Language Theory, Epistemology, and Aesthetics of Jean Le Rond d'Alembert.* Studies on Voltaire and the Eighteenth Century. Oxford, 1976.

Folkierski, Wladyslaw. *Entre le classicisme et le romantisme: Étude sur l'esthétique et les esthéticiens du XVIIIe siècle.* Paris, 1925.

Gilman, Margaret. *The Idea of Poetry in France: From Houdar de la Motte to Baudelaire.* Cambridge, Mass., 1958.

Grimsley, Ronald. *Jean d'Alembert.* Oxford, 1963.

Müller, Maurice. *Essai sur la philosophie de Jean d'Alembert.* Paris, 1926.

Pappas, John N. *Voltaire and d'Alembert.* Bloomington, Ind., 1962.

Pappas, John N. "D'Alembert et la querelle des bouffons d'après des documents inédits." *Revue d'histoire littéraire de la France* 65 (1965): 479–484.

Le Ru, Véronique. *Jean Le Rond d'Alembert philosophe.* Paris, 1994.

Saisselin, Rémy G. *The Rule of Reason and the Ruses of the Heart: A Philosophical Dictionary of Classical French Criticism, Critics, and Aesthetic Issues.* Cleveland, Ohio, 1970.

GITA MAY

ALIENATION, AESTHETIC. The thesis of aesthetic alienation is that as a result of art's becoming an autonomous practice, the domain of the aesthetic is separated, alienated, from its own cognitive and normative potential; or, more simply, modern autonomous art and aesthetic discourse are alienated from truth. Arguably, aesthetic alienation is the governing idea in three major twentieth-century philosophies of art: Martin Heidegger's "The Origin of the Work of Art," Hans-Georg Gadamer's *Truth and Method,* and Theodor Adorno's *Aesthetic Theory.* These works share a sense that there is a manifest loss, to art and to truth, when the experience of works of art becomes noncognitive.

Sometimes theories pronouncing on the radical separation between art and truth that occurs in the modern world are talked about in terms of "the death of art." But the primary concern of theories of aesthetic alienation is not with the death of art but with the distortion to cognitive and rational activity that transpires when particular aspects of experience are isolated, excluded, and then marginalized into an autonomously constituted domain of art.

It is useful to consider the thesis of aesthetic alienation as composed of a neutral historical claim and a more contentious conceptual claim. Historically, with the arrival of modernity, art *becomes* an autonomous domain of practice with rules and norms uniquely appropriate to it. Works of art, tendentially, are made and judged in terms—harmony,

beauty, sublimity, elegance, power, depth—that abstract from religious or secular contents in order that they be more purely works of art. Hence, the primary experience of works of art now is conveyed through judgments of taste of the form "It is beautiful." In making such judgments, we are concerned with works' formal integration of their materials, with how the elements in works are combined. To consider works of art in this manner is to consider them "aesthetically." The rules and norms that orient our attention to the formal properties of works and spell out the appropriate terms for judgments of taste can be regarded as forming "a grammar of the aesthetic." This grammar is now normative for art practices.

The conceptual component of the thesis of aesthetic alienation is difficult to state simply. Minimally, the claim is that although the grammar of the aesthetic does indeed orient attention to an aspect of experience, that aspect is misunderstood and deformed when taken in isolation. Ideally, the aesthetic aspects of experience, including sensuous immediacy, should be fully integrated into our everyday cognitive and ethical encounters with the world. This view reverberates back onto the historical thesis: If the conceptual thesis is true, then the emergence of an autonomous grammar of the aesthetic does not amount to the discovery of the essence of art and aesthetic experience. On the contrary, the production and reception of artworks in terms of the grammar of the aesthetic are but a fallible historical determination of the meaning of art that should be displaced.

An explicit version of the thesis of aesthetic alienation is put forward by Gadamer. He argues that works of art from premodern societies were not intended for free acceptance or rejection; rather, such works lodged an immediate truth claim, for example, about the gods, or the nature of human suffering. In abstracting from what such works say and present, and attending solely to their formal features, "aesthetic consciousness" is alienated from the full cognitive experience these works can provide. Aesthetic consciousness is formed through an effort of differentiating the formal, aesthetic qualities of a work from its substantive features; as a consequence, Gadamer claims, aesthetic consciousness is always secondary to the immediate truth claim that proceeds from the work. Two theses are implied by Gadamer's claim: first, that it is the historical grammar of the aesthetic itself that is responsible for the abstraction of works' formal from substantive features; second, given the dominance of the grammar of the aesthetic, the experience of alienation is the experience of the gap between a work's original truth claim and the availability of only an aesthetic response (e.g., "It is beautiful") to that claim. The experience of that gap, the experience of works of art saying or wanting to say more than aesthetic discourse permits them to say, is the experience of the aesthetic as alienating works from their own cognitive potentiality.

The theory of aesthetic alienation is not a straightforward thesis about truth in art because it is conceded that the grammar of the aesthetic is now historically dominant: to deploy artworks as cognitive instruments transgresses what is now proper to art. It is the business of the natural and social sciences, not art, to lodge and validate truth claims. Hence, the belief that through the experience of a particular work of art we are given a fuller, truer, more adequate understanding of some phenomenon than could be had through any other route is now necessarily illusory. We possess no practices of judgment and criticism that would license regarding works as providing unique forms of access to aspects of experience, or, equally, regarding the aspects of experience constituted through the grammar of the aesthetic as essential ingredients in cognition.

Like other conceptions of alienation, the idea of aesthetic alienation must ultimately depend upon the truth of a strongly counterfactual thesis, namely, that despite the fact that the cognitive and the aesthetic are now utterly separated from one another, they belong together. Because the alienation of the aesthetic from the cognitive is of historical provenance, the intelligibility of the thesis requires placing it within a wider historical setting.

Modernity as the Separation of Spheres. The theory of aesthetic alienation arises not only as a critique of a false theory of artistic production and reception, but also as a critique of enlightened modernity in which the grammar of the aesthetic has become dominant. What characterizes enlightened cultural modernity is the separation of the substantive reason found in premodern religious worldviews and metaphysics into the three autonomous spheres of science, morality, and art, with each of these spheres possessing its own specific aspects of validity: truth, normative rightness, and beauty. Within this categorial system, truth is identified with scientific knowing, where scientific knowing is understood as fundamentally concerned with causal laws ordered within a hierarchy of theories, each of which is ideally derivable from a theory of simpler entities. Although trivially this denies any epistemic aspect to moral and aesthetic experience, more significantly it excludes purposive, creative, and irreducibly singular episodes from being objects of knowledge under those three descriptions. Arguably, however, it is those three predicates that best typify what is most distinctive about human experience. Insofar as that is the case, then what is most distinctive about human experience necessarily remains unknowable.

Conversely, the grammar of aesthetic production and judgment is designed, as it were, to cope with objects manifesting just those three features, albeit in a manner that is now nonepistemic. Objects that are novel, internally purposive, and irreducibly singular are a perfect match for judgments geared to examining harmony, integrity, and the like. Implicitly or explicitly, most accounts of aesthetic alienation take Immanuel Kant's analyses of aesthetic reflective judgment and genius as mapping out the modern grammar of aesthetic reception and production, respectively. Equally, most accounts regard Kant's critical system, as manifest in his separate critiques of pure reason, practical reason, and judgment, to be the exemplary defense of the division of reason into three autonomous spheres. Thus arises the general strategy of using Kant's aesthetics against the divisions of the critical system and the restriction of truth to the discerning of mechanical relations between objects.

For example, in the urtext of the aesthetic critique of modernity, the "Oldest System Programme of German Idealism" of 1796, the author(s) carefully first subordinate physics (theoretical reason) to morality (practical reason), because even a mechanistic physics is the creation of free and rational beings who practice science under the governance of competing normative ideas of order concerning the natural world, and then subordinate truth (physics) and goodness (morality) to beauty, because each human creation must synthesize its diverse elements into a purposive and orderly whole. Beauty is now understood to be the synthetic unity of truth and goodness, the thought of which leads to the call for a new mythology of reason, that is, a conception of "pure" reason that would be powerfully joined with the affective and sensuous elements of experience. However crude, the clear implication of the "Oldest System Programme" is that rationality requires an entwining of the three spheres, and that only under the sign of that entwinement, as represented by the mythology of reason to be, can the promise of the Enlightenment ideals of freedom and equality be satisfied.

It is, then, the defense of the differentiation and abstractive achievements of modern reason, most explicitly worked out in the philosophies of Kant and Jürgen Habermas, that constitutes the conception of modernity challenged by the theory of aesthetic alienation. Aesthetic alienation itself must thus be taken as a symptom and exemplar of the wider forms of alienation, fragmentation, and nihilism besetting modern societies that are the direct consequence of its rationalization. If aesthetic alienation is regarded as a symptom and clue to the problematic status of modernity, it follows that the difficulties of modern societies are to be understood as involving more than, say, radical inequalities in wealth and power. The rationalized and fragmented character of modern societies and all the social ills that follow from that fragmentation—variously identified as caused by capitalist relations of production, technology, and instrumental rationality—have their logical or categorial source in the differentiation of reason into three autonomous spheres. Contesting modernity requires deploying the experience of aesthetic alienation, the experience of works of art as saying "more" than what the grammar of the aesthetic permits, to contest the fragmentation of reason. It is, in broad terms, this set of logical relations connecting problems in aesthetic rationality as tokened by the experience of aesthetic alienation with the analysis of the fragmented character of modern societies that best explicates the familiar aesthetic critique of modernity that runs from early German idealism and romanticism through to philosophers as different as Heidegger, Gadamer, and Adorno.

Creating Works and Disclosing Truth. If the idea of aesthetic alienation is to be philosophically intelligible, what must be shown is that the features of experience designated as merely aesthetic are amenable to and vital for cognition. Our prephilosophical intuitions do not bode well for this claim: science discovers truth, while art creates works; cognitive advance occurs when particulars are subsumed under some universal, whereas the judgment of aesthetic particulars is a matter of taste.

From these prephilosophical intuitions follows the most persistent error in understanding the aesthetic critique of modernity, namely, that it means to pose the irrational powers of the will and the imagination against the analytic powers of truth-only cognition. Of course, some aesthetic critiques of modernity do attempt to overthrow the sovereign character of truth and put in its place the kind of valuing and organizing of experience that we find exemplified in the creation and judgment of works of art. A dominant strand of the thought of Friedrich Nietzsche implies such a view. But this reversal of the hierarchical relation between art and truth salvages the aesthetic dimension of experience at the expense of the cognitive. Thus Nietzschean claims about the essentially created and aesthetic character of language leave human experience as unknown and unknowable as before. The complaint against modernity lodged by aesthetic alienation theories is not that scientific rationality intrudes where it does not belong, but that reason itself becomes irrational in virtue of its becoming differentiated into separate spheres. Rationality requires more than what narrow truth-only cognition allows.

If the argument is to be sustained that artworks in modernity carry with them a defused potentiality for cognition that is representative of a general conception of truth or reason that has been suppressed, then some characterization of that potentiality is called for. The characteristic of artworks most routinely pointed to as adumbrating an epistemic potential disenfranchised by truth-only cognition is that they are created objects. If creativity is viewed from the perspective of truth-only cognition, it gets reduced to being a psychological prelude to cognition proper: only the logic of justification, the logic guiding the evaluation of existing theories against the facts, is amenable to cognitive handling, whereas the logic of discovery, the creation of ideas or theories, belongs to the arational background against which scientific thought emerges. Regarding creation as being of only psychological significance directly entails all the central elements that distinguish the grammar of truth-only

cognition from the grammar of the aesthetic while handing priority over to the former.

If the activity of creation is withdrawn from consideration, then in each case types or universals or theories will come to be regarded as logically and ontologically prior to tokens or particulars. It is this priority that leads to the joint beliefs that truth is timeless or nonhistorical, and that being true involves a correspondence with always already-given facts. It is worth noting that although this conception of truth elegantly mirrors our beliefs about the nature of the physical universe, and is thus a good match for it, it becomes much less compelling when the object to be known is itself historical and changing, as in the case of biology.

The dark question left unanswered by the two beliefs about truth is: independently of the created item, what explains the accessibility of facts to cognitive inspection? If the accessibility of facts to cognitive inspection only becomes available through created items, then either cognitive space is made possible by what is itself noncognitive, entailing skepticism, or created items can themselves be cognitive. In order to maintain the nonskeptical limb of this either/or, one must depart from the correspondence theory of truth because the relevant facts only become available through what is created. The notion of truth at issue here is that of truth as disclosure. If truth as disclosure occurs through creations, works, then particulars must have a priority over universals, and truth must be viewed as historical. These ideas first emerge through reflection on modern art.

Through the history of artistic modernism, we have become accustomed to the thought that art cannot be defined in a priori terms, that there is no general essence or universal that can define what it is for a thing to be a work of art. Rather, what art *is,* what music or painting or literature *is,* is reconfigured and disclosed through artistic practice, through what art becomes. Artistic performance, so to speak, the token, brings into being and reveals the always historical essence. Kant sketched the logic of this movement in his conceptualization of genius as the creating of exemplary items. For the theory of aesthetic alienation, Kant's and modernity's localization of exemplarity or truth as disclosure in art, the domain of fiction and semblance, is its alienation or disenfranchisement. It is this localization that is a consequence of sphere differentiation that makes truth as disclosure unavailable for everyday worldly purposes, a fact registered and protested against in the practices of those avant-garde projects that sought to bridge the gap separating the art world from the everyday world.

From this angle, one can perceive that the guiding thought behind Heidegger's seminal essay "The Origin of the Work of Art" is the contrast between the localization of truth as disclosure in the art world and the capacity of past works of art—Heidegger instances a Greek temple—to reveal or disclose a "world," to provide the categorial shape or look of a particular historical form of life. Gadamer follows Heidegger in conceiving of truth as disclosure prior to truth as correspondence, but diverges from Heidegger in two important respects: (1) Gadamer conceives of world-disclosure as accomplished not through individual works but through tradition, the sedimented concatenation of works, as it were; and (2) as a consequence, Gadamer believes that particular works disclose features or aspects of experience. For Heidegger, disclosure is primarily epochal and macrological, whereas for Gadamer disclosure is micrological, an ongoing transformation of experience. Nonetheless, in both cases truth is historical.

The most potent argument against conceiving of creation as cognitive derives from an intrinsic feature of the logic of exemplarity, namely, that the litmus test of exemplarity is succession. An item is exemplary and hence makes *original* sense only if it is succeeded by works that draw on the paradigm of sense making it establishes. But from this it follows that exemplary works are neither explicable in terms of their antecedents nor autonomously self-validating. If this is the case, then in themselves exemplary works are cognitively opaque and indeterminate in their meaning: they logically and conceptually exceed their antecedents (if they did not, they could not be making original sense) and license what follows from them while nonetheless being dependent on that succession for their claim to exemplarity (because that they make original sense is only revealed and confirmed retrospectively). The reciprocal determination of exemplary items and their successors might be just a way of conceiving of meaning without presupposing transparent foundations or anterior determinacy. It is thus that the opaque aspects of truth as disclosure cohere with the idea that human truth must be finite and historical. Even if correct, does not pointing to the ultimately opaque nature of truth as disclosure entail conceding to the very skeptical worry that truth as disclosure was meant to resolve? And would not that concession give force to the rationalist thesis that justification, but not discovery (creation), is susceptible to cognitive handling?

Sensuous Particularity and Reflective Judgment. The idea of truth as disclosure aids the thesis of aesthetic alienation by showing how within the activity of artistic creation hibernates a cognitive function that, arguably, even natural science requires. Can something equally applicable to cognition generally be salvaged from the receptive side of aesthetic experience, the making of judgments of taste? Is this activity equally deformed when made merely aesthetic? And is cognitive judgment in need of an aesthetic dimension?

At this juncture, another aspect of the priority of types over tokens enters. Being in possession of a type, say, a concept or a theory, permits an individual to subsume individual cases under it, and those cases thus become tokens of the type. In judgment, this is the model of judgment as subsumptive: bringing intuitions under concepts, to employ

Kant's familiar terms of art. Aesthetic judgments, however, are not subsumptive, and therefore not determinate, but reflective: the inspection of a particular in its own right and not for the sake of the already determinate concept falling under it; hence, the thought that the works of art are unique but nonsubsumable objects of contemplation. Although there is a complex story to be told about reflective judgment, for present purposes the most salient fact about it is that it is a necessary ingredient even in determinate judgments because particulars do not emerge into consciousness with conceptual labels attached. Rather, in order to determine which concept to apply in a particular case, we must employ our capacities as reflective judgers, and the more novel the cases the more explicit this reflective effort becomes.

Again, the field of artistic modernism is telling: each new artistic adventure has rightly been challenged with the question "But is it art?" Hence, the very idea or meaning of "art" is permanently indeterminate or vague, forever dependent on the very objects it is supposed to classify, identify, and individuate. In a sense, modernist art has been nothing but the reiterated attempt to impress upon us the distinctiveness of its grammar of creation and reflective judgment; that, at least, is Adorno's understanding of this art. For him, radically modernist works aim to be works in excess of everything we had previously believed art to be. In responding to them, we must give up existing beliefs and concepts about art and yet find ourselves required to judge that "this too is art." If these judgments are valid, then there exist possibilities of meaningfulness that are nonsubsumptive in character. Moreover, such nonsubsumptive judgments find this meaningfulness in items that are both irreducibly singular and, apparently, purely sensuous in character. For Adorno, the model of purely sensuous meaning is the music of Arnold Schoenberg, whereas more recent debates have concerned the paintings of the American Abstract Expressionists.

With respect to reflective judgment too the skeptical question arises as to whether it is to be regarded as merely a psychological prelude to the cognitive business of subsumption or as cognitive and meaningful. If reflective judgment is taken as only psychological, then an absolute abyss opens between concept and sensuous particular. Only if reflective judgment is taken as cognitive, albeit without being fully discursive, and sensuous particulars as protomeaningful, can the skeptical doubt be answered. And although perspicuously reflective judgments, say, judgments of taste, are not demonstrable, they are criticizable; and that provides a good reason for believing them to be, even now, protocognitive.

The form of argumentation being used to defend the grammar of the aesthetic as general is weakly transcendental: truth as correspondence and determinate judgment exist; how are they possible? Truth as correspondence presupposes truth as disclosure and determinate judgment presupposes reflective judgment; truth as disclosure and reflective judgment presuppose and mutually determine one another; hence, truth as disclosure and reflective judgment provide the necessary conditions for the possibility of standard forms of cognition. Truth as disclosure and reflective judgment share the feature of integrating language (meaning) into the world, or the world into language.

Even if valid, this argument contains within it an unacknowledged pathos, because if the thesis of aesthetic alienation is true, then socially significant action that would make the grammar of the aesthetic an explicit element of everyday cultural practice remains as unavailable as before. It is this fact that best explains the negativity and pessimism that appears to be such a curious aspect of the thought of Heidegger and Adorno. It is equally the source of the even more curious call for a new mythology of reason by the young author(s) of the "Oldest System Programme."

[*See also* Adorno, Epistemology and Aesthetics; Gadamer; Heidegger; Kant; Schoenberg; *and* Truth.]

BIBLIOGRAPHY

Adorno, Theodor W. *Philosophy of Modern Music* (1948). Translated by Anne G. Mitchell and Wesley V. Blomster. London, 1973.

Adorno, Theodor W. *Aesthetic Theory* (1970). Translated by Robert Hullot-Kentor. Minneapolis, 1997.

Bell, David. "The Art of Judgement." *Mind* 96.2 (April 1987): 221–244.

Bernstein, J. M. *The Fate of Art: Aesthetic Alienation from Kant to Derrida and Adorno.* University Park, Pa., 1992.

Bernstein, J. M. *Recovering Ethical Life: Jürgen Habermas and the Future of Critical Theory.* London and New York, 1995.

Bowie, Andrew. *Aesthetics and Subjectivity: From Kant to Nietzsche.* Manchester, 1990.

Caygill, Howard. *Art of Judgement.* Oxford and Cambridge, Mass., 1989.

Dupré, John. *The Disorder of Things: Metaphysical Foundations of the Disunity of Science.* Cambridge, Mass., 1993.

Gadamer, Hans-Georg. *The Relevance of the Beautiful and Other Essays.* Edited by Robert Bernasconi, translated by Nicholas Walker. Cambridge and New York, 1986.

Gadamer, Hans-Georg. *Truth and Method* (1960). 2d rev. ed. Translation revised by Joel Weinsheimer and Donald Marshall, New York, 1989.

Habermas, Jürgen. "Philosophy as Stand-in and Interpreter." In *After Philosophy: End or Transformation?* edited by Kenneth Baynes, James Bohman, and Thomas McCarthy, pp. 296–315. Cambridge, Mass., 1987.

Heidegger, Martin. "The Origin of the Work of Art." In *Poetry, Language, Thought,* translated by Albert Hofstadter, pp. 15–87. New York, 1971.

Kant, Immanuel. *Critique of Judgment* (1790). Translated by Werner S. Pluhar. Indianapolis, 1987.

Nehamas, Alexander. *Nietzsche: Life as Literature.* Cambridge, Mass., 1985.

Thesis Eleven 37 (1994).

J. M. BERNSTEIN

ALISON, ARCHIBALD (1757–1839), eighteenth- to nineteenth-century associationist and empiricist. The Reverend Archibald Alison's *Essays on the Nature and Principles of Taste* was published at Edinburgh in 1790. It did not receive the attention it deserved until 1811, when the second, enlarged edition appeared. Alison gives what is arguably the most complete account of aesthetic experience to be found in the associationist tradition of British empiricism.

Alison argues that beauty is not a quality of objects but rather a feeling in the perceiver's mind. The feeling of beauty consists of a simple emotion that elicits a drawn-out association of ideas performed by the imagination—a process that intensifies the original emotion. These reveries, or "trains of taste," are caused by certain "affective qualities" in objects. Affective qualities, such as vivacity or danger, are qualities that are capable of inspiring emotions in sentient creatures.

Alison supports his claim that trains of taste are essentially emotional in character by noting that it is impossible to *describe* objects of taste without mentioning the feelings they inspire. Not only do we tend to justify our judgments of taste by pointing to some affecting quality of the object, but we also would find it absurd if someone were to assert that "some object, though positively indifferent or uninteresting, is yet beautiful." Alison is aware that sometimes we do admire objects for their formal features alone, but he claims that in such cases we are not concerned with their beauty as much as with their harmony or color, which he takes to be distinct from beauty.

The second component of the feeling of beauty—an association of ideas undertaken by the imagination—consists in a train of thought that is unified by the simple emotion first evoked. Although each of the ideas which compose this train is accompanied by some emotion (Alison terms them "ideas of emotion"), each individual emotion must, in order for the feeling of beauty to arise, be consistent with the character of the original one. For example, a painting depicting a grieving face must exclude the rosy cheek of joy or the elevated eyebrow. Trains of taste are thus distinguished from other trains of thought by the fact that they consist of ideas of *emotion* that achieve *regularity* through their relation to one underlying mood.

Alison's claim that trains of taste are distinguished from other trains of thought by their regularity needs explanation. Is it not conceivable that a beautiful object might evoke contrasting and even conflicting emotions? Such a juxtaposition is highly effectful, but it is far from clear that it involves a regular train of thought. Alison's insistence on unity of character must be understood in conjunction with his view that in aesthetic experience we not only exercise, but also *cultivate,* our emotions. The feelings of taste can refine and crystallize our emotions, but they do so only by bringing a simple emotion to its full-blooded particularity. If a given emotion is *enhanced* by means of a contrasting one, the requirement of unity of character has not been violated, because the simple emotion that originated the train of thought is still in command. It is only if contrasting emotions *detract* from the original emotion that the regularity of the train of thought is destroyed. The criterion of unity of character should not, then, be taken to exclude the presence of suitably contrasting emotions, because "suitably contrasting" just means "having a tendency to enhance the emotion which underlies the train of association."

It follows that aesthetic delight need not be based on *pleasurable* emotions. The feeling of beauty has less to do with pleasure than with the fact that the object brings on a rich or "interesting" train of associations. For example, when we view the melancholy scenes of autumn, we are led to contemplate "that inevitable fate, which is to bring on the decay of life, of empire, and of nature itself." Because the feeling of beauty is essentially characterized by such drawn-out reveries, we can see why an ugly or repellent object is unfit to bring on a train of taste: we simply do not *want* to linger over it.

Having considered the components of the feeling of beauty, let us turn to his account of how material objects can evoke emotions, given his belief that "dead" matter is inherently incapable of evoking any kind of emotion. Alison believes that a material quality can evoke an emotion only by being *associated* with another quality that is "fitted, by the constitution of our nature" to produce an emotion. Such a quality is "affective."

On Alison's theory, a material quality comes to evoke an emotion by being *associated* with an affective quality. This association is based on the constant conjunction we find between the material quality and the abstract quality that evokes the emotion: the material quality (the sound of thunder) becomes the *sign* of a more abstract quality (danger), which evokes an emotion (fear). Given a sufficiently constant connection, we become disposed "to attribute to the sign that effect which is often produced only by the quality signified"; hence, we call thunder "fearful." Similarly, the sun is likely to make us joyful because it is uniformly associated with warmth, a quality that evokes joy. Warmth is associated with joy in virtue of a certain "resemblance between our sensations and emotions"—another type of association to which we are led "by the constitution of our nature."

The connection between material and affective qualities is by no means invariable. The farmer who, after a long drought, hears the sound of thunder is not afraid but overjoyed, because the thunder in this case indicates the prospect of a bountiful harvest. Thus, the sound of thunder does not invariably inspire fear. Conversely, the sound of a rattling cart can be mistaken for the sound of thunder, and thereby produce the same feeling of fear as the thunder would by its association with danger—a feeling that disappears as soon as the mistake is discovered. This is taken to show that the thunderous sound is not fearful in itself, but only as a result of the images or qualities we associate with it, providing further evidence for Alison's claim that material qualities are not beautiful in themselves, but only by being associated with affective qualities; indeed, his entire theory is an inductive demonstration of this claim.

Alison explains difference in taste in terms of divergence in, or absence of, associations that produce trains of taste. The sheer absence of associations is the most frequent cause of difference in taste. Failure to indulge in trains of taste arises in times of trouble or worldly concerns: "The seasons of care, of grief, of business, have other occupations, and destroy, for the time at least, our sensibility to the beautiful and the sublime, in the same proportion that they produce a state of mind unfavorable to the indulgence of imagination." Such times not only make the imagination unreceptive to feelings of beauty; they can also render repugnant objects that one would ordinarily consider beautiful: "The sound of the hunting horn, so extremely picturesque in seasons of gaiety, would be insupportable in hours of melancholy." Only those who are unoccupied by pressing concerns are in a position to make aesthetic judgments. We might call this the condition of *disinterestedness* in aesthetic judgments, because it requires that one withdraw from one's private cares and abandon oneself to the emotions that scenes of beauty inspire.

The condition of disinterestedness explains how one person might fail to see beauty where others in more receptive moods see it. But it cannot explain how two parties can disagree about what *makes* an object beautiful. Alison explains the latter by reference to private and/or local associations. Different upbringings, literary backgrounds, and so forth can make people see objects as beautiful because they evoke childhood memories, images from particular poems, and so on. Judgments of taste that are based on local associations are not, in Alison's mind, less legitimate than those based on universal associations. Local associations are by nature less permanent, however, and therefore should not be used by artists if they want their works to have lasting appeal. Good artists are distinguished precisely by the fact that they are able judiciously to combine natural signs—material qualities uniformly associated with particular affective qualities—and thereby to evoke universal associations that produce emotions fuller and stronger than the ones received from nature herself. This intensification of emotions can be seen as the ultimate source of aesthetic delight in Alison's theory: the more intense an emotion, the more vivid the activity of the imagination that accompanies it, and the greater our general delight in the object.

[*See also* Beauty; Blair; Emotions; Gerard; Priestley; *and* Taste, *article on* Modern and Recent History.]

BIBLIOGRAPHY

Work by Alison

Essays on the Nature and Principle of Taste (1790). Hildesheim, 1968.

Other Sources

Craig, R. Cairns. "The Continuity of the Associationist Aesthetic: From Archibald Alison to T. S. Eliot (and Beyond)." *Dalhousie Review* 60.1 (Spring 1980): 20–37.

Hipple, Walter John. *The Beautiful, the Sublime, and the Picturesque in Eighteenth-Century British Aesthetic Theory.* Carbondale, Ill., 1957.

Kivy, Peter. *The Seventh Sense: A Study of Francis Hutcheson's Aesthetics and Its Influence in Eighteenth-Century Britain.* New York, 1976.

Stolnitz, Jerome. "On the Origins of 'Aesthetic Disinterestedness'." *Journal of Aesthetics and Art Criticism* 20.2 (Winter 1961): 131–144.

Townsend, Dabney. "Archibald Alison: Aesthetic Experience and Emotion." *British Journal of Aesthetics* 28.2 (Spring 1988): 132–144.

JOSEFINE NAUCKHOFF

AMERICAN AESTHETICS. *See* Abstract Expressionism; Arnheim; Beardsley; Black Aesthetic; Cavell; Danto; Dickie; Emerson; Goodman; Greenberg; Harlem Renaissance; Kahn; Langer; Locke; New Criticism; Peirce; Pop Art; *and* Santayana.

ANALYTIC AESTHETICS. *For examples of the types of entries characteristic of Analytic Aesthetics, which is derived from twentieth-century Anglo-American philosophy (and which is often contrasted with Continental Aesthetics, which is derived from nineteenth- and twentieth-century European philosophy of the continent, exclusive of Great Britain), see, for example,* Appreciation; Attitude; Definition of Art; Emotions; Evaluation; Expression Theory of Art; Fiction; Formalism; Imagination; Intention; Interpretation; Metaphor; Ontology of Art; Perception; Qualities, Aesthetic; Representation; *and* Universals.

ANTHROPOLOGY AND AESTHETICS. From the time of its inception in the late nineteenth century until the rise of postmodern criticism a hundred years later, the discipline of anthropology developed principally within the paradigm of Western science. Most of its practitioners and the public at large tended to see it either as a branch of the social sciences (for the subdisciplines of sociocultural anthropology, archaeology, and anthropological linguistics) or as a biological science (for the subdiscipline of physical anthropology). Anthropologists generally strived to base their work on empirical data and to emulate the methodology of the sciences rather than the humanities. Sometimes there was little choice in the matter. For example, the form and decoration of a prehistoric ceramic vessel may affect the contemporary Westerner, providing grist for theorists grounded in Western traditions of art and aesthetics. Nevertheless, the pot's meaning and its status as "art" in its society of origin are probably lost forever, forcing the archaeologist to relegate the artifact to the quotidian domain of "material culture" and allowing the pursuit of only certain kinds of questions, such as the cataloging of stylistic traits, chemical analysis of materials, and so on—issues hardly at the center of modern aesthetic discussion.

Nevertheless, anthropologists—especially sociocultural anthropologists—have perennially pursued, at least sotto voce, some issues of relevance for aesthetics. Thus, the first generation of anthropologists was fascinated by questions of cultural evolution. What, they asked, were the primal forms of kinship, law, religion, and so on, and how did they change down through the millennia of prehistory to produce the institutions of today? Applied to the arts, this line of inquiry leads to questions regarding the evolution of motifs in the visual arts. Two schools of thought soon emerged on the subject. One group (including the Americans W. H. Holmes, Frank Cushing, and Otis Mason) used archaeological and ethnographic data from the American Southwest to argue that the earliest human efforts at art making took the form of nonrepresentational designs, some of which eventually evolved into representational figures. The Swedish anthropologist Hjalmar Stolpe, however, used data from Polynesia to argue that evolution had taken place in exactly the opposite direction, from representational figures to nonrepresentational patterns.

If the debate could have been resolved, it might have had interesting ramifications for the turn-of-the-century controversy regarding the relative merits of figurative versus abstract painting and sculpture in Western art. Instead of settling the issue, however, most of the next generation of anthropologists rejected the whole project of cultural evolutionism. In the United States, Franz Boas led the assault on the cultural evolutionists, showing that much of the data used to support their theories was of dubious accuracy and that they held the untenable ethnocentric assumption that modern, Western institutions are qualitatively better than their non-Western counterparts.

In *Primitive Art* (1927, but extant in lectures as early as 1903), Boas used art to argue the case against the cultural evolutionists. Marshaling information gathered from the best field studies then available, he showed how, with the passage of time, some art styles had indeed changed in the direction hypothesized by Holmes et al., whereas other arts had followed the pattern suggested by Stolpe. Subsequent evidence has supported Boas's claim: although he had access only to sparse and temporally shallow prehistoric data, it is now known that figurative and abstract designs both reach back at least thirty thousand years.

In retrospect, Boas's pioneering work clearly established several parameters and assumptions that most subsequent sociocultural anthropologists have adopted in their study of art and aesthetics. For one thing, Boas helped establish a methodological precedent by basing his analysis on information that he and others had collected through careful, in-depth fieldwork. Of necessity, this limits the field of inquiry for sociocultural anthropologists to the arts of living—or recently living—peoples. The remarkable cave paintings of the European Upper Paleolithic, the subtle stone carvings made two and a half millennia ago by the Olmecs of Mesoamerica, and the rich and diverse performing arts of the peoples who lived in what is now the eastern United States before the time of Christopher Columbus's arrival—all are subjects as intriguing as they are inaccessible to indepth cultural analysis. (These examples—intentionally selected from painting, sculpture, and the performing arts—reveal another Boasian precedent, namely, the inclusion of *all* expressive media within the domain of study.)

In addition, Boas demonstrated that any insights we might have into the artistic creations of other peoples are contingent on our understanding their integration into a larger sociocultural setting. Art affects and is affected by religious, ideological, political, familial, jural, educational, and other systems of belief and practice. It is generally accepted within sociocultural anthropology that studies that wrench art out of its context are incomplete at best, mistaken at worst.

Finally, Boas approached non-Western art with the same respect previously reserved for Western fine arts. This brings us to a point, however, at which contemporary art anthropologists generally take exception with him. Although he adamantly opposed ethnocentrism in the comparative study of art, we now hear a lapse in his reference to "primitive" art. The word "primitive" still appears in some anthropological writing (e.g., Price, 1989), but usually only with the author's express awareness that it carries such unacceptable connotations as "inferior," "backward," and "undeveloped"—some of the very qualities that most anthropologists from Boas onward have been at pains to remove from the Western study of non-Western art (cf. Anderson, 1979, pp. 5–8; 1989, pp. 2–8).

Operating within the Boasian model, sociocultural anthropologists produced a substantial literature on non-Western art, as summarized in surveys of the field such as Richard Anderson (1979, 1989), Anderson and Karen Field (1993), Evelyn Payne Hatcher (1985), Carol Jopling (1971), Robert Layton (1991), and Charlotte Otten (1971). They have, for example, demonstrated in great detail and with myriad case studies the multitude of ways in which art performs a variety of functions within human cultures. Some such functions are overt, as illustrated by Daniel Biebuyck's account (1973) of the role of art in male initiation ceremonies among the Lega of Central Africa: To enter the highest levels of the Lega *bwami* association, initiates had to swear to obey numerous aphorisms for good behavior. Rather than merely verbalizing these sayings at the time of initiation, a variety of objects, including carved human and animal figures, were used to illustrate the ideas. In this case, as in countless others in which the visual, literary, and performing arts are incorporated into traditional rituals, intangible concepts become more arresting by being given sensuous, aesthetic embodiment.

Of greater interest to aestheticians may be the many anthropological studies of art expressing deeper—albeit often tacit—sociocultural postulates. For example, F. Alan Hanson (1983) noted a distinctive form of symmetry not only in Maori (New Zealand) wood carving but also in Maori architecture, myth, poetry, and love songs, all of which he related to principles regarding unity and separation, concepts that structurally underlay many components of Maori culture. If Hanson is correct, then Maori art's function goes far deeper than its obvious use in religion and ritual, providing, as it were, a sensory mode through which Maori individuals apprehend their culture—a premise that informs most studies that examine the ways in which art reflects traditional values.

These references to the communicative function of art lead directly to issues of iconography and symbolism. Much non-Western art represents specific subject matter, with even supernatural spirits typically being given distinguishing characteristics. In some instances, such as the well-known Benin bronzes from precolonial West Africa, likenesses are very precisely executed; in others, stylization is so extreme that interpretation is virtually impossible for the uninitiated, even if they are members of the societies in which the art is produced. Thus, two dimensions may be distinguished regarding the communicative function of art. One continuum runs from representational through stylized to abstract art; another, from public through private to personal art. Works that embody all combinations of these two variables are found among the visual arts of the non-Western world; and the performing and literary arts may be conceptualized in like manner. (It should be noted that in most non-Western settings, art's function is culturally conservative, tending to perpetuate traditional values, beliefs, and power arrangements.)

Another fertile topic for anthropological investigations of art and aesthetics has been artists themselves (cf., e.g., d'Azevedo, 1992). Much is known about cross-cultural variations in the training of artists, non-Western conceptions of artistic talent and genius, patterns of gender difference, and the diverse social roles of the mature artist, which range from good-for-nothing pariah to disciplined and hardworking aristocrat, and from creative iconoclast to paragon of wisdom. (Whatever their status, artists in non-Western societies are rarely, if ever, untutored naives, idiosyncratically expressing themselves through artistic media.)

During the first three-quarters of the twentieth century, anthropologists focused mainly on the questions outlined here. With the emergence of the numerous critiques that fall under the rubric of postmodernism, many anthropologists have broadened their purview to include issues that little troubled earlier generations of scholars. The status of anthropology as a science has been questioned by several practitioners, and the complex and multivalent relationship between the West and the Other has become an active site for analysis.

One vector of interest in recent art anthropology has focused on the many ways in which Western and non-Western cultures, arts, and aesthetics have influenced each other during the colonial and postcolonial eras. Specialists have long rejected the image of non-Western art as being timeless and unchanging, a notion well refuted by John Adair's classic account (1944) of the inception (around 1859) and development of Native American silversmithing in the American Southwest, and in the essays collected by Nelson Graburn (1976). But as study has continued, the picture has become more, rather than less, complex. For example, Bennetta Jules-Rosette (1984) has documented the sophistication of several African traditions that previously were dismissed as "tourist art"; and Sally Price (1989) has cataloged the varied ways in which covert ethnocentrism still colors Western framing of non-Western arts, even among those with special training in the field.

Another dimension of current critical debate questions one of the seminal assumptions that Boas unquestioningly accepted. On the first page of *Primitive Art*, Boas confidently asserted that "aesthetic pleasure is felt by all members of mankind" and that art is found "among all the tribes known to us." Although these ideas underlie Boas's whole treatment of art, he failed to define the crucial terms *aesthetic* and *art*. Issues of definition and universality bring anthropologists closer to problems that have perennially dogged aestheticians.

Resolution has yet to be reached in the debate concerning the universality of aesthetic principles and the cross-cultural usefulness of the concept of "art" itself. At the minimum, fieldwork-based ethnoaesthetic reports make clear that although non-Western philosophies of art differ in detail, art typically plays a central role in the intellectual lives of many other peoples. It is not so much that non-Western cultures in some vague way are intrinsically artistic; rather, art's relevance lies in its performing specific functions that are profound, abstract, and vital.

Pre-Columbian Aztec culture provides a vivid example (cf. Léon-Portilla, 1963). Aztec myths asserted that the world would be created and destroyed five times, that four such cycles had already taken place, and that the fifth and final cataclysm was imminent. Many Aztecs may have taken such forecasts literally, but Aztec intellectuals had more abstract interpretations and agonized over such questions as, Are all humans and all their creations ephemeral, destined to disappear into nothingness? They concluded that one thing was indeed genuine and lasting, namely, "flower and song," a figure of speech that referred to *art*. By dedicating to the deities the finest art and the blood of human sacrifice, the Aztec priests reasoned that the ultimate destruction of the world might be temporarily forestalled. Some seem to have seen the mechanism as a simple quid pro quo, with the

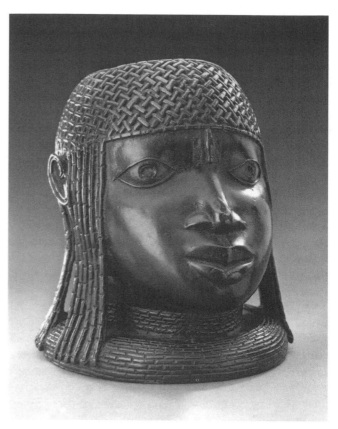

ANTHROPOLOGY AND AESTHETICS. *Memorial Head of an Oba*, Nigeria (sixteenth century), brass, 9 1/8 inches (23.2 cm) high; Nelson-Atkins Museum of Art, Kansas City, Missouri (Purchase: Nelson Trust). (Photograph used by permission.)

gods receiving art in return for postponement of the final destruction of the earth. A few, however, had deeper explanations. For example, the priest Azuiauhtzin reasoned that a deeply felt engagement with art can make time subjectively stand still; and if time stops, then so does the otherwise inevitable progression toward time's end. These and other indigenous aesthetic theories were sufficiently compelling to prompt the Aztecs to create great quantities of art, work that in a sense has given them the immortality they sought, since it is largely through their art (and their warfare) that the Aztecs are now remembered.

The Aztecs are not unique in possessing an aesthetic system that is at once independent of Western systems and insightful regarding art. For example, working in Nigeria, the art historian Robert Farris Thompson (1973) identified scores of Yoruba art critics, individuals whom the Yoruba themselves consider to be connoisseurs of carved wooden statuettes. As a result of his extensive interviews, Thompson described the subtle and integrated set of criteria used by Yoruba critics in appraising and rigorously discussing the statuettes. (For a broad survey of the anthropology of non-Western aesthetic systems, see Anderson, 1990.)

But descriptions of non-Western aesthetic systems aside, some have questioned the epistemological basis of art anthropology itself. It is a truism that some—perhaps most—languages lack words that translate even approximately as *art*. Similarly, some—probably most—cultures have no tradition of using disinterested, theoretical principles to discuss the relative merits and fundamental nature of art; that is, they have no explicit, clearly articulated aesthetic philosophy. These problems are addressed in various ways by different scholars. For example, in her study of performances among the Kono of Liberia, Kris Harden emphasizes the "aesthetic response." The event she describes is significant, she feels, not because it exemplifies what English speakers might call "dance," but because of its salience in Kono thought, where the "adherence to and successful re-presentation of principles . . . elicits positive aesthetic response. The primary mechanism here is one of redundancy" (1988, p. 37).

The aesthetic response is even more central to the work of Jacques Maquet (1986). Admittedly, within the mainstream of Western aesthetics the concept of aesthetic response is now often viewed as highly problematic; and, moreover, it is such an elusive and ephemeral subjective state that its application to non-Western art is at best difficult (cf. Anderson, 1979, pp. 14–17). Nevertheless, Maquet has made a significant contribution to the field by providing sensitive analyses of the capacity of non-Western art sometimes to evoke an aesthetic response in some Western viewers.

But if Morris Weitz's approach (1956) to defining art has informed the work of many late-twentieth-century Western aestheticians, a parallel approach is found in most anthropological writing, either tacitly or explicitly (as in Anderson, 1990, 1992). By analogy, one might note that all cultures certainly have systems of thought regarding the supernatural, despite the fact that some have no words that translate directly into the English terms *religion* and *magic*. Similarly, although an equivalent to *art* is not found in most languages, all cultures seem to recognize as being special certain material and behavioral artifacts of human creation that manifest most or all of the following features: they convey significant cultural meaning; they are created with exceptional manual and/or mental skill; they are produced in a public medium; they are intended to create a sensuous effect; and they share stylistic conventions with works of proximate geographic and temporal origin. Although few peoples have coherent, explicit philosophies of art, all seem to recognize many distinctly aesthetic principles, variously expressed in myths or stories of origin, in standards for ritual behavior, in taste for secular adornment, or, perhaps most interesting of all, articulated within the idiom of art itself.

Thus, although anthropologists long labored within the paradigm of science, their writing is of relevance for aestheticians in several ways. Working under the banner of Boasian empiricism, they produced descriptions of non-Western art that provide a valuable antidote to the persistent tendency (trenchantly noted by Eliot Deutsch, 1975, pp. x–xi) of most aestheticians to equate "art" with "Western art" and as a consequence to produce theories that are closely tied to their own "historical placement." In addition, recent scholars have broadened the range of aesthetic possibilities by documenting philosophies of art in numerous non-Western cultures and by problematizing the very foundation of aesthetic inquiry. One hopes that future years will see increasingly fruitful cross-pollination between the disciplines of anthropology and aesthetics.

[*See also* Artifact; Comparative Aesthetics; Craft; *and* Tribal Art.]

BIBLIOGRAPHY

Adair, John. *Navajo and Pueblo Silversmiths.* Norman, Okla., 1944.
Anderson, Richard L. *Art in Primitive Societies.* Englewood Cliffs, N.J., 1979. 2d ed. published as *Art in Small-Scale Societies* (Englewood Cliffs, N.J., 1989).
Anderson, Richard L. *Calliope's Sisters: A Comparative Study of Philosophies of Art.* Englewood Cliffs, N.J., 1990.
Anderson, Richard L. "Do Other Cultures Have 'Art'?" *American Anthropologist* 94 (1992): 926–929.
Anderson, Richard L., and Karen L. Field, eds. *Art in Small-Scale Societies: Contemporary Readings.* Englewood Cliffs, N.J., 1993.
Biebuyck, Daniel P. *Lega Culture: Art, Initiation, and Moral Philosophy among a Central African People.* Berkeley, 1973.
Boas, Franz. *Primitive Art* (1927). New York, 1955.
Deutsch, Eliot. *Studies in Comparative Aesthetics.* Monograph of the Society for Asian and Comparative Philosophy, no. 2. Honolulu, 1975.
d'Azevedo, Warren L., ed. *The Traditional Artist in African Societies* (1973). 2d ed. Bloomington, Ind., 1992.
Graburn, Nelson H. H., ed. *Ethnic and Tourist Arts: Cultural Expressions from the Fourth World.* Berkeley, 1976.
Hanson, F. Alan. "Art and Maori Construction of Reality." In *Art and Artists of Oceania,* edited by Sidney M. Mead and Bernie Kernot, pp. 220–225. Mill Valley, Calif., 1983.
Harden, Kris. "Aesthetics and the Cultural Whole: A Study of Kono Dance Occasions." *Empirical Studies of the Arts* 6.1 (1988): 35–57.
Hatcher, Evelyn Payne. *Art as Culture: An Introduction to the Anthropology of Art.* Lanham, Md., 1985.
Jopling, Carol F., ed. *Art and Aesthetics in Primitive Societies: A Critical Anthology.* New York, 1971.
Jules-Rosette, Bennetta. *The Messages of Tourist Art: An African Semiotic System in Comparative Perspective.* New York, 1984.
Layton, Robert. *The Anthropology of Art* (1981). 2d ed. Cambridge and New York, 1991.
Léon-Portilla, Miguel. *Aztec Thought and Culture: A Study of the Ancient Nahuatl Mind.* Translated by Jack Emory Davis. Norman, Okla., 1963.
Maquet, Jacques. *The Aesthetic Experience: An Anthropologist Looks at the Visual Arts.* New Haven, 1986.
Otten, Charlotte M., ed. *Anthropology and Art: Readings in Cross-Cultural Aesthetics.* Garden City, N.Y., 1971.
Price, Sally. *Primitive Art in Civilized Places.* Chicago, 1989.
Thompson, Robert Farris. "Yoruba Artistic Criticism." In *The Traditional Artist in African Societies,* edited by Warren L. d'Azevedo, pp. 19–61. Bloomington, Ind., 1973.
Weitz, Morris. "The Role of Theory in Aesthetics." *Journal of Aesthetics and Art Criticism* 15.1 (September 1956): 27–35.

RICHARD L. ANDERSON

ANTI-AESTHETICS. *See* Anti-Art; Essentialism.

ANTI-ART. An obviously paradoxical neologism, anti-art, like art, is composed of many elements in shifting combinations, and paradox dogs its definition. Although the exact relationship between art and anti-art is always one of contradiction, any recognizable pattern in this opposition is gained by hindsight, meaning that the fact and form of its appearance is entirely unpredictable.

Anti-art is an anarchic aesthetic, in a broad sense of the term, an anarchy that includes both Michael Bakunin and Buster Keaton and that informs, among other trends, the fractal psychedelia of Chaos Theory, King Mob, Hakim Bey's Poetic Terrorism, Richard Neville's Play Power, and Paul Feyerabend's theory of scientific progress, where anything goes. It is an aesthetic most easily discerned in the modern era, and although it may extend before and after, it has a history that often mirrors and interacts with modernism.

There is more to anti-art than simple transgression of cultural boundaries, although such violations, with corollaries of outrage, sensation, and even crime, are often associated with anti-art activities. Therefore, although Impressionism revolted against visual norms, and its supporters called for the abolition of official beauty, it is difficult to imagine anti-art flourishing under Claude Monet. The anti-art value of shock, however, is proven by Alfred Jarry, whose antihero Ubu Roi launched a tradition of insult with a barely disguised expletive. Although disgusting and suitably offensive, Père Ubu is ultimately less important to an understanding of anti-art than is Jarry's concept of *'pataphysics*. The *épater le bourgeois* approach, although a continuing staple of anti-art, has become a cliché that requires increasing doses of irony in order to be effective.

'Pataphysics (preceded by an apostrophe so as to avoid a simple pun) is the philosophy of exceptions, a science of absurd solutions, which Jarry postulated most cogently through the mouthpiece of Dr. Faustroll. It must be understood as a product of nineteenth-century scientific excess, pseudoreligious inquiry, and Symbolist melodrama, a combination that Jarry suicidally exemplified in his daily life. As a model for anti-art, however, such exercises as defining God through algebra retain considerable contemporary power: taking a conventional belief and applying relentless logic to it until it assumes a bizarre, absurd, or even malevolent complexion is a method used throughout the twentieth century. It is another appropriate paradox that anti-art developments should become models for art production, from the Theater of the Absurd to Minimalism.

Because anarchy has gradually assumed political connotations, anti-art activities often coincide with political-cultural movements. This is clearly demonstrated by Italian Futurism, whose germinal anti-art reflected the political heterodoxy of its anarchist, socialist, and ultimately fascist members. It is evident from the voluminous production of manifestos that accompanied their activities that they were engaged in a direct political process. It also becomes apparent on reading their texts that, far from agitating for the dissolution of art as it was currently understood, Futurists were intent on ultimately transforming art to suit their sociocultural purposes. The utopias they imagined still reserved a place of glory for their monstrous, Futurist, artist; even though the art they proposed was so radically different from contemporary practice as to constitute an opposition, and the demands that they made were violently antiestablishment, they wanted to change art, not destroy it. Some of the techniques they used, however, particularly simultaneity and bruitism, were rapidly appropriated and refined by Dada, which seized upon them as ideal generators of confusion, irritation, and chaos.

It is Dada, the explosive movement that first developed in neutral Zurich during World War I, that is perhaps most closely associated with anti-art. Dada was the crucible in which many of the recognizable attributes of anti-art were formed, and Dada is responsible for some of the confusion that still surrounds—and is perhaps inevitably a part of—anti-art. A complex alchemy in which antiauthority protest was distilled from a romantic, even Expressionist impatience with the stolidity of the art establishment, transmuted through chance operations, and sublimated by a poetic anarchist philosophy, the 'pataphysical argument of Dada might be schematized as an attempt at total rejection of the culture that led to the massive devastation of World War I: if logic led to such lunacy, could chance-based irrationality lead to anything worse? Tristan Tzara reiterated the impetus of Dada as disgust, a disgust that is almost spiritual in its all-encompassing scope:

> Dada applies itself to everything, and yet is nothing, it is the point where the yes and the no and all the opposites meet, not solemnly in the castles of human philosophies, but very simply at street corners, like dogs and grasshoppers.
> Like everything in life, Dada is useless.
> Dada is without pretension, as life should be.
> Perhaps you will understand me better when I tell you that Dada is a virgin microbe that penetrates with the insistence of air into all the spaces that reason has not been able to fill with words or conventions   (as quoted in Motherwell)

The founders of Dada only briefly, if ever, shared a coherent set of tactics, or even a program. Only through the plethora of contemporary and subsequent contradictions identified within the Dada program is it possible to see, if not a distinct stratagem, then at least a vague unity in the direction of their opposition: a preference for chance over choice or reasoned decision; a general antipathy to logic, to bourgeois compromise (whether over material, philosophical, or aesthetic assumptions), and to the constraints—formal and metaphysical—that logic and bourgeois values combine to enforce. Any convention, whether philosophical, political, moral, or social, was a valid target for Dada. Its activities moved outside traditional academic study, to linger on the fringes of accountability, or even sanity, like Johannes Baader's bid for the presidency of the Weimar Republic. This accounts, perhaps, for another of the paradoxes associated with anti-art: the successful anti-artist may never be "discovered" by official culture, and may disappear, like Arthur Cravan; or, as in the case of Marcel Duchamp's mythical cessation of art, the reality may lie hidden from history for years.

Duchamp, anti-art's missionary of insolence, is credited with coining the term, and his contributions to anti-art are manifold. They sprang from his refusal of the merely retinal justification for art; his extension of chance-based operations as a method of working; his use of industrially mass-produced objects chosen, avowedly, with indifference to aesthetic emotions; his investigation of puns and the paradoxes inherent in language, particularly in combination with imagery. Thus, on the simplest level, without recourse to psychology or occult readings, his proposal of an unaltered mass-produced bottle rack or pissoir as a work of art distilled the venomous cacophony of Dada into a refrain of deceptively simple questions, loaded with ironic ramifications: if a work of art is inevitably composed of aesthetic decisions, whose should they be, what should determine their limits, and how much control can artist or audience claim over effect or meaning, given the remarkable shifts in potential caused by context or other external variables?

Duchamp's contributions to anti-art were revitalized after World War II by John Cage, who, although never labeled an antimusician, effected such a radical reappraisal of music as to be clearly open to the accusation. Apart from introducing Duchamp to a new generation of artists, and, by way of the *Yi jing* and Zen Buddhism, providing a plausible set of alternatives to the prevalent Western, modernist aesthetic, Cage's influence on anti-art stems from his refusal to countenance conventional aesthetic hierarchies. He not only eschewed qualitative judgment—arguing that the difference between good and bad was an uninteresting distinction that offered little explanation, analysis, or understanding of a work—but he also expanded on a proposition made earlier in the century by the Italian Futurist Luigi Russolo, who noted that the difference between noise and music was an arbitrary, socially driven distinction, which was therefore open to modification. Cage championed a return to chance-based operations, best exemplified in his most famous work, *4′33″*, an interval that is filled only, but inevitably, with ambient sounds and the audience's imagination. The proposition formed by *4′33″*—that music is where any individual chooses to hear it—has been applied subsequently in other anti-art areas.

On 27 November 1960, French painter Yves Klein declared that every act in the world during that day was part of his Théâtre du Vide; and in a work of 1961, Piero Manzoni placed the world on a pedestal *(Le Socle du Monde)*, thus including the entire planet in a sculpture: these ambitious individual attempts portended an exhilarating decade of anti-art activity in many disciplines, and for many different reasons, whose reverberations are still being felt. Manzoni's other anti-art gestures included a limited edition of his feces, canned, with a signed label; his breath was also for sale, packaged in balloons; and he developed a system for authenticating people as works of art—by Manzoni. In a similar vein, Klein successfully marketed a number of apparently empty spaces, filled only with his Immaterial Pictorial Sensitivity. It is here, however, defending their authority as artists, that both men return from the zone of paradox, while their actions, alongside Cage's and Duchamp's, serve as new benchmarks for the ubiquity of aesthetic experience—and thus its negation. After these eloquent arguments—each of which was quickly accepted as affirmative evidence, and thus orthodox—simple absence of an object can no longer guarantee anti-art status: conceptual art stands as witness to this fact.

This interplay between anti-art and art depends on an understanding of art as an open concept that functions in some connection to power. Marxism proved to be a useful and convincing method of revealing the existence—if not the nature or the workings—of the connection, and many anti-art ideas have depended on modifications of Marxist arguments. Situationists, beginning from this base in post–World War II Europe, argued that bourgeois domination of artistic values had robbed Dada and Surrealism of meaning, leaving only a reactionary shell of spectacle that promoted passivity and conspired against freedom. Their solution, a transcendance of art through its simultaneous abolition and realization, was, as articulated by the French Situationist International, dense in theory and rarely specific; the basic elements involved applying modified Dada techniques of collage and Surrealist notions of the unconscious to everyday life. They experimented with unfettered physical and psychic behavior under conditions of urban existence, incited provocations, and believed themselves to be the theoretical motor and aesthetic fuel of the tumultuous uprisings in Paris during May 1968.

The rapid cultural changes that occurred during the 1960s provided energy and occasion for many varieties of anti-art argument, some of which have yet to surface. The compound fracturing of authority that occurred throughout the decade led to myriad splinters that have ossified at different rates, leaving more or less jagged edges—the most obvious of which exist where anti-art activity stands in direct negation of art tenets: however *art* might be defined, anti-art contradicts the definition. Therefore, because one essential element of art is creation, anti-art revels in destruction, as witnessed by the 1966 Destruction in Art Symposium, whose attendees celebrated the cathartic effects of violence to the body and idea of art through literal demonstration (including the burning of artworks, books, and so on) and symbolic gestures (as when an audience was invited to cut the clothing off Yoko Ono's motionless body). In an era where gesture dominates and the "radical heterogeneity" of collage is standard, destruction can certainly be manipulated into a creative act: and if inspired creation is central to art, then automatic destruction will be its shadow.

Again, if art is permanent—in the sense of *ars longa vita brevis*—then anti-art finds meaning in change and the opportunity for brief life. Fluxus, a collective that blossomed with the 1960s, was named for change and became the century's most coherent site of anti-art since Dada—with which it is often compared. Fluxus might be characterized as an international constellation of poets, musicians, intermedia experimenters, and anti-artists who combined a general disdain for conventional kinds of art practice with radical strategies to attack art in favor of lived experience. Although few among them fully believed the published call to "Purge the world of dead art, imitation, artificial art, abstract art, illusionistic art, mathematical art" (as quoted in Maciunas), and few more actively undertook the program, to replace art with Fluxus art-amusement (the former of necessity appearing complex, profound, serious, intellectual, inspired, skillful, significant, the latter antidote being simple, amusing, etc.), they nevertheless attacked art on three basic levels, and did in some ways "promote living art, anti-art." First, the use of a corporate name, under which individual personalities would be subsumed, was a vain, but nonetheless sincere assault on the notion of the artist as hero, touched by genius. Without an identifiable creator, without the possibility of personalizing the product, connoisseurship would be threatened, mythologizing histories would be prevented, and audiences would more readily concur that their role in the completion of the work was literally vital: Fluxists understood in the early 1960s that author and authority are inextricably linked. Their attempt to counter what they saw as the parasitical and elitist status of the artist, although quickly doomed, has subsequently been modified and retried by correspondence artists and "Neoists." Second, Fluxus works defied categorical norms: deliberately intermedial, they operated in the interstices between and around conventional disciplines—between poetry and music, between sculpture and theater, between reality and reflection—creating hybrids that not only reinforced Duchamp's disparagement of the object, but that continue to outwit the careful schemes of museums and other conventional classifying systems. By contradicting all the usual apparatus of art-ness, replacing unique, precious, discrete objects with cheap, ephemeral, multiples that were difficult to characterize and that welcomed interpretations, Fluxists aimed to deny the fixity of art and celebrate instead the process of experience. Although their practices failed to preserve them from eventual museum status, the idea of art

as process was an enormous influence on following generations. Third, Fluxus was deliberately not serious, and called for an emphasis on playfulness of approach, whether in works, in analyses, in the serious business of history, in measures of significance, or in aesthetic paradigms. Using humor almost as a weapon to puncture intellectual and theoretical pretension also served to temporarily preserve Fluxus pieces from the purportedly deadening effects of art-historical analysis. This antipathy to the serious also meant that, for Fluxists, purpose, solidity, and the immortality conferred by history were suspect, leading them not only to celebrate vaudeville and the gag, but to startling developments in live art, initiating performative events that by definition were ephemeral, deliberately open to endless emendation, and often ludicrously funny.

Playfulness and laughter were also recommended by Fluxus contemporary Allan Kaprow as escape routes, not only from the dead hand of history but eventually, slyly, from the discrete category of art-ness. Kaprow has reported that he deliberately set out to do whatever what art was not, and by this process, paradoxically, nurtured and named a whole new direction in art—in the Happening. In subsequent theoretical texts, he laid out what amounts to a program for creating the opposite to art, arguing that, given the criteria for aesthetic experience, all the best opportunities lay outside the purview of art. Hence, conversations between ground control and astronauts are "better" than poetry, lint from the bedroom floor is "more engaging" than contemporary sculpture, the drama of real life is "richer" than theater. Kaprow is careful to point out that these are examples of "nonart," a category he distinguishes from anti-art—and from what he calls art art—by virtue of the former's lack of intent. Aware of the paradox that implies the presence of art within anti-art, subsequent plans toward the phasing out of art superseded his initial formal rule breaking, introducing ideas and actions that ignored almost all the conventions of art, defining a new territory that he called "un-art."

New territories and new titles also play a part in the anti-art concerns of Henry Flynt, whose philosophical efforts to reject art led to the proposal that *brend*—his term for purely subjective experiences that parallel, but precede aesthetic experiences—should be recognized as offering far superior insights than does art. Flynt's argument—that art and the experiences it offers are the result of social conditioning—meant that, for him, modern art should be rejected because the distance between the object and the aesthetic experience was unnecessarily great. Once a population had been trained to locate and develop its own "brend," that is, once it had isolated its own subjective affinities (he referred to these as "just-likings"), then art would be redundant, everyone would be personally more fulfilled, and the intellectual fraud of art—whereby other people's subjective experiences are presumed to have a higher value than one's own—would cease. This transference of value onto the object, simply because of its social position, was an affront to Flynt, partly because of the intellectual sleight of hand involved, but more so because he regarded modern art as increasingly filled with irrelevancies, waste, and superficial prestige garnered as a result of worthless innovation.

This hostile conception of art as a frivolous fraud at the expense of purportedly genuine experience, which is, perhaps, an echo of Dada disgust, resounded throughout the 1960s, and could be illustrated with a multitude of further examples ranging in intensity from physical assault to complete withdrawal—from the Guerilla Art Action Group's visceral attacks on the fabric of the museum world to Gustav Metzger's call for an industrial-style, three-year-long art strike. That anti-art activity disappears—or is much less visible—for more than a decade after this might be explained by some of the effects of sixties activism: ecology-minded Process Art, feminism, Correspondence Art, the trend toward consumer-friendly museum education—each provided some relief from, or appeared to answer some element of the anti-art argument. The pluralist veneer of the 1970s allowed less scope for overt contradiction of a visual norm, although the oppositional nature of individual efforts did not lessen, they went underground or became an anti-art element in more general works.

The apparent diffusion of anti-art in the polystylistic disorder of the 1970s—which has yet to be thoroughly historicized—conforms to ideas about the dearth of antiliterature. As Jules Laforgue suggested in the 1880s, if artists were allowed the stylistic freedom and solitude of writers, then perhaps "official" beauty would cease to exist. Certainly, literature had no parallel to Duchamp or Cage until William Burroughs and Bryon Gyson injected new life into Dada's moribund cutup, extending the method into prose. Despite an embryonic antitheater at the turn of the century, and the best efforts of Futurists, the world of letters seems more familiar with—and thus less vulnerable to—anarchy. Language has been subverted variously throughout the modernist era: *lettristes* sought to replace it with icons, and concrete poets continued the dispersal of text into image begun before the twentieth century. These rarely amount to a consistent negation, and are closer perhaps to Marcuse's idea of desublimation than to an attack on the principles of writing.

The most obvious anti-art influence after 1968 surfaced in music, where punk erupted in ranting, furious anger against the status quo. Following the contradictory tenets of anti-art, punk opposed the complex, artificial, specialized music of the early 1970s with post-Elvis noise in which energy surpassed ability, emotion outweighed reflection, and simple experience meant more than messages or motifs. Punk's original thrust, which is most clearly articulated in brutal generalizations, proposed an aggressive anarchy, individual action and ironic ad hoc-ism—Situationism, but without the theory, and more fun. Despite the popularity of

insolent defiance, and a successful translation into American, punk as a music and lifestyle was rapidly repackaged as a commercially viable entity, and diluted into a studied nihilism, almost indistinguishable from old-fashioned teenage angst. Punk did, however, at least contrive to expose these commercial developments even as they were happening—it added appropriate injury to the insult—and, continuing a situationist heritage, this seditious honesty offers a clue to current trends in anti-art.

Given the current connection between art education, art history, and art production, it is inevitable that the dissident strain within modernism should infect contemporary practice, and should spread quickly to art history and theory, whether or not it undermines the idea of an avant-garde. Thus it seems that the virus of discontent should become a diffuse but palpable presence throughout the body cultural. It may be diagnosed in benign stylistic refusals—as in "bad painting"—or in more exotic strains, such as Stewart Home's playful appropriation of Gustav Metzger's proposed art strike. Home provides a shrewd palliative for the paradoxical complications of anti-art history by hilarious and well-informed invention, presented in the same deadpan manner as his other research, so that history, theory, fiction, pornography, and even prophesy become indistinguishable. Otherwise, despite published threats to develop an anti-aesthetic, postmodern theory has fallen for the "ruse of reason," and has largely failed to surpass the frank refusal of belief that constitutes genuine opposition.

It almost goes without saying that as anti-art becomes the subject of historical scrutiny—or definition—it becomes suspect. Perhaps, like duration, anti-art suffers as soon as it is described, becoming a trite metaphor, a grain of sand in an oyster, a mutant cell, a theoretical root system that invites hypothetical evaluations but that simultaneously must acknowledge the insufficiency of rhetoric. Endlessly oppositional, the paradox of anti-art may unfortunately be reducible only to the elemental discrepancy between relative and absolute conceptions of existence—at which point anti-art returns the argument to its rightful realm: metaphysics.

[*See also* Cage; Dadaism; Duchamp; Essentialism; Futurism; *and* Situationist Aesthetics.]

BIBLIOGRAPHY

Bergson, Henri. *An Introduction to Metaphysics.* Translated by T. E. Hulme. Indianapolis, 1949.
Flynt, Henry. *Blueprint for a Higher Civilization.* Milan, 1975.
Graver, David. *The Aesthetics of Disturbance: Anti-Art in Avant-Garde Drama.* Ann Arbor, 1995.
Gray, John. *Action Art: A Bibliography of Artists' Performance from Futurism to Fluxus and Beyond.* Westport, Conn., 1993.
Home, Stewart. *The Assault on Culture: Utopian Currents from Lettrisme to Class War.* London, 1988.
Hulten, Pontus. *Futurism and Futurisms.* New York, 1986.
Hulten, Pontus, ed. *Marcel Duchamp: Work and Life.* Cambridge, Mass., 1993.

In the Spirit of Fluxus. Minneapolis, 1993. Published on the occasion of the exhibition "In the Spirit of Fluxus" organized by Elizabeth Armstrong and Joan Rothfuss.

Kaprow, Allan. *Essays on the Blurring of Art and Life.* Edited by Jeff Kelley. Berkeley, 1993.

Knabb, Ken, ed. *Situationist International Anthology.* Berkeley, 1981.

Kostelanetz, Richard, ed. *John Cage: An Anthology.* New York, 1991.

Lippard, Lucy R., ed. *Six Years: The Dematerialization of the Art Object from 1966 to 1972.* New York, 1973.

Maciunus, George. "Manifesto" (originally published by Fluxus [no date]). In *happening + fluxus,* edited by H. Sohm. Cologne, 1970.

Marcus, Greil. *Lipstick Traces: A Secret History of the Twentieth Century.* Cambridge, Mass., 1989.

Meyer, Ursula. "The Eruption of Anti-Art." In *Idea Art,* edited by Gregory Battcock. New York, 1973.

Motherwell, Robert, ed. *The Dada Painters and Poets: An Anthology.* 2d ed. Reprint, Cambridge, Mass., 1989. Originally published as "Conference sur dada" Merz. 2 no. 7:68 January 1924. Translated and published as Tristran Tzara: Lecture on Dada. 1922.

Richter, Hans. *Dada: Art and Anti-Art.* London, 1965.

Shattuck, Roger. *The Banquet Years: The Origins of the Avant-Garde in France, 1885 to World War I.* Rev. ed. New York, 1968.

Stansill, Peter, and David Zane Mairowitz, eds. *BAMN: (By Any Means Necessary): Outlaw Manifestos and Ephemera, 1965–1970.* Harmondsworth, England, 1971.

Vaneigem, Raoul. *The Revolution of Everyday Life.* 2d rev. ed. Translated by Donald Nicholson-Smith. Seattle, 1994.

SIMON ANDERSON

ANTI-ESSENTIALISM. *See* Essentialism.

APOLLINAIRE, GUILLAUME. *See* Breton; Surrealism.

APPRECIATION. The term *appreciation* is used in literary and art criticism for the act apprehending a work of art with enjoyment. In art theory and literary theory, the concept of appreciation is not distinguished systematically from "interpretation." This often has a debilitating effect on the discussion of interpretation as a way of apprehending a work of art, for the concept of appreciation is different from the concept of interpretation in subtle ways.

Appreciation is conceptually linked to perception and to reflection. It is a kind of perception. One takes a sip of a cup of Darjeeling First Flush and appreciates its taste *in tasting it.* What distinguishes appreciation from other kinds of perception is that it is a perception of a value, positive or negative. The arrival of Darjeeling First Flush is eagerly awaited every year, almost as eagerly as the arrival of the Beaujolais Nouveau. Appreciation is not untrained perception, but is the outcome of a long process of initiation and practice. Someone who has only drunk Typhoo tea will not be able properly to appreciate a First Flush, though he or she may perceive that it is a good tea. This process of initiation is partly a process of training one's sensibility and partly a

process of learning how to apply a certain vocabulary that embodies the discriminations involved in the kind of appreciation one is trained in. The two processes are not really distinguishable: one trains one's sensibility by learning to apply the vocabulary. This is the point that T. S. Eliot somewhat obscurely tried to make when he wrote that "the perceptions do not, in a really appreciative mind, accumulate as a mass, but form themselves as a structure; and criticism is the statement in language of this structure; it is a development of sensibility" (Eliot, 1923, pp. 14–15). One becomes a connoisseur of wine by learning to use the language embodying the discriminations made by connoisseurs.

The element of reflection in appreciation enters with the application of the vocabulary embodying these discriminations. This does not mean that appreciation involves two kinds of judgment, an act of perception and an act of reflection. One may have to *decide* what one's perceives, to reflect before it becomes clear what it is that one perceives, but this involves only *one experience:* the reflection constitutes the perception. One *tastes* the goodness of the Darjeeling First Flush. The quality is identified *in* the perception.

The element of reflection is strengthened by the fact that appreciation does not take place in a vacuum but in a context of knowledge that extends further than to a wide experience of the kind of object one aims to appreciate. Appreciating wine involves knowledge of wine districts, their soils and climate, types of grapes, traditions of wine making, and so on, and discriminating palates can place a wine in time and geographically, sometimes identifying both the year and the winery. Thus, appreciation is not only developed through a training of sensibility but also by acquiring theoretical knowledge. For different kinds of object of perception, this body of knowledge will not be merely different but also of different kinds. The knowledge one needs to appreciate a tennis match is different in kind from the knowledge one needs to appreciate a great work of architecture.

Appreciation is a mode of apprehension through which those features of an object that make it worthy of appreciation are identified. This means that appreciation is constituted by a set of expectations that define a perspective on the object of appreciation and direct the attention of the person involved. The expectation and the type of attention are defined through the discriminations made possible through the vocabulary of, and the knowledge defined as relevant for, appreciation. *Aesthetic appreciation* identifies those features that make an object aesthetically worthwhile, that is, the features that make the object a work of art. Thus, there is a conceptual link between the notion "work of art" and the notion of "aesthetic appreciation." In P. F. Strawson's words, "it would be contradictory to speak of judging something *as a work of art,* but not from the aesthetic point of view" (Strawson, 1974, p. 183). The conceptual link between "work of art" and "aesthetic appreciation" has as a consequence that any suggestion to give up the "ideology of the aesthetic" is really a suggestion to the effect that one should dispense with art.

The concept of interpretation is different from the concept of appreciation in that it is usually linked to the notion of "understanding": it is taken to be "uncontentious and perhaps not very informative to say that in [cases of interpretation] the critics are trying to understand the work" (Barnes, 1988, p. 7). Linking the concept of "interpretation" (of a work of art) with the concept of "understanding," however, does not provide an adequate characterization of the *kind of apprehension* that is invited by a work of art qua work of art. There is no conceptual link between the notion of understanding and the notion of value, aesthetic or other; the reason one takes the trouble to interpret works of art is to recover their value, to experience them as valuable. Consider, for example, the following comments on Regine Engstrand, the parlor maid in Ibsen's *Ghosts*:

> With regard to one of the other characters of the play, Regine, we know for certain that Ibsen's description rests on particular and direct observation. In Munich the Ibsen family employed a parlour-maid whom the writer quietly and carefully observed; she interested him as a phenomenon—Mrs Ibsen related—since she had connection with two different classes and two different worlds: she was from Bohemia and spoke dialect with her equals, but with her employers high German *(Hochdeutsch),* mixed with a number of French words and expressions—she had spent some time in Paris. Regine's speeches show that Ibsen used his ears well, just as Oswald's accounts of the artists' lives in Paris both in form and content derive from what Ibsen heard in Munich and Rome.
> (Francis Bull, "Introduksjon" to *Ghosts* in the centenary edition of Ibsen's works; reprinted in Francis Bull, Halvdan Koht, and Didrik Arup Seip, *Ibsen's Drama*   [Oslo, 1972], pp. 108–109)

This information about Regine contributes to our *understanding* of the play, an understanding of how Ibsen composed it, where he collected his material, and, in particular, it explains why Regine has the particular characteristics that she has in the play. This understanding, however, does not help the reader to apprehend *Ghosts* as a dramatic work of art. It does not involve in any way an apprehension of the contribution made by the Regine character to the aesthetic value of the work. An apprehension of this contribution is constituted by a structured experience of the various scenes of the play itself in which Regine appears, the structure of this experience being in part determined also by the information the play provides about Regine's past and origins. Here is the ghost scene in *Ghosts*:

> *(From the dining-room comes the sound of a chair being overturned; simultaneously a voice is heard.)*
> REGINE'S VOICE *(in a sharp whisper):* Oswald! Are you mad? Let me go!
> MRS ALVING *(stiffening with horror):* Ah . . .!
> *(She stares wild-eyed towards the half-open door. Oswald can be heard coughing and humming. A bottle is uncorked.)*

> MANDERS *(agitated):* What on earth was that! What's the matter, Mrs Alving?
> MRS ALVING *(hoarsely):* Ghosts! Those two in the conservatory . . . come back to haunt us.
> MANDERS: What do you say? Regine . . .? Is she . . .?
> MRS ALVING: Yes. Come. Not a word . . .!
> *(She grips Pastor Manders by the arm and walks unsteadily towards the dining-room.)*
> *(The Oxford Ibsen,* vol. 5 [Oxford, 1961], translated by James Walter McFarlane. All quotes are from this translation.)

A member of the audience must structure an experience of this scene by help of the vocabulary and the conventions acquired as a reader of literature and a watcher of plays; must perceive two different generations represented by the two groups of *characters;* must see Captain Alving's son repeating in the dining room his father's action a generation before, and repeating it, not with a mere parlor maid but with his half sister, and with Mrs. Alving in the same spot listening, as a generation before. The substitution of the half sister for the parlor maid is important. Previously in the act, Mrs. Alving has described how Captain Alving's infidelities and excesses moved from outside into their home:

> MRS ALVING: I put up with things, although I knew very well what was going on in secret outside this house. But when it came to scandal within these very walls . . .
> MANDERS: What's that you say! Here!
> MRS ALVING: Yes, here in our own home. In there *(points to the first door right)* in the dining-room, that's where I first got wind of it.

This is where Mrs. Alving moved in and took charge and contained, even though she could not put a stop to, Captain Alving's excesses:

> MRS ALVING: I had to put up with a lot in this house. To keep him at home in the evenings . . . and at nights . . . I had to join him in secret drinking orgies up in his room. I had to sit there with him, just the two of us drinking, and listen to his obscene, stupid remarks, and then struggling with him to get him dragged into his bed. . . .

What the member of the audience witnesses when Oswald makes his pass at Regine is the Captain's "excesses" moving even closer, into the very core of the family. This perception of what is happening anticipates the revelation that Captain Alving's excesses have penetrated as deeply as they can come into the family, into Oswald's very brain: he is dying from syphilis inherited, or transferred to him, from his father. It is such a structured perception of the scene, a perception conditioned by knowledge of the characters from other parts of the play, that constitutes an adequate apprehension of the scene as making a contribution to the aesthetic value of the play. One *experiences* the scene as a part of a dramatic work of art.

To characterize this form of apprehension, the concept of "understanding" is not merely inadequate; it is the wrong concept altogether. The concept of "interpretation," insofar as it is used to denote activities and results aimed at clarifying the qualities of a work of art, cannot be satisfactorily explained in terms of understanding but must be explained in terms of appreciation. Understanding has nothing to contribute to the identification of the aesthetic value of a work of art, whereas interpretation of a work of art qua work of art is aimed at defining a perception of the work of art as valuable. Appreciation is essentially different from understanding in that it is constituted by a structured perception of value and it must be recognized as a mode of apprehension different from understanding. The two modes of apprehension are similar in many respects, but the notion of understanding lacks the reference to an experience of value. One must consequently reject the view that when critics interpret a work of art they are "trying to understand the work." If they are interpreting it as a work of art, they are trying to *appreciate* it. Linking the concept of interpretation to the concept of aesthetic appreciation is to tie interpretation to a purpose that will then govern the activity and be aimed at a certain kind of result. The purpose of aesthetic appreciation is governed by a set of conventions and a vocabulary just like any other kind of appreciation. Aesthetic appreciation is, however, the most complex form of appreciation there is, and it engages—just as does the creation of works of art themselves—the imagination and the emotions as well as the intellect, to the full extent of the reader's powers.

[*See also* Evaluation; Interpretation; Nature, *article on* Japanese Appreciation of Nature; Perception; Qualities, Aesthetic; Sports Aesthetics; *and* Value.]

BIBLIOGRAPHY

Barnes, Annette. *On Interpretation: A Critical Analysis.* Oxford, 1988.
Danto, Arthur C. "The Appreciation and Interpretation of Works of Art." In *The Philosophical Disenfranchisement of Art,* pp. 23–46. New York, 1986.
Danto, Arthur C. "Deep Interpretation." In *The Philosophical Disenfranchisement of Art,* pp. 47–67. New York, 1986.
Eliot, T. S. "The Perfect Critic." In *The Sacred Wood,* pp. 1–16. London, 1923.
Hampshire, Stuart. "Logic and Appreciation." In *Aesthetics and Language,* edited by William Elton, pp. 161–169. Oxford, 1954.
Olsen, Stein Haugom. "Criticism and Appreciation." In *The End of Literary Theory,* pp. 121–137. Cambridge and New York, 1987.
Scruton, Roger. *Art and Imagination: A Study in the Philosophy of Mind.* London, 1974.
Strawson, P. F. "Aesthetic Appraisal and Works of Art." In *Freedom and Resentment and Other Essays* pp. 178–188. London, 1974. Originally in *Oxford Review* 3 (1966).
Wilsmore, S. J. "The Appreciation and Perception of Easel Painting." *British Journal of Aesthetics* 33 (July 1993): 246–256.

STEIN HAUGOM OLSEN

APPROPRIATION. [*To explain how artists have appropriated (that is, explicitly and accurately copied) work by other artists and presented it as their own, this entry includes two essays:*

> Historical Overview
> Appropriation Art and Copyright Law

The first essay explains what appropriation art is and what its history has been, especially in the twentieth century. The second explains the legal issues that arise when people whose work has been appropriated press legal charges against artists who have done the appropriating. For related discussion, see Artist; Collage; Creativity; Intention; *and* Pastiche.]

Historical Overview

In the parlance of the art world of the late twentieth century, *appropriation* refers to the conscious use of material (images, for example, in the case of the visual arts, sounds, in the case of music) that derives from a source outside the work. To appropriate an image in this sense is to incorporate it intentionally into the context of one's own body of work.

Copying, faking, plagiarism, borrowing, reproduction, and other practices that involve appropriation in one way or another have been central practices in the arts for as long as the arts have existed. No artist starts from scratch; every artist derives material from the past. In many cultures, in fact, motifs are ritually prescribed, and an authentic artist is precisely one who is capable of reproducing the traditional forms accurately and in the proper spirit of reverence. Mechanical reproduction of images has taken many forms, from printmaking to the massive dissemination of images and words in books, magazines, radio, film, and television (see Benjamin, 1969). Mark Twain is reported to have said: "Good writers borrow; great writers steal." Nevertheless, at least since Romanticism, the West has made a cult of originality and an obsession out of tracing origins. The reputations of such artists as Ludwig van Beethoven, T. S. Eliot, and Jackson Pollock are largely based on the belief that these figures are stunningly original, that they originated entire cultural movements. Such figures are often held to be incomprehensible to their contemporaries, ahead of their time, and so forth, precisely because of their production of unprecedented forms. Indeed, the concept of "genius," central to the discourses surrounding art in modernity, trades on notions of origin and originality.

Such notions are difficult to sustain even for the material they were designed to account for (see Krauss et al., 1986). Associated with the artistic and cultural movement known as "postmodernism," artists and theoreticians have attempted a systematic subversion of the notion of originality (especially understood as the production of new forms), and hence of "genius," being "ahead of one's time," and a host of related notions. One tactic in this subversion has been appropriation. Such artists as Sherrie Levine, Elaine Sturtevant, George Condo, Mark Bidlo, Gretchen Bender, Philip Taafe, Jeff Koons, and many others have engaged in elaborate appropriate projects. Sometimes (as with some of Levine's work) this takes the form of a mechanical reproduction (Levine, for example, has photographed reproductions of photographs by such masters as Walker Evans and displayed them as her own works). In other cases, the artist copies the appropriated work by hand, but as closely as possible, even attempting to use the identical materials (much of the work of Sturtevant and Bidlo fits this description). Such works have given rise to some of the most vituperative criticism imaginable (see Kuspit, 1988, and Schjeldahl, 1988, on Bidlo's *Picassos*). In yet other cases, the appropriated image is altered or distorted in different ways (much postmodern art consists of such practices). Many familiar or banal images may be combined, a single image may be edited or trivialized or repeated over and over, or, as in some of Koons's work, an image may be transferred from one medium to another.

The practice has given rise to serious controversies regarding the copyright of images and other artistic materials. [*See* Appropriation, *article on* Appropriation Art and Copyright Law.] It has also given rise to a critical backlash that holds such works to be trivial, dishonest, or a symptom of the general decline of civilization.

The practice of appropriation reached its apex in the 1980s, but it has deep roots within modern art practice itself. For example, Marcel Duchamp's ready-mades, such as *In Advance of the Broken Arm,* which consisted of a snow shovel, are directly appropriated from the culture at large. The Dadaists and Surrealists made wide use of pirated or copied images, often systematically decontextualized or distorted. The practice of collage, associated with such figures as Georges Braque, Pablo Picasso, and Kurt Schwitters, likewise relies on the incorporation into art of items from outside of art. Such practices constantly raise the possibility that the distinction between art or high culture and the culture at large might break down and that various laws might be violated. That possibility is raised even more emphatically and consciously by the Pop art movement of the early sixties. Here, as a direct response to the cult of originality that attended such Abstract Expressionists as Jackson Pollock and Willem de Kooning, figures like Andy Warhol and Roy Lichtenstein appropriated images from popular culture into the fine arts. Warhol used movie stills, advertisements, and product packages, whereas Lichtenstein appropriated images from romance and combat comic books. Lichtenstein also produced comic book versions of works by Claude Monet, Pablo Picasso, and other arch modernists. Even contemporary popular music, in the practice of "sampling," or literally incorporating bits of sound from other sources, employs appropriative strategies. This is particularly true of the African-American musical form known as hip-hop, which has snatched everything from bits of James Brown and George Clinton to television theme songs and advertising jingles. This practice became more and

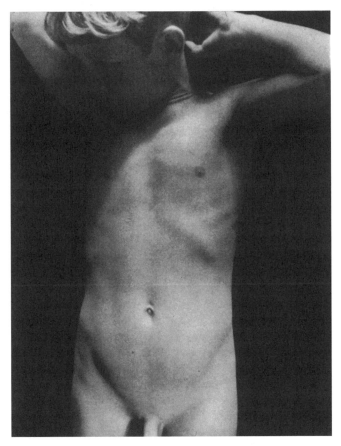

APPROPRIATION. Sherrie Levine, *After Edward Weston #1* (1980), black and white photograph, 10 × 8 inches. (Courtesy of the artist and Margo Leavin Gallery, Los Angeles.)

more pervasive in the popular music of the mid and late 1990s.

Perhaps the first figure to directly appropriate images from other high-art practitioners and display the result as her own high art was Elaine Sturtevant, who began this practice in the mid-1960s (see Cameron, 1988). Interestingly, she chose artists who were themselves in some sense engaged in appropriation, such as Warhol, Jasper Johns, Lichtenstein, and Duchamp. Warhol even gave her silk screens of his own work. Sturtevant said: "If you go back before the pop artists, you have the abstract expressionists, who were obsessed with the idea of creating a new imagery, and it was really an obsession to create something new. And then when you had the pop artists, and they came up with incredibly startling, forthright, dynamic imagery, it was a further step in that direction, but it was still concerned with imagery. That seemed to me rather flat, because it's limiting if you are only involved with creating an image" (Cameron, 1988, p. 77). So Sturtevant understood her own practice as an extension of Pop and perhaps also as a critique of Pop, because she apparently did not regard her own work as creating images in the same way that the Pop artists did. We might also understand Sturtevant's work as a movement toward or into conceptualism, where the character of the object is de-emphasized in favor of an understanding of its philosophy, or the conceptual process that it embodies.

Postmodern artists practice appropriation in many different ways and for many different reasons, but two dogmas of modernism seem to be the particular targets: the claim that important artists are original, and the claim that aesthetic value inheres in the form of the work. These claims are related in that originality is itself often understood as being embodied in the production of new forms. Nevertheless, appropriation is much more successful in attacking the second dogma (critical formalism) than in attacking the first. This is because, despite the treatment of some thinkers (see Krauss, 1986), appropriation has itself been effortlessly appropriated into the discourse of originality. For example, Sturtevant, as exemplified above, has been lionized as the originator of the practice. Leo Castelli says that Sturtevant's early appropriative practice "was really at that time an incredibly original idea" (as quoted in Cameron, 1988, p. 76). One suspects that that was precisely why Castelli, in his capacity as a gallery owner, represented Sturtevant. One suspects as well that when there is no more originality to be milked from the practice, it will cease to be a dominant presence in the art market. That may already be the case.

On the other hand, the critique of formalism that is embodied in the practice of appropriation has been devastating. To see this, let us compare in some detail Sherrie Levine's *After Egon Schiele* to Schiele's *Self-Portrait Nude II*. Despite the fact that they have virtually the same form, these two works are extremely different aesthetically. This shows that aesthetic properties do not inhere only in form. One conspicuous fact about the Schiele is that it is a self-portrait. A self-portrait is a work that depicts the artist of that work. But Levine's work does not depict its artist; it depicts Schiele.

And here is another interesting fact, on which Levine places great weight: the artist of *Self-Portrait Nude II* is a man, while the artist of *After Egon Schiele* is a woman. Schiele's self-portraits are often described as "erotically charged," and that is certainly true of this one. Levine only appropriates the works of male artists, and she describes the works she appropriates as "expressions of male desire." But what does a work by a woman, which is indistinguishable from a work expressing male desire, express? Certainly not male desire! An interview of Levine by Jeanne Siegel contains this exchange:

SL: A lot of what my work has been about since the beginning has been the difficulty of situating myself in the art world as a woman, because the art world is so much an arena for the celebration of male desire.

JS: So his desire becomes yours in order to make this explicit? Then it's in the nature of a critique, really.

SL: I prefer the word "analysis."   (Siegel, 1985, p. 141)

There is all the difference in the world between a direct expression of male desire and an analysis of male desire.

Despite their formal identity, the expressive qualities of *Self-Portrait Nude II* are just the opposite of those displayed by *After Egon Schiele*. The Schiele is a "hot" work, charged with an almost unbearably intense self-expression. There is little thinking; the expression is absolutely immediate, which is one reason the work is a masterpiece. It is violent, agitated, aggressive. All this stands in the starkest contrast to the Levine. Levine and her ilk have often enough been condemned as "cool," as emotionally arid. This charge is not misplaced. Levine's work is all intellection and no expression. It is knowing, sophisticated, utterly mediated. And it stands in such absolute, dramatic aesthetic contrast to the Schiele, not in spite of, but precisely because of, its visual similarity.

This demonstrates that the aesthetic interest and value of the works do not reside in their form, in the arrangements of lines and colors. If there were formal differences, this would render the works more, rather than less, aesthetically similar. If they diverged, there might be something of Levine's emotional expression in her work, and that would compromise her "analysis," and bring her work together with Schiele's as expression. The vast aesthetic differences between them *depend* on their visual similarity.

[*See also* Duchamp; Forgery; Originality; Pop Art; *and* Postmodernism.]

BIBLIOGRAPHY

Benjamin, Walter. "The Work of Art in the Age of Mechanical Reproduction" (1936). In *Illuminations,* edited by Hannah Arendt, translated by Harry Zohn, pp. 217–251. New York, 1969.

Cameron, Dan. "A Conversation: A Salon History of Appropriation with Leo Castelli and Elaine Sturtevant." *Flash Art* (International Edition) 143 (November–December 1988):76–77.

Krauss, Rosalind E. "The Originality of the Avant-Garde." In *The Originality of the Avant-Garde and Other Modernist Myths,* pp. 151–170. Cambridge, Mass., 1985.

Krauss, Rosalind E., Benjamin H. D. Buchloh, Molly Nesbit, Stephen Z. Levine, Linda Nochlin, and Michael Fried. "College Art Symposium on Originality as Repetition." *October* 37 (Summer 1986): 35–97.

Kuspit, Donald. Review of Mark Bidlo at Leo Castelli. *Artforum* 26.9 (May 1988): 141.

Schjeldahl, Peter. "Bidlo's Pablo." *Art in America* 76.5 (May 1988): 173–174.

Siegel, Jeanne. "After Sherrie Levine." *Arts* 59.10 (June 1985): 140–143.

CRISPIN SARTWELL

Appropriation Art and Copyright Law

Many artists are oblivious to copyright, even as it relates to their own works, so they are often surprised to learn that copyright law might stand as a barrier to their use of another artist's (or another person's) image in their own work.

Visual artists' somewhat casual attitude about copying or borrowing from other artists' works—at least compared with text authors, for whom plagiarism is anathema—may be reinforced by the long tradition of borrowing images from, and copying or mimicking, the work of earlier artists as an exercise for developing certain drawing or painting skills. Édouard Manet's *Olympia,* for example, clearly comments on Giorgione's *Sleeping Venus;* Pablo Picasso's *Las Meninas* refers to Diego Rodríguez de Silva y Velázquez's *Las Meninas;* and Marcel Duchamps's *L.H.O.O.O.,* a mustachioed version of the *Mona Lisa,* blatantly incorporates Leonardo da Vinci's painting.

All of these works might have been challenged for copyright infringement but for the fact that, measured under any copyright law, the earlier works had long ago entered the public domain. In the last part of this century, however, copyright issues have become prominent among visual artists because of the merging of fine art and popular culture, in which artists incorporate—by design, although not necessarily for the same reasons—copyrighted images into their own works. These range from the collage that combines copyrighted material with other images and media to form a new work; to the works of artists such as Roy Lichtenstein or Andy Warhol that incorporate images of copyrighted characters (e.g., Mickey Mouse); to works that are faithful photographs of copyrighted photographs (e.g., Sherrie Levine's photographs of photographs of Edward Weston nudes that are so faithful that the unpracticed eye cannot distinguish the original photograph from Levine's photograph of it). (Artistic works also incorporate symbols and words—the logos and slogans used to identify commercial sponsorship—that are protected by trademark law. Use of well-known trademarks by artists is governed by other legal principles and is not addressed here.)

Copyright Primer. Understanding the copyright issues artists face when appropriating the work of others requires understanding some basic copyright law. Copyright rights in any given country are determined by the law of that country, regardless of the author's nationality or the country where the work was first created or published. For example, the copyright rights accorded an Englishman's work in the United States are determined by U.S. law; English and French law govern the rights accorded the work in England and France.

The authority for copyright in the United States arises from the Constitution, which authorizes a federal copyright (and patent) law for the purpose of "promot[ing] the Progress of Science and useful Arts." The word *Science* has been interpreted broadly in keeping with its etymological origins and has been interpreted to include visual expression. Under the United States Copyright Act (17 U.S.C. §§ 101 et seq.), copyright registration is not required in order to obtain a copyright. Copyright arises in original works of authorship (including visual works) at the moment they are fixed in any tangible medium of expression (id., at § 102[a]). A copyright gives the author of a visual work the exclusive right to reproduce, distribute, and publicly display the copyrighted visual work and, especially relevant to appropriation, to prepare derivative works based on the copyrighted work (id., at § 106).

What this last right means is that the copyright owner generally has a legal right to control whether another artist may incorporate the copyrighted work into a new or "derivative" work and, if permission is granted, to demand payment as a condition of that use. If the first artist gives permission (a license) to create a derivative work (for example, to reproduce a work as part of a collage or a painting or to create a long narrative work in pictures based on a single painting), then the second artist acquires a copyright in whatever original material he or she has added to create the new work, but acquires no independent rights in the underlying work. In copyright terms, an artist who uses the work of another artist to create a new work is creating a "derivative work." As explained above, the copyright owner of the underlying work ordinarily has the right to decide whether to authorize the creation of derivative works.

What Copyright Does Not Protect. Not every reference to an earlier work amounts to copyright infringement. An essential concept in copyright law is that copyright does not protect ideas or facts, but only the particular expression the artist gives to them. To allow protection of ideas or facts would give the first artist to produce a work far too broad a monopoly that would squelch other artistic expression. If a painter looks at Rembrandt van Rijn's *Potato Eaters* and makes an entirely new painting inspired by the idea of it, as Robert Colescott did with his *Eat Dem Taters,* there is no copyright infringement because even if the idea of the two paintings is (vaguely) the same, the expression certainly is not. Copyright law is implicated only if the second artist has used the *expression* of the first artist, which can include the detailed composition of a work as well as its specific elements. Although this threshold determination of what has been taken is critical, making the determination is not always easy. As the second artist's taking moves farther away from the first artist's specific expression, the closer the second artist comes to having used only the first artist's idea, but there are no bright lines for deciding when that has happened.

Another way that copyright law safeguards against one artist's monopolizing an image is that before a court will find copyright infringement, it must find that the infringer *copied* a work and that the copy is "substantially similar." If both Manet and Claude Monet paint the same pastoral scene, their two paintings may be substantially similar, but that is because both were painting the same subject. Even if they produced identical paintings of the scene, there could be no copyright infringement, so long as neither copied the other's work.

Fair-Use Doctrine. An artist desiring to use or appropriate a work (or elements of it) of another artist in a new work can avoid all copyright problems by securing permission—a license—to do so. Artists who are aware of their copyright rights and are hostile to the unauthorized use of their own works recognize that protecting the copyright in their own works carries the reciprocal obligation to respect the copyright in other artists' works. But a license may not always be given, and there are certain kinds of uses for which it is highly unlikely that the first artist will give a license, such as biting parody or satire.

If the right to use a copyrighted work (or elements of it) were controlled too tightly, the original purpose of copyright—the promotion of science and the useful arts—would be defeated. A book reviewer could not quote a passage of the book; a composer interviewed on a television talk show could not sing a line from a popular song to illustrate a point; and a film arts professor could not show movie clips to her class. Allowing a copyright owner to forbid all uses of his or her work might also defeat the right of free speech protected under the First Amendment of the Constitution. In recognition of these problems, U.S. copyright law incorporates the doctrine of "fair use," a doctrine originally developed by the courts.

The fair-use doctrine allows use of a work for purposes "such as criticism, comment, news reporting, teaching, scholarship, or research" (17 U.S.C. § 107). Whether a particular use is a fair use is both a legal and a factual determination and requires a court to consider in each case such factors as (1) the purpose and character of the use, including whether it is of a commercial nature; (2) the nature of the copyrighted work; (3) the amount and substantiality of the amount borrowed, measured both quantitatively and qualitatively; (4) the effect of the use on the potential market for or value of the copyrighted work. A factor that can also be considered is whether the work has ever been published. Under the copyright law, if the use is a fair use, then it is not infringing.

The problem with copyright law's fair use test is that it is not very predictive. Because it requires the balancing of several factors, depending on the specific appropriation, it is not always safe to make predictions about future cases from earlier ones. What one can do is to observe what factors the courts have considered important and consider whether they are likely to be as important when applied to new cases.

Judicial Application of the Legal Principles. Artists, including well-known artists, have been sued for their use of copyrighted images owned by others, but often these cases have been settled and have not resulted in judicial decisions. In the early 1990s, however, a series of cases involving appropriation artist Jeff Koons and a 1994 U.S. Supreme Court case involving a music parody of a well-known rock/country song, *Oh, Pretty Woman,* provided insight into how courts are likely to treat the appropriation of art that is protected by copyright. Because the cases analyzed the appropriation of copyrighted works under the fair-use doctrine, it is important to study the courts' analyses of the fair-use factors. That analysis shows that the courts have not shown any particular willingness to deviate markedly from the statutory specifications of fair use, even if they do not accommodate the long tradition of appropriation in the visual arts.

Jeff Koons. Koons was found to have violated the copyright law in three cases brought by other artists claiming that his work appropriated their works without authorization, that is, that the Koons works infringed theirs. All three cases arose from a single show of Koons's works at a New York gallery in 1988, which Koons called the Banality Show, because the works were meant to be a "critical commentary on conspicuous consumption, greed, and self indulgence." In *Rogers v. Koons,* the only case that was appealed, the infringing work at issue was a large sculpture titled *String of Puppies,* which depicted a couple displaying eight puppies. To create the work, Koons had taken a black-and-white photograph titled *Puppies* by the photographer Art Rogers, which had been reproduced on a note card; torn off the back of the card, which bore Rogers's copyright notice; sent the photo to craftsmen in Italy; and directed them to copy the image, on several occasions giving explicit directions that the work should be "just like photo" or "per photo." Koons's work duplicated the original with the following differences: it was produced in a different medium and on a much larger scale; the woman had daisies behind her ears, the man had one on the top of his head; and the sculpture was in color, including blue puppies.

Art Rogers prevailed in the trial court. That Koons had copied Rogers's original work was not disputed, and the trial judge found that the Koons sculpture was "substantially similar" (the test for copyright infringement) to original expression in the plaintiff's work and that, measured under the four-factor test described above, Koons could not show that use of the plaintiff's work was a "fair use." In addition to having to pay damages, Koons was ordered to turn over to Rogers any infringing copies of Rogers's work, including any copies of the sculptures that Koons had not yet sold.

On Koons's appeal, the United States Court of Appeals for the Second Circuit affirmed the conclusion that Koons's *String of Puppies* infringed Rogers's *Puppies* photograph. If Koons had simply taken the *idea* of a couple showing off a new litter of puppies, but depicted it in a new way, Rogers would have had no claim, because copyright does not protect ideas. The problem, in the court's view, was that Koons's work came too close to Rogers's expression, which was hardly surprising, as the court of appeals pointed out, since Koons had repeatedly instructed the artisans to make the sculpture "just like the photo."

The court of appeals also rejected Koons's defense that his use of Rogers's *Puppies* was a fair use. The court observed that he had copied virtually the entire work (third fair-use factor), rather than some excerpt from it, and that conclusion was not affected by the fact that the Koons work was in a different medium and much larger in scale. The court was apparently unmoved by the point, noted by some critics of the decision, that the figures in Koons's work, especially with the added daisies, have a ridiculous expression, unlike the figures in Rogers's original photograph. That the work Koons copied was a creative work of art weighed against Koons (second fair-use factor) because such works are usually accorded more copyright protection than are works based on uncopyrightable facts. The court was also critical of Koons's purpose and conduct (first fair-use factor), noting that he had removed Rogers's copyright notice and that he had used the original photograph primarily for profit-making purposes. The court paid lip service to the fact that creating a work for commercial gain, which is a motive of nearly all creators of copyrighted works, cannot by itself be controlling. Yet, it nevertheless weighed particularly heavily against Koons the fact that he had created his work for sale ("Knowing exploitation of a copyrighted work for personal gain militates against a finding of fair use").

The court was particularly unpersuaded by Koons's effort to bring himself within the fair-use doctrine's requirement that the derivative work be created for purposes such as comment, criticism, and teaching (17 U.S.C. § 107). To meet that standard, Koons had claimed that his sculpture was a satire or parody of society at large. His work was an example, Koons explained, of the artistic school to which he belonged of "American artists who believe the mass production of commodities and media images has caused a deterioration in the quality of society" and that members of this artistic tradition propose "through incorporating these images into works of art to comment critically both on the incorporated object and the political and economic system that created it."

The court acknowledged that parody and satire are valued forms of criticism, which are encouraged because they foster the sort of creative commentary that copyright is intended to encourage. It also recognized that parody and satire necessarily must borrow from the original if they are to achieve their goal of making ridiculous the original work's style and expression. The problem for the court was that Koons's work was not, even in part, a parody of the underlying work itself, but only of modern commercialized society. Although that was a legitimate object of comment, the controlling law required that the copied work be, at least in part, an object of the parody. Without that requirement, said the court, there would be no limitation on the copier's use of another's work to comment on society at large and no practical limitation to the fair-use defense.

Finally, the court of appeals concluded that Koons also lost on the fourth fair-use factor—the effect of Koons's use on the market value of the original. Describing this as the most important fair-use factor, the court explained that it balances the benefit gained by the copyright owner when the copyright is found to be an unfair use and the benefit the public gains when the use is held to be fair. If the adverse impact on the copyright owner is low, then less public benefit need be shown to sustain noncommercial fair use. The court scored this factor against Koons again because he had created his works with the intent of selling them for commercial gain. Under those circumstances, the court said, "some meaningful likelihood of future harm is presumed." A copyright owner prevails on this last factor by showing that if the "unauthorized" use becomes widespread, it would prejudice the potential market for the owner's work. The court concluded that to hold Koons's sculpture a fair use would prejudice Rogers's market to license the rights to other sculptures; it might also dampen Rogers's market for licensing his photo for note cards if photos of Koons's work were permitted to compete in the marketplace.

One of the more troubling aspects of the *Koons* decision was the heavy emphasis it placed on the fact that Koons had created his artistic works for ultimate sale. What book author, musician, painter, or other creator of copyrighted works does not create works with the expectation that they will be not only critically but commercially successful, purchased by readers, listeners, and collectors? Indeed, the very premise of the U.S. copyright law is that allowing an author a limited financial monopoly is the best method for fostering creative work. If the commercial goal of a work is overly emphasized in the fair-use balance, it threatens always to be the deciding factor.

Legions of cases recognize the problem of overemphasizing in the fair-use analysis the fact that most creative works are ultimately sold. Why, then, one wonders, did this factor play such a prominent role in the court's analysis in the *Koons* case? Why is this factor dismissed in some cases, but weighed so heavily in others? One disturbing answer is that courts adjust the importance of the commercial nature of the work depending on their judgment of the quality or content of the works, a factor that is supposed to play no role in copyright analysis. Thus, the commercial nature of the work is emphasized when courts are hostile to the infringing artist and/or the work that the artist has created.

Some basis exists for believing that the *Koons* court's application of the fair-use test was skewed by its disapproval of Koons, his art, and his conduct in the case. The court noted that Koons had concealed the copyright notice on Rogers's note card before sending it to the Italian woodcarvers who executed it; the parody/satire motive that he advanced as the heart of his fair-use defense had been only a "faint suggestion" in the district court, leaving the impression that it was an after-the-fact rationale for his conduct; and he had violated the district court's order to turn over a copy of the work by sending it abroad, an act for which he was held in contempt. One is left wondering whether the court would have weighed the fair-use factors in the same way and with the same lack of sympathy had Koons conducted himself and presented his case differently.

The Supreme Court's 1994 decision in the *Oh, Pretty Woman* music parody case suggests that the *Koons* analysis may not be the model for future cases. Unfortunately, the Supreme Court's change in analytic emphasis may still not give much encouragement to appropriation artists.

2 Live Crew and Oh, Pretty Woman. In 1994, two years after *Koons,* the U.S. Supreme Court in *Campbell v. Acuff-Rose Music, Inc.* clarified and revised the fair-use analysis that the *Koons* court and other courts had been applying in ways that shed new light on how courts might evaluate appropriation art. *Campbell* involved the appropriation of a preexisting musical composition to create a rap parody, but the application of the fair-use principles the court discussed apply equally to the appropriation of a visual image that is incorporated in a new visual work.

In *Campbell,* the music publisher that owned the copyright in the popular rock/country ballad *Oh, Pretty Woman* sued the rap group 2 Live Crew, claiming that its rap-parody version of the song infringed both the music and lyrics of the musical composition. There were some distinct differences between *Campbell* and *Koons.* First, Luther Campbell, 2 Live Crew's lead vocalist, had testified from the start that he had written the parody as an attempt to satirize the original song and the court assumed that that had been his intent, whereas Koons's parody defense had not been at the heart of his case in the trial court. Second, the song that was parodied in *Campbell,* unlike Rogers's photograph, was a rock classic, well known to most listeners of Campbell's new version.

But there was one striking similarity. Overturning the district court's conclusion that Campbell's parody was a fair use, the appellate court in *Campbell,* like the appellate court in *Koons,* emphasized the commercial aspects of the 2 Live Crew recording and found that factor nearly dispositive in concluding that the Campbell rap parody was not a fair use of the underlying song. It agreed that the commercial purpose of the derivative should not be controlling but thought that the trial court had given it insufficient emphasis. To reach this conclusion, the appellate court relied on earlier Supreme Court cases holding that "every commercial use of copyrighted material is presumptively an unfair exploitation of the monopoly privilege that belongs to the owner of the copyright." A strict interpretation of this language would be fatal to almost all uses of copyrighted work in new works.

The Supreme Court reversed the court of appeals's holding that 2 Live Crew's rap-parody song was not a fair use of the underlying *Oh, Pretty Woman.* Although the incomplete factual record prevented the court from making a final determination that the use was fair, the Supreme Court refined its interpretation of how the fair-use test should be applied in ways that should provide guidance for artists' appropriation of other works. In particular, the court emphasized that the four statutory fair-use and other equitable factors must be considered on a case-by-case basis without bright-line rules. It also faulted the court of appeals's presumption on both the first and fourth fair-use factors that the commercial nature of 2 Live Crew's work precluded a finding of fair use.

The court emphasized that unless the case involves mere duplication of the underlying work for commercial purposes, presumptions relating to the commercial value are improper. If the derivative work has changed or "transformed" the underlying work to create a new work, then a court considering the first factor (nature and character of the use) must weigh whether that transformation advances the copyright goals of promoting science and the arts to an extent that justifies de-emphasizing the commercial nature of the work. Similarly, when considering the fourth factor (the effect of the use on the value of or market for the original), a court must consider the effect that the transformation of the work has on the market for the work. If the work is so transformed that it does not serve as a substitute for the original, it may not detract from the value of the work; on the other hand, it might diminish the market for other derivative works, depending on the nature of the derivative work.

The court also clarified that to qualify for the fair-use defense as a parody, the parody must parody the underlying work (and not some other work), and the underlying work must be known to the appropriator's audience. This double requirement is likely to disqualify from fair-use consideration many appropriations that artists formally have justified as parodies.

Finally, the court suggested a variation on remedies that is a departure in the copyright world. In general, a finding of copyright infringement entitles the copyright owner to an order (injunction) prohibiting the further reproduction, display, and distribution, as well as the seizure and destruction of all copies, of the infringing work. That means that if artist A is found to have infringed the copyright of artist B by appropriating B's image into A's work, A's work is likely to be confiscated and A will be prevented from ever reproducing, selling, or displaying the work. The court suggested, however, that an automatic injunction might not be an appropriate remedy where there is a close, but unsuccessful, claim of fair use by a parodist because the remedy would thwart the copyright goal of stimulating the creation and publication of new works. This approach would, of course, deprive the copyright owner of one of his or her rights, namely, the decision whether to authorize derivative works in the first place. Nevertheless, while commenting that denial of injunctive relief would not be the usual course, the court observed that the balance between the copyright owner's interests and the public interest in publishing the second work might be better served by an award of money damages only.

Fair Use and Appropriation Art after Campbell. Would Jeff Koons have fared any better after *Campbell?* Probably not, but the Supreme Court's decision would have forced a reevaluation of the balance of the factors, especially the emphasis on the commercial nature of Koons's work. Koons would still probably have lost on the first factor: his work was created for a commercial purpose. As *Campbell* clarified, that might not be a disqualifying factor for a work that had "transformed" the original in the creation of a new, original work. However, because copyright cases do not usually consider a change of size or medium or slight changes in composition to be particularly original, it is not likely that Koons's work, which reproduced the original photograph in a large wood three-dimensional work, would have been thought to have been sufficiently "transformative" to diminish the commercial purpose of the work. The Supreme Court's stricter requirements for a parody would have been fatal to Koons's claim that he was entitled to the fair-use defense, because he conceded that his work was not meant as a parody of Rogers's particular work but of the general artistic milieu that encourages such works; in addition, it was unlikely that Koons's audience was familiar with Rogers's work.

The second factor, the nature of the original work, would remain unchanged—in Rogers's favor. The third factor, the extent of the copying—would probably still be weighed against Koons because he copied all of the principal figures in the Rogers photograph.

It is the last factor (the effect on the market for the original) that is most difficult to evaluate. The inquiry must consider not only the harm to the market for the original work but also harm to the market for derivative works. The more transformative the second work, the less likely it will serve as a substitute for the original and harm the market for it. It is difficult to believe that anyone who wanted one of the photographs would have been satisfied with one of Koons's enormous sculptures. On the other hand, the *Koons* appellate court speculated that photographic reproductions of the Koons work might interfere with Rogers's market for photographic reproductions of his work. Moreover, if there were a market for sculptural versions of the Rogers work, then finding that Koons's use was a fair use would detract from that market. It is this loss of licensing potential that usually tips the fourth factor in favor of the plaintiff, unless the defendant's work involves a market that the plaintiff cannot or would not exploit. Although fair use is not simply a matter of scoring each factor and then adding them up, it is unlikely, even with *Campbell's* de-emphasis of the com-

mercial nature of the new work, that the *Koons* case would have been decided any differently.

Under the fair-use test as clarified by *Campbell*, it is unlikely that photographs such as Sherrie Levine's exact photographs of existing Edward Weston photographs would be found to be fair use. Most important, there is nothing about Levine's production of the new photographs that appears to be "transformative" in the sense that the Supreme Court seems to mean. But does that mean that Levine is prevented from taking extremely exact photographs of other photographers' work in order to question the nature of authorship? No, it simply means that she must use photographs that are already in the public domain. That both permits her to make her artistic point and fosters the ultimate copyright aim of encouraging the creation of new work, sometimes building on earlier work that has passed out of its term of copyright protection into the public domain. Indeed, when Levine's use of the Weston photographs was challenged, she simply turned to the work of Walker Evans that had been created when he was working for the Works Progress Administration (WPA), much of which was in the public domain. (Although not the subject of this essay, there is considerable question whether Levine would be able to claim a derivative copyright in her photograph of a Walker Evans photograph, titled *After Walker Evans.* To challenge the notion of authorship, it is important to Levine's work that she photograph the underlying photograph with utmost accuracy, without introducing any creative element that would detract from a faithful representation of the original. The difficulty is that to claim a copyright, including a copyright in a derivative work, an author must demonstrate the contribution of some minimal level of originality. Although Levine's use of an underlying public domain photograph might solve fair-use problems, the lack of originality—i.e., in a copyright sense—might bar her claim that her new work is entitled to a copyright.)

The kind of reuse of a visual work that is most likely to satisfy the Supreme Court's new fair-use analysis is Picasso's use of Velázquez's *Las Meninas* (assuming for the moment that Velázquez's work were still protected by copyright). The essential elements of the original are all present and easily recognized by anyone familiar with it. Indeed, that recognition is probably essential to Picasso's purpose of showing his Cubist approach to the same subject. Knowing that the viewer is already familiar with a representational version of the subject gives Picasso the freedom to demonstrate his new view of the same subject.

But if, despite the transformative use of the original, Picasso's purpose in using the earlier work is not to comment on the earlier work, but simply to use a well-known image as a vehicle that his viewers will recognize, then the derivative use might not satisfy the fair-use doctrine's requirement that the borrowing be for purposes such as comment, criticism, and teaching. If, however, the work were judged to have infringed on that ground alone—without having caused much damage to the value of the copyright in the original—a court might choose to exercise the extraordinary remedy the Supreme Court hinted at. It might find an infringement, award the original artist some damages for the copying, but not enjoin the display, reproduction, or distribution of the new work. It would, in effect, be granting the second artist a compulsory license for the derivative use. It cannot be assumed that this license will be used routinely; not only does it deprive a copyright owner of the long-cherished right not to authorize derivative works, but, if used excessively, it would foster infringements by those who would risk the infringement in the hope of being granted the compulsory license, thereby gutting the copyright owner's right altogether.

The potential compulsory license was probably the Supreme Court's effort to mitigate the harsh result of destroying a derivative work that had failed, however slightly, to satisfy the fair-use factors. But one can see that such a dispensation could be misused. The Supreme Court offered no guidance about the circumstances that would warrant granting such a license. It is not hard to imagine that such a resolution might be manipulated in the same way that courts formerly manipulated their evaluation of the commercial nature of the work, withholding the compulsory license from those works (and artists) that displease the courts, regardless of how transformative the derivative work is and how little likely it is to interfere with the value of the copyright in the original artist's work. One can hope that courts will invoke this compulsory license carefully, but vigilance is necessary to see that they do.

[*See also* Law and Art.]

BIBLIOGRAPHY

Constitution and Statutes

U.S. Constitution, Article I, § 8, cl. 8
17 U.S.C. §§ 101 *et seq.*

Cases

Acuff-Rose Music, Inc. v. Campbell, 972 F.2d 1429 (6th Cir. 1992).
Campbell v. Acuff-Rose Music, Inc., 114 S. Ct. 1164 (1994).
Campbell v. Koons, 1993 WL 97381, 1993 U.S. Dist. LEXIS 3957 (S.D.N.Y. 1993).
Feist Publications, Inc. v. Rural Telephone Service Co., 499 U.S. 340 (1991).
Rogers v. Koons, 751 F. Supp. 474 (1970), *amended,* 777 F. Supp. 1 (S.D.N.Y. 1991).
Rogers v. Koons, 960 F.2d 301 (2d Cir. 1992).
United Feature Syndicate, Inc. v. Koons, 817 F. Supp. 370 (S.D.N.Y. 1993).

Other Sources

"Beyond Rogers v. Koons: A Fair Use Standard for Appropriation." *Columbia Law Review* 93 (1993).
Buskirk, Martha. "Commodification as Censor: Copyrights and Fair Use." *October* 60 (Spring 1992): 82–109.

Carlin, John. "Culture Vultures: Artistic Appropriation and Intellectual Property Law." *Columbia-VLA Journal of Law and the Arts* 67 (1988).
Gastineau, John. "Bent Fish: Issues of Ownership and Infringement in Digitally Processed Images." *Indiana Law Journal* 95 (1991).
Ginsburg, Jane C. "Exploiting the Artist's Commercial Identity: The Merchandizing of Art Images." *Columbia-VLA Journal of Law and the Arts* 19 (1995).
Greenberg, Lynne A. "The Art of Appropriation: Puppies, Piracy, and Post-Modernism." *Cardozo Arts and Entertainment Law Journal* 11 (1992).
Hamilton, Marci A. "Appropriation Art and the Imminent Decline of Authorial Control over Copyrighted Works." *Journal of the Copyright Society of the U.S.A.* 42 (1994).
Leval, Pierre. "Toward a Fair Use Standard." *Harvard Law Review* 103 (1990).
Patry, William, and Shira Perlmutter. "Fair Use Misconstrued: Profit, Presumptions, and Parody." *Cardozo Arts and Entertainment Law Journal* 11 (1993).
Wang, Elizabeth H. "(Re)Productive Rights: Copyright and the Postmodern Artist." *Columbia-VLA Journal of Law and the Arts* 14 (1990).

GLORIA PHARES

AQUINAS, THOMAS (1225–1274), medieval Italian philosopher and theologian. Aquinas was a Dominican friar and studied with Albertus Magnus in Cologne, and subsequently taught in Paris and Rome, among other places. *Summa Theologiae* (1266–1273), his major work, was still uncompleted at his death but contains his mature thought in systematic form. He was canonized in 1323.

The writings of Thomas Aquinas figure prominently in almost all scholarly discussions of medieval aesthetics. In *Gothic Architecture and Scholasticism* (1951), for example, Erwin Panofsky invokes Thomas to ground the "genuine cause and effect relationship" he sees to obtain between the scholastic method and the architectural principles of the Gothic cathedral. Panofsky links cathedral architecture to certain general features of Aquinas's argumentative style. More philosophically minded writers on aesthetics, such as Umberto Eco and Francis J. Kovach, take Aquinas's writings in aesthetic theory as their points of departure. Both are convinced that one can speak meaningfully of Aquinas's "writings in aesthetics"—that they constitute a discrete and important unit of his thought. Thus, in the Foreword to the new edition of *The Aesthetics of Thomas Aquinas* (1988), Eco describes his goal as the presentation of the aesthetic theory of Thomas Aquinas as a constitutive, coherent, and self-contained element of his larger philosophical system.

When following the path of texts gathered by such authors, one notices immediately that beauty is nowhere neatly thematized in Aquinas's work; it is treated in passing, if at all. Chapter 4 of Aquinas's commentary on Pseudo-Dionysius's *De divinis nominibus* represents an exception. Of all Aquinas's writings, his commentary on this treatise by an enormously influential anonymous Neoplatonist of the sixth century contains his most extensive remarks on the beautiful. His commentary on the *De divinis nominibus* is generally not invoked in attempts to reconstruct his philosophical aesthetics but is treated as something of a special case in the pertinent literature.

Theoreticians of Aquinas's aesthetics make much out of his "formal definition of the beautiful"—his effort to characterize beauty in its "objectivity," with reference to its "autonomous appearance." A thing is called beautiful, according to Aquinas, when it delights its beholder (*pulchra enim dicuntur, quae visa placent* [*S.th.* I q. 5 a. 4 ad 1]). A glance at the larger hermeneutical context of this description—that is, Aquinas's teaching about the nature of God and of the good (*bonum*) in the *Summa theologiae*—points to the incomplete character of this definition, and thereby calls into question certain standard approaches to his aesthetics. Following the view of Pseudo-Dionysius that the good, on account of its relation to the beautiful, has the character of a formal cause, Aquinas speaks of good in its proper sense as an object of the appetitive power of the soul. The beautiful, however, is an object of the rational power, when one considers its attractiveness qua object of knowledge. It is in this context that one finds Aquinas's remark about the beautiful as that whose vision "delights its beholder." Aquinas is clearly defining the concept in a very special sense. The beautiful is, to a certain extent, defined a posteriori, through an analogy to the good. Just as it belongs to the notion of the good, that in it all desire finds rest, so it belongs to the notion of the beautiful, that in being regarded or thought (*in eius aspectu seu cognitione*), intellectual desire finds rest. Aquinas begins by asking what, at the level of sense (*sensus*)—at the level of being struck and attracted in an initial and unmediated way by an object of knowledge—draws the cognitive power (*vis cognoscitiva*) to an object of knowledge. Being "struck" and "attracted" by a thing is seen as constituting the initial form of knowledge (*cognitio*) of that thing. The senses are drawn by the well-proportioned character (*debita proportio*) of an object of knowledge, for in this *debita proportio*, a kind of likeness (*similitudo*) is recognized (*S.th.* I q. 5 a. 4 ad 1). Aquinas thus first speaks of the beautiful and its modes of expression at the level of sensitive knowledge—that is, well before it acquires the character of a judgment, much less of an aesthetic judgment. In effect, he expands the cognitive power in general, by incorporating both the cognitive (*visa*) and the appetitive (*placent*) elements of the definition in his own account. Every act of knowledge occurs by means of assimilation (*per assimilationem*). Every similarity, however, is in reference to form. By means of this analysis, Aquinas confirms the Dionysian claim that the beautiful is related in a certain way to the formal cause.

Pseudo-Dionysius's claims about the beautiful also figure prominently in a second classic text traditionally invoked in reconstructions of Aquinas's aesthetics. In the *Summa the-ologiae*, in the midst of his discussion of the Trinity, Aquinas lists three sets of "notes of the beautiful": first, "integrity" (*integritas*) or "perfection" (*perfectio*); second, "right proportion" (*debita proportio*) or "harmony" (*consonantia*)—both terms are taken from Pseudo-Dionysius, as are their parallels, "commensurate character" (*commensuratio*) and "convenience" (*convenientia*); and third, "clarity" (*claritas*) (*S.th.* I q. 39 a. 8 c). Clarity (*claritas*) and harmony (*consonantia*), which come together in the notions of the beautiful (*pulchrum*) and the honorable (*honestum*), are traced by Aquinas, with reference to book 4 of *De divinis nominibus*, to the notion of God as cause of the beautiful (*S.th.* II–II q. 145 a. 2 c; In *de div. nom.* IV, lect. 5, 339). God is called beautiful insofar as God is the cause of the harmony and clarity of all being. A body is called beautiful when it has well-proportioned members and a "clear" (i.e., healthy) color. A soul is called beautiful that makes well-ordered use of its spiritual gifts, in accord with the spiritual clarity of reason. In the same context, Aquinas undertakes to exposit the two definitions of "comeliness or beauty" (*species sive pulchritudo*)—attributed to the Son by Hilary of Poitiers—and of "beauty or perfection" (*pulchritudo sive perfectio*) to illustrate how the Son truly and perfectly possesses the nature of the Father. Both definitions express Hilary's intended affirmation, by means of the concept of the image (*species sive imago sive pulchritudo*), of the perfect agreement in essence shared by Father and Son. Their close association to the systematic context of Aquinas's teaching on the divine nature, which itself finds confirmation in similar associations within the tradition, renders suspect the claim that this definition can be treated as a "material" definition of beauty divorced from its larger context.

The teaching of beauty as transcendental offers another starting point for the reconstruction of a medieval aesthetics (see Aertsen, 1991). With the help of this teaching, one might hope for a systematic comparison, on the metaphysical level, of beauty with other goods. As Aertsen notes, however, beauty is missing from Aquinas's most complete enumeration of the transcendentals; it is missing from his list of the most common attributes of being (*Quaestiones disputatae de veritate.* 1,1), and thus apparently holds no special place among transcendentals. It is only in connection with his teaching about the divine nature that Aquinas speaks of the beautiful alongside the good. The beautiful adds something to the notion of the good—a certain orderedness to the intellectual powers. It adds nothing to the concept of being. The good and the beautiful are really identical because both are grounded in the form qua common subject of predication. On this point, Aquinas upholds the Dionysian formula of their identity—"the good is praised as beauty" (*bonum laudatur ut pulchrum*)—although he modifies it in the sense mentioned above, through his extension of the good to the true, reiterating that the beautiful adds to the good a certain orderedness to the intellectual powers.

In a similar vein, we may question the assumption that *artistic beauty, art,* and *artist* correspond neatly in meaning to the Latin terms *pulchrum/pulchritudo, ars,* and *artifex,* respectively. The argument for a neat parallelism between both conceptual fields assumes that the same sorts of objects be characterized as "art" and as "beautiful" that the medievals spoke of with their terms *ars* and *pulchrum.* The differences between modern and medieval aesthetic sensibilities manifest themselves with particular acuity with respect to the understanding of *ars* and *artifex.* The nearest equivalents of these terms within our modern vocabulary designate, first and foremost, an *individual creative subjectivity* that (1) is conscious of itself as such; and that (2) understands artistic beauty as autonomous.

Should one seek an equivalent in Thomas Aquinas for this creative and autonomous kind of production, one will find that such activity is reserved to God alone; only the divine will is capable of creation out of nothingness (*creatio ex nihilo*). On Aquinas's view, this unique way of "bringing forth" is to be distinguished from two other ways: (1) the work of nature, which, in a way that is bound to matter, generates substantial forms; and (2) bringing forth as making in general, *facere* (*S.th.* I q. 45 a. 2 c). Aquinas explicates this second notion by appealing to the example of the *artifex* who is constrained by the limits both of his matter and of substantial form in general. He is constrained, one might say, by the limits of nature; by the matter and form of the thing to be made, which for the *artifex* assume the character of principles (*S.th.* I q. 45 a. 2 c, In II *Phys.*, lect. 1, 145). This is actually the systematic context in which Aquinas makes his well-known remarks about *ars* as the imitation of nature (*imitatio naturae*). The *artifex* remains bound to the conditions of creaturely being—it is in this sense that he "imitates" nature. Stated more precisely, *ars* is the application of right reason to something makable (*applicatio rationis rectae ad aliquid factibile* [*S.th.* I–II q. 47 a. 2 ad 3]). Consequently, as a habit of action (*habitus operativus*), it applies its powers, in conformity with its design and with the laws of production, to the task to be accomplished alone, and not on the *uses* of the thing produced or the *intentions* of its user(s). Accordingly, *ars* encompasses, in accordance with the Aristotelian distinction between *praxis* and *poiesis,* a knowledge of making but not of use/doing. *Ars* is thus, for Aquinas, primarily of a productive/technical nature, as in building or operating (*S.th.* I–II q. 57 a. 4 c). It is, then, of a necessarily *particular* nature, ordered to a certain defined and thus particular end, namely, the work to be realized, and employing certain limited means (*determinata media*) to reach this end. *Ars* only rises above its concrete, technical domain through its association with the wider horizon of human goal setting.

This understanding of *ars* derives from Aristotle and is itself an expression of that epochal turn in medieval intellectual history from Plato to Aristotle occasioned by the thirteenth-century reception of the Aristotelian corpus in its entirety. Influenced by Aristotle, Aquinas lays emphasis on particular elements of the complex *ars* concept he inherits. Through its association with the ancient educational program of the *septem artes liberales, ars* had been understood as encompassing the entire spectrum of human knowledge. The differentiation of the complex *ars* concept undertaken in the thirteenth century understood the term as mediating, on the theoretical plain, between experience (*experientia/empeiria*) and knowledge (*scientia/epistéme*). Consequently, an *artifex* became distinguished by his field-specific expertise, directed toward particular subjects. The differentiation of meanings within the *ars* concept known to Aquinas followed upon another epochal change: the loss of the notion of a theory of the sciences encompassing all human knowledge and activity, as well as of the speculative certainty, affirmed well into the twelfth century (most tellingly in the *Didascalicon* of Hugh of St. Victor), of the deep unity of the technico-productive, scientifico-philosophical, and theological bodies of knowledge. On this older view, all human knowledge was seen as ordered unconditionally to the one highest wisdom. Beauty is in this respect an expression of the anagogic character of the *artes* of this period, as well as of their objects.

The relative autonomy of "artistic knowledge" (*ars*) with respect to scientific knowledge (*scientia*), as it is articulated by Aquinas, led to the loss of the conception of beauty in this sense of an "anagogic way" (*mos anagogicus*). Nevertheless, a more restricted *ars* concept is one of the presuppositions of theoretical reflection within the specific domain of a particular art. With this reflection, which is of such a nature as to be capable of grounding its judgments, the meanings of aesthetic notions associated with individual arts began to grow. This development led finally to a modern scheme of the fine arts, which itself saw further theoretical elaboration in the Renaissance.

Such an understanding of aesthetics is not to be found in the Middle Ages; the statements of Thomas Aquinas about "art" and "beauty" must not be taken in this sense. Paul Oskar Kristeller (1965) rightly suggests that the attempt to conceptualize an aesthetics in accord with scholastic principles is a modern projection. The multiple meanings of artistic activity in the Middle Ages, each deriving from particular and diverse conceptions of beauty, can only be understood when read with respect to a general hermeneutical reservation. This does not amount to a general denial of the category of the aesthetic, whose function certainly does not consist in the manifestation of supratemporal properties of being, but is rather heuristic; it consists of an encounter, across diverse horizons of understanding, which themselves are located in this diversity of interests. It is in this respect that the enterprise of developing an aesthetic paradigm that is faithful to the medieval understanding proves valid; the enterprise must proceed reconstructively, guided by the following questions: How was that entity that we identify within modern paradigms as "art" perceived and experienced by the people of the Middle Ages? Might that entity also have been the subject of theoretical reflection and interpretation? This, I submit, is the appropriate background against which to reconsider the contribution of Thomas Aquinas to a history of aesthetics.

[*See also* Aristotle; Augustine; Beauty, *article on* Medieval Concepts; *and* Maritain.]

BIBLIOGRAPHY

Works by Aquinas

In librum beati Dionysii De divinis nominibus expositio. Edited by Ceslai Pera. Turin, 1950.
Summa Theologiae. In *S. Thomae Aquinatis Doctoris Angelici Opera Omnia iussu impensaque Leonis XIII P. M. edita,* vols. 5–12. Rome, 1889–1906. Translated by the Blackfriars in 60 Volumes. (New York, 1964–1976).

Other Sources

Aertsen, Jan A. "Beauty in the Middle Ages: A Forgotten Transcendental." *Medieval Philosophy and Theology* 1 (1991):68–97.
Aertsen, Jan A. "Die Frage nach der Transzendentalität der Schönheit im Mittelalter." In *Historia Philosophiae Medii Aevi: Studien zur Geschichte der Philosophie des Mittelalters,* edited by Burkhard Mojsisch and Olaf Pluta, pp. 1–22. Amsterdam, 1991.
Binding, Günther, and Andreas Speer, eds. *Mittelalterliches Kunsterleben nach Quellen des 11. bis 13. Jahrhunderts.* Stuttgart, 1993.
Bruyne, Edgar de. *Études d'esthétique médiévale.* 3 vols. Brugge, 1946.
Eco, Umberto. *Art and Beauty in the Middle Ages.* Translated by Hugh Bredin. New Haven, 1986.
Eco, Umberto, *The Aesthetics of Thomas Aquinas.* Translated by Hugh Bredin. Cambridge, Mass., 1988.
Kovach, Francis J. *Die Ästhetik des Thomas von Aquin: Eine genetische und systematische Analyse.* Berlin, 1961.
Kristeller, Paul Oskar. "The Modern System of the Arts." *Journal of the History of Ideas* 12.4 (October 1951):496–527; 13.1 (January 1952):17–46. Reprinted in *Renaissance Thought II: Papers on Humanism and the Arts.* (New York, 1965), pp. 163–227.
Panofsky, Erwin. *Gothic Architecture and Scholasticism.* Latrobe, Pa., 1951.
Speer, Andreas. "Thomas von Aquin und die Kunst: Eine hermeneutische Anfrage zur mittelalterlichen Ästhetik." *Archiv für Kulturgeschichte* 72.2 (1990):323–345.
Speer, Andreas. "Kunst und Schönheit: Kritische Überlegungen zur mittelalterlichen Ästhetik." In *Scientia und ars im Hoch- und Spätmittelulter,* edited by Ingrid Craemer-Ruegenberg and Andreas Speer, Miscellanea Medievalia 22.2, pp. 945–966. Berlin and New York, 1994.
Tatarkiewicz, Wladyslaw. *History of Aesthetics,* vol. 2, *Medieval Aesthetics.* Edited by C. Barrett. The Hague, 1970.

ANDREAS SPEER

ARAB AESTHETICS. In keeping with the traditional exegetical and normative method of Quranic and philological sciences, early aesthetic thought in Islam pursued a validation that might be called "argument by example and illustration." These sciences justified the validity of particular examples by finding an original accepted model of excellence and showing that the example bore significant analogies with that model. In this mode, literary critics advanced an account of the nature of poetry by examining the grammatical and philological rules present in works that were accepted as models of good poetry. Although these rules also refer to the different mental states of subjects, the play of different causal factors, or the play of imagination, they nonetheless remain dependent on linguistic factors where, in effect, if a work fails grammatically because it differs from accepted usage, lacks significant analogies with an accepted model, and fails to generate consensus through the responses of its audience, then it fails to be poetry at all.

In this context, the critics' analysis of the same examples provides a body of exemplary cases that establish what is good poetry. Analysis displays what their value consists in, why newer works are also good so far as they use these or analogous rules, and how members of the audience can appreciate the work and come to agree, by having for themselves, in response, feelings of calm and peace as factors that beautify. (See, for example, al Qāḍī al-Jurjāni, 1966, p. 320).

Poetry was arguably the premier art form in Arab Islamic culture, and among the concepts central to understanding and explaining the nature of poetry are *majāz* or figurative language and *istiʿāra* or metaphor. In *al-Bayān wa'-l-tabyīn* (1948–1950), al-Jāḥiẓ explains *istiʿāra* as calling one thing by the name of something else because of a similarity between two terms based on their contiguity and resemblance. He maintains that it concerns single words or stylistic devices, and warrants its legitimacy by analyzing its linguistic structure. Ibn Qutaybah proposes that *majāz* or figurative language underpins poetry, and in *Ta'wīl Mushkil al-Qur'ān* (1959) explains the term through such linguistic terms as *istiʿāra*, inversion, omission, and repetition.

Thaʿlab, in *Qawāʿid al-Shiʿr* (1966), analyzes the transference of meaning in *istiʿāra* in terms of mental imagery, which he explains through the language poets use to articulate imagery. He argues that "the meaning borrows a mental representation" and constitutes *istiʿāra*, for example, by borrowing "the mental image of the camel, and thus contains all the properties of the camel from which the appropriate ones can be selected to establish the [relevant] analogy." Similarly, when in *Kitāb al-Badīʿ* (1935) Ibn al-Muʿtazz sets out seventeen apparently new figures, his radical innovation is tempered by the fact that, first, earlier writers had already set out nine of these figures and in the other eight he proposes distinctions already present, if inadequately identified, in established and exemplary instances, and, second, he explains the figures by reference to the grammatical and philological rules governing their use.

In *al-Muwāzana bayn shiʿr Abu Tammām wa-l-Buḥturī* (1961–1965), al-Āmidī argues that because the purpose of discourse is to communicate something, if the borrowed word or phrase is not useful it also lacks justification and

ARAB AESTHETICS. *Amr, Disguised as a Doctor, Treating Sorcerers in a Courtyard,* page from a *Hamza-nama* series, India, Imperial Mughal style (Akbar period, 1562–1577), opaque watercolors and gold on cotton, sheet: 31 × 25 inches (78.8 × 63.5 cm), image: 26 3/4 × 20 5/8 inches (68 × 52.4 cm); Brooklyn Museum (Museum Collection Fund). (Photograph used by permission.)

cannot claim to be aesthetic. In order to preserve the intersubjective validity of poetic discourse, he says, first, one cannot make poetic comparisons by using *isti'āra* that are far-fetched, and, second, one must use familiar and traditional personification because, third, the audience must be able to grasp the point of any similarity. Otherwise, putative poetic discourses become simply subjective, idiosyncratic, and incapable of general appreciation. In a parallel move, in *al Wasāṭa bayn al-Mutanabbī wa-khuṣūmih* (1966), al-Qāḍī al-Jurjānī treats *isti'āra* as part of "the perfection of the artistic treatment" and of the creative ability of the poet, which makes it a fundamental element of aesthetic discourse, as contrasted with literal or cognitive expression.

In addition to the linguistic analysis of works, critics argue that the evaluation of poetic discourse must refer to the soul's response—the calm and peace it evokes or the antipathy it causes, where the latter is supervenient on the former. Thus, in *Kitāb al-Badī'*, Ibn al-Mu'tazz distinguishes the presence of *isti'āra*, which makes the use of language agreeable or disagreeable and shows that language is figurative rather than literal, from the deployment or absence of

maḥāsin al kalām, or factors that beautify literary discourse. Similarly, al-Āmidī validates the communicable meaning of poems by relying on analogies (*qiyās*) with accepted usages but insists on *ijma'* or agreement in subjects' responses to explain their aesthetic value.

With theorists like Ibn Farīs, al-Tha'labī, and Ibn Rashiq, the philological character of their discussions consciously stems from issues raised in Quranic exegesis. In any case, these critics relied on the linguistic exegetical method because that was a guarantee of validity provided by philology. This grammatical analysis came to compete with another in which aesthetic validity had a distinctive logical cast. The principal representatives of this approach are the Aristotelian philosophers al-Fārābī, Ibn Sīnā (Avicenna), and Ibn Rushd (Averroës). They limited grammar and philology to examining the rules of a particular language; by contrast, logic examined the rules for reasoning generally, and because they considered poetics to be a part of reasoning, logic would provide a justification of poetic thought generally.

[*See also* Aristotle; Comparative Aesthetics; al-Fārābī; Ibn Rushd; Ibn Sīnā; *and* Islamic Aesthetics.]

BIBLIOGRAPHY

Āmidī, al-. *al-Muwāzana bayn shi'i Abu Tammām wa-l-Buḥturī.* 2 vols. Edited by A. Sakr. Cairo, 1961–1965. See vol. 1, p. 135.
Ibn al-Mu'tazz. *Kitāb al-Badī'.* Edited by I. Kratchkovsky. London, 1935.
Ibn Qutaybah. *T'awīl Mushkil al-Qur'ān.* Edited by A. Sakr. Cairo, 1954.
Jāḥiz, al-. *al-Bayān wa'-l-tabyīn.* 4 vols. Edited by A. M. Harun. Cairo, 1948–1950. See vol. 1, pp. 153ff.
Jurjānī, al-Qāḍī al-. *al Wasāṭa bayn al-Mutanabbī wa-khuṣūmih.* 4th ed. Edited by A. M. al-Bajjawi and M. A. F. Ibrahim. Cairo, 1966.
Tha'lab. *Qawā'id al-Shi'r.* Edited by 'Abd al-Tawwab. Cairo, 1966.

SALIM KEMAL

ARCHITECTURE. [*This entry contains only a few of the many essays on architectural aesthetics in this encyclopedia:*

Early Greek Aesthetics
Italian Renaissance Aesthetics
Modern Overview
Modernism to Postmodernism

The first essay explores the earliest stages of architecture's long-standing relationship with the philosophy of art. The second essay describes a pivotal period in architectural aesthetics—the Italian Renaissance. The third essay surveys the history of modern architectural aesthetics since Immanuel Kant and ends by discussing architecture's ethical-aesthetic function. The last essay traces the twentieth-century transition from modernist to postmodernist architecture. For the full picture of architectural aesthetics within philosophy and architectural theory alike, see also Autonomy, *article on* Autonomy and Architecture; Baroque Aesthetics; Bötticher; Constructivism; Durand; Futurism;

Early Greek Aesthetics

"Why are there essents rather than nothing?" This "first of all questions," according to Martin Heidegger—the "fundamental question of metaphysics"—had its earliest known formulation in the Ionian Greek city of Miletus on the west coast of Asia Minor in the mid-sixth century BCE, where Greek philosophy began. The material specificity of time and place is crucial, for the identity—and, as Jean-Pierre Vernant has argued, the thinking—of each of the early Greek philosophers was inextricably linked to that of a city: Anaximander is "of Miletus," Pythagoras, "of Samos," Heracleitus, "of Ephesus," and so on. Cities positioned philosophers: Socrates, later, in the Athenian agora and in the craftsmen's workshops that surrounded it; Stoics, later still, in the portico of the Stoa Poecile at the western edge of this same agora; Epicureans, who repudiated civic engagement, in the garden beyond the city walls.

Second after Thales of the Ionian naturalists, Anaximander of Miletus is generally looked upon as the first real philosopher and his thought as the watershed in the transition from myth to philosophy. His *floruit* of about 560 BCE coincides with the construction of two of the largest Greek temples ever built: the Ionic Temple of Hera at Samos and that of Artemis of Ephesus, both near his native city of Miletus, known in the early Greek world as the "mother of colonies." Anaximander himself is said to have led a colonizing expedition to Apollonia on the Black Sea, which was one of the colonies.

It is in the Anaximander fragment, which is all that survives of what appears to have been a considerable body of written work, that Heidegger's "fundamental question" was first articulated. The traditional reading of this fragment has been that something called "the Boundless" *(to apeiron)* is the source out of which existing things (or "essents") come to be—a "boundless" fathomable, perhaps, only as Heidegger's ineffable "nothing" is fathomable—the limit, as he says, of the question that takes in everything that ever was or will be.

Close reading of the Greek original, however, reveals that what Anaximander said was that "some other boundless nature" gives rise to the heavens and the *kosmoi* (plural "orders") within them, but not, in fact, to existing things as such. Existing things *(ta onta)* do not arise from "the Boundless," or even from "some other boundless nature," but from *kosmoi*. What exists exists because of *kosmos*, and there are many possible *kosmoi*.

Kosmos, deriving from the verb *kosmeo,* I "arrange, order, adorn," is both order and ornament—not one *or* the other but, interchangeably, both, for indeed "cosmetic" comes from *kosmos.* Cosmetic *kosmos* was visible order in a world where visibility was the evidence for existence.

The fragment attests that Anaximander wrote about order. He also, it would appear, built order: a cosmic model about which very little is known but whose several parts included a celestial sphere, a circular map of the world, and a sun clock, whose pointer, the *gnomon,* he introduced to Greece from Babylon: heaven, earth, and time, beyond which there is indeed, ineffably, nothing. If one takes his assembly of real, concrete parts into a three-part artifact (sphere, map, *gnomon*) as the genesis of his cosmology, it was its very construction or ordering *(kosmon)* that brought the entire universe (cosmos) into visible existence as an image that endured for more than two thousand years.

His model, once made, was recognized as having coherence, and confirmed the configuration of a universe known from (Greek) experience to have Earth at its center and Greece, with its navel-stone at Delphi, at the center of a seabound Earth. Because of this, and because there were no others, Anaximander's became *the* model: in Plato's *Timaeus,* written a century and a half later, the *paradeigma* or template for a divine craftsman *(demiourgos)* whose creation of *kosmos* was no longer a question of making a world appear, but a matter of representing one through the duplication of an immutable pattern.

Daedalus, legendary craftsman and mythical first architect, whom Socrates claimed as his ancestor, was also a *demiourgos,* one of a class of people who, in early Greece, included heralds, prophets, doctors, bards, lawgivers, and magistrates, as well as builders—people through whose work or creative work*ing (ergon)* the *polis* and civilization itself were brought into being. According to Homer, the one-eyed Cyclopes, savage creatures who lived alone in caves, were uncivilized because they had no assemblies and because "there are no shipwrights in their land who might build them well-benched ships, which should perform all their wants . . . craftsmen who would have made of this isle also a fair settlement."

Among the cosmic/cosmetic creations of the legendary Daedalus were statues so animated with divine life that they had to be bound in chains, a mechanical cow that facilitated Queen Pasiphaë's conception of the Minotaur—the bull-man who, after his birth, was sequestered in the Cretan labyrinth, which Daedalus also built—the dancing floor *(choros)* at Knossos that was the labyrinth's mirror image, and, of course, wings, the means of Daedalus's escape from Crete, which, according to some sources, may have taken place in boats.

The feature common to all artifacts generically known as *daidala* was that they were assemblies of cutout pieces: constructions that were *areros,* well adjusted or perfectly fitted

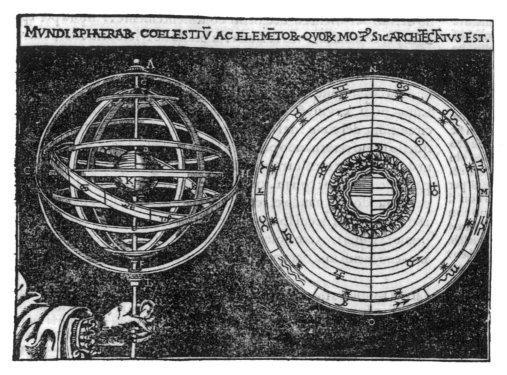

ARCHITECTURE: Early Greek Aesthetics. *The Celestial Sphere of the Cosmos and Its Parts Which are Set in Motion as if by an Architect,* folio CXLIX recto, from a translation (Como, 1521) of *De architectura* by Marcus Vitruvius Pollio, Rome, active first century BCE; woodcut, 10.4 × 14.5 cm; collection Centre Canadien d'Architecture, Montréal. (Photograph used by permission.)

together, whence, both etymologically and experientially, the Greek word *harmonia,* in Homer a shipbuilding term with specific reference to the joints. Textiles could also be *daidala,* and were so qualified if they were tightly woven—*areros,* like a ship's joints—and had a luminous sheen.

Anaximander's model, like the creations of Daedalus, or like the boat Odysseus builds in book 5 of the *Odyssey,* must also have been *areros,* in the oldest sense of the term, and it was primarily because, as a construction, it was *areros* that was able to reveal all that other unseen harmony. The coherence of the system devolved upon the coherence of the artifact, and the invisible harmonies that Pythagoras alone was said to have been able to hear were grounded in the built ones that first brought them into visible being.

This is not to say that *kosmos* was "nothing but" an arbitrary human fabrication that was subsequently projected as celestial order. In Homer, things that are orderly are *eu kata kosmon,* "well according to order"; disorderly things are *ou kata kosmon,* "*not* according to order." Early Greek assessments of order invariably assumed a standard of rightness external to itself, but the criteria, which were not yet fixed (there were many *kosmoi* in Anaximander's heaven), were not known (*eidos:* "seen") until the *ergon* of a *demiourgos,* whether builder, bard, or legislator, had set them before people's eyes.

The craftsman found *kosmos* through the artifact. If one understands the craftsman as a *demiourgos* in the wider Greek sense of the term while retaining the notion of craft in its more limited, physical sense, as the early Greeks did when they claimed that there was no community, no civilization, without such craft, then it becomes quite clear that the emergence of the Greek city state in the eighth and seventh centuries BCE hinged on the craft tradition. The agora where citizens assembled and philosophers questioned was, literally, brought into spatial existence by the craftsmen's workshops that defined its periphery.

What is noteworthy about the new *poleis,* in contrast to the old Mycenaean cities destroyed during Dorian invasions of the twelfth century BCE, is the presence of sanctuaries, which had never existed in Mycenaean civilization, apart from the hearth of the quasi-divine king-father located in the *megaron,* or great hall, of the Mycenaean palaces. The sequential building of these sanctuaries at strategic points of urban center and territorial limit, together with the subsequent ritual processions that wove together into spatial and political unity the distances that separated them, were, as François de Polignac has shown, indispensable for bringing the archaic Greek polis into visible and viable existence. The first appearance of orthogonal plans in colonial foundations with gridded street layouts is concomitant with the appearance of the *poleis* so woven.

In weaving, which entails the interlacing of evenly spaced warp and weft threads at right angles to one another, orthogonality is fundamental. Skewed or unequally distributed threads will produce a loosely woven fabric full of holes, and a textile with a loose weave cannot be, so to speak, "harmonious." Neither, it would appear, could a new Greek city. If the order of orthogonal street layouts was a cosmic one, intended to square the position of the citizen with the geometric configuration of the cosmos, as Joseph Rykwert has argued, it became so because, long before either the cosmos or city streets were geometrical, the experience of weavers had already revealed to them that equally spacing warp and weft threads and interlacing them at right angles made a cloth that was *eu kata kosmon,* "well according to order."

The principal feature of the sanctuaries that brought these early Greek *poleis* into existence was usually, although not always, a temple. At first a freestanding *megaron,* divorced from its palace context, it very soon afterward became the prototypical "Greek" temple, with its *naos,* the dwelling place of the cult statue, surrounded by a peristyle of evenly spaced columns. When, in the eighth and seventh centuries, the Greek temple became peripteral, it acquired *ptera,* wings.

The Greeks had always been a seafaring nation, but in the eighth and seventh centuries—the colonization period when the polis was brought into being by its agora and its temples—boats and navigation played a particularly important role. When a colonizing expedition set out from a mother city like Miletus, and before it arrived at its destination, it was the ship itself that, for the duration of the voyage at least, was the city: a ship that, in the early Greek imagination, sped through the waves like a bird through the air, propelled, as the poets would have it, by "well-shaped oars that are as wings unto ships." *Naus* (ship), moreover, is only a vowel away from *naos* (sanctuary), and sounds almost the same, not a negligible factor in a culture where troping of this kind was endemic. The columns (*ptera,* analogous to oars) were people, too, of course, an assumption that remained uncontested in architectural theory until just three hundred years ago. In the peristyle of a temple, these "people" were brought to stand, equally spaced, around a sanctuary as the visible model for more abstract notions of civic harmony. The craftsmen's workshops that framed the agora created the place of assembly. The temple, or temples, most craft-intensive, largest, and by far most visible of a Greek city's built productions, set before the citizens who constituted that assembly their own incorruptible presence as essential constituents of the very shrine of the divinity who ruled them.

The building of the temple concentrated both the making and the discovery of *kosmos,* which, at least from Hesiod onward, was explicitly understood as the province of the divine. Thus, the temples that testified to the indissociability of craft and community also replaced the caves and sacred groves of earlier divine epiphanies to become the place where the presence of the god or goddess was revealed. In Athens, as in many other cities, chief among the divinities whose appearing was so propitiated was Athena, polis goddess of craft and of wisdom.

Citizens enriched the sanctuaries of temples with votive offerings, but they did not enter them. Sacrificial altars stood in front of temples, not inside them. Temples, once built, were objects of contemplation, of *theoria.* They only became places of assembly much later when the altars moved inside, along with the columns that lined the naves (from the Latin *navis,* ship) of early Christian basilicas, and when the city of God replaced the city of men as the focus of devotion.

The peripteral temple, and the emerging polis of whose making the temple was both an essential constituent and an emblem, did not appear *with* the birth of theory in sixth-century Ionia. Their appearing took place over the two-hundred-year period that *preceded* it. Anaximander, like his contemporaries the Ionian architects Rhoikos and Theodoros, who wrote the earliest architectural treatise mentioned by Vitruvius, on the colossal Ionic temple of Hera at Samos, theorized the order of a work already built. The architectural treatise does not survive, but the answer to Heidegger's "fundamental question" would have been as obvious to its authors, as it was to Anaximander: if there are "essents" rather than nothing at all, it is because of *kosmos.*

In the European West, architecture preceded philosophy. Monumental building was not, at least not initially, the embodiment of ideas or abstractions—the infusion of brute matter with ideal Platonic form or Pythagorean number mysticism made concrete. Plato and Pythagoras were Anaximander's successors, just as Anaximander himself succeeded the first temple builders, whose pupil, in a sense, he was. Initially, the artifact generated the idea and not vice versa; theory was the contemplation of something already built. Post-Vitruvian architectural theory reversed this order, with Renaissance architects such as Leon Battista Alberti and Donato Bramante becoming self-conscious imitators of a cosmic order understood to be unalterably fixed. It was not, of course. The discoveries of Nicolaus Copernicus and Galileo Galilei contributed, in turn, to a post-Cartesian theory that was reduced to a set of arbitrary, inflexible rules. With the cosmic referent abolished altogether, ornament eventually became mere decoration whose superfluity, once identified, resulted in the stripped, self-referential forms of twentieth-century modernism. Current recognition that both architectural and philosophical order are *made* have led to the self-castigating deconstruction of both. But the relationship between them persists.

[*See also* Plato.]

BIBLIOGRAPHY

Barber, E. J. W. *Prehistoric Textiles: The Development of Cloth in the Neolithic and Bronze Ages with Special Reference to the Aegean.* Princeton, N.J., 1991.

Burford, Alison. *Craftsmen in Greek and Roman Society.* London, 1972.

Casson, Lionel. *The Ancient Mariners: Seafarers and Sea Fighters of the Mediterranean in Ancient Times.* 2d ed. Princeton, N.J., 1991.

Coulton, J. J. *Ancient Greek Architects at Work.* Ithaca, N.Y., 1977.

Frontisi-Ducroux, Françoise. *Dédale: Mythologie de l'artisan en Grèce ancienne.* Paris, 1975.

Heidegger, Martin. *An Introduction to Metaphysics.* Translated by Ralph Mannheim. New Haven, 1959.

Hersey, George. *The Lost Meaning of Classical Architecture: Speculations on Ornament from Vitruvius to Venturi.* Cambridge, Mass., 1988.

Hurwit, Jeffrey M. *The Art and Culture of Early Greece, 100–480 B.C.* Ithaca, N.Y., 1985.

Kahn, Charles H. *Anaximander and the Origins of Greek Cosmology.* New York, 1960.

Kirk, G. S., J. E. Raven, and M. Schofield. *The Presocratic Philosophers: A Critical History with a Selection of Texts.* 2d ed. Cambridge and New York, 1983.

Lawrence, A. W. *Greek Architecture.* 4th ed. Revised by A. W. Lawrence. Harmondsworth, England, 1983.

McEwen, Indra Kagis. *Socrates' Ancestor: An Essay on Architectural Beginnings.* Cambridge, Mass., 1993.

Morris, Sarah P. *Daidalos and the Origins of Greek Art.* Princeton, N.J., 1992.

Polignac, François de. *Cults, Territory, and the Origins of the Greek City-State.* Translated by Janet Lloyd. Chicago, 1995.

Rausch, Hannelore. *Theoria.* Munich, 1982.

Rykwert, Joseph. *The Idea of a Town: The Anthropology of Urban Form in Rome, Italy, and the Ancient World.* 2d ed. Cambridge, Mass., 1988.

Rykwert, Joseph. *The Dancing Column: On Order in Architecture.* Cambridge, Mass., 1996.

Vernant, Jean-Pierre. *The Origins of Greek Thought.* Ithaca, N.Y., 1982.

INDRA KAGIS McEWEN

Italian Renaissance Aesthetics

All architectural discourse in the Renaissance is indebted in some sense to Vitruvius's *De architectura* (first century BCE), the only text on architecture to have survived from antiquity. Although Vitruvius offers an epitome of the treatises of the Hellenistic period rather than an original theory, he provides a mass of information on all aspects of building and design, and was particularly appreciated by Renaissance architects for his discussion of the orders and ornament on one hand, and of building techniques and machinery on the other. His three essential elements of the work of architecture—*utilitas, firmitas* (structural strength), and *venustas* (beauty)—were adopted throughout the Renaissance. But he was a frustrating master: his language was obscure, and many technical terms remained unexplained; his illustrations had been lost, and it was hard to check his observations against the monuments, because most of the accessible remains were of later—Imperial—date. Although theorists of the figural arts in the Renaissance sought to build their principles and vocabulary from Pliny the Elder's history of ancient art and, more profitably, from the many ancient texts on rhetoric, those sources were only moderately helpful in constructing a base for an architectural aesthetic.

The first, and in many ways the most brilliant and influential, architectural theorist of the Renaissance was the Florentine humanist and architect Leon Battista Alberti (1404–1472), who had published small essays on painting and sculpture—as well as literary works and treatises on many other subjects—prior to the completion of *De re aedificatoria* around 1452 (first printed in Florence in 1485). This book, written in Latin and therefore addressed to patrons and intellectuals rather than to architects, followed Vitruvius's work in its general structure and in its focus on antique forms, but is much more cohesive in its concepts. Alberti attempts to provide rational grounds for architecture based on his conception of the laws of nature. His rational orientation is expressed in his definition of beauty: "when you make judgments on beauty, you do not follow mere fancy, but the workings of a reasoning faculty that is inborn in the mind." He proposes that the harmony of the universe is expressed in mathematical terms that can be emulated in architecture; thus architectural design should be based on three principles: number, proportion, and distribution. The proper employment of these three results in *concinnitas*; "it is the task and function of *concinnitas* to arrange according to precise laws parts that otherwise by their nature would be distinct from each other, so that they appear to be in a reciprocal relationship." Alberti's proof of the universality of nature's harmony is in the fact that the numerical proportions required in musical theory to produce consonances (e.g., 2:3, a fifth) also produce pleasing ratios in architecture, and he applies them extensively to plans and elevations, for example, at the Palazzo Rucellai in Florence, where he covered with an intricately proportioned facade a row of inharmonious old houses (Vitruvius had also employed musical consonances, but only in relation to acoustics in the theater).

Proportion based on musical consonances remained important throughout the Renaissance: the treatise of Andrea Palladio (*I quattro libri dell'architettura*, Venice, 1570) reflects a more developed musical theory, the adaptation of which he demonstrates in many woodcuts illustrating his own buildings, often with measurements that harmonize more perfectly than those of the buildings themselves (figure 1; proportional system indicated by numbers). The Venetian nobleman and church dignitary Daniele Barbaro left the most scholarly application of musical theory to architectural design in his commentary on Vitruvius. At the close of the sixteenth century, proportion was given a preeminent role in the Neoplatonic theories of two painters who addressed architectural design in terms of the *Idea*, or principle, of divinely inspired form: Gian Paolo Lomazzo and Federico Zuccaro (founder of the Roman Accademia del Disegno).

Alberti did not join other fifteenth-century writers such as Antonio Averlino, called Filarete (unpublished treatise of around 1461–1464), and the author of the *Life* of Filippo Brunelleschi, and Andrea Palladio (in a letter on the completion of the Gothic church of San Petronio in Bologna) in attacking the irrationality of the Gothic style that dominated the built environment of their time, and indeed wrote a sympathetic description of the Gothic cathedral of Florence. Nor did he, like Vitruvius, emphasize the human body as the primary source of architectural proportions, as did the Sienese Francesco di Giorgio (treatise in two principal versions, of which the last was around 1490), who proposed that not only the orders, but also the elevations and plans of buildings, could be based on the body. At the same time, Leonardo da Vinci drew his famous illustration of the Vitruvian passage deriving a square and a circle from the body of a man with outstretched hands and legs. Michelangelo, whose only statement of architectural principles appears in a letter, says that architects must first be figural artists because buildings, in their symmetry and apertures, imitate the form and orifices of the human body; he was resolutely opposed to proportional systems, as was his student Vincenzo Danti.

In discussing architectural types, Alberti is particularly concerned with the design of churches (which he calls "temples"), because they embody the highest aspirations of the society. He favors the central plan, and particularly the circle (project for San Francesco in Rimini, 1450), for which there were many antique precedents of the post-Vitruvian period, most notably the Pantheon in Rome), since it is a perfect Platonic form and reflects natural forms such as trees. Later writers, particularly Serlio and Palladio, also emphasize circular and polygonal plans for similar reasons, although they are poorly adapted to the Christian liturgy, and records of clerical opposition begin with Alberti's own circular tribune for the church of SS. Annunziata in Florence.

Theorists and architects of the early sixteenth century became committed to a more intensive examination of ancient architecture in an effort to visualize what ruined buildings may have looked like originally and to accommodate this knowledge to the Vitruvian text. The change is documented in the appearance of masses of measured drawings of ancient buildings (much more numerous than project drawings) and in a letter of 1516–1518 written to Pope Leo X by Raphael and Baldassare Castiglione proposing a systematic survey of the remains of ancient Rome and calling for legislation to preserve them from further destruction. The architecture of the period followed suit—Bramante's new Saint Peter, Raphael's Villa Madama in Rome—employing Roman structural techniques, and achieving a mass and volumetric grandeur not realized previously.

No theoretical writing appeared in the early years of the sixteenth century in either architecture or the figural arts, though—or maybe because—this was a time of great creative activity. The first printed architectural treatise after Alberti's was that of Sebastiano Serlio, composed of several books published from 1537 to 1575. Serlio's work was based on the ideas of his mentor, the Sienese architect Baldassarre Peruzzi, who had succeeded Raphael as architect of Saint Peter in the Vatican. Serlio's *Tutte le opere dell'architettura* introduces a polarity and tension in the aesthetics of architecture between decorum and license. *Decorum* was a Vitruvian term defining propriety, but one Alberti and Francesco di Giorgio associated primarily with ornament (*decor*ation). Later Renaissance writers, however, used it to fuse the observance of tradition with the adjustment of architectural design to the purpose of a building, the character and status of a client, or the attributes of the deity or saint to whom a religious building is dedicated, whereas license was the freedom of invention without which a design could be only conventional. Serlio writes of a *prima forma* that establishes the

ARCHITECTURE: Italian Renaissance Aesthetics. *Rustic Gateway* (1551). Reproduction from *Tutte l'opere d'architettura et prospetiva* by Sebastiano Serlio (Venice, 1587). (Courtesy of James Ackerman.)

base from which license departs; his *Estraordinario libro* (Lyons, 1551) is a book of gate designs that explicitly illustrate license (figure 2). Other writers were more wary; Giorgio Vasari, author of the extraordinary cornucopia of biography, art history, and criticism, the *Vite dei pittori, scultori ed architettori* (1550; 2d ed., 1568), says that license is essential to innovation in the arts, but warns of the dangers of excess, which he fears the work of Michelangelo—the Medici Chapel in Florence, Porta Pia in Rome—might encourage. Palladio includes a chapter on "abuses" (examples would be the pediment with a broken peak, a favorite device of Michelangelo, and the column bound in by stone bands, a favorite of Serlio's) in which he writes: "Though variation and new things ought to please everyone, one should not do what is contrary to the precepts of art and against what reason shows us, when one sees that even the ancients varied [their designs]; but never departed from certain universal and necessary rules."

In the atmosphere of the Counter-Reformation, a new kind of decorum appeared in the literature on ecclesiastical architecture. The major contribution was that of Saint Carlo Borromeo, whose *Instructiones fabricae et supellectilis eccleasiasticae* (Milan, 1577) was intended as a manual for bishops involved in the construction or reconstruction of churches; in mandating forms supportive of the liturgy and expressive of Christian dogma—and incidentally in opposing Renaissance practices that impeded these goals—it represents a kind of Catholic functionalism, reflected in the work of Pellegrino Tibaldi, such as San Fedele in Milan and the Collegio Borromeo in Pavia.

Serlio treats architectural expression as a matter of language, and proposes that the treatment of architectural elements—assembled according to a syntax—evokes the use of the building, as, for example, a rusticated facade expresses defensive strength and is thus mandated for fortification and city gates, as illustrated in Michele Sanmicheli's gates in Verona and fortifications for Venice and its colonies. Palladio enunciates a version of the imitation of nature (the principle of imitation being at the core of Renaissance criticism in all the arts) in which he calls on the architect to design the parts of the order to evoke the stresses created by gravity—for example, the swellings of the columnar base express the downward pressure of the columnar shaft, which itself, in its entasis (the curved profile diminishing the diameter toward the top), represents not the human body, as in the Vitruvian tradition, but again the response to weight. Vincenzo Scamozzi (*Idea dell'architettura universale*, 1615) further develops Palladio's principle of imitation, adding a psychological aspect anticipating early modern architectural aesthetics (e.g., Geoffrey Scott, *The Architecture of Humanism*, 1914), and describing elements in anthropomorphic terms ("weak," "solid," "swelling"); the viewer experiences the mechanical stresses of the building as if they were his or her own. Scamozzi also puts more emphasis than his predecessors on form as perceived by the senses, discarding the interpretation of decorum as the affirmation of tradition. Scamozzi sees architecture as being primarily representational, and therefore gives decorum a rhetorical character, as a kind of public address. But, as implied by his adoption of the Neoplatonic concept of the *Idea*, design must follow the "order" of nature and must avoid subjectivity.

In establishing a canon of the orders—a prime enterprise of sixteenth-century theory—Serlio fixed the parameters. Vitruvius's description of the orders had permitted only a partial visualization of the Doric, Ionic, and Corinthian, had failed to define the Tuscan, and did not discuss the Composite (which had emerged in Imperial architecture). Fifteenth-century writers were not clear or consistent on the subject. Serlio set proportions for each order and provided detailed illustrations of the component parts and a plate showing the five columns and entablatures together. His canon arbitrarily combined Vitruvian measurements with those taken from a variety of ancient monuments, and others selected for convenience. It was not rationalized by a mathematical rule, as was that of Giacomo Barozzi, called Vignola, who published a book in 1562 exclusively devoted to *Regole delli cinque ordini d'architettura*, consisting of engraved plates (which afforded greater precision and detail than the woodcut illustrations of most other texts). Vignola, who admitted that he had not arrived at his canon by following the best examples of ancient practice but "according to where my judgment took me," coordinated the proportions of the orders within a uniform formula, explicitly deciphered only recently, that removed them still farther from Vitruvius and Roman precedent and solidified the canon for classical architecture of all later time. It is paradoxical that a convention of ornament should have been established by way of license. Vignola's plates were copied in innumerable editions into the twentieth century; they influenced the canon of Daniele Barbaro and Palladio, who did not, however, preserve his proportional formula.

The principal architectural publications of northern Europe during the Renaissance were devoted to the orders and to models of—mostly domestic—design or ornament (in Germany, Hans Blum, 1555; Wendel Dietterlin, 1598). The most substantive theoretical contribution was Philibert Delorme's *Le premier tome de l'architecture* (Paris, 1567; he announced a second book on proportion but died before it was finished), which attempted to impart professional stature to the architect at a time when design was still in the hands of master masons (though Delorme still included a chapter on stereotomy [stone cutting], exemplified curiously in his château at Anet, that rarely figured in Italian treatises). He breaks from the Italian canon of the orders by adding a sixth, "French" order, claiming that because the orders evolved from nature they could not be fixed in number. He promotes a theory of proportion based on the dimensions of buildings treated in the Bible. Delorme's utilitarian approach to design foreshadows the work of the most innovative architectural theorist of the seventeenth century, Claude Perrault (*Ordonnance des cinq espèces de colonnes selon la méthode des anciens,* Paris, 1683; *Les dix livres d'architecture de Vitruve,* Paris, 1684).

In summary, writers of the fifteenth and sixteenth centuries formulated consistent themes in architectural discourse sparked by the treatise of Vitruvius, and focused on the polarity of decorum and license with respect to ancient precedent, but failed to match theorists of the figural arts in defining an overall aesthetic.

[*See also* Alberti; *and* Renaissance Italian Aesthetics.]

BIBLIOGRAPHY

Ackerman, James S. "The Tuscan/Rustic Order: A Study in the Metaphorical Language of Architecture." *Journal of the Society of Architectural Historians* 42.1 (March 1983): 15–34.

Alberti, Leon Battista. *On Painting and On Sculpture.* Edited and translated by Cecil Grayson. London, 1972.

Alberti, Leon Battista. *Momo o del principe.* Edited by Nanni Balestrini. Genoa, 1986.

Alberti, Leon Battista. *Dinner Pieces.* Translated by David Marsh. Binghamton, N.Y., 1987.

Alberti, Leon Battista. *On the Art of Building in Ten Books.* Translated by Joseph Rykwert, Neil Leach, and Robert Tavernor. Cambridge, Mass., 1988.

Blunt, Anthony. *Artistic Theory in Italy, 1450–1600.* Oxford, 1940.

Germann, Georg. *Einführung in die Geschichte der Architekturtheorie.* Darmstadt, Germany, 1980.

Guillaume, Jean, ed. *Les traités d'architecture de la Renaissance.* Paris, 1988.

Günther, Hubertus. *Deutsche Architekturtheorie zwischen Gotik und Renaissance.* Darmstadt, Germany, 1988.

Kemp, Martin. "From 'Mimesis' to 'Fantasia': The Quattrocento Vocabulary of Creation, Inspiration and Genius in the Visual Arts." *Viator* 8 (1977):347–398.

Klotz, Heinrich. "L. B. Albertis 'De re aedificatoria' in Theorie und Praxis." *Zeitschrift für Kunstgeschichte* 32 (1969): 93–103.

Kruft, Hanno-Walter. *A History of Architectural Theory.* Translated by Ronald Taylor, Elsie Callander, and Antony Wood. London and New York, 1994.

H. Millon. "The Architectural Theory of Francesco di Giorgio." *Art Bulletin* 40 (1958): 257–261.

Pagliara, Pier Nicola. "Vitruvio dal testo al canone." *Memoria dell'antico nell'arte italiana,* vol. 3, edited by Salvatore Settis, pp. 7–85. Turin, 1986.

Panofsky, Erwin. *Idea: Ein Beitrag zur Begriffsgeschichte der älteren Kunsttheorie.* Leipzig, 1924. Translated by Joseph J. S. Peake as *Idea: A Concept in Art Theory* (Columbia, S.C., 1968).

Payne, Alina. "Between *Giudizio* and *Auctoritas*: Vitruvius' *Decor* and Its Progeny in Sixteenth-Century Italian Architectural Theory." Ph.D. diss., University of Toronto, 1992.

Schlosser, Julius von. *La letteratura artistica.* 2d Italian ed. Revised by Otto Kurz. Florence, 1956.

Smith, Christine. *Architecture in the Culture of Early Humanism: Ethics, Aesthetics, and Eloquence, 1400–1470.* New York and Oxford, 1992.

Summers, David. *Michelangelo and the Language of Art.* Princeton, N.J., 1981.

Tafuri, Manfredo. "Discordant Harmony from Alberti to Zuccari." *Architectural Design* 49 (1979): 36–44.

Tafuri, Manfredo. *Teorie e storia dell'architettura.* Bari, 1968. Translated by Giorgio Verrecchia as *Theories and History of Architecture* (London, 1980).

Thoenes, Christof. "Vignolas 'Regola delli cinque ordini'." *Römische Jahrbuch für Kunstgeschichte* 20 (1983): 345–376.

Wittkower, Rudolf. *Architectural Principles in the Age of Humanism.* London, 1949.

JAMES S. ACKERMAN

Modern Overview

The philosophy of architecture has developed as part of the philosophy of art; the philosophy of art again has come to be all but identified with aesthetics: thus the widespread tendency to consider the "philosophy of architecture" a branch of aesthetics—Roger Scruton's *The Aesthetics of Architecture* (1979) is a good example. According to Scruton, the aesthetics of architecture "aims to capture the essence, not the accidents, of architectural beauty," where beauty is understood as the object of a distinctive kind of pleasure.

Insistence on the autonomy of aesthetic interest has helped to define aesthetics ever since Immanuel Kant. But if often used that way, "aesthetics" should not be understood as just a synonym for "philosophy of art": understanding the philosophy of art first of all as aesthetics reflects a specific approach to art that, even though it has a long prehistory going back to the Renaissance and indeed to antiquity, triumphed only in the eighteenth century over an older approach that assigned art a religious, social, or ethical function. The birth of aesthetics as a philosophical discipline belongs with that triumph.

To insist on the autonomy of aesthetic delight means that aesthetics has to deny art what Georg Friedrich Wilhelm Hegel considered its highest function: to be a privileged way of expressing humanity's deepest interests. The rise of the aesthetic approach is thus of a piece with Hegel's much-discussed claim that for moderns, art in its highest sense is a thing of the past.

More than the other arts, architecture, involved as it is with the whole of life, resists such marginalization. This helps to explain why from the very beginning aesthetics treated architecture as a stepchild. Kant already noted that architecture has difficulty rising to the purity found in the other arts, for, he observed, "the suitability of a product for a certain use is the essential thing in an *architectural work.*" But only a concern for beauty elevates a mere building into a work of art. Committed to the aesthetic approach, Nikolaus Pevsner thus begins his *An Outline of European Architecture* (1943) with this seemingly self-evident observation: "A bicycle shed is a building; Lincoln Cathedral is a piece of architecture." A work of architecture "is designed with a view to aesthetic appeal": work of architecture = building + aesthetic component.

In support of this distinction between building and architecture, one could cite Vitruvius, who demanded that the architect build "with due reference to durability, convenience, and beauty." That these conditions do not form a harmonious set was pointed out by Geoffrey Scott: the world is too much with the architect. The autonomy and completeness traditionally demanded of the aesthetic object require that the observer keep his or her distance from it. But so understood, aesthetic objects are essentially uninhabitable. It is thus hardly surprising that, with the rise of the aesthetic approach in the eighteenth century, architecture, caught between the conflicting claims of engineer and artist, entered a period of uncertainty and crisis from which it has not yet emerged. The aesthetic approach has to lead to an understanding of the work of architecture as a compromise between essentially unrelated concerns that must violate the demands of both beauty and utility.

To be sure, architectural modernism refused such a compromise: once more, architecture was to be all of a piece—consider Walter Gropius's dream of "the complete building," a dream that, looking back to medieval craft, refuses to accept the distance of art from the reality in which we work and live, thus challenging the aesthetic approach in a way that invites comparison with Martin Heidegger's related challenge. But the promise of that challenge, which necessarily also challenges Hegel's thesis of the death of art, remains unrealized. Although modernism created works of a new kind of strength and integrity, their strength often turned out to be that of modernist megasculptures. Refusing the halfhearted embrace of technology represented by the nineteenth century's decorated sheds, architectural modernists ended up embracing the aesthetic object, and in the process violated the requirements of dwelling far more resolutely than did the decorated sheds of nineteenth-century architecture, which, condemned no longer, today hint at possibilities of a more humane dwelling.

The term *decorated shed* is Robert Venturi's. But what he and his associates called for was not so much a return to aesthetic decoration as to architectural symbolism. Once again, architecture was to carry messages, to speak to us; the comparative muteness of much modernist architecture is linked to the muteness of aesthetic objects, which are supposed not to mean, but be. Whereas architectural modernism wanted space to triumph over communication, *Learning from Las Vegas* (1977) sought to invert that triumph by celebrating "the dominance of signs over space." Such dominance, however, is parasitic on established discourse and sense. Thus it cannot restore to architecture what Hegel considered it highest function and it accepts the marginalization of art. It cannot restore to architecture its own voice.

The same concern to restore to architecture its lost voice also shows itself in the proliferation of semiotic, poststructuralist, and deconstructive approaches to architecture. The fact that for two or three decades now architecture and architectural theory have been so fascinated by language and linguistics invites questioning. As Manfredo Tafuri points out, "the emergence, within architectural criticism, of the language problem" answers, not just to a sense of crisis in architecture, but to a widespread conviction that this is a language crisis." Is it? As Scruton observes, buildings do not make assertions as sentences do. However, to conclude that "the whole 'science' of semiology is" therefore "founded upon a mistake" is to presuppose an overly reductive understanding of language that cannot do justice even to the language of poetry, where what is said matters less than how it is said, than its distinctive style. The style of a building, too, can communicate a particular stance toward persons and things. Not that such "saying" relies on or can be translated without significant loss into spoken or written words. Architecture's proper language reaches beyond words, beyond reason.

As Heidegger has shown, this "language" has its foundation in the way human beings exist in the world, embodied and mortal, bound to the earth and open to the sky; it is bound up with experiences of rising and falling, of getting up and lying down, of self-assertion and surrender, of shelter and exposure, of height and depth. Buildings speak to us because our experience of space and therefore of particular spatial configurations cannot but be charged with meanings. In this sense, one can speak of natural symbols, "natural" because they are rooted in the nature of human beings in the world to which architecture helps to recall us. We have learned to be suspicious of appeals to "nature" or "essence." All too often they endow what is merely conventional with a false aura. Marc-Antoine Laugier's appeal to the primitive hut may serve as an example. What lifts architecture beyond mere building on Laugier's view is its power of representation, where he has in mind a double representation: representing a Greek temple, architecture represents at the same time an ideal building, an imaginative construct, supported, so Laugier thought, by reason and nature. Representing the primitive hut, works of architecture recall us to the essence of building. To speak of this essence, architecture makes conspicuous elements of building that are usually taken for granted and hardly noticed. The Greek temple that furnishes Laugier with his paradigm is supposed to have accomplished this by translating wooden vertical supports into columns of stone, the supported horizontal members into entablatures, the inclined members that carry the roof into pediments. Such translation represents the translated element, rendering conspicuous its essence. The idea of re-presentation invites us to reconsider Pevsner's claim that what distinguishes a work of architecture from a mere building is the addition of features that give it an aesthetic appeal. Sometimes something commonplace is transfigured into an aesthetic object simply by being brought into a new environment. Such displacement represents what is displaced in a way that invites us to linger, to look again. Re-presentation makes visible. Modern artists have made conspicuous the power of re-presentation. What moves us when we look at a painting by Jackson Pollock is first of all not what the painting represents, but the way paint and canvas have been re-presented. One can speak here of a realism of materials. Such realism has its counterpart in buildings that do not just use up steel and glass, concrete and stone, brick and wood, but re-present them and thus make them speak, where what they "say" will depend on the connotations carried by what is thus re-presented. Consider once more a Greek temple's translation of posts into columns of gleaming marble, which is at the same time a re-presentation of the stone that lets it speak to us with its own voice, so very different from the voice of dark granite or red brick. Representing a post, the column also represents itself as a post, as a building element whose function it is to support the lintel's heavy horizontal, now transformed into an entablature. That this particular configuration of vertical and horizontal speaks to us presupposes the natural language of space, as the re-presentation of building architecture re-presents and thereby makes conspicuous and lets us attend to that speech. Good architecture lets all buildings speak more loudly.

What Laugier took to be the authority of reason and nature owed all too much to the prejudices of his own day, to his historical situation. But if our being in the world is inevitably historical, it is not equally historical in all its aspects: we have to recognize the many different strands or themes that make up our world, some of quite recent origin, others as old as humanity as we know it. If there is a sense in which Greek temple and Gothic cathedral belong to worlds that have perished, this is not to say that the temple's fluted columns or the cathedral's diaphanous walls speak to us only of what has perished.

What should architecture speak of? Laugier suggests that it should recall us to the arche of building: architecture speaks as arche-tecture. As such it recalls an essential dwelling. So understood, architecture has not so much an aesthetic as an ethical function. "Ethical" derives from "ethos." A person's ethos refers to his or her character, nature, or disposition. Similarly, a community's ethos refers to the spirit that presides over its activities. "Ethos" here names the way human beings exist in the world: their way of dwelling. The ethical function of architecture names its task to help articulate and support a shared ethos.

Sigfried Giedion claimed such an ethical function for today's architecture when he called for an architecture that would speak to us of a way of life valid for our period. To be sure, we heirs of a whole series of Copernican decenterings and deconstructions have been taught to be on guard before appeals to some communal ethos, appeals inevitably shadowed today by the National Socialist specter. But it is precisely the absence of an effective common sense that opens the door to totalitarianism and a totalitarian architecture.

Needed is a very different architecture, an architecture that, preserving inevitable tensions, balances the rights of the community with those of the individual, the seductive magic of place with the promise of open space, the need for roots with the claims of freedom. Laugier's primitive hut and Heidegger's very different and yet related eighteenth-century farmhouse are constructs that lie behind us. Different is our sense of community, different our relationship to nature, to space, and to time. Science and technology have transformed our way of being in the world, our mode of dwelling, and thus the voices of space. Not that we can or should simply affirm this process: for that it has shown us too many questionable and increasingly frightening sides. But neither should we simply reject it in a vain attempt to return to the security of premodern, supposedly more primordial, modes of dwelling. We have to recognize the legitimacy of technology and at the same time put it in its place. And so should our architecture. Only in this way can it speak of a way of life valid for our period.

[*See also* Bauhaus; Kahn; Mies van der Rohe; *and* Modernism, *article on* Modernity and Tradition in Architecture.]

BIBLIOGRAPHY

Giedion, Sigfried. *Space, Time, and Architecture.* 5th rev. ed. Cambridge, Mass., 1967.

Harries, Karsten. *The Ethical Functions of Architecture.* Cambridge, Mass., 1996.

Hegel, Georg Wilhelm Friedrich. *Philosophy of Fine Art.* Translated by F. P. B. Osmaston. London, 1920.

Heidegger, Martin. "The Origin of the Work of Art." In *Poetry, Language, Thought,* translated by Albert Hofstadter, pp. 17–87. New York, 1971.

Heidegger, Martin. "Building, Dwelling, Thinking." In *Basic Writings,* edited by David Farrell Krell, translated by Albert Hofstadter, pp. 323–339. New York, 1977.

Kant, Immanuel. *Critique of Judgment.* Translated by J. H. Bernard. New York, 1951.

Laugier, Marc-Antoine. *An Essay on Architecture.* Translated by Wolfgang Herrmann and Anni Herrmann. Los Angeles, 1977.

Pevsner, Nikolaus. *An Outline of European Architecture* (1943). 7th ed. Harmondsworth, England, 1963.

Scott, Geoffrey. *The Architecture of Humanism: A Study in the History of Taste* (1914). London, 1980.

Scruton, Roger. *The Aesthetics of Architecture.* Princeton, N.J., 1979.

Tafuri, Manfredo. *Theories and History of Architecture.* Translated by Giorgio Verrecchia. New York, 1980.

Venturi, Robert, Denise Scott Brown, and Steven Izenour. *Learning from Las Vegas: The Forgotten Symbolism of Architectural Form.* Rev. ed. Cambridge, Mass., 1977.

Vitruvius. *The Ten Books of Architecture.* Translated by M. H. Morgan. New York, 1960.

KARSTEN HARRIES

Modernism to Postmodernism

In the first few years of the twentieth century, the Viennese architect Adolf Loos drew an analogy between ornament and decadence, between tattooing, that emblem of crime and instance of bodily ornament, and degeneracy. In his essay "Ornament and Crime" (1908), he says, "The modern man who tattoos himself is a criminal or a degenerate. There are prisons in which eighty per cent of the prisoners are tattooed. . . . If someone who is tattooed dies in freedom, then he does so a few years before he would have committed murder." From this social commentary, Loos arrives at a general historical principle: "I have discovered the following truth and present it to the world: cultural evolution is equivalent to the removal of ornament from articles in daily use." For Loos, architecture was not art, but more properly, a utilitarian occupation.

Modern architecture, the story, like the theoretical history of modernism itself, can tolerate various beginnings. But Loos's point of provocation, ornament and the call for its removal, is a good place to begin, because it generates hosts of relevant issues and is alternatively expressed in a variety of ways. It should be kept in mind how strikingly bare and denuded Loos's residences looked to his contemporaries, how lonely they appeared on the landscape of the "good" neighborhood—how astonishing for his time and class, while seeming so plain or ordinary in our own. As the architectural historian Sigfried Giedion, looking back on the beginnings of modern architecture, wrote in 1954: "many things nowadays taken for granted were only brought to birth with great difficulty and by deep personal devotion after defeats, suspicion and threats."

The call for the removal of ornament became a kind of Occam's razor for modern forms, spaces, and facades. It is a central maxim in the representation of modern architecture, in plan and perspective, for buildings built as well as for those that are a part of the history of architecture on paper alone. As Ludwig Wittgenstein, another Viennese and onetime architect put it in his *Tractatus Logico-Philosophicus* (1921), "If a sign is *useless,* it is meaningless. That is the point of Occam's maxim." (With Paul Englemann, Wittgenstein, in 1926, designed a town house for his sister that is considered a classic of bare-bones modernism.) The Occam principle was definitionally incorporated in mechanics and embodied in the machine, which was utilized by many of the masters of modernism as a paradigm for their own work. The idea of ornament as merely unnecessary in a mechanical sense was intuitively recognized as encumbrance, as hindrance, as distraction and concealment, even as a mode of dishonesty by drawing attention away from the structural and the functional and hence from what was held to be essential aspects of architecture. Modern architecture is, then, in a sense, a kind of Platonic rendering of the perceived essence of architecture—stripping away accidents as much as possible.

A decade or so after Loos's essay, the paradigmatic role of machines was reflected in Le Corbusier's (né Charles-Édouard Jeanneret) 1923 *Vers une Architecture,* published

two years after Wittgenstein's first seminal work. Le Corbusier's slogans, "A chair is a machine for sitting in" and "A house is a machine for living in," were specific aspects of what he called in general his Engineers' Aesthetic. The *clarity* in language that Wittgenstein was famous for requiring philosophically, Corbusier saw generated by the machine in his *The Decorative Art of Today* (1987 [1925]). There, in his chapter "The Lessons of the Machine," he writes: "With the machine the test is immediate; this one runs, that one does not. . . . Broadly, one can say that every machine that runs is a present truth. It is a viable entity, a *clear organism.* I believe that it is towards this clarity, this healthy vitality that our sympathies are directed." Adhering to the limits of functional building gave modern architecture an affinity with technology and hence allied it to the forces of development and progress.

"Less is more," Ludwig Mies van der Rohe, the last director of the Bauhaus, the famous design school founded by Walter Gropius et al. in 1919, said famously. Functionalism required minimalism. But minimalism also took on a minimalist *appearance.* No matter how complex were the threshold requirements of an architectural project, minimalism was the *look* of modern architecture—clean empty spaces and bare geometrical forms. Simple forms in juxtaposition. It was a high-school geometry one could enter. The plan also was to instantiate the idea that a building could not look good in three dimensions if it did not look good in two. Plans tended to be asymmetrical but maintained a Mondrianesque balance. In plan, the modernist emblem of the lateral grid became prominent: graphlike layouts that could be expanded upon by adding elements or adjusted downward by subtracting boxes. It was comparable in plan to what modularism was in actual building: prefabricated construction materials that could be produced en masse in the factory and transported to the building site and arranged in any desired manner.

The emphasis on geometry was also important for its universality. Geometry belonged everywhere and nowhere: it was as valid in ancient Athens as it is in contemporary Atlanta. It was ahistorical, timeless, and, in principle, unrelated in content to traditions and mores. Non-Euclidean geometries aside, geometry seemed a tie to a kind of singleness of voice, as Jean-François Lyotard was later to put it, while at the same time hooking it to a stable foundation. The fragile link with history was only through the latest innovations in manufactured materials, in steel, glass, or reinforced concrete. But modern architecture did not advocate or display the avant-gardism of some other modern art forms, despite its Cartesian ground-zero-type of universal abstraction.

The idea of functionalism was already at work in everyday life, and modern designers were drawn to ordinary building—anonymous architecture, so to speak—that made no pretenses to being art. There, specifically, in the American landscape, in the form of grain elevators and water towers, stood structures of unadorned, functional, geometric forms. The 1913 yearbook of the German Werkbund, *Art in Industry and Trade,* pictured grain silos and American factories, and Walter Gropius writes of their "unacknowledged majesty." Le Corbusier's *Vers une Architecture* contained dozens of photographs of such industrial entities and his own buildings reflected them, for example, the bell tower in his church at Ronchamp and American farm silos.

The machine idea was architecturally relevant as a kind of minimalism, not simply in building material but in simplicity of lifestyle. It was, in part, a reaction to a modern world that, at least in the urban capitals of Europe, was expanding ontologically and thus suffered from an overpopulation of ideas, activities, and objects as well as people, transforming an older, more stable society into an attractive, but perhaps superficial way of life. Modern life brought about the "intensification of nervous stimulation," as Georg Simmel put it in 1903, five years before Loos's essay. "The metropolis exacts from man as a discriminating creature a different amount of consciousness than does rural life," Simmel says not entirely disapprovingly. Perhaps ironically, modern architecture was something of a reaction against the new busyness, a shelter from the storm of too much and too many, a simplification of life as an antidote to a new and powerful eclecticism that had left behind a culture of an older, more unified character.

In that response, architecture was certainly not alone. There was a general spirit of matter-of-factness on the Continent even before World War I seemed to confirm that something warranted a rethinking of modern life. As Franz Schulze says in his biography of Mies: "The *neue Sachlichkeit* was destined to win the day in Germany. It was, in fact, related to a larger movement gaining ground everywhere on the Continent, a tendency away from the riot of dada, the antiart of the futurist, and the subjective indulgence of expressionism, toward a cooler, more exacting, and order-conscious mood in all the arts." As Wittgenstein turned toward Tolstoy and romanticized peasantry, architecture could look toward the clarity of forms in distinct relationships as a way of getting back to basics in public and private life alike. The *neue Sachlichkeit* contained the double edge of morality and aesthetics.

The idea of universality manifested itself in part in a theory that was to go beyond objects of architecture to all objects in everyday use, just as Loos had put it. Thinking of the binary opposition utilitarian/art, architecture for Loos was properly considered nonart. In contrast, the Bauhaus ideal, growing out of Henry van de Velde's School of Arts and Crafts in Weimar, among other sources, was that art should be everywhere, especially in objects of daily use. Hence, there resulted a blurring of the border between the high and the low, or at least between elitist or unique objects and those used by almost everyone and manufactured by mass production. It was the smaller and daily analogue to prefabricated construction. The Bauhaus did textiles, coffee cups, and furniture, as well as painting and sculpture.

Loos, in his essay on ornament, had understood the relationships among ornament, price, and labor—the additional work necessary to decorate an object upped its price and sometimes, for that reason alone, its status for the consumer. Even if Loos was attempting only to straighten the way of the "aristocrat," the affordability of unadorned building using modular building units was an early modern theme. A postulate of Gropius's Bauhaus was that the working person had the most to gain by low-cost, simple housing. Gropius's row houses at Toerten, Dessau, in 1926 and various full-scale models at international exhibitions exemplified his idea that many things considered luxuries, can, with the proper design, be made commonplace. In addition to working-class homes, the workplace itself was an object of modern projects, including Behrens's AEG factory in Berlin (1909), Gropius's Fagus shoe factory and his "Fabrik," Werkbund Exhibition, Cologne (1914) (a glass-walled office building, workshops, and a roof garden with a covered terrace for dancing).

In thinking about the theoretical aspects of modern architecture, it should not be forgotten that war and architecture make strange bedfellows. World War I brought building to a halt, only later, out of necessity and as a result of destruction, to provide the opportunity for new architects to work on projects that would never otherwise have been constructed in the sweeping dimensions that were called for in the postwar period.

In France, the Congrès Internationaux d'Architecture Moderne (CIAM), an organization with ideas analogous to the Bauhaus, met to reestablish the place of architecture in its proper social and economic sphere. In particular, its Charter of Athens (1933), adopted at its sixth congress, proposed "to work for the creation of a physical environment that will satisfy man's emotional and material needs and stimulate his spiritual growth." Whatever the intentions, the move to town planning where innovations of modern architecture were transferred to large-scale projects was later understood as one of the more telling, perhaps most notorious, aspects of modern architecture. The Bauhaus's Ludwig Hilberseimer *(Architecture of the Metropolis),* for example, and even Le Corbusier's Radial City, displayed a kind of clean-slate mentality in envisioning the ideal city that tended to favor an a priori idea of efficiency over maintaining the traditions of the old neighborhoods. One had to imagine vast superblocks, sometimes taking the form of towering rows of identical apartment houses placed strategically in parklike surroundings. This vision was seen as a cure for urban ills and found its way from idea to structure in many of the anonymous low-income housing projects for hundreds of simultaneously dislocated families.

Like much of modern art generally, then, modern architecture was not immune to a criticism of elitism. But, especially when public housing was at stake, where the effects were immediate, practical, and long-term, that "accusation" was particularly acute with respect to architects who would never live in the publicly owned buildings of their own design. With its emphasis on formalism and functionalism, matched with the removal of "down-home" decoration, modernism in architecture often ignored the dozens of small but significant features that made a typical social, public space a "human" place to live—or so the criticism goes. Worse, older neighborhoods that constituted the social fabric of lower-income families often were destroyed, only to be replaced by the very architectural "experiments" designed by powers that did not know what those neighborhoods really were. Modern architecture was thus critically conceived as a manifestation of rational utopianism with unwarranted political implications.

However the founders of modern architecture saw things, modern architecture was first understood as a style. It was brought to the United States in an exhibit curated by Philip Johnson, himself one of the contributors to modern architecture (as he was later, with his AT&T building in New York, to postmodern architecture), in an influential Museum of Modern Art exhibit (1932) featuring the name "International Style."

Modern architecture succeeded beyond the wildest imagination of any of its early participants. After World War II, "late" modern architecture simply became architecture itself. Architecture had come to a closure. The powerful institutions bought it and the schools taught it. It was analogous to the way knowledge had become science itself, speaking with a single voice—a male voice, some would say—the voice of reason and efficiency and progress, uncontaminated by ordinary human activity. Architecture had just become modern architecture.

With Robert Venturi, a Philadelphia-based architect, a turning point can be located in architectural history, an opening provided for radical architectural change. In his 1966 *Complexity and Contradiction in Architecture,* Venturi once again made ornament a point of contention, this time proposing a new definition of architecture based on its central role. "Architecture," Venturi says, "is building with decoration on it." Distinguishing the decorated shed from a duck (conceived after a Long Island restaurant shaped like one), he noted that the duck idea contained the modern singularity of form that impacted a viewer all at once. But the *shed* covered with ornament, including signs of commerce, was allied, Venturi thought, with the premodern past in structures like the great cathedrals whose walls held advertisements for God and the church, restraining the expression of power and monumentality with humanist detail.

Venturi's colleagues made liberal use of recognizable fragments from architectural history, a strategy precluded by a modernism that nevertheless chose its formal constituents from industrial design. But Venturi also sought to *learn,* as he put it, from contemporary anonymous scenes such as Las Vegas, Main Street, or the fast-food strip with their vitality of ordinary displays of two- and three-dimensional advertising pasted up against its exteriors or put forth prominently in storefront windows or parking lots. The strip, in particular, displayed an eclecticism that was immediately recognizable, completely unserious in character, and contained an architectural diversity that mirrored America's taste and diversity. "Main Street is almost all right," was a characteristic slogan, and Venturi claimed to prefer the "ugly and ordinary" over the "heroic and original."

Many of Venturi's first buildings were far tamer than his prescriptions. His Guild House, apartments for senior citizens in Philadelphia, although it embodied some of his prescriptions, took the brunt of the "ugly and ordinary" critique. His most characteristic work was an unbuilt proposal for a college football hall of fame in Princeton. The building itself was hidden from view by a giant electronic billboard, recalling a scoreboard, that could change its message. Ornament was literally superficial in that it was appliqué, applied to and replacing aspects of a surface that it was intended to enhance or destroy. But it was also perceived as an opportunity to mark a sense of the presentness of the building and to communicate with the local gentry. It reversed the technological/formal limitations, the universality/geometricity of building in favor of one that allowed, for example, a building in Dallas to say something about Texas and one in Singapore to say something about Asia or British colonialism.

Writers on postmodern architecture, most notably Charles Jencks, began to see in the decorative use of architectural elements a kind of textuality or use of signs and syntax, easily "read" by the public but already concealing some aspects of its meaning for a more elitist interpretation, apparently by those familiar with the history and theory of architecture. Jencks thought of this as double or multiple coding and found it in the fragmented appropriations on the exteriors and interiors of architects such as Arata Isosaki, Michael Graves, Aldo Rossi, James Stirling, and Charles Moore.

Venturi's writings, and to a certain extent his architecture, were significant for what they did in opening the closure of modern architecture. Other formerly modern purists began to acknowledge the self-imposed limits of modernism, its distant if not inhuman ambiance, its celebration of global economy, and rediscovered in their own historical perspective the genius and richness, the integration with life and times, of past architectural strategy and resourcefulness. To the extent that postmodernism turned toward an architectural vernacular, it was something of a manifesto, prompting architects to respect popularism in its various material manifestations.

ARCHITECTURE: Modernism to Postmodernism. Peter Eisenman, *Wexner Center for the Arts,* Ohio State University Campus in Columbus, Ohio. (Photograph copyright by Jeff Goldberg/Esto, Mamaroneck, New York; used by permission.)

In the summer of 1988, New York's Museum of Modern Art hosted an exhibit called, "Deconstructivist Architecture." "Deconstructivist Architecture" was curated by Philip Johnson and Mark Wigley and was Johnson's first major museum project since his 1932 landmark show that introduced the International Style to America. The exhibit brought under one umbrella seven important architects who by some stretch of the imagination could be called "deconstructivists." Not merely a variation of *deconstructionist,* the term *deconstructivist* refers back to the constructivist art born in prerevolutionary Russia. Those architects whose works were exhibited—Frank Gehry, Daniel Libeskind (who is retracing a Jewish Berlin through a museum), Rem Koolhaas (who has turned toward an older Coney Island for inspiration), Peter Eisenman, Zaha Hadid (the only woman), Coop Himmelblau, and Bernard Tschumi—each challenged some of the more central traditional aspects of architecture, among them unity, stability, harmony, comfort, and function. Deconstruction in architecture may be seen as a vital response to the historically necessary, but more facile, architectural postmodernism (as defined by Venturi and others), as well as to classical/modern architecture in the broad sense of those terms. But it must be kept in mind that far from being the name of an architectural movement or school, *deconstructivism* refers at best to the practices of a loose set of diverse members, many of whom would justifiably resist that or any other label. Eisenman, perhaps the most theoretical of the seven, and one of two Americans in the MOMA show (the other was Frank Gehry), is no exception.

With the possible exception of Libeskind, Eisenman's work seems more in tune than the others with Jacques Derrida's brand of deconstructionist philosophy (Eisenman and Derrida collaborated on the design of an unbuilt vegetationless garden at a larger Tschumi La Villette project outside Paris). Eisenman came to recognize a paradox in architecture that he articulated as follows: "In order to be, it must always resist being. . . . This is the paradox of architecture. Thus, in order to reinvent a site . . . the idea of site must be freed from its traditional places, histories, and systems of meaning. This involves the dislocation of the traditional interpretation of its elements." Eisenman's work (his Wexner Center for the Arts in Columbus, for example) constitutes an architecture that is somehow removed from an unreinvented architectural milieu, one requiring an architect who will break with architecture's own hierarchical presuppositions. Eisenman's concern is not so much about whether good or interesting work can be produced within architecture's traditional presuppositions; rather, he is skeptical about whether a more "speculative," exploratory architecture, an architecture that investigates its own assumptions, can be designed within the limits of traditional tastes, beliefs, and principles. His architecture, like the collected works of other postmodernists, is less interested in provided answers to questions (e.g., what is a church? a bookstore? a home?) than in generating questions, conversations, about what such questions might mean and in what new ways they might be approached.

On Eisenman's view, modern architecture merely *assumed* the role of nonreferential "objectivity." However, "In reality . . . their 'objective' forms never left the classical tradition. They were simply stripped down classical forms or forms referring to a new set of givens (function, technology)." Some of Eisenman's strategies aimed to "surgically open up the Classical and the Modern to find what is repressed." His architecture is a recognition that the apparent essence/accident conception of architecture itself has generated certain binary oppositions, structure/ornament being one, privileging or celebrating one side of a duality while devaluing or repressing the other. In his projects, Eisenman has tried to work "between" the suspended domains of architecture's traditional oppositions, such as architecture/landscape, outside/inside, center/periphery, product/process, and stability/instability.

In several of his writings (for example, his work on metaphor), Derrida has turned his strategies to the structure/ornament hierarchy. In *The Truth and Painting* (1987), Derrida investigates the stance on ornament taken by Immanuel Kant in his *Critique of Judgment,* in which the structure/ornament demarcation is a working assumption, ornament being merely a supplement to the primary work. Derrida's strategy is to problematize the "border" or *parergon* between the work, *ergon,* and what is outside the work *(hors d'œuvre),* in order to disturb the peripheral role of ornament as a mere adjunct, not an intrinsic constituent of a work. It should be emphasized that Derrida tries to *suspend* rather than reject such oppositions, working during the "suspense" between the two. Hence, Derrida calls into question the inside/outside opposition in Kant's main work on aesthetics. But Derrida, who explores the architectural metaphor in philosophy generally, also sees the presence-presentation-representation hierarchy in metaphysics as analogous to the ground-structure-ornament connection in architecture, with similar devaluings, concealments, or repressions.

How these repressions are part of bourgeois taste, economic power, or anthropocentrism is not a topic from which architecture need be removed. Such an architecture would refuse to acknowledge the stability of the concept of architecture, which is buttressed by a grounding metaphysics of essentiality and which in turn allows for the misleading appearance of the timeless self-evidence of architecture's so-called essential features. "Deconstruction," Derrida has said, "is first and foremost a suspicion directed against just that kind of thinking—'what is . . . ?' 'what is the essence of . . . ?'" Again, the aim is to work *between* the oppositions generated by traditional architecture, thereby suspending the hierarchical privileging or monumentality of a traditional architectural essence that celebrates stability or comfort, function or structure.

In the sense that many aspects of Eisenman's work have embodied a refusal to build monumentality, his strategies can be understood as examples of what Gianni Vattimo has called *il piensiero debole*—weak thinking. Weak architectural thinking is, in a sense, architecture against architecture, that is, against architecture as a manifestation of wealth and power, as a teller of grand historical narratives, and as an architecture that builds in ways that attempts to celebrate the often repressive traditional values of gender, race, class, and so on, as they are displayed, fetishized, and passed on in enduring works of art.

Derrida reminds us:

> This architecture of architecture has a history, it is historical through and through. Its heritage inaugurates the intimacy of our economy, the law of our hearth *(oikos),* our familial, religious and political "oikonomy," all the places of birth and death, temple, school, stadium, agora, square, sepulcher. It goes right through us *(nous transit)* to the point that we forget its very historicity: we take it for nature. It is common sense itself.

As Derrida puts it, the result of opening the closure of architecture, in a way that may take architecture to philosophical depths while helping to uncover the architectural metaphor in philosophy, would aid in "letting other voices speak." It would be a way of removing both the architect of tradition and the traditional history of architecture as a resistance in the investigation and embodiment of new ways of meaning. It would allow architecture to take its own place beside other art forms in the history of ideas.

The break from modern architecture was consistent with a general postmodern condition: eclecticism and diversity, multiplication of voice, repetition of previous forms, fragmentation and localization, a greater tendency toward textuality and self-referentiality, and an inclusion of play and accident. But the accomplishment of postmodern architecture and whatever followed it may have been to allow architecture to play with a full deck of strategies and to make it, again, vitally placed, in mind and body, within the culture of everyday life.

[*See also* Bauhaus; Derrida; Mies van der Rohe; Minimalism; Postmodernism, *historical and conceptual overview article; and* Wittgenstein.]

BIBLIOGRAPHY

Bayer, Herbert, Walter Gropius, and Ise Gropius, eds. *Bauhaus, 1919–1928.* New York, 1938.

Derrida, Jacques. "Point de Folie—Maintenant l'architecture." *AA Files* 12 (20 February–22 March 1986): 65–71.

Derrida, Jacques. *The Truth in Painting.* Translated by Geoff Bennington and Ian McLeod. Chicago, 1987.

Eisenman, Peter. "The End of the Classical." *Perspecta: The Yale Architectural Journal* (Cambridge, Mass.) 21 (Summer 1984): 54–172.

Eisenman, Peter. *Houses of Cards.* New York and Oxford, 1987.

Giedion, Sigfried. *Space, Time and Architecture.* 5th ed. Cambridge, Mass., 1967.

Goldblatt, David. "The Dislocation of the Architectural Self." *Journal of Aesthetics and Art Criticism* 49.4 (Fall 1991): 337–348.

Jencks, Charles. *The Language of Post-Modern Architecture.* New York, 1977; 6th ed., New York, 1991.

Johnson, Philip, and Mark Wigley. *Deconstructivist Architecture.* New York, 1988.

Kipnis, Jeffrey. "Nolo Contendere." *Assemblage* 11 (1990): 54–57.

Kolb, David. *Postmodern Sophistications: Philosophy, Architecture, and Tradition.* Chicago, 1990.

Koolhaus, Rem. *Delirious New York: A Retroactive Manifesto for Manhattan.* New York and Oxford, 1978; new ed., New York, 1994.

Le Corbusier (Jeanneret, Charles-Édouard). *Towards a New Architecture.* Translated by Frederick Etchells (1927). New York, 1986.

Le Corbusier (Jeanneret, Charles-Édouard). *The Decorative Art of Today.* Translated by James Dunnett. Cambridge, Mass., 1987.

Lerup, Lars. *Planned Assaults.* Cambridge, Mass., 1987.

Loos, Adolf. "Ornament and Crime." In *Programs and Manifestoes in Twentieth-Century Architecture,* edited by Ulrich Conrads, translated by Michael Bullock, pp. 19–24. Cambridge, Mass., 1970.

Rabinow, Paul. *French Modern: Norms and Forms of the Social Environment.* Cambridge, Mass., 1989.

Rossi, Aldo. *A Scientific Autobiography.* Translated by Lawrence Venuti. Cambridge, Mass., 1981.

Schulze, Franz. *Mies van der Rohe: A Critical Biography.* Chicago, 1985.

Tafuri, Manfredo. *Architecture and Utopia: Design and Capitalist Development.* Translated by Barbara Luigia La Penta. Cambridge, Mass., 1976.

Venturi, Robert. *Complexity and Contradiction in Architecture.* 2d ed. New York, 1977.

Venturi, Robert, Denise Scott Brown, and Steven Izenour. *Learning from Las Vegas: The Forgotten Symbolism of Architectural Form.* Rev. ed. Cambridge, Mass., 1977.

Wigley, Mark. *The Architecture of Deconstruction: Derrida's Haunt.* Cambridge, Mass., 1993.

DAVID GOLDBLATT

ARISTOTLE. [*This entry comprises five essays on one of the principal philosophers to write on art long before the ages of art and aesthetics:*

Survey of Thought
Aristotle on Mimesis
Aristotle on Form and Unity
Reception of Aristotle in Antiquity
Reception of Aristotle in Modernity

The first essay is a survey of Aristotle's philosophy as a whole and his poetics in particular. The next two essays discuss three major concepts in his poetics, mostly concerning tragedy: "mimesis" (imitation), "form," and "unity"—all of which have had a profound influence on the history of aesthetics. The final two essays concern the reception of his poetics in antiquity and modernity, respectively, where his influence in aesthetics has been significant despite the fact that he, like the Greeks and most other cultural traditions prior to the eighteenth century, did not have a concept of art or engage in what since the eighteenth century has been called aesthetics. See also Arab Aesthetics; Aquinas; Augustine; Comedy; Creativity; Metaphor; Morality and Aesthetics; Perception; *and* Representation.]

Survey of Thought

Aristotle (384–322 BCE) made substantial contributions to virtually every field studied in his day, including logic, metaphysics, history of philosophy, political science, history, ethics, poetry, music, rhetoric, biology, astronomy, physics, and theology. Some two hundred works were attributed to him in antiquity, most of which do not survive. Among the works on poetry attributed to him were *On Poets; Treatise on the Art of Poetry; Homeric Problems; Poetics; Victories at the Dionysia; On Tragedies; Didaskaliae; Hesiodic Problems; Cycle on Poets; Problems from Archilochus, Euripides, Choerilus; Poetical Problems; Poetical Explanations.* (See catalog of Aristotle's works in Barnes's Oxford translation.) Aside from some fragments, the only one of these works to survive is the first book of the *Poetics.* Aristotle's other extant works, however, can help to illuminate many topics in the *Poetics.* For example, *Rhetoric* and *On the Soul* contain material on the emotions, *Politics* discusses music, the biological works are helpful for an understanding of biological analogies in the *Poetics,* and the *Nicomachean Ethics* contains numerous ethical examples taken from tragedy.

The *Poetics* is a short work, containing only forty-six pages in the standard Greek text (Kassel, 1966). The unique source is a single manuscript, codex Parisinus 1741, of the tenth or eleventh century. It is generally thought to be a late work, although this has been disputed. (See discussion in Halliwell, 1986, Appendix 1.) Internal evidence indicates close connections between the *Poetics* and the *Rhetoric.* The standard method of citing passages in the *Poetics* and other works of Aristotle is by page, column, and line number in Bekker's 1831 edition (e.g., 1450a2).

The *Poetics* presents numerous difficulties for the reader. There are many signs that our text is incomplete. The opening chapter announces a discussion of *poiētikē* in general, with its several genres, but our text deals almost exclusively with only two genres, epic and tragedy. The beginning of chapter 6 states: "Concerning the craft of imitation in hexameters [that is, epic], and concerning comedy we will speak later." Epic is discussed in chapters 23–26, but the promise to discuss comedy later in the *Poetics* is never kept. Moreover, there is some indication in manuscripts, and in other ancient and medieval sources, that a second book, including a discussion of comedy, originally followed. (For a recent attempt at reconstruction, and evaluation of the evidence for a second book, see Janko, 1984.) The text of the *Poetics* also contains numerous lacunae and other textual difficulties, many real or apparent inconsistencies, and frequent obscurities. Whether or not it is a series of lecture notes, as many scholars believe, it is certainly not a polished work written for the general public. The elliptical style leaves many terms and concepts in need of explanation. Aristotle notoriously fails to explain *katharsis* (catharsis), merely stating, in the definition of tragedy, that tragedy accomplishes catharsis. The explanations he does offer may be unclear. For example, Aristotle defines *peripeteia*, "reversal," as "a change to the opposite of the things done," but he does not say what kind of change is involved or who is affected by it. Moreover, the examples he provides are frequently drawn from works no longer extant. These and other difficulties have helped to create disagreement on virtually everything in the *Poetics*. The reader must keep in mind that all translations contain a large element of interpretation, that any statements by scholars about major issues are likely to be highly controversial, and that not everything that has been attributed to Aristotle is actually in the *Poetics*.

Poetics: Subject and Scope. The Greek title, *peri poiētikēs,* is more accurately translated as "On the poetic craft," although the word *poiētikē* is more inclusive than English "poetry." It is cognate with the verb *poiein,* "to make," and is sometimes used by Aristotle to refer to the productive crafts in general. In the *Poetics,* it is not clear what specific crafts are included in *poiētikē*. After saying that he will discuss the kinds of *poiētikē*, Aristotle proceeds instead to a consideration of the kinds of imitation *mimēsis* (mimesis), including music, dance, and painting as well as "poetry." After these introductory remarks, however, the range of the *Poetics* is much narrower than that of "poetry," for this work deals primarily with only a single, highly formalized genre: tragedy. The works Aristotle discusses were all written during the fifth and fourth centuries BCE for performance at competitive dramatic festivals in Athens, at which many aspects of performance and composition, including the number of actors and choral singers, length of performance, and subject matter, were governed by explicit rules of competition, or by generally accepted conventions.

In evaluating his critical theories, it is important to remember that Aristotle's knowledge of the tragedies and of the dramatic festivals vastly exceeds our own. We now have, aside from a few fragments, only thirty-two complete tragedies by three authors (Aeschylus, Sophocles, and Euripides), but Aristotle had access to all or most of the entire corpus of hundreds of plays by numerous authors. It is generally agreed that our extant records of plays produced at the dramatic festivals are based to some extent at least on his lost *Didaskaliae*. The *Poetics* alone mentions some fifty plays by at least thirteen authors, and Aristotle's other works contain many more references. Aristotle's knowledge was also impressively detailed. For example, the text of line 727 of Euripides' *Iphigenia among the Taurians* is established by Aristotle's quotation in *Rhetoric* 3.1407b34–35.

The *Poetics* begins with a programmatic introduction of the subject matter: (1) the poetic craft studied in itself, (2) its forms and their powers, (3) how to organize plots, and (4) quantity and quality of parts (1.1447a1–13). Chapters 1–3 then provide a general discussion of imitation. Epic, tragedy, music, painting, and dance are all imitations, differing in three respects: objects imitated, medium, and manner of imitation. Tragedy imitates the actions of people who are better than us, in the medium of sound (words, rhythm, and harmony) and in the manner of enactment without narration. *Poetics* 4 discusses the causes and origins of imitation and the development of the poetic craft. Although Aristotle grounds the imitative arts in a human nature common to all, stating that the human being is the most imitative of all animals and that all people learn from and take pleasure in imitation, he holds that people with special aptitudes for imitation helped to create and perfect the different genres of poetry. Aristotle's outline of the development of poetry is partly historical and partly teleological. After an early improvisational stage, poetry divided into two branches, one of which led from hymns and encomia to Homer's *Iliad* and *Odyssey,* and finally culminated in tragedy. The other branch developed from blame poetry to Homer's lost *Margites* and ended in comedy. Chapter 4 also provides some tantalizing but puzzling clues to the more recent development of tragedy "from those leading off the dithyramb" and from a "satyric" origin. Chapter 5 begins with a brief discussion of comedy, and then compares epic and tragedy. In chapter 6, Aristotle turns to his main subject, tragedy. He defines tragedy as "imitation . . . by means of pity and fear accomplishing katharsis of these kinds of emotions." He then discusses the six qualitative parts of tragedy. These are, in order of importance: plot (*muthos,* "the composition of events"), character (*ēthos,* "that which indicates what kind of choice someone makes"), thought (*dianoia,* by means of which "people make a demonstration or reveal an opinion"), speech (*lexis,* "expression by means of language"), song, and spectacle. Aristotle distinguishes plot from character and stresses the primacy of plot. Plot is the imitation of action, not of life or of human beings; it is, as it were, the soul, and the first principle of tragedy, whereas character is only second in importance, like the colors added to an outline drawing. Aristotle even asserts that there could be no tragedy without plot, though there could be without character. It is disputed how literally this last statement is to be taken, especially since chapter 6 also states that action is caused by character and thought.

With the exception of the brief and possibly spurious chapter 12, on the quantitative parts of tragedy (prologue, episode, exodos, parados, and stasimon), chapters 7–14 focus on the tragic plot. A good plot is one, whole, and complete, and proceeds from beginning to middle to end, according to probability or necessity. It deals with "the universal," as opposed to "the particular," which is the subject of history. The tragic plot moves either from good to bad fortune or from bad to good fortune. The three parts of the plot are *pathos* ("a destructive or painful event"), reversal (*peripeteia,* "the change to the opposite of the things done"), and recognition (*anagnōrisis,* "a change from ignorance to knowledge, leading either to friendship or to enmity, of those defined with respect to good or bad fortune"). All plots, both simple and complex, have *pathos,* but only the best plots, the complex, have reversal, recognition, or both. Chapters 13 and 14 give rules for the construction of plots, though the two accounts are difficult to reconcile with one another other. In chapter 13, Aristotle writes that the best kind of plot is one like that of Sophocles' *Oedipus the King,* in which a stage figure goes from good to bad fortune, because of a mistake *(hamartia),* whereas plays that end happily are inferior. In chapter 14, however, the best kind of plot is said to be like that of Euripides' *Iphigenia among the Taurians,* in which *philos* (the Greek word means "kin," or "friend") is about to harm *philos,* in ignorance of the relationship, but recognizes the relationship before acting. In this chapter, the *Oedipus* plot, in which *philos* harms *philos* in ignorance, and later recognizes the relationship, is only second-best. After a discussion of character in chapter 15, Aristotle returns to plot, discussing kinds of recognition (chapter 16), and more rules for composing plots (chapter 17).

Chapter 18 contains many miscellaneous remarks, the most important of which is the distinction between the two parts of a tragic plot: complication *(desis),* that part of tragedy from the beginning until just before the change to good or bad fortune occurs, and resolution *(lusis),* that part from the beginning of the change to the end. After a brief discussion of thought at the beginning of chapter 19, chapters 19–22 contain a lengthy, and often obscure, discussion of another part of tragedy, speech. This section deals with such topics as grammatical terms, usage, and metaphor. *Poetics* 23–24 discuss epic, constantly comparing it with tragedy. Chapter 25 focuses on poetical problems and solutions, and chapter 26 concludes our *Poetics* with a comparison of epic and tragedy, arguing that tragedy is superior.

Aristotle and Plato. Plato has a very low opinion of most poets and other imitators, holding that they are mere makers of images, products "third from the truth" on the ontological scale, and ethically base as well, capable of corrupting the souls of even the best people. He consequently excludes most poets from his ideal state, welcoming only the imitators of the good, who make hymns and encomia. Plato does, however, invite lovers of poetry to speak in prose on her behalf, if they can show that poetry is not only pleasant but also beneficial to cities and individuals (*Republic,* book 10). Many scholars believe that Aristotle takes up this challenge in the *Poetics.* They argue that Aristotle refutes Plato's ontological criticisms by attempting to show that the poet's art is a true *technē,* a craft with definite skills and goals, and objective criteria by which its products may be evaluated. Plato's ethical criticisms, it is held, are refuted primarily by Aristotle's theory of catharsis, according to which poetry purges, purifies, or clarifies undesirable psychic elements, rather than strengthening them. Although these arguments are plausible, it is important to recognize that they are based on inferences from few explicit statements in the *Poetics.* Aristotle gives rules, whether normative, prescriptive, or both, for a *technē* of poetry, and he connects imitation in general with a pleasure in learning that is characteristic of philosophers (chapter 4). He also holds that tragedy imitates people "better than us" (chapter 3), and appeals to a "better audience" (chapter 26). On the other hand, Aristotle never mentions Plato and he says little about the specific ethical, psychological, or intellectual effects that tragedy has on its audience. Although Aristotle was undoubtedly influenced by Plato's aesthetic views, his concerns in the *Poetics* are very different from those of his predecessor. Aristotle's primary goal is not to defend poetry on ethical or metaphysical grounds, but to give a detailed account of the specific ways in which each genre accomplishes its own goals.

Imitation (mimesis). Plato holds that imitations are mere images, like those produced mechanically and passively by a mirror. For Aristotle, however, imitation is a much more active and creative process, producing objects that have a kind of life of their own. Aristotle frequently uses biological analogies, comparing plot to a living animal, or to the soul of an animal. He also gives imitation an important role in education and learning, and he holds, as noted earlier, that it has an essential connection with human nature itself, because humans are the most imitative of all animals (chapter 4). Unfortunately, Aristotle nowhere gives a detailed theoretical account of imitation, but leaves us to draw inferences from scattered remarks in the *Poetics* and elsewhere. In the *Poetics,* imitation includes a wide range of activities. Among the imitative crafts are music, dance, painting, and poetry; among the objects of imitation are characters, emotions, and actions (chapter 1), and "things as they were or are, things as they are said and seem to be, or things as they should be" (chapter 25). It is imitation rather than meter that makes the poet (chapter 1). Unlike the historian, who relates particular events that actually happened, the poet as imitator relates things that are probable or necessary (chapter 9). In other works (e.g., *Physics* 199a), Aristotle states that "craft imitates nature." Although Aristotle's concept, or concepts, of imitation are hard to pin down, it is clear that imitation is neither simply representation, nor representation plus similarity—although imitations in some sense stand for, and are similar to, the objects they imitate. Perhaps the best that can be said is that imitation is a human activity that, like natural processes, creates products with intelligible structures organized for the sake of an end *(telos)*. [*See the following article for an extended discussion of mimesis.*]

Catharsis. Catharsis is the most widely known and discussed of all Aristotle's aesthetic concepts, and it is also the one about which he says least. In the *Poetics,* the term occurs only twice, once in the definition of tragedy as "imitation . . . by means of pity and fear accomplishing the katharsis of such emotions" (chapter 6), and once in chapter 17, where it refers to a ritual purification. The complete absence of explanation has led to much speculation about the philosopher's meaning. Some argue that a lost second book contained a discussion of catharsis. They see evidence for this in a statement in book 8 of Aristotle's *Politics:* "What we mean by katharsis we will state now in general terms, but again in the works on the poetic craft we will speak of it more clearly" (1341b). Others deny that this is a reference to our *Poetics,* and argue that, in any case, the subjects and goals of the *Politics* are very different from those of the *Poetics.*

Many translations and interpretations of the term have been proposed. The following categories are among the most important. (1) *Medical.* According to Jacob Bernays ("Aristotle on the Effect of Tragedy," in Barnes, Schofield, and Sorabji, 1979), catharsis is a *purgation* analogous to a medical purge. *Politics*, book 8, where Aristotle compares catharsis to a medical treatment, is frequently cited in support of this view. (2) *Ethical.* According to G. E. Lessing (quoted by Bernays), catharsis is a *purification* of the emotions, by means of which undesirable elements are removed from them. In favor of an ethical view of catharsis, Richard Janko cites *Politics* 8, where catharsis is said to reduce excessive emotion, as well as many post-Aristotelian ancient sources in which poetry is said to produce ethical and intellectual virtue. (3) *Intellectual.* In the view of Leon Golden (1992), catharsis is an *intellectual clarification.* In support of his view, Golden cites chapter 4 of the *Poetics,* where Aristotle states that people learn by means of *mimesis.* (4) *Structural.* According to Gerald Else (1957), catharsis does not operate on the emotions but on the pitiable and fearful events of the plot. In favor of his view, Else cites the absurdity of holding that pity and fear can produce, homeopathi-

cally, a catharsis of pity and fear. Else is one of the few modern scholars to challenge the now dominant homeopathic interpretation. In the Renaissance, however, many scholars, such as Vincenzo Maggi, held that catharsis is not homeopathic but allopathic, in that pity and fear purge the soul of emotions unlike themselves: anger, greed, lust. I have recently argued for an allopathic view of catharsis (Befiore, 1992). In the complete absence of explicit internal evidence, all interpretations of catharsis must rest on a combination of inherent plausibility, consistency with the *Poetics,* and a judicious use of external evidence.

Hamartia. In chapter 13, Aristotle states that the best plot represents someone changing from good reputation and good fortune to bad fortune, not because of vice, but because of a great *hamartia.* Aristotle does not explain *hamartia,* but merely cites Oedipus as an example. Because his statement is ambiguous, it is disputed whether the Oedipus example illustrates the whole pattern, including *hamartia,* or only the fall from good fortune. Although *hamartia* is often identified with the "tragic flaw" of pride, this is not what the Greek term means, for *hamartia* is cognate with the verb *hamartanō,* "miss the mark," and it refers to a mistake, whether intellectual, ethical, or both. Most scholars agree that *hamartia* in the *Poetics* cannot be a seriously vicious error, for Aristotle states that a vicious person cannot arouse pity, and he explicitly contrasts vice and *hamartia.* There is disagreement about nearly everything else, however. *Hamartia* is taken to refer either to a nonvicious ethical error, or to an intellectual mistake, or to include both kinds of errors. Aristotle's example, Oedipus, raises new difficulties, for there is no agreement about the nature of Oedipus's mistake in Sophocles' *Oedipus the King.* Those who argue for the ethical interpretation of *hamartia* argue that Oedipus's irritable temper led him to kill his father, or that his skepticism about the oracle is impious. Others argue that his error is instead purely cognitive, a failure to recognize his parents. Still others deny that Aristotle connects Oedipus with *hamartia* at all, and argue that he is merely cited as an example of a person who changes to bad fortune from great good fortune. Whatever *hamartia* means, it is clear that it is not an essential part of every play, but is found only in some plays with unhappy endings.

Influence of Aristotle's Poetics. The *Poetics* was lost sometime during antiquity. No indisputable trace of its influence is found in Hellenistic literature or in such Roman aesthetic works as Horace's *Ars poetica.* After its reappearance in Renaissance Italy, however, the *Poetics* has been the single most influential work on aesthetics in the Western tradition. Every study must in some way take its ideas into account, whether to accept, reject, or adapt them. Nor is the influence of the *Poetics* limited to aesthetics. Catharsis as a psychological term has become part of our everyday speech. The idea, now widespread in many fields, that stories or narratives are an important way of constructing reality undoubtedly owes much to Aristotle's views on the primacy of plot. On the other hand, textual difficulties and conceptual obscurities in the *Poetics* can easily lead to misunderstandings about what the philosopher actually says. Although the three "unities" of French seventeenth-century drama are often thought to be derived from Aristotle, only unity of action is firmly grounded in the text; unity of place has no foundation in the *Poetics,* and unity of time is based on a controversial interpretation of an obscure passage. The common view that every Aristotelian "hero" has a "tragic flaw" is based on a very questionable interpretation of *hamartia.* The pyramid, drawn on many a high-school blackboard, of action rising to a climax and falling to a catastrophe is often associated with Aristotle's distinction between complication and resolution. However, Aristotle does not mention a dramatic climax, and he has no concept of rising and falling action. The pyramid is derived from Gustave Freytag's imaginative adaptation of Aristotle (trans., *Freytag's Technique of the Drama,* New York, 1894). *Catharsis* is commonly used today to refer to a relief, produced by art or therapy, from painful, excessive, or unhealthy emotional states. This idea is not derived directly from Aristotle, but from a Freudian interpretation of the *Poetics.* Freud was no doubt influenced by his father-in-law, Bernays, whose "purgation" theory of catharsis is only one of many. Finally, modern attempts to apply Aristotelian principles to modern genres, such as the novel or the film, often fail to take into account the fact that the philosopher was not concerned with all possible kinds of literature, but with a very limited range of genres, and that in most of the *Poetics,* he was dealing with only the single genre of Greek tragedy.

[*See also* Katharsis; Plato; Poetics; *and* Tragedy, *article on* Greek Tragedy.]

BIBLIOGRAPHY

Works by Aristotle

Aristotelis De arte poetica liber. Edited by Rudolfus Kassel. Oxford, 1966.
Aristotle on the Art of Poetry. Translated and edited by Ingram Bywater. Oxford, 1909; reprint, New York, 1980.
The Complete Works of Aristotle: The Revised Oxford Translation. 2 vols. Edited by Jonathan Barnes. Princeton, N.J., 1984.
Poetics. Edited by D. W. Lucas. Corr. ed. Oxford, 1972.
Poetics I with the Tractatus Coislinianus, a Hypothetical Reconstruction of Poetics II, The Fragments of the On Poets. Translated by Richard Janko. Indianapolis, 1987.

Other Sources

Barnes, Jonathan, Malcolm Schofield, and Richard Sorabji, eds. *Articles on Aristotle,* vol. 4, *Psychology and Aesthetics.* New York, 1979.
Belfiore, Elizabeth S. *Tragic Pleasures: Aristotle on Plot and Emotion.* Princeton, N.J., 1992.
Else, Gerald F. *Aristotle's Poetics: The Argument.* Cambridge, Mass., 1957.
Golden, Leon. *Aristotle on Tragic and Comic Mimesis.* Atlanta, 1992.
Halliwell, Stephen. *Aristotle's Poetics.* London, 1986.

Janko, Richard. *Aristotle on Comedy: Toward a Reconstruction of Poetics II.* London, 1984.
Jones, John. *On Aristotle and Greek Tragedy.* New York and Oxford, 1962; reprint, Stanford, Calif., 1980.
Lesky, Albin. *Greek Tragic Poetry.* Translated by Matthew Dillon. New Haven, 1983.
Pickard-Cambridge, Arthur. *The Dramatic Festivals of Athens.* 2d ed. Revised by John Gould and D. M. Lewis. Oxford, 1988.
Rorty, Amélie Oksenberg, ed. *Essays on Aristotle's Poetics.* Princeton, N.J., 1992.

ELIZABETH BELFIORE

Aristotle on Mimesis

Aristotle's *Poetics* opens with an analysis that differentiates tragic drama from other species of poetry and music as distinct forms of *mimēsis* (mimesis), while leaving mimesis itself in the dark. Its meaning begins to emerge when Aristotle turns to consider the natural source of the art of poetry and locates it in a distinctively human imitative capacity: the living being who is at once the unique possessor of logos—language and reason (*Nicomachean Ethics* 1097b30–98a4)—and the "political animal," whose potential is to be realized by living together with others (*Politics* 1253a3–10), is at the same time "the most mimetic" of all animals (*Poetics* 4.1448b7). That this is no mere coincidence is suggested by the twofold notion of mimesis in which the roots of the poetic art are to be found.

On the one hand, from childhood on we are inclined to imitate and the first things we learn are by imitating (4.1448b4–8): the process by which we acquire our native language, or that by which we form our dispositions of character, testifies at once to our being by nature imitative, sociable, and potentially rational. In such behavioristic mimicry, we assimilate ourselves to another; a certain distance, on the contrary, is required for the natural experience associated with mimesis in another sense, that is, the special pleasure that accompanies contemplation of an image.

Even, or especially, when the object of such a representation is in itself something painful to see—such as "shapes of the most dishonorable beasts," Aristotle suggests, or corpses—there is a peculiar pleasure in contemplating the most precise possible likeness of it (4.1448b9–12). Aristotle explains this experience by referring, once again, to learning, which is most pleasant, he grants, not only to philosophers but even to others—to whatever small extent they share in it; only this kind of learning, productive of pleasure, is not a matter of habituation, but the recognition that results from seeing an image and inferring. "This is that" (4.1448b12–17). Aristotle suggests what is at stake in such a recognition when, in *Parts of Animals,* he encourages the study even of "the more dishonorable animals," which, however repulsive to perception, furnish immense pleasure to one who is able to "recognize the causes," that is, one who is by nature philosophical; for if we appreciate images of such creatures that manifest the artfulness of the crafts-man, surely we should enjoy contemplating the organism it-self, where nature exhibits the beautiful through the fitting-ness of parts to whole and the absence of chance (*Parts of Animals* 645a6–24). Tragic drama, if it is analogous, would produce its peculiar pleasure by transforming the ugliness of the action it represents; unless a sequence of events could have in itself the teleological design of an organism, tragedy would accomplish this transformation, not by the uncover-ing of a hidden order of nature, but by the construction of one through its mimetic art.

Although our experience of contemplative pleasure may be as natural as our imitative inclination, the mimetic repre-sentation that produces it is not. The subordination of one of these senses of mimesis to the other—the natural to the artful—guides the argument of the *Poetics* as it moves through three stages. In the first, an analysis differentiating the species of poetry within the genus of mimetic art (chap-ters 1–3) prepares for a genetic account of tragedy and com-edy as expressions of the distinctive natures of the poets (chapters 4–5). Once tragedy has been differentiated from the outside and observed in its coming into being, the argu-ment moves, in a second stage, to analyze its "being" or "substance" (chapters 6ff.), as determined by plot, the inter-nal principle that makes the mimetic work one and a whole. The seemingly self-enclosed mimetic work has, however, as a third stage of the argument reveals, a function *(ergon)* that involves its effect on the spectator (chapters 13–14); but this effect, far from reinstating the mimetic assimilation of our-selves to another, results, rather, from our contemplation at a distance of the beautifully constructed plot.

It is the first stage of the argument of the *Poetics* in which mimesis as a natural inclination for imitation is most at home. Employing, like other species of poetry and music, rhythm, harmony, and logos as the means by which its mimesis is carried out (chapter 1), tragedy is separated from epic on the basis of the manner in which the poet ex-presses himself—in drama he never speaks in his own voice but remains hidden behind his characters (chapter 3), and from comedy on the basis of the character type that is the object of the poet's mimesis (chapter 2), for "the imitators imitate those acting" (1448a1). This ambiguous statement might seem to fit best the actors on stage, in their impersonation of dramatic characters. "The imitators" must refer in the first place, though, to the poets, for it is to a difference in their natures that the split between two kinds of drama is being traced: at the outset, the more serious poets repre-sented beautiful actions and characters, the inferior poets actions of the inferior (4.1448b24–26). But insofar as the characters of tragedy are divided from those of comedy in being "better than us" or worse, while both may have to be in some respects "such as ourselves" (2.1448a1–5, 15.1454b9–12), it is we, the audience, who provide the stan-dard; if we in turn, then, emulate, in the case of tragedy, the

superior figure through which the poet has already pro-jected his own nature, we too would count as imitators who "imitate those acting" and mimesis would proceed, not just from the real person to the fictional image, but in the oppo-site direction as well.

The notion of a mimetic chain that passes from the poet through his dramatic character to the spectator (cf. Plato's *Ion* 535e–536d) disappears almost without a trace once the argument of the *Poetics* turns, in its second stage, to the ques-tion of what tragedy is in itself. The primary sign of this turn, for that reason, is a change in the identification of the object of mimesis: tragedy, according to the definition of its being, is the representation of an action and it is only because it is the mimesis of a *praxis*, Aristotle argues at this point, that tragedy must represent those who are acting (6.1450b3–4). What makes the drama's representation of an action one, complete, and a whole is the "arrangement of the incidents" or plot *(muthos)*. Character must be as subordinate to plot, therefore, as color is to outline in a painted representation. Plot is the "end" *(telos)* of the drama (6.1450a21–22) because it is "as it were, the soul" of it (6.1450a37–38), and the soul, according to Aristotle, is the same in a sense as the whole ani-mal whose life principle it is.

In unfolding the ways in which plot confers on a sequence of events a unity and completeness analogous to that of a sin-gle organism, Aristotle makes it clear that tragedy's mimetic representation cannot be a passive "mirror of nature." The limits plot sets on the action it represents—a beginning that does not follow from anything else and an end from which nothing else follows—constitute a frame imposed by art that no sequence of incidents in life would seem capable of sup-plying. The action that plot represents is rendered beautiful not only by its order, but also by its magnitude: whereas events in life are apt to be like the very small animal, of which our view is confused, or like one so gigantic that we cannot take in the whole, the mimesis of action in tragic drama aims at a magnitude that makes manifest its articulated parts and the whole to which they belong (7.1450b34–1451a6). By its own logic, plot binds together the sequence of incidents it represents in accordance with necessity or probability (9.1451a36–38): probability seems to be a standard for the correspondence of the representation to our expectations about reality—how certain sorts of persons would act in cer-tain sorts of situations—whereas necessity must be a stan-dard for the coherence of the representation in itself, of which no part could be transposed or removed without de-stroying that whole. Because in reality chance is inelim-inable, and even the improbable has its place, both principles serve to transform the contingency of life into the teleologi-cal design of the mimetic work. This transformation makes poetry the mimesis of that which could or would happen, and in this respect "more philosophical" than history, whose proper object is that which has actually happened (9.1451a36–b7).

The account of tragedy as a self-contained whole, with plot as its internal *telos,* is initiated by the formal definition of tragedy as the representation of action (chapter 6), for which Aristotle claims to have gathered up the material from the preceding discussion. Nothing prepared, however, for the concluding element of that definition, which establishes not what tragedy is but what it does, in "accomplishing through pity and fear the katharsis of such passions" (6.1449b27–28). In this function lies tragedy's power to "lead souls" (*psychagogei,* 6.1450a32–34). The introduction of this function in the definition of tragedy anticipates a third stage of the argument, in which the mimetic work comes to be understood in some relation to its audience, and it is this relation that in fact provides the requisite criterion for evaluating the formal whole of tragic plot.

In the midst of criticizing episodic plots, which violate the principles of probability or necessity, Aristotle recalls that tragic plot must be a mimesis, not just of complete action, but of that which is fearful and pitiable. That requires a sequence of incidents arranged one as the consequence of another, but at the same time contrary to expectation. Aristotle offers, in illustration, the story of the statue of Mitys at Argos: while being contemplated by the murderer of Mitys, it suddenly fell on his head and killed him. Even what does come about by chance, Aristotle comments, seems most wondrous when it appears to have occurred in a providential way (9.1452a1–11). The most beautiful construction of such a sequence of incidents is the accomplishment of a privileged plot structure—"complex" as opposed to "simple." Its distinctive features are "reversal," when the action turns not just on a change of fortune—every drama has that—but on a moment that leads to precisely the opposite outcome from what was intended by it, and "discovery," when the logic of events that brought about that unintended result comes to be recognized by the character involved in it (chapters 10–11). In a complex plot, the action of the whole, in which the tragic character's intention is embedded, reveals who he is in a way that his own intention could not; such a plot, in being mimetic of pitiable and fearful things, accomplishes most beautifully the function of tragedy (13.1452b30–33).

Plot can be the *telos* of drama without sealing it off from any relation to its audience because it is the arrangement of the incidents in itself, ideally, that contains tragedy's power to "lead souls." The effect produced on the spectator, referred to in the definition of tragedy, without further explanation, as a matter of "catharsis," seems to be one with, or necessarily accompanied by, the "peculiar pleasure" tragedy aims to produce "from pity and fear through mimesis" (13.1453b10–14). If, in actual experience, pity is a luxury that the state of fear precludes (*Rhetoric* II.8), what allows both to affect us together must be our perspective as spectators, who identify with the tragic character enough to fear while standing back to pity what we think of as his un-

deserved suffering. The mimetic assimilation of oneself to another is not entirely suppressed, then, by plot as the representation of an action; it is the natural response that has been harnessed in the service of plot, so that tragedy can achieve the function of arousing its peculiar pleasure. Such a pleasure was illustrated, originally, by the experience of contemplating the precise image of a repulsive animal and coming to recognize, "This is that": this ugly and unintelligible creature is beautiful when mind discovers its hidden design or order. If the tragic character, in his discovery, comes to recognize his unintentional crime as belonging to some design of the gods or fate, what the spectator discovers, with his double vision, is not that, or not only that, but the design of the plot as the product of the mimetic art of the poet.

[*See also* Mimesis; *and* Plato, *article on* Mimesis.]

BIBLIOGRAPHY

Works by Aristotle

Aristotle's Theory of Poetry and Fine Art. 4th ed. Translated and edited by S. H. Butcher. Reprint, New York, 1951.
Poetics. Edited by D. W. Lucas. Corr. ed. Oxford, 1972.

Other Sources

Belfiore, Elizabeth S. *Tragic Pleasures: Aristotle on Plot and Emotion.* Princeton, N.J., 1992.
Benardete, Seth. "On Greek Tragedy." In *Current Developments in the Arts and Sciences: The Great Ideas Today.* Chicago, 1980.
Davis, Michael. *Aristotle's Poetics: The Poetry of Philosophy.* Lanham, Md., 1992.
Else, Gerald F. *Aristotle's Poetics: The Argument.* Cambridge, Mass., 1957.
Else, Gerald F. "'Imitation' in the Fifth Century." *Classical Philology* 53 (1958):73–90.
Golden, Leon. *Aristotle on Tragic and Comic Mimesis.* American Classical Studies, no. 29. Atlanta, 1993.
Goldstein, H. D. "Mimesis and Catharsis Reexamined." *Journal of Aesthetics and Art Criticism* 24 (1966):567–577.
Halliwell, Stephen. *Aristotle's Poetics.* London, 1986.
Koller, Hermann. *Die Mimesis in der Antike.* Bern, 1954.
McKeon, Richard P. "Literary Criticism and the Concept of Imitation in Antiquity." In *Critics and Criticism: Ancient and Modern,* edited by R. S. Crane, pp. 147–175. Chicago, 1952.
Rorty, Amélie Oksenberg, ed. *Essays on Aristotle's Poetics.* Princeton, N.J., 1992.
Trench, W. F. "Mimesis in Aristotle's *Poetics.*" *Hermathena* 48 (1933): 1–24.

RONNA BURGER

Aristotle on Form and Unity

Concepts of form and unity are fundamental to Aristotle's understanding of mimetic works of art and our experiences of them. His remarks on the subject are terse but pregnant: they convey a position whose mature poise renders it a still valuable and influential reference point in aesthetics. Some of these remarks, however, have often been considered too much in isolation, with the result that Aristotle's stance has frequently been misconstrued as formalist, where that denotes a doctrine of self-sufficient form that is independent of representational, referential, or expressive value.

In the general terms of Aristotelian philosophy, form is what makes an entity essentially what it is. Form is the structure or organization that gives something its specific nature and allows it to fulfill its function. But since the world is not encountered simply as a collection of discrete individuals, form can also be grasped as that which makes something a certain *kind* of thing (a man, a tree, a tragedy). Form is a property of particular things, but a property that embodies the common nature of classes of things. Aristotle sometimes uses a work of art to illustrate this area of his thought: he distinguishes, for example, the form that makes a statue a recognizable artifact from the material of which it is made (*Physics* 7.3, 245b9–16, *Metaphysics* 7.7, 1033a5–23, 1035a1–9). To apprehend a statue is not to identify its physical composition but to perceive the intelligible design that it possesses. We should therefore expect Aristotle, when addressing representational art in its own right, to treat form not as an autotelic principle, but as a major dimension of how mimetic works, both as particulars and as instances of types (genres), can be meaningfully interpreted. That is indeed what we do find.

Aristotle's most explicit remarks on artistic and aesthetic form occur in the *Poetics*. Especially illuminating is the following: "A beautiful object, whether an animal or anything else with a structure of parts, should have not only its parts ordered but also an appropriate magnitude: beauty consists in magnitude and order, which is why there could not be a beautiful animal which was either minuscule . . . or gigantic. . . . So just as with our bodies and with animals beauty requires magnitude, but magnitude which allows coherent perception, likewise plots require length, but length that can be coherently remembered" (*Poetics* 7.1450b34–51a6).

This compressed passage allows us to observe several key aspects of Aristotle's thinking. First, form is a principle that applies equally to artifacts and to organisms; but that hardly makes Aristotle an organicist, since he conceives of artistic form not as developing quasi-spontaneously from within, but as imposed by the maker's rational control: "by art/craft *(technê)* come the things whose form is in the soul [of the maker]; and by 'form' I mean the essence and primary substance of things" (*Metaphysics* 7.7, 1032a32–b2, cf. 1.6, 988a2–4). Second, not all forms are beautiful, but only those whose structure is matched by an appropriate size or scale. Scale, as *Politics* 7.4, 1326a33–b5, makes clear, is related to function; that is why Aristotle states the appropriate size for tragedy in terms of its defining concern with certain kinds of human happening ("the size which permits a transformation to occur . . . from adversity to prosperity or prosperity to adversity," *Poetics* 7.1451a12–14). Third, the conditions of beauty do not amount to an a priori prescrip-

tion; they are extrapolated from the parameters of human perception and judgment: a gigantic animal cannot be beautiful insofar as *we* cannot see beauty in it (because "contemplation of it has no cohesion, but those who contemplate it lose a sense of unity and wholeness," *Poetics* 7.1450b39–51a2). Finally, unity is construed as nothing other than wholeness and perfection of form.

Form, then, is simultaneously an intrinsic property of a work of art and the unifying principle of its representational nature. To discern form is to discern significance. But whereas some modern aestheticians have used "significant form" to denote a completely autonomous aesthetic feature, independent of reality in general and fitted for disinterested contemplation, the significance of form within Aristotelian aesthetics is inseparable from the mimetic character of works of art. For reasons rooted in the Greek tradition, Aristotle scarcely reckons with purely abstract artistic or aesthetic features (though *Poetics* 4.1448b18–19 alludes to their existence). Form consists of an organization of parts, but an organization that functions as the bearer of meaning. The form and unity of a work of art cannot be explicated, on Aristotle's model, without at least implicit reference to the world. Thus unity is not a self-contained condition, but implies a certain kind of imagined reality: "Just as in the other mimetic arts [including music, dance, and the visual arts] a unitary mimesis has a unitary object, so too the plot [of tragedy], since it is mimesis of an action, should be of a unitary and indeed whole action" (*Poetics* 8.1451a30–32). The object of mimesis need not be some identifiable particular in the world; indeed, the finest poetry, which is Aristotle's main concern, aspires to the philosophical condition of conveying universals (*Poetics* 9.1451b5–10). But the point remains that form and unity inside the work of art constitute a structure whose intelligibility connects it to the world outside the work. In a passage of the *Politics*, Aristotle states that pleasure and pain in the experience of mimetic art are closely related to pleasure and pain felt toward actuality, and he writes: "For example, if someone enjoys contemplating a portrait of someone for no other reason than the depicted form, he is bound to find it pleasant to contemplate the person who is the subject of the portrait" (*Politics* 8.5, 1340a23–8). Although the example is deliberately simple, and ignores the possible complexity of aesthetic pleasure (cf. *Poetics* 4.1448b10–17), it confirms that the form of a representational work, and the way in which it is interpreted, cannot be divorced from the kind of reality that is the subject of the work.

In the case of tragedy, where Aristotle puts his principles most fully into practice, form and unity are analyzed as features of plot *(muthos)*. Aristotle calls plot "the first principle and, as it were, soul of tragedy" (*Poetics* 6.1450a38–9): just as soul is the "form," the organizing principle, of a natural body (*De anima* 2.1, 412a19–21), so plot is the essential form of a tragedy. When discussing tragic plot, Aristotle makes many technical points about the shapes of plays: he distinguishes "simple" from "complex" plots, for example, and employs concepts such as "reversal," "recognition," "episode," "complication," and "dénouement." But these and other details are all defined in terms that call for reference to the human subject matter of drama: what counts as an episode, for example, depends on the judgment of what is or is not integral to a certain sequence of action. Moreover, the identification of generic components and plot patterns is subordinate to the guiding thesis that unity of plot, beauty of tragic form, is constituted by the representation of "a unitary object," that is, an action that can be followed and understood as a coherent pattern of events (of the appropriate, fear-and-pity-inducing kind). That is why Aristotle repeatedly invokes the criteria of "necessity and/or probability" (*Poetics* 7.1451a12–13), for these supply the standards of causal, logical, and explanatory connection by which we find, or fail to find, intelligibility in human life and the world in general, and by which the dramatic representation of action must consequently also be appraised.

To judge artistic form is not, however, to measure it in some straightforward way against common or average reality. On the contrary, Aristotle repeatedly allows for divergence between the representational field of mimesis and ordinary experience of the world: the life of a particular individual, for instance, may lack the degree of unity that is desirable in a tightly knit plot structure (*Poetics* 8.1451a16–19); and the mimetic arts as a whole are not restricted to depicting types of reality that are known to have occurred (*Poetics* 9.1451b4–5, 25.1460b8–11). This means that what will count as necessary or probable depends very much on both generic conventions and the particular context. The application of criteria of coherence or unity will always start from relationships within the work itself, and will accommodate the genre-related expectations of consistency that cultural tradition has established. But coherence in a mimetic art will ultimately, on the Aristotelian account, require reference to canons of sense that cannot themselves be exclusively artistic: the interpretation of form and unity must draw on notions of what the world is really like.

Everything said so far points to the conclusion that a distinction between form and content is difficult in Aristotelian terms. Of course it is possible to generalize content discursively, in the sense that we can speak, say, of a myth that has been used by several poets, and comment on the different forms that they have given it. Equally, works on different subjects can, at a certain level of abstraction, be considered as having the same, or very similar, form: hence Aristotle's remark that "it is right to count plays as different or the same principally by plot: that is, 'the same' means having the same complication and dénouement" (*Poetics* 18.1456a7–9). But in the case of any given work, form and content will be closely interlocked. This is implicit in the concept of a tragic plot structure, which is defined as "the mimesis of the action, . . . the construction of events" (*Poetics* 6.1450a3–5). In the strictest sense, the form of a tragedy *is* its plot-structure—the design embodied in its depiction of a nexus of action.

Unity is not something over and above form; it is completeness and perfection *of* form. In the case of tragedy, completeness is defined in terms of the sequence, "beginning, middle, and end" (*Poetics* 7.1450b26–7), and in elucidating this formula Aristotle again invokes the principles of necessity and probability. What matters for unity of structure and form is not just *any* sense of closure, but a certain sort of plausibility, a plausibility based (for drama) on the connections between a play's constituent events. True beauty of form entails the integration of the parts; it cannot be achieved by individual or discrete elements: "a painter would never allow a figure to have a foot that was disproportionate, however beautiful it might be in itself" (*Politics* 3.13, 1284b8–10). Proportion, *summetria*, is an important source and aspect of beauty (cf. *Metaphysics* 13.3, 1078a36–b1), but the discernment of aesthetic proportion rests on cognitive attention to a work's figurative, narrative, or dramatic substance.

The views presented here amount to a paradigmatic model of "closed" form, in the sense of form that leaves little room for open-ended or unresolved significance. But the closed form that Aristotle advocates is not an ideal of autonomy or independence but of complete and lucid intelligibility. In this light, it is a mistake to interpret Aristotle as a prescriptive formalist in aesthetics, because to do so overlooks the link between his concepts of form and beauty and his mimeticism. The subtlety of Aristotle's position has long suffered, moreover, from confusion with certain reductive and rule-bound products of neoclassicism, especially the Renaissance doctrine of the three unities. Aristotle can fairly be said to have emphasized one kind of unity at the expense of others, but he did so not through doctrinaire inflexibility but from a considered perspective on aesthetic understanding. Schiller was therefore right, in his letter to Goethe of 5 May 1797, to contrast Aristotle both with those who overvalue purely external form in art and with those who ignore form altogether.

[*See also* Formalism.]

BIBLIOGRAPHY

Work by Aristotle

Poetics. Translated and edited by S. Halliwell. In *Aristotle Poetics, Longinus on the Sublime, Demetrius on Style.* Loeb Classical Library. Cambridge, Mass., 1995.

Other Sources

Belfiore, Elizabeth S. *Tragic Pleasures: Aristotle on Plot and Emotion.* Princeton, N.J., 1992.
Halliwell, Stephen. *Aristotle's Poetics.* London, 1986.

Heath, Malcolm. *Unity in Greek Poetics.* Oxford, 1989.
Cherniss, Harold F. "Form and Its Relation to Matter." In *Aristotle's Criticism of Plato and the Academy,* chap. 3, pp. 174–479. Reprint, New York, 1962.

STEPHEN HALLIWELL

Reception of Aristotle in Antiquity

Aristotle's aesthetic theory, now rightly recognized as lying at the root of modern aesthetics, semiotics, and art theory, was taken at face value in antiquity as applying only to literature, and specifically poetry. It was known during most of antiquity not from the *Poetics,* his difficult lecture notes (in two book rolls), but rather through other works of his, now lost, principally the dialogue *On Poets* in three "books." Indeed, his lecture notes were mostly unpublished until Cicero's time, whereas his dialogues always circulated widely, being, like Cicero's dialogues, popularizing works intended for a general audience. Even so, the *On Poets* contained, as well as biographical material about poets, an account of Aristotle's own poetic theory, overlapping considerably with parts of the *Poetics.* From a refutation in the *On Poems* IV of the Epicurean poet and aesthetic theorist Philodemus (c.110–35 BCE), we now know that it *(a)* distinguished between comedy and tragedy according to the characters represented (cf. *Poetics* 2), *(b)* argued that tragedy is superior to epic (cf. *Poetics* 5), and *(c)* claimed that tragedy achieves its effect through speech, not through song *(melos).* Elsewhere in *On Poems* Philodemus summarizes *(d)* Aristotle's theory of tragic and comic catharsis, another topic of the *On Poets,* as the Neoplatonists reveal (see later in this article). From other fragments we know that in it Aristotle *(e)* defined poetry according to mimesis, as including mime and Socratic dialogue (cf. *Poetics* 1), *(f)* discussed faults in poetry, using some of the same examples as in *Poetics* 15, and *(g)* reviewed the origins of the major poetic genres, including epic, elegiac, and didactic verse, dithyramb, tragedy, and comedy (cf. *Poetics* 4–5, but with poetic quotations and more historical detail).

Aristotle's dialogue was fundamental to literary biography and scholarship in the Hellenistic period, which was dominated by Peripatetic approaches; above all, the Homeric and tragic critic Aristarchus (d. c.144 BCE) was deeply Aristotelian in his assumptions and procedures. Yet it is uncertain even whether he knew Aristotle's *Homeric Questions,* a major work of literary interpretation of the Homeric epics (in six or nine "books"). The *On Poets* was also basic to early Hellenistic poetics, together with the cognate views of Aristotle's contemporaries Heraclides Ponticus and Theophrastus. Heraclides, however, argued that Homer aimed at both truth and entertainment, a crude dichotomy that Aristotle avoided, and Theophrastus drew a distinction between poetry and truth; also, the latter's definitions of the major genres lack the overarching cohesion of Aristotle's. The *On Poets* is lost, so we cannot reconstruct its influence in detail; nonetheless, it is clear that there was eventually a strong reaction against Aristotelian aesthetics. Thus, the scholar-poet Callimachus (d. c.240 BCE) favored epic over tragedy, shorter over longer poems, and small topics over bigger ones, but still upheld Aristotelian ideals of unity and representation.

That the Hellenistic period was rife with multifarious critical theories has recently become clear from the writings of Philodemus, whose *On Poems,* in which he critiques them, is at last being reconstructed. Radical theorists generally went to one extreme or the other of the polarities that Aristotle had balanced so skillfully. Thus, Eratosthenes (c.274–194 BCE) held that the purpose of Homer's poetry was sheer entertainment, discounting the element of learning in Aristotelian *katharsis* (catharsis) through *mimēsis* (mimesis). Neoptolemus of Parium (c.200 BCE), on whose theory Horace is alleged to have based the *Ars poetica,* recast Aristotle's views in a more rigid manner, dividing poetics into *poesis* (plot construction), *poema* (versification), and *poetes* (the composer); this method of treating the subject, effectively separating form from content, became widespread. Others, the so-called *kritikoi* (Andromenides, Pausimachus, and Heracleodorus) broke completely with Aristotelian mimesis by arguing that the excellence of a poem lies solely in its sound, which can be appreciated by the trained ear alone; the sense is irrelevant. Some felt that word choice was paramount, others word order, but all insisted on that basic separation of form from content that Aristotle's theory had transcended. Crates of Mallos (d. c.150 BCE) advanced a similar theory, combining it with a search for allegorical interpretations of Homeric poetry.

By about 50 BCE, a reaction in favor of Aristotelian theory began, marked by the work of Philodemus. As an Epicurean, Philodemus insisted that poetry must bring pleasure, but he combatted euphonist theories vigorously; it is the mind that must be pleased, not the ear. For him, as for Aristotle, form and content are inseparable; if the words are altered, so is the sense. But the sense matters more. Philodemus's pupils included the greatest poets of Augustan Rome—Virgil and Horace. Under his influence, Virgil combined the attention to fine detail characteristic of Hellenistic poetry with an Aristotelian conception of great literature as being about significant human action to create the *Aeneid;* and Horace, in his *Ars poetica,* made an Aristotelian case for the need for Roman tragedy to match that of the Greeks, both in grandeur and in polish. The *Ars poetica* is thoroughly Aristotelian in its principles, although such direct parallels as there are may derive from Aristotle's *On Poets* rather than his *Poetics.* However, Pseudo-Longinus's *On the Sublime* may also be Augustan in date; although it takes the same side as Horace in calling for great, if imperfect, literature, it displays few signs of Aristotle's influence.

This revival of Aristotelian aesthetics had little to do with the publication of Aristotle's lecture notes, including the entire *Poetics*, by Andronicus of Rhodes (c.50 BCE). The *Poetics* always had a limited circulation, and the corrupt state of its text confirms that it was rarely read; moreover, no Greek or Roman scholar ever wrote a commentary on it. Between the Augustan age and the third century CE, traces of Aristotelian aesthetics are rare. Aristotle's lecture notes began to be studied intensively in the philosophical schools, however, which eventually ensured their survival at the expense of his other works. The latest author who knew the *Homeric Questions* is Porphyry (c.234–304 CE). The *On Poets*, but not the *Poetics*, is still cited by Macrobius (c.430 CE) and Proclus (412–485 CE). The Neoplatonists attempted to reconcile the teachings of Plato and Aristotle while upholding the spiritual value of such classics of pagan literature as the Homeric epics. Proclus accepted that poetry was a mimesis of universals, but not in Aristotle's sense of generalized patterns of human action; instead, poetry could imitate the Platonic Forms directly.

The Neoplatonists also supply our clearest information about Aristotle's theory of tragic and comic catharsis. Aristotle's response to Plato's attack on poetry had also been a response to Plato's hostility to the emotions. In his *Ethics*, Aristotle argues that a disposition can be developed to feel emotion correctly, that is, in the proper circumstances and to the right degree; emotions, combined with understanding, then become a guide to right action. Poetry need not induce us to indulge emotions that should be suppressed, as Plato held (*Republic* X 605d–606d); on the contrary, it can help to habituate us to feel the correct emotional responses, and thereby to approach the mean between the extremes, where virtue lies. Here Aristotle's theory of mimesis is crucial: by watching a representation of the actions and sufferings of others, we can benefit from experiencing emotions that could be harmful if they were based on reality—painful feelings like pity and fear in the case of serious genres like tragedy and epic, and pleasant ones like laughter in the case of nonserious genres like comedy and invective:

> When listening to representations *(mimēseis)*, everyone comes to share in the emotion, even apart from the rhythms and songs in themselves. Since *mousikē* (i.e. literature and music) happens to belong among pleasant things, and virtue is concerned with feeling delight correctly and loving and hating correctly, clearly one should learn, and become habituated to, nothing so much as judging correctly, i.e. feeling delight in decent characters and fine actions. Rhythms and songs contain especially close likenesses *(homoiomata)* of the true natures of anger and mildness, bravery, self-restraint and all their opposites, and of the other character-traits: this is clear from the facts—we are moved in our soul when we listen to such things. Habituation to feeling both pain and delight in things that are like [reality] is close to being in the same state regarding reality.
>
> (Aristotle, *Politics* VIII.5, translated by R. Janko)

We would hardly recognize this as the theory of catharsis mentioned in *Poetics* 6 and *Politics* VIII.7 if we lacked the testimonies of Philodemus, Iamblichus (c.280–340 CE), and Proclus:

> A poet represents a complete action. . . . Poetry is useful with regard to virtue, purifying, as we said, the [related] part [of the soul].   (Philodemus, *On Poems*, papyrus 1581, frag. I Nardelli)
>
> By observing others' emotions in both comedy and tragedy, we can check our own emotions, make them more moderate and purify them.   (Iamblichus, *On the Mysteries* I.11)
>
> It has been objected that tragedy and comedy are expelled [from Plato's *Republic*] illogically, if by means of them one can satisfy the emotions in due measure and . . . keep them tractable for education. . . . It was this that gave Aristotle and the defenders of these kinds of poetry in his dialogue against Plato most of the grounds for their accusation against him.
>
> (Proclus, *Commentary on Plato's* Republic; Kroll p. 49)

Aristotle's equally important theory of comedy has also remained obscure until very recently. Remarks by him prove that he discussed catharsis, comedy, and the kinds of humor in *Poetics* book 2. Although quoted by Porphyry, book 2 now survives only in a brief, anonymous, and untitled summary, the *Tractatus Coislinianus*, in a Byzantine manuscript of around 920 CE, together with a fuller text of a limited portion of it in manuscripts of Aristophanes. Book 2 resembled book 1 in structure, including a recapitulation of the theory of mimesis, a definition of comedy, a distinction between comedy and invective (like that between tragedy and epic), and a survey of the qualitative and quantitative parts of comedy, which are the same as those of tragedy. It focused on humor rather than plot as the main feature of comedy, however, replacing the discussion of unity with that of the different types of humor. As *Poetics* 3 leads us to expect, Aristophanes is here the leading comic poet, as good as Homer and Sophocles in their respective genres, who attains a mean between the excessive buffoonery of earlier poets and the seriousness of later ones. Comic laughter concerns errors of body or spirit that are not painful or destructive (cf. *Poetics* 5). Comedy achieves a catharsis of the emotions concerned with pleasure, leading, for instance, to a mean between buffoonery and boorishness (cf. *Nicomachean Ethics* IV 1128a4–7, b5–9), or to that between boastfulness and understatement. Aristotle's discussion of the purpose of comedy and tragedy, catharsis, corresponds to his account of the origins of those genres in *Poetics* 4–5. The identification of this summary as deriving from *Poetics* book 2 is controversial: critics complain that parts of it are too like Aristotle, and other parts too unlike him, but they cannot have it both ways, and a better identification has yet to be advanced.

The full text of *Poetics* book 2 evidently disappeared in late antiquity; because the Neoplatonists placed the *Poetics* last in the corpus of Aristotle's *Organon*, it was vulnerable to loss. *Poetics* book 1 survived to be translated into Syriac, probably around 700 CE, and thence into Arabic by Abū Bishr Mattā in

932 CE. It became influential in the Islamic world, with commentaries by Ibn Sīnā (Avicenna, 980–1037 CE) and Ibn Rushd (Averroës, 1126–1198 CE). The Greek text survives in only two Byzantine manuscripts, one tenth-century, the other fourteenth-century, in date. Although William of Moerbeke had translated it into Latin in 1278 CE, it remained unknown in the West until the Aldine edition of 1508 CE. Book 2 remained wholly lost until the discovery of the *Tractatus Coislinianus* by J. A. Cramer in 1839 CE.

[*See also* Katharsis; Mimesis; *and* Poetics.]

BIBLIOGRAPHY

The *On Poets*

Aristotle. *Poetics I with the Tractatus Coislinianus, a Hypothetical Reconstruction of Poetics II, The Fragments of the On Poets.* Translated by Richard Janko, pp. 56–65, 175–195. Indianapolis, 1987.
Janko, Richard. "Philodemus' *On Poems* and Aristotle's *On Poets.*" *Cronache Ercolanesi* 21 (1991):5–64.

Hellenistic Literary Theory

Lamberton, Robert, and John J. Kearney, eds. *Homer's Ancient Readers: The Hermeneutics of Greek Epic's Earliest Exegetes.* Princeton, N.J., 1992.
Montanari, Franco, ed. *La Philologie grecque à l'époque hellénistique et romaine.* Entretiens sur l'Antiquité classique, 40. Geneva, 1994.

Philodemus and Horace

Horace. *Horace on Poetry:* vol. 1, *Prolegomena to the Literary Epistles* and vol. 2, *The 'Ars Poetica.'* Edited by Charles O. Brink. Cambridge, Mass., 1963–1971.
Obbink, Dirk, ed. *Philodemus and Poetry: Poetic Theory and Practice in Lucretius, Philodemus, and Horace.* New York and Oxford, 1995.
Proclus. *Commentary on Plato's Republic: In Platonis rem publicam Commentarii,* Vols. 1–2. Edited by W. Kroll. Leipzig, 1899–1901.

The Neoplatonists and Catharsis

Coulter, James A. *The Literary Microcosm: Theories of Interpretation of the Later Neoplatonists.* Columbia Studies in the Classical Tradition, 2. Leiden, 1976.
Eden, Kathy. *Poetic and Legal Fiction in the Aristotelian Tradition.* Princeton, N.J., 1986.
Janko, Richard. "From Catharsis to the Aristotelian Mean." In *Essays on Aristotle's Poetics,* edited by Amélie Oksenberg Rorty, pp. 341–358. Princeton, N.J., 1992.
Sheppard, Anne D. R. *Studies on the 5th and 6th Essays of Proclus' Commentary on the Republic.* Hypomnemata 61. Göttingen, 1980.
Sorabji, Richard, ed. *Aristotle Transformed: The Ancient Commentators and Their Influence.* Ithaca, N.Y., 1990.

Theory of Comedy

Heath, Malcolm. "Aristotelian Comedy." *Classical Quarterly* 39 (1989): 344–354.
Janko, Richard. *Aristotle on Comedy.* London, 1984.
Nesselrath, Heinz-Günther. *Die attische mittlere Komödie.* Berlin and New York, 1990. See pp. 65–187.

The *Poetics* in Arabic and Latin

Aristotle. *Die arabische Übersetzungen der Poetik des Aristotles und die Grundlage der Kritik des griechischen Textes.* 2 vols. Edited by Jaroslaus Tkatsch. Vienna, 1928–1932.
Aristotle. *Aristoteles Latinus XXXIII: De Arte Poetica.* 2d ed. Edited by L. Minio-Paluello. Brussels, 1968.
Brams, Jozef. "Guillaume de Moerbeke et Aristotle." In *Rencontres de cultures dans la philosophie médiévale: Traductions et traducteurs de l'antiquité tardive au XIVe siècle,* edited by Jacqueline Hamesse and Marta Fattori, pp. 317–336. Louvain, 1990.
Kemal, Salim. *The Poetics of Alfarabi and Avicenna.* Leiden, 1991.
Rushd, Ibn. *Averroes' Middle Commentary on Aristotle's Poetics.* Translated and edited by Charles E. Butterworth. Princeton, N.J., 1986.

RICHARD JANKO

Reception of Aristotle in Modernity

The *Poetics* of Aristotle has exerted its influence in the twentieth century in two important ways: first, as the subject of continuing scholarly inquiry that, after centuries of debate, has begun to reach a significant degree of consensus in the interpretation of key concepts; and second, as an important guide and stimulus for modern critics who are sympathetic to Aristotelian doctrine. Thus, Aristotle's famous definition of tragedy has taken on a different interpretative shape in the twentieth century from the one that dominated discussion in earlier centuries. The italicized phrases in the definition below have especially significant theoretical importance and have profited from insightful interpretation or reinterpretation by modern scholars:

> Tragedy is a representation *(mimēsis)* of an action involving characters worthy of respect *(praxeōs spoudaias)* and one that is complete and has magnitude; it is presented in language that has been made pleasurable by each of the kinds of pleasurable enhancement separately employed in the various parts of the play; it is a representation of characters acting and is not presented through narration; by means of *pity and fear* it accomplishes the *katharsis* of such emotions.

At the center of the Aristotelian theory of tragedy as well as at the core of the modern reinterpretation of Aristotelian literary theory is the key concept of *katharsis* (catharsis). In this regard, as Kevin Crotty, writes (1994, p. 15, n. 32): "A consensus seems to be forming that tragic catharsis has to do with the increased understanding, or 'clarification,' of the emotions brought about by the tragic performance and the experience of emotion in response to it." The history of this significant interpretative development represents one of the major advances offered by twentieth-century scholarship in our understanding of Aristotelian aesthetics.

In his important edition of the *Poetics* published in 1909, Ingram Bywater included an appendix on the various translations of the term *katharsis* that had appeared from 1527 to 1899. Two interpretations of the term almost exclusively control these translations: *medical purgation* and *moral purification.* A thorough examination of medical purgation as a homeopathic or allopathic process has been made by Elizabeth Belfiore (1992). In 1979, Donald Keesey noted that many modern critics of tragedy had abandoned Aristotle's key critical term because they found the dominant philological interpretations of catharsis totally unpersuasive as an account of tragic effect. He was, however, also able to report on the development of a new "cognitive" interpretation of catharsis that then was only known to him through the work of L. A. Post and Leon Golden, but which, in time, has won additional adherents. Such cognitive views of catharsis, Keesey (1978–1979) writes, were "in most respects consonant with several main lines of modern criticism" and would, "if accepted, make Aristotle's 'catharsis' once again a respectable critical term." Keesey specifically cites John Gassner, who had argued that "enlightenment," which brings about "an understanding of cause and effect," was *the* decisive feature of catharsis. Other critics, not mentioned by Keesey, also recognized an important cognitive goal in artistic experience. Francis Fergusson identified "perception" as the climactic stage of the audience's aesthetic experience; James Joyce used the term *epiphany* to describe the point at which an audience discovers the inner coherence of a work of art; and Austin Warren used the phrase "rage for order" to designate the goal of the poet and the aspiration of the reader of poetry.

In 1991, Mathias Luserke edited a series of nineteenth- and twentieth-century interpretative essays on the nature of catharsis. His volume reflects the powerful influence of Jacob Bernays, who revived the "purgation" theory of catharsis in the nineteenth century and extended its influence widely. The contributions of Schadewaldt, Flashar, and Pohlenz, included in Luserke's work, which he correctly judges still to be highly influential, operate in the shadow of Bernays's emphatic insistence on the role of medical purgation in the aesthetic response to tragedy. Luserke, however, included in his anthology two twentieth-century studies (Leon Golden, "The Clarification Theory of *Katharsis*" [and] Christian Wagner-Salzburg, "'Katharsis' in der Aristotelischen Tragödiendefinition") which argued for catharsis as "clarification."

What has occurred in the twentieth century in regard to catharsis is analogous to what Thomas Kuhn has called a "paradigm shift" in the natural sciences. Kuhn pointed out that scientific theories maintain their influence so long as their explanatory power remains broad and powerful. Whenever data are discovered that begin to subvert the explanatory power of a theory, and this happens with a certain regularity in the natural sciences, the possibility opens up for new theories to supplant the previously orthodox one. Not finding any definition of catharsis in the *Poetics* itself, scholars, over several centuries, sought guidance from (1) the use of that term in Aristotle's *Politics* to mean "medical purgation" and (2) the process of "purification" of such emotions as pity from excess and deficiency that is described in the *Nicomachaean Ethics*. The "purification" theory has had few defenders, but the interpretation of catharsis as "medical purgation" has been extremely popular.

Gerald Else (1957) called attention to serious weaknesses in this theory when he pointed out that the medical interpretation derived from the *Politics* "is inherently and indefeasibly *therapeutic*" and "presupposes that we come to tragic drama . . . as patients to be cured, relieved, restored to psychic health." Else correctly asserts that there is not a single word in the *Poetics* to support such a view.

Although Else offered persuasive criticisms of the "purgation" theory, the view he himself presented of catharsis as a substitute for it has not gained wide acceptance. The interpretation that has emerged to challenge the dominance of "purgation" and "purification" is the "clarification" theory, which has its roots in philology, Platonic aesthetics, the history of medicine, and psychoanalytical theory. Crotty, cited earlier as discerning a developing consensus for the interpretation of catharsis as "clarification," lists Golden, Halliwell, Janko, and Nussbaum among the adherents of that view. Several uses of the term *katharsis* in Greek texts testify to the fact it bears the meaning "intellectual clarification," but an especially powerful demonstration of this fact is found in Plato's *Theaetetus* 230 D–E, where *elenchos*, the Socratic process of cross-examination, is described as the "greatest and most authoritative of all forms of *katharsis*." That *katharsis*, in the sense of "intellectual clarification," best meets the requirements of Aristotle's argument about the essential nature of poetry in the *Poetics* is clearly seen from his statement in chapter 4 that the fundamental pleasure and final cause of all artistic activity is the pleasure of "learning and inference." Neither "purgation" nor "purification" are close rivals to "clarification" in establishing a relevant and consistent bond with this requirement. Support for the clarification theory has also been provided by the work of the medical historian Pedro Laín Entralgo (1970) and the psychiatrist and classical scholar Bennett Simon (1978). Laín Entralgo persuasively argued that catharsis must be understood as an intellectual phenomenon rather than a somatic one because the "agent of tragic catharsis is not a material purgative, nor even a melody, but rather that airy, invisible, material and immaterial reality that we call the 'word'" (p. 235). Simon linked the cognitive aspects of tragedy and psychotherapy when he wrote that in drama "the tragic figures in the plays struggle with their relationships and obligations to those in their past, present, and, future. The audience acquires a new sense of the possibilities in being human and in coming to terms with forces that are more powerful than any one individual," while "in therapy we also expect an enlarged view of the possibilities that are open in relationships to the self and to others" (p. 144).

Mimēsis. In the twentieth century, much work has been done by Else, Koller, D. W. Lucas, McKeon, Sörbom, and others in unraveling the meaning of *mimēsis* (mimesis) in Greek philosophical thought. Lucas (1972, Appendix I, pp. 258–272) extrapolates from this material an accurate view of Aristotle's doctrine of mimesis by correctly noting that the term can be rendered in different contexts as "imitate, represent, indicate, suggest," or "express." He accurately perceives that for Aristotle the appropriate mimetic form for a work of art is a "causally united structure" and understands that when the parts of a work of art are "in a necessary causal relationship with each other and the whole," then the work of art *"reveals something about the nature of an action under the conditions obtaining in our world"* (my emphasis). When one speaks of mimesis in the *Poetics,* then, one must understand a representation involving a causally connected sequence of action that leads to some sort of epiphany or clarification. This would be fully consistent with Aristotle's assertion in chapter 4 of the *Poetics* that the essential pleasure of mimesis is the intellectual pleasure of "learning and inference."

The translation here of the phrase *praxeôs spoudaias* as "an action involving characters worthy of respect" follows the perceptive judgments of Lucas (p. 66) and Rostagni (1945, p. 32), who connect it to Aristotle's explicit identification of tragedy as a mimesis of superior kinds of human beings in his discussion of tragic character in chapters 2 and 4. The far more common translation of the phrase as "serious action" is based on a distinction between serious and nonserious literature that Aristotle nowhere makes in the *Poetics.*

Pity, Fear, Hamartia. Aristotle himself explicitly discusses the nature of pity and fear in chapter 13 of the *Poetics.* Pity, he says, refers to the emotion we feel when we observe someone unjustly suffering misfortune, and fear to the emotion we experience when we observe that it is someone like ourselves who suffers this unjust misfortune. Lucas (1972, Appendix II, pp. 273–275) recognizes that pity is an easily understood and widely shared emotion. Aristotelian "fear" *(phobos),* he correctly notes, is an experience that reveals "the precariousness of the human condition" and makes "men fear for themselves." What must also be connected to this discussion is the term *hamartia* (treated by Lucas in Appendix IV, pp. 299–307), which has been subject to considerable dispute but whose precise meaning in Arisotle's *Poetics* has been significantly clarified by twentieth-century scholars such as van Braam (1912), Hey (1927), Bremer (1969), and Dawe (1967). These scholars have shown that *hamartia* in the context of Aristotle's definition of tragedy cannot mean what it often means in other contexts: "a flaw of character." A serious "flaw of character" would subvert the status of the tragic protagonist, who must remain "worthy of respect" *(spoudaios)* to earn pity and fear in Aristotle's sense of those terms. Aristotelian *hamartia* must, rather, represent an *intellectual* error that could cause a fall from happiness to misery as required in tragedy without undermining the moral stature of the tragic hero.

Aristotelian Influence in the Twentieth Century. In addition to the scholarly reassessment of key terms in Aristotle's theory of tragedy, a strong neo-Aristotelian move-

ment within the field of literary criticism and theory has emerged in the twentieth century. This movement arose in the mid-1930s among a group of scholars at the University of Chicago in the departments of English, Philosophy, and Modern Languages. The most prominent of the originating members of this group were R. S. Crane, W. R. Keast, R. P. McKeon, E. Olson, N. Maclean, and B. Weinberg. A manifesto stating their beliefs and demonstrating their methods was issued in 1952 and edited by R. S. Crane. The "Chicago School" was attracted to the *Poetics* by its rigorous methodology and because Aristotle, in Crane's words, "made available, though only in outline sketch, hypotheses and analytical devices for defining literally and inductively, and with a maximum degree of differentiation, the multiple causes operative in the construction of poetic wholes of various kinds and the criteria of excellence appropriate to each" (p. 17). Neither they nor their second- and third-generation successors as neo-Aristotelian critics felt compelled to follow the strict "word" of Aristotle. Unlike the scholars discussed in the first part of this article, who have striven to understand the precise meaning of Aristotle's actual text and doctrine, the neo-Aristotelian critics have labored under a generalized Aristotelian inspiration with the license to adopt, adapt, or modify Aristotelian positions as they find it useful or necessary.

Great progress made in the twentieth century in developing a consensus on the interpretation of the key terms catharsis, mimesis, *hamartia* in the *Poetics,* although by no means is there yet universal agreement on the meaning of these concepts. On the basis of the work that has been done, it is very likely that continuing progress will be made in understanding the original significance of the aesthetic doctrines of the *Poetics,* just as it is most probable that neo-Aristotelian critics, by their skillful adaptations of Aristotelian theory, will continue to find new and imaginative ways to maintain the vitality and authority of that theory.

[*See also* Katharsis; *and* Mimesis.]

BIBLIOGRAPHY

Works by Aristotle

Aristote: La Poétique. Edited by Roselyne Dupont-Roc and Jean Lallot. Paris, 1980.

Aristotle on the Art of Poetry. Translated and edited by Ingram Bywater. Oxford, 1909; reprint, New York, 1980.

Aristotele: Poetica. Edited by Augusto Rostagni. Turin, 1945.

Aristotle's Poetics: A Translation and Commentary for Students of Literature. Translated by Leon Golden, commentary by O. B. Hardison, Jr. Englewood Cliffs, N.J., 1968; reprint, Tallahassee, Fla., 1981.

Poetics. Edited by D. W. Lucas. Corr. ed. Oxford, 1972.

Poetics I with the Tractatus Coislinianus, a Hypothetical Reconstruction of Poetics II, The Fragments of the On Poets. Translated by Richard Janko. Indianapolis, 1987.

Other Sources

Belfiore, Elizabeth S. *Tragic Pleasures: Aristotle on Plot and Emotion.* Princeton, N.J., 1992.

Bernays, Jacob. *Zwei Abhandlungen über die aristotelische Theorie des Drama* (1880). Darmstadt, 1968.

Bernays, Jacob. *Grundzüge der verlorenen Abhandlung des Aristoteles über die Wirkung der Tragödie* (1857). Hildesheim, 1970.

Braam, P. van. "Aristotle's Use of Hamartia." *Classical Quarterly* 6.4 (October 1912): 266–272.

Bremer, J. M. *Hamartia: Tragic Error in the Poetics of Aristotle and in Greek Tragedy.* Amsterdam, 1969.

Cooper, Lane. *An Aristotelian Theory of Comedy.* New York, 1922.

Crane, R. S., ed. *Critics and Criticism: Ancient and Modern.* Chicago, 1952.

Crotty, Kevin. *The Poetics of Supplication: Homer's Iliad and Odyssey.* Ithaca, N.Y., 1994.

Dawe, R. D. "Some Reflections on Ate and Hamartia." *Harvard Studies in Classical Philology* 72 (1967): 89–123.

Else, Gerald F. *Aristotle's Poetics: The Argument.* Cambridge, Mass., 1957.

Flashar, Hellmut. "Die medizinischen Grundlagen der Lehre von der Wirkung der Dichtung in der griechischen Poetik." *Hermes* 84 (1956): 12–48.

Golden, Leon. *Aristotle on Tragic and Comic Mimesis.* Atlanta, 1992.

Halliwell, Stephen. *Aristotle's Poetics.* London, 1986.

Hey, O. "Hamartia." *Philologus* 83.2 (1927): 37–163.

Janko, Richard. *Aristotle on Comedy: Toward a Reconstruction of Poetics II.* London and Berkeley, 1984.

Keesey, Donald. "On Some Recent Interpretations of Catharsis." *The Classical World* 72.4 (December 1978–January 1979): 193–205.

Koller, Hermann. *Die Mimesis in der Antike.* Bern, 1954.

Laín Entralgo, Pedro. *The Therapy of the Word in Classical Antiquity.* Edited and translated by L. J. Rather and John M. Sharp. New Haven, 1970.

Luserke, Mathias, ed. *Die Aristotelische Katharsis.* Hildesheim, 1991.

McKeon, Richard P. "Literary Criticism and the Concept of Imitation in Antiquity." In *Critics and Criticism: Ancient and Modern,* edited by R. S. Crane, pp. 147–175. Chicago, 1952.

Post, L. A. *From Homer to Menander.* Berkeley, 1951.

Simon, Bennett. *Mind and Madness in Ancient Greece: The Classical Roots of Modern Psychiatry.* Ithaca, N.Y., 1978.

Sörbom, Goran. *Mimesis and Art: Studies in the Origin and Early Development of an Aesthetic Vocabulary.* Stockholm, 1966.

Stinton, T. C. W. "Hamartia in Aristotle and Greek Tragedy." *Classical Quarterly* 25.2 (December 1975): 221–254.

LEON GOLDEN

ARNHEIM, RUDOLF. [*To explore the work of Arnheim, a contemporary psychologist of art, this entry comprises two essays:*

Survey of Thought
Dynamics of Art

The first is an overview essay about Arnheim's psychology of art and its relationship to aesthetics. The second essay is by Arnheim, who here introduces a basic idea—dynamics—through which he proposes to understand some features common to all the arts. See also Perspective; *and* Tribal Art.]

Survey of Thought

Rudolf Arnheim (b.1904) has been a long-standing proponent of a perceptualist approach to (primarily visual) art based on Gestalt psychology. His central work is *Art and Visual Perception: A Psychology of the Creative Eye,* published in 1954 and revised in 1974. Arnheim uses the central thesis of Gestalt psychology—visual organization—as a guide to the fundamental meaning of the work of art. Every work, whether figurative or nonfigurative, has what Arnheim calls a "structural skeleton," and the configurations that constitute this skeleton disclose the work's meaning. "Structure" and "organization" have both phenomenal and physical meanings, for in Gestalt psychology's drive toward a kind of monism within which value may be naturalized, perceptual states have been hypothesized to bear a formal or "isomorphic" structure to the underlying brain processes supporting them.

Arnheim's approach mitigates against obscure iconographic symbolism because this is seen to deal only in accidental, historical significances rather than "universal" spontaneous symbolism. For Arnheim, in fact, a true symbol is something that tells us something about its referent through its own appearance. Confronted with an *Annunciation,* for example, Arnheim would care little about the attributes of the angel and the Virgin; more interesting would be their bearing to one another, whether they share the same space, the means by which the artist might differentiate their realms. Arnheim's theory raises several problems for aesthetic theory. As a primarily psychological theory, how relevant is it to aesthetics? Is Arnheim's understanding of the nature of art useful? Are his theories of expression and representation enlightening? And, finally, can a perceptualist approach do justice to the variability of the historical reception of art?

Arnheim always identifies himself as a psychologist and perhaps shares the natural scientific antipathy to philosophical hairsplitting of his teachers, Max Wertheimer (1880–1943) and Wolfgang Köhler (1887–1967). As a specifically *psychological* theorist, what can Arnheim contribute to the *philosophy* of art? Arnheim might have helped matters if he had underscored the gestalt idea that phenomenological description is a necessary propaedeutic to psychological explanation. Regardless of his conclusions, Arnheim's writings could then be situated in a broadly phenomenological tradition, and, like phenomenological aestheticians, this descriptive phenomenology could be subjected to ontologizing. Gestalt psychology, however, has a delicate relation to the phenomenological/physical distinction. When Arnheim points to the "stresses" and "strains" in visual configurations, he is appealing to phenomenological facts, but when he appeals to brain dynamics underlying such percepts, it seems to undercut the authority of the phenomenological (Beardsley, 1980).

Although Arnheim has reflected on such problems (1966, pp. 51–73), the purported novelty of speaking in both objective and psychological senses has to be addressed. He might have relied on the efforts of Maurice Mandelbaum

(1964), also influenced by Köhler, in particular the notion of a "radical critical realism," which does not assume *any* relationship between stimulation and perception. Only when the ambiguities of this situation are worked out could the true role of phenomenology be understood, because the role of this phenomenology would have been situated within the psychology.

In contrast to his most important competitor in psychological aesthetics, E. H. Gombrich, Arnheim easily discusses decoration, design, and ornament in the context of painting and sculpture and does not tend to produce a dichotomy between high and low art. He is also quite able to discuss traditional and East Asian forms of art. In this, his ideas of art are rather democratic. At the same time, critics like David Carrier (1986) have expressed doubts that Arnheim's theory is able to handle nonstandard works that are neither easel pictures nor freestanding sculptures. Once again, Arnheim's theory suffers from a lack of clarification of its fundamentals. Technically, his idea of art is both formal, focusing on the qualities of the artifact, and relational, requiring that works of art be made intentionally for artistic purposes. But the underlying ontological idea is unclear. On inspection, it is evident that Arnheim considers works of art as inherently lacking in the completeness of aspects or qualities enjoyed by real objects. In detail, this is essentially similar to the much more explicit framework provided by the phenomenologist Roman Ingarden in his discussions of "indeterminacies" of purely intentional (artistic) objects.

In such a more explicit framework, it is much easier to understand Arnheim's discussions of the distinctions between spatial and temporal works of art (1986, pp. 78–89), and the properties of individual media such as sculpture (1992, pp. 82–91) and architecture (1977). Carrier's contention that Arnheim is essentially unable to consider what is essentially "postperceptualist" art should be made in the context of Arnheim's collaboration with the artist-theorist Robert Sowers (1923–1990), who made much more explicit Arnheim's ideas about the various spatial modalities. Sowers (1984, 1990) outlined three abstract modalities—image, object, and habitation—that suggest a way in which an underlying core of invariants can be discerned amid seeming superficial differences. Judging from the more contemporary examples he is able to cite, Sowers's efforts seem promising. But they cannot be said to have solved the applicability of a perceptualist framework to postmodern concerns.

Arnheim's familiarity with perceptual psychology is promising for his discussions of both representation and expression. To represent, in gestalt perspective, is to offer a pithy, clear-cut ("prägnant") equivalent of an object. Neither bearing a true resemblance to the object, nor a simple denotative relationship, such an equivalence recalls Gombrich, but there is a difference. Arnheim's idea has tied up with it the nature of the medium into which the translation

of equivalence is made (1974, pp. 139–144). Depending on the medium—painting, for example—the kinds of limited resemblances that can be equated are broad and elementary. In contrast, when Gombrich stresses equivalence, he stresses an almost literal substitution in which there is confusion ("illusion") between the object and the representation. The success of Arnheim's alternative version depends on the rigidity with which he affirms this resemblance. Although he is most often thought to affirm it assertively, it is significant that Gombrich, well known for his critique of the "innocent eye," criticized Arnheim for the seeming relativization of perception suggested by his system.

Arnheim's contribution to the debate over the conventionality of perspective serves to illustrate his views on representation. Almost all involved in the debate either affirm (J. J. Gibson, Gombrich) or deny (Nelson Goodman) the validity of central perspective. Arnheim agrees that perspective is conventional and that it is not privileged in some way. But he still retains a privileging by affirming the importance of "inverted perspective" (1986, pp. 159–185). Inverted perspective is that system of rendering space that follows the demands of the medium and thereby resists perspective deformations and displays all relevant details (instead of overlapping) and suggests pictorial importance by size. Since "realistic" or "mimetic" painting attempts to counteract the medium, and ambiguously portray three dimensions on two, it is subject to variable reception, adaptation, and habituation. Whereas the central perspective debate becomes one over the critical fortunes of primarily Western art, Arnheim culls his examples of successful representations from all geographies and historical periods.

Arnheim's reading of expression is perhaps less promising, if only because it seems to demand an objectivity. Arnheim is a cognitive theorist of expression, and has never assumed a literal arousal of emotion by art (1966, pp. 302–319). In this his theory should be seen in the context of the cognitive theories of Susanne Langer and Carrol Pratt, who have influenced contemporary aesthetics. Once again, the expressive component of a visual percept is a part of its rich phenomenology; it cannot really be differentiated from so-called secondary qualities. But centralizing expression in this way, and making it as theoretically viable as, say, color, also precariously places expectations on the critical agreement found in expressive judgments ascribed to works of art. Arnheim, of course, is confident that, with the proper controls, such judgments can be confirmed (1986, pp. 297–326). Another angle that Arnheim follows is the understanding of the cause of the expression physically, in the physiology of perceiving. However, either a philosophy of critical agreement or a realist ontology of expressive properties is notoriously difficult to defend.

All of Arnheim's extremely interesting and promising ideas presented thus far seem to suffer from an appropriate limitation or staking of boundaries within which they can be assumed to operate. The ambiguous relation of Gestalt psychology to sociology might contain the heart of the matter. After consistently denying that past experience, emotion, personality, social class, and especially culture can alter perception, Gestalt psychology might seem to have left no room for the social at all. In the case of the perceptions of different cultures, the fact that the human nervous system *can* adapt to the differing conditions obtaining in either culture is assumed to resolve the fact that at certain times it *does not*. Such a "psychologism" becomes trivial when it does not link up with the importance of the *causes* of such conditions.

A reasonable philosophy of science might portray the problem in the following way. Psychological knowledge as directed to the arts attempts to give (among other things) explanation to aspects of perceiving common to all perceivers. It has nothing to say about the way in which an institution arose utilizing some aspect of perceiving in contrast to a different institution that arose utilizing a different aspect of perceiving. The fact that perception is found in both instances is tautologous and bound only to the definition of psychology. In this sense, psychology is inherently incomplete in dealing with the ways in which perceivers apprehend works of art. All is not lost, however, for the Arnheimian. A scientific realist might still try to combine sociological laws with psychological laws in order to make explanatory statements about the ways in which people perceive works in different societal contexts.

By working extensively with the findings of one school of psychology, Rudolf Arnheim has enlightened many aspects of art, and especially the ways in which formal means give rise to meaning in works of art. Although many of his assumptions about perceiving, representation, and expression rise or fall with the fortunes of this school, those that are phenomenological can be said to provide important material for any philosophical approach to art to take into account. Those strictly psychological assumptions concerning the same phenomena can be maintained if they are communicated within their present semistable social context, and could only begin to be accorded some sort of universality if contextualized within some theory of social institutions.

[*See also* Psychology of Art.]

BIBLIOGRAPHY

Works by Arnheim

"Experimentell-psychologische Untersuchungen zum Ausdrucks-problem." *Psychologische Forschung* 11 (1928):2–132.
Film als Kunst. Berlin, 1932. Translated by L. M. Sieveking and Ian F. D. Morrow as *Film* (London, 1933); first half reprinted as *Film as Art* (Berkeley, 1957).
Rundfunk als Hörkunst. Munich, 1979. Original German manuscript completed in 1935; translated by Mary Ludwig and Herbert Read as *Radio* (London, 1936); reprinted as *Radio: An Art of Sound* (New York, 1971).
"Nuovo Laocoonte." *Bianco e Nero 8* (31 August, 1938): 3–33. Translated by Arnheim as "A New Laocoön: Artistic Composites and the Talking Film" in *Film as Art* (Berkeley, 1957), pp. 199–230; original German manuscript, "Neuer Laokoon: Die Verkoppelung der künstlerischen Mittel," in *Kritiken und Aufsätze zum Film,* edited by Helmut Diederichs (Munich, 1977), pp. 81–112.
Art and Visual Perception: A Psychology of the Creative Eye. Berkeley, 1954; new exp. rev. ed., Berkeley, 1974.
Toward a Psychology of Art: Collected Essays. Berkeley, 1966.
Visual Thinking. Berkeley, 1969.
Entropy and Art: An Essay on Disorder and Order. Berkeley, 1971.
The Dynamics of Architectural Form. Berkeley, 1977.
The Power of the Center: A Study of Composition in the Visual Arts. Berkeley, 1982; new version, Berkeley, 1988.
New Essays on the Psychology of Art. Berkeley, 1986.
To the Rescue of Art: Twenty-Six Essays. Berkeley, 1992.
The Split and the Structure: Twenty-Eight Essays. Berkeley, 1996.

Other Sources

Beardsley, Monroe. "The Role of Psychological Explanation in Aesthetics." In *Perceiving Artworks,* edited by John Fisher, pp. 185–212. Philadelphia, 1980.
Carrier, David. "Theoretical Perspectives on the Arts, Sciences and Technology." *Leonardo* 19 (1986): 251–254.
Ingarden, Roman. *The Literary Work of Art.* Translated by George G. Grabowicz. Evanston, Ill., 1973.
Mandelbaum, Maurice. "Toward a Radical Critical Realism." In *Philosophy, Science, and Sense-Perception: Historical and Critical Studies,* pp. 171–245. Baltimore, 1964.
Sowers, Robert. "A Theory of Primary Modalities in the Visual Arts." *Journal of Aesthetics and Art Criticism* 42.3 (Spring 1984): 271–276.
Sowers, Robert. *Rethinking the Forms of Visual Expression.* Berkeley, 1990.
Smith, Ralph, ed. *Essays in Honor of Rudolf Arnheim. Journal of Aesthetic Education* 27 (special issue) (1993): 1–189.
Verstegen, Ian. "The Thought, Life, and Influence of Rudolf Arnheim." *Genetic, Social and General Psychological Monographs* 122 (1996): 197–213.

IAN VERSTEGEN

Dynamics of Art

Dynamics, the primary quality of artistic form, is emerging in aesthetic theory only now and quite hesitantly. Aesthetic theory has been dominated by the axiom that visual art deals essentially with objects. These objects differ in size and shape as well as in their spatial position. Secondary, formal analysis considers the mutual relations of objects and their capacity to change and to move from place to place. All these aspects of sensory reality derive from the objects and their defined shape.

This aesthetic approach reflects the practical way in which people handle the material world. The world consists of objects, desirable and undesirable ones, needed for use or to be avoided as obstacles. To a considerable extent, this practical approach determines our way of experiencing the world. Yet it is not the most spontaneous and ultimately decisive quality of experience. Spontaneously as well as ultimately, the world impresses us as a constellation of forces. These forces are not secondary properties of things, but they are what strikes us first. The world is given as occupied by forces that deal with us and are dealt with by us. Coping with them is what life is ultimately about. Children and "naturals," who are least monopolized by practical function, experience forces most directly, and artists emphasize them as themes of their visions.

Human direct experience is limited to what the senses receive. Therefore, perceived forces are but images of physical forces. A hammer striking an anvil is heard as a sound or seen as a motion. The information received is indirect. It is a translation, partial and indirect, as all translations are. The least indirect communication with the physical world is haptic, by touch or kinesthesia, that is, by the sensations of pressure or tension produced by the nerves of muscles, tendons, and joints. The actions of our bodies and the impact they suffer from outer forces are perceived as being generated and received "by us." Hence, dance and pantomime are the most elementary media of art.

It is essential for the present argument that performing art is not only the most elementary but also a most abstract form of artistic statement. What dancers experience kinesthetically when they stretch their arms or bend their bodies is not behavior of shapes but of pure forces. Only secondarily are these forces attributed to the body in motion. The forces occupying the body are perceived by the performer as a constellation, limited by no contour but only by the range of their power and possessing no other shapes but the directions in which they reach. They are pure, abstract dynamics.

To be sure, dancers and actors control their behavior not only by their kinesthetic sensations but also by what they see their bodies doing. This correspondence between two different modalities of perception is taken for granted in practice but is far from obvious in theory. It relies on what psychologists call an isomorphic relationship, made possible by the abstractness of perceptual dynamics. The abstract qualities of dynamics are essentially the same in the various perceptual areas, which makes them relatable.

Isomorphism also enables the audience of a performance not simply to see what is happening on the stage but also to experience the dynamic qualities enlivening the images of the performing bodies. This evocation of dynamics through perception will be continuously central to the following discussion. What needs to be said here is that any perception of dynamic forces is a reflection of physical forces, generated in the cortical centers of the perceiver's brain. Very little is known so far about the physiology of these processes; but they must be assumed to exist, if it is true that no conscious sensation is without its physical equivalent.

When we move from visual performance to the other medium reflecting physical forces of the outer world least indirectly, we come to the experience of music. Music as such—that is, music apart from language and performance—has mostly been dealt with as an expression of human emotion, and there is indeed a close affinity between music

and human feelings, experienced in our minds or made audible in speech. Emotion is also one of the motives for making and seeking music. Even so, one ignores the very nature of music when one treats it as a mere secondary reflection of human feelings. In and of itself, music is the purest but also the most abstract medium of auditory dynamics. Detachable even from any generating body—when we listen to music without the use of our eyes—the nature of music has been most tellingly defined by Arthur Schopenhauer in book 3 of his *Die Welt als Wille und Vorstellung*. What he means by his key concept, the will, is precisely what is discussed as dynamics in the present essay. The dynamics of music are conveyed, for example, in diatonic music, by the tension and distension created by the relation between the tonic and the other tones of the scale, which strain toward the tonic as a base or strive away from it. Similarly, discord strives for resolution, and the rising and descending in melodic sequence expresses the overcoming of gravitational weight or the giving in to the relaxation of repose. The regular beat as against the withholding and impulsive forward push of syncopation conveys the expressive dynamics of rhythm in the progression of time.

It is the inherent abstractness of the musical medium that invites its application to all human experiences involving dynamics. Our perception of the forces of physical events may find its repercussion in the musical representation of violence, and especially in the forces that animate human passions. Dynamics is the decisive feature distinguishing life from death, and as the arts endeavor to represent life they rely on dynamics as their principal means of expression.

Only because dynamics is so abstract was it possible, as Johann Wolfgang von Goethe did in a conversation with Johann Peter Eckermann, to compare music with architecture. Among the visual media, architecture is the one that displays the dynamic forces most purely. Although architecture is visual, whereas music is aural, they are both detached from the representation of natural objects and share similar dynamic forces.

Buildings, dwelling in three-dimensional physical space and in interaction with human users, display dynamic expression in two different ways. First, they are experienced as sequential. In this respect, there is a basic difference between a procession walking along the peristyle of the Parthenon around a central, inaccessible sanctuary and the straight approach to the altar of a basilica. Similarly, the sequence of spatial sights revealing the various areas of a palace as one walks from its entrance through its halls, corridors, and rooms, from the ground floor to the top, represents the time dimension of architecture, not unlike a symphonic structure in music.

In its atemporal visual aspects of the three dimensions of space, a building displays a powerful abstract dynamics first of all by rising from the ground and challenging thereby the attractive force of gravity. Like the shapes of all atemporal media, however, those of architecture work in two opposite directions. Read from the ground upward, a building displays an increasing detachment from its base, that is, with a decreasing effect of gravitational attraction. Read from the top down, dynamics is reversed. This is particularly evident in a pyramidal shape. A pyramid contracts as it grows from the base to the top. It unfolds with increasing impact from the peak down.

Apart from the force of gravity, the shapes of architecture display in and of themselves a rich action and interaction. Tension is created by the contrast between large and small or between straightness and the curvature of arches or the volutes of Ionic capitals. The principal generator of dynamics is the deviation from the "keynote," the vertical-horizontal framework. The leaning campanile of Pisa owes its dynamics to its deviation from the plumb line, not only physically but also visually. The obliqueness of a gable or pediment crowns the static cube of a building with a lively completion. But even a straight wall is described incompletely by its geometrical parameters. To do justice to its expression, one must perceive it as the resultant of equal, but opposite forces that push it from both sides and thereby keep it in balance.

Despite creating this lively world of visual images, however, architecture's sturdy immobility in a mobile setting stands as a counterweight of security and permanence. The visual arts of sculpture and painting serve a similar function, although with lesser power. Their timelessness enables them to function as an effective elaboration of architecture and is supported in turn by architectural settings. The visual arts synchronize events and by confronting them display their interaction in a synoptic, uniting presence. But while excluding the dimension of time, they cannot do without the representation of dynamics. They are unwilling to ignore life.

To account in theory for the presence of dynamics as the principal generator of expression, it has often been maintained that the arts replace absent movement with what is remembered from experience in actual space. It is said that when we see a picture of a bird in flight we know that it is in motion and endow it with imagined mobility. But dynamics need not rely on motion. As in architecture, the appropriate qualities of shape evoke, in the viewer's perception, the sensations of directed tension in a much more immediate way. As mentioned earlier, these sensations are conscious reflections of processes in the nervous system. They respond with dynamic configurations to the stimulus patterns conveyed to them by the sense organs.

In the particular case of representational art, past experience does act as a source of dynamics. The mental images of the objects of reality remembered by viewers interact with the images offered by the artist. The slim figures of the sculptor Alberto Giacometti are normally seen in relation to the known proportions of the human body, and the synchrony of the two sources of optical experience produces a deviation from the norm. Deviations make for dynamic tension.

Similarly, color creates tension through the coexistence of perceptual factors. The contrast between known natural colors, such as the pink of skin or the green of foliage, and the deviations from such norms often preferred by artists creates tension. So does any dissimilarity between a pattern of shape and a pattern of color in the same objects: where there is coherence of shape, there may be detachment of color, and vice versa. Furthermore, within the organization of color schemes there is the tension of discord and the distension of concord, analogous to what happens in music. And just as in music a leading tone strains toward the tonic, tertiary color mixtures strain toward the primary color that is dominant in the mixture.

Like architecture, sculpture shares three-dimensional space with the viewer, and because the viewer's access to space depends on two-dimensional projections on the retina, perceiving a piece of sculpture comes about as a synthesis of various perspective aspects, as the viewer walks around the work; but because these aspects vary from each other, to fuse them as the same object creates considerable tension. Here again, the different aspects are perceived as deviations from one another.

Even so, such a "composite" experience adds up to the presence of immobile objects, sharing the dwelling place with the viewers. Sculpture, however, lacks the practical interaction with consumers who, in architecture, occupy a building and use it as a facility. Sculpture is an object of contemplation, and as such it partakes in the function of the visual arts to synthesize the sequence of represented action in a single, lasting image. Because such an image is to depict life, however, it must express the dynamics of directed tension. In architecture, there is a fairly clear distinction between the vectors enlivening the shapes of walls and the vectors accompanying the action from the outside toward the inside and vice versa. In sculpture, there is no such distinction. The carriers of dynamic shape animate the various volumes all around and in all directions. This is particularly true for much modern sculpture, where the traditional distinction between the mass of the body and the forces mobilizing it is often replaced with a network of almost disembodied strivings, operating in much empty space. One is reminded of modern physics, where the distinction between mass and energy has given way to mere configurations of forces.

Painting limits itself to the second dimension. When it depicts three-dimensional space, it squeezes depth into a surface, thereby obtaining a dynamic effect. This effect is perceived as the effort to unfold distances where none are actually given. The compressed surface pattern, however, has a compositional organization and meaning of its own, and this surface image interacts in a dynamic counterpoint with the composition of the objects occupying the three-dimensional arena.

In all arts, the "structural skeleton" of the dynamic forces carrying expression is not identical with the shapes actually presented by the artist. The skeleton presents the configuration of forces, as it were, "in the nude" of pure abstraction. To make an expressive theme perceivable, the artist discovers and stresses the structural skeleton of, say, the human body in its more elaborate actual appearance. For the same reason, beauty does not really reside in the proportions and shapes as such, as has been traditionally maintained, but in the vitality and harmonious interrelations of the directed tensions generated by the proportions and shapes.

Finally and briefly, literature appeals directly to the senses only through the musical and rhythmical expression of sound. It profits thereby from the dynamic qualities of sound, referred to earlier. But being essentially a referential medium, which makes use of the perceptual world by the mental images it evokes, literature refers in an indirect fashion to the dynamic qualities inherent in sensory experience.

[*See also* Dance, *article on* Contemporary Thought; *and* Perception.]

BIBLIOGRAPHY

Arnheim, Rudolf. "Dynamics." In *Art and Visual Perception* (1954), new exp. rev. ed., chap. 9. Berkeley, 1974.

Arnheim, Rudolf. "Visual Dynamics." *American Scientist* 76.6 (November–December 1988): 585–591.

Bartenieff, Irmgard, and Dori Lewis. *Body Movement: Coping with the Environment.* New York, 1980.

Kivy, Peter. *The Corded Shell: Reflections on Musical Expression.* Princeton, N.J., 1980.

Langer, Susanne. "On Significance in Music." In *Philosophy in a New Key,* 3d ed., chap. 8. Cambridge, Mass., 1957.

Lipps, Theodor. *Raumaesthetik und Geometrisch-optische Täuschungen.* Leipzig, 1897. See sec. 1, "Zur Aesthetik der schönen Raumform."

Meyer, Leonard B. *Emotion and Meaning in Music.* Chicago, 1956.

Torroja Miret, Eduardo. "Phenomena of Stressing." In *Philosophy of Structures,* translated by J. J. Polivka and Milos Polivka, chap. 2. Berkeley, 1958.

Wölfflin, Heinrich. "Prolegomena zu einer Psychologie der Architektur" (1886). In *Kleine Schriften,* edited by Joseph Gantner. Basel, 1946.

Zuckerkandl, Victor. *The Sense of Music.* Princeton, N.J., 1959.

Zuckerkandl, Victor. *Die Wirklichkeit der Musik: Der musikalische Begriff der Aussenwelt.* Zurich, 1963.

RUDOLF ARNHEIM

ARNOLD, MATTHEW (1822–1888), English Victorian poet and critic. Arnold's career can be divided into four distinct phases: a period of youthful discontent during which he wrote most of his poetry; a decade during which he formulated the main ideas of his cultural theory; an eight-year period devoted almost exclusively to religious themes and biblical studies; and a final decade in which he

returned to the more balanced concerns of his early criticism. The works written during his religious phase, *St. Paul and Protestantism, Literature and Dogma,* and *God and the Bible,* had an immense influence during his own time but have been little read or valued by later critics. Their basic argument is that religion can be reduced to moral sentiment illuminated by ideas that should be understood as "poetry" rather than as factual propositions. The prose works by which he is now chiefly known are the essays written before and after the religious books. These essays number in the dozens and engage a range of topics that includes education, politics, religion, classical studies, history, philosophy, and, most important, literary criticism. Arnold never lived by his writing. For most of his adult life, he served as an inspector of schools, and toward the end of his life he received a modest pension from the government in acknowledgment of his contributions as a writer.

Arnold's career seems almost to have been designed to dramatize the spiritual crisis of the Victorian age. He is at one with Thomas Carlyle, John Stuart Mill, George Eliot, and many others in giving expression to the sense of distress at living in "an age of transition," without settled beliefs, facing the need to create a new spiritual basis. The nadir of this experience, as Arnold describes it in his poem "Stanzas from the Grande Chartreuse," is a sensation of helpless suspension, "Wandering between two worlds, one dead, / The other powerless to be born." Unlike his youthful friend and fellow poet, Arthur Hugh Clough, Arnold was constitutionally indisposed to remain long in any such condition of helplessness. In one of his early essays, "On the Modern Element in Literature" (1857), he declares that "the human race has the strongest, the most invincible tendency to *live*, to *develop* itself" (vol. 1, pp. 29–30; all citations from Arnold's essays are to R. H. Super's edition of the prose).

In his first published essay, the 1853 preface to his poems, Arnold's own instinct to survive and develop gets off to a false start. He renounces all engagement with the concerns of his age, both its spiritual travail and its enthusiasm for material progress and social reform. As an alternative, he recommends that the poet take refuge in the study of ancient literature so that he can "delight himself with the contemplation of some noble action of a heroic time" (vol. 1, p. 14). This position is an anomaly in Arnold's work. The aesthetic standards of classicism remain an elementary component of his total worldview, but at no other point in his career does he ever again recommend simply withdrawing from his own contemporary world. What he recommends instead, during the second phase of his career, is that the writer formulate a comprehensive understanding of the historical progression of Western civilization. He calls this sort of understanding "an intellectual deliverance" (vol. 1, p. 19), and he anticipates that it will provide both fulfillment and peace of mind. "The deliverance consists in man's comprehension of this present and past. It begins when our mind begins to enter into possession of the general ideas which are the law of this vast multitude of facts. It is perfect when we have acquired that harmonious acquiescence of mind which we feel in contemplating a grand spectacle that is intelligible to us" (vol. 1, p. 20). In the period of his religious preoccupations, in the 1870s, Arnold turns away from the idea of an intellectual deliverance and seeks salvation instead through moral earnestness emotionally charged with the "poetry" of traditional religion. Ultimately, the effort to save religion by treating it as poetry undercuts itself, and Arnold concludes by replacing religion with poetry. He declares that "the strongest part of our religion to-day is its unconscious poetry. The future of poetry is immense, because in conscious poetry, where it is worthy of its high destinies, our race, as time goes on, will find an ever surer and surer stay" (vol. 9, p. 63). In his final decade, he returns to the cultural theory worked out in the 1860s. He polishes and refines it, without altering its fundamental structure, and he applies it, with undiminished wit and force, to important topics like those discussed in "Literature and Science," "The Study of Poetry," and his revaluations of the Romantic poets.

The "general ideas" through which Arnold seeks an intellectual deliverance are not merely objective laws of history, whatever laws those might, on dispassionate, scientific inquiry, turn out to be. Like other Victorians, Arnold regarded history as a quasi-providential, teleological progression leading, through a sequence of necessary phases, to human "perfection"—both a perfected order of society and a perfected state of individual human development. In its perfected state, the individual human mind would replicate the larger order of Western cultural history, harmoniously integrating its dichotomous elements. The two ideas, a teleological cultural development and a perfected human consciousness, are interdependent. Culture achieves its immanent purpose in producing human perfection, and humanity achieves perfection by assimilating culture. Arnold defines "culture" as "*a study of perfection*," and he defines perfection as "a harmonious expansion of *all* the powers which make the beauty and worth of human nature" (vol. 5, pp. 91, 94). A liberal education thus becomes a process of acculturation within a transcendent, ideal order that has been progressively manifested in the course of Western civilization.

The central motive in Arnold's main constructive phase, from "The Modern Element" through *Culture and Anarchy*, is to work out in detail the relations among the components within the larger order of Western cultural history. He delineates a system of the human faculties and aptitudes and correlates these elements with the major cultural phases of Western history. The largest dichotomy within Arnold's system is the distinction between "Hebraism and Hellenism": the moral earnestness of the Judeo-Christian ethos and the

intellectual spontaneity of the Hellenic temper. In Arnold's historical scheme, these concepts are associated with dynamic formal properties and set in dialectically alternating sequence. Hellenism is associated with "expansion" and Hebraism with "concentration." Ages of expansion are exploratory and creative, adapting to changed circumstances and formulating new knowledge. Ages of concentration reaffirm the established structures of belief and value within a culture and emphasize the importance of "conduct" and character.

Periclean Athens establishes the central norms for Arnold's intellectual and aesthetic values, but for the sake of his dialectic he concedes that even the high Hellenic age lacked sufficient moral earnestness. In its degenerate, Hellenistic phase, the ancient world reduces itself to a light and frivolous play of "the senses and the understanding," and it thus gives rise, by dialectical counteraction, to a medieval phase in which the dominant faculties are "the heart and imagination" (vol. 3, pp. 223, 225). The stultification of intellect in the Christian Middle Ages is succeeded by the rebirth of Hellenic curiosity in the Renaissance, itself counterpointed by a Hebraic Reformation. The Enlightenment and the French Revolution, as assertions of intellectual freedom, generate a reaction of political and intellectual conservatism. Arnold's own age, he thinks, is just emerging out of this conservative phase, and it is invested with peculiar significance as a culminating moment of self-consciousness within the whole progression. Like many Victorians, Arnold has a foreshortened historical vision of a neatly ordered dramatic sequence in which his own time constitutes the climactic moment. He clearly expects that within a generation or so the historical process will have reached a final point of poise, a point at which each individual and the culture as a whole will be working in synchronized effort to produce that "harmonious expansion of *all* the powers which make the beauty and worth of human nature."

Arnold's idea of perfection provides a theoretical link between two seemingly divergent aspects of his thought: his democratic political orientation and his cultural elitism. Presupposing that civilized people are endowed with charitable social motives, he maintains that "individual perfection is impossible so long as the rest of mankind are not perfected along with us" (vol. 5, p. 215). In this case, compassion joins hands with enlightened self-interest. A cultural elite depends on the energy generated by a nationally diffused enthusiasm for the life of the mind. Arnold invokes this principle of social energy to account for such peculiarly favored cultural epochs as Periclean Athens, Renaissance Italy, and Elizabethan England. When "high culture" pervades a large body of the community, "individual genius gets its proper nutriment, and is animated to put forth its best powers" (vol. 2, p. 316). Athens in particular offers an example of a community in which high culture is the culture of a whole people. It offers the spectacle of "the middle and lower classes in the highest development of their humanity that these classes have yet reached. It was the *many* who relished those arts" (vol. 2, p. 25).

If there is no such "national glow of life and thought," Arnold thinks it might still be possible for a large intellectual elite to construct an intellectual substitute, a circulation of ideas that will provide "a quickening and sustaining atmosphere" (vol. 3, p. 263). The Weimar of Johann Wolfgang von Goethe and Friedrich von Schiller offers a model for this alternative. In his own efforts to achieve perfection through culture, Arnold wavers between the alternatives presented by Athens and Weimar. At times, he seems to believe it possible to educate and elevate the whole British population, and at other times he spurns the common public and seeks salvation only among and for the cultivated few.

In his later works, Arnold identifies four "powers" or faculties of civilization: conduct, intellect, social life, and beauty. The first two powers are those of Hebraism and Hellenism. The power of social life makes itself felt in his acknowledgment that great eras of artistic creation depend on a general circulation of cultural energy within a larger social order. As his definition of human perfection suggests, the idea of beauty exercises a crucial regulative function in all of his thinking. The final condition by which one can judge the adequacy of an intellectual deliverance is that it be "harmonious." His judgments of the three classes of British society—barbarians (aristocrats), philistines, and populace—are based in large part on the aesthetic qualities of each class. And even his preoccupation with Hebraic moral rectitude is closely associated in his own mind with his devotion to the poetic power of traditional religious worship.

Arnold's aesthetic standards are largely constituted by the interaction between his conceptions of the classical and the Romantic. Throughout his career, he takes classicism as the prototype for unity and formal symmetry in works of art. In the most thoroughgoing statement of a classicist aesthetic, the 1853 preface to his poems, Arnold contrasts this prototype with all of modern literature, and especially with the literature of the Romantic period. Tacitly invoking a well-established tradition in the battle between the ancients and the moderns, he affirms that the ancients are concerned with grand actions and elementary passions and that they construct coherent designs in which all expression is subordinated to a "unity and profoundness of moral impression" (vol. 1, p. 12). Modern writers, in contrast, are said to occupy themselves with introverted and intellectualized reflections, and in matters of design they are led astray by "attractive accessories" such as "single thoughts," "richness of imagery," and "abundance of illustration" (vol. 1, p. 9). In other works, and especially in his later essays, Arnold acknowledges that Romantic literature is itself much concerned with elementary passions. In his own experience of literature, the Romantic poets, and above all William Wordsworth, evoke his deepest emotional responses. In his best-known treatment of poetic taste and value, the late essay on "The Study of Poetry," Arnold rises above any simple opposition between the classic and the Romantic. His illustrative instances of "high and excellent seriousness" (vol. 9, p. 176) include passages from Homer, William Shakespeare, Dante Alighieri, and John Milton, and the criteria with which he judges them are concordant with those by which he offers positive revaluations, in other essays, of Wordsworth, George Byron, and John Keats.

For about seventy years after his death, Arnold served as the preeminent authority in England and America for the idea of "culture," a term that in his use meant primarily the study of great works of literature from Western civilization. He witnessed and felt personally the collapse of Christian orthodoxy as the basic doctrinal framework for his civilization, and more than any other Victorian he was himself responsible for establishing the study of "culture" as the main substitute for this framework. Northrop Frye (1972), who is widely regarded as one of the most important literary theorists of this century, observes that "Arnold's doctrine in general was, for most humanists of my generation, the shadow of a rock in a weary land." T. S. Eliot (1951), the most prominent poet-critic of the first half of the century, rightly regarded Arnold as a threat to Eliot's own religious traditionalism, and he accordingly deprecated Arnold's authority; nonetheless, he referred to Arnold more often than to any other predecessor in cultural theory. In his own most general theoretical formulations, Eliot remained heavily dependent on Arnold, sometimes acknowledging this dependence, sometimes not. In the first half of the century, the two most influential evaluative and canonical critics, F. R. Leavis (1938) in Britain and Lionel Trilling (1939) in the United States, took Arnold as their chief model for cultural criticism. Trilling began his career by writing an intellectual biography of Arnold, and Leavis, despite his near-idolatrous deference to Eliot, vigorously defended Arnold against Eliot's strictures.

In one of his essays, the poet Wallace Stevens (1989) remarks that "to see the gods dispelled in mid-air and dissolve like clouds is one of the great human experiences." A historian contemplating the fate of Arnoldian humanism in the past three or four decades might have an experience similar to that which Stevens describes. In the early 1970s, a metaphysical revolution took place in the literature departments of American and British universities. The doctrines that animated this revolution are variously designated as "postmodern" or "poststructuralist," and they are intimately affiliated with more specific critical schools such as deconstruction, New Historicism, reader-response criticism, and the cultural study of science. The two leading divinities of the new dispensation are Jacques Derrida and Michel Foucault, and it has a pantheon of lesser gods such as Stanley Fish, Stephen Greenblatt, and Fredric Jameson.

In its fundamental tenets, poststructuralism runs directly counter to Arnoldian humanism. Whereas Arnold invested the canonical texts of Western civilization with numinous value, current authorities tend to regard Western civilization itself as an engine of arbitrary power, and they take the canonical texts either negatively, as media for the propagation of this power, or positively, as countermines designed to subvert it. And whereas Arnold and his acolytes focused on the cultivated individual sensibility as a central locus of creativity and value, current authorities deprecate the individual as a mere medium for the self-realization of language or of autonomous cultural epistemes. Arnold remains a common point of reference in cultural theory, but he appears now almost exclusively in the role of foil for antihumanist polemic. Among the critics and theorists who hold positions of influence at a level equivalent to those once held by Frye, Leavis, and Trilling, not one would now identify himself closely with Arnold, and indeed, few would have even a respectful word to say about him.

The vicissitudes of Arnold's influence are a boon to intellectual historians, for they correlate with the main movements of cultural thought since the Victorian period. The recent disappearance of Arnoldian humanism was presaged, less spectacularly but no less decisively, by the disappearance of the humanism practiced by Arnold himself. Although he was the founding father of humanism in the modernist age, he was not himself modern. He was among the last of the great Victorians, representative in his own time, but influential on later generations only by means of adaptations that tacitly, and for the most part unconsciously, altered the fundamental structure of his thought. He relied on metaphysical assumptions about the nature of mind and history that have not been tenable since his own time and that were not shared by the most prominent among his descendants. The fact that Arnold could have exercised such influence as he did offers strong evidence that his perceptions and judgments are compatible with intuitive beliefs not limited to the peculiarly Victorian structure of his ideas. These intuitive beliefs are decidedly not compatible with the assumptions of the current poststructuralist paradigm, but the tectonic shifts that have taken place in cultural theory since Arnold's time should make us cautious about assuming that our current dispensation has any final and definitive validity.

Arnold's legacy can be detected in modern views of art or poetry as a numinous object, in the ideal of personal cultivation through the study of literature, and in the humanist belief in the central social function of liberal education. As they have been transmitted through the differing personalities and ideologies of other critics, Arnold's beliefs and attitudes have undergone major transformations, some of which would have been wholly unpalatable to Arnold himself.

Arnold's substitution of poetry for religion can be associated with the efforts of at least two major modern poets, William Butler Yeats and Wallace Stevens. In his Byzantium poems, Yeats sought to invest the poem itself with mystical, magical powers—to make of it a medium through which he could gain entry to an eternal aesthetic realm. Stevens's whole career orients itself to the production of a Grand Poem, a "supreme fiction" that would, he explains, take the place of God. Arnold himself would very likely have recoiled at Yeats's mystical reification of the poetic object. What he anticipated was that poetry would serve as the medium of a religious reverence, not that poetry would itself become a sacred object. Stevens's project, as an extension of the Romantic visionary mode, would perhaps have been more congenial to Arnold, but Arnold distances himself from the more visionary aspects of Wordsworth's poetry. Instead, he concentrates his attention on "the joy offered to us in the simple primary affections and duties" (vol. 9, p. 51).

In his declaration that "the future of poetry is immense," Arnold might have seemed, in the first half of the twentieth century, to have been prophetically inspired. He regarded his own age as an age of prose and criticism that would create the "order of ideas" (vol. 3, p. 261) within which great poetry could later be written, and it might have seemed, at one point, that the whole of modernist literature, prose and poetry, was answering to the mission with which he had entrusted it. The peculiar intensity and iconoclastic fervor of modernist literature imply high ambitions, and in the same period the critical commentaries of the professional academic class, especially the New Critics, have about them an air of priestly, sacerdotal reverence for the objects of their study. In the perspective presented by the history of poetry since World War II, Arnold's prophetic stature seems considerably diminished. No contemporary poets hold a canonical status even remotely close to that of the great modernist poets, or, for that matter, of the great Victorian poets. At no other time in the past several centuries has poetry been so little regarded as a cultural force. Moreover, literature in general has not tended toward creating an atmosphere of religious reverence equivalent to that of traditional religion.

The most influential aspect of Arnold's work has been the ideal of the cultivated individual sensibility. Among the critics who have adopted the ideal of literary cultivation, and who have cited Arnold as an authority for it, very few have ever accepted the two central premises of his cultural theory: the idea that there are objective, universally valid laws of moral and aesthetic judgment, and that these laws have progressively manifested themselves in the course of Western civilization. Indeed, almost none of Arnold's commentators have even recognized the systematic character of his own thought or the crucial role he gives to the idea of a total, coherent cultural order. In the commentaries that grew out of Leavis's defense of Arnold, the one main point of consensus is that Arnold is not to be regarded as a systematic or coherent thinker. He is to be regarded, rather, as the proponent of a delicate humanist sensibility, a "temper of mind" that finds its central merit in "flexibility." In the absence of a larger system of ideas, the notion of individual cultivation tends to deteriorate into a cult of the "self." In Leavis, the fiction of D. H. Lawrence provides a temple for the mystical adulation of the individual identity. In Trilling's early work, Arnoldian "culture" serves as a medium for a "liberal" social ideal, but by the end of his career, Trilling's cultivation of the Arnoldian sensibility has virtually inverted itself, and Trilling has become a high priest of the neurotic Freudian inner identity—a form of personal force that he sets in opposition to the repressive force of civilization.

When the ideal of personal cultivation is combined with the idea of art as an end in itself, the result is the kind of "aestheticism" associated with Walter Pater, Arnold's first major disciple. Pater is the patron saint of "art for art's sake" and a primary source for at least two prominent aesthetes, Oscar Wilde and George Santayana. Henry James's idolization of art as an end in itself affiliates him with the Paterian school, but James responded much more directly and favorably to Arnold than to Pater, and James, like Arnold, would have roundly rejected the proposition that the hedonistic exploitation of artistic "sensations" could serve as the central motive in life.

Arnold's concept of a canonical humanist education has survived through much of this century because our civilization has felt the value of a shared body of literary experience. If we can no longer accept the transcendental theory through which Arnold tried to secure the authority of the canon, we can still recognize the need for what he called a "full humanity" (vol. 8, p. 286), and for many people the study of great literature will continue to satisfy this need. The desire for normative cultural values will probably survive the adversarial ethos that currently animates the professional academic class. If it does, Arnold will continue to be read, for he is a highly capable guide to "the best that is known and thought in the world" (vol. 3, p. 282).

[See also Cultural Studies; and Literature, article on Literary Aesthetics.]

BIBLIOGRAPHY

Works by Arnold

The Complete Prose Works of Matthew Arnold. 11 vols. Edited by R. H. Super. Ann Arbor, 1960–1977.
The Note-Books of Matthew Arnold. Edited by Howard Foster Lowry, Karl Young, and Waldo Hilary Dunn. London, 1952.
The Poems of Matthew Arnold (1965). Edited by Kenneth Allott, 2d ed. revised by Miriam Allott. London and New York, 1979.
Selected Letters of Matthew Arnold. Edited by Clinton Machann and Forrest D. Burt. Ann Arbor, 1993.

Other Sources

Carroll, Joseph. The Cultural Theory of Matthew Arnold. Berkeley, 1982.
Culler, A. Dwight. Imaginative Reason: The Poetry of Matthew Arnold. New Haven, 1966.
DeLaura, David J. Hebrew and Hellene in Victorian England: Newman, Arnold, and Pater. Austin, Tex., 1969.
Dudley, Fred A. "Matthew Arnold and Science." PMLA 57 (1942): 275–294.
Eliot, T. S. "Arnold and Pater." In Selected Essays. 3d ed., pp. 431–443. London, 1951.
Frye, Northrop. "The Critical Path: An Essay on the Social Context of Literary Criticism." In In Search of Literary Theory, edited by Morton W. Bloomfield, pp. 91–93. Ithaca, N.Y., 1972.
Leavis, F. R. "Arnold as Critic." Scrutiny 7 (1938): 319–332.
Machann, Clinton. The Essential Matthew Arnold: An Annotated Bibliography of Major Modern Studies. New York, 1993.
Madden, William A. Matthew Arnold: A Study of the Aesthetic Temperament in Victorian England. Bloomington, Ind., 1967.
Stevens, Wallace. Opus Posthumous (1957). Edited by Samuel French Morse. Rev. enl. corr. ed. Edited by Milton J. Bates. New York, 1989.
Trilling, Lionel. Matthew Arnold (1939). Rev. ed. New York, 1958.

JOSEPH CARROLL

ART, DEFINITION OF. See Definition of Art.

ART, END OF. See Baudrillard; Blanchot; Danto, article on Danto's End of Art Thesis; Hegel, article on Hegel's Conception of the End of Art; and Heidegger.

ART FOR ART'S SAKE. The notion of art for art's sake, or l'art pour l'art, was employed beginning with the French Romantics to encapsulate several key aspects of Romantic and high modernist aesthetics. The phrase conveys the idea that art should not be evaluated primarily by the standards of morality or religion: that there is an autonomous and incommensurable realm of aesthetic value. In this sense, it in part represents the Romantic attack on neoclassicism, which insisted above all on "content" of a moral/historical variety. At its most extreme, the doctrine of art for art's sake holds that art is of no use whatever, that it has no real-world application, and that it is the appropriate object of an absolutely "pure" regard. The notion has been fundamental both to the Romantic liberation of the imagination and the creation of the avant-garde. But the ideology it represents has also been at the heart of the deeply problematic nature of modernism and the twentieth-century avant-garde's attempts at self-destruction.

John Wilcox (1953) traces the origin of the phrase to a garbled reading of Immanuel Kant's aesthetics by French intellectuals of the early nineteenth century. It is generally agreed that the first use of the phrase in something like its present sense appeared in the diaries of Benjamin Constant in 1804. Constant was a French/Swiss novelist and political writer (also famous as the lover of Madame de Staël) who visited Weimar in the winter of 1803–1804, where he frequented the circle of Johann Wolfgang von Goethe, Johann Christoph Friedrich von Schiller, and Friedrich von

Schelling. In his diary, he wrote: "I have a visit with Robinson, pupil of Schelling's. His work on the *Esthetics* of Kant has some very forceful ideas. *L'art pour l'art* without purpose, for all purpose perverts art" (as quoted in Wilcox, 1953, p. 360). To say that this is a simplified version of Kant is an understatement. Nevertheless, the notion that art should be created and appreciated for the sake of art alone has its origins in Kantian disinterestedness. This is true also of its use by the brilliant teacher Victor Cousin, who taught a course in aesthetics at the Sorbonne in 1818. [*See* Cousin.] The course was eclectic, but focused on (roughly) Kantian notions of free beauty and the independence of artistic from religious, moral, and practical value. Cousin's course was highly influential on the next generation of French thinkers including Théodore Jouffroy, and, through him, the critic Charles-Augustin Sainte-Beuve. (The most thorough discussion of the German sources of the notion in Kant, Goethe, Schelling, Johann Gottlieb Fichte, and others is Egan [1921, 1924].)

These were, however, only intermittent outbreaks, though they expressed the emerging Romantic sensibility toward beauty. The phrase entered general circulation in France in 1834 with the publication of Théophile Gautier's *Mademoiselle de Maupin*. In the preface, he wrote that "Only those things that are altogether useless can be truly beautiful; anything that is useful is ugly, for it is the expression of some need, and the needs of man are base and disgusting" (Gautier, 1835, p. 22; trans. Jenkins 1968, p. 110). The phrase and the sensibility it embodied (often termed "aestheticism") were taken up by such figures as Gustave Flaubert, Charles Baudelaire, and Stéphane Mallarmé. [*See* Baudelaire; *and* Mallarmé.] A particularly clear statement of the view is provided in Flaubert's correspondence with George Sand, in which Flaubert asserts against Sand the claims that art need not be morally uplifting, that beauty is opposed to utility, that style can be distinguished from content, and so forth (Flaubert and Sand, 1993). (The definitive account of the development of the notion in French Romanticism is Cassagne, 1906).

The view was taken up as well by British aesthetes, most famously by Oscar Wilde and Walter Pater. [*See* Pater; *and* Wilde.] Pater, for instance, argued passionately that the deepest human wisdom is found in the immediate enjoyment of experiences for their own sake rather than in the conceptual reconstruction of experience. Here are the final lines of Pater's *The Renaissance* of 1868: "Of such wisdom, the poetic passion, the desire of beauty, the love of art for its own sake, has most. For art comes to you proposing frankly to give nothing but the highest quality to your moments as they pass, and simply for those moments' sake" (Pater, 1873, p. 239). The appreciation of art was supposed by Pater to immerse one in the present moment, to call one from the arenas of life in which everything is held to moral standards or historical significance and into an intense experience of sheer presence within the experience. This suggests, among other things, a suspension of instrumental or technological rationality, in which all human action and experience are supposed to be ordered toward ends. It is no coincidence that the aesthetics of art for art's sake emerges with, and perhaps declines with, the industrial revolution: art and industrial production are held to be polar opposites, and within the view of someone such as Pater, the exaltation of aesthetic experience is contrasted with the base labor and technology of manufacturing.

Among the consequences of art for art's sake as a mode of regarding art is the claim that art is not to be appreciated for what might be termed its anecdotal value, its value as a representation. This is in part because the representation of human action, or even of natural scenery, always seems to possess a moral or religious dimension. Even the still lifes and landscapes of seventeenth-century Holland, for instance, have been read as elaborate religious allegories. This in turn suggests (a notion that appears, albeit qualifiedly, in Kant) that the aesthetic properties of a work of art, the properties that are relevant to an experience and assessment of it qua art, are the formal properties, the arrangement of lines and colors, rhythms and tones, masses and curves. Pater's account surely suggests, in fact (though Pater himself drew this implication only inconsistently), that the representational content of a work is at best of secondary value; for the point in Pater is the immediacy of a sense experience: the value that is yielded on an analysis of representational content, or what we can see through the work to, is not "immediately" experienced in this sense.

This move into aesthetic immediacy, so beautifully captured in Pater's prose, had massive implications for the history of art and thought about art in the West. In art history, it led directly to the development of elaborate formal analysis of the sort most famously exemplified by Heinrich Wölfflin's *Principles of Art History*. In painting, it resulted in the development, first, of ever-greater representative distortion in the work of the late Impressionists and Postimpressionists, and finally, in the second decade of this century, in the development of pure abstraction. In literary theory, one product was the "New Criticism," which attempted to consider text without context. [*See* New Criticism.] In aesthetics, the result was the virulent formalism of such figures as Clive Bell, Roger Fry, and, to some extent, Clement Greenberg. Bell, for example, wrote that "to appreciate a work of art we need bring with us nothing from life, no knowledge of its ideas and affairs, no familiarity with its emotions" (Bell, 1914, p. 27).

The avant-garde art world of this century has persistently attempted to put the ideology of art for art's sake into operation, and the ideology itself persists. In 1993, for example, the abstract painter Ellsworth Kelly wrote, regarding a blockbuster Henri Matissse exhibition at the Museum of Modern Art in New York: "Personally, I believe in *art for art's sake* and I believe Matisse did also. He only painted to please himself, not to please the world, nor to change the world" (Kelly, 1993, p. 76).

It is necessary to point out, however, that the art of the twentieth century has been marked by an equally persistent effort to eradicate the ideology of art for art's sake and to expunge the distinction between art and life. Marcel Duchamp's ready-mades, for instance, were, among other things, attempts to ridicule the notion of art for art's sake in just the context in which that notion had reached its greatest intensity: the high modernist art exhibition. One could look at Duchamp's urinal with disinterest, but one would have to take oneself awfully seriously not to feel ridiculous doing so. In its vivid demonstration that anything could be art, the practice of the ready-made called into question many of the assumptions of aestheticism. Similarly, the Russian avant-garde of the 1920s operated on the slogan "art into life"; great artists such as Kazimir Malevich and Aleksandr Rodchenko attempted to destroy the autonomous realm of art (constructed from the ideology of art for art's sake) by designing propaganda materials and packaging for the Soviet regime. Or consider Pop. Here, artists attempt to bring the products of the debased culture (movies, comic books, and tabloid newspaper photographs, for example) into the museum in an attack on formalism, aesthetic autonomy, snobbery, and the rest of the notions associated with the doctrine of art for art's sake. Roy Lichtenstein went so far as to ridicule the history of modernist painting by turning its great masterpieces into comic-book images. The 1993 Whitney Biennial was another case in point. Here much of the art expressed a political view, or affirmed an identity articulated in ethnicity, gender, and sexual orientation. The Rodney King beating video played over and over on an endless loop. These were, among other things, comments on the political implications of insulating art from the full-fledged cultural environment in which it is all the time embedded.

In one way or another, then, the notion of art for art's sake has deeply informed Western art for 150 years. The avant-garde constructed and then deconstructed itself within this notion. It is worth holding on to some of the original motivations for the notion. For example, there can be more to art than sheer didacticism or edification. The demand that art be pedagogical or edifying was rightly felt as an arbitrary restraint by the Romantics, and the notion of art for art's sake played its part in a liberation from philistinism. On the other hand, the notion itself is highly problematic. We know enough to be suspicious at this point of the claims of *any* human endeavor to escape the exigencies of class, politics, and morals: even the withdrawal from the political is a political act. Certainly, Bell's claim that to understand art we need bring with us nothing from life is baldly ridiculous. We always do bring with us something

from life, and if we were able to jettison life completely we could understand nothing whatever.

It is important also to keep in mind that the notion of art for art's sake only ever had currency in a very small arena of artistic production: primarily European and European-oriented high art of the nineteenth and twentieth centuries. In the popular arts, in the crafts, and in various religious or ceremonial arts of world cultures during the same period, the notion was ignored and art continued to provide practical, moral, and religious applications. Navajo sand paintings, African-American gospel music, Yoruba festival masks—none of these are art for art's sake, and yet they are among the most absorbing and important artistic productions of the same era.

The Romantic and high modernist withdrawal from life into "abstraction" may have represented an impulse that was (and is) fundamentally fearful of and hostile toward human life and the world as a whole. Just as the defining moment of Romanticism may have been the suicide of Werther, so art's withdrawal into itself may have expressed the aesthete's extreme sensitivity to a harsh reality. Finally, the attempt to turn art always back in on itself renders art narcissistic, concerned only with itself and with insulating itself from the disruptive encounter with the real. If high art has become less and less relevant to more and more people in the last two hundred years, it is largely because of the ascendency of the notion that the purpose of art is itself. Arthur Danto argues that art is at an end, because art simply consists of the search for itself: art ends when it becomes its own philosophy (Danto, 1986). This is to take the ideology of art for art's sake into the final moment of its self-destruction, when art, infinitely concerned only for itself, gazes at the mirror and finds it empty.

[*See also* Aestheticism; Autonomy; *and* Disinterestedness.]

BIBLIOGRAPHY

Bell, Clive. *Art.* London, 1914.

Cassagne, Albert. *La Théorie de l'art pour l'art en France chez les derniers romantiques et les premiers réalistes.* Paris, 1906.

Danto, Arthur C. "The End of Art." In *The Philosophical Disenfranchisement of Art,* pp. 81–115. New York, 1986.

Egan, Rose Frances. "The Genesis of the Theory of Art for Art's Sake' in Germany and in England." *Smith College Studies in Modern Languages* 2.4 (July 1921): 5–61; continued in 5.3 (April 1924): 1–33.

Flaubert, Gustave, and George Sand. *Flaubert-Sand: The Correspondence.* Translated by Frances Steegmuller and Barbara Bray. New York, 1993.

Gautier, Théophile. *Mademoiselle de Maupin.* Paris, 1835.

Jenkins, Iredell. "Art for Art's Sake." In *The Dictionary of the History of Ideas,* edited by Philip P. Wiener, vol. 1, pp. 108–111. New York, 1968. See p. 110.

Kelly, Ellsworth, et al. "Matisse: A Symposium." *Art in America* 81.5 (May 1993): 74–87.

Pater, Walter. *The Renaissance.* Oxford, 1873.

Wilcox, John. "The Beginnings of *L'art pour L'art.*" *Journal of Aesthetics and Art Criticism* 11 (June 1953): 360–377.

Wölfflin, Heinrich: *Principles of Art History: The Problem of the Development of Style in Later Art.* Translated by M. D. Hottinger. London, 1932.

CRISPIN SARTWELL

ART HISTORY. *Key concepts, persons, and theories in art history are discussed in many entries: see especially* Alberti; Baroque Aesthetics; Canon; Classicism; Diderot; Feminism, *article on* Feminist Art History; Gombrich; Gothic Aesthetics; Historicism, *article on* Historicism in Art History; Iconography and Iconology; Kant, *article on* Kant and Art History; Museums; Narrative; Panofsky; Perspective, *overview article;* Renaissance Italian Aesthetics; Riegl; Semiotics, *article on* Semiotics as a Theory of Art; Vasari; Winckelmann; Wittkower; Wölfflin; *and* Worringer.

ARTIFACT. In its literal sense, an artifact is an intentionally produced object (or possibly, event). Its Latin etymology is from *ars,* by art or craft, and *factum,* to be made. This characterization equates an artifact with a tool (cf. Dipert [1993]). Because no object is wholly an artifact, one might more precisely speak of *artifactual features:* properties of an object that have been contemplated and intentionally left alone or have been intentionally modified. (One might further wish to stipulate that these properties are "intensional" or description-sensitive according to the way the modifier of the properties conceived them.) Certainly not all features of an artifact need be modified or even contemplated for modification by an agent, and it is anachronistic to describe an artifactual feature in terms other than (as closely as one can) how it was originally conceived.

Nevertheless, suspicions may arise that this precise philosophical formulation evades certain issues, including widely used technical senses for the term in anthropology and art history. For example, consider a piece of unmodified flint that is discovered on a known trail from a flint source to an ancient hunting area. This simple example presents an interesting problem for the philosophical definition. An anthropologist might well consider it an "artifact," by which he or she presumably means that it provides evidence of past human behavior. More precisely, it is a concrete product of human behavior (perhaps unintentional) that thereby gives us evidence of the nature of this behavior. The behavior that such an artifact indicates may be further used as evidence for the habits, beliefs, customs, or even intentions, thoughts, and emotions that spawned it. What distinguishes this anthropological-historical sense of artifact from its philosophical-etymological sense is that an artifact might be viewed as evidence of behaviors (or their causes) that are products of a culture or society, rather than of an individual with precise individual thoughts and intentions. Edmund Husserl (1977) speaks of "cultural objects" in roughly this sense and Randall Dipert (1993) calls them "historical-cultural objects." For example, the precise identity of the hunter who dropped the piece of flint is of no particular interest to the anthropologist, nor his exact thinking when he did so. In fact, it is an anthropological artifact in spite of the fact that the piece of flint betrays no intentional modifications and that even its location, namely, where it was accidentally dropped, is unintentional. At most, one might propose that its conveyance along the path from flint source to hunting ground was intentional—although this seems like a diminishingly small respect in which the object itself is an artifact in the philosophical sense. In yet another way, such an object may not be an artifact in the philosophical sense: it may be a product of a culturally inherited behavior pattern that is in no clear sense an *intention* of the individual who modified it (here, merely spatially); that is, the anthropological sense of artifact may lack any commitment to the claim that an artifactual feature was consciously considered, or deliberated about, by a member of a human society.

Some of this distancing can also be discerned from individuality and intentionality in current artistic uses of the term *artifact.* In fact, one might conjecture that the anthropological and the artistic senses of artifact have interconnections that have been further strengthened by the injection of "primitive" art into the visual arts of the early twentieth century, and that both approaches are partially antithetical to the strict philosophical sense. The artistic usage of artifact suggests that it is an object (or event) that is a product of human thought or feelings, and that then evokes in others thoughts or feelings. The first part of this definition—namely, being a *product* of human thought and feelings—is an essential part of virtually all current notions of "artistic" artifacts, and indeed of artworks. This distinguishes such entities from purely natural objects and events. Not even interpretative radicals such as Jacques Derrida seem equally interested in nonartifactual, natural objects. It is also noteworthy that most "found" artworks *(objets trouvés)* were themselves originally artifacts; and even repositioned or "displayed" natural objects seem to suggest, or are regarded as, a product of some human intention, thought, or feeling in this displaying; that is, their presentation is an artistic gesture. This is a central and useful insight of the Institutional Definition of Art.

The umbrella term *human thoughts and feelings* that spawns artifacts and that may be caused in the latter's perceivers is broad in ways that contemporary philosophy of mind has only begun to investigate and classify. The phrase may include conceptualized and nonconceptualized elements, and a variety of mental states that range from beliefs to hopes, desires, emotions and moods. Conceptual states of mind are those directed at a thought-object, usually only describable in language, and not at a predominantly immediate and sensuous object; they would typify human, as opposed to animal, experience. Nonconceptual experience and behavior are predominantly undigestedly perceptual and immediate, even instinctual. The full list of states of mind may include, but is not restricted to, the banal list of such states that has been the primary focus of modern philosophy since René Descartes, namely, beliefs, perceptions, sensations, and sometimes wants, goals, and intentions. Artistic practice and theory have for centuries, or even millennia, recognized moods and emotions, from Plato and Aristotle to the *Affektenlehre* of the eighteenth century. Modern artistic practice, especially since the theories of Carl Jung and Sigmund Freud, would not restrict artistic artifacts to *intentional* products of thoughts and feelings: they might include outpourings and other (products of) relatively uncalculated, indeed, allegedly primal or spontaneous, gestures. Some traditional "high" art may more closely approximate a philosophical definition of art, in which artists are focused, for example, on intentionally creating products that cause in others, or express, mental states. There is of course reason to question whether all purportedly spontaneous outpourings of thought and feeling are indeed uncalculated, or whether "apparent spontaneousness" is just part of the intended effect—or indeed whether such spontaneous (seeming) outpourings are possible, or why they are valuable.

The ability of art to evoke in even a sophisticated or a cynical spectator some valuable effects that are difficult to describe (including an impression of beauty or of shock), and the inability of artists or theorists to explain how this is possible in some of its more impressive instances, suggest at least that there might well not be a conscious setting of a goal by the artist, and thus no achievement of this goal through calculation. Otherwise, it should have proven much easier to describe what precisely this artistic intention was, and how an artist reasoned that it was to be achieved. (Possibly, this goal was not fully conceptualized or, while broadly conceptual, is not easily expressible in words.) Additionally, many in the Romantic era, and continuing into the contemporary scene suggested that art must, by definition, transcend an ability to describe its goals, means, or content; when it does not do so, it falls into being craft or technology. Such views are quite pronounced in John Ruskin, Leo Tolstoy, and Robin Collingwood. This thesis—which hints at the essential obscurity of art—would more readily explain why the philosophical sense of "artifact," with its intimation of precisely conceived goals and intentions, would be greeted as overly rationalistic and unwelcome.

The second part of a core artistic notion of artifact—the evocation in others of thoughts and feelings—has been far more subject to debate and interpretation. Artworks of the late nineteenth and twentieth centuries have sometimes gloried in not being directed at audiences: this is usually described as a "self-expression" or therapeutic function of art, and has occasionally erupted into tantrums that are described as antiaudience, or antimarket. (Again, one might suspect that in some cases this is simply shrewd marketing.) Despite these denials, there is a certain sense in which art essentially remains a social phenomenon of one group (artists) knowingly producing objects or events that another, usually distinct, group (spectators) then experiences. This latter experience consists in a wide range of mental states precipitated by the artwork. Modern artistic theory (especially antiintentionalism) balks at admitting that the thoughts and feelings of the producing artist are related in any substantive way—especially whether they are identical—to the thoughts and feelings elicited in members of the audience experiencing the artwork. This is in part to reject an (intentionally) communicative function of these artifacts as artworks, in part to reject the hegemony of an artist to determine the proper reaction, and to promote originality, nonpassivity, and individuality in interpretation. Modern artistic conversation has, especially in its more anticapitalist forms, also balked at attributing any "calculated" intentions of the artist toward the audience; the thoughts and feeling provoked in others by the artifact are somehow incidental to the noneconomic creative impetus. Given the realities of the economics of art, this seems improbable or irrational, although it may well be a sincere belief of some artists.

Although the anthropological and the artistic senses of *artifact* may agree in not being concerned with the precise intentions of the agents that create artifacts, most modern art has remained studiedly individualistic (at the same time, the history of art, urged on by Georg Wilhelm Friedrich Hegel and Karl Marx, has sometimes moved in the opposite, anthropological direction: seeing artworks as indicative of their time and milieu); that is, artists themselves seek to express a distinctive array of thought and feelings, and art critics and theorists often still look for an individual message or style. Most Western contemporary artists would be dissatisfied with merely expressing the perspective of their period or milieu, and many art critics would be unsatisfied with such "generic" art (although for an anthropologist, this is not only useful but the very goal). Again, one suspects economic concerns at work: it may be impossible to sustain oneself if, in an era of mass-reproducibility one expresses a generic rather than a "unique" and timely style or gesture.

A further difference between the philosophical (and anthropological) conception of artifact on the one hand, and the artistic on the other, is more interesting and philosophical, although hardly clear: artists and artistic theory have sometimes balked at the "objectification" of the artifact or artwork that the philosophical definition of artifact seems to presuppose. Artists seem to reject the idea of a well-defined, discrete, and especially physical entity being the precise bearer of their artistry. In part, this may be a repulsion for contemporary theories of objects, especially in Anglo-American philosophy, that reduces any object worthy of the name to a physical or material body, event, or configuration thereof. It may also reflect political inclinations of artists to separate themselves from what they see as the metaphysical underpinnings of capitalism—materialism in the popular and philosophical sense. But, the "phenomenal" approaches of Husserl and Roman Ingarden, and the Idealist theories of Benedetto Croce and others, have often not fared any better with the art world. Here the problem may be an artistic dedication to the obscure and a suspicion that even these "phenomenal" approaches, although not proposing a reduction of all artistic phenomena to physical terms, talk about art and artistry in analytic terms. In these artistic obscurantists—like their brethren who oppose the possibility of computational intelligence—one has reason to suspect a humanist-artistic desire to save basic, essentially mysterious, human phenomena in the face of precise language, in the face of a dehumanizing language of "technology." (This also resonates with the rejection of the means-ends vocabulary of goals and intentions in the philosophical definition of artifact.) It could be that this is little more than a self-serving antirationalism. It may also, however, underscore the implausible and thinly computational theory of "mind" that has become the vogue in Anglo-American philosophy, as well as a chronic lack of attention to the "marginal" mental states of desire, mood, and emotion in modern philosophy, and the often superficial theories of mental and emotive content that fail to acknowledge the "embedded," historical, and relational nature of large-scale human practices such as language, artistic styles, and perhaps all artistic gestures and artifacts.

[*See also* Anthropology and Aesthetics; Craft; Definition of Art; *and* Institutional Theory of Art.]

BIBLIOGRAPHY

Adams, William Y., and Ernest W. Adams. *Archaeological Typology and Practical Reality: A Dialectical Approach to Artifact Classification and Sorting.* Cambridge and New York, 1991.

Davidson, Donald. *Essays on Actions and Events.* Oxford, 1980.

Dipert, Randall R. *Artifacts, Art Works, and Agency.* Philadelphia, 1993.

Dipert, Randall R. "Some Issues in the Theory of Artifacts: Defining 'Artifact' and Related Notions." *The Monist* 78.2 (1995): 119–35.

Doepke, F. "The Structure of Persons and Artifacts." *Ratio* 29 (1987): 36–51.

Fletcher, James J. "Artifactuality Broadly and Narrowly Speaking." *Southern Journal of Philosophy* 20 (1982): 41–52.

Husserl, Edmund. *Phenomenological Psychology: Lectures, Summer Semester, 1925.* Translated by John Scanlon. The Hague, 1977.

Ingarden, Roman. *The Literary Work of Art: An Investigation on the Borderlines of Ontology, Logic, and Theory of Literature.* Translated by George G. Grabowicz. Evanston, Ill., 1973.

Ingarden, Roman. *Ontology of the Work of Art: The Musical Work, the Picture, the Architectural Work, the Film.* Translated by Raymond Meyer and John T. Goldthwait. Athens, Ohio, 1989.

Kalish, Charles W. "Essentialism and Graded Membership in Animal and Artifact Categories." *Memory and Cognition* 23 (1995): 335–353.

Malt, Barbara, and Eric Johnson. "Do Artifact Concepts Have Cores?" *Journal of Memory and Language* 31 (1992): 195–217.

Margolis, Joseph. *Culture and Cultural Entities: Toward a New Unity of Science.* Dordrecht and Boston, 1984.

Schwartz, Stephen P. "Putnam on Artifacts." *Philosophical Review* 87 (1978): 566–574.

Stalker, Douglas. "The Importance of Being an Artifact." *Philosophia* 8 (1979): 701–712.

Workman, Michael E. "The Artifact as Evidence: So What?" *Technology and Culture* 27 (1986): 118–120.

Wylie, Allison. Review of William Y. Adams and Ernest W. Adams, *Archaeological Typology and Practical Reality: A Dialectical Approach to Artifact Classification and Sorting. Current Anthropology* 33 (1992): 486–491.

RANDALL DIPERT

ARTIFICIAL INTELLIGENCE. [*This entry explains the meaning of artificial intelligence and how it both relates to traditional aesthetic theories and challenges them.*]

Artificial intelligence (AI) is an area of research and design of "intelligent" computer hardware and software. The term *artificial intelligence* was coined for a conference at Dartmouth College held in the summer of 1956 (Gardner, 1985). The Dartmouth conference brought together the majority of researchers who are today considered the founders of the field including John McCarthy, Marvin Minsky, Herbert Simon, Allen Newell, and others. Although AI has primarily been a concern of computer scientists, its multidisciplinary membership (including also mathematicians, philosophers, engineers, and social scientists) was evident even at the time of the Dartmouth conference. AI did not have a name before the Dartmouth conference, yet it participates in older intellectual and design traditions that have investigated mechanical and symbolic systems and human cognition and perception for centuries. Consequently, as an area of design concerned with cognition and perception, AI can be understood as the latest manifestation of certain views of aesthetics that have their roots in older philosophical, scientific, and artistic projects.

The purpose of this article is to give a short history of AI that highlights its relations with a Kantian view of aesthetics. Its purpose is *not* to give a comprehensive overview of AI (see instead Shapiro, 1992 for one such overview). Instead, this article's focus is the intersection of AI and aesthetics (cf. Haase, 1996), and thus it supplements, but does not largely overlap, two different histories that have been repeatedly told about (1) AI and science and (2) AI and art. A history of AI concerned with its scientific roots would emphasize its relations to the development of calculating machines, logic, and mathematics (e.g., Gardner, 1985). An art history of AI (cf. McCorduck, 1979, pp. 3–29) would, by contrast, detail its similarities and differences with ancient and modern myths, literatures, and depictions of robots, cyborgs (González, 1995), and artificially (re-)created humans like Frankenstein's monster. For expository purposes, these other histories (of AI, art, and science) are mostly left to the side so that a single, streamlined story, focusing on AI and aesthetics, can be told. At the end of this article, the "streamlining" is questioned by examining some of AI's relationships to other (i.e., non-Kantian) aesthetics.

Early AI. Throughout its—now more than forty-year—history, AI has never been a discipline without internal differences. Nevertheless, until about the mid-1980s it was possible to say that a large majority of AI researchers were concerned with the elaboration of a *rationalist* understanding of cognition and perception (Winograd and Flores, 1987). Within the rationalist tradition, human identity and the thinking, calculating mind tend to become conflated. AI's rationalist bent can be understood by examining it as a reaction against behaviorism (Skinner, 1953), the approach that dominated the social sciences for most the first half of the twentieth century in the United States, and an outgrowth of cybernetics (Wiener, 1948), an interdisciplinary effort born during World War II to study social, biological, and electromechanical systems as systems of control and information.

Behaviorism and AI. Behaviorists' preference for studying external, empirically observable behaviors rather than, for example, a method of introspection or the analysis of verbal reports of others' thinking, effectively divided psychology (and other social sciences) from closely related disciplines such as psychoanalysis that were founded on the postulation of internal, mental structures and events. As computers became more and more common, the behaviorists' hegemonic position in American social science began to wane. Behaviorists were unwilling to postulate the existence of intentions, purposes, and complicated internal, mental mechanisms. Yet, during and after World War II, as computers were built to do more and more complicated tasks, not only computer engineers, but also the popular press began to call computers "electronic brains" and their internal parts and functions were given anthropomorphic names (e.g., computer "memory" as opposed to, for instance, the synonymous term the *store* of the computer). Concomitantly, some social scientists began to take seriously the analogy between the workings of a computer and the workings of the human mind (Turkle, 1988). This set of social scientists went on to found AI and cognitive science as a whole, the area of science that includes AI and a variety of other "computationally inspired" approaches to cognition in linguistics, anthropology, psychology, and neurophysiology (Gardner, 1985).

Cybernetics and AI. At the same time—that is, during and immediately after World War II—the science of cybernetics gained increased prominence. Cybernetics differs from most work done within the confines of a strict behaviorism in at least two ways: (1) whereas behaviorists postulated linear relationships between an external stimulus and an organism's response, cybernetics introduced the ideas of recursive (i.e., circular) relations between perception or sensation and action known as positive and negative feedback circuits; (2) although behaviorists avoided labeling any behavior "goal-directed" (because it would imply the postulation of internal representations), cyberneticians (re)introduced teleology into scientific descriptions of behavior (Heims, 1991, p. 15).

Subsequently, the earliest work in AI elaborated on the cyberneticians' usage of "goal-directed behavior" and de-emphasized external contexts and empirically observable stimuli, the preoccupation of the behaviorists. Consequently, AI immediately began to diverge from cybernetics as a result of AI's neglect of an analysis of feedback from the environment. Some contemporary work addresses this early neglect, but early work in AI—for example, the work of Newell, Shaw, and Simon (1963) on the General Problem Solver (GPS)—only explored feedback insofar as the "external world" could be internalized in the computer. To work, GPS required that a full and accurate model of the "state of the world" (insofar as one can even talk of a "world" of logic or cryptoarithmetic, two of the domains in which GPS solved problems) be encoded and then updated after any action was taken (e.g., after a step was added to the proof of a theorem). This assumption—that perception was always accurate and that all of the significant details of the world could be modeled and followed—was incorporated into most AI programs for decades and resulted in what became known to the AI community as the "frame problem," that is, the problem of deciding what parts of the internal model to update when a change is made to the model or the external world (see Martins, 1992, p. 111). Not surprisingly, AI robots built around strict internal/external divisions sometimes exhibited extremely erratic behavior when the robots' sensors were even slightly inaccurate in the measurement of the external world.

AI as a Kantian Endeavor. Early AI's antibehaviorist, inward turn to focus on internal representations (like "goals") led to what can be understood as the reinvention of philosophical rationalism's problems and "solutions." Or, because AI has routinely been concerned with the difficulties and sometimes the limits of rationality (expressed, for example, in Herbert Simon's notion of "bounded rationality" [Simon, 1996]), its "reinventions" more specifically resemble not rationalism per se but philosophical responses to rationalism such as, for example, Immanuel Kant's *Critiques*. [*See* Kant.] Indeed, the rationalist approach to perception and cognition pursued by a large majority of AI researchers until the mid-1980s can be explained in Kantian terms.

The following explanation of AI using Kantian terms relies on a well-known reading of Kant formulated by the philosopher Gilles Deleuze (Deleuze, 1984). [*See* Deleuze.] Deleuze's interpretation is akin to several other readings of Kant (notably, the work of Jean-François Lyotard [Lyotard, 1994]) that, collectively, might be viewed as the "poststructuralist" response to Kant. [*See* Lyotard.]

Kant's comparison of aesthetic and teleological judgment (Kant, 1969) provides a framework for narrating how AI's original preoccupations with teleology and neglect of aesthetics caused a series of crises for the field in the mid-1980s that initiated an "aesthetic turn" (Sack, 1997) in research, motivating AI scientists and designers to pay increasing attention to issues of the body, the senses, and physical and social environments. Although Kant's vocabulary provides a convenient means of describing the problems and achievements of AI, within the literature of AI Kant is rarely mentioned, or, if mentioned, then only represented as formative of AI's parent discipline, cognitive science (cf. Gardner, 1985; Brook, 1994). Here it is argued that Kant's vocabulary of aesthetics (as "spoken" by poststructuralism) is equal to the task of describing many important research issues in AI. No argument is offered to support the opinion that some sort of "equivalence" exists between AI and Kant's critical project.

In conflict with rationalists (such as René Descartes), Kant argued for a limited role for teleological principles to supplement mechanical explanations (Caygill, 1995, p. 388). Likewise, cyberneticians—in conflict with most behaviorists—argued for a limited use of teleology in coordination with the vocabulary of physics to describe the behavior of complex, nonlinear systems. In the 1950s, when AI took up the vocabulary of teleology (i.e., "final cause") from cyberneticians, what was repressed—or at least foreclosed—for AI was the problematic status of the posited goals and purposes used to understand the behavior of complex systems. For Kant, teleological principles were considered to have no explanatory significance (Kant, 1969, para. 61). Instead, teleological judgment—in Kantian terms—was seen as a response to an apparent purposelessness of aesthetic judgment: "purpose" is a projection of the cognitive subject on nature, not an intrinsic property of nature itself. In contrast to Kant's careful reintroduction of teleology within a nuanced discussion of aesthetics—where teleology was seen as a *product of cognition,* but not necessarily an artifact useful for communication and explanation—AI researchers took teleology as a *basis for their scientific explanations of cognition,* problem solving, and learning. This difference of opinion concerning the explanatory significance of goals and purposes is so large that one might assume that any continued narration of AI as a type of "Kan-

tianism" (as AI's history is here described) would be fruitless. However, the way in which AI has struggled with the questions of teleology (e.g., For whom do posited goals and purposes signify something meaningful?) is strikingly Kantian in its (AI's) recurrent appeal to "common sense," a faculty of great importance to Kant's critical philosophy.

Kant and Common Sense. *Faculty* (e.g., a "faculty of common sense") is a crucial yet ambiguous term in Kant's writings. For present purposes, it suffices to say that a Kantian "faculty" is a potential or power to realize some end (Caygill, 1995, p. 190). Computational approaches to philosophy, like those championed by AI, often equate "powers" with "computational processes" or (to use a less theoretical term) "computer programs." Thus, to draw an analogy between the writings of Kant and the writings of AI researchers, it is necessary to imagine that Kant's "faculties" could be reexpressed in a variant, textual form: as computer programs with specific data structures, data flow, and control flow. Although this metaphoric comparison of the human cognitive faculties to computer programs may seem outlandish to many, it is a hallmark not only of AI but of all contemporary cognitive science (Gardner, 1985, p. 6). To compare Kant's work to the research goals of AI, it is not necessary to believe that this metaphor (mind as machine) is "true." Rather, it is only necessary for the reader to be able to imagine that AI researchers consider this metaphor to be true; or, if not true, then at least extremely useful.

Kant discusses three cognitive faculties: understanding, reason, and imagination. In the terminology of AI, one might explain these faculties as classification (understanding), inference (reason), and schema or pattern matching (imagination). In addition to the three cognitive faculties, Kant describes three sorts of common sense: two legislated and one engendered (cf. Deleuze, 1984, pp. 49–50). The ways in which the three faculties described by Kant (of understanding, reason, and imagination) interrelate with one another are referred to as (1) *logical common sense* and (2) *moral common sense* when, respectively, (1) understanding, and (2) reason legislate over the two other complementary faculties. In contrast with these two legislated sorts of common sense, (3) *aesthetic common sense* is engendered when none of the faculties are regent, but when they all, nevertheless, work together even as they function autonomously and spontaneously. In the vocabulary of contemporary computer science, one might say that the differences between these three kinds of common sense are differences in "control structure," that is, differences concerning which (or whether) one computer program, program statement, or "faculty" is directing the others.

Kant's theories of *reflective judgment* (which includes both *aesthetic reflective* and *teleological reflective judgment*) function with the support of an engendered, aesthetic common sense. This common sense is engendered when, for example, the faculty of reason compels the faculty of imagination to confront its limits by attempting to schematize a perception of the formless or the deformed in nature (a state referred to as the *sublime*). According to Deleuze, the aesthetic common sense should not be understood as a supplement to logical and moral common sense but as that which gives them a basis or makes them possible, because the faculties of understanding and reason could not take on a legislative role if it were not first the case (as in the accord of an aesthetic common sense) that they are each capable of operating in free subjective harmony (Deleuze, 1984, p. 50). The implications for AI of this conceptualization of common sense—like Kant's aesthetic common sense—will play an important role in the discussion that follows.

AI and Common Sense. The neo-Kantian Jean-François Lyotard draws an analogy between Kant's description of *reflective judgment* (a mode of thought that works from the particular toward the universal, as opposed to *determinant judgment,* which proceeds in the inverse direction) and AI researchers' (especially Marvin Minsky's) descriptions of "frame-based" thought and perception (Lyotard, 1991, p. 15). Minsky's "frames" proposal (Minsky, 1981) was an attempt to describe common sense thought in humans and its possibilities in computers. Minsky, McCarthy (1990), their students, and colleagues in AI were concerned with the following question about common sense: What is the structure and content of common sense such that it allows one to quickly draw useful conclusions from a vast array of existing knowledge and perceptional data? One of the immediate outgrowths of this research was a series of "frame-based" computer programming languages with control-structure statements very unlike previous programming languages (e.g., Roberts and Goldstein, 1977). From this AI point of view, common sense is a legislative faculty, that is, a control (or controlling) structure that allows a system to turn its attention away from nonsense so that it can concentrate on the sensical or what is implied by the commonsensical. In other words, in Kantian terms, AI's analysis of "common sense" was largely (and still is in some circles) limited to "legislated common sense"—"logical common sense" and "moral (i.e., 'reason-legislated') common sense"—and had (until recently) completely neglected "aesthetic common sense," an unlegislated state of relations between understanding, reason, and imagination.

AI and Nonmilitary Concerns. Such was the case until the mid-1980s, when two "events" motivated a reappraisal within AI of the issues of aesthetics, including the role of the body and the senses in cognition. The first "event" was the commercial success of a genre of AI computer programs called "expert systems" (Feigenbaum and McCorduck, 1983). For the first thirty years of its existence (in the United States) AI was mostly academic research funded by the military. Then, in the mid-eighties, business concerns began funding the development of expert systems

to automate a variety of white-collar work. Whereas the U.S. Department of Defense had been content to finance long-term research in which it was presumed that theoretical work might, one day, be of practical interest, the new benefactors of AI demanded empirically evaluated, immediate results. What soon became clear was that many expert systems were "brittle," that is, they performed competently within a narrow domain of problems, but if the problems were posed in a slightly different manner, or if slightly different types of problems were posed to the systems, the systems responded in erratic and erroneous ways. Moreover, it was noted by users of the systems that the systems were difficult to communicate with: one needed to pose problems in a specially constructed, artificial language and, often, after receiving a solution from a system it was impossible to get the system to explain the rationale for its solution. Expert system adherents claimed that the problem was simply that more rules needed to be added to the "brittle" expert systems to make them "flexible." Expert system opponents, often using a philosophical vocabulary of (Martin Heidegger's) phenomenology, claimed that rules were inadequate to the task of articulating the means of human expertise, and thus no number of rules could allow a machine to match the skills of a human expert. [*See* Phenomenology.]

The second "event" was the U.S. military's loss of funding in the late-eighties as a result of the end of the cold war with the Soviet Union. Both "events" pushed AI researchers to look for new funding sources and "applications" in finance, advertising, and entertainment.

Two Strands of Aesthetic AI Research. This exodus from the isolated, military-industrial-funded laboratories fostered two strands of research. One strand is attributable to a diverse collection of researchers who, for the purposes of this article, will be called the "neo-Encyclopedists." The second strand of researchers will be called the "computational phenomenologists." Both of these strands have longer histories of existence, even within the lifetime of AI itself, but they were given more funding and attention after the two above-mentioned "events." One of the major distinctions between these two strands of researchers is this: whereas the neo-Encyclopedists (or at least their predecessors in symbolic AI; e.g., Minsky) feel that "common sense" can be catalogued as a system of rules with intentional content (cf. Dreyfus and Hall, 1982, p. 23), the computational phenomenologists do not believe that "common sense" can be articulated in the structure of rules.

The "rules" under scrutiny by the computational phenomenologists can be understood as a certain specialized form of computer program articulated as a series of "if-then" statements (e.g., "If the water is steaming and bubbling, then its temperature is probably 100 degrees Celsius"). But, the term *rules* can also be understood as synecdochically referring to a larger class of computer programs (including, for example, Minsky's "frames," and what others have called "schemata" or "scripts" [Schank and Abelson, 1977]).

The Neo-Encyclopedists. Motivated by the observation that most AI programs do not contain enough schemata or rules to deal with unforeseen circumstances (cf. the "brittleness" of expert systems mentioned earlier), the neo-Encyclopedists are attempting to produce huge catalogs of "common sense" (i.e., computer programs and databases). Some of these efforts are largely accomplished "by hand" whereby dozens of people are employed for years to encode myriad mundane details and rules (e.g., "water is a liquid," "what goes up must come down"). Other efforts are aided by statistical and machine learning techniques to augment or build such catalogs. The most well known of these efforts has been a ten-year project called CYC (originally short for enCYClopedia) financed largely by corporate sponsors (Lenat and Guha, 1990). CYC and a handful of other efforts are the contemporary offspring of Minsky's (1981) and McCarthy's (1990) proposals for representing common sense, oftentimes referred to as "symbolic AI."

Although work in symbolic AI has always stressed the importance of teleological and "intentional" representation, however, newer work in "computational linguistics" (a field that intersects with the AI subfield of "natural language processing") contributes to the neo-Encyclopedists' efforts without necessarily ascribing the same importance to teleology. Computational linguistic, neo-Encyclopedist work is often described as the latest extension to the long-standing field of lexicography, the discipline that has historically been responsible for the construction of encyclopedias, dictionaries, and thesauri (Wilks et al., 1996). This turn away from teleology in recent neo-Encyclopedist work might be seen as a renewed interest in the freedom of the (Kantian) imagination and its power to schematize without any concept (Kant, 1969, para. 35), that is, an interest in the basis for an aesthetic common sense (taste). One difference, however, is, for instance, the dependence of much recent computational linguistic work on the form of very simple "schemata" or "rules" (e.g., the form and limitations of Markov models) versus the postulation of no schematic influence whatsoever by Kant.

The Computational Phenomenologists. Although computational phenomenology can be understood to be in opposition to the project of the neo-Encyclopedists, the neo-Encyclopedists' turn away from teleology (in favor of lexicography) makes it clear that this opposition is more of a tension than an unbridgeable gap. In fact, the two strands can both be understood as pursuing different forms of phenomenology, one more Edmund Husserl-inspired (i.e., transcendental) and the other more Martin Heidegger-inspired (i.e., existential).

Disbelief in structured rules with intentional content has spawned several different research paradigms, some of which will here be subsumed under the label "computational phenomenology." One paradigm, known as "connectionism" (McClelland and Rumelhart, 1986), is an attempt to replace rules with digitally simulated "neural nets." Another paradigm, "situated action" (e.g., Agre and Chapman, 1987) or "behavior-based AI" (e.g., Brooks, 1991), couples the "neural nets" of connectionism to robotic (hardware and software) bodies with sensors. The research agenda of the latter group is, in many ways, a direct descendant of cybernetics insofar as it insists on the employment of feedback circuits and the disruption of internal representation versus external world dichotomies created in and by early AI work. Finally, what is here labeled "computational phenomenology" is also meant to encompass recent work in "distributed AI" (Gasser, 1991) and "multiagent systems"; such work takes its metaphors of interaction from social systems (e.g., the systems of various scientific communities for the publication and archiving of journal articles) instead of the metaphors of the isolated thinker preferred by early AI researchers.

The Aesthetic Turn. The work of the computational phenomenologists constitutes an "aesthetic turn" (Sack, 1997) in AI research because they focus attention on the aesthetic dimensions of cognition, including the senses, the body, and the social and physical environment of perception. Although the neo-Encyclopedists might be seen as an outgrowth of an older, "symbolic AI," computational phenomenology has been formulated in opposition to symbolic AI. Pivotal to the computational phenomenologists' position has been their understanding of common sense as a negotiated process, as opposed to a huge database of facts, rules, or schemata. This position is often repeated by the computational phenomenologists: "It should come as no surprise that the area in which [symbolic] artificial intelligence has had the greatest difficulty is in the programming of common sense. It has long been recognized that it is much easier to write a program to carry out abstruse formal operations than to capture the common sense of a dog. This is an obvious consequence of Heidegger's realization that it is precisely in our 'ordinary everydayness' that we are immersed in readiness-to-hand" (Winograd and Flores, 1987, p. 98). In other words, common sense is a faculty engendered by our encounters with "nature" and others—that is, that said by Kant (according to Deleuze [1984]) to engender an "aesthetic common sense."

Husserl, Heidegger, and AI. The references to Martin Heidegger by the computational phenomenologists can be seen as a contemporary manifestation of a debate between AI software designers that began as a philosophical debate initiated by Hubert Dreyfus (Dreyfus, 1972). [*See* Heidegger.] Dreyfus and several of his colleagues (especially John Searle) have been critiquing AI (particularly symbolic AI) for more than three decades. Dreyfus has pointed out the close philosophical affinities between the projects of symbolic AI and Edmund Husserl's transcendental phenomenology and its differences from a Heideggerian existential phenomenology (cf. Dreyfus and Hall, 1982, pp. 2–27). [*See* Husserl.] In particular, Dreyfus details the relationship between Husserl's philosophical project and Marvin Minsky's "frames" proposal for encoding common sense (ibid., pp. 19–22).

Given Husserl's deep intellectual debts to Kant, it is understandable that Lyotard would compare Minsky's proposal to Kant's idea of reflective judgment (Lyotard, 1991, p. 15). Thus, these philosophical critiques of AI (e.g., of Dreyfus and Lyotard) give one a means of seeing how symbolic AI's proposals to encode common sense (e.g., Minsky's proposal) inherit the limitations of Kant and Husserl; and, also, the critiques illustrate how Heidegger's critique of Husserl is reflected in the computational phenomenologists' critique of symbolic AI. Despite the frequent citation of Heidegger's work within the literature of computational phenomenology, however, it is not clear whether computational phenomenology is a Heideggerian project. In many ways, computational phenomenology is a self-contradictory (cf. Coyne, 1995, p. 177) effort to "enframe" (Heidegger, 1977) Heidegger's critique of Husserl in a set of technologies (cf. Dreyfus, 1992).

AI and Cultural Difference. When AI has been dependent on a Kantian-influenced vocabulary (e.g., the terms *schema, common sense,* and *teleology*), its inability to articulate cultural difference is reminiscent of Kant's own limitations or oversights (e.g., with respect to gender differences). For example, in AI discussions of common sense, few researchers have asked *whose* common sense is under consideration, preferring instead to assume that common sense is common to all humans and not culturally specific.

Even with the "aesthetic turn" in AI, practically no work has been done in AI on cultural difference (e.g., the [re]production of differences of gender, sexuality, class, race, and nationality). A belief in aesthetics as culturally invariant is obviously a useful one for a liberal, Enlightenment politics to which Kant's theories of universal subjectivity contribute. AI and cognitive science, in general, are very much in the vein of Kant's cosmopolitan universalism in their hypothesis of universal cognitive mechanisms "executable" on all sorts of (silicon- and carbon-based) "hardware." What this hypothesis of a universal subjectivity leaves unthought is that significant differences between people do exist and, furthermore, the introduction of powerful technologies, like AI, can change people even more by changing their day-to-day lives. As a result, AI and its critics have largely been blind to the ethical implications of AI (Sack, 1997) and its implications for post-Kantian aesthetics.

Nevertheless, some AI work has been done addressing what could be *interpreted* as cultural difference. For instance, ideological difference has been modeled (e.g., Abelson and Carroll, 1965; Carbonell, 1979) as a difference of teleology (that is, a difference of goals and the interrelationships between goals); expert/novice differences in education and learning have been modeled as differences of number, detail, type, and interrelationships of rules and schemas (e.g., Wenger, 1987); differences between the mentally healthy and the mentally ill (e.g., Kenneth Colby's [1981] simulation of a paranoid mind) have been computationally modeled as differences of beliefs and intentions. Although such work does engage the problematics of such important cultural phenomena as ideology, education, and mental illness, it implicitly assumes that differences of culture are personal differences by attempting to represent them exclusively with "mental," "internal" constructs such as goals, plans, beliefs, and intentions. Such work reduces the public to the private by ignoring the ways in which social interaction can be (re)productive of cultural difference.

This weakness of AI is not surprising given that the central metaphor of the discipline has been not *minds,* but *mind*-as-machine. Marvin Minsky's more recent work (1986) stretches this metaphor by hypothesizing that a mind is composed of a society of "agents." This work is a shift away from a Kantian vocabulary to a vocabulary of psychoanalysis (cf. Elizabeth Grosz [1990] for a description of "agents" and Freud's "realist" model of the ego). Other, newer work in distributed artificial intelligence (e.g., Bond and Gasser, 1988), multiagent systems (e.g., Fagin et al., 1995), artificial life (e.g., Brooks and Maes, 1994), computational models of discourse (e.g., Grosz and Sidner, 1986), and computer-supported cooperative work (cf. Winograd and Flores, 1987) stretches the central metaphor of AI further by making groups and communities (rather than the mind of a single individual) the object of study. Increasingly these new offshoots of AI are not simply stretching the boundaries of AI but, rather, creating independent disciplines.

Even within these newer disciplines, however, little attention has been paid to the issue of cultural difference. Instead, what is predominantly stressed is consensus and questions like the following: Within a community of agents, how can significant difference and miscommunication be overcome to allow for coordination, agreement, and "common knowledge"? (cf. Fagin et al., 1995).

Turing's Imitation Game. Ironically, cultural difference (specifically gender) is central to what is considered by most AI researchers to be the founding essay of AI. In his essay "Computing Machinery and Intelligence" (Turing, 1950), Alan Turing proposes a Wittgensteinian language game, the "imitation game," to replace what he sees as the meaningless question "Can machines think?" Turing's "imitation game" includes a proposal to program a computer to play the role of a man attempting to imitate a woman—an intriguing proposal concerning the reproduction and representation of gender difference in computational, networked media. Turing's "imitation game" is usually renamed in the

AI literature as the "Turing Test" and renarrated to exclude any mention of gender difference (Genova, 1994; Sack, 1996).

Turing describes the imitation game as follows:

> It is played with three people, a man, a woman, and an interrogator who may be of either sex. The interrogator stays in a room apart from the other two. The object of the game for the interrogator is to determine which of the other two is the man and which is the woman. . . . It is [the man's] object in the game to try and cause [the interrogator] to make the wrong identification. . . . The object of the game for [the woman] is to help the interrogator. . . . We now ask the question, "What will happen when a machine takes the part of [the man] in this game?" Will the interrogator decide wrongly as often when the game is played like this as he does when the game is played between a man and a woman? These questions replace our original [question], "Can machines think?" (Turing, 1950, pp. 433–434)

Within the AI literature, discussions of Turing's imitation game have focused on the role of the machine and the role of the interrogator. The role of the woman has been almost entirely ignored. Yet, if one looks more closely at the woman's role in Turing's game, it is clear that variants of this role have been reiterated in popular art and performance for thousands of years. The woman's role, in Turing's game, is to compete with the machine for an identity that is properly hers to begin with (i.e., the role of "woman"). The frequently reiterated, popular fears surrounding AI and its cultural and specifically artistic precedents are the fears of this sort of role, that is, the fears of loss of identity, fears of replacement by machine, fears of disfiguration, dismemberment, and death.

AI and Aesthetics of the Uncanny. In short, these fears of an AI machine are, specifically, the fears of the "double" as it has been explored in psychoanalytic theory (e.g., Rank, 1971) and in the arts, for instance, in literature (e.g., "The Sandman" by E. T. A. Hoffmann [1855]) and film (e.g., *The Student of Prague* written by Hanns Heinz Ewers and directed by Paul Wegener [1912]). More generally, these fears can be described as those associated with the *uncanny aesthetic* discussed by Sigmund Freud (1955) and others (e.g., Julia Kristeva, 1991; Anthony Vidler, 1992). Fears of the uncanny are often associated with machines, automata, and artificially produced "doubles."

Julia Kristeva has written that "uncanniness occurs when the boundaries between imagination and reality are erased" (Kristeva, 1991, p. 188). Some AI researchers have tried to disavow association between their "real" work and the imaginative, artistic tradition that explores the fears of uncanny aesthetics (e.g., Hayes and Ford, 1995, p. 976). Yet, any review of AI and aesthetics would be incomplete without mentioning AI's relationship to the aesthetics of the uncanny because popular perception (e.g., as reflected in film, television, literature, and journalists' stories about AI) is often dominated by questions of "doubling": Will machines replace people?

Conclusion. A poststructuralist view of Kant provides a means of understanding some of the relationships between aesthetics and issues central to AI research (e.g., common sense and teleology). Newer offshoots of AI research tend to engage a larger variety of post-Kantian, philosophical, and critical vocabularies (e.g., those of Heideggerian phenomenology and psychoanalysis). But, although newer work might move AI outside the limits of a Kantian-inspired aesthetics, the newer work is *not* independent of a larger discourse of aesthetics that includes issues beyond the beautiful and the sublime (e.g., the uncanny).

[*See also* Computer Art; Creativity; Cyberspace; Hypertext; Multimedia; *and* Virtual Reality.]

BIBLIOGRAPHY

Abelson, Robert P., and J. D. Carroll. "Computer Simulation of Individual Belief Systems." *American Behavior Scientist* 8 (1965): 24–30.

Agre, Philip, and David Chapman. "Pengi: An Implementation of a Theory of Activity." In *Proceedings of the Fifth National Conference on Artificial Intelligence*, pp. 268–272. Los Altos, Calif., 1987.

Bond, Alan H., and Les Gasser, eds. *Readings in Distributed Artificial Intelligence.* Los Altos, Calif., 1988.

Brook, Andrew. *Kant and the Mind.* Cambridge and New York, 1994.

Brooks, Rodney. "Intelligence without Representation." *Artificial Intelligence* 47 (1991): 139–160.

Brooks, Rodney A., and Pattie Maes, eds. *Artificial Life IV: Proceedings of the Fourth International Workshop on the Synthesis and Simulation of Living Systems.* Cambridge, Mass., 1994.

Carbonell, Jaime. "Subjective Understanding: Computer Models of Belief Systems." Ph.D. thesis, Yale University, 1979.

Caygill, Howard. *A Kant Dictionary.* Oxford and Cambridge, Mass., 1995.

Colby, Kenneth Mark. "Modeling a Paranoid Mind." *Behavioral and Brain Sciences* 4 (1981): 515–534.

Coyne, Richard. *Designing Information Technology in the Postmodern Age.* Cambridge, Mass., 1995.

Deleuze, Gilles. *Kant's Critical Philosophy: The Doctrine of the Faculties.* Translated by Hugh Tomlinson and Barbara Habberjam. Minneapolis, 1984.

Dreyfus, Hubert L. *What Computers Can't Do: A Critique of Artificial Reason.* New York, 1972.

Dreyfus, Hubert L. *What Computers Still Can't Do: A Critique of Artificial Reason.* Cambridge, Mass., 1992.

Dreyfus, Hubert L., with Harrison Hall, eds. *Husserl, Intentionality, and Cognitive Science.* Cambridge, Mass., 1982.

Ewers, Hanns Heinz. *Der Student von Prag.* Directed by Paul Wegener. Essex Films, 1980. Videocassette release of the 1912 German motion picture.

Fagin, Ronald, J. Y. Halpern, Y. Moses, and M. Y. Vardi. *Reasoning about Knowledge.* Cambridge, Mass., 1995.

Feigenbaum, Edward A., and Pamela McCorduck. *The Fifth Generation: Artificial Intelligence and Japan's Computer Challenge to the World.* Reading, Mass., 1983.

Freud, Sigmund. "The 'Uncanny.'" In *Standard Edition of the Complete Psychological Works of Sigmund Freud*, edited by James Strachey, vol. 17, pp. 217–252. London, 1955.

Gardner, Howard. *The Mind's New Science: A History of the Cognitive Revolution.* New York, 1985.

Gasser, Les. "Social Conceptions of Knowledge and Action: Distributed Artificial Intelligence and Open Systems Semantics." *Artificial Intelligence* 47 (1991): 107–138.

Genova, Judith. "Turing's Sexual Guessing Game." *Social Epistemology* 8.4 (1994): 313–326.

González, Jennifer A. "Envisioning Cyborg Bodies: Notes from Current Research." In *The Cyborg Handbook,* edited by Chris Hables Gray with Heidi Figueroa-Sarriera and Steven Mentor, pp. 267–279. New York and London, 1995.

Grosz, Barbara, and Candace Sidner. "Attention, Intentions, and the Structure of Discourse." *Journal of Computational Linguistics* 12.3 (1986): 175–204.

Grosz, Elizabeth A. *Jacques Lacan: A Feminist Introduction.* London and New York, 1990.

Haase, Kenneth B. "A Model of Poetic Comprehension." In *Proceedings of the Thirteenth National Conference on Artificial Intelligence,* pp. 156–161. Cambridge, Mass., 1996.

Hayes, Patrick, and Kenneth Ford. "Turing Test Considered Harmful." In *Proceedings of the Fourteenth International Joint Conference on Artificial Intelligence,* pp. 972–977. Los Altos, Calif., 1995.

Heidegger, Martin. *The Question Concerning Technology and Other Essays.* Translated by William Lovitt. New York, 1977.

Heims, Steve Joshua. *The Cybernetics Group.* Cambridge, Mass., 1991.

Hoffmann, Ernst Theodor Amadeus. *Hoffmann's Strange Stories.* Translated by L. Burnham. Boston, 1855.

Kant, Immanuel. *Kritik der Urtheilskraft* (1790). In *Kant's gesammelte Schriften,* vol. 5, pp. 165–485. Berlin, 1969.

Kristeva, Julia. *Strangers to Ourselves.* Translated by Leon S. Roudiez. New York, 1991.

Lenat, Douglas, and R. Guha. *Building Large Knowledge-Based Systems: Representation and Inference in the Cyc Project.* Reading, Mass., 1990.

Lyotard, Jean-François. *The Inhuman: Reflections on Time.* Translated by Geoffrey Bennington and Rachel Bowlby. Stanford, Calif., 1991.

Lyotard, Jean-François. *Lessons on the Analytic of the Sublime: Kant's Critique of Judgment.* Translated by Elizabeth Rottenberg. Stanford, Calif., 1994.

Martins, J. "Belief Revision." In *Encyclopedia of Artificial Intelligence,* 2d ed., edited by Stuart C. Shapiro, vol. 1, pp. 110–116. New York, 1992.

McCarthy, John. *Formalizing Common Sense.* Edited by Vladimir Lifschitz. Norwood, N.J., 1990.

McClelland, James L., and David E. Rumelhart, eds. *Parallel Distributed Processing: Explorations in the Microstructure of Cognition.* 2 vols. Cambridge, Mass., 1986.

McCorduck, Pamela. *Machines Who Think: A Personal Inquiry into the History and Prospects of Artificial Intelligence.* San Francisco, 1979.

Minsky, Marvin. "A Framework for Representing Knowledge." In *Mind Design: Philosophy, Psychology, Artificial Intelligence,* edited by John Haugeland. Cambridge, Mass., 1981.

Minsky, Marvin. *The Society of Mind.* New York, 1986.

Newell, Alan, J. C. Shaw, and Herbert A. Simon. "GPS, A Program That Simulates Human Thought." In *Computers and Thought,* edited by Edward A. Feigenbaum and Julian Feldman, pp. 279–293. New York, 1963.

Rank, Otto. *The Double: A Psychoanalytic Study.* Translated by Harry Tucker, Jr. Chapel Hill, N.C., 1971.

Roberts, R. Bruce, and Ira P. Goldstein. "The FRL Manual." Massachusetts Institute of Technology, 1977.

Sack, Warren. "Painting Theory Machines." *Art and Design* 48 (May 1996): 80–92.

Sack, Warren. "Artificial Human Nature." *Design Issues* (Spring 1997).

Schank, Roger C., and Robert P. Abelson. *Scripts, Plans, Goals and Understanding: An Inquiry into Human Knowledge Structures.* New York, 1977.

Shapiro, Stuart C., ed. *Encyclopedia of Artificial Intelligence.* 2 vols. 2d ed. New York, 1992.

Simon, Herbert A. *The Sciences of the Artificial.* 3d ed. Cambridge, Mass., 1996.

Skinner, B. F. *Science and Human Behavior.* New York, 1953.

Turing, Alan. "Computing Machinery and Intelligence." *Mind* 59.236 (1950): 433–460.

Turkle, Sherry. "Artificial Intelligence and Psychoanalysis: A New Alliance." *Daedalus* 17.1 (Winter 1988).

Vidler, Anthony. *The Architectural Uncanny: Essays in the Modern Unhomely.* Cambridge, Mass., 1992.

Wenger, Étienne. *Artificial Intelligence and Tutoring Systems: Computational and Cognitive Approaches to the Communication of Knowledge.* Los Altos, Calif., 1987.

Wiener, Norbert. *Cybernetics: Or, Control and Communication in the Animal and the Machine.* Cambridge, Mass., 1948.

Wilks, Yorick A., Brian M. Slator, and Louise M. Guthrie. *Electric Words: Dictionaries, Computers, and Meanings.* Cambridge, Mass., 1996.

Winograd, Terry, and Fernando Flores. *Understanding Computers and Cognition: A New Foundation for Design.* Reading, Mass., 1987.

WARREN SACK

ARTIST. [*To explain the concept of the artist in the Western aesthetic tradition, this entry comprises two essays:*

History of the Concept of the Artist
Sociology of the Artist

The first essay explains the history of the concept of the artist, and the second surveys past and (especially) present modes of research about artists in sociology, psychology, and other fields. For related discussions, see Appropriation; Intention; *and* Museums.]

History of the Concept of the Artist

In contemporary discourse, the artist is separated from other categories of human beings by virtue of what s/he does: s/he makes art. The concept of "art" and the activity "art making" are the preconditions for the concept "artist." The artist has often been said to reside in the work of art; or the intentions of an individual artist have been said to be visible in, or concealed within, a particular work of art. With the concept "artist," the work of art is "individualized as a product of an original mind which imposes its unique imprint upon it" (Nahm, 1956).

The original mind of the individual maker can be understood to be operating in the "invention" of the artist. This is the way that artists and their work have been distinguished from one another by criticism and the art market since the early modern period (Summers, 1987; Hughes, 1990). However, the theoretical proposition that the work of art is a product of an original mind that imposes its unique imprint on it has been widely accepted in Western culture since the Greeks. Thus, the modern concept of the artist, born in Renaissance Italy, entails the concept of the original work of art. Both concepts indicate a dialectical relationship between the maker and the art object whose importance in the following discussion cannot be overemphasized.

The practices of traditional connoisseurship, or the judgment of the work of art by experts according to a system of evaluation that seeks to define the "unique imprint" of the individual artist, support the theoretical proposition, just as they rely on it. In the work of art, particularly paintings, drawings, and wax and clay models, the sign or mark of the artist is often called the "hand" of the artist. A connoisseur notes particularities of technique, details of execution, and treatment of subject matter in works of art common to a majority of the individual's production. In this way the connoisseur helps to establish an artist's oeuvre, or total production.

The characterization of an individual artist's oeuvre in terms of his "hand" is known as the "style" of the artist. Style relies on a rational organization of the works by an individual maker so that the manner developed by that maker can be discerned by or articulated in discourse. A key aspect of that rational organization is chronology, the arrangement of the works of art according to when they were made during the individual artist's life. (*Provenance,* on the other hand, is the chronology of the work of art subsequent to its separation from the artist and according to its ownership.) A chronological organization allows the works of art to be tied to events in the life of a particular historical individual. Traditionally, this arrangement has allowed for a history of art where works and makers were interpreted according to the biological model of time, that is, the life of the artist from birth to death determines and supports an account of the works from early to late style. This is the model of writing about the artist and his work that can be found in biographies of artists beginning in the early Renaissance and continuing today. The later professional genre of the monograph of the artist that developed with the rise of art history in the late nineteenth century follows this model of pinning a chronologically rational catalog of the works of the artist to his or her biography.

This model of art's history according to the *bios,* or lived life of the individual artist, converges significantly with the view of the material object found in archaeological discourse beginning with J. J. Winckelmann's *History of Ancient Art* (1764). Here, the object's, monument's, or image's existence—whether partial or complete—persists over long periods of time, regardless of the individual maker's life. The outcome in archaeology is the understanding of the object from the past as a document with evidentiary and truth-revealing qualities concerning the history of the culture that produced it, rather than the individual who made it. According to such historicist interpretations, the material object bears the distinctive but anonymous marks of time rather than the purposeful signs of the individual maker.

Anthropology has appropriated this view of the human artifact from archaeology in response to the problem of interpreting the products of a tribe or group where individualized making does not pertain. Today, however, some cultural anthropologists explore the contradictions that arise when this definition of the artifact is put to the test by the global market for art in which contemporary tribal makers appropriate the Europeanized concept of the maker as artist (Myers, 1994). In any case, when the object, art, is thought to persist over time *and* is known by its maker, the artist, its interpretation will require a knowledge of the artist's historical existence. Art's history depends on the survival of one or many objects known as art and on a verbal tradition, either oral or written, that associates particular works with the lives and social situations of individual makers. These are the prerequisites for art history, which seeks to know objects according to style (whether defined on an individual, school, period, or geographic basis) as well as historical context. The mutually supportive conditions of the concepts art and artist in the European tradition can be seen in the written record extending back at least as far as the fourth century BCE (Webster, 1939; Pollitt, 1974).

The Greeks had a plethora of differentiations for visual media and their techniques, particularly those associated with sculpture, but they lacked an encompassing term for "art" (Donahue, 1988). They also lacked a term for the visual "artist." For the Greeks, distinctions were made on the basis of medium (marble sculpture/sculpture; encaustic painting/encaustic painter; singing/singer; horsemanship/horseman, etc.), not on the basis of a generalized practice or a category of people tied to art making. As Jerome Pollitt has noted, the Greek term *technē,* understood to be the closest to our term *art* and similar to the Latin term *ars,* "might be translated as 'organized knowledge and procedure applied for the purpose of producing a specific preconceived result,' or simply 'rational production,'" neither of which corresponds to the later understanding of the term *art.* It must be seen as key to any history of the artist that there is no term for the maker corresponding to *technē.* Even in poetry, according to Aristotle, the medium exists without the writer or speaker posited as "artist" or "creator."

Aristotle notwithstanding, the Platonic tradition uses the term for genius-creator to refer to the poet who writes poetry for nonpractical ends (Mason, 1993). The creator, unlike the encaustic painter, was "free" from practical concerns. Plato established for the concept of the creator in the Western tradition a freedom from the usual social constraints or rational thinking deemed necessary for the success of other kinds of human activity and intellection. Plato's idea of poetry focused on the poet, in whom the concept of the divine creator existed together with a theory of inspiration in which the poet could mimic the creative powers of God—in *furor poeticus.* Milton Nahm (1956) has argued that when this absolute freedom can be recognized in the work of art and practiced by the figure known as the artist, it is constitutive of the aesthetic.

ARTIST: History of the Concept. Albrecht Dürer, *Self-Portrait* (1500), oil on panel, 26 1/4 × 19 1/4 inches (66.3 × 48.9 cm); Alte Pinakothek, Munich. (Photograph courtesy of Foto Marburg/Art Resource, New York.)

Historically and in philosophical discourse, the aesthetic emerges as a category of knowledge in the eighteenth century. However, the conditions necessary for the aesthetic required that the ancient discourse on media and techniques pertaining to visual culture be brought into alignment and justified discursively with the idea of the creator and his freedom. These adjustments in the classical arguments concerning the poet and his invention and visual media and their techniques took place from the fourteenth through the seventeenth centuries in the European, particularly Italian and French, literature on art.

Wollheim (1980) has argued that questions of definition regarding media and their critical terminology follow from art's constitution conceptually. According to him, these discussions appear later, indicating a more developed phase of the discourse on art *even though they may be most often raised in regard to the origins of art*. Such "post-art" discussions, particularly those stories about the origins of various media, would appear to require the maker as well, and this hypoth-

esis is borne out by an investigation of the earliest Greek discourse on the history and origins of sculpture, where makers are invariably named in the discussions of both the various sculptural media (bronze sculpture, marble sculpture, etc.) and the techniques associated with them (Donohue, 1988). In the later Greek and Roman literature, the names of the makers are modified and amplified by the medium or technique of what they make.

This earliest written tradition consists of anecdotes, little narratives revelatory of the character of the maker and a particular work of art, which appear inserted in larger, historical narratives, such as Pliny's *Natural History* (Isager, 1991). In this literature, the narrative form of the "artist anecdote" serves to name the "inventors" of various techniques and/or styles and to tie the creators of these to particular works of art. Indeed, anecdotes about makers can be found in other cultures, such as that of China, from earliest recorded times. The apparent universality of the "artist's anecdote" in cultures with very ancient written traditions and rich artistic heritages has led some to conclude that the rhetorical form itself is the identifying characteristic of "artist," at least insofar as s/he is represented historically (Kris and Kurz, 1979).

The emphasis in the early Greek discourse on the specificity of medium and associated techniques used in making, denoted by an extensive critical vocabulary but lacking a generalized term for maker, or the present-day "artist," persisted from antiquity until the late seventeenth century. In the Middle Ages, the various *ars, artes,* or crafts had been separated from each other into guilds whose practitioners bore the name of the medium and/or techniques they practiced. Beginning with the Renaissance in Italy (c.1350), these guilds were gradually amalgamated and in some cases renamed, but the separation according to medium continued even after the institution of the court artist during the period of absolute monarchies (mid-thirteenth century [Warnke, 1993]) and the introduction of the academies of art in the middle of the sixteenth century (Pevsner, 1940). In 1550, Giorgio Vasari, for example, published his famous biographies of painters, sculptors, and architects, designated by the medium each practiced and *not* called biographies of "artists." This is the case with Vasari, as well as with all other sixteenth- and seventeenth-century *Lives* of artists, such as those by Giovanni Pietro Bellori (1674) and Fillippo Baldinucci (1682).

Whether in ancient writers, such as Pliny or Vitruvius, or early modern writers, such as Vasari or even Winckelmann, the arts are separated from each other according to medium, that is, kinds of painting, kinds of sculpture, and architecture. The term *artist,* then, must be understood to have emerged when it was necessary to distinguish "makers" of art from other kinds of makers of things or products rather than from each other. This process of delineation began discursively in Italy in the fourteenth century. It can be tied to a complex set of circumstances pertaining historically to the Tuscan vernacular and its usage in historical writing and poetry; the position of painters, sculptors, architects, humanists, goldsmiths, and so on in society; the technical advances being made in a variety of media; and the conditions necessary for the expression of these in a discrete narrative form, that is, the biography of the artist (Soussloff, 1997). When the first kinds of narratives devoted exclusively to makers—that is, the genre of the biography of the artist—emerged in fifteenth-century Florence, the anecdote persisted as the essential rhetorical element, along with the description and discussion of the work of art according to technique. Thus, when we encounter the maker and the works discussed extensively together and in a separate genre for the first time, we also encounter a fully formed discourse for that discussion signaling—using Wollheim's logic—not a beginning of an idea about what is the artist and what is art, but rather a society already possessing at least the outlines of our understanding of these terms (Baxandall, 1971).

The first maker to emerge discursively as something other than only a maker is the architect. Not surprisingly, then, in fourteenth-century Italy architecture was the earliest of the visual media to become associated with the term for art *(arte)* instead of being understood as a vocation *(mestiere)* (Ettlinger, 1977). In the earliest biography of an artist, Antonio Manetti's *Life of Brunelleschi* (c.1478–1485), the architect is credited with reviving the "rules" of architecture, known to him via the *Ten Books on Architecture* by the Roman architect Vitruvius. According to Manetti, Brunelleschi reinvented the aspects of architecture crucial to its status as art: order, measure, and the imprimatur of the classical model via methods of building known to but forgotten since antiquity. In addition, Manetti credited Brunelleschi with having invented the "science" of perspective, echoing a similar attribution made for Brunelleschi by the Florentine humanist Leon Battista Alberti in his influential treatise *On Painting* (1435). Hubert Damisch (1994) has argued that the invention of perspective functions as the central trope for a "beginning" of art's (in this case, painting's) history, lending further credence to Wollheim's conclusion that the discussion of media and techniques occurs in the context of art's origins but *after* art. [*See* Perspective.]

Martin Jay (1993) similarly locates the invention of perspective as central to the discourse about art and the artist. He argues that the invention of perspective in the fifteenth century allowed the separation of the object from the corporeal, or the depicted object from the body of the artist. This separation having to do with the nature of the artist's subjectivity in relationship to the world he represents resulted, according to Jay, in the possibility of envisioning an art object removed from the historical space that it once inhabited, a characteristic of art theorized by eighteenth-century aesthetics in terms of both art's universality and

its immutability. Whether one agrees or not with Jay's contention regarding the centrality of the imposition and metaphor of perspective, its emergence in discourse and art theory at exactly the same moment as the genre of the biography of the artist-architect indicates a similarity in effect on the issue of the subjectivity of the artist. This special subjectivity, one in which the artist comes to be liberated from the rest of society and its rules, resulted finally in the concept of the artist that is found in aesthetics. Clearly, however, this concept of the artist could not exist, even in its earliest locus, without the art object *and* the invention of the artist.

Concerning subjectivity, Bernard Williams has observed that the body is a precondition of individual identity. The individually identified artist has a body whose existence is different from all others because its identity resides in the work of art. In the early biographies of the artist, the body of the artist becomes a major subject and miraculous or unusual events or attributes are associated with it, such as when Vasari reports that even twenty-five days after death,

ARTIST: History of the Concept. Cindy Sherman, *Untitled #138* (1984), color photograph, 77 × 48 1/2 inches. (Courtesy of the artist and Metro Pictures, New York.)

Michelangelo's body appeared "so perfect in every part, and so free from any noisome odour . . . the features of the face were exactly as in life." In much of the discourse on the artist since Vasari, the body of the artist may commonly be fetishized, just as the work of the art may be endowed with spiritual or miraculous properties. [*See* Vasari.]

The name of the artist is central here, for it refers both to the body and to its place in history, that is, in the work of art and in discourse, indicating how the artist is individualized in history. In the European tradition, we receive a name as a given or natural part of "the self," thereby causing the name to be emblematic of "the self" (Kripke, 1980). If the body is essential to the personal identity of the individual, a name is essential to the representation of the body and the identity in historical discourse. The naming of the artist-genius in general in historical discourse is already emblematic of what is already given, the work of art. The naming of the artist in a specifically art-historical discourse also concerns specialized issues, such as connoisseurship, the attribution of works of art, and the definition of personal style.

The biography of the artist, firmly established as a genre during the Renaissance period, ensured that discourse on art and the individualized artist—on the named painter, sculptor, architect, or whatever—would be inseparable. Indeed, Holquist (1989) has argued that a characteristic of the normative paradigm of the heroic type established by biography qua genre "rubs smooth" the differences between praxis and ethos. The early discourse on artists found in biography and its central rhetorical structure, the anecdote, conjoins the description of what the artist does or makes with discussion of his moral and ethical behavior as a professional craftsman and as an individual. This discourse in content and form paves the way for the freedom of the artist-genius from the rules and ethics governing other individuals and hypothesized for the artist in aesthetics.

The timeless and idealized position of the artist in culture persists today, therefore, because that position has been maintained by the discourse and arguments of aesthetics and art history concerning the artist and the work of art. The maintenance of the separation of the two categories, art and artist, from each other within the realm of aesthetics— what could be called a "splitting" of artist/object—finds its earliest and most powerful articulation in Immanuel Kant's *Critique of Judgment.* The absolute artist, also known as "genius," "creative genius," or "artistic genius," parallels the autonomy from direct determination by economic or social forces commonly understood to belong to the category art *(Encyclopedia Brittannica).* With the birth of the concept of the artist-genius, the term *artist* could be applied to any producer of culture considered art, that is, the composer, the writer, the director, as well as to the visual artist. The possibility of the infinitude of interpretation bestowed by culture on works of art, such as the Sistine Chapel or *Hamlet,* and artists considered "great" by the culture, such as

Michelangelo or William Shakespeare, constitutes a key aspect of the operation of the dialectical relationship between the two terms of the aesthetic.

The fact that even today there exists no clear-cut definition of the term *artist* (see, e.g., the *Oxford English Dictionary*) attests to the absolute status of the artist and the autonomy of his or her activity and products from other social practices and norms, including epistemological endeavors by history, philosophy, and anthropology to define, and thereby limit, the "artist." Today, this understanding of *artist* is used everywhere, without regard to specific historical or social contexts. Absent epistemological definition or critical evaluation, it can fairly be said that at the deepest of theoretical levels, the term *artist* denotes that knowing excludes the creator. The absence of critique about the artist in philosophy and art history since the eighteenth century when the term first had widespread use signals the epistemological status of this figure in culture (Woodmansee, 1994). Structuralist and poststructuralist positions calling for the "death" of the author in literary studies (Wimsatt and Beardsley, 1954; Barthes, 1977; Foucault, 1977); and the revision of the concept of auteur in film studies (Caughie, 1981) have barely touched the traditional concept of "artist" either in art history specifically, or in the culture as a whole.

When the category "artist" has been examined, usually from within an idealist philosophical tradition, it has been in order to claim unconditional freedom for the artist, resulting in his or her release from the conventional criteria of judgment, such as truth or falsehood (Croce, 1992), and from the imposition of ethical concerns seen to pertain to activities other than art making and categories of humans other than artists (Hegel, 1975). The generalized meanings attributed to "artist" today as well as the tensions and stakes inherent in distinguishing one class of practitioners from another that occurred in the eighteenth century coincide with (1) the taxonomies of culture undertaken with the scientific revolution (Kemp, 1990); (2) the refinements of the discourse on art found in the philosophy of aesthetics (Kant, 1951) and art criticism (Crow, 1985); and (3) the emergence of the public for art, or the "art market," in England and France in the earliest days of the industrial revolution (Habermas, 1989; Barrell, 1986; Solkin, 1995).

We can now understand how eighteenth-century thinkers separated the "artist" from other kinds of practitioners, such as physicians, also said in the early modern period to be practicing "art," that is, the new "science" of biology or medicine. The difference in the concepts of "artist" and "scientist" can be explained on the basis of differences in subjectivity attributed to the identity of each, although both terms rely on a concept of the immutability of their productions, that is, art and science. It would be absurd today to call the physician an "artist." So too, as the use of the word *artist* spread and the concept spread, it came to be more and more understood by the inseparability of the maker and the "object," located in and persisting immutably through history and commerce (i.e., the "art market"). Today, the word *artist* refers more often than not to the maker in the visual arts, rather than to musicians, poets, and others, although it must be said that any time an absolute conception of the maker is required by society, the artist will be there.

Paradoxically, given the desire for communal making expressed at the time by participants, the "happenings" of the mid-1960s reinforced the position of the individual artist and the interpretation of art according to style by doing away with the archaeological ideal of the object as permanent and evidentiary. Today's performance and installation art, like the earlier happenings, accept an opposite premise: that art can be temporary, occasional, or a unique event. Temporary or not, the entailment of the singular artistic event or even the illusory or virtual object with the artist, ensures that the concept of the artist contains within it the work of art, just as the concept of art requires "an original mind which imposes its unique imprint upon it."

[*See also* Creativity; Genius; *and* Originality.]

BIBLIOGRAPHY

Alberti, Leon Battista. *On Painting and On Sculpture.* Edited and translated by Cecil Grayson. London, 1972.

Barrell, John. *The Political Theory of Painting from Reynolds to Hazlitt: "The Body of the Public."* New Haven, 1986.

Barthes, Roland. "The Death of the Author." In *Image, Music, Text,* edited and translated by Stephen Heath, pp. 142–148. New York, 1977.

Baxandall, Michael. *Giotto and the Orators: Humanist Observers of Painting in Italy and the Discovery of Pictorial Composition, 1350–1450.* Oxford, 1971.

Caughie, John, ed. *Theories of Authorship: A Reader.* London and Boston, 1981.

Croce, Benedetto. *The Aesthetic as the Science of Expression and of the Linguistic in General.* Translated by Colin Lyas. Cambridge and New York, 1992.

Crow, Thomas. *Painters and Public Life in Eighteenth-Century Paris.* New Haven, 1985.

Damisch, Hubert. *The Origin of Perspective.* Translated by John Goodman. Cambridge, Mass., 1994.

Donahue, A. A. *"Xoana" and the Origins of Greek Sculpture.* Atlanta, 1988.

Ettlinger, Leopold D. "The Emergence of the Italian Architect during the Fifteenth Century." In *The Architect: Chapters in the History of the Profession,* edited by Spiro Kostof, pp. 96–123. New York and Oxford, 1977.

Foucault, Michel. "What Is an Author?" In *Language, Counter-Memory, Practice: Selected Essays and Interviews,* edited by Donald F. Bouchard, translated by Donald F. Bouchard and Sherry Simon. Ithaca, N.Y., 1977.

Habermas, Jürgen. *The Structural Transformation of the Public Sphere: An Inquiry into a Category of Bourgeois Society.* Translated by Thomas Burger with Frederick Lawrence. Cambridge, Mass., 1989.

Hegel, G. W. F. *Aesthetics: Lectures on Fine Art.* 2 vols. Translated by T. M. Knox. Oxford, 1975.

Holquist, Michael. "From Body-Talk to Biography: The Chronobiological Bases of Narrative." *Yale Journal of Criticism* 3 (1989): 3–40.

Hughes, Anthony. "The Cave and the Stithy: Artists' Studios and Intellectual Property in Early Modern Europe." *Oxford Art Journal* 13 (1990): 34–48.

Isager, Jacob. *Pliny on Art and Society: The Elder Pliny's Chapters on the History of Art.* London and New York, 1991.

Jay, Martin. *Downcast Eyes: The Denigration of Vision in Twentieth-Century French Thought.* Berkeley, 1993.

Kant, Immanuel. *Critique of Judgment.* Translated by J. H. Bernard. New York, 1951.

Kemp, Martin. *The Science of Art: Optical Themes in Western Art from Brunelleschi to Seurat.* New Haven, 1990.

Kripke, Saul A. *Naming and Necessity.* Cambridge, Mass., 1980.

Kris, Ernst, and Otto Kurz. *Legend, Myth and Magic in the Image of the Artist: A Historical Experiment.* New Haven, 1979.

Manetti, Antonio di Tuccio. *The Life of Brunelleschi.* Edited by Howard Saalman, translated by Catherine Enggass. University Park, Pa., 1970.

Mason, John Hope. "Thinking about Genius in the Eighteenth Century." In *Eighteenth-Century Aesthetics and the Reconstruction of Art,* edited by Paul Mattick, Jr., pp. 210–239. Cambridge and New York, 1993.

Myers, Fred. "Beyond the Intentional Fallacy: Art Criticism and the Ethnography of Aboriginal Painting." *Visual Anthropology Review* 10 (Spring 1994): 10–43.

Nahm, Milton. *The Artist as Creator: An Essay of Human Freedom.* Baltimore, 1956.

Pevsner, Nicolaus. *Academies of Art, Past and Present.* Cambridge, 1940.

Pollitt, Jerome J. *The Ancient View of Greek Art: Criticism, History, and Terminology.* New Haven, 1974.

Solkin, David H. *Painting for Money: The Visual Arts and the Public Sphere in Eighteenth-Century England.* New Haven, 1993.

Soussloff, Catherine M. *The Absolute Artist: The Historiography of a Concept.* Minneapolis, 1997.

Summers, David. *The Judgment of Sense: Renaissance Naturalism and the Rise of Aesthetics.* Cambridge and New York, 1987.

Vasari, Giorgio. *Lives of the Most Eminent Painters, Sculptors, and Architects.* 10 vols. Translated by Gaston du C. de Vere. London, 1912–1914.

Warnke, Martin. *The Court Artist: On the Ancestry of the Modern Artist.* Translated by David McLintock. Cambridge and New York, 1993.

Webster, T. B. L. "Greek Theories of Art and Literature Down to 400 B.C." *Classical Quarterly* 33 (1939): 166–179.

Williams, Bernard. *Problems of the Self: Philosophical Papers, 1956–1972.* Cambridge and New York, 1973.

Wimsatt, William K., Jr., and Monroe C. Beardsley. *The Verbal Icon: Studies in the Meaning of Poetry.* Lexington, Ky., 1954.

Winckelmann, J. J. *The History of Ancient Art.* 4 vols. Translated by G. Henry Lodge. Reprint, New York, 1969.

Wollheim, Richard. *Art and Its Objects.* 2d ed., with six supplementary essays. Cambridge and New York, 1980.

Woodmansee, Martha. *The Author, Art, and the Market: Rereading the History of Aesthetics.* New York, 1994.

CATHERINE SOUSSLOFF

Sociology of the Artist

One reason that artists are so interesting as workers is that there are so many attitudes toward categorizing them. Whether the purpose of such categorization is government policy, grassroots advocacy, social welfare, or the justification of a personal system of belief, artists seem to run the gamut from what the United States census calls fifty- to fifty-two-week-a-year employees to Miller's definition of hustlers in *Dimensions of Work:*

The most basic feature of workers who hustle for a living is that they do not have full-time conventional jobs. . . . Sometimes they may work at low-paying, temporary jobs, but at other times they may do any number of other things to earn income. . . . a more important factor than their unconventionality is the uncertain nature of their work. . . . As a result, their histories reflect frequent job changes, and outsiders often describe them as unstable.   (As quoted in Hall, 1986, pp. 32–33)

Further, as Judith Adler states, not only is the comparability of artists' occupations to other trades and professions difficult, but the analysis may not accurately reflect appropriate comparisons:

A study of the job market experience of professional plumbers does not need to be overly concerned with distinguishing its population from people who fix washers in their spare time with uncertain competence. A study of artists in society in which occupational membership is (fortunately) not defined or restricted by a guild, an academy, or a state system of licensing can neither comfortably ignore problems of occupational definition nor resolve them.   (Adler, 1983, pp. 177–178)

And we must not forget the legacy of the artist who, often cast in life as well as literature and opera as a romantic (but starving) bohemian, was relegated to being at best a traveling troubadour and at worst a vagrant. According to Theodore Bikel in the *Journal of Arts Management and Law,* in Britain, in the nineteenth century,

when the great actor and entrepreneur Henry Irving was honored with a Knighthood, dubbing him Sir Henry Irving, he received the honor solely for his work in the theatre. However, an act of Parliament in Britain called the "Rogues and Vagabonds Act" held that actors could not be counted as proper members of society. Therefore Henry Irving was knighted not as an actor, God forbid, but as a "meritorious householder."
                (Bikel, 1986, pp. 20–21)

Appropriate categorizations become even more difficult when the subject of professionalism is introduced. One of the most inclusive definitions of artists is the one endorsed by the United Nations Educational, Scientific, and Cultural Organization (UNESCO) in 1980, admitting anyone who seeks acknowledgment as an artist. A definition based completely on self-assessment, it emphasizes the individual's commitment to artistic creation, and encompasses the amateur as well as the professional. Other organizing agencies that put forward a response to the question of who attains professional status as an artist include:

1. Funding agencies, such as the National Endowment for the Arts (NEA), which distribute guidelines stipulating that they do not fund amateurs; yet they never define professionals.
2. Artists' unions, such as Actors' Equity Association and the American Federation of Musicians that proselytize

by arguing that membership in a formal artists' union confers the mantle of professionalism.
3. Some educational institutions, especially those that provide graduate degrees in the fine, applied, and performing arts, which often espouse their educational training as the standard of professionalism.

In *Dimensions of Work,* Paul Harr recalls that the development of established professions such as law and medicine have a relatively short history in the United States and that scholars have been arguing for some time about what constitutes professional status of any workers. This essay will present an overview of the various kinds and scope of research on artists. For the purposes of clarity, these are grouped into the following categories, even though in individual cases there is undoubtedly some overlap: Status of the Artist Research, Census-Based Research, Economic Studies, Information and Advocacy Studies, Sociological Studies, Psychological Studies, Special Interest Studies, and Observational Comments.

Status of the Artist Research. A number of UNESCO-based artist studies and studies in other countries focus on the status of the artist. In 1980, the UNESCO General Conference in Belgrade created the first regulatory instrument on the status of artists. *Research about Artists* (1993, p. 28) described this as one that set out "principles and guidelines designed to promote the artist's social and economic status, employment, working and living conditions and role in cultural policies and development."

Although the lack of information on artists around the world is great, the lack of comparable information is even greater. In addition, such information appears under different auspices in different countries, and sometimes is found in a number of different agencies in one country alone—ministries, research units, provincial governments. A conference in 1992 in Hanasaari, Finland, produced a summary of major issues and findings. This European Symposium on the Status of the Artist also produced a number of motions and resolutions on a wide range of issues including the social protection of artists and social security, the state's role in aiding individual artists, the education and training of artists, dissemination of art and the "intrusion of market forces," and taxation of artists.

Canada and Australia are two countries that have been pursuing status of artist research for over a decade. In 1986, the Canadian Department of Communications published *The Status of the Artist* and moved into closer collaboration with the Canada Council's Research Division and Statistics Canada. Most interesting in Canadian research is the inclusion of artists who are identified as working in freelance employment as well as those who work in traditional employment in the arts. *Research about Artists* (1993) reports that, in 1992, Employment and Immigration Canada, the Department of Communications, the Canada Council, and the

Canadian Conference on the Arts began the Cultural Labour Force Project to provide detailed benchmark data about individuals in the arts, the cultural industries, and the heritage sectors.

In Australia, in 1982 the Australia Council mandated a Committee for the Individual Artists Inquiry chaired by cultural economist David Throsby. The committee's findings culminated in periodic surveys of individual artists, and occasional comparison of the results with Australian census data and data from other outside studies.

Census-Based Research. For most countries, the most logical place to look for information on employment, earnings, geographic trends, and gender in regard to any occupation is the census. In the United States and England, for example, the census is conducted once every ten years, but in the United States it is conducted in the year following the decade mark with information pertaining to the decade year (the 1990 census was taken in 1991 and its data reflect information from 1990); in England, the census is taken during the year of the decade mark and information is for the preceding year (the 1990 census was taken in 1990 and its data reflect information for 1989). In the United States, respondents are characterized according to their employment in the "reference week," normally the week preceding the census. Therefore, an artist who earns a living driving a taxi during the reference week is categorized as a taxi driver by the census.

For comparisons of artists, this situation is complicated by the categorization of different kinds of artists: (1) several different kinds of artists are lumped into a single category; for example, actors and directors are one category, as are painters, sculptors, craftspeople, and artist printmakers in the United States; (2) even these categories have undergone revision from one decade to the next; in the United States, actors in 1970 became actors and directors in 1980; (3) in some countries, certain kinds of artists do not seem to be identified at all—dancers, for example, in the census in England.

In the United States, advantages of census data include the following: (1) a large database is available that is relatively good for comparison and that allows for comparison with other nonartist occupations surveyed by the census; (2) the census database is the most comprehensive one available; (3) the census can give a firm hold on the central tendencies of a large number of artists, which can give a broad general picture of the census's artist population; (4) the census can provide an answer to the question, how many artists?—a question that is used time and time again by policymakers, funders, and arts groups, particularly in times of scarce resources.

In the United States, the disadvantages to artists being represented by the census include the fact that (1) the census lumps together different kinds of artists in one category,

mentioned earlier; (2) the census does not acknowledge artists who work in more than one art form (painter-musician, for example); (3) the census does not recognize artists who work at more than one job (it is well known that many artists hold two or more jobs simultaneously, but the census limits the artist's occupation to the one during which the survey was taken); (4) the census does not reflect the multiple-career phenomenon that is quickly becoming a part of contemporary life, therefore, one has no sense of whether the current occupation of an artist (or anyone else) is one of a series of careers, whether these careers are consecutive or simultaneous, or what influence earnings and employment have on these occupations' growth or decline; and (5) the census actually provides cross-sectional, but not longitudinal, data, which is a limitation of almost all existing surveys of artists.

In the United States, the National Endowment for the Arts, since its founding in 1965, has developed a series of monographs, research notes, reports, and other mechanisms to extrapolate artists' data from the census and, in its 1990 census analysis, encouraged the additional information and analysis of independent artist studies to shed greater light on census findings. Additionally, other census-related surveys exist such as the Current Population Survey (a monthly survey of fifty-seven thousand households that covers cases where one or more members of a household self-identify as artists) and the Bureau of Labor Statistics, which provides monthly surveys regarding unemployment. Recent historical data are also available in the files of the Comprehensive Employment and Training Act (CETA), a program of the Employment and Training Administration of the U.S. Department of Labor that provided substantial support for artists during the 1970s.

Economic Studies. The Association of Cultural Economics International (ACEI) is a newly reconstituted version of an organization that began to hold annual conferences and create a journal collectivizing information in this new discipline around 1980. The tension between those who would deem artists a special breed and therefore unresponsive to economic incentives or even analysis and those who would define artists in the labor market as consumers and in other ways, often isolated the economists' findings to their academic colleagues. Almost all economists looking at American artists used the census as the basis for their theories, "counting what can be counted." Occasionally, surveys would be commissioned, such as the 1980 New England Foundation for the Arts survey by Neil Alper, Gregory Wassall, and Rebecca Davidson, which resulted in a publication called *Art Work* (Alper, Wassall, and Davidson, 1983) that is highly readable and quite useful. Rarely however, were arts practitioners, arts managers, or artists seen at the economists' meetings or in their publications. As economic impact studies became more and more prevalent through the

1970s and 1980s, arts practitioners became more aware of the possible economic role of the arts and the subject of "cultural economics" found some credence in larger arts service organizations, programs in arts administration, and among those responsible for running arts institutions. In the United States, caught between a desperate battle to secure money for programs and the production of art, the practitioners were often skeptical of "yet another study," no matter what kind. By the 1990s, severe cutbacks in public funding seemed to direct even a marginal interest in economic investigations only toward those that could lose more dollars. In England in the 1980s, the Calouste Gulbenkian Foundation published *The Economic Situation of the Visual Artist* in the United Kingdom and in 1994 the Crafts Council in the United Kingdom brought out *Crafts in the 1990s,* "an independent socio-economic study of craftspeople in England, Scotland and Wales" (Knott, 1994). This report followed up on 1981 research, called *Working in Crafts.* In 1995, the Scottish Arts Council published *A Socio-Economic Study of Artists in Scotland* based on research by the Departments of Sociology, Social and Economic Research at the University of Glasgow. As Bruce A. Seaman (1992) observes, measurement problems plaguing the discussion of the economic importance of the arts that include the "ambiguity of terminology" ("What is an Artist?") and the "vagaries of self-reporting" have parallels in all occupations and industries. For economists, a major debate about individual artists centers on "the intrinsic enjoyment of artists in their work that might induce them to accept lower monetary compensation in exchange for the opportunity to engage in such satisfying activity" (Seaman, 1992, p. 12). Aside from the fact that many artists are not being included in the census count, for reasons already described, Seaman says there is a debate among economists about "the extent to which the income of those who *are* being counted as employed in the arts is lower than it otherwise would be if the arts were not so intrinsically enjoyable (the so-called 'starving artist' syndrome)" (ibid., pp. 44–45).

Almost all the studies described in this essay have an "economic piece," especially in regard to artists' earnings, but the studies in this category are driven by an economic approach that, when too narrowly focused, ignores aspects that would give these studies resonance. What they do provide is analysis that is quantified, often formula-based, "hard numbers" that are used for assorted reasons, including increasing tourism through regional development and as ammunition for more grant money for individual artists.

Information and Advocacy Studies. These studies use many of the tools described elsewhere in this essay, but their purpose is directly tied to the specific character and mission of the organizations that commission them. For example, Actors' Equity Association keeps detailed annual records on its membership's employment—length of con-

tracts, earnings, comparisons with previous years. These data can be valuable in comparative studies such as those done by Ruttenberg and associates in the 1980s and 1990s, which used data from several performing arts unions to ascertain geographic and employment trends.

All the major discipline-based arts service organizations collect annual data on their members—the American Symphony Orchestra League, Opera America, the Theatre Communications Group, Dance/USA, the American Association of Museums—but their members are institutions, so very little data, if any, are collected on artists. National artists' organizations, such as the National Association of Artists Organizations (NAAO), do sporadic surveys of their individual members.

For national service organizations such as the National Assembly of State Arts Agencies (NASAA) and the National Assembly of Local Arts Agencies (NALAA), data on the number of individual artist grants or regrants at the state and local level are documented by state or community. For NASAA, these include money in the form of fellowships, works in progress, workshops, conferences, awards, technical assistance, travel, and "other." For example, in 1992, 2,450 grants were given by state arts agencies to individual artists totaling $6.7 million, and although the number of grants did not vary greatly, the amount of grant dollars decreased significantly from the three previous years.

Funding agencies occasionally commission an analysis of their funding categories by outside contractors; this has been done in the visual artist fellowship category at the NEA, for example. The New York Foundation for the Arts commissioned an attitudinal study of the artists applying for individual grants/fellowships and designed a group of advocacy posters and postcards using the data. The data in these studies provide members and constituents, especially political constituents, with hard numbers about artists in a very general sense.

Informational studies have also been created by the Research Center for Arts and Culture at Columbia University, including Information on Artists (IOA), a study of ten thousand artists in ten U.S. locations in 1989, and the Artists Training and Career Project (ATC) a study of four thousand craftspeople, two thousand painters, and six thousand actors that looked at a combination of sociological, economic, and psychological realities. The center's survey instruments have been reproduced domestically by regional and local arts councils and agencies, and internationally by the Portuguese Club for Arts and Ideas in the first artists' survey in Portugal. The center's information, which can be used as an advocacy tool by other organizations, investigates issues of social services for artists—health care, pensions, legal and financial aid, copyright protection, profit and nonprofit marketplace mechanisms (grants, sales), and career stages of "validation" and "resistance" eliciting responses about seminal events in artistic careers. The ATC surveys were informed by oral history narratives of 150 artists and related experts.

The studies make a singular contribution to the discussion of professionalism by asking artists to identify themselves and others according to a dozen categories, which include a Marketplace Definition (the artist earns/intends to earn a living as an artist), an Education and Affiliation Definition (the artist is formally trained; the artist belongs to a union, a guild), and a Self and Peer Definition (the artist has an inner drive; the artist spends substantial time at his or her art). The greatest limitation in these and all noncensus-based surveys is the absence of a commonly accepted, defined universe of artists from which to select a representative random sample. Obviously, each survey has taken pains to define its own universe, usually through organizational memberships or affiliations, which, like the census, probably omits a significant number of artists.

Sociological Studies. Cultural sociology as a field of study has blossomed over the last three decades and with it concerns that have been described by Rosanne Martorella and colleagues as less with "organizational analysis, social problems, criminology, items of substantive research" and more with "new vocabularies, theoretical orientations, methodologies" (Martorella et al., 1989, p. 1). This has been good news for artists, because some of the most eminent sociologists have looked at the sociology of artistic careers (Diana Crane, Elliott Friedson, Vera Zolberg, Rosanne Martorella), and the artist and the marketplace, both historically (Harrison and Cynthia White) and in contemporary times (Raymonde Moulin in France). American guru Howard Becker deals with the most fundamental concepts of being an artist as well as subjects of distribution, the role of the state, and, relevant to this essay, aesthetics. As Becker describes them, "Aesthetic principles, arguments and judgments make up an important part of the body of convention by means of which members of art worlds act together" (Becker, 1982, p. 131). Those who create and develop aesthetic systems may be specialists like critics and philosophers, participants in those art worlds, artists themselves, or all of these. Consensus of these participants' points of view results in a shared aesthetic value, but it is clear that there are many competing styles and schools within an art world that demand attention. According to Becker:

> Artists produce new work in response not only to the considerations of formal aesthetics but also in response to the traditions of the art worlds in which they participate, traditions which can profitably be viewed . . . as sequences of problem definitions and solutions; in response to suggestions implicit in other traditions, as in the influence of African art on Western painting; in response to the new possibilities contained in the new technical developments; and so on. (1982, p. 138)

Becker's and others' work on the artist's reality includes the artist's relation to the distributors of his or her product, the audience for that product, the role of specialists in aesthetic judgments, and the organizations that represent this work in the world as well as the different players that keep the "machinery" of the art world working.

According to Becker, aestheticians (although these are clearly not the only ones entitled to an opinion in Becker's view) provide "the rationale by which art works justify their existence and distinctiveness, and thus their claim to support. Art and artists can exist without such a rationale, but have more trouble when others dispute their right to do so" (ibid.). To cite one example, it was just this kind of "aesthetic rationale" that acquitted Dennis Barrie, executive director of Cincinnati's Contemporary Art Center, from charges of pornography and obscenity in displaying the works of Robert Mapplethorpe, on tour in the exhibition "The Precious Moment."

Psychological Studies. Studies about the larger scope of learning include a focus on creativity and multiple intelligences, such as those of Howard Gardner with his Project Zero at Harvard and innumerable studies of creativity, including those by Howard Gruber, work by psychiatrist Lawrence Kubie, extended discussions of child prodigies (many of whom are artists) like those in David Feldman's *Nature's Gambit,* and, of course, many individual biographies and autobiographies of artists that contribute to the general discussion of artists and how they develop.

Of prime importance for artists is the longitudinal study of Mihaly Csikszentmihaly with his partners Jacob Getzels and Stephen P. Kahn, who, in 1981, followed up a study of fine artists who studied at the Art Institute of Chicago in 1963. *The Creative Vision* is the book resulting from their first study; "Talent and Achievement" (1984) is the unpublished report containing findings from their follow-up study almost twenty years later. It explains the study's purpose as "to find out the extent to which various cognitive abilities . . . perceptual abilities, values, and personality characteristics are involved in the making of art that is thought to be creative." Csikszentmihaly's work, and the work of students of his such as Joanna Stohs, complement routine socioeconomic data with other information about motivation, career satisfaction, personal goals, and inner challenges that deepens any discussion of artists.

Special Interest Studies. In the 1970s, organizations in several U.S. cities conducted studies on the development of combined living and working spaces for artists. This was, in part, a response to the growing artist gentrification of areas like Soho in New York where artists rented loft and other spaces zoned for commercial use, rehabilitated the spaces at their own cost, and gentrified the area, greatly increasing the value of the real estate, and were then forced out by those who could pay to own those spaces. The Artists Foundation in Boston and groups in Minneapolis and Seattle, among others, explored various options for resident-controlled ownership of space, including condominiums, cooperatives, nonprofit corporations, limited partnerships, and contractual agreements. In the Boston case, the Artists Foundation actually became the bridge between the artist and the space, using its resources as collateral for artists to become owners.

In the 1980s, the American Council for the Arts conducted a study to determine the kinds and amounts of health insurance held by artists. This study served as background for the National Endowment for the Arts, which has since convened a health-care and insurance task force. These two examples illustrate information about artists tied to very specific agendas and are very much a function of their time and place.

Observational Comments. Although usually not sources of hard numbers, assorted cultural commentators often have much to offer those interested in finding out more about artists. An interesting phenomenon of the last decade has been the emergence of private foundations created from individual artists' estates whose primary function is to help other artists, of which Robert Rauschenberg's Change, Inc. was a definite precursor. The Adolph and Esther Gottlieb Foundation, the Pollock-Krasner Foundation, the Keith Haring Foundation, and the Robert Mapplethorpe Foundation provide emergency aid, AIDS relief, and other kinds of help to artists. Their overseers have solid information on their applicants and their grantees, but, more important, they bring an important real-life perspective to the discussion of the contemporary artist.

Artists themselves have not only become cultural commentators but have taken the researchers' instruments into their own hands. In 1994, an article in the *Nation* described a survey by artists Vitaly Komar and Alexander Melamid as the first "scientific nationwide poll of what Americans want in art." This telephone survey of 1,001 Americans in forty-eight states observed scientific data collection rules in an attempt to create "a real pop art, a real art of the people." Using the consumerist tool of the statistical poll, Komar and Melamid also used focus groups, and then, following the highest statistical responses as to color, shape, subject matter, and so on, created a painting "on commission from the entire American people."

The idea itself as well as its execution sets out to defy the shared aesthetic of the art world that Howard Becker described. Surprisingly, however, perhaps it reinforced just that because the "most wanted picture" that the artists created was very close to "classic 19th century American painting . . . a landscape with people, showing harmony with nature, or the conquest of nature" (as quoted in "Painting by Numbers: The Search for a People's Art." the *Nation*, 14 March 1994, p. 343). As tongue-in-cheek as this survey may have been, it does set the audience or the "consumer" thinking and it does pull the artist roughly out of the

nineteenth-century stereotype of alienated, starving genius, something that much of the other aforementioned research has done as well. Indeed, in Becker's terms, Komar and Melamid, *as* artists, are behaving exactly in response to the traditions of the art worlds in which they participate, and are doing what artists do best—making us look again.

[*See also* Art World; *and* Sociology of Art.]

BIBLIOGRAPHY

Adler, Judith. "Artists' Job Market Experience." *Journal of Arts Management and Law* 13 (Spring 1983): 177–183.

Alper, Neil, Gregory Wassall, and Rebecca Davidson. *Art Work: Artists in the New England Labor Market.* Cambridge, Mass., 1983.

Becker, Howard S. *Art Worlds.* Berkeley, 1982.

Bikel, Theodore. In "Labor Relations and the Arts," edited by Joan Jeffri. Special issue of *Journal of Arts Management and Law* 16, (Spring 1986).

Csikszentmihalyi, Mihalyi, Jacob Getzels, and Stephen P. Kahn. "Talent and Achievement." Unpublished report. Chicago, 1984.

Gardner, Howard. *Multiple Intelligences: The Theory in Practice.* New York, 1993.

Hall, Richard H., ed. *Dimensions of Work.* Beverly Hills, Calif., 1986.

Irjala, Auli, ed. *European Symposium on the Status of the Artist.* Finnish National Commission for UNESCO. No. 64. Helsinki, 1992.

Jeffri, Joan, ed. "Labor Relations and the Arts." Special issue of *Journal of Arts Management and Law* 16 (Spring 1986).

Jeffri, Joan, ed. *Information on Artists.* New York, 1989.

Jeffri, Joan, ed. *The Artists' Training and Career Project.* New York, 1990.

Jeffri, Joan, and Robert Greenblatt. "Artists Who Work with Their Hands: Painters, Sculptors, Craftspeople and Artist Printmakers: A Trend Report, 1970–1990." In *Artists in the Work Force: Employment and Earnings, 1970–1990,* by Neil Alper et al., National Endowment for the Arts, Research Report no. 37, pp. 59–84. Santa Ana, Calif., 1996.

Jeffri, Joan, and David Throsby. "Professionalism and the Visual Artist." *European Journal of Cultural Policy* (Switzerland) 1.1 (1994): 99–108.

Knott, Cherry Ann. *Crafts in the 1990s.* London, 1994.

Martorella, Rosanne, et al., eds. *Course Syllabi, Resources, and Instructional Material on the Sociology of Culture.* Washington, D.C., 1989.

"Painting by Numbers: The Search for a People's Art." *Nation* (14 March 1994): 334–348.

Research about Artists: Summary Report of August 1993 Roundtable. Washington, D.C., 1993.

Ruttenberg, Friedman, Kilgallon, Gutchess, and Associates. "A Survey of Employment, Unemployment and Underemployment in the Performing Arts." Washington, D.C., 1978.

Ruttenberg, Friedman, Kilgallon, Gutchess, and Associates. "Working and Not Working in the Performing Arts: A Survey of Employment, Unemployment and Underemployment among Performing Artists, 1980." Washington, D.C., 1981.

Ruttenberg, Kilgallon, and Associates. "Employment and Earnings of Performing Artists: 1970–1990." Washington, D.C., 1995.

Seaman, Bruce A. "The Economic Contributions of the Arts." Washington, D.C., 1992.

Throsby, C.D., and D. Mills. *When Are You Going to Get a Real Job? An Economic Study of Australian Artists.* Sydney, 1989.

Throsby, C.D., and B. J. Thompson. *But What Do You Do for a Living? A New Economic Study of Australian Artists.* Sydney, 1994.

UNESCO. *Recommendations concerning the Status of the Artist.* Adopted by the General Conference at it twenty-first session. Belgrade, 27 October 1980.

JOAN JEFFRI

ART LAW. *See* Law and Art.

ART MARKET. To consider the art market is to view art in terms of its exchange, consumption, economic valuation, and prestige rather than in terms of the qualities of individual works, the careers of artists, or the history of movements. Aesthetic judgments may play a part in determining value, but they are contingent and variable.

History. A historical survey of the art market reveals that different qualities and types of objects were valued at different times, and that the basis for judgment frequently had more to do with a display of wealth or knowledge than with aesthetics. References to the art market in ancient times indicate that the Romans put an emphasis on precious objects that could be indicators of prowess at war or of wealth. Decorative objects in rare or precious materials seem to have commanded the highest prices. Gerald Reitlinger (1982), in a study of the auction prices from the eighteenth century to the 1960s, found that items of conspicuous display, such as furniture and decorative arts, commanded the highest prices until the late nineteenth century. There was no consensus over time as to what constituted greatness, at least as measured in financial terms.

In the Middle Ages, "art" was not a primary category by which objects were identified, and the exchange of works of art as commodities was limited. Works were usually commissioned for a specific purpose by the church, which was the primary patron, or at court. Works of art were sold at fairs in commercial centers such as Antwerp and Bruges in the late Middle Ages, however, and in 1640 the Antwerp fair spawned the first showroom expressly for the exhibition and sale of works of art in post-classical Europe.

The distinction between works of art and household furnishings and other useful or decorative objects was slow to emerge. According to Richard Goldthwaite (1993), in the course of the Renaissance, art created consciously as such emerged as a specific kind of object, but was still within the context of material culture. As options become available, aesthetics might be involved in the criteria for selection of one producer over another, or one object over another. In the early modern period, these criteria are difficult to deduce from existing documents such as inventories, wills, and contracts. The language used in descriptions of works tends to draw on literary topoi rather than on a vocabulary of terms that might give clues to characteristics involved in aesthetic valuation.

In the fifteenth and sixteenth centuries, art was still produced primarily for specific patrons. Artists in Renaissance Italy belonged to the households of the rich and the noble, or worked on commissions for churches, city edifices, princely courts, and wealthy burghers. The market for ready-made works was still narrow and underdeveloped in northern Europe as well.

Artists who produced paintings or sculptures without a commission usually sold them directly; classical objects and rare curiosities, however, could not be obtained from their makers. Initially, collectors seem to have approached the owners of antiquities directly, but toward the end of the fourteenth century there are records of agents whose job it was to find specimens of ancient art as well as coins, gems, medals, manuscripts, or other works for collectors. Less frequently, agents had a stock of paintings or sculpture for sale, mostly small devotional pictures.

Although international trade was hampered by risky modes of transportation, with no insurance, records of a few dealers indicate that there was an international market for paintings and rare objects. Collections of members of the nobility who had fallen on hard times provided one source of more ancient and more recent works. Although modern modes of classifying emphasize the art in great collections of the early modern period, contemporary documents indicate that they contained many different kinds of precious objects and curiosities such as animal, plant, and mineral specimens, fossils, and antiquities. Rarity outweighed aesthetic criteria, and in the category of "artificial things" what is now classified as art came relatively low on the scale of value.

In Holland in the seventeenth century, where the lack of centralized authority and a wider distribution of wealth were associated with the development of a free market, the first art market identifiable in modern terms emerged. Although the accounts of English and French travelers exaggerate the extent to which Dutch houses were "full of paintings," works by guild-registered masters did penetrate into middle and lower strata as they probably had not before seventeenth century, and still had not in France, England, or Italy. However, most of the works of art appear in inventories of the richest third of the population.

John Montias's (1982) detailed study of economic aspects of art in Delft provides evidence on the nature of the art market in the Protestant northern Netherlands in the seventeenth century. Faced with the loss of their traditional sources of income, painters had no alternative but to work "for the market." Sculptors still largely depended on commissions, but Montias found that for painters of easel pictures the growth of the market for individual consumption more than picked up the slack left by the decline of public patronage. Many outlets existed for ready-made works. Artists could sell from their studios or in guild exhibitions or through dealers who sold books and prints, luxury goods, or paintings exclusively. Auctions and estate sales were an important source of paintings, which could still be considered household furnishings.

The lack of direct patronage produced a situation where, in theory, artists were free to produce what interested them. In practice they had to anticipate the wishes of their buyers. The types of paintings produced in Holland were different from those produced in Catholic countries, where court patronage was still influential. They were frequently small in scale, far less likely to show religious subjects, and more likely to depict genre scenes, landscape, and still life.

Wills and other documents provide little evidence of aesthetic criteria used for valuation, although it is clear that artists' names carried weight. Svetlana Alpers (1988) controversially argues that Rembrandt was innovative in creating a modern market in works that depended on the aura of individuality, and for which the artist's execution was a key feature.

Holdings in Holland tended to be modest in contrast to the great collections formed by Philip IV of Spain, Cardinal Richelieu and Cardinal Mazarin in France, Archduke Leopold Wilhelm of Hapsburg, and especially Charles I of England during the seventeenth century. Such collections were in some sense involved in a market, especially in the subsequent sale of that of Charles I by his creditors; however, most of the paintings, furniture, horse trappings, and other precious objects were not bought in an open market. Some were commissioned, and princely agents benefited from a period of economic decline in Italy to purchase entire collections such as that of the Gonzaga.

In the eighteenth century, especially in France and England, collecting increased as a form of recreation and a means of distinction. Dealers became essential middlemen as the number of collectors grew. New institutions also facilitated the circulation of works of art and set the terms for aesthetic discourse. In contrast to northern Europe, where more sophisticated markets were developing, the Italian market was mainly a one-way system in which existing rich stocks were sold off to collectors on the Grand Tour or to agents from northern Europe. Market-related publications such as auctions and sales catalogs were less common than in France and England, and advertisement and discussion of art in literary journals started later than in France, England, and Germany.

At this time "the arts," especially the "fine arts," came to be thought of as a distinct domain. Eighteenth-century commentators minimized the element of craftsmanship in favor of inspiration and in doing so emphasized the notion of the original genius of the author. Martha Woodmansee (1994) discusses ways in which debates about aesthetics, particularly in literature, can be seen as motivated by financial interests such as those involved in copyrights. Such writings provided new criteria for characterizing works of art and played a part in setting terms of discussion for participants in the market.

Louise Lippincott's (1983) study of Arthur Pond, active in London between 1720 and 1758, documents the changing role of a dealer from an agent to an entrepreneur who sold paintings and prints from his stock, and who could be a connoisseur and a promoter of particular kinds of art. In England, there was a gradual shift in political and cultural power from a landed and mainly aristocratic group to a new class of collectors whose money came from colonization, foreign trade, and manufacturing. Prints provided an alternative for those who lacked the means to buy paintings. Pond and others supplied paintings for gentlemen's country houses and made copies to satisfy the demand for works by Italian artists such as Claude Lorrain. Although authenticity was not a concern for such works, it was becoming one in other cases. At a time when forgeries were common, Pond was also an active and knowledgeable promoter of European old masters and encouraged a taste for northern paintings.

Wars, unstable supplies, and fear of forgeries all contributed to uncertainty in the market in old masters. According to Haskell (1976), in the eighteenth century Dutch and Flemish cabinet pictures were more popular with most collectors than were large-scale Renaissance and baroque works. Until the end of the nineteenth century, the admiration for old masters did not include the hierarchies and notions of permanent value associated with the canon.

The print trade in eighteenth-century England, along with auction houses such as Christie's, were the fastest-growing sectors of the art world. Print selling moved from the artist's workshop and bookseller's stock into the world of commerce, attracting many new buyers. Pond and other dealers turned to commercial techniques of booksellers, including advertising, distribution through retail shops, and emphasis on novelty through serial publications.

In the eighteenth century, the art market was bound up with developing institutions for presenting art to a public. Auctions gave buyers a mechanism for influencing prices, as well as allowing the public a view of works that were otherwise in private collections. Regular public exhibitions, and the development of criticism and public discussion of art, were instrumental in forming and consolidating a public for art in both England and France. Consumption of culture increasingly went beyond purchasing works of art. It could include attendance at events, buying reproductions, or buying or reading critical and historical writings. Jürgen Habermas argued that the eighteenth century witnessed nothing less than the invention of culture per se, as a commodity to be consumed ostensibly for its own sake, through the medium of rational discussion.

According to David Solkin (1993), a characteristic of eighteenth-century British culture was the heretical proposal that the general good might be served by a pattern of acquisitive behavior driven entirely by personal desires. His discussion of how a visual culture came to be shaped by and for the purposes of commerce emphasizes the way in which market-driven institutions allowed painting to gain significant access to the spaces of public life while cultivating viewers' awareness of their shared interests. At exhibitions before auctions, regular exhibitions by the Royal Academy and the Society of Artists, as well as at proliferating galleries, people could examine a wide range of works by contemporary painters and sculptors, which were also offered for sale.

In France, Edne François Gersaint, through the sign painted by Antoine Watteau, and through printed notices and sales catalogs, was one of the first dealers to create a persona, an image of expertise and breeding. Although he also sold paintings, his stock was dominated by the luxury goods demanded by wealthy buyers who, after the decline of Versailles, wanted to display their status through paintings and furnishings for their *hôtels*.

Salon exhibitions mounted by the Academy of Painting and Sculpture began as regular events in 1737 and were an important public entertainment as well as a display of works for sale. The salon was in some sense the precedent for both museums of modern art and sales galleries, but the restrictions on other sales by academicians indirectly encouraged the development of institutions that eventually undermined the academy's aesthetic authority and place in French art world. Festivals, shops, and boutiques provided alternate sites for sales, and other spaces in Paris provided places where "low" audiences used the materials of high culture for their own ends.

Thomas Crow (1985) discusses the way in which salons gave birth to a normative practice of art criticism, which introduced a new class of professional writers to the regular operations of determining quality and taste. They set standards that were outside of the control of academicians and paid attention to artists outside of the "grand tradition." Similarly, an independent market, catering to different segments of the population, presented a challenge to the abstract notion of artistic value. In contrast to the state's interest in the political utility of French art for domestic and foreign propaganda, consumers chose subjects and types of works that suited their private purposes.

The state and civic museums established in the eighteenth and nineteenth centuries had an ambiguous relation to the market. Many of them were princely collections made public and did not depend on the market for acquisitions. In the United States, however, unlike Europe, a connection was established in the late nineteenth and early twentieth centuries between collectors who worked for the establishment of museums and bought works to give them outright or who willed them their collections. Museums asserted the prestige of art and increasingly set the terms for its historical and aesthetic evaluation.

The shift in modes of organizing information associated with collections accessible to the public had implications for the market. Systematic descriptions in guidebooks meant that the information could be retrieved easily and become part of a pool of knowledge. The hanging of collections by national schools, motivated by nationalism, was part of a movement toward more rigorous consideration of history and connoisseurship. Buyers and sellers of art could increasingly refer to publications in judging works.

In England in the 1840s and 1850s, the market for modern art flourished as that for old masters collapsed. Worries about authenticity on the one hand, and promotion of the national school and an appeal to the interests of manufacturers and other new buyers without classical education on the other, led to an enthusiasm for contemporary works showing modern subjects.

In the United States, the mid-nineteenth-century emergence of an art market where one had hardly existed was connected with the growth of an urban population as well as of art unions, reproductions, and coverage of art by journals and general periodicals, and with a more international outlook. In the late nineteenth century, the art market had become truly international. The circulation of objects from Asia and colonized territories testified to the links between economic power and the commerce in art.

Dealers. Who is the producer of value—the painter or the dealer? According to Pierre Bourdieu (1984), who asks this question, the ideology of creation, which makes the author the first and last source of the value of his work, conceals the fact that the cultural businessman (art dealer, publisher, etc.) is both the person who exploits the labor of the "creator" by trading in the "sacred" and the person who, by putting it on the market, exhibiting, publishing, or staging it, consecrates a product that he has "discovered" and that would otherwise remain a mere natural resource.

In the nineteenth century, especially in France, dealers and galleries emerged as important forces in the art world alongside auction houses state-sanctioned exhibitions. Active entrepreneurial dealers, who sold works of contemporary artists by shaping public opinion to their purposes, began to take a position comparable to that in the current market by mid-century. Robert Jensen (1994) points to Adolph Goupil, Paul Durand-Ruel, and Francis Petit in Paris, and William Agnew and Ernest Gambart in London, as key figures in the new market. They were overtly competitors but were linked in a cooperative net of purchases, loans, and contracts that spread from Paris to London, Brussels, and New York. They reorganized their businesses in the 1850s, from relatively passive concerns growing out of shops that had combined artists' supplies, frames, and prints with a variety of old and new art and art objects, into more highly specialized enterprises.

Jensen writes of the ideological refashioning of the commercial gallery from the equivalent of book dealers and antiquarians to rivals of museums. As eighteenth-century dealers such as Pond had already begun to do, they turned the business lessons learned in the print trade, with its mass-market audiences, to the promotion of "high" art objects. In contrast to the traditional sales method of showing individual pictures to clients, entrepreneurial dealers began to hold special exhibitions to draw the attention of the public and press to the gallery.

The Impressionists and their dealers were the most visible participants in a new system that shifted from a centralized state apparatus for showing and selling works to a complex and more commercially oriented system. By mid-century, conservative critics and artists felt that the salon had become commercially debased, appealing to tastes of the public rather than being true to the noble calling of art. The Impressionist exhibitions have been viewed as rebellious acts by a revolutionary minority, but they can also be seen as part of a response to structural problems in the official system for presenting art, which also included an effort by dealers to take advantage of the new possibilities for selling art. Patricia Mainardi (1993) views the desire of the Impressionists and other independent artists to exhibit their work in smaller, less "incoherent" contexts than the salon, and in "sympathetic groupings," as part of a much larger trend, which was motivated more by economic than by aesthetic concerns.

Nicholas Green (1987) characterizes the change in focus on the part of dealers as one of dealing in temperaments rather than in works that corresponded to received standards of craftsmanship. With the arrival of "nature" painters, the singular masterpiece gave way to myriad productions from an artist's hand. To market these works, dealers needed to draw on the support of critics who focused on evidence of the artist's individual response rather than on academically endorsed criteria for excellence. Rapid execution could be seen as a mark of personality; it could also mean that many works were produced quickly, which suited a growing market. Audiences of the 1870s and 1880s became accustomed to measuring the value of a work of art in its worked surfaces, regardless of subject. The habit of reading personality through the artist's touch would only be translated into a theoretical system with Expressionism, but it became a feature of the appreciation of art in this period, closely connected with the market for avant-garde works.

Critics played an essential part in establishing new criteria. Harrison White and Cynthia White (1965) referred to the consumer-oriented market of the late nineteenth century as the "dealer-critic system." According to Jensen, the critic Théodore Duret's equation of genius with market value inverted the two-centuries-old effort on the part of European academies to preserve many features of traditional patronage in the face of a growing market economy. But if the system opened new markets, it was comparatively unsuccessful in selling modernist paintings inside France until the end of the century; Germans, and especially Americans, were the most important early buyers of modernist works.

With respect to the mechanics of modern art dealing, Nicholas Green (1987, 1989) argues that the market developed across a range of institutions, and that auctions became the fulcrum of an emergent speculative strategy. In the 1840s and 1850s, a growing body of collectors, disenchanted with the high prices and dubious quality of mainstream collecting areas and attracted by the rising prices of modern works, gravitated toward contemporary pictures.

Auctions have continued to play an important part in the market, setting prices for modern works. As the supply of old masters has diminished, they have focused on Impressionist and modern art, and increasingly on contemporary art. The sale in 1914 of *La peau de l'ours* by a group of collectors who had pooled funds demonstrated to speculators that avant-garde art could appreciate in value in a relatively short time and established auctions as a viable mode for sales of contemporary art in the early twentieth century. The Scull auction in 1973, with its record prices for works by living artists, would have an even more dramatic effect on the art market in the 1970s and 1980s.

The relation between dealer and artist established in the late nineteenth century has in many respects remained stable. Dealers try to have an exclusive arrangement with the artists in their "stable," while the artists may try to be shown as widely as possible. In return for the percentage retained for each work sold (recently, half its price or more), the dealer "introduces" the artist and his or her work into ever more select company (group exhibitions, solo shows, museums), and ever more sought-after placements (prestigious collections and museums). Dealers rely on their reputation for aesthetic and financial acumen (their "symbolic capital," in Bourdieu's [1984] terms), and on their connections. Rather than overt advertising, the most successful dealers rely on discreet forms of "public relations"—receptions, society gatherings, judiciously placed confidences—as well as on their contacts with writers and the press. They are actively involved in shaping aesthetic judgments.

According to Raymonde Moulin (1989, 1992), the classic problem of economics of how much to produce takes the form: what painters to choose? how many? She proposes that the dealer's ability to make rational predictions ends where the artist's creative freedom begins. The dealer's initiative is limited to such areas as allocation of capital resources for publicity as opposed to acquisition, to the limitation of supply, and to the manipulation of prices. She claims that it is possible to make a rational choice among alternatives based on aesthetic judgment, but that the dealer must weigh whether to act while the work happens to correspond to some contemporary interest, or to wait if he or she feels sure that the work will ultimately find its place in the hierarchy of values recognized by history. Durand-Ruel, the primary dealer of the Impressionists, succeeded ultimately because he bought a huge stock of paintings and held on to them for many years. Because few dealers can afford to operate in this way, most work actively to promote a particular point of view.

The dealer's judgment may extend to encouraging particular kinds of work by an artist, or collaborating with the artist to cultivate an image. Michael FitzGerald (1995) documents the cooperation between Pablo Picasso and Paul Rosenberg in selecting and presenting work to the public. A dealer also has an interest in working with critics and museums to attempt to influence the writing of history. Some New York dealers who were first successful in promoting Abstract Expressionism, and subsequently Pop art, including Sidney Janis, Leo Castelli, and Betty Parsons, gained a reputation for picking artists partly because "their" artists were featured in modernist art criticism.

The market context has affected the appearance and presentation of art. The display of isolated works in a neutral gallery space is an innovation of the art market that has come to seem natural. It tends to detach works from any context and to present them as autonomous objects. The gallery and museum have also provided an impetus for the creation of works of art, from Géricault's *Raft of the Medusa* to contemporary installations and works on a massive scale, which are not adapted to individuals' homes, but which may contribute to the prestige of a gallery.

With the success of the art market, the number of dealers has increased dramatically in the twentieth century, especially after World War II, while the number of artists has increased even faster than the exhibition spaces that could show their work. Much of this growth has been in traditional centers like Paris and New York; however, new museums (which can hope to amass only a limited quantity of old works), expanded teaching of art in universities, and generally an extended art infrastructure mean that contemporary art is very widely shown and sold.

According to Diana Crane (1987), economic theories of market behavior suggest that when a large number of small firms compete with each other, there is likely to be a high level of competition and a wider diversity of products than when, as the markets increase in size, a few organizations establish positions of leadership, limiting the competition. She claims that dealers' strategies in the 1960s and subsequently, in identifying and promoting new styles in collaboration with other dealers, art magazines, and art museums, tended to focus the market on a limited number of new developments. From the point of view of the market, the turnover of artistic movements makes short-term commercial operations highly speculative. Dealers in contemporary art are in a position of constantly presenting new things, but they have a strong incentive to control the history into which their "discoveries" are inserted.

Artists working in other styles, in nontraditional ways, or who are members of underrepresented groups frequently have been excluded, and in some cases have turned to "alternative spaces." The dynamics of the art world make it difficult for such artists to sell their work and to affect the terms of discussion. Some, such Hans Haacke, have been successful in presenting work that deals centrally and critically with the economics of art in mainstream venues.

The art market became a matter of interest outside of art circles in the 1980s with the enormous prices attained by Impressionist, modern, and contemporary works. When new collectors and financial institutions bought on speculation, their choices were not made primarily on aesthetic grounds. The art market is now described in terms drawn from financial markets, such as *boom, crash, appreciation,* and *quotation.* During the boom in the art market in the 1980s and the subsequent decline and slower revival, books and articles on art as investment offered analyses of works based on their potential for appreciation or as part of undervalued market segments. Certain collectors, such as Charles Saatchi, became tastemakers because of their reputation for picking winners. Although some buyers have made very large profits, analyses of the movements of prices over the very long term show that the return for art, on the average, is less than that for stocks and bonds. Periods of euphoria and the phenomenal rise in prices of individual works have to be looked at in the context of downturns and the fate of nonfamous works.

Liquidity of art as an investment depends on a consensus. In seventeenth-century Holland, according to John Montias (1982), paintings, silver, and fine furniture were all relatively liquid valuables, because standards of quality were fairly uniform among large groups of people, at least of the same social class. The relative illiquidity of many works today is a reflection of the wide disparity of tastes even among individuals in a given income group, and of the difficulty in locating the rare customer willing to pay the highest price. Nevertheless, the possibility of financial gain continues to attract both buyers and artists.

For artists, however, the power of the market is frequently problematic. In the late twentieth century, a resistance to the commodification of art has affected both its form and its content. Especially since the 1960s, artists producing earthworks, installations, conceptual art, and performance art have made works that are not easily consumable, or that, on the contrary, attempt to undermine the rarity of the unique work. To some extent, documentation and by-products of these works have been marketed and collected; however, the economic underpinnings for such production also depend on noncommercial institutions such as university art programs and granting agencies. Although not completely independent of the market, such institutions offer in theory an alternative approach, considering the theoretical implications or social relevance of art rather than specific qualities of individual works.

Writing about the Art Market. Writings on the art market have provided an alternative approach to studies of art focused on individual artists, styles, or movements. Early writings that assembled data and looked at historical trends have been supplemented by detailed studies of individual periods in which the art market is viewed as a participant in a dynamic process of negotiating cultural meanings.

A consciousness of the market has involved a challenge to the notion of pure art, but also to that of disinterested scholarship. Books and exhibitions can stimulate interest in artworks. The "discovery" and the reconstruction of artists' careers, and especially the authentication of works of art, inevitably affect market values. Commercial galleries have sponsored the research and publication of recent catalogues raisonnés.

The retrospective exhibition involves an overlapping of historical research or critical formulations and the marketplace. Not only is it almost always done with the collaboration of commercial galleries, whether it involves contemporary works or works from much earlier periods, but it also has usually been preceded, at least in the case of contemporary works, by smaller exhibitions in galleries, publicity, and critical writing. The notion that an artist's exhibition record consists of independently arranged, usually one-person shows in rented spaces or commercial galleries and subsequently in museums is taken for granted. Historians or writers on aesthetics who take the art market into account must recognize the contingency of aesthetic judgments and their own involvement in the networks that make them.

Value. To investigate the art market is to analyze objects without prices. The valuation of art depends on something other than the cost of materials and the labor that went into its making (although materials and labor can be a factor, especially in decorative arts). The value of a work of art is a function of exchange, a social construct produced by a relational system, rather than something "natural." Factors such as provenance, which have nothing to do with its characteristics or quality, can add to the monetary value of an object. Its worth can fluctuate dramatically over time. Only when the work reaches a museum from which it will not be sold does it become "priceless." Both aesthetic judgments and monetary ones can determine the "value" of a work, but the relation between aesthetic and market value is not a simple one. Aesthetic worth may be used to justify a price, and high sales prices may be held up as evidence of aesthetic value, but such claims are inherently unstable. [*See* Evaluation; *and* Value.]

The idea of evaluating works of art in monetary terms implies the possibility of ownership, which tends to focus attention on individual objects. The appreciation and consumption of objects defined as art has sometimes reshaped them in terms set by Western capitalism. For instance, discussions of cultural heritages, especially with respect to the archaeological past, tend to be framed as debates over ownership of cultural properties. The aesthetic appreciation of non-Western art has been associated with its collection and sale, and increased demand has led to extensive pillaging of sites and smuggling.

How art, if it were a commodity like any other, could acquire a status that removed it from a price system based on the cost of labor and materials is a question that requires an understanding of ways in which art operates in a social context, as a bearer of meaning or as a signifier of wealth or status. When art is exchanged, its function changes from being an object of some particular use in a religious or secular setting, to a commodity whose use and value can vary according to the interests and tastes of the buyer. Further shifts in use or appreciation may be involved in the revival of artists or types of art. Francis Haskell (1976) points out that the "discoveries" of artists such as Orcagna, Vermeer, El Greco, Botticelli, Piero della Francesca, and the Le Nain brothers between 1790 and 1870 depended on the notion that qualities of the works, once thought to be inevitably connected with religion or some particular concept of art, could be considered separately.

Bourdieu's (1984) notion of distinction as a function of class segment can be a helpful one in considering how a market sets value. The valuation of art depends on distinctions between works of high value and those of low value. Expensive and rare art always coexists with alternatives. Bourdieu (1993) maintains that the field of cultural production is structured by an opposition between subfields of restricted product, "high" and a more inexpensive or widely available product. Inexpensive works, such as "sofa art" in the twentieth century or "paintings by the dozen" in Holland in the seventeenth century, for a poorer group of buyers, presumed to be unsophisticated, have long been at the bottom of the market. Works in multiple versions such as prints and reproductions, or bibelots, also present alternatives to the unique expensive work. [*See* Bourdieu.]

Rarity, however, does not in itself indicate high value. The social value of high art depends on the existence of a distinction between high and low culture, and on further differentiations among alternatives. The choice of one type or style of work rather than another takes on meaning within a social context. In *Distinction* (1993), Bourdieu defines "cultural capital" as a form of knowledge, an internalized code or a cognitive acquisition that equips the social agent with empathy toward, appreciation for, or competence in deciphering cultural relations and cultural artifacts. The purchase of a work of art can be an indicator of cultural competence, evidence of cultural capital accumulated through social formation, education, and social institutions. But the work of art has meaning and interest only for someone who possesses the cultural competence to appreciate it, someone who understands the code into which it is encoded. Simply paying a very high price for a work of art does not automatically confer the status of amateur on rich buyers, but associations, which Jensen (1994) refers to as "the fetish gloss," can allow them to achieve cultural capital.

Whereas traditionally works of art were more likely to bring cultural rather than financial capital to their buyers, the speculative buying of art, especially in the latter half of the twentieth century, has brought other criteria for judging value into play. In terms of the market, it is not possible to separate "pure aesthetics" from a sociological understanding of the arts. Art participates in a larger economic and social context, both as a commodity and as a creator of meanings.

Consideration of the market in relation to aesthetics necessarily draws on a sociological critique of traditional aesthetics such as that offered by Janet Wolff (1993). Whereas the sociology of the arts considers all cultural products, discussions of the art market are usually limited to consumable and exchangeable objects, especially those that are unique or produced in small quantities: in effect, paintings, sculpture, prints, photographs, objets d'art, and furniture. Publishing and performance arts such as literature, music, dance, and film play an important part in the economics of art, but their products are not valued as objects of exchange in the same way.

A focus on the art market challenges the centrality of concerns with the nature of art and aesthetic experience and with aesthetic judgment as absolute or unchangeable. In contrast to Kant's claims that the distinguishing characteristic of the judgment of taste is that it is "disinterested," a consideration of the market necessarily views judgments about art as variable and motivated by external interests. A work is not beautiful in an absolute sense but is desirable to a particular person at a particular time. The market fosters and legitimates such desires and provides a means for their satisfaction. Although Institutional Theory of Art has nothing to say about the nature of the aesthetic experience, it can explain why certain works or groups of works are considered appropriate objects for aesthetic attention. From this point of view, aesthetic value arises from the consensus of participants in an art world, and the market is an important participant in forging that consensus.

[See also Art World; Ideology; and Sociology of Art.]

BIBLIOGRAPHY

Alpers, Svetlana. Rembrandt's Enterprise: The Studio and the Market. Chicago, 1988.

Alsop, Joseph W. The Rare Art Traditions: The History of Art Collecting and Its Linked Phenomena Wherever These Have Appeared. New York, 1982.

Becker, Howard S. Art Worlds. Berkeley, 1982.

Bourdieu, Pierre. Distinction: A Social Critique of Judgement of Taste. Translated by Richard Nice. Cambridge, Mass., 1984.

Bourdieu, Pierre. The Field of Cultural Production: Essays on Art and Literature. Edited by Randal Johnson. New York, 1993.

Crane, Diana. The Transformation of the Avant-Garde: The New York Art World, 1940–1985. Chicago, 1987.

Crow, Thomas E. Painters and Public Life in Eighteenth-Century Paris. New Haven, 1985.

FitzGerald, Michael C. Making Modernism: Picasso and the Creation of the Market for Twentieth-Century Art. New York, 1995.

Goldthwaite, Richard A. Wealth and the Demand for Art in Italy, 1300–1600. Baltimore, 1993.

Green, Nicholas. "Dealing in Temperaments: Economic Transformations of the Artistic Field in France during the Second Half of the Nineteenth Century." Art History 10 (March 1987).

Green, Nicholas. "Circuits of Production, Circuits of Consumption: The Case of Mid-Nineteenth-Century French Art Dealing." Art Journal 48 (Spring 1989).

Harris, Neil. The Artist in American Society: The Formative Years, 1790–1860. Reprint, Chicago, 1982.

Haskell, Francis. Rediscoveries in Art: Some Aspects of Taste, Fashion, and Collecting in England and France. Ithaca, N.Y., 1976.

Jensen, Robert. Marketing Modernism in Fin-de-Siècle Europe. Princeton, N.J., 1994.

Lippincott, Louise. Selling Art in Georgian London: The Rise of Arthur Pond. New Haven, 1983.

Mainardi, Patricia. The End of the Salon: Art and the State in the Early Third Republic. Cambridge and New York, 1993.

McClellan, Andrew. "Watteau's Dealer: Gersaint and the Marketing of Art in Eighteenth-Century Paris." Art Bulletin 78 (September 1996).

Montias, John Michael. Artists and Artisans in Delft: A Socio-Economic Study of the Seventeenth Century. Princeton, N.J., 1982.

Moulin, Raymonde. Le marché de la peinture en France. New ed. Paris, 1989. Abridged English translation by Arthur Goldhammer published as The French Art Market: A Sociological View (New Brunswick, N.J., 1987).

Moulin, Raymonde, with Pascaline Costa. L'Artiste, l'institution et le marché. Paris, 1992.

Pears, Iain. The Discovery of Painting: The Growth of Interest in the Arts in England, 1680–1768. New Haven, 1988.

Reitlinger, Gerald. The Economics of Taste: The Rise and Fall of Picture Prices, 1760–1960. 3 vols. Reprint, New York, 1982.

Solkin, David H. Painting for Money: The Visual Arts and the Public Sphere in Eighteenth-Century England. New Haven, 1993.

Wallis, Brian, ed. Art after Modernism: Rethinking Representation. New York, 1984.

Wallis, Brian, ed. Hans Haacke: Unfinished Business. Cambridge, Mass., 1986.

White, Harrison C., and Cynthia A. White. Canvases and Careers: Institutional Change in the French Painting World. New York, 1965.

Wolff, Janet. Aesthetics and the Sociology of Art. 2d ed. Ann Arbor, 1993.

Woodmansee, Martha. The Author, Art, and the Market: Rereading the History of Aesthetics. New York, 1994.

GRACE SEIBERLING

ART THEORY. See Theories of Art; and Theory, History of.

ART WORK. See Art World; Definition of Art; Essentialism; Historicism; and Ontology of Art.

ART WORLD. Art is the product of collective action, of many people cooperating in the many activities without which particular works could not come into existence or continue to exist. They cooperate by means of shared understandings—conventions—that allow them to coordinate these activities easily and efficiently. When such cooperation is carried on repeatedly, even routinely, by the same people, or by people similar enough to be considered the same, we can speak of an *art world.*

The production of any art object or performance requires that many activities be carried out in order that the work appear as it finally does. The form of this division of labor is variable, finely divided in such arts as film or opera, much less so in more solitary arts such as painting or poetry. In the limiting case, only one person is involved, that person doing everything that needs doing.

When no one is available to do some of these activities, they will go undone and the resulting work will differ in form and substance from what it would have been had such help been present. If no one makes a light-sensitive paper of platinum salts that some photographers want, they will make it themselves or, more likely, use a silver-based paper, and the resulting photograph will lack the distinctive tones of a platinum print. If no one does the work of finding financial support, the artist will have to take time out from other work to raise the money, losing time that might have been spent painting or writing. If no one has invented a musical instrument that plays forty-two tones between the octaves, a composer like Harry Partch will have to invent it and the notation for music made from a forty-two tone scale. Most composers, finding that such resources are not readily available, will content themselves with the standard twelve-tone chromatic scale of Western music.

Some of these activities—providing materials or financing, or arranging for distribution, exhibition, or sale, for instance—are defined by everyone involved as *support* activities, which may be done by any competent person. Others—composing or performing music, writing, directing or performing a play, painting a picture, or making a photograph—are seen as core *artistic* activities, which may be done only by those specially gifted people called artists. Yet another crucial activity is that of consuming art: reading the book, listening to the music.

This differentiation between support and artistic personnel and audience members is not given in the nature of the materials an art form works with, but is instead entirely conventional. In some versions of music, such as composing for symphony orchestra, the composer is seen as one of the crucial artistic collaborators; in others, such as jazz, the composer of a song has only provided a vehicle for the real artists who will improvise on that foundation.

Wherever people cooperate to produce works of art, conflict may arise, as a result of the differing motives and interests of the cooperating parties. Technical support staff may refuse to follow an artist's orders to do something that would reflect badly on their own professional skills or produce legal trouble (as when a gallery or printer refuses to deal with material that may legally be held to be obscene or libelous). Institutions may refuse to give a place to work that does not fit into its standard ways of doing things: sculptures that are too big, symphonies that require too many players, plays that last too long. Most artists find it convenient to create and even to envision work that will not make trouble with those whose cooperation they need.

The cooperation between people necessary to the production of an artwork might be achieved by full discussion of every point: in the case of music, for instance, what notes and harmonies will be allowable, what instruments will be used, how long the pieces will be, and so on. But it is clearly more efficient to rely for the most part on already achieved understandings, within which small adjustments and innovations can be made. As the term *convention* implies, what the understandings are can be quite arbitrary; there is no inherent reason for an orchestra to tune to an A that is 440 vibrations per second rather than 444 or 436. Conventions allow audiences to know what is likely to happen in an artwork. That provides the background against which an artist can create emotional effects by delaying or frustrating audience expectations.

Art worlds, to arrive finally at a definition, consist of all the people whose activities are necessary to the production and reception of the characteristic works that that world, and perhaps others as well, define as art. Members of art worlds coordinate the activities by which work is produced by referring to a body of conventional understandings embodied in common practice and in frequently used artifacts. The same people often cooperate repeatedly, even routinely, in similar ways to produce similar works, so that we can think of an art world as an established network of cooperative links among participants. Works of art are not the product of individual, gifted makers but are rather joint products of all the people who cooperate via an art world's characteristic conventions to bring works like that into existence.

"Art" is an honorific title that, bestowed on a work, gives it a value it does not have without it. Aestheticians study the premises and arguments people use to justify classifying things and activities as "beautiful," "artistic," "art," "not art," "good art," "bad art," and so on. They construct systems with which to make and justify both the classifications and specific instances of their application.

Members of highly developed art worlds rely on these systems as resources in arriving at collective lines of activity. Critics apply aesthetic systems to specific art works and arrive at judgments of their worth and explications of what gives them that worth. These judgments produce reputations for works and their artists. Distributors and audience members take reputations into account when they decide what to support emotionally and financially, and that affects the resources available to artists to continue their work. Artists use aesthetic systems as a guide to making the innumerable small decisions that go into the production of a work. As a result, aesthetic systems have practical consequences for the kinds of work people make, the support they receive, and the way work is received.

Aesthetic value thus arises not from inherent qualities of a work but rather from the consensus of participants in an art world, from their agreement to accept and use the same criteria to make those distinctions. To the degree that such a consensus does not exist, shared value does not exist: judgments of value not held jointly by members of an art world do not provide a basis for collective activity premised on those judgments, and thus do not affect activities very much. Work becomes good, therefore valuable, through the achievement of consensus about the basis on which it is to be judged and through the application of the agreed-on aesthetic principles to particular cases.

Many aestheticians and critics find the analysis above too relativistic for their taste. Leaving everything to the consensus of art-world participants, it provides no way to make the distinctions and judgments aestheticians want to make. From such a standpoint, how can we tell art from nonart? The theories of Arthur Danto and George Dickie, for example, seem designed to preserve the justification for such judgments while recognizing the realities of art-world organization.

Art is too crude a concept to capture what is at work here. Like other complex concepts, it disguises a generalization about the nature of reality. When we try to define it, we find many anomalous cases, cases that meet some, but not all, of the criteria implied or expressed by the concept. When we say "art," we usually mean something like this: a work that has aesthetic value, however that is defined; a work justified by a coherent and philosophically defensible aesthetic; a work recognized by appropriate people as having aesthetic value; a work displayed in the appropriate places (hung in museums, played at concerts). In many instances, however, works have some, but not all, of these attributes. They are exhibited and valued but do not have aesthetic value, or have aesthetic value but are not exhibited and valued by the right people. The generalization contained in the concept of art suggests that these all co-occur in the real world; when they do not co-occur, we have the definitional troubles that have always plagued the concept.

The definition of art worlds proposed here is empirical and inductive, derived from the inspection of specific cases of conventionally recognized arts and of marginal arts of many kinds, rather than a priori and analytic, based on deduction from agreed-on general principles. The definition does not aim to produce logical neatness, careful distinctions, and mutually exclusive categories, but rather to describe the term's meaning in the practices of those who use it.

Empirically, art cannot be distinguished from nonart in any clear-cut way. To the sociologist studying art worlds, it is as clear as, but no clearer than, it is to the participants in them whether particular objects or events are "really art" or whether they are craft or commercial work, the expression of folk culture, or the embodied symptoms of a lunatic. Yet,

if we are concerned with art worlds, we should be able to distinguish them from other worlds that are not concerned with art. How can one theorize about something, or study it, if one cannot say what it is and distinguish instances of it from instances that are not it?

One can easily study activities whose definition as art is not widely contested. One looks for groups of people who cooperate to produce things that they, at least, call art; finding them, one looks for other people who are also necessary to that production, gradually building up as complete a picture as possible of the entire cooperating network radiating out from the work in question. One looks for when, where, and how participants draw the lines that distinguish what is and what is not art, what is and is not their kind of art, and who is or is not an artist. One is not misled by the arguments between establishments and avant-gardes over whether the work of one or the other group is "really" art.

But to limit the analysis to what would not be widely contested leaves out too much that is interesting: all the marginal cases in which people seek but are denied the title of "art," as well as those in which people do work that outside observers can see might meet the definition but whose makers are not interested in that possibility (e.g., folk or so-called naive artists). That would allow the process of definition by members of the society, which is the subject of study, to set its terms. To include everything that might conceivably be defined as art includes too much; almost anything might meet such a definition, if it were applied ingeniously enough. Sticking to the marginal cases makes the process of definition a central arena of investigation.

[See also Art Market; Bourdieu; Danto; Dickie; Institutional Theory of Art; and Sociology of Art.]

BIBLIOGRAPHY

Becker, Howard S. *Art Worlds.* Berkeley, 1982.

Bourdieu, Pierre. *Photography: A Middle-brow Art.* Translated by Shaun Whiteside. Stanford, Calif., 1990.

Candido, Antonio. On *Literature and Society.* Translated and edited by Howard S. Becker. Princeton, N.J., 1995.

Danto, Arthur. "The Artworld." *Journal of Philosophy* 61.19 (15 October 1964): 571–584.

Dickie, George. *Art and the Aesthetic: An Institutional Analysis.* Ithaca, N.Y., 1974.

Finnegan, Ruth. *The Hidden Musicians: Music-Making in an English Town.* Cambridge and New York, 1989.

Gross, Larry, ed. *On the Margins of Art Worlds.* Boulder, Colo., 1995.

Hennion, Antoine. *La Passion musicale.* Paris, 1993.

Menger, Pierre-Michel. *Le Paradoxe du musicien: Le compositeur, le mélomane et l'État dans la société contemporaine.* Paris, 1983.

Meyer, Leonard B. *Emotion and Meaning in Music.* Chicago, 1956.

Moulin, Raymonde. *Le marché de la peinture en France.* Paris, 1967.

Rosenblum, Barbara. *Photographers at Work: A Sociology of Photographic Styles.* New York, 1978.

Smith, Barbara Herrnstein. *Poetic Closure: A Study of How Poems End.* Chicago, 1968.

Sudnow, David. *Ways of the Hand: The Organization of Improvised Conduct.* Cambridge, Mass., 1978.

Vianna, Hermano. *O Mundo Funk Carioca.* Rio de Janeiro, 1988.

Wilder, Alec. *American Popular Song: The Great Innovators, 1900–1950.* Edited by James T. Maher. New York and Oxford, 1972.

HOWARD S. BECKER

ASSOCIATIONISM. *See* Alison; Blair; Gerard; *and* Priestley.

ATTITUDE. [*To explain the meanings and history of the concept of attitude, this entry comprises two essays:*
Aesthetic Attitude
Pictorial Attitude
The first essay traces the history and critique of the notion of "aesthetic attitude," that is, the particular psychological or mental attitude that some theorists believe we adopt when we experience art or make aesthetic judgments. The second essay analyzes the notion of pictorial attitude from the point of view of contemporary cognitive psychology.]

Aesthetic Attitude

Aesthetic attitude theories are designed generally for the purpose of explaining those situations where on one occasion an individual attends to a particular object or event in a way that creates an aesthetic experience, and on another occasion attends to the same object in a way that does not. Attitude theories are constructed to explain what it is that the individual does, what sort of attitude the individual adopts, that brings about aesthetic experience. For example, one may pass a spring flower bed on the way to the office and enjoy its beauty, and, on the way home, pass that same flower bed and consider only the allergy-promoting pollen that it is producing. Yet throughout, the control as to whether the experience is aesthetic or not lies with the individual. The aesthetic attitude can be "turned on" or "turned off" at will.

Traditionally, the aesthetic attitude is defined as an attitude or state of mind that is entered into, voluntarily and consciously, by an individual making that individual receptive to having an aesthetic experience. First, in adopting the aesthetic attitude, it is the individual's purpose to have an aesthetic experience. Second, the object or event under consideration can be any object or any event; it is the adoption of the aesthetic attitude by the individual that transforms the object into an aesthetic one. Third, the adoption of the aesthetic attitude is traditionally always under the control of the individual; it is a voluntary and conscious act on the part of the attender. In traditional theorizing about the aesthetic attitude, it has been necessary to maintain a rigid subject-object distinction in order to preserve the subjective control and the "on-off" feature of aesthetic attention (that an object can be viewed aesthetically at one moment and nonaesthetically the next).

This definition, however, covers only what is traditionally common to most aesthetic attitude theories. It does not define the content or substance of the aesthetic attitude. This is where theorizers differ, and this is what makes aesthetic attitude theorizing interesting. The next section will review these specific views in an account of the history of attitude theorizing.

History of the Aesthetic Attitude. The historical foundations of the aesthetic attitude theories lie in two places. The first is Britain in the eighteenth century. The second is Germany in the late eighteenth and early nineteenth centuries. Those who first contributed to the establishment of the tradition of the aesthetic attitude are known as the British Taste Theorists. By and large, they worked in a spirit of growing empiricism in Britain (British empiricism being committed to the exclusive use of the senses for the acquisition of knowledge).

Over the course of aesthetic attitude theorizing, the attitude of disinterest has been the single most prevalent candidate for what the aesthetic attitude truly is. Anthony Ashley Cooper, Earl of Shaftesbury (1671–1713) is credited with being the first to utilize the notion of disinterestedness in a way comparable with later attitude theorizers. [*See* Cooper; *and* Disinterestedness.] Lord Shaftesbury's motivation in developing his aesthetic attitude theory was part of a larger ethical project to counter Thomas Hobbes's ethical egoism. He adopted a Platonic position, holding that there are extramental, extranatural absolutes. The epistemological access to these absolutes is through the adopted attitude of disinterest. Here *disinterest* has primarily a negative or privative meaning: "not motivated by self-concern or personal advantage." It is this negative sense that forms the cornerstone of the way in which the term was used from Shaftesbury up to today. But it is important to understand that the term had a positive side as well. *Disinterest* does not mean "uninterest." Disinterest allows for an interest on the part of the agent, but that interest is not motivated or informed by issues relative only to that attender herself. By taking on a posture of disinterest, the agent could assure herself that she would judge just as any other person would, or so Lord Shaftesbury, and those who followed him, concluded.

Francis Hutcheson (1694–1746) was to some extent a mirror of Lord Shaftesbury, especially with regard to disinterest. [*See* Hutcheson.] Significant differences exist between the two, however, Hutcheson was not a Platonist; he was a relational realist, one who believes that aesthetic properties exist in a combination or relationship of subjective and objective states. This metaphysical position allowed Hutcheson to ground the universality that both he and Shaftesbury sought not in extranatural objects, or even in the objective world, but in the subject and her faculty of taste, an innate ability to sense and judge beauty. The faculty of taste, which Hutcheson called the "internal sense," functions like other senses: as one with working and practiced senses sees something yellow and recognizes the color as yellow, so when one sees an object whose properties trigger in one the experience of beauty, one recognizes the experience as beauty. And just as one can go wrong perceptually, one can misperceive beauty. Proper disposition for the correct functioning of the faculty of taste is when one's attitude is disinterested.

Joseph Addison (1672–1719) reacted to Hutcheson's claim that there was such a thing as a special faculty that accounted for the universality of taste, that one would judge the same as another if each is properly disposed. [*See* Addison.] Addison's account may be seen as an attempt to explain Hutcheson's description of aesthetic experience and judgment as a function of such a faculty. Addison studied aesthetic judgments and found that there are three qualities that, when in the object, produce in the spectator a pleasant experience and a favorable judgment: that which is great, that which is uncommon, and that which is beautiful. To judge correctly, one must be pleased with the *proper* qualities of what one is perceiving. It is the adoption of an attitude of disinterest on the part of the spectator that assures that one is judging properly. One is then appropriately disposed to react not out of one's own concerns and interests, but out of a pure appreciation of the object.

Archibald Alison (1757–1839) stressed disinterestedness more than Addison did, and expressed it in a way that is still closer to the way it is used today by attitude theorists. [*See* Alison.] Alison thought that the having of an aesthetic experience is a matter of the exercise of imagination and the recollecting of certain associations. However, one must be disposed in a certain way in order to experience an object aesthetically; personal or practical interests will interfere with one's attention to the object. The ideal state of the mind, he says, is to be "vacant and unemployed." With the addition of any practical or personal concerns, the experience of beauty may be lost.

This brings us to the second primary location where aesthetic attitude theories were being developed. Immanuel Kant was motivated to determine how it is that aesthetic judgments can be true or false while still accounting for the problem, raised by David Hume, that judging is a subjective phenomenon, which apparently gives rise to a large amount of disagreement between judgments of different agents. (Here *subjective* means that the judgment is grounded not in the properties or states of objects but in the subject or the person making the judgment; this seems to lead to the difficulty that there is nothing to ensure that the judgment of one person will be comparable to that of another. If, on the other hand, a judgment is "intersubjective," which is how Kant describes aesthetic judgments, that judgment is grounded in the subject but is universally

shared among all those properly disposed and attending to the same object.)

Kant determined that the key to correct aesthetic evaluation lay in two things: (1) that human beings each have the same faculties for understanding the world, and (2) that if each aesthetic evaluator were motivated in his or her evaluation by an appreciation of the object *merely* as it is an object of contemplation—with no regard for its actual existence—then insofar as one would be judging disinterestedly, one would be judging *that* particular object just as every other properly disposed aesthetic evaluator would judge it.

The other thinker who contributed heavily to the history of the aesthetic attitude was Arthur Schopenhauer (1788–1860). [*See* Schopenhauer.] His theory of the Will as a domineering and negative force that enslaves all, a force brought about by worldly desire, led him to look for escape. His escape took two forms, one permanent, one transitory but more accessible. The permanent escape was to deny desire, to adopt asceticism and take up the life of pure contemplation. The second escape was through art. Through art, the individual could understand not just the phenomenal world, but also the world of Platonic Ideas, the world of universal, immutable, perfect formal objects. In rising to this higher level of understanding, one escapes desire. To release oneself from desire, one must appreciate the art from a disinterested viewpoint, contemplating the object for the object's sake, and for no other (practical) end.

In the twentieth century, Edward Bullough articulated an aesthetic attitude theory in an article originally published in 1912 in the *British Journal of Psychology* titled " 'Psychical Distance' as a Factor in Art and as an Aesthetic Principle." [*See* Bullough.] For one to adopt an attitude of distance is to remove practical concerns from one's focus. Unlike traditional accounts of attitudes of disinterest, where one is either disinterested or not, Bullough's conception of gaining distance admits of degree. Bullough's *Antinomy of Distancing* says that in order for the fullest or best aesthetic experience to take place, one must seek not only to distance oneself from the work, but that distance must be kept to an absolute minimum. The best aesthetic experiences are had when one achieves the least possible amount of distance, without its total collapse.

In 1914, Clive Bell published *Art*. There he describes what it is in objects that makes them art. An object is an art object if it contains "significant form." "Significant form" is a relation of the formal properties of the object under consideration. Unlike other formalists, Bell does not describe the properties that make up significant form in objective terms; instead he says that we recognize significant form in objects under our consideration when those objects arouse in us the experiences of "aesthetic emotion." Bell's arousal theory is not squarely in the aesthetic attitude tradition for two reasons: first, his theory is about the identification of objects as art objects; traditional attitude theories are about aesthetic experience and, second, about aesthetic judgment; they are generally not about classifying objects as art. Second, Bell's theory is an arousal theory, where the properties of the object under consideration act on us to trigger the aesthetic emotion. Traditional attitude theories stress the subjective control of the individual over whether her experience is aesthetic or otherwise. On the other hand, Bell's work does continue the tradition that one must be properly disposed for the object to induce an aesthetic emotion.

Within the last three decades, the banner for disinterestedness has been most prominently carried by Jerome Stolnitz. Two things distinguish Stolnitz from the Germans: he does not have a metaphysical structure in which the disinterestedness is supposed to fit, and he does not specifically address aesthetic evaluation in his description of disinterestedness, as did Kant. The goal of adoption of the aesthetic attitude, for Stolnitz, is simply the having of an aesthetic experience. Stolnitz begins his account by noting that attention is selective. One focuses routinely, either consciously or not, on different aspects of what one senses, and one dismisses those aspects that are not relevant to the purpose of viewing. If one's purpose is to mow the lawn, the focus is on the function of the lawn mower, on whether it is gassed up, and so on. If the purpose is to fix a broken lawn mower, then the focus is on the wires, valves, and plugs. The state of attention in the absence of purpose is that state where one focuses on the object as an aesthetic object, paying attention only to its perceptible properties. Stolnitz defines the aesthetic attitude as "disinterested and sympathetic attention to and contemplation of any object of awareness whatever, for its own sake alone" (Stolnitz, 1961). If one is to appreciate the object, one must accept it "sympathetically," attentively, and on its own terms, one must be willing to engage attention on the phenomenal characteristics in a serious way, not haphazardly or nonchalantly.

The task of another theorizer, Vincent Tomas, was to make clear the distinction between the ordinary way of seeing objects and the aesthetic way. Tomas says that when one sees objects ordinarily, one sees them classificatorily; for example, I see the person approaching me along the hall as the philosopher, the woman, my friend, Andrea. The aesthetic way of looking at objects is the preclassificatory way. Looking at the object under consideration without adding to it any labels or classifying it is to see the object as *just* itself. Viewing aesthetically puts the individual out of the normal relation with the world; it puts her in a preanalytic, prescientific, preclassificatory, pre-"use" relationship. Because viewing aesthetically is viewing prior to doing anything with the object, it follows that the first, or logically prior, viewing is the aesthetic viewing, and that, further, it takes no act of will or adoption of particular attitude to view an object aesthetically. Rather, viewing aesthetically takes the privative stance of simply ceasing to view the object naturally.

The motivation of another philosopher, Virgil Aldrich, was to bring to the notion of aesthetic viewing more objectivity than had been captured in other accounts. First, Aldrich wanted to put more emphasis on the empirically accessible properties of the object; second, he was concerned that with undue emphasis on the subjective, the danger of rampant relativism would present itself. Aldrich, like Tomas, posits two separate ways of viewing. The first way is "observation," by which Aldrich means the sort of viewing where patterns and commonalities are seen, where one is in the position to use the objects observed in purposeful ways. Aesthetic viewing, on the other hand, is what Aldrich calls "viewing aspectually," "prehending" or "prehension." The aesthetic viewer *prehends* the object by seeing the *objective* qualities of the figure, *but* seeing them aspectually, impressionistically, or "seeing [them] as" they are representative of something that is different but that has objectively the same visual qualities. Through viewing the one set of properties differently, one prehends in the objective properties different objects. When one looks at a cloud, one might apply the label "cloud," but one might also apply other labels, such as "dragon," "train," or "frog" to what is (visually) *objectively* seen. One is able to apply these other labels impressionistically to the objective properties seen.

Attitude Theory Criticism. The evidence relied upon for the existence of an aesthetic attitude has been largely pretheoretical. One may believe, based on numerous examples generated from everyday life, that a special attitude can be adopted toward any object or event, and in so doing one may appreciate it aesthetically; that is, one can have an aesthetic experience through proper attention to that object. Critics of the existence of an aesthetic attitude must make their claims against this kind of evidence. Without answering clearly why it is that common experience includes the ability to turn aesthetic viewing on and off at will, the critic's case will be incomplete.

George Dickie's motivation for questioning the existence of an aesthetic attitude is, at least in part, a matter of ontological economy. [*See* Dickie.] Dickie sees in the most representative attitude theories the excess of having two kinds of attitudes—ordinary and aesthetic—giving rise to two kinds of experiences where one kind of object is transformed into another kind. This excess, he believes, is a mistake. One of his attacks is on the apparent absence, in his experience and that of others, of any shift of attitude from an ordinary attitude to an aesthetic attitude. A famous criticism of Psychical Distance, discussed by Suzanne Langer, focuses on the aesthetic engagement of children while watching *Peter Pan*. When Tinkerbell is about to die from poison, the children are entreated to clap to make Tinkerbell live. The vast majority of children have no difficulty breaking down the invisible fourth wall, entering into the action of the situation, and clapping vigorously. This is clearly a case of breaking distance as Bullough conceived it (supposing the children were distanced from the play), yet with aesthetically beneficial consequences. Dickie cites this as a case where no shift, no change in attitude, is had. The children's involvement in watching the unfolding of the play, their feelings of suspense at the incidence of Peter being saved from the poison by Tinkerbell, and their concern with her well-being are not different *in kind* from their involvement with assisting in the well-being of Tinkerbell by clapping and shouting.

Dickie draws a distinction between what it means to have the way of attending itself brought about by a certain attitude, different ontologically from the ordinary, nonaesthetic, attitude taken toward things, and what it means to have the way of attending motivated by certain foci but still being ordinary attendance, which is, Dickie says, the only way to attend. This (ontologically) different *kind* of attitude, then, would give rise to a(n ontologically) different *kind* of experience. Dickie suggests that one may be interested, as in an object as a tool, or one may be disinterested, as in not interested in an object for any end other than the simple viewing of, say, the phenomenal properties of the object. But this only applies to *why* one attends to the object and to the purposes that one has in attending. The motives of attending, then, do not make the attending itself different in character from any other attending. The motives simply make one attentive to different aspects or different properties of the object and inattentive to other aspects or properties, those that do not correspond to one's purposes and motives (consider the parallel to Stolnitz here).

Apologists for the existence of an aesthetic attitude might argue that the things that are most central to the aesthetic attitude tradition can remain even if Dickie is correct that shifts in *kinds* of attitude do not occur, that the only shifts that occur are shifts in the focus of one's attention. Apologists might say that this is sufficient to provide for the subject's control of moving from aesthetic viewing to nonaesthetic that is at the heart of theories of the aesthetic attitude. Those accounts in the history of the aesthetic attitude that are marked by ontological shifts in attitude or shifts in the status of objects from ordinary to aesthetic, then, may be defeated by Dickie's criticism. Aesthetic attitude theorizing need not add, in any serious respect, to the ontological furniture. Ontological economy can coexist with attitude theorizing in such a way that no sacrifice of common experience or economy is necessary.

Yet another problem with the aesthetic attitude is to explain the phenomenon of beauty "breaking in upon us" or "striking us." Perhaps most people have had the experience of being, so to speak, minding their own business and suddenly being struck with the beauty of some part of nature. These experiences are not planned nor are they such that one freely, consciously, or volitionally enters into them.

They occur without preparation, much less the adoption of a special attitude. And they are not uncommon. If the evidence used to justify belief in the possibility of an aesthetic attitude is the pretheoretical description of common phenomenon, then one is obliged to consider the phenomenon of beauty striking one unexpectedly, another aspect of common experience. In that case there can be no talk about subjective control or about the agent's adoption of anything. Although adoption of the aesthetic attitude may be sufficient for aesthetic experience, it may not be necessary.

Other problems for aesthetic attitude theories may be found in contemporary criticism. Questions can be raised regarding the purity of perception that might characterize orthodox conceptions of attitudes of disinterest. Although associations and the workings of the imagination, as in the case of Alison, may coexist with a disinterested attitude, questions concerning the comparability of perceptions of those of different cultures or even different backgrounds may still be raised in the case where adoption of a disinterested attitude is sufficient for comparability of judgment. However, apologists for the tradition may consider such criticisms anachronistic.

BIBLIOGRAPHY

Addison, Joseph (and Richard Steele). "On the Pleasures of the Imagination." In *Selections from The Tatler and The Spectator*, edited by Robert J. Allen, numbers 411–421. New York, 1957.

Aldrich, Virgil C. *Philosophy of Art.* Englewood Cliffs, N.J., 1963.

Alison, Archibald. *Essays on the Nature and Principles of Taste.* Hildesheim, 1968.

Bullough, Edward. *Aesthetics: Lectures and Essays.* Edited by Elizabeth M. Wilkinson. Stanford, Calif., 1957.

Cooper, Anthony Ashley, Earl of Shaftesbury. *Characteristics of Men, Manners, Opinions, Times.* New York, 1964.

Dickie, George. "Bullough and the Concept of Psychical Distance." *Philosophy and Phenomenological Research* 22.2 (December 1961): 233–238.

Dickie, George. "The Myth of the Aesthetic Attitude." *American Philosophical Quarterly* 1.1 (January 1964): 56–65.

Dickie, George. "Attitude and Object: Aldrich on the Aesthetic." *Journal of Aesthetics and Art Criticism* 25.1 (Fall 1966): 89–91.

Dickie, George. "Stolnitz' Attitude: Taste and Perception." *Journal of Aesthetics and Art Criticism* 43.2 (Winter 1984): 195–203.

Fenner, David E. W. *The Aesthetic Attitude.* Atlantic Highlands, N.J., 1996.

Hutcheson, Francis. *An Inquiry into the Original of Our Ideas of Beauty and Virtue.* New York, 1971.

Stolnitz, Jerome. *Aesthetics and Philosophy of Art Criticism.* Boston, 1960.

Stolnitz, Jerome. "On the Origins of 'Aesthetic Disinterestedness.'" *Journal of Aesthetics and Art Criticism* 20.2 (Winter 1961): 131–143.

Stolnitz, Jerome. "'The Aesthetic Attitude' in the Rise of Modern Aesthetics." *Journal of Aesthetics and Art Criticism* 36.4 (Summer 1978): 409–422.

Tomas, Vincent. "Aesthetic Vision." *Philosophical Review* 68.1 (January 1959): 52–67.

DAVID FENNER

Pictorial Attitude

The term *pictorial attitude* has two related meanings: (1) It can refer to seeing the world as one sees a picture; and (2) it can mean holding certain beliefs or other attitudes toward pictures themselves. The attitude in the first sense is directed to ordinary perceptual objects; in the second sense, to pictures.

The first meaning concerns a way of perceiving that is typically acquired by looking at pictures and extended to undepicted objects. For instance, any scene viewed with a pictorial attitude might appear as a static array of visual elements that can be isolated and made the focus of attention. The effect of adopting a pictorial attitude in this sense will be specified in terms of a theory of picture perception; and different theories will specify different results. But, in general, the implication is that this sort of pictorial attitude, once acquired, can be deployed as an alternative to everyday perceptual attitudes. It then affects the way we see the world.

The second meaning of the term concerns a way of conceiving the nature or function or aim of pictorial representation, especially as it is used in art. Various construals are possible. The aim of pictures may be to depict objects as they really are, to represent the pure appearances of objects, or to represent the perceiver's knowledge or beliefs about the appearance of objects (and other beliefs as well). These construals are most naturally described as theories or beliefs about pictures, but they can also be called simply *concepts* or ways of conceptualizing pictures, to leave open the possibility that the attitudes may take forms other than belief.

These two senses of *pictorial attitude* are related, because the psychological states to which they refer can causally interact. Attitudes toward pictures will affect how the pictures are perceived. And picture perception, in turn, will affect ordinary perception. Thus, beliefs about pictorial functions can indirectly affect everyday perception. Furthermore, in practice, attitudes about pictorial functions will themselves often be derived from looking at pictures. To that extent, everyday perceptual experience can be changed, again indirectly, by the prior perception of pictures.

As psychological states, pictorial attitudes of either kind can take different forms, in accordance with different theories. Specifically, they may be treated either as internal, mental representations, or as behavioral dispositions or abilities. Moreover, when the attitudes are taken to be mental, their contents can be embodied in representations of different types.

Thus, on the one hand, pictorial attitudes could simply be propositional attitudes—for example, beliefs about pictures or produced by seeing pictures. A propositional attitude is an intentional or content-bearing entity, which is "about" an object or event. On one current theory, an attitude consists in a relation between a person and a mental sentence (in the "language of thought"). It is the proposition expressed by that sentence that provides the content of the attitude. Different attitudes (e.g., desires and beliefs) can have the same content, but consist in different relations to the sentence that bears it. On this model, then, pictorial attitudes would express propositions about pictures or propositions acquired by a careful visual study of them.

On the other hand, however, pictorial attitudes are sometimes said to have a distinctive form. For instance, they can be embodied in mental images or gestalt configurations. If pictorial attitudes do have a special form, we might want to say that any mental state with that form is a pictorial attitude. Thus, to "see the world as one sees a picture" would simply amount to seeing the world by means of a mental picture when the latter has a certain causal history (e.g., is acquired by looking at paintings). But having a pictorial attitude in this sense will also require generating and processing the mental pictures in certain ways: attending to them as one would attend to a perceived picture, scanning, magnifying, or exaggerating certain elements of them. And that makes pictorial attitudes consist in *relations* to images, in a way that is strictly analogous to the relational model of propositional attitudes. The difference is that the content embodied in such pictorial attitudes will be nonpropositional. So construed, different pictorial attitudes could be identified with different types of image, functionally defined: schemas or prototypes, mental pictures that emphasize transient visual details (using exemplars), expressive configurations, and so on. Of course, such mental representations will not be found only in picture perception, and their presence does not always imply that ordinary objects will be seen as if they had pictorial properties. But the point is that pictorial attitudes in the sense of (1) and (2) above can be treated as a species of what might be called nonpropositional or iconic attitudes—for example, mental images produced by exposure to visual art or used to emphasize selected features of perceived objects.

As psychologically real phenomena, however, pictorial attitudes do not have to be mentalistic in any sense. Nonmentalistic attitudes can be either behavioral dispositions or abilities to extract information from light, where those abilities require no mediation by inferential or interpretative mechanisms. For example, when James Gibson (1966, 1979) speaks of pictorial attitudes, he means native perceptual abilities that have been enhanced by looking at pictures. No special learning mechanisms or informational properties are involved, only a cultivation of attentional skills.

Why, then, are pictorial attitudes important? Their significance comes from their roles in visual education and art history. In the work of Ernst Gombrich (1969), Rudolf Arnheim (1969), and Gibson (1966, 1979), representing three different psychological traditions, an individual's experience in perceiving pictures is said to change his or her perceptual experience or abilities. In addition, Gombrich and

Arnheim try to account for the history of various artistic movements in terms of the attitude toward pictorial functions that was dominant in each period. These three theories can be described briefly as a prelude to discussion of more recent accounts.

For Gombrich, all perception is theory laden, and pictures employ schemata or techniques for encoding perceptual hypotheses. This view suggests an account of art history, namely, in terms of the evolution of representational techniques as perceptual knowledge grows. On Gombrich's account, however, art history also depends on changing attitudes about the purpose of representation. For example, Impressionists tried to represent pure appearances, rather than to depict objects or visual hypotheses. Later, the goal of representation was abandoned altogether. When the conception of art varies in this way, then the development of a style cannot be understood simply as the addition of another schema. Instead, styles reflect pictorial techniques adopted to express hypotheses about observations made under guidance of a theory. The techniques can be imaginative and the observations informative, even if the theory is false. Thus, perceivers can learn from art even when the attitude that produced it was misbegotten. Art is like science in this respect; there can be progress toward truth by showing the falsity of proposed theories. [*See* Gombrich.]

On Arnheim's gestalt approach, perceptual experience is largely a mental construct; but what the mind contributes are organizational forms, not hypotheses and theories. The forms of perceptual experience, which cannot be reduced to more primitive elements, are the result of brain events that are isomorphic to them. But the relevant features are structural and expressive of dynamic forces, rather than being particular shapes or contours that could be represented by figures that resemble them. That is important because it allows Arnheim to hold that the forms can be more or less abstract and thus to rebut Berkeley's argument against mental images as a medium for cognition. While admitting the obvious possibility of incomplete or partial images, Berkeley denied that images could ever be truly generic: even partial images will always include attributes not shared by all members of the relevant class. But, Arnheim argued, this is to ignore that expressive capacity that lines and forms possess, which can be described in terms of gestalt principles of organization. Thus, on Arnheim's account, perception is a form of thought, and purely visual concepts are used in "visual thinking." [*See* Arnheim.]

These visual concepts are essentially attitudes of three types: one focuses primarily on implicit form, to the exclusion of momentary appearance; another reduces appearance to momentary aspects, to the exclusion of common form; and a third combines the two. Although Arnheim refers only to the last concept as the "aesthetic attitude," and calls the first and second attitudes "practical" and "reductive," respectively, all three types of attitude can find

their way into art. So-called primitive and children's art emphasizes forms that are common to perceptual experience, ignoring transitory differences. These same forms are at the heart of the everyday or practical attitude. And, as an example of the second attitude, Impressionism calls attention to appearances to which perceptual experience might be reduced. However, Arnheim holds that several different styles of painting have the potential to reveal form under varying conditions. Even Impressionism can manifest the aesthetic attitude in this way, albeit through changes in color rather than by emphasizing a constant object shape. What is important, according to Arnheim, is the presentation of an aspect or appearance of an object that contains *renvois,* or references to other aspects or appearances. These are projected by the gestalt law of "good continuation." While some art (e.g., Egyptian murals) lacks *renvois,* the latter are not limited to perspectivist paintings. They can be found, for instance, in Cubist work as well. Thus, although there is no simple movement from practical to reductive to aesthetic attitudes, there can be progress in art, namely, when new techniques for presenting perceptual aspects with *renvois* are discovered.

In contrast to both Arnheim and Gombrich, Gibson holds that perception is direct, unmediated by any mental representation. Perceivers have a native ability to pick up information about contours and distances from texture gradients found on all surfaces. These constitute properties of various sorts that are invariant across changes in perspective. In his early work, Gibson relied on the idea that the relevant information is contained in static arrays. This information is captured best by perspective paintings, which use techniques that depend on the compression of texture over distance. As a result, on Gibson's early account, such paintings have a special place in the history of art. He used the term *pictorial attitude* to refer to the education of attention as the result of examining perspectivist art. In this case, adopting the pictorial attitude meant, not acquiring a concept or theory, but being guided by certain types of pictures to notice the textural elements in which perceptual information is contained.

In his later work, however, Gibson recognized the importance of motion as a source of information that is sometimes necessary to disambiguate static scenes. Ambiguity is found even in perspectivist art. Therefore, the latter should not be singled out as the one successful pictorial technique, even if it does convey the most information. Unfortunately, movement by the perceiver is ineffective in disambiguating pictures; the pictures impose a point of view. It is thus not clear how one could learn to see the world as one sees a picture merely by attending to the details of pictures, if that means picking up invariant properties in a visual array; for the invariant properties are not apparent in pictures.

Some work in perceptual psychology and cognitive science makes use of notions similar to pictorial attitude. For example, Margaret Hagen (1980) has proposed an eclectic "generative" account of picture perception in which elements of Arnheim's and Gibson's views are combined. She claims that the notion of *renvois* should be taken to refer to aspects represented in pictures that exhibit canonical perceptual forms. The latter function as rules for generating the represented aspect as well as related ones. These rules or generative structures can be accessible in all sorts of art, and the aesthetic attitude is a conception of pictures as capable of representing them. In that respect, there really is no progress from primitive to modern art; any style can exhibit canonical form. Moreover, aesthetic sophistication or education is not required to detect the presence of rules or canonical forms; perception of them is, to that extent, direct. Not even the training of attention is required.

In light of the difficulties with Gibson's direct account (on which the generative model draws), however, it seems necessary to ground perceptual generative theory on native computational abilities that depend on psychologically real, rulelike components that are independent of, and unaffected by, background knowledge or beliefs. This would push the generative model in the direction of David Marr's theory of vision, which has itself been called computational Gibsonism (1982). Marr explained vision in terms of distinct stages of information extraction, by means of which a more and more complete representation of a scene is constructed. The process at each step (e.g., edge detection or shape representation) is described by an algorithm, and the mental construction draws on a vocabulary of visual forms and relations that is common to all perceivers. Given the right rules and vocabulary, Marr believed, it is possible to explain how we recognize objects, even when they are presented in unusual ways, as in a Picasso painting.

Another new approach to pictorial attitudes is found in the work of Paul Churchland (1995). He argues that there are several types of nonpropositional attitude: *numerical, figurative,* or *vectorial.* The objects or contents of such attitudes are, respectively, numbers or shapes or vectors. These can be used in various ways. For example, "has a length n" and "has a velocity n" are two different attitudes with the same content, n. By extension, when seen in different ways, an ambiguous figure (such as a duck-rabbit or a Necker cube) is the object of two different perceptual attitudes, but with the same figural content. Quite apart from any subsequent beliefs or higher-order concepts applied to the image, to see a shape as a duck first implies that the shape can be used in certain ways and not others; it has a certain computational potential. To be disposed to use the image in those ways is to adopt an attitude toward it.

On Churchland's connectionist model, the content of such nonpropositional attitudes is supplied by internal representations in the form of *prototypes*, that is, stable, neural activation patterns. These are analogous to concepts that can be more or less abstract. So described, nonpropositional attitudes are unrelated to either picture perception or the effect of picture perception on ordinary observation. Nonetheless, the model can be extended to these concerns; indeed, the model has the potential to shed light on art history. Churchland has claimed that there are specifically aesthetic prototypes; hence, there could be nonpropositional aesthetic attitudes on his account. In that case, attitudes that are distinctively pictorial might be those nonpropositional attitudes that are directed at or derived from visual art. The challenge, then, is to use the resources of neuroscience and connectionist computer models to explain more precisely how these attitudes are produced when pictures are perceived.

Churchland has also argued that perception is theory-laden and used that idea to explain the history of science. This claim of theory ladenness could be understood in terms of the effects of nonpropositional attitudes (specifically, pictorial and aesthetic ones) and used to account for the history of art. The theories in question will consist of sets of prototypes and will themselves be nonpropositional. Against Gombrich, who makes art, like science, on a Popperian model of inference and hypothesis testing, the result will be an account of pictorial attitudes as paradigms (using Thomas Kuhn's notion of paradigm), and of new stylistic movements as radical paradigm shifts.

A third source of ideas similar to those discussed here comes from recent work on mental imagery. Stephen Kosslyn (1994) has developed both a computational and a neurological model of images as iconic representations that play essential roles in perception. By extension, the content of mental images will at least partly determine the content of perceived pictures. Kosslyn has not worked out the aesthetic implications of his imagery research, but a concept of pictorial attitude can be applied to his model. (See Rollins, 1989.) Attitudes are relations to mental images; the relations consist in perceptual processes such as scanning or rotation. The images will be constructed from a vocabulary of components—*internal* canonical forms—drawn from the visual system. Relations among the images can vary depending on how schematic or prototypical the images happen to be. Thus, there will be a variety of possible pictorial attitudes. These can figure in the perception of both pictures and ordinary objects, the former affecting the latter in significant ways.

[*See also* Perception; *and* Psychology of Art.]

BIBLIOGRAPHY

Arnheim, Rudolf. *Visual Thinking.* Berkeley, 1969.
Churchland, Paul M. *The Engine of Reason, the Seat of the Soul: A Philosophical Journey into the Brain.* Cambridge, Mass., 1995.
Gibson, James J. *The Senses Considered as Perceptual Systems.* Boston, 1966.

Gibson, James J. *The Ecological Approach to Visual Perception.* Boston, 1979.

Gombrich, E. H. *Art and Illusion: A Study in the Psychology of Pictorial Representation* (1960). 2d rev ed., New York, 1961; reprint, Princeton, N. J. 1969.

Hagen, Margaret A., ed. *The Perception of Pictures.* 2 vols. New York, 1980.

Kosslyn, Stephen M. *Image and Brain: The Resolution of the Imagery Debate.* Cambridge, Mass., 1994.

Marr, David. *Vision: A Computational Investigation into the Human Representation and Processing of Visual Information.* San Francisco, 1982.

Rollins, Mark. *Mental Imagery: On the Limits of Cognitive Science.* New Haven, 1989.

MARK ROLLINS

AUERBACH, ERICH (1892–1957). A Romance philologist with wide-ranging scholarly interests, Erich Auerbach wrote extensively on European literature and culture from antiquity through the twentieth century, which is to say, from the classics of Greco-Roman antiquity through assorted masterpieces of European modernism. The scope of his interests can be readily ascertained in his best-known book, *Mimesis: The Representation of Reality in Western Literature* (published in German in 1946 and translated into English in 1953). The first chapter in the book examines a section of the *Odyssey* and the last a few pages in Virginia Woolf's *To the Lighthouse*. His literary scholarship has acquired a special patina because of the correspondences between major events in world culture in the 1930s, 1940s, and 1950s and the main movements in his own life: forced out of Germany because of the racial laws, he served as a professor from 1936 to 1947 at the Turkish State University before coming to the United States and eventually being appointed as a professor at Yale University from 1950 until his death in 1957.

Although the term *aesthetic* seldom appears in his writings, Auerbach engaged constantly in the critical reflection on art and culture that is characteristic of aesthetics. In the 1950s and 1960s, he was criticized sometimes for having been drawn too much toward a sociological rather than a literary understanding, but in his own opinion his approach was historicist. Even so, his particular brand of historicism emphasized a careful consideration of individual episodes in literary texts, that is, a close appreciation of *aesthetic* qualities and techniques. Partly for this very reason, Joseph Engels, a philologist who assessed Auerbach's scholarship in 1953, disqualified Auerbach's writings as philology and classified them instead as aesthetics and literary criticism. Last but not least, Auerbach merits inclusion in an appraisal of twentieth-century aesthetics because of the unique artfulness in his manner of writing. In one review of the English translation of *Mimesis*, the literary historian René Wellek stated that "it must be judged as something of a

work of art, as a personal commonplace or rather uncommonplace book" (1954, p. 300). In another review, Charles Muscatine put his finger on the same quality of *Mimesis:* "The book contains a wealth of historical data, and repeated recommendations of historicism, yet it is itself only semi-history. At its center is something intuitive and creative, aesthetic, even moral" (1955–1956, p. 456). A more recent article by Wilhelm Wolfgang Holdheim has made much the same assertion: "his very way of writing history (in *Mimesis*, for example) is strikingly aesthetic" (1981, p. 143).

Auerbach averred that he would have liked to avoid all generalities and to restrict himself to a suggestive account of particulars, by which he meant particular passages in particular texts; but despite this declaration, he demonstrated a knack for deriving general principles and observations from specific texts. He combined sensitivity to individual works of art with awareness of the historical contexts in which they originated. He was a particularist in that he identified authors as individual people creating art at particular cultural moments in particular media, and yet a determinist in that he saw cultures as having basic styles that writers transfer into their texts, whether wittingly or not.

Despite having written only a few essays (most notably "Vico's Contribution to Literary Criticism" and "Introduction: Purpose and Method" in *Literary Language and Its Public* [1993]) that could properly be called *theoretical* as the term is now used in literary studies, Auerbach conveyed in considerable detail the nature and sources of his historicism (sometimes translated as *historism*)—and he labeled this historicism explicitly an *aesthetic* historicism. According to Auerbach, the breadth of a culture's aesthetic horizons stood in direct proportion to the extent of its historicism. In his view, the broadening achieved through historicism was "a precious (and also a very dangerous) acquisition of the human mind" ("Vico and Aesthetic Historism," 1959, p. 184). The peril of historicism was that, in the form it took among the Romantics in Germany, it would lead from an "interest in the individual roots and forms of the folk genius, in folklore, national traditions, and the national individuality in general" to something worse: "an extremely nationalistic attitude toward their own fatherland, which they considered as the synthesis and supreme realization of folk genius" (ibid., p. 187).

In the evolution of aesthetic historicism, Auerbach singled out the eighteenth century as having been singularly important. At one end stood Giambattista Vico (1668–1744), whose *scienza nuova* (1725) Auerbach viewed as having anticipated extraordinarily those principles of historicism that attained wide acceptance only at the other end of the century in Johann Gottfried von Herder and the German Romantics. [*See* Herder; *and* Vico.] Those principles arose in reaction against the French classicism associated with René

Descartes (1596–1650), with its constrictive aesthetic absolutes that favored the imitation of models.

Throughout his career, Auerbach consistently devoted substantial energies to the aesthetic historicism of Vico: he published more than a dozen essays and books concerned with Vico. From Vico, Auerbach derived what he defined as "historical perspectivism." This historical outlook entailed a distinctive aesthetics, namely, "the conviction that every civilization and every period has its own possibilities of aesthetic perfection; that the works of art of different peoples and periods, as well as their general forms of life, must be understood as products of variable individual conditions, and have to be judged each by his own development, not by absolute rules of beauty and ugliness" (ibid., pp. 183–184).

Alongside his engrossment in Vico, Auerbach cultivated lifelong interests in Dante Alighieri (1265–1321) and Benedetto Croce (1866–1952), in the translation of whose book on Vico he collaborated and whose absolute historicism complemented and complicated Vico's aesthetic historicism. Already during the five years (1924–1929) in which Auerbach was employed as a librarian in the Prussian State Library in Berlin and which marked the real beginning of his academic career, he made these three authors points of reference by which he triangulated to his own intellectual positions: he brought forth an abridged translation of Vico's *La scienza nuova* (1924), a collaborative translation of Croce's introductory study of Vico (1927), and his first book on Dante (1929).

Through his studies of Vico, Croce, and Dante, Auerbach evolved approaches that he applied again and again in his scholarship. In particular, he developed the habit of taking an aesthetic problem—especially that of the levels of style—as his primary point of departure (Holdheim, 1984, p. 144). Here Auerbach was especially influenced by two scholarly movements of his day, namely, "idealism" and what has been tagged the "New Stylistics." Both can be seen as having been special branches of philology.

Auerbach conceived of philology as an exceptionally broad and important approach to human culture. It encompassed the interpretation of all texts, not solely of literature in the restricted sense of belles lettres. More important, philology was regarded by Auerbach as a powerful tool to achieve insights into the presiding spirits of peoples or cultures.

Idealism was formulated in Romance philology by Croce in Italy and by Karl Vossler (1872–1949) in Germany. According to idealism as set forth by Vossler, language is "not an independent, ready-made system, subject to mechanical laws, but a human activity" (Christmann, 1981, p. 260). The product of a people's spirit, language reveals the distinctive thoughts and feelings of a people. At the same time, the idealists demanded attention not only to the language of a people as a whole but also to the idiolects of the individuals who together constitute the people; for distinctiveness of thought

and feeling will be nowhere more strikingly apprehensible than in texts created by individuals.

Idealism is not the sole movement with which Auerbach has been affiliated. Along with Leo Spitzer (1887–1960), Auerbach has also been considered a representative of what has been called the "New Stylistics"—a movement that was likewise tied closely to Croce and Vossler and that employed the methods of stylistics toward the end of *Kulturforschung* (cultural research) (Catano, 1988, pp. 37, 38, 56–57, and 62–64). Both Spitzer and Auerbach evolved methods of deriving meaning from words and phrases that went beyond mere *Wortphilologie* to achieve broad insights into culture. Auerbach's essays on *figura, sermo humilis, la cour et la ville,* and *passio* convey well the scope of his stylistics, which verges on being a history of literary styles and forms of literary expression.

One of Auerbach's chief aims in his scholarship was to find "points of departure" that provided insight into very large literary or cultural developments, which he treated explicitly as aesthetic developments. Two examples will suffice: In the case of *figura*, the movement was nothing less than the separation between classical and Christian forms and attitudes. In an essay titled "The Aesthetic Dignity of the *Fleurs du Mal*" (1959), Auerbach endeavored to show that the nineteenth century changed the basis of a correlation between style and content that had held in European culture for more than two millennia thanks to the enduring power of classical aesthetics.

The influence of Auerbach's approaches and insights in late-twentieth-century aesthetics has followed a fascinating course. In one sense, there have been very few scholars anyone would be inclined to call Auerbachian: no "school of Auerbach" has ever existed or is likely ever to exist. It could be argued that Auerbach, despite the success of *Mimesis*, reached his peak at the wrong moment in history: precisely when he and Ernst Robert Curtius (1886–1956) brought the age of philology to its apex with tomes of literary history that became best-sellers, the age of theory was poised to begin. In another sense, Auerbach's writings, especially but not just *Mimesis*, have continued to occupy such a central place in twentieth-century literary criticism that critics and theorists of many stripes have shown a gritty determination to affiliate him with one vogue or another. As Claus Uhlig (1996, p. 48) has demonstrated succinctly, Auerbach has been subjected to deconstruction and has been related to the chic Bakhtinian concept of the *chronotope*—and to these two treatments of Auerbach could be added Michael Holquist's (1993, pp. 373 and 390), which has made *Mimesis* into a foundational document of cultural criticism and Auerbach himself into a cultural figure well suited to Democratic politics in the United States of the 1990s: "great singer of diversity, subtle opponent of all homogenizing forces."

A solid basis for the present-day reception of Auerbach lies in his own farsighted pronouncements on the consequences of aesthetic historicism on the responses of Westerners to world literature: "Not only the scholars and critics among us, but also a large and steadily growing section of the general public, have ceased to be frightened by the diversity of peoples and epochs. This willingness to see things in their proper perspective, it is true, ceases as soon as politics becomes involved; but in the esthetic field our power of adaptation to diverse cultural forms or epochs is constantly brought into play" (Auerbach, 1993, p. 11). This capacious ideal of aesthetic historicism, rooted ostentatiously in Vico's philosophy of history, would seem well suited to exercise a growing appeal (Uhlig, 1996, pp. 48–49).

[*See also* Historicism, *article on* New Historicism in Literary Theory; *and* Mimesis.]

BIBLIOGRAPHY

Works By Auerbach

Mimesis: The Representation of Reality in Western Literature (1946). Translated by Willard R. Trask. Princeton, N.J., 1953.

"Philology and *Weltliteratur*" (1952). Translated by Maire Said and Edward Said. *Centennial Review* 13 (1969): 1–17.

Literary Language and Its Public in Late Latin Antiquity and in the Middle Ages (1958). Translated by Ralph Manheim. New York, 1965; reprint, Princeton, N.J., 1993.

"The Aesthetic Dignity of the *Fleurs du Mal*." In *Scenes from the Drama of European Literature: Six Essays*, pp. 201–226. New York, 1959.

"Vico and Aesthetic Historism." In *Scenes from the Drama of European Literature: Six Essays*, pp. 183–198. New York, 1959.

"Vico's Contribution to Literary Criticism." In *Gesammelte Aufsätze zur romanischen Philologie*, edited by F. Schalk, pp. 259–265. Bern, 1967.

Other Sources

Breslin, Charles, "Philosophy or Philology: Auerbach and Aesthetic Historicism." *Journal of the History of Ideas* 22 (1961): 369–381.

Catano, James V. *Language, History, Style: Leo Spitzer and the Critical Tradition*. Urbana, Ill., 1988.

Christmann, Hans Helmut. "Idealism." In *Trends in Romance Linguistics and Philology*, vol. 2, edited by Rebecca Posner and John N. Green, pp. 259–281. The Hague, 1981.

Engels, Joseph. "Philologie romane-Linguistique-Études littéraires." *Neophilologus* 37 (1953): 14–24.

Holdheim, Wilhelm Wolfgang. "Auerbach's *Mimesis:* Aesthetics as Historical Understanding." *CLIO* 10 (1981): 143–154. Reprinted in *The Hermeneutic Mode: Essays on Time in Literature and Literary Theory* (Ithaca, N.Y., 1984), pp. 211–225.

Holquist, Michael. "The Last European: Erich Auerbach as Precursor in the History of Cultural Criticism." *Modern Language Quarterly* 54 (1993): 371–391.

Muscatine, Charles. Review of *Mimesis. Romance Philology* 9 (1955–1956): 448–457.

Uhlig, Claus. "Auerbach's 'Hidden' (?) Theory of History." In *Literary History and the Challenge of Philology: The Legacy of Erich Auerbach*, edited by Seth Lerer, pp. 36–49. Stanford, Calif., 1996.

Wellek, René. "Auerbach's Special Realism." *Kenyon Review* 16 (1954): 299–307.

Ziolkowski, Jan M. "Foreword." In Erich Auerbach, *Literary Language and Its Public in Late Latin Antiquity and in the Middle Ages*, pp. ix–xxxix. Reprint, Princeton, N.J., 1993.

JAN ZIOLKOWSKI

AUGUSTINE (354–430), early church father and philosopher. Among the few truly revolutionary philosophers of art, Augustine's theories fundamentally changed the way art is interpreted, made, and used. While the imitation theories of Plato and Aristotle rely on metaphors drawn from mathematics, biology, and politics, Augustine's thought rests on the new religion (Christianity) and its texts, the Hebrew scriptures and the Greek New Testament. His concerns are with the process and method of interpretation, with reading, allegorizing, discovering continuities and secrets hidden in texts, and his obsession directs his inquiries to answering the riddle of divine intention, providence, and the world to come. These questions are asked and pursued in the context of a growing and ever more powerful institution, the church, whose relationship to the city becomes problematic in the sense that human destiny now is seen to have an otherwordly component. Political obligations, as defined in classical philosophy, no longer exclusively determine the goals of action. And therefore the philosophy of art no longer rests on pagan presuppositions. Yet the pagan world must be recognized, cited, and reinterpreted for the purposes of religion as it is becoming established under the life of Christ. Augustine stands as the great interpreter who would bring into one grand synthesis Athens, Jerusalem, and Rome. As each city had its forms of art, the arts of the temple, the agora, and the forum call for reinterpretation according to a new set of principles.

Augustine's model, then, is a new conception of the purpose and function of art, and a new conception of the self, based on two great paradigms: the life of Christ as told in the New Testament, and the life of Aeneas as told in Virgil's epic, the *Aeneid*. Although it may not at first appear to be a primary essay on art as we think of it, Augustine's *Confessions* subtly explicates his basic point of view and establishes foundational arguments that are set into more philosophical mode elsewhere. (See the bibliography for the basic texts.) The story of the life of Augustine as he tells it is key to all his thought, and its influence on philosophy is revealed in the writings of Blaise Pascal, René Descartes, Jean Jacques Rousseau, Jean-Paul Sartre, Martin Heidegger, and Ludwig Wittgenstein.

Augustine's internalization of Virgil's *Aeneid* establishes some basic metaphors that provide insight into the aesthetic theory of this church father. Despite his insistence that the interests of the church exercise control over all the arts, Augustine recognizes the aesthetic needs and the fantasy life of individual persons whose lives, although to be modeled on the life of Christ, are unfulfilled without aesthetic experience and the glorious escape from self that the arts afford. Augustine represents himself as the hero in his quest to establish a New City; it is clear that he imagines himself a Virgilian pious, yet fleshly, yet God-driven founder of a holy precinct: for Aeneas it is Rome, for Augustine it is the City of God. Both heroes almost succumb to the debauchery of Carthage; both are directed to their proper goals, both "saved" by their mothers (for Augustine it is his mother, Monica; in Aeneas's case it is the goddess Venus). Virgil and Augustine each create a text that incorporates all of history, and both present the reader with a method that opens up texts to an understanding of depths below mere story. As close reader and interpreter of the Latin epic (in his young years he earned his bread as a rhetorician), Augustine perfects his doctrine of the means whereby the manifest content of a text—that which it literally and obviously asserts—yields and reveals the inner latent content, its deeper spiritual meaning. Because every text has this duality of presence, all biblical as well as all pagan writings require philosophical interpretation to arrive at the hidden inner depths, often discovered to be a covert representation of divine purpose. All church-sponsored and church-consumed art must be structured in this way to discover and thus ultimately exhibit a spiritual reference.

This sets Christian art (as contrasted with pagan art) in a context that creates special philosophical-aesthetic issues for it and for all art it would draw into its circle of acceptable works.

1. The status of art: its function and purpose are to be evaluated by reference to the Christian faith.

2. Production and consumption of art are to be sponsored by the church. (This led Augustine to propound arguments on both sides of what came to be the iconoclastic controversy in the tenth century, when both sides turned to Augustine for arguments. Representations of saints can intensify faith, but also can act as a diversionary surrogate for the real thing, and therefore Augustine was always ambivalent about the place of icons in worship.)

3. The artist as a "knower" is judged by reference to faith and approved church doctrine; art must reinforce faith and the Book; thus, artists' works are judged by moral and spiritual truths that are theologically established.

4. Art must reinforce and strengthen worship. (This leads Augustine to be ambivalent toward music, for although it reveals and stands as a perfect metaphor for God's design and sense of proportion and harmony throughout the created order, it is also seductively sensuous.)

Christian philosophy of art as conceived by Augustine must confront three basic conflicts: Christian versus pagan; nature versus art; imitation versus symbol.

Christian versus Pagan. Augustine argues that many of Plato's doctrines can be given Christian interpretations. He thought of Plato as in a later age Dante thought of Virgil: one who carried a lantern that cast a light for others who came afterward, though Plato (like Virgil) walked in the dark. Thus, Socrates had deep insights into the nature of representation, "for he understood that all natural works produced according to the laws of Providence are far preferable to human works and the undistinguished works of artisans, and that therefore they are more worthy of divine honor than objects worshipped in temples" (*On the True Religion*, 1953, Book II, Section 2). Yet pagan beliefs are preferable to heretical. (See *Confessions*, Book III, Section 6).

Nature versus Art. God is the supreme artist; humans must come to understand their relationship to nature in their art, and the ways in which human art making differs from divine creation; for, Augustine argues, "The artist is not like God, though he draws his creative power from God. God creates ex nihilo, by means of his wisdom; the artist creates in and by means of a material. The proportions and harmonies of line which by a bodily action they realize in an object, these they receive from God's wisdom which is realized in the consummate art and proportions of nature created ex nihilo. If one becomes too closely attached to these lesser objects made by human art, one is drawn away from the essential and eternal forms of God's artistry. Those who make a cult of images are drawn away from the truth" (*De Diversis Questionibus, 83*, no. 78). Augustine's reflections on the distinction between creation and mere making establish boundaries that are metaphysical as well as theological, and constitute a challenge to pagan classical thought that nevertheless draws on Pythagorean number mysticism and shares to some extent Plato's suspicions about the dangers of art, for the arts draw us away from primary commitments: in Plato's case, political life, in Augustine's, the world to come.

Imitation versus Symbol. Although Augustine's epistemology of art objects rests on classical imitation theory, his doctrine of inner hidden meaning leads him to allegorize all works of art and nature itself, because nature stands to God as art stands to humans. His conception of allegory includes levels of complexity and strands of meaning that endow all artworks with symbolic powers that only one trained in Augustine's interpretative method can come to recognize. Augustine must necessarily reject and reinterpret Platonic theory: thus, the theory of ideas is replaced by a divinity that in some manner emanates ideas; and the Greek belief in creator as *dēmiurgos* working with a preexistent eternal combination of forms and matter becomes God creating from nothing, yet somehow structuring matter with ideational mind talked about simply as "Wisdom." The Augustinian interpretation sees all created things in nature as images of ideas whose prototypes are in God's mind. Individual objects *participate* in divine ideas. If art is to both imitate and reflect this truth, it must pattern itself on the harmony and "number" found in nature. Degrees of closeness to God, who created the heavens and the earth, are expressed in numerical relationships. Those closest to God participate in the idea of unity; those farther away constitute a hierarchy of number falling away into more and more remote ratios. The *beauty* of a thing depends on its likeness to and closeness to God.

Augustine inspired by a kind of Platonic dualism must introduce Christian theological categories and thereby in ef-

fect double the Platonic theory of imitation: The Son participates in the absolute perfect likeness to God the Father,
and the created order attempts to *imitate* this *likeness*. The
artist achieves beauty in the work of art insofar as the artist
imitates the participation of nature in the likeness of Son to
Father. This is best expressed through number ratios, and
therefore music comes closest to divine likeness and of all
the arts is closest to perfection. But once more Augustine's
ambivalence enters: the arts, because of their beauty, are apt
to draw human perception and contemplation away from a
proper fixation on God. Therefore, art ought to be used as
steps toward fuller recognition of religious truths and
church doctrine, but because of art's very closeness to
God's beauty, works of art detain us in their isolating power.
No philosopher in the West has expressed an epistemology
of art and beauty so consistently shot through with ambivalence, and for that very consistency of contrariness, Augustine is a rich mine of arguments about all of the arts in every
aspect of their creation, expression, and interpretation.

Augustine's Method of Interpretation. Although Augustine's method of interpretation establishes principles
that appear in our own time as fragments embedded in theories to which critics have given such familiar names as
"reader reception theory," "deconstruction," "hermeneutics," his own interpretative metaphysics expresses a reversal of the biblical observation in the Fourth Gospel: "And
the Word was made flesh and dwelt among us" (John 1:14).
Augustine reverses the metamorphosis in his interpretative
strategy, as if he were to say, "And the flesh was made Word
and thereby escaped its sinfulness." Interpretation transforms the body and the mind as it transforms the text. It
may even be said that the *Confessions* teaches us that; for, if
we truly attend and truly understand Augustine's life, we
will be changed to this extent, that we will make the first
transitional step toward possible salvation. The next steps
require us to read and interpret in the manner he teaches,
and by this mediation, the fleshly self undergoes transfiguration (figuratively speaking) into a possibility for ultimate
redemption. The arts, then, do provide a means to salvation,
but the way is fraught with dangers of aesthetic seduction.
The method to be applied is rigorous, and in its outline goes
as follows:

There are four distinct ways of reading Scripture (and
this may be applied to pagan writings as well).

1. Historical exegesis: one reads for what is written as having happened as history.
2. Etiological exegesis: one reads to find the cause of an
   event, an action, a description.
3. Analogical exegesis: one reads to establish continuity between the Hebrew scriptures and the New Testament
   texts of the Bible. And for each book of the Bible Augustine produced, or planned to pen, an interpretative reading according to this method.

4. Allegorical exegesis: one reads to demonstrate and to establish the figurative (symbolic) meaning of a book or
   passage or act or word.

Once the level of the figurative or symbolic has been
reached, it in its turn opens out into a set of new and higher
levels of revelation of inner meaning.

1. Literal meaning should now be established by the previous inquiries, although literal meaning in some texts, especially the Hebrew and the Greek pagan texts, present
puzzles that require extensive scholarly knowledge. Thus,
for example, Augustine is troubled by the fact that Socrates
swears "By the Dog." What can that mean? *We* know that it
meant that Socrates was swearing by the Dog Star. Augustine concludes that it must mean that Socrates realized that
it is better to swear by something in nature than by something created by humans, because the natural is at least
God's work.

2. Allegorical (to speak otherwise) meaning refers to
truths in relationship to humanity as a whole, but especially
to Christ as the head of humanity. Thus, allegory reveals the
inner meaning of the Logos, the Word that was made flesh.

3. Tropological (to turn) refers to the moral lesson contained within the textual event, which always leads us to
contemplate the inner moral life of human beings. In the
Confessions, great emphasis is placed on this level of at first
hidden meaning, for Augustine argues that in the case of his
own life he never understood its meaning and its direction
until he interpreted it in his writing the very text we read.
And we must create a text out of our own lives in like manner. Thus, the flesh becomes word.

4. Anagogical (elevation or leading up) refers to the ultimate spiritual truth to be found in the passage under interpretation. Ultimate truths on this level burst upon us as revelations, and grow in depth and revelatory power as we
apply a receptive mind to the text. We may be helped in discovering ultimate spiritual truth by human works of art, especially by icons and by music. But again, there lurks a dangerous seduction.

An example often given of Augustine's method is the following: Abraham's sacrifice of Isaac (1) literally presents a
true story, as told in *Genesis;* (2) allegorically, it is to be read
as Christ's sacrifice for man; (3) tropologically, it tells of the
sacrifices humans must make in actions and choices subordinate to the divine will; (4) anagogically, it symbolizes the
ultimate sacrifice the human race makes in its collective desire and need to be joined to God in salvation and redemption.

Augustine's method of reading and interpretation could
be described as moving from a prefigured world to a transfigured world through the mediation of a configured world.
There is a divine structure and purpose antecedent to human history; humans do not grasp God's will at first, but
only through stages of representation, which begins with

the Bible. That in turn exfoliates like a complex flower into the history of representations, best illustrated by a great poem like the *Aeneid*. Once we learn to allegorize in the sense that encompasses all the levels outlined above, the world in its material presence, the City of Humankind, is glimpsed in its ultimate transfiguration into the City of God.

Augustinian method and the huge accumulation of interpretations created thereby remain central to a tradition of art and beauty seen today in the architectural proportion theory of Le Corbusier, in the critical doctrines of idealism (Hegel, Nietzsche, Freud), in the interpretative techniques of "reader-response theory" (Wolfgang Iser), and in the hermeneutical tradition with roots deep in the past that now attaches itself not only to all religious textual readings but also to the most modern self-conscious "difficult" experiments, and to the "creative" deconstruction of texts in the French tradition. In Western philosophy of art, Augustine stands between the classical philosophies of art of Plato and Aristotle and modern idealism, which picks up and transforms the medieval Christian symbolism with a new purpose: it introduces the idea that art, which through the ages has enjoyed centrality in cultural life, may now be moved to a museumlike preservation as philosophy takes on itself the act of giving meaning to art. But even in Augustine that idea is shadowed forth in the exasperating distance he establishes between his literal scholarly exegetical readings and his symbolic extravagances. As Henri-Irénée Marrou has noted, "one is struck by the confident tone with which Saint Augustine (and all the church fathers) set forth their most fanciful symbolic interpretations. This dogmatic manner on Augustine's part contrasts most especially with the extreme prudence he demonstrates toward literal readings. The second case is a matter of pure science; but the first is an action that we can only call an element of sport" (*Saint Augustin et la fin de la culture antique*, 1938).

This inconsistency in Augustine's interpretative soundness reflects a deep insecurity in his evaluation of the arts as they are often conceived today—that is, as the creative originality of the artist embodied in an object—and compares them to the ceremonial repetitions of a growing institutional set of practices. Ritual seems secure and comforting; art threatens with its openness to private expression that may be willful and even heretical. Ritual *prescribes* every aspect of performer and performance; no deviation is allowed and certainly never encouraged. Yet, those who contribute to ceremonial occasions may be gifted artists who, like Augustine himself in his symbolic extravagances, would express the self in its absolute uniqueness. In reading Augustine's interpretations and theory of art, one is struck by his need to express himself as a masterful artist while at the same time he reins in his originality on behalf of an unplumbed conservatism. Despite that, however, he himself is a great artist. As E. R. Dodds observed, "Augustine is the last *orig-*inal master of Latin eloquence, and at the same time the first writer of modern romantic prose" (1927).

[*See also* Interpretation; Plato; *and* Religion and Aesthetics.]

BIBLIOGRAPHY

Works by Augustine

On Divine Order (386). Library of Christian Classics. London, 1953.
Selections from *De Ordine* (386). In *Philosophies of Art and Beauty: Selected Readings in Aesthetics from Plato to Heidegger*, edited by Albert Hofstadter and Richard Kuhns, translated by Robert P. Russell, pp. 173–185. Chicago, 1976.
Selections from *De Musica* (387). In *Philosophies of Art and Beauty: Selected Readings in Aesthetics from Plato to Heidegger*, edited by Albert Hofstadter and Richard Kuhns, translated by W. F. Jackson Knight, pp. 185–202. Chicago, 1976.
De Diversis Questionibus, 83 (On 83 Questions, 388).
On the True Religion (390). Translated by John H. S. Burleigh. Philadelphia, 1953.
On the Usefulness of Belief (391). Translated by John H. S. Burleigh. Philadelphia, 1953.
The Confessions (398). Translated by R. S. Pine-Coffin. New York, 1961.
On the Trinity (399). Library of Christian Classics. London, 1953.
The City of God (426). 2 vols. Translated by John Healey. London, 1945.
On Christian Doctrine (427). Translated by D. W. Robertson. Indianapolis, 1958.

Other Sources

Brown, Peter. *Augustine of Hippo: A Biography*. Berkeley, 1967.
Bruyne, Edgar de. *Études d'esthétique médiévale*. 3 vols. Bruges, 1946.
Dodds, E. R. "Augustine's Confessions: A Study of Spiritual Maladjustment." *Hibbert Journal* 26 (1927): 459–473.

RICHARD KUHNS

AUTHENTICITY. [*To clarify the concept of authenticity in aesthetics, this entry comprises two essays:*
Conceptual Overview
Authenticity in Music
The first essay explains what authenticity means and how it has been understood in aesthetics; the second essay discusses the particular meaning of authenticity in the field of music, where it has been especially important.]

Conceptual Overview

Theater, dance, opera, and music are the main performing arts. Most works of these types are instanced by live performances. A given work might have no instances, because it has never been performed, or it might have many instances, being often performed. By contrast, oil paintings and hewn sculptures have single instances that are for presentation, not performance. In some cases, performance is involved in the creation of a work that is not for live performance. This is so for movies and for musical pieces whose definitive form is a recording or video. These works are for screening or playing; their multiple instances are cloned from a master print or tape by a technological process. In what follows, only works that are intended for live performance are considered.

In classical music, the "authentic performance movement" has become both prominent and controversial since the 1950s. In playing works composed in earlier times (usually, those written prior to about 1850), advocates of this approach employ period instruments and closely adhere to the composer's instructions, as well as to the performance practices of the work's time. By purporting to be "authentic," such performances claim a special legitimacy, one that questions the credentials of the orthodox practice that uses modern instruments and musical styles in performing the music of earlier eras. The claims made on behalf of "authentic" performances have been criticized: their advocates mistake composers' wishes and suggestions for mandatory commands, the resulting performances are stilted and unappealing, the pursuit of "authenticity" is only one among many viable options for interpretation, and, anyway, the modern audience cannot experience the music as composers' contemporaries would have done. The discussion that follows addresses at a general level the force and relevance of many of the issues raised by such criticisms.

For works such as tragedies, symphonies, and ballets, an authentic performance is one that is faithful to the work. What can be required in the name of authenticity depends on the nature of the work in question. For instance, if a musical piece is (merely) a note sequence, the successful production of that note sequence will result in an authentic performance of the work, no matter whether it is produced on bells, recorders, or a sound synthesizer. On the other hand, if the instrumentation is included within the work, only a performance using the appropriate instruments could be authentic. Similarly, if a play consists (merely) in a word sequence, any performance of it that preserves the words and their order will be authentic, even if in one the characters wear space suits and speak the words with a heavily ironic tone while in the other they wear contemporary dress and seem sincere in what they say. What, then, is the nature of works for performance?

In creating a work for performance, the artist often prepares a set of instructions intended for execution by the work's performers. These instructions—scores and scripts, for instance—specify some of the work's contents and/or contain directions for making an instance of the work. In other cases, the artist supplies a model instance that the performer is to emulate; this is common in ballet. The model is not to be slavishly copied but, rather, to be interpreted as encoding instructions like those that might be notated. The artist's instructions are to be read in terms of the conventions that surround the practices involved. For instance, in a musical score, an accidental (an added sharp or flat) in a

measure applies not only to the note it precedes but to subsequent notes at the same pitch within the bar. Moreover, some of the notations in the score, such as keyboard fingerings, might be recommendatory rather than mandatory, and others, such as precise metronomic tempo indications, are to be read as indicating a range of acceptable alternatives. Only a musician who understands the conventions can read the instructions presented by way of the notation, because not everything that is required is notated and not everything that is notated is obligatory. Departures (whether accidental or deliberate) from the artist's mandatory instructions result in performances that are less than ideally authentic. An attempted performance might be so inauthentic that it fails to qualify as of the given work.

What kinds of things are mandated by artists' instructions for the authentic performance of their works? This question has no easy, single answer. Unless the performer worked under the artist's direction, the latter was not in a position to require much from the performer by way of detail until the (comparatively recent) advent of professional ensembles, of troupes of given sizes and types, and of standardized venues. Frequently, artists took control whenever they could do so and the status of the artist, as against that of the performer, rose accordingly. Thus, for instance, classical musical works of the late nineteenth century are performed authentically only where the specified instruments are used, the indicated phrasing is observed, and so on, whereas there is more freedom in the practices concerning such matters in the sixteenth century. In the case of other types of performing art, the performer has retained a greater liberty. The musician who plays a jazz standard is constrained by conventions and musical practices but has much more freedom in determining note sequence and rhythm than does his or her counterpart in classical music. Similarly, the pantomime performer is freer than an actor presenting a play by Harold Pinter. Some types of musical, dramatic, and dance works include parts or elements that are to be improvised by the performer.

Even in those art forms that give considerable control to the artist, the instructions produced underdetermine artistically important decisions and actions that must be taken and done by the performer in deriving an instance of the work from its text, score, or script. For instance, a line of a play might be spoken with many different inflections and little or no indication of the intonation to be adopted is likely to be offered by the artist, yet the line must have *some* articulation if it is to be spoken at all. Because an authentic performance is one faithful to the artist's determinative instructions, and since these underdetermine the outcome of performance, performances might differ in many respects while being equally and ideally authentic. It is in the gap between what is mandatory and the full detail of an instance of the work that the performer (or the person who directs the performers) exercises creative and interpretative freedom.

The performer "interprets" the work in exercising this liberty; different performances might instance not only the work but a given interpretation or production of it, provided they involve the same decisions and executions.

Although the focus thus far has been on authenticity in the performance of works, other types of authenticity can be considered. (As already hinted at, one might evaluate a performance's authenticity with respect to a given interpretation.) Authenticity is discussed in relation to styles and genres, as well as works; a performance that is correct or faithful in conforming with the conventions specifying the requirements of a style or genre is authentic as an instance of that style or genre. Where performance takes place in the absence of works—for instance, where all aspects of the performance are freely improvised—authenticity is pursued, if at all, only with respect to styles and genres. One other kind of authenticity is worth noting. A presentation might be faithful with respect to a tradition of performance, where, for example, E studied with D who studied with C who studied with B who studied with the artist, A. If authenticity of this kind is valued, presumably it is because it leads to authenticity of the primary kind discussed earlier, for it reveals a link between the present performer and the practices and conventions applying to the work's delivery at the time of its creation. These two kinds of authenticity might conflict, though. Many small innovations over time might produce contemporary performances that are very different from earlier renditions despite an unbroken chain, recognized as a tradition, linking performances in the two eras.

Is Authenticity in Performance Possible? One might wonder if authenticity in performance, as characterized above, is attainable except in the case of works of the day created in styles and genres with which performers are at home. It might be suggested that we cannot know how to authentically interpret texts or conventions from another time because we cannot view such things from any perspective other than a modern one. And even if we could achieve this mode of interpretation, our experience of the work could not be the appropriate one because we do not share the values, attitudes, and beliefs of the work's intended audience. On this view, works from the past are inaccessible to us as objects of interpretation or of experience.

There is reason to be skeptical of such objections to the possibility of authentic performance. As the disciplines of history and anthropology testify, both the past and other cultures are accessible to us. We can understand and appreciate the past and other cultures, just as we can understand and communicate with others without having to get "inside their heads" and despite differences between their beliefs and values and our own. Like a person who makes suitable adjustments in moving with ease between jazz and contemporary classical music, or between Arthur Miller's plays and the Theater of the Absurd, we can approach the art of the past in terms of the expectations and familiarities appropriate to it.

This is not to deny that lack of knowledge is a bar to authentic performance on many occasions. Sometimes we do not know what conventions to apply or how to read the notation. For instance, many uncertainties stand in the way of authentic performances of plays from ancient Greece. Where the artist is anonymous, it is obvious that the piece cannot be considered as of an oeuvre, but only as of a period, style, and genre. Many subtle aspects of past performance practice might not be known, or might be conjectured rather than established as fact. As a result, claims to authenticity in the performance of works from the period will be questionable. Despite these concessions, however, it can be denied that uncertainties are inevitable and unavoidable. Claims to authenticity can possess credibility.

The epistemic worry dismissed above might be replaced with a more practical one. Performance, if it is to be natural and idiomatic, must be spontaneous. Now, even if one is aware of the conventions and performance practices of the past, the self-conscious application of that knowledge in the name of authenticity is likely to produce a stilted, inauthentic result. Better, then, to rely on the integrity of the living performance tradition than to revive a zombie-like pursuit of lost performance practices.

The worry expressed here has some force, but surely is exaggerated. It might not be possible, for instance, to perform musical works from the distant past without using instruments that are no longer current, or without finding some way of filling in the gaps left for decorations or a figured bass, so that an interest in performing the works inevitably commits one to some concern with authenticity. Moreover, although attempts at authenticity often have been wooden and lifeless, experience suggests that performers often do master the special demands of outdated instruments and performance practices, so that a performance can be both authentic and vibrant. Indeed, it can be predicted that authenticity in performance, where it can be achieved, much more often than not will bring life and interest to the work in question, because most works will be at their most artistically rewarding when presented as they were intended to be.

Is Authenticity Desirable in Performance? Now, if authentic performance might be possible, is it a goal worth adopting? Is it just one among many equally legitimate strategies that might be followed, or should it be the preferred route? It might be thought that the heterogeneity of performance practices counts against claims for the special value of "authenticity." As implied earlier, if one wants to perform the artist's work, one must be committed to the pursuit of authenticity. The work is specified by the artist's instructions as interpreted in light of the relevant conventions, so a performance that willfully departs from those instructions thereby departs from the artist's work. One might accept this while challenging the assumption that the goal of performance is the presentation of the artist's work (or of any work as such). If there are no definitive "texts," if there are interpretations only, the target at which authenticity aims is chimerical. In that case, the performer need not (and might not) place special significance on the artist's authority; the performer might choose to depart from the artist's instructions, or might read those instructions in terms not of the conventions that the artist understood and used, but of others. Anyway (it might be said), our major concern—one probably shared by artists—is that the work should be interesting and relevant. A work should be approached with a view to what will appeal to the contemporary audience, not with the focus on artists' directions that were written with some other audience in mind. Where the audience is a modern one and the work is old, it may be that the work can be made interesting only by rejecting the artist's prescriptions. If then the piece is not strictly the one the artist created, so much the worse for the original work and on with the new!

The sentiments just expressed are perhaps misguided, but there are ways of recasting them that might capture much of what they are after.

Aesthetic satisfaction is provided by artworks more often than by other things; artworks are satisfying because they are very carefully and skillfully made to be so, and that it would be surprising if they were satisfying as often or as deeply if no special regard is paid to the features they are designed to display. As a result, an interest in artists' works is primary. Without that concern, we would not have the concept of art as we know it. (The history of the performing arts might be mapped as a battle for preeminence between, on the one hand, artists who see performers merely as tools for the presentation of their achievements and, on the other, performers who see artists merely as providing the means by which they put their talents on display. Although, in this battle, the artist's cause seems more compelling, the practice gives a close result between the two when it comes to the audience's affections.) Once the aesthetic regard is established, though, it can be applied counterfactually to naturally occurring things and to items made for nonartistic purposes (in which use it might not be rewarded so readily). In a similar vein, performers might ignore the instructions of artists. When they do so, their skills can produce an artistically satisfactory result but often will not do so—by no means are all actors good playwrights or all musicians good composers, especially when forced to create on the spot. Performance practice takes many forms, but that which accords primacy to realizing the artist's instructions faithfully (yet creatively) is fundamental in giving point to the creation and presentation of works for performance.

With all this said, it also is true that a work should be brought to life through its performance. Authenticity, even if it is a primary one, is by no means the only goal of performance. Performances are the better for being stimulating and revealing, other things being equal. One consequence of this is that if its authentic performance must kill a work for the contemporary audience, performers might experiment with the piece to make it more attractive, producing something based on the original in preference to consigning it to oblivion. (This case is doubtless not a common one because art often deals with common human concerns and these are not radically different now from what they were several hundred years ago.) A more frequent and important corollary is the following: the interest of a work can pall through repetition; we look to performances for different, challenging interpretations. Accordingly, where performers present a well-known work, it is appropriate that they explore novel, not prosaic, interpretations. This is not because authenticity is irrelevant to performance but because the requirements it imposes might be satisfied by prior renditions, leaving the present performers more free than they would be were they offering the work for the first time or to an audience of novices. This explains the toleration shown to the many eccentric, idiosyncratic interpretations of William Shakespeare and Ludwig van Beethoven. There is no reason to suppose that the same freedom would be appropriate in performing for the first time the new play of a contemporary playwright.

One can conclude that authenticity is a primary virtue in the performance of works. Unless it were taken as a goal, the performing arts could not have attained their presently high status, because their continuing aesthetic value and interest depend ultimately on a successful commitment to the faithful presentation of artists' works. But authenticity is not the only goal and, with these art forms established, performers sometimes pursue other priorities. Moreover, these other values might properly take precedence where the character of the given work already has been made apparent within the performance tradition.

[*See also* Performance.]

BIBLIOGRAPHY

Davies, Stephen. "Authenticity in Musical Performance." *British Journal of Aesthetics* 27.1 (Winter 1987): 39–50.

Davies, Stephen. "The Ontology of Musical Works and the Authenticity of Their Performances." *Noûs* 25.1 (March 1991): 21–41.

Dipert, Randall R. "The Composer's Intentions: An Examination of Their Relevance for Performance." *Musical Quarterly* 66.2 (April 1980): 205–218.

Godlovitch, Stan. "Authentic Performance." *Monist* 71.2 (April 1988): 258–277.

Kivy, Peter. "Live Performances and Dead Composers: On the Ethics of Musical Interpretation." In *Human Agency: Language, Duty, and Value*, edited by Jonathan Dancy, J. M. E. Moravcsik, and C. C. W. Taylor, pp. 219–236. Stanford, Calif., 1988.

Kivy, Peter. "On the Concept of the 'Historically Authentic' Performance." *Monist* 71.2 (April 1988): 278–290.

Kivy, Peter. *Authenticities: Philosophical Reflections on Musical Performance*. Ithaca, N.Y., 1995.

Levinson, Jerrold. "Evaluating Musical Performance." *Journal of Aesthetic Education* 21.1 (Spring 1987): 75–88.

Levinson, Jerrold. "Authentic Performance and Performance Means." In *Music, Art, and Metaphysics: Essays in Philosophical Aesthetics,* pp. 393–408. Ithaca, N.Y., 1990.

McFee, Graham. *Understanding Dance.* New York and London, 1992.

Sparshott, Francis. *Off the Ground: First Steps to a Philosophical Consideration of the Dance.* Princeton, N.J., 1988.

Thom, Paul. *For an Audience: A Philosophy of the Performing Arts.* Philadelphia, 1993.

Young, James O. "The Concept of Authentic Performance." *British Journal of Aesthetics* 28.3 (Summer 1988): 228–238.

STEPHEN DAVIES

Authenticity in Music

In Western art music today, the word *authentic* usually refers to a class of performances that seek historical verisimilitude, typically through using period instruments and attempting to re-create period performance idioms. Such performances have covered music ranging from pre-Gregorian plainchant to Arnold Schoenberg. Since the late 1960s, they have become increasingly influential; they have also been unwaveringly controversial. The issues raised about them have gone beyond specific debates over performance practices to deeper aesthetic questions.

History. Before the nineteenth century, musicians rarely performed music of the past, with the exceptions usually involving sacred music; but by the middle of the nineteenth century, performances of secular music from earlier generations had become commonplace. This change reflected various forces, such as the era's growing awareness of history and the emerging idea of a canon of great masterpieces in music as well as in other arts. Lydia Goehr (1992) argues that the nineteenth century brought a further shift: musical practice began to be governed to an unprecedented extent by the concept of the musical "work." Earlier eras had been more likely to conceive of a piece of music as an act of performance, a carrier of a text, or a functional part of some other event such as a church service; but the "work" concept elevates a piece of music to the status of an autonomous, enduring, integral work of art. This can lead to a demand that performers be true or faithful to the works they play.

From that, it is a short (though not necessary) step to a concern for their honoring the performance intentions of the work's composer. The ideal of serving the composer's intentions might also have gained strength simply from the increasing division of labor between composers and performers. In music, the composer has come to control the performer's actions to a degree rarely approached in other performing arts. For whatever reasons, admonitions to honor the composer's performance intentions are recorded as early as the fifteenth century, but they become common

in the nineteenth century (Bowen, 1993) and dominant in the twentieth.

One can go a step further and insist on playing music with the instruments and styles that past composers used, but few nineteenth-century musicians took this step. One possible reason is that it does not follow necessarily from the ideal of being faithful to the work and its maker: many performers have believed that musical works possess an ahistorical essence, which does not depend on the accidents of period performance practice. Another reason may be the nineteenth century's general faith in technological progress, evident in the redesign of musical instruments. Most musicians believed that they could serve works and composers best by using the latest instruments. But, over the course of the twentieth century, a growing minority of musicians have believed otherwise, and have taken the step of exploring period instruments and styles. Again, the change of attitude might result from various causes. One might be an increasing disillusionment with modern life and with technological progress (the latter documented in Heilbroner, 1995). Another might be the rise of modern attitudes in hermeneutics and historiography, which could cast doubt on the assumption that modern playing styles and instruments are improvements, because one's preference for them is considered to be historically contingent rather than neutral and objective (John Butt, personal communication, 1996). Also, Robert Morgan (in Kenyon, 1988) argues that the post–World War I advent of radical styles of musical composition, which seemed discontinuous with the past, contributed to a sense that the music of the past was no longer part of a living tradition and thus should be played in the current style, as most nineteenth-century musicians believed. Instead, masterworks of the past began to seem like heirlooms best preserved by being played in their own periods' styles. (Other proposed motivations are discussed below.)

Attempts at historical performance began to occur regularly around the turn of the twentieth century, and became increasingly prominent over the century's course (Haskell, 1988). Historical performance gained commercial visibility in the 1960s and 1970s, by which time it had become widespread enough to be known as the "early-music movement." In the 1980s and 1990s, it produced best-selling recordings of Bach, Handel, and even Beethoven; and a few of its performers succeeded in bringing medieval and Renaissance music to a much larger audience than it had generally reached before.

As historical performers began to play Bach, Beethoven, and Brahms, "disputes over turf" arose with mainstream players (Kerman, 1992). These disputes sometimes exemplify what psychologists call in-group/out-group psychology (Brewer and Kramer, 1985). Some of the kinds of thinking one finds in ethnic warfare can be found in both the mainstream and early-music camps: both have been known to describe the other camp with simplistic stereotypes, and to impute maleficent strength to it and beleaguered virtue to one's own camp (Sherman, 1997, p. 5). The self-righteousness of in-group psychology may contribute in part to the moral tone of much argument for and against the early-music movement. In recent years, however, the turf disputes have softened, at times giving rise to what Alfred Brendel calls "true cross-fertilization" (1990, p. 224).

Dispute has also arisen over the aesthetic underpinnings of the early-music movement, often within the movement itself. The most influential critic has been Richard Taruskin (1995), a musicologist who for many years was a professional viola da gamba player and Renaissance choral director. The rest of this article will examine the issues raised by Taruskin, the gambist/musicologist Laurence Dreyfus (1983), the keyboardist/scholar John Butt, the scholar and pianist Charles Rosen, the philosopher Peter Kivy (1995), and a number of others.

Debates over Authenticity. The use of the term *authentic* to describe historical performance may have originated by analogy to the term's usage in musicology, where it refers to the assignment of authorship: this piece is authentic Bach, that piece spurious. But, applied to historical performance, it is "a baleful term which has caused endless acrimony" (Kerman, 1985, p. 192). The arguments against applying the term to historicism in performance have been influential enough that early-music performers now almost always enclose it in quotation marks to indicate that they know better than to use the term naively (for convenience, I will use it without quotation marks). Critics have attacked not only the terminology, but also the goals and assumptions, of historicist musicians. The critiques have taken many forms, but can be classified into three groups: those that question the possibility of historical authenticity, those that question its desirability, and those that examine the motivations of performers (Sherman, 1997, pp. 8–20).

Possibility. Some authors believe that it is impossible nowadays to perform music just as it was done in its own era. In a few cases, such as the use of castrati singers, it is obviously impossible (or repellent) to re-create a known practice. But more generally, evidence about period performance practice is almost never complete, so performers must go beyond what scholars can certify as historically accurate. This involves the use of the performers' imaginations—and modern musical imaginations inevitably differ from those of previous centuries (Taruskin, 1995). The incompleteness of the evidence could short-circuit attempts even to re-create only the audible parameters of a period performance, with no concern for how context affects musical communication.

But contextual factors do figure prominently in many other arguments against the possibility of authenticity. For example, one type of argument points to differences between modern and period experience in such realms as economics, politics, religion, and science; it argues (sometimes convincingly, sometimes not) that such factors affect how we play and hear music. Another contextual barrier to true historical re-creation is that our contexts of performance and listening—CDs, radios, and concert halls—are usually quite different from those of the past, such as feasts, church services, and salons. This affects the nature of performance; one plays differently for one's private edification in a music room than for critics in Carnegie Hall (Rosen, 1990). Also, the advent of recordings increased audiences' demands for technical perfection, as well as performers' concerns with literalness and accuracy (Philip, 1992).

Such factors may limit the historical veracity even of performances that are embedded in "historical reconstructions"—for example, concerts that stage the liturgical ceremonies for which the featured sacred music was written. Liturgical reconstructions, moreover, face another type of barrier to historical authenticity: the audience. At such reconstructions, most audiences know that they are at a concert to be entertained or edified, rather than at a service to worship, and few audiences share the emotional or theological associations that period audiences felt toward specific texts and plainchant melodies. This is an example of another argument for impossibility: historically authentic audiences do not exist today.

Desirability. Regardless of whether historical accuracy is possible, some authors doubt that it is an artistically worthy goal; they especially deny that it is a valid standard by which to judge performances. If one's goal is to play exactly as was done in the period, these critics argue that period performances cannot be assumed to have been better in any meaningful way than modern, unhistorical ones. If one's goal is to re-create period sounds, Charles Rosen (1990) points out that sound per se was usually not as central to the conception of early music as it often is to that of later music. (An objection sometimes made to this argument is that period instruments are often valued not as means of re-creating period sound per se, but as means for gaining a feeling for the articulation of musical phrases, or for gaining insight into the constraints that led the composer to write as he or she did; Levinson, 1990, pp. 390–408, makes a related case for period instruments.)

As mentioned earlier, the ideal of historical authenticity does not follow inevitably from the ideal of serving the composer's performance intentions. Most mainstream performers espouse the "composer's intention" ideal as strongly as most historical performers do (though the degree to which either truly aspires to the ideal has been questioned by John Butt). And some historical performers seek not to serve the composer's intentions so much as to revive period performance practices. But many link the ideals, so arguments against the desirability of historical performance often reconsider the "composer's intention" ideal. Some critics argue that the composer's performance intentions are rarely clear or fixed (Taruskin, 1995, pp. 54–55), and that even when precise they cannot be assumed to be superior to anyone else's (ibid., pp. 190–193; Kivy, 1995, pp. 162–169). Dipert (1980) distinguishes between the composer's "high-level" performing intentions (such as aesthetic effects) and "low-level" ones, which include the means for making those aesthetic effects audible; when these levels conflict, he says, the high-level ones should be given priority. Kivy (1995, pp. 30–46) distinguishes between the composer's strong intentions and his mere wishes, suggestions, and weak intentions, which may include many details of performance. Sometimes a composer's stronger intentions—such as wanting the most effective possible performance of his work for each audience and concert situation—might be served best by *not* using the means available in his era. Another argument is that the performer's main duty is not to the composer, who forfeits "ownership" upon publication, but to the modern audience (Taruskin, 1995, p. 47). Modern audiences, as already noted, may have different aesthetic backgrounds than period audiences; thus, they may be better served by unhistorical performances. Furthermore, "period ears" might not necessarily be preferable to modern ones for listening to old music (Kivy, 1995, pp. 214–217)—modern audiences may understand the music better in some cases, if not in others. Arguments based on pleasing the audience can, however, be problematic in certain respects (Butt, 1996); for example, they raise the specter of performers who must serve a "dictatorship of the marketplace." Kivy (1995, p. 184) shows that utilitarian arguments can be used to defend a performer's *not* simply catering to modern audiences— although, without audience approval, he notes, a performance style will never prevail. Kivy also says that it is understandable in our "culture of the author" that we expect performers to begin their musical preparation by considering the composer's performance intentions, even if they end up rejecting those intentions when other solutions seem to them to work better (ibid., pp. 185–186).

In practice (and sometimes in theory), many historical performers determine on a pragmatic, case-by-case basis whether it is desirable to use period performance practices. Admittedly, some try to use as much of the evidence as possible, and believe that this produces better musical results (though Taruskin argues [see below] that even these performers are unconsciously selective); but other performers distinguish between historical practices that seem to them beneficial or important to a successful performance, and historical practices that seem insignificant or even harmful. In a few repertoires, a consensus exists over the desirability of historical practices, but such repertoires are rare. As this demonstrates, determining which historical practices are desirable is not an objective process, but is influenced by the performer's (and the era's) priorities and concepts of music.

A further reason that consensus is rare may be that an informed choice between modern and period practices or instruments often involves making trade-offs. Period styles and instruments usually have both advantages and disadvantages, as do modern instruments and styles. A fortepiano, for example, has a wider variety of articulations than a modern grand, but a narrower dynamic range. Which instrument one prefers will depend in part on which costs and benefits concern one most. Again, such valuation is generally influenced by one's aesthetic priorities and beliefs, and not simply by the demands of the music.

Motivation. Some critics have looked not at the justification for the authenticity enterprise, but at the reasons why so many musicians undertake it. The most obvious reason is that the musicians are convinced that historical practice yields better performances; and in some cases (such as French Baroque music) this explanation is widely accepted. But critics have posited other, more complex motives. Some have already been mentioned—disillusionment with technological progress, the rise of modern hermeneutics, and a sense of separation from the past—but a variety of other proposed motives exist. One is competition: if great performers have already fully explored the mainstream style and repertoire, one way to make one's mark is to stake out new and unconquered musical territory. A related but less cynical formulation sees historical performance as an attempt to inject novelty into an ailing concert life, whose circumscribed repertoire and performance styles were leading to atrophy. Many contemporary works had, since World War I, been unpalatable to the majority of listeners, so could not offset this trend, but the early-music movement could provide both approachable new repertoires and new ways of playing familiar works.

The most widely discussed motivation hypothesis is that of Taruskin. He posits a discrepancy between the conscious and the hidden motives of early-music performers. Although performers think that they are trying to use musicological scholarship to re-create the sounds of the past, what unconsciously motivates them, he believes, is the creation of a style of performance that expresses modern tastes. He illustrates this with examples of artists using historical evidence selectively, privileging evidence that accords with modern taste while ignoring or dismissing evidence that does not. Although Taruskin occasionally condemns instances of these processes, his defining position is to praise them: he says that they give historical performance its artistic relevance. It is a vastly greater thing, he says, to be the "true voice of one's time" than to be the "assumed voice of history" (1995, p. 166).

Another idea is that historical performance motivates performers by giving them special latitude. This view argues that Western art music today places authoritarian demands on performers—above all, that they must honor the composer's authority as embodied in the written score—but that these demands conflict with our artistic ethos of individual creativity and expression. Because period idioms are often believed to involve inflecting the music in ways not indicated in the score (for example, by adding embellishments), historical performance may let a performer innovate without being censured for ignoring the authority of the composer (see Dulak, 1993, 1995; Sherman, 1997, pp. 19–20). Others argue, however, that historical performance might actually increase the authoritarian demands placed on performers, by adding (or, at times, substituting) the authority of musicology to the other demands already present (Dreyfus, personal communication, 1995).

Despite their contradictions, all the motivations above may operate simultaneously, perhaps even within a single musician. In addition, other motives have been suggested. For example, Butt (quoted in Sherman, 1997, p. 175) says that he is concerned as a performer with historical issues to the degree that they help him understand the composer's creative process.

The Future of Historical Performance. It is, of course, impossible to know what future eras will make of our era's authenticity movement (or, as its practitioners are far more likely to call it now, "historically informed performance"). Even some of the most distinguished historical performers speculate that their own work will someday appear to reflect the tastes of the late twentieth century rather than of the historical eras being reconstructed. Perhaps the very concern with historical verisimilitude will appear a peculiarity of our time. On the other hand, some of the historical performers' work might well be considered to have improved the performance of some repertoires, and some may even come to be regarded as historically accurate; and certain trends in historical performance have influenced at least some mainstream performance. Other trends promise to do so; the revival of the art of improvisation, in music ranging from medieval instrumental pieces to Mozart concertos, may become influential and, if so, would be a significant legacy. This may be the sort of legacy that Goehr (1992, p. 284) has in mind when she speculates that the early-music movement may be well positioned to provide modern musical life with an alternative to the "work" concept. (Taruskin [1995, p. 13] complains that historicist performers have often applied the "work" concept anachronistically to music from eras that did not themselves possess it; he particularly welcomes these experiments in improvisation [ibid., pp. 284–289].)

Some historicist performances might be remembered for musical excellence, unrelated to historical accuracy. Even the critics mentioned earlier have often lavished praise on specific performers. The most important legacy of the historical performance movement may be those performances that attain authenticity in the deepest sense: that of conviction, self-knowledge, spontaneity, and emotional honesty.

[*See also* Music, *historical overview article; and* Performance.]

BIBLIOGRAPHY

Bowen, José A. "Mendelssohn, Berlioz, and Wagner as Conductors: The Origins of the Ideal of 'Fidelity to the Composer'." *Performance Practice Review* 6 (1993): 77–83.

Brendel, Alfred. *Music Sounded Out: Essays, Lectures, Interviews, Afterthoughts.* London, 1990.

Brewer, Marilyn, and Roderick M. Kramer. "The Psychology of Intergroup Attitudes and Behavior." In *Annual Review of Psychology*, vol. 36, edited by M. Rosenzweig and L. Porter, pp. 219–243. Palo Alto, Calif., 1985.

Brown, Howard Mayer, and Stanley Sadie, eds. *Performance Practice: Music after 1600.* London, 1989.

Butt, John. "Acting Up a Text." *Early Music* 24 (1996): 323–332.

Dipert, Randall. "The Composer's Intentions: An Examination of Their Relevance for Performance." *Musical Quarterly* 66 (1980): 205–218.

Dreyfus, Laurence. "Early Music Defended against Its Devotees." *Musical Quarterly* 69 (1983): 297–322.

Dulak, Michelle. "The Quiet Metamorphosis of Early Music." *Repercussions* 3 (Fall 1993): 31–61.

Dulak, Michelle. "The Early Music World Circles Its Wagons Again." *New York Times*, 11 June 1995, sec.C, p. 24.

Goehr, Lydia. *The Imaginary Museum of Musical Works: An Essay in the Philosophy of Music.* Oxford, 1992.

Haskell, Harry. *The Early Music Revival: A History.* London, 1988.

Heilbroner, Robert. *Visions of the Future: The Distant Past, Yesterday, Today, Tomorrow.* New York and Oxford, 1995.

Kenyon, Nicholas, ed. *Authenticity and Early Music.* New York and Oxford, 1988.

Kerman, Joseph. *Contemplating Music: Musicology in Context.* Cambridge, Mass., 1985.

Kerman, Joseph. Introduction to "The Early Music Debate." *Journal of Musicology* 10 (Winter 1992): 113.

Kerman, Joseph. *Write All These Down: Essays on Music.* Berkeley, 1994.

Kivy, Peter. *Authenticities: Philosophical Reflections on Musical Performance.* Ithaca, N.Y., 1995.

Levinson, Jerrold. *Music, Art, and Metaphysics: Essays in Philosophical Aesthetics.* Ithaca, N.Y., 1990.

Morgan, Robert. "Tradition, Anxiety, and the Current Musical Scene." In *Authenticity and Early Music,* edited by Nicholas Kenyon, pp. 57–82. New York and Oxford, 1988.

Philip, Robert. *Early Recordings and Musical Style: Changing Tastes in Instrumental Performance, 1900–1950.* Cambridge and New York, 1992.

Rosen, Charles. "The Shock of the Old." *New York Review of Books,* 19 July 1990, 46–52.

Sherman, Bernard D. *Inside Early Music: Conversations with Performers.* New York, 1997.

Taruskin, Richard. *Text and Act: Essays on Music and Performance.* New York and Oxford, 1995.

BERNARD D. SHERMAN

AUTHOR. *See* Artist; Barthes; Creativity; Foucault; Intention; Law and Art; *and* Originality.

AUTONOMY. [*To explain the philosophical concept of autonomy (that is, self-legislation or freedom), this entry comprises four essays:*

Historical Overview
Critique of Autonomy
Autonomy and Its Feminist Critics
Autonomy and Architecture

The first is an overview essay of the meaning, origins, and history of the concept of autonomy and its particular application in aesthetics. This is followed by two critiques of autonomy: first, from the perspective of critical theory (of the Frankfurt School variety; see here Adorno and Marcuse); and, second, from that of feminism. Because autonomy is a concept that has had varying significance in the different arts and architecture is not discussed in the other essays, the final essay analyzes how the concept of autonomy has developed in that particular field. See also Aestheticism; Art for Art's Sake; Disinterestedness; and Romanticism.]

Historical Overview

The idea of autonomy has been a centerpiece of traditional aesthetic thinking, and of Western humanist thought generally, since the eighteenth century. At the same time, it has moved increasingly in recent decades to the center of a range of debates among philosophers and historians of art, critics, and artists about the claim of philosophical aesthetics (or philosophy of art) itself to be an autonomous inquiry with a distinctive subject and methodology. The most basic connotation of "autonomy" in aesthetics is the thought that aesthetic experience, or art, or both, possess a life of their own apart from other human affairs, where under the latter heading are included the objects and processes of moral, social, political, psychological, and biological inquiry. This proposition reflects *autonomy*'s general meaning of "self-rule" or "self-legislation," signifying a condition attaching to some object of analysis insofar as it is self-dependent, or, less strongly, independent of other objects of analysis in various context-relative ways. Subjects of aesthetic inquiry traditionally described as autonomous include aesthetic judgments, the mental faculties responsible for aesthetic experience, artworks, formal qualities and meanings inherent in artworks, the actions and purposes of artists, the development of styles, genres, or media in art history, and the practices or institutions that sustain artistic activity in society.

Of the welter of more specific connotations *autonomy* has acquired in aesthetics since its explicit appearance in the late eighteenth century (see Hermerén, 1983), two are particularly basic and will inform this discussion. The first connotation affirms the uniqueness of art, or aesthetic experience, or both, as a *source of value*, and their logical irreducibility to other sources of value. Art, aesthetic experience, or both are here characterized as autonomous in a *jus-tificatory* sense. A "heteronomist" view in this context would, in contrast, make the values of art and aesthetic experience, construed as ends, conditional on the value of further ends—for example, morality, utility, or truth. The second connotation affirms the *causal independence* of artistic or aesthetic phenomena, qua artistic or aesthetic phenomena, from influences of, for example, a psychological, biological, economic, social, or political nature. Here autonomy is attributable to aesthetic or artistic phenomena in an *explanatory* sense. A heteronomist view, in contrast, would place emphasis on how such phenomena are shaped by, and hence demand explanation in terms of, influences such as those just mentioned. All of the positions just sketched, it need hardly be said, are idealizations: in practice, writers on aesthetic subjects typically advance arguments that aim to synthesize autonomist and heteronomist considerations in various respects.

Early History. The early ancestry of modern discussions of autonomy in aesthetics is discernible in classical discussions of subjects such as beauty, the form and function of mimetic artifacts, and the sources of artistic creativity. Recall, for example, Plato's characterization of poets and other practitioners of mimetic *techné* as possessed by a "divine madness" that separates their activity from the rational analyses of philosophers and as specializing in the production of illusion or "mere appearances." These descriptions, though not meant entirely as flattery, anticipate later accounts of the artist as guided by a distinctive form of intelligence, as well as later accounts of the ontological differences between artworks and other kinds of natural and cultural objects. Aristotle further develops these themes in characterizing the work of tragic poetry as possessing a form that is *kálliste* (from *to kalón*, roughly translatable as "beauty") and "complete unto itself," and that in consequence aspires to a kind of organic unity and a perfection internal to the tragic genre. Aristotle further suggests that tragedy affords a grasp of human experience that exceeds that of historiography and approaches that of philosophy.

We thus find in Aristotle a clear ancestor of the modern autonomist theme that art plays a unique positive role in society, even though this is tempered by his Greek tendency to construe the value of all artifacts instrumentally. Such value is construed in terms of how the direct experiences afforded by imitative artifacts promote ends beyond themselves, for example, the good of the individual or of society. Yet, there are intimations of autonomist thinking in Aristotle and Plato, insofar as both have occasion to characterize philosophical contemplation as the consummate human activity, enjoyable and valuable in itself. By the end of the classical period, a synthesis of both lines of thought would begin to appear in allusions by writers such as Plotinus to the contemplation of divine beauty as an end in itself. A few centuries later, Augustine would tie such contemplation expressly to the Christian idea of a perfect, self-sufficient (hence, in a sense autonomous) being. In this context, he would employ a distinction between loving something for itself and loving it for the sake of further ends, anticipating the modern distinction between the intrinsic value of aesthetic contemplation and the instrumental values of more worldly forms of experience.

The story of the emergence of modern aesthetics is to some extent the story of how the idea of what pleases in—and is supremely valuable for—itself would evolve from these theologically inflected discussions into a secular idiom, retaining all the while the core theme of the transcendence of worldly experience; hence, in the eighteenth century, the emergence of philosophical accounts of fine art and aesthetic experience that emphasized their transcendence of worldly affairs in the justificatory and explanatory senses noted at the beginning of this essay.

Eighteenth Century. Two developments in eighteenth-century thought and culture would exercise a particular influence on the further history of autonomy in the history of aesthetics. First, there was the emerging recognition of painting, sculpture, poetry, architecture, and music as comprising a basic kind of cultural practice, now known as "fine art," that does not depend, in the way that the individual arts did in earlier periods, on religious or political institutions for its justification or patronage. Second, the resulting reconfiguration in the categories of cultural description—with fine art now understood in logical opposition to, for example, craft and entertainment—was further reflected at the level of theory with the emergence of a new subdiscipline of philosophy, christened "aesthetics" by Alexander Baumgarten in 1735 and devoted to the systematic elucidation of the aesthetic experience of culture and nature.

Increasing emphasis was now placed in the aesthetic literature on the independence of aesthetic experience, understood as a universal feature of psychological and social life and a distinctive source of value, from other kinds of experience associated with everyday practical affairs. This theme evolved on a number of specific fronts. For example, it became increasingly common to speak of aesthetic experience as free from practical interest or "disinterested." This notion, which underlies later accounts of the aesthetic "attitude" or "point of view," was given initial formulation in the work of British writers such as Anthony Ashley Cooper, earl of Shaftesbury. It would be taken up by later German writers such as Karl Philipp Moritz, who wrote in 1785 that "In contemplating a beautiful object . . . I roll the purpose back into the object itself: I regard it as something that finds completion not in me but in itself and thus constitutes a whole in itself and gives me pleasure for its own sake. . . . Thus the beautiful object yields a higher and more disinterested pleasure than the merely useful object" (Moritz, 1973). [*See* Moritz.] Moritz here conjoins the theme of disinterestedness with the distinction, noted earlier in connection with Augustine, between contemplating an

object for itself and for further ends, and with the idea that the aesthetic object possesses its purpose within itself. In a later essay, he would expand the scope of the idea of the poem as a "heterocosm"—a fictional world possessed of its own internal structures and purposive organization—as formulated earlier by Baumgarten and others.

Kant. All these ideas underwent further refinement in the seminal work in aesthetics of the eighteenth century, Immanuel Kant's *Critique of Judgment* (1790), which would become the common reference point for all subsequent discussions of autonomy in aesthetics. A principal aim of this work is to describe the transcendental conditions of taste, as represented in the ways human beings judge various natural and cultural objects to be beautiful. Central to Kant's argument is the idea that the pleasure human beings take in beauty is disinterested and "free." This means broadly that aesthetic pleasures are of a different order from ordinary day-to-day desires and satisfactions. In Kant's technical idiom, it also means that when we issue a judgment of taste, our faculty of understanding stops short of applying a determinate empirical concept to an object. In this sense, aesthetic judgment stops short of being a form of *cognitive* judgment, implying that to experience an object aesthetically is different from knowing it in a scientific or philosophical sense. Kant also argues that the natural and cultural objects we find beautiful exhibit "purposiveness without purpose"; that is, we apprehend all the sensuous details of a beautiful object as if they were deliberately created to conform to the requirements of human cognition even while they elude conception under ordinary design-descriptions; this leads to our pleasurable sense that the object somehow contains its purpose within itself. In arguing along these lines, Kant departs from the view, common to Shaftesbury and other British theorists, that aesthetic and moral sensibilities share a common basis in mental activity. Instead, he assigns aesthetic judgment to a separate faculty of taste within the transcendental economy of mental activity, and takes the further step of arguing that taste enjoys a special a priori basis as a faculty of judgment. These last two moves would be of fundamental importance for subsequent aesthetic theory, in that they claim for aesthetic judgment an unprecedented logical independence, hence a kind of autonomy, with respect to the activities of practical and theoretical reasoning—that is, broadly, with respect to morality and science. Kant's characterization of his aesthetic theory as a transcendental rather than an empirical inquiry similarly paves the way for later defenses of the self-sufficiency of aesthetics as a discipline whose methods and data are irreducible to those of empirical projects such as a sociology of art and taste.

Kant essentially introduced the systematic usage of the concept of autonomy (he generally uses *Autonomie*) into modern aesthetics, just as he had done with the term earlier in ethics. In the *Critique, Autonomie* is reserved for characterizing the self-legislative operation of the faculty of taste; the faculty of judgment engages in a more narrowly self-legislative activity termed "heautonomy" (*Critique of Judgment*, Introduction) Kant never applies *Autonomie* to the creative imagination or to fine art; yet it may be generally said that he regards the creative imagination and hence, by implication, fine art as *free from* certain kinds of external determining influence, as when he refers to the imagination as "productive and exerting an activity of its own." Another source of Kant's alleged autonomism is his formalist thesis that in all the visual arts, "*design [Zeichnung] is what is essential*" (ibid., section 14). By *Zeichnung* Kant means qualities of line and spatial composition as contrasted with the "charm" of coloration; in musical perception, the counterpart to *Zeichnung* is the awareness of melodic and harmonic structure, as contrasted with a more sensuous apprehension of "the agreeable tone of an instrument." The point of this distinction is not, as one might first think, to theoretically purge art's essence of all referring or semantic functions. Rather, it is to exclude from the aesthetic characterization of art aspects of artworks occasioning sensations that are inextricably tied to lower, more bodily based satisfactions, sensations that cannot provide a basis for the universal rational communication about pleasure that genuine taste, for Kant, requires. Many readers will understandably feel that this appeal to universal communicability projects an unreasonably bleak, not to mention dualistic, picture of the relationship between aesthetic experience and the life of the body. Kant's theory is indeed more austere in this regard than the views of later formalists in visual art criticism such as Clive Bell, Roger Fry, and Clement Greenberg. At the same time, it is more generous regarding the relationship between an artwork's aesthetic value and its semiotic aspects, so that he can be a formalist about perception yet also consistently hold that beautiful objects express "aesthetic ideas" and are hence "symbols of morality" (ibid., section 59). In the end, then, the *Critique* stops short of advancing an art-for-art's-sake-type view, striking as it does a balance between the autonomist impulse to picture the aesthetic as an independent source of mental activity and value and the heteronomist impulse to subordinate aesthetic values in an instrumental sense—as all nonmoral values must finally be subordinated for Kant—to the unconditional value of the moral will. This in turn reflects Kant's Enlightenment humanist conviction that the value of all higher culture lies ultimately in its promotion of moral community (ibid., sections 44 and 60).

Schiller. Friedrich Schiller's influential *On the Aesthetic Education of Man in a Series of Letters* (1793–1795; hereafter, *Letters*) would carry the autonomist impulse in Kant's argument an important step further. Schiller views aesthetic experience as the key to healing the condition of emotional and intellectual fragmentation that he identifies as a consequence of modern life. At the center of the argument of the *Letters* is the idea of "aesthetic semblance" *(ästhetischen Schein)*, whose instances include artworks and objects of everyday experience. Echoing Kant's thesis that the experiences of the aesthetic and the sublime arise from a "free play" between the imagination and the understanding, Schiller argues that our aesthetic lives revolve around the activity of a "play drive" that at once unifies and transcends the ordinary operations of our sensuous and cognitive faculties. "As soon as the play-drive begins to stir," he writes, "it will be followed by the shaping spirit of imitation, which treats semblance as something autonomous" *(Selbständiges,* from *Selbständigkeit)*. He continues a few paragraphs later: "In whatever individual or whole people we find this honest and autonomous kind of semblance, we may assume both understanding and taste, and every kindred excellence. There we shall see actual life governed by the ideal, honour triumphant over possessions, thought over enjoyment" (Letter 26). These words bespeak an oft-noted tension in Schiller's argument between a characteristically Enlightenment tendency to construe the values of aesthetic semblance as instrumental to higher ends of a moral, social, and political nature, and a more Romantic tendency to redescribe the highest condition to which we may aspire as itself an aesthetic condition. The *Letters* thus epitomize in their way a question that would haunt aesthetic debate throughout the nineteenth century: Are aesthetic values subordinate to the values of life, or vice versa—or are the two entirely separate?

Nineteenth and Twentieth Centuries. In the nineteenth century, two developments were of particular consequence for the development of autonomist themes. One was the narrowing of the central focus of aesthetic inquiry to include fine art and to exclude nature, epitomized in Georg Wilhelm Friedrich Hegel's equation of "aesthetics" with "the philosophy of fine art" early in the century. The other was the growing sense that given the failures of science and religion to address and remedy the forms of psychic fragmentation and social alienation that were now increasingly associated with modern experience, the arts have a unique redemptive mission in modern social life.

Both developments figured in the general philosophical outlook of Romanticism, whose main initial contributions to aesthetics came from German writers such as Friedrich Wilhelm von Schelling and August Wilhelm Schlegel. The sense that art offers an alternative to everyday experience found its most radical expressions in the spin-off Romantic aestheticist movement known as "art for art's sake." The phrase *l'art pour l'art* was apparently first used by Benjamin Constant in 1804 in connection with the Kantian doctrine of the "purposiveness without purpose" of beautiful objects. In subsequent decades, the phrase became a slogan for diverse artists and critics, first primarily in France (including such writers as Victor Cousin, Théophile Gautier, and Gustave Flaubert) and later in England (including such writers as John Keats, Walter Pater, and Oscar Wilde). Particularly in its early phases, this movement represented a reaction against the utilitarian thinking and conventional tastes of bourgeois culture; proponents held that art is authentic only when it is not beholden in style and substance to convention, especially concerning matters of morality. This attitude went hand in hand with the paradigmatic modern shift from "mimetic" to "expressive" understandings of the basic nature and purpose of media like painting or poetry, whereby the latter were now held to be in their essence freely expressive of the artist's inner experience.

It was now common to hear metaphorical references to art and aesthetic experience as a "realm" of practice and value structured according to "inner" principles. This way of talking in turn reinforced the idea of artistic values as intrinsic values or ends in themselves (autonomy in a justificatory sense) and the idea that artistic practices, qua artistic practices, enjoy a special exemption from determining influences affecting other areas of culture (autonomy in an explanatory sense). These themes would take on further articulation and local emphasis from a succession of movements in the nineteenth and twentieth centuries of which only a brief survey is possible here.

Literary studies, for example, would see a growing trend in the twentieth century toward understanding the literary text as an organically unified and self-sufficient linguistic object from whose aesthetic interpretation all direct reference to the external world or to the author's intentions are properly excluded. This line of thought culminated at mid-century in the Anglo-American movement known as the New Criticism, which met with severe criticism for its autonomist leanings from various quarters, notably from the French-inspired poststructuralist movement known as deconstruction. (Yet, it is striking that the theme of the self-enclosed linguistic object would reappear in the writings of deconstructionists themselves, this time as a thesis about language as a whole, as expressed in the slogan "there is nothing outside the text.") In musical aesthetics, nineteenth-century philosophers such as Arthur Schopenhauer and critics such as Eduard Hanslick emphasized the metaphysical transcendence and formal purity of music; this trend would continue in the formalist New Music movement of the twentieth century. Another main site for autonomist development was art history, whose academization toward the end of the nineteenth century was pioneered by a number of "critical" writers influenced by the historical-developmental vision of Hegel. These included Alois Riegl, who argued for an "artistic volition" *(Kunstwollen)* that guides the artistic productions of periods, schools, and individuals and is irreducible to individual artists' intentions or collective ideologies, and Heinrich Wölfflin, who held that successive styles in the history of the visual arts possess internal laws of formal development demanding a logic of explanation apart from that of general history. This internalist emphasis carried over into visual art criticism, where formalism was increasingly in vogue, as represented by writers like Clive Bell and Roger Fry. The antirepresentationalist impulse in their work culminated in the post–World War II movement known as Modernist Criticism, whose leading spokesman was the American critic Clement Greenberg. [*See* Greenberg.] Greenberg put forward the influential, and subsequently much contested, hypothesis that each fine-art medium has historically striven, consciously or unconsciously, toward a self-critical and self-purifying awareness of its essence as a unique medium. Greenberg was primarily concerned to show this in connection with painting, which in his view had, with the advent of Impressionism, cast aside older representationalist ideals in recognition of its essentially two-dimensional or "flat" character. Yet, like many others, Greenberg believed that analogous and contemporaneous developments were evident throughout the fine arts. Under modernism, a medium like architecture, music, poetry, dance, or sculpture need no longer seek its material in such allegedly extra-aesthetic realms as nature, or human psychology, or social life; its "subject," as in painting, is essentially just itself. In philosophical aesthetics, finally, the concern with explanatory autonomy running throughout the movements above would be reinforced by writers emphasizing a Kantian-style insulation between transcendental and empirical inquiries into aesthetic subjects, such as Benedetto Croce, Robin G. Collingwood, and Suzanne Langer. Many of their concerns continue to be carried forward today by representatives of the post–World War II movement of "analytic" aesthetics, whose work characteristically recasts the Kantian transcendental/empirical distinction in the idiom of post-Wittgensteinian philosophy of language.

Critiques of Autonomism. All of the movements above have generated extensive critical literatures. It is hardly possible here to do justice to the details of specific debates, but two general patterns of philosophical critique recurring throughout such discussions deserve mention.

One line of critique addresses the justificatory logic of autonomist thinking. It argues that views of artistic autonomy that overemphasize the purity and intrinsic value of aesthetic experience have the effect of theoretically disconnecting art from the ends of life as actually lived by most people, whose tastes and pleasures are of a piece with the fabric of day-to-day experience. One recent version of this line of argument questions the very intelligibility of the idea that works of art, or selected defining features of the latter such as formal properties, are ends in themselves in the strong sense of possessing an intrinsic value requiring no reference to extra-aesthetic ends for their justification. Here the critic of autonomism can proceed by arguing that the idea of aesthetic value-making features of artworks makes little sense without reference to the ability of such features to promote aesthetic experience. If so, the critic continues, strong claims about the artwork's intrinsic value become incoherent; for such value is now made logically dependent on the "external" end of aesthetic experience, and to this extent the artwork's distinguishing value turns out to be a form of instrumental, not intrinsic, value. The critic might now continue by arguing that the idea of aesthetic experience is itself incoherent without reference to larger means-end relationships, including social relationships, within which practices of artistic production and reception have a place. This style of argument is common to the literatures of Marxist and pragmatist aesthetics, and can be further developed in various directions. For example, critical attention may be given to linkages between the rise of the modern idea of the aesthetic as an autonomous realm of intrinsically valuable objects and the rise of lifestyles organized around the passive enjoyment and marketing of commodities, within and without the art world. Or, further scrutiny may be directed to how strict distinctions between autonomous and nonautonomous cultural values can function to legitimize the tastes of certain social groups over those of others in morally and politically questionable ways.

A second line of critique approaches autonomist thinking from an explanatory, sociology-of-culture perspective, and has figured centrally in recent debates about the status of aesthetic canons, the relationship between "high" and "popular" cultural practices, and the validity of modernist accounts of the histories of the arts. First, it is observed that various judgments about the aesthetic merits of specific cultural objects (e.g., "classic" works of art), along with higher-order beliefs in autonomy and other doctrines of aesthetic theory, claim universal validity but are in fact the local product of specific cultures. Second, the critic might argue that it is reasonable to inquire into the local (e.g., social, economic, political) causes of such beliefs, just as it is reasonable to do so with, say, moral or religious beliefs. Pressing the latter analogy, the critic might then note that the lower-order aesthetic judgments cannot be validated without appealing to the higher-order beliefs, but that these beliefs are in turn peculiarly resistant to falsification. It is then open to the critic to argue for "nonrational" explanations of the appeal of autonomist doctrines on analogy to empirical explanations of religious belief by some secular critics. The doctrines in question may be given an "institutional" analysis, which construes them, for example, as ideological projections onto the cultural field that consciously or unconsciously promote the interests of specific economic, gender, or ethnic orientations. Moderate variants of this sociological style of argument typically draw on the deeper premises of philosophical naturalism: a good example of this is John Dewey's *Art as Experience*. They may also, as in the work of Marxist writers such as Herbert Marcuse and Theodor Adorno, append to the foregoing critique further arguments about how art in some contexts exhibits a restricted form of autonomy, as in the case of artworks that resist assimilation to, or "negate," mass social consciousness, and so facilitate the realization of progressive political ideals. Less moderate variants occur in recent postmodern syntheses of neo-Marxist, poststructuralist, and pragmatist arguments characteristic of the Cultural Studies movement, where the very distinction between distinctively aesthetic and nonaesthetic modes of cultural production is subjected to symptomatic empirical analysis.

These critiques suggest, in conclusion, both that the debate about autonomy in aesthetics has become increasingly interdisciplinary in recent years and that the modern struggle between the philosophical impulses to separate aesthetic phenomena from, and assimilate them to, larger contexts of valuation and explanation has hardly come to an end. What can be said is that, at the turn of the twenty-first century, the more moderate of the critical arguments presented here have left their imprint on even the more conservative practitioners of disciplines like philosophical aesthetics, art criticism, and art history, who affirm the distinctiveness of art as an aesthetic practice while increasingly understanding their subjects and methods in historical terms. What remains unclear is how the more uncompromisingly contextual, and skeptical, of the arguments will shape such disciplines in the future and, no less important, how they will shape future understandings of the practices still generally called the fine arts; for, carried to its logical extreme, skepticism about the attempt to define an institutionally distinctive set of cultural practices as aesthetic and autonomous is ultimately skepticism about belief in the existence of a separate aesthetic realm of practice and value—a belief that has, by and large, been exempt from serious critique in the history of aesthetics until now.

[*See also* Genius; Kant; Marxism; *and* Schiller.]

BIBLIOGRAPHY

Abrams, M. H. "Art-as-Such: The Sociology of Modern Aesthetics." In *Doing Things with Texts: Essays in Criticism and Critical Theory,* edited by Michael Fischer, pp. 135–158. New York, 1989.

Abrams, M. H. "From Addison to Kant: Modern Aesthetics and the Exemplary Art." In *Doing Things with Texts: Essays in Criticism and Critical Theory,* edited by Michael Fischer, pp. 159–187. New York, 1989.

Adorno, Theodor W. *Aesthetic Theory* (1970). Edited by Gretel Adorno and Rolf Tiedemann, translated by Robert Hullot-Kentor. Minneapolis, 1997.

Bell, Clive. *Art* (1914). Edited by J. B. Bullen. New York and Oxford, 1987.

Bell-Villada, Gene H. *Art for Art's Sake and Literary Life: How Politics and Markets Helped Shape the Ideology and Culture of Aestheticism, 1790–1990.* Lincoln, Nebr., 1996.

Bourdieu, Pierre. *The Rules of Art: Genesis and Structure of the Literary Field* (1992). Translated by Susan Emanuel. Stanford, Calif., 1996.

Bürger, Peter. *Theory of the Avant-Garde* (1974). Translated by Michael Shaw. Minneapolis, 1984.

Dahlhaus, Carl. *Foundations of Music History* (1977). Translated by J. B. Robinson. Cambridge and New York, 1983.

Dewey, John. *Art as Experience.* New York, 1934.

Diffey, T. J. "Aesthetic Instrumentalism." *British Journal of Aesthetics* 22 (Autumn 1982): 337–349.

Frascina, Francis, and Jonathan Harris, eds. *Art in Modern Culture: An Anthology of Critical Texts.* New York, 1992.

Fry, Roger. *Vision and Design* (1920). Edited by J. B. Bullen. New York and Oxford, 1981.

Hermerén, Göran. *Aspects of Aesthetics.* Lund, 1983.

Kant, Immanuel. *Critique of Judgment* (1790). Translated by Werner S. Pluhar. Indianapolis, 1987.

Moritz, Karl Philipp. *Werke in Zwei Bänden.* Edited by J. Jahn. Berlin, 1973.

Müller, Michael, et al. *Autonomie der Kunst: Zur Genese und Kritik einer bürgerlichen Kategorie.* Frankfurt am Main, 1972.

Podro, Michael. *The Critical Historians of Art.* New Haven, 1982.

Schiller, Friedrich von. *On the Aesthetic Education of Man in a Series of Letters* (1793–1795). Translated by Elizabeth M. Wilkinson and L. A. Willoughby. Oxford, 1967.

Smith, Barbara Herrnstein. *Contingencies of Value: Alternative Perspectives for Critical Theory.* Cambridge, Mass., 1988.

Wood, Paul, et al., eds. *Modernism in Dispute: Art Since the Forties.* New Haven, 1993.

Woodmansee, Martha. *The Author, Art, and the Market: Rereading the History of Aesthetics.* New York, 1994.

CASEY HASKINS

Critique of Autonomy

To speak of the autonomy of art, or of the artwork, is, for various reasons, anything but unequivocal. For one thing, the concept is historical, but it is again and again treated by prominent theoreticians of aesthetics as if it were timeless, which gives rise inconsistencies. For another, it makes a difference where one situates autonomy, whether one speaks of the autonomy of art or of the artwork (for although both are connected, they are not the same). A historical reconstruction might shed some light on the obscurity of the use of this concept.

It is well known that the arts—the collective singular "art" as an encompassing designation for poetry, music, visual arts, and architecture is only established later—were, in the feudal and absolutist society of the seventeenth century, still in no way autonomous. Molière (Jean-Baptiste Poquelin) had to struggle for years to have his *Tartuffe* performed publicly. In this dispute, it was a question of more than a single play, namely, of whether the author of a comedy should have the right to thematize essential problems of social coexistence, or whether this right should belong solely to the church. If Molière finally triumphed after a long dispute, he owed his success not only to his own stubbornness, but above all to the intervention of the king on his side. The *Querelle du Tartuffe* is significant in more than one respect.

It shows that Molière did, in fact, maintain the autonomy of the theater, which consists in the right of a comic author to take positions regarding society in his plays. Autonomy means here something quite different from the idea of *l'art pour l'art* in the aesthetic programs of the nineteenth century.

Molière may only assert himself against the power of the church by appealing to absolutist central power. The autonomy that he thereby attains remains a relative one. Nonetheless, he does not simply exchange one form of dependency for another, but reaches more freedom; for the functions that absolutism assigns to the theater—the representation of kingly grandeur and the divertissement of the courtly society—indeed leave the author, within these set limits, a certain measure of formal freedom.

Nor did the Enlightenment of the eighteenth century yet know the modern concept of autonomous art. The article "Beaux-Arts" from the *Encyclopédie* makes art responsible for social usefulness, and thereby for the practice of moral behavior; at the same time, it distinguishes itself from the conception of art connoted by courtly society: "Weak or frivolous minds repeat incessantly that the arts are only destined for our amusements." For the history of the concept of autonomy, it is extremely revealing that the author of this article never regards usefulness as the original feature of the arts. Rather, he takes his point of departure in the idea that they had spontaneously arisen out of life praxis, much as the shepherd ornaments his crook, or as the nomad builds a well-proportioned hut. For the author, there exists therefore "a beauty that is independent of its usefulness." Formulations in which the "particular charm" and the "magical force" of the art work is discussed point in the same direction. One should certainly not overvalue these remarks, but they show that the Enlightenment surmised potentials of spontaneous sensuality in art that it wanted not only to make useful, but also to keep under control. From this urge stem also the suggestions, in this same article in the *Encyclopédie,* for a restrictive cultural policy that would make the admission to artistic activity dependent on a preceding examination of the applicant in history, the faculty of judgment, and moral integrity. To be sure, views were formulated in Denis Diderot's circle that clearly point beyond a moral and educatory function of the arts. This is above all true of the concept of genius, with the help of which, since the mid-eighteenth century, the artist is understood as an exceptional human being whose actions are subordinate to no rules. In the relevant article of the *Encyclopédie,* the work of the genius is characterized as follows: "it must have an air of neglect about it, appear irregular, rocky, savage." The rejection of the normative poetics that were valid in France until well into the nineteenth century could hardly be expressed more clearly. The autonomy of art is thus found first as the autonomy of the artist regarding rules, and thus is in relation to the rational moment in the conception of art held in courtly and feudal society. This may be difficult to understand at first glance, because we are used to assuming a connection between the rise of the bourgeoisie and the establishment of the principle of rationality in society, even if this is done from a simplifying sociological viewpoint; for, with the concept of genius, the same bourgeoisie creates a position that defines itself against rationality.

The writings of Johann Wolfgang von Goethe's friend Karl Philipp Moritz, which were written in the years before the 1789 French Revolution, show particularly well why, in the transition to a modern society, art came into a relation of tension with rationality. [*See* Moritz.] If the Encyclopedists had been concerned with making the arts into useful tools of social progress, then Moritz defines the beautiful in opposition to the useful. "We may thus recognize the beautiful in general in no other way than by opposing it to the useful and distinguishing it as sharply as possible from the latter," he writes in his essay "On the Plastic Imitation of the Beautiful" (1788). Even more clearly than later in Kant, Moritz's texts betray the social conditions that have called up this definition of the beautiful. In the essay "The Noblest in Nature" (1786), he notes: "The dominant idea of the useful has gradually repressed the noble and beautiful—for one regards even grand and sublime nature only with the eyes of state finance *[Kameralistik]* and finds its sight only interesting insofar as one can calculate the profits of its products" (1973, vol. I, p. 263). For a society that tends to see nature only as the object of exploitation, nothing is more important than to keep open the possibility of another form of converse with nature. This relation to nature is the aesthetic one, which keeps itself as free of any considerations of usefulness as it does from immediately moral judgments. Transposed onto artistic beauty, there results from this the idea of the artwork's freedom from goals and its definition as a whole that exists for itself; for whereas the category of usefulness always refers an object to other things and sees it only as a part, the goal-free eye stays longer with the object of its contemplation and thus demands that it be a whole.

With this autonomy of art arises also a new, contemplative attitude of reception, which Moritz sketches as follows: "While the beautiful draws our contemplation entirely into itself, it also draws it away from ourselves for a time, and effects our self-loss in the beautiful object; and it is just this self-loss, this forgetting of ourselves, which is the highest degree of the pure and unselfish pleasure that beauty may offer us. We give up in the moment our individual and limited existence to a kind of higher existence" (1973, vol. I, p. 206). Aesthetic experience appears here to be radically separated from everyday experience, so radically that the subject loses itself. The analogy here between the experience of beauty and religious experience is extremely clear. Such an understanding becomes possible at a historical point in time where the loss of validity of religious worldviews awakens a longing for a metaphysical experience of a different sort, which will find its admittedly ever precarious fulfillment in autonomous art.

One might sum up as follows: the postulate of autonomy in the last third of the eighteenth century responds to central problems of incipient bourgeois capitalist society, and

for this reason retains its validity in the two centuries to come, however disputed that validity will come to be. The problems to which this new definition of art reacts are called forth by the transition from a traditional to a modern society and by the changes in attitudes and patterns of life that this conditions. One may also characterize these problems as a loss of a dimension of meaning of human existence, just as much as a nascent perception of increasing alienation between individuals who are directed to egotistical goals of action. To this individual, who is in conflict with himself and his fellow humans, and is abandoned by God, autonomous art opens a world that lets him experience perfection as reality, although only at the cost of the strict separation of this from any life praxis.

What makes Kant's *Critique of Judgment* (1790) the fundamental text of modern aesthetics is above all the fact that the separation of art from its life-practical relations is here reflected on with extreme conceptual precision: "If someone asks me whether I find the palace I see before me beautiful, I may indeed say: I don't care for such things which are made only for gawking at; or, like the Iroquois *sachem,* I might say that I like nothing in Paris better than certain kinds of cakes; I could also whittle down the vanity of the great in good Rousseau-like fashion, for this vanity wastes the sweat of the people on such unnecessary things. . . . One may admit and approve of all of this, yet this is not the question here. One wants only to know whether the mere representation of a thing in me is accompanied with pleasure" (*Critique of Judgment,* section 2). [*See* Kant.] The quote makes clear what Kant understands by "disinterestedness." Both the interest of the Iroquois sachem, which is directed to immediate gratification of need, and the practical interest of reason of a Rousseau-like critic of society lie outside the domain that Kant circumscribes as the object of aesthetic judgment. It is not Kant's purpose to make statements about the essence of art or the laws of construction of artworks; he wants only to isolate a specific mode of contemplation, while admitting that the object in question could be considered otherwise. The oft-cited definitions of disinterested pleasure, of purposefulness without goal, and of a generally valid pleasure without concepts are, for Kant, definitions of the judgment of taste, and not judgments on the work of art. "Art [*schöne Kunst*], on the contrary," he writes, "is a mode of representation, which is for itself purposeful" (ibid., section 44). But after Kant has first completely restricted himself to the definition of the judgment of taste, he then transposes the characteristics he has found onto the work of art and thus lays the foundation stone for a metaphysics of art that, even today, frames the context of what we call aesthetic experience.

The debate about the autonomy of art is taken up in France in the nineteenth century. The mutually contradictory positions are not easy to disentangle. For instance, the Saint-Simonians take up the Enlightenment idea that assigns to art the task of making sensual abstract ideas and acquiring thereby mass effectiveness; on the other hand, this same group inclines to see a religious function in art, and to view the artist as bearer of revelation. Théophile Gautier, in contrast, disappointed by the outcome of the July Revolution, already in the 1830s proclaims the turning away of the artist from society. His polemic against the principle of usefulness in art, in the preface to *Mademoiselle de Maupin* (1835), is well known: "There is nothing truly beautiful except that which serves no end; everything that is useful is ugly, for it is the expression of some need. . . . The most useful place in a house is the latrine." Not only the aggressivity of this polemic, but also the endless series of immorality trials (those of Charles Baudelaire and Gustave Flaubert are only the most famous), show that freedom from moral claims may indeed have been theoretically permitted to art but was denied to it in practice. This contradiction leaves its stamp on the concept of art of Victor Cousin, whose *Cours de la philosophie* (1836) can hardly be overestimated in its influence on the notions of art of the educated bourgeoisie in nineteenth-century France. [*See* Cousin.] Cousin does insist on the autonomy of art: "art is no more in the service of religion and of morality than it serves the agreeable and the useful"; (Cousin, 1836, pp. 224, 261) but since he also departs from the unity of the true, good, and beautiful he finally subordinates art again to morality.

There can be no doubt that the failure of the 1848 revolution crucially encouraged the radicalization of the autonomy of art. To the degree that social engagement became as good as impossible, the autonomy principle's inherent tendency to purity of the aesthetic had actually to establish itself. "One sees finally, toward the end of the nineteenth century, the accentuation of a remarkable will to isolate definitively Poetry from any other essence than its own (Valéry, 1957, vol. I, p. 207). Valéry's statement holds true not only for poetry, but also, with corresponding temporal delays, for visual art.

There are, however, different interpretations of the principle of autonomy. Flaubert dreamed of a "book about nothing," but his two most important books live precisely from the tension between their formal claims and the ugly everyday world of his age. The same is true of Baudelaire's *Fleurs du mal*. It is Stéphane Mallarmé who first renounces this tension, in order to drive the autonomy of art into that vertiginous height where the "absolute" is recognized as made by men, and where it coincides with the "game." "We know, captives of an absolute formula that, certainly, is nothing but what is. Incontinent to put aside nonetheless, under the pretext, the trap, would accuse our inconsequence, denying the pleasure that we want to have: for this beyond is its agent, and the motor, I should say, if I did not find it distasteful to operate, in public, the impious disassemblage of fiction and consequently of the literary mechanism, to spread out the principal element or nothing. But, I

venerate how, by trickery, one projects—to some forbidden elevation of lightning!—the conscious lack in us of that which explodes up there. What aim does this all serve—a game (Mallarmé, 1945, p. 647).

Mallarmé here pursues the destruction of the belief in the substantiality of art ("the impious disassemblage of fiction" [ibid.]), even when he pretends not to do so. The argument is simple: only that which is exists, nature and the world of material objects. Humans may add nothing to this ("nature has taken place, one will not add to it" [ibid.]). The belief in art as an absolute is only a bait, certainly a necessary one, if there is to be aesthetic pleasure. This latter depends on a mechanism (Mallarmé carries through his technological metaphor consequently here) whose particularity consists in the fact that that which keeps it moving is nonexistent. More precisely: that which moves this mechanism is only the projection of a lack, thus a deception. Mallarmé unveils the metaphysical ground of art as an empty postulation, without this last's losing any of its value; for he discovers at the same time in "an ennui regarding things if they establish themselves solidly and preponderantly" the force that generates the longing for the ideality of art. Art is thus simultaneously the absolute *and* an empty game.

The importance of Mallarmé for the history of the autonomy of art cannot be overemphasized. On the one hand, he unveils the secret of art as a vacant arcanum; on the other hand, the principle of autonomy, in his work, takes hold of the artwork itself. Flaubert's idea of a "book about nothing" is thus elevated as if to a principle; that is, the semantic relations that tie the artwork to social reality are broken off. This was not yet the case in the original concept of autonomy as it was developed at the end of the eighteenth century. There, autonomy means, as we have seen, the status of art within society, its independence relative to moral claims and demands for social utility. Art is thereby understood as an institution in which the principles of that which is theoretically true and morally right have no application (or at least no immediate one). For the artwork, a domain of freedom is thereby opened up—also one for the theoretization of social problems. This domain is only limited by the principle of the unity of the work. Under the impression of the irreconcilability of art and modern society, this position is now radicalized in such a way that the work of art may only express its own impossibility. From the perspective of the artist, Mallarmé formulates this in a conversation with Jules Huret: "For me, the case of a poet in this society which does not permit him to live is that of a man who isolates himself to sculpt his own tomb" (Mallarmé 1945, p. 869).

The historical avant-garde movements such as Futurism, Dadaism, and Surrealism react to this situation in the crisis period around World War I. However divergent the programs and political positions of these individual movements may be, they are unanimous in their fundamental questioning of the autonomy of art. At least in their heroic phase, it is, for the Surrealists, not a question of producing works of art, but rather of revolutionizing life itself. The formula "to practice poetry" from the first *Manifesto of Surrealism* (1924) preserves this intention: it is not a matter of writing poems, but rather of letting poetry become practical: for example, to return the potential of world-forming, which in autonomous art is severed from the world, back to the latter. [*See* Surrealism.] Out of despair over a world that mutilates individuals and in which art consequently remains impotent, the avant-garde drew a radical consequence: only through an attack on the autonomy of art itself did they believe that they could unleash the forces contained in art and use them for a revolutionary change in society.

The attack of the historical avant-garde movements on the institution of art led neither to art's sublation nor to the revolutionizing of the everyday; rather, the nonworks of the avant-garde have been absorbed into the canon or into the museum. It would be false, however, to draw from this failure the conclusion that the avant-garde had no effect. Its effect is very considerable, but it affects less the relation of art and life than the self-understanding of art. Since Marcel Duchamp, in 1917, sent a factory-produced urinal to a nonjuried exhibition, the question of what a work of art is has become a necessary moment of artistic production. The avant-garde movements have robbed autonomous art of its self-evidence, and bequeathed to every post-avant-garde artist who wants to be up to the demands of the time doubts as to the meaningfulness of his or her actions (this may be already read in the text of Mallarmé cited earlier). Even beyond this, the avant-garde has confronted the artist with the question of what it is that one does when one produces works of art. The necessity of always seeking anew an answer to this question—a question that emanates from the avant-garde movements onto the art of the entire twentieth century—and of pursuing this search not alongside artistic production, but as an integral part of the latter, deeply alters the problem of autonomy.

This may be best explained with the example of Josef Beuys, who has depotentialized traditional oppositions. [*See* Beuys.] Beuys knows that in bourgeois society art will never be other than art, and that social ineffectiveness is the flip side of autonomy. Based on this insight, he seeks to leave the ghetto of art. Thereby he meets with the avant-garde project of leading art back into lived praxis, and also to this project's failure. His position is aporetical. He can neither "return" to the production of autonomous works (for thereby he would betray the claims formulated by the avant-garde) nor take up the project of the avant-garde (which has failed). He must thus attempt to bind the mutually contradictory, that is, to create works, but in such a way that these latter are absorbed in an intention that goes beyond them. He must invent a new place for art, which is neither within nor outside of art, but on the edge that separates artistic action from other forms of social action. It is an impossible place, which exists nowhere, but rather must in each case be created in the moment. In this movement, the autonomy of art is both always assumed and overstepped. Instead of exposing a weakness in Beuys's position, this contradiction proves to be the most precise answer so far given to the aporetical situation in which art finds itself after the historical avant-garde movements.

[*See also* Avant-Garde; *and* Mallarmé.]

BIBLIOGRAPHY

Bénichou, Paul. *Le Temps des prophètes: Doctrines de l'âge romantique.* Paris, 1977.
Cousin, Victor. *Cours de philosophie.* Paris, 1836.
Mallarmé, Stéphane. *Œuvres complètes.* Edited by Henri Mondor and G. Jean-Aubry. Paris, 1945.
Moritz, Karl Philipp. *Werke in zwei Bänden.* 2 vols. Edited by J. Jahn. Berlin, 1973.
Valéry, Paul. *Avant-propos à la connaissance de la déesse.* In *Œuvres,* edited by Jean Hytier, vol. 1. Paris, 1957.

PETER BÜRGER

Autonomy and Its Feminist Critics

Aesthetic autonomy is an ideal with a distinguished lineage, its roots lying in the eighteenth-century works of British empiricists (interested in the psychological effects of art and aesthetic experience) and Immanuel Kant's *Critique of Judgment* (1790). Commitment to this notion—that works of art are valuable in their own right as objects of aesthetic contemplation—plays an essential role in modernism and formalist theories of art. Additionally, this idea has largely defined the discipline of Anglo-American aesthetics.

In recent decades, however, theories of aesthetic autonomy have come under attack by feminist aestheticians, art historians, and art critics. Feminists are not the first to object to traditional autonomous aesthetics, but the grounds of objection are new. Central among many arguments is the claim that an autonomous aesthetic—and the Kantian tradition out of which it grows—operates with an unacknowledged gender bias that infects purportedly impartial standards of evaluation and distorts judgments about which works of art and artists are significant. As a result, women have been consigned to the minor leagues of art history—not for lack of talent or ability, but because the standards by which they have been judged are discriminatory.

The effects of this critique have been striking. Feminist thinking has prompted a widespread examination of the established understanding of artistic production, reception, and evaluation. Even within mainstream Anglo-American aesthetics, the Kantian model no longer holds the place it once did: its advocates now find themselves forced to defend assumptions and methods once taken for granted. Furthermore, feminist criticisms of aesthetic autonomy merit scrutiny not only for their impact on contemporary aesthetic theory and the light they throw on Anglo-

American aesthetic tradition, but for their intrinsic interest. Before undertaking this investigation, however, it is necessary first to get clear about *what* is being rejected. What, then, is the theory of aesthetic autonomy?

Aesthetic Autonomy. The terms *aesthetic autonomy* and *autonomy of art* are used in a variety of ways. Who or what is "autonomous"? The artist? The work of art? The institutions in which art is displayed? The standards by which it is evaluated? And what does it mean to call any or all of these autonomous? Is the basic idea that works of art are valuable in their own right? "Separate from life"? Independent? Politically disengaged? Or that they—the artists or the institutions of the art world—*should* be?

These questions are difficult to answer for two reasons: first, these terms are used in a variety of different ways, and second, none of those who make claims in the name of aesthetic autonomy—formalist art critics such as Roger Fry and Clive Bell, literary figures such as Oscar Wilde, and a variety of aestheticians working within the Anglo-American philosophical tradition—have provided a fully worked-out, systematic account of what allegiance to autonomy comes to. Nonetheless, it is possible to formulate the idea of aesthetic autonomy as two separate, but related, claims: a claim about the nature of art and a claim about appreciation and evaluation.

The first, the "nature of art" claim states that works of art are independent, intrinsically valuable, and universal. "Independent" means that works of art are not mere copies of nature; "intrinsically valuable" means that their value resides in themselves, not in some extra-artistic end; and "universal" means that art—at least great art—transcends its originating influences, speaking not only for its particular author or culture but "for all mankind."

According to the second claim, the "appreciation and evaluation" claim, the proper experience of art requires a disinterested attitude, that is, one disengaged from the needs and wants of everyday life; art's evaluation requires the application of exclusively aesthetic criteria. The idea of a disinterested attitude has its origins in Kant's *Critique of Judgment*; a related, but popularized variant—the notion of "psychical distance"—was introduced by Edward Bullough in 1912 to exclude what he termed "practical" interests in the work of art, for example, an interest in its origins, influence, or purpose, its market value or moral effect. Putting aside these practical, nonaesthetic interests makes possible attention to, and detached reflection on, the work of art "in its own right," that is, *as* a work of art. This in turn involves appreciating and judging the work in strictly aesthetic terms. [*See* Attitude, *article on* Aesthetic Attitude; Bullough; Disinterestedness; *and* Kant.]

These claims reflect a way of thinking that arose in the eighteenth century with the emergence of a concept of "fine art," a concept associated with the Western European tradition of high art. This outlook assigns an elevated status to the object of art. As it develops, this tradition comes to see the work of art as a unique object, a product of genius, an "original." Its appeal is timeless and universal, its appreciation and evaluation purely aesthetic matters.

Historically speaking, this understanding of the nature of art and the demands of aesthetic evaluation is associated with formalism. Formalism is a theory of aesthetic value and a theory about art and artists. The formalist theory of aesthetic value begins by defining the aesthetic in terms of formal properties. Formal properties are the perceptually available features of an object's external form (the line, color, and shape of a painting, for example) as distinguished from its content (e.g., what the painting represents, what its subject is). It is these formal properties that make art *art* and give it value *as* art—and it is to these properties that the properly engaged spectator attends. [*See* Formalism.]

Formalists regard aesthetic value, so defined, as utterly distinct from other kinds of value and hold that it alone properly determines artistic quality. On this account, it is a work's formal properties that evoke and sustain a state of noninstrumental, contemplative attention—a state thought to be valuable in its own right. Considerations other than formal merit (e.g., of a work's historical origins, political content, or social effect) are either irrelevant or of merely secondary importance.

The formalist theory about art and artists can be captured in the slogan "art is separate from life." At the core of the loose configuration of ideas to which this slogan refers is the idea that works of art belong to a separate domain, that they are, and should be, understood in terms drawn not from everyday life but from the world of art itself. In practice, this has come to mean appreciating and evaluating works of art not as cultural objects with complex relations to politics, religion, economics, and so on, but as isolated objects of strictly aesthetic contemplation.

Formalist theory thus provides a rationale for the two broad claims of aesthetic autonomy: that works of art have a special nature and require for their appreciation and evaluation a distinct attitude, one disengaged from everyday needs and wants.

The proposition that making or enjoying art is a special form of human activity, in need of no external justification, and that aesthetic experience has an important—perhaps unique—role in human experience, is an attractive one. Equally, the insistence that works of art should be judged on artistic grounds, not on practical or moral or political grounds, appears to have a strong claim on our assent. Why then, and on what grounds, do feminists reject the theory of aesthetic autonomy?

Why Feminists Reject Aesthetic Autonomy. Feminism's main quarrel with the doctrine of aesthetic autonomy is a quarrel with formalism. Its feminist critics reject both the picture of art and the theory of aesthetic value advanced by formalism. They argue that the formalist picture of art is false; the formalist model of appreciation and standards of evaluation is, they contend, too narrow. What is needed is a revised conception of evaluative standards and a broader understanding of what art is and can be.

Feminist theorists maintain that formalism misunderstands the relationship between works of art and other social and cultural forces. This misconception arises from a deeper misunderstanding of the nature of art. Work of arts are not "separate from life." They are rooted *in* life, outgrowths of larger social, religious, economic, and other cultural forces and the immediate concerns of the time and place in which they were created. This view returns the work of art from a separate realm of pure aesthetics (and the removed institutional setting of the museum and gallery) to the everyday world of social and political praxis. Art is no longer the revered product of individual genius, best experienced by individuals in a state of disinterested contemplation, but part of a complex, tightly woven cultural fabric. Social and cultural conditions frame both its production and its reception.

Seen from this perspective, feminists argue, works of art are not correctly characterized as universal. Works of art are not timeless; they are historically rooted in evolving cultural practices. Far from speaking to or for human beings generally, works of art—especially those esteemed by the European tradition of high art—typically speak the language of a mostly male, educated elite. This language must be learned, and learning it involves access to institutions and practices that historically have excluded women and members of other disenfranchised groups. The feminist reexamination of the history of art finds that, contrary to traditional claims for its universality, art is typically created not for "man," but for men.

Finally, feminists question the intrinsic value of art. Art, it is pointed out, is not uniformly enlightening and liberating. Even highly esteemed art (canonical "greats" such as Mark Twain, D. H. Lawrence, and Norman Mailer) is often exclusionary in ways that many find alienating, degrading, and dispiriting. For some feminists, the implicit or explicit misogyny or racism of these works undercuts or outweighs their literary or strictly aesthetic value. For others, the existence of such works points to the need to enlarge the category of the aesthetic to accommodate consideration of a work's moral or political point of view, social effect, and so on. Common to both perspectives is the thought that the value of the work of art—aesthetic or otherwise—cannot simply be assumed.

This brings us to feminist critiques of the formalist model of appreciation and evaluation. About appreciation, feminists make a simple but telling point: even the most sophisticated formal analysis is inadequate in understanding many works of art, particularly works of political art, for example, Francisco José de Goya's *Caprichos,* Judy Chicago's *Dinner Party,* Maya Lin's *Vietnam War Memorial,* or Robert Mapplethorpe's *X Portfolio.* These works *can* be looked at as formal configurations of line and color, but when viewed in such terms, they cannot be properly understood. In the case of political art, to leave aside nonformal considerations such as historical setting, political content, or the work's intended audience is, feminists argue, to disregard important features of the *work of art* itself. The same argument is made with respect to many other categories of art: religious art such as Dante Alighieri's *Inferno,* John Milton's *Paradise Lost,* folk art, Marcel Duchamp's ready-mades. From a feminist perspective, then, the recommendation that we look at art by setting aside such nonformal matters is wholly misguided.

Feminist criticisms of formalist evaluation are more complicated. Much of the discussion here is motivated by recent work in art history and centers on the actual practices of formalist evaluation. These evaluative practices involve classifying and ranking works of art according to formal success or failure. Evaluation on these grounds is meant to be purely formal and hence objective in the sense of being independent of particulars such as the artist's gender, race, training, artistic stature, marital status, and so on. The objection here is that these practices are biased. While purporting to be objective and impartial, formalist judgments reflect and advance preferences that have little or nothing to do with formal significance and technical achievement.

Art historian Linda Nochlin (1988) argues, for example, that an allegedly "purely aesthetic" preference for large-scale historical painting—a type of painting that from the Renaissance through most of the nineteenth century epitomized the highest category of art—effectively excluded women from the ranks of great painters. Women during this period, she points out, were banned from attending life drawing classes, thus making them ill equipped to handle the large-scale human figures demanded by history painting in the grand style represented by Eugène Delacroix. The "domestic" genres of painting that women could and did master, such as small-scale still lifes, reputedly fell lower in the hierarchy of art-historical importance.

An unfair and unacknowledged gender bias operates not only in the way art gets evaluated, but also, it is claimed, in the way art gets defined. Because, for the formalist, art means "fine art," certain kinds of artistic activity (pottery making, quilting, weaving), certain materials (cloth rather than paint, for example), and certain artistic ends (e.g., practical or decorative rather than formal ones) tend to get placed outside the designation of art altogether. These categories of "applied art" or craft, are precisely those in which women have traditionally worked. Thus, whatever technical mastery or formal achievement women have historically demonstrated, a formalist definition of art renders most of their artistic labor invisible.

In brief, its critics charge, prevailing formalist standards of classification and evaluation are discriminatory: the product of male-defined assumptions about gender roles (e.g., how women think, how they paint, what they find interesting) and art itself (e.g., what is artistically important or valuable, what is appropriate subject matter, what kind of experience art is meant to provide).

It is worth noting that although this line of objection establishes the gender bias of much formalist evaluative *practice*, it is not a cogent argument against the formalist *theory* of aesthetic value. From the fact that formalist practice often departs from purely formal considerations, it does not follow that there is anything wrong with the ideal of formal assessment. It sometimes looks, however, as if feminists are drawing just that conclusion, holding that evaluating works of art in terms of color and line (or other strictly formal terms) is inherently a gender-biased process. If this is the claim, then one wants to know in what exactly the gender-bias consists—in the preference for work of formal significance or in the exclusion of women from the opportunities for training and practice necessary to achieve formal mastery? Historically, of course, even color and line have tended to be characterized in gendered terms (the bold, jutting lines of the masculine; the soft, curved lines of the feminine, and so on), and this feminists rightly find objectionable. The legitimate target of this objection, however, is not formalist assessment, but the contingent practices of its implementation.

Although its feminist critics have not established the gender bias of formal assessment per se, they are correct in pointing to the narrowness of formalism's conception of art and its theory of aesthetic value. Much of the world's art, including many canonical works, cannot be fully understood or appreciated in strictly formal terms. This is not, of course, a specifically feminist point. What is specifically feminist is the claim that the particular ways art gets defined and evaluated tend to exclude or denigrate most women's art. But it is a mistake to explain this exclusion in terms of formalism alone. Its sources are much broader, pervading traditional art history and aesthetic theory—formalist and otherwise.

What is needed to rectify this imbalance is nothing less than a *new* conceptual framework for the definition and evaluation of art. What that framework would look like—whether it would be gender-neutral or properly gendered—and whether it would be commensurable with the old are important, but as yet unanswered, questions.

What to Make of the Feminist Critique. The feminist critique of autonomy (which largely amounts to a critique of formalism) has two welcome features. First, it has opened the way for a more complex and nuanced conception of art: a conception of art better able to account for the many different forms art takes, the varied roles it plays in human experience, and the complex reasons we have for valuing it. Second, the questioning of autonomy has broadened the framework of artistic appreciation and evaluation. Some art

is best approached from a state of disinterested contemplation; some is not. With many works, a variety of other responses—historical, sociological, political, religious, personal—may be useful and desirable, even essential. These other responses are not mere propaedeutic to appreciation; they are inextricably part of it. Although feminist theorists have yet to provide a full-fledged theory of criticism, they have articulated the issues to which any adequate alternative to a formalist theory must respond.

But if the rejection of aesthetic autonomy has these beneficial results, it also runs two risks. The first is that in emphasizing the social and political character of art, critics of autonomy may lose sight of or underestimate the elements that make art *art*. It would be difficult, if not impossible, to give a definitive list of these "art-making" elements, but the general idea is familiar enough. One need not be a formalist to want to talk not only about "what" the work says, but "how." This will include attention to formal matters, but also to such nonformal matters as the use of symbolism or genre conventions. The worry is that once the traditional distinction between aesthetic and nonaesthetic considerations is blurred, the evaluation of art will be reduced to the straightforward analysis of social and political content.

Nonetheless, the concern that art might be reduced to propaganda ought not to be exaggerated. Acknowledging that works of art may have political content and political consequences does not entail that political considerations are the *only* factors relevant to their evaluation—nor does it imply that political considerations must invariably take priority. Formalist theories of art render the political irrelevant to the evaluation of art, but the reverse is not the case: a view that recognizes the political character of art—feminist or otherwise—need not deny the relevance of art's formal features. The possibility of analyzing art in a broadened social and cultural context *and* remaining sensitive to its formal features is demonstrated by the sophisticated feminist criticism of Nochlin, Lucy Lippard (1976), Rita Felski (1989), and others.

The second risk feminists run is that of unwittingly exposing art to political interference. Might they not be reopening the door to censorship that formalism helped to close? Historically, the separation of the aesthetic and the political has provided an argument both against artistic censorship, narrowly defined, and what John Stuart Mill called "the tyranny of the majority." When threatened with interference, artists and their supporters simply appealed to the idea of the "autonomy" of art, claiming the illegitimacy of any evaluative criteria other than the purely aesthetic. But having abandoned strictly "aesthetic" (i.e., formal) criteria in favor of a wider set of political and social considerations, feminist critics of autonomy need a principled basis for distinguishing legitimate from nonlegitimate grounds of evaluation. If a work's misogyny may be relevant to its assessment as art, then why not its failure to promote the "family values" demanded by Senator Jesse Helms and others on the political right?

It thus appears that aesthetics faces a dilemma: *either* adopt a theory of autonomy that protects art from the exigencies of political fashion but isolates it from life, *or* opt for a political conception of art that integrates art with life at the price of compromising its independence.

The Proper Understanding of Aesthetic Autonomy. This impasse can be escaped by revising the notion of aesthetic autonomy. Aesthetic autonomy, properly understood, is the idea that works of art deserve a protected space, a special normative standing. "Protected space" does not refer to the obvious safeguards, such as velvet ropes, railings, and alarm systems needed to preserve works of art from vandals and the overly curious. Nor does granting such a "space" require art's isolation from the social and political world. The idea of aesthetic autonomy has historically come to be associated with formalism and "nonpolitical" art, but it need not be. Nothing about logic or the nature of art or the aesthetic requires this connection. (One thing that unites formalists and feminists is precisely their failure to disentangle these notions.) Autonomy simply requires that works of art—be their concerns political, "purely" aesthetic, or somewhere in between—remain under the control of artists and the institutions of the art world in which they work. It is this figurative space (this special normative standing) that the literal spaces of the museum and gallery symbolize. Understood in these terms, the aim of aesthetic autonomy is not to isolate artists or to separate art from the rest of life, but to protect art and artists from political interference.

The idea that art deserves special protections is traditionally defended by appealing to the special character of art's formal properties, but it is also possible to defend on straightforward political grounds. The basic idea here is that works of art deserve protection not because they are detached from life or disconnected from social forces, but precisely because they often play an important social and political role: pushing beyond or challenging existing ways of seeing and thinking about the world. This characterization of art as an independent, critical voice—as a mirror to catch the conscience of kings—is an important strand of the tradition of aesthetic autonomy, though one for the most part overshadowed by the historical association of autonomy with formalism. The key to preserving the idea of aesthetic autonomy is to free the notion from its association with formalism.

One can both insist on the importance of granting art a protected space, as autonomy's defenders do, *and* acknowledge, with many feminists, the wrongheadedness of the proposition that art must be apolitical or disengaged. One of the best reasons for endorsing the principle of autonomy is precisely the thought that art can play an important political role. The fact that art—that particular works of art—can

play this role provides a reason for thinking that art in general deserves protection. For it is precisely the progressive political role that art can play—a role that formalism asks us to set aside—that frequently places works of art in jeopardy. The idea that art should be free to put itself in jeopardy and that when in jeopardy it should be protected is, of course, a liberal one. But it is an idea that feminists (whatever their other quarrels with liberalism) have a special *political* reason to accept.

[*See also* Feminism.]

BIBLIOGRAPHY

Bell, Clive. *Art.* London, 1914.

Brand, Peggy Zeglin, and Carolyn Korsmeyer, eds. *Feminism and Tradition in Aesthetics.* University Park, Pa., 1995.

Bullough, Edward. "'Psychical Distance' as a Factor in Art and an Aesthetic Principle." *British Journal of Psychology* 5 (1912–1913): 87–118.

Devereaux, Mary. "The Philosophical and Political Implications of the Feminist Critique of Aesthetic Autonomy." In *Turning the Century: Feminist Criticism in the 1990s,* edited by Glynis Carr, pp. 164–186. Special issue of *Bucknell Review* 36.2 (1992).

Devereaux, Mary. "Protected Space: Politics, Censorship, and the Arts." *Journal of Aesthetics and Art Criticism* 51.2 (Spring 1993): 207–215.

Duncan, Carol. *The Aesthetics of Power: Essays in Critical Art History.* Cambridge and New York, 1993.

Felski, Rita. *Beyond Feminist Aesthetics: Feminist Literature and Social Change.* Cambridge, Mass., 1989.

Fry, Roger. *Vision and Design.* Edited by J. B. Bullen. New York and Oxford, 1981.

Hein, Hilde, and Carolyn Korsmeyer, eds. *Aesthetics in Feminist Perspective.* Bloomington, Ind., 1993.

Kant, Immanuel. *Critique of Judgment* (1790). Translated by Werner S. Pluhar. Indianapolis, 1987.

Korsmeyer, Carolyn. "Pleasure: Reflections on Aesthetics and Feminism." *Journal of Aesthetics and Art Criticism* 51.2 (Spring 1993): 199–206.

Lippard, Lucy R. *From the Center: Feminist Essays on Women's Art.* New York, 1976.

McClary, Susan. *Feminine Endings: Music, Gender, and Sexuality.* Minneapolis, 1991.

Mulvey, Laura. "Visual Pleasure and Narrative Cinema." In *Visual and Other Pleasures,* pp. 14–26. Bloomington, Ind., 1989.

Nochlin, Linda. *Women, Art, and Power, and Other Essays.* New York, 1988.

Pollock, Griselda. *Vision and Difference: Femininity, Feminism, and the Histories of Art.* London and New York, 1988.

Wilde, Oscar. Preface. *The Picture of Dorian Gray.* Paris, 1910.

Wolff, Janet. *Aesthetics and the Sociology of Art.* 2d ed. Ann Arbor, 1993.

MARY DEVEREAUX

Autonomy and Architecture

The argument for the aesthetic autonomy of architecture—the notion that architecture is a self-enclosed cultural project in continual search for purely immanent meaning—might, at first gloss, be seen as just an extension of similar arguments of Clement Greenberg (1961) in the visual arts. And yet, whereas Greenberg's call for autonomy was Kantian in its derivation and, at least in part, a direct response to social conditions during World War II, the issue of autonomy reemerged in architecture theory as the developments in structuralism were assimilated in the 1960s and 1970s. And whereas Greenberg's call for the rigor of a removed, autonomous practice was a defense against a bereft and impoverished mass culture, architecture's autonomy thesis never made the same strong distinction between "high" architecture and anonymous buildings or the spaces of popular culture. Architecture's most felt threat came not from an external "kitsch" but from its own utilitarian legacy.

By the 1960s, the doctrine of functionalism—the intersection of brute facts of utility with objective design methodologies and standardized means of production—had given rise to positivist inquiries of the behavioral sciences, sociology, and operations research that sought to quantify architecture's characteristics, to explain architecture away in terms of something else. The contemporaneous importation and transformation of European structuralist criticisms were thought by many architects and theorists to offer potential frameworks and strategies for thinking architecture back into its own as a discipline, a practice, and a mode of knowledge.

Aldo Rossi, whose influential *L'architettura della città* (1966) helped launch the contemporary autonomy argument, explicitly draws on Claude Lévi-Strauss and Roman Jakobson in his insistence that "the explanation of urban facts in terms of their function must be rejected when it seeks to illustrate their constitution and form. Such an explanation is repressive rather than enlightening because it inhibits the study of forms and a knowledge of the world of architecture according to its own authentic laws" (Rossi, 1982). Like structural anthropologists, Rossi treats the city as an artifact in which one can find fixed structures and laws of transformation. An architecture based on an analysis of these typological laws was asserted as a counterideological form of resistance to the demands placed on architecture as a commercial service industry as well as to positivist science.

Peter Eisenman, perhaps more than any contemporary architect, has sought a space for architecture outside the traditional parameters of the economical, the utilitarian, and even the built, in what may properly be called a conceptual architecture—one that seeks through an aesthetic withdrawal to replace the built object with a diagram of its formative procedures, "laying bare the device," investigating and exposing the most basic disciplinary conventions of architectural practice while at the same time liquidating the last vestiges of sensuous architectural experience. Between 1967 and 1978, influenced primarily by structuralist linguistics, Eisenman's writings and projects were concerned almost exclusively with isolating and elaborating the architectural elements and operations that would ensure autonomy and self-reflexivity of the architectural object so that the object could

verify and purify itself in resistance to all encircling determinants of architectural form. Eisenman's notion of "cardboard architecture" refuses material as a meaningful attribute of the object; "postfunctionalism" shifts our engagement with form from utilization and even inhabitation to a consideration of architectural elements as the material support of signals or notations for a conceptual state of the object; and his emphasis on the syntactic over the semantic dimension of form proposes an underlying system of architectural principles and rules of organization—deep, conceptual structures from which various architectures can be generated independent of contextual contingencies (1970, 1976, 1987).

If Rossi and Eisenman—who are practicing architects as well as theorists—represent the position that, in the "pure" materials of architecture, one might find a source of counterideological resistance, the historian Manfredo Tafuri (1976, 1987) represents that position's most radical inverse: that architecture, *when it is most itself*—most pure, most rational, most attendent to its own techniques—is *then* the most efficient ideological agent of capitalist planification and unwitting victim of capitalism's historical closure. Historicizing architecture's intellectual project, from the Enlightenment to the present, in the agonized matrix of the bourgeois metropolis, Tafuri formulates the entire cycle of modernism as a unitary development in which the historical avant-gardes' visions of a social and formal utopia come to be recognized as an idealization of capitalism, a transfiguration of the latter's rationality into the rationality of autonomous form. Like the blasé personality of Georg Simmel, bourgeois art and architecture essentially and contradictorily register the very forces that assure their ineffectual functioning in the system that sponsored them. Having first been exploded by the shock and distress of the metropolis (Expressionism), and then, with a sardonic detachment, taken an inventory of its surrounding remains (Dadaism), bourgeois thought must conclude that "the subject" itself—the individual, art, or architecture—is the only impediment to the smooth development of the fully rationalized technocratic plan that was to become the total system of capital. One had to pass from Edvard Munch's cathartic, expressionist *Scream* (1895) to Ludwig Hilberseimer's metropolitan machine (1924) to Peter Eisenman's houses of cards—the ultimate architectural sign of self-liquidation through the autonomy of formal construction—wherein the homeostatic regulation of form becomes the ideological training ground for life in the desacralized, distracted, posthumanist world. "Among all the avant-garde movements, autonomy of formal construction no longer necessarily meant controlling daily experience through form. They were now disposed to accept the idea that it is experience that dominates the subject. The problem was *to plan the disappearance of the subject,* to cancel the anguish caused by the pathetic (or ridiculous) resistance of the individual to the structures of domination that close in upon him, to indicate the voluntary and docile submission to those structures of domination as the promised land of universal planning" (Tafuri 1976, p. 73).

Thus does architectural ideology resolve the contradiction between the internal, subjective shock of modern experience and the external, structural totality of the production system: this is its utopia. For Tafuri, that utopianism—against whatever other aims and local concrete effects it may have—ends up ushering into being the universal, systemic planification of capitalism, all the while concealing that fundamental function behind the rhetoric of its manifestos and within the purity of its forms. The struggle of architecture to "purify" itself, to rationalize itself through autonomous formal operations, alerts us not to architecture's success but to the historical moment as a limiting condition, one that shuts down certain social functions that architecture previously performed.

Although Tafuri writes from a Marxian position, his analysis is not incommensurate with that of contemporary architecture's other ur-theorist, Colin Rowe, who is a comparatively pure formalist. Rowe agrees that the historical architectural avant-garde shared common ideological roots with Marxism and, also, a Marxian philosophical ambition to interfuse "form" and "word"—variously articulated as expression and content, system and concept, practice and theory, building and politics. That the fusion process ultimately failed for reasons that are integral to the history of modernization itself entailed a shift, Rowe reasons, in the terms in which the experience of modernity was thought: a shift from modernity, fully developed, as the essential desired achievement of architecture to *modernity as architecture's limiting condition.*

Feeling the force of this shift, Rowe forthrightly exposes what seems to him to be the only possible choice for the neo-avant-garde: adhere to the forms, the "*physique*-flesh" of the historical avant-garde and relegate the "*morale*-word" to incantation; for, if the latter has been reduced to "a constellation of escapist myths," the former "possess an eloquence and a flexibility which continues now to be as overwhelming as it was then" (Rowe, 1972, pp. 6, 7). The measure of architecture no longer lies in the efficacy with which it prefigures a new and better social world, but rather in its achievement, within the contingent historical conditions of the modern, of meeting the demands of the flesh, as it were, of elevating form as its own language without reference to external sentiments, rationales, or indeed, social visions. Rowe rewrites Lévi-Strauss's concept of the bricoleur, over and against the engineer or the scientist, as a technique of architectural "collage," in which the history of architecture and painting constitutes a repository of formal material available for recombination. The plastic and spatial inventions of Cubism and Constructivism, Giuseppe Terragni and Le Corbusier, remain the standard specific to the ideologically indifferent medium of architecture. But it is through acceptance of that standard and the repetition of

just those simulacra that the contemporary architect aspires to be intelligible. From Rowe's position, the true potential of architecture lies not in the prospect of its popular or technological relevance, but in the possibility of its autonomy. And, for both Tafuri and Rowe, the struggle of architecture to rationalize itself through autonomous formal operations signals not architecture's success, but the way it comes to grief against its historical situation, which has shut down certain social and aesthetic functions that architecture previously performed.

For all its advances since the early formulations of Rossi, Eisenman, Tafuri, and Rowe, architecture theory remained largely within the dialectic between the universality of autonomous form and the universality of form's historical contingency until the mid-1980s, when a younger generation of theorists effected a shift from the structuralist- and semiotics-based problematic dominant in the 1970s to new affinities with cultural criticism (including concerns with textual strategies, constructions of subjectivity and gender, power and property, geopolitics, and other themes). Although considerations of the internal, autonomous workings of architecture were never completely abandoned, attempts were made to transcode architecture's effects into various other discourses, to recalibrate them according to what was sayable or thinkable in the idiolects of deconstruction, psychoanalysis, complexity theory, and other imported systems. These systems were not merely yoked together with architecture; rather, something of a shift of perspective and level took place in which the specific autonomous forms, operations, and practices could now more clearly be seen not as simply determined by a specific historical context, nor as free from any contextual constraint, but rather as reciprocally producing concepts whose ultimate horizon of effect lay outside of architecture's internal systems of meaning construction.

What recent discussions of the autonomy thesis have realized is that, to the extent that a theory like Tafuri's succeeds in its uncovering of the ideological imperative, or a theory like Eisenman's succeeds in its predicting of the counterideological effects of a building, both types of theory also fail, because the more powerful the model constructed, the less chance of any resistance or transformation or excess on the part of the architecture. One might say that a more "true" autonomy thesis must reserve for the architectural object the chance to provoke radically new responses not anticipated by a prior reading instrument that would try in vain to account for it in advance or even describe it afterward. In other words, an adequate autonomy thesis must partially undo itself in order to acknowledge what the building does differently.

Architecture theory's phobia of a language of *sentiments* that might register the desires and pleasures of things, images, and experiences suggests that the autonomy thesis be understood as a "reaction formation" during a "latency period" of architectural theory. Theory has handed architecture the fig leaf of autonomy and channeled architecture's libido into historical imperatives and counterideological resistances. However much these theories of autonomy are in advance of older forms of sublimation (historicism, functionalism, and the like), to read architecture as an isomorph of the categories and operations of theory can be as reductive as those readings that trace architecture to an inevitable reflection of a wholly predictable technological or economic context, that give no reciprocal force to architecture as a social production. In our successful theorizing of autonomy we have theorized ourselves out of the means to see architecture as exceeding our theories.

[*See also* Architecture; *and* Ideology.]

BIBLIOGRAPHY

Autonomous Architecture. Special issue of *Harvard Architecture Review* 3 (Winter 1984).

Bedard, Jean-François, ed. *Cities of Artificial Excavation: The Work of Peter Eisenman, 1978–1988.* New York, 1994.

Eisenman, Peter. "Notes on Conceptual Architecture: Towards a Definition." *Design Quarterly* 78–79 (1970): 1–5.

Eisenman, Peter. "Post-Functionalism." *Oppositions* 6 (Fall 1976).

Eisenman, Peter. *Houses of Cards.* New York and Oxford, 1987.

Greenberg, Clement. *Art and Culture: Critical Essays.* Boston, 1961.

Moneo, Rafael. *The Solitude of Buildings.* Cambridge, Mass., 1986.

Rossi, Aldo. *L'architettura della città* (1966). Translated by Diane Ghirardo and Joan Ockman as *The Architecture of the City.* Cambridge, Mass., 1982.

Rowe, Colin. "Introduction." *Five Architects: Eisenman, Graves, Gwuthmey, Hejduk, Meier,* pp. 3–7. New York, 1972.

Rowe, Colin, and Fred Koetter. *Collage City.* Cambridge, Mass., 1978.

Silvetti, Jorge. "The Beauty of Shadows." *Oppositions* 9 (Summer 1977): 43–61.

Solà-Morales, Ignasi de. "From Autonomy to Untimeliness." In *Differences: Topographies of Contemporary Architecture,* translated by Graham Thompson, edited by Sarah Whiting, pp. 73–92. Cambridge, Mass., 1997.

Tafuri, Manfredo. *Architecture and Utopia: Design and Capitalist Development.* Translated by Barbara Luigia La Penta. Cambridge, Mass., 1976.

Tafuri, Manfredo. *The Sphere and the Labyrinth: Avant-Gardes and Architecture from Piranesi to the 1970s.* Translated by Pellegrino d'Acierno and Robert Connolly. Cambridge, Mass., 1987.

Whiteman, John, Jeffrey Kipnis, and Richard Burdett, eds. *Strategies in Architectural Thinking.* Cambridge, Mass., 1992.

— K. MICHAEL HAYS

AVANT-GARDE. [*This essay offers a critical theory interpretation of the avant-garde and its legacy in modern and postmodern art. For discussion of avant-garde art, see* Constructivism; Cubism; Dadaism; Expressionism; Modernism; Suprematism; *and* Surrealism.]

The use of the concept *avant-garde* is not a consistent one. Many authors use it to mean nothing more than whatever the newest literary and artistic appearances may be, insofar as they make claims to modernity. Even Theodor Adorno, in his *Aesthetic Theory,* uses the term occasionally in this broad sense, but knows also along with it another, more specific usage, according to which the avant-garde aims for the "abolition of art." "Avant-garde disturbances of aesthetically avant-garde events are as illusionary as the belief that they are revolutionary" (Adorno, 1970, p. 372). Adorno here sets the broader concept (for "aesthetically avant garde": that which works on the most advanced artistic material) polemically in opposition to the specific meaning of the term. This latter usage will, in this essay, be differentiated from the concept of the modern and clarified in its aporias, taking as its point of departure a short conceptual history.

Saint-Simon and his early socialist cocombatants in the 1820s were the first to apply the concept of the avant-garde to art. In the hope that the society of atomized individuals that had emerged from the French Revolution would be overcome by the utopia of an organic society, they saw in artists those who "would call out the future of the human species." "It is we artists who will serve you as an avant-garde: the power of the arts is in fact the most immediate and the fastest" (Rodrigues, 1964, p. 210). This is proclaimed, in a Saint-Simonian dialogue, by the artist against his conversation partners, a scientist and an industrialist. On the one hand, art receives the function of being the motor of social change. On the other, art becomes dependent ("who will serve") on a historico-philosophical project.

The artists in this conception are not avant-gardists because they develop artistic forms. They are in fact not so because of their works at all, but only because they bring about the reality of utopia by awakening enthusiasm for the idea of a harmonious society of working citizens. After the collapse of Christian faith, according to the belief of the Saint-Simonians, only art may again establish that unity of convictions that is necessary in order to overcome the isolation of egotistically acting individuals.

When Paul Bénichou (1977) determines that contemporary artists and poets had no interest in Saint-Simon's appeal, he overlooks Heinrich Heine (1896), who ends his report on the Paris painting exhibition of 1831 by letting political reality break into the text. The author (according to the fictive writing situation that Heine sketches here) is distracted from his art-critical endeavor by the street noise of a crowd that is mourning the repression of the Polish uprising: "Warsaw has fallen! Our avant-garde has fallen!" Avant-garde means here the political avant-garde of the democratic and revolutionary movement. Heine allows it, the "raw noise of life," to question the "undisturbed pleasure in art." He forces an opposition: confronted with the interests of social progress, art is inessential, a triviality that inflates itself. "Current art must perish, for its principle is rooted in the extinct ancien régime, in the past of the Holy Roman Empire." But: "the new age will also give birth to a new art, which will be in enthusiastic unison with the former." Here the Saint-Simonian motif of an art that is no longer subjectivistically divided against itself, but rather harmonizes with a new social reality, is clearly sounded. But, as one can hardly expect otherwise from Heine, this supposedly sure faith in the future of art is immediately put in doubt: "Or will there be a sad end both for art in general and with the world? That dominant spirituality which manifests itself now in European literature is perhaps an omen of imminent extinction."

Heine does not speak of an avant-garde art or literature, but under the catchword of an "end of the period of art," he considers the possibility of a political art that is involved in the reality of democratic society. The failure of the 1848 revolution puts an end to such hopes. Charles Baudelaire, the disappointed revolutionary who became a cynical anarcho-conservative, criticizes not only the idea of progress ("this grotesque idea"), but also the love of the French for military metaphors such as "the combat poets" and "the avant-garde literati" (Baudelaire, 1954, p. 1219). These metaphors point out, for Baudelaire, a spirit made for discipline and conformism. To the degree that the utopian project of the early socialists pales, the concept of the avant-garde retains only its moment of dependency. Baudelaire, who criticizes the social-reforming connotations of the concept of the avant-garde literati, himself develops the outlines of a concept of modern art. He projects an aesthetic of the sketch, which corresponds only to the ephemerality of perceptions in the life of the modern metropolis, poses the question of the representability of modern life, and insists on the inclusion of the repulsive and ugly in art. In this concept there is no question of the political engagement of the artist, but only of the capacity to make something enduring from the perishable: "to draw the eternal from the transitory" (Baudelaire, 1954, p. 892). Baudelaire's concept of modernity is conceived from the point of view of the work of art, not from that of a social function of art.

For the concept of a literary avant-garde to become important again, another revolutionary situation was necessary. During the Paris Commune, Arthur Rimbaud develops his idea of the seer *(voyant)*, in which it is again a question of giving the poet a social function. After Rimbaud has devalued all of Occidental poetry as a diversion *(délassement)*, an entertainment that serves convalescence, he opposes to this his idea of a poetry that intervenes: the poet would define the quantity of the unknown that awakens in his time in the universal soul: "he would be truly a *multiplier of progress*" (Rimbaud, 1960, p. 347). The early socialist hopes for a resonance between the poet and his time return here, along with the thought that a poet might become a driving force of social change. Thus Rimbaud claims for poetry the position of an advance post. Poetry will not only, as in ancient Greece, rhythmically accompany deeds, but it will be in advance of the latter. "Poetry will no longer make action rhythmic; it will be *in advance*." In one point, how-

ever, Rimbaud's poet as seer *(poète voyant)* is distinct from the idea of the avant-garde artist projected by the early socialists; he is not dependent on a preexisting philosophy of history, but makes the claim to be both the great outcast and the "highest" scientist ("the great cursed one—and the supreme Knower!"). This claim is taken up by the Surrealists, who also understand themselves as a vanguard of a science that explodes the bounds of rationality.

In this sketch, one may detect *one* concept of avant-garde art that means more than just the latest and most up-to-date art of modernity. The preposition *avant* means not, or at least not primarily, the claim to be in advance of contemporary art (this is first true of Rimbaud), but rather the claim to be at the peak of social progress. The artist's activity is avant-gardist not in the production of a new work but because the artist intends with this work (or with the renunciation of a work) something else: the realization of a Saint-Simonian utopia or the "multiplication" of progress, a task that Rimbaud assigns to the poet of the future.

Inasmuch as avant-garde artists go beyond the sphere of art, they stand in a relation of tension to the principle of aesthetic autonomy. The Saint-Simonians polemicized against the idea of *l'art pour l'art*, Heine was amused by the "uprisings" of the Young Germans against Goethe, and Rimbaud condemned all of Western poetry as mere entertaining game. The avant-garde needs autonomous art in order to protest against it.

The tendencies mentioned here will develop and be radicalized in the historical avant-garde movements (Futurism, Dadaism, Surrealism). From the Saint-Simonian polemics against *l'art pour l'art* and Heine's farewell to the "idea of art" of Goethe's time, there comes the direct attack on the institution of art. Out of the stress on the social function of the artist will arise either anarchist revolt or engagement for the revolution.

What begins to emerge in Rimbaud's "letter of the seer" is the longing to break out of the institution of art, and this means to make artistic production into an act that forms reality. This longing becomes the impulse of the historical avant-garde movements in the period of crisis around World War I. However divergent the programs and political positions of the individual movements may be, they all share the questioning of the autonomy of art, for example, the protest against an art that has removed itself from life praxis. The expressions this protest takes are admittedly very different. With the Italian Futurists, the breakout from the ghetto of art takes place via an aestheticization of technology and of war, and thereby also a subordination of art under the most aggressive forms of a life stamped by modernization. The Dadaists, on the other hand, who, coming from various European countries, fled from the genocide of the world war to Zurich, abandon art to laughability in happening-like performances, including their own activity in this rejection. The Surrealists, finally, develop from this

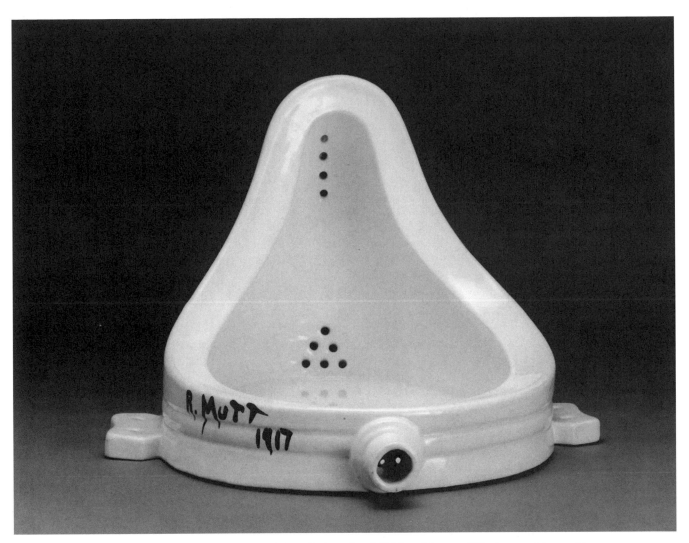

AVANT-GARDE. Marcel Duchamp, *Fountain* (1917/1918 Edition Schwarz, Milan), porcelain, 14 × 19 5/16 × 34 5/8 in. (35.5 × 49.1 × 62.5 cm); Indiana University Art Museum, Bloomington, Indiana (Partial Gift of Mrs. William Conroy). (Photograph by Michael Cavanagh, Kevin Montague, courtesy of the Indiana University Art Museum. Copyright Estate of Marcel Duchamp/Artists Rights Society, New York/ADAGP, Paris; used by permission.)

gesture of total negation the thought that the productive potential of art, which through autonomy has been severed from life, should be used for the renewal of life praxis. "One must only make the effort of *practicing poetry*," André Breton wrote in the first Surrealist manifesto (Breton, 1988, p. 322). If, at the end of the eighteenth century, the predication of art's autonomy had signified its separation from the domain of knowledge as well as that of morality, then the Surrealists claim to question the institution of art. They also claim to explore unknown areas of the human psyche and to live according to the principles of a morality that draws its strength from the refusal of bourgeois existence.

Both aspects of the avant-garde project—the attack on the institution of art and the revolutionizing of life—belong to-gether. If one adds to this that the avant-garde movements (with the sole exception of Dadaism) never abandon aesthetic claims, despite their anti-aesthetic attitude, then one sees the aporias in which these movements had to become entangled in the process of trying to realize their project. We may distinguish between a political and an aesthetic dilemma.

The political dilemma arises wherever revolutionary engagement is serious, as it must lead to a collaboration with radical left or right parties or groups. From this there arises for the avant-gardes the dilemma of either being sublated into the political movement they support (as certain of the Italian Futurists were into fascism) or, as a result of insisting on their independence, coming into an irresolvable conflict with the political movement (as some of the Surrealists did with the Communists).

The aesthetic dilemma is connected to the fact that the institution of art survives the avant-garde attack on it. In a text titled *From a Paris Diary,* Peter Weiss noted in 1962 about an exhibit of avant-garde art:

> The revolt had been tried once, and in three simultaneous exhibitions their results have been preserved. The mere fact that they were here hung, framed, or stood on pedestals or lain in exhibition cases was opposed to their original intent. These works, which wanted to tear down the ordinary, which wanted to open people's eyes to a free way of living, which mirrored the questionability and the delirium of external norms, were here presented in well-maintained spaces and could be contemplated from the vantage point of comfortable armchairs. The order they attacked, made ridiculous, and exposed in its hypocrisy had well-meaningly taken them up into itself.   (Weiss, 1968, p. 83)

In this respect, one can speak of the failure of the avant-garde. To talk of failure here leads to misunderstandings, however, not because the avant-garde project could be unproblematically renewed, but because it conceals the fact that that which has failed has not simply disappeared, but continues to exert influence precisely in its failure.

Our concepts are constructions that help us to make evident contexts and oppositions; they are not the mirror of reality. This holds true also of the concept of the avant-garde proposed here. It has been objected that this concept excludes relevant phenomena of literature and art of the early twentieth century, such as German Expressionism; yet, the concept in fact assigns Expressionism its proper place, namely, outside of the avant-garde. As opposed to other constructions (for instance, one that would emphasize the connection between Surrealism and Romanticism), the sketch presented here has the advantage of making recognizable common elements in otherwise opposing movements. Whereas Surrealism, with its critique of rationality, may actually be placed in a Romantic tradition, this is precisely not true for avant-gardes that are favorable to reason and technology, such as the Dutch de Stijl movement or Russian Constructivism. Yet the "end of the separation of art and life" belongs to the fundamental principles of Surrealism as much as it does to that of de Stijl. But whereas the Surrealists expect the realization of this project from untrammeled subjectivity, the de Stijl group demands the "suppression of subjective arbitrariness in the means of expression" (as quoted in Bächler and Letsch, 1984, pp. 55, 53).

The aim here is not to define a supposedly "correct" concept of the avant-garde against "false" ones, but only to direct attention to the fact that our concepts are constructions. Thus, simply to ask the question of the relation between modernity and avant-garde would be naive. Rather, one should reformulate the question: How does the concept of avant-garde outlined here relate to the construction of modernity that is familiar to us from Adorno's aesthetic theory?

Adorno's concept of modernity is centered on the category of the work of art. The work—and not its producer, nor its recipient—is the acting center of the artistic process. In it, mutually exclusive positions, such as mimesis and rationality, chance and calculation, meet in a unity that may not be theoretically anticipated and that is nevertheless necessary. The work of art is neither object nor subject, but in a peculiar way both at once, for its thing-like quality allows a subjective moment to appear within it that is not identical with the subjectivity of the artist, but inheres rather in the work itself. In short, the artwork is a bit of metaphysics that we ourselves have effected: the last form of metaphysics after the death of God.

The avant-gardes seek to break through the aporias that, in this concept of the modern work of art, arrive at an equilibrium that is both charged with tension and precarious. These movements want to take seriously the promise that autonomous art always contained, and they want to actively intervene in the real world. The avant-gardists do not understand their own texts and images as works of art, but either as actions meant to effect something or as protocols of an experience. It is a question of revolutionizing life, not of creating forms that are destined to become the object of aesthetic contemplation. When the artwork is at the center of artistic modernity, then at the center of the avant-garde is the action of those who no longer understand themselves as artists, but rather as scientists and revolutionaries.

These remarks might mislead one into seeing the avant-gardes as a movement opposing artistic modernity. That would, however, be wrong, for the avant-gardes not only draw their force from the critical potential of modernism, but they also base their revolutionary hopes on the assumption that the aesthetic metaphysics of modernism may be historically realizable. Breton's strong statement that it is a matter of practicing poetry—of living according to the principles of fantasy and not those of purposive rationality and strategic action—expresses this. It would be both simplistic and inappropriate to see only a pretty illusion in this idea. The work of Joseph Beuys shows what force one may still release even from the failure of the avant-garde project. Beuys takes up the project of the avant-garde after its failure in full consciousness of the aporia in which he thereby is caught. As an avant-gardist, he cannot define himself as an artist; but because the avant-gardes have failed, he cannot define himself outside of their project either. He may find a place neither within the institution of art nor outside of it, but only in an impossible realm "in between." He may only link his work back to the historical avant-gardes, and thereby remain on a level with his own time, in the paradox of constant self-contradiction: "I have really nothing to with art, and this is the only possibility to do anything for art."

The radicality of the avant-garde critique of the existing order is the result of an unbroken confidence in the possibility of living without anxiety and restructuring social reality. Wherever this confidence—which, however fragile, still stamps the work of Beuys—is lost, whenever the future is darkened, the avant-gardes enter a zone of extreme peril. This is shown in the suicides of Vladimir Mayakovsky and René Crevel. It is no accident that today authors such as Georges Bataille, Maurice Blanchot, and Jacques Lacan should be at the center of the interest of young intellectuals who keep a wakeful eye on our own time. All three of these authors attempt to realize something like a Surrealism without illusions, which circles around the impossible experience of one's own death. Where one has recognized that the hope of "a finally inhabitable world" (Breton) is an illusion, the avant-garde project has lost its compass and gets lost in ecstasy (Bataille), in the endless movement of writing (Blanchot), or in the insane recognition of the paranoia of all knowledge (Lacan).

BIBLIOGRAPHY

Adorno, Theodor W. *Ästhetische Theorie.* Edited by Gretel Adorno and Rolf Tiedemann. Frankfurt am Main, 1970. Translated as *Aesthetic Theory* by Robert Hullot-Kentor. Minneapolis, 1997.

Bächler, H., and H. Letsch, eds. *De Stijl: Schriften und Manifeste.* Leipzig, 1984.

Baudelaire, Charles. "Le Peintre de la vie moderne." In *Œuvres,* edited by Y.-G. Le Dantec. Paris, 1954.

Baudelaire, Charles. "Mon Cœur mis a nu." In *Œuvres,* edited by Y.-G. Le Dantec. Paris, 1954.

Bénichou, Paul. *Le Temps des prophètes: Doctrines de l'âge romantique.* Paris, 1977.

Biermann, Karlheinrich. *Literarisch-politische Avantgarde in Frankreich, 1830–1870: Hugo, Sand, Baudelaire und andere.* Stuttgart, 1982.

Breton, André. *Œuvres complètes.* Edited by Marguerite Bonnet. 2 vols. Paris, 1988–1992.

Bürger, Peter. *Theorie der Avantgarde.* Frankfurt am Main, 1974.

Bürger, Peter. "Everydayness, Allegory and the Avant-Garde: Some Reflections on the Work of Joseph Beuys." In *The Decline of Modernism,* translated by Nicholas Walker, pp. 147–161. Cambridge, 1992.

Drijkoningen, F. "Dada et anarchisme: Quelques réflexions préliminaires." *AvantGarde* (1987): 69–82.

Heine, Heinrich. "Französische Maler." In *Sämtliche Werke,* edited by Ernst Elster, vol. 4, pp. 69–73. Leipzig, 1896.

Rimbaud, Arthur. Letter to Paul Demeny of 15 May 1871. In *Œuvres,* edited by Suzanne Bernard, pp. 344–350. Paris, 1960.

Rodrigues, Olinde. "L'Artiste, le savant et l'industriel: Dialogue." In *Œuvres de Saint-Simon et d'Enfantin* (1865–1879), vol. 39. Reprint, Aalen, 1964.

Weiss, Peter. *Rapporte,* vol. 1. Frankfurt am Main, 1968.

PETER BÜRGER

AVERROËS. *See* Ibn Rushd.

AVICENNA. *See* Ibn Sīnā.

B

BACHELARD, GASTON (1884–1962), variously viewed as a philosopher of science, an analyst of the imagination, and a literary critic. Bachelard was clearly at home in the "two cultures" of science and the humanities.

Born in Bar-sur-Aube in the Champagne region southeast of Paris, the young Gaston Bachelard served as a postal clerk with an interest in telegraphy and engineering. Following World War I, he taught physics and chemistry at a secondary school in Bar-sur-Aube, eventually turning to the teaching of philosophy after obtaining the *agrégation* in that field. Upon completion of his doctorate in the history and philosophy of science in 1927, Bachelard began teaching at the University of Dijon, where he was named to the chair of philosophy in 1930. Most of his works during this period focused on the epistemology of science, but he began an exploration of the poetic imagination that would become his central, though never his exclusive, focus after his appointment to the chair of history and philosophy of science at the Sorbonne in 1940. In 1961, he was awarded the Grand Prix National des Lettres, a rare honor for a philosopher. At the time of his death, Bachelard had written twenty-three books and numerous essays, almost equally divided between the epistemology of science and the poetic imagination.

In his early work on the epistemology of science, Bachelard sees a "'Copernican revolution' of abstraction" (1937, p. 139) in the way reason and its relation to reality are transformed by the practice of contemporary science. New discoveries are of such epistemological consequence that they bring about a new scientific mind where "the world in which we think is not the world in which we live" (1940, p. 95) and where scientific reality is a function of the means of knowing. Concerned with the pedagogical implications of the new scientific spirit in *La formation de l'esprit scientifique* (The development of the scientific mind, 1938), Bachelard seeks to eradicate elements from a common intellectual past that might block objective knowledge and form "epistemological obstacles" (*La formation de l'esprit scientifique*, 1938, p. 19).

In a companion book, curiously titled *The Psychoanalysis of Fire* (1938, 1964), Bachelard sets out to "psychoanalyze" the scientific mind in order to identify unnoticed images that pose an obstacle to objective knowledge. Like any good psychoanalyst, his purpose is to bring these unrecognized images to awareness in order to free the scientific mind

from their power. Far less concerned with the depths of the unconscious revealed in the dream *(rêve)* than with the semiconscious imaginative responses of daydream *(rêverie)*, Bachelard focuses on fire as one of the most common objects of such reveries. Convinced that, when it comes to fire, "personal intuitions and scientific images are intermingled" (*The Psychoanalysis of Fire*, 1964, p. 3), he sets out to keep "the axes of poetry and science . . . opposed to one another" (ibid., p. 2), yet "to make poetry and science complementary, to unite them as two well-defined opposites" (ibid.). Liberally inventing new "complexes" to account for various subjective attitudes toward fire, Bachelard proposes his celebrated four-part classification of the imagination, "the four categories of souls in whose dreams fire, water, air, or earth predominate" (ibid., p. 89). He is "not dealing here with matter," he explains, "but with orientation" (ibid., p. 90). His focus is on the subject by way of the object.

Before exploring further the link between the four elements and the imagination, Bachelard writes a monographic essay titled *Lautréamont* (1939), pen name of nineteenth-century poet Isidore Ducasse. With its reliance on both the methodological perspective of contemporary science and its identification of key explanatory images, this book anticipates Bachelard's dual approach for much of his subsequent writing on the literary imagination. The brutal imagery of Lautréamont's *Les chants de Maldoror*, in Bachelard's view, abandons the space-conscious *form* of traditional descriptive poetry in favor of a dynamic poetry of time-conscious *function*. Bachelard brings to Lautréamont's poetry a thorough familiarity with the revolutionary power of contemporary science that rejects rigid determinism and a priori outlooks. Thus, despite Lautréamont's profound irrationalism, Bachelard gives a sympathetic reading to this aggressive attack on dogmatic formalism.

In *Water and Dreams* (1942), Bachelard distinguishes between images of clear reflective water, which he associates with the superficial world of visual contemplation, and images of a more palpable viscous water, such as those found in Edgar Allan Poe's work. Overly conceptual, visual water images are seen as weak imitations of what is perceived. In Bachelard's estimation, the power and creative force of water images are best expressed verbally rather than visually. This preference for words over visual form leads to Bachelard's differentiation between the formal and the material imagination. Matter and the material imagination, as opposed to the mere surface object, are seen as the source of poetic reverie.

Bachelard's aesthetics of the imagination share with his epistemology of science an aversion to surface reality. In both cases, the object of interest is beyond the immediate. Yet, the importance accorded to matter over form betrays an unscientific, naive realism in which the surface qualities of objects mask an underlying substance. Unlike the scientist, whose apprehension of reality is a function of his or her descriptive method, the poet, like the alchemist of old, dreams directly of substance.

The rational knowledge associated with Bachelard's epistemology demands an escape from subjectivity. But the imagination, which is both subjective and objective, leads us back, through reverie, to what is particularly human within ourselves. Imagination and reverie make of life a human reality that is as nondeterministic as the constructed reality of contemporary science. Reverie is to everyday life what scientific reason is to the physical world. Both transcend immediate reality—reason, in the direction of a constructed, objective reality, inseparable from the means of knowing; reverie, in the direction of a subjective reality, inseparable from its means of expression. Thus, reverie serves an ontological function by transposing everyday life into human terms. Indeed, the association of reverie with language makes it appropriate to speak of a symbolic ontology in Bachelard's work on the imagination.

As Bachelard's epistemology yields to ontological considerations in the works on the four elements, nondeterministic, transcendent openness remains a constant theme. Moreover, Bachelard's notion of the imagination itself is not limited to a static material imagination. There is what Bachelard calls a *"coefficient of adversity"* (1983, p. 159) between the imagination and matter. The imagination does not remain neutral toward a substance. It is "a fundamental law of *material imagination*" (ibid., 142), he writes, to give value to substance and to assign it the will to act. Thus "material imagination is transformed into dynamic imagination" (ibid., 143) and both repudiate the more superficial formal imagination.

Air and Dreams (1943) considers dreams of flying and images of physical phenomena such as sky, stellar space, and wind. While continuing to focus on questions of ontology, Bachelard becomes increasingly interested in the specifically literary aspect of the psychology of the imagination. Apparently unable to find a satisfactory common ground for both philosophy and literature, he writes two conclusions—one on the literary image, the other on the philosophy of motion.

The dual conclusions of *Air and Dreams* follow upon Bachelard's two major goals in this work. The first, indicated by the subtitle—*An Essay on the Imagination of Movement*—is to attempt to follow the movement of the imagination in its journey "from the real to the imaginary" (1988, p. 4). Unlike water, which evokes a prescientific ontology based on naive realism, air, with its dynamism and immateriality, is especially suited to designate an escape toward the imaginary. Yet, as Bachelard writes, "the way in which we escape reality gives a clear indication of our inner reality" (p. 7). Thus the ontological orientation remains, but the ground has shifted. Bachelard's first objective is to examine that dynamic continuity from the real to the imaginary which allows the inner reality to be known.

His second goal is to "limit [himself] further to a study of the *literary* metaphors of air" (p. 238; emphasis added). The imagination, Bachelard writes, displays a "will to logos" (p. 245) and poetry grows out of this will to speak. Any study of the movement of the imagination from reality to irreality must, therefore, also require an examination of the verbal expression that makes such movement possible. The metaphor of "sublimation" that Bachelard uses to describe the upward motion of most aerial images allows him to portray the aerial imagination as working independently of practical logic. Reason might suggest, for example, that dreams of flying presuppose wings. But such images strike Bachelard as inauthentic. Instead, he proposes the "principle that in the dream world we do not fly because we have wings; rather, we think we have wings because we have flown" (p. 27). Such precedence of function over form is consistent with his earlier perspective on the material and dynamic imagination and his disdain for the formal imagination.

The dynamic aerial imagination with its upward motion readily conveys the aspirations of human will. Although Bachelard is careful not to suggest that images of falling are of less *aesthetic* value than images of ascent, he does see different ontological consequences for each: "everything that *rises* becomes awakened to and involved in being. Conversely, everything that falls is dispersed into empty darkness and becomes part of the void" (p. 74). Emphasizing the importance for human well-being of an "unreality function" (p. 7), Bachelard unabashedly argues for the ontological legitimacy of subjective being.

Bachelard labels the idea of placing "dream before reality" (p. 101) a "Copernican revolution of the imagination" (p. 101). As with the Copernican revolution of abstraction, Bachelard calls attention to a revolutionary transformation in the relationship of subject and object. In both science and poetry, the mind, whether reason or the imagination, determines how external reality is perceived. The difference is that in science the determining factor is how we know, whereas for poetry it is who we are. As Bachelard sees it, in poetry not only is the subjective state primordial, it is necessarily verbal for "there is no reality that precedes the literary image" (p. 249). For Bachelard, the creation of the literary image is a fundamental human activity, one that is essential to the dynamism of the imagination. At the moment it is formed, the literary image expands the possibilities of language and "is inscribed like a new crystal in the soil of language" (1988, pp. 265–266). Imaginative and intimate, the literary image is also verbal and public. It is a subjective yet communicable reality.

Bachelard continues to explore the interplay of the dynamic and material imaginations in his two books on the element of earth. In the introduction to both earth books that opens *La terre et les rêveries de la volonté* (Earth and reveries of will, 1948), Bachelard acknowledges the differences between the "introverted" material imagination that associates the world with inner subjectivity and the "extroverted" dynamic imagination that moves outwardly toward the world. Yet, he cautions against making too sharp a distinction, for both types of imagination overcome the division of subject and object through the image: "It is through the image that the imagining being and the imagined being are closest" (1998, p. 5).

Focusing in particular on the encounter between the dynamic imagination and the resistant element of earth in which "the *human being* is revealed as the *counter being* of things" (p. 119), Bachelard considers that "the image is always an advancement of being" (p. 20). Being increases when the human imagination imposes its will on matter through work, whereas "an arrested dynamism" brings about "a diminution of being" (p. 374). Bachelard finds his examples for the dynamic imagination of earth in the literary image and its "differential of newness" (p. 6). He emphasizes the autonomous nature of the literary image as an originator of language whose purpose is to create being through beauty. Convinced that "when someone speaks to you of the *interior* of things, you are sure of hearing disclosures of his own inner secrets" (p. 233), Bachelard again attributes ontological status, in the form of a symbolic ontology, to a subjective being that transcends immediate concrete reality through the literary image.

Subtitled an *Essay on the Images of Intimacy,* Bachelard's second book on the element of earth, *La terre et les rêveries du repos* (Earth and reveries of repose, 1948) explores literary images pertaining to the interior of things where "the imagination reaches an *ontology of struggle*" (p. 75). Whether it is a question of tension, as in the case of intimate images of refuge such as the house, the belly, and the cave, or a question of contention, as with images of the serpent and the root, dynamism is a constant feature of earthly reveries for Bachelard.

Bachelard's exploration of intimate earth images in *La terre et les rêveries de repos* demonstrates that, even in the most material images of repose, the imagination's dynamism is attributable to the verbal expression of such images. Literary images awaken Jungian archetypes that make them communicable, but, for the communication to take place, we must "attempt to read texts more slowly still than they were written, as slowly as they were dreamed" (p. 136).

Through such reading, Bachelard endeavors to recapture the reverie that preceded the narration; for it is in keeping with Bachelard's notion of a Copernican revolution of the imagination that reverie should precede narration, just as subjectivity precedes perception. This attention to reading as reverie marks a new emphasis in Bachelard's thinking that he will develop in his last two major works on the imagination, *The Poetics of Space* (1957) and *The Poetics of Reverie* (1960).

In *The Poetics of Space,* Bachelard considers the possibility that a "philosophy of poetry" (1969, p. xi), unlike one of science, would be based not on axiomatic principles but on a renewal of each image through a "phenomenology of the imagination" (p. xiv). Although a phenomenological approach is not altogether new to Bachelard, he is now inclined to discount as reductive references to psychology and psychoanalysis. In keeping with his goal of examining the literary or *poetic* image, as he now calls it, he places a renewed emphasis on the centrality of reading—including the slow, deliberate reading suggested in *La terre et les rêveries du repos.*

Bachelard calls his exploration of a space that is given value by the poetic image a "topoanalysis" (p. 8). An adaptation of the term *psychoanalysis, topoanalysis* is meant to apply to the daydream rather than the dream. In practice, it becomes a phenomenological analysis of space, a means of inquiry into how space is imagined, without regard to causal questions. The related term, *topohilia* (p. xxxi), recognizes that, unlike the subjectively neutral space of geometry, imagined space always acquires a quality for the imagining subject. When reverie replaces reason as an integrating principle, Bachelard remarks, a corner has the makings of a house and a house can become a universe.

Although Bachelard's avowed purpose is to consider the poetic image phenomenologically, from the perspective of a naive reader, the philosophical frame of reference remains. Setting out to "found a metaphysics of the imagination" (p. xiv) and to study the "direct ontology" (p. xii) of the image, in which the reader is asked to consider the "specific reality" (p. xv) of the poetic image, Bachelard reveals a substratum of ontological questions that will undergird both *The Poetics of Space* and *The Poetics of Reverie.* The role of phenomenology, in this situation, is to serve as a means of apprehending the image without destroying its specific reality.

In *The Poetics of Reverie,* Bachelard continues his attempt to develop "an ontology of images and a phenomenology of the imagination at the same time" (1971, p. 209). Now more secure in his phenomenological approach, he unhesitatingly makes use of the lessons of Jungian psychology not to reduce images to a hidden reality but to examine the "absolute sublimation" (p. 58) or idealized transformation of that reality into the words of the poem. Returning to the Jungian androgynous basis of the human psyche—the *animus* and its conceptual disposition to organize, and the *anima* and its inclination to imagine and daydream—Bachelard is particularly drawn by the openness and receptivity of the latter. He finds the *anima* principle especially well suited to a phenomenological approach and, more particularly, to an exploration of poetic reverie. As a facet of the human psyche, the *anima* principle gives psychological legitimacy to a reverie on reverie implied in Bachelard's phenomenology.

For Bachelard, anything that excluded the *anima* principle would be too rigid to preserve the special reality of the image. Only a nonconceptual, phenomenological approach seems suitable. Unlike the nocturnal dream, reverie does not exclude consciousness and it can be communicated. Reverie's ability to be conscious of itself makes it an ideal phenomenological tool because subjective consciousness is a sine qua non of phenomenological activity. Reverie also links the daydreaming subject and the world through words. "Thus there are cosmic words, words which give man's being to the being of things. . . . Through reverie, words become immense" (1960, p. 189).

Bachelard's consideration of reverie leads him, once again, to a preoccupation with ontological considerations. Whether it be the "antecedence of being" or "penumbral ontology" (p. 111) of childhood reverie, the "differential ontology" (p. 167) that would take into account the interpenetration of subject and object in reverie, or the "ontology of the imagination" (p. 200) associated with cosmic reverie, it remains a symbolic ontology based in philosophical idealism. Bachelard takes his examples from literature precisely because the poet transforms reality into an idealized image, which then has the power to idealize objective reality for the reader. The idealizing reverie associated with that expanding verbal image is free from immediate common-sense experience, and because reverie creates the subject along with the world, one can speak of a subjective idealism in Bachelard.

In his final years, Bachelard returned to the element of fire, with a short book of reverie titled *The Flame of a Candle* (1961) and with a project for a longer book variously titled *The Experience of Fire, A Poetics of Fire* and, in a later, truncated form, *The Poetics of the Phoenix*. Initially conceived as part of *The Poetics of Fire, The Flame of a Candle* stands on its own as an in-*anima*, solitary meditation on candleflame whose concerns range from "an ontology of solitary existence" (1961, p. 9) to the literary imagination and to personal reveries on the writer's work. The longer project anticipated a study of "the two poles of the imagination, fire and warmth, through the dialectics of *anima* and *animus*" (1988, p. xiii), but Bachelard died in 1962 with the project very much incomplete. Major portions appeared in 1988 as *Fragments of a Poetics of Fire*, where, in an introduction, Bachelard hopes to explain "how reverie works one's inner being" (1988, p. 9).

Reverie's idealism beyond commonsense experience may bring to mind the counterintuitive, constructed object of science discussed in Bachelard's epistemological work; for although Bachelard invariably insists on the difference between the rationalism of science and the reverie of poetic imagination, an examination of the "two more or less independent halves" (1988, p. 8) reveals the constancy of his philosophical idealism. Without clouding his understanding and respect for the distinction between science and poetry, Bachelard, in effect, applies a common philosophical approach to both. Having begun as a rationalist who is concerned with the epistemological issues posed by science, he explores the imagination from an ontological perspective. Having learned from science the lesson that philosophy should tread lightly on the object of its inquiry, Bachelard develops a philosophy of the imagination based in phenomenological reverie rather than the overpowering concept. Thus, it might be said that Bachelard's phenomenology is his "epistemological" response to literature, his means of *knowing* the literary image. For Bachelard, it turns out, both science and literature require not only their own ontology but their own epistemology.

Not quite a theoretician of literature, because he eschews rational approaches in favor of reverie; not truly a literary critic, because, with the exception of *Lautréamont*, he writes no sustained piece on any writer and neglects the whole work in favor of the imagistic part; unconventional as a thinker, because his works on the imagination forsake system, Bachelard must be understood as a philosopher of science whose epistemological interests are so profound that they inevitably provide the context for his work on the imagination. Despite his effort to keep science and poetry apart, Bachelard transfers the most essential lessons of one realm to the other without denying the distinctiveness of each.

Having amply demonstrated in his epistemology of science his ability to apply rigorously conceptual approaches, Bachelard comes to favor phenomenological reverie when writing on the imagination because the object of his scrutiny, the literary image, requires it. Such a view is perfectly consistent with his epistemology of science, in which philosophy must learn from the object of its analysis and must avoid imposing a priori categories. Bachelard's choice of reverie as a method is grounded in his conviction that the image is fundamental to literature. Coming from a recognized conceptual philosopher, Bachelard's respect for image makes an original and powerful statement about how philosophy might approach the literary imagination.

[*See also* Imagination; Poetics; *and* Science and Aesthetics.]

BIBLIOGRAPHY

Works by Bachelard

Le nouvel esprit scientifique. Paris, 1934. Translated as *The New Scientific Spirit* by Arthur Goldhammer (Boston, 1984).
L'expérience de l'espace dans la physique contemporaine. Paris, 1937.

La formation de l'esprit scientifique: Contribution à une psychanalyse de la connaissance objective. Paris, 1938.

La psychanalyse du feu. Paris, 1938. Translated as *The Psychoanalysis of Fire* by Alan C. M. Ross (Boston, 1964).

Lautréamont. Paris, 1939; new ed., Paris, 1951. Translated by Robert S. Dupree (Dallas, 1986).

La philosophie du non: Essai d'une philosophie du nouvel esprit scientifique. Paris, 1940. Translated as *The Philosophy of No: A Philosophy of the New Scientific Mind.* by G. C. Waterston (New York, 1968).

L'eau et les rêves: Essai sur l'imagination de la matière. Paris, 1942. Translated as *Water and Dreams: An Essay on the Imagination of Matter* by Edith R. Farrell (Dallas, 1983).

L'air et les songes: Essai sur l'imagination du mouvement. Paris, 1943. Translated as *Air and Dreams: An Essay on the Imagination of Movement* by Edith R. Farrell and C. Frederick Farrell (Dallas, 1988).

La terre et les rêveries de la volonté: Essai sur l'imagination des forces. Paris, 1948. Translated as *Earth and Reveries of Will* by Kenneth Haltman (Dallas, 1998, forthcoming).

La terre et les rêveries du repos: Essai sur les images de l'intimité. Paris, 1948.

La poétique de l'espace. Paris, 1957. Translated as *The Poetics of Space* by Maria Jolas (reprint, Boston, 1969).

La poétique de la rêverie. Paris, 1960. Translated as *The Poetics of Reverie: Childhood, Language, and the Cosmos* by Daniel Russell (reprint, Boston, 1971).

La flamme d'une chandelle. Paris, 1961. Translated as *The Flame of a Candle* by Joni Caldwell (Dallas, 1988).

Le droit de rêver. Paris, 1970. Translated as *The Right to Dream* by J. A. Underwood (New York, 1971; reprint, Dallas, 1988). Posthumous collection of essays.

On Poetic Imagination and Reverie. Rev. ed. Translated and edited by Colette Gaudin. Dallas, 1987.

Fragments d'une poétique du feu. Edited by Suzanne Bachelard. Paris, 1988. Translated as *Fragments of a Poetics of Fire* by Kenneth Haltman (Dallas, 1990).

Other Sources

Caws, Mary Ann. *Surrealism and the Literary Imagination: A Study of Breton and Bachelard.* The Hague, 1966.

Lecourt, Dominique. *Marxism and Epistemology: Bachelard, Canguilhem, and Foucault.* Translated by Ben Brewster. London, 1975.

McAllester, Mary, ed. *The Philosophy and Poetics of Gaston Bachelard.* Washington, D.C., 1989.

McAllester Jones, Mary. *Gaston Bachelard, Subversive Humanist: Texts and Readings.* Madison, Wis., 1991.

Smith, Roch. *Gaston Bachelard.* Boston, 1982.

Tiles, Mary. *Bachelard: Science and Objectivity.* Cambridge and New York, 1984.

ROCH C. SMITH

BAKHTIN, MIKHAIL MIKHAILOVICH (1895–1975), Russian essayist and theoretician. Born south of Moscow, Mikhail Mikhailovich Bakhtin grew up in Vilnius, a Lithuanian town called "the Jerusalem of the North" because of its rich Jewish intellectual heritage. He studied philology and classics at Petrograd University from 1914 to 1918, and later lived in small Russian cities—Nevel, Vitebsk, Kustanai, Saransk, Savelovo—as well as Leningrad and Moscow, where he was active in both literary and philosophical circles. In the mid-1920s, he contracted os-teomyelitis and, throughout the rest of his life, was subject to periods of acute pain and infirmity. During the harshest periods of Stalinist repression, Bakhtin and his wife, Elena Aleksandrovna, were exiled from Moscow; he alternately taught high school and worked as a bookkeeper. Although his writing consistently began to appear in print in the 1960s, only since his death has Bakhtin's oeuvre become widely known throughout the world.

Bakhtin's four earliest essays, in *Art and Answerability* and *Toward a Philosophy of the Act,* were written between 1919 and 1926 and before he developed a consistent emphasis on language and discourse that would pervade the rest of his work. Here he articulated a nascent philosophy of creativity with concepts such as answerability, outsideness, and unfinalizability. Books and essays written between 1929 and 1971 contain many useful categories that have aided literary theorists, critics, and historians. In fact, his name is most often associated with his theories of genre and the novel and with specific concepts from this period: the dialogic or dialogism, carnival, and technical terms used in literary analysis such as chronotope, monologism, polyphony, and heteroglossia *(Problems of Dostoevsky's Poetics, Rabelais and His World,* and the essays published in *The Dialogic Imagination).* His last essays *(Speech Genres and Other Late Essays)* return to many of the themes he had addressed in the 1920s, such as the difference between dialectics and dialogics and other ideas related to Kantian philosophy and aesthetics. Bakhtin's circle included writers such as Valentin N. Voloshinov *(Marxism and the Philosophy of Language* [1986] and *Freudianism: A Critical Sketch* [1987]) and Pavel N. Medvedev *(The Formal Method in Literary Scholarship* [1985]), whose books are sometimes attributed to Bakhtin, but this essay will only address works that are firmly established as having been written by him. Bakhtin's essays and books are significant for aesthetics in two primary ways: first, in relation to Kantian and neo-Kantian aesthetic theories with which he was familiar and entered into dialogue; and second, in terms of his aesthetic categories, many of which emerged out of the context of his specific literary readings.

Although there is no clearly defined and universally understood definition of aesthetics in the twentieth century, Mikhail Bakhtin was an inheritor of modern aesthetic theories. He actively refuted Kantian aesthetics from two directions. First, he challenged "impressive" theorists such as Konrad Fiedler, Adolf Hildebrand, Eduard Hanslick, and Alois Riegl, who, in his view, centered too heavily on the creating consciousness and the artist's interaction with the material. Second, he was convinced that "expressivist" theories were limited because they were based on the idea that art is an expression of feelings and the inner self. Expressivist aesthetics takes the human being as the primary subject and object and therefore is decidedly anthropocentric; everything—even lines and colors—is given human attributes. Within expressive aesthetics, the goal of aesthetic perception and the aesthetic act is to experience the object as if from within; the contemplator and the object literally coincide. There is no juxtaposition of an I and an other, which in Bakhtin's view was essential to the aesthetic process. Bakhtin placed a diverse group of writers—Theodor Lipps, Herman Cohen, Robert Vischer, Johannes Volkelt, Wilhelm Wundt, Karl Groos, Konrad Lange, Arthur Schopenhauer, and Henri Bergson—in this category and tried to develop an alternative and more adequate approach.

Unlike both Kantians and neo-Kantians, however, Bakhtin shunned orderly systematic thought, preferring instead to muse, to work out ideas by following the circuitous and often fragmentary meanderings of imagination. Most aesthetic theories are concerned with the category of beauty, which is visible in both nature and art, yet invisible in moral and intellectual activity. Some give priority to the aesthetic object or work of art. Others privilege the perceiving subject, the viewer who looks and experiences. Bakhtin brings us back to the aesthetics of the creative process itself, back to the activity of the artist or author who creates.

Since the 1730s, when Alexander Baumgarten coined the term, *aesthetics* has remained ambiguous. For Baumgarten and for Kant after him, aesthetics had to do with sensory knowledge or sensory cognition, which included but was not limited to the problem of beauty. In a broad sense, Bakhtin's understanding of aesthetics fits into such a definition. He was concerned with how humans give form to their experience: how they perceive an object, text, or another person, and how they shape that perception into a synthesized whole. But rather than focusing on beauty, he developed an unusual vocabulary for describing the process by which we literally "author" one another, as well as artifacts such as texts and works of art.

Still, Bakhtin never explicitly defined aesthetics. Like Kant, he treated the aesthetic as a sphere in which the cognitive-theoretical and ethical-practical spheres may be brought together. But he pressed further than Kant in defining their activity. According to Bakhtin, each of these spheres approaches reality differently. By assuming primacy, cognition tends to separate itself from ethical evaluation and the aesthetic organization of reality. Cognition assumes a unitary world of knowledge that is always open, though separated from the world. The realm of ethical action differs from the cognitive, because here one meets with conflict over moral duty or obligation. As a result, neither cognition nor action alone can provide a foundation for philosophy.

Turning to artistic creation and the aesthetic sphere, Bakhtin stated that this sphere is fundamentally different from the other two, precisely because here reality and life interpenetrate with art. "Art celebrates, adorns, and recollects this preveniently encountered reality of cognition and action (nature and social humanity). It enriches and completes them, and above all else *it creates the concrete intuitive unity of these two worlds*. It places man in nature, understood as his aesthetic environment; it humanizes nature and naturalizes man" (Bakhtin, 1990.) This statement is a key to why Bakhtin focused on the aesthetic dimension of life. By establishing a unity of nature and humanity (and of cognition and action) in society, aesthetics could become the basis for a new approach to philosophy.

Bakhtin understood aesthetics as a subcategory of the broader category of architectonics, as Michael Holquist has observed (in ibid.). Like aesthetics, architectonics is not a strict formal cognitive structure, but it is an activity that describes how relationships between self and other, self and object, self and world are structured. The uniqueness of Bakhtin's approach to aesthetics is that it is based not on categories such as the aesthetic attitude, aesthetic object, or aesthetic values (truth, goodness, or beauty), but on the phenomenology of self-other relations, relations that are embodied—in actual bodies—in space and in time.

Certainly, Bakhtin did treat traditional aesthetic categories such as detachment, empathy, isolation, and the aesthetic object, as well as theories of art and the relationship of art and morality. But his discussions of all of these categories and topics were grounded in the unique human being, located spatially and temporally and thus having a particular relationship to all other persons, objects, and events in the world. As humans struggle to express and to shape perception and experience, they engage in creative aesthetic activity. Bakhtin called such activity "authoring." His interpretation of authorship was not limited to literary texts, but he saw this as a process involving other persons, nature, and works of art. To author, in Bakhtin's vocabulary, is to create.

Just as he avoided clear definitions of aesthetics and creativity, however, Bakhtin never produced a systematic theory of the creative process. In fact, his early essays are both an implicit and explicit critique of unified and ordered systems. In *Toward a Philosophy of the Act* (1993), Bakhtin used the term *theoretism* to describe his aversion to unified and orderly structures or systems. Like his writing on other topics, Bakhtin's critique of theoretism was neither sustained nor systematic. On the one hand, he was convinced that theory cannot provide the basis for responsible action in the world. Theory does not directly translate into everyday life and experience. On the other hand, a specific act or deed *(delo* or *postupok)* does provide a basis for assessing what is most meaningful, and for creating an adequate orientation in life. Nevertheless, his resistance to all forms of theoretism did not preclude writing theoretical texts.

Three ideas from Bakhtin's writing of the 1920s—answerability, outsideness, and the degree of finalizability or unfinalizability of a creative act—are a meditation on the crucial links between creativity and religious and moral issues. Along with ideas developed later, they form the core of his extended, if fragmentary, aesthetic theory.

Developing the concept of answerability, Bakhtin emphasized that we are not obligated by theoretical norms or values (theoretism), but by real people in real historical situations. A genuine life, and genuine art, can only be realized in concrete responsibility or answerability. This concept became the basis for his later development of dialogism. Central to Bakhtin's interpretation of answerability are other ideas such as the aesthetic event, and a fascinating account of soul and spirit. In his writing, the architectonics of the deed has three moments or aspects: I-for-myself (*dukh*, spirit), another-for-me, and I-for-another (*dusha*, the soul). An event, perceived by a person as a living, concrete, graphically unified whole, may be oriented toward one of these moments, which do not necessarily occur in order. For Bakhtin, spirit and soul are simultaneously technical terms for arranging people in space, and ways of describing how one's inner and outer selves are expressed in artistic creativity.

With the concept of outsideness, Bakhtin criticized and tried to balance the notion of aesthetic empathy and identification, understood from a neo-Kantian perspective. For Bakhtin, aesthetic and moral activity only begin after empathy, which he interpreted as a kind of living-oneself-into the experience of another person. Only with the return into the self do we begin to form and consummate the experience derived from projecting the self into another's position. Creativity itself is only possible on and because of boundaries between persons, events, and objects. In Bakhtin's words, "A cultural sphere has no inner territory. It is situated entirely on boundaries; boundaries go through it everywhere. . . . Every cultural act lives on boundaries: in this is its seriousness and significance" (Bakhtin, 1990.) The meaning of a creative act evolves in relation to the boundaries—the inside and outside—of the cognitive, ethical, and aesthetic spheres of culture. Indeed, creative activity must be understood in relation to the unity of culture and to life itself. As Bakhtin repeated many times in subsequent writings, text and context are inseparable.

Unfinalizability is a core concept in all of Bakhtin's writing, as Gary Saul Morson and Caryl Emerson have shown (1990). Unfinalizability results from the fact that we are finite human beings and have finite knowledge. What we apprehend are constructions, and inevitably conflicts arise over these constructions. Therefore, no one person or group can contain the truth. We simply cannot see the whole, everything that is. Ultimately, the unrepeatability and open-endedness of a creative act makes transformation possible. In the early essays, Bakhtin was ambiguous about the degree of finalization that is necessary. On the one hand, he differentiated between the problematic and even immoral attempt to finalize another person, except in death. To do this would deny the other the possibility of full becoming as a soul, an "I-for-myself." On the other hand, he emphasized the multifarious ways in which we need the

other to create and finalize ourselves. In artistic creativity, aesthetic finalization is essential. By the early 1970s, when he wrote his "Response to a Question from the *Novy Mir* Editorial Staff" and "Toward a Methodology for the Human Sciences" (in *Speech Genres and Other Late Essays* [1986]), the valence had shifted clearly toward the unfinalizability of creative activity.

As noted earlier, Bakhtin's aesthetic ideas also developed out of the context of specific literary readings, of Fyodor Dostoevsky, Leo Tolstoy, Johann Wolfgang von Goethe, and François Rabelais. Scholars have commented on the inaccuracies and fragmentary nature of Bakhtin's literary analysis. He did not engage in close readings of particular writers or literary works, but was more interested in examining philosophical problems concerning self-other relations or the spirit of a time through the work—for instance, the Renaissance through Rabelais, the second half of the nineteenth century through Dostoevsky (Emerson, 1989).

Certainly, there are different ways of describing the structure of Bakhtin's ideas that evolved between the late 1920s and the 1960s; various interpreters have concentrated on the literary, ideological, or philosophical dimensions of his essays and books. One approach is to interpret notions such as dialogue and polyphony, the chronotope, and carnival as parts of, or models for, his theory of the novel and of genre types more generally. Genre, for Bakhtin, provided evidence of a specific mode of thought or a particular realm of experience. From this perspective, much of his work can be seen as a veering between the contextualization of literary categories and their generalization as exemplary genre types.

Bakhtin used the concept of dialogue and the dialogic in many contexts and in at least three distinct ways in his book on Dostoevsky, as well as in other essays (Morson and Emerson, 1990). First, and most specifically, dialogue refers to the fact that every utterance is by nature dialogic. An utterance can never be abstract, but must occur between two consciousnesses, a speaker and a listener, a creator and an audience.

Second, dialogue in this first sense either can be monologic or dialogic. Although Bakhtin's discussions sometimes lack clarity—for instance, he introduced complicated concepts of active and passive/single and double-voiced discourse—monologism means that dialogue becomes empty and lifeless. As he wrote in "Notes Made in 1970–71" concerning dialectics as a form of monologism, "Take a dialogue and remove the voices (the partitioning of voices), remove the intonations (emotional and individualized ones), carve out abstract concepts and judgments from living words and responses, cram everything into one abstract consciousness—and that's how you get dialectics." For Bakhtin, truth could be monologic or dialogic, and he argued that modern thought has been dominated by monologic conceptions of truth. Dostoevsky, he observed

(Bakhtin, 1984), was the first truly "polyphonic" writer, who thought and spoke through paradoxes, differing points of view, and unique consciousnesses. To be polyphonic, verbal communication and social interaction must be characterized by contestation rather than automatic consensus. Polyphony, however, is distinct from heteroglossia, which describes the diversity of speech styles within a particular language. All utterances are heteroglot, insofar as they occur within particular set of social, historical, physiological, and other conditions. Polyphony has more to do with the position of the author and with the nature of dialogue and truth in the work.

Bakhtin's concept of polyphony, although he never explicitly defined it in the Dostoevsky book or elsewhere, describes a way of thinking and visualizing that presupposes the third, most general sense of dialogue. Bakhtin understood life itself as dialogue, as he articulated in his 1961 essay on Dostoevsky: "To live means to participate in dialogue: to ask questions, to heed, to respond, to agree, and so forth. In this dialogue a person participates wholly and throughout his whole life: with his eyes, lips, hands, soul, spirit, with his whole body and deeds. He invests his entire self in discourse, and this discourse enters into the dialogic fabric of human life, into the world symposium" (Bakhtin, 1984.) Dialogue, therefore, is epistemological: only through it do we know ourselves, other persons, and the world.

Where dialogue describes the process and practice of communication and relationship among selves, the concept of the chronotope describes the time/space nexus in which life exists and creativity is possible. This intrinsic connectedness of temporal and spatial relationships is aesthetically expressed in literature, especially through literary genre. For instance, the epic is characterized by a chronotope that values a national heroic past, rooted in tradition; temporal distance separates it from the present. By contrast, the novel—with a world (and worlds) still in the making, rooted in experience and multilayered consciousness, and where knowledge and practice evolve not in relation to past traditions but to contemporary realities—expresses profoundly different chronotopes. Subject and genre boundaries are open in the novel, which may use fictional events, moral confessions, philosophical manifestos, rhetoric, letter or diary forms. The chronotope of the novel expresses a new relationship to future. But with this concept Bakhtin was not articulating a phenomenology, which would objectify time and space; rather, he sought to describe how experience is made palpable. The chronotope is not a concept in a Kantian or Hegelian sense, but a formal heuristic notion that demonstrates the impossibility of constructing seamless totalities.

In his study of Rabelais, Bakhtin hoped to move away from moralistic nineteenth-century readings and toward a reconstruction of the folk culture of carnivalesque laughter.

He had also explored themes of laughter and folk culture in earlier essays such as "Forms of Time and of the Chronotope" (in *The Dialogic Imagination*), but in *Rabelais and His World* (1968) carnival became another example of a genre type. In carnival, and in folk culture more generally, official institutions as well as definitions of the sacred are transcended or reversed, at least for a time. Although Bakhtin's reading of Rabelais cannot be understood as a historical study of carnival, he sought to show that the world is a place where the drama of the body—its physicality through birth, coitus, eating, drinking, evacuation, death—is played out. In analyzing phenomena such as laughter, masks, grotesque images of the body, what he called "images of the material bodily lower stratum," and various forms of debasement, Bakhtin created an encyclopedia of folk culture, showing that the body is actually the foundation of society and of our relationships to nature.

In the late essays and notes, written in the 1970s, Bakhtin returned to themes related to his early essays. For instance, he touched on issues such as creative understanding, great time (related to Fernand Braudel's *longue durée*), intertextuality, the uniqueness of the humanities, and a broad interpretation of genres that emphasized the ways in which they offer diverse approaches to seeing and interpreting the world.

Bakhtin's ideas—answerability, outsideness, unfinalizability, dialogue, monologism, polyphony, heteroglossia, chronotope, and the carnivalesque, to name but a few—offer contemporary scholars categories for aesthetics in general and for analysis of the breakdown of genres and the reemergence of new narrative structures in contemporary art and literature. His work can also aid critics and historians in creating taxonomies for interpreting works of verbal and visual art in relation to one another. With ideas such as unfinalizability, as well as his emphasis on the importance of individual particularity and situatedness, his interpretation of the ways in which narrative and fiction structure history, and his understanding of the interpenetration of text and context, Bakhtin's work predates and anticipates a variety of ideas within literary and cultural movements such as neohistoricism and various strands of poststructuralism and postmodernism.

Aesthetic theory can describe *what happens when we look.* Such a theory of looking is not just phenomenological, but, as Bakhtin's oeuvre shows, it must describe a genuine encounter of one consciousness with another. Visual or aesthetic theory can also function to describe, literally and formally, *what one sees.* To see another life for its significance qua life—this should be the goal of aesthetic experience and of art, according to Bakhtin. Perhaps the most significant contribution of Mikhail Bakhtin's aesthetics to contemporary cultural theory, however, is his affirmation that art must exist in an integral relationship with life, that art for its own sake is mere artifice. His ideas offer renewed appreciation for the world-forming potential of the artist's creative vision and creative voice.

[*See also* Grotesque; Poetics; Russian Aesthetics; *and* Text.]

BIBLIOGRAPHY

Works by Bakhtin

Art and Answerability: Early Philosophical Essays. Translated by Vadim Liapunov and Kenneth Brostrom, edited by Michael Holquist and Vadim Liapunov. Austin, Tex., 1990.

The Dialogic Imagination: Four Essays by M. M. Bakhtin. Edited by Michael Holquist, translated by Caryl Emerson and Michael Holquist. Austin, Tex., 1981.

Problems of Dostoevsky's Poetics. Edited and translated by Caryl Emerson. Minneapolis, 1984.

Rabelais and His World. Translated by Helene Iswolsky. Cambridge, Mass., 1968; reprint, Bloomington, Ind., 1984.

Speech Genres and Other Late Essays. Translated by Vern W. McGee, edited by Caryl Emerson and Michael Holquist. Austin, Tex., 1986.

Toward a Philosophy of the Act. Translated by Vadim Liapunov, edited by Vadim Liapunov and Michael Holquist. Austin, Tex., 1993.

Other Sources

Clark, Katerina, and Michael Holquist. *Mikhail Bakhtin.* Cambridge, Mass., 1984.

Emerson, Caryl. "The Tolstoy Connection in Bakhtin." In *Rethinking Bakhtin: Extensions and Challenges,* edited by Gary Saul Morson and Caryl Emerson. Evanston, Ill., 1989.

Haynes, Deborah J. *Bakhtin and the Visual Arts.* Cambridge and New York, 1995.

Holquist, Michael. *Dialogism: Bakhtin and His World.* London and New York, 1990.

Medvedev, Pavel N. *The Formal Method in Literary Scholarship.* Translated by Albert J. Wehrle. Baltimore, 1978; reprint, Cambridge, Mass., 1985.

Morson, Gary Saul, and Caryl Emerson. *Rethinking Bakhtin: Extensions and Challenges.* Evanston, Ill., 1989.

Morson, Gary Saul, and Caryl Emerson. *Mikhail Bakhtin: Creation of a Prosaics.* Stanford, Calif., 1990.

Voloshinov, V. N. *Marxism and the Philosophy of Language.* Translated by Ladislav Matejka and I. R. Titunik. New York, 1973; reprint, Cambridge, Mass., 1986.

Voloshinov, V. N. *Freudianism: A Critical Sketch.* Translated by I. R. Titunik, edited in collaboration with Neal H. Bruss. Bloomington, Ind., 1987.

DEBORAH J. HAYNES

BAROQUE AESTHETICS. Like *Gothic, baroque* is at once a qualitative term and a historical concept. In everyday discourse, the term *baroque* is used pejoratively to mean overwrought, complex, and excessive. At the same time, *Baroque* describes a cultural movement of the seventeenth century, defined by characteristic styles in the visual arts, music, and literature. Its most common usage is as a reference to the period spanning around 1580 to 1720–1750, depending on the art form. As an overall aesthetic concept, a quality, a sensibility, or a style, *baroque* is notoriously difficult to analyze, because its two applications are in many ways inextricable and interdependent. The most fruitful understanding of *baroque* demands an overview of both the concept's development and the aesthetic ideals of the Baroque period itself.

History of the Term. Over the past two centuries the term *baroque* has undergone a number of transformations that reflect not only changing fashions in aesthetics but shifts in critical theory as a whole. Even its etymology has been disputed. The most popularly cited derivation, acknowledged during the eighteenth century when the term was first used, is from the Spanish *barrueco,* and Portuguese *barroco,* from the Latin *veruca,* or wart, referring to the irregularly shaped pearls favored in sixteenth- and seventeenth-century jewelry design; *barroco* is still used among jewelers today. Another derivation, suggested by Benedetto Croce during the 1920s, is *baroco,* a mnemonic term devised during the fourteenth century for a complex figure in formal logic. Sixteenth- and seventeenth-century Italian writers would use the phrase *argomento in baroco* to designate the pedantic, convoluted thinking of late-medieval logic. The tradition of two derivations is understandable because they are in fact similar in connotation.

By the mid-eighteenth century, *baroque* or *barocco* had become a convenient, and always derogatory, term for the grotesque, bizarre, excessive, or absurd, applied indiscriminately to artistic, architectural, and musical styles. This is largely because of the classicist bias of much contemporary aesthetics. In 1746, the French philosopher Noël-Antoine Pluche distinguished *musique baroque* (mutable, speedy, audacious, artificial, technically demanding of the performer) from *musique chantante* (unforced, melodic in a manner attuned to the human voice, natural and artless). He also described performances, as well as the music itself, as *baroque* (*Spectacle de la nature,* 1746, vol. 7). Jean-Jacques Rousseau's *Dictionnaire de la musique* (1778) defines baroque music as dissonant, confusingly intricate, and with impetuous changes in tempo and harmony. Meanwhile, in Denis Diderot's *Encyclopédie* (1772), *baroque* referred to bizarre forms of architecture. Interestingly enough, what is now called Baroque art—that is, post-Renaissance art—was severely criticized during the eighteenth century. Millizia, in his *Dizionario delle Belle Arti e del Disegno* (1797), applies the term in its sense of "bizarre" to the work of architects such as Francesco Borromini and Guarino Guarini.

Baroque as a Period Style. The art historian Jakob Burkhardt (1855) was the first to designate Baroque as an artistic style associated with a particular historical period. Continuing the term's tradition of opprobrium, he defined the baroque as "a corrupt dialect" of the Renaissance. Indeed, some art historians under the influence of Burkhardt and his fellow partisans of the Italian High Renaissance, Croce and Bernard Berenson, used *baroque* as a generic aes-

BAROQUE AESTHETICS.   Peter Paul Rubens, *Venus Holding Back Mars* (1637), oil on canvas; Palazzo Pitti, Florence. (Photograph courtesy of Alinari/Art Resource, New York.)

thetic concept meaning the decadent, grotesque late stage of a given style, without reference to a particular historical period. Thus *Roman Baroque* was occasionally used to refer to late antiquity, and *Gothic Baroque,* for the expressive distortions of fifteenth-century German art.

Baroque was finally rescued from opprobrium by Heinrich Wölfflin in *Renaissance und Barock* (1888), a study of sixteenth- and seventeenth-century architectural form. Wölfflin insisted on eliminating the term's pejorative associations in an effort to clarify seventeenth-century style. Baroque style, according to Wölfflin, was not decadent but "a great phenomenon": an inevitable shift from the classical stability, harmony, and clarity of the High Renaissance to a heavy, unarticulated, massiveness, shot through with light, dissonance, and movement.

By 1915, in *Kunstgeschichtliche Grundbegriffe,* Wölfflin had definitively isolated the distinction between Renaissance and baroque style, in painting and sculpture and architecture, according to his famous formal dichotomies: linear/painterly, plane and recession, closed form/open form, multiplicity/unity, clearness and unclearness. This theory of stylistic evolution based on opposing forces is strikingly similar to Friedrich Nietzsche's proposal of Dionysian and Apollonian principles in *Die Geburt der Tragödie* (1870).

Wölfflin's pairs of opposites are meant as absolute, inevitable polarizations in all of art, and are not limited to a particular time period. Thus, his comparisons of Renaissance and Baroque paintings, prints, and sculptures isolate patterns of evolution in the essentials of representation: lines and shadows, composition, the treatment of space, which operate independently of differences among native traditions, or modes appropriate to the work's subject matter or context. Instead, his deterministic notion of style is historicized in a more global, abstract manner, claiming that Baroque style arose from larger historical and social forces and visualizing a new zeitgeist. [*See* Wölfflin.]

Thereafter, studies in seventeenth-century art continued in the wake of Wölfflin's rehabilitation of the Baroque. The term lost its pejorative associations, as well as its original meaning, over the centuries; it has become a loose definition of the period between Mannerism and Rococo, spanning the late sixteenth century to the mid-eighteenth century. As a historical phenomenon, the Baroque began to be defined more fully in relation to both psychological and social concepts. Erwin Panofsky, in his lecture "What Is Baroque?" (1935), defined its stylistic tendencies as a transformation of the formal, emotional, and even religious conflicts of the High Renaissance and Mannerism into "subjective emotional energy" (Panovsky, 1995). The limits of the Baroque, for Panofsky, extend to the industrial revolution. [*See* Panofsky.*] Some scholars have treated the Baroque as a purely Italian phenomenon, driven by the evangelical demands of Catholic institutions in a spirit of renewal and reform. Others have reintroduced the element of classicism, which Wölfflin omits, reclaiming for the Baroque academically inclined artists such as the Carracci brothers and Nicolas Poussin. More recently, with the increase of specialization within the discipline, art historians have taken *Baroque* as a given, focusing their scholarly view on specific examples of Baroque art to trace local traditions rather than the character of the *baroque* in general.

Two notable exceptions are Germain Bazin (1968) and John Rupert Martin (1977), who offer surveys of Baroque art as a whole by integrating art of several cultures in several media. Bazin's bold, all-embracing strategy, organizing his discussion around "principles," "styles," "modes" and "themes," is exhilarating but ultimately confusing. "Principles," for example, includes not only philosophical and aesthetic issues but different social institutions and milieus; Baroque "style" encompasses Gothic, Mannerist, and Classical as well as baroque. Martin follows this brilliant example in a more lucid manner, taming the unruly concept by organizing his discussion around larger themes such as "space," "time," and "light," as well as naturalism, allegory, and antiquity.

In the history of music, the definition of Baroque as a historical period has been fairly straightforward, presumably because it demarcates the evolution of specific, easily identifiable forms and structures. The most important structural change is a shift toward chordal harmony, the splitting of equal-voiced counterpoint into a treble line carrying the melody and an accompanying continuo. This was accompanied by a free use of dissonance; greater variation in rhythm, now liberated from the precision and consistency of the Renaissance *tactus;* and the use of measures to regulate patterns of beats. New forms based on these structural changes include recitative and opera, the concerto, the prelude, and the fugue. There is general consensus about the beginnings of Baroque (about 1580), though more dispute about its end, or emergence into the "classical" period in the mid-eighteenth century.

The progress of Baroque as a period concept in literary studies has been far more troubled. In *Renaissance und Barock,* Wölfflin had encouraged the application of the term to literature, comparing the opening stanzas of Ludovico Ariosto's *Orlando Furioso* (1532) and Torquato Tasso's *Gerusalemme Liberata* (1575). He evokes the shift in these verses from the light and easy grace of the Renaissance to seriousness and dignity—pompous, rustling splendor as an analogy to changes in pictorial and architectural form. His association of style and zeitgeist was likewise popular among scholars in other fields, and made them especially receptive to his ideas. Taking their cue from his formal dichotomies, literary scholars began applying the concept of Baroque to literature during the 1920s.

In some cases, the term was adopted as easily as in art history. The success of Baroque as an art-historical concept in Germany prompted literary scholars to accept the term readily. Scholars of Spanish literature likewise adopted the term fairly quickly, encompassing specific tendencies of the native tradition such as *cultista* and *conceptismo,* in contrast to a more sober classical style. The term was slower to win approval in England, where period designations tend to correspond to political eras (e.g., Elizabethan, Jacobean), which in turn overlap stylistic modes such as "metaphysical." This was also the case in France, where, as is clear from the critical writings of the eighteenth century, there has always been a strong classicist disapproval of the Baroque aesthetic.

Nonetheless, on an international scale, the entry of Baroque into the field of literature has created a tradition of thorny debate, revealing the enormous difficulty of adapting an art-historical term to literary studies. Several generations of scholars have proposed and refined various definitions of Baroque poetry, prose, and drama, as well as arguing the merits and problems of the term itself. Many critics have attempted to consider a unified Baroque style throughout the arts, whereas others have remarked on the inadequacy of this endeavor, focusing instead on the origins of Baroque style within literary tradition itself, or on themes and subject matter, rather than styles, common to Baroque literature and visual arts. The literary debate flourishing since the postwar period suggests that no specific style can be appropriately applied across the arts.

What has proved far more useful in literary studies is the art-historical approach to the Baroque as an agglomeration of styles and modes, whereby the various arts are subsumed under a more general discussion of Baroque culture. Such is the case with surveys by Peter Skrine (1978) and Giancarlo Maiorino (1990), who associate works of literature with visual art according to similarities of theme, mode, and subject. In general, the term's enormous convenience as a historical designation, even a catchphrase, has outweighed and perhaps resolved its past problems of definition and scope. Carl Friedrich's (1952) survey of Baroque culture, arts, politics, and war anticipates the approach of most contemporary scholars, for whom Baroque is not only a seventeenth-century cultural movement, but a sensibility. Indeed, since the early 1970s, the unwieldy nature of the concept has proved an asset rather than a liability: Baroque has become an appealing subject for the interdisciplinary approach popular in late-twentieth-century critical methodology. The art-historical model of Baroque permits an analysis of various styles, produced by often widely divergent artists in various media, who nonetheless share certain themes, modes, and preoccupations.

Political and Social Origins of the Baroque. Since the 1920s, studies of the origins and character of the Baroque have inevitably addressed religion and cultural history as well as elements of style. Wölfflin's use of the zeitgeist model has been replaced—or rather, refined—to analysis of the relation between the arts and specific religious and political institutions during the seventeenth century. The most persistent theory associates Baroque arts with the Counter-Reformation, which demanded great emotional intensity in the arts as a way of inspiring religious faith. In comparative studies, Richard Crashaw and Gianlorenzo Bernini are commonly invoked as representatives of this trend; yet, this association does not account for the many other artists, poets, and patrons who were neither Catholic nor concerned with religious subject matter. Another useful but limited theory links the development of the Baroque with the cultivation of the arts at the absolutist courts. More recently, market and patronage studies have explored cultivation of the arts among the rising bourgeoisie, the development of secular genres to suit this new audience, the influence of academies in France and Italy on the nature of artists' styles and careers, and the changing social status of artists and poets, who no longer needed to be members of court in order to practice and find an audience for their work.

A crucial element of Baroque is its international flavor. Extraordinary economic expansion enabled an unprecedented degree of cultural exchange among the new nation-states. Both Bernini and Peter Paul Rubens, for example, developed an enormously successful style that earned them the status of international celebrities. This sensuous and grandiloquent manner, enlivening classical models with naturalistic observation, eroticism, and raw emotion, was equally well suited to allegorical, mythological, religious, and political art. Painting and sculpture in this mode became a desirable commodity among aristocratic and royal patrons throughout Europe and England.

An important factor in the dissemination of Baroque styles was the rise of art collecting. In addition to the aristocracy, bourgeois collectors began to acquire paintings, prints, and drawings in record numbers. Drawing in particular became a valued medium in its own right, as an index of an artist's personal style, direct, free, and untrammeled by detail and finish. (This is also true of the preparatory oil sketch, which Rubens promoted through his own practices.) Meanwhile, the increase in the publication and sales of prints gave both artists and amateurs greater access to a variety of styles, and abetted the international spread of local traditions. Rembrandt's collection of prints, paintings, and plaster casts of antique sculpture offered such an abundance of visual material that he once famously remarked that he had no need to visit Italy.

Another fruitful area of historical analysis links the Baroque arts with an expanding knowledge of the world engendered by new developments in science, exploration, and technology. The inventions of the telescope and the microscope increased the awareness of an infinitude beyond the limits of the visible world. Galileo's confirmation of Copernican theory established an Earth in motion along with other planetary bodies, inspiring a preoccupation with the transience of human life. The pendulum clock and the spiral watch spring, invented by Christiaan Huygens, created a systematic regulation of time by which institutions could function and individuals could live and work. Finally, voyages of discovery during the sixteenth and seventeenth centuries brought the artifacts of new cultures into the environment of the wealthy European.

Accordingly, Baroque artists explored formal and thematic means of articulating this expanded awareness of space, time, and motion. One common aim was to dissolve as much as possible the barrier between the work of art and the real world, pushing their media to the limits of physical possibility. Painters employed sophisticated trompe l'oeil devices to make their two-dimensional works spring to life, and sculptures were designed in the round to interact directly with the observer's space. Architects expanded their manipulation of space and scale into entire environments. In theater, stage design was coordinated with the surrounding space rather than isolated by a proscenium. The access to foreign cultures made possible by broadening geographic horizons inspired a trend toward exotic fantasy that would find expression in the fine and decorative arts. At the same time, the interest in geographic expansion was nourished by the prospering cartography business; in the Netherlands, for example, maps hung alongside pictures in every home.

Another new Baroque theme was the passage of time. This is strikingly evident in the sense of arrested movement captured in painting and sculpture. The aesthetic of sponaneity, in fact, can be seen as responsible for the new valuation of the sketch as a work of art in its own right. Likewise, artists developed new subjects illustrating the themes of transitoriness and mutability, such as still life and landscape, the four seasons, and allegories of vanity. Finally, the dramatic power of light was exploited to an unprecedented degree, central to both the tenebrous dramas of Michelangelo da Caravaggio and the reflecting pools and mirrors of Versailles.

Baroque Aesthetics. The theoretical movement with the greatest influence on the aesthetics of the period was the great interest among philosophers in emotions and behavior, what might be called Baroque psychology. Central to these philosophical inquiries is the theory of the affections, or passions, developed during the late sixteenth century. The concept of the affections is based on an Aristotelian concept of fear, anger, sorrow, joy, and so on as discrete separate states. The affections are animal spirits and vapors that live in varying combinations in the body. Internal or external sensations stimulate the body to alter the spirits; hence, a new "affection" or "passion" results. An important text for this theory is René Descartes's *Passions of the Soul* (1649), which validated many ideas already in circulation regarding the passions. Thomas Hobbes writes in *Leviathan* (1651) that the passions are essential for human life, being evidence of man's "perpetual and restless desire of power." From the late sixteenth century onward, arousing the affections became the main objective of the arts. Artists sought to transport their audiences to a higher level of feeling, whether religious or political awe, amusement, astonishment, or terror. Effects of wonder and surprise dominated the visual, dramatic, and literary arts: masques, with their eye-popping extravagance and sudden "turns" or revelations; the statues suddenly appearing around a bend in fantasy-garden; the elaborate conceits and spasms of emotion in metaphysical poetry; and the enveloping sound of Venetian polychoral music.

Baroque theory, expressed in the form of didactic essays, lectures and handbooks, and biographies, linked all the arts through the long-standing humanist theory of ut pictura poesis. Theorists emphasized the importance of audience, viewer, or reader response, recommending various modes and devices best suited to stirring the passions. To some extent, this involved a rejection of Mannerism or *maniera,* which by 1600 had taken on a pejorative sense of "mannered" and divorced from nature. In general, the aim of art, to echo Aristotle, was to instruct and delight—that is, to give abstract ideals the most persuasively physical form. An important aid favored by writers on art and literature alike was the emblem book. Since the late sixteenth century, these visual repositories of moral and spiritual themes were produced all over Europe. Much of their immense appeal was in providing a pictorial repertoire of philosophical, amorous, and political formulas, which could acquire physical authority and emotional resonance through the transforming arts of poetry, painting, and sculpture.

One commonly noted feature of Baroque aesthetics is a bifurcation of emotional intensity (often associated with Counter-Reformation ideals) and the balance and restraint of classicism, one of several theoretical problems in discussions of the term. Yet, many seventeenth- and eighteenth-century writers encouraging emotional expression in painting were deeply committed to a classicist aesthetic. In fact, the study of the affections, that is, an interest in emotional immediacy, dovetailed with the continued reverence for antiquity, still an ideal as it had been during the Renaissance. During the seventeenth century, theory emphasized making classical models more dramatically present and psychologically acute. Didactic writings stressed the importance of copying ancient sculpture (often included in the rubric "drawing from life") as an ideal of beauty and heroism on which to build stirring dramas. There was an established canon of Roman antique sculptures, which artists used over and over in different ways according to their tastes. Antiquities, like nature itself, were to be copied and then improved upon; the artist's task was to bring them to colorful life. Two characteristic essays stressing the practical and theoretical aspects of antique models are Rubens's "On the Imitation of Statues" (published by De Piles in 1708), and Giovanni Bellori's *L'idea del pittore, dello scultore, e dell'architetto* (1674), in many ways the definitive statement of classicism.

Thus, theorists also emphasized the importance of invention, or the artist's own imagination, combining an eye for historical authenticity with a flair for anecdote and immediacy. The resulting powerful narratives not only captivate the viewer but ennoble the painter. Taking Leon Battista Alberti's governing principle of *istoria* to a new level of intensity, Baroque theorists encouraged painters to engage the viewer as vigorously as possible. Gérard de Lairesse, in his *Groot Schilderboeck* of 1711, recommends organizing a narrative scene so that the denouement strikes the observer "just as a cannonball, shot from a distance, hits a nearby bulwark and scatters everything in its path."

Roger De Piles, in his *Cours de peinture* (1708), and Samuel van Hoogstraten, in his *Inleyding tot de hooghe schole der Schilderkonst* (1678), express related views in their hierarchies of genres. This categorization favored the multifigured historical scene as the greatest subject for painting, permitting the greatest exploitation of the painter's choreographic and dramatic skills. At the same time, the "lesser" genres such as still life, landscape, and genre scenes, reflecting the interests and tastes of new patrons, were also opportunities to display one's talents for lively anecdote and mimetic scrutiny.

This concern for vividness, linking "classical" and "emotional" modes of expression, and "high" and "low" subjects, was often manifested in the systematic study of expression. The means of expressing the passions through gesture and facial expression had already been formulated by Renaissance artists and theorists using Aristotle and the ancient rhetoricians as their guide. Both Alberti and Leonardo da Vinci had considered the study of expression to be vital to the history painter. During the Baroque period, the range of experience to be depicted in visual art was expanded. Poussin applied theories of ancient rhetoric to painting, believing that the depiction of gestures and facial expressions could move the spectator emotionally just as an orator would do. Echoing Quintilian, he claims that without the language of the body, line and color are likewise useless. Charles Le Brun, who carefully studied Descartes's treatise, created a strict codification of the passions. He illustrated his renowned lecture on expression (published in 1698) with drawings of faces. Forming a literal catalog of expressions, they are grouped in pairs that express contrasting emotions, such as hope and fear, accompanied by descriptions echoing the Cartesian system of opposites.

Naturalism and the Model of Rhetoric. Poussin's invocation of rhetorical theory, and Le Brun's classification of the passions, are similar to the adaptations of rhetoric in literature and music. Baroque poetry and prose, with their complexity, ingenious metaphors, and shifts of tone, were strongly influenced by the practices and ideas of rhetoric. Likewise, composers used systematically codified musical "figures," such as sudden rhythmic or harmonic changes, extended ornamentation of a line or a cadence, or unexpected chromatic notes, to illustrate or emphasize the meanings of words.

This close association with rhetorical models is the force behind the importance of naturalism in Baroque aesthetics. Hand in hand with the use of classical models is the repeated injunction to represent the world and its objects as they appear, as a means of persuasion. (These seemingly divergent standards, the "classicist" and the "realist," were not necessarily in conflict as they came to be during the nineteenth century.) The Dutch theorists were particularly concerned with achieving what they called *houding*, fusing drawing, composition, color, and shadow to create a legible, convincing space, as Willem Goeree wrote: "receding or advancing naturally to the eye, as if it were accessible to one's feet" (*Grondlegginge der Teykenkonst*, 1670). Similarly, the portrayal of individual character required special concentration. Portraitists strove for more dynamic compositions along with greater psychological penetration, which also spurred the invention of caricature.

Naturalistic effects likewise appealed to the passions in the other arts. In theater, realism replaced allegory, both in stage design (in the transition from a medieval flat facade to the modern illusionistic stage) and in the plays themselves. Plays became increasingly mimetic, expanding from allegories to more realistic tragedy and farce. The French concept of the three dramatic unities codified this mimetic tendency into an official mode. Similarly, in baroque music, the dominant aim of composers and performers was the expression of a text. Hence, the invention of recitative, or quasi speech, whereby the words governed the musical rhythm. Writers on music at the time acknowledged the theatricality of recitative: the singer was supposed to move the audience with the same skills as an orator.

Baroque Today. While *Baroque* has settled into its current comfortable niche as a designation of a period style, the word has persisted as a pejorative term. In critical discourse, it is still used to describe an artistic style characterized by extravagance and bombast. Jean Baudrillard, in "L'effet beaubourg" (1981), uses *baroque* to refer to what he sees as the worst excesses of postmodern architecture. Similarly, in everyday conversation, the generic adjective *baroque* is used to characterize objects, institutions, systems, procedures, and rituals that strike one as convoluted and overly theatrical. Interestingly, it has overtones similar to

those of *gothic* and *byzantine*. All three terms, evoking the aesthetics of the past, serve equally well to describe something excessive and tortuously complex, a fact that attests to their tenacity in our cultural imagination.

[*See also* Style.]

BIBLIOGRAPHY

Bazin, Germain. *The Baroque: Principles, Styles, Modes, Themes.* Translated by Pat Wardroper. London, 1968.
Brusati, Celeste. *Artifice and Illusion: The Art and Writing of Samuel van Hoogstraten.* Chicago, 1995. See pp. 218–227.
Bukofzer, Manfred F. *Music in the Baroque Era.* New York, 1947.
Filipczak, Zirka Zaremba. *Picturing Art in Antwerp, 1550–1700.* Princeton, N.J., 1987.
Friedrich, Carl J. *The Age of the Baroque, 1610–1660.* New York, 1952.
Haskell, Francis. *Patrons and Painters: A Study in the Relations between Italian Art and Society in the Age of the Baroque.* Rev. enl. ed. New Haven, 1980.
Lee, Rensselaer W. *Ut Pictura Poesis: The Humanistic Theory of Painting.* New York, 1967.
Maiorino, Giancarlo. *The Cornucopian Mind and the Baroque Unity of the Arts.* University Park, Pa., 1990.
Martin, John Rupert. *Baroque.* New York, 1977.
Palisca, Claude V. *Baroque Music.* 3d ed. Englewood Cliffs, N.J., 1991.
Panofsky, Erwin. *Idea: A Concept in Art Theory.* Translated by Joseph J. S. Peake. Columbia, S.C., 1968.
Panofsky, Erwin. "What Is Baroque?" In *Three Essays on Style,* edited by Irving Lavin. Cambridge, Mass., 1995. A previously unpublished lecture, delivered in 1935.
Pevsner, Nikolaus. *Academies of Art, Past and Present.* Cambridge, 1940.
Pigler, A. *Barockthemen, eine Auswahl von Verzeichnissen zur Ikonographie des 17. und 18. Jahrhunderts.* Budapest, 1956.
Praz, Mario. *Studies in Seventeenth-Century Imagery.* 2d ed. Rome, 1964.
Skrine, Peter N. *The Baroque: Literature and Culture in Seventeenth-Century Europe.* New York, 1978.
Steadman, John M. *Redefining a Period Style: "Renaissance," "Mannerist," and "Baroque" in Literature.* Pittsburgh, 1990.
Warnke, Frank J. *Versions of Baroque: European Literature in the Seventeenth Century.* New Haven, 1972.
Wellek, René. "The Concept of the Baroque in Literary Scholarship." *Journal of Aesthetics and Art Criticism* 5 (1946): 77–109. This entire issue contains a number of articles devoted to the baroque as a stylistic concept in various arts.
Wölfflin, Heinrich. *Principles of Art History: The Problem of the Development of Style in Later Art.* 6th ed. Translated by M. D. Hottinger. London, 1932; reprint, New York, 1950.

MARTHA HOLLANDER

BARTHES, ROLAND (1915–1980), French essayist and critic. Barthes charted the course run in mid-twentieth-century France from structuralism to a poststructuralism that included his search for a science of the individual predicated on revision of traditional conceptions of the human subject. His reconception is distinctive in marking a turn from the semiological to the causal and in repositioning the subject with respect to time as well as to language. Barthes's desire was always to discover what was beyond the languages of any time, and in the last years of his life his interest was increasingly in what could not be said but nonetheless was felt and lived.

Barthes was among the first to apply Ferdinand de Saussure's structural model of language to literature and cultural systems. *Writing Degree Zero* (1953) distinguishes modern poetry from a perfectly neutral, undivided, and unambiguous language by characterizing two poles: language, displayed along a horizontal axis because spoken over time, and style, displayed along a vertical axis because rising from the depths of the unconscious, the seat of the instincts whose energy drives the organism. Algebra is pure language: its symbols, context-dependent, are transparent to their determinate meanings. Modern poetry is pure style: its words, context-free, are pregnant with all the words and, hence, all the meanings there are. Writing, as Barthes understands it, is an operation on language in which, perforce, choices are made among words. No choice is necessary in algebraic operations because the symbols operated on are perfectly determined by their context. No choice is necessary in poetry because its symbols, rich with all the associations that a creative imagination can make, are not limited by their setting. Writing, therefore, is at zero degree in these pure states. Recognizing that language penetrates passions and actions, beliefs and desires, Barthes saw writing as the quintessential human activity because through it individuals become producers rather than consumers of the "intelligible unities" carved out by the languages of a time. "Writing" is not the exclusive possession of literature, for literature is just one species of writing, not different in kind from others. Writing itself is one species of signifying, and until 1970 Barthes sought to uncover the common structures in various signifying systems: cultural phenomena (*Mythologies,* 1957), French literature (*On Racine,* 1963), fashion (*The Fashion System,* 1967), and other cultures (*Empire of Signs,* 1970). A primer, *Elements of Semiology* (1964), introduced the new science, while the book on Racine inspired the academic critic, Raymond Picard, savagely to attack the New Criticism. Barthes's reply in *Criticism and Truth* (1966) was a triumph of structuralism over the criticism entrenched in the academy. The science of structure soon gave way, however, to an emphasis on the performance of the subject structured by the signifying systems.

The activity of structuring is what interested Barthes. He characterized this activity as consisting in the fragmentation of almost anything whatsoever and the recombination of the fragments according to certain codes. Only the unique individual is excluded from the process. The given can in principle be fragmented in any way, no a priori nature determines its fault lines, and the units can be associated along whatever lines pragmatic criteria suggest. Barthes's examination of the construction and the consequences of the science of various structures soon gave way, however, to exploration of the *per-*

formance of the subject that both does the structuring and is itself structured by the signifying systems. *S/Z* (1970) is the fragmentation of a Balzac story into an arbitrary number of lexemes (least units of significance) that demonstrated a creative, productive *writerly* reading that unsettles the reader's comfortable beliefs about language. The lexemes are organized by a number of codes, and the reader may follow whichever of them she chooses for however long she wills. She may freely move among them all in many rhythms and patterns. Saussure's structure has been set in motion by being operated by a writerly reader. This new kind of reading had been demanded by avant-garde texts that made no sense when read in the familiar *readerly* way, and although not demanded by tradition's texts, writerly readings of them produce a "little cataclysm" in the reader's set of beliefs. The notion of the writerly is parasitic on a conception of language according to which, first, language is an infinite network of horizontal and vertical axes, directionless, with no prescribed entry points and no end, and, second, particular works are homologues of the network. The reader's interpreting a given lexeme with a given code invests it with a meaning that lasts as long as the reading does, and the reader's interweaving the one code with another proceeds neither by rules nor by anything actual in her or the text. It is a pure performance that dissolves the reader into the text she is reading. This is Barthes's first ecstasy, and its possibility defines his poststructuralism.

The *Pleasure of the Text* (1973) characterizes the ecstasy of the writerly as an erotic tracing of the course of the reader's desire and inaugurates a trio of books on love: *Roland Barthes by Roland Barthes* (1975), *A Lover's Discourse: Fragments* (1977), and *Camera Lucida: Reflections on Photography* (1980). In the first, Barthes identifies himself as characters in a novel, plural and made out of words. This is to say that not even from the first person point of view is there a unifying and enduring soul or self that constitutes him; there is not even a set of characteristics true of him and constant over time that comprises an identity. There are only words, material and mobile. Barthes is one for whom words are dense and have weight, for whom they are not ready vehicles for the transmission of ready-made thoughts, for whom the *acts* of language (speaking, writing, etc.) preempt their issue (what is spoken, written, etc.). In the second of the trio, *A Lovers's Discourse,* Barthes identifies whomever he loves as what cannot be classified but only designated by blank words, *thus, so.* The beloved is neither spoken (of) nor speaking: love is outside of language, its discourse solitary, and the lover is identified by his wordless designation of the objects of his love. Because each designation is sheer act, sheer affirmation, it is unique and unrepeatable, and the lover is the site of all such acts. Nothing is spoken, written, read, or heard: in the discourse of love, language is all act and no issue.

In the final book, *Camera Lucida,* human subjects' writing with words yields to nature's writing with light on the camera's photographic plate, and the lover's wordless designation of the beloved yields to the camera's designation of the past real. The second ecstasy, whose possibility defines Barthes's postmodernism, is the dissolve of a photograph's spectator into the past time when the photograph was taken. The photograph recalls the spectator to the time of its taking, when the object was there before the camera to pattern the light the camera captured. The causal efficacy of the process proves the past reality of the object as nothing can prove a present reality. Two points must be made. First, the photograph does not prove the past reality by triggering the spectator's memory, for memory is vulnerable to distortion by the spectator's beliefs, desires, emotions, moods, and states of mind. Rather, it proves it in the same way that any effect proves the existence of its cause: if the existence of X is necessary for Y to exist, and Y exists from time T, then X existed at T. On the assumption that a photograph has not been deliberately falsified, its object wholly fabricated in the course of taking or processing the film, then, at the time the photograph was taken, an object had to have been in front of the camera to bend the rays of light that imprinted themselves on the photographic plate. Notice that it is not claimed that the object in the photograph is exactly as it was at the time of the picture's taking but only that an object was there: existence, not essence, is what is proved. Second, perception does not prove the reality of the object perceived, for familiar reasons. Like memory, it is vulnerable to distortion. Also, a photograph of a present object is never perfectly contemporary with the object, for however fast the camera, there is always time between the taking and the presentation of the photograph.

What the camera records is not inflected by language as what the eye sees is. What the eye sees is the *studium,* the culturally coded in the photograph. Because the photograph is a causal trace of the past reality of the object, what the camera records is the past presence of the photographed physical object. The object, or something about it, can break through the field of the *studium* to touch the photograph's viewer. This intrusion of the past object into the coded image is the photograph's *punctum,* evidence for the viewer of the reality of the past, whereas reality for Barthes is what is primitive, raw, outside of language. The primitive is what has not been tamed by culture's codes and classifications. Innocent and naive, it is not independent of the network of language but is what has not been captured by the net. Barthes wrote in *S/Z* that such poor freedom as we have is the freedom to produce meaning by reading in the writerly way, where the ecstasy occasioned by such reading does not release the reader from language but from the tyranny over her of its present and customary meanings. The freedom promised by the primitive, however, releases the spectator touched by a photograph's *punctum* from the culturally coded altogether, not just from settled and familiar meanings, and from the secure haven of present and immediate experience. The *punctum* can bring madness when, in punctuating the photograph's *studium,* it juxtaposes the camera's impersonal indirect proof of past existence with the direct proofs of present existence afforded by the viewer's immediate experience, when it penetrates the scrim of consciousness, language, and culture to touch what in the viewer is brute, dumb, and raw, and when, in embracing the past, he gives up the present. The last words of Barthes's final book, *Camera Lucida,* are that between the madness threatened by the *punctum* and its taming by the *studium,* "the choice is mine."

The book that ends this way tells the story of Barthes's refinding his mother, shortly after her death, in a photograph of her taken in a winter garden when she was a little girl. In looking at it, he was in the presence of the imprint of light reflected by her child's body, there with her brother in the garden years before Barthes was born. The winter garden photograph showed him *both* how a photograph can break through what the culture has made of its viewer *and* how it can give him knowledge of its object, which is, perforce, an individual. Aristotle observed that an individual can only be perceived because only the general can be known. Bertrand Russell asserted that knowledge of an individual is by acquaintance or description. Barthes, however, claims that certain photographs afford a knowledge of their (individual) objects that is neither by acquaintance nor by description. This knowledge of the individual through its photograph is not by acquaintance because one is not acquainted with the photographed physical object itself but only with its effect on the light rays that touch it. Nor is it by description, because knowledge by photography requires perception of physical traces of the known object, whereas knowledge by description does not. The spectator knows the object when its photograph pierces him, producing an ecstasy: what he knows cannot be said, but it can be resisted. The knowledge can bring wildness, and it is between this and Aristotle's tameness that Barthes said he can choose.

[*See also* Fashion, *article on* Fashion and Philosophy, Photography; Poststructuralism; Semiotics, *article on* Semiotics as a Theory of Art; *and* Text.]

BIBLIOGRAPHY

Works by Barthes

Writing Degree Zero (1953). Translated by Annette Lavers and Colin Smith. New York, 1967.
Michelet (1954). Translated by Richard Howard. New York, 1987.
The Eiffel Tower and Other Mythologies (1957). Translated by Richard Howard. New York, 1979.
Mythologies (1957). Translated by Annette Lavers. New York, 1972.
On Racine (1963). Translated by Richard Howard. New York, 1964.
Critical Essays (1964). Translated by Richard Howard. Evanston, Ill., 1972.
Elements of Semiology (1964). Translated by Annette Lavers and Colin Smith. New York, 1967.

Criticism and Truth (1966). Translated by Katrine Pilcher Keunemen. Minneapolis, 1987.

The Fashion System (1967). Translated by Matthew Ward and Richard Howard. New York, 1983.

Empire of Signs (1970). Translated by Richard Howard. New York, 1982.

S/Z (1970). Translated by Richard Miller. New York, 1974.

Sade, Fourier, Loyola (1971). Translated by Richard Miller. New York, 1976.

New Critical Essays (1972). Translated by Richard Howard. New York, 1980.

The Pleasure of the Text (1973). Translated by Richard Miller. New York, 1975.

Roland Barthes by Roland Barthes (1975). Translated by Richard Howard. New York, 1977.

Image-Music-Text. Translated by Stephen Heath. New York, 1977.

A Lover's Discourse: Fragments (1977). Translated by Richard Howard. New York, 1978.

Writer Sollers (1979). Translated by Philip Thody. Minneapolis, 1987.

Camera Lucida: Reflections on Photography (1980). Translated by Richard Howard. New York, 1981.

The Grain of the Voice: Interviews, 1962–1980 (1981). Translated by Linda Coverdale. New York, 1985.

Responsibility of Forms: Critical Essays on Music, Art, and Representation (1982). Translated by Richard Howard. New York, 1985.

A Barthes Reader. Edited by Susan Sontag. New York, 1983.

The Semiotic Challenge (1985). Translated by Richard Howard. New York, 1988.

The Rustle of Language (1986). Translated by Richard Howard. New York, 1986.

Incidents (1987). Translated by Richard Howard. Berkeley, 1992.

Other Sources

Brown, Andrew. *Roland Barthes: The Figures of Writing.* New York and Oxford, 1992.

Burke, Sean. *The Death and Return of the Author: Criticism and Subjectivity in Barthes, Foucault, and Derrida.* New York, 1993.

Calvet, Louis-Jean. *Roland Barthes: A Biography.* Translated by Sarah Wykes. Bloomington, Ind., 1995.

Culler, Jonathan. *Barthes.* New York, 1983.

Lavers, Annette. *Roland Barthes: Structuralism and After.* Cambridge, Mass., 1982.

Lombardo, Patrizia. *The Three Paradoxes of Roland Barthes.* Athens, Ga., 1990.

Moriarty, Michael. *Roland Barthes.* Stanford, Calif., 1991.

Rylance, Rick. *Roland Barthes.* Englewood Cliffs, N.J., 1994.

Thody, Philip. *Roland Barthes: A Conservative Estimate.* Atlantic Highlands, N.J., 1977.

Ungar, Steven. *Roland Barthes: The Professor of Desire.* Lincoln, Nebr., 1983.

Wiseman, Mary Bittner. *The Ecstasies of Roland Barthes.* London and New York, 1989.

MARY WISEMAN

BATAILLE, GEORGES (1897–1962), French novelist, philosopher, and writer. The secret of art, according to Georges Bataille, resides in the following proposition: like sacrifice, it removes its object from the realm of *things.* But it is no secret that the motor force of the Bataillian opus resides in demonstrating that an essential part of human nature seeks to extricate itself from an exclusive subordination to work, production, and accumulation. Irrespective of a culture's level of material riches, humanity in all times and places has manifested the urge to expend and direct its energies and resources toward constructive goals. It is possible to argue that the need for loss is as powerful as the acquisitive instinct, and reflects the experience that extreme expenditure can provide pleasure of a violent sort. This is what Bataille's prolific outpouring of novels, poems, economic and political treatises, philosophical meditations, essays, and reviews—covering virtually every facet of culture and intellectual endeavor—proclaim. Their widespread influence testifies to the discontent wrought by modernity and the challenge to cultural theory that it poses—that an increase in material wealth has exacerbated servility to, rather than emancipation from, the imperatives of production. Yet the Bataillian experience of sovereignty has little to do with material objects—laughter, eroticism, and effervescence explore collective modes of expenditure that simulate the effects of sacrifice through a radical modification of the subject. Isolated in a world according to things—where the horrors of death and destruction are occulted—individuals seek to transmute their anguish into the ecstasy of the sovereign instant. Eschewing the feudal model of sovereignty in which expenditure ultimately reinforced class privilege, the idealism for which he rebuked the Surrealists, or the aestheticizing solution of "art for art's sake," the perspective of Bataille's self-described Copernican revolution considers forms of giving that seek no return. In its most systematized expression, the theory of a general economy posits a menacing, "cursed" reserve destined for destruction at the center of a point of view of human activity so capacious that it claims as much relevance to artists as to economists.

Art, however, does not provide privileged reference points within the labyrinth of Bataillian writings. Few artists are discussed in any sustained way other than Édouard Manet, about whom Bataille wrote a study commissioned in the mid-1950s. The problematic status of art was indeed set forth early, when Bataille aggressively argued that even if individual artists offer local examples of rebellion, the place of art in Western culture is more accurately assessed by the pervasive role fulfilled by architecture in monumentalizing the principles of domination and authority. His global indictment encompasses all manifestations of *construction*—whether evidenced in physiognomy, dress, music, or painting—as testaments to the moral straightjacket of idealism. Thus, *Documents*, the eclectic review that Bataille edited between 1929 and 1931, leveled an iconoclastic, innovative, and subtly scandalous assault on the hierarchy within the arts in Western society. Assisted by fellow excommunicates from Surrealism—Michel Leiris and Jacques Baron—as well as the ethnomusicologist André Schaeffner, Carl Einstein, and the ethnographer Marcel Griaule, among others, Bataille contributed texts whose impact was bolstered by their symbiosis with the surrealistic photographs of Eli Lotar and

Boiffard. *Documents,* as Michel Leiris noted, was an "impossible" undertaking—a glossy journal of commentary on modern art in the minds of its backers, at odds with Bataille's determination to explore the impossible underside of bourgeois civilization. Yet the results undoubtedly stand among the outstanding contributions to cultural criticism in the twentieth century. Bataille was responsible for a critical dictionary, whose entries applied scholarly references to seemingly banal or everyday objects and, when isolated and then juxtaposed with esoteric figures, created an effect that critics have compared to the sensation of the "uncanny" (Fer, 1995) or, for its defamiliarization, to an "ethnographic surrealism" (Clifford, 1988). Roland Barthes admired Bataille's ability to reinterpret icons of industrial civilization and even the body—one thinks of the big toe as well as the factory chimney—in affective terms that managed to resist both the psychoanalytic "police" and the temptation to aestheticize. Instead, the Hegelian *Aufhebung* was revised so that the opposition between material objects and their ideal models was not supserseded by means of a higher synthesis. Idealization is occluded by the introduction of a *third* term, whose transgressive function is to disrupt the very foundation on which hierarchical dualisms were based, as well as to pose an alternative to the usual inversions that would leave their theological underpinnings intact. Materialism, for instance, presented the dilemma of how to conceptualize something other than "dead" matter—a passive derivative from idealism. Bataille's *base* materialism is defined as an active, creative force, historically comparable to that of the early gnostics, encompassing a scatological predilection for the filth, waste, and detritus shunned by metaphysics.

Art's uneasy place within the Bataillian corpus is, therefore, symptomatic of the dramatic revisions in the act of "seeing" needed for expenditure to emerge from its occultation by utilitarian criteria. The instant of sacred communication resists representation, just as the impulse to communicate through the dismantling of individual boundaries and overcome the "suffocation" of imposed thing-ness in the world of homogeneous relations, defies the conventions of a discursively determined reality. Both requirements lead to a characteristic innovation of Bataille's early writing practice: his "operation" on certain privileged metaphors, notably the sun. The need for expenditure is paradoxically obscured by the light of reason, a rationality whose economy of energies is primarily—if not exclusively—directed toward production. Within the dominant Ocularcentric paradigm (Jay, 1993), aesthetics privileges sight over the other senses and facilitates the appropriation of objects. By redefining the sun in terms of its task or *besogne*—as Bataille argued all words should be understood—to generate combustion and noxious gases as well as boundless energy, a second sun appears whose blinding force provides the requisite insight into expenditure at the limit of destruction.

This re-vision of the privileged metaphors of Western metaphysics entails a reinscription of the disembodied senses, but in the shocking form of a "pineal" eye (*pine* being a slang word for *penis* in French) jutting from the head, or the automutilations inflicted by a dazzled Vincent van Gogh.

The exorbitant sun of the general economy circulates within an alternative paradigm determined by visual as well as linguistic homologies—especially with the eye and the egg—relayed by their obscene status in relation to the conscious mind. By staging enactments of transgression involving their migration to the body's orifices, Bataille's narrative traces unconscious associations that provide an erotic jolt at the limits of sexuality. Unlike conventional pornography, his texts play with images derived from the archetypes of classical myths, especially Prometheus, Icarus, and the Minotaur. "Sacred horror," not titillation, is the desired effect. Admittedly religious in its inspiration, the Bataillian sensibility seeks contact with the "divine" forces of death and destruction.

One of Bataille's earliest published texts—a review of the 1928 exhibition of pre-Columbian art in Paris—suggests the connection between art and sacrifice that would remain a constant throughout his career. The introduction to Aztec society reinforced his understanding of sacrifice at odds with the utilitarian premise that an initial relinquishment is made in view of some ultimate recompense. Projected into the realm of the divine, the sacrificial victim mediates the collectivity's encounter with the menacing forces segregated by religion as sacred. In accord with Émile Durkheim, the sacred is located negatively in relation to the profane, and envisioned as entirely *other,* incommensurable with the homogeneity founded on identity and equivalence. Further distinctions introduced by Robert Hertz expand the traditional sacred associated with law, order, and the right, to encompass a *left* sacred as well, whose virulent, often malevolent, force signals the distinctive experience and repertoire of heterological elements that Bataille sought to reactivate within a postsacred society. The sacred's demise is not the inevitable consequence of heightened rationality, he argued, but a reflection of the pandemic fear of confrontation with suppressed horrors. In sacrifice, violence is liberated, and the discontinuity separating individuals momentarily obliterated, so that the intimacy of "continuity" may be recaptured in the sacred instant.

Bataille's writing practice is distinguished by the realization that sovereignty is intuited on condition that the subject submit to the same dramatic transformations—strained to the limit of destruction—as the object it is willing to immolate. The experience of extreme expenditure is never an end point, but an interminable process. As with the sacred, it is impossible to predict when sovereignty will erupt or can be identified within a work of art. Manet's exploration of the possibility for an annulment of the subject within painting is described as an "impersonal subversion." Yet, Bataille also acknowledged the paradox of the author or artist who contributes to the accumulation of things through the investment of energy into the production of works. Although logically insuperable, this tension reappears when devising safeguards against the perversion of sovereignty, as manifested in the abuse of the other by means of acts ultimately directed toward acquisition or profit, rather than loss. It also explains Bataille's insistence on a certain congruence between writer and text, or artist and work, that may otherwise appear as a retrograde facet of his art criticism.

In its parallel function to the analytic model, painting provides a concrete index of those areas critical to the development of the unconscious within the evolution of civilization, including modernism. From the trans- or de-formation of classical figures applauded in the painting of Joan Miró and Pablo Picasso, for instance, emerges the history of art as revelation of the "optical unconscious" (Krauss, 1993). Bataille's idiosyncratic survey focuses on "figures" whose appearance within a particular historical juncture serves as a marker for the nature of the relation of the general economy of expenditure to the restricted one; namely, how the repressed "need" for annihilating *dépense* inhabits and subverts the strictures dictated by the equally powerful solicitation for production and rationality. Among those featured in his prewar atheological pantheon, an Aztec priest kneels at the base of a temple dedicated to sacrifice and raises a still-beating heart to the blinding sun; in the acephalic figure designed by André Masson, the head reappears as a skull in the place of genitals, right hand holding a flaming heart, the left a sword, and the abdomen revealing the intestines in the form of a labyrinth; and the photos of Chinese torture reveal the "ecstatic" smile of the lacerated victim. Similarly, the study of the Lascaux caves not only claims that they witnessed the birth of art but that their paintings testify as well to the emergence of a new being, not actually represented, but the imagined artistic *homo ludens* responsible for the drawings. Manet's canvases usher in modernity (also credited to some facets of Goya's work), while his maieutic method brings forth a seductive creature whose movements are "indifferent" to the demands of conventional beauty. In both inaugural moments, innovation is attributed to transgression.

In the beginning was art, or nearly so, because art coincides with the festival, when the worker that he first was, and still is, homo sapiens threw down the tools by which he transformed nature. In so doing, he demonstrated the capacity to break the very rules or prohibitions he had imposed on himself, and through which he sought protection from the disorder of death and sexuality. Transgression marks the moment when necessity is transformed into abundance, and the products of human labor are sacrificed, when sexuality's proximity with death is replaced with erotic pleasure that knows no end other than its own, and

play prevails over purposeful activity. One of the most challenging moments of Bataillian anthropology is undoubtedly this view of prohibitions as an *enabling* structure, so that "transgression exists only from the moment when art itself is manifested, and that more or less, the birth of art coincides . . . with the tumultuousness of play and the festival, which is announced in the depths of the caverns where figures explode with life, where transgression supersedes and completes itself in the play between death and birth" (Bataille, 1979, p. 41; all translations from French are mine). Art emerges when the thing-ness of an object is sacrificed, its utilitarian significance annulled, and communication in the strong sense of sovereignty is realized. Sacrifice is a crime at odds with the common morality prohibiting killing and destruction. By attributing to art the status of a transgressive act, Bataille lauds its instantiation of a "hypermorality" beyond good and evil, or beauty and ugliness.

Within the history of aesthetics since Immanuel Kant and Friedrich Nietzsche, which situates art at the antipodes to utility, and morality within the realm of taste, Bataille also figures as heir to the ethical imperative promoted by the Surrealists that art be produced by all, not one. In the absence of ritualized sacrifice, he followed Durkheim in seeking the sacred in moments of collective effervescence that the sociologist credited with the production of major cultural—including religious—forms. Bataille's numerous collective endeavors reflect his conviction that aesthetic, moral, and political displacements take place within a larger network or community. By the time of the postwar writings on Lascaux and Manet, the possibility for community was translated into the affinity experienced for certain artworks or artists, and this connection was placed under the sign of friendship. It encompasses intimate collaborations with the artists André Masson and Jean Fautrier, for instance, or is enlisted to describe the sovereign "presence" of the figure that emerges from the work's sacrificial operation. In Lascaux, the viewer is moved by the lone representation of a human—a paltry stick figure in erection discovered at the base of a shaft hidden deep within the cave's recesses—because its sacrifice releases the elation of the artist who, through the "negation of the negation" of unmediated animal sexuality and of his own death-fearing self, attains the sovereign majesty of the magnificent creatures depicted. The daily intensity of the friendship between Manet and the poet Stéphane Mallarmé consecrated their shared aesthetics of "indifference" to the bourgeois subjugation of art to social ends and to the replacement of ancien régime majesty by bourgeois morality.

More than three decades have elapsed since Bataille's death in 1962, when Malraux banned his posthumous last book, *The Tears of Eros* (1961). Its collection of images, encompassing prehistoric statues with visual sexual puns to the photo of Chinese torture, serve as visual support for

Bataille's final epiphany: death and sexuality meet, just as the most beautiful and horrific find their encounter in art. While exploring the relation of art to cruelty, earlier essays had warned against the aestheticization of areas intended to provoke a sense of sacred terror. The stated goal of *The Tears of Eros* is to expand consciousness of their presence without aspiring to emancipation from their obsessive effects. Rather than aesthetic criteria, the basis for inclusion compares with the typology proposed for literary texts—those to which their authors had been "constrained." Bataille's recurrent illustration is his own sexual arousal at the sight of a dead body—including his mother's. The shock quotient of the Bataillian aesthetic is thus intensified by its willingness—as well as its ability—to depict states of being that escape volition, but to which the subject bears witness.

By the mid-1970s, the Bataillian reworking of certain categories and "notions" in relation to excess—whether sovereignty and heterogeneity, or *dépense* and the *part maudit*—pervaded the critical discourse of disciplines committed to deconstructing their foundational basis. Bataille also figured at the forefront of analyses subverting the economy of reading and writing derived from the classical mimetic model. The repercussions for art criticism of his "antiarchitecture" (Hollier, 1989) were equally wide-ranging, proposing nothing less than a rebuttal to the Vitruvian premise that representative art originated with the reflection of Narcissus and in the "light" of architectural verticality (ibid.). Lascaux offered an alternative mythological space, led by the charging Minotaur in labyrinthine obscurity. Despite the increased availability of his work, however, references to Bataille in architecture and art criticism initially lagged in comparison with acknowledgments of his preeminent influence on contemporary Continental philosophy. Some works have filled the lacunae in the United States (Krauss, 1986, 1993; Jay, 1993; Tschumi, 1994), where art historians had not been attentive "to how his alternative mythological practice . . . unravels the neat categories of a too formulaic modernism" (Krauss, 1986, p. 153). Indeed, the disruptive effects of a sacrificial aesthetic reasserting the necessity for prohibitions—rather than their lifting—must be situated within a resistant postmodernism that commits art to the interminable task of rescuing its object from the forces of appropriation, while subjecting it—as the eloquent formula inspired by Manet's painting insists—to a "ravishment without repose."

[*See also* Surrealism, *article on* Surrealism and Literature.]

BIBLIOGRAPHY

Works by Bataille

Œuvres complètes, vol. 1. Paris, 1970.
Œuvres complètes, vol. 9. Paris, 1979.
Œuvres complètes, vol. 11, *Articles I, 1944–1949.* Paris, 1988.
Œuvres complètes, vol. 12, *Articles II, 1950–1961.* Paris, 1988.
The Tears of Eros (1961). Translated by Peter Connor. San Francisco, 1989.

Other Sources

Barthes, Roland. "Les sorties du texte." In *Le bruissement de la langue: Essais critiques IV,* pp. 271–283. Paris, 1984.
Clifford, James. "On Ethnographic Surrealism." In *The Predicament of Culture: Twentieth-Century Ethnography, Literature, and Art,* pp. 117–151. Cambridge, Mass., 1988.
Fer, Briony. "Poussière/Peinture: Bataille on Painting." In *Bataille: Writing the Sacred,* edited by Carolyn Bailey Gill, pp. 154–171. London and New York, 1995.
Hollier, Denis. *Against Architecture: The Writings of Georges Bataille.* Translated by Betsy Wing. Cambridge, Mass., 1989.
Jay, Martin. *Downcast Eyes: The Denigration of Vision in Twentieth-Century French Thought.* Berkeley, 1993.
Krauss, Rosalind E. "Antivision." *October* 36 (Spring 1986): 147–154.
Krauss, Rosalind E. *The Optical Unconscious.* Cambridge, Mass., 1993.
Tschumi, Bernard. *Architecture and Disjunction.* Cambridge, Mass., 1994.
Wilson, Sarah. "Fêting the Wound: Georges Bataille and Jean Fautrier in the 1940s." In *Bataille: Writing the Sacred,* edited by Carolyn Bailey Gill, pp. 172–192. London and New York, 1995.

MICHELE H. RICHMAN

BATTEUX, CHARLES. *See* French Aesthetics, *article on* Eighteenth-Century French Aesthetics.

BAUDELAIRE, CHARLES. [*To explain the significance of one of the first poets and theorists of modernity, this entry comprises two essays:*

Survey of Thought
Baudelaire and Art

The first essay discusses Baudelaire's general aesthetics, and the second analyzes his art criticism in particular. See also Aestheticism; Caricature; Difficulty, Aesthetics of; Fashion; Poetics; *and* Symbolism.]

Survey of Thought

Charles Baudelaire (1821–1867), French symbolist poet and art critic. He had only a slight knowledge of academic philosophy; he knew nothing about the emerging science of art history, as it was being developed by German scholars. Because he traveled very little after his youthful trip around Africa, his knowledge of painting was essentially limited to what could be seen in Paris. Even as a historian of his own time, Baudelaire is limited. He wrote at length about one great artist, Eugène Delacroix, who was briefly his friend. He was close to Honoré Daumier, Édouard Manet, and—at one time—Gustave Courbet, but published only brief accounts of them. His greatest essay, "The Painter of Modern Life" (1859), was devoted to a minor illustrator, Constantin Guys. Yet, despite these limitations, Baudelaire presents a highly sophisticated aesthetic theory, whose full significance and importance remain to be understood.

The standard biography (Pichois and Ziegler, 1987) tells his life. This essay focuses on the aspect of his work of obvious philosophical interest: his theory of beauty. According to the traditional Neoplatonic theories, standards of beauty are universal and unchanging. Artistic beauty is grounded in nature. "The work of art is inferior to nature, insofar as it merely imitates nature . . . and . . . superior to nature because, improving upon the deficiencies of nature's individual products, art independently confronts nature with a newly created image of beauty" (Panofsky, 1968, p. 14). But this belief in the objectivity of beauty, as found in the High Renaissance art of Michelangelo and Raphael, could not easily withstand the European discovery of other cultures, and the introduction into the museum of pre-Renaissance European art.

Already in 1855, Baudelaire anticipated this result. What, he asks, would "a modern Winckelmann" say "if faced with a product of China—something weird, strange, distorted in form . . . ? And yet such a thing is a specimen of universal beauty" (Baudelaire, 1965, p. 121). A beautiful Roman sculpture and a Raphael Madonna are similar; but what do they have in common with beautiful Japanese paintings, Persian miniatures, Peruvian sculpture, and Romanesque carvings? One possible response to this question is a subjective theory of beauty. "The Painter" presents a different, more original argument.

Already in his "Salon of 1846" Baudelaire imagined an art depicting beautiful contemporary scenes. "The life of our city is rich in poetic and marvellous subjects. . . . there is a new element—modern beauty" (Baudelaire, 1965, p. 119). This was a bold prophecy, for Manet was then only fourteen. "The Painter" presents in much more detail an account of modernism. Contemporary Paris, Baudelaire says, provides great subjects for painters. His description of those subjects interests art historians. But he also gives a philosophical argument.

All beauty, he argues, has two components: "*general* beauty, as it is expressed by classical . . . artists," and "*particular* beauty" (Baudelaire, 1964, p. 1), which is presented by a visual journalist like Guys. Without the second element, a beautiful picture would be impossible to enjoy; lacking the first element, an artwork could not remain of lasting interest. Images of modern life are beautiful because, while showing the present, they also contain general beauty. Baudelaire links the duality of beauty to the dual nature of man. Just as humans are body and soul, so successful artworks have these two aspects. Baudelaire's view that standards of beauty are historically variable was anticipated, he notes, by Stendhal, who asserted that beauty is the promise of happiness. But Stendhal did not develop a theory of modernism.

Baudelaire introduces two important themes: the attractiveness of fashion and pleasure of the present. Fashion images showing earlier styles are interesting for their historical value; images of contemporary beauty are interesting for a different reason. "The pleasure which we derive from the representation of the present is due not only to the beauty with which it can be invested, but also to its essential quality of being present" (Baudelaire, 1964, p. 1). Perhaps because the remainder of "The Painter" so brilliantly anticipates Impressionism, little attention has been devoted to this statement. Yet, there is a real puzzle here. It is easy to understand why images of Manet's depictions of nineteenth-century Paris attract our attention today. But why does Baudelaire think that this quality of "being present" is pleasurable?

This question can be answered by asking another: How does Baudelaire think that the two aspects of beauty are combined in successful artworks? Normally, understanding unity requires identifying the elements that are unified into one whole. To speak, for example, about the unity of a representational painting presupposes that one can recognize the separate depicted figures. By comparison, the unity of beautiful Baudelairean images is difficult to characterize in a positive way because there seems no way to identify the separate components, relative and absolute beauty. One can know that a beautiful modernist image has two elements—both an unchanging component and beauty of the present—only when it is no longer of the present.

When it is of the present, the beautiful image has unity. Later, it ceases to be unified. Images of modern beauty seem to change because one stops looking at them for a while. If one could watch an image of modern life during an extended time period, one would see it cease to be a unified beautiful picture. It is as if this eye movement, a flicker of attention toward, then away, and finally back to the picture, destroys the unity of beautiful images of the present. Ceasing to have perfect unity, images become records of past styles of beauty. That movement shows *what was* modern beauty. Here, the past tense is important; one can only know that there were two components later, when they come apart. One can *know* that a beautiful modern image is beautiful, but one cannot *see* how it achieves unity; that is knowable only when it no longer is beautiful. To analyze beauty, it is sometimes said, destroys it; what time does automatically, this account suggests, is destroy the unity of beautiful images.

How does one picture contain two such components of beauty? Arthur C. Danto's (1981) account of period style suggests a further way of describing this experience. Modern beauty, like a period style, is invisible until its era has passed. "What would have been transparent to Giotto's contemporaries," Danto writes, "almost like a glass they were seeing through to a sacred reality, has become opaque to us, and we are instantly conscious of something invisible to them but precious to us—Giotto's style" (1981, p. 162). One beautiful picture does not have two components, but only two descriptions. An image of modern life might be described first as "beautiful in itself" and then as "showing the beauty of contemporary dress." Danto's way of thinking moves us away from Baudelaire's suggestion that these two components of beauty are somehow added together.

One can identify this unity of modern beautiful images only after they have come apart, or, and this amounts to the same thing, only by comparing them to beautiful pictures from other periods, which now fail to achieve such unity because they are of the past. The perfect unity of images of modern life can be seen as a unity only when it no longer exists. One discovers the presentness of an image only when it has disappeared.

Baudelaire's theory really describes the *experience* of consciousness of presentness and of pastness, not the unity at one moment of two aspects of *one image*. One's present consciousness is of this moment; later, one remembers that moment. The oneness of present consciousness is succeeded by this doubleness of memory because when one remembers, one does two things in one act: one *reexperiences* one's awareness of that departed moment, and *experiences that moment as past,* that is, no longer present. Are there two elements in that one moment of consciousness? Normally, one is just conscious; in remembering, one is conscious that one is thinking of the past, but there are not two separable elements present at once. The present moment simply is; when recollected, that moment has this more complex identity. Consciousness is always of the present, whether engaged entirely in the present moment or recollecting earlier times.

The presence Baudelaire describes is impossible to identify in isolation. There can be no pure presence because every experience carries traces of other earlier experiences. There can be no way of picking out a "here and now," separating it off from everything past and future, without appeal to a language, a system of representation that contains traces of other temporal moments. It is impossible that such a "self-presence . . . be produced in the undivided unity of a temporal present so as to have nothing to reveal to itself by the agency of signs" (Derrida, 1973, p. 60). No picture can be absolutely present because every image must be understood in relation to the entire system of images.

A psychoanalytic account might explain why Baudelaire is so attracted to the beauty of presence. "The image," John E. Jackson has suggested, "far from being always for him a mere representation, rather is valorized in itself, and with a rare intensity, in a manner that gives his 'cult of pictures' its proper foundation" (Jackson, 1982, p. 102). Perhaps his account of beauty thus has roots in his unhappy erotic life. As Baudelaire explains in "The Painter," much art of modern life is devoted to woman; she is "the object of the keenest admiration and curiosity that the picture of life can offer its contemplator" (Baudelaire, 1964, p. 30).

For the present-day art writer, Giorgio Vasari and Denis Diderot seem to be historically distant figures. By contrast, Baudelaire speaks immediately to us. Danto explains how

"standing at an intersection" with used-car lots and "brash signs proclaiming unbeatable deals, crazy prices, insane bargains," a scene he would have found "intolerably crass and tacky when I was growing up as an aesthete," he came to understand how "Pop redeemed the world in an intoxicating way" (Danto, *Beyond the Brillo Box*, 1992, p. 140). That scene would not surprise Baudelaire. As Fredric Jameson (1985) observes, many "postmodernist" concerns were anticipated by Baudelaire. But what would surprise him is that our critics no longer speak much about beauty. In the "cultural convulsion we have been living through," Danto says, "beauty seems all at once irrelevant to the aims of art" (Danto, 1992, "What Happened to Beauty," p. 418).

A proper account of Baudelaire's theory of beauty would need to link political and psychoanalytic analysis with an examination of the strictly philosophical significance of his argumentation. Such an analysis could connect the concerns of the aesthetician with the work of the art critic and historian.

[*See also* Modernism, *overview article and article on* Modernism in Literature.]

BIBLIOGRAPHY

Works by Baudelaire

Art in Paris, 1845–1862: Salons and Other Exhibitions. Translated and edited by Jonathan Mayne. London, 1965.
Œuvres complètes. 2 vols. Edited by Claude Pichois. Paris, 1976. This standard French edition contains the above texts in vol. 2.
The Painter of Modern Life and Other Essays (1863). Translated and edited by Jonathan Mayne. London, 1964.

Other Sources

Carrier, David. "Baudelaire's Philosophical Theory of Beauty." *Nineteenth-Century French Studies,* forthcoming.
Danto, Arthur C. *The Transfiguration of the Commonplace: A Philosophy of Art.* Cambridge, Mass., 1981.
Danto, Arthur C. "What Happened to Beauty." *Nation* (30 March 1992):418–421.
Danto, Arthur C. *Beyond the Brillo Box: The Visual Arts in Post-Historical Perspective.* New York, 1992.
Derrida, Jacques. *Speech and Phenomena and Other Essays on Husserl's Theory of Signs.* Translated by David B. Allison. Evanston, Ill., 1973.
Jackson, John E. *La mort Baudelaire: Essai sur* Les Fleurs du Mal. Neuchâtel, 1982.
Jameson, Fredric. "Baudelaire as Modernist and Postmodernist: The Dissolution of the Referent and the Artificial 'Sublime.'" In *Lyric Poetry: Beyond the New Criticism,* edited by Chaviva Hosek and Patricia Parker, pp. 247–263. Ithaca, N.Y., 1985.
Panofsky, Erwin. *Idea: A Concept in Art Theory.* Translated by Joseph J. S. Peake. Columbia, S.C., 1968.
Pichois, Claude, and Jean Ziegler. *Baudelaire.* Paris, 1987.

DAVID CARRIER

Baudelaire and Art

Modern literary criticism has assigned Charles Baudelaire with more "lives" than are generally attributed to the cats he so admired, judging by the various personae of the poet that have emerged from successive representations of the man and his oeuvre since the last century. Over the years, Baudelaire has been read as a damned perverse poet and a damned fine poet, as different versions of the *poète maudit* would have it. He has been labeled a Romantic poet, a Symbolist poet, a modernist poet, and a postmodern poet, according to different versions of nineteenth-century French poetics. His poetry has been interpreted as the work of an alienated genius, of a victim of a hostile bourgeois world, and of a sexually dysfunctional neurotic voyeur. He has been deemed a profoundly apolitical poet and, more recently, a profoundly political poet.

For an author whose poetic output consists of fewer than two hundred published poems, it is remarkable just how many myths and discourses have surrounded both the man and his work. Ross Chambers has suggested that the continuous interpretative activity that has surrounded Baudelaire's work since his death has made his oeuvre the very prototype for poetry, modern poetry, or literature. As such, it has been judged the "worthy" text par excellence for raising and testing the broadest questions of literary theory and method. One is indeed struck by the way that Baudelaire's work has become something of a commodity fetish for modern critical discourses and schools. It would appear that each new critical envoy to the twentieth century has had to deliver credentials in the form of a selective reading of Baudelaire. The "test cases" include René Laforgue's early literary psychobiography, the first such Freudian analysis devoted to a French author (*The Defeat of Baudelaire: A Psychoanalytical Study of the Neurosis of Charles Baudelaire* [1932]); Walter Benjamin's sociological investigations of art and modernity (*Charles Baudelaire: A Lyric Poet in the Age of High Capitalism* [1973]); Jean-Paul Sartre's first existential psychoanalysis (*Baudelaire* [1950]); Roman Jakobson and Claude Lévi-Strauss's famous structuralist example ("'Les Chats' de Charles Baudelaire" [1980]); Hans Robert Jauss's hermeneutic essay on the aesthetic of reception ("The Poetic Text within the Change of Horizons of Reading: The Example of Baudelaire's 'Spleen II'" [1982]); Paul de Man's deconstruction of Baudelaire's programmatic sonnet "Correspondances" ("Anthropomorphism and Trope in the Lyric" [1984]); and Richard Terdiman's historico-political analysis ("Baudelaire's 'Le Cygne': Memory, History, and Sign" [1993]). Each critical mission has, not surprisingly, singled out a particular Baudelairian poem or set of poems to be its "text," that is, the touchstone for articulating a set of critical suppositions about poetry, language, and art.

Thus, for instance, in the mid-1970s, at the height of structuralist controversies, Baudelaire's verse poems—and especially the incidental poem "Les chats"—provided the pretext for a generalized debate on poetics and semiotics. Baudelaire exemplified then the principles and skills of an inspired linguist and versifier, for whom the composition of poetry overrode any interaction with the nonpoetic worlds of action and ideas, history and philosophy. Literary criticism of the 1980s, on the other hand, emphasized a more political and a more rhetorically self-conscious Baudelaire. Poststructuralist readings of the poet concentrated largely on the Baudelaire who reflects alternately on the stresses of "modernity" in the Haussmannized streets of Paris and the representational impasses of modern art with its related detours of meaning. The works most often cited in this context came from the prose poems (*Le spleen de Paris* [Paris spleen]) and the urban verse poems of the *Fleurs du mal*, such as "Le cygne" (The swan), published in the section "Tableaux parisiens" (Parisian scenes). Unlike the structuralist versifier who masterfully created a poetic order and coherence that surmounted—or bypassed—the existential and epistemological crises of his time, the poststructuralist Baudelaire, on the contrary, derives his poetry from the inescapable disorder, incoherence, and crisis of his day, which he reflects and replicates. Beyond the illusions of structure and meaning, his is a poetry of discontinuities and discord that anticipates and comments on our own postmodernity. More recent criticism of Baudelaire has followed in this vein, compounded by the insights of gender criticism that reflect on Baudelaire's sexual politics, his misogyny, and his poetic "lesbianism."

If Baudelaire's poetry has been used, selectively and successfully, to illustrate so many different critical positions, it is not only because of its extraordinary variety (this despite the relatively small output) and its unmistakable quality (Baudelaire was an uncanny and meticulous self-editor), but, ironically, because of the relatively few critical statements he devoted directly to poetics. To be sure, the poetic premises gleaned from Baudelaire's writings come principally from the poems themselves, from occasional journal entries, and especially from the essays on painting that he wrote throughout his career; for, indeed, it was as an art critic rather than a poet that Baudelaire began his career as an author. If there is a coherent aesthetic position to be discerned from his critical writings, it is an aesthetic of Impressionism, stemming from his reflections on painting.

To the extent that Baudelaire's literary reputation has been for the most part confounded by the Symbolist label he earned for the *Fleurs du mal*, it may be surprising to see his aesthetic stand assimilated with principles of Impressionism. That the two terms are mutually and historically exclusive, however, is not at all certain, as Richard Shiff convincingly demonstrated in *Cézanne and the End of Impressionism* (1984). Shiff argued that the popular association of Symbolism and Impressionism with expressions of subjectivity and objectivity, respectively, is a reductive falsification of the theoretical premises of each movement. Indeed, both theories rely on a dialectical exchange between subject and object, in which each effects an imprint ("impression') on the other to privilege ultimately the imaginative eye of the spectator: the active observer of nature who becomes the artist and, by extension, the active observer of art who becomes the critic.

To be sure, Baudelaire's art criticism, like much of his poetry, presupposes the governing imagination of the spectator as its center of consciousness. In an early review essay of 1846, "*Prometheus Delivered* by L. de Senneville," Baudelaire announces: "the poetry of a painting must be made by the spectator" (Baudelaire, 1976, vol. 2, p. 9). This statement, which Baudelaire expanded in the "Salon of 1846," provides us with the terms that serve to constitute the major considerations of Baudelairean aesthetics: observation (the spectator), creation (making), poetry, and painting. It furthermore justifies the many different interpretations of Baudelaire: each critic or critical movement fashioning the poetry of Baudelaire according to its own idiosyncratic view.

From the start, the "Salon of 1845" (Baudelaire's first published work) cast him in the role of a critical spectator who chooses, exceptionally, not to describe the paintings in objective, exhaustive detail, but rather to examine the relationship in which they engage the viewer. "We shall speak of everything that attracts the eye of the crowd and of the artists; our professional conscience obliges us to do so," he declares (Baudelaire, 1965, p. 2). In the "Salon of 1846," Baudelaire, repeating some of these ideas, insisted once again that the poetry of a picture is not something the artist conceives, but rather "the result of the art of painting itself; *for it lies in the spectator's soul*, and it is the mark of genius to awaken it there" (ibid., p. 98). In short, Baudelaire displaced the critical focus from the intentional *expressive* relationship of the artist to his work onto the *impressive* effects of the painting on the spectator. Art enters into a dialogue with the spectator, and that dialogue becomes the basis of the text of criticism. Hence, Baudelaire's observations in the famous second chapter of the "Salon of 1846," "What Is the Good of Criticism?":

> I sincerely believe that the best criticism is that which is both amusing and poetic: not a cold, mathematical criticism which, on the pretext of explaining everything, has neither love nor hate, and voluntarily strips itself of every shred of temperament. But seeing that a fine picture is nature reflected by an artist, the criticism that I approve will be that picture reflected by an intelligent and sensitive mind. . . . I hope that the philosophers will understand what I am going to say. To be just, that is to say, to justify its existence, criticism should be partial, passionate, political, that is to say, written from an exclusive point of view, but a point of view that opens up the widest horizons.   (Ibid., p. 44)

Rather than describe and judge the technical merits of paintings exhibited at the Salon, Baudelaire seeks to translate his partial, passionate "impressions" of them. "You will often find me appraising a picture exclusively for the sum of ideas or of dreams that it suggests to my mind," he explains in his review of the 1855 Universal Exposition (ibid., p. 125). Similarly, as he strolls through Paris, he is drawn to images and street scenes that spark those sums of ideas and dreams that will become poems.

Much of Baudelaire's poetry is organized around the impressions of a "seeing I" who scrutinizes the world and his own existential condition, framing its fleeting images into discrete tableaux. The lexical frequency of references to eyes and looking far outweighs any other image-cluster in Baudelaire's poetry and invests it with a strategy of aesthetic gazing that is one of the dominant motifs of the later poetry and art criticism. The lyric persona of Baudelaire's "Tableaux parisiens," like the central persona of Baudelaire's collection of prose poems, *Le spleen de Paris*, is characterized as a *voyeur* and a *flâneur* who wanders through Paris gathering impressions from its streets that he then composes into the language of poetic speculation. One need only think of the prose poem of 1863, "Windows," a poem that anticipates in the urban voyeurism of its artist-persona films by Alfred Hitchcock and Brian De Palma:

> Looking from outside into an open window one never sees as much as when one looks through a closed window. There is nothing more profound, more mysterious, more pregnant, more insidious, more dazzling than a window lighted by a single candle. What one can see out in the sunlight is always less interesting than what goes on behind a window pane. In that black or luminous square life lives, life dreams, life suffers.
> Across the ocean of roofs I can see a middle-aged woman, her face already lined, who is forever bending over something and who never goes out. Out of her face, her dress and her gestures, out of practically nothing at all, I have made up this woman's story, or rather legend, and sometimes I tell it to myself and weep.   (Baudelaire, 1970, p. 77)

Baudelaire's identification of the modern artist with the voyeuristic *flâneur*, a motif investigated by Walter Benjamin, is most fully developed in the 1863 essay "The Painter of Modern Life," in which he celebrates Constantin Guys (a contemporary, journalistic artist) as the exemplary artist of modernity. In chapter 3 of that essay, "The Artist, Man of the World, Man of the Crowd, and Child," Baudelaire presents a day in the life of Monsieur G., the "perfect flâneur" and "passionate spectator," all of whose waking hours are spent busily roaming the streets of Paris. The rapid succession of scenes and events that the painter encounters on his daily *flânerie* are organized in terms of "light," "illumination," and "harmony" by the expert eye that "sees," "looks," "marvels," "gazes," "delights in," "spots," "examines," and "analyzes." Indeed, with the exception of the one magnificent "And off he goes!" at the start of the passage, all the verbs that relate Guys's day are verbs of perception. It is only at night, "when others are asleep," that the painter returns home to capture on paper the scenes that have seeped through his imagination all day. "And the external world is reborn upon his paper, natural and more than natural, beautiful and more than beautiful, strange and endowed with an impulsive life like the soul of its creator" (Baudelaire, 1964, p. 12).

The modern artist, as characterized and admired here by Baudelaire, is the man in the crowd who filters through his "acute, magical perception" visual impressions of urban life that contain suggestions of profound universal insights; for the beauty Baudelaire seeks is, by his own definition, always double: containing at once something of the eternal and the ephemeral. Baudelaire had stated this conviction in the "Salon of 1846," and he restates it again in "The Painter of Modern Life." It is one of the fundamental principles of his aesthetic.

Beauty is always and inevitably of a double composition, although the impression that it produces is single. . . . Beauty is made up of an eternal, invariable element, whose quantity is excessively hard to determine, and of a relative, circumstantial element, which will be, if you like, whether severally or all at once, the age, its fashions, its morals, its emotions. Without this second element, which might be described as the amusing, enticing, appetizing icing on the divine cake, the first element would be beyond our powers of digestion or appreciation, neither adapted nor suitable to human nature.   (Ibid., p. 3)

The impressionist artist, with his acute powers of vision, is the man who is able to appreciate the timely beauty of a surface detail and to speculate about the timeless abstractions he discerns beyond it. Visual contact with the objective, natural world (what Baudelaire calls in this essay "modern life") is the point of departure of art. But it is only the point of departure, for the successful artist, Baudelaire tells us, is the man—Baudelaire assumes the artist to be male—who distills and expresses the truth of these images through his subjective temperament. "As a matter of fact," Baudelaire insisted, "all good and true draughtsmen draw from the image printed on their brains, and not from nature" (ibid., p. 16). This singling out of the image written on the brain (the definition of the *impression*), an image that mediates the aesthetic relationship between subject and object, also characterizes the Impressionist aesthetic of Baudelaire's poetry.

The poems in Baudelaire's "Tableaux parisiens," for example, constitute the private picture album of a lyric persona who wanders through the streets of Paris, isolating fleeting images of the city and its inhabitants that he elaborates into reflections on (modern) life. The opening of the seventh poem of the series, "Les petites vieilles" (The little old women), provides a characteristic mise-en-scène:

In the sinuous folds of old cities
where everything—even horror—turns magical,
servile to my fateful moods, I look out for
unusual people, both charming and decrepit.

The active verb in this stanza, as is so often the case in these poems, is a verb of seeing, more precisely *staring* (*guetter*).

The persona identifies himself as a voyeur spying on some decrepit old women whose appearance evokes in his mind images of a mythical past that transcends the particular moment to evoke a universal tradition of mortal indignity:

These dislocated monsters were women once,
Eponine or Laïs! We must love these pathetic freaks,
hunchbacked and crippled!—for they still have souls. . . .

The poem then expands the poet's furtive, distant view of these women—"Oh! how many little old women I have followed!"—into a larger, alienated vision of the human condition, in which his own fate is assimilated to theirs:

Poor wizened spooks, ashamed to be alive,
you hug the walls, sickly and timorous,
and no one greets you, no one says good-bye
to rubbish ready for eternity!

But I who at a distance follow you
and anxiously attend your failing steps
as if I had become your father—mine
are secret pleasures you cannot suspect!

I see first love in bloom upon your flesh;
dark or luminous, I live your vanished days;
my teeming heart exults in all your sins
and all your virtues magnify my soul.
                              (1976, vol. 1, pp. 89–91)

The vicarious move from "I see" to "I live" (*je vois—je vis*) in the penultimate verse of the poem (the last stanza above) actualizes the transition from an objective observed reality to the subjective surreality (Baudelaire's word) of the poet's imagination, a move that is familiar in much of Baudelaire's poetry and, indeed, in much of the art of Baudelaire's time. What Baudelaire appreciates in Guys's journalistic prints and aquarelles of modern life, for instance, is precisely the energy that emerges from the dialectical encounter between the "historic" and the "poetic," the aesthetic vibration between objective and subjective realities. In his adamant refusal of any unique, absolute standard of beauty, Baudelaire articulates a modernist, Impressionist stance that can be further assimilated to the artistic ambitions of yet another contemporary Parisian artist and an intimate friend, Édouard Manet.

Like Baudelaire, Manet's reputation has been conditioned by an apocryphal mythology that credits him with the invention of modern art. It is significant that the myth of Manet imitates the model of the modern artist sketched out by Baudelaire in "The Painter of Modern Life": Manet's modernity as an artist is as much a factor of his commitment to modern subject matter as it is an expression of personalized style, the translation of an individual imagination. Numerous anecdotes are told of the young artist's aggressive attachment to "modern reality" while still a pupil in the studio of Thomas Couture. Antonin Proust tells of the young Manet's constant arguments with the models who took on "outrageous" poses for his class. "Can't you be more natural?" Manet would exclaim. "Is that how you stand when you go to buy a bunch of radishes from the grocer?" When the famous professional model, Dubosc, responded that, thanks to him, more than one artist had won the coveted Prix de Rome, Manet defiantly proclaimed: "We are not in Rome, and we don't want to go there. We are in Paris: and we're staying here!"

Like Baudelaire, again, the taste for modern subject matter as the point of departure for art (posing as at a fruit stand, rather than as a Greek statue) drew Manet to the streets of Paris, where, in the frequent company of the poet, he assumed the role of flaneur, strolling the boulevards and jotting in his notebook "a nothing, a profile, a hat, in a word, a fleeting impression *[une impression fugitive]*" (Proust, 1913, p. 29). Like Baudelaire and Guys, Manet also demonstrated in his art a particular fascination with the most ephemeral of modern details, fashion. As Baudelaire declared of the "painter of modern life," "he makes it his business to extract from fashion whatever element it may contain of poetry within history, to distil the eternal from the transitory" (Baudelaire, 1964, p. 12). Some of that taste for sketches of contemporary fashionability is apparent in the 1861 painting *La musique aux Tuileries* (The concert in the Tuileries Gardens), a painting that depicts Baudelaire in a stylish Second Empire crowd.

The picture, and a rather mischievous Manet staring out from the lower left corner, challenge the viewer to read it historically, poetically, or both. The viewer faces a casual assembly of fashionable Parisians, some of whom stare back blankly. Among them are artists and musicians, friends and associates of Manet. The picture is at once a document of a bourgeois Parisian milieu in 1861 and an imaginative evocation of Manet's private social world. Among the more readily identifiable faces on the left side of the painting is an orange blotch of color under a distinctive top hat, whom critics have always recognized to be Baudelaire. Although critics have occasionally argued about the dates and degree of friendship between the two men, none have commented on the fact that one recognizes Baudelaire *at all* in that blotch of color. An obvious answer is that he is recognizable because of other portraits Manet did of him in subsequent years, but that is a circular argument based on retrospection. It would appear that in this case, in a very Baudelairean way, the spectator is indeed being called on to write the text of that orange brush stroke—that is, in the literal identification of a poetic presence (Baudelaire) who exists only in the eye and memory of the beholder, the spectator here *produces the poetry of the painting*. Similarly, it would seem that the ultimate irony of this painting, titled *The Music [or Concert] in the Tuileries,* is that there is no music represented in the picture. It is only the suggestion of the title that makes the spectator "guess" the presence of a band-shell in the blurry background of the painting. The specta-

tor thus becomes engaged as an active participant in the completion of that sketchy background, whose legibility relies on the imaginative eye of the viewer for its meaning. The viewer joins in the voyeuristic exercise of the artist, as a flaneur in the crowd, creating the poetry of a painting, free to indulge the imagination and the eyes in what, a full century later, another Impressionist critic, Roland Barthes, would call "the pleasure of the text."

This, perhaps, is the ultimate legacy of Baudelaire's Impressionist aesthetic to contemporary readers and spectators: the privilege to make poetry and to find pleasure and meaning in the art that they not only confront, but in which they participate—like the many different critics enumerated at the beginning—as active players.

[*See also* Criticism.]

BIBLIOGRAPHY

Works by Baudelaire

Art in Paris, 1845–1862: Salons and Other Exhibitions. Translated and edited by Jonathan Mayne. London, 1965.
Les fleurs du mal (1857). Translated by Richard Howard. Boston, 1982.
Œuvres complètes. Edited by Claude Pichois. 2 vols. Paris, 1976.
The Painter of Modern Life and Other Essays (1863). Translated and edited by Jonathan Mayne. London, 1964.
Paris Spleen (1869). Translated by Louise Varèse. New York, 1970.

Other Sources

Barthes, Roland. *The Pleasure of the Text.* Translated by Richard Miller. New York, 1975.
Benjamin, Walter. *Charles Baudelaire: A Lyric Poet in the Era of High Capitalism.* Translated by Harry Zohn. London, 1973.
Burton, Richard. *Baudelaire in 1859: A Study in the Sources of Poetic Creativity.* Cambridge and New York, 1988.
Chambers, Ross. "Du temps des 'chats' au temps du 'cygne'." *Œuvres et critiques* 9.2 (1984): 11–26.
Chambers, Ross. "Memory and Melancholy." In *The Writing of Melancholy,* translated by Mary Seidman Trouille, pp. 153–173. Chicago, 1993.
de Man, Paul. "Anthropomorphism and Trope in the Lyric." In *The Rhetoric of Romanticism,* pp. 239–262. New York, 1984.
Godfrey, Sima. "Baudelaire's Windows." *Esprit Créateur* 22 (Winter 1982): 83–100.
Jakobson, Roman, and Claude Lévi-Strauss. "'Les chats' de Charles Baudelaire." In *"Les chats" de Baudelaire: Une confrontation de méthodes,* edited by Maurice Delcroix and Walter Geerts, pp. 9–35. Paris, 1980.
Jauss, Hans Robert. "The Poetic Text within the Change of Horizons of Reading: The Example of Baudelaire's 'Spleen II'." In *Toward an Aesthetic of Reception,* translated by Timothy Bahti, pp. 139–185. Minneapolis, 1982.
Johnson, Barbara. "Gender and Poetry: Charles Baudelaire and Marceline Desbordes-Valmore." In *Displacements: Women, Tradition, Literatures in French,* edited by Joan de Jean and Nancy K. Miller, pp. 163–181. Baltimore, 1991.
Kamuf, Peggy. "Baudelaire au féminin." In *Signature Pieces,* pp. 123–144. Ithaca, N.Y., 1988.
Laforgue, René. *The Defeat of Baudelaire: A Psychoanalytical Study of the Neurosis of Charles Baudelaire.* Translated by Herbert Agar. London, 1932.

Pichois, Claude, and Jean Ziegler. *Baudelaire*. Translated by Graham Robb. London, 1989.

Proust, Antonin. *Édouard Manet: Souvenirs*. Paris, 1913.

Sartre, Jean-Paul. *Baudelaire*. Translated by Martin Turnell. New York, 1950.

Shiff, Richard. *Cézanne and the End of Impressionism*. Chicago, 1984.

Terdiman, Richard. "Baudelaire's 'Le Cygne': Memory, History, and Sign." In *Present Past: Modernity and the Memory Crisis*, pp. 106–147. Ithaca, N.Y., 1993.

SIMA GODFREY

BAUDRILLARD, JEAN (b. 1929), French theorist and contemporary critic of society and culture who has had a central role in French postmodern theory. As a prolific author who has written more than twenty books, Baudrillard's reflections on art and aesthetics are an important, if not central, aspect of his work. Although his writings exhibit many twists, turns, and surprising developments as he moved from synthesizing Marxism and semiotics to a prototypical postmodern theory, interest in art remains a constant of his theoretical investigations and literary experiments.

A professor of sociology at the University of Nanterre from 1966 to 1987, Baudrillard has paid attention to art as an important and distinctive mode of objects since the beginning of his work in the 1960s. In his early studies, *The System of Objects* (1968) and *The Consumer Society* (1970), Baudrillard analyzed art objects as important artifacts in the system of objects that constitute everyday life. For Baudrillard, Pop art represents the dramatic transformations of art objects in the early twentieth century. Whereas previously art was invested with psychological and moral values that endowed its artifacts with a spiritualistic-anthropomorphic aura, by the twentieth century art objects "no longer live by proxy in the shadow of man and begin to assume extraordinary importance as independent elements in an analysis of space (cubism, etc.)" (Baudrillard, 1970, p. 33; translations from French are mine). Soon after the moment of Cubism, art objects exploded to the point of abstraction, were ironically resurrected in Dada and Surrealism, were destructured and volatized by subsequent movements toward abstract art, yet today "they are apparently reconciled with their image in New Figuration and Pop Art" (ibid.).

Pop art is of essential significance for Baudrillard in that it exemplifies the reduction of art to flat, nonsignifying image, thus replicating what he sees as the logic of contemporary (postmodern) society: "Whereas all art up to Pop was based on a vision of the world 'in depth,' Pop on the contrary claims to be homogeneous with its industrial and serial production and so with the artificial, fabricated character of the whole environment, homogeneous with this *immanent order of signs:* homogeneous with the all-over saturation and at the same time with the culturalized abstraction of this new order of things" (ibid.). Pop therefore signifies the end of depth, perspective, evocation, testimony, and the concept of the artist as active creator of meaning and iconoclastic critic.

Pop art thus constitutes a turning point in the history of art for Baudrillard whereby art becomes quite simply the reproduction of signs of the world, and in particular the signs of the consumer society, which itself is primarily a system of signs. Pop thus represents for Baudrillard the triumph of the sign over its referent, the end of representational art, the beginning of a new form of art that he will privilege with his term *simulation*. From this perspective, art henceforth becomes mere simulation of the images and objects of the contemporary world. Baudrillard thus insists that it is wrong to criticize Pop art for its naive Americanism, for its crass commercialism, for its flatness and banality, for precisely thereby it reproduces the very logic of contemporary culture.

Developing a more general semiotic perspective on art in *For a Critique of the Political Economy of the Sign* (1981), Baudrillard takes the painting as a signed object (signature) and as a gestural object, the product of artistic gestures or practices. In particular, he sees art as exemplary of how objects in the consumer society are organized as a system of signs. The painting for Baudrillard only becomes an art object in today's art world with the signature of the painter, with the sign of its origin, which situates it as a "*differential* value" within the system of signs, the series of works, which is that of the oeuvre of the painter (Baudrillard, 1981, p. 102). Baudrillard argues that copies or even forgeries previously were not as denigrated as in the contemporary world in part because art was more the collective product of artists' studios and because today art is supposed to be the "authentic" product of an individual creator as part of her or his oeuvre.

For Baudrillard, "modernity" in painting begins when the work of art is not seen as a syntax of fragments of a general tableau of the universe but as a succession of moments in the painter's career, as part of a series of works: "We are no longer in space but in time, in the realm of difference and no longer of resemblance, in the series and no longer in the order [of things]" (ibid., p. 104). It is the act of painting, the collection of the painter's gestures in the individuality of the oeuvre, that is established with the painter's signature, which produces the sign value of the work as a differential item in the series whereby the work is inserted into the system of art and receives its place (and value).

Painters such as Robert Rauschenberg and Andy Warhol who produce almost identical series of works present "something like a truth of modern art: it is no longer the literality of the world, but the literality of the gestural elaboration of creation—spots, lines, dribbles. At the same time, that which was representation—redoubling the world in space—becomes repetition—an indefinable redoubling of the act in time" (ibid., p. 106). In other words, precisely the seemingly peculiar gestures of Pop artists of repeating almost identical works in series point to the very nature of modern art, which establishes itself not as a presentation of the world but as a series of gestures, as the production of signs in the series of an oeuvre. This practice also reveals the naïveté, Baudrillard believes, of believing that the function of art is to (re)grasp the world, to refresh ways of seeing, to provide access to the real, for such art, all art, is merely a set of signs, the product of "the subject in its self-indexing" within a series (ibid., p. 107).

Thus, Baudrillard interprets painting as emblematic of sign culture, of the reduction of culture to a system of signs within which "art" often plays a privileged role. Art is subject to the same rules and system of signification as other commodities and follows as well the codes of fashion, determination of value by the market, and commodification, thus subverting its critical vocation. Modern art is thus for Baudrillard an *art of collusion vis-à-vis* the contemporary world. It plays with it and is included in the game. It can parody this world, illustrate it, simulate it, alter it; it never disturbs the order, which is also its own" (ibid., p. 110).

Pop art and ultrarealist trompe l'oeil paintings for Baudrillard illustrate the ways that simulacra came to replicate reality and the process whereby it became increasingly difficult to tell the difference between simulacra and reality, in which hyperreal models came to dominate and determine art and social life. These theories of art as simulation and hyperreality developed in studies in the mid-1970s and early 1980s, collected in *Simulations* (1983) and *Simulations and Simulation* (1994), came to influence new movements in the art world. Consequently, Baudrillard himself was taken as a leading theoretical figure in the world of contemporary art, becoming an icon who was increasingly referred to and cited in discussions of the art scene.

In addition, his theories of stages of representation and simulacra were applied to art history and his analyses of simulations to artworks, thereby providing him a certain currency in avant-garde art scenes and periodicals. In particular, the trend of simulation art seemed to embody his theory of simulations, while hyperrealist art movements illustrated his theory of hyperreality. The hyperrealist, simulationist, or neo-geo artists such as Peter Halley do not attempt to represent any objects or social reality, but simply reproduce hyperreal models or simulations through abstract representations of signs that simulate/pastiche former paintings—abstract and representational; or they attempt to represent scientific paradigms or models, or those of cybernetic languages, or simulate commodity and image production. Baudrillard distanced himself from such movements, but was nonetheless frequently proclaimed as a prophet of such postmodern simulation art.

As he turned to metaphysics in the 1980s, Baudrillard soured a bit on art; believing that it had exhausted itself, he became associated with the "end of art" theory. In the interview "Game with Vestiges" (1984), Baudrillard claims that in the sphere of art every possible artistic form and every possible function of art has been exhausted. Furthermore, against Walter Benjamin, Theodor Adorno, and other cultural revolutionaries, Baudrillard claims that art has lost its critical and negative function. Art and theory for Baudrillard became a "playing with the pieces" of the tradition, a "game with vestiges" of the past, through recombining and playing with the forms already produced.

Baudrillard continued his speculations on the end of art in *The Transparency of Evil* (1994), where he projected a vision of the end of art somewhat different from traditional theories, which posit the exhaustion of artistic creativity, or a situation in which everything has been done and there remains nothing new to do. Baudrillard maintains both of these points, to be sure, but the weight of his argument rests rather on a metaphysical vision of the contemporary era in which art has penetrated all spheres of existence, in which the dream of the artistic avant-garde for art to inform life has been realized. Yet, in Baudrillard's vision, with the realization of art in everyday life, art itself as a separate and transcendent phenomenon has disappeared.

Baudrillard calls this situation "transaesthetics," which he relates to similar phenomena of "transpolitics," "transsexuality," and "transeconomics," in which everything becomes political, sexual, and economic, so that these domains, like art, lose their specificity, their boundaries, their distinctness. The result is a confused condition in which there are no more criteria of value, of judgment, of taste, and the function of the normative thus collapses in a morass of indifference and inertia. Thus, although Baudrillard sees art proliferating everywhere, and writes in *The Transparency of Evil* that "talk about Art is increasing even more rapidly" (1994, p. 14), the power of art—of art as adventure, art as negation of reality, art as redeeming illusion, art as another dimension and so on—has disappeared. Art is everywhere but there "are no more fundamental rules" to differentiate art from other objects and "no more criteria of judgement or of pleasure" (ibid., p. 14). For Baudrillard, contemporary individuals are indifferent toward taste and manifest only distaste: "tastes are determinate no longer" (ibid., p. 72).

Yet, as a proliferation of images, of form, of line, of color, of design, art is more fundamental than ever to the contemporary social order: "our society has given rise to a general aestheticization: all forms of culture—not excluding anti-cultural ones—are promoted and all models of representation and anti-representation are taken on board" (ibid., p. 16). Thus, Baudrillard concludes: "It is often said that the West's great undertaking is the commercialization of the whole world, the hitching of the fate of everything to the fate of the commodity. That great undertaking will turn out rather to have been the aestheticization of the whole world—its cosmopolitan spectacularization, its transformation into images, its semiological organization" (ibid.).

In the postmodern media and consumer society, everything becomes an image, a sign, a spectacle, a transaesthetic object—just as everything also becomes transeconomic, transpolitical, and transsexual. This *"materialization* of aesthetics" is accompanied by a desperate attempt to simulate art, to replicate and mix previous artistic forms and styles, and to produce ever more images and artistic objects. But this "dizzying eclecticism" of forms and pleasures produces a situation in which art is no longer art in classical or modernist senses but is merely image, artifact, object, simulation, or commodity (Baudrillard is aware of increasingly exorbitant prices for artworks, but takes this as evidence that art has become something else in the orbital hyperspace of value, an ecstasy of skyrocketing values in "a kind of space opera" [ibid., p. 19]).

Thus, Baudrillard emerges as a prophet of the end of art, whose Gallic world-weariness and pessimism, obsessive repetition of previous ideas, and nihilistic evacuation of value end up disabling critical thought and inquiry. Consequently, although art and aesthetics are definitely changing in response to the mass media, new technologies, and new cultural forms, it is precisely these changes that require fresh theories and analyses. From this perspective, Baudrillard's dismissal of art and aesthetics blocks the necessary work that needs to be done. Although his analyses are certainly a provocation to new thinking and practice, one must go beyond Baudrillard to make his insights productive for aesthetic theory and practice today.

[*See also* Pop Art; Postmodernism, *overview article; and* Semiotics, *article on* Semiotics as a Theory of Art.]

BIBLIOGRAPHY

Works by Baudrillard

America. Translated by Chris Turner. London and New York, 1988.
"The Ecstacy of Communication." Translated by John Johnston. In *The Anti-Aesthetic,* edited by Hal Foster, pp. 126–134. Port Townsend, Wash., 1983.
For a Critique of the Political Economy of the Sign. Translated by Charles Levin. Saint Louis, 1981.
Forget Foucault. Translated by Nicole Dufresne. New York, 1986.
"Interview: Game with Vestiges." *On the Beach* 5 (Winter 1984): 19–25.
In the Shadow of the Silent Majorities: Or, the End of the Social, and Other Essays. Translated by Paul Foss, Paul Patton, and John Johnston. New York, 1983.
The Mirror of Production. Translated by Mark Poster. Saint Louis, 1975.
Simulacra and Simulation. Translated by Sheila Faria Glaser. Ann Arbor, 1994.
Simulations. Translated by Paul Foss, Paul Patton, and Philip Beitchman. New York, 1983.
La société de consommation. Paris, 1970.
Symbolic Exchange and Death. Translated by Ian Hamilton Grant. London, 1993.
Le système des objets. Paris, 1968.
The Transparency of Evil: Essays on Extreme Phenomena. Translated by James Benedict. London and New York, 1994.

Other Sources

Best, Steven, and Douglas Kellner. *Postmodern Theory: Critical Interrogations.* New York, 1991.
Frankovits, Andre, ed. *Seduced and Abandoned: The Baudrillard Scene.* Glebe, N.S.W., 1984.
Genosko, Gary. *Baudrillard and Signs: Signification Ablaze.* London and New York, 1994.
Kellner, Douglas. *Jean Baudrillard: From Marxism to Postmodernism and Beyond.* Stanford, Calif., 1989.
Kellner, Douglas, ed. *Jean Baudrillard: A Critical Reader.* Oxford and Cambridge, Mass., 1994.
Pefanis, Julian. *Heterology and the Postmodern: Bataille, Baudrillard, and Lyotard.* Durham, N.C., 1991.

DOUGLAS KELLNER

BAUHAUS. Founded in 1919 in Weimar, Germany, and closed in 1933 in Berlin, the Bauhaus was one of the most concentrated and seminal pedagogical experiments in art, architecture, and the reform of everyday life in the twentieth century. It was instrumental in forging the modern concept of design as a comprehensive theory of cultural production for mass society. Its mission was nothing less than a new, all-embracing cultural and environmental paradigm—a new architecture, a new vision, and a new way of living that would be commensurate with the social and technological challenges of modernization. The school's celebrated "foundation course," its geometric formalism and expressive functionalism, prototypes for furniture and household objects, as well as exemplary buildings, graphic design, typography, photography, and advertising, were disseminated throughout the world through publications, exhibitions, performances, and events, as well as the commercial promotion of its products and designs. The Bauhaus attracted students from across Europe and later the world, and became one of the most widely recognized institutions of the avant-garde during the interwar period and one of the touchstones for the transformation of avant-gardism into mainstream international modernism beginning in the late 1920s.

The story of the Bauhaus is typically told in stages defined by the sequence of directors (Walter Gropius, Hannes Meyer, Ludwig Mies van der Rohe), locations (Weimar, Dessau, Berlin), and key teachers (Johannes Itten, László Moholy-Nagy, Josef Albers, Marcel Breuer, Ludwig Hilberseimer, Lilly Reich). The dominant image of the school, however, was derived largely from works, events, and publications of the period from 1923 to 1928, with which Gropius—its most effective spokesperson—most strongly associated himself afterward. Focusing on these five years, which straddle the closing of the school in Weimar and its rebirth in Dessau, effectively rendered the Bauhaus more monolithic than it had actually been. Gropius's claims for the systematic character of its pedagogy, which privileged a strategic selection of teachings and works, was equally important to the creation of this dominant image. Yet, the history of events at the Bauhaus reveal diverse—at times irreconcilable—positions among the teachers, numerous internal disagreements, crises, and transformations, and external tensions around the implicit and explicit politics of the school, which on three occasions led to its closing. Only since the 1970s have the different periods, positions, and accomplishments within the school been treated more evenly, giving recognition to its founding "Expressionist" years (suppressed by Gropius), the directorships of Meyer (1928–1930) and Mies van der Rohe (1930–1933), and the contributions of women previously neglected, especially Ani Albers, Marianna Brandt, Gertrud Grunow, Lucia Moholy, Lilly Reich, and Gunta Stölzl.

Recognition of the Bauhaus as a tentative coalition of artists, craftspeople, architects, and designers raises the question of what commonalities and continuities brought and held the school together. In addition to certain stylistic and formal tropes, which were often denied, it may be said that the school was structured by the common goal of a new cultural unity to be achieved through a form of societal expression that would be direct and unmediated, unimpeded by prior conventions. Overlaps and intersections among the diverse agendas of Bauhaus teachers, as well as inheritances from one iteration of the program to the next, produced a complex web of affiliations and differences around this general aim. The premises of aesthetic theory, announced in the late eighteenth century and rendered scientific during the late nineteenth and early twentieth centuries, were central to this agenda, even in its most radically anti-aesthetic form under Meyer. The educational program of the Bauhaus may, in fact, be seen as the site of shifting and competing claims for operationalizing the pedagogical implications of modern aesthetics.

Responding to the Enlightenment imperative to rethink art and architecture in relation to the authority of reason and sensation, modern aesthetics harbored a reformist agenda that required the simultaneous de-education and retraining of artists and audiences alike. By 1900, the powerful desire for a new and broadly generalizable art and architecture—nonmimetic, organic, and objective—had aligned itself with several aspects of modernization that had taken up aspects of the aesthetic project. The founding of the German Werkbund in 1907 gave momentum to Germany's acceptance of industrialization for manufacturing in the decorative and applied arts, under way since the early 1890s. It served to link the applied arts and architecture and redefined culture and society in relation to mechanical production. At the same time, psychophysiological research by scientist-aestheticians, such as a Hermann von Helmholtz, Wilhelm Wundt, and Theodor Lipps, offered scientific explanations of human perception and aesthetic experience that became a new foundation for the arts, reinforcing emerging preoccupations with abstraction, elemental form, color, contrast, rhythm, and geometric mediation. Assuming the authority of science for the project of aesthetic retraining became strategic for efforts aimed at a new style that would be the counterpart to the reform of subjectivity and everyday life made necessary by the psychological, physiological, and nervous trauma engendered by modernization and metropolitanization. Educational reformers in the nineteenth and early twentieth centuries, notably Heinrich Pestalozzi, Friedrich Fröbel, Maria Montessori, and Georg Kirschensteiner, placed new emphasis on bringing out and developing children's inherent gifts through a guided process of free and playful activity, learning through doing, and creative expression. The abstract and geometric nature of toys developed for learning linked elemental forms and combinative geometries with the nurturing of creative imagination. The reformer Alfred Lichtwark argued in the 1880s for art education to become central to life for nonartists as well as professionals. He called for a moral renewal of life with art as the centerpiece of all education, promoting inner discipline within an atmosphere of greater outward freedom. At the turn of the century, these trajectories converged in the founding of new schools of art and applied art throughout Germany, including the School of Arts and Applied Arts established in Weimar by the influential Belgian architect Henry van de Velde in 1902. Forced by the war to leave Germany in 1915, van de Velde recommended Walter Gropius (1883–1969) as his successor and discussions began that led finally to Gropius's appointment in 1919.

Gropius's "founding" of the Bauhaus may itself be taken as symbolic of the aesthetic project, considered especially in relation to the legacy of Romanticism. The institutional structure of the new school proclaimed a new beginning for working progressively toward a new unity through the merger of opposites: the union of the Weimar Academy of Fine Art with van de Velde's School of Arts and Applied Arts. Renaming the school the Staatliche Bauhaus affirmed the promise of overcoming the antinomies of modernity by returning "salon art" to its origins in craft proficiency, an ur-position from which the potential fusion of all the arts in "a new structure of the future" could be announced. However, in the absence of teachers who were equally skilled in craft and art, the educational program of the school maintained this division until 1926. As students proceeded through the program in stages from "apprentice" and "journeyman" to "master," they studied in two streams—in workshops dedicated to different materials and skills, each run by a "workshop master," and in courses concerning basic design and theory, directed by "masters of form," artists who also had workshop affiliations. This double structure was only abandoned once some of the most talented students had graduated to become teachers. Gropius considered these "young masters" to be a new breed of designers—"new men" and "new women" such as Marcel

Breuer (1902–1981), Josef Albers (1888–1976), Herbert Bayer (1900–1985), and Gunta Stölzl (1897–1983)—doubly gifted and doubly skilled, capable of confronting the challenges of modernity with childlike creativity, scientific precision, and heroic vigor.

Insisting that a new architecture was the goal of the Bauhaus, Gropius's initial pedagogy emphasized that it would only emerge by delineating a common foundation among the arts. Where, in 1911, Gropius had privileged the naïveté of engineers over the learning and academicism of architects, now he sought to foreground the spontaneous creativity of the artist for its potential to generate a pure architectonics that could then be developed into a comprehensive environmental paradigm. His first appointments at the Bauhaus were all artists: the pedagogue Johannes Itten (1888–1967), the sculptor Gerhard Marcks (1889–1981), and the painter and printmaker Lyonel Feininger (1871–1956). Between 1920 and 1922, he appointed five more artists: the well-established Paul Klee (1879–1940) and Wassily Kandinsky (1866–1944), along with the younger Oskar Schlemmer (1888–1943), Georg Muche (b. 1895), and Lothar Schreyer (1886–1966).

The influential *Vorkurs* or "foundation course" emerged from the theory course introduced by Itten, at Gropius's request, to correct the lack of discipline among the school's initial students. During its six months (quickly expanded to one year), students were taken through improvisatory and constructive exercises in both two and three dimensions and in various media. They prepared exact, detailed drawings from human figures and of materials and textures in order to heighten their perception and develop rendering skill. They studied color, elementary form, and contrast, as well as the structure and rhythm of old master paintings. For Itten, training the senses, the hand, and the emotions was essential for the effective communication of inner experiences. The importance of this self-discipline led him to incorporate breathing exercises, meditation, and diet into his lessons. Having begun by teaching children in Vienna, he now carried the tradition of educational reform for children into that for adult artists. His teaching was infused with a pervasive yet vague idealism that combined aspects of Western empathy theory with Eastern mystic beliefs in the affinity between subject and object, spirit and matter, mediated only by intuition. The paradox of nurturing unimpeded expression through systematic discipline remained central to the dynamic of Bauhaus pedagogy.

A split between Gropius and Itten emerged at the end of 1921 over differences in philosophy brought to the fore by Itten's increasing influence. The quasi-religious aura around him had attracted a strong following among students, and the centrality of his teaching and workshop responsibilities began to rival that of the director. Itten focused exclusively on the self-discovery and empowerment of the students and eschewed the notion of art as a preliminary to the design of commodities. He had no commitment to craft training for the artist and took Gropius's desire to bring actual projects into the workshops as damaging of the quietude and harmony necessary for creative expression. For Gropius, on the other hand, this was essential for regrounding art and architecture, integrating theory and practice, and maintaining support from government sponsors. Itten's teaching also lacked any systematic theory of structure, pictorial space, or composition. His mystic privileging of subjective expression led to criticism by influential outsiders, notably Theo van Doesburg, who introduced the discourse of objectivity and collective societal expression then emerging among the European avant-garde, which became important to post-Expressionist art and architecture during the mid-1920s.

On Itten's resignation in 1922, Gropius hired the young Hungarian Constructivist László Moholy-Nagy (1895–1946) to transform and systematize the foundation course together with Josef Albers. Overemphasis on the differences between the Itten and the Moholy-Nagy years, however, neglects the continued importance of theories of expression and empathy, which were transferred from the expression of the subject to the expression of the inner nature, effective form, and purpose of objects. The quest for direct expression and empathetic congruence between subject and object continued, but it assumed a purified, sober, and geometric form that was thought to be universal, fit for manufacturing, and appropriate to the function of object. Albers's first-semester course on materials incorporated tours of manufacturing plants and emphasized the expressive potential of materials rationally manipulated, as in his exercises on the structural properties of folded paper or his own work in stained glass. Moholy-Nagy's second-semester course on materials and organization in space focused on the constructive assembly of elemental components in dynamic equilibrium, which pointed to a technologically based architecture of light, floating transparency, and virtual volumes exemplified by Moholy-Nagy's paintings, photograms, photographs, sculptures, stage sets, and films; his course (summarized in his book *Von Material zu Architektur* [1929]) also informed the work of the metal studio, which he reoriented to include modern materials and to focus on the production of standardized household objects. Marianna Brandt's metalworks of 1923, Alma Buscher's toy blocks of 1924, Karl Jucker and Wilhelm Wagenfeld's table lamp of 1923–1924, and Marcel Breuer's tubular metal furniture became signature works of the school in this period. It was this systematized iteration of the course under Moholy-Nagy and Albers, augmented by Paul Klee's courses in visual thinking and pictorial structure and Wassily Kandinsky's in analytic drawing (from 1922) and color (from 1925), that came to underpin the school's program of aesthetic reform as the necessary prerequisite to an education in architecture and design. Its purpose was to release stu-

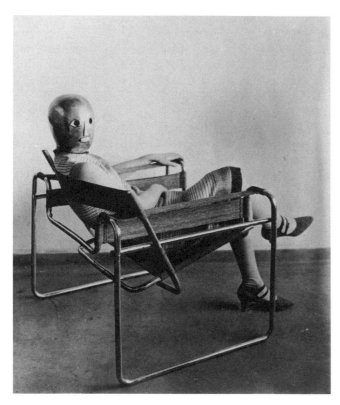

BAUHAUS. Marcel Breuer, *Tubular Steel Armchair (known as the "Wassily Chair") with a Sitter (Inge Schwollmann, Ise Gropius, or Lis Beyer) with a Mask by Oskar Schlemmer* (1925/26); Bauhaus-Archiv, Berlin. (Photograph by Erich Consemüller; copyright by Stephan Consemüller; used by permission.)

dents from ingrained customs so as to discover their own latent creative abilities, to learn the properties of diverse materials and techniques, and to understand what were thought to be the universal basic elements and principles of art as an objective grounding for individual work in all media and at all scales.

Another aspect of Gropius's aesthetic project concerned the dynamic production of a new unity that would avoid the codification associated with "style"—a new totality figured alternatively as *Gesamtkunstwerk* (total work of art), *Einheitskunst* (art of unity), and *Gestaltung* (form creation, or design). Whereas prior to World War I, the advocates of bringing together the various fine arts, applied arts, and architecture had invoked the idea of the *Gesamtkunstwerk* first proffered by Richard Wagner for his operatic productions in 1851, Gropius referred to the medieval *Bauhütte* in his initial program for the Bauhaus, evoking a more egalitarian ideal for the production of collective work (the future cathedral) in which artists, architects, sculptors, and craftspeople would come together in the humble understanding of their work as part of a common task and idea. The productions of the theater workshop were the principal vehicle within the school for this. Led initially by Lothar Schreyer, the pu-

rification of the theater into elementary forms, colors, sounds, and movements was extended by Oskar Schlemmer in the figural abstractions of his "Triadic Ballet"—a hybrid of dance, costume, pantomime, and music—and in student productions such as the "Mechanical Cabaret" of 1923 in which people disappeared into a choreography of abstract colored planes. Kandinsky's ambition for synthesis, especially for his own theatrical projects, was also expressed in terms of a *Gesamtkunstwerk*. Outside the school, the building commissions of Gropius's architectural office with Alfred Meyer provided opportunities for collaborative works, such as the Sommerfeld House (1920–1921), the Municipal Theater at Jena (1922–1923), and the Haus am Horn (designed by Georg Muche for the Bauhaus Exhibition of 1923).

Alfred H. Barr, Jr., noted in 1938 that the idea of a Bauhaus style or a Bauhaus dogma as something fixed and permanent was at all times merely the inaccurate conclusion of superficial observers. Gropius's conception of design education for a new organic society was based on the principle of dynamic growth and ever-renewed creativity operating in relation to a changing external world. His slogan for the Bauhaus exhibition of 1923, "Art and Technology—A New Unity," rearticulated the new paradigm under the sign of *Bauen* (building or construction) and *Gestaltung* (design). In 1923, the principal instrument of Gropius's *Einheitskunst* was still a geometric and abstract formalism, whereas the organic principle of *Gestaltung*—common to theory in the life sciences, human sciences, technology, and art—became increasingly central as the Bauhaus discovered that pure forms often made for dysfunctional objects. Functionalist theory was based on the proposition, taken from biology, that the form of an object, like that of a plant, is the outward expression of inner life forces that may be understood scientifically and reproduced through technology. This shift was exemplified in Gropius and Meyer's design of the new building for the Bauhaus when it was forced to leave Weimar in 1925 and relocated in Dessau. Each part of the building complex was given a distinctive form specific to the spatial needs of its use; in Gropius's words, "the building bodied itself forth" as the direct expression of inner purpose in concrete masses that remained unadorned save for a coat of white paint. Its pinwheel configuration with a street running through it appeared to seize the dynamics of pure becoming and hold it like frozen motion or a still from a film. The furniture and fittings of the new building marked the shift from craft *Gesamtkunstwerk* to the serial production of functional objects for society at large. In moving to Dessau, the Bauhaus assumed the subtitle Hochschule für Gestaltung (Institute for Design), which institutionalized its move toward professional training and scientific studies. Masters were redesignated professors, apprentices became simply students, and the school was able to grant diplomas for the first time. The strategic value of the idea of *Gestaltung* for forging a modernist mainstream was reinforced by its common usage among the other branches of German Constructivism during the 1920s (the circles around the magazines *De Stijl, G,* and *ABC*); after World War II, it became widely accepted as the German word for design.

In the shift from *Gesamtkunstwerk* to *Einheitskunst* and finally to *Gestaltung,* attitudes changed toward the organization and production of the workshops, as well as the relationship between the workshops and courses. The material-based workshops of the early years were gradually reorganized into functionally based ones and redirected toward the integration of teaching and production. In 1925, the number was reduced to six—joinery (cabinetry), metal, mural painting, textiles, book and art printing, and sculpture. In 1928, the cabinet-making and metal shops were combined into the design of furniture and household equipment under Marcel Breuer. The pottery workshop had been the school's first commercially successful operation, but it had been run on a quasi-independent basis and was not transferred to Dessau. The weaving workshop, whose training program was initially incomplete, was redirected in 1925 toward the industrial design of textiles as Gunta Stölzl introduced a comprehensive three-year training at the interface of design and technology. The workshops had from the start enabled students to support themselves by selling their work, but they were gradually turned toward production that would benefit the school as well. Patents, royalties, and sales became an important independent source of income. By 1924, forty-three objects had already been designed for production, including tea caddies, dishes, pots, ashtrays, coffee and tea services, and lamps. The school issued a catalog of designs and participated in exhibitions and trade shows. This shift proved to be so successful that Gropius formed the company Bauhaus GmbH in 1925. In the following years, the school bought another 183 works by students and faculty, including the rights for reproduction.

Gropius's use of the workshops to promote the programs and work of the school developed, over the years, into a comprehensive publicity program that sponsored the institutionalization of graphic design. In 1922, the print workshop was already replaced by graphic printing whose production included prints and portfolios, notably the "Bauhaus Masters Portfolio" of 1923. In the same year, Moholy-Nagy launched the Bauhaus in the design of new elemental typography and the exclusive use of lowercase letters "to save time," and give the school a new graphic identity in black, white, and red. Lucia Moholy became instrumental as the school's unofficial publicist and photographer from 1923 to 1928, and her photographs contributed greatly to its dynamic image. After attempting unsuccessfully to found a publishing house in 1923, Gropius established the Bauhaus book series in 1926 under the direction of Moholy-Nagy and in conjunction with the publisher Albert Langen in Munich. Launched with Gropius's own *International Architecture* in 1925, the series was to be a comprehensive portrait of contemporary architecture and design operating in relation to problems of art, science, and technology. It also aimed at drawing together the various Constructivist avant-gardes into a united modernist mainstream. In 1926, the print workshop became graphic art production under Herbert Bayer and was expanded to include layout, typography, and advertising. With the opening of the new building in Dessau the same year, the school inaugurated its journal, *bauhaus,* which continued until 1931. In conjunction with the promotion of Bauhaus products through catalog and exhibitions, these initiatives constituted a concerted campaign to reform the system of mass consumption in tandem with the reform of production. Moholy-Nagy's efforts to chart the characteristics and potentials of a new vision and sense of motion, mediated by mechanical instruments and means of reproduction, were key to forging this link between production, media, and publicity.

Gropius's initial efforts to incorporate architectural training remained tentative, limited by the mandate of an Arts and Crafts school, the skepticism of faculty, and the economic conditions of the time. From 1922 to 1925, his partner Adolf Meyer taught courses in technical drawing that included studies in proportion and projective geometries. With the move to Dessau and the redesignation of the school, Gropius was finally able, in 1927, to create an architecture department and appointed the Swiss architect Hannes Meyer (1889–1954) to direct it. The program of the school was completely reorganized to focus on architecture, which was taught in two sections: building *(Bau)* and interior decoration *(Inneneinrichtung).* A diploma in architecture was introduced and, although the initial number of students was small, the new emphasis quickly established itself, bringing with it, however, a steady decline in the number of women students. Advertising appeared next in the order of priority, combining the printing, sculpture, and photography workshops. Theater took third place, which was a higher rank than it had ever held. As the unifying and comprehensive art of architecture assumed centrality, Gropius's earlier rejection of traditional art classes relaxed under pressure from both Klee and Kandinsky to teach "free painting classes." Paradoxically, this marked the end of the strategic importance of art in the curriculum. Having installed the school in its new building, formalized the link between design, production, and publicity, and launched an architectural curriculum, Gropius resigned in 1928 to dedicate himself to his growing practice, which also prompted the departure of Moholy-Nagy, Breuer, and Bayer.

Taking a categorical stand against the advertising theatricality of the previous Bauhaus, Meyer advocated design based on social needs, economics, technology, and science and quickly implemented another overhaul of the school's internal structure. The preliminary course was expanded and further systematized. A compulsory lettering class was introduced by Joost Schmidt, and Schlemmer developed classes in life drawing and "Man" in which he proffered the triple unity of humanity's physical, emotional, and psychological nature as the basis for a metaphysical harmony in space. An alternative student-initiated theater emerged known as the "Young Group," its collectivism aligned more with the political theater of Erwin Piscator and Bertolt Brecht than with Schlemmer. For Meyer, this set of program consolidated the "artistic pole" of the Bauhaus curriculum. The systematic knowledge of hygiene, anatomy, biology, sociology, psychology, physics, chemistry, acoustics, lighting, and color constituted the "scientific pole." The resolution of this opposition came to rest with the students. The timetable of the workshops called for an eight-hour workday in order to emulate industry, and Saturdays were dedicated to sport. The overall duration of the program was extended to seven semesters. The architecture department was reorganized into theory and practice sections over a nine-semester program, and Ludwig Hilberseimer (1885–1967) was hired in 1929 to teach architectural theory and city planning. The workshops were changed once more, amalgamating metal, textiles, joinery, and mural painting into interior decoration under the direction of Alfred Arndt (1898–1976). The advertising studio absorbed printing, publicity, exhibitions, photography, and plastic design. In photography, Walther Peterhans (1897–1960) rejected Moholy-Nagy's productive photography and light design in favor of technical perfection and precise detailing in halftones.

Although workshop production had been somewhat successful under Gropius, the school failed to meet his income targets. During the directorship of the more radical Meyer, however, the marketing of Bauhaus products became (paradoxically) more successful through their "proletarianization." From the outset, Meyer was critical of the *sachlich* formalism of primary colors and elementary forms as well as the lack of research in determining what would be produced. Affiliated with the Swiss cooperative movement and Marxist collectivization, he redirected the approach to design from forms presumed to have universal validity to the analysis of social needs and opportunities in manufacturing. He abandoned workshops that were commercially ineffective and moved to eliminate actual production in the workshops in favor of designing prototypes that would be produced by manufacturers. Lamps, wallpaper, and floor coverings proved to be especially popular, production in the workshops grew, and revenue increased for both students and the school.

Meyer's position, which he developed during these years not only at the Bauhaus but also as editor with Mart Stam and Hans Schmidt of the journal *ABC. Beiträge zum Bauen*, was more radical than Gropius's in every respect. Whereas Gropius eschewed overt politics, Meyer promoted active engagement by architects not only in the system of production but in the politics of social transformation. Whereas Gropius sought a synthesis between art and technology, Meyer rejected the very concept of art as sustaining bourgeois false consciousness. His "new world" demanded the "dictatorship of the machine" as the inexorable mediation of "the possibilities and tasks of all our lives." Although Meyer's conception of building coincided in part with Gropius's rhetoric, he pushed pure construction to an extreme, favoring the rational side of the binary opposition that Gropius had struggled to resolve in a new unity. "All things in this world," he wrote in 1928, "are the product of the formula: (function times economy)" and "building is nothing but [deliberate] organization: social, technical, economic, psychological organization." Combining metaphors of machine and organism, he held that building was a biological rather than aesthetic process organizing and giving shape to the functions of life. Its products were biological apparatuses serving the needs of body and mind. Meyer also offered his own version of the *Gesamtkunstwerk* ideal by suggesting that the new architecture would be realized through the cooperative effort of craftspeople and inventors operating in a working community. His design for the League of Nations competition in 1927 and the Trade Union School in Bernau of 1928–1930 are demonstrative of this approach, distinguished from Gropius's Bauhaus at Dessau by their material and technical sobriety, utilitarian rigor, and systematic use of repetition. Moreover, these projects exemplified the proposition that aesthetic practice was a form of social production that could actively intervene in the organizational structure of the productive cycle. Meyer's anti-aesthetic and antihumanist depletion of the object of bourgeois values aimed at sublating art into life, while self-reflexively reinscribing traces of production into the material presence of the object.

As the political tide in the Weimar Republic continued to turn toward the right, Meyer's explicit affiliation with the left and the emergence of a student cell of the Communist Party within the Bauhaus gave rise to attacks on the school by local politicians and eroded confidence in Meyer's directorship. Undermined from the inside as well, especially by Kandinsky, Meyer resigned in 1930 and was replaced at Gropius's recommendation by the architect Ludwig Mies van der Rohe (1886–1969). Mies's orchestration in 1927 of the Werkbund's housing exhibition in Stuttgart, the Weissenhofsiedlung, and his German Pavilion at the Barcelona World Exposition of 1929, had by then confirmed his leading position among the modernist avant-garde. His first task was to restore the political neutrality that Gropius had himself struggled to maintain.

Mies kept most of Meyer's curriculum, but he instituted a number of strategic transformations that moved the school toward a more normative professional model for training architects and reiterated the negotiation between material-ism and idealism that structured his own work. Whereas Meyer advocated nothing more than *bauen*, Mies promoted architecture as *Baukunst* (art of building), an art in its own right neither dependent on the other arts nor adequately de-fined as mere technique. Grounded nevertheless in the technical and material knowledge of fabrication, *Baukunst* was, for Mies, an art of formation *(Gestaltung)*, which he characterized as "the spatial execution of spiritual decisions *[geistiger Entscheidungen]*" by which to "illuminate, make visible, and direct the currents of the spiritual situation in which we stand." He challenged his students, as he had his colleagues in the Weissenhofsiedlung, to respond individu-ally to the conditions and opportunities of the epoch. Whereas Gropius's conception of totality focused on the in-tegration of the arts and Meyer's on materially registering the systematization of production, Mies interpreted the given conditions of material culture in clear and effective formations that could be understood as symbols of a poten-tial and emergent totality.

In taking over Meyer's curriculum, Mies redefined it as the base level of his own, dedicated to imparting systematic knowledge of techniques, materials, physical science, human psychology, and urban planning. He exempted students with prior training from the *Vorkurs*, which was criticized as overly subjective, and redefined the school's purpose as providing the highest stage in the "handicraft, technical and artistic training of students." Working exclusively with Mies in the fi-nal two semesters, the students used their skills in building technique and functional design, acquired in previous se-mesters, as a platform for more abstract, ideal tasks of design in which proportions, the combination of materials, the cre-ation of dynamic spatiality, and disciplined judgment were emphasized. Mies also conducted courses during these final semesters in free architectural sketching as the essential vehi-cle for the search for form. In finally eliminating production from the workshops, reducing their number even further, amalgamating furniture, metalwork, and wall painting into interior design under Lilly Reich (1885–1947), and remov-ing the last residues of apprenticeship, Mies changed the re-lation between theory and practice. Some have argued that these changes corroded the Bauhaus idea of integrating the-ory and practice, which Gropius had claimed for his concept of design and whose social effectiveness Meyer had sought to advance, but Mies's acceptance of modern professional-ism may be understood as transferring the problem more fully from the school into the world. His curriculum effec-tively sought to transform the given system of production by reasserting, in modern guise, the traditional role of the archi-tect as artistic director of the building enterprise—giving form to life "in its entire fullness, in its spiritual and concrete interconnection."

The architectural curriculum under Mies consisted of three stages. Technical and scientific knowledge was im-parted over the first four semesters, taught largely by out-side engineers and scientists who had been brought into the school by Meyer. Courses included the study of building law, materials, projective geometry, statics, heating and ven-tilation, physics, chemistry, mathematics, psychotechnics, and psychology. In the second year, Ludwig Hilberseimer taught architectural theory under the title "Seminar for Apartment and Town Planning." Hilberseimer's instruction focused on systematic estate planning guided by the princi-ples of uniform sun-orientation, mixture of low and tall buildings, variety of building types and designs, and the in-tegration of efficient infrastructure. Lilly Reich, one of the most gifted and successful women designers of the Weimar period, aligned the weaving and interiors workshops more with architecture, focusing on exercises in the combination of materials and colors, and the design of patterns suitable for textile prints and wallpaper. Long affiliated with the German Werkbund, Reich had developed a formid-able understanding of the German manufacturing industry through her designs for manufacturing exhibitions, as well as furniture and interiors, frequently undertaken in collabo-ration with Mies.

Despite Mies's efforts to stabilize the relationship of the Bauhaus to its municipal host, the school became the victim of increasing political polarization between left and right in the wake of the world Depression of 1929. The elections of 1930 brought Adolf Hitler's National Socialists their first majority; and although the state of Thuringia Landtag (provincial diet) and the city of Dessau were also quick to elect Nazi governments, the Bauhaus remained a center for left-wing forces. Lobbying against the school by Nazi politi-cians and the Nazi-approved architect and author Paul Schultze-Naumburg remained frustrated until a petition to close it was finally successful in August 1932. Able never-theless to retain the furniture, inventory, patents, and regis-tered designs, Mies reopened the school in Berlin as a pri-vate teaching and research institute in a disused telephone factory. The school continued to be accused of harboring Communists and Jews, however, and was closed again in April 1933. Determined to rectify the injustice to the school, Mies lobbied to reopen it, only to decide, once per-mission was granted in July, to close voluntarily. This ges-ture of intellectual freedom, made in conjunction with his remaining colleagues, was indicative of his decisionist ap-proach to the art of life as well as building, exercising choice in the face of historical challenges.

Although teaching at the Bauhaus was, in retrospect, not as unified as Gropius had presented it, the school brought the program of transforming everyday life into aesthetic ex-perience to a level of articulation, institutionalization, and publicity that allowed it to become widely disseminated. Paradoxically, the diffusion of Bauhaus teaching, especially in the United States, led to the codification of "Bauhaus style" and "Bauhaus form" in which the quest for authentic, vital, and ever-creative expressions of life collapsed into a formal system and "machine aesthetic." Once absorbed into the system of mass production and consumption, the idea of simplified, unornamented, and functional forms became a recipe with unprecedented commercial success. Without the utopian moment of its initial neo-Romantic avoidance of formalization, however, the "Bauhaus aesthetic" simply served to aestheticize commodity production and legitimate manufacturing efficiencies. Criticism of Bauhaus "good design" quickly followed and by the 1960s its eclipse had signaled the end of the problematic intersection of aesthetic purification with the logic of industrial capitalism.

Equally disturbing to the received image of progressive Bauhaus modernism, recent scholarship has shed light on the history of relations between a broad array of modernists (including Gropius and Richard Döcker as well as Mies) and the early years of the National Socialist regime, revealing accommodations on both sides and unexpected commonalities between their respective programs for cultural renewal. Efforts to insist on the inherent ideological value of modernist form in distinction to its Fascist counterparts— so central to maintaining the flame of modernism during the war and after 1945—were confounded by shared aims and assumptions that served to link the extreme ends of the political spectrum below the surface of consciousness. Both right and left operated within post-Enlightenment intellectual traditions, embraced modernization, and aestheticized technology; both subscribed to determinist theories of history and strategies of *Gesamtkunstwerk* for their potential to usher in a new organic society and culture; both celebrated *Sachlichkeit*, objectivity, and the return to origins in the belief that (pure) outer form was the necessary physiognomic expression of (pure) inner essence (figured by conservatives as neoclassical architecture and by progressives as unornamented construction); and both sought to reforge the human subject through the aesthetic reform of the environment for everyday life. These realizations have been further reinforced by historians demonstrating the continued influence and practice of Bauhaus design deep into the Nazi period, from which it was earlier presumed to have been entirely expunged.

The transformation of aesthetics into the programmatic reform of society, whether for profit, power, or redemption, entailed a politics of control at a mass scale that subjugated freedom to a higher necessity. In this regard, the differences between the aesthetic aims and pedagogical strategies of the Bauhaus's three directors remain of consequence. In Gropius's Bauhaus, freedom resided in the openness of creative expression, the play of beginning each task anew, and the self-realization of objects. For Meyer, on the other hand, freedom was understood in terms of class struggle and cooperative association, which led him to reposition the school within the larger world, hoping to transform it from within into a system of freedom. Mies's insistence on architecture

as an artistic practice confronting, interpreting, and directing the material conditions of the epoch avoided the totalitarian implication of comprehensive new visions, syntheses, and universal subject formations without abandoning the theorization of totality and the quest for organicity. For Mies, each situation demanded a fresh response to the challenges and constraints of the era, giving rise to singular works of art that delineated the space of freedom in tense and contingent configurations of irresolution between affirmation and negation, openness and closure, transparency and opacity, union and estrangement.

[*See also* Archicture, *overview article;* Constructivism; Design; Mies van der Rohe; Modernism, *article on* Modernity and Tradition in Architecture; *and* Suprematism.]

BIBLIOGRAPHY

50 Jahre Bauhaus. Stuttgart, 1968. Exhibition catalog.

Banham, Reyner. *Theory and Design in the First Machine Age.* London, 1960.

Bauhaus-Archiv Museum für Gestaltung: Sammlungs-Katalog: Architektur Design Malerei Grafik Kunstpädagogik. Berlin, 1981.

Bax, Marty. *Bauhaus Lecture Notes, 1930–1933.* Amsterdam, 1991.

Bayer, Herbert, Walter Gropius, and Ise Gropius, eds. *Bauhaus, 1919–1928.* New York, 1938.

Dearstyne, Howard. *Inside the Bauhaus.* Edited by David Spaeth. New York, 1986.

Droste, Magdelena. *Bauhaus, 1919–1933.* Cologne, 1990.

Experiment Bauhaus. Berlin, 1988. Exhibition catalog.

Feininger, T. Lux. "The Bauhaus: Evolution of an Idea." *Criticism: A Quarterly for Literature and the Arts* 2.3 (Summer 1960): 260–277.

Franciscono, Marcel. *Walter Gropius and the Creation of the Bauhaus in Weimar: The Ideals and Artistic Theories of Its Founding Years.* Urbana, 1971.

Gropius, Walter. *The New Architecture and the Bauhaus.* Translated by P. Morton Shand. New York and London, 1936.

Hahn, Peter, ed. *Bauhaus-Berlin: Auflösung Dessau 1932, Schliessung Berlin 1933, Bauhäusler und Drittes Reich.* Weingarten, 1985.

Hays, K. Michael. *Modernism and the Posthumanist Subject: The Architecture of Hannes Meyer and Ludwig Hilberseimer.* Cambridge, Mass., 1992.

Hüter, Karl-Heinz. *Das Bauhaus in Weimar: Studie zur gesellschaftspolitischen Geschichte einer deutschen Kunstschule.* Berlin, 1976.

Itten, Johannes. *Mein Vorkurs am Bauhaus: Gestaltungs- und Formlehre.* Ravensburg, 1963.

Krauss, Rosalind. "Jump over the Bauhaus." *October* 15 (Summer 1982): 103–110.

Lupton, Ellen, and J. Abbott Miller. *The ABCs of the Bauhaus and Design Theory.* New York, 1991.

Moholy-Nagy, László. *Von Material zu Architektur.* Munich, 1929. Translated by Daphne M. Hoffmann as *The New Vision: From Material to Architecture* (New York, 1938).

Naylor, Gillian. *The Bauhaus Reassessed: Sources and Design Theory.* New York, 1985.

Nerdinger, Winfried, ed. *Bauhaus-Moderne im Nationalsozialismus: Zwischen Anbiederung und Verfolgung.* Munich, 1993.

Neumann, Eckhard, ed. *Bauhaus und Bauhäusler: Bekenntnisse und Erinnerungen.* Berlin, 1971; rev. ed., Cologne, 1985. Translated by Eva Richter and Alba Lorman as *Bauhaus and Bauhaus People* (New York, 1970; rev. ed., New York, 1993).

Nyberg, Folke. "From Baukunst to Bauhaus." *Journal of Architectural Education* 45.3 (May 1992): 130–137.

Schlemmer, Oskar, László Moholy-Nagy, Farkas Molnár. *Die Bühne im Bauhaus.* Munich, 1925; reprint, Berlin, 1965.

Steckner, Cornelius. *Zur Ästhetik des Bauhauses: Ein Beitrag zur Erforschung synästhetischer Grundsätze und Elementarerziehung am Bauhaus.* Edited by Sigfried Albrecht and Erwin Herzberger. Stuttgart, 1985.

Tafuri, Manfredo, and Francesco Dal Co. *Modern Architecture.* Translated by Robert Erich Wolf. New York, 1979.

Whitford, Frank. *Bauhaus.* London, 1984.

Wick, Rainer. *Bauhaus Pädagogik.* Cologne, 1982.

Wick, Rainer, ed. *Ist die Bauhaus-Pädagogik aktuell?* Cologne, 1985.

Wingler, Hans M. *Das Bauhaus, 1919–1933: Weimar, Dessau, Berlin und die Nachfolge in Chicago seit 1937.* 3d ed. Bramsche, 1975. Translated by Wolfgang Jabs and Basil Gilbert as *The Bauhaus: Weimar, Dessau, Berlin, Chicago,* edited by Joseph Stein (3d rev. ed., Cambridge, Mass., 1976).

Winkler, Klaus-Jürgen. *Die Architektur am Bauhaus in Weimar.* Berlin, 1993.

Wolsdorff, C. *Der vorbildliche Architekt: Mies van der Rohes Architekturunterricht, 1930–1958, am Bauhaus und in Chicago.* Berlin, 1986. Exhibition catalog.

DETLEF MERTINS

BAUMGARTEN, ALEXANDER GOTTLIEB

(1714–1762), German philosopher who was influential as the author of the textbooks on metaphysics and ethics on which Immanuel Kant lectured. Baumgarten's significance for aesthetics lies not only in his coinage of the term aesthetics for the philosophy of art but also in his creation of a paradigm for understanding art that was profoundly influential in his own time and has continued to be so, although indirectly, down to the present.

Born in Berlin and educated in the Pietist orphanage and university of Halle, Baumgarten studied the philosophy of Christian Wolff after the banishment of its author, and left Halle for a professorship in Frankfurt an der Oder in 1740, the year of Wolff's rehabilitation and return; thus, he cannot be considered a personal disciple of Wolff. Yet, through his *Metaphysica* (1739) and *Ethica* (1740), he was a major transmitter of Wolffianism to subsequent generations, while through his two works in aesthetics, the 1735 dissertation *Meditationes philosophicae de nonnullis ad poema pertinentibus* (Philosophical meditations on some matters pertaining to poetry) and the two volumes of his incomplete *Aesthetica,* published in 1750 and 1758, he was also the major revisionist in the Wolffian tradition.

Baumgarten first defined *aesthetics* in 1735 as "the science of how things are to be cognized by means of the senses," a definition amplified in 1750 as "the theory of the liberal arts, the logic of the lower faculty of cognition, the art of thinking beautifully, the art of the analogue of reason." Passing comments in other works suggest that he sometimes envisioned an "empirical aesthetics" or a logic of empirical data as a propaedeutic for logic in the traditional sense, but in his aesthetic writings he had in mind a study of the perfection of and pleasure in the exercise of sensibility for its own sake, as manifested in the production of works of artistic beauty. Thus, whereas Wolff had associated beauty with the sensory perception of perfection (a definition reiterated in Baumgarten's *Metaphysica*), sensory perception being viewed as a confused and inferior form of intellection, in his aesthetics Baumgarten subtly but crucially redefined beauty as "the perfection of cognition by means of the senses as such," or as the perfectly realized potential of sensory representation rather than a merely imperfectly realized form of conceptualization. The subtlety of Baumgarten's revision escaped many readers of the time, including his own disciple Georg Friedrich Meier and perhaps Kant as well, who may have relied on Meier's German popularizations rather than Baumgarten's own intricate and lengthy Latin magnum opus.

In the *Meditationes,* Baumgarten restricts himself to the case of poetry, which he defines as "perfect sensate discourse" *(oratio sensitiva perfecta).* The special perfection of sensitive, as contrasted to intellectual, discourse consists in the poem's manifestation of "extensive" rather than "intensive clarity," or in its suggestion of a wealth of striking but densely packed imagery and ideas—the perfection of sensibility as clear but confused perception—rather than in the abstract analysis of ideas sought in ordinary logical and scientific discourse. Extensive clarity is optimally realized through the presentation of individuals in all of their determinacy rather than through abstract ideas.

The extant portion of the *Aesthetica* amplifies this approach in tremendous detail. The work was originally supposed to consist of two halves, dealing with theoretical and practical aesthetics, the first of which was in turn to be divided into three parts—heuristics, methodology, and semiotics—dealing, respectively, with the content or materials, the order and arrangement, and the means of expression in works of art in general (although still largely illustrated by poetry). Of this grand plan, only five of the six intended chapters of the heuristics were produced. Nevertheless, in these chapters, Baumgarten illuminates the original idea of extensive clarity as the basis of artistic beauty by developing the categories of aesthetic richness *(ubertas),* magnitude or gravity *(magnitudo),* truth *(veritas),* clarity *(claritas, lux),* and certainty *(persuasio, certitudo);* the sixth chapter was to have dealt with *vita cognitionis,* or the moving effects of art. These categories are by no means all original to Baumgarten, often deriving from the humanist tradition of rhetoric; but Baumgarten exploits them with great skill to provide a sense of the very different sort of knowledge of human experience that can be afforded by art rather than science.

Although few seem ever to have read the *Aesthetica* firsthand (it did not have a second printing until the twentieth century), its influence has been enormous. Through Moses Mendelssohn, it provided the conceptual framework for Gotthold Efraim Lessing's *Laocoön;* Kant's conception of aesthetic ideas as the paradigm for works of artistic genius is his reconstruction of Baumgarten within his own system;

the emphasis on the richness of individuals as opposed to abstractions was crucial to Friedrich von Schiller's idea of aesthetic education; and Baumgarten's conception of sensitive cognition was vital to the idealist aesthetics of Friedrich Wilhelm von Schelling and Georg Wilhelm Friedrich Hegel, although the latter's subordination of art to philosophy in Absolute Knowing represents a return to Wolffian priorities. More recently, the cognitivist aesthetics of Ernst Cassirer and Susanne Langer, the "concrete universal" of William K. Wimsatt and the New Critics, and especially Nelson Goodman's explorations of semantic and syntactic variety in *Languages of Art* all stand under the aegis of Baumgarten.

[*See also* Kant; *and* Origins of Aesthetics.]

BIBLIOGRAPHY

Works by Baumgarten

Meditationes philosophicae de nonnullis ad poema pertinentibus. Halle, Germany, 1735. Translated into modern German by Heinz Paetzold as *Philosophische Betrachtungen über einige Bedingungen des Gedichtes* (Hamburg, 1983). Translated as *Reflections on Poetry* by Karl Aschenbrenner and William B. Holther (Berkeley, 1954).

Aesthetica (1750, 1758). 2 vols. Hildesheim, 1961. Modern Latin Edition, Bari, 1936. Reprinted with German translation and commentary in Hans Rudolf Schweizer, *Ästhetik als Philosophie der sinnlichen Erkenntnis* (Basel, 1973). Reprint without commentary in Alexander Baumgarten, *Theoretische Ästhetik* (Hamburg, 1983).

Texte zur Grundlegung der Ästhetik. Edited by Hans Rudolf Schweizer. Hamburg, 1983.

Other Sources

Cassirer, Ernst. *The Philosophy of the Enlightenment.* Translated by Fritz C. A. Koelln and James P. Pettegrove. Boston, 1955.

Franke, Ursula. *Kunst als Erkenntnis: Die Rolle der Sinnlichkeit in der Ästhetik des Alexander Gottlieb Baumgartens.* Studia Leibnitiana, supp. vol. 9. Wiesbaden, 1972.

Gregor, Mary. "Baumgarten's *Aesthetica.*" *Review of Metaphysics* 37.2 (December 1983): 357–385.

Nivelle, Armand. *Kunst- und Dichtungstheorien zwischen Aufklärung und Klassik.* Berlin, 1960.

Poppe, Bernhard. *Alexander Gottlieb Baumgarten: Seine Bedeutung und Stellung in der Leibniz-Wolffischen Philosophie und seiner Beziehungen zu Kant, nebst Veröffentlichung einer bisher unbekannten Handschrift der Ästhetik Baumgartens.* Münster, 1907. Contains partial transcription of Baumgarten's lectures on the *Aesthetica* in German.

PAUL GUYER

BAZIN, ANDRÉ (1918–1958), French film critic and theorist. In a life that spanned only forty years, Bazin became the most influential film theorist of his time without ever making, or wanting to make, films, and without a university post. He did so as a full-time critic, writing for daily, weekly, and monthly magazines, attending film festivals, and organizing film clubs. A brilliant student of French literature and philosophy, Bazin in fact had hoped to teach, but a speech impediment cost him that opportunity in 1942, the year he founded a successful *ciné-club* at the Sorbonne. His earliest writings, which are notes from this *ciné-club*, show that he had already worked out a program to study cinema comprehensively, that is, from a variety of organized perspectives. Before the war was over he had composed the essay that launched this project, "The Ontology of the Photographic Image." By the time it appeared in print late in 1945, Bazin was making certain that cinema would play a role in the rebuilding of French culture. In the following years, he would operate on two fronts. On the one hand, he helped upgrade the status of cinema, bringing this art into places formerly reserved for painting and literature. With Jean Cocteau, he started "Objectif 48," a rather refined club that met at the elegant Théâtre Champs-Élysées, where such directors as Orson Welles, Roberto Rossellini, and Robert Bresson would screen and discuss their latest work. On the other hand, Bazin, a left-wing Catholic, set up networks of film clubs in labor unions and cultural centers not just in Paris, but throughout France, and even in North Africa. Largely to make a living, but also to do what he could to improve movies by raising the standards and expectations of viewers, he began reviewing films several times a week for the undistinguished newspaper *Le Parisien libéré*, something he continued to do throughout the rest of his life. His larger, more speculative essays initially came out in *L'écran Français,* until 1949 when he found himself fighting tuberculosis as well as an ugly political battle brought on by that journal's Stalinist response to the Marshall Plan. After a year of recuperation, Bazin returned in full strength to Paris, cofounding *Cahiers du cinéma* (first issue, April 1951) and soon writing regularly for such influential new publications as *L'observateur* and *Télérama.* He always reserved his most substantial essays for the Catholic intellectual monthly *Esprit.* All told, Bazin signed close to three thousand pieces in fourteen years, many of them, it is true, ephemeral notes and reviews. To date, his reputation has rested on the approximately two hundred articles that have been kept in circulation.

In the final year of his life, Bazin selected the best of his writing for inclusion in four small volumes bearing the overall rubric *Qu'est-ce que le cinéma?* (What is Cinema?). He lived to see the first of these appear, *Ontologie et langage.* For Bazin the word *ontology* refers to the mode of being of the photographed image, including not only its physical properties but also the psychology of spectators, who can be said to give it its existence in looking at it. *Language* involves both the general way the cinema is capable of making sense and communicating and the specific strategies and codes it has built up in its "evolution" throughout the century. The second of the four French volumes steps outside the medium to define it in its relation to the other arts. The third volume concerns *Cinéma et sociologie,* something Bazin was not alone in recognizing to be crucial to this mass medium. Here he examines genres (the Western, above all) and such subjects as eroticism and the treatment of children on the screen. The final volume provides a case study of Italian neorealism, the most vital form of cinema in the immediate postwar years, and a development that ratified his own understanding of the virtues of the medium. Neorealism supported Bazin's view of cinema's evolution, and its achievements were clarified by the principles he had developed in the first three volumes. In 1975, the entire collection was consolidated into a single, slightly abridged edition. The English translation, organized in two volumes but representing less than half the original, came out in 1967 and 1971, where it had immediate impact in the growing university study of cinema in the anglophone world. During the 1970s, a number of other collections were assembled from Bazin's essays, some of which appeared in English translation. Except for the volume on Orson Welles (an early version of which dates from 1950) and the one on Jean Renoir (that he was working on literally up to the day of his death), these are the compilations of friends and disciples, particularly François Truffaut and the editors of *Cahiers du cinéma*. Given the ample archive of his routine criticism, most of it still unexamined, one can imagine future collections of Bazin's writings on topics such as "television" (to which he consecrated a great many pieces). In short, nothing approaching the complete Bazin is yet available.

But even if all his writings were in print, no one should expect to discover a different Bazin, for his consistency is seldom doubted. Eric Rohmer, in a 1958 review of *Qu'est-ce que le cinéma?* said: "Each article, but also the whole work, has the rigor of a real mathematical proof. . . . All of Bazin's work is centered on one idea, the affirmation of cinematic 'objectivity,' in the same way that geometry centers on the properties of the straight line" (Rohmer, 1958). The objectivity axiom is precisely the topic of that foundational essay already mentioned, "The Ontology of the Photographic Image." Bazin defines photography not as a particular sort of object but as a type of representation that functions in relation to the spectator's belief in its "automatic" mode of production. Cinema's specificity is based on this photographic substratum to such an extent that Bazin should exclude animation from film, or at least from his theory of film; for, even though animated pictures may come on reels of celluloid to be projected at twenty-four frames a second onto a reflecting screen, their "ontology" by his account would be related to the traditional arts of drawing and design, because the spectator senses these to be their genesis. Thus Bazin's ontology is bound up in viewer psychology, something Jean-Marie Schaeffer names the *arché*. The *arché* of the photograph has nothing to do with its physical form, but rather with the way it came into being, or, more accurately, the way the spectator believes it to have come into being (through the imprinting of light from an object on a chemically treated substance). The photographic image, for Bazin, is specifically and essentially an "index," to

invoke C. S. Peirce's tripartite division of signs. Earlier theorists treated cinema for its "iconic" value (notably, Rudolf Arnheim and Vsevolod Pudovkin) and concerned themselves with the look of the image in relation to the look of visible reality. Occasionally, a theorist discussed the possibility of cinema as a "symbolic" sign system, as when Sergei Eisenstein related film language to Japanese graphic script or when he imaged adapting Karl Marx's *Das Kapital* to the screen. Bazin explicitly opposed turning cinema into a conventional symbolic language (hence his antipathy to coded editing strategies that viewers learn to "read"). He also remained relatively indifferent to cinema's presumed propensity to deliver an icon or picture of reality (the icon is Peirce's sign based on "similarity" to the referent). Bazin did not know Peirce's work, but all his key metaphors for cinema relate it to Peirce's index, which is the type of sign motivated by a physical or existential connection to the referent. He spoke of film as a "fingerprint," a "death mask," the "veil of Veronica," and so forth. Bazin, following Jean-Paul Sartre, considered this to be part of the psychology of the image, psychology alerting us to the way a sign is taken in terms of belief or distance or the like.

Bazin reasoned that "if the history of the plastic arts is less a matter of their aesthetic than of their psychology" then the issue of realism can be said to be its central and endemic problem. Realism, in Bazin's special sense of the term, is once again related more to the genesis than to the mimesis of a sign. "The quarrel over realism in art stems from a misunderstanding . . . between the aesthetic and psychological" (Bazin, 1967, p. 12). Photography and cinematography may serve communicational, symbolic, and aesthetic functions; but beneath any of these functions lies their indexical link to the moment light imprinted the appearances of an object or a scene on celluloid, for motion pictures carry the photographic *arché* within them like DNA. Bazin's notion of realism need not encompass subject matter or genre; it has little to do with the literary or pictorial movements and manifestos bearing the name *realism*. Instead, it designates a condition of experience whereby the viewer first regards what is on the screen as the actual trace of something whose impression is now seen, and second that perceives this trace using many of the same presuppositions that govern the routine of everyday perceptual acts (searching, recognizing, verifying impressions, etc.).

Whereas most earlier theories of film associated the new medium with one or another of the traditional arts, or with the art function itself, especially in its mimetic or iconic guise, Bazin valued photographs and films precisely because they are not primordially related to art. "A very faithful drawing may actually tell us more about the model [than a photo] . . . but it will never have the irrational power to bear away our faith. . . . [Still,] no matter how fuzzy, distorted, or discolored, no matter how lacking in documentary value the [photographic] image may be, it shares by virtue of the very process of its becoming, the being of the model of which it is the reproduction" (ibid., p. 14). The way an image comes into being, then, utterly alters the way one takes it in, and in this psychological rather than aesthetic sense photography "satisfied our appetite for illusion by a mechanical reproduction in the making of which man plays no part" (ibid., p. 12).

Bazin's position has been sustained and elaborated by such important writers as Roland Barthes in *Camera Lucida* (1981) and Jean-Marie Schaeffer in *L'image précaire* (1987). Stanley Cavell's *The World Viewed* (1979) presents a theory of film that begins from principles parallel to those of Bazin, whom he is careful to cite. The many arguments aiming to refute the "objectivity axiom" can be grouped into two types: the categorical and the historical. The first proposes that the process by which a photograph becomes a representation of a scene or an object is only a variant of picture-making processes that go on in all the visual arts. The hand of the artist may not be evident in the taking of the photograph, but it is surely there in the selection and arrangement of the subject, and it is indisputably there in the optical and chemical processes that result in the particular focus, composition, illumination, and color that re-present the subject on a screen. This type of objection must still explain the authority that the photographic media claim (over drawings or other man-made images) as evidence in scientific experiments, law cases, and insurance reports.

The historical argument against the objectivity axiom is more recent, triggered by technological developments that have, for instance, reduced the authority of photographs in court cases. Photography and other technologies producing analogue images may have dominated the era usually termed "modernity" (and which Régis Debray, following Walter Benjamin and many others, dates from the early nineteenth century), but this reign has now been cut short by digital images. Digital images, the argument goes, are capable of unusually detailed illusion that can be produced entirely without relation to a referent in the world. A disciple of André Malraux, Bazin might have treated this development as a step in the evolution of images in culture, a step potentially demoting the social standing of cinema. A disciple of Jean-Paul Sartre, he would have described the psychology of image perception entailed by fully synthesized representations. In "The Myth of Total Cinema," he forecast with enthusiasm technological developments that may permit the increasingly perfect "reproduction" of the visual world. Synthetic, digitalized images, he could have argued, imitate rather than reproduce the world. They may amaze the spectator with trompe l'oeil effects but, being fabrications rather than imprints, they are not to be trusted or studied as guides to the world they depict.

The objectivity axiom would seem to place the documentary at the center of the types of cinema that Bazin ex-

plored, and he did in fact write about many forms of this mode. But it would be a mistake to assume that he held a parochial interest in any one mode or genre, for nearly every type of film is affected by the remarkable property whereby light stamps its information on a durable support. This includes, for example, films about paintings, films taken from novels, and films that restage theatrical events such as operas and plays. The second volume of *Qu'est-ce que le cinéma?* suggests time and again the peculiar advantages of the hybrids that result when cinema's "materialism" (capturing whatever the lens takes in, planned or not) confronts cultural artifacts (physical ones such as paintings or mental ones such as novels). Ridiculing the temptation to disassemble masterpieces of other arts so as to reassemble them according to some purported notion of "the cinematic," Bazin praised those instances when cinema makes use of culture as it does of phenomena in nature, photographing plays or paintings as it might animals or social rituals. In the case of making a movie using paintings as material, the filmmaker operates "as in any ordinary documentary . . . [with] a realism once removed, following upon the abstraction that is the painting" (Bazin, 1967, pp. 166–167). The result may itself become, or be taken as, an artwork in its own right, as in the case of Alain Resnais's *Guernica* (1951) or Cocteau's film from his own play, *Les parents terribles* (1949), for the filmmaker, while presenting the original in its material density (as a canvas or as a play rather than as a film) may "read" the original work in a particularly insistent or insightful, hence artistic, manner.

The opposition between cinema's inherent material objectivity and the subjectivity commonly attributed to the mode of being of art is often phrased by Bazin in the idiom of his day as an opposition between symbolism and realism, particularly in his crucial history of film style. This history proceeds by means of a dialectic between two opposed cinematic traditions: "I will distinguish," he wrote, "between two broad and opposing trends: those directors who put their faith in the image and those who put their faith in reality" (Bazin, 1967, p. 24). Gathering evidence from current and older films to stage this contest in several essays he stitched together under the title "Evolution of the Language of Cinema," he looked for continuities between directors working on both sides of the sound barrier. The dominant Hollywood side he characterized as dedicated to psychological montage, the breaking down of events into convenient and legible fragments reassembled according to rules of perceptual and narrative logic. This standard system in fact has much in common with the silent art cinemas of Germany and the Soviet Union, both of which readily dispensed with the integrity of the profilmic event in an effort to create an eloquent cinematic statement or experience. The Germans deformed reality so as to manipulate the "plastics of the image," whereas the Soviets built up sequences of associations and metaphors out of fragments of shots that "alluded to" but did not deliver the referent. All three forms worked to overcome reality through art.

Bazin declared that the modern cinema had reversed that trend, beginning with the 1939 *La règle du jeu*. Jean Renoir, followed by Welles, neorealism, and the early New Wave, emphasized shooting in depth and mise-en-scène. Pointing to such precursors as Robert Flaherty, F. W. Murnau, and Eric von Stroheim, Bazin championed directors who operate within rather than upon profilmic space. The modern cinema, or at least Bazin's view of it, derives from a dual process: cinema brings to the screen in its material clutter and detail the complexities of a natural or cultural moment; this is presented, however, through the consciousness of a director who takes a stance toward it, filtering the facts, but not altering them. In a famous example, he claimed that Bresson illuminates rather than transforms the great novel of Georges Bernanos, *Le journal d'un curé de campagne*. Bresson cut some scenes from the novel and lingered unduly on others, but, by eliminating the intermediate stage of the scenario (often termed *adaptation*), he filmed nothing but the novel. This attitude, similar to that of Resnais's films of paintings, flourished after Bazin's death in the work of Jean-Marie Straub and Danièle Huillet *(Othon, The Chronicle of Anna Magdelena Bach),* Jacques Rivette *(La religieuse),* and other confirmed modernist filmmakers. Jean-Luc Godard is known for pressing this attitude to the limit, leaving chunks of cultural sources undigested within his films.

This demotion of "adaptation" and of all intermediate phases between a subject and its representation on the screen led Bazin to declare that Bresson and other postwar directors had become the equal of the novelist. No doubt under the influence of Sartre's "Situation of the Writer in 1948," he argued that modern filmmakers carved stories out of a complex space (whether found on location or built as the space of fiction in the studio). Attentive to the material distinctiveness of the situation being filmed, the modern director aims to bring to the screen both a significant block of reality (natural or cultural) and a significant view of that reality. As for the spectator, the complexity of the world represented in the modern style (often rendered in long take) seems to extend beyond the view of it that the filmmaker holds out, producing the effects of "ambiguity" and sometimes of "mystery" that were prized in the postwar ambience of existentialist humanism. Bazin's views were to suffer a setback after this Sartrean tradition had been supplanted by structuralism in France in the 1960s, particularly because his existentialism was infused with a philosophical Catholicism that was easy for opponents to target in their attacks. Bazin claimed that the greatest films (Renoir, neorealism) make visible a "conscience" in stark contact with a "mysterious" world," producing a "moral vision" that encourages the spectator to make choices while watching. But opponents could claim that his ideas urge complacency among spectators. *Ambiguity* and *mystery* are

Bazin's limit terms, and they are liable to result in reverential contemplation, not social critique or action. Opponents could readily point to the rather sentimental criticism penned by followers of Bazin in the 1950s, as well as to early films of the New Wave, which could be said to turn on the conversion of the individual soul (whether that of the main character or of the spectator) rather than promoting the social understanding of what are finally social constructions of reality.

Bazin's preference for the long-take tradition flows from his central tenets but need not relegate his theory to any particular style or ideology. Nor is the auteur theory (implicit in the idea of a director taking a stance toward reality) a necessary corollary of his ideas, although, as promulgated by his disciples at *Cahiers du cinéma*, auteurism did single out those directors who dispensed with scenarists and who evinced a particularly strong filtering temperament. Bazin in fact was ambivalent about this "policy," which he never took to be a theory at all, but rather a convenient way to organize and evaluate the hundreds of films he and his colleagues watched. Auteurism celebrates the genius of the director but neglects what Bazin termed, in a famous phrase, "the genius of the system." Studio, genre, cultural source, and national style—all these forces shape the auteur and govern the impact of every film produced, although they do so in tension with the brute facts of the imprinted referent that the film bodies forth. As a critic, Bazin and his followers preferred films that accentuate this tension, that call themselves and the world they image into question. His theory, however, as distinct from his critical taste, concerns the relation of the photographic image to dynamic cultural issues and forces, no matter what form they take.

Bazin's overall aesthetic may be best distinguished from earlier views through a consideration of the issue of cinematic purity. The classical period (including both Hollywood and artistic alternatives such as the German Expressionist and Soviet Montage schools) worked toward a pure cinematic experience that could overcome the resistance of subject matter and of the physical world with which every project must begin. Even André Malraux, whom Bazin admired, declared that only editing had allowed cinema to become an art capable of delivering pure experiences of cinema by de-realizing the recalcitrant image and locking it into a pattern willed by the cineast's imagination. Bazin, on the other hand, authored an essay titled "For an Impure Cinema," promoting the medium not as merely another art but as something with which the artistic impulse must struggle. His modernism stems from his belief in the important interplay of the artistic imagination against the recalcitrance of source material and of the physical world.

The "principle of recalcitrance" comes out in the best of Bazin's criticism, for instance, in his reflections on the familiar figure of Charlie Chaplin. The slightly sour taste that *Monsieur Verdoux* and *Limelight* left on viewers of the day derives precisely from the conflict of the familiar "Charlot" cast against himself (against the person of Charles Chaplin). This disorienting effect follows on the work of cinema that over the years has kept before viewers the tracings of light that permit them to see Chaplin age from one film to the next, an effect that Chaplin's genius understood and exploited. Here Bazin may be contributing to the auteurist cult of genius, but, unlike many of his followers (and despite misrepresentations of his position after his death), he kept in mind the constant cinematic complexities of directorial idea, system of production, integrity of source material, and the recalcitrance of the physical world.

Bazin is more vulnerable to the sorts of objections posed after 1968 by the emergent school of cine-semiotics, a school of film theory that came to the fore partly in reaction to the prevalence of Bazin's ideas. Convinced that vision, as well as cinema, is culturally coded, socially constructed, and thus alterable, these thinkers regarded Bazin's ideas as naive and as inculcating the complacent or reverential viewing of films. Although he never forgot that "cinema is also a language" and that "there is only one way to produce realism and that is by style," Bazin's obsession with the imprint of the visual contour of the referent on celluloid kept him from focusing on the concatenation of images, except when he wrote about the negative effects of editing. In the semiotic terms of Roman Jakobson, often called upon in the 1970s, one might say that Bazin theorized the metonymic pole of the cinematic sign system, refusing to countenance the metaphoric pole and its potential to induce more abstract significations through montage. In "The Virtues and Limitations of Montage," Bazin isolated certain laws that attend any film operating in the genre of "the marvelous." Analyzing several children's films, he proved that no matter how convenient it might be or how advantageous in developing the plot or moral of such a story, a director cannot cut into what might be called the space of the marvelous without paying the price of believability. In extending his photographic axiom to corollaries that restrict the use of montage in certain genres, Bazin tried to adjust the scales to make up for the overemphasis that earlier theories had given to montage.

Aside from what might be seen as the critic's evaluation of one form of film over another, Bazin's demotion of montage can be seen today as an effect of his insistence on the prelinguistic substratum of cinema's photographic base. Although most theorists (classical as well as postmodern) define cinema as they would any other art or medium of communication, Bazin holds that cinema really is something different, a phenomenon that fascinates precisely because it makes the viewer continually assess its intermediate status between ontology and language, between being and meaning. His film theory insistently draws attention to the effects of the photographic substratum in movies of all sorts, whether they take advantage of it or not. His criticism aims to bring out the dialectic, visible in the most telling of films, between cultural meaning (what he and many semioticians call "language") and a perceptual and experiential plenum saved by the medium from disappearing completely into the past. He was the theorist of the impure amalgam of the modern cinema.

[*See also* Film.]

BIBLIOGRAPHY

Works by Bazin

Bazin at Work: Major Essays and Reviews from the Forties and Fifties. Translated by Alain Piette and Bert Cardullo, edited by Bert Cardullo. New York and London, 1997.
Cinema of Cruelty: From Buñvel to Hitchcock. Edited by François Truffaut, translated by Savine d'Estrée with Tiffany Fliss. New York, 1982.
Essays on Chaplin. Edited and translated by Jean Bodon. New Haven, 1985.
French Cinema of the Occupation and the Resistance: The Birth of a Critical Aesthetic. Edited by François Truffaut, translated by Stanley Hochman. New York, 1981.
Jean Renoir. Edited by François Truffaut, translated by W. W. Halsey II and William H. Simon. New York, 1973.
Orson Welles: A Critical View. Translated by Jonathan Rosenbaum. New York, 1978.
Qu'est-ce que le cinéma? 4 vols. Paris, 1958–1962. Abridged "definitive edition" in one volume (Paris, 1975).
What Is Cinema? 2 vols. Edited and translated by Hugh Gray. Berkeley, 1967, 1971.

Other Sources

Andrew, Dudley. *André Bazin.* New York, 1978.
Barthes, Roland. *Camera Lucida: Reflections on Photography.* Translated by Richard Howard. New York, 1981.
Carroll, Noël. *Philosophical Problems of Classical Film Theory.* Princeton, N.J., 1988.
Cavell, Stanley. *The World Viewed: Reflections on the Ontology of Film.* Enl. ed. Cambridge, Mass., 1979.
Graham, Peter, ed. *The New Wave: Critical Landmarks.* Garden City, N.Y., 1968.
Rohmer, Eric. "La 'somme' d'André Bazin." *Cahiers du Cinéma* 91 (December 1958). Translated by Carol Volk in Rohmer, *A Taste for Beauty* (New York, 1989), pp. 93–104.
Rosen, Philip. "History of Image, Image of History: Subject and Ontology in Bazin." *Wide Angle* 9.4 (Winter 1987).
Schaeffer, Jean-Marie. *L'image précaire: Du dispositif photographique.* Paris, 1987.

DUDLEY ANDREW

BEARDSLEY, MONROE (1915–1985), American philosopher and writer who had broad humanist interests that were centered in philosophy, and aesthetics in particular. Born and raised in Bridgeport, Connecticut, and educated at Yale University, Monroe Beardsley taught at a number of American universities, including his alma mater, but most of his career was spent at Swarthmore College and Temple University.

Beardsley is best known for his work in aesthetics, but he also published articles in various areas of philosophy, including the philosophy of history, action theory, and the history of modern philosophy. Indeed, his interests were not confined to "pure philosophy" or even to philosophy broadly conceived. *Practical Logic* (1950), his first book, was one of the first informal logic, or critical thinking, texts of the contemporary era, and *Thinking Straight,* a related book, saw four editions over a period of twenty-five years. Outside of philosophy, he wrote literary criticism and books and articles on style, writing, and the humanities.

Beardsley's first article in the philosophy of art is probably his best known. In "The Intentional Fallacy" (1946; written with W. K. Wimsatt), he argues that "the intention of the author is neither available nor desirable as a standard for judging the success of a work of literary art." Nor, he adds, is the intention of the author relevant to judging what a literary work means. When generalized to all the arts, what this amounts to is that an artist's intentions are irrelevant to the interpretation and evaluation of his or her work. Statements about the meaning or value of a work of art are one thing, Beardsley insists, and statements about an artist's psychological state quite another. The latter have to do with the artist, not the work of art, and thus have no bearing—no evidential bearing—on what the work means, or how good or bad it is. In a companion piece, "The Affective Fallacy" (1949; again, with W. K. Wimsatt), Beardsley takes a similar position in regard to the emotional responses of a reader to a literary work. The affective responses of a reader say something about the reader but nothing about the work. Once again, the thesis can be generalized to all the arts. The interpretation and evaluation of works of art are thus independent of what, for a critic of the Romantic school, are of the essence: the intentions of the artist and the emotions of the art critic.

Beardsley's entire philosophy of art is, in fact, anti-Romantic through and through. The school of art criticism that he is associated with, and rightly, is the so-called New Criticism.

Aesthetics: Problems in the Philosophy of Criticism (1958), Beardsley's first book in aesthetics, might even be read as a philosophical defense of the New Criticism. It is, without a doubt, and for a number of reasons, one of the most important books of twentieth-century aesthetics. First, it is informed with an extensive knowledge of the arts, art criticism, and the philosophy of art. Beardsley knew and loved the arts and was, as he once wrote, addicted to art criticism. But his knowledge of the philosophy of art was just as broad and just as profound. Second, *Aesthetics* is philosophically sophisticated and argumentatively dense in a way that few preceding books on aesthetics were and, for that matter, few subsequent ones have been. In the main, Beardsley writes as an analytic philosopher, and is intent on making distinctions, mapping out positions—which entailed extracting, from massive amounts of very disparate art-critical and philosophical material, common and comprehensible argu-

ments and principles—and arguing for and against those positions. One wag once called him the C. D. Broad of aesthetics for his ability to make distinctions, organize material, and expose and critique arguments. Whatever the justice of the comparison—one important difference between the two is that Beardsley came to a definite conclusion on virtually every topic he wrote on—Beardsley is not exclusively an analytic philosopher. Deweyan pragmaticism makes it way into *Aesthetics,* as does phenomenology. Third, and most important, *Aesthetics* presents and defends a truly comprehensive philosophy of art. Virtually every major issue of aesthetics is discussed in it, and the results are woven into a consistent, unified whole. It is for that reason that almost every major philosopher of art in the Anglo-American tradition writing after Beardsley has had to reckon with him, and respond to his arguments.

One issue broached in *Aesthetics* is the ontology of art—or "aesthetic objects," Beardsley's preferred term at the time. Aesthetic objects are classified as "perceptual objects," or entities (in the broad sense of the term that includes both buildings and dances) at least some of whose properties are sensuously perceivable. Distinctions between the productions, performances, and presentations of aesthetic objects lead Beardsley in the direction of phenomenalism, the view that critical statements about aesthetic objects can be translated into statements about their presentations, that is, their appearances to particular people at particular times. Obviously inspired by empiricist, indeed, logical positivist, theories of perception that seemed promising at the time, Beardsley later repudiated phenomenalism and embraced a form of "nonreductive materialism." Works of art are physical objects, he came to think, or—and this is a second alternative he seriously considered—some works of art are physical objects, and some are kinds of physical object. The latter category may be necessary because multiple instances of one and the same work are possible in some of the arts, such as lithography.

An issue studiously avoided in *Aesthetics* is the definition of art. At the time, and for a variety of reasons, Beardsley thought a head-on discussion of the issue ill-advised. Later, however, he joined in the fray, and both proposed his own definition and criticized the art-historical and institutional definitions of others. His own considered view is that a work of art is an arrangement of conditions intended to be capable of affording an experience with marked aesthetic character. Basically, a work of art is an artifact created with an aesthetic intention. Although there might be some temptation to think otherwise, this definition does not run afoul of the intentional fallacy, according to Beardsley, for the intentional fallacy concerns the interpretation and evaluation of art, not the definition of art.

Literature, music, and the visual arts are all considered in *Aesthetics,* but literature, and especially poetry, was always closest to Beardsley's heart. Explication, elucidation, and interpretation are distinguished by him, though all are concerned with what a text means. Explication operates on the local level, so to speak, and is contextual. To declare "the meaning of a metaphor, the connotation of a work, [or] the implications of a fragment of ambiguous syntax" (Beardsley, 1958) is to engage in explication. Elucidation involves forming hypotheses, based on textual evidence, to account for things and events explicitly reported in a text. It is, Beardsley says, "simply causal inference" applied to literary works; we elucidate when we "fill in the gaps" needed to make a story, poem, or essay comprehensible. Finally, interpretation is a semantic relation between a literary work and something outside it. Paradigmatically, to interpret is to state, based on reasons, the theme or thesis of a work. Given his emphasis on interpretation, and given his views of what interpretation consists in, it is not surprising that Beardsley held that literature is defined as discourse in which an important part of the meaning is implicit. Literature, and again especially poetry, is basically semantically rich discourse. Speech act theory, which Beardsley later incorporated into his aesthetics and especially his philosophy of literature, helps to bolster the case for this view, he thinks. A poem, he says in *The Possibility of Criticism* (1970), is a complex imitation of a compound illocutionary act. Properly understood, this is close to the "final and familiar formula: poems are distinguished by their complexity of meaning" (1970). This, however, provides only the genus of poetry, he admits, and not the differentia.

Interpretation is only one of three basic critical activities in Beardsley's philosophy of art, the other two being description and evaluation. It is an especially important activity, though, if only because many art critics and more than a few philosophers play fast and loose with the concept. For one thing, and despite the lax use of *interpretation* by some critics, interpretation is not the same thing as superimposition (a term introduced in *The Possibility of Criticism*). To superimpose is to use a work to illustrate a pre-existent system of thought, not to dig out meaning. To "interpret" *The Merry Wives of Windsor* as a Marxist fable, for example, is really not to interpret at all. Marxist meanings—the use of Marxist concepts and references to Marxist themes and theses—simply are not in the play. Neither, of course, are authorial intentions or readers' emotions.

But, contrary to some dissenting remarks from critics and philosophers, there is such a thing as the correct interpretation of a literary work. Interpretations are true or false, in other words, and one can, in most if not all cases, know whether an interpretation is correct. Disputes among critics can be resolved if close attention is paid to the "potentialities of meaning" in a text. Determining what those potentialities are requires knowing the lexical meanings of words and phrases that existed at the time of composition, and knowing the rules of syntax operative at that time, so one may well have to go outside a text in order to find what it means, and what interpretation of it is correct. Still, the sources one consults are not narrowly biographical ones, or psychological or sociological ones. They are sources that tell what a language allows, both actually and potentially, at a given time. Interpretation is thus an objective activity, and the critic's duty, like that of any other objective investigator, is to get at the truth. If, after all is said and done, multiple meanings remain, and such meanings do not conflict with one another, they can all be accepted, Beardsley thinks, for they would only enrich the text. On the other hand, if they conflict, ineliminable ambiguity (in the bad sense of the term) is the result, and it is simply impossible to decide among competing interpretations. Generally speaking, however, Beardsley thinks that this will seldom be the case. Contextual factors, especially those having to do with the interaction of word and phrase meanings, will eliminate almost all ambiguity.

Metaphor is another topic that Beardsley had a keen interest in, and he returned to it a number of times over the years, sometimes modifying his views slightly, but always maintaining essentially the same theory. Indeed, returning to an issue, surveying recent literature, rebutting or accepting criticism, and modifying his position while remaining very much in the same camp—that is characteristic of Beardsley's approach to aesthetics. In *Aesthetics,* he argues for what he calls the Controversion Theory of metaphor, but essentially the same theory appears as the Verbal Opposition Theory in "The Metaphorical Twist" (reprinted in *The Aesthetic Point of View* [1982]). According to this theory, a metaphor is not an elliptical simile, nor does it work by comparing two objects. Rather, metaphor is "a special feat of language, or verbal play, involving two levels of meaning in the modifier" (1982) that is, in the term to be taken metaphorically. When a predicate is metaphorically adjoined to a subject, "the predicate loses its ordinary extension because it acquires a new intension—perhaps one it has in no other context. This twist of meaning is forced by inherent tensions, or oppositions, within the metaphor itself" (ibid.). There are metaphorical as well as literal senses, then, and in metaphor a term can acquire a new sense, perhaps even a nonce sense. But, contrary to the view he originally proposed, Beardsley came to hold (in "The Metaphorical Twist" and the "Postscript, 1980" to the 1981 edition of *Aesthetics*) that "the meaning of a metaphorical word cannot be limited to its pre-existing connotations: the metaphor transforms what were previously [known or believed] contingent properties of the things referred to [by the metaphorical modifier] . . . into meanings [of that modifier]." Metaphors thus have cognitive value, and help to extend the language.

Beardsley's views on literature in general also hold for his views on one species of literature, namely, fiction: in being subsumed under speech act theory, the positions he argues for in *Aesthetics* are not abandoned, he says, but are subsumed, reinforced, and enriched. [*See* Fiction.] A fictional text is the representation or depiction of an illocutionary action, with this meaning, to use a comparison to help make the position clearer, that a kiss in a work of fiction stands to a real kiss in much the same way that a painting of a cow stands to a real cow, or a murder committed in a play stands to a real murder. One reason that fiction is not a record of actual illocutionary acts, according to Beardsley, is that fictional sentences "fail . . . to connect with the real world in a certain way: the weddings narrated in the novel never took place, the names of the characters do not belong to real persons, and so forth." "Mr. Pickwick" and other fictional names do refer, however, even though there is no Mr. Pickwick. What "Mr. Pickwick" refers to is, quite simply, Mr. Pickwick. One can refer to what does not exist (or subsist), in other words, with one principal reason for holding to this admittedly minority view being that if one did not, it would be very difficult to explain certain fundamental facts about fiction, such as that one can refer to the same fictional character with different tokens of the same name. As for the truth-values of fictional sentences, such sentences—those in a fiction—are neither true nor false, Beardsley thinks. A critic's sentences about a fiction, however—those about Othello or King Lear, for example—are a different story. They are either true or false.

Expression theories of art are handled very roughly in *Aesthetics,* and Beardsley never did retreat from his view that such theories are fundamentally misdirected. Central to expression theories is "the assumption that artworks—or successful artworks—are created by a process in the course of which an artist expresses his emotions, and that the special character and value of an artwork is the result of its having been brought into being in this way" (1958). All of this is an evident hangover from Romanticism, and none of it is correct. An artist need not express his or her emotions in the course of creating a work of art, successful or not; and expressing emotions in creating a work of art does not guarantee anything at all, aesthetically speaking. "The special character and value" of a work of art—roughly, its aesthetic qualities and aesthetic value—are at best contingently related to the emotional state of its creator, and aesthetic qualities (e.g., vivacity) can be accounted for quite independently of any assumptions about a work's origin or manner of production. In a nutshell, the principal problem with expression theories is that they try to explain what a work of art expresses (e.g., majesty, remoteness) in terms of what the artist expressed, when explanation should run in exactly the opposite direction. In other words, according to expression theories, the act or process of expression is basic, and statements about the expressive qualities of a work derivative, because they carry with them "an implicit reference to the expressing agent." In point of fact, things have to be understood the other way around. An artist's act of expression is conceptually derivative, and has to be understood in terms of the act of creating something expressive. As always with Beardsley, the work of art and its qualities are primary.

Aesthetic qualities are not, as such, discussed in *Aesthetics,* but something in the near neighborhood is, namely, regional qualities. A regional quality is a quality that a complex (an object having proper parts) has as a result of the characteristics of its parts and the relationships among them. The restfulness of a Kandinsky painting is obviously a regional quality of it, and it is also an aesthetic quality of it. Not all regional qualities are aesthetic qualities, though. Squareness, for example, is a regional quality, but not an aesthetic quality. More promising is the suggestion that aesthetic qualities are human regional qualities, a human regional quality being a regional quality designated (perhaps metaphorically) by a term that also applies to human beings. Splendor, charm, wit, dignity, and relentlessness are all human regional qualities, and all are also aesthetic qualities. Beardsley's considered view, however, is that aesthetic qualities need not be confined to human regional ones, even metaphorically. Rather, an aesthetic quality is a quality that counts directly for a judgment of aesthetic value (goodness) or disvalue (badness). Aesthetic qualities supervene on nonaesthetic qualities, just as all gestalt qualities do, and, a few exceptions aside, Frank Sibley is right in maintaining that aesthetic terms do not have conditions of application—that is, necessary or sufficient conditions for their application—and are not applied in accordance with rule-governed criteria. Taste is required for their application, as Sibley says, but taste is not a mysterious faculty. It is simply the ability to make fine and sensitive discriminations by using one's usual perceptual equipment. One hears, in the usual sense of the term, the agitation of a musical composition; and one sees, again in the usual sense of the term, the delicacy of a Ming vase.

Even conceding that the art critic qua art critic engages in, or at least might be required to engage in, as many activities as Beardsley thinks—description, explication, elucidation, interpretation, exposition of aesthetic qualities and their bases, and so on—there is still, he thinks, one essential critical task as yet unmentioned: critical judgment or evaluation, saying how good or bad a work of art is. The evaluation of works of art as works of art—and they can certainly be evaluated from other perspectives, as, say, propaganda or moral instruction—is aesthetic evaluation, in Beardsley's view. The evaluative judgments of critics, then—and a critic qua critic must evaluate—are judgments of aesthetic value; or, better, they are estimates of aesthetic value, the latter term being preferable because quantifiable accuracy is usually impossible in critical judgment, and confidence may be lacking as well. Negatively, this implies that critical judgments are not many things: they are not predictions of what others will like or appreciate; they are not statements of the tendency of a work of art to have "sticking power" or attract people; they are not verdicts, or statements involving a choice or a decision tied to social consequences; they are not propaedeutic aids to call attention to something, to open people's eyes or ears, or to tell them how to look or listen or read in some preferred way; and they are not personal endorsements, or the critic "giving his word" for the benefits of spending time with a work of art. They are estimates of aesthetic value, and necessarily call for support with objective reasons, reasons that cite features found in the work itself. Such reasons can cite a work's simple qualities, its relational properties, its meanings, its references, its aesthetic properties, and so on, for all can figure as criteria of critical judgment. On a higher level of generality, though, there are three primary reasons, three general criteria or general canons, as Beardsley calls them in *Aesthetics,* of critical judgment, which lower-level reasons factor into, and which are the ultimate bases for critical judgment. Unity, complexity, and intensity of regional quality, Beardsley argues, hold across the board, for all the arts, as general standards of critical judgment, or general criteria for estimates of aesthetic value. Thus, Beardsley, never a critical skeptic, not only thinks that criticism is based on reason and that the reasons it is based on are objective, but he also thinks that there are fundamental standards of evaluation common to all the arts, and, as he should, he supplies them, and argues for them.

Hinted at in much of the preceding discussion are two themes at the core of Beardsley's aesthetics: the independence or autonomy of the work of art, and the primacy of the aesthetic. The autonomy of works of art can be seen in their descriptive, interpretative, and evaluative independence from their creators and from their immediate audience, and their stubborn possession of whatever descriptive, interpretative, and evaluative properties they have, once created, across different contexts, cultural and otherwise. That is why criticism is a search for truth, according to Beardsley, and why the critic is an objective investigator. A being (a supernatural being, if that is required) may create a rock, but once created, the rock has the properties it has. Those properties are in the rock, and the job of the geologist, an objective investigator, is to discover those properties and report the truth about the rock. That truth will not change, and is not a function of what concepts the geologist possesses, or whether different geologists come to different assays of the rock, or whether the rock is displayed and analyzed in different cultures. Rocks are independent or autonomous objects. They are just like works of art, in Beardsley's view.

No less important to Beardsley's aesthetics is the primacy of the aesthetic. The main reason that art is so important is that it is one of the main sources of a distinct and very important kind of value, aesthetic value. Aesthetic value may be available to use outside the arts—Beardsley would be the last to deny that nature supplies us with aesthetic value—but works of art are our principal sources of aesthetic value, and one of our most certain ones as well. We can count on

works of art to deliver the goods, aesthetically speaking, and the goods they deliver are often concentrated, intense ones.

In fact, in a sense, Beardsley's whole aesthetics both leads up to and is founded on the notion of the aesthetic. Criticism is founded on an interest in the aesthetic, and its job is to detect and explain aesthetically relevant properties of works of art. Ultimately, it must issue, and justify, a judgment of aesthetic value. A vital issue for Beardsley, then, is, What is aesthetic value?

Beardsley is committed not just to providing an answer to that question but to characterizing aesthetic value as a distinct sort of value, not reducible to other kinds of value, such as moral, historical, or cognitive value. In addition, he has to ground *aesthetic value* in terms that are not ultimately aesthetically laden; for, if the concept were defined in aesthetic terms, and those terms were themselves defined in aesthetic terms, and so on, the result would be an unhelpful circular explication. In *Aesthetics,* the aesthetic is grounded by isolating and describing, in general terms, "certain features of experience that are peculiarly characteristic of our intercourse with aesthetic objects" (1958). That done, aesthetic value is defined in terms of this kind of experience, aesthetic experience. Aesthetic experience, Beardsley argues, is experience characterized by unity (coherence and completeness), intensity ("concentration of experience"), and complexity ("diversity of distinct elements"). Aesthetic value is simply "the capacity to produce an aesthetic experience of fairly great magnitude."

Over the years Beardsley came to think that, although his earlier definition of *aesthetic experience* was basically sound, it failed to capture a broader notion of the aesthetic that is "important, indeed essential, to introduce." This is the notion of the aesthetic in experience, or the aesthetic character of experience. An experience, Beardsley says, has aesthetic character if and only if it has the first of the following five features and at least three of the others:

1. *Object directedness.* A willingly accepted guidance over the succession of one's states by phenomenally objective properties (qualities and relations) of a perceptual or intentional field on which attention is fixed with a feeling that things are working or have worked themselves out fittingly.

2. *Felt freedom.* A sense of release from the dominance of some antecedent concerns about past and future, a relaxation and sense of harmony with what is presented or semantically invoked by it or implicitly promised by it, so that what comes has the air of having been freely chosen.

3. *Detached affect.* A sense that the objects on which interest is concentrated are set a little at a distance emotionally—a certain detachment of affect, so that even when we are confronted with dark and terrible things, and feel them sharply, they do not oppress but make us aware of our power to rise above them.

4. *Active discovery.* A sense of actively exercising constructive powers of the mind, of being challenged by a variety of potentially conflicting stimuli to try to make them co-here; a keyed-up state amounting to exhilaration in seeing connections between percepts and meanings, a sense (which may be illusory) of intelligibility.

5. *Wholeness.* A sense of integration as a person, of being restored to wholeness from distracting and disruptive influences (but by inclusive synthesis as well as by exclusion) and a corresponding contentment, even through disturbing feelings, that involves self-acceptance and self-expansion. This passage is from *The Aesthetic Point of View* (1982), Beardsley's last book. The title of the book is a good indication of Beardsley's overall approach to art, the philosophy of art, and the aesthetic; and the passage, in its eloquence, sensitivity, and eminently humanist understanding of an important sector of human experience, is characteristic of his entire philosophy of art.

[*See also* Criticism; Intention, *overview article;* Interpretation; Metaphor; *and* New Criticism.]

BIBLIOGRAPHY

Works by Beardsley

"The Intentional Fallacy." *Sewanee Review* 54.3 (Summer 1946): 468–488. Collaboration with W. K. Wimsatt, Jr.
"The Affective Fallacy." *Sewanee Review* 57.1 (Winter 1949): 31–55. Collaboration with W. K. Wimsatt, Jr.
Aesthetics: Problems in the Philosophy of Criticism. New York, 1958; 2d ed. with postscript, Indianapolis, 1981.
Aesthetics from Classical Greece to the Present: A Short History. New York, 1966; reprint, Tuscaloosa, Ala., 1975.
The Possibility of Criticism. Detroit, 1970.
The Aesthetic Point of View: Selected Essays. Edited by Michael Wreen and Donald Callen. Ithaca, N.Y., 1982.

Other Sources

Aagaard-Mogensen, Lars, and L. De Vos, eds. *Text, Literature, and Aesthetics: In Honor of Monroe C. Beardsley.* Amsterdam, 1986.
Fisher, John, ed. *Essays on Aesthetics: Perspectives on the Work of Monroe C. Beardsley.* Philadelphia, 1983.

MICHAEL J. WREEN

BEAUTY. [*To explain the complex history of the role of beauty in philosophy and aesthetics, this entry comprises three essays:*

Conceptual and Historical Overview
Classical Concepts
Medieval Concepts

The first essay is an overview of the distinct periods in the history of the concept of beauty both before and since it became part of Western aesthetics in the eighteenth century. The second and third essays concern two main stages of this history—classical and medieval—when beauty was a significant philosophical concept, though not yet an aesthetic concept. The discussion of beauty in the eighteenth century, when it was a central concept, is to be found in the following entries: Alison, Blair, Burke, Cooper, Gottsched, Herz, Heydenreich, Home, Hume, Hutcheson, Kant, Meier, Moritz, Price, Reid, Reynolds, Smith, Sulzer, *and* Winckelmann. *Despite the common association of aesthetics with beauty (and of* aesthetic *with* beautiful*), there is comparably little discussion of it in the nineteenth century. Here see* Art for Art's Sake, Baudelaire, Coleridge, Cousin, Gurney, Hegel, Nietzsche, *and* Schiller. *For further discussion, see* Aestheticism; Daoist Aesthetics; Eco; Gadamer; Glass; Ibn Sīnā; Islamic Aesthetics; Japanese Aesthetics; Landscape; Picturesque; Pleasure; Santayana; *and* Ugliness.]

Conceptual and Historical Overview

Ideas of beauty can be found in almost every culture and at almost every time in human history, with many similarities. Many of these have been preserved throughout the economic, industrial, epistemological, and artistic transformations of the past two or three centuries throughout the world. Yet, such transformations have also promoted changes in ideas of beauty and its relations to nature and art that make many of its historical resonances difficult to comprehend.

In the earliest cultures known, before written history, and in China, Egypt, the Islamic world, and sub-Saharan Africa, beauty was and still is a term of great esteem linking human beings and nature with artistic practices and works. Human beings—men and women—their bodies, characters, behaviors, and virtues are described as beautiful, together with artifacts, performances, and skills, and with natural creatures and things: animals, trees, and rock formations. In such cultures beauty, goodness, and truth are customarily related. Ancient Greece and China were no exceptions. In the Confucian tradition, Kongzi (sixth to fifth century BCE) emphasized social beauty, realized in art and other human activities. Two centuries later, Daoism united art and beauty with natural regularity and purpose, and with human freedom.

Beauty here carries a double meaning, inclusive and exclusive. In the exclusive, restricted sense, it pertains to how things appear, their manifestations, and to the joys human beings experience when presented with beautiful things: human bodies, artifacts, natural creatures, and things. Relevant questions here are always what kinds of things are beautiful and what are not, what qualities make something beautiful. In the inclusive sense, beauty pertains to anything worthy of approbation, to human virtues and characters, to nobility and goodness, to hidden things and truths, to the natural and the divine worlds. Almost anything may be regarded as beautiful, and beauty may include almost any quality. In the exclusive sense, it is important to distinguish what is beautiful from what is not. In the inclusive sense, beauty resists binary oppositions, joins disparate and opposing terms. As different as these two meanings may seem today, they have not traditionally been kept distinct.

From the time of the earliest Greeks, in the fifth and sixth centuries BCE and before, among the Hebrews, the idea of beauty was inseparable from ideas of goodness and the divine. The Greeks did not distinguish beauty and the beautiful, *kallos* and *to kalon*, from the good, *agathon*. The Delphic oracle describes the most just as the most beautiful. Sappho says that what is beautiful is good, and what is good will soon be beautiful. The Old Testament speaks of the beauty of holiness, perfection, and the Lord. In Genesis, when God "saw the light, that it was good," it could have been described as beautiful. More than any other term, *beauty* expressed unqualified approbation, beyond conflict and opposition. It linked the finite, human world with the infinite and divine.

The term for *beauty* in Greek expressed preeminent perfection, nobility, and worth. Nature and natural things were beautiful, as were divine things and acts; so were human beings, their thoughts, characters, and bodies; and so were social institutions, laws, and works of art. Even so, the Greeks usually restricted beauty to visible works; poetry and music were seldom described as beautiful, though they were called good. Roman poets, Horace and Lucian, spoke far more frequently of beauty (*pulchrum*) in poetry.

For the Greeks, the concept of beauty was complex and resonant, linked with many of the concepts at the center of philosophical thought for much of European history: knowledge, truth, goodness, nature or being, and art. Throughout much of this history, beauty has represented both a quality of things that might allow them to be called beautiful and something preeminent beyond qualitative distinctions and linguistic categories. Beauty expressed what is finite, perceivable in form, and what is infinite, beyond form, linking what is measurable with what is immeasurable. Beauty linked the human world with nature and the divine, all related to the good, expressing what is ethical, invaluable in all things, measurable and immeasurable, limit and unlimit.

Much of this can be seen in Heracleitus, who claims that "to god all things are beautiful and good and just, but men suppose some things to be just and others unjust." He relates beauty, justice, and goodness with the divine, belonging to all things. In the human, finite world, things are divided into just and unjust, good and bad, beautiful and ugly.

Similar thoughts can be found in Plato, for example, in the *Symposium*, where Diotima describes a "nature of wondrous beauty (*phusin kálon*) . . . beauty absolute, separate, simple, and everlasting, which without diminution and without increase, or any change, is imparted to the ever-growing and perishing beauties of all other things." Beauty here is infinite, unchanging, beyond all opposition and distinction, beyond measure. And when Socrates suggests in Plato's *Republic* that the idea of the good is the cause of knowledge and truth, perhaps of being, Glaucon responds that it is "an inconceivable beauty (*kallos*)." In *Hippias Ma-*

jor, Socrates suggests that beauty is identical with the good but independent of sense—sight and hearing—and of pleasure. In different places in his dialogues, Plato speaks of nature, gods, things, human beings, the good, being, and the world as beautiful, as well as of beauty itself. What we do, Plato suggests, is for the sake of the good, inseparable from beauty.

Plato is traditionally read as criticizing art, especially the visual arts, as presenting but a semblance of this wondrous beauty. Yet, the historical relation of beauty with art suggests that art may bear an important relation to this inconceivable beauty in all things, beyond measure, linking nature and humanity to the good and the divine. Here no disciplinary distinction can be sustained between knowledge of the human and natural worlds and art, or between art and ethics. In the finite world of measure, the human world, these are distinct. In relation to the gods, infinite and immeasurable, such distinctions cannot be maintained. In Romanticism and later, this understanding of art and beauty became a central theme.

For the Greeks, beauty was understood in the following ways:

1. as wonderful and supreme;
2. as beyond all measures and distinctions, related to unlimit;
3. as pertaining to all things;
4. as pertaining to the gods and to nature and natural things as well as to human beings and their works, including works of art;
5. as pertaining to finite things, shapes, colors, sounds, thoughts, customs, characters, and laws;
6. as inseparable from goodness and excellence (*aretē*).

In this form, beauty eludes many of the traditional distinctions that define philosophical reflection: disciplinary distinctions between philosophy and art, poetry and ethics; philosophical distinctions between appearance and reality, truth and value, mind and body, humanity and nature, reason and emotion, virtue and pleasure; and so on. Similarly, to the extent that beauty is closely linked with art, including poetry, these express the undivided, infinite, and supreme values of the natural and divine worlds. Artistic beauty expresses something immeasurable in finite things.

For the Greeks, however, beauty was also understood in the following ways, derived in part from the Pythagoreans, who believed in a cosmic harmony of numbers, a music of the spheres:

7. as pertaining to light and visible things more than to poetry and music: early Greek poets speak of beautiful songs, words, men, and deeds; classical poets speak of beautiful figures, buildings, statues, and shapes;
8. as order, pertaining to the arrangement and proportion of parts;

9. as harmony, symmetry, measure;
10. as that which is pleasant to sight and hearing.

Beauty as the highest value, associated with the infinite, immeasurable, and divine, and beauty as perceived order, harmony, and proportion, appear on a modern view to be distinct. Yet, for nearly two thousand years, they were regarded as inseparable.

Greek thought and practice gave rise to many issues involving beauty and art, further complications of their role in Greek life. Many of these foreshadowed later controversies:

11. The Sophists argued that what is beautiful is what gives pleasure, through hearing and sight, that nothing is beautiful in itself apart from pleasure and perception. Works of art are made to give such pleasure. Several questions arise:
12. Is beauty a property of things, which apprehended, gives us pleasure?
13. Is beauty, given by perception, primarily subjective in nature?
14. Is artistic beauty distinct from natural beauty, perhaps in the subjective conditions of its production and reception?
15. Is beauty distinct from goodness? Is something beautiful because of its function, aptness, and purpose? Are beauty and goodness different from aptness and purpose?
16. What is the relation between beauty as a quality of things and works and the creation, the making, of those works?

The Greeks spoke of making in relation to art as *poiēsis*, and spoke of art as both *technē* and *mimēsis*. *Poiēsis* was understood as creating, the bringing forth of being from nonbeing, frequently allied with nature and the gods as well as art. *Technē* was understood in terms of acting, making, to an end, with a purpose, related to form. *Mimēsis*, imitation, was given two different meanings, both present in Plato's *Republic*. One is the reproduction of ordinary things, for example, a statue of a man, a painting of a bed; the other is the presentation of fictional and imaginative characters and things as if real, later described by Aristotle as the kind of thing that might happen and by Immanuel Kant as the production of another nature. Much of the subsequent European artistic tradition can be understood to trace the beauty of nature and the divine in relation to the beauty of works of art in terms of making, accomplishing an end, and creating an imaginative world, linking *poiēsis, technē*, and *mimēsis*. This idea of an imaginative beauty presents works of art as created and performed for the sake of something of utmost value, which is not the fulfillment of a purpose.

Aristotle largely departed from the infinite, immeasurable, and supreme sense of beauty found in his predecessors, especially Plato, and restricted beauty to size, order, and proportion, to harmony and symmetry on the one hand, to function, aptness, use, fulfillment of a purpose on the other. He associated beauty predominantly with form, understood in terms of two related spheres of meaning: one related to figure, shape, appearance, and apprehension; the other related to function, excellence, and utility. More perhaps than any other distinction central to Aristotle's thought is that beauty is measured, always more and less. Things are more or less beautiful as they are more or less orderly, fulfill their formal purposes more perfectly, give more or less pleasure in their apprehension. Aristotle represents the dominant European tradition of ideas of beauty through the Renaissance, still present today in Thomist thought, linking beauty with order and with pleasure and its apprehension.

Even so, Aristotle links beauty with excellence in his *Nicomachean Ethics*. And he expands the Delphic oracle's maxim in his *Eudemian Ethics* to say that "happiness is at once the most beautiful and best of all things and also the pleasantest." He barely speaks of beauty in his *Poetics*, except to say that it is "a matter of size and order." Yet, his *Rhetoric* is filled with references linking beauty to useful practices, stature, and implements, to fitness and aptness of purpose, to excellence, to figure, shape, sounds, and meanings, and to language: "the materials of metaphor must be beautiful to the ear."

From the third and fourth centuries BCE through the end of the seventeenth century in Europe, the following views and adumbrations of beauty could be found:

Epicurus (fourth to third centuries BCE) equated beauty with what was pleasurable.

The Stoics (fourth to first centuries BCE) equated beauty with goodness and virtue—*kalon, agathon, aretē*—understanding them in terms of harmony and proportion. They took the world and all its living creatures to be beautiful, expressing cosmic harmony and order. Cicero (first century BCE) also understood the world to be excellent and beautiful. He divided beauty into *dignitas* and *venustas*—dignity and comeliness—and described them as male and female principles throughout nature, an example of the long tradition in which the world was divided by gender and in which the female principle was subordinated to the male. Women's beauty was regarded as both an object of great desire and inferior to higher beauties.

Distinctions among kinds of beauty proliferated until the end of the Renaissance. The view of nature and the world as beautiful and good continued from Stoicism into Hellenistic thought and Roman poetry, then into Christianity, understood as reflecting the perfection of the divine.

Longinus (third century) in *On the Sublime (Peri Hypsous)* addressed the theme of lofty, great, exalted writing. At the time, sublimity was regarded as part of beauty. In later writers such as Edmund Burke and Immanuel Kant, beauty and sublimity were separated, contributing to the decline in the role of beauty in relation to art and nature associated with the growth of the cult of artistic genius.

Plotinus (third century), perhaps with exaltation in mind, argued that beauty should not be identified with symmetry, harmony, and proportion alone, but is related to the Ideal, beyond sense. Simple things can be beautiful, not in the order of their parts but in the ideal that illuminates them. Beauty is the revelation of spirit in matter.

Augustine (fifth century) and Boethius (sixth century) strongly emphasized proportion, harmony, congruence, and consonance, especially in relation to music, which Boethius understood in Pythagorean terms to be regulated by number. Augustine also understood beauty in Neoplatonic terms, after Plotinus, as regularity and simplicity, promoting a conflict in later writers between a beauty of quality and a beauty of quantity. For medieval writers, as for Augustine, light, color, radiance, brilliance, and clarity all were beautiful, testaments to the unity of God. Unity in multiplicity but also unity as such were regarded as beautiful.

Robert Grosseteste (twelfth to thirteenth centuries) and Saint Bonaventure (thirteenth century) took light to be beautiful in itself, in its simplicity, understanding identity as perfect proportion with itself. Bonaventure also took light to be the principle of all beauty because it is the source of its luminosity. The beauty of light represents the beauty of the visible reality of the world.

Abūꞌ Alī al-Husayn Ibn Sīnā (known in the West as Avicenna), in Islamic medieval philosophy, followed Plotinus in associating beauty with spirit. Beauty, erotic and worldly, provides a ladder for ascent to the good.

Pseudo-Dionysus (fifth century) followed by Johannes Scotus Erigena (ninth century) and Hugh of St. Victor (eleventh to twelfth centuries) developed a theory of beauty based on a world filled with reminders and symbols of the divine. Things reflect, refer to, allude to each other; the world together with human works is filled with symbols and allegories. Everything answers to everything else, a beauty that everywhere reveals the hand of God in the world as divine maker, poet, and creator. Eternity, infinity, and perfection shine everywhere as beauty. This Plotinian thought was a Christian expression of the revelation of divine spirit in things everywhere as profusion and multiplicity. It produced a poetry of prophecy and prefiguration.

Thomas Aquinas (thirteenth century) marked a watershed in ideas of art and beauty, as he did in many other areas of philosophy and theology, gathering together different ideas of beauty into a more coherent whole. With respect to the appearance required for beauty to show itself, and the pleasure given by beautiful things, Aquinas defined beauty as that whose very apprehension pleases. Yet, although beauty is apprehended and pleases immediately, it does not reside in the apprehension or the pleasure, but in the beautiful object's form. Aquinas rejected the view that the divine is present everywhere in things through the proliferation of

allegories and symbols, and took these to exist only in the mind. Joined with the rational order of a universe intelligible to understanding is an infinite play of metaphors, symbols, and figures in the mind, filling it with exhilaration.

Aquinas equated beauty with form and, consequently, with goodness. Goodness is related to the end, the form as final cause. Beauty is related to proportion, figure, and form as formal cause. Here Aquinas addressed a view of beauty present throughout medieval thought, the beauty of being in general, metaphysical, or transcendental beauty. Being is resplendence of form, and form is both good and beautiful. This relation of beauty and form went against the link of beauty with infinity, multiplicity, and profusion, beyond end or measure.

Aquinas synthesized the empirical side of beauty in apprehension and pleasure with its presence in form. He offered a synthetic resolution of the question of whether beauty is subjective or objective. Similarly, he integrated beauty as harmony—integrity, proportion, and clarity—with Aristotle's understanding of form as order, purpose, and substantial essence into a synthetic understanding of proportion. Beauty is numerical, quantitative, the arrangement of parts, integrated into the unity and essentiality of the substance, which cannot be separated from its purpose or end.

The sculptor Lorenzo Ghiberti (fourteenth century), the architect Leon Battista Alberti (fifteenth century), and the painter Nicolas Poussin (seventeenth century), spoke of beauty in terms of order, measure, and form. Thomas Hobbes (sixteenth to seventeenth centuries), discussed the beauty of the universe in terms of order and perfection. René Descartes (sixteenth century) described the beauty and perfection of God's works and the divine light. As late as the eighteenth century, beauty retained its relation to divinity and perfection, expressed in art.

Even so, with Descartes and his time a transformation of the world began that included alterations in the practice and understanding of art and in the thought of beauty and beautiful things. Several themes may be noted:

1. the rise of modern science, replacing the vision of a beautiful universe apprehended in its perfection by an orderly universe apprehended through knowledge of its laws;
2. the separation of the knowing, perceiving subject or mind from the corporeal and visible parts whose arrangements constituted beauty;
3. the replacement of a sense of order related to unity and multiplicity by one related to scientific method, dividing into simple parts, recombining into complex aggregates;
4. the separation of humanity from nature based on the unique possession of reason by human beings.

In a universe made by God, the beauty and perfection of the world are immediate and infinitely important. In a universe available to be known, approachable through science, beauty and perfection of form fade in value. Knowledge and reason took precedence over perfection and resplendence. The successes of science, the opening of the world to exploration, all were presented as revelations of truth and understanding. Despite continuing recognition that the world revealed to understanding was beautiful in remarkable ways, beauty faded as a category central to human relations to the world. Science divided itself from art as humanity divided itself from nature and reason divided itself from emotion and perception.

Moreover, in response to Cartesian rationalism, to ideas of universal principles present in reason and applicable to the world, empiricism turned to human experience as source of both knowledge and feeling. The place of the knowing subject was occupied by an experiencing and feeling subject. Ideas of art and beauty underwent further transformations as a consequence of these changes and changes in artistic practices.

Eighteenth-century British writers such as Joseph Addison, Francis Hutcheson, Henry Home, and Archibald Alison, and much more prominent figures such as David Hume, Edmund Burke, and Adam Smith, all turned to a very different sense of beauty and experience as a result of changing developments in science and art. They understood beauty in art as neither proportion nor harmony, but as absence of regularity, vitality, and expressiveness, suggesting that beauty either cannot be defined or is subjective, in the mind. A better term for this subjective relation was *taste*, though it also carried suggestions of superiority and inferiority, reflecting British class distinctions. Beauty was there for all to behold. Taste was possessed by few—the height of subjective judgment. Taste, feeling, sentiment, and pleasure became the dominant ideas of art.

Hume spoke of a *delicacy of taste* as differing from person to person, together with judgments of beauty. The beauty lies not in the poem but in the sentiment or taste of the reader. "Beauty is no quality in things themselves. It exists merely in the mind which contemplates them" (Hume, 1987). What was novel was not that beauty is subjective, but that a new and powerful knowledge of the natural world was taken to be objective in contrast with the subjectivity of beauty and goodness. Hume understood science, ethics, and art all to be products of the laws of human nature. Yet, although the achievements of science made his psychologistic views of natural knowledge implausible, the proliferation of arts in Europe and other cultures opened by exploration made a subjectivist view of art increasingly plausible.

Kant followed, marking another watershed in ideas of art and beauty, responding to suggestions in Hume that the subjectivity of taste made universal judgments of beauty impossible. Much more similar to Hume in his earlier work, *Observations on the Feeling of the Beautiful and Sublime,* Kant pursued a very different line of thought in his last Critique,

the *Critique of Judgment,* where he presented a theory of beauty as universal satisfaction or delight, a theory that to many of his followers gave support to the production and admiration of beautiful art, leading to Romanticism.

The *Critique of Judgment* is divided into two parts: "Critique of the Aesthetical Judgment," related to the beautiful and the sublime, and "Critique of the Teleological Judgment," related to order in nature. The term *aesthetics* had been introduced by Alexander Baumgarten only fifty years before Kant wrote his third Critique to name a science of beauty. Kant departed from Baumgarten's emphasis on sense and perception, yet greatly contributed to the growing acceptance of *aesthetics* as the term defining reflection on the values of art, presupposing art's autonomy.

Kant defines beauty together with taste in terms of four negative moments. (1) Taste is disinterested satisfaction; beauty is the object of such a satisfaction. (2) Beauty pleases universally without requiring a concept. (3) Beauty is the form of the purposiveness (or finality) of an object without representation of a purpose. (4) Beauty is the object of a necessary satisfaction independent of a concept. In other words, beauty falls under no concept, scientific or ethical; pleases disinterestedly, without a purpose; pleases universally; consequently, it is the universal object of a subjective universality, taste.

The structure of these moments is negative—what beauty is not—and paradoxical. How Kant is read depends on how a reader judges his success at resolving the contradictions. Yet, Kant responds to many traditional understandings and values of beauty in rich and complex ways. For example, he understands the purposiveness or finality of objects, of works of art, not as their aptness or function, but as their formal orderliness, *as if* made to an end. He extends this notion to nature, under teleological judgment, to speak of the order of nature, not made to serve an end, but formed as if to an end. He praises free over dependent beauty, where the latter expresses a purpose or end while the former represents perfection of form without the idea of a purpose. Moreover, while beauty is distinguished from goodness as the object of a disinterested satisfaction (goods are ends of interest and desire) beauty is a symbol (*hypotyposis*) of the good. In all these ways, Kant links beauty with ethics and nature while defending the autonomy of aesthetic judgment.

Kant also distinguishes the beautiful from the sublime, describing beauty as formal order, proportion, and harmony, satisfied in taste, and sublimity as exceeding sense, measure, and order. What is great beyond sense can appear in works of art, giving delight. In relation to the sublime, Kant speaks of artistic genius, beyond rules; of a productive imagination, beyond mere reproduction; and of an imaginative freedom distinct from moral freedom. Yet, he subordinates genius to taste, the sublime to beauty. In Kant, beauty retains the marks of order, perfection, and form; the sublime retains the marks of what surpasses order, end, and form. Beauty, not the sublime, is a symbol of the good.

Kant's followers divided along these lines of demarcation, frequently in complex ways, influenced by and contributing to developments in philosophy and art. Romantics emphasized the productive imagination and the transcendence of the sublime, insisting on the immeasurable depths and heights of art. Epistemological philosophers gave privilege to the formation of concepts, suggesting that art, aesthetic judgment, and beauty were unamenable to philosophical reflection. Aesthetics became the appreciation of art and the theory of that appreciation. With twentieth-century developments in art such as modernism, beauty as order appeared an outmoded term from the standpoint of artists themselves. Genius conflicted with beauty. The sublime took precedence over beauty.

These developments did not eliminate beauty from philosophic or artistic discussion. Samuel Taylor Coleridge (1949) defined beauty in ways that linked post-Kantian Romanticism with medieval symbols and allegories—"The Beautiful, contemplated in its essentials . . . is that in which the *many*, still seen as many, becomes one"—meticulously analyzing beauty in relation to form, shape, grandeur, and the sublime. In his lectures on aesthetics, published after his death in 1831, Georg Wilhelm Friedrich Hegel spoke of beauty as the Ideal, the Idea in its spirituality and universality given determinate form: the immediate unity of the Concept immediately present in sensuous appearance (Hegel, 1974–1975). He understood beauty to be inseparable from truth and goodness, all of them related to the Ideal. But the Ideal as beauty requires sensuous appearance, whereas the Ideal as truth is realized in thought.

This distinction leads to one of Hegel's most remarkable claims, found in the *Critique of Judgment* but largely undeveloped there, directly relevant to the history of ideas of art and beauty; for he claims that art no longer expresses the highest realization of Spirit, that Romantic art emphasized the subjectivity of Spirit, unbalancing the unity of the Ideal. A century later, Martin Heidegger powerfully expressed Hegel's thought as a question: "Is art still an essential and necessary way in which that truth happens which is decisive for our historical existence, or is art no longer of this character?" (Heidegger, 1971). Is beauty still an expression of the highest ideals of human historical life? The answer suggested to many artists and philosophers today, after the development of modern art and philosophical aesthetics, is that it is not. Heidegger's own answer is that "Beauty is one way in which truth occurs as unconcealedness" (ibid.). He preserves the historical affinity of beauty with truth, though not with the good. More to the point, Heidegger wonders whether a world shaped by modern technology—far from the ideality of Spirit—might make beauty no longer relevant. Such a possibility belongs to what Heidegger calls the forgetting of Being, under the pressure of the picture of the modern world shaped by instrumentality and measure, oblivious to both the endless possibilities in Being and the historicality of their realization. Hegel and Heidegger both insist on the historical expression of beauty in art and nature as something that arrives on the scene and that may depart. Art may no longer produce works of beauty, either as formal order and perfection or as immeasurable expressions of ideality.

After Kant and Hegel, under the pressures of Romanticism and modernism, joined by the successes of the physical sciences and the growth of industrial society, the ambiguous nature of the idea of beauty worked to its detriment as a term that expressed the nature and value of art, though none of its competitors were free from comparable difficulties. Beauty as order and perfection conflicted with the sense that Romantic artists sought sublimity, that ugliness served artistic ends. Beauty as a quality, subjective or objective, conflicted with the sense of the authority of the artist, the adulation for genius that contributed so strongly to Romanticism. On the other hand, beauty as a term of unqualified approbation did not support growing disciplinary classifications. It applied to human beings, nature, and mathematics as well as art.

Aesthetics—understood as the theory of art, its criticism and value—was derived from sensibility and perception and was an awkward term in relation to poetry and literature. It presupposed disciplinary distinctions, so that its relation to ethics, science, and philosophy was problematic. Even more difficult was the relation of aesthetic values to nature, mediated by sensibility and experience. Nature could not be said to be aesthetic, though human beings may experience it aesthetically. Expression was similarly understood to be restricted to human experience and language. Form failed to express either poetic value or disorder and disruption.

Friedrich Nietzsche's famous response in *The Birth of Tragedy* to Hegel's claim concerning the end of art was that "art represents the highest task and the truly metaphysical activity of this life" (1968). Nietzsche's insistence that Greek tragedy was originally both Apollonian and Dionysian associated the Apollonian with order, perfection, appearance, and light, the Dionysian with rapture, frenzy, intoxication, and terror, closer to the sublime. Tragedy requires both. By a certain symmetry, as Nietzsche later understood the Apollonian to include a frenzy for order, beauty may be understood to include rapture and frenzy, to include the excesses of the sublime. The distinction between Apollonian and Dionysian art, beauty and sublimity, can then be understood to collapse, bringing beauty back to infinity as excess, beyond measure.

To Nietzsche, the gesture in which Western philosophy separated science and ethics from art was the same gesture in which Apollo triumphed over Dionysus in Greek, and later European, thought. The issue was the idea of reason that came to govern ethics and science. One response is that beauty is the idea and art the practice that have most resisted this separation—understanding beauty in its inclusive sense. Beauty is also the idea that most expresses the responsibility repeatedly experienced by artists and audiences to pursue freedom and resist political oppression through art. In both cases, beauty means something more than appearance, but pertains to something fundamental in works and things.

Throughout the nineteenth and twentieth centuries, as the cult of the artist arose, as artists insisted that art is to be pursued for its own sake, as economic development transformed the beauties of nature, beauty lost its place of honor in relation to nature and art. Even so, many twentieth-century philosophers and artists continued to speak of beauty, in three ways. One way drew from Kant and Hegel, sometimes from Aquinas, bypassing the Romantic ascendancy of the sublime. Beauty is that whose apprehension pleases; pleasure and perception are the central terms. Writing early in the century, George Santayana defined beauty as "pleasure regarded as the quality of a thing" (1955), preserving many of Kant's distinctions, with an emphasis on the experience rather than the quality. More recently, Mary Mothersill (1984) has reevoked the idea of beauty in terms of perception and pleasure. Jacques Maritain (1960) and other Thomist philosophers retain Aquinas's understanding of the objective and transcendental nature of beauty within the pleasure of its appearance.

The second way in which beauty continues to be spoken of in relation to art pursues its traditional link with nature, goodness, and the divine. Writing early in the century, Samuel Alexander (1968) related beauty with values inherent throughout nature. John Dewey (1934) emphasized the aesthetic experience, unified without holes or seams, understanding beauty as the pervasive quality of such an experience, joining nature and the ideal. Alfred North Whitehead (1933) spoke of beauty in relation to truth throughout a universe filled with evil. Beauty here remains the term of approbation that least calls for qualification. Much Asian, Islamic, and African thought retains this sense of beauty.

The third way continues to pursue the traditional link of beauty with truth and the good, reinvoked and deeply problematized after Nietzsche in the name of Dionysian principles, questioning the values of order and perfection. Heidegger speaks of beauty as one way in which truth appears, neglecting ethics. Yet, truth appears for him as freedom, evoking the good. Theodor Adorno (1996) includes ugliness within beauty and insists on the link between beauty and freedom. Jean-François Lyotard defines postmodernism in terms of the sublime, as that which, "in the modern, puts forward the unpresentable in presentation itself, that which denies itself the solace of good forms" (1984). Postmodernism presents what is unpresentable, excessive, regardless of order and perfection: the postmodern sublime. Yet, Lyotard understands politics as that unpresentable.

Postmodern art and postmodern politics are intimately related in the name of the sublime, reevoking its relation to art. The role of the unpresentable in Lyotard is not to reinstate order and perfection but to interrupt the rule of form in the name of multiplicity and heterogeneity, to resist the tyranny of neutrality. The issues are ethical and political, an immeasurable responsibility to give form to what escapes form, to give voice to those who have been silenced, a responsibility frequently borne by art.

The possibility then remains of retaining the inclusive and unqualified sense of beauty in art, relating it to truth and the good, resisting its restriction to perfection and order, relating it to nature's abundance and multiplicity. Postmodern beauty is Dionysian as well as Apollonian, detached from the rule of genius, inseparable from rapture, terror, and disorder, linked with the sublime, all expressions of profusion and heterogeneity. Beauty here links nature and art with the good, with an endless ethical and political responsibility to resist—to interrupt—the tyranny of form in caring for the multiple and heterogenous individuals and their worlds that suffer violence under the rule of categories and distinctions. Art here, though not art alone, interrupts the forms and distinctions that philosophers have come to accept as governing their conceptual and practical worlds. Such an interruption is profoundly ethical, an ethics beyond ethics, perhaps, linking art with truth and nature, resisting neutrality. Art can show us promises and possibilities in human and natural worlds that vanish in the categories of disciplinary distinctions. These reevoke the nature of wondrous beauty beyond binary distinctions, understood as an ethical critique of all such distinctions, resisting their neutrality. Such an inclusive sense of beauty and of art can be found in *The Gift of Beauty* (1996), where Stephen David Ross speaks of beauty, in art and nature, as given from the good, expressing abundance, interrupting disciplinary distinctions, resisting neutrality and the tyranny of form. In this way, beauty continues to express the infinite—excessive, immeasurable—side of finite things, linking art with nature and the good.

Despite repeated efforts to restrict its meaning, *beauty* continues to express unqualified and inclusive values in art and nature as no other term of artistic value can, linked with truth and goodness. With the understanding that ugliness, disruption, fascination, frenzy, rapture, violence, and terror all belong to art and nature, together with order and perfection, and with the possibility that beauty can be understood to include these extremes within an understanding of humanity, nature, and the divine, then reflections on art may continue to be expressed in terms of beauty, resisting every attempt to deny truth and goodness to art. *Beauty* is a term of utmost value that resists classification, together with art, nature, truth, and the good, contributing to the endless questions that human beings bring to nature and art.

BIBLIOGRAPHY

Adorno, Theodor W. *Aesthetic Theory.* Edited by Gretel Adorno and Rolf Tiedemann, translated by Robert Hullot-Kentor. Minneapolis, 1997.

Alexander, Samuel. *Beauty and Other Forms of Value.* Reprint, New York, 1968.

Aquinas, Thomas. *Summa Theologiae.* 22 vols. Translated by English Dominicans. Reprint, New York, 1981.

Aristotle. *Eudemian Ethics, Nicomachean Ethics, Poetics, Rhetoric.* In *The Complete Works of Aristotle,* 2 vols, edited by Jonathan Barnes. Princeton, N.J., 1984.

Burke, Edmund. *A Philosophical Enquiry into the Origin of Our Ideas of the Sublime and Beautiful.* Rev. ed. Edited by James T. Boulton. Reprint, Oxford and New York, 1987.

Coleridge, Samuel Taylor. *Biographia Literaria.* Edited by J. Shawcross. Reprint, London, 1949.

Dewey, John. *Art and Experience.* New York, 1934.

Eco, Umberto. *Art and Beauty in the Middle Ages.* Translated by Hugh Bredin. New Haven, 1986.

Hegel, G. W. F. *Aesthetics: Lectures on Fine Art.* 2 vols. Translated by T. M. Knox. Oxford, 1975.

Heidegger, Martin. "On the Origin of the Work of Art." In *Poetry, Language, Thought,* translated by Albert Hofstadter, pp. 15–87. New York, 1971.

Hume, David. *Essays, Moral, Political, and Literary.* Rev. ed. Edited by Eugene F. Miller. Indianapolis, 1987.

Kant, Immanuel. *Critique of Judgment.* Translated by J. H. Bernard. New York, 1951.

Kant, Immanuel. *Observations on the Feeling of the Beautiful and Sublime.* Translated by John T. Goldthwait. Berkeley, 1960.

Lyotard, Jean-François. "What Is Postmodernism?" Translated by Régis Durand. In *The Postmodern Condition: A Report on Knowledge,* translated by Geoff Bennington and Brian Massumi, pp. 71–82. Minneapolis, 1984.

Maritain, Jacques. *Creative Intuition in Art and Poetry.* Reprint, New York, 1960.

Mothersill, Mary. *Beauty Restored.* Oxford, 1984.

Nietzsche, Friedrich. *Basic Writings of Nietzsche.* Translated and edited by Walter Kaufmann. New York, 1968.

Osborne, Harold. *Theory of Beauty: An Introduction to Aesthetics.* New York, 1953.

Plato. *Ion, Hippias Major, Phaedrus, Republic, Symposium.* In *The Collected Dialogues of Plato,* corr. ed., edited by Edith Hamilton and Huntington Cairns. Princeton, N.J., 1963.

Ross, Stephen David. *A Theory of Art: Inexhaustibility by Contrast.* Albany, N.Y., 1983.

Ross, Stephen David. *The Gift of Beauty: The Good as Art.* Albany, N.Y., 1996.

Santayana, George. *The Sense of Beauty: Being the Outline of Aesthetic Theory.* Reprint, New York, 1955.

Tatarkiewicz, Wladyslaw. *History of Aesthetics.* 3 vols. Edited by C. Barrett. Translated by Adam and Ann Czerniawski (vol. 1); R. M. Montgomery (vol. 2); Chester A. Kisiel and John F. Besemeres (vol. 3). The Hague, 1970–1974.

Tatarkiewicz, Wladyslaw. *A History of Six Ideas: An Essay in Aesthetics.* Translated by Christopher Kasparek. The Hague, 1980.

Whitehead, Alfred North. *Process and Reality.* (1929) Corr. ed. Edited by David Ray Griffin and Donald W. Sherburne. New York, 1978.

Whitehead, Alfred North. *Adventures of Ideas.* New York, 1933.

Zhu Liyuan and Gene Blocker, eds. *Contemporary Chinese Aesthetics.* New York, 1995.

STEPHEN DAVID ROSS

Classical Concepts

The analysis of classical concepts of beauty begins here with Plato.

Plato. In light of Plato's assault on poetry, and some of his remarks about painting, sculpture, and music, his very willingness to think theoretically about beauty signals the distance that he will keep between it and art. Beauty hardly matters to Plato's discussion of art, though it matters decisively to his metaphysics and epistemology.

The *Hippias Major* is Plato's sustained attempt to define beauty. One of the aporetic dialogues, it rests with no single definition. Still, three features of its argument are worth noting. First, the beauty under investigation resembles the entities that Plato later calls Forms. The Form of any property F will be an unvarying exemplar of the property: that is, the Form of F can in principle be defined so as to capture the F-ness that turns up in any particular F thing; and the Form of F, by its "presence" in things, makes them F as well. Beauty in the *Hippias Major* works in the same way (esp. 286d, 289d, 292c, 297b). Second, beauty is agreed to bear some close relationship to the good, even though Socrates argues against their identity (e.g., 296eff., 303eff.). Third, both Socrates and Hippias appeal to artworks as examples of beautiful things—especially fitting examples once the conversation turns to pleasures of the eye and ear—but they never treat them as the central cases (290a–b, 297e–298a). Even if the *Hippias Major* was written, as many believe, by someone besides Plato, these aspects of its argument describe the parameters for Plato's views on beauty. He treats it as an intelligible if ambiguous quality; he veers toward equating it with the Form of the good; and he conducts his inquiry into beauty at a distance from his quite differently flavored inquiry into art.

Beauty and art. Aside from the *Hippias Major,* the *Symposium* contains Plato's only specific account of beauty, in the climax to Socrates' discourse on love. Diotima calls beauty the object of love's longing, and clarifies the philosophical soul's progressive approach to ever-purer beauty, from one body to all, then through all beautiful souls, laws, traditions, and kinds of knowledge, up to universal beauty (210a–211d). It is remarkable that in all this talk of beauty, with its acknowledgment of beauty's varied manifestations, only two passing remarks suggest that artworks count as beautiful, even in the lowly sense that a human body is beautiful (209a, d). Comparably, the *Philebus's* examples of pure sensual beauty explicitly exclude pictures, admitting only certain colors, simple geometrical shapes, and "series of pure notes" (51b–d).

If art rarely shows up when the subject is beauty, beauty remains fixedly outside when Plato turns to art. Socrates might grant the beauty of poems (*Ion* 534a), but not in the spirit of imagining such beauty to be part of art's nature.

The *Sophist* admits some beauty to exist in mimetic works, but only as a sign that those works are false representations, hence judged by a standard like beauty that is extraneous to the standard of truthfulness (235e–236a). More significantly, the *Republic's* arguments against poetry contain several reminders that Plato does not want to associate it with beauty. The dialogue's first discussion of poetry, whose context is the guardians' education, censors poems and poetic genres that corrupt the young (377b–398b); yet, elsewhere in its remarks on education, the *Republic* insists that young souls are trained by exposure to what is beautiful (401b–d; cf. 403c). Why should Plato have seen the effect of beauty on education and not raised the subject in his criticisms? Why could not this part of the *Republic* so much as concede that false and pernicious poems affect the young through their beauty? It feels as if Plato's categories for explaining poetry—truth and falsehood, narrative and mimesis—make for an entity to which beauty can be at most an addendum.

In book 10, after having ridiculed the ignorance of poets, Socrates compares their sayings to the attractive but not really beautiful faces of young men when they lose the bloom of youth (601b). Poetry looks beautiful (602b) and exercises charm (601b), but stripped of language and rhythms it sounds trivial. Thus, the beauty in poetry can be separated from the otherwise humdrum claims that poets have to offer. Beauty seems to have attached itself accidentally to artworks. At the same time, the argument in book 10 falters for omitting it; for the argument's vehemence implies not only that poetry is ignorant and misguided, but fundamentally that it seduces its audience. As poetry's seductiveness is linked to its beauty, there is an opportunity here for an account like the *Phaedrus's*, with its appeal to the divine madness that makes every good poem attractive (245a; cf. *Ion* 533d–534e). Why has Plato not expanded his critique here with some account of beauty?

The form of beauty. The brief answer is that Plato has no quarrel with beauty, properly conceived. "Beauty itself," the Form or Idea of beauty, makes its greatest appearance in the *Symposium* (210d–212a), where it stands atop a hierarchy of beautiful items but surpasses them all, as Forms are wont to surpass their instances. The *Symposium* speaks of no other Form, preferring to heap its considerable praise on beauty's head alone. True philosophers meet this beauty in a simultaneously mystical and intellectual experience, in which they both consummate their deepest love and attain the loftiest knowledge. Such elevation for beauty prohibits it from sharing in art's shame.

Without gesturing toward quite the *Symposium's* worship of beauty, many passages in Plato repeat its claim that beauty has a Form (*Cratylus* 439c, *Euthydemus* 301a, *Laws* 655c, *Phaedo* 65d, 75d, 100b, *Phaedrus* 254b, *Parmenides* 130b, *Philebus* 15a, *Republic* 476b, 493e, 507b). Indeed, Plato mentions beauty as often as any other quality that ad-

mits of intelligible understanding. He conceives of an absolute beauty whose nature can be articulated without recourse to the natures of particular beautiful things—not because they lack all beauty, but because true beauty's essence consists in properties not shared by visible objects. Certain objects of sense might be intrinsically beautiful (*Philebus* 51b), thanks to what gets called their own proportion and unity (*Philebus* 64e, 66b, *Statesman* 284b, *Timaeus* 87c–d), but even this situation of beauty in the world of appearance does not deny that its grounds lie in the intelligible realm, where proportion and unity themselves get precise and unconditioned definitions.

Beauty's penchant for turning up in rosters of the Forms follows from its bearing the marks of a classic Form: *beauty* is an evaluative term as much as *justice* or *courage*, and suffers as much as they do from disputes over its meaning. As the theory of Forms mainly exists to guarantee stable meanings for disputed evaluative terms, then if anything has a Form, beauty will.

A Platonic Form F differs from an individual F thing in that F may be predicated univocally of the former (the Form F *is* F), only equivocally of the latter (the F thing both is and is not F: *Republic* 479a–c). In Plato's dialogues, equivocal predication sometimes means that individual F things are F at one time and non-F at another (e.g., *Cratylus* 439d–e); sometimes that they are F in one part and non-F in another; sometimes that they are F to one observer and non-F to another; sometimes that they are F in one context and non-F in another (*Symposium* 211a). To call the corresponding Form univocally F is therefore to deny every equivocality in F things. Beauty makes a perfect example of such a property, because Plato's analyses of individual F things recall observations that everyone makes about beautiful objects. They fade and break. They require an offsetting unattractive detail (the face's mole, the song's unmelodious bridge) to bring out their splendor. People disagree about them. The objects lose their beauty outside their proper context (adult shoes on childish feet).

The ordinariness of these worries about beautiful things points to the second way in which beauty is a paradigm for Platonic Forms: vividly physical beauty makes Platonic recollection more plausible than most other examples do. The philosophical merit of equivocally F things is that they come bearing signs of their incompleteness, so that the inquisitive mind responds with the desire to know more (*Republic* 523c–524b). But whereas large or unequal items typically prompt questions from minds with abstract bents, and the perception of examples of justice or self-control presupposes moral development, beautiful things affect every soul. So, again, do their inconstancy, complexity, and controversiality. Therefore, beauty promises more effective reflection than any other property of things. It is for this reason that the *Phaedrus* (250d–256b) and the *Symposium* ignore other experiences when they describe the first move-ment toward philosophy. Neither dialogue promises that insight will always follow from the sight of beauty. The *Phaedrus* makes clear that vulgar souls respond vulgarly to physical comeliness (250e); elsewhere, Plato says that lovers of beauties need to be weaned from particulars with a dialectical exposé of the equivocation in claims to beauty (*Republic* 476–480). Nevertheless, beautiful things attract our attention and remind us of their mystery as no other visible objects do, and in his optimistic moments Plato welcomes our attention to them.

Beauty's pedagogical effects make one reason for Plato's repeated testimonies to its goodness and good consequences, sometimes its identity with goodness (*Laws* 841c, *Philebus* 66a–b, *Republic* 401c, *Symposium* 201c, 205e). They also explain the great gulf between beauty and art. Where beauty may or may not lead its viewer into dialectics, art only misleads: all but a very few get corrupted by it (*Republic* 605c). Because artworks systematically mislead, no feature of the experience they offer can serve as a bridge to philosophical knowledge. If the study of art were centrally about beauty, artworks would stand in Plato's system alongside just acts and wise laws: respectable in themselves, as far as ordinary people are concerned, and stimulations to higher knowledge. Since artistic mimesis, as Plato conceives it, bends rather toward the quirky and grotesque (*Republic* 395d–396b, 605a), it lacks that defense.

Aristotle. Given Aristotle's un-Platonic view of poetry and mimesis, it is natural that his *Poetics* refers freely to what is beautiful. Tragedies, their plots, their language, their characters, and their characters' actions can all deserve the adjective, which in one form or another occurs nineteen times in this brief treatise. Plato may see the charms in poetry as cosmetic embellishments that entice the unwary; when Aristotle calls a tragedy or its elements beautiful, he means instead that it does just what it should, that it has found its right form.

Beauty and art. Yet nearly all the *Poetics'* references to beauty frustrate the reader's attempt to find its definition. The work's definition of tragedy (1449b24–28) leaves out references to beauty. Aristotle may urge the inclusion of beautiful characters in tragedy (1454b11), and praise some plots as more beautiful than others (1452a10, 1453a12), but with only one exception makes that word a compliment to what has been properly accomplished, rather than a defining criterion of art. That exception comes when Aristotle proposes an appropriate length for tragedies, that they be neither too long to surpass what the memory can hold nor too short to stand as serious (*Poetics* 1451a4–15). Tragedies need the right size in order to be beautiful, just as living creatures do. As beauty is a matter of magnitude and proportion, it cannot belong either to minuscule animals whose attractiveness is imperceptible, or to things so gargantuan that their form grows incomprehensible (1450b34–1451a4).

This passage appears to assume a definition of beauty as adequate scale and proportion. Other passages in Aristotle's corpus bear out the suggestion; though he never sets out to define beauty, he does mention, for example, that an artwork's beauty requires proportion (*Politics* 1284b8–10), and that mathematics belongs in the study of beauty thanks to its concern with "order, symmetry, and definiteness," the basic elements of beauty (*Metaphysics* 1078a31–b5).

Such remarks clearly make beauty a real property of beautiful things: "beautiful" is not a cheer given at the sight of objects one finds pleasing, but a perception of some quality in them. But Plato's conception of beauty, while asserting its reality, further demands a definition for it that stands independent of the definitions of any particular beautiful things. The question that remains regarding Aristotle is whether he likewise means beauty to possess that sort of definition. Are order and symmetry characteristics that turn up in every beautiful individual? The passages cited do not settle the question. Order may vary with types of objects. The organization of an orderly intestine would look haphazard if transferred to the plumbing of a house. A river may follow a definite path and thus look beautiful, but a shoemaker's treatment of leather needs much sharper cuts before it is definite. The magnitude that the *Poetics* called a prerequisite for beauty (cf. *Nicomachean Ethics* 1123b7) may sound like a standard applicable equivalently to all objects; but then Aristotle's *Categories* specifies that magnitude is a relative concept, a small mountain and a large millet grain being so by virtue of mountains' and millet grains' natures (5b15–29; see *Politics* 1326a34–39 on beauty, scale, and function). Aristotle's criteria thus remain at best ambiguous between absolute and relative standards for beauty.

Within the *Poetics,* some help on this subject comes from Aristotle's claims about the pleasure found in a tragedy. Although tragedy's visual effects do possess allure, they have less to do with the art (*technē*) of tragedy than any other element does (1450b17). We should not demand every variety of pleasure from a tragedy, but only the pleasure proper to it (1453b11). Here the pleasing quality of a thing only counts as its own if that pleasure derives from the thing's essential nature, what the object must be like to count as a member of its species. If beauty bears a relation to pleasure (see *Topics* 146a22–30, *Rhetoric* 1388b13–14, and the probably inauthentic *Problems* 896b10–26), perhaps Aristotle similarly admits beauty into the study of art only as the beauty specific to tragedy, comedy, painting, and so on. Then art theory does not begin with a general concept of beauty, but comes to the beauties it speaks of by way of separate inquiries into each art form's nature.

Aristotle's treatment of mimesis confirms this suspicion. Even when a corpse or unseemly animal is painful to look at, the skillful rendering of it brings joy (*Poetics* 1448b10–13; also *Parts of Animals* 645a11). Aristotle would call such a picture beautiful (see *Poetics* 1450b1–3); but then the beauty of the mimesis derives from its success as a likeness, which is to say its success at its proper task. Because art is fundamentally mimetic, it does not have to be beautiful in the same sense that nonrepresentations are. Mimesis trumps beauty—or rather, the beauty of good mimesis trumps that will-o'-the-wisp beauty in general.

Beauty in general. Other passages outside the *Poetics,* while few and mostly inconclusive, support these assessments of Aristotle's view. Several of his references to beauty vanish after mentioning it (e.g., *Metaphysics* 1013a22; *Nicomachean Ethics* 1115b12, *Rhetoric* 1405b6–8); the word and its definitions arise several times in the *Topics,* but merely as examples of more general claims about definition, hence uncertain guides to Aristotle's considered position (102a6, 135a12–14, 146a22–30). But three short discussions confirm the interpretation that Aristotle takes beauty to inhere in the beautiful object: he argues that the cause of all things may rightly be called beautiful (*Metaphysics* 1072b32–35), claims some objects to be beautiful in themselves (*Problems* 896b10–26), and—most relevantly—distinguishes what really is beautiful from what only gets perceived as good for the perceiver, so that beauty-claims refer to more than an observer's desire (*De Motu Animalium* 700b26–35). It is safe to conclude that Aristotle and Plato agree about the reality of beauty.

Regarding the trickier matter of whether this real property is also a univocal one, identically characterized in every manifestation, two telling passages separate Aristotle's view from Plato's. The *Rhetoric* distinguishes different meanings of human beauty for the different stages of life, depending on whether the body is fit for feats of speed and strength, for warfare, or for bearing up under the pressures of age (1361b7–14); and in *Parts of Animals,* Aristotle urges his students not to despise the gruesome details of biology. Whatever one thinks of certain animals, each reveals something beautiful; for living things display organization fitted to a purpose, and that quality of design counts as beauty (645a23–25). Philosophers look past their preconceptions about beauty to discover unsuspected attractions in the means by which every plant and animal feeds and reproduces itself. Then the markers of beauty ought to be understood heuristically. Alone they do not define what makes a fly or fungus beautiful: that information emerges from empirical study, which will show where the fly's order and the fungus' definiteness reside.

Such dependence of beauty on its context explains why Aristotle could neither admit the existence of a Platonic Form of beauty nor put it to Platonic work. The first point may be cast in familiar terms. Beautiful things share no kind of property. They belong not only to different species (dog, tree, house), but also to different categories (substance, position, etc.: *Categories* 1b25–2a5), and no property can be univocally predicated of items in different categories. Aristotle's decisive argument against a Platonic Form of the good depends on this principle: "good" might apply to both God and reason, but once it covers both of those *and* the virtues *and* the relation of usefulness, it ceases to designate any single essence of the sort that Forms were made to capture (*Nicomachean Ethics* 1096a18–28). So much for the Form of the good, and so much too for any Form of beauty. The wide-ranging predication of beauty implies not (as Plato would have it) the universality of the property, but its hopeless ambiguity in the absence of any more specific content.

For the same reason, Aristotle would say that even if a Form of beauty existed, it could not induce the experience Plato describes, in which unschooled shudders at the sight of a good-looking face lead upward to knowledge. The dependence of beauty-claims on species-claims means that the experience of beauty must be mediated by knowledge, in the sense that one cannot call this a beautiful X until one knows what it is to be X. Thus, what Aristotle considers philosophical knowledge is logically prior to experiences of beauty, and that indeterminate quality that Plato found so compelling loses its pedagogical function.

Despite these profound differences between Plato and Aristotle, it is worth reiterating that neither makes beauty a foundational principle for the study of art, despite, for example, Gerald Else's claim that beauty is the *Poetics'* "master-concept." Their agreement concerning tragedy helps explain why: Aristotle's defense of the genre shares with Plato's attack the assumptions that poetic works deserve praise or blame depending on (1) their ethical effects on their audience and (2) their ability to contain and impart philosophically legitimate knowledge. Plato's determination that tragedy fails on both counts renders its comeliness at best a distraction. Just as naturally, when Aristotle praises tragedy for being morally serious and educational, he cannot ground his encomium in appeals to beauty, but will instead call a given tragedy beautiful only because it succeeds at its defining purpose.

Plotinus. Plotinus has proved more influential in the creation and criticism of art than either Aristotle or Plato, though some of that influence has resulted from later Neoplatonic elaborations of his position. Two treatises spell out Plotinus's account of beauty: *Enneads* I.6, "On Beauty," and V.8, "On the Intelligible Beauty." The former, a freestanding early piece, develops the basic lines of Plotinus's analysis, more clearly situating his theory between Plato's and Aristotle's. The latter, which properly belongs with three other treatises in a long metaphysical work, embeds its account of beauty in broader discussions of knowledge and the realm of the Forms.

A sensitive and imaginative reader of Plato, Plotinus relies on Platonic vocabulary in unfolding his definition of beauty. For him, too, beauty represents a universal principle, and beautiful objects can inspire an intellectual ascent to knowledge. But Plotinus leaves his stamp on Platonism. He extends the range of beautiful objects one learns from to include artworks, and also expands the place of beauty within the intelligible realm, transforming it (along somewhat Aristotelian grounds) from one discrete Form among others into an essential characteristic of all Forms.

Beauty is form. Plotinus begins by denying physical objects' essential possession of their beauty. There is no beauty in a body without its being perceived by a human soul (see *Ennead* V.8.2.34–35). In the same vein, Plotinus attacks the Stoic definition of beauty as proportion (I.6.21–54). Because proportion does inhere in a body, calling this beauty would return the property to the material thing it appears in. Plotinus makes his point clear, in Platonic style: "The same bodies appear sometimes beautiful, sometimes not beautiful; so to be bodies is one thing, to be beautiful another thing" (I.6.1.14–17).

Locating beauty in the perception of it by no means implies, however, that beauty reduces to individual mental experience. Plotinus rather infers, as Plato had, that when the soul finds itself attracted to bodies' beauty, it must be perceiving a reminder of something soul-like, hence higher, in those bodies (I.6.2.3–11). Beauty is form (I.6.2.19–22, V.8.2.14, V.8.3.1–3, V.8.9.43–47, V.9.2.14–15), an essential characteristic of the intelligible Forms (V.8.5.23, V.8.10.25–27), and a product of the general divine principle that Plotinus calls Intellect (*nous:* V.8.3.20–22). It occurs in the objects of sense when their guiding form has overcome matter's inclination toward chaos, so that what the perceiving soul delights in when it calls a physical object beautiful, is the successful rout of the object's antecedent matter (I.6.2.19–22). For Plotinus as for Plato, the soul's joy at the sight of beauty instigates its turn toward form, that is, toward everything philosophical (I.3.1, V.9.2). Like Plato, Plotinus is impressed by beauty's status as the nearest thing to a visible abstraction.

There is an Aristotelian element to this account, inasmuch as the thing's beauty depends only on the presence in it of its own proper form, not also on an infusion of the Form of beauty. In this specific sense, there is no Form of beauty on a par with the other Forms (but see the suggestions of such a Form at V.1.11.1–3 and V.9.2.17–19). Beauty's definition in any particular case proceeds from the definition of the thing in question, much as animals' beauty in *Parts of Animals* proceeded from their capacity to be what they were supposed to be. But Plotinus's development of this idea does not sound Aristotelian in the least; for beauty becomes a defining presence in the intelligible realm, a principle essential to every other.

Elevating beauty to the rank of a general feature of all lesser intelligibles makes it begin to resemble the Form of the good, and at times Plotinus speaks as though he has identified the two supreme Forms of Plato's *Symposium* (210e–211e) and *Republic* (507a–509b). Beauty is the good (I.6.7.1–5); because being is beauty (V.8.9.37–42), both beauty and goodness serve as names for the highest intelligible being. The absolute equation of beauty and the good cannot be sustained, and at several points Plotinus restates their relationship (see I.6.9.37–45, V.8.13.11–12, and esp. V.5.12.9–38). But in every version, whatever the precise priority, beauty transcends any individual Form, as the good also does (III.8.11). This act of lifting beauty above the other Forms bears fruit for Plotinus. He simplifies the Platonic quest to define beauty by eschewing appeals to a narrowly defined Form that must apply to all beautiful things; and rather than retain the Platonic distinction between the universally and the particularly beautiful, he reads that distinction into his dualism of soul and matter, by attributing beauty to every victory of the former over the latter.

Beauty and art. If beauty ranks higher for Plotinus than for Plato, it also can be found in lower places, namely, in works of art. Plotinus lets some artworks, above all music and statues, serve as his examples of beautiful particulars (I.3.14–34, I.6.1.3, I.6.1.35–37, V.8.1.9–10, V.8.1.15). As bodies, such works can boast of no more intrinsic beauty than other bodies have, and are similarly left behind by the philosophical soul, which might otherwise find them distracting (see I.3.1 on the musician turned philosopher, and V.5.12). Artworks nevertheless deserve prima facie attention, because—contra Plato—mimesis captures more than the look of its object. The mimetic artist works from insight into the intelligible principles that inform nature (V.8.1.33–38). Every created item, whether natural or artificial, is made by wisdom; hence, the artist and the artisan possess wisdom too (V.8.5.1–5, V.9.11.13–17; cf. the unexpected reference to poets' *sophia* at *Republic* 605a). Even when Plotinus treats mimetic artists less kindly (V.9.11.1–13), he seems to object less to what they can do than to what most have proved prone to do.

Plotinus does not explicitly draw the conclusion that art is the mimesis of Forms, but it lies waiting to be drawn from these comments, and he came to be seen as proposing such a defense of art. But because Plotinian beauty, like the sort Aristotle alludes to, inheres in all achievements of form, even this much apology for art leaves beauty outside aesthetics. Art neither possesses a special claim to beauty nor makes beauty its subject. If anything, beauty rather belongs to the study of ethics, as it only vaguely had for Plato and explicitly had not for Aristotle (see *Metaphysics* 1078a33): to Plotinus, the soul's beauty becomes indistinguishable from its virtue (I.6.5; cf. V.8.13.19–25).

Conclusion. This discussion has one principal omission, the Stoics after Aristotle, who defined beauty explicitly as symmetry and proportion and developed a theory of its relationship to moral goodness. Although extended Stoic discussions of beauty are hard to find, a good single source to their thought is Cicero, *Tusculan Disputations* IV. The Stoics serve in *Ennead* I.6 as Plotinus's major opposition, whom he must refute before looking elsewhere for beauty. Their ethical use of beauty, broadly comparable to Plotinus's, also invites study for its elaboration of a possibility only latent in the Stoics' predecessors.

The small role for beauty in ancient art theory follows from a mode of analysis of art that may almost be called anthropological. Art belongs in the social realm, so these philosophers' discussion centers on the human contribution to art objects and experience of them. For both Plato and Aristotle, mimesis implies a function for artworks, whether or not they approve of that function. Beauty, as a natural quality inhering in natural objects as well as in artificial ones, is not a component of any mechanism that performs a specifically human function. Of the three philosophers, only Plotinus allows for the possibility that art is made to work by being beautiful; thus, only he even gestures toward the modern conception of objects that lack a social function.

[See also Aristotle; Hellenistic Aesthetics; Plato; and Plotinus.]

BIBLIOGRAPHY

Annas, Julia. "Plato on the Triviality of Literature." In *Plato on Beauty, Wisdom and the Arts,* edited by Julius Moravcsik and Philip Temko, pp. 1–27. Totowa, N.J., 1982.

Anton, John P. "Plotinus's Refutation of Beauty as Symmetry." *Journal of Aesthetics and Art Criticism* 23 (1964): 233–237.

Aristotle. *Poetics.* Translated and edited by Richard Janko. Indianapolis, 1987.

Armstrong, A. H. "Beauty and the Discovery of Divinity in the Thought of Plotinus." In *Kephalaion: Studies in Greek Philosophy and Its Continuation Offered to Professor C. J. de Vogel,* edited by J. Mansfield and L. M. de Rijk, pp. 155–163. Assen, 1975.

Butcher, S. H. *Aristotle's Theory of Poetry and Fine Art.* 4th ed. London, 1907; reprint, New York, 1951.

Cicero. *Tusculan Disputations.* Rev. ed. Translated by J. E. King. Loeb Classical Library. Cambridge, Mass., 1966.

Edwards, M. J. "Middle Platonism on the Beautiful and the Good." *Mnemosyne* 44 (1991): 161–167.

Else, Gerald. "Aristotle on the Beauty of Tragedy." *Harvard Studies in Classical Philology* 49 (1938): 179–204.

Gould, Josiah B. *The Philosophy of Chrysippus.* Albany, N.Y., 1970.

Griswold, Charles. "The Ideas and the Criticism of Poetry in Plato's Republic, Book 10." *Journal of the History of Philosophy* 19 (1981): 135–150.

Grube, G. M. A. "Plato's Theory of Beauty." *Monist* 37 (1927): 269–288.

Gulley, Norman. "Aristotle on the Purposes of Literature." In *Articles on Aristotle,* edited by Jonathan Barnes et al., vol. 4, pp. 166–176. London, 1979.

Halliwell, Stephen. *Aristotle's Poetics.* Chapel Hill, N.C., 1986.

Lodge, Rupert C. *Plato's Theory of Art.* London, 1953.

Nehamas, Alexander. "Plato on the Imperfection of the Sensible World." *American Philosophical Quarterly* 12 (1975): 105–117.

Plato. *Hippias Major.* Translated by Paul Woodruff. Indianapolis, 1982.

Plato. *Symposium.* Translated by Alexander Nehamas and Paul Woodruff. Indianapolis, 1989.

Plotinus. *Enneads.* 7 vols. Translated by A. H. Armstrong. Loeb Classical Library. Cambridge, Mass., 1966–1988.

NICKOLAS PAPPAS

Medieval Concepts

Beauty in the Middle Ages is not related primarily to art or human culture. The notion of "fine arts" is unknown in this period. The medieval accounts of beauty belong to ontology or theology and are informed by two different traditions. In the line of the Platonic-Pythagorean tradition mediated by Augustine and Boethius, mathematical proportion or harmony is considered an essential condition of beauty. This tradition acquired even greater authority in the Middle Ages through its connection with a Christian motive. In their reflections on the beautiful, many authors appeal to a text from the book of Wisdom (11.21): "You, O Lord, have ordered all things according to measure, number and weight." The world was created by "divine art" as an ordered whole and is therefore beautiful. The second tradition that informed medieval views of beauty goes back to Pseudo-Dionysius the Areopagite (sixth century), a thinker strongly influenced by Neoplatonism. Characteristic of this tradition is that it regards not only harmony but also clarity (*claritas*) as essential to beauty, and identifies the beautiful with the good.

Proportion and Harmony. Augustine describes expressively in his writing *On True Religion* (*De vera religione,* c.32) the way to insight into what beauty is. He wonders why an architect constructs an edifice in a particular way. When he has put up one arch, why does he proceed to make a second, similar one opposite it? His answer will probably be: "To let similar components of the edifice correspond." Augustine then asks just why he prefers to do so. The architect will say that this is beautiful, but the question remains why that is so. The answer Augustine suggests is that things are beautiful "because the parts are like each other and work together in harmony through some connection." They form a unity.

In Augustine's reflection on beauty, the notion of unity is central: unity is the measure of beauty. Because unity is the principle of all numbers, number determines beauty. Harmony and proportion are forms of a numerical order. Augustine therefore defines beauty (*De musica* VI.13.38) as "equality determined by number [*aequalitas numerosa*])," a definition adopted verbatim by Bonaventure in the thirteenth century (*Itinerarium* II.5).

The other mediator of the Platonic-Pythagorean conception is Boethius. His widely read *The Consolation of Philosophy* contains a hymn that paraphrases Plato's dialogue the *Timaeus,* which describes how the Demiurge creates order in matter. Boethius invokes the "Father of all things" (*De musica* III.9.6–10):

> All things Thou bringest forth from Thy high archetype:
> Thou, height of beauty [*pulcherrimus*], in Thy mind the
> beauteous world
> Dost bear, and in that ideal likeness shaping it,
> Dost order perfect parts a perfect whole to frame.
> The elements by harmony Thou dost constrain.

The study of the harmony in reality belongs to the domain of *musica,* because this science concerns itself, as Boethius writes (*De musica* I.3), with *consonantia,* that is, "the agreement of different sounds that have been brought to unity." "Music" was one of the *artes liberales.* The "musical" conception, which regards proportion and harmony as essential to beauty, therefore also influenced the Middle Ages through education in the liberal arts.

Clarity. In his *On the Divine Names* (*De divinis nominibus*), Dionysius the Areopagite deals with the predicates attributed to God in Scripture that express God's causality with respect to creatures, such as "Good," "Being," "Life," and "Wisdom." The primary among these names for Dionysius, is the "Good." One of the divine names that he elucidates in chapter 4 is "Beautiful." The divine is called "Beauty" because it confers beauty on all things according to their proper natures. It is the cause of the harmony and clarity of all things. Here Dionysius names two features of the beautiful: in addition to the traditional notion of harmony, he mentions "brightness" or clarity. This condition is closely associated with "light," which he had discussed directly before the beautiful.

In their definitions of the beautiful, many medieval authors refer to this passage from Dionysius. His exposition is the source, for example, of Aquinas's analysis of the conditions of the beautiful. In his *Summa theologiae* (I.39.8), Aquinas enumerates three things that are required for beauty: first, integrity (*integritas*) or perfection, for "those things which are impaired are by that fact ugly"; second, due proportion or harmony; and third, clarity, which notion is explained by an example: "whence things are called beautiful which have a bright color." In other places (e.g., II–II.145.2), Aquinas mentions only the two Dionysian conditions. The first enumerated requirement, "perfection," is a general condition that connects the beautiful to the good, for the mark of the good as good is that it has attained its end.

The close connection between the good and the beautiful is a basic idea in the Dionysian tradition. Dionysius even claims identity between the good and the beautiful. In this respect, there is a difference from the conception of beauty mediated by Augustine, in which beauty is connected mainly with "unity." One of Dionysius's arguments for the sameness of the good and the beautiful is that "there is no being that does not participate in the good and the beautiful" (*De divinis nominibus* 4.7). With his thesis of identity, the Areopagite is a typical representative of Greek culture, for already in Homer the beautiful (*kalos*) and the good (*agathos*) had been brought together in a single notion: the *kalokagathia.*

Is the Beautiful a Transcendental Attribute? In the thirteenth century, Dionysius was the most important authority for medieval thought on beauty. *De divinis nominibus* was commented on by, among others, Albertus Magnus and Aquinas, who elaborated two aspects in particular of the Dionysian doctrine: the first is his statement that there is no being that does not participate in the beautiful and the good; the second is the thesis of the identity of the beautiful and the good.

Dionysius's assertion that every being participates in beauty posits the universal extension of the beautiful. This view makes possible the connection with a doctrine that was developed in thirteenth-century thought, the doctrine of the *transcendentia.* "Transcendentals," such as "being," "one," "true," and "good," exceed the particular modes of being that Aristotle called the "categories" (substance, quantity, or quality, etc.), because they are common to all things. Transcendentals are universal attributes of being; "one," "true," and "good" are coextensive with "being." Given the extension of the beautiful to all being posited by Dionysius, it is understandable that in the thirteenth century the question arises of whether the beautiful can be incorporated in the doctrine of the transcendentals. If that should be the case, the consequence is that the beautiful "acquires a metaphysical worth, an unchanging objectivity, and an extension which is universal" (Eco, 1988, p. 22).

Is, however, beauty regarded as a distinct transcendental in the Middle Ages? This question is answered by most modern scholars in the affirmative. Umberto Eco, for example, believes that Scholastic aesthetics succeeded in integrating beauty with other forms of values on the metaphysical level and thereby resolved the problem of the transcendental character of beauty. Yet, it is striking that thinkers such as Alexander of Hales, Bonaventure, Albertus Magnus, and Aquinas do not include the beautiful in the series of transcendentals. In his most complete exposition of the transcendentals (*De veritate* 1.1), Aquinas does not mention the beautiful. The only exception is an anonymous thirteenth-century treatise (edited by Dieter Halcour in *Franziskanische Studien* 41 [1959]). In this work, it is asserted that there are four general "conditions" of being, namely, one, true, good, *and* the beautiful. But this statement is not representative for the thirteenth century.

Dionysius's thesis of the identity of the beautiful and the good is modified by his medieval commentators. In his commentary to *De divinis nominibus* (c. 4, lect. 5, p. 356), Aquinas observes that although the beautiful and the good are the same in reality, they nevertheless differ in concept, "since the beautiful adds to the good a relation to the power that is able to know." In a text in the *Summa theologiae* (I–II.27.1), he elaborates on this difference. It pertains to the notion of the good that the appetite comes to rest in it. In contrast, it pertains to the notion of the beautiful that desire comes to rest in the knowledge of it. "Good" therefore refers to that which pleases the appetite absolutely (*simpliciter*), whereas the beautiful refers to that whose knowledge (*apprehensio*) is pleasing.

What is new about the beautiful in medieval thought compared to Greek thought is the emphasis on the relation of the beautiful to knowledge. This relation to knowledge finds expression in Aquinas's definition of the beautiful, which is often cited in modern times: "Those things are called beautiful which please when they are seen" (*S.th.* I.5.4 ad 1). The emphasis on the relation to knowledge culminates in the fifteenth century with Dionysius the Carthusian (1402/3–1471). In his *De venustate mundi et pulchritudine Dei* (On the loveliness of the world and the beauty of God), he presents a definition of beauty from which the moment of "pleasing" has disappeared completely. His definition of beauty is "that which all behold or know" (*quod omnia adspiciunt vel cognoscunt*). The modification of the identity of the beautiful and the good that began in the thirteenth century results in the Carthusian in a purely cognitive definition of beauty.

The emphasis on the cognitive aspect leads to a shift of the place of beauty in the direction of "truth," for truth is the transcendental property that expresses that things are related to an intellect and are intelligible. When characterizing the classical traditions of thought about beauty, one can say that in Augustine beauty is related to "unity" and that in Dionysius it is identical with "goodness." In the Middle Ages, the relationship with the good is generally not denied, but beauty is related at the same time to "truth." In his commentary on *De divinis nominibus* (c. 4, n. 72), Albertus Magnus connects the beautiful with the true, but not with truth as such. He distinguishes two forms of truth, which he traces back to two kinds of knowledge. The first is the knowledge of theoretical reason, which is directed at truth as such; the other is the knowledge of practical reason, which arises through the "extension" of the true to the good. The beautiful is the true that has acquired the character of good.

Medieval Aesthetics? Scholastic authors reflect on the question whether the beautiful is a transcendental attribute of being and on the beautiful as a divine name. The context of Aquinas's analysis of the three conditions of beauty in the *Summa theologiae*, for example, is the doctrine of the Trinity. Aquinas asks whether the property "beauty" is correctly ascribed to the second Person of the Trinity, the Son. His analysis is not intended as an aesthetic theory. It is therefore misleading to speak of a "medieval aesthetics" or the "aesthetics of Thomas Aquinas." [*See* Aquinas.]

Only after the Middle Ages is a philosophical aesthetics established in which beauty is given an independent place beside truth and goodness. In modern scholarship there is a tendency, inspired by the French philosopher Jacques Maritain (1930), to project this modern development backward into the past. Attempts are made to construct a philosophical aesthetics based on Scholastic principles. As a result of this interest, beauty acquires a place that, historically, it never had in Aquinas's own thought.

[*See also* Aquinas *and* Maritain.]

BIBLIOGRAPHY

Primary Sources

Albertus Magnus (Albert the Great). *Super Dionysium De divinis nominibus.* Edited by P. Simon. In *Opera omnia,* vol. 37.1. Münster, 1972.

Anonymous (Assisi, Biblioteca Comunale, Codex 186). *Tractatus de transcendentalibus entis conditionibus.* Edited by D. Halcour. *Franziskanische Studien* 41 (1959): 41–106.

Aquinas. *In librum beati Dionysii De divinis nominibus expositio.* Edited by Ceslai Pera. Turin, 1950.

Aquinas. *Summa theologiae.* In *S. Thomae Aquinatis Doctor's Angelici Opera Omniu iussu impersaque Leonis XIII P. M. edita,* vols. 5–12. Rome 1889–1906. Translated by the Fathers of the English Dominican Province in 5 vols. as *Summa Theologica: Complete English Edition* (Westminster, Md., 1981); also translated by the Blackfriars in 60 vols. as *Summa Theologiae* (New York, 1964–1976).

Augustine. *De vera religione.* Corpus Scriptorum Ecclesiasticorum Latinorum, vol. 77. Vienna, 1961.

Boethius. *The Consolation of Philosophy.* Edited and translated by S. J. Tester. Loeb Classical Library. Cambridge, Mass., 1978. See also the translation by V. E. Watts (Harmondsworth, England, 1969).

Boethius. *De musica.* In *Patrologia latina,* edited by J. P. Migne, vol. 63. Paris, 1882.

Dionysius the Areopagite (Pseudo-Dionysius). *Pseudo-Dionysius: The Complete Works.* Translated by Colm Luibhead and Paul Rorem. New York, 1987.

Dionysius Cartusiensis. *De venustate mundi et pulchritudine Dei.* In *Opera omnia,* vol. 34. Monstrolii, 1907.

Other Sources

Aertsen, Jan A. "Beauty in the Middle Ages: A Forgotten Transcendental?" *Medieval Philosophy and Theology* 1 (1991): 68–97.

Assunto, Rosario. *Die Theorie des Schönen im Mittelalter.* 2d ed. Cologne, 1987.

Eco, Umberto. *Art and Beauty in the Middle Ages.* Translated by Hugh Bredin. New Haven, 1986.

Eco, Umberto. *The Aesthetics of Thomas Aquinas.* Translated by Hugh Bredin. Cambridge, Mass., 1988.

Kovach, Francis J. *Die Ästhetik des Thomas von Aquin: Eine genetische und systematische Analyse.* Berlin, 1961.

Maritain, Jacques. *Art and Scholasticism.* Translated by J. F. Scanian. New York, 1930.

Tatarkiewicz, Wladyslaw. *History of Aesthetics,* vol. 2, *Medieval Aesthetics.* Edited by C. Barrett. The Hague, 1970.

JAN A. AERTSEN

BELL, ARTHUR CLIVE HOWARD (1881–1964), an early architect of contemporary analytic aesthetics (aesthetics of the twentieth-century Anglo-American philosophical tradition). Clive Bell's work as an art theorist, critic, and successful champion of the Post-Impressionists has secured his philosophical and cultural importance, an importance independent of his link to the intermittently voguish Bloomsbury group. His formalist theory of art (this article's focus) has become one of the classics of twentieth-century philosophical aesthetics. The now canonical text is his earliest book, *Art,* especially the first of its fifteen chapters ("The Aesthetic Hypothesis"), and, to a lesser extent, the third ("The Metaphysical Hypothesis"). Bell alleges in his Preface that his hypotheses explain what he considers a universal human phenomenon, that "Everyone in his heart believes that there is a real distinction between works of art and all other objects" (1914). Never daunted by the members of the art world who saw this distinction as purely conventional, Bell spent his creative life convinced of the real uniqueness of aesthetic objects and even of their momentous value for an ethical human life. Bell's formalism, then, is a version of aesthetic realism in that he finds in artworks an essential property that provides the truth conditions for many aesthetic claims, both descriptive and evaluative.

Before examining Bell's formalism more closely, it is necessary to glance at the widely discussed provenance of his theory, both philosophical and artistic. Bell, as a student at Cambridge in 1899 and then as an original Bloomsbury, had social ties to G. E. Moore and those in his philosophical circle. Many commentators on Bell note two theoretical connections between Bell's aesthetics and G. E. Moore's ethical intuitionism. They interpret Bell as applying Moore's conception of value to aesthetics. (See Bywater, 1975; Dickie, 1965; Ekman, 1970; Gould, 1994; Lang, 1964; and Meager, 1965.) As others have noted (most recently, Jeffrey Dean [1996]), Bell seems to validate his own commitment to the moral value of aesthetic experience by appealing to Moore's ethics, tenuous though his grasp of that may be. (Dean and William Bywater have questioned the depth of Bell's understanding of Moore.)

Although Bell's work clearly owes much to its philosophical milieu, it emerges equally from his passionate involvement with art, especially the art of his contemporaries. He draws on Cambridge philosophy at least in part to articulate a theoretical foundation for his defense, not to say virtual deification, of those artists moving toward abstraction and his denigration of those aiming for physical or psychological verisimilitude. As a critic and a collaborator with Roger Fry on the 1910 and 1912 Post-Impressionist exhibitions, he worked assiduously to transform the public sensibility, to reveal the genius of such artists as Paul Cézanne, Pablo Picasso, Henri Matisse, and Duncan Grant to admirers of academic art, of sentimentalized art, and to those who saw the Renaissance as the pinnacle of artistic progress.

Thus, Bell takes as aesthetically inconsequential representational content, ethical significance, psychological penetration, and technical virtuosity; however helpful this last quality may be in producing aesthetic interest, he disparages the mere "illusionists and masters of craft," "the virtuosi . . . who might have been artists if painting had not absorbed all their energies . . . setting themselves technical acrostics and solving them," these along with the "dunces" whom he counts as most of the artists "who flourished between the high Renaissance and the contemporary movement." Bell's critical assessments and art-historical analyses (some considered eccentric) arise from his formalism, the

key to which is his distinctive idea of significant form as the defining element of an artwork or aesthetic object.

Conceptually, Bell's theory rests on three axioms, two explicit, the third not: (1) He begins from a frankly experiential claim that sensitive people respond to artworks with a phenomenologically unique kind of experience. He calls this the "aesthetic emotion," an infelicitous term because he construes it more as a perception than as an emotion, as demonstrated in Carol Gould (1994). (2) He assumes that all such experiences arise from the same sort of quality, which must be the essence, the "quality common and peculiar to" an artwork. (3) In delineating this essential feature, he implicitly presumes a clear distinction between the form and the content of a work of art. All three beliefs—in the existence of the aesthetic experience, in essence, and in the form/content distinction—have faced virulent attacks in the twentieth century, but such assaults have not been aimed specifically at Bell's theory.

More problematic for Bell in particular and more philosophically intriguing is his notion of significant form as the essential feature of artworks. Significant form is what elicits the aesthetic experience, but it exists in the work independently of the viewer. For Bell, aesthetic experience differs from ordinary experience, and significant form is rooted in properties peripheral, if anything, to everyday life. He describes it as arising from "relations and combinations of lines and colours," "lines and colours combined in a particular way, certain forms and relations of forms [that] stir our aesthetic emotions." To put it more technically, significant form supervenes on the formal—and only the formal—elements of an artwork. Bell avers that an even inspired copy of an artwork can possess significant form and move the viewer no less than the original (1914, pp. 49–50). For Bell, the aesthetic nature and value of a work are so detached from its cultural, historical, and personal origins that he would have to grant that a well-executed forgery of, say, a Cézanne, would be equal in value to an original. Significant form is internal to the work and, as he often observes, no historical, biographical, or psychological knowledge from life is needed to grasp this aesthetic property.

One discerns significant form noninferentially, immediately, and intuitively. One may see the lines, colors, and shapes visually, but must focus on them and their relations in order to have an intuitive grasp of significant form.

The responsible critic guides the viewer to this discernment by perspicuously describing the formal properties of an artwork. This may dispose one to detect more readily significant form. The good critic might be compared to an astute music teacher who helps a student develop a sense of pitch by drawing the student's attention to subtle differences in the same note executed several times on a violin. If the student is tone-deaf or limited in capacity, however, years of training will prove futile. Bell seems to think that most people do have aesthetic sensibilities that can be cultivated, but he clearly does not think that nature has endowed them equally with aesthetic powers. Bell's appeal to an aesthetic sensibility has opened him up to the charge of elitism (see Lang, 1964, for example). But he views aesthetic obtuseness as more recalcitrant than irreversible: it is recalcitrant because the viewer so directly looks to the psychological, moral, representational, historical, or literary features of an artwork and disregards the fact that art is not about "human business and passion . . . the chatter and tumult of material existence."

What, then, is art about? Significant form, for Bell, does, in an important sense, *signify.* As he explains in his metaphysical hypothesis, significant form represents some ultimate reality. In some passages, he seems to mean by *reality* a visual reality stripped of interpretation, a reality that evokes the aesthetic response in the artist, who represents it for us. In other passages, however, he seems to construe *reality* in a plainly romanticist sense as that "which lies behind the appearance of all things—that which gives to all things their individual significance, the thing in itself, the ultimate reality." One cannot help but conclude that the urgency of Bell's practical concerns made him construct rather hastily the metaphysics that he thought necessary to undergird his aesthetic theory.

In any case, if one allows that Cézanne, Giovanni Cimabue, and the Ravenna mosaicists all represent ultimate reality (whatever that may be) by means of significant form, Bell then has his own riddle of style. Given especially Bell's ahistorical approach to art, how does one account for the different stylistic idioms for conveying significant form? Bell himself seems inchoately aware of this matter, for he introduces, and in his later works develops, his notion of "the artistic problem" and the correlative "artistic conventions" that are necessary to give contour to the artist's vision. As Thomas M. McLaughlin (1977) insightfully argues, Bell does evince (especially in his more mature work) considerable sensitivity to the importance of artistic traditions.

Interestingly, in affirming the "absolute necessity" of artistic conventions, Bell uses a literary example (1914, p. 51). This leads one to wonder whether Bell is offering a unified aesthetic theory designed to cover all of the arts. His notion of significant form applies easily to music, arguably nonrepresentational by nature; in fact, Bell refers to his own occasional oblivion to significant form in music. But literature poses special problems for Bell's theory, for it is an art of language, which by nature represents. Moreover, much literature derives some value from its dread ethical dimension. In *Art,* Bell betrays some ambivalence about significant form in literature, making such remarks as "Literature is never pure art" (1914, p. 107), but then "In great poetry it is the formal music that makes the miracle" (p. 110). He never specifies the literary correlates of such visual elements as line and color, yet he insinuates that they exist. This is even more evident in his widely, and perhaps justly, ignored work on Proust (1928).

Undeniably, the most serious charge against Bell's theory is the traditional objection that it is circular. Bell, his critics allege, defines significant form as that which causes the aesthetic emotion and the aesthetic emotion as that experience caused by significant form. The problem, discussed most incisively by Noël Carroll (1989), entails that the theory is unfalsifiable. Could one have a nonveridical aesthetic experience, as one might, say, a visual experience of red? Various tests can confirm whether the appropriate sort of object is causing a person's sensation of red. But how can one test for significant form? Presumably, Bell would respond, by the aesthetic emotion. Although this criticism, if cogent, would be a damaging indictment of his theory, Bell has been variously defended against it (for example, by Ekman [1970], Meager [1965], Bywater [1975], and Gould [1994]). Bell's theory has also raised questions about the logical status of an aesthetic theory, an issue on which Beryl Lake (1954) reflects.

Bell's theory, though beset with problems and long superseded by more sophisticated versions of formalism, remains engaging and philosophically compelling. However many dimensions one might find worth examining in an artwork—historical, psychoanalytical, ethical—one cannot read Bell's impassioned *Art* and some of his more carefully wrought critical essays without speculating on whether the aesthetic is one of those dimensions and whether it indeed has more value for human life than it is now fashionable to think. Bell also forces one to consider the very nature of the artistic enterprise. He was eager to deflate the idea that the painter should be "either a photographer or an acrobat." Today, the question must be framed differently. In his 1948 "Preface to New Edition" of *Art,* Bell unfairly, and with some embarrassment, ascribed to his youthful work mainly historical interest. But its author's vitality, range of questions, and insistence on connecting philosophical aesthetics to the art world have all earned it a central place in the philosophical canon rightly denied to other texts with more rigor and less ardor.

[*See also* Bloomsbury Group; Definition of Art; Essentialism; *and* Formalism, *overview article.*]

BIBLIOGRAPHY

Works by Bell

Art. London, 1914; reprint, New York, 1958.
Since Cezanne. London, 1922; reprint, Freeport, N.Y., 1969.
Civilization: An Essay and Old Friends. Chicago, 1973. Both published originally in 1928 and 1956, respectively.
Proust. London, 1928.

Other Sources

Bell, Quentin. *Bloomsbury Recalled.* New York, 1995.
Bywater, William G., Jr. *Clive Bell's Eye.* Detroit, 1975.
Carroll, Noël. "Clive Bell's Aesthetic Hypothesis." In *Aesthetics: A Critical Anthology,* 2d ed., edited by George Dickie, Robert Sclafani, and Ronald Roblin, pp. 84–95. New York, 1989.

Dean, Jeffrey T. "Clive Bell and G. E. Moore: The Good of Art." *British Journal of Aesthetics* 36 (1996): 135–145.

Dickie, George T. "Clive Bell and the Method of *Principia Ethica.*" *British Journal of Aesthetics* 5 (1965): 139–143.

Ekman, Rosalind. "The Paradoxes of Formalism." *British Journal of Aesthetics* 10 (1970): 350–358.

Fishman, Solomon. *The Interpretation of Art: Essays on the Art Criticism of John Ruskin, Walter Pater, Clive Bell, Roger Fry, and Herbert Read.* Berkeley, 1963.

Gould, Carol S. "Clive Bell on Aesthetic Experience and Aesthetic Truth." *British Journal of Aesthetics* 34 (1994): 124–133.

Laing, Donald A. *Clive Bell: An Annotated Bibliography of the Published Writings.* New York, 1983.

Lake, Beryl. "A Study of the Irrefutability of Two Aesthetic Theories." In *Aesthetics and Language,* edited by William Elton. Oxford, 1954.

Lang, Berel. "Intuition on Bloomsbury." *Journal of the History of Ideas* 25 (1964): 295–302.

McLaughlin, Thomas M. "Clive Bell's Aesthetic: Tradition and Significant Form." *Journal of Aesthetics and Art Criticism* 35 (1977): 433–443.

Meager, Ruby. "Clive Bell and Aesthetic Emotion." *British Journal of Aesthetics* 5 (1965): 123–131.

Read, Herbert. "Clive Bell." *British Journal of Aesthetics* 5 (1965): 107–110.

Schork, R. J. "Additions to the Bibliographies of Clive Bell, E. M. Forster, and Virginia Woolf." *Notes and Queries* 39 (1992): 194–196.

CAROL GOULD

BENJAMIN, WALTER. [*To clarify the aesthetics implicit in Benjamin's literary and critical theory: this entry comprises three essays:*

Survey of Thought
Benjamin and Surrealism
Benjamin's Writing Style

The first essay is a survey of his thought in general, and his role in the Frankfurt School tradition of critical theory. The second is a discussion of a particular art movement—Surrealism—that is important in understanding his aesthetics. The third is an analysis of (a) his writing style as an integral, if difficult, part of his thought and (b) the philosophy of language that underlies his aesthetics.]

Survey of Thought

Walter Benjamin (1892–1940), an early twentieth-century German philosopher and critical theorist. Although his career was marked by numerous false starts and failed ambitions, and cut tragically short by the rise of National Socialism, Benjamin's work nevertheless has proved to be pathbreaking for a wide range of contemporary currents of literary theory and criticism.

Born into a well-to-do assimilated Jewish family in Berlin in 1892, Benjamin was sent to the most progressive schools, and early on became a significant figure in the German-Jewish wing of the short-lived German Youth Movement in the years leading to World War I. Many of his earliest published essays are impassioned appeals to "Youth" as a meta-physical category of spiritual purity and historical consciousness. Benjamin's thought developed in an intellectual milieu of secular German Jews who consciously rejected the assimilationist mentality of their bourgeois parents, plunging themselves into radical intellectual and political currents of various kinds: into a newly recovered Judaism, often with deeply existentialist motifs, reacting to the soullessness and rationalism of the earlier generation; into Zionism and communism as political alternatives to the perceived failure of the liberal versus illiberal political dyad; and, increasingly, into newly emerging forms of radical cultural criticism.

By the early 1920s, Benjamin had written a sober dissertation on the genesis of the concept of literary criticism in the German early Romanticism, essays on Friedrich Hölderlin, Fyodor Dostoyevsky, on the ontology of language and philosophy, and a brilliant study of Johann Wolfgang von Goethe's novel "Elective Affinities." In the early 1920s Benjamin labored on his *Habilitationsschrift*, or second scholarly dissertation, a full-length study of the forgotten and reviled genre of German Baroque *Trauerspiel* or "mourning-play," with which he hoped to win a place in the university. The book, *The Origin of German Tragic Drama*, was a brilliant, eccentric, often impenetrable work of literary criticism, in which Benjamin argued against seeing the awkward and overblown German dramas of the seventeenth century as degenerate or failed forms of classical tragedy, and insisted instead that the distinctness and autonomy of the genre had to be rescued from its oblivion within the context of a falsely progressive literary history. Applying a distinction that he had developed in his earlier work, Benjamin began with a historical "commentary" on the contextual situation of the "ruined" genre of *Trauerspiel*, arguing that the concrete historical experiences of the seventeenth century—general war, extreme physical violence and ruin, and a deep crisis in traditional conceptions of sovereignty—formed the necessary context and material for the genre of the *Trauerspiel*, its dramatic action, its characterology, its grammar and diction, and ultimately the melancholic typology that determined the image of creative authority for the genre. Having reconstructed the historicity of the genre and thus freed it from being seen as a degenerate form of tragedy, the second half of the study turned to "critique": moving from history to theology, Benjamin recovers the theological essence of the genre of *Trauerspiel*. Focusing on the genre's use of allegorical practice, Benjamin argues that allegory—in which one thing "stands for" another by the conventional assignation of meaning—provides a portal to glimpse a foundational crisis of meaning and subjectivity, the specter of an arbitrary and hence meaningless subjective existence, and the implicit promise of God's redemptive return. In the image of the corpse, so prevalent in the exaggerated violence of the *Trauerspiel*'s dramatic action, Benjamin finds a final allegory in which the dead body, at once subject and object, "means" the very meaninglessness of allegorical intention itself and hence reverses itself—the corpse, in the Counter-Reformation dramas, becomes the material signifier of the promise of eternal life. Hence, the "origin" or "primal leap" (*Ur-sprung*) of the genre is the graphic image as the theological core of the dramas. The image, as Idea, is precisely what is constructed, via redemptive criticism, from out of the constellation of fragments of text that are wrested from their consignment to literary oblivion, and exists not in the dramas themselves but in the redemptive moment that obtains between the concrete historical moment of the seventeenth-century dramas and Benjamin's own time.

The rejection of *The Origin of German Tragic Drama* at the University of Frankfurt led to the final ruin of Benjamin's academic plans, and for the remainder of his life he would earn an unsteady living as an occasional reviewer and essayist, from the sale of books, and, in exile, from a tiny stipend paid by the Institute for Social Research in New York. Already in the mid-1920s, however, Benjamin had begun moving away from the highly esoteric and theological language of his early works under the influence of Marxist theories of literary production. Throughout the second half of the 1920s and into the 1930s, Benjamin's typically iconoclastic reading of Marxist theory (with little interest in political economy, Benjamin appears to have read Marx virtually entirely as a theory of culture and as a doctrine of political decision) fueled the project of producing a genuinely materialist version of literary criticism. Signal works such as *One-Way Street and Other Writings,* a collection of lapidary essays, glosses, and observations on his own Weimar-era Berlin, essays on Surrealism, Bertolt Brecht, and "The Author as Producer" challenged the traditional institution of literature and demanded an integration of the category of literary production (and literary criticism) into the broader context of social production. (Although Benjamin never joined the Communist Party, he never rejected the basic premises of historical materialism, but typically transformed them in ways that would have been quite foreign to a doctrinaire Marxist.) At the same time, Benjamin's early theological and esoteric notions of language and history, far from eliminated, were increasingly incorporated into his critical work. The result was a distinctive, indeed inimitable, critical practice in which cultural formations—not only literary works, but increasingly the marginal and indeed the trivial cultural products of society—could be regarded both as textualities containing the physiognomy of capitalist modernity within them in encoded form and as precious and unique expressions of a "truth content" demanding recognition and redemption in their own right.

The 1930s saw influential essays on Marcel Proust, Franz Kafka, Karl Kraus, Brecht, and other literary figures; radio plays; essays on photography, film, and contemporary theater; and keenly observed autobiographical sketches. After relocating to Paris following the National Socialist seizure

of power, Benjamin spent the remainder of his life laboring on what was to be his central work: tentatively titled the *Passagen Werk* or the "Arcades Project," it was to have been a study of the cultural, literary, and cognitive prehistory of capitalist modernity, and was named after the Parisian arcades, the protomalls of the mid-nineteenth century in which the earliest uses of iron and glass as architectural and design elements combined to form private galleries, cutting straight through city blocks, as showcases for new commodities. The project's complex theoretical framework was intended to disappear invisibly beneath the surface of the text, which was to have consisted virtually entirely of a careful, montage-like construction of quotations and excerpts, descriptions, observations, and historical data. Taken as a whole, such a construction out of facts would, according to Benjamin's intention, capture the gradual rise of capitalism as a "dreamtime," as a form of mythic thralldom in which the extraordinary creativity of capitalist production gave rise to new cultural forms. By satisfying the imperative for perpetual newness, theses forms in fact served to renew or re-present archaic collective fantasies and images. Benjamin hoped to show that this "dreamtime" of the commodity culture, if traced to its political and geographical heart (to its *Ursprung*), could be revealed as containing the elements for a possible revolutionary wakening as well as the mythic or dreamlike perpetuation of the ever-the-same. In the very phantasmagorical apparitions of high capitalism, Benjamin thought, in the moments of relatively unguarded—hence, unintentionally critical—self-reflection such as panoramas, world exhibitions, utopian fantasies, advertisements, gambling and prostitution, and the like, the nineteenth century revealed the dialectical relation between newness and the primally old, and hence revealed the commodity itself as a site in which collective wishes and fantasies (for example, for material abundance or a world without fear) were both graphically represented and yet denied any possibility for real, collective fulfillment. The "Arcades Project" was to have constructed such "sites" for the graphic disclosure (or self-disclosure) of the phantasmagoric aspect of capitalist modernity, sites whose graphicness and concreteness led Benjamin to describe them as *dialectical images.* This term—half methodological practice, half theological event of mystical disclosure of a concrete moment of the past—has rightly come to be regarded as a central, if centrally ambiguous, component of Benjamin's practice of cultural criticism.

As readers such as Susan Buck-Morss (1989) have described, Benjamin's interest in the Parisian Arcades centered on the transformation of their status as they declined, from the height of urban fashion to their tawdry twilight as refuges for cheap consumer goods, disreputable and transitory businesses, and prostitution in the decades prior to their disappearance in the massive urban projects of Baron von Haussmann in the 1860s. Benjamin's insight was that *dialectical images* could be constructed, as in a montage, out of the very material that capitalism consigned to oblivion—the shopworn and forgotten stuff of everyday use, bric-a-brac, out-of-fashion styles, and slightly antiquated commodities. This insight focused critical attention for the first time on the curious fact that the aging of commodities also established them as moments of critical resistance to capitalism itself—a fact, as Benjamin points out, that was first recognized by the Surrealists but that needed to be transposed from artistic insurrection to the practice of historical materialist criticism. Margaret Cohen (1993) explores the concrete use Benjamin made of the Surrealists, the manner in which he gradually made Surrealist practice central to his own understanding of critical activity, and the way in which this adoption determined the contours of the "Arcades Project."

Much of Benjamin's best work from the 1930s was written either as direct or indirect efforts to contribute to the "Arcades Project": essays on Baudelaire and "Paris, Capital of the Nineteenth Century" were meant as précis of the project; other works, such as the famous essay "The Work of Art in the Age of Mechanical Reproduction," were written with the "Arcades Project" directly in mind, as ways of clarifying Benjamin's theoretical convictions. Yet, the "Arcades Project" itself never appeared. Amassing an ever-increasing treasure trove of meticulously cross-referenced notes and material (the notes to the project, published as the two-part fifth volume of Benjamin's collected works in German, run to well over a thousand closely printed pages), Benjamin was increasingly unable to wrestle the mass of material into a single coherent text. Impoverished and increasingly vulnerable, he nevertheless refused to leave the city that he regarded as the only possible source for his work. Having delayed his flight from Paris until 1940, Benjamin was briefly confined at an internment camp in France and, on his release, attempted to flee to Spain in preparation for his arranged emigration to the United States. Detained at the Spanish border without proper papers, Benjamin took his own life in September 1940. His last work, the "Theses on the Philosophy of History" (in *Illuminations*), written in confinement, marks a profound return to the overt theology of his earlier, "pre-Marxist" work in the context of an apocalyptic Marxism. The theses demand a form of materialist historical criticism that will constitute a redemptive struggle for the "oppressed past" as it summons a revolution understood as an apocalyptic break with historical time, and call for a form of remembrance that will resist the Fascist horror by forming an unbreakable solidarity with the generations of the oppressed. The theses thus reaffirm Benjamin's oldest concerns—the juxtaposition of the time of history with the time of redemption in images of ruin, devastation, and an infinitely postponed redemption of the material world; the creative tension between Marxism and Jewish theology; the shocking disclosure of literature as a hidden repository

of historical truth; a love of the historical detail and the fragment; the summoning forth of suppressed powers of collective remembrance under the sign of historical justice. In the rightly famous ninth thesis, Benjamin describes a "Klee painting named *Angelus Novus*" (which Benjamin himself owned and to which he attached a deep personal significance), which

> shows an angel looking as though he is about to move away from something he is fixedly contemplating. His eyes are staring, his mouth is open, his wings are spread. This is how one pictures the angel of history. His face is turned toward the past. Where we perceive a chain of events, he sees one single catastrophe which keeps piling wreckage upon wreckage and hurls it in front of his feet. The angel would like to stay, awaken the dead, and make whole what has been smashed. But a storm is blowing from Paradise; it has got caught in his wings with such violence that the angel can no longer close them. This storm irresistibly propels him into the future to which his back is turned, while the pile of debris before him grows skyward. This storm is what we call progress.
> (Benjamin, 1968, pp. 257–258)

Images such as this one are "critical" in a way that fulfills Benjamin's earlier ambition: insofar as one is still capable of being moved (struck) by them, one recognizes that they insist on a criticism that has re-created itself as a genre—but not necessarily a genre that one can or ought to transform into a new school of thought. Like so many of Benjamin's texts, the image is utterly sui generis, and it may well be this that Benjamin had in mind.

As stated earlier, Benjamin's crucial intellectual influences are to be found in a distinctive cultural milieu in which the children of the assimilated German-Jewish middle class sought to express their own recognition of the soullessness of contemporary society and the failure of the assimilationist ideal by the appropriation of a number of currents of radical thought: Zionism, Marxism, Jewish mysticism, anarchism, *Lebensphilosophie,* and neo-Romanticism. Although Benjamin was clearly a product of this milieu of radical thought, his reception of it left its various traditions transformed utterly. Like peers such as Ernst Bloch, Benjamin saw Jewish theology and literary Romanticism as traditions that provided the conceptual tools both for a radical critical confrontation with cultural modernity and for new forms of literary critique. In his early philosophy of language, for example, Benjamin made open use of theological categories such as the Fall, and of an "Adamic" originary language of pure signification, sketching out a boldly speculative theory meant both as a critique of the decay of language into a mere instrumental mode of communication within rationalized, industrialized modern civilization and as a foundation for a style of literary criticism that would be based on an ontology of language. So too Benjamin's lifelong notion of historical time: borrowing from Judaic notions of messianic time, exile, rupture, and catastrophe, Benjamin developed a powerful critique of the prevailing ideology of historical progress and insisted instead on a messianic model of historical time in which a continuum of mythic repetition and fixity was, under the critical gaze, revealed to be seeded with "chips of messianic time," as he would put it in his last work, the "Theses on the Philosophy of History" (Benjamin, 1968, p. 263), moments of discontinuity or rupture in the mythic continuum of repetition that marked sites of sudden legibility between a present and a concrete, material past. The recovery and representation of such moments of rupture, contained monadically in what Benjamin would later refer to as *dialectical images,* formed the core of a deeply theological sense of "redemptive criticism."

Along with Benjamin's lifelong interest in an ontology of language and a messianic conception of historical time, a third aspect should be mentioned, although it is much harder to characterize: Benjamin's persistent and utterly idiosyncratic materialism, his fascination with things, which entered into a highly unusual constellation with his theological concerns. Benjamin's deep interest in the material level of cultural history led early on to his theories concerning the materiality of the signifying process in Baroque allegory, and would in his mature writings emerge as a startlingly literal reading of "dialectical materialism." His most powerful critical works (for example, his essays on Charles Baudelaire) pay particular attention to the interactions between poetic form and the range of material objects in which the text is embedded. His work on the Parisian Arcades constitutes the attempt to marshal a fascination with ornament, detail, fragment, junk, collections, and the entire tide of material existence of a newly emerging commodity economy into a new form of critical reading, in which the range of objects themselves—and above all the small, lost, or insignificant objects—appears as the enciphered text of capitalist modernity. Parallel with Benjamin's material fascination is a rejection of argumentative, and indeed conceptual, thought in favor of imagistic thinking and graphic description, a practice that imparts a distinctive sense of concreteness and often a magical sense of surprise and fascination to his texts themselves.

"The goal I have set for myself," Benjamin wrote in 1930, ". . . is that I be considered the foremost critic of German literature. The problem is that literary criticism is no longer considered a serious genre in Germany and has not been for more than fifty years. If you want to carve out a reputation in the area of criticism, this ultimately means that you must recreate criticism as a genre" (Benjamin, 1994, p. 359). This startlingly ambitious self-definition is utterly characteristic of Benjamin's extraordinary career as a literary critic, theorist, and essayist. It was a career marked as much by the unlikely theoretical and cultural traditions that Benjamin drew from—and that often remained in open antagonism with one another in his work—as by Benjamin's success in re-creating the genre of criticism. Even the context in which Benjamin's claim is made contains in minia-

ture the kinds of theoretical and personal polarities that underlie both his remarkable creativity as a theorist and stylist and the odd, occasionally frustrating scope of his mature work as a critic: it comes in a letter, in French, written to his great lifelong friend Gershom Scholem, as a way of justifying Benjamin's final refusal to fulfill an old promise to emigrate to Palestine and begin an intensive confrontation with Jewish thought, in favor of his decision to remain in Europe and continue his iconoclastic critique of the cultural origins of capitalist modernity, a project theoretically underwritten by (among others) Karl Marx, Sigmund Freud, Surrealism, and a good deal of esoteric theological speculation.

Moreover, Benjamin's confidence that he was indeed revolutionizing the genre of criticism did not ignore, but in fact seems to have depended on, his own understanding of the extent of his previous failures measured against the conventional criteria of the professional literary scholar. By 1930, Benjamin had failed in his attempt at an academic career and had seen most of his grand projects for essays, books, and journals end without publication; a noted and respected literary reviewer and essayist, he would nevertheless hardly have been regarded as a likely candidate as the "foremost critic of German literature." His personal life was in ruins, and he had been largely unsuccessful in his efforts to align himself with more established persons or schools of critical thought in Germany and France. By 1930, Benjamin was eking out a meager living as a professional journalist and book reviewer for the better Weimar left-oriented publications, and within a few short years he would settle into an uneasy and impoverished exile in Paris, where he would spend his remaining years laboring on his never-completed magnum opus, in English usually referred to as the "Arcades Project," a Sisyphean task that would keep him in Paris until just after the last possible moment for escape. Refused passage into Spain, Benjamin committed suicide in the border village of Port Bou in the Pyrenees in 1940, as he fled agents of the Gestapo.

Although he failed utterly to accomplish his goal in his lifetime, Benjamin has in fact surpassed even its most ambitious side in the posthumous reception of his works. More than a half century after his death, he is widely regarded as the most original and influential German literary critic of the twentieth century. Since the first readily available collections of his essays were published in German in the 1950s, his reputation has steadily grown; the contemporary academic world has dedicated a veritable mountain of publications to him and his work, with no end in sight. Moreover, Benjamin's popularity cuts across disciplinary boundaries that otherwise are quite tightly patrolled in contemporary scholarship. He has long been a central figure in the critical social theory of the Frankfurt School, and his Marxist works of the 1920s and 1930s are canonical for critical social theory. His earlier essays on language, translation, and figures such as Goethe and Hölderlin have become deeply influential in the fields of contemporary literary criticism; his notion of allegory and its connection to the "natural history" of ruin and fragmentation remain vital sources for literary deconstruction, as in the work of Paul de Man. Benjamin's later work on media and the transformation of modes of experience in modern urban life, on the material aspects of modernity, and on the dominative aspect of literary and historical traditions have made him an important source of inspiration for the nascent field of cultural studies.

At the same time, however, the posthumous achievement of Benjamin's programmatic ambition—to be recognized as the foremost critic of German literature—is double-edged, as Benjamin's own rather deliberately ambiguous formulation already implies. Although Benjamin is indeed so recognized, there is little consensus among contemporary readers of his work as to how his achievement should be understood. His influence is still growing for contemporary literary theory (and not just in Germany), but Benjamin did not leave behind any coherent or consistent theoretical approach. Although he has become one of the most cited and imitated writers of his age, he left behind no school, no doctrine, and (with the possible exception of Theodor W. Adorno) no disciple. In effect, his 1930 prediction has come true, but in a distinctly Benjaminian fashion: not at all the way even he would have expected, and in a manner that calls into deep question the historical nature of the terms—*criticism,* above all—in which the prediction was made. There is no "Benjaminian" reading of a contemporary literary text or cultural formation, no one brand or variety of critical praxis that would serve to define what a new, Benjaminian criticism would be. In this sense, Benjamin's achievement came about, characteristically, via a combination of personal skill and imagination, or character, and of the vagaries of the many historical processes of transmission, loss, deferral, misinterpretation, and accident by which texts, critical no less than literary, detach themselves from their authors and their ambitions and intentions to reemerge in a present that interprets them in its own light according to its own needs. The contemporary reception of Benjamin, in other words, fulfills one of Benjamin's own most deeply held convictions: there is no progressive history of art or art criticism, but there is a historical phenomenon of loss, recognition, and transformation; texts are not ageless, but rather, one can first discern the truth content of the work as one observes the process in which it ages and decays, and in which the concrete concerns of a particular period of the past can, through a critical reception, win an unexpected and explosive relevance for the present.

BIBLIOGRAPHY

Works by Benjamin in English Translation

Charles Baudelaire: A Lyric Poet in the Era of High Capitalism. Translated by Harry Zohn. London, 1973.

The Correspondence of Walter Benjamin, 1910–1940. Edited by Gershom Scholem and Theodor W. Adorno, translated by Manfred R. Jacobson and Evelyn M. Jacobson. Chicago, 1994.
Illuminations: Essays and Reflections. Edited by Hannah Arendt, translated by Harry Zohn. New York, 1968; reprint, New York, 1969.
One-Way Street and Other Writings. Translated by Edmund Jephcott and Kingsley Shorter. London, 1979.
The Origin of German Tragic Drama. Translated by John Osborne. London, 1977.
Reflections: Essays, Aphorisms, Autobiographical Writings. Edited by Peter Demetz, translated by Edmund Jephcott. New York, 1978.
Selected Writings, vol. 1, 1913–1926. Edited by Marcus Bullock and Michael W. Jennings. Cambridge, Mass., 1996.
Understanding Brecht. Translated by Anna Bostock. London, 1973.

Other Sources

Buck-Morss, Susan. *The Dialectics of Seeing: Walter Benjamin and the Arcades Project.* Cambridge, Mass., 1989.
Cohen, Margaret. *Profane Illumination: Walter Benjamin and the Paris of Surrealist Revolution.* Berkeley, 1993.
Eagleton, Terry. *Walter Benjamin: or, Towards a Revolutionary Criticism.* London, 1981.
Handelman, Susan A. *Fragments of Redemption: Jewish Thought and Literary Theory in Benjamin, Scholem, and Levinas.* Bloomington, Ind., 1991.
Jennings, Michael W. *Dialectical Images: Walter Benjamin's Theory of Literary Criticism.* Ithaca, N.Y., 1987.
McCole, John. *Walter Benjamin and the Antinomies of Tradition.* Ithaca, N.Y., 1993.
Mehlman, Jeffrey. *Walter Benjamin for Children: An Essay on His Radio Years.* Chicago, 1993.
Pensky, Max. *Melancholy Dialectics: Walter Benjamin and the Play of Mourning.* Amherst, Mass., 1993.
Scholem, Gershom. *Walter Benjamin: The Story of a Friendship.* Translated by Harry Zohn. Philadelphia, 1981; reprint, London, 1982.
Smith, Gary, ed. *On Walter Benjamin: Critical Essays and Recollections.* Cambridge, Mass., 1988.
Witte, Berndt. *Walter Benjamin: An Intellectual Biography.* Translated by James Rolleston. Detroit, 1991.
Wolin, Richard. *Walter Benjamin: An Aesthetic of Redemption.* New York, 1982; reprint, Berkeley, 1994.

MAX PENSKY

Benjamin and Surrealism

Walter Benjamin placed an engagement with Surrealism at the core of the "cycle of production" that was to occupy him from the late 1920s until his death in 1940 (Benjamin, 1994, p. 322). In this cycle, Benjamin sought to untangle the interrelations among economic modes of production, aesthetics, politics, technology, mass culture, and everyday life, particularly its phantasmic dimensions, characterizing high capitalist modernity; Benjamin understood high capitalism predominantly in Frankfurt Marxist terms.

Benjamin's cycle on high capitalist modernity was inaugurated by *One-Way Street,* his "first attempt to come to terms with" Paris (ibid., p. 325). He pursued this attempt in the cycle's centerpiece: the uncompleted work on nineteenth-century Paris whose existing notes and fragments have been published as *Das Passagen Werk* (the Arcades Project). Benjamin wrote two résumés of the Arcades Project, in 1935 and 1939, and their common title sums up the intellectual grounds for his choice to focus his study of high capitalism on Paris: "Paris, Capital of the Nineteenth Century." In 1928, Benjamin told Gershom Scholem that to overcome "an all too ostentatious proximity to the surrealist movement [that] might become fatal," the Arcades Project would need to "take possession of the *inheritance* of surrealism . . . with all the authority of a philosophical Fortinbras" (ibid., p. 342). In 1935, Benjamin was still grappling with the Arcades Project's relation to the inheritance of Surrealism: "The work represents . . . the philosophical application of surrealism—and thereby its sublation" (ibid., p. 505).

The diverse aspects of Surrealism's contribution to Benjamin's high capitalist cycle of production all turn around Benjamin's interest in the fundamental Surrealist moment of "unchaining" (*désenchaînement*) or, as it was also called, the "encounter," to use the term of the movement's leader, André Breton. In this moment, Surrealist activity succeeded in dismantling some aspect of the dominant order (whether ideological, aesthetic, political, or epistemological) by bringing together pieces of this order that the reigning conceptual structures habitually held apart. The Surrealists understood it to release restorative hidden forces, which they conceptualized in psychic and/or collective terms: as repressed libidinal energy and/or as oppressed social classes or groups. Bringing to light occulted, highly charged energy that was potentially simultaneously constructive and destructive, Surrealist unchaining shared much with the notion of the uncanny that Sigmund Freud had articulated in a 1921 essay of the same name (Breton, moreover, played an important role in introducing Freud's writings into France). Benjamin's term for the Surrealist moment of disruption was the *profane illumination* in his 1929 "Surrealism, the Last Snapshot of the European Intelligentsia."

Benjamin made use of the Surrealist profane illumination in a number of ways. Most frequently, critics have commented on his rhetorical interest in Surrealist aesthetic strategies. "After you, my beautiful language," wrote Breton, and Benjamin too sought to harness the disruptive powers of the signifier in order to dismantle the clichés of bourgeois poetics. Like the Surrealists, Benjamin explored the rhetorical effect of poetic "encounters," what Breton called "the light of the image" that flashed from "the fortuitous juxtaposition" of two seemingly incompatible terms (Breton, 1969, p. 37). Like the Surrealists, Benjamin also pursued the disruptive encounter in a fashion that went beyond the Dada and Constructivist avant-gardes' understandings of montage as conflict, collision, and opposition. As Max Ernst's collages in *Une semaine de bonté* and *La femme cent têtes* demonstrate, in Surrealist montage the disjunctive pieces not only collide but also create uncanny, new syntheses nowhere available in everyday experience.

Benjamin's engagement with the Surrealist encounter permeated his thinking as well as his rhetorical practice. At a time when other European avant-gardes (the German Bauhaus, the Soviet Constructivists, the Dutch De Stijl, L'Esprit Nouveau in France) were glorying in the power and beauty of modernity, Surrealism was drawn to junk, kitsch, cultural debris, the outmoded. Arguably the first postmodernists, the Surrealists staged the encounter of high art with the low, whether the low took the form of tawdry mass culture, urban sites that were the location of marginal social activity, or the fleeting, liminal psychological states of everyday life.

Benjamin seized the full importance of the Surrealist fascination with cultural debris, with "everything that we have experienced on mournful railways journeys (railways are beginning to age), on Godforsaken Sunday afternoons in the proletarian quarters of the great cities, in the first glance through the rain-blurred window of a new apartment" (1978, "Surrealism," p. 182). "No one before these visionaries and augurs perceived how destitution—not only social but architectonic, the poverty of interiors, enslaved and enslaving objects—can be suddenly transformed into revolutionary nihilism" (ibid., pp. 181–182). Benjamin understood this fascination as part of Surrealism's liberating destruction of the clichés of bourgeois society, which ranged well beyond the bourgeoisie's paradigm of beauty to include its humanist notions of the subject and freedom; its allegiance to technology, scientific objectivity, and historical progress; and the general privilege it accorded the new. "Balzac was the first to speak of the ruins of the bourgeoisie. But only Surrealism exposed them to view" (1978, "Paris," p. 161).

The "profane illumination did not always find the surrealists equal to it," was Benjamin's opinion and he represented himself as providing the sustained materialist critique of the bourgeois ideologemes that Surrealist nihilism uncovered in fits and starts (1978, "Surrealism," p. 179). One successful example of this critique is Benjamin's expansion of the Surrealist interest in decay and debris. In the Arcades Project, Benjamin discusses in depth early cultural expressions of high capitalist modernity that once were state-of-the-art but now seem quaint, if not dilapidated (the arcades, the panoramas, the daguerreotype, the first World's Fairs, utopian socialism). In doing so, he shows how innovation and the outmoded are two faces of the modern ideology of novelty, which itself is an effect of the commodity form. If commodity fetishism reifies a relation among people as a relation among inorganic things, novelty is one primary way in which the members of commodity society experience that reification. Novelty "is the quintessence of false consciousness, whose indefatigable agent is fashion," Benjamin asserts, and he cites Charles Baudelaire's demystifying the fascination with the inorganic underlying the lure of novelty in the last poem of *Les fleurs du mal:* "Oh death, old captain, it is time, let us weigh anchor . . . To the depths of the unknown, there to find something new" (1978, "Paris," 157).

Another Surrealist dimension to Benjamin's excavation of high capitalist modernity is the material from which he planned to construct his own Parisian arcades. "I won't filch anything of value. . . . Only the trivia, the trash" (Benjamin, 1989, pp. N, 1a, 8). Thus, when Benjamin sought to understand the way in which the commodity structure affected the artwork, he focused on commercial art forms like photography, rather than on painting, the medium that was at the top of the fine arts hierarchy in the nineteenth century (see, for example, "The Work of Art in the Age of Mechanical Reproduction" [1969]). Benjamin is true to Surrealism not only in his fascination with the low but in his commitment to stage its encounter with the high. His Arcades Project folders intersperse notes on the great men and deeds of history (Karl Marx, Victor Hugo, barricade fighting, and Baudelaire) with notes on the eccentric visionaries of utopian socialism, on petty, professional conspirators, on popular optical technologies, on boredom, advertising, fashion, and prostitution.

Benjamin also turned to Surrealism when he groped in the 1930s for an alternative model of historical process to the linear, progressive model of bourgeois history that continued to permeate orthodox European Marxisms. In particular, he was interested in the Surrealists' psychoanalytically informed understanding of the present as haunted by the repressed ghosts of personal and collective history; the movement's substitution of a "political for a historical view of the past" (1978, "Surrealism," p. 182). Staging his own unorthodox conceptual "encounter," Benjamin brought together this Freudian-Surrealist notion of historical process with the redemptive schemas of messianic Judaism and the Marxist dialectic. Benjamin speculated that the violence of history made it a process characterized by multiple layers of repression. Lost chips of the past would flare into view when they were sparked by some relevant experience in the present and the historian had to seize this chance for "rescue" or it might pass forever. Benjamin called the moment of potential redemption the "'Now of recognizability,' in which things put on their true—surrealist—face" (1989, pp. 3a, 3).

Benjamin characterized the material rescued at such a moment as "the dialectical image": "It isn't that the past casts its light on the present or the present casts its light on the past: rather, an image is that in which the Then (*das Gewesene*) and the Now [*das Jetzt*] come into a constellation like a flash of lightning. In other words: image is dialectics at a standstill," wrote Benjamin, using the rhetoric of lightning that the Surrealists had coined in formulating the "encounter" (ibid., pp. 2a, 3). Benjamin also associated the dialectical image with the experience of the dream and the Freudian notion of overdetermination, or, as he termed it,

"ambiguity": "Ambiguity is the pictorial image of dialectics, the law of dialectics seen at a standstill. This standstill is utopia, and the dialectical image therefore a dream image" (1978, "Paris," p. 157).

As these citations suggest, Benjamin's notion of the dialectical image is ambiguous and has been a long-standing source of critical dispute. From the time of Theodor W. Adorno's first harsh letters on the Arcades Project in the mid-1930s, Frankfurt School thinkers have attacked it for fixing the dynamic and demystifying critical process of dialectics in a static expressive form associated with an illusionistic phenomenology; for succumbing to the lure of bourgeois psychology; for displaying Benjamin's allegiance to reenchantment as well as to disenchantment. As an antidote to such potential mystification, this lineage proposes to do away with the imagistic side of the dialectical image and counsels Benjamin to make it all dialectics.

Benjamin refused this solution to the dialectical image's ambiguities. In his musings on the concept, he makes evident that he couched it in a Surrealist rhetoric of light and dream because of its Surrealist conceptual inheritance. As the Surrealist view of historical process as repression indicates, the Surrealists too turned to psychoanalysis to revise aspects of orthodox Marxism mired in positivism. Thus, Breton defended Surrealism's serious Marxist ambitions against the French Communist Party by appealing to the psychoanalytic view of historical causality as overdetermination and of expression as a form of action. In a similar way, the renegade Surrealist Georges Bataille challenged orthodox Marxism's instrumental notion of labor by invoking the psychoanalytic notion of the drive. Interested both in Breton's "modern materialism" and Bataille's' "base materialism," Benjamin speculated rather inconclusively throughout the Arcades Project on how the cultural products of the superstructure might be the expression of a historicized collective unconscious. Likening the dialectical image to a collective dream, he suggested that it might be a cultural product where the hopes and fears of a collective were particularly accessible. Such cultural forms, he surmised, might very well occur at the inception of a mode of production, in this case high capitalism: "The arcades and interiors, the exhibitions and panoramas . . . are the residues of a dream world. The realization of dream elements in waking is the textbook example of dialectical thinking" (1978, "Paris," p. 162).

The dream is only one example of a liminal psychic state that Benjamin redeemed with the help of Surrealism. In Benjamin's work on high capitalist modernity, other important liminal psychic states include the experience of distraction, which he explores in his discussion of the positive political potential of cinema in "The Work of Art in the Age of Mechanical Reproduction." They also include the experience of intoxication, whether it is the intoxication of "the reader, the thinker, the loiterer, the *flâneur*" or of "the opium eater, the dreamer, the ecstatic" (1978, "Surrealism," p. 190). In their attention to liminal psychic states, both Benjamin and the Surrealists show their interest in psychoanalysis, which appreciated the rich material contained, as Freud put it in 1901 in *The Psychopathology of Everyday Life*. In their specific attention to intoxication, they also manifest their continuity with a Romantic visionary lineage predating psychoanalysis (and informing it). Benjamin explores the psychopathology of everyday life not only in his Arcades Project, but also in his own autobiographical writings, notably *One-Way Street,* and his writings on cities and drugs from the late 1920s and 1930s.

The historical details of Benjamin's personal relations with the high Surrealists are unclear; his letters to André Breton "have been lost or cannot be located" (Benjamin, 1994, p. xii). In contrast, Benjamin had well-documented personal contact with Bataille during the seven years that he lived in Paris. Benjamin encountered Bataille in the context of his work at the Bibliothèque Nationale; he attended the meetings of Bataille's Collège de Sociologie on a regular basis from its inception in 1937; and it was to Bataille that Benjamin confided the notes and fragments of the Arcades Project when he fled Paris with the fall of France in 1940.

[*See also* Surrealism.]

BIBLIOGRAPHY

Selected Surrealist Texts Important for Benjamin

Aragon, Louis. *Traité du style*. Paris, 1928.
Aragon, Louis. *Nightwalker (Le paysan de Paris)*. Translated by Frederick Brown. Englewood Cliffs, N.J., 1970.
Bataille, Georges. *Visions of Excess: Selected Writings, 1927–1939*. Edited and translated by Allan Stoekl. Minneapolis, 1985.
Breton, André. *Nadja*. Translated by Richard Howard. New York, 1960.
Breton, André. *Manifestoes of Surrealism*. Translated by Richard Seaver and Helen R. Lane. Ann Arbor, 1969.
Breton, André. *Communicating Vessels*. Translated by Mary Ann Caws and Geoffrey T. Harris. Lincoln, Nebr., 1990.

Representative Writings by Benjamin Informed by Surrealism

"N [Re the Theory of Knowledge, Theory of Progress]." Translated by Leigh Hafrey and Richard Sieburth. In *Benjamin: Philosophy, Aesthetics, History*, edited by Gary Smith. Chicago, 1989. Selection from *Das Passager–Werk*.
Charles Baudelaire: A Lyric Poet in the Era of High Capitalism. Translated by Harry Zohn. London, 1973.
Correspondence of Walter Benjamin, 1910–1940, edited by Gershom Scholem and Theodor W. Adorno, translated by Manfred R. Jacobson and Evelyn M. Jacobson. Chicago, 1994. See the letters on the Arcades Project.
Das Passagen Werk. 2 vols. Edited by Rolf Tiedemann. Frankfurt am Main, 1983.
"The Task of the Translator." In *Illuminations: Essays and Reflections.* edited by Hannah Arendt, translated by Harry Zohn, pp. 69–82. New York, 1969.
One-Way Street. In *One-Way Street and Other Writings*, translated by Edmund Jephcott and Kingsley Shorter. London, 1979.
"Marseilles" and "Hashish in Marseilles." In *Reflections: Essays, Aphorisms, Autobiographical Writings,* edited by Peter Demetz, trans-
lated by Edmund Jephcott, pp. 131–136 and 137–145. New York, 1978.
"Paris, Capital of the Nineteenth Century." In *Reflections: Essays, Aphorisms, Autobiographical Writings,* edited by Peter Demetz, translated by Edmund Jephcott, pp. 146–162. New York, 1978.
"Surrealism, the Last Snapshot of the European Intelligentsia." In *Reflections: Essays, Aphorisms, Autobiographical Writings,* edited by Peter Demetz, translated by Edmund Jephcott, pp. 177–192. New York, 1978.

Selected Secondary Writings on Benjamin and Surrealism

Adorno, Theodor W. "Benjamins 'Einbahnstrasse'." In *Über Walter Benjamin*. Franfkurt am Main, 1968.
Bloch, Ernst. "Revue Form in Philosophy." In *Heritage of Our Times,* translated by Neville and Stephen Plaice, pp. 334–337. Berkeley, 1990.
Buck-Morss, Susan. *The Dialectics of Seeing: Walter Benjamin and the Arcades Project*. Cambridge, Mass., 1989.
Bürger, Peter. *Der französische Surrealismus*. Frankfurt am Main, 1971.
Cohen, Margaret. *Profane Illumination: Walter Benjamin and the Paris of Surrealist Revolution*. Berkeley, 1993.
Foster, Hal. *Compulsive Beauty*. Cambridge, Mass., 1993.
Furnkäs, Josef. *Surrealismus als Erkenntnis*. Stuttgart, 1988.
McCole, John. *Walter Benjamin and the Antinomies of Tradition*. Ithaca, N.Y., 1993.
Pensky, Max. *Melancholy Dialectics: Walter Benjamin and the Play of Mourning*. Amherst, Mass., 1993.
Wisman, Heinz, ed. *Walter Benjamin et Paris*. Paris, 1986.
Wolin, Richard. *Walter Benjamin: An Aesthetic of Redemption*. New York, 1982; reprint, Berkeley, 1994.

MARGARET COHEN

Benjamin's Writing Style

If, as Walter Benjamin once remarked, "style is the jump-rope [*Sprungseil*] thought must take in order to push forward into the realm of writing" (1986, p. 202), it is worth noting how little attention has been paid to Benjamin's own style of writing in the massive amount of secondary literature that his work has elicited. Perhaps the rest of his unpublished fragment "Thought and Style" suggests why this is so: "Thought must pull all its forces together. But style [must] meet it halfway and [yet] stay supple, like the rope in the hands of the children swinging it as one of them gets ready to jump" (ibid.). "Style" must both respond to the most extreme concentration of thinking and yet at the same time stay loose in its recurrence, never rigidifying into regularity, always leaving room for the *Sprung*: the *leap*, to be sure, but also the *crack*.

If a leap or crack is the way Benjamin describes the way "thinking" gains access to the "domain of writing," one rather unusual stylistic trait that recurs throughout his writings may help readers "push forward" into the labyrinthine realm of his thought. It is the tendency to formulate certain key concepts in nouns that employ the suffix *-ability* or *-ibility* (in German, *-barkeit*). What are these "key" concepts? Here is a partial list: *communicability* (*Mitteilbarkeit*) in his early essay "On Language in General and on Human

Language" (or "On Language as Such and on the Language of Man" [1915]; *criticizability* (*Kritisierbarkeit*) in his doctoral dissertation, "The Concept of Criticism in German Romanticism" (1920); *translatability* (*Übersetzbarkeit*) in "The Task of the Translator" (1923); *reproducibility*, in "The Work of Art in the Age of its Technical Reproducibility" (or "The Work of Art in the Age of Mechanical Reproduction" [1936]); and *knowability* (*Erkennbarkeit*) in the posthumously published notes "On the Concept of History" (or "Theses on the Philosophy of History" [1940]). The list could easily be extended, but in the limited space of this article there will be room only for a brief discussion of the first and last of the terms mentioned. This discussion should suffice to indicate certain essential aspects of Benjamin's thought and of the "jump rope" by which it articulates itself.

Before turning to Benjamin's use of these terms, however, it might be helpful to reflect briefly on some of the more general implications of the suffix *-ability/-ibility*. Nouns formed in this way refer to a *possibility* or a *potentiality*, to a *capacity* rather than to an actually existing *reality*. Communic*ability*, for instance, does not refer to an accomplished act as does *communication;* the same holds true for *knowability*, which is by no means equivalent to *knowledge*. Benjamin himself discusses this difference in introducing the notion of the "translatability" of works, which, he emphasizes, does not depend on the empirical fact of whether or not a work has or ever will be actually translated. Benjamin's *-abilities*, then, refer to what Jacques Derrida, writing in "Limited Inc." (1988). Of his quasi concept, "iterability," called "structural possibilities," the necessity of which does not depend on actual fact or probable implementation.

This emphasis on a *possibility* that is structurally *necessary* without being necessarily *real* disposes Benjamin to make use of such terms, even where they are rather uncommon. In "On Language as Such and on the Language of Man," Benjamin distinguishes "linguistic" from "spiritual" being by defining it in terms of "communicability": "That in a spiritual being which is communicable is its linguistic being" (1978). This is tantamount to saying that the "being" (or "essence": Benjamin uses the German word *Wesen*, which can mean both) of language does not have the character of a determinate, self-contained entity. It is precisely in order to highlight this difference between spiritual, intellectual, or semantic being on the one hand, and that of language on the other, that Benjamin makes emphatic use of the suffix *-ability*, which is stressed in the text: "It is not that whatever is communicable in a spiritual being *appears* most clearly in its language . . . but rather that this communic*able* [*dieses Mitteilbare*] is immediately [*unmittelbar*] language itself" (ibid.). The *-ability* that distinguishes language from spirit or intellect has less to do with a *what* than with a *how*. "Language," although a noun, names something that is more like an adjective or an adverb: a property or attribute

that is not self-contained but that requires something else in order to be, just as every *how* requires a *what*. Language, in short, names a *modality* rather than a *substance* or a *substantive*. It describes the possibility of a particular *way* of being: that of *being communicated*, of "communicability."

But the English word *communicability* is not the only translation possible of the German word used by Benjamin, *Mitteilbarkeit*. Another, perhaps more literal, translation would be *impartibility*. This rendering would be more literal for several reasons. First, its root, like the German word, stresses the *partiality* of the process of *Mit*-teil-*ung*, something that does not necessarily come across in the English *communication*. The being of language, which is to say the particular *way of being* that constitutes language, has more to do with parts, and indeed with *partitioning*, than with wholes. Second, that way of being involves not simply "communicating," if by that word is meant conveying a meaning by *means* of something else. If Benjamin insists not simply that "impartibility" is what constitutes language, but that it constitutes it "immediately" (*unmittelbar*), it is in order to highlight the decisive relationship between two German words that sound and look almost identical although they mean very different things: between *mitteilbar* (impartible) and *unmittelbar* (immediate[ly]). The difference is decisive because *unmittelbar* means not just "immediate(ly)" but also, more literally, *without means* or instrumentality. Language, in short, is to be understood not as a "means" to some other goal, but as the immediate possibility of *being imparted:* "This impart*ible is* language itself."

But this ability can never be found in a vacuum, all by itself. It is not a thing, not a substance, nothing that could be aptly designated by a straightforward substantive. In other words, it requires something else in order to be: it requires beings. Language requires beings and yet is not essentially determined by them; for what language "communicates" is nothing but itself: it communicates, or better, im-parts itself. In this way, language operates as a "medium": "Each language imparts itself *in* itself, it is in the purest sense the 'medium' of communication. The medial, which is to say, the *immed*iacy [Unmittel*barkeit*] of all spiritual communication—that is the basic problem of the theory of language" (ibid.). The reason such "immediacy" defines a "problem," and indeed even a "paradox"—the "paradox of all theory of language"—is that Benjamin will not resort to the expedient of saying that "the medium is the message." The fact that the medium operates in an "immediate" manner signifies, for Benjamin, that an essential understanding of *medium* must above all else avoid confounding it with the notion of *message*. It is this irreducible difference that his notion of "impartibility" seeks, in however preliminary a fashion, to articulate.

Benjamin's insistence, in this essay of 1916, on the irreducible mediality of language qua impartibility indicates that his concern with the "media" originates not in his later studies of radio, film, and photography, but rather in his effort to elaborate a noninstrumental conception of *language*. It is this that leads Benjamin to insist on the irreducible *immediacy of the medial*. The "medial" is "immediate" in the sense of not being instrumental. The *media* must above all be distinguished from the *means*. It is characteristic that Benjamin should seek to elucidate this distinction through the use of prepositions with strong *spatial* connotations. Considered as a "means" of communication, language would be something "through" which something else was conveyed; language would be a more or less neutral vehicle of something essentially external to it. But, as a "medium," language is itself a dynamic space "in" which something happens. Yet, what happens tends to disrupt the usual meaning of *in;* for this ostensibly well-defined, containing, and *self-contained* space of the *medium* consists precisely in the *self parting company from itself by im-parting itself.* In thus refusing the instrumentalist conception of language as a medium through which *something* is communicated by *someone* to *someone else,* Benjamin does not introduce an alternative version of immanence or identity—for instance, the medium itself as the message. Rather, he opens a highly volatile space in which all "spiritual being"—which is to say, all *identity,* whether of subjects, objects, things, or meanings—appears only *in and through* the process of parting company with itself, and in so doing, *imparting* itself to *others.* It is only in *parting company with itself,* in im-parting itself, that com-munication can take place. The "com-" of communication thus presupposes the *parting* of *imparting,* which alone opens up the space "in" which relations, whether social, semantic, or semiotic, can "take place."

It is precisely the ambivalent ramifications of "the immediacy of the medial," that is, of the *originating crack* or fracture first described as *imparting,* that drive Benjamin's thinking and writing. They are marked by a double (or "cracked") tone: on the one hand, that of melancholy, sadness, and mourning (*Trauer* is a leitmotif from first to last); on the other hand, however, inseparable from the first because its consequence, that of energetic engagement, militancy, and hope, because the very same fracture that is felt as loss also opens up the (linguistic) possibility of this *loss itself being lost,* im-parting and thus altering itself and thereby keeping the way open for something radically different.

This is how the ostensibly neo-Kantian transcendentalism of Benjamin's -*abilities* comes to acquire historical, political, and cultural significance. Everything that contributes to dislodging that which is, by forcing it into a mode of self-imparting, self-departing, wrenching it free from its established sites, is *both* painful, creating a sense of loss—that of the "aura," for instance, provoked by the spread of techniques of "reproducibility"—and *at the same time* the bearer of messianic hope.

This ambivalent movement of imparting is perhaps nowhere more striking than in one of Benjamin's last writings, where it seizes on the notion of "time" itself, or rather on the key concept that has traditionally determined how time has been construed: that of the "present" or the "now." As "now," Benjamin reveals the -*ability* of time to *part company* from itself, thereby opening up nothing less than a messianic space in which mourning and melancholy converge in vengeful hope. It is in the context of Benjamin's discussion of the "concept of history" that he elaborates what will be his last -*ability:* "knowability."

It should be added, however, that this question was one that occupied Benjamin from his very earliest writings on. In the 1918 essay "On the Program of the Coming Philosophy," for instance, he called for a critical transformation of the Kantian philosophical heritage through renewed reflection on the "singular temporality" of finite experience and its significance for cognition. The direction such reflection should take, he urged, was toward the "systematic" elaboration of "a certain non-synthesis of two concepts in one another," which was to be one of the most urgent tasks of the "coming philosophy." The "coming philosophy," in short, would be the philosophy of a certain "coming"—and going.

In a certain sense, all of Benjamin's writing and thinking can be productively studied in the light of the task of elaborating the "non-synthesis of . . . concepts in one another." Probably the most extended attempt of this is to be found in the "epistemo-critical Preface" to his major published work (and unsuccessful *Habilitationsschrift*), *The Origin of the German Mourning Play* (or, *The Origin of German Tragic Drama*). By replacing the consecrated philosophical and Kantian term *epistemological* with the neologism "epistemo-*critical*" in the title of that Preface, Benjamin indicates that his task is not simply that of reflecting on the conditions under which cognition is produced, but rather that of exploring the way his writing questions the notion of knowledge itself. His (Nietzschean) determination of all knowledge as a "having," and his effort to develop the mourning play not as a concept in which phenomena are subsumed under universals, but as an "idea" in which their distinctive singularity is saved through a "configuration" of "extremes," constitute a practical effort to develop a "nonsynthetic," nonsubsumptive form of knowledge. It is significant that this effort culminates in a discussion of "philosophical style," a form of "presentation" characterized by discontinuity, interruption, and renewed effort.

These considerations return in Benjamin's discussion of the "knowability" of history and the status of historical knowledge. The following passage from section 5 of "Theses on the Philosophy of History" or "On The Concept of History" indicates the manner in which the question is framed: "The true image of the past rushes by. Only as an image that just barely flashes its nevermore in the instant of its knowability can the past be retained" (1969). As is clear, or should be, from this turn of phrase, Benjamin's often noted penchant for figural language has little to do with illustration or elucidation. Rather, what he describes here as the "nevermore" (*Nimmerwiederschen*) of the image that disappears so rapidly that it can only be glimpsed in—and with—an *Augenblick* articulates practically, *graphically,* the "singular temporality" of the "coming philosophy." Benjamin, so far removed in so many ways from the United States, treats the notion "phenomenon" in a sense accorded the word by American slang, as a manifestation of the extraordinary ("it's phenomenal!"), whose coming to light converges with its disappearance.

If Benjamin designates this image as "dialectical," it is less with reference to Hegel than to his own earlier demand, in the "Program," that the "coming philosophy" introduce "a certain non-synthesis" into the Kantian triad, one that, however, would "hardly lead to a quartet [*Vierheit*] of relational categories." Benjamin's "dialectical image" thus heightens precisely what Hegelian dialectics seek to overcome: the "disjunctive relation" of the "synthesis." The dialectical image does this by *arresting* the forward flow of time, but it can only accomplish this by interrupting its "own" intentionality qua representation and signification. In short, the "dialectical" image disrupts the horizon of expectation to which it ostensibly responds and thereby makes way for something *else*.

Such an interruption does not therefore install the *nunc stans* of a mystical *kairos*. Rather, it dislocates the self-perception of "the present" as unified and self-identical. In a fragment not included in the published version of "Theses on the Philosophy of History" or "On the Concept of History," titled precisely, "The Now of Knowability," Benjamin quotes Turgot: "Before we are able to inform ourselves about a given state of things, it has already changed many times. Therefore we are always too late when we learn what has transpired. And thus one can say that politics is obliged, as it were, to predict the present." For Benjamin, it is "just such a concept of the present that must be the basis of the actuality of genuine historiography."

The "now of knowability" thus presupposes an awareness of time not as a medium of becoming but as one of alteration and passing; what Benjamin calls the "image," therefore, is not simply the stable representation of a self-identical content but an allegorical figure that explodes the semblance of teleological progression by bringing its movement to a standstill while simultaneously moving in a different, less linear manner: as signification and repetition. Its temporality is that of the "calendar," which Benjamin distinguishes from that of "clocks." The time of the calendar, unlike chronological time, is neither homogeneous nor irreversible. Rather, it is *commemorative,* discontinuous, repetitive. But such repetition turns out to be as ambivalent as all of Benjamin's other *-abilities*. It opens the possibility of deadening routine no less than that of messianic redemption, at times even leaving the impression that the two possibilities may not be entirely separable.

Such ambivalent *-abilities*—splinter of a word—endow Walter Benjamin's writings with much of the enigmatic fascination that has made them increasingly difficult to ignore but even more difficult to respond to. Melancholic and yet revolutionary, sober and yet scholarly, his texts invite readers to measure their certitudes and prowess in a strange game of jump rope that they solemnly and prosaically reenact.

[*See also* Style.]

BIBLIOGRAPHY

Works by Benjamin

"On the Program of the Coming Philosophy." In *Benjamin: Philosophy, History, Aesthetics,* edited by Gary Smith, pp. 1–12. Chicago, 1989.

"The Concept of Criticism in German Romanticism." In *Gesammelte Schriften,* vol. 1. Frankfurt am Main, 1980.

"Thought and Style." In *Gesammelte Schriften,* vol. 6, *Fragmente vermischten Inhalts,* edited by Rolf Tiedemann and Hermann Schweppenhäuser. Frankfurt am Main, 1986.

"The Task of the Translator." In *Illuminations: Essays and Reflections,* edited by Hannah Arendt, translated by Harry Zohn, pp. 69–82. New York, 1969.

The Origin of German Tragic Drama. Translated by John Osborne. London, 1977.

"On Language as Such and on the Language of Man." In *Reflections: Essays, Aphorisms, Autobiographical Writings,* edited by Peter Demetz, translated by Edmund Jephcott, pp. 314–322. New York, 1978.

"Theses on the Philosophy of History." In *Illuminations: Essays and Reflections,* edited by Hannah Arendt, translated by Harry Zohn, pp. 253–264. New York, 1969.

"The Work of Art in the Age of Mechanical Reproduction." In *Illuminations: Essays and Reflections,* edited by Hannah Arendt, translated by Harry Zohn, pp. 217–251. New York, 1969.

SAMUEL WEBER

BERENSON, BERNARD (1865–1959) American connoisseur, critic, and aesthetic theorist. Born in Lithuania, Bernard Berenson grew up in Boston and entered Harvard in 1884. He departed for Europe following graduation and, after several years of travel, settled in Italy, which became his permanent residence. From 1900 to his death, Berenson lived on a large estate in Settignano, outside of Florence. At his residence, the Villa I Tatti, with its eclectic art collection, enormous library, and formal gardens, Berenson received the artists, intellectuals, and European dignitaries who composed his vast network of social contacts, as well as the American millionaires who sought his advice in the formation of their personal collections.

Berenson was a chief practitioner of scientific connoisseurship, a method of attributing works of art (pioneered by the Italian critic Giovanni Morelli) based on the careful scrutiny of morphological detail. His early reputation rested on extensive knowledge, acquired through years of careful study and maintained through a vast collection of photographic reproductions, of the stylistic particulars of Italian

Renaissance painting. As a professional connoisseur retained by the well-known art dealer Joseph Duveen, Berenson routinely adjusted incorrect attributions and assigned authorship to, or authenticated, unattributed works. In his scholarly writing, he also sought to construct artistic personalities through the collective examination of paintings attributed to the same hand. Although many of Berenson's attributions have been challenged by subsequent scholars, his contribution to the systematic study of Italian painting is undisputed. In recent years, however, Berenson's legacy has been tainted by a nagging suspicion that the practice of connoisseurship might have served his financial interests to the detriment of his scholarship.

Although he upheld the fundamental importance of connoisseurship to the writing of art history, Berenson grew dissatisfied with the practice as he came to question its value in the appreciation of art. This skepticism was fueled, in part, by a growing sense that the efficacy of connoisseurship stood in inverse proportion to the originality of the artist in question. Over the years, he became increasingly susceptible to the suggestion, voiced by his detractors, that scientific connoisseurship was largely a specialized research tool that too often yielded uninteresting information about unimportant paintings.

Berenson's stature as a connoisseur derived from a series of essays on the regional schools of Italian Renaissance painting (published between 1894 and 1907; consolidated into a single volume in 1930) that were accompanied by lists of correctly attributed works. In these early essays, critical and historical appraisals of individual artists are interspersed with discursive passages on the nature of art and aesthetic experience. *The Drawings of the Florentine Painters* (1903), Berenson's magnum opus and his most important contribution to the historiography of Renaissance art, was also written during these years. In the ensuing decades, while acting as adviser on Italian art to the Duveen firm (c.1907–1937), Berenson undertook periodic revisions of the lists and wrote almost exclusively on technical matters.

Although Berenson's fame and legacy rest largely on his reputation as a connoisseur, his intellectual interests extended well beyond these professional activities. Especially at the beginning and end of his career, Berenson often addressed issues of aesthetic theory and art appreciation in the context of his specialized writing. After the death of his wife and collaborator, Mary Costelloe Berenson (1864–1945), and the termination of his relationship with Duveen, Berenson published a series of books dealing with broader issues within art history and aesthetics, as well as several volumes consisting of excerpts from a personal diary he began to keep during World War II. The latter contain considerable insight into the idiosyncratic nature of his thought (more aphoristic than analytic) and the extraordinary range of his interests.

Berenson's originality as a critic rested on the distance he placed between himself and the followers of John Ruskin, whose literary approach to art was the dominant critical mode of late-nineteenth-century England and of the United States. As a young critic, Berenson was eager to disengage aesthetic judgment from discussions of ethical and moral value, and especially from the concept of Christian virtue that was at the heart of Ruskin's criticism. Berenson placed his emphasis instead on the importance of viewer response to the artistic properties of Renaissance painting, what he called "decoration," a position that encouraged devaluation of representational subject, or in his words, "illustration," as the primary purveyor of significance in pictorial art.

Berenson's general theories, with their emphasis on salient artistic properties and the uniqueness of aesthetic emotion, were rooted in the principles of psychological aesthetics current in the late nineteenth century. His understanding of aesthetic experience was greatly influenced by William James, with whom he studied at Harvard, and by German theorists such as Heinrich Wölfflin and Theodor Lipps. Fundamental to Berenson's thinking was his assumption that human beings respond physically, with unconscious self-identification or empathy, to certain formal elements in art. His theoretical tenets derive from the protoformalist view that visual images can be analyzed and broken down into discrete components such as sensations of touch, movement, and space. Aesthetic pleasure, which he understood as the experience of being reminded of primary physical sensations in an acute and facilitated manner, can be accounted for by identifying the "ideated sensations" produced by art and linking them with specific formal elements.

The concept of "tactile values," developed in Berenson's early essays and thereafter associated with his thinking, refers to those properties (manifest in visual images) that stimulate the viewer's sense of touch. Introduced in a discussion of the Tuscan painter Giotto (di Bondone), whom Berenson praised for his ability to render mass and material presence, it became the benchmark of his critical method. Berenson's admiration for quattrocento Florentine painting, and for the work of more recent artists such as Paul Cézanne and Edgar Degas, turned on this suggestion that the primary task of the painter is to create "tactile values." By linking the enjoyment of art to the viewer's apprehension of mass and the material significance of objects, Berenson provided not only a useful guide for the appreciation of Renaissance painting, but also potential encouragement, albeit inadvertent, for modern pictorial conventions such as Cubism.

Belief in the autonomy of art and the possibility of disinterested aesthetic pleasure was fundamental to Berenson's critical outlook. His aestheticism, which manifests itself in epicurean idealism and in a critical method that relied on an intense awareness of his own sensations, has its origins in

Walter Pater and the art for art's sake milieu. These convictions firmly align Berenson with the most progressive artists of his youth and, in his early writings, it was Berenson's habit to consider Renaissance painting in light of what he most admired in the present. Similarly, Berenson's approach to the study of art and the writing of art criticism, which privileged formal qualities over interpretative issues, was an important precursor of modern formalism, especially as it was articulated in the writings of English-language critics such as Roger Fry and Clive Bell.

In spite of the relative modernity of his early critical method, throughout his life Berenson insisted on the superiority of Western art in the classical tradition and he was openly antagonistic to all forms of nonrepresentational painting in the twentieth century. Berenson believed that formalist criticism, when applied to modern painting, had the effect of diminishing the human content of art in favor of intricate discussions of visual detail as a self-sufficient goal. Although his appreciation of Renaissance painting had turned on an acute sensitivity to intrinsic formal qualities, his distaste for modern art prompted him to redirect attention in his later writing to the extrinsic or associative qualities embedded in representation.

In his early books, Berenson had described aesthetic empathy as a mechanism for the achievement of intensified life through art. His concept of "life enhancement" functioned initially in the rather narrow context of explicating aesthetic pleasure in terms of sensate experience. But, as Berenson shifted his critical emphasis to the affective qualities of representation as well as form, life enhancement assumed a pivotal role in a broader discourse on the civilizing power of art. By linking life enhancement to humanist imperatives, Berenson moved toward a position more appropriately described as moral than aesthetic.

Most of Berenson's last books, although ostensibly concerned with art and theory, are thinly concealed indictments of what he regarded as the decadent state of modern culture. The rhetoric of humanism under siege, which dominated these publications, was informed by an apocalyptic view of the present as an age of cultural barbarism drifting toward purely technological and egalitarian interests. Berenson's vision of modern painting, particularly abstraction, as symptomatic of cultural decay stimulated his interest in the theme of artistic decline, a concern that occupied him for half a century and to a large extent shaped the contents of his personal library.

Berenson's antipathy to modern art was inconsistent with his critical method and, to a certain extent, his aesthetic theories. Because it embodied a tacit judgment of generative cultural and social conditions, the conclusions he drew with respect to twentieth-century art involved precisely the kind of reasoning he had discouraged in the study of historical art. Furthermore, Berenson's demand that aesthetic experience finds its moral justification in classical humanism,

heard repeatedly in his last years, reflects a way of thinking that he went out of his way to discredit in his youth and ultimately separates him from the school of formalist criticism he helped to establish.

[*See also* Aestheticism; *and* Formalism.]

BIBLIOGRAPHY

Works by Berenson

The Italian Painters of the Renaissance (1894, 1896, 1897, 1907). Oxford, 1930.
"Rudiments of Connoisseurship." In *The Study and Criticism of Italian Art*, Second Series. London, 1902.
The Drawings of the Florentine Painters (1903). 3 vols. Chicago, 1938.
Aesthetics and History in the Visual Arts. New York, 1948.
Sketch for a Self-Portrait. New York, 1949.
Rumor and Reflection, 1941–1944. New York, 1952.
Seeing and Knowing. New York, 1953.
The Arch of Constantine; or, The Decline of Form. New York, 1954.
The Selected Letters of Bernard Berenson. Edited by A. K. McComb. Boston, 1963.
Sunset and Twilight: From the Diaries of 1947–1958. Edited by Nicky Mariano. New York, 1963.

Other Sources

Barolsky, Paul. "Walter Pater and Bernard Berenson." *New Criterion* 2 (April 1984): 47–57.
Brown, David Alan. *Berenson and the Connoisseurship of Italian Painting*. Washington, D.C., 1979.
Calo, Mary Ann. *Bernard Berenson and the Twentieth Century*. Philadelphia, 1994.
Freedberg, Sydney. "Berenson, Connoisseurship and the History of Art." *New Criterion* 7 (February 1989): 7–16.
Maginnis, Hayden B. J. "The Role of Perceptual Learning in Connoisseurship: Morelli, Berenson, and Beyond." *Art History* 13 (March 1990): 104–117.
Mariano, Nicky. *Forty Years with Berenson*. New York, 1966.
Samuels, Ernest. *Bernard Berenson: The Making of a Connoisseur*. Cambridge, Mass., 1979.
Samuels, Ernest. *Bernard Berenson: The Making of a Legend*. Cambridge, Mass., 1987.
Schapiro, Meyer. "Mr. Berenson's Values." *Encounter* 16 (January 1961): 57–65.
Simpson, Colin. *Artful Partners: Bernard Berenson and Joseph Duveen*. New York, 1986.

MARY ANN CALO

BERGSON, HENRI-LOUIS (1859–1941), French philosopher. Henri Bergson became an international celebrity following the 1907 publication of *Creative Evolution;* elected to the French Academy in 1914, he received a Nobel prize in literature in 1927. His other major books include *Time and Free Will* (1889), which described the temporal dimension of human consciousness as synonymous with creative freedom, and *Matter and Memory* (1896), a philosophical analysis of the relation of mind to body. In addition, he published more specialized studies, the most notable being *Duration and Simultaneity* (1922) and *The Two Sources of Morality and Religion* (1932); other writings were later collected in his *Mélanges* (1972). Bergson's influence on the writers and artists of his generation has been the subject of numerous studies, as has his legacy in political thought.

Central to his philosophy was an instrumental conception of the intellect and an attempt to define intuition as a mode of cognition informing both artistic and scientific endeavor. By asserting that intuition established an immediate relation between sign and signified, Bergson and his followers proclaimed their ability to create "natural" signs, signs whose temporal properties were anterior to and at the origin of all conventional sign systems. Under the rubric of the natural or "transparent" sign were numbered all those signs whose properties were deemed "qualitative," rhythmic, and organic, as opposed to "quantitative," nonrhythmic, and mechanical. Thus, the differentiation that Bergson's followers made between intuitive and intellectual signs entailed a radical schism between the immediate and the mediated, the natural and the conventional, the temporal and the spatial, the spiritual and the material.

In Bergson's philosophy, artistic perception "has no other object than to brush aside the utilitarian symbols, the conventional and socially accepted generalities" to "enter into immediate communion with things and ourselves" (Bergson, 1900, p. 162). In the case of the fine arts, a work by "a Corot, a Turner" will reveal "a brilliant and vanishing vision" that "the pale and colourless vision of things that is habitually ours perceived without seeing." As beholders, we declare such works to be "true" because they reveal the subliminal perceptions that utilitarian thought veiled from us. Painting, then, not only encompasses self-expression but also "imitation," and "the great painters are people who possess a certain vision of things that has or will become the vision of all people." With regard to painting, Bergson suppresses the expressive component of his theory and emphasizes the imitative one, comparing a painter's vision to the chemical bath that operates as the "revealing agent" for a photographic image.

In his writings, Bergson equivocated over whether the various arts—music, poetry, or painting—should be expressive or imitative in their aims. His reason for doing so relates in part to his differentiation between the arts and their mediums, based on a hierarchy of perceptual faculties. He consistently privileges the sense of hearing above sight, describing the latter faculty as a perceptual tool serving utilitarian needs (Antliff, 1993, pp. 64–66; Jay, 1993, 149–209). Bergson's predilection for sound over sight is most obvious in his comparison of *durée* to a melody, and his deprecation of recourse to images in describing duration, a habit, he says, that usually succeeds in dividing and "intellectualizing" time. In *Creative Evolution,* Bergson describes the intellectual faculty as preferring to study a subject's surface appearance rather than focusing on its inner being, as the "inner eye" would. If "our faculty of seeing is tied to our faculty of willing," that is, if we see empathetically, our "in-

ner" and ocular sight would be made one and vision would transcend its utilitarian function to discern inner duration, the melody of the soul (Bergson, 1907, p. 259). Unlike the artist, we are not used to "listening to the uninterrupted humming of life's depths" because "our auditory perception has acquired the habit of absorbing visual images," of dividing this unbroken melody into "befores and afters," a "juxtaposition of distinct notes." Because intuitive vision is native to artists, they alone can perceive the durational cadence for which harmony of color and form are the material or "surface" equivalent (Bergson, 1900, p. 159). Artists alone replace the Cartesian light of reason with an intuitive grasp of the mystical, inner light of being (Antliff, 1993, pp. 12, 16–36). Auditory perception is naturally attuned to the soul's inner music and optical vision to the intellect's divisive biases.

The question thus arises as to whether music is superior to the plastic arts by virtue of its focus on pure temporality rather than the inner harmony manifest in outer appearances. That implication is present when Bergson describes musicians in contrast to poets or painters as delving "deeper still" to grasp "certain rhythms of life and breath that are closer to man than his own feelings" (Bergson, 1900, p. 131). Unlike the artist, who "applies himself to colours and forms," or poets, who reveal an emotional state "by the rhythmical arrangement of words," musicians delve "beneath these joys and sorrows which can, at a pitch, be translated into language [to] grasp something that has nothing in common with language," namely, those "rhythms of life" mentioned previously (ibid., p. 161). There is, then, an artistic hierarchy in Bergson's theory, based on his association of each art form with the "natural" disinterestedness of a particular sense (ibid., pp. 157–158 and 160–161).

Bergson labeled all forms of life material manifestations of a vital impulse (élan vital) resulting in the rhythmic unfolding of temporality into extensity, Bergson's term for spatial form. By defining extensity as a quality, Bergson hoped to defuse the intellectual prejudice that would identify the inextensive with quality and extensive with quantity (Antliff, 1993, pp. 100–105; Deleuze, 1988, pp. 73–113). In reality, Bergson states, concrete extensity is composed of nothing more than changes of tension and energy, in short, qualitative movement. To Bergson's mind, "these movements, regarded in themselves, are indivisibles which occupy duration, involve a before and after, and link together the successive moments of time by a thread of variable quality which cannot be without some likeness to the continuity of our consciousness" (Bergson, 1896, p. 268). This tension, therefore, is comparable to a melody, a linear succession of tones that cannot be divided. Even if a melody is stopped "it would no longer be the same sonorous whole, it would be another, equally indivisible" (Bergson, 1889, p. 104). Indeed, all that distinguishes the melody of matter from that of our own duration is the faster rhythm of the latter in comparison to the former. Our duration has its own determined rhythm, and because all movements possess a rhythm, "it is possible to imagine many different rhythms which, slower or faster, measure the degree of tension or relaxation of different kinds of consciousness, and thereby fix their respective places on the scale of being" (Bergson, 1896, p. 275). In Bergson's cosmology, matter itself possesses a latent consciousness, taking its place as the slowest rhythm on the scale of being whose degrees of rhythmic tension are a function of the degree of freedom inherent in their activity. It is rhythm, manifest in sensations of melody, harmony, or degrees of tension that an artist translates into a work of art.

Bergson expanded this thesis in *Creative Evolution,* where he applied his concept of rhythmic extensity to his definition of qualitative as opposed to quantitative differences. Duration is made up of the former, because it is composed of qualitative sensations bound together by a particular rhythm. Each rhythm is itself a quality, so that the universe is made up of slower or faster rhythms. Quantitative differentiations do not take account of qualitative differences, with the result that our intellectual biases cause us to subsume all durational rhythms into a single, homogeneous time or arbitrarily divide the extensive continuum. Bergson describes the distinct outlines delineating an object—the surfaces and edges of things—as a product of our utilitarian need to act on them (Bergson, 1907, pp. 11–12). Such clearcut outlines are arbitrary divisions in a continuum of colors and shapes that would otherwise be resolved into a harmonious whole. Thus, artists, in Bergson's philosophy, perceive the inner life of things by grasping the "original harmony" of "forms and colours" that binds them into an ensemble (Bergson, 1900, p. 15).

Quantitative divisions are imposed on the extensive continuum from without, but there are systems whose differentiation is the product of their internal structure, the rhythm of their duration. Such, for example, is the case with the living organism, which, as the product of creative evolution, has been separated by nature itself, given a particular rhythm, and composed of parts that form an undivided whole (Bergson, 1907, pp. 11–13). Having compared duration to a melody in *Time and Free Will,* Bergson went on to liken time to "a living being whose parts, although distinct, permeate one another just because they are so closely connected" (ibid.). Despite their apparent closure, however, durational organisms are not separate; rather, they are joined by their sympathetic relation to each other. Bergson finds evidence of this sympathy in a mother's relation to her child, which proves that "the living being is above all a thoroughfare, and that the essence of life is in the movement by which life is transmitted" (ibid., 128). As the product of an intuitive act, a painting is also "internally" organized, just like the organisms that creative evolution has produced. But an artist's ultimate raison d'être is to convey this creative capacity to others, by way of one's intuitive reaction to paintings. Thus, an artist's relation to the public is not unlike the relation of the élan vital to its organisms, for, in Bergson's words, "everything leads us to believe that the role of each individual is to create, as if a great artist had produced, as his works, other artists" (Bergson, 1972, p. 1071).

Yet, the terms of this organicist discourse bear the seeds of their deconstruction, for the organic metaphor itself is a linguistic term that posesses a determinant logic that overruns the powers of origination that it is said to embody. Organic form is typified in Bergsonian criticism by its creative freedom, its continual invention, whereas mechanical form is predetermined, a lifeless fabrication. There is an inherent contradiction in this system, however, for, although artistic invention is not mechanically predetermined, its relation to the organicist metaphor of growth or self-generation constitutes another determinant (Culler, 1981, pp. 153–154). When Bergson declared human creativity a manifestation of the cosmic élan vital, he bracketed artistic creativity as both the product and the producer of a metacreative process. Far from being a unique evolutionary force, the creative activity of each individual was part and parcel of a supracreative universe, a single tone in an ongoing durational melody. In short, the personality was decentered as the origin of creativity, for, as an instance of the materialization of the élan vital, our organic form bore within it a creative force that did not originate with us. To enter into intuitive relation to the self was, paradoxically, to dissolve self-presence altogether, and become immersed in the rhythmic pulse of the élan vital.

An analysis of Bergson's theory of the personality demonstrates that within Bergson's system there is no pure vital impulse prior to its spatialization into form, with the result that distinctions between natural and conventional signs become blurred. Indeed, when one scrutinizes Bergson's metaphysics, it becomes clear that no radical break separates the temporal from the spatial; as already mentioned, there are only gradations of "extensity" linking the intensive and extensive, pure durée and its material manifestations. The fluctuant mixture of time and space that extensity embodies results in an ambiguous dialectic of the élan and form, wherein the élan is not an observable reality in its pure state. When Bergson confronted this ambiguity in his book *Matter and Memory,* he acknowledged that his distinction between intuitive and intellectual signs was an ideal one, for, in the realm of concrete experience, every form, even the most quantified, contains within it a trace of the durational rhythm that created it. Thus, forms of mediation and determination are inscribed into the élan from the very start, and hard distinctions between types of spatial form become arbitrary, a matter of *social* rather than metaphysical determination. To uncover the power relations implicit in such authorization is to reveal the transparent sign's ideological import: that is the project undertaken by those who have considered the political implications of Bergson's notion of intuition.

[*See also* Creativity.]

BIBLIOGRAPHY

Works by Bergson

Time and Free Will (1889). Translated by F. L. Pogson. New York, 1910; reprint, New York, 1960.

Matter and Memory (1896). Translated by Nancy Margaret Paul and W. Scott Palmer. London, 1911; reprint, New York, 1988.

Laughter (1900). Translated and edited by Wylie Sypher. Garden City, N.Y., 1956; reprint, Baltimore, 1980. In a volume with George Meredith's *Comedy*.

Creative Evolution (1907). Translated by Arthur Mitchell. New York, 1911; reprint, New York, 1938.

The Creative Mind. Translated by Mabelle L. Andison. New York, 1946.

Mélanges. Paris, 1972.

Other Sources

Antliff, Mark. *Inventing Bergson: Cultural Politics and the Parisian Avant-Garde.* Princeton, N.J., 1993.

Arbour, Romeo. *Henri Bergson et les Lettres Françaises.* Paris, 1955.

Culler, Jonathan. "The Mirror Stage." In *High Romantic Argument: Essays for M. H. Abrams,* edited by Lawrence Lipking, pp. 149–163. Ithaca, N.Y., 1981.

Douglass, Paul. *Bergson, Eliot, and American Literature.* Lexington, Ky., 1986.

Deleuze, Gilles. *Bergsonism* (1966). Translated by Hugh Tomlinson and Barbara Habberjam. New York, 1988.

Gillies, Mary Ann. *Henri Bergson and British Modernism.* Montreal, 1996.

Jay, Martin. *Downcast Eyes: The Denigration of Vision in Twentieth-Century French Thought.* Berkeley, 1993.

Quirk, Tom. *Bergson and American Culture: The Worlds of Willa Cather and Wallace Stevens.* Chapel Hill, N.C., 1990.

MARK ANTLIFF

BERKELEY, GEORGE (1685–1753), Irish philosopher and cleric. Both a student and a critic of John Locke and a forerunner of David Hume, Berkeley is best known for his theory of vision (*A New Theory of Vision,* 1709), in which he developed the empiricist argument that what we take to be visual cues for distance do not represent distance innately, but have to be learned to be associated with kinesthetic cues (sensations of moving), and for his idealism (defended in *A Treatise on the Principles of Human Knowledge* [1710] and *Three Dialogues between Hylas and Philonous* [1713]), in which he argued not merely that matter is unknowable but that its very idea is incoherent, and that all that can exist is ideas and the spirits, finite spirits and God, that have ideas. His contribution to aesthetics was limited to one argument in his last substantial philosophical work, *Alciphron, or the Minute Philosopher* (1732), but this argument played an important and influential part in a debate that was to last until the time of Immanuel Kant, and it should be remembered.

Alciphron attacks the unorthodox theism of the early-eighteenth-century freethinkers led by Anthony Ashley Cooper, third earl of Shaftesbury. A main target of Berkeley's attack is the moral sense theory of ethical judgment, which eliminates the traditional conception of moral rules as divine commands known by revelation. Because Francis Hutcheson, who presented himself as a follower of Shaftesbury, had offered his account of the sense of beauty as an introduction to his theory of the moral sense, Berkeley extended his attack to Hutcheson's aesthetics. Hutcheson had argued for what subsequently came to be called the disinterestedness of aesthetic judgment by asserting that our response to beauty is analogous to other sensory responses in its immediacy, and that because it is immediate it cannot depend on any rational reflection of the use of its object to satisfy any interest, because there literally is no time for such reflection (*An Inquiry concerning Beauty, Order, Harmony, and Design* [1725], section I, paragraphs XII–XIII). Berkeley controverted Hutcheson by arguing that the perception of beauty plainly does involve the recognition of fitness and usefulness—in particular, the proportionateness of the parts and form of an object to its intended use—and that because the recognition of such matters requires the use of reason, the response to beauty must involve reason and cannot be merely sensory. In the dialogue form of *Alciphron,* his spokesman Euphranor says that in a beautiful object, the parts are "in true proportions . . . so related, and adjusted to one another, as that they may best conspire to the use and operation of the whole"; that "the comparing of parts with one another, the considering of them as belonging to one whole, and the referring this whole to its use or end, should seem the work of reason"; and that "Consequently beauty . . . is an object, not of the eye, but of the mind" (*Alciphron,* dialogue III). To extend this argument—which is ironically closer to the view of Shaftesbury than Hutcheson's own view—to the domain of the fine arts, Berkeley adds that our response to beauty need not always be a response to actual usefulness, but is sometimes a response to the *appearance* of usefulness; Greek columns, for instance, are tapered to *look* stable even though they would actually be stable without being tapered.

In a note appended to the fourth edition of his *Inquiry* (1738), Hutcheson riposted that fitness to a use could not be a sufficient condition for beauty, because a chair with legs in four different styles would hold people up as well as one with four uniform legs, or a coffin-shaped door would let people pass as well as one of the usual shape, but neither of these objects would be beautiful. He also argued that knowledge of function could not be a necessary condition of beauty, because we can discern beauty "in Plants, in Flowers, in Animals whose Use is to us unknown," a remark that may have influenced Kant's conception of "free judgments of beauty" half a century later (*Critique of Judgment,* Section 16). Thus, Hutcheson maintained his view that judgment of beauty is a sensory response to a formal relation between variety and uniformity independent of any consideration of use. But his response to Berkeley hardly settled this fundamental issue of whether beauty is a purely formal property known by the senses or a functional property judged by reason. In book 2 of his *Treatise of Human Nature,* published the year following Hutcheson's reply to Berkeley (1739), Hume took Berkeley's side, arguing that although there are some beauties of form (or mere *species*), the great majority of cases of beauty are cases of fitness or the appearance of fitness to use. Two decades later, the issue was still very much alive when Burke made his famous objection to the Berkeleian position that the snout of a swine is eminently useful to it but certainly not beautiful (*A Philosophical Enquiry into the Origin of Our Ideas of the Sublime and Beautiful* [1757], part 3, section 6). Another three decades later, Kant was still trying to reconcile the two sides to this debate with his distinction between free and dependent judgments of beauty; thus, the issue that Berkeley raised remained a live one for aesthetic theory until its radical transformation in the post-Kantian period.

BIBLIOGRAPHY

Works by Berkeley

Alciphron, or the Minute Philosopher. Edited by T. E. Jessop. In *The Works of George Berkeley, Bishop of Cloyne,* edited by A. A. Luce and T. E. Jessop, vol. 3. London, 1950.

Primary Sources

Burke, Edmund. *A Philosophical Enquiry into the Origin of Our Ideas of the Sublime and Beautiful.* Edited by J. T. Boulton. London, 1958.
Hume, David. *A Treatise of Human Nature.* 2d ed. Edited by L. A. Selby-Bigge, revised by P. H. Nidditch. Oxford, 1978.
Hutcheson, Francis. *An Inquiry into the Origin of Our Ideas of Beauty and Virtue, in Two Treatises.* 4th corr. ed. London, 1738; facs. ed. Farnborough, England, 1969. The only modern edition of Hutcheson's *Inquiry,* edited by Peter Kivy (The Hague, 1973), although based on the fourth edition, unfortunately omits Hutcheson's reply to Berkeley.

Other Sources

Guyer, Paul. *Kant and the Experience of Freedom: Essays on Aesthetics and Morality.* Cambridge and New York, 1993. See chapter 2.
Kivy, Peter. *The Seventh Sense: A Study of Francis Hutcheson's Aesthetics and Its Influence in Eighteenth-Century Britain.* New York, 1976.
Urmson, J. O. "Berkeley on Beauty." In *Essays on Berkeley: A Tercentennial Celebration,* edited by John Foster and Howard Robinson, pp. 227–232. Oxford, 1985.

PAUL GUYER

BEUYS, JOSEPH (1921–1986), German artist who worked in various mediums and created installations. Born in Krefeld in the Lower Rhine region of Germany, from 1947 through 1952 Beuys studied at the State Art Academy in Düsseldorf, where in 1961 he was appointed professor for monumental sculpture. In 1972, he was dismissed from his post over an incident involving the unlawful occupation of the academy's administrative offices, but was later reinstated to his professorial title and the use of his office. He died in Düsseldorf of heart failure, his health having been compromised for many years by injuries received during his wartime military service.

Beuys's artistic career spans the development of the Federal Republic of Germany, from its postwar origins through the "economic miracle" and the student revolt to the emergence of the ecological movement as a social and political force. Although his entire work can be seen in relation to Germany's past and present history, he became increasingly active in politics beginning in the late 1960s, initially in university politics, then in the extraparliamentary oppositional movement, and finally in the Green Party, which he cofounded. Beuys considered his political activities to be an integral part of his artistic work.

Beuys worked in many media. From the late 1940s on, he produced thousands of drawings, many of them grouped into cycles. His earliest works in sculpture were religious monuments. After an intellectual and emotional crisis in the mid-1950s, he emerged with a conception of art, the "plastic theory" *(plastische Theorie),* which was to provide the foundation for his entire subsequent work in drawings, sculptural objects, performances *(Aktionen),* installations, vitrines, and multiples, as well as lectures and discussions. The range as well the growth of Beuys's artistic endeavors is best reflected in his increasingly monumental representation at five *documenta* exhibitions (III in 1964, IV in 1968, V in 1972, VI in 1977, VII in 1982).

The scale of Beuys's works ranges from intimate drawings to room-filling sculptures and temporally extended educational and environmental processes. For the most part, Beuys employed ordinary materials, which were then subject to often elaborate artistic processes. Beuys favored the use of fat, felt, and copper in his sculptural objects, installations, and actions. A large part of his work draws on the world of animals and prehistoric human life, represented in such figures as the hare, the stag, and the priestess.

Although Beuys's art shows affinities to a number of modern and contemporary artistic traditions, most notably the ready-made and Fluxus, he himself claimed the influence of German idealist and Romantic thought on his work. Beuys expressed special indebtedness to the German Expressionist sculptor Wilhelm Lehmbruck (1881–1919), and to the founder of the anthroposophic movement, Rudolph Steiner (1861–1925), whose doctrinaire didacticism he mitigated with a good dose of Rhenish humor.

Beuys's reputation grew steadily from local recognition through political notoriety in Germany to international artistic stature. His auratic personal presence, innovatory spirit, tremendous productivity, and sweeping intellect have made Beuys the most influential German artist in the second half of the twentieth century and the last great representative of the modernist avant-garde. His works are for the most part gathered in German museums (Berlin, Bonn, Darmstadt, Düsseldorf, Kassel, Krefeld, Schloss Moyland, Stuttgart), with additional major Beuys holdings in New York and Paris. Among his many students are Anselm Kiefer and Jörg Immendorf.

Beuys's theory and practice of art are philosophically significant in regard to the conception of art, the role of the artist, the nature of the work of art, and its relation to the public. The various aspects of Beuys's vision are held together by the notion of the plastic. Beuys distinguishes between sculptural processes, in which some material (e.g., marble) is formed by subtractive activities (e.g., hammering away), and plastic processes, in which some material (e.g., clay) is formed additively (e.g., clumping together). Beuys likens the latter process to organic formation from within *(Bildung)*. The plastic process is seen as a threefold unity in which material is subject to movement resulting in form.

For Beuys, the plastic is not only a specific artistic technique but the overall character of art and, by a further extension, of all human activity. Viewed most generally, the plastic process consists in the transition from chaos to order. Order and chaos are not simply juxtaposed. Rather, the former is developed out of the latter such that the product represents as much the potential of the material as the influence of the formative activity.

According to Beuys, the procedural, formative nature of artistic activity introduces the elements of time and energy into the plastic work of art. Plastic processes are temporally extended and impart temporal character to their products. Moreover, plastic processes involve the transformation of energy from a "warm" source to a "cold" product. For Beuys, warmth is the basic manifestation of energy with the potential to be consumed in formative activity.

Beuys's art consists in the multiform exhibition of the formative and specifically thermal nature of the plastic process. To begin with, Beuys chooses his materials with an eye toward their plastic quality. Fat and felt have distinct thermal qualities, one generating heat, the other retaining it. Copper is a conductor of heat. Moreover, fat is malleable, and can be put to formative use, as in Beuys's notorious "fat corners." Beuys's actions address the temporal element of the plastic process by enacting the formation in real time. His sculptural objects and installations often have the status of generators or batteries designed to create or retain energy or warmth. His extended lecture and discussion activity aims at the (in)formation of audience and interlocutors. The corpus of his drawings can be seen as Beuys's extended, lifelong formation process. Taken individually, their evocative, haunted character renders most palpable the transitional nature of the artistic process between the unformed and the formed. Finally, Beuys's total immersion in his work is itself a process of exhaustive transformation of life resources into art, as conveyed in the stamped inscription, "I know no weekend" *(Ich kenne kein Weekend),* which he affixed to a copy of Immanuel Kant's *Critique of Pure Reason* in one of his multiples.

It should be noted that, with few exceptions, Beuys's chrono-thermal sculptures are not machines that actually function at a physicochemical level. Nor should they be taken to simply represent such concrete functioning. Rather, the sculptures are designed to enact at the most elementary level universal transformative processes. Beuys's emphasis on the concrete, material dimension of his work is matched by a claim to the widest application of the plastic theory.

For Beuys, the main employment of the conceptual apparatus provided by the plastic theory is the interpretation of human life, in both its individual and its social forms. Beuys sees the human organism as a formative process involving the chaotic energy of the will channeled by the movements of feeling and emotion to the production of the order of thought. Analogously, the social organism is seen as a triad of economic, legal, and spiritual realms. Given the paradigmatic role of the artistic process, Beuys casts individual as well as social human reality in terms of creative processes.

The linear model of chaos (warmth) being transformed by means of movement (consumption) into order (cold) is further complicated by the dimension of deformation that complements the role of formation in Beuys. Order and form are not stable but are subject to change that includes their decline and destruction. Beuys's work is centrally concerned with the mutual relation between life and death, in which death is both the end of old life and the beginning of new life. The interplay between growth and decline in the phenomena of injury or wound and healing assumes central importance.

For Beuys, the organic nature of the plastic process manifests itself most prominently in human history. In general terms, the plastic historical process consists in the migration of human beings from "warm" Asia to "cold" Europe. Beuys's work shows a continuing fascination with the nomadic life forms of the central Asian steppes and the historical as well as mythical presence of old European cultures, especially the Celts. In Beuys's Eurasian perspective on history, institutional Christianity belongs together with scientific and technological progress in a process of Europe's gradual emancipation from its Asian origins.

Although Beuys does not argue with the progressive, outright liberating potential of the European civilizational process, he is mindful of the limitations of "Western man" *(Westmensch)* as manifested in contemporary materialist culture and the hegemony of economic life over other forms of human self-realization. Many of Beuys's works enact a return to Europe's Eurasian roots. For Beuys, the reintegration of Europe's historic and prehistoric past is not a matter of nostalgic re-creation but an issue concerning the future of humanity. His own political activities, which center on the replacement of representative democracy with more direct, plebiscitarian forms of political life, must be placed in this wider context of a world-historical process.

With its sustained theoretical dimension and its sweeping range of cultural and political issues, Beuys's work leaves behind the historically limited philosophical category of the aesthetic. Not even the wider term *philosophy of art* seems suitable to cover the comprehensive, anthropological scope of Beuys's thinking in and through art. The extra-aesthetic status of Beuys's artistic thought is matched by the very appearance of his works, which seem to belong to the present time in terms of their material substrates, while conveying a magical, almost prehistorical, aura and issuing an appeal to the shaping of the future.

The radical alterations in matters of art involved in Beuys's work operate at several levels. Most important, there is the "extended conception of art" *(erweiterter Kunstbegriff)* that includes formative processes of all kinds, to the point of aspiring to the formation on an invisible revolutionized political body or "social sculpture" *(soziale Skulptur)*. Beuys considered the transformations involved at the individual and at the social level to be a "parallel process" *(Parallelprozess)*.

The emphasis on the process character of art brings with it a shift from an object-centered conception of art to one centered on action, both in its actual performance and in its preparatory and subsequent stages. For many of Beuys's works, this raises serious issues about the possibility and adequacy of their museum presentation. To a large extent, the ingredients of Beuys's sculptural objects, installations, vitrines, and multiples are relics of earlier performances. The reuse of materials lends an aura of celebratory self-reference to many of Beuys's works, which is further enhanced by his frequent self-presentation in the guises of Christian and pagan religiosity. For Beuys, such historical and cultural images are not references to the past but vehicles that transport toward humanity's open future.

The radically revised conception of art goes together with an expanded concept of the artist, as expressed in Beuys's oft-quoted statement, "Every human being is an artist." For Beuys, the artist is not a specialist dealing with specific materials and techniques but the human being as such. Accordingly, Beuys relates to the audience of his works not as aesthetic contemplators but as ideal participants in a common superartistic project.

Beuys's work represents a unique, creative amalgamation of diverse artistic and cultural influences. His thought continues the German double tradition of aesthetic revolution and social critique with its central tenet of the redemptive power of art. Specific affinities can be established between Beuys and Johann Christoph Friedrich von Schiller's project of an "aesthetic education of humanity" *(ästhetische Erziehung des Menschen)*, Friedrich Wilhelm Joseph von

Schelling's conception of a "mythology of reason" *(Mythologie der Vernunft)*, and Wagner's project of a comprehensive, aesthetico-political work of art *(Gesamtkunstwerk)*. Moreover, Beuys shares the individualist orientation of much of German ethicosocial thought, to be found in Kant and Johann Gottlieb Fichte as well as Arthur Schopenhauer and Friedrich Nietzsche, according to which social change has to originate in the individual and its efforts toward moral self-determination.

It is in light of Beuys's German idealist heritage that the shortcomings and dangers of his artistic thinking become most apparent. The inclusion of all human activity in a totalized conception of art obliterates crucial differences between specifically diverse human pursuits such as artistic, scientific, legal, or economic activities, which may well have different sets of rules and criteria. Furthermore, the radical expansion of the concept of art eliminates the critical distance of art from the other manifestations of human life and undermines the adversarial impetus of art. Finally, the other spheres of human life subsumed under the expanded concept of art may undergo an aestheticization that transforms their genuine reality into objects of artistic manipulation.

Given these implications of a completed Beuysian program, it should be stressed that Beuys's lifelong work was itself a process that remained incomplete and open. It would seem quite in line with his own plastic theory that what ultimately mattered was the radical formative activity itself rather than some completed, ready form of thinking or societal order. Instead of looking at Beuys's art as part of his wider politics, one would seem justified in viewing his politics, including his political self-interpretation, as an ingredient of his art. In its very effort to extend the confines of art to new extremes, Beuys's work remains faithful to the role of art as the shadow cast upon life by a brighter future that cannot yet be seen directly.

[*See also* Conceptual Art, *overview article; and* Contemporary Art.]

BIBLIOGRAPHY

Bezzola, Tobia, and Harald Szeemann, eds. *Joseph Beuys.* Zurich, 1994.

Eva, Wenzel, and Jessyka Beuys, eds. *Joseph Beuys: Block Beuys im Hessischen Landesmuseum Darmstadt.* Munich, 1990.

FIU-Kassel (Stephan von Borstel et al.), eds. *Die unsichtbare Skulptur: Zum erweiterten Kunstbegriff von Joseph Beuys.* Stuttgart, 1989.

Götz, Adriani, Winfried Konnertz, and Karin Thomas. *Joseph Beuys.* Rev. exp. ed. Cologne, 1994. Translation by Patricia Lech of an earlier edition published as *Joseph Beuys: Life and Works* (Woodbury, N.Y., 1979).

Harlan, Volker. *Was ist Kunst? Werkstattgespräch mit Joseph Beuys.* Stuttgart, 1986.

Harlan, Volker, Rainer Rappmann, and Peter Schata. *Soziale Plastik: Materialien zu Joseph Beuys.* 2d ed. Achberg, 1980.

Heiner, Bastian, ed. *Joseph Beuys: Skulpturen und Objekte.* Munich, 1988.

Kuspit, Donald. "Beuys: Fat, Felt, and Alchemy." In *The Critic as Artist: The Intentionality of Art*, pp. 345–358. Ann Arbor, 1984.

Kuspit, Donald. *The Cult of the Avant-Garde Artist.* Cambridge and New York, 1993. See pp. 83–99 and 103–106.

Loers, Veit, and Pia Witzmann, eds. *Joseph Beuys: Documenta, Arbeit.* Kassel, 1993.

Oman, Hiltrud. *Die Kunst auf dem Weg zum Leben: Joseph Beuys.* Weinheim, 1988.

Schneede, Uwe M. *Joseph Beuys: Die Aktionen.* Ostfildern-Ruit bei Stuttgart, 1994.

Stachelhaus, Heiner. *Joseph Beuys.* Düsseldorf, 1987.

Stüttgen, Johannes. *Zeitstau: Im Kraftfeld des erweiterten Kunstbegriffs von Joseph Beuys.* Stuttgart, 1988.

Temkin, Ann, and Bernice Rose. *Thinking Is Form: The Drawings of Joseph Beuys.* New York, 1993.

Theewen, Gerhard. *Joseph Beuys: Die Virtrinen.* Cologne, 1993.

Tisdall, Caroline. *Joseph Beuys.* New York, 1979.

Verspohl, Joachim. "Beuys, Joseph." In *Allgemeines Künstlerlexikon: Die bildenden Künstler aller Zeiten und Völker,* vol. 10, pp. 295–306. Munich, 1995.

Vischer, Theodora. *Beuys und die Romantik: Individuelle Ikonographie, individuelle Mythologie?* Cologne, 1983.

Vischer, Theodora. *Joseph Beuys: Die Einheit des Werkes.* Cologne, 1991.

Wiegand, Wilfried, et al. *In Memoriam Joseph Beuys: Obituaries, Essays, Speeches.* Translations by Timothy Nevill. Bonn, 1986.

Zweite, Armin, et al. *Joseph Beuys: Natur, Materie, Form.* Munich, 1991.

GÜNTER ZÖLLER

BHARATA. *See* Abhinavagupta; *and* Rasa.

BLACK AESTHETIC. The foundations of the black aesthetic can be traced back to the nineteenth century and to a tradition of earlier writings, social and cultural movements, and literary manifestos extending into the first three decades of the twentieth century. The emergence and flowering of the Black Aesthetic movement, however, can be placed roughly between 1964, the year of the passing of the Civil Rights Act, and the end of the Vietnam War in 1975 (Martin, 1988, p. 25). During that period, the movement served both as a critique of the mainstream criteria on the basis of which all modes of evaluative criticism of literature, art, and music were carried out and as a vehicle for the introduction of a set of countercriteria. These new criteria, in turn, inspired a range of politically activist poetry, plays, drama, and essays, as well as further experiments in "free jazz" and a new approach to the visual arts, collectively known as the Black Arts movement. The activities of both of these movements had been realized in the context of both the black civil rights and the black power nationalist movements by means of a network of rapidly improvised, black-controlled organizations. These included a chain of writing and theater workshops, journals (which focused on poetry but comprised other genres, including theoretical and political essays), and several black-owned publishing houses. Among the most memorable of the workshops was the Black Arts Repertory Theatre School in Harlem, which was headed by Amiri Baraka and others and opened in the Spring of 1964. The range of activities of this school consisted centrally in the staging of a series of plays written by Baraka that dealt with one of the major imperatives of both movements. This imperative was the transformation of consciousness from being "Negro," in the negative term defined by the dominant society, to being self-defined positively as "Black," with the effecting of a Negro-to-Black conversion experience (Van Deburg, 1992, pp. 33–54).

Specifically, the proposals for new counterevaluative criteria for an aesthetic criticism appropriate to the new drama, poetry, and fiction then emerging were put forward in a wide range of nonmainstream journals and anthologies. Central to the former was the *Negro Digest*, later *The Black World*, edited by Hoyt Fuller. Fuller, with a group of contributors who included, among others, Don L. Lee and Carolyn Gerald, were among the leading nonacademic proponents of the need for new standards of writing, art, and music, able to displace those of the mainstream in all fields of artistic creativity. The literary critical aspect of the black aesthetic, in its academic form, was introduced into the English departments of the mainstream universities, however, by a group of literary scholars, among them Addison Gayle, Jr., Stephen Henderson, and Houston A. Baker, Jr. This group soon began to interact with, and in some cases cross over into, by means of joint appointments, the new black studies programs/departments that were established toward the end of the 1960s. The struggle for the academic institutionalization of black studies was fought primarily by a recently enlarged group of black students and younger faculty at mainstream universities who had begun to mount a challenge—on the basis of what they saw as the exclusion and denigration of the black historical experience and the "white orientedness" of the university as a whole—to the reputed universal applicability of the truth of the mainstream order of knowledge, and to call for "something other than truth in an abstract universal sense" (McWhorter, 1969, p. 67).

The challenges of Black Aesthetic/Black Arts movements to the reputed universality of the mainstream's evaluative aesthetic criteria were also developed in a series of anthologies, among them *The New Black Poetry* (1969) edited by the poet Clarence Major, one of the first theoreticians of the movements. Other important anthologies included Nikki Giovanni's *Night Comes Softly: Anthology of Black Female Voices* (1971), Abraham Chapman's *New Black Voices* (1972), and collections such as Amiri Baraka's essays on art, *In Raise, Race, Rays, Raze: Essays since 1965* (1971), and Ishmael Reed's *19 Necromancers from Now* (1970). The two anthologies that were to be the definitive foundational texts of the movement, however, were LeRoi Jones (later Amiri Baraka) and Larry Neal's *Black Fire: An Anthology of Afro-American Writings* (1968) and the collection of theoretical essays edited by Addison Gayle, Jr., *The Black Aesthetic* (1971). Both of these can now be seen to have crystallized the creative practice and dominant theoretical tendencies of the movements in what were to be, from 1968 to 1971, their apogee years. During the same epoch of heightened intellectual questioning, what was to become the foundational text of the black studies movement was also published: the proceedings of a symposium organized by the Black Student Alliance at Yale, financed by the Yale administration, and held at the university in the Spring of 1968. Titled *Black Studies in the University*, the proceedings were published in 1969, the same year that *Black Fire* came out in paperback.

A "Cultural Revolution in Art and Ideas," an Alternative Aesthetic Tradition, and a New Standard of Being, of Beauty. Larry Neal, coeditor with Amiri Baraka of *Black Fire*, proposed in a series of essays that, because the Western aesthetic had "run its course," what had to be worked toward was "a cultural revolution in art and ideas" (Neal, 1971, p. 272). The Black Arts movement as "the aesthetic and spiritual sister of the Black Power Movement" had to envision not only "an art that speaks directly to the needs and aspirations of Black America," but also one that would effect a "radical reordering of the Western cultural aesthetic" on the basis of the creation of a "separate symbolism, mythology, critique, and iconology" (ibid.). The "main tenet of Black Power" had been the "necessity for Black People to define the "world in their own terms," and now the Black artist should make the same point in the context of aesthetics, doing so outside and beyond the premises of the "mythological configurations" of Western culture, of its "unique construal of what life is, of what art is" (Neal, 1968, p. 648).

If some fifteen years later, in 1983, the anthropologist Clifford Geertz was to point out that although the contemporary culture of the West is a local culture and that such a recognition was still a "fugitive truth" that needs urgently to be taught (Geertz, 1983, p. 16), Neal had placed the emphasis, correctly, on the fact that it was also a culture that was unique in human history—correctly because, as can now be seen, it had been precisely in the terms of this uniqueness that the issue of the aesthetic (i.e., the "construal of what . . . art is") had become central, from the nineteenth century onward, to the overall struggles both of the peoples of sub-Saharan Africa and to those of its diaspora. Within the overall process of the secularization of human existence by the humanist intellectual revolution of the Renaissance, the later Enlightenment's rupture with all forms of religious authority had led to the elaboration of a new form of authority. The projection of an aesthetic criterion adapted from Greek classical sculpture as a criterion ostensibly determined by universally applicable laws of nature was to enable a new principle of classification, that of "beauty" (the Greek Ideal type construct) and of "ugliness" (its projected countertype), to come to serve as as much "a principle of human classification as a material factor of measurement, climate, and the environment" (Mosse, 1985,

p. 11). As a result, within the emergence of an overall climate of opinion based on the thesis that a true soul could reside only in a perfect human form, with the Greek Ideal type (whose physical referent was the color and physiognomy of the Indo-European peoples) thereby coming to be posited as the standard of beauty and of being to which all mankind should relate, the Negroid physiognomy of the large majority of African peoples—the human hereditary variation most different from that of the Europeans—had been taken not only as "proving" a greater degree of closeness of black peoples to monkeys and apes rather than to the human race, but also as the extreme marker of "ugliness." This essentialized bioaesthetic equation was to be further developed by the pseudoscientific discourse of phrenology, whose founding premise of a "measurable" *facial angle* that identified the Greek Ideal type as a biologically determined norm of beauty (because it was ostensibly the "facial angle" most distant from that of the ape) also identified the "facial angle of the Negroid countertype as ostensibly the closest to the ape's. If, in the wake of Charles Darwin's theory of evolution, the "facial angle" of the represented Ideal type of the European physiognomy now became projected as the marker of the most evolved mode of being and of beauty, and at the same time that of the black Bantu countertype came to be represented as the marker of the least evolved modality of the human—the nadir, therefore, of being as of beauty (ibid., pp. 10–15)—this same evolved/nonevolved schema would lead to the systemic stigmatization of the cultural creations of sub-Saharan Africa and of its New World diaspora. They too were to be stigmatized as nonevolved, and therefore "backward," as creations of the lowest of the "lower races."

As a result, within the hegemonic context of this principle of classification and its essentialized equation, all precursor attempts of black writings and literary movements to grapple with the systemic negation instituting this principle—from (1) the mid-nineteenth-century fiction and nonfiction of a Martin Delaney; to (2) the 1903 collection of essays *The Souls of Black Folk* by W. E. B. Du Bois (with its classic identification of the conflicted nature of the consciousness of the "American Negro" as a "double consciousness" in which, in order to realize himself as an "American" he had both to see and evaluate his "Negro" self in terms of the negative criteria of the dominant world), together with its setting in train of the aesthetic revalorization of the spirituals of or "sorrow songs" that had been created by black slaves (Du Bois, 1965, pp. 213–216); to (3) the diaspora-wide Garveyite movement (one of whose platform's major provisos was the call for black peoples to learn to love, rather than to continue to despise their skin color, Negroid facial features, hair, and Afro-European modalities of speech, as the negative images of the dominant world induced them to do); to (4) the first literary cultural movement of the Harlem Renaissance in the 1920s (whose manifesto written by Alain Locke called for a new art for the "New Negro"); to (5) the 1930s movements of negritude in the francophone Africa and the Caribbean (whose avatar figures were the poet/thinkers Aimé Césaire and Léopold Sédar Senghor), as well as of the Afro-Cuban movement (whose key figure was the poet Nicolás Guillén)—were to be compelled to adopt a dual approach. The approach involved working to effect the revalorization of black being, its skin color, and Negroid physiognomy, as well as that of the equally stigmatized black cultural forms, while also directing these revalorizations to an even more central purpose. It was therefore this dual approach and primary purpose— that of the effecting of the transformation of the mode of consciousness, in which all black peoples had come to see and to respond to themselves in the prescriptively negative terms in which they, like their white peers, as Frantz Fanon would point out in the sixties, had been socialized as subjects of our contemporary order (Fanon, 1967, pp. 13–14)—that was now to define Neal's more comprehensive formulations in response to the same issue with which his precursors had grappled.

The thrust of the four-page table summary that Neal contributed to Gayle's *Black Aesthetic* anthology therefore supported his revalorizing thesis of the existence, in the Americas, of an alternative aesthetic tradition to that of the Euro-American mainstream and identified the origin of the black aesthetic in the African-derived tradition that had been carried by the nonformally educated lower-class black Americans, the creators of the achieved forms of black music. He then traced a line of descent for black music both from the mythological system of traditional African religions (the spirit worship of the Orishas or loas) and from the syncretized Afro-Christian forms that these religions had taken to the New World, such as the religions of voodoo and macumba (both of which syncretized with Catholicism), as well as the Afro-Protestant forms in whose context priests had been transformed, in the secular U.S. world, into "preachers, poets, blues singers, macdaddies, politicians" (Neal, quoted in Gayle, 1971, pp. 13–16). Black music, like black dance in the New World, he further argued, was the expression of a "memory" born of both Africa and the Middle Passage, the slave trade, slavery, and segregation, and had come to express quite different aesthetic imperatives to those of the mainstream. At the same time, however, in his Afterword to the *Black Fire* anthology, Neal emphasized that the primary goal of any literature of revolt or revolutionary aesthetic should be to ensure the destruction of the "double consciousness" that W. E. B. Du Bois had identified, because it was this "double consciousness" that had, inter alia, induced black artists to despise their own African-derived alternative cultural tradition, making them oblivious not only to the originality and creative force of black music, but also to the fact that it would be only on the basis of the aesthetic criteria similar to those expressed in black music

that the achieved perfection of a truly great black art could be attained.

If Neal was the major theoretician of the Black Arts movement, it was LeRoi Jones/Amiri Baraka who, as the artist-activist of the movement, put the theories into a conjoined creative and political praxis. For Baraka, who, at this stage, saw himself as a poet-artist who was also a black nationalist, art and poetry were a central site of the cultural revolution. In addition, his creative work, especially his poetry, had come to be defined by an intimate and long-standing relationship with black music. This relation (besides his 1963 book *The Blues People*, he had also published *Black Music* in 1969) had led him to be among the first to call for a black poetics that should seek to model itself on black music. He himself became a practitioner of this attempt to effect a shift in black written poetry by the use of the rhythmic imperative of black music, as well as by means of a turn both toward the speech patterns of the hitherto despised African inflected vernacular of Black English, and toward the dynamic of its fast-paced urban street colloquialisms. A 1973 poem, "Food for Thought," written by Val Ferdinand (Kalamu Ya Salaam), canonizes Baraka as the "bird [the analogue of the great jazz musician Charlie Parker] of black poetics" (quoted in Chapman, 1973, p. 379).

At the beginning of the sixties, Baraka (then LeRoi Jones) had been an established avant-garde Greenwich Village writer, with two published collections of poetry, one of essays, and a novel to his credit (Van Deburg, 1992, p. 176). With his conversion to black nationalist politics, however, he turned his back on his earlier modernist poetic practice and set out, through his poetry and plays, as well as through the institutions he founded, to effect Neal's call for a "radical reordering of the Western cultural aesthetic." With his change of name from LeRoi Jones to Imamu (spiritual leader) Amiri (prince) Baraka (blessed one), he himself became the living example of that Negro-to-Black conversion experience whose process, in the case of others, it was the function and goal of his series of revolutionary plays, staged at the Theatre School in Harlem, to effect and propagate. These plays, including *Dutchman, Experimental Death Unit #One, Black Mass,* and *Jello,* as well as his earlier play *The Slave,* all foregrounded the issue of black America's need to grapple with its own internalized consciousness, as well as with the negation of blackness that that consciousness entailed, if its members were to unify with each other in a revolutionary struggle to ensure the psychic emancipation and the material well-being of their mostly impoverished community.

The linkage of this consciousness-transformation goal to the fundamental issue of the mainstream's aesthetic criteria was forcefully captured by the popular slogan "Black is Beautiful!" which served as the common thread unifying the continuum of approaches to the quest for a black aesthetic. These approaches ranged from the more political, which saw the aesthetic as a mere function of the broader struggle, to the purely aesthetic, which saw aesthetics as the central site of the struggle. Embodying the former thrust, Maulana Karenga (head of the Black Nationalist Organization) would have the most direct and widespread impact on a broad spectrum of black Americans. Because Karenga saw the aesthetic issue only as a part of the larger issue of a "black cultural renaissance" that was essential to a revolutionary struggle for Black Power, he and his organization, US, were in the forefront of the popular aspects of this "renaissance." Leading the West Coast "back to black" movements in clothing and hairstyles, his organization championed the teachings of Swahili as a "nontribal" language of "self-determination," sponsored community-based arts events, and inaugurated the celebration of black holidays, such as Uhuru Day (August 11, commemorating the 1965 Watts riot) and Kuzaliwa (May 19, celebrating Malcolm X's birth) (Van Deburg, 1992, p. 171). Although he saw himself, in the terms of his adopted African name, as the "keeper" of the black community's tradition, he nevertheless saw this tradition as one whose origin was in agrarian Africa, and as a tradition reinterpreted by him, rather than as the empirical one reinvented over the centuries by lower-class popular initiatives in the Americas and in the Caribbean. As a result, although he borrowed eclectically from several traditional African cultures in order to develop a set of seven value principles (i.e., the *Nguzo Saba*) by means of which black people were from here on to order their relations and live their lives (the invented Christmas holiday, Kwanzaa, which was to outlive the demise of the movement and to take its place as a "multicultural" holiday promoted by corporate consumer culture, had its origin here), Karenga dismissed the musical tradition of the blues. Because the "blues" preached resignation, he wrote in an essay, they were a hindrance to the revolutionary struggle and would have to be given up (Karenga, 1971, p. 482). On this point, however, Karenga encountered opposition from some black writers, among them James Cunningham. In a 1972 essay titled "Hemlock for the Black Artist: Karenga Style," Cunningham pointed out that Karenga's viewpoint on the arts derived from a position of black cultural nationalism, which posited a contradiction between the individual and the collective. Yet, "when Ray Charles sings the blues, he is also a product of the cultural form that is the blues," a cultural form that not only "allows him to be a real individual," but also bridges the gap between the individual and the collective. If Karenga wanted revolutionary change, what better witness to this change could there be than "the spectacle, the drama of a man, changed and charged, and tuned into the mysterious power of the vocabulary and a grammar called the blues"? Karenga, therefore, only rejects the blues together with what he defines as "his people's past ways of thinking," because a black nationalist cannot "reasonably define his own goal" as being that of "the develop-

ment of a culture *for* his people" without "first rejecting as mistaken the stubborn belief that Black people already have a culture, a tradition, of which both the Negro's speech and abundant musical expression are a definitive and irrefutable part." This is the assumption that had come to bolster the "shepherd complex of the leaders of the movement" (Cunningham, 1972, pp. 484–487).

Those for whom, unlike Karenga, the aesthetic was *the* site of the struggle, and who also belonged to this first extra-academic phase, included the poet Clarence Major. Major proposed that the issue of the mainstream aesthetics and its evaluative criteria was inseparable from the issue of the culture that gave rise to them, that therefore the real target of black writing should be Western culture itself. The role of "black poetic energy" should be to overthrow "the Western ritual and passion, the curse, the dark ages of this death, the original sin's impact on a people and their unjust projection of it upon us Black people." In addition, this focus on Western culture itself and the negative projections that it imposed on black people by means of its aesthetic criteria was also developed during this first, extra-academic phase of the Black Aesthetic movement by Hoyt Fuller. Fuller, who, as editor of the *Negro Digest* (later *The Black World*), was both the promoter and a theoretician of the aesthetics-as-a-central-site-of-the-struggle tendency, contributed an essay to the *Black Aesthetic* anthology, in which he challenged Euro-America's (Greek Ideal type) "reference standard of being" and of beauty, and called for these standards to be reinvented (Fuller, 1971, pp. 7–8). In the same context of a proposed war over *"the control of the image."* Carolyn Gerald, one of the contributors to the journal, in a seminal essay published first in the *Negro Digest* and then in *The Black Aesthetic*, traced the way in which the negative images of the Black projected by Western art and literature played and plays a direct role in the control of the behaviors of black Americans, leading them to acquiesce in their own group subordination. She ended her essay with a poem, which began with the cry: "Dress the Muse in black / No, kill her!" (Gerald, 1971, p. 335). Gerald's and Fuller's thesis of a "war over the control of the image" was also central to the theoreticians of the second wave, which began in the early 1970s "when the Black Aesthetic Movement was appropriated and expanded by Black academics" (Martin, 1988, p. 20). Its members included, among others, Stephen Henderson, Houston Baker, Jr. (in his first literary-critical phase), and, centrally, Addison Gayle, Jr., whose writings were to become synonymous with the Black Aesthetic movement as it related to literary criticism.

Literary Criticism: The "White Aesthetic" and the Call for a New "Table of the Laws," for an "Ars Poetica for All." Gayle articulated the major theses of his own approach to a literary criticism based on the black aesthetic: in his introduction to and two essays in *The Black Aesthetic* (1971) and *The Way of the New World: The Black Novel in*

America (1975). In *The Black Aesthetic,* Gayle identified what the goal of such an aesthetic must be. Like Major, who had earlier argued that the "writing of a poem should serve some useful human-edifying function" (quoted in Martin, 1988, p. 20), Gayle proposed that, unlike the art-for-art's-sake goal of mainstream literary and artistic criticisms, the new goal of both black literary criticism and the new black writing must be to "aid men to become better than they are" (Gayle, 1971, p. xxiii). After tracing the "racial" textual politics by means of which Euro-American writers had portrayed black Americans in terms that equated them with evil and ugliness, Gayle saw this racialized textual politic as the result of a mainstream aesthetic whose reputed universalism was really that of a "white aesthetic." White critics argued that because "Americans of all races, colors, and creeds share a common cultural heredity" (that of the "one predominant culture—the American culture"), and because, in this context, literature, as the most important by-product of this cultural monolith, knows "no parochial boundaries," there could be no "black aesthetic" given that there is no "white aesthetic" (ibid., p. 39). But the facts belie this claim; for nowhere is this hegemonic "white aesthetic" more to be seen at work than in the way its prescriptive criteria have led to the cultural strangulation of black creativity. The goals of a black aesthetic should, therefore, be to unleash this creativity. Because historical reality has led to two different experiences—one white, the other black—with each "unique experience" leading to the production of "unique cultural artifacts," the "unique art derived from the unique cultural experience of Black America mandates unique critical tools for evaluation" (ibid., p. xxiv). The role of the black literary critic should be to refuse the assimilationist tradition of the mainstream in order to bring about a new black literature (ibid., pp. 445–453). The role of black writers should be to create a new literature that, turning its back on the earlier "literature of assimilation," would now redirect its art "to the strivings within the race."

In a later book, *The Way of the New World: The Black Novel in America* (1976), Gayle shifted his position somewhat. Rather than attack the idea of the universal as he had done earlier, he reclaimed the universal in the context of the call for a general social transformation. Calling for a battle to be waged against the imagists of the mainstream, whom he now defined as being as much black as they were white, Gayle proposed that a central criterion should be placed at the core of black aesthetic ideology, as the criterion to be used for the evaluation of all art. This criterion was based on the question: "How much better has the work of art made the life of a single human being on this planet, and how functional has been the work of art in moving us toward that moment when an *ars poetica* is possible for all?" On the basis of this criterion, the issue was not only that of the mainstream aesthetic having to be displaced and re-placed. The world to which it belonged had also to be remade: "before beauty can be seen, felt, heard, and appreciated by a majority of the earth's people, a new world must be brought into being; the earth must be made free and habitable for all men" (Gayle, 1975, p. 379).

The contradiction that Cunningham had pointed to in the case of Karenga with respect to the blues was also at work in Gayle's proposed new prescriptive guidelines. This contradiction lay in the gap between the ideology and aesthetics of black nationalism (essentially an ideology and aesthetics of the radical, black intelligentsia) and the reality of the aesthetic tradition and poetics of liminality of the lower-class black Americans who had been the autonomous creators of an alternative *ars poetica.* Ishmael Reed, who represented the most maverick wing of the Black Aesthetic movement, had even earlier noted and attacked this contradiction. Putting forward the alternative of a "neo-hoodoo aesthetic"—a term adopted from the African-derived popular black culture itself in the place of the black aesthetic—Reed called into question what he saw as the totalitarian nature of the prescriptive criteria of both black aesthetic and Marxist critics. In spite of Reed's projected neo-hoodoo aesthetic, however, his own largely satirical work, which harnessed the African-derived belief system of magic to its own radical intelligentsia purposes, was not itself to escape Cunningham's insight into the fact that the fundamental challenge to the mainstream and to its class (and local culture) aesthetics was being carried not by a Black poetics, but rather by the liminalist poetics of the "grammar and vocabulary of the blues," one whose alternative aesthetic tradition places it outside the terms of the mainstream aesthetics with its standard of beauty and of being.

The Funky Low-down Aesthetics and the Rise of Rap in the Place of a Black Poetics. In an essay in *The Black Aesthetic* titled "The Changing Same (R&B and New Black Music)," Baraka pointed out that the songs of the popular singer James Brown had come to "identify an entire group of people in America," that the music of these songs made an "image," thereby bringing into existence and revealing a "world powered by that image." Furthermore, because the "world James Brown's images power is the lowest placement (the most alien) in White American social order," it is the "Blackest and potentially the strongest" (Baraka, quoted in Addison, 1971, p. 123). The term *blackest* here signifies that the group whose world James Brown's song images served and serves as the ultimate negative reference point, not only in terms of *race* (and thereby "blackest" in the sense defined by black cultural nationalism), but also as the ultimate negative reference point in terms of *class.* Given that its creators and their primary audience comprise both the working class and the most extreme form of casually employed or endemically jobless members of the underclass, and as such the most liminally deviant category of the lower classes, the musical culture produced by this dually proscribed group had come to serve, in the terms of Lawrence Levine, as the lowest of the lowbrow to the high-brow ideals specific to the aesthetics of the now culturally hegemonic bourgeoisie. After making the point, in his book *Highbrow/Lowbrow: The Emergence of Cultural Hierarchy in America* (1988), that the value terms *highbrow/lowbrow* were taken from the pseudoscientific discourse of phrenology (the same discourse that had earlier given rise to the "facial angle" index), Levine shows how this "brow" index was to enable the cultural hegemony of the bourgeoisie to be ef-fected through the elaboration of new, class-specific canons in all the arts. Central to these was that of the literary canon, which comprised the works of "highbrow" figures such as William Shakespeare, John Milton, and Charles Dickens, who were then projected as the iconic bearers of an ostensi-bly superior, because highly evolved, form of life along with musical, visual, and literary forms (Levine, 1988, pp. 221–231).

Because the term *highbrow* could serve as a value term only by each canon's relation of refusal and exclusion of all forms of art and music that provided the popular entertain-ment enjoyed by the lower classes (Bourdieu, 1984, p. 486), all such forms were negatively iconized by being mapped onto the ostensibly "pitifully lowbrow of alien races." As a result, if this new system of value categorization served to separate the "artistic" cultural forms of the bourgeoisie from those of the lower classes, and, indeed, of the "lower races," nowhere was the signifier of the ultimate lowbrow to be more totally inscribed than in the "mere entertainment" forms of black music, in the soul/funk aesthetics and poetics of its rhythm and blues. "Rhythm and blues music," as "the prevailing popular music in Black America by the 1940's," was carried by "stripped-down urban combos" and was de-fined by "dance rhythm, scat rhythm, tap rhythm, horn solo rhythm," because the "high energy and low overhead of these small black hands made them the center of Black folks' entertainment"; it was out of this existential interac-tional process that alternative criteria of what aesthetic force and beauty were being established (Vincent, 1996, pp. 40–41). "People who worked all day," Vincent points out, "needed good, hard, loud soulful music to get them through a rough night of dancing and carousing." The criteria here were those of "a heartfelt scream, a billowing saxophone, a rocking guitar, pulsing rhythms and singers who were sin-cere," criteria that ensured that "the hard Black troubles of the day would go away." Vincent cites Jones/Baraka to the effect that its very vulgarity "assured its meaningful emo-tional connection with people's lives" (ibid.) and trans-muted the pain of their proscribed deviance and liminality from "normal" being, at the level of both their racial/cul-tural and their class/underclass status, into forms that moved outside the parameters of the mainstream, trans-valuing aesthetic value rather than inverting it. There was, therefore, to be an incommensurability between the forms

produced out of the dually *race/class* proscription of the black lower classes and the genre of contemporary written poetry, whether written by whites or by the most radical proponents of a black poetics.

Baraka had emphasized this crucial difference in his book *The Blues People,* when he located the origin of black music in the difference of worldviews between the traditional African cultural system that the slaves brought with them and that of the Western mainstream, as well as in the ex-cluded role that had been assigned to its bearers and cre-ators in the social structure of both pre- and the postaboli-tion United States. Because of the continued existence of a "border beyond which the Negro could not go whether mu-sically or socially," it was out of this proscribed situation that the genre of black music would be born. Because the lower-class "Negroes" who were its creators—unlike mid-dle-class black artists, who, although marginalized on the grounds of *race,* could nevertheless make use of the cultural forms of the dominant culture—had no access to these highbrow forms, they had been forced to resort to "other resources, whether African, sub-cultural, or hermetic" (Jones, 1963, p. 80). The paradox here is that it was the *race/class* proscription of the lower-class black tradition that would ensure that, among the aesthetic traditions carried by the multiple groups who came as free settlers and immi-grants to the Americas, only those traditions that are African-derived have been brought into the modern world on their own terms. Thus, if, as the art historian Robert Far-ris Thompson (whose paper at a Yale Symposium docu-mented the continued existence of African wood-carving traditions in the United States [Farris Thompson, 1969]) has further pointed out (in his 1983 book *Flash of Spirit: African and Afro-American Art and Philosophy*) that much of the contemporary popular music of the world has had its source in Afro-America, and increasingly on the African continent itself, and that this can only be understood by the fact that since "the Atlantic slave trade ancient African or-ganizing principles of song and dance have crossed the seas from the Old World to the New," he at the same time at-tempted to identify these principles and the aesthetic crite-ria to which they give rise as ones that move entirely outside the terms of the aesthetic criteria of the West. In his com-mentary on the photograph of a terra-cotta head created between the tenth and twelfth centuries by master Yoruba sculptors, who were producing work of high quality at a time when nothing of comparative quality was being pro-duced in Europe, Farris Thompson explains the way in which the criteria that the head embodies—criteria that would be transplanted in the Americas—were specific to the Yoruba aesthetic tradition. Because, in the Yoruba religion, the spirits are seen as messengers and embodiments of *Ashé* (a vital spiritual force and energy of which the supreme God, Olorum, is the quintessence), all artistic creation is as-sessed according to the degrees of "freshness and improvisation" with which they express this vital force, as well as the spiritual command that it embodies, its power to make things happen (Farris Thompson, 1984, p. 5). The terracotta head's aesthetic perfection, rather than the result of the represented universalism of the Greek Ideal type criterion, was the criterion of *Ashé*—in this case, that of "spiritual alertness (the searching gaze), of self-discipline and discretion (the sealed lips)" (ibid., p. 4).

Because of their proscribed and segregated status, therefore, the lower-class descendants of the slaves would find themselves in a situation in which they were provided with an aesthetic and "ontological" ground that, while itself also becoming secularized, was one that was quite different from that of the dominant culture. At the same time, however, it was a "ground" that, unlike that of the elite heroic traditions of African art, had been refashioned by the slaves and their nonelite descendants (Farris Thompson, 1969, p. 165) in the new terms of the historico-existential reality of their group experience of subordination to another culture in the terms of whose aesthetic norms theirs were the negation, the noncriteria of lowbrow "field niggerism." Yet, it was through their existential anchoring in "field niggerism" that the lower-class descendants of the slaves in the Americas and the Caribbean were to effect the syncretic fusion of two dominant world traditions, that of pagan Africa and that of Judeo-Christian Western Europe, as a fusion out of which emerged the secular *sermo humilis* of the spirituals, gospel, the blues, jazz, rhythm and blues, samba, salsa, mamba, zouk, reggae, and rap, together with the continuum of new global popular forms to which they gave rise. Hence the paradox that, whereas jazz, during the sixties, could renew itself as "free jazz" by returning to the atonal traditions of the "shouts" and "hollers" of the archaic forms of the blues (Berendt, 1975, p. 26), the very virtuosity with which Baraka and other practitioners of a black poetics were seeking to bring written poetry close to the now audiovisually carried oral structure and rhythmic dynamic of black music, was, at the same time, signaling the end of black written poetry as a meaningful activity. In spite of the dynamic quality of the poetry written on the basis of the call for a black poetics (as in the case of Baraka's own poetry, that of a group of women poets including Sonia Sanchez, Mari Evans, Jayne Cortez, Sherley Anne Williams, and Nikki Giovanni, as well as the recordings made by the group The Last Poets, who set their revolutionary poetry to the drum rhythms of black music), they were still the expression—to make use of a distinction put forward by José Luis González—of popularist models from above that seek to harness the creative energies of a lower-class stratum to its own "elite" dynamic, as distinct from "models from below" in which creative artists from that stratum impose their own criteria (González, 1980, pp. 99–100). As a result, when Larry Neal, in *Black Fire,* put forward the challenge of the new criterion that was to be ultimately defining of the black poetics (i.e., "can a Black poet write a poem the way James Brown screams?"), this challenge would soon be moot, overtaken by events.

Although the struggle of the Black Aesthetic and Black Arts movements had been to unify the black middle class and the masses in a common struggle within the overall context of the black civil rights and Black Power movements, one of the contradictory effects to which these movements led was the splitting off and separation of these interests. In place of a black poetics, a new form would arise out of the difference of situation between, on the one hand, a vastly expanded, socially mobile and increasingly suburban black middle class, and, on the other, the third of the population that were now being pushed even further into endemic joblessness and poverty, with many trapped in the increasingly physical isolation of crime- and drug-ridden ghettos. This new form was rap, and it was the direct progeny of James Brown's "blackest" music, which, as Vincent points out, had come to speak to and for the black masses who now found themselves dispossessed by the decline of the movements of the 1960s. Brown's "Black Power" messages were powerful, yet secondary to the sounds with which he powered his message, sounds of "a furious and unrelenting barrage of stripped-down rhythmic R&B, a primordial funk groove" that turned rhythmic structure on its head, emphasizing the downbeat—the "one in a four bar"—while driving "the furious bluesy fatback drumbeats all around the twos and fours to fill up the rhythms, never leaving any blank space" (Vincent, 1996, p. 8).

Rap had its origin *both* in Brown's stripped-down rhythmic R&B and in reggae music, which had been born out of a similar jobless ghetto situation in Kingston, Jamaica. As Houston Baker notes, it was as Brown's sounds began to be routinized by the disco craze that rap was put into play by disk jockeys, first in the reggae/sound systems scene in Jamaica, and then in the United States, as a form of toasting or ongoing political and cultural commentary. By their appropriation of the two-turntable technology of disco, thereby transforming the turntables into a sound system, and then adding a beat box and a heavy amplification headphone, the disk jockeys created the new medium in which the poetics of rap was created (Baker, 1993; pp. 88–90). In spite of the contradictions arising from the rapid commercialization of the genre (and thereby the emphasis being placed on one of its variants, gangsta' rap, and on the frequent brutality and misogyny that marked its lyrics), rap was instantly, by the very nature of its underclass political thrust and new post-print-medium, to become an international and metropolitan form expressed in multiple languages, syncretizing with indigenous popular musical styles—in effect, an *ars poetica* for all. But the "essentialized equation" was not to go away. Rap, like its major creators, jobless black males of the ghetto (who, as the Other to the also bourgeois ideal of the human as economic breadwinner, were now made to occupy the extreme Human Other place formerly taken by the black population as a whole), would now find itself as systemically stigmatized as the "grammar and vocabulary of the blues" had been prior to the sixties.

The Decline of the Movements: From a "Black" to an Ethnic, Multicultural Aesthetic. At the end of their decade of flowering, in spite of the far-flung and interlocking nature of their activities, the decline of the Black Aesthetic and Black Arts movements (unlike the black studies programs, which were incorporated into the mainstream of academia in new and domesticated terms such as "ethnic" and/or multicultural studies) was precipitous. This decline coincided with several larger factors, including the tapering off of the black civil rights movement following passage of civil rights laws that ensured the ending of overt segregation in the South, the instituting of federally guaranteed voting rights and affirmative action policies for nonwhite "minorities" and Euro-American women, and the subsiding of radical New Left politics subsequent to the end of the Vietnam War. Another factor was the blow given to the Black Aesthetic movement by the "defection" of the most creatively original practitioner of the "Black Arts" movement, Amiri Baraka, following his conversion from cultural nationalism to Marxism-Leninism and his call for Marxist criteria, rather than the prescriptive criteria and guidelines posited by the Black Aestheticians for a new black writing, as "the only possible guidelines for acceptable writing . . . which would aid the people" (Martin, 1988, p. 35).

Two additional factors also contributed to the movement's demise. The first was the emergence of a new field of black feminist fiction, in the context of a newly emergent black feminist criticism, which, as part of the increasingly hegemonic Euro-American feminist movement, displaced and subsumed the creative ferment of the Black Aesthetic and Black Arts movements, replacing the earlier nationalist imperative with their own, primarily gender, issues and concerns. The second factor was the elaboration of a new mainstream literary-critical thrust put forward by a successor generation of academics who had been hired in English departments in significant numbers in response to earlier struggles. Against the claim of the earlier movement to a black aesthetic with its own evaluative criteria as distinct from those of the mainstream, including those of literary criticism, the goal of this group was to integrate the study of black literature (redefined in ethnic terms first as "Afro-American," then as "African-American") into a new multicultural liberal pluralist framework. This new goal was most clearly expressed in the work of two scholars, Houston Baker, Jr., and Henry Louis Gates, Jr. As a young beginning scholar, Baker, in a 1971 anthology, *Black Literature in America,* had himself put into practice some of the major literary-critical tenets of the black aesthetic. A decade later, arguing that the term *black aesthetic* should more properly

be defined in ethnic terms, as "Afro-American Aesthetics," he put forward the idea of a descriptive "anthropological" approach to literary criticism, whose aim, rather than to effect an aesthetic revolution, was to seek to identify and describe a ceremonial pattern that was distinctive in Afro-American narrative events. He achieved this aim with the publication of his *Afro-American Poetics: Revisions of Harlem and the Black Aesthetic* in 1988.

Over the same period, Gates, using a multicultural and poststructuralist approach, even more decisively refuted the goals of the earlier two movements. Where they had sought above all to "unfix the nation of Blackness from the traditional color symbology of the West," as one in which blackness was equated "with ugliness, evil, corruption, and death," Gates accused them in deconstructionist terminology of having become entrapped in a "racial essentialism," a definition of "blackness" that had come to depend "on the absent presence of the Western framework it sets out to subvert" (Dubey, 1994, pp. 28–29). Poststructuralist critical activity, like all contemporary critical activity, however multicultural, must itself depend on the very same cultural-aesthetic framework in whose logic blackness continues to be portrayed in negative terms that are themselves essentialized. This fact was overlooked by its practitioners, but that did not detract from the success of the later generation's attacks on the earlier movements. As a result, although the dismissive charge of a "Black essentialism" became commonplace, the "essentialism" of the premises of the mainstream framework that the movements had "reversed" (in order to challenge the premises by which the equation of blackness with evil was, and is, inseparably linked to its aesthetic equation with "ugliness") was strategically ignored.

Conclusion. Both the impact and the legacy of the Black Aesthetics and Black Arts movements lay not in the answers that their theoreticians and artists gave, but in the central questions that they posed to the larger society. These questions had, and still have, to do with the phenomenon of the aesthetic in general (its possible relation to consciousness, the relation of both to Geertz's "local cultures," the question posed by the prison poet Etheridge Knight as to whether aesthetic criteria are necessarily also moral, or socially egalitarian) as well as questions specific to contemporary mainstream aesthetics and to its posited acultural universality; that is, these questions are still valid, and still have to be answered, even where some of the premises they had challenged have been transformed, even sanitized, in the postmodern age.

In this context, a point made by Mikhail Epstein is apposite. Epstein argued, in the same vein as Fanon, that we are reciprocally created as humans by the cultures that we create. We are, therefore, neither supernatural creators nor purely biologically and evolved beings. Consequently, in the same way as the phenomenon of culture freed us from the imperatives of nature, only a transcultural perspective can free us from the absolutist imperatives of "any one culture" (Epstein, 1993, pp. 109–110). The central contribution of the Black Aesthetic and Black Arts movements was, therefore, linked to the revalorizing turn they made to the hitherto despised African-derived tradition, and their recognition of it, as in the case of Neal's four-page summary, as an alternative cultural and aesthetic tradition. Their claim to a black particularism—a claim made against the ostensibly supracultural universal of the mainstream aesthetic and as a function of their challenge to the metaphysical burden of nonbeing imposed on the "Negro" to ensure its signifying role as the countertype to the latter's reference standard of being and of beauty—opened up the possibility of providing a transcultural perspective from which the "local culture" (Geertz, 1983, p. 16) nature of both our present "highbrow aesthetic" and the specific conception of the human with which it is interrelated can be recognized and its Geertzian "fugitive truth" grasped. Because these movements challenged this aesthetic, its related inscription of the human, and the "essentialized equation" of their premises in black nationalist terms, and thereby in the context of the same, if now inverted (from "white-as value/black-as-nonvalue" to "black-as-value/white-as-nonvalue"), biocentric principle of classification that they were in the process of calling into question, they closed this possibility off—the possibility, that is, of going beyond what the black writer James Weldon Johnson anguishedly identified in his 1933 autobiography as the "Man/Negro duality" (Johnson, 1933), and thereby beyond present-day culture's construal of "what life is, what art is." It is the challenge of going beyond this construal, on the basis of a transcultural perspective, rather than the now fashionable challenge of multiculturalism, that is the intellectual legacy that they, and their precursors, have handed down to contemporary scholarship.

[*See also* African Aesthetics; Harlem Renaissance; *and* Locke.]

BIBLIOGRAPHY

Baker, Houston A., Jr. *Afro-American Poetics: Revisions of Harlem and the Black Aesthetic*. Madison, Wis., 1988.

Baker, Houston A., Jr. *Black Studies, Rap, and the Academy*. Chicago, 1993.

Berendt, Joachim. *The Jazz Book: From New Orleans to Rock and Free Jazz*. Translated by Dan Morgenstern, Helmut Bredigheit, and Barbara Bredigheit. New York, 1975.

Bourdieu, Pierre. *Distinction: A Social Critique of the Judgement of Taste*. Translated by Richard Nice. Cambridge, Mass., 1984.

Chapman, Abraham, ed. *New Black Voices: An Anthology of Contemporary Afro-American Literature*. New York, 1972.

Cunningham, James. "Hemlock for the Black Artist: Karenga Style." In *New Black Voices: An Anthology of Afro-American Literature*, edited by Abraham Chapman. New York, 1972.

Dubey, Madhu. *Black Women Novelists and the Nationalist Aesthetic*. Bloomington, Ind., 1994.

Du Bois, W. E. B. "Of Our Spiritual Strivings." In *The Souls of Black Folk*. Chicago, 1903. Republished in *Three Negro Classics* with an Introduction by John Hope Franklin (New York, 1965).

Epstein, Mikhail. "Post-Communist Post-Modernism." *Common Knowledge* 3.3 (1993): 103–118. Interview with Ellen E. Berry, Kent Johnson, and Anesa Milla-Pogachor.

Fanon, Frantz. *Black Skin, White Masks*. Translated by Charles Lam Markmann. New York, 1967.

Farris Thompson, Robert. "African Influence on the Art of the United States." In *Black Studies in the University: A Symposium*, edited by Armstead L. Robinson, Craig C. Foster, and Donald H. Ogilvie. New Haven, 1969.

Farris Thompson, Robert. *Flash of the Spirit: African and Afro-American Art and Philosophy*. New York, 1983.

Fuller, Hoyt. "Introduction: Towards a Black Aesthetic." In *The Black Aesthetic*, edited by Addison Gayle, Jr. Garden City, N.Y., 1971.

Gates, Henry Louis, Jr. "Preface to Blackness: Text and Pretext." In *Afro-American Literature: The Reconstruction of Instruction*, edited by Dexter Fisher and Robert B. Stepto, p. 48. New York, 1978.

Gates, Henry Louis, Jr. "The Blackness of Blackness: A Critique of the Sign and the Signifying Monkey." In *Black Literature and Literary Theory*, edited by Henry Louis Gates, Jr., pp. 285–321. New York and London, 1984.

Gayle, Addison, Jr., ed. *The Black Aesthetic*. Garden City, N.Y., 1971.

Gayle, Addison, Jr. *The Way of the New World: The Black Novel in America*. Garden City, N.Y., 1975.

Geertz, Clifford. *Local Knowledge: Further Essays in Interpretive Anthropology*. New York, 1983.

Gerald, Carolyn. "The Black Writer and His Role." In *The Black Aesthetic*, edited by Addison Gayle, Jr., pp. 370–378. Garden City, N.Y., 1971.

González, José Luis. *El país de cuatro pisos y otros ensayos*. Río Piedras, Puerto Rico, 1980.

Johnson, James Weldon. *Along This Way: The Autobiography of James Weldon Johnson*. New York, 1933.

Jones, LeRoi (Amiri Baraka). *The Blues People: Negro Music in White America*. New York, 1963.

Jones, LeRoi (Amiri Baraka), and Larry Neal, eds. *Black Fire: An Anthology of Afro-American Writing*. New York, 1968.

Karenga, Maulana Ron. "Black Cultural Nationalism." In *The Black Aesthetic*, edited by Addison Gayle, Jr. Garden City, N.Y., 1971.

Levine, Lawrence W. *Highbrow, Lowbrow: The Emergence of Cultural Hierarchy in America*. Cambridge, Mass., 1988.

Martin, Reginald. *Ishmael Reed and the New Black Aesthetic Critics*. New York, 1988.

McWhorter, Gerald. "Deck the Ivy Racist Halls: The Case of Black Studies." In *Black Studies in the University: A Symposium*, edited by Armstead L. Robinson, Craig C. Foster, and Donald H. Ogilvie, pp. 55–74. New Haven, 1969.

Mosse, George L. *Toward the Final Solution: A History of European Racism*. Reprint, Madison, Wis., 1985.

Neal, Larry. "And Shine Swam On: An Afterword." In *Black Fire: An Anthology of Afro-American Writing*, edited by LeRoi Jones and Larry Neal, pp. 637–656. New York, 1968.

Neal, Larry. "Some Reflections on the Black Aesthetic and Black Arts Movement." In *The Black Aesthetic*, edited by Addison Gayle, Jr., pp. 12–15, 370–378. Garden City, N.Y., 1971.

Pandian, Jacob. *Anthropology and the Western Tradition: Toward an Authentic Anthropology*. Prospect Heights, Ill., 1985.

Van Deburg, William L. *New Day in Babylon: The Black Power Movement and American Culture, 1965–1975*. Chicago, 1992.

Vincent, Rickey. *Funk: The Music, the People and the Rhythm of the One*. Foreword by George Clinton. New York, 1996.

SYLVIA WYNTER

BLAIR, HUGH (1718–1800), Scottish divine and rhetorician who was the first person to occupy the distinguished Regius Chair of Rhetoric and Belles Lettres at the University of Edinburgh (1762). Blair was part of the *literatia* circle of Edinburgh, which included David Hume, Lord Kames, and Adam Smith. A popular preacher and instructor, Blair wrote *Lectures on Rhetoric and Belles Lettres* (1783), widely used as a text in both the United States and Great Britain for more than a century. The work saw more than sixty subsequent English-language editions and more than fifty abridgments (Schmitz, 1948).

Blair played a key role in the controversy surrounding the publication of the poems of Ossian, allegedly translated from ancient Gaelic documents by James Macpherson. Along with John Home, Blair persuaded Macpherson to publish two collections of these poems: *Fingal* (1762) and *Temora* (1763). Suspicions about their authenticity began to surface early from Dr. Johnson and eventually from Hume, but through it all Blair remained supportive (Burton, 1846, pp. 462–480). In *A Critical Dissertation on the Poems of Ossian* (1763), Blair likened the ancient poet to a Scottish Homer, and considered the epics as prime examples of the classical style. An 1805 report by the Highland Society of Scotland, however, found that the poems were forgeries (Schmitz, 1948).

Like most members of the Scottish Enlightenment, Blair was an empiricist and a proponent of associationism. For these philosophers, aesthetic values are merely expressions of sentiment. Thus, Blair writes that taste is "ultimately founded on an internal sense of beauty, which is natural to men, and which, in its application to particular objects, is capable of being guided and enlightened by reason" (*Lectures*, vol. 1, p. 30). Although subjective, "taste is far from being an arbitrary principle, which is subject to the fancy of every individual," for there is a uniformity with respect to the operations of our perceptions (ibid., p. 34). Consequently, art that is truly beautiful will be recognized as such through the ages. "That which men concur the most in admiring, must be held to be beautiful. His taste must be esteemed just and true, which coincides with the general sentiments of men" (ibid., p. 30). In this way, taste is subject to an objective, empirical standard.

Although the standard is the "general sentiments of men," this does not mean that good taste is determined by majority rule, for one's sentiments must be properly tuned through education and practice. Blair's theory "supposes our natural sense of beauty to be refined by frequent attention to the most beautiful objects, and at the same time to be guided and improved by the light of understanding" (Cohen, 1958, p. 269). Reason plays an important role in judgments of taste and such judgments are open to improvement. This is important because "moral beauties" are classified among the objects of taste. "A cultivated taste increases sensibility to all the tender and humane passions" (Blair, *Lectures*, vol. 1, p.

12; Brinton, 1992, p. 40). Hence, as our aesthetic sentiments improve, so do our moral sentiments.

Many will note in Blair a similarity between his views and those of Hume, but the theory just sketched owes as much to the thoughts of Alexander Gerard and Edmund Burke. Moreover, Blair was adverse to Hume's ideal critic because "there is no such living standard, no one person to whom all mankind will allow such admission to be due" (Blair, *Lectures*, vol. 1, p. 30).

Blair's attitudes about the sublime were also heavily influenced by Burke. He notes some typical examples: "infinite space"; "the burst of thunder or of cannon"; "the grandeur of earthquakes and burning mountains"; "darkness, solitude, and silence"; "a Gothic cathedral" (ibid., pp. 45–52). The remaining question is whether there is "some one fundamental quality in which all these different objects agree" (ibid., p. 54). Blair considers some suggestions, including one he attributes to Burke, "that terror is the source of the sublime" (ibid., p. 55). This position is flawed given that vast, open spaces and the starry sky are not in any way terrifying (ibid.). In the end, Blair endorses a skepticism about finding a single feature essential to the sublime, though he favors the quality of "mighty power or force" above others (ibid., p. 56; see Hipple, 1957, p. 127).

One of Blair's more interesting categories is that of the "moral, or sentimental sublime" (*Lectures*, vol. 1, p. 52). Virtues, like courage, are a source of moral sublimity because "they produce an effect extremely similar to what is produced by the view of grand objects in nature; filling the mind with admiration, and elevating it above itself" (ibid., pp. 52, 54). The previously noted connection between aesthetic and moral values is contained in this example of the sublime (Brinton, 1992, pp. 36 ff.)

BIBLIOGRAPHY

Works by Blair

A Critical Dissertation on the Poems of Ossian, the Son of Fingal. New York, 1970. First published anonymously in 1763 and with Blair's name in 1765. This is a facsimile of the 1765 edition.
Sermons. 5 vols. London, 1777–1801. James Finlayson also edited a five-volume edition in 1801 that included "A Short Account of the Life and Character of the Author." See Schmitz (1948) for information about subsequent editions.
Lectures on Rhetoric and Belles Lettres. 2 vols. Carbondale, Ill., 1965. Edited by Harold F. Harding. First published in London in June 1783, and in Edinburgh in July 1783. See Schmitz (1948) for a complete list of other editions.

Other Sources

Bator, Paul G. "The Formation of the Regius Chair of Rhetoric and Belles Lettres at the University of Edinburgh." *Quarterly Journal of Speech* 75 (1989): 40–64.
Bowers, John Waite. "A Comparative Criticism of Hugh Blair's Essay on Taste." *Quarterly Journal of Speech* 47 (1961): 384–389.
Brinton, Alan. "Hugh Blair and the True Eloquence." *Rhetoric Society Quarterly* 22 (1992): 30–42.

Burton, John Hill. *Life and Correspondence of David Hume.* 2 vols. Edinburgh, 1846.

Chapman, R. W. "Blair on Ossian." *Review of English Studies* 7 (1931): 80–83.

Cohen, Herman. "Hugh Blair's Theory of Taste." *Quarterly Journal of Speech* 44 (1958): 265–274.

Golden, James L., and Edward P. J. Corbett. "Introduction." In *The Rhetoric of Blair, Campbell, and Whately.* New York, 1968.

Greig, J. Y. T., ed. *The Letters of David Hume.* 2 vols. Oxford, 1932.

Hipple, Walter John, Jr. *The Beautiful, the Sublime, and the Picturesque in Eighteenth-Century British Aesthetic Theory.* Carbondale, Ill., 1957.

Irvine, James R., and G. Jack Gravlee. "Hugh Blair: A Select Bibliography of Manuscripts in Scottish Archives." *Rhetoric Society Quarterly* 13 (1983): 75–77.

Monk, Samuel H. *The Sublime: A Study of Critical Theories in Eighteenth-Century England.* New York, 1935; reprint, Ann Arbor, 1960.

Schmitz, Robert M. *Hugh Blair.* New York, 1948.

Sheppeard, Sallye. "Blair and Emerson on the Sublime: A Question of Influence." *Lamar Journal of the Humanities* 11 (1985): 19–25.

Stephen, Leslie. "Hugh Blair." In *Dictionary of National Biography,* vol. 5, pp. 160–161. London, 1882.

JOSEPH KEIM CAMPBELL

BLANCHOT, MAURICE (b. 1907), French fiction writer and literary critic. Blanchot began his career in the 1930s as a political journalist for right-wing periodicals, but during the Occupation he published chiefly essays on literary topics (for example, "How Is Literature Possible?") in addition to two novels, *Thomas l'obscur* (1941) and *Aminadab* (1942). His first volume of critical essays, *Faux pas,* appeared in 1943. After the Liberation, Blanchot began contributing essays and reviews regularly to *Critique* and *La nouvelle revue francaise.* In 1949, a second collection of essays appeared, *La part du feu* (The Work of Fire), which includes one of his most important theoretical pieces, "Littérature et le droit à la mort," in which literature—or, more exactly, writing *(l'écriture)*—is characterized as an interruption or refusal of the discursive movement that produces meanings, propositions, narratives, and works of art. In subsequent essays, particularly those collected in *L'espace littéraire* (The Space of Literature; 1955), *Le livre à venir* (1959), and *L'entretien infini* (The Infinite Conversation; 1969), Blanchot came to think of writing as an anarchic event of fragmentation or "worklessness" *(désœuvrement).* After the appearance of his last novel, *Le très-haut* (The Most High; 1948), his fiction became increasingly minimalist, austere, and enigmatic, and in 1962 he published *L'attente, l'oubli* (Awaiting Oblivion), a work composed of intersecting fragments of dialogue and narrative. Thereafter, the fragment became his distinctive mode of writing, especially in *Le pas au-delà* (The Step Not Beyond; 1971) and *L'écriture du désastre* (The Writing of the Disaster; 1980).

Blanchot's poetics of the fragment is important for aesthetics because it entails both a theory of literary language and a phenomenology of aesthetic (or, perhaps more accurately, poetic) experience. The starting point for the theory of literary language is a certain picture of Hegel's dialectic derived from Alexandre Kojève's famous lectures on *The Phenomenology of the Spirit* in Paris during the 1930s. Here the dialectic is understood as a movement of negation that annihilates things by turning them into objects of consciousness. This concept of negation is foundational for Blanchot's poetics, which can be thought of as an extended critique of Hegel and the idea that language or speech, the production of meaning or the formation of concepts, is a transformation of what is singular and irreducible into what is universal and intelligible. Following Kojève, Blanchot has one word for this event: death—"the infamous death that is the beginning of the life of the spirit." As Blanchot puts it in "Literature and the Right to Death," "when I speak, death speaks in me. My speech is a warning that at this very moment death is loose in the world, that it has suddenly appeared between me, as I speak, and the being I address: it is there between us as the distance that separates us, but this distance is also what prevents us from being separated, because it contains the condition for all understanding. Death alone allows me to grasp what I want to attain; it exists in words as the only way they can have meaning. Without death, everything would sink away into absurdity and nothingness." But, for Blanchot, "a death that results in being represents an absurd insanity, the curse of existence." Poetry is a refusal of this absurd insanity, a lifting of this curse.

Blanchot's thesis is that poetry or literature is language that remains on the hither side of the "speech of death." It is a refusal of "the terrible force that draws beings into the world and illuminates them." How is this possible? As Blanchot puts the question: "How can I . . . turn around and look at what exists *before,* if all my power consists in making it into what exists *after?*" After all, literature is a discourse like any other. Narrative, for example, is "turned toward the movement of negation by which things are separated from themselves and destroyed in order to be known, subjugated, communicated." But for Blanchot the language of literature is always in excess of its discursive logic. Because of "the materiality of language," literature (whatever its designs) always remains an event of *l'écriture:* "A name ceases to be the ephemeral passing of nonexistence and becomes a concrete ball, a solid mass of existence; language, abandoning the sense, the meaning which was all it wanted to be, tries to become senseless. Everything physical takes precedence: rhythm, weight, mass, shape, and then the paper on which one writes, the trail of ink, the book." Poetry in this sense, that is, as *l'écriture,* is a mode of exteriority. "It is not beyond the world, but neither is it the world itself: it is the presence of things before the *world* exists, their perseverance after the world has disappeared." In "Literature and the Right to Death," Blanchot characterizes this exteriority by appropriating a concept from the philosopher Emmanuel Levinas's *Existence and Existents* (1948): the *il y a* (there is), the materiality of being or "existence without existents." The *il y a* is not nothing; it is the event of existing on the hither side of every determination of being, that is, on the hither side of the dialectic or of the sovereignty of the cognitive subject. Blanchot calls it "existence without being, as poetry tries to recapture it behind the meaning of words."

Understood in this way, poetry is perhaps less intelligible as a form or entity than as an event or experience. For Blanchot, at any rate, the work of writing never takes the form of an aesthetic object; it is irreducible to a genre description. It thus resembles the work of art in Martin Heidegger's aesthetics, where work is to be understood as something that happens as well as something that is created. In Heidegger's "The Origin of the Work of Art" (1933–1935), the work of the work of art is an event of disclosure, the opening up of a world and the introduction of time and history. But the work is also made of earth, and for Heidegger the earth is something like an absolute horizon that marks the limit of the world. Thus, if the work of art opens up the world, its earthly character means that the work will itself always remain on the hither side, as if without room in the world. In formal terms, this would mean that the work of art always remains opaque vis-à-vis the world. In virtue of its materiality, it is always excessive with respect to the world and its projects, so that the experience of the work of art will always be in some sense an experience of exteriority. Heidegger expresses this by emphasizing the strangeness and, indeed, the inhumanness of the work. The work exists, purely and simply, in a kind of ontological solitude. We can only enter into its proximity, but to do so is to find ourselves turned inside out, no longer subjects of cognition or of conceptual mastery and control. Thus, the work is never an object for us. It is as if our relation to the work of art were one of exposure.

These are insights that Blanchot develops explicitly and in various ways in *The Space of Literature*, a work that shows a detailed understanding of Heidegger's aesthetics. Literary space is not a formal property of the literary work (not "spatial form" or a description of literary structure). Blanchot characterizes it initially as an "essential solitude." This solitude is ontological, not subjective or private in the manner of Walt Whitman's "solitary singer." It describes the mode of being of the work of art. What is it to experience this mode of being? This is the regulating question of *The Space of Literature*. What makes Blanchot's poetics unique is that he pursues this question from the standpoint of the writer (Stéphane Mallarmé, Franz Kafka, Rainer Maria Rilke) rather than that of the audience, reader, spectator, critic, or philosopher of art. What is the writer's experience of writing? Put simply, it is a reversal of consciousness or, indeed, of subjectivity itself. Kafka, Blanchot notes, called it the loss of "the power to say 'I'" and both Kafka and Mallarmé thought of the event as a kind of interminable dying, a limit-experience in which one loses all mastery of the present and future. The writer's relation to the work of writ-

ing is not one of agency and cognition; rather, it is analogous to an experience of fascination when the act of seeing is gripped as if the gaze were seized from the outside and held in suspension. "Whoever is fascinated," Blanchot says, "doesn't see, properly speaking, what he sees." It is like the gaze of Orpheus when he turns back from the world to look at the vanished Eurydice (one must imagine him transfixed with horror, exposed to something like the *il y a*). Likewise, writing belongs to the radical passivity of an ego turned inside out as a "subjectivity without a subject" (a condition dramatized in many of Blanchot's *récits* and which he returns to obsessively in all of his writings). As Blanchot says, "To write is to let fascination rule language."

In this event, writing ceases to be a discursive function that makes possible the construction of propositions, narratives, or conceptual contexts. On the contrary, it is an interruption or, as Blanchot likes to say, the "impossibility" of this function. "To write," Blanchot says, "is to withdraw language from the world, to detach it from what makes it a power according to which, when I speak, it is the world that declares itself, the clear light of day that develops through tasks undertaken, through action and time." Writing is a deprivation of the world of knowledge and speech, action and achievement, but (as in Kafka's case) this deprivation is not a negative condition; it is an entry into the mode of being of the work of art. "For art is linked, precisely as Kafka is, to what is 'outside' the world." This outside is not another world; it is, Blanchot says, "the other of all worlds." It is the space of the *il y a*, of existence without being on the hither side of the movement or labor of the spirit that produces concepts, works, epochs, and the end of history.

Indeed, in contrast to the productive and progressive movement of the spirit, the movement of writing is one of errancy or wandering. Literary space is a space of exile, which becomes for Blanchot a principal metaphor of poetic experience or the mode of being of the one who writes: "The poet is in exile; he is exiled from the city, from regular occupation and limited obligations, from everything connected to results, substantive reality, power." The poet "belongs to the foreign, to the outside which knows no intimacy or limit." The poem "makes the poet a wanderer, the one always astray, he to whom the stability of presence is not granted and who is deprived of a true abode. And this must be understood in the gravest sense: the artist does not belong to the movement of the true because the work is itself what escapes the movement of the true. For always, whatever our perspective upon it, it revokes the true, eludes signification, designating the region . . . where man withstands that which the true must negate in order to become possibility and progress."

In his later writings, Blanchot translates this condition into temporal terms, where the exteriority of the poet is figured as the *entre-temps*, the meanwhile or between-time that separates past and future: the interminable time of fascination, insomnia, attention, suffering, and vigilance for a messiah who never arrives or toward a history that never ends (and is therefore never redeemed). In the time of writing, the work of writing can never be concluded; the work remains unfinished and unfinishable, as if beginning and beginning again in an eternal return of a present that endures without a future and from which there is no exit. This interval is Blanchot's *le pas au-delà* (the step not beyond). In *The Writing of the Disaster*, Blanchot expresses this in typically anti-Hegelian style: the interminable, incessant *entre-temps* interrupts the dialectic and "renders the *Aufhebung* null and void."

The time of literature is infinite according to the temporality of the infinitive. In this temporality, language ceases to work systematically; rather, it can be thought of on the model of a conversation that starts and stops but properly has neither beginning *(arché)* nor end *(telos)*. In *The Infinite Conversation*, Blanchot says that the conversation gives us "a nondialectical experience of speech." The essence of the conversation is to drift; it is errant, self-interrupting, anarchic discourse in the nature of the case. It is, Blanchot says, an example of "plural speech," not just in the sense that there are two or more participants in conversation, but in the sense that speech in this event is irreducible to a subject, that is, it belongs neither to one nor the other of the interlocutors. It is speech of the between: no one's speech. It is refractory to concepts of unity or the subordination of parts. A conversation cannot issue in a "work." Thus, it is an instance of what Blanchot calls *désœuvrement:* worklessness, or "the fragmentary." For Blanchot, the insubordination of the fragmentary is captured incisively by Herman Melville's Bartleby the Scrivener: "I prefer not to." An interview would not be a conversation. Nor would an interrogation, especially one that issues in a confession. For Blanchot, the worse thing is to force someone to speak.

For Blanchot, the fragmentary or *désœuvrement* is both a poetic and a political and historical concept. On the one hand, the fragmentary recalls Mallarmé's idea that a poem is made of words, not ideas. Poetry is made of language but is not a use of it; that is, it is made of words but not of any of the things we use words to produce: meanings, concepts, statements about the world, descriptions, narratives, rules. Poetry in this respect is a refusal of what Blanchot calls "the violence inherent in speech." In *The Infinite Conversation*, Blanchot writes: "When I speak, I always exercise a relation of force *[puissance]*. I belong, whether I know it or not, to a network of powers of which I make use, struggling against the force that asserts itself against me. All speech is violence, a violence all the more formidable for being secret and the secret center of violence; a violence that is already exerted upon what the word names and that it can name only by withdrawing presence from it—a sign . . . that death speaks (the death that is power) when I speak." Poetry is nonviolent speech that refuses power and sovereignty over the world. It is speech that is responsive to things in their singularity and irreducible strangeness. It is a discourse of freedom, where freedom is not the negative freedom of the rational subject but the ontological freedom of things—Jean-Luc Nancy, in *The Experience of Freedom*, calls it "the free dissemination of existence."

Freedom is the link between a poetry and a politics of *désœuvrement*. In *The Unavowable Community*, Blanchot envisions a community that is not organized as a hierarchical system in which power flows from the top down to form a rational order of things but is rather like a network through which power flows from point to point without concentrating itself at any one site. Such a community will resemble a nomadic movement rather than a statelike structure. Thus, there is no one thing that counts as community, which is always plural and heterogeneous. In the modern nation-state, such communities are possible only at the micropolitical level of "acephalic" (literally, headless) relations that we associate with friendship, love, the exchange of gifts, and the sharing of practices. Such communities are not defined by the occupation of territories. As Blanchot says in *The Infinite Conversation*, "the order of realities in which we become rooted does not hold the key to all the relations to which we must respond." Such relations are always local and are experienced as movements and gatherings rather than as constituted entities—artistic communities, civil rights groups, feminist movements, uprisings whose purpose is not to take power but to resist it (May 1968, Tiananmen Square). Indeed, for Blanchot community is not a utopian concept but a concept of exteriority. It is a name for whatever cannot be assimilated into a totality.

The most radical concept of exteriority in Blanchot's oeuvre is that of the "disaster." In *The Writing of the Disaster*, Blanchot says that the disaster "is foreign to the ruinous purity of destruction, so the idea of totality cannot delimit it." If history is a dialectical movement, the disaster is an event of separation that this movement cannot overcome. Thus, in one sense the disaster is not simply a synonym for catastrophe. But in another sense it describes the temporality of an event like the Holocaust, which for Blanchot is a tragedy that exposes the history of the spirit for what it is, namely, the work of death. The Holocaust is a caesura in the history of the spirit. It is not just a catastrophe that is now over and done with; it interrupts history as an interval of memory that cannot be closed. This means, among other things, that the Holocaust cannot be conceptualized or reduced. Our relation to it is not one of knowing and doing but one of responsiveness and acknowledgment. Henceforth, survival is our mode of being historical.

In Blanchot's later thinking, poetry (that is, the writing of the disaster) is not the speech of death but the speech of memory. This does not mean that poetry is a form of mediation that brings memory into the field of representation. Memory is always singular and irreducible; it is refractory to history conceived as a world-historical narrative composed from the standpoint of the end. Like poetry, memory is not so much a mode of cognition as one of obsession, as if our relation to memory were traumatic in the nature of the case. Thus, for Blanchot memory is not opposed to forgetting; on the contrary, memory turns forgetfulness toward those historical forms of time that make up the life of the spirit. One might think of forgetfulness as symmetrical with the gaze of Orpheus. In any event, *The Writing of the Disaster* asks us to imagine, among other things, a forgetting of the future, a vigilance toward the past, and a history that cannot be terminated because it is "as zigzagging as it is dialectical." This would be a history from below, a history of singular events or a history in fragments articulated in the mode of responsibility or witness. In this respect, Blanchot's thinking is coherent with the work of the poet Paul Celan, whose austere, increasingly fragmentary texts are deeply shadowed by the Holocaust.

Blanchot's influence on French intellectual culture, especially since the 1960s, is pervasive and complex, and still in need of close study. All the major themes of poststructuralist thinking are fully in place in Blanchot's writings from the 1940s and 1950s: the critique of subject-centered rationality and instrumental control, the materiality of *l'écriture*, the insistence on finitude, the irreducibility of the singular in the face of categories and distinctions, the priority of historicity over systems, concepts, rules, and (above all) history conceived as a totality immanent in its effects. The notions of language that turn up in the writings of Jacques Lacan, Jacques Derrida, Michel Foucault, and Gilles Deleuze are directly traceable to Blanchot. Yet, for all that, Blanchot remains basically an existentialist preoccupied with the experience of extreme situations. Some of his work suggests an attempt to develop an explicitly non-Sartrean or, in any event, a nonsubjectivist conception of freedom. Of particular importance is Blanchot's relationship with the philosopher Emmanuel Lévinas, with whom he maintained a friendship lasting more than half a century, and whose ethics of responsibility is powerfully informed by Blanchot's concepts of exteriority, passivity, and anarchy. Interestingly, in the English-speaking world Blanchot's influence has been principally among poets and writers, many of whom translated Blanchot's writings into English for the first time.

[*See also* Death and Aesthetics; *and* Literature, *article on* Literary Aesthetics.]

BIBLIOGRAPHY

Works by Blanchot

Thomas l'obscur (1941). New edition. Paris, 1950. Translated by Robert Lamberton as *Thomas the Obscure* (Reprint, Barrytown, N.Y., 1988).
Faux pas. Paris, 1943.
L'arrêt de mort. Paris, 1948. Translated by Lydia Davis as *Death Sentence* (Barrytown, N.Y., 1978).
Le très-haut. Paris, 1948. Translated by Allan Stoekl as *The Most High* (Lincoln, Nebr., 1996).

La part du feu. Paris, 1949. Translated by Charlotte Mandell as *The Work of Fire* (Stanford, Calif., 1995).
Lautréamont et Sade. (1949). Rev. ed. Paris, 1963.
Au moment voulu. Paris, 1951. Translated by Lydia Davis as *When the Time Comes* (Barrytown, N.Y., 1985).
Celui qui ne m'accompagnait pas. Paris, 1953. Translated by Lydia Davis as *The One Who Was Standing apart from Me* (Barrytown, N.Y., 1993).
L'espace litteraire. Paris, 1955. Translated by Ann Smock as *The Space of Literature* (Lincoln, Nebr., 1982).
Le dernier homme. Paris, 1957. Translated by Lydia Davis as *The Last Man* (New York, 1987).
Le livre à venir. Paris, 1959.
L'attente, l'oubli. Paris, 1962. Translated by John Gregg as *Awaiting Oblivion* (Lincoln, Nebr., 1997).
L'entretien infini. Paris, 1969. Translated by Susan Hanson as *The Infinite Conversation.* (Minneapolis, 1993).
L'amitié. Paris, 1971.
Le pas au-delà. Paris, 1973. Translated by Lycette Nelson as *The Step Not Beyond* (Albany, N.Y., 1992).
L'écriture du désastre. Paris, 1980. Translated by Ann Smock as *The Writing of the Disaster* (Lincoln, Nebr., 1986).
The Gaze of Orpheus and Other Literary Essays, Edited by P. Adams Sitney, translated by Lydia Davis. Barrytown, N.Y., 1981.
La folie du jour. Montpellier, 1973. Translated by Lydia Davis as *The Madness of the Day* (Barrytown, N.Y., 1981).
The Sirens' Song: Selected Essays. Edited by Gabriel Josipovici, translated by Sacha Rabinovitch. Bloomington, Ind., 1982.
Après-coup, précédé par le réssassement éternel. Paris, 1983. Translated by Paul Auster as *Vicious Circles: Two Fictions and "After the Fact"* (Barrytown, N.Y., 1985).
La communauté inavouable. Paris, 1983. Translated by Pierre Joris as *The Unavowable Community* (Barrytown, N.Y., 1988).
The Blanchot Reader. Edited by Michael Holland. Oxford and Cambridge, Mass., 1995.

Other Sources

Bruns, Gerald L. *Maurice Blanchot: The Refusal of Philosophy.* Baltimore, 1997.
Clark, Timothy. *Derrida, Heidegger, Blanchot: Sources of Derrida's Notion and Practice of Literature.* Cambridge and New York, 1992.
Collin, Françoise. *Maurice Blanchot et la question de l'écriture.* Paris, 1971.
Critchley, Simon. *Very Little . . . Almost Nothing: Death, Philosophy, Literature.* London and New York, 1997.
Derrida, Jacques. *Parages.* Paris, 1986.
Foucault, Michel. "Maurice Blanchot: The Thought from Outside." In *Foucault/Blanchot,* translated by Jeffrey Mehlman and Brian Massumi, pp. 7–60. New York, 1987.
Gill, Carolyn Bailey, ed. *Maurice Blanchot: The Demand of Writing.* London and New York, 1996.
Gregg, John. *Maurice Blanchot and the Literature of Transgression.* Princeton, N.J., 1994.
Kofman, Sarah. *Paroles suffoquées.* Paris, 1987.
Lévinas, Emmanuel. *Sur Maurice Blanchot.* Montpellier, 1975. Included as "On Maurice Blanchot" in Lévinas, *Proper Names,* translated by Michael B. Smith, pp. 125–170 (Stanford, Calif., 1996).
Libertson, Joseph. *Proximity: Levinas, Blanchot, Bataille, and Communication.* The Hague and Boston, 1982.
Schulte-Nordholt, Anne-Lise. *Maurice Blanchot: L'écriture comme expérience du dehors.* Geneva, 1995.
Ungar, Steven. *Scandal and Aftereffect: Blanchot and France since 1930.* Minneapolis, 1995.

GERALD L. BRUNS

BLOOMSBURY GROUP. The term *Bloomsbury* was taken around 1910 as a sobriquet for a group of young intellectuals living in the London neighborhood of that name. Although its roots were at Cambridge University, where most of Bloomsbury's men studied, the group is notable as the last British intellectual contingent to sustain itself outside of an academic institution. This fact reflects certain of the group's characteristics: (1) its very specific place within the professional sector of the English ruling class, with its belief in individual freedom and legacy of continuing liberal reform (well analyzed by Raymond Williams [1980]), and (2) the wide range of Bloomsbury's interests, which transcend the boundaries of academic disciplines. Bloomsbury's core included the economist John Maynard Keynes, historian Lytton Strachey, political activist and commentator Leonard Woolf, novelist Virginia Woolf, art critic Clive Bell, painter and critic Roger Fry, and the painters Vanessa Bell and Duncan Grant. But these professional labels are misleadingly limited, for both as a group and individually, Bloomsbury's members worked across many fields, and all of Bloomsbury's members were interested in aesthetics and involved in the arts. The group contributions are most significant in two fields within modern aesthetics: formalism and feminism.

Until the recent rise of interest in feminism, Bloomsbury's contribution to the history of aesthetics was associated primarily with the formalist theories articulated by Roger Fry and Clive Bell. Bell's highly influential 1914 book, titled simply *Art,* codified ideas that Fry developed in his journalistic writings and set the terms for anglophone aesthetic debate for the following half century. In *Art* (1914), Bell argued that what makes an object "art" is the presence of "significant form"—a composite of line, mass, proportion, chiaroscuro, and color—which arouses the viewer's "aesthetic emotion." This argument allows the term *art* to include a wide array of objects. Bell's examples included, in addition to famous paintings, the Hagia Sophia in Istanbul, the windows at the cathedral of Chartres, Mexican sculpture, Persian ceramics, and Chinese carpets. At the same time, the argument undercuts conventional Victorian aesthetic hierarchies based in the hortatory value of subject matter. Bell denied the status of art to many—even most—Victorian paintings, including works that are simply displays of detailed realism, sentimental scenes designed to evoke patriotism or pathos in the viewer, "portraits of psychological or historical value," and images that offer ersatz possession of some desired commodity or erotic object.

These formalist ideas did not originate in Bloomsbury. The French painter and critic Maurice Denis in 1890 famously proclaimed that "a picture, before it is a warhorse, a naked woman, or some anecdote, is essentially a flat surface covered by colors assembled in a certain order." Fry and Bell led other British critics in the knowledge and admiration of the Parisian avant-garde, and their accomplishment was to provide a coherent explanation of modern French

art and aesthetics for English speakers. Early in 1910, Fry translated a lengthy essay on Paul Cézanne by Denis for the *Burlington Magazine,* inaugurating terms such as *plastic* and *classic,* which are closely associated with Bloomsbury formalism (see Shiff, 1984). Bloomsbury's presentation of recent French aesthetics to English audiences accompanied the group's introduction to London of work by painters such as Henri Matisse and Pablo Picasso, who were featured in the two "Post-Impressionist" exhibitions (an influential term coined by Fry) in 1910 and 1912. Many of Fry's original essays, on which *Art* is based, were written during the controversies over these shows; some of these essays were collected by Fry in the 1920 *Vision and Design;* a more complete selection may be found in *A Roger Fry Reader* (1996). Books such as Bell's *Art* and Fry's *Cézanne* (1927) introduced the terms of this debate along with reproductions of modern French art to readers throughout the anglophone world.

Bloomsbury's background in French art and aesthetics was not always matched by commentators constrained by conventional academic disciplines to contextualize the group primarily in relation to movements in English intellectual history: the aestheticism of Walter Pater and J. A. M. Whistler or the Arts and Crafts activism of John Ruskin and William Morris. Fry did cite Morris's precedent when in 1913 he (along with Grant and Bell) founded the Omega Workshops, an atelier for the production of modernist decorative arts. But even this connection was filtered through France, where the ideas of Ruskin and Morris influenced such projects as Paul Poiret's École Martine, a precedent Fry also cited in his publicity for the Omega. It is, nevertheless, with the Omega (1913–1919) that Bloomsbury's artists reveal their heritage in the English Arts and Crafts tradition that united the fine and decorative arts, offering a far more sustained exploration of modern art's implications for design than any in France at the time.

Much closer to formalist aesthetic theory are the "art for art's sake" doctrines of the Aesthetes, who are frequently cited as constitutive influences, though Bloomsbury disavowed their legacy. Ignoring Pater and Whistler, many in Bloomsbury—including Clive Bell in *Art*—credited their influential Cambridge teacher G. E. Moore, author of the *Principia Ethica,* with valuing awareness of beauty as a state of mind that is good in itself, independent of any educational or documentary purpose. Fry, in the autobiographical conclusion to *Vision and Design,* cited Leo Tolstoy's *What Is Art?* as his source for the idea that "art was not the record of beauty already existent elsewhere, but the expression of an emotion felt by the artist, and conveyed to the spectator." Such notions are basic to the formalist indifference to subject matter in favor of aesthetic criteria based in the emotive potential of form.

Ultimately, debates about the roots of Bloomsbury's formalism are of dubious historical value, because many new ideas about art were "in the air" at the turn of the century, with their precise source unknown to people at the time and unquantifiable today. What is of historical interest are the reasons why Bloomsbury's members cited the sources they did—that is, how they constructed from the diversity of influences a particular historical legacy to defend and explain their work. This is particularly clear in Fry's invocation of Tolstoy, which, as he acknowledged, ignores Tolstoy's strange conclusion that the value of a work of art corresponded to the moral value of the emotion expressed. Because this conclusion is what distinguishes Tolstoy's aesthetics from other broadly Romantic ideas of art as the outpouring of the artist's emotion, Fry's citation of his Russian progenitor seems motivated by Tolstoy's status within a foreign avant-garde. Tolstoy's name connoted the highest level of artistic accomplishment; he was "the greatest of all novelists," said Virginia Woolf. Moreover, like the French painter/critic Denis, he exemplified an alternative to Englishness. More specifically, Tolstoy was renowned for his rejection of convention (including his aristocratic title) and his commitment to social change. Influential members of foreign avant-gardes, thinkers who combined creative and critical work, charismatic teachers—these were the figures Bloomsbury chose as models in its collective effort to bring a modernist sensibility to a wide range of endeavors (including architecture, dance, and art exhibition and education, as well as painting and design) and audiences.

Bloomsbury's aspirations for formalism are exemplified not just in the forerunners it cited, but also—perhaps most clearly—in those they abjured. The group denied its derivation from the Aestheticism of Pater and Whistler not so much because of their ideas but because of these Aesthetes' social roles. This dynamic is especially clear in Fry's writings on Whistler. The same autobiographical essay that upholds Tolstoy dismisses Whistler as an influence, criticizing the way he "too cavalierly" ignored the ethical questions of art's value. Fry's meaning is illuminated by a return to his early art criticism, which dealt extensively with Whistler (see *A Roger Fry Reader*). Here Fry condemned the way Whistler "refused to persuade" the public, "spoke only ephemeral witticisms in the press," and "took a vicious pleasure in being misunderstood." He contrasted Whistler's isolated self-righteousness to the attitude of the French Impressionists, among whom, "in spite of vivid contrasts of temperament, we find a tendency to formulate a common style, to fight a common battle, to combine forces in a 'movement'" (1996). The story is much the same with Pater. Bloomsbury dismissed the example of this timid and reclusive Oxford scholar who responded to attacks on his work by disclaiming and eliminating passages that challenged the Victorian insistence on morally uplifting themes in art. For Bloomsbury, Pater was particularly disappointing because he raised so many of the issues of concern to

the group, only to deal with them unsatisfactorily. This was true not only of his writings on art, but also in the way he related aesthetics to sexuality and gender. The homosexual men in Bloomsbury mocked with the phrase "the higher Sodomy" the anguished homoerotic relationships suggested and then denied in Pater's fictional paean to the aesthetic life, *Marius the Epicurean,* as in his scholarly studies of figures like Winckelmann and Michelangelo. Virginia Woolf likewise condemned Pater's misogyny, which was manifest in his opposition to the admission of women to Oxford. For Bloomsbury, the bid to free art from imperatives to approved subject matter into a realm of pure form was part of a movement to challenge Victorian habits of thought, including norms of sexuality and gender.

Because formalism and feminism are often seen as separate, even antagonistic, the connections between these aspects of Bloomsbury's work have been widely overlooked. For Bloomsbury, however, the two were, at least initially, complementary. Much of the misunderstanding stems from the differences between Bloomsbury feminism and the feminism of the 1970s. Whereas the latter often concentrated exclusively on women's bodies and experiences, Bloomsbury's feminism was part of its broader liberal ambitions, inseparable not only from its embrace of male homosexuality but also from the political and economic activism now associated primarily with the careers of Leonard Woolf and John Maynard Keynes. Virginia Woolf, the group's most articulate feminist, makes this point in her manifesto *Three Guineas* (1938), which is written as three letters to organizations that appealed to her for funds: a pacifist group, an anti-Fascist government, and a women's college. Woolf explains to each how its cause depends on the success of the others.

Despite their differences, the more strictly identity-based feminism of the late twentieth century focused attention on Bloomsbury's theorization of sexuality and gender, propelling Virginia Woolf to the center of discourses on feminist aesthetics. Woolf's major novels of the 1920s—*Jacob's Room, To the Lighthouse, Mrs. Dalloway*—combine attention to women's lives with such modernist narrative techniques as indeterminate narrative voice and plots that focus on the seemingly insignificant. Woolf's many essays on women in fiction and on individual women writers, along with her book-length *A Room of One's Own* (1929), specifically address the material and aesthetic conditions of women's self-expression. Personifying literary convention as "some powerful and unscrupulous tyrant" who insists on "plot," Woolf grounds her writing in her gender: "When a woman comes to write a novel, she will find that she is perpetually wishing to alter the established values—to make serious what appears insignificant to man and trivial what is to him important."

The parallels between formalism and feminism, as conceived within Bloomsbury, are clear. Under the banner of modernism, both propose to free art from conventions designed to give the viewer/reader the illusion of unmediated access to a subject matter assessed as valuable according to the standards of the dominant (patriarchal) culture. Thus, Woolf argues that writers betray what she calls "the *form* of the novel" (emphasis added) by using it to "preach doctrines, sing songs, or celebrate the glories of the British Empire," while Bell, in *Art,* complains about the prevailing aesthetic theory in which "a beautiful picture is a photograph of a pretty girl, beautiful music, the music that provokes emotions similar to those provoked by young ladies in musical farces; and beautiful poetry, the poetry that recalls the same emotions felt, twenty years earlier, for the rector's daughter" (1914). Woolf's experimental fiction is openly indebted to the aesthetics of her colleagues in Bloomsbury's visual arts contingent. In her memoirs (posthumously published as *Moments of Being*), she wrote: "We are under the dominion of painting. Were all modern paintings to be destroyed, a critic of the twenty-fifth century would be able to deduce from the works of Proust alone the existence of Matisse, Cézanne, Derain, and Picasso" (1976). Her own experimental fiction, most notably the short stories in which she first tried out new narrative techniques, was published with Vanessa Bell's woodcut illustrations in modernist style, sometimes interwoven so that lines of text wrap around the images (for a detailed analysis, see Diane Gillespie's *The Sisters' Arts* [1988]). In certain short stories and in *To the Lighthouse,* the narrator is compared with a painter who adheres explicitly to the formalist aesthetics proposed by Bell and Fry.

Fry, who was deeply interested in literature, was especially influential for Woolf. The connections between the two often have been misunderstood by literary historians who compare her fiction from the 1920s with his most accessible writings on aesthetics, which date from the previous decade. In fact, by the 1920s, Fry had abandoned his partnership with Bell, and joined instead with the French intellectual Charles Mauron (who was later to develop *psychocritique,* a mode of textual analysis) to turn formalism away from the study of abstract forms and toward the analysis of "psychological volumes" created by the play of themes and subjects. In this, Bloomsbury's aesthetic theory paralleled the development of its art, for, after a brief period of experimentation with abstract painting around 1915, Fry, Grant, and Bell returned to figuration in their work, often with explicit historical references that anticipate something of the playfulness of postmodernism. This period of Bloomsbury's formalism was of scant interest to later modernists, especially after World War II, when "Greenbergian formalism" reasserted the primacy of abstraction in twentieth-century art. Overlooked by a subsequent generation of artists and critics, however, Bloomsbury's late criticism fascinated Woolf, whose writing engaged a similar play with subject matter.

By the 1930s, the division that later generations would come to see between formalism and feminism began to appear in Bloomsbury. Through its evolution, formalism in Bloomsbury maintained that artistic dynamics—whether the play of form or of themes—must be motivated for aesthetic, rather than hortatory, effect. This belief informs Woolf's injunctions to women novelists in the 1929 *A Room of One's Own:* "It is fatal for a woman to lay the least stress on any grievance; to plead even with justice any cause; in any way to speak consciously as a woman." Under the threat of fascism, however, Woolf's writing began to deal more overtly with social issues. Her unfinished novel-essay, *The Pargiters*—part of which became the exhilaratingly partisan *Three Guineas* (1938)—and her angry last novel, *Between the Acts* (1941), both flout the warnings of *A Room of One's Own* that "books will be deformed and twisted" if a woman "will write in a rage where she should write calmly." Although formalism was initially empowering in developing modernist forms of writing resistant to the imperatives of convention—including patriarchal convention—it came to seem limiting to Woolf. Woolf's biography of Fry (1940), itself a testament to their friendship, was written simultaneously with *Between the Acts* and reveals her struggle with his legacy. Ultimately, she concludes that, "when we read him, we never feel shut off alone in a studio; morality and conduct, even if they are called by other names, are present" (1940). She saw formalism's refusal of the urge to possess, both materially and sexually, echoed in Fry's generosity, which "ask[ed] nothing for oneself." In the final analysis, Woolf reasserts Bloomsbury's vision of aesthetics as a category that transcends traditional disciplinary boundaries to become a regimen for life itself.

[*See also* Aestheticism; Bell; Feminism; *and* Formalism.]

BIBLIOGRAPHY

Bell, Clive. *Art.* London, 1914.

Collins, Judith. *The Omega Workshops.* Chicago, 1984.

Fry, Roger. *Vision and Design.* London, 1920.

Fry, Roger. *Cézanne.* London, 1927; reprint, with an Introduction by Richard Shiff, Chicago, 1989.

Fry, Roger. *A Roger Fry Reader.* Edited by Christopher Reed. Chicago, 1996.

Gillespie, Diane Filby. *The Sisters' Arts: The Writing and Painting of Virginia Woolf and Vanessa Bell.* Syracuse, N.Y., 1988.

Gillespie, Diane Filby, ed. *The Multiple Muses of Virginia Woolf.* Columbia, Mo., 1993.

Shiff, Richard. *Cézanne and the End of Impressionism: A Study of the Theory, Technique, and Critical Evaluation of Modern Art.* Chicago, 1984.

Watney, Simon. *The Art of Duncan Grant.* London, 1990.

Williams, Raymond. "The Significance of 'Bloomsbury' as a Social and Cultural Group." In *Keynes and the Bloomsbury Group,* edited by Derek Crabtree and A. P. Thirlwell. London, 1980.

Woolf, Virginia. *A Room of One's Own.* London, 1929.

Woolf, Virginia. *Three Guineas.* London, 1938.

Woolf, Virginia. *Roger Fry: A Biography.* London, 1940.

Woolf, Virginia. *Moments of Being: Unpublished Autobiographical Writings.* Edited by Jeanne Schulkind. New York, 1976.

Woolf, Virginia. *Women and Writing.* Edited by Michèle Barrett. London, 1979.

Zwerdling, Alex. *Virginia Woolf and the Real World.* Berkeley, 1986.

CHRISTOPHER REED

BOAS, FRANZ. *See* Anthropology and Aesthetics.

BODY. *See* Beauty; Censorship; Dance; Emotions; Fashion; Katharsis; Models, Artists'; Origins of Aesthetics; Performance Art; Pleasure; Sensibilité; Sexuality; Taste; *and* Theater.

BOILEAU-DESPRÉAUX, NICOLAS (1636–1711), French poet and critic. Introduced to literary circles by his brother Gilles, who was a member of the Académie Française, from the first, Boileau found literature to be the perfect arena in which to satisfy the "pleasure" that he confessed he took in denouncing the vices of his day. As part of the morally based attack he mounted against various forms of hypocrisy and affectation, Boileau—who would go on to be considered the "Legislator of Parnassus"—took aim at "mediocre" writers in his first seven satires (published in their definitive form in 1666). In this work, as in all of Boileau's writings, personal grievances mingled with remarks on good taste in literary matters. Until the very end of a long career during which he made several enemies, Boileau praised the qualities of intellectual independence and sincerity that had inspired him to become a writer. In his last satire, "Sur l'équivoque" (1705), he reformulated the essence of his philosophy by denouncing "fraudulent speech" and "ambiguous thinking," which he saw as the source of all the "evils" and "errors" that plagued the world; the moral order of the universe had, Boileau argued, been perverted by the "cunning malice" of equivocation.

The first edition of Boileau's *Œuvres diverses* (Collected works), which appeared in 1674, included his *Satires* I–IX and *Epîtres* I–IV (Epistles), as well as the first part of the mock-heroic poem *Le lutrin* (The lectern), a translation of the *Treatise on the Sublime* by Longinus, and *L'art poétique* (The art of poetry). *The Art of Poetry,* long considered the ultimate expression of classical aesthetics, reflected Boileau's distinctive polemical bent: mediocrity and "false rhetorical dazzle" were attacked in order to define the criteria for poetic excellence. The ideal that Boileau expounded in this text—in which he distinguished himself above all by skillfully expressing theory in verse—drew on most of the precepts that had already been accepted and applied by his contemporaries. *The Art of Poetry* was conceived as a work of popularization: it presented a coherent synthesis of both the debates that were then raging among the major theoreticians (e.g., Jean Chapelain, François Hédelin d'Aubignac, René Rapin) and the literary practices of the day. In his presentation of tragedy, for example, Boileau reformulated the "rules" of dramaturgy (verisimilitude, *bienséance* [decorum], and unity of action, space, and time), while also invoking the doctrine of imitation. Moreover, his discussion of the various literary genres (in cantos 2 and 3) underscored the importance of both pleasing and instructing the public.

Boileau devoted cantos 1 and 4 of this work to some general considerations on poetic creation. Inspiration, he declared, is essential to writing but should be controlled by an assiduous and scrupulous "work" on the part of the poet that would be based on the application of precise techniques. The writer, who should strive for clarity and naturalness, was instructed first and foremost to follow "reason"—the principle from which all rules derived, and which would protect him from any excessive flights of fancy. Along with these prescriptive remarks, Boileau described the poet as a "man of faith" and virtue who was more concerned with glory than with personal profit. The poet, Boileau explained, should be sensitive to the opinion of both friends and the public, the latter being the ultimate judge of the value of a literary work.

Boileau's respect for the Ancients clearly stands out in *The Art of Poetry.* From 1687 onward, three years after being named to the Académie française, Boileau took a stand against Charles Perrault and assumed the role of defender of the Greeks and Latins in the "Quarrel of the Ancients and the Moderns." Taking this position gave him the opportunity to clarify a concept that he had already expounded in his translation of Longinus's *Treatise on the Sublime,* in which imitation of the Ancients was justified as a means of paving the way to artistic "enthusiasm." In 1694, Boileau published the first nine *Réflexions critiques sur quelques passages du rhéteur Longin* (Critical Reflections on Some Passages of the Rhetorician Longinus). This reply to Perrault's *Parallèle des Anciens et des Modernes* (A Parallel between the Ancients and the Moderns) shifted the debate of the famous quarrel: Boileau aimed to determine the nature of "the marvelous element" *(le merveilleux)* that had "for so many centuries" prompted admiration for Homer, Plato, Cicero, and Virgil. As Boileau put it, those who did not "feel" what other men "felt" on reading these authors had neither taste nor genius.

It is undoubtedly in his remarks on the definition of the sublime, "which forms the excellence and supreme perfection of discourse," that Boileau expressed the most original side of his aesthetic principles. Thanks to him, the concept of the sublime was separated from rhetoric: it was no longer associated with an elevated style and no longer implied an effect of persuasion. In fact, maintained Boileau, this ultimate manifestation of the "beautiful" could be discerned in "the simplest words," because it was based on a mode of thought that acted primarily on the emotions. That "discursive force" exerted an effect of "rapture" and "transport" on the reader. The sublime was just as likely to arise from "greatness of thought" and "nobleness of sentiment" as from "magnificence of words" or a "vivid and harmonious turn of phrase which enlivens expression"; the "perfect sublime" joined these three qualities. The preface to the *Collected Works* of 1701 provided Boileau's most precise definition of the *"je ne sais quoi,* which one can far more easily feel than articulate": it consisted essentially in "never presenting to the reader anything but true thoughts and proper expressions . . . therefore, given that a thought is only beautiful inasmuch as it is true, and that the inevitable effect of truth—when it is well expressed—is to be striking, it follows that anything that is not striking is neither beautiful nor true." By reconciling intellectual and emotional appreciation in this manner, a literary work could arouse the "general taste" and approval of the audience.

During the eighteenth century, Boileau's influence in England took the form of an aesthetics of sentiment based in part on the work of Longinus; in France, by contrast, his authority grew but was fixed in the image he held as the "artisan of classicism." His reputation has long been attached (too exclusively) to the precepts of *The Art of Poetry.* Yet, the notion of the sublime that Boileau conveyed and interpreted went far beyond the dogmatic system of the classical age. One might say, therefore, that the main contribution that the "Legislator of Parnassus" made to the aesthetics of his period was to have shown the interplay between two fundamental principles: the imperatives of reason, and the demands of the "je ne sais quoi"—a principle that could not be understood in terms of rules, but that constituted, in Boileau's mind, the essential force underlying both artistic creation and the "pleasure" of the reader.

[*See also* Classicism; *and* Poetics.]

BIBLIOGRAPHY

Works by Boileau-Despréaux

Complete Works. 3 vols. London, 1711–1713.
Œuvres complètes. Edited by Antoine Adam and Françoise Escal. Paris, 1966.
The Poetical Works of Dryden. Rev. enl. ed. Edited by George R. Noyes. Boston, 1950. This edition includes a reprint of Sir William Soame's translations from Boileau (1683), revised by Dryden.
Selected Criticism. Translated by Ernest Dilworth. Indianapolis, 1965.
The Works of Monsieur Boileau. 2d ed. 2 vols. Translated by Nicholas Rowe et al. London, 1736.

Other Sources

Adam, Antoine. *Histoire de la littérature française au XVIIe siècle.* See vol. 3, pp. 49–156; vol. 5, pp. 58–84. Paris, 1956.
Beugnot, Bernard. "Boileau et la distance critique." *Études Françaises* 5.2 (1968): 195–206.
Beugnot, Bernard, and Roger Zuber. *Boileau: Visages anciens, visages nouveaux, 1665–1970.* Montreal, 1973.
Borgerhoff, E. B. O. *The Freedom of French Classicism.* Princeton, N.J., 1950. See pp. 200–212.
Bray, René. *La formation de la doctrine classique en France.* Paris, 1963.
Brody, Jules. *Boileau and Longinus.* Geneva, 1958.
Clarac, Pierre. *Boileau.* Paris, 1964.
Clark, Alexander F. B. *Boileau and the French Classical Critics in England, 1660–1830.* Paris, 1925.
Davidson, Hugh M. "The Literary Arts of Longinus and Boileau." In *Studies in Seventeenth-Century French Literature: Presented to Morris Bishop,* edited by Jean-Jacques Demorest, pp. 247–264. Ithaca, N.Y., 1962.
Edelman, Nathan. "L'art poétique: Longtemps plaire et jamais ne lasser." In *Studies in Seventeenth-Century French Literature: Presented to Morris Bishop,* edited by Jean-Jacques Demorest, pp. 231–246. Ithaca, N.Y., 1962.
Gillot, Hubert. *La querelle des anciens et des modernes en France.* Champion, 1914.
Grimal, Pierre, et al. "Boileau et le débat critique sous Louis XIV." In *Critique et création littéraires en France au XVIIe siècle,* edited by Marc Fumaroli, part 4, pp. 183–250. Paris, 1977. Articles by Pierre Grimal, Slobodan Vitanovic, Bernard Tocanne, Gaston Hall, Jules Brody, and Ronald Tobin.
Joret, Paul. *Nicolas Boileau-Despréaux: Révolutionnaire et conformiste.* Paris, 1989.
Litman, Théodore A. *Le sublime en France, 1660–1714.* Paris, 1971.
Marin, Louis. "Le sublime dans les années 1670." *Papers on French Seventeenth-Century Literature* 25 (1986): 185–201.
Pocock, Gordon. *Boileau and the Nature of Neo-Classicism.* Cambridge and New York, 1980.
Wood, Allen G. *Literary Satire and Theory: A Study of Horace, Boileau, and Pope.* New York, 1985.
Wood, Theodore E. B. *The Word "Sublime" and Its Context, 1650–1760.* The Hague, 1972.

MARTINE DEBAISIEUX

BÖTTICHER, KARL GOTTLIEB WILHELM

(1806–1889), German architectural theorist. Bötticher was born in Nordhausen and arrived in Berlin in 1827 to study architecture at the Allgemeine Bauschule. In 1832, he obtained a teaching position at the newly founded Gewerbeinstitut and later taught architectural history at the Akademie der Künste and ornamental design at the Allgemeine Bauschule, where he was appointed professor of architecture in 1844. During the 1830s, Bötticher wrote several handbooks on ornamental principles in classical design and architecture. Between 1840 and 1852, he published a series of articles and a book on the theory of architectural tectonics. In these latter writings—"The Development of the Forms of Greek Tectonics" (1840), *The Tectonics of the Greeks* (1844, 1852), and "The Principles of Greek and German Building Methods" (1846)—he explained his aesthetic.

Bötticher is best known for his theory of tectonics, an attempt to integrate approaches to function, structure, and symbolism within architectural design. Tectonics is perhaps the greatest contribution made by German architectural theorists during the nineteenth century. It preoccupied Karl Friedrich Schinkel, Bötticher's colleague in Berlin, and led Gottfried Semper to write the monumental *Style in the Technical and Tectonic Arts or Practical Aesthetics* (1860).

From the outset, it is important to emphasize that theories of tectonics were not just about construction. Rather, they were attempts to construe an architectural aesthetic in light of the dramatic changes reverberating throughout Europe during the early phases of industrialization. Tectonics was an architectural philosophy for the post-Hegelian age, a dialectical offspring from the discipline's new cross-purposes of disinterested pleasure and purposive fabrication. Opposition to the fragmentation of the architectural discipline was common to all theories of tectonics. But, whereas Semper's tectonics gave priority to reintegrating the fine and practical arts, Bötticher strove to create a composite architectural identity from Romantic imagination and classical rule. His tectonics preoccupied itself with surmounting the polarization between classical Greece and Romantic medievalism that had agitated German culture since the late eighteenth century.

This reading explains the importance that Bötticher attached to an association between technological innovation and artistic continuity, or, more specifically, evolutionary iron engineering (seen as an outgrowth of medieval structure) and architecture's most enduring vocabulary of signification—the ornamental language of classical Greece. Paradoxically, Bötticher's tectonics suggested a rationale for ends-oriented, mimetic representation (commonly shared classical forms) in a world increasingly dominated by imaginative instrumentalism (ranging from the individual psyche to iron engineering).

The roots of Bötticher's tectonic aesthetics extend from the demise of Vitruvian architectural theory during the late eighteenth century. In the projects of innovators such as Friedrich Gilly, Vitruvian *Ordinatio*—the harmonious, symmetrical, and proportional unification of all parts of a building into a whole—gave way to a concept of architecture as a simulacrum of nature for the sake of subjective reflection. What was now of utmost importance in respect of the Greek temple was not the relation of the parts to each other, but the impression that a framework of support and bearing made on the observer. By the time Schinkel's teachings and writings on tectonics during the 1820s and 1830s, the term had come to be associated (via Johann Gottlieb Fichte's philosophy) with a clarification of the unconscious beauty of nature within the absolute ground of the subjective mind.

Like Schinkel, Bötticher argued that architecture must develop an expressive language to communicate the endless variation and emotional impact of experienced nature. If his tectonics advanced the thought that architecture embodied the construction of artifice out of brute matter, it would be critical nonetheless to restrain the boundlessness and potentially destabilizing forces of that creation. Structural forces (building nature) must be symbolized by ornament (an expressive language) as the ultimate culmination of the architectural act. In philosophical terms, tectonics attempted to resolve architectural *Mannigfaltigkeit* (the variety and complexity of the mechanical forces of building) in an *Einheit* (unity) possible only in art.

In these and other instances, Bötticher's theory may be seen as an architectural reaction to the aesthetic enshrinement of art as the highest subjective ideal. During the eighteenth century, new concepts of originality, sensations, and imagination were developed to release artistic judgment from the restraints of imitation and rule. These aesthetic theories reoriented reflection on architecture's artistic qualities from the passive apprehension of objects to the active unfolding of the imaginative faculties of the mind. The subjective perception of art and nature, however, separated architecture's mechanical essence from its artistic symbolism. Ornament, as the culmination of a subject's imaginative drive to bring unity to the manifold of natural forces, became a higher artistic level. This implied a lower level for the functional and structural relations of architecture. By the time of Georg Wilhelm Friedrich Hegel's and Arthur Schopenhauer's aesthetics, architecture was depicted as the lowest of all the arts.

Bötticher's tectonics reversed this aesthetic hierarchy. Like aestheticians, he accepted that the essence of architecture lies in functional needs and constructive forces. But he did not concur with the sublimation of these utilitarian aspects to artistic transcendence. Indeed, his attempt to harmonize the muscular passion of architectural materiality and statics with the objectivity of art is quite different from Immanuel Kant's or Friedrich Schiller's concept of *Architektonik*-beauty as the marshaling of the subjective senses toward objective reality. Instead, like Schinkel, Bötticher argued that art must refer back to utility and external nature. Within tectonics, the hierarchies of the aesthetic *Architektonik* are reversed. The beauty of architecture is precisely an explication of mechanical concepts.

Unlike most earlier architectural theory, which focused on the imitation of objects (either directly or through analogies), tectonics investigated architecture through the manifold processes that make up building. In the introduction to *The Tectonics of the Greeks*, Bötticher explicitly stated that architecture's first principle is the enclosure of space. Thus, instead of starting design with a model in mind, he recommended that architects begin with an analysis of social and physical forces: the needs that instigate plan, roof covering, and vertical supports, and result in the creation of architectural form and space. Here was an integrated system of architectural expression based first on considerations of plan and structure, and only then on the symbolism of structure in ornamental forms.

Furthermore, the amplification of mechanical necessity through artistic symbolization promised an integration of the modern complexities of materials, statics, and everyday needs with the universal unities of beauty and truth. Bötticher interpreted ornament as the communication of themes intrinsic to building. In a historical sense, he envisioned a medievalist armature of material and structural forces represented by an explanatory language of Greek ornamental forms. The harmony of the Greek temple, its correspondence of part to whole through intricate ornamental relationships, confirmed for him the timeless value of the Greek contribution to the architectural art. As was the case with Alois Hirt and Johann Joachim Winckelmann, Bötticher looked to Greece as a model of order with which to combat contemporary social disunity. In the later tectonics, while moving from an analysis of medieval stone vaulting to one of modern iron structure, Bötticher held fast to his belief that Hellenic ornament was the best language to depict the actively changing technological forces of building.

Like all dialectical programs, however, Bötticher's tectonics created initial divisions that always threatened to undermine the final synthesis. Thus, in the effort to establish a thoroughgoing organic unity between structure and ornament, Bötticher first had to divide architecture into radical core form (the material or mechanical function) and conservative art form (the historical expression of function). His radical promotion of iron architecture only aggravated doubts that the Hellenic art form could illuminate the entirely new range of building actions in the industrial age.

As might be expected of so divisive a theory of unity, Bötticher's suturing of classical mythology onto technological modernity aroused quite distinct reactions in later years. During the late nineteenth century, in movements such as the *Jugendstil* and Moderne, his tectonics provided part of the grounds for investigations into a merger of industry with appropriate contemporary art forms—resulting in an aesthetic of the iron line. By contrast, the twentieth-century Modern movement seems to have been more influenced by Bötticher's discussion of the differences between *Werkform* (structure) and *Kunstform* (ornament). Although Bötticher took architecture apart in order to put it back together, the legacy of his initial opposition produced unintended consequences, among which was the creation of an architectural aesthetic (e.g., the *Neue Sachlichkeit*) solely out of the technological and material *Werkform*. Finally, in postmodern times, the irresolute relationship between *Werkform* and *Kunstform* has taken on an interest in and of itself. Absent earlier longings for either absolute unification or a decisive choice between these two forces, contemporary theorists are interested in understanding architecture through its oppositions and endlessly contesting alterities.

[*See also* Architecture.]

BIBLIOGRAPHY

Works by Bötticher

Die Holzarchitectur des Mittelalters. Berlin, 1836.
Ornamenten-Schule: Ein Studien-Cursus für die Zeichnung und Erfindung des Ornamentes, nach dem von der antiken Kunst gegebenen Karakterisierungsprinzipe architectonischer Formen. Berlin, 1838.
"Entwicklung der Formen der hellenischen Tektonik." *Allgemeine Bauzeitung* 5 (1840): 316–340.
Die Tektonik der Hellenen (1st partial ed. 1844, 1st complete ed. 1852). 2 vols. Berlin, 1874.
"Polemisches-Kritisches." *Allgemeine Bauzeitung* 10, Beilage n. 18 (1845): 218–320.
"Das Prinzip der hellenischen und germanischen Bauweise." *Allgemeine Bauzeitung* 11 (1846): 111–125.
Der Baumcultus der Hellenen. Berlin, 1856.
Bericht über die Untersuchungen auf der Akropolis von Athen im Frühjahre 1862. Berlin, 1863.
"Mittheilungen aus der Sammlung der Sculpturen und Gypsabgüsse des königlichen Museums." *Archäologische Zeitung* 3 (1871): 59–64.
"Tektonische Untersuchungen auf der Akropolis von Athen im Frühjahre 1878." *Zeitschrift für Bauwesen* 30 (1880): 71–88, 209–228.

Other Sources

Blankenstein, Hermann. "Karl Bötticher, Sein Leben und Wirken." *Centralblatt der Bauverwaltung* 9 (1889): 315–317, 326–329.
Herrmann, Wolfgang, ed. *In What Style Should We Build? The German Debate on Architectural Style*. Santa Monica, Calif., 1992. Contains a translation of "The Principles of the Hellenic and Germanic Ways of Building with Regard to Their Application to Our Present Way of Building," pp. 147–168.
Jacobsthal, E. *Rückblicke auf die baukünstlerischen Prinzipien Schinkels und Böttichers*. Berlin, 1890.
Schwarzer, Mitchell. "Ontology and Representation in Karl Bötticher's Theory of Tectonics." *Journal of the Society of Architectural Historians* 52 (September 1993): 267–280.
Skerl, Joachim. "Zur Architekturtheorie Karl Böttichers." In *Karl Friedrich Schinkel und die Antike*, edited by M. Kunze. Leipzig, 1985.

MITCHELL SCHWARZER

BOULEZ, PIERRE (b. 1925), French contemporary composer and conductor. Boulez's visibility as conductor and Parisian musical bureaucrat have tended to veil his primary significance as one of the most important composers since 1945. If this combination of conducting and composing recalls Gustav Mahler, Boulez is, in addition, with Robert Schumann and Richard Wagner, one of the most articulate composers in music history.

Compositions and Career. More than any other twentieth-century composer, Boulez exemplifies the modernist imperative that the artist be not merely the tool of blind natural genius or tendency of the time, but rather, historically and aesthetically self-conscious. In his own words, "creation is in some part analytical" (Boulez, 1976, p. 188). His polemical and theoretical writings offer a cogent synthetic view of music aesthetics and history often close to that of Theodor W. Adorno, whom he personally knew. Boulez's role as programmatic polemicist of music may thus be compared with that of Clement Greenberg or Leo Steinberg in art. If his work has been less influential than Wagner's outside of music, this is only because the twentieth century has not been as fascinated with music as queen of the arts as was the nineteenth.

Boulez's career began directly in 1945–1946, when, after studies with Olivier Messaien, his first important works were written: the flute sonatina, the first piano sonata, and his first settings of the poet René Char. These pieces are marked by an extreme and dramatic Expressionism at times informed by early Arnold Schoenberg. At the time of Schoenberg's death, in 1951–1952, Boulez inaugurated, with *Structures I* for two pianos, what would be variously known as post-Webernism, total serialism, and later the Darmstadt school. Here the idea of the total rationalization of all musical materials (or parameters, in the parlance of the time) by one formula was drastically carried through: Webern's mathematization of pitch being extended to rhythm, register, and timbre as well. (Messaien had anticipated the idea with his study *Mode de valeurs et d'intensités* not long before, as had, in the United States, Milton Babbitt; yet, neither composer would provide this technique with as elaborate and articulate an ideology as would Boulez.) It is precisely this total rationalizing of the musical material that Adorno's *Philosophy of New Music* had proleptically criticized a few years earlier, and in response to the subsequent wave of total serial works, Adorno returned to the attack with "The Ageing of Modern Music."

Boulez had, however, already drawn his own consequences from the aporias of total *ordo;* his most famous piece, *Le marteau sans maître,* followed soon after (1954–1955) as a self-critique of the aridities of musical rationalism. The work, again a setting of texts of Char, consciously evokes the chamber cantata of Schoenberg's *Pierrot Lunaire,* interweaving vocal movements with instrumental commentaries in a decentered cycle (and thus anticipating Karlheinz Stockhausen's later *Momentform*); its most influential aspect was its instrumentation, with prominent vibraphone, marimba, and unpitched percussion. The new concept of flexible form combining openness and development exemplified in this work is not far from that espoused in Adorno's later essay "Vers une musique informelle." Later in the 1950s Boulez would discover the poetry of Stéphane Mallarmé, devoting another great vocal setting to him: *Pli selon pli,* written between the late 1950s and the early 1960s. The engagement with Mallarmé was accompanied by a concern with the role of chance in music (Boulez himself, with characteristic elegance, coined the term *aleatoric*). Although Boulez had known John Cage's work, and Cage personally, since the late 1940s, it was not until a decade later, when the possibilities of total control seemed exhausted, that randomness would become central to advanced compositional practice.

By this point, musical fashions had turned against the fastidious polish and consummate control of Boulez's aesthetic; the 1960s saw a rise of musical neo-Dadaism, theater pieces, and politicization, tendencies all alien to Boulez, whose compositional output began to dwindle as he turned to conducting in the hope of combating the fossilization of orchestra repertory and the marginalization of modernity by market and mass culture. The majority of his compositions begun from the late 1950s on have remained incomplete until the present (a matter still discreetly passed over in silence by official exegetes); this seems due less to a deliberately modernist aesthetics of the fragment than to external distractions. A planned reorganizing of French musical life with Boulez in command was frustrated by a conservative cabal around André Malraux in 1966; after terms at the BBC and New York Philharmonic orchestras, and a debut at Bayreuth with *Parsifal* in 1966 (the Chereau Ring would follow in 1976), Boulez finally made his triumphal return to Paris as the director of IRCAM (Institut pour la Recherche et Coordination Acoustique-Musique) in 1976. The central work for this period is *Répons,* for electronics, soloists, and orchestra (1981–): in it, as in his work at IRCAM's electronic research center, Boulez takes up again the cause of technological experiment, in which Stockhausen had outpaced him in the late 1950s and 1960s.

The technical hallmarks of Boulez's compositions may be summed as a brilliant orchestral palette, partly derived from Messaien in its prominence given to percussion and winds at the expense of the nineteenth-century string choir; highly virtuosic piano writing, using novel effects such as silently depressed sounding keys (but eschewing more drastic sounds not played on the keyboard); an idiosyncratic and more literary than graphic use of notation; extreme structural and formal density; an approach to text setting that breaks drastically from all operatic parlando naturalism or *stile rappresentativo;* and a floridly ornamented vocal writing that might well be described as twelve-tone bel canto. Boulez's compositions synthesize the technical acquisitions of the first half of the twentieth century—Viennese serialism, Stravinskyan rhythms, Varese's percussion, Messaien's Orientalism—much as Wagner drew together the inheritance of early Romanticism. His work and his writing have provided the dominant musical paradigm in Europe, one that has survived subsequent short-lived fashions such as Minimalism and neo-Romanticism. It is to be expected that a break with so powerful a presence will eventually be as necessary as was the turn away from Wagner in the 1920s.

Aesthetics: History and Technique. Although Boulez is not trained as a philosopher or aesthetician and his theoretical pronouncements tend to follow from rather than direct his artistic praxis, his view of the history of modernism—one, moreover, informed by a broad range of reference to literature, painting, and science—is so close to Adorno's that it is instructive to contrast the two. (Boulez hardly knew the older man's work before the mid- to late 1950s; any question of influence would have to mean that of Boulez on Adorno.) In fact, Adorno himself would agree in the *Aesthetic Theory* that aesthetic considerations divorced from considerations of technique can lead only to bankruptcy—as also with Boulez's repeated polemic against the idea of "style."

Boulez's view of musical history has an underlying inheritance from Marx in its idea of a progressive unleashing of productive forces; yet, this belief is also limited by a skepticism regarding linear teleologies or anonymous "laws of necessity" (Boulez, 1976, p. 33). In opposition to any form of historicist conservativism, Boulez believes that history, in its monumental form, is "not a history of conservation but a history of destruction" (ibid.). History can thus be present only as a negative trace in a work that has parricidally liquidated its ancestors. Boulez saw serialism as a consequence of Wagnerian chromaticism, of innate "tendencies of the material." Music has no natural language not subject to historical variation (ibid., p. 188). Boulez therefore also rejected Stravinskyan neoclassicism; the vehemence of his early polemics from circa 1950 were due, like the polemical tone of Adorno's *Philosophy of New Music*, to the international dominance of that style during the 1930s and 1940s. Boulez, however, articulately defended the early, pre-Pulcinella Stravinsky. The key document is the long and magistral rhythmic analysis of *The Rite of Spring* ("Stravinsky Remains," in *Notes of an Apprenticeship* [1968]). In fact, Boulez concurred in Adorno's criticisms of that work's harmonic conservativism and the limits of its static, mosaic-like form. Yet, Boulez develops here an entirely different view of the role of rhythm in music than Adorno. Unlike the latter, whose musical culture was largely limited to European music after Bach, Boulez evoked medieval isorhythmic techniques and those of Indian and Balinese music in defense of Stravinsky's independence of rhythm from melodically expressive subjectivity. Thus, Boulez criticized Schoenberg's later work as being in its own way as restorative and backward-looking as Stravinsky's historicism: most vigorously in the manifesto "Schoenberg Is Dead" of 1951 (in *Notes of an Apprenticeship*). It is indicative of the difference between Boulez and Adorno that the former preferred Bach to Beethoven, while reading Bach in decidedly modernist fashion. Unlike the by now predictable association of Bach with fugue, Boulez cites Bach's organ chorales as models of developmental technique. Boulez, too, moved toward an increasing appreciation of the work of Alban Berg over that of the other two Viennese; for Boulez, disinterested in neat architectonic formal symmetries, preferred to continue the tendency to Nominalism or "musical prose" that Adorno saw in Wagner and Schoenberg in Brahms.

Boulez came to be increasingly suspicious of what he called the "fetishism" of technological novelty for its own sake. Interest in new techniques could not, for him, override the ultimate question of musical meaning (Boulez, 1976, p. 188). Thus, for all his fascination with the poetics of the fragment, Boulez never abandoned the idea of a cogent, unitary work of art. In this he stands diametrically opposed to the aesthetics of ephemerality, effect, and improvisation developed by Stockhausen, in a way somewhat analogous to action painting, in the 1960s (cf. Glock, 1986, p. 19). The measured consideration of practical performance realizability and the hermeneutical limits of listener comprehension constantly check any utopian fantasies in his writing. Nor has Boulez cared for the secret conformism of shock techniques, collage, or neo-Dadaist attacks on the institution of art, as his overt contempt for Erik Satie (Cage's favorite composer) testifies. His distaste for popular culture is equal to Adorno's (and extends to much of nineteenth-century bourgeois concert repertory such as Pyotr Ilich Tchaikovsky and Italian opera); he has thus never made any use of quotation of pop or everyday materials in his work.

At the center of Boulez's aesthetic writings is a concern with judgment, but a judgment that, unlike Immanuel Kant's, is one not only of the beholder but also of the artist. An irreducible moment of intuition and irrationality remains here, defying the modernist urge to rationalization: "revolutions must be not only constructed, but also dreamed" (Boulez, 1976, p. 28). The aesthetic subject for Boulez is not only one of *ratio* and construction. The mechanization of art implied both in total serialism and in electronics must fail in its attempt to exclude an element of subjective freedom. (Thus, Boulez's own writing style, for all its pursuit of didactic rigor, consciously evades the formulaic and normative, preferring an allusively literary mode of presentation influenced by Claude Debussy and Paul Valéry's *Monsieur Teste*.)

Aesthetics: The Musical Subject. Boulez shares with French literary modernism a general distaste for the Greco-Roman inheritance, and a corresponding interest in the Orient. This accompanies a novel notion of musical subjectivity, the point where he differs most sharply from Adorno. One of Boulez's favorite references is to Antonin Artaud's idea of "organizing delirium"; another frequently encountered notion is an aesthetics of hermeticism and anonymity, developed on the basis of Mallarmé's poetics. (Boulez's discovery of Mallarmé in the late 1950s places his project in historical proximity to structuralism.) Already *Structures I* was compared by Boulez himself to Roland Barthes's "writing degree zero" (Boulez, 1976, p. 51). Yet, the obliquity of the subject would survive the end of extreme functionalism in Boulez's work in the mid-1950s.

Because Boulez does not write in the language of philosophical aesthetics, one must extrapolate this idea of the subject from hints made often in technical discussions. Adorno, in *The Philosophy of New Music*, correctly saw the spatialization of time as a central aspect of modernity. Boulez is also interested in this phenomenon, as the central discussion of space and time relations in *Boulez on Music Today* (1971), informed both by science and by an implicit awareness of phenomenology, testifies. Beyond any simple attempts at arresting time in static frozenness or repetition, however, Boulez has subtler ideas about the perception and execution of time. In opposition to usual pulsated time, the time of repetitive meter (which in Georg Wilhelm Friedrich Hegel's *Aesthetics* was at the origin of the musical subject),

> there is also a kind of musical time that can do entirely without pulsations—a music that seems to float, and in which the writing itself makes it impossible for the performer to keep in time with a pulsed tempo: grace notes, ornaments, or a profusion of differences in dynamics will make the performer give so much attention to what is happening that temporal control recedes into the background. At such times the activity itself is more important than its control, so that at times mensural notation is no more than a visual aid. Such notation will not be respected because it cannot be.   (Boulez, 1976, p. 69)

The musical subject sketched in here is close to that of Artaud's "affective athletism": it is at once an absolute subject and a dissolved, acephalous, unrepresentable one. The overloading of local detail—ornament, loudness, attack—in the writing leads to a breakout of pure gesturality. Against any scholastic fixation on the "text," the writing seems to abolish itself in the spontaneity of *actus purus*. One might say that here the musical subject opens up to its other, to its nonidentity, through the destruction of the representation of historically continuous time. This is very different from Igor Stravinsky's insistence on the severe rhythmic precision of the dancer—for there is nothing here of the disciplinary aspect that Adorno detected in Stravinskyan ballet—and yet Boulez has reached this via Stravinsky's autonomy of rhythm from melody. Thus, unlike Cage (and Stockhausen in his later chance pieces), Boulez never abandoned the tension between subjective choice and objective chance in favor of the latter alone. As Boulez puts it, "the concept of tempo is a concept of error" (ibid., p. 71)—that is, tempo, subjective time, is what cannot be mechanized; it is experienced and not chronological time. The central role of chance and intuition in Boulez's poetics thus emerges as tied up with his gestural, unrepresentational notion of musical subject. The athematicism of Boulez's work contributes also to this loosening of the subject (one may recall that for Adorno in *The Philosophy of New Music*, the musical subject was inseparable from a thematic kernel or *Einfall*). In this insistence on the ultimate impossibility of closing any totalizing and impersonal structure, in the idea of the subject as what falls out of or disturbs mechanism, Boulez's aesthetic resembles that of certain forms of poststructuralism (Jacques Lacan's in particular). An important essay on chance in music, "Alea" (Boulez, 1976, p. 51), ambivalently evoked killing the Artist a decade before this became a rallying cry in literary theory—yet, the irony with which this is

done precludes any obvious taking of sides or certainties on the matter.

The question of a musical subject as impersonal and absolute as Mallarmé's or Artaud's suggests a metaphysical dimension to Boulez's aesthetics. Boulez was too aware of Debussy's sarcasms on the pseudophilosophical bombast of Richard Strauss to venture any overt programmatical statements on this matter. It is, however, not hard to detect a poetics of negativity at work here that is solidly in the line of Franz Kafka, of Schoenberg, and of Adorno as well. One might suggest that, just as, in his vocal writing, Boulez broke with the tradition of naturalist, mimetic declamation that had dominated opera from Claudio Monteverdi to the nineteenth century, so his poetics is closer to one of a cosmic, Pythagorean *musica mundana* than to the individual expressivity of *musica humana* (or *reservata*) that began in the mid-sixteenth century.

The tendency of philosophical aesthetics to see this metaphysical reference of music as a constant is an ahistorical generalization from Arthur Schopenhauer and Friedrich Nietzsche; it should be recalled that both the late eighteenth century and many aspects of the twentieth (among them neoclassicism, *Gebrauchsmusik*, politicized music, Dada happening, and cabarettism) explicitly broke with this inheritance. Boulez, here as often elsewhere, evinces, as does Adorno, aspects of a conservative radical. In a historical period where music has lost the paradigmatic role it had for Romanticism, and where (as Boulez himself has noted) music has often tended to lag behind or borrow from other arts rather than anticipate them, Boulez has, both in his writings and in artistic practice, returned music a metaphysical dignity it has otherwise retained largely in the works of philosophers and theoreticians.

[*See also* Adorno, *article on* Adorno's Philosophy of Music; Modernism, *article on* Modern Music; *and* Music, *historical overview article*.]

BIBLIOGRAPHY

Works by Boulez

The Boulez-Cage Correspondence. Edited by Jean-Jacques Nattiez, translated by Robert Samuels et al. Cambridge and New York, 1993.

Boulez on Music Today. Translated by Susan Bradshaw and Richard Rodney Bennett. Cambridge, Mass., 1971. Translation of *Penser la musique aujourd'hui.*

Conversations with Celestin Deliege. London, 1976. Translation of *Par volonté et par hasard.*

Jalons pour une décennie. Edited by Jean-Jacques Nattiez. Paris, 1989.

Notes of an Apprenticeship. Edited by Paule Thevenin, translated by Herbert Weinstock. New York, 1968. Translation of *Relevés d'apprenti.*

Orientations: Collected Writings by Pierre Boulez. Edited by Jean-Jacques Nattiez, translated by Martin Cooper. Cambridge, Mass., 1986. Translation of *Points de repère.*

Other Sources

Breatnach, Mary. *Boulez and Mallarmé: A Study of Influence.* Aldershot, 1996.

Glock, William, ed. *Pierre Boulez: A Symposium*. London, 1986.

Golea, Antoine. *Rencontres avec Pierre Boulez*. Paris, 1958.

Häusler, Josef, ed. *Pierre Boulez Festschrift*. Vienna, 1986.

Hirsbrunner, Theo. *Pierre Boulez und sein Werk*. Laaber, 1985.

Jameux, Dominique. *Pierre Boulez*. Translated by Susan Bradshaw. Cambridge, Mass., 1991.

Koblyakov, Lev. *Pierre Boulez: A World of Harmony*. Chur, Switzerland, 1990.

LARSEN POWELL

BOURDIEU, PIERRE. [*To examine Bourdieu's critique of Aesthetics, This entry comprises two essays:*

Survey of Thought

Artistic Field

The first essay explains Bourdieu's sociology of art, which has influenced museology or the study of museums. The second essay examines in depth a key concept—artistic field—that Bourdieu introduces into discussions of aesthetics.]

Survey of Thought

Pierre Bourdieu is a contemporary French sociologist who writes mainly about art and culture. Bourdieu's first published writings in the late 1950s concerned the Algerian peasantry and working class, in relation both to "traditional" society and to the nationalist revolution. The early sixties saw his first application of anthropological methods to his own milieu, that is, to students and their relations with professors. In 1965, he published a study of photography as a class-differentiated social practice; this was followed a year later by *The Love of Art*, an analysis of art museums and their visitors. From then on, his gigantic bibliography has been dominated by studies of European "high culture," academic and artistic, along with works on the methodology of social science. Bourdieu is professor of sociology at the Collège de France and director of the Center for European Sociology at the École des hautes études en sciences sociales.

Strictly speaking, it would be incorrect to list Bourdieu's studies of art and culture under the rubric "aesthetics." A series of important works deals with such matters central to the tradition of aesthetics as taste, the definition of art and its value, the autonomy of art as a sphere of activity, and aesthetic experience. But Bourdieu has consistently made an effort to investigate these matters from a point of view that might be described as external to that of aesthetics, in the sense that it takes the fundamental categories of that discourse as open to question. On the other hand, he has insisted on the need to transcend the opposition of "internal" and "external"—or "subjective" and "objective"—viewpoints that has so consistently structured the methodology of the social sciences. He stresses both that the members of a society are in general unaware of important determinants of their social behavior and that their modes of action cannot be understood without reference to their representa-

tions of their own practices. Accordingly, although sociological analysis must construct its own categories of description and interpretation, if it is not to be limited to restating the self-understanding of those it studies, those categories must allow one to make sense of that self-understanding and the actions it determines. In the case of modern aesthetics, this means that its basic assumptions—of the existence of a specifically aesthetic experience, of the value of artworks, and of the potential universality of their meaning—cannot be taken for granted but must be themselves explained. This explanation, given the nature of social practices, must be at once sociological (referring to the social conditions and consequences of such assumptions) and historical (referring to the processes by which these conditions came into existence and are preserved—or not). The result, as Bourdieu has carried out this program, is not so much a debunking of aesthetic judgments as a historical and social delimitation of their validity, which explains both their matter-of-fact quality for some and their incomprehensibility for others.

"The question of the conditions that make it possible to experience the work of art (and, in a more general way, all cultural objects) as at once endowed with meaning" does not arise for those who have this experience because "the culture that the originator puts into his work is identical with the culture . . . which the beholder brings to the deciphering of the work" (Bourdieu, 1993, p. 216). Hence, the aesthetic experience seems natural to those who have it, and determined directly by the work itself. In contrast, "faced with scholarly [or artistic] culture, the least sophisticated are in a position identical with that of ethnologists who find themselves in a foreign society" (ibid., p. 217), except that they come to this position, in general, not with an attitude of scientific curiosity but with the sensation of having wandered into an area of their own society in which they do not belong.

From the viewpoint of the possessors of what Bourdieu calls "cultural competence," those who do not possess it are not just different but deficient. Although the deficient themselves tend to respect the norms of official culture, their attitude to that culture is commonly also one of "reluctance or refusal." This reflects an orientation toward experience characterized by "the subordination of form to function, or, one might say, the refusal of the refusal which is the starting point of the high aesthetic, i.e., the clear-cut separation of ordinary dispositions from the specifically aesthetic disposition" founded on emotional and practical distance from the object of appreciation (Bourdieu, 1984, p. 32). The contrast between what Bourdieu calls the "taste of freedom" and the "taste of necessity" corresponds to the difference between the modes of life of those who are and those who are not, given their economic resources and social power, in a position to perceive life as a matter of choices, to be made on stylistic (or formal) grounds. The aesthetic disposition (and the artistic competence that it makes possible), though in appearance an individual attribute, is in reality an attribute of social class.

Possession of the aesthetic attitude is not, according to Bourdieu, simply a matter of the money and leisure required to acquire cultural competence, though these are certainly important circumstances. As crucial is the sense of entitlement that fosters the acquisition of competence. This is learned in the home, from childhood on, and is reinforced (or counteracted) by the experience of schooling and other institutions. It is embodied in what Bourdieu calls "habitus," a structure of behavior embedding "what some would mistakenly call *values* in the most automatic gestures or the apparently most insignificant techniques of the body—ways of walking or blowing one's nose, ways of eating or talking, "and thereby constituting "taste" as "a practical mastery of distributions [of goods and opportunities] which makes it possible to sense or intuit what is likely (or unlikely) to befall—and therefore to befit—an individual occupying a given position in social space" (ibid., p. 466). Family-derived habitus interacts with the experiences (and expectations) of movement from one class position to another that Bourdieu calls "trajectory" to produce taste as a system of classifications applied, beyond the strictly "aesthetic sphere," to the totality of objects and practices (food, sports, clothing, modes of speech, etc.) encountered in social life. Embodied in reactions of attraction or discomfort and visible linguistically in such oppositions as those between high and low, fine and coarse, light and heavy, distinguished and common, brilliant and dull, this system represents the internalization of social distinctions. For this reason, its employment in classifying objects at the same time classifies the classifier: the person able to appreciate a piece of "high" art is marked as culturally superior herself, just as those who prefer "coarse" and "heavy" foods thereby betray their low position on the social scale. The value hierarchy immediately suggested by the descriptive vocabulary is present in the tendency, definitive of the taste of freedom, to attend to style in all spheres of life. "This affirmation of power over a dominated necessity always implies a claim to a legitimate superiority over those who, because they cannot assert the same contempt for contingencies in gratuitous luxury and conspicuous consumption, remain dominated by ordinary interests and urgencies" (ibid., p. 56).

As Bourdieu observes, "a dominant culture owes its main features and social functions—especially that of symbolically legitimizing a form of domination—to the fact that it is not perceived as such" (Bourdieu, *The Logic of Practice*, 1990, p. 129). The class aesthetic appears as the sensitivity of superior individuals to the finer things. What is essential in the system of taste is not the particulars it classifies but the relations it establishes between them. Classifications shift over time; thus Vivaldi's *Four Seasons*, which in France

had high social value in 1963, had by 1967 been "pulled towards 'middle-brow' culture by popularization" (ibid., p. 601), its place as a marker of educated taste to be taken by some more recondite piece of music. At any given moment, however, the system of tastes is discernible in the form of preferences in clothing, furniture, food, friends, movies, music, and pictures, such as those elicited by the questionnaire whose use provided the data utilized in Bourdieu's magnum opus of 1979, *Distinction*. On the basis of these data, Bourdieu demonstrated statistically the fit between social origin and trajectory, on the one hand, and the range of lifestyle choices, on the other (showing, for example, that the tastes of factory foremen were closer to those of the workers from whose ranks they came than to office workers who earned the same salaries but aspired to movement upward—perhaps by their children—into management or the professions).

His analysis demonstrates in particular that, "of all the objects offered for consumers' choice, there are none more classifying than legitimate works of art, which, while distinctive in general, enable the production of distinctions ad infinitum by playing on divisions and sub-divisions into genres, periods, styles, authors, etc." (Bourdieu, 1984, 16). The aptitude for aesthetic experience, appearing as a personal rather than a learned attribute, serves at once as a sign and as a justification (because those unable to appreciate the finer things clearly do not deserve them) of the gross division of society into dominant and dominated classes. It also structures a division within the dominant class, between those whose social power is based on the ownership of economic capital and those who possess relatively greater quantities of what Bourdieu calls "cultural capital," a familiarity, based in habitus and developed through education, both with the objects and practices that constitute the world of culture and with the categories necessary to classify and so fully perceive and respond to them.

He uses the term *capital* in this context both to suggest an analogy to capital in the normal sense, as a matter of resources "subject to exclusive appropriation" that "yield a profit in distinction, proportionate to the means required to appropriate them" (ibid., p. 228), and because cultural capital can be converted into economic capital, whose name has primacy as the basic form of social power in modern society. (For example, an upward class trajectory can take the form of familial investment of money, and time, in the education of a child, who can later make a claim to higher social position and access to money on the basis of cultural competence, as certified, say, by a law degree or a master's degree in business administration). A literate culture is essential for the formation of cultural capital, as it makes possible the concentration of social knowledge in a form that can be appropriated by a few, but this form of capital "is given the conditions of its full realization only with the appearance of an educational system, which awards qualifications durably consecrating the position occupied in the structure of the distribution of capital" (*The Logic of Practice*, 1990, p. 125). Of course, access to cultural capital is, as we have seen, open differentially to those with the appropriate habitus, reflective of upper-class parentage. Thus, "the literary and artistic fields attract a particularly strong proportion of individuals who possess all the properties of the dominant class *minus one:* money" (Bourdieu, 1993, p. 165).

Despite their kinship, cultural and economic capital are in competition as principles of social superiority. This has led, with the development of capitalism, to the elaboration of what Bourdieu calls the autonomous "field of cultural production," the ensemble of social positions—such as, in the visual arts, those of artists, dealers, critics, collectors, museum personnel, and the art public at large—jointly involved in the production, valuation, and circulation of cultural goods. This field is autonomous in the sense that the activities constituting its life are governed by standards independent of economic value, such as artistic quality and originality. But just as there is a tension, within cultural fields, between cultural value (as exemplified by the noncommercial masterpiece) and the pressures of the market, which incarnates the fundamental principle of modern social life, so in society as a whole the two forms of capital live in a conflicted embrace. This is discernible in Bourdieu's statistical survey in the form of structures of taste (with respect to such matters as decor, dress, and—above all—cultural goods themselves) that distinguish those who live by culture from the bourgeoisie proper, even while other patterns of preference unite them in contrast to the working classes.

Artists, writers—and professors—thus form what Bourdieu calls the "dominated fraction of the dominant class," subordinated to the possessors of economic power by the systemic logic that decrees that they too must work for capital, but participating in domination both (when all goes well) economically and (above all) by the symbolic profits drawn from their mastery of the dominant forms of culture. This has consequences for cultural production. "The structural ambiguity of their position in the field of power leads writers and painters, those 'penniless bourgeois' in Pissaro's words, to maintain an ambivalent relationship with the dominant class within the field of power, those whom they call 'bourgeois,' as well as with the dominated, the 'people'" (ibid., 165). In this way, Bourdieu suggests, one can account for many features of the positions taken by intellectuals and artists in their professional activity—that is, for important episodes in the history of art. What is important, he insists against more simpleminded class determinisms, is that the social shaping of cultural production be understood as not simply direct (say, via patronage, or the influence of specific political institutions) but as mediated by the peculiar character of the cultural field. In particular, this approach helps us understand a phenomenon like the self-reflexive art of formalist modernism, exemplifying at once the bourgeois "taste for freedom" and the particular interest of the dominated fraction of the dominant class, as an aspect of the development of modern society. Generally, Bourdieu's analysis reveals how in all its forms the aesthetic attitude, rooted in habitus, becomes the basis for a systematic misrepresentation of social power as cultural aptitude.

Bourdieu's work is rich in detail as well as in theoretical power, and this account can only suggest its interest. In particular, *Distinction* contains a novel and suggestive approach to the nature of social class, here represented as "the unity hidden under the diversity and multiplicity of the set of practices performed" in different areas of life, and revealed in the choices regulated by habitus produced by relatively "homogeneous conditions of existence" (1984, p. 101). This both indicates the way in which social structure constrains and makes possible active modes of class formation, and illuminates such phenomena as the ambivalent relation of cultural workers to the primary holders of social power. Interestingly, Bourdieu seems unable to imagine the possibility of the dominated forming themselves into a social power capable of calling class domination into question. At the same time, he seems overly ready to believe in the ability of social scientists, and artists, to transcend the ideological orientation that defines their specific social power, and asserts that "the specific interests of cultural producers, in so far as they are linked to fields that, by the very logic of their functioning, encourage . . . the transcending of personal interest in the ordinary sense, can lead them to political or intellectual action that can be called universal" (Bourdieu, *In Other Words*, 1990, p. 146). It must be said that such hopes, like Bourdieu's addiction to a conventionally academic prose style, are exactly what his own theory would predict for someone operating in his area of social life.

[*See also* Photography; *and* Taste, *article on* Modern and Recent History.]

BIBLIOGRAPHY

Works by Bourdieu

Un art moyen, essai sur les usages sociaux de la photographie. Written with L. Boltanski, R. Castel, J.-C. Chamboredon, and D. Schnapper. Paris, 1965; rev. ed., Paris, 1970. Translated by Shaun Whiteside as *Photography: A Middle-Brow Art* (Stanford, Calif., 1990).

L'amour de l'art, les musées d'art et leur public. Written with Alain Darbel and Dominique Schnapper. Paris, 1966; rev. ed., Paris, 1969. Translated by Caroline Beattie and Nick Merriman as *The Love of Art: European Art Museums and Their Public* (Stanford, Calif., 1990).

La distinction: Critique sociale du jugement. Paris, 1979; rev. ed., Paris, 1982. Translated by Richard Nice as *Distinction: A Social Critique of the Judgement of Taste* (Cambridge, Mass., 1984).

Le sens pratique. Paris, 1980. Translated by Richard Nice as *The Logic of Practice* (Stanford, Calif., 1990).

In Other Words: Essays Towards a Reflexive Sociology. Translated by Matthew Adamson. Stanford, Calif., 1990.

The Field of Cultural Production: Essays on Art and Literature. Edited by Randal Johnson. New York, 1993.

Other Sources

Garnham, Nicholas, and Raymond Williams. "Pierre Bourdieu and the Sociology of Culture: An Introduction." In *Media, Culture and Society: A Critical Reader,* edited by Richard Collins et al., pp. 116–130. London, 1986.

Lamont, Michèle, and Annette Lareau. "Cultural Capital: Allusions, Gaps and Glissandos in Recent Theoretical Developments." *Sociological Theory* 6 (1988): 153–168.

Wilson, Elizabeth. "Picasso and Pâté de Foie Gras: Pierre Bourdieu's Sociology of Culture." *diacritics* 18.2 (1988): 47–60.

PAUL MATTICK

Artistic Field

The concept of artistic field *(champ artistique)* elaborated by Pierre Bourdieu is the central tool of a distinctive sociological approach to aesthetics. From its minting in the mid-1960s to its varied applications through the 1990s, it has played a pivotal role in Bourdieu's dissection of the peculiar logics of the universes of literature, painting, poetry, theater, high fashion, and germane "symbolic goods" (Bourdieu, 1966, 1975, 1977, 1979, 1987 ["L'institutionalisation"], 1992, 1993). Its chief aim is to revoke the perennial oppositions that have splintered the understanding of artistic practices and products—between text and context, individual innovation and collective constraint, essence and history, as well as between interpretation and explanation—so as to found a *historicist science of cultural works* capable of reconciling the social necessity these embody with the potential they hold for expressing transhistorical truths and values.

A recent feature of modern society, the artistic field is this particular arena, or *structured space of positions and position takings,* wherein individuals and institutions compete for monopoly over artistic authority as the latter becomes insulated from economic, political, and bureaucratic powers. Within the relatively autonomous sphere of action and contention thus constituted, the logic of the economy has been suspended, nay, inverted; properly aesthetic standards of judgment are affirmed over and *against* commercial criteria of profit; and participants wage an incessant internecine fight to establish the worth of their work according to the prevailing principle of artistic perception. The field thus produces and reproduces through its very functioning the unquestioned belief, shared by active and aspiring members alike, that art is a "sacred" realm, separate from and transcendent to mundane conduct and material interests (Bourdieu, 1979, 1983, 1987 ["Historical Genesis"]).

Like any other field, the artistic field, or the "field of cultural production" more broadly (Bourdieu, 1993), is first a *field of forces,* that is, a network of objective determinations that bear upon all those who perform in it. For instance, a young poet entering into the literary field of 1880s France faces a "set of probable constraints" that limit his options and orient his practices in the form of a hierarchy of literary crafts and schools, topics and styles, accepted *problématiques* and a pantheon of exemplary personas (Bourdieu, 1992, pp. 330–331). Second, the artistic field is also a *battlefield:* a terrain of struggle in which participants seek to preserve or overturn evaluative standards or, to use Bourdieu's conceptual idiom, to alter the relative weight of different species of "artistic capital." Those who occupy the dominant positions in the existing distribution of artistic capital will be inclined to strategies of conservation (orthodoxy) while holders of dominated and marginal positions will tend to pursue strategies of subversion (heterodoxy or even heresy). These conflicts are the engine of the specific history of the field: struggle is the "generative and unifying principle" whereby "the latter temporalizes itself" and abstracts itself, to a degree, from environing determinations (ibid., p. 199).

An analysis of cultural works in terms of field entails three indispensable and closely interlinked operations. The first is locating the artistic (literary, poetic, musical, etc.) microcosm *within the "field of power,"* that is, the web of institutions wherein circulate the economic, political, and cultural powers that the ruling class strives to arrogate. Based on his recapitulation of the invention of the modern figure of the writer by Gustave Flaubert, Bourdieu (1992) contends that the present-day field of cultural production forms the dominated pole of the field of power and that, as a consequence, it is the site of an ongoing battle between two opposed principles of hierarchization: an autonomous criterion ("art for art's sake") and heteronomous criterion favoring those who preponderate within the field economically and politically ("bourgeois art").

The second moment of field analysis consists in drawing a *topology of the internal structure* of the artistic field in order to disclose the patterning of the relations (of supremacy and subordination, distance and propinquity, complementarity and antagonism) that obtain, at a given moment, between the agents and institutions—major and minor artists, schools and journals, salons and coteries, academies and galleries—competing for artistic legitimacy. This reveals a hierarchy of producers and products based on a dynamic opposition between the subfield of "restricted production" (by and for specialists, evaluated according to properly aesthetic standards) and the subfield of "generalized production," in which works are aimed at lay audiences and achievement is measured by commercial success.

The third and final step involves constructing the social *trajectories* of the individuals who come to vie within the field so as to uncover the socially constituted system of dispositions (habitus) guiding their conduct and representations in and out of the artistic sphere. It is via these embodied schemata of understanding that artists will actualize (or not) the potentialities inscribed in the positions they hold. Artistic practice cannot be deduced from structural location alone; nor does it spring singly from individual propensities;

rather, it arises from their turbulent dialectic. A particular art piece is precipitated by "the superposition of redundant determinations" born of the "more or less 'felicitous' encounter between position and disposition" (Bourdieu, 1993, p. 207), between social and individual history sedimented in the habitus of the artist on the one side, and the history of aesthetic struggles inscribed in the structure of the field on the other.

Bourdieu proposes that a close correspondence or *homology* exists between the place of the artist in the field and the artistic stances he or she adopts, such that the former governs the latter through the mediation of habitus. The proper task of a science of art, then, is to elucidate this two-way "relationship between two structures, the structure of objective relations between positions in the field of production (and between the producers who occupy them) and the structure of objective relations between position-takings *[prises de positions]* in the space of works" (Bourdieu, 1992, p. 325). This necessitates a *double historicization*, of the diverse social universes of artistic production and of the changing categories of aesthetic perception, which together make up modern art as mutually complicitous gaze and institution (Bourdieu, 1987 ["Historical Genesis"]).

The concept of field thus breaks with both "pure" and "materialist" theories of art while trying to preserve the strengths of each (Jurt, 1995). Against all variants of *internalist* analysis propounded by neo-Kantian aesthetics, the Russian formalists, and structuralists from Roman Jakobson to Michel Foucault, Bourdieu rejects the conflation of the space of works with the space of objective positions constitutive of the field. Unless one wishes to absolutize artworks, one cannot sever the aesthetic order from the institutions that underpin it and the power struggles that traverse them. Against *externalist* analysis (as illustrated by the Marxist theories of literature of György Lukács and Lucien Goldmann or the *marxisants* refurbishings of Terry Eagleton and Fredric Jameson), the notion of field reminds us that works cannot be directly derived from the social properties of their creator or audience. Such a "short-circuit fallacy" omits the crucial mediation of the field of cultural production.

The artistic field acts in the manner of a prism that filters and refracts external forces according to its own logic and structure. The greater the autonomy of an artistic field and its ability to exclude outside factors and criteria of judgment, the more exacting the work of sublimation it requires of its members, and the more its history will be cumulative and therefore capable of transmuting mundane interests into self-referentially aesthetic motives and deeds. Artistic originality is thus achieved, not by the charismatic gift of the artist, but through this collective "transcendence of institution" made possible by the social machinery of the field (Bourdieu, 1992, pp. 375–380).

Finally, the notion of artistic field differs also from that of "art world" as used by Arthur Danto (1964) and Howard Becker (1982). Instead of fastening on concrete, observable *interactions* between the diverse agents who cooperate to produce and evaluate artworks, Bourdieu's *champ* focuses on the *structure* of objective positions and invisible relations of power that unite and bind contending agents. Agonistic competition and symbolic imposition, not collaborative forms of "collective action," are for him the stuff of artistic life.

The concept of artistic field has demonstrated its heuristic value in such varied empirical studies as the "birth of the writer" in the classical age (Viala, 1985), the formation of the literary society of mid-nineteenth-century France (Ponton, 1977; Charle, 1979), the consecration of avant-gardes (*Actes de la recherche*, 1991; Simonin, 1994) and the marginalization of regional literatures (Thiesse, 1991), the crystallization of the social type of the intellectual (Charle, 1991), and the relations between writing, gender, and politics (Moi, 1994; *Actes de la recherche*, 1996). It has been trained not only on literature but also on music (Menger, 1983; *Actes de la recherche*, 1995), painting and iconography (Verger 1987; Christin 1991), and the life and works of such singular artists as Odilon Redon and Vincent van Gogh (Gamboni, 1989; Heinich, 1996). As part of a broader theory of practice (Bourdieu, 1980), it has permitted the drawing of contrasts with, and the fruitful transfer of results from parallel inquiries into, the logic of other fields of cultural production, such as religion, science, law, journalism, education, and philosophy (Bourdieu, 1971, 1986–1987, 1988, 1991, 1994; Ringer, 1992; Fabiani, 1988; Boschetti, 1988; Pinto, 1995).

[*See also* Sociology of Art.]

BIBLIOGRAPHY

Works by Bourdieu

"Intellectual Field and Creative Project" (1966). In *Knowledge and Control: New Directions for the Sociology of Education*, edited by Michael F. D. Young, pp. 161–188. London, 1969.

Genesis and Structure of the Religious Field." *Comparative Social Research* 13 (1971): 1–43.

"Le couturier et sa griffe. Contribution à une théorie de la magie." *Actes de la recherche en sciences sociales* 1 (January 1975): 7–36. Written with Yvette Deslaut.

"The Production of Belief: Contribution to an Economy of Symbolic Goods." *Media, Culture and Society* 2 (July 1977–1980): 261–293. Reprinted in *The Field of Cultural Production* (New York, 1993).

Distinction: A Social Critique of the Judgement of Taste (1979). Translated by Richard Nice. Cambridge, Mass., 1984.

The Logic of Practice (1980). Translated by Richard Nice. Stanford, Calif., 1990.

"The Field of Cultural Production, or the Economic World Reversed." *Poetics* 12 (November 1983): 311–356. Reprinted in *The Field of Cultural Production* (New York, 1993).

"The Force of Law: Toward a Sociology of the Juridical Field." *Hastings Journal of Law* 38 (1986–1987): 209–248.

"The Historical Genesis of a Pure Aesthetics." *Journal of Aesthetics and Art Criticism*, special issue on the topic "Analytic Aesthetics," edited by Richard Schusterman (1987): 201–210. Reprinted in *The Field of Cultural Production* (New York, 1993).

"L'institutionalisation de l'anomie." *Cahiers du Musée national d'art moderne* 19–20 (June 1987): 6–19. Reprinted in *The Field of Cultural Production* (New York, 1993).

The Political Ontology of Martin Heidegger (1988). Translated by Peter Collier. Stanford, Calif., 1991.

"The Peculiar History of Scientific Reason." *Sociological Forum* 5–2 (Spring 1991): 3–26.

The Rules of Art: Genesis and Structure of the Literary Field (1992). Translated by Susan Emanuel. Stanford, Calif., 1996.

The Field of Cultural Production: Essays on Art and Literature. Edited by Randal Johnson. New York, 1993.

"L'emprise du journalisme." *Actes de la recherche en sciences sociales* 101–102 (March 1994): 3–9.

Other Sources

Actes de la recherche en sciences sociales. Thematic issue: "Les avant-gardes." 88 (June 1991).

Actes de la recherche en sciences sociales. Thematic issue: "La musique et les musiciens." 110 (December 1995).

Actes de la recherche en sciences sociales. Thematic issue: "Littérature et politique." 111–112 (March 1996).

Becker, Howard S. *Art Worlds.* Berkeley, 1982.

Boschetti, Anna. *The Intellectual Enterprise: Sartre and "Les Temps modernes"* (1985). Translated by Richard C. McCleary. Evanston, Ill., 1988.

Charle, Christophe. *La crise littéraire à l'époque du naturalisme: Roman, théâtre et politique.* Paris, 1979.

Charle, Christophe. *Naissance des "intellectuels," 1880–1900.* Paris, 1991.

Christin, Olivier. *Une révolution symbolique: L'iconoclasme huguenot et la reconstruction catholique.* Paris, 1991.

Danto, Arthur. "The Artworld." *Journal of Philosophy* 61.19 (15 October 1964): 571–584.

Fabiani, Jean-Louis. *Les philosophes de la République.* Paris, 1988.

Gamboni, Dario. *La plume et le pinceau: Odilon Redon et la littérature.* Paris, 1989.

Heinich, Nathalie. *The Glory of Van Gogh: An Anthropology of Admiration.* Translated by Paul Leduc Browne. Princeton, N.J., 1996.

Jurt, Joseph. *Das literarische Feld: Das Konzept Pierre Bourdieus in Theorie und Praxis.* Darmstadt, Germany, 1995.

Menger, Pierre-Michel. *Le paradoxe du musicien.* Paris, 1983.

Moi, Toril. *Simone de Beauvoir: The Making of an Intellectual Woman.* Oxford and Cambridge, Mass., 1994.

Pinto, Louis. *Les neveux de Zarathoustra: La réception de Nietzsche en France.* Paris, 1995.

Ponton, Rémi. *Le champ littéraire en France de 1865 à 1905.* Paris, 1977.

Ringer, Fritz. *Fields of Knowledge: French Academic Culture in Comparative Perspective, 1890–1920.* Cambridge and New York, 1992.

Simonin, Anne. *Les Éditions de Minuit, 1942–1955: Le devoir d'insoumission.* Paris, 1994.

Thiesse, Anne-Marie. *Écrire la France: Le mouvement régionaliste de langue française entre la Belle Époque et la Libération.* Paris, 1991.

Verger, Annie. "L'art d'estimer l'art: Comment classer l'incomparable." *Actes de la recherche en sciences sociales* 66–67 (1987): 105–121.

Viala, Alain. *Naissance de l'écrivain: Sociologie de la littérature à l'âge classique.* Paris, 1985.

Loïc Wacquant

BOURGEOIS, LOUISE (b. 1911), contemporary American artist and sculptor. The American feminist critic Lucy Lippard observed in 1975 that "it is difficult to find a framework vivid enough to incorporate Louise Bourgeois's sculpture" (Lippard, 1976). Since the first exhibitions of her sculpture in the late 1940s, critics have underscored the resistance of Bourgeois's diverse production to any fixed position within the history of mid-twentieth-century art. As Deborah Wye noted in the catalog to the first retrospective exhibition of the artist's work, held at the Museum of Modern Art in New York in 1982, it is an oeuvre that comprises an almost unparalleled range of form, material, and scale, "from a tiny four-inch fetish pincushion to a room-size environment" (Wye, 1982). Recent scholarship on Bourgeois, and revisionist histories of modernism itself, have suggested that an adequate account of her practice demands a rethinking of the formalist basis of twentieth-century sculpture. In particular, a reassessment of the privileged status of the abstract in the critical reception of modern sculpture has been deemed necessary to articulate the interrelations between Bourgeois's oeuvre and a range of historical frames that encompasses Surrealism and its American reception, Abstract Expressionism, and the American feminist art movement.

Louise Bourgeois began her artistic career in Paris in the 1930s, under the sign of Surrealism. As a student at the École des beaux-arts, living near André Breton's gallery Gravida, she moved in a circle that included Breton and Marcel Duchamp. In 1938, following her marriage to the American art historian Robert Goldwater, Bourgeois emigrated to New York, where she exhibited as a painter and printmaker with artists who would come to define the Abstract Expressionist generation, including William Baziotes, Adolph Gottlieb, Robert Motherwell, Jackson Pollock, and Mark Rothko. Then, in the mid-1940s, Bourgeois abruptly turned her attention to sculpture, exhibiting a series of simple carved wood figures titled *Personages* at the Peridot Gallery in New York in two solo exhibitions in 1949 and 1950.

Explaining this shift, the artist has remarked that she was not satisfied with painting's "level of reality," claiming that the move from two dimensions into three made possible the materialization of "fantastic reality." Marking her connection to Surrealist practices, this phrase invokes Surrealism's desire to inscribe fantasy in the matrix of the real, to project the unconscious into the world. In Bourgeois's formulation, however, phantasmic projection explicitly embraces the materiality of the body and of objects. "Fantastic reality," therefore, distinguishes itself from Surrealism in its enactment of fantasy as bound up in physical existence, as a function of the body rather than a work of the unconscious mind.

As the five decades of Bourgeois's sculptural production clearly demonstrate, the reality that painting failed to materialize was this: the experience of the body in the grip of fantasy. In her essay "Louise Bourgeois: From the Inside Out" (1976), Lippard offered the provocative suggestion that Bourgeois's work did not represent the body as seen from without, but enacted its physicality as experienced from within. Focusing on an inside-out logic in the construction of key works from the 1960s, including a series of pieces titled *Lairs,* Lippard proposed a reading of those objects as projections of the body's internal states.

In 1991, Rosalind Krauss discussed this desublimatory and phantasmic logic of the body in Bourgeois's work in relation to Surrealism. If modernist abstract sculpture contracted the body to the forms of ovoid, sphere, and column, Krauss argued, Bourgeois's work, like such Surrealist precedents as Alberto Giacometti's *Suspended Ball* or *Disagreeable Object,* reduced it instead to its organs and drives. In psychoanalytic terms, the organ that is the object of the drives is termed a part-object and is associated principally with infantile experience, in which the body is felt to be not a unitary whole but a discontinuous accumulation of parts. A part-object-based analysis, as Krauss observed, therefore shows Bourgeois's oeuvre to enact an insistent dismemberment of the body: into breast (*Breasted Woman* [1949–1950] and *Trani Episode* [1971–1972]); penis (*Sleeping Figure* [1950], *Fillette* [1968], *Harmless Woman* [1969], and *Fragile Goddess* [1970]); vagina (*Janus Fleuri* [1968]); and uterus (*Homage to Bernini* [1967] and *The Destruction of the Father* [1974]). Often, the parts are multiplied in phallic clusters (*Germinal* [1967] and *The Fingers* [1968]) or conflated, as in the viscous penis/breast conjunction of *Unconscious Landscape* (1967).

This part-object model of the body, grounded in Surrealist practices of fracture and dissolution, counters the abstract logic of much modernist sculpture, in which the bodily fragment, termed the partial figure, instead stands synecdochically as a substitute for the whole. An analogue of the body, the partial figure is seen to retain, even to accentuate, the figure's completeness precisely through the reductive process of abstraction. In contradistinction to the part-object, which it serves to repress and which historically has been subsumed within it, the partial figure therefore reinforces the stability of the phallic figure, the fragment standing not for a fracturing of the body into recognizable parts, but for its distillation into an abstract whole.

Fundamental to the process of abstraction, as Albert Elsen observed in his canonical account of modernist sculpture, was the "elimination of the distinguishing features of specific bodily parts" (Elsen, 1969). Bourgeois's production has most often been located within this logic, understood to generate, as Elsen writes of Constantin Brancusi, "associations with other forms in nature having a similar generalized structure." Applying Elsen's analysis to Bourgeois's production, William Rubin (1969), for example, distinguished between works by Bourgeois in which the body was sublimated and those in which its distinctive features were displayed. The "phallic character" of works such as *Sleep* (1967) could, he argued, be "savored and absorbed, like the sexuality of Brancusi and Arp, within the framework of the

appreciation of the work as a whole," whereas in other works, such as *Fated Portrait* (1963–1964, now titled *Torso/Self-Portrait*), "themes of sexuality are pressed too literally" (Rubin, 1969). Yet, in demonstrating how *Torso/Self-Portrait,* with its frontal summary of breasts, ribs, and labia, resists sublimation, this reading points up the very elision signaled by Krauss: namely, modernist art history's misrecognition of the part-object, or object of the drives, as partial figure. For in Krauss's revisionist account of modernism, the abstract formal logic of the partial figure is read as radically incompatible with the literalizing, fixating logic of the part-object.

Through her deployment of the part-object, Bourgeois can be seen to align herself with a counterformalist history of modern sculpture grounded in Surrealism. And nowhere is this stance toward modernist abstraction more evident than in a 1968 work called *Fillette,* or little girl, a two-foot-long latex phallus that invokes Giacometti's own phallic prop, *Disagreeable Object* of 1931. A carved wood portable phallus fitted with spikes and grooves, *Disagreeable Object* was an object "sans base," as Giacometti described it, a sculpture without a base. Hung from a hook slightly overhead, Bourgeois's *Fillette* was similarly detached from a supporting pedestal. In a series of photographs by Robert Mapplethorpe, taken on the occasion of her 1982 New York retrospective, Bourgeois further demonstrated that *Fillette,* like *Disagreeable Object,* was also made to be held in the arms.

In the most famous image from that photographic session, Bourgeois, wearing a tufted coat of fake monkey fur, clasps *Fillette* under her right arm and grins broadly, a smile reported again and again in the widening crinkles of her face. As her fingers firmly grasp the tip, behind her elbow nestle the big, shiny balls. Physically enacting a charged relation between the artist and *Fillette,* Mapplethorpe's photograph underscores the status of the piece as part-object. Intended to commemorate the moment in which her production of four decades was to be assembled for the first time in a retrospective exhibition, the photograph suggested that, contrary to its prevailing art-historical reception, her work was often less abstract, or even figural, than literal. Further, the picture seemed to suggest that if works like *Fillette* and *Torso/Self-Portrait* recast the bodily fragment as an object of psychic fixation, they did so by evoking precisely the graphic properties of such precedents as Brancusi's *Princess X* and *Torso of a Young Man,* or Giacometti's *Disagreeable Object.*

Surrealism is the movement—the set of practices and the circle of artists—to which Bourgeois's sculptural practice most closely relates. A pivotal problem for the interpretation of her oeuvre, therefore, is that the transgressive sexual imagery that made Bourgeois an iconic figure for the American feminist art movement in the 1970s was grounded in a practice, notorious for its insistent fragmentation of the female

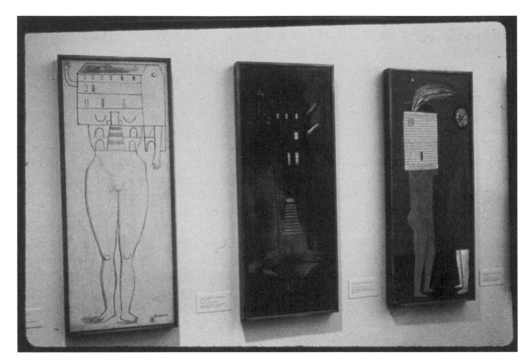

BOURGEOIS, LOUISE. Louise Bourgeois, three *Femme Maison* paintings (1946/47). (Courtesy of the artist and the Robert Miller Gallery, New York.)

body (as in, for example, Giacometti's *Woman with Her Throat Cut* of 1932), that has frequently been interpreted as misogynist. Further, Bourgeois's engagement with Surrealism was perhaps most intensive in the 1960s and 1970s, during the period of her active participation in feminist politics. Works from this period include *Trani Episode,* with its enactment of round phallicism; *Hanging Janus* (1968), its suspended format and ambiguous conflations of sexual organs suggesting Giacometti's *Suspended Ball;* the clitoris-like *Femme Couteau* (Knife Woman, c.1969–1970), its ambivalent conjunction of blade and delicately enfolded flesh an even more marked allusion to *Disagreeable Object* than the slightly earlier *Fillette;* and *Femme-Pieu* (Stake Woman, c.1970), its double evocation of prone vulnerability and prickly menace making it, too, a disagreeable kind of object.

In analyzing Bourgeois's complex relation to Surrealism, some feminist art historians have argued that this engagement can be read as parodic excess, restaging Surrealism's fragmentation of the female body in relation to a feminist politics. M. Catherine de Zegher, for example, has suggested that Bourgeois's work articulates "the problematics of bodies reduced to pieces, partial objects" via critical exaggeration (de Zegher, 1996). In the poses she struck in the Mapplethorpe photographs, and in such performances as the "Banquet/Fashion Show of Body Parts" staged in 1978, in which male and female actors paraded in gowns encrusted with teatlike protuberances, Bourgeois has seemed to reinforce this suggestion that through burlesque and par-

ody her work embodies feminist resistance to phallocentrism.

A feminist critique of Surrealism first appeared in Bourgeois's work, however, in the 1940s, long before it is possible to invoke feminist art in a historical sense. It arose in the context of her close contact with the circle of Surrealist artists who emigrated to New York during the war years, including, in addition to Breton and Duchamp, Yves Tanguy, Roberto Matta, and André Masson. Conceiving her own work as a "rebuttal" to Surrealist production, and a repudiation of the offensively patriarchal attitude she attributed to those artists, Bourgeois's feminist appropriation and subversion of Surrealist representations of the female body was acknowledged even by critics at the time.

The *Femme-Maison* painting series of 1946–1947, in which female figures combined with houses to produce the aggregate construction woman-house, reproduced the stylistic discontinuity of Surrealist painting to critique the role of female subjects within patriarchy. Evoking Surrealist modes of collective production such as the exquisite corpse, the part-to-part concatenation of the woman-house assumed an architectural logic: stories were placed atop one another to produce the body as an assembly of parts, rather than a unitary whole. The theme of the woman's body caged, of the head trapped and effaced by the house, however, also reworked this Surrealist-based fragmentation of the female body in relation to a feminist politics. The encaged head of the woman-house might, for example, be seen as a revision of André Masson's mannequin-with-head-in-birdcage, made for the Surrealist exhibition of 1938. The woman-house thus demonstrated how the part-to-part organization of Surrealist images could be used to enact not only a phantasmic shattering of the female body, but also the alienation of the female subject within patriarchy.

De Zegher has argued that Bourgeois's work, like that of other female artists active during the 1930s and 1940s, deployed fragmentation to represent not only the alienation of the female subject in phallocentric culture, but also the violent oppression of racial and ethnic otherness in prewar Europe. In this analysis, the work of Bourgeois, Hannah Höch, Claude Cahun, and Carol Rama, among others, is seen to engage problems of difference in representation while "diverging in an ironic way from the then-current" Expressionist and Surrealist uses of primitivism.

Although critics responding to Bourgeois's early sculptures frequently described the upright wooden poles as totemlike, marking their resemblance to African and Oceanic tribal objects, the problematic of primitivism in her work has not been closely examined. Through her connection to Surrealist circles in Paris and New York in the 1930s and 1940s, as well as through her relationship with Robert Goldwater, whom she met in Paris while Goldwater was writing his influential study *Primitivism in Modern Art* (1967), Bourgeois became intimately familiar with a wide range of tribal art and its modernist appropriations. De Zegher's suggestion that allusions to tribal art in her work of the 1930s and 1940s operated within a framework of feminist resistance to the patriarchal construction of difference remains to be more fully explored.

When Bourgeois turned from painting to sculpture in the 1940s, this shift was mediated by another process, engraving. An action that delved into three dimensions, engraving edged her production away from the image and toward the object, from a Surrealist-automatist model of projecting the unconscious into image to sculptural processes of enacting fantasy as a bodily operation. Embracing the physical demands of this process that, as she observed to Wye (1982), is "a muscular statement," Bourgeois implied a connection between engraving and sculpture at the level of cutting.

Her earliest sculptures, produced through techniques of gouging, digging, and incising specifically transposed from printmaking techniques, can be read as projections of the architectonic structures of her contemporaneous engravings. Consisting of simple motifs paired with short texts depicting what Marius Bewley described as "tiny tragedies of human frustration" (Bewley, 1949), a portfolio titled *He Disappeared into Complete Silence* (1947) juxtaposed architectonic and machinic setups, isolated in shallow stagelike spaces, with flat, affectless vignettes like this one: "Once a man was telling a story, it was a very good story too, and it made him very happy, but he told it so fast that nobody understood it."

Initiating processes of sculptural production, *He Disappeared into Complete Silence* demarcated a break with the logic of painting. It was not, however, simply a matter of a physical process—a cutting action that registered lines by scratching, digging, or biting into the metal plate—anticipating its own more complete realization in the sculptural operations of carving; for if automatism, which Bourgeois investigated in her painting and graphic work, was a Surrealist system of generating images from the unconscious, cutting was instead a system through which to produce objects via the drives, through what might be thought of as a corporeal unconscious.

Bourgeois's first sculptural installation, exhibited at the Peridot Gallery in 1949, consisted of fragile, attenuated posts of balsa wood scaled to the human body and arranged in pairs and knots around the room. Called *Personages*, these figures stood for people, enacting, as she explained to interviewer Susi Bloch in 1976, a concrete reconstruction of the past. The works had, she said, "nothing to do with sculpture, they meant physical presences. That was an attempt at not only re-creating a past, but controlling it" (quoted in Bloch, 1976).

A striking feature of Bourgeois's debut sculpture exhibition was its installation. The pieces were set directly on the floor, without bases, and installed in specific relation to the space of the gallery, or, as Bourgeois explained to Bloch, "instead of displaying pieces the space became part of the piece" (ibid.). This staging of the figures recalled Giacometti's elimination of the sculpture's base in the 1930s, shifting the object from an aesthetic plane to the extra-aesthetic register of table and floor, and then making the object itself coextensive with the base, or all base. The installation of the Personages so as to articulate a social space continuous with that of the viewers reinforced this connection.

The terms of a specifically feminist reworking of Surrealist sculpture were broached in a second exhibition of *Personages* at the same gallery the following year. This time, the works appeared under titles such as *Figures Who Talk to Each Other without Seeing Each Other* that signaled their status as anonymous types, rather than individuals. Detached from identities like Jean-Louis and C.Y. assigned to the earlier series, and given instead generic titles like *Figure Leaving the House*, they were subsumed in a roll call of figure types that, as Krauss has suggested, invite comparison with the generic figures of the bachelor apparatus in Duchamp's *The Bride Stripped Bare by Her Bachelors, Even*. Moreover, the suddenly organlike, graphic morphology of the second series of Personages, casting them in more literal, bodily terms, suggested a connection with Duchamp's enactment of the body as a system of desiring parts, a bachelor machine. The work now called *Breasted Woman*, for example, a carved post articulated by the stacking of swelling pendulous breasts, demonstrates the reductive logic of the part-object, initiating the inventory of organs that comprises the central project of Bourgeois's oeuvre.

In perhaps the best-known work from this series, *Figure endormie (Sleeping Figure)* (1950), purchased by Alfred Barr in 1951 for the Museum of Modern Art, the contingency of the phallic figure was explicitly staged. An attenuated upright figure with legs tapering to points, the work is trussed on either side by tall, movable poles. The distinctly phallic, cleft head of the female figure, encased in a long dresslike garment, foreshadowed Bourgeois's subsequent preoccupation with the crossing up of gender. In later works such as *Fillette*, or the contemporaneous series of Januses, this instability of gender was enacted in the suspension of the phallus from a cord hung from the ceiling, a device that also recalled Giacometti's *Suspended Ball*. *Figure endormie*, however, displayed instead an erosion of the figure from below, an undermining of the erect posture of the body that threatened to precipitate its collapse. A sleeping figure propped up in an erect pose, a female figure crowned with a phallic head, this work materialized the elision of gender binaries that Bourgeois was on the verge of enacting in 1950, a collapse foretold in *Figure endormie* by the instability of what might be called simply the figure—the vertically oriented body dominating a surrounding horizontal field.

In 1964, at the Stable Gallery in New York, Bourgeois presented a new body of work that rejected the verticality of the figure as abruptly as her early Personages had turned away from painting. Described by the artist as a "change from rigidity to pliability," this shift announced that the psychic field into which the figure would now finally fall was to be not only horizontal and nonhierarchical, but liquescent and low. Turning to plaster and latex and forsaking the vertical armature of the Personages, Bourgeois now produced objects in which not only the phallic hierarchy of the figure but the structure of difference itself was radically elided. Thus, figure abruptly succumbed to the condition of liquid.

As Daniel Robbins observed at the time, "these new sculptures seemed to have the capacity to quiver and ooze," adding that "no longer would one immediately associate them with figures" (Robbins, 1964). The devolution of form into a viscous field, its subsuming in a lumpy plaster flow or a sticky deliquescence of brackish rubber, however, pressured not only the category of the figure, but also its supporting structure of gender. The shift from figure to organ, from the upright wooden pole to the blistered latex flow, was mediated by a number of developments in this period, including the move from the totemic structures of sculpture in the 1940s and 1950s (the period dominated by Abstract Expressionism) to the expansion of the sculptural field and the use of more flexible materials and processes in much work of the 1960s and 1970s. Lucy Lippard's "Eccentric Abstraction" exhibition, mounted in New York in 1966, for example, presented Bourgeois as a precursor for contemporary work "devoted to opening up new areas of materials, shape, color, and sensuous experience" (Lippand, 1966). But for Bourgeois herself, the expansion of the sculptural field and the multiplication of materials and processes seems to have served primarily to facilitate a more radical deployment of the part-object, and that was to destabilize gender difference.

In Bourgeois's production of the 1960s, differences—of inside and outside, horizontal and vertical, figure and ground, male and female—dissolved in roiling surfaces, hanging nests, and molten flows. Organlike, spackled by thick, scrofulous skins or coated in a mucuslike film, these pieces enacted the breakdown of the figure into the part-object body of the drives. *Portrait* (1963), in its glistening viscosity and shapelessness, evoked not the architecture of a body but the fluidity of its internal matrix. In a related work, *Soft Landscape* (1963), a grainy surface of cement applied to a peaked whorl of sticky yellow-orange latex marked the interface of inside and outside, grit sealing the bodily ooze like a poultice. *Le Regard* (1966), a glutinous latex sac stiffened by burlap, was slit open to reveal a cluster of bumps and knobs nestled organlike inside and bathed in the same gummy latex.

In its striking diversity and hybridity, the work Bourgeois exhibited in 1964 convulsed an oeuvre previously structured by discrete series and types. At the level of material, whereas she had earlier worked almost exclusively in wood, beginning in about 1960 Bourgeois employed plaster, clay, cement, plastic, rubber latex, and, slightly later, marble and bronze. The new work was similarly discontinuous in form. A wood *Still Life* (1962) appeared alongside a knotted length of plaster-coated tubing (*Spiral/Summer*, 1960), a suspended nest (*Fée Couturière*, c.1963), and the series of *Lairs*, inert coils and spirals enfolding labyrinthine interiors.

"Throughout Bourgeois's oeuvre," Lippard noted, "shapes and ideas appear and disappear in a maze of versions, materials, incarnations" (Lippard, 1976). As many critics have observed, the nonlinear unfolding of her production—its material eclecticism, its shifting among formal modes, its range of scale and theme, and above all its conflations of sex and gender—are powerfully subversive of late modernism's principles of sublimatory abstraction, medium specificity, and formal consistency.

[*See also* Installation Art; Sculpture; *and* Surrealism.]

BIBLIOGRAPHY

Bewley, Marius. "An Introduction to Louise Bourgeois." *Tiger's Eye* 1.7 (15 March 1949): 89–92.

Bloch, Susi. "An Interview with Louise Bourgeois." *Art Journal* 35.4 (Summer 1976): 370–373.

Cole, Ian, ed. *Louise Bourgeois*. Museum of Modern Art Papers, vol. 1. Oxford, 1996.

de Zegher, M. Catherine. "Introduction: Inside the Visible." In *Inside the Visible: An Elliptical Traverse of 20th Century Art in, of, and from the Feminine*, pp. 19–41. Cambridge, Mass., 1996.

Elsen, Albert E. "Notes on the Partial Figure." *Artforum* 8 (November 1969): 58–63.

Gibson, Ann. "Louise Bourgeois's Retrospective Politics of Gender." *Art Journal* 53.4 (Winter 1994): 44–47.

Goldwater, Robert. *Primitivism in Modern Art.* Enl. ed. Cambridge, Mass., 1986.

Gorovoy, Jerry. *The Iconography of Louise Bourgeois.* New York, 1980. Exhibition catalog, Max Hutchinson Gallery.

Krauss, Rosalind. "Portrait of the Artist as *Fillette*." In *Louise Bourgeois*, pp. 210–216. Otterlo, Netherlands, 1991. Exhibition catalog, Rijksmuseum Kroller-Muller.

Lippard, Lucy R. "Eccentric Abstraction." *Art International* 10 (20 November 1966): 28, 34–40.

Lippard, Lucy R. "Louise Bourgeois: From the Inside Out." In *From the Center: Feminist Essays on Women's Art*, pp. 238–249. New York, 1976. Reprinted from *Artforum* 13.7 (March 1975): 26–33.

Nixon, Mignon. "Pretty as a Picture: Louise Bourgeois's *Fillette*." *Parkett* 27 (March 1991): 48–54.

Nixon, Mignon. "Bad Enough Mother." *October* 71 (Winter 1995): 71–92.

Pincus-Witten, Robert. *Bourgeois Truth.* New York, 1982. Exhibition catalog, Robert Miller Gallery.

Robbins, Daniel. "Sculpture by Louise Bourgeois." *Art International* 8 (20 October 1964): 29–31.

Rubin, William S. "Some Reflections Prompted by the Recent Work of Louise Bourgeois." *Studio International* 8 (20 April 1969). 17–20.

Storr, Robert. *Louise Bourgeois Drawings.* New York, 1988. Exhibition catalog, Robert Miller Gallery.

Strick, Jeremy. *Louise Bourgeois: The Personages.* Saint Louis, 1994. Exhibition catalog, Saint Louis Museum of Art.

Wye, Deborah. *Louise Bourgeois.* New York, 1982. Exhibition catalog, Museum of Modern Art.

Wye, Deborah, and Carol Smith. *The Prints of Louise Bourgeois.* New York, 1994. Exhibition catalog, Museum of Modern Art.

MIGNON NIXON

BRAQUE, GEORGES. *See* Collage; Cubism; *and* Picasso.

BRECHT, BERTOLT (1898–1956), German playwright and poet. Brecht was born into a well-to-do family of the managerial class in Augsburg. He studied medicine and science at the University of Munich, took an active role in the short-lived Bavarian Revolution of 1918, and (also in 1918) wrote his first plays, *Baal* and *Spartakus*. Not performed for several years, these two wild and extravagant pieces caught the notice of influential theater critics in Berlin—because the never shy Brecht brought them to their attention. This led to his first successful theater production, *Drums in the Night*, in Munich in 1922. In 1923, the same year as Adolf Hitler's Munich beer-hall putsch, Brecht's publication of a poem satirizing right-wing nostalgic idealizations of fighting in World War I earned him the undying hatred of the National Socialists. In 1924, Brecht moved to Berlin, shortened his first names from Eugen Berthold Friedrich to simply Bertolt, and, with the staging of his *In the Jungle* and *Edward II*, plunged into the cultural politics of the late Weimar Republic.

A summary of Brecht's work in Berlin between 1924 and 1933 includes two collections of poems, collaboration with Erwin Piscator and others in mounting a stage production based on Jaroslav Hašek's *Good Soldier Schweik*, the financially successful collaboration with Elisabeth Hauptmann and Kurt Weill on *Die Dreigroschenoper* (*The Threepenny Opera*), a series of didactic theater pieces (the *Lehrstücke*) with Hauptmann, Weill, and Hanns Eisler, a film called *Kuhle Wampe* (the only left-wing film to get by the Weimar censors), and *St. Joan of the Stockyards*, again with Hauptmann. (The latter, one of the major plays of the Brechtian corpus, did not see a production until 1959.) The canny character of Schweik was to become the very model for Brecht's handling of controversial situations both before and after he fled Germany in February 1933 on the day after the Reichstag fire.

In exile from 1933 to 1948 in Denmark, Finland, the United States, and Switzerland, Brecht wrote four of his six most famous major plays: *Mother Courage, The Good Woman of Setzuan, Galileo,* and *The Trial of Lucullus*. He struggled, largely without success, to break into the theater world of the United States. His only real success was a 1947 collaboration with Charles Laughton in a production of *Galileo*. His writings did prompt a subpoena to appear before the House Un-American Activities Committee, however, in October 1947. Brecht's long-professed Schweikian faith in the virtue of cowardice was not needed here: his accusers were not familiar enough with his work to make a convincing case, and he confused and confounded them by doing what he called "adhering strictly to the untruth." Despite what many of his friends regarded as a complete victory, Brecht left the United States at his first opportunity.

In 1949, Brecht finally returned to the East quarter of a divided Berlin. Despite his longtime left-wing politics, he took several years to finally decide to do this; and even after having done so, he seemed to hedge his bets by taking Austrian citizenship in 1950. But, from 1949 until his death in 1956, Brecht directed the famous Berliner Ensemble that he founded. His last great work, *The Caucasian Chalk Circle*, was conceived in the middle of the Berlin uprising of 1953 and produced in 1954.

The director Peter Brook wrote that Brecht is the key figure of our time, and all theater work today at some point starts or returns to his statements and achievement. Brook's remark can be extended; however Brecht is understood, his influence is detectable not only in theater theory and practice, but also in film and music theory and practice. Yet, the nature and extent of that influence remain a complicated matter. Disagreements over what Brecht's statements mean and what his achievement was (if any) still mark the reception of his writing and production history.

The initial reception was not smooth. In the West, in an intellectual environment colored by cold-war politics and a highly developed analysis of what a theory is, Brecht was frequently castigated for writing overheated and self-contradictory rhetoric in place of theory. It came to be almost a platitude that Brecht, who was acknowledged to be a pretty good theatrical director, if not a genius, and a first-rate playwright, rejected his own theories upon entering the doors of the theater. His theory would not work, it was said, and, when he worked as writer or director himself, he knew it. Only in the last decade has there been an attempt to reevaluate the matter, looking at Brecht in the context of his development both as a playwright/director and as a writer about theater practice. In this way, what appeared to be contradictions in his theory now appear to some in a more nearly dialectical relationship to each other and to the needs of theater practice that called forth Brecht's reflections.

In the East, the initial reception was, if anything, even more fraught by ideological struggles. In this case, the struggles were among the like-minded for the correct aesthetic doctrine, and Brecht's was not among the official winners in the struggle. Brecht and Ernst Bloch, on the side of Expressionism and the Russian Formalists, clashed with the defenders of Socialist Realism, primarily György Lukács, in a series of essays between 1932 and 1933 in the Moscow-based German-language journal *Das Wort*. Lukács charged that Formalism, Abstraction, and Expressionism did not allow artists to pursue the contradictions in life in their interconnections with any immediacy for the viewer; he championed instead naturalistic Victorian models in painting and theater. In these Expressionism/Realism debates, as they have come to be known, Brecht first articulated a concept of "realism" that focused on what the audience for a work of art could take away rather than on what it was presented. If the audience is enabled to grasp the reality represented, he thought, the work is realistic, even if the style (or form) is abstract. *Grasp* here means both to understand and to be able to seize on the reality in order to change it. In these terms, the choice of a naturalistic and mimetic style in a work is actually a *formal* aspect of the work. Although this usage appeared at the time to be a perverse and self-serving technique for defending what he had been calling "epic theater" since about 1926, analogous philosophical positions have been worked out subsequently by Nelson Goodman and others. Such positions rest on criticisms of resemblance theories of representation and seek to develop instead accounts of representation that take more seriously the conventional nature of styles, including those styles that strike us as more naturalistic or realistic because of our particular cultural education. Brecht's contributions to the debate were to come back to bedevil him when, after World War II, he returned to the German Democratic Republic and attempted to convince a skeptical Communist Party to fund further theatrical endeavors.

Brecht was eventually successful, apparently on the strength of a stunning new production of his own *Mother Courage and Her Children*. But his stance against Socialist Realism, already officially endorsed by Stalin at the time of the debates, was never completely forgiven.

A further measure of what Brechtian theory involves and how it changed as Brecht worked with it can be gained by considering two concepts with which he worked for most of his career, *Gestus* and *Verfremdungseffekt*. Brecht began to use the term *Gestus* in conjunction with his experiments with didactic theater in the late 1920s and early 1930s. In the most general sense, Brecht uses the term to denote the physical manifestation of an attitude. But Brecht's interest in the physical manifestation is never pictured as a clue to an otherwise hidden psychological attitude; rather, he approaches the manifestation as a sign of the social relationships it expresses. This point might be put as follows: we have the attitudes we have, expressed in this or that characteristic physical manifestation, because of our histories and the social roles we occupy. In this way, we can see why Brecht was often at pains to distinguish his use of *Gestus* from conventional notions of "gesture" or "gesticulation," which seemed to suggest a psychological interest. He sometimes (somewhat confusingly) offered instead a distinction between *Gestus* and "social *Gestus*" to make essentially the same point, namely, that he was calling attention not to psychological motivations, conceived as themselves having purely psychological antecedents as causes, but to social relationships.

There is something fairly natural about this. Gestures *can* be thought of in two ways—as outward expressions of something inner and in terms of the audiences they assume. Gestures, moreover, imply various kinds of audiences: those at whose attention, entertainment, or edification a gesture is aimed, those gestured to, those gestured at, and so forth. If we are able to see that each gesture and each mode of gesturing implies as well a very particular social relationship between the one gesturing and the kind of audience the auditor is, we are very close to the notion in which Brecht was interested. In this way, we can also see something of how the notion is fruitful for thinking about what is happening in a play. In trying to understand the action of a play, actors and directors are wont to look for those places that might be called its "joints," the places at which it can be sectioned off both for rehearsal purposes and for purposes of audience understanding. Brecht regarded the occurrence of distinct *Gesten* as the signal for such sectioning. This afforded him a rehearsal technique as well; study the scene to determine its essential social *Gestus* and then practice it until that *Gestus* becomes clear for an audience. This also implies an idea about what is happening between the performers and the theater audience.

Brecht began to use the terms *Entfremdung, Verfremdung*, and *Verfremdungseffekt* after his visit to Moscow in the spring of 1935. In Moscow, he had come into contact with the Russian Formalists. Particularly important in this context was Viktor Shklovsky, whose term *priem ostrannenija* is now thought most likely to be what Brecht was trying to translate or otherwise capture by the Hegelian term *Entfremdung* and other related terms. Initially, Brecht used these new terms to contrast what he had wanted to happen in what he was already calling "epic theater" with that empathic identification in Naturalism to which he had already objected in earlier writing. In this sense, he was perhaps offering not much more than would be caught by translating these terms as "negation" or "distantiation." As he worked out the implications of these notions, however, their impact and meaning shifted. It is fair to say that in his mature thinking in the 1940s, Brecht had come to see that the real issue in theater is how to make visible that which is hidden either because it is too familiar *or* because it is *already too strange.* The "V-effects" were, he began to say, aimed at "showing," making visible. Thus, in contrast to his earlier theory and practice, where the aim was often a cold and "distanced" rationality, in the mature practice he was able to incorporate moments of deep empathic identification in his productions when, by such a moment, the audience would come to grasp the essential *Gestus* of the particular scene.

Many of the techniques used earlier to achieve distance remained. Placards, background projections of films and photographs, scene titles, the use of choruses and choral elements, verses spoken or sung between scenes, songs instead of dialogue carrying the scene, and various devices by which the actor called attention to the fact she was playing a role still filled the typical Brechtian production. But the dominant method of explaining these "V-effects" came to be the picture of an eyewitness explaining to other bystanders an accident he had seen just moments before. In such an explanation, there is never any question that the eyewitness is "being" anyone other than himself. Yet, he will now play the role of the victim, now the role of the careless driver, and now perhaps even the role of the car crashing into a streetlight or the role of the streetlight being hit and bending and falling over. There are no strictures here against momentary empathic identification; for, where the criterion of success is that the bystanders get a clear picture of what happened, that the reality is made visible, no such restrictions are necessary. Indeed, they might even hinder. For this reason, an assessment of Brecht's notion of *Verfremdung* is decidedly not assisted by translating it as initially suggested, as "negation" or "distantiation," and much less as "alienation."

This cursory review reveals several aspects to the development of the Brechtian theoretical vocabulary. In one connection, Brecht was building up a set of terms with which both to give instructions to actors and directors as to how to go about achieving what he wanted to achieve in the theater, and to articulate what it was he wanted to achieve, especially as regards the change he sought in the relationship between performer and audience. In another connection, Brecht was sometimes seeking simultaneously to redefine the relationship between what is performed and the audience before whom it occurs and to find words, consistent with that newly defined relationship, for analyzing the elements of any playscript. These initial two were the first, and always the primary, connections in which Brecht worked out the terminology of what has come to known as "Brechtian Theory." At certain other times, Brecht was writing primarily to make connections between the practice of theater as he conceived it and his mostly Marxist philosophical and scientific commitments, sometimes in order to defend his practice in difficult political environments. The additional fact that his views changed as his experience (and experiments) grew and changed has made it difficult to get a single fix on what he was after with regard to any of the concepts he deployed over the years. Thus, beyond the one enduring feature—that theater is capable of providing representations that can enable people to understand reality in such a way as to take hold of it to change it—it would probably be a mistake to try to get a univocal fix on what Brecht meant by any of his quasi-technical terms.

Add these facts to the waning influence of Brecht everywhere in the 1990s except, perhaps, England and one might well wonder whether there is likely to be any lasting contribution derivable from Brecht. Perhaps his plays, even acknowledged masterpieces like *Mother Courage* and *The Life of Galileo,* and his theory are going to become mere exhibits in the museum he so decried in his many diatribes against what he called "culinary theater." Perhaps, then, there is no reason to try to sort out what is meant by the terms in the Brechtian lexicon. Indeed, if one looks to Brecht's work for solutions to the problems he set, one is likely to get this result. Seen as sets of questions, however, analysis of Brecht's theory can continue to stimulate helpful discussion about still-unresolved issues in both practical theater aesthetics and about philosophical accounts of artistic representation.

At the very least, consideration of these matters affords material for the arsenal of questions that any actor or director can bring to any scene, any script. Even if the answers given are not always Brecht's, the questions alone are a fundamental addition to the actor's and the director's crafts. The fact that questions like these were rarely explored in the Naturalistic theater that Brecht confronted—and continue to go unasked in most North American theater today—suggests just how dominant the hold has been of individualistic psychologism in theater theory and practice since the rise of Naturalism. Moreover, considerations like these could be useful as an antidote to a kind of actor training that puts certain kinds of theater beyond the actor's reach. Because this applies to the plays of most periods preceding the advent of Naturalism in the late nineteenth century—

including the plays of Sophocles and Shakespeare, for example—this is no small matter. Thus, as for the practical matters in theater aesthetics, Brecht's need to invent a specific vocabulary for articulating the goals of his theater continues to point to fundamental questions about the nature, goals, and possibilities of theatrical enactment. This is true even if one does not adopt a Brechtian answer to such questions, and even if one cannot determine uniquely and univocally what a "Brechtian answer" actually is.

Finally, Brecht's understanding of how to achieve theater that was "realistic" but not mimetic raises important questions about mimetic accounts of representation. Of course, if not even "realism" needs mimesis, for the reasons Brecht offers, one has further reason for abandoning resemblance theories of artistic representation. But even if something like a resemblance theory is reconceived as applying not to the relation between work and world but to that between viewing of a work and viewing of the world, as Kendall Walton has, Brecht's theory and practice continue to pose real problems. Where the criterion of "realism" is that the reality is made clear to an audience in such a way that it can seize upon it to change it, resemblance between how auditors look at the representation and how they look at that represented drops out as unnecessary, and perhaps is not even helpful at all.

[*See also* Marxism; Poetics; *and* Theater.]

BIBLIOGRAPHY

Works by Brecht

Gedichte. Frankfurt am Main, 1960–1976.
Schriften zum Theater. Edited by Siegfried Unseld. Berlin, 1957.
Stücke. Berlin, 1953–1959.

Works by Brecht in English Translation

Brecht on Theatre: The Development of an Aesthetic. Edited and translated by John Willett. New York, 1964.
Collected Plays. Edited by Ralph Manheim and John Willett. New York, 1970–.
Poems. 2d ed. Edited by Ralph Manheim and John Willett. London, 1979.

Other Sources

Barthes, Roland. "Diderot, Brecht, Eisenstein." In *Image, Music, Text*, edited and translated by Stephen Heath, pp. 69–78. New York, 1977.
Benjamin, Walter. *Versuche über Brecht*. Edited by Rolf Tiedemann. Frankfurt am Main, 1966.
Bentley, Eric. *The Brecht Memoir*. New York, 1985.
Eckhardt, Juliane. *Das epische Theater*. Darmstadt, Germany 1983.
Esslin, Martin. *Brecht: das Paradox des politischen Dichters*. Frankfurt am Main, 1962.
Esslin, Martin. *Brecht: The Man and His Work*. New rev. ed. Garden City, N.Y., 1971.
Esslin, Martin. *Brecht: A Choice of Evils: A Critical Study of the Man, His Work, and His Opinions*. 3d rev. ed. London, 1980.
Fowler, Kenneth. *Received Truths: Bertolt Brecht and the Problem of Gestus and Musical Meaning*. New York, 1991.
Fuegi, John. *Brecht and Company: Sex, Politics, and the Making of the Modern Drama*. New York, 1994.
Hecht, Werner, ed. *Bertolt Brecht: Sein Leben in Bildern und Texten*. Frankfurt am Main, 1978.
Kleber, Pia, and Colin Visser, eds. *Re-interpreting Brecht: His Influence on Contemporary Drama and Film*. Cambridge and New York, 1990.
Lellis, George. *Bertolt Brecht, Cahiers du Cinéma, and Contemporary Film Theory*. Ann Arbor, 1982.
Mews, Siegfried, ed. *A Bertolt Brecht Reference Companion*. Westport, Conn., 1997.
Mueller, Roswitha. *Bertolt Brecht and the Theory of Media*. Lincoln, Nebr., 1989.
Pike, David. *Lukács and Brecht*. Chapel Hill, N.C., 1985.
Reinelt, Janelle. *After Brecht: British Epic Theater*. Ann Arbor, 1994.
Rouse, John. *Brecht and the West German Theater: The Practice and Politics of Interpretation*. Ann Arbor, 1989.
Thomson, Peter, and Glendyr Sacks, eds. *The Cambridge Companion to Brecht*. Cambridge and New York, 1994.
Walsh, Martin. *The Brechtian Aspect of Radical Cinema*. Edited by Keith M. Griffiths. London, 1981.
Willett, John. *The Theatre of Bertolt Brecht*. 4th rev. ed. London, 1977.
Willett, John. *Brecht in Context Comparative Approaches*. London, 1984.
Wright, Elizabeth. *Postmodern Brecht: A Re-presentation*. London and New York, 1989.

JAMES R. HAMILTON

BRETON, ANDRÉ (1896–1966), French poet, theorist, polemicist, essayist, movement leader, editor, and founder of Surrealism. Breton is the foremost embodiment of the aspirations and accomplishments of the Surrealist movement, an arts movement, born in Paris in 1924, that sought to expand the application of poetic experience to include all forms of expression. Breton drew from a diverse array of sources to shape Surrealism: primitive art, ancient philosophy, gnosticism, alchemy, spiritualism; Romanticism, Symbolism; Georg Wilhelm Friedrich Hegel, Sigmund Freud, Karl Marx, anarchism, as well as contemporaneous avant-garde movements that had similar reaction formations, such as Futurism, Expressionism, and, more specifically, Dada, out of which Breton launched Surrealism.

In addition, many writers and artists from all over the world came to participate in Breton's order in disorder movement and influenced his development of Surrealism's premises. At its outset, Surrealism, which Breton defined as "psychic automatism," was offered as a means to tap an interior reality, what he termed "the huge indeterminate area over which the protectorate of reason does not extend." The Jewish diaspora in Spanish-speaking countries, America, and the Caribbean, however, would help Breton expand Surrealism in terms of heightened importance given to elemental nature and tribal arts. One of the highpoints of Breton's stay in America during the war years (1941–1946) was his visit with the Pueblo Indians. Above all, Surrealism, as envisioned by Breton, was anti-aesthetic, in the conventional sense of the term. In fact, concern with aesthetics constituted a major "heresy." About the poet Paul Éluard, Breton complained: "aesthetics, which we meant to prohibit, passes through the door with the greatest of ease." Yet,

Breton had also worshiped the Symbolists, who made a religion of aesthetics: "They glided down the slippery slope of reverie," he wrote; on the other hand, the desperate mood that World War I had created tore "certain young men, myself included, . . . from their aspirations and flung [them] into a cesspool of blood, mud, and idiocy." Traditional "critical sense" was considered by Breton, "public enemy number one." The technique of automatic writing, which Breton was astute to initially frame more generally in the *Manifesto* of 1924 as "psychic automatism . . . by which one proposes to express—verbally, by means of the written word, or in any other manner—the actual functioning of thought . . . in the absence of control exercised by reason, exempt from any aesthetic or moral concern," lured artists as well as writers. In fact, Surrealism was nowhere more successful than in the visual arts, where the talents of Max Ernst, Pablo Picasso, Salvador Dalí, René Magritte, André Masson, Marcel Duchamp, Alberto Giacometti, Frida Kahlo, Toyen, Alexander Calder, David Hare, and many others indicated the elastic possibilities of such an approach.

In certain respects, Breton's theory of Surrealism was a variant of the ancient spiritual belief in poetry as a form of divine possession or inspiration. Breton stated that the Surrealists were above all interested in re-creating trancelike states. Indeed, poets and artists of his generation were among the last to unabashedly refer to the *spirit* (one thinks of Guillaume Apollinaire's *esprit nouveau* or Breton's essay by virtually the same name, or even Wassily Kandinsky's theoretical masterpiece, *Über das Geistige in der Kunst* (Concerning the Spiritual in Art). This zeal for spirit, however, was balanced by the avowals of atheism and the hostility toward any system that stood on a principle of authority. Nowhere was the conflict more full-blown than in Surrealism, where the author/authority is rejected, as is the concept of *plot*. Rejecting the end, Breton, along the lines of other avant-garde movements, made of Surrealism an ideology of commencement. The spirit of poetry, in a sense, is pitted against the spirit of prose, as the spirit of childhood is pitted against the spirit of adulthood.

Breton had a strong prosaic side as well. His prose works, in fact, outstripped the verse poetry in quantity and influence—one thinks of his manifestos, for instance, more readily than any of his poetry collections. Although it was his poetry that caught the attention of Paul Valéry and Guillaume Apollinaire, "literature" was not enough. Breton's exhortation to "*practice* poetry" and his categorization of Surrealism as a philosophy, "based on the belief in the superior reality of certain forms of previously neglected associations," seemed dedicated to provoking a poetic way of living and expressing oneself. The means of such a provocation were diverse and above all transliterary: the most poetic figure for André Breton was Jacques Vaché, who never wrote a poem but was a poet in his nonconformist lifestyle. To "practice poetry" was to live according to the dictates of

spirit rather than form. Form had come to be perceived as a cenotaph. In some of the more violent fantasies regarding classical forms, Filippo Tommaso Marinetti, the Italian Futurist, advocated the blowing up of museums and libraries, which he compared to cemeteries. Breton presented his own version of "breaking the form." The rejection of the notion of aesthetics, which was already evident in the Dada movement's anti-art orientation, took the shape of an attack on what Breton called "the ready-made human type" presented in novels. Instead, Breton referred to Surrealists as "humble recording instruments."

Breton began by constructing his theory via Freud. Inspiration was introduced as a privately induced psychological phenomenon triggered by surfing along rapidly moving waves of thought. In the *Manifesto* of 1924, Breton boasted that "the Surrealist voice that shook Cumae, Dodona, and Delphi is nothing more than the voice that dictates my less irascible speeches." The paradox here is that he and his group were also keenly interested in the divinatory arts, which were the hallmark of supernatural primitive religions and their myths, whether Celtic, Greek, African, Indian, or Oceanic. Can a theory based on divination and inspiration survive the loss of faith in divinities and in the concept of spirit?

Initially, Breton differentiated Surrealism from other compelling contemporary movements that had also rejected Realism, such as Cubism and Expressionism, as well as movements whose aesthetics was turned into a type of political theater, such as Futurism and Dada. The 1920s were certainly the decade of the avant-garde movement. This was also the decade of the philosopher-poet: Marinetti, Apollinaire, and Tristan Tzara were poets who became polemical theorists with an increasing influence in the visual arts. Breton took as points of departure Marinetti's violent juxtaposition of imagery and the urgent tone of his manifesto, as well as his innovations in typography and his invective manner; Apollinaire's posture of the flaneur and his glorification of eros and the adventure of the Paris streets; and Tzara's attack on logic, as well as his use of collage.

The increased emphasis on the double or splintered image to express the multiple reality of the inner self was embodied by collage, which Breton was to fuse with the more obsessive, desire-ridden products of psychic automatism. Breton called for a "convulsive beauty" or "a truly living form of beauty," as an antidote to what he saw as the serene coyness of art: "The need to know and make known, predominated over the need to please and be admired."

Breton also differentiated Surrealism by emphasizing the importance of the dream. As a young medic in the army who treated soldiers returning with mental disorders from the front during World War I, he fortified his belief in the soluble and elastic nature of external reality. Breton felt that the dream should be given more opportunity to shape reality, whereas Freud saw dream material as the domain of for-

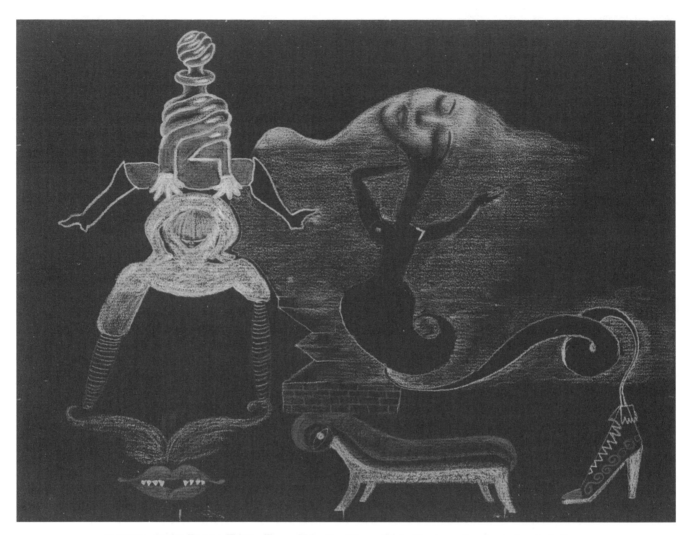

BRETON. André Breton, Tristan Tzara, Valentine Hugo, Greta Knutsen, *Landscape* (c.1933), from the series Exquisite Corpse (Cadavre exquis), composite drawing: colored chalk on black paper, 9 1/2 × 12 1/2 inches (24.1 × 31.7 cm); Museum of Modern Art, New York (Purchase). (Photograph copyright 1998 by the Museum of Modern Art; used by permission.)

bidden wishes and thoughts that had to be continually neutralized and sublimated. Breton thought in terms of channeling the dream into reality.

Most of Breton's work—automatic writing, manifestos, poetry, poetic prose works, and essays—first appeared in periodicals of which he was editor or in which he had a strong editorial say: *Littérature* (1919–1924), *La révolution surréaliste* (1924–1929), *Le surréalisme au service de la révolution* (1930–1933), *Minotaure* (1933–1939), *Clé* (1939), *VVV* (1942–1944), *NÉON* (1948–1949), *Médium* (1953–1955), *Le surréalisme, même* (1956–1959), *La brèche* (1961–1965). No other modern movement had as rich or as steady a journalistic unfolding as Surrealism. Breton was such an anchoring point that Surrealism became a main port for all kinds of fellow travelers in the arts. Many artists

and writers in fact used Surrealism to escape the closing net of censorship in the 1930s. Fascism and zealous nationalism closed in on Europe by the mid-thirties. The hermetic component of Surrealism allowed it to often bypass censorship because of its obscure syntax and meaning. This was to be a sticking point with the Communists, whose support Breton so coveted and, for a brief moment, achieved. Yet, he was consistent throughout in his attack on Realism, distinguished from documentation, which he encouraged, as long as it was an authentic, impassioned rendering of an event. Thus, under the banner of freedom from aesthetic and moral considerations, as well as freedom from logic, a variety of techniques, if not a general style, emerged.

The Surrealist movement also offered the loose subculture of the artists' society as an extended family alternative to the increasingly nuclear middle-class family and its various norms, whose implementation was based on repression and social censorship. The scandals of Surrealism, aimed at denouncing official culture, were attacked in the press above all for their "bad form."

Yet, Breton also retained, perhaps as a further antidote to bourgeois life, certain elements of Symbolism in Surrealism, in particular, its hostile view of *reality*. The spirit of negation and unsatisfied longing, as well as the dandyism that permeated Symbolism, helped shape Paris Dada and Surrealism. The big leap from Symbolism to Surrealism occurred in the rejection of art as an end in itself. "We have no taste," proclaimed Breton.

Breton was not, however, totally free himself of the business of art. He advised the collector and famous couturier Jacques Doucet on purchases of painting and rare books, and courted the most important literary and artistic figures of his day, such as Paul Valéry, Apollinaire, and Picasso in a traditional type of artistic social climbing. He was also a close guardian of the reputation of Surrealism and demanded of participants adherence to shared ideals. His strict sense of morals, manifested as a type of puritanicalness in response to members of the movement who were perceived to have sold out or to be disloyal earned him the ironic title of "pope of Surrealism" (see the *Second Manifesto of Surrealism*, 1930, for a firsthand introduction to this phenomenon).

Psychic automatism was a process that emphasized dredging more than constructing: this was conveyed in the peekaboo form that Surrealist images and words manifested. The interplay between enclosure and opening, and obscurity and illumination, was influenced by the alchemical rebus, where an image either dissolved into or emerged out of another. This splitting of the image led to an expansion of the application of the principle of poetic analogy, as a large array of hybrid fusions was generated under the auspices of automatism by individual artists and by collective experiments, such as the Surrealist prose poem, poem-object, collage, automatic writing, Exquisite Corpse, frottage, decalcomania, fumage, heatage, Rayogram, ready-made, Surrealist object (see Pierre [1974] for a description of each of these). Frottage, for instance, was made by placing a piece of paper over the wood surface and rubbing with crayon or pencil. Discovered by Max Ernst, this process revealed unexpected images in the wood grain; Breton's poems and automatic writing texts achieved a similar sense of emerging form.

André Breton's poetic orientation was initially shaped by the decadence and Symbolist poets: Joris-Karl Huysmans, Charles Baudelaire, Arthur Rimbaud, Stéphane Mallarmé, and Valéry were mentors in a quality of poetry that he was to consider crucial—*insularity*, where the mind, detached from all external preoccupations becomes absorbed with its own life. Breton also admired the heroic obscurity and detachment of these men. In fact, Mallarmé's call to artists was to be disdainful, to go on strike *(en grève)* against society, to treat art as the magnum opus. Baudelaire's plea "to go anywhere out of this world" and Rimbaud's "disordering of the senses" found an echo in Breton's "existence is elsewhere" and "disorientation of sensation."

Aesthetically, Breton's early poems were Symbolist in tone and imagery. The poetry from his first collection, *Mont de Piété* (Pawnbroker; 1916), conjured Breton as a salvager of literary curiosities and rarities. The poems manifested Symbolist influence in the setting of words as if they were rare gems, in the anagrammatic and euphonic internal rhyme schemes, in their thematic emphasis of recovery of pristineness. The prose poem, "Âge," for instance, from this collection, recalled Rimbaud's "Aube" (Dawn): "Dawn, adieu, I'm leaving this haunted wood; facing the torrid crossroads. Blessed boughs are my perdition. August is as seamless as a mill" ("Aube adieu! Je sors du bois hanté; j'affronte les routes, crois torrides. Un feuillage bénissant me perd. L'août est sans brèches comme une meule"). Compare Rimbaud's "Aube" to Breton's "Âge": "I embraced the summer's dawn. Nothing moved at all along the palace wall. Dominions of shadows lingered on the woodland path. I walked waking warm vivid breaths; and the precious stones will share our gaze, and the wings raise themselves without a sound" ("J'ai embrassé l'aube d'été. Rien ne bougeait encore au front des palais. L'eau était morte. Les camps d'ombres ne quittaient pas la route du bois. J'ai marché, réveillant les haleines vives et tièdes; et les pierreries regardèrent, et les ailes se levèrent sans bruit").

The fugue or chase of images that Rimbaud created, as dawn, personified as goddess and virgin, was pursued with her many veils and massive body to the city—"Then, I lifted one by one her veils" ("Alors je levai un à un les voiles")—then back to the edge of the wood before the dreamer wakes, conveyed a pristine adoration that would become increasingly erotic in the poetry of Breton, who departed from the same haunted wood, so to speak, as Rimbaud but arrived with greater excitement at the crossroads. "I will pick a precarious niche" ("Je vais m'élire une enceinte précaire"), wrote Breton in another line of this poem. The play of language led him to want to re-create the verbal moment in physical experience. Increasingly, he would move away from the abstract sparseness and lyrical subtlety of Symbolist imagery and replace it with the spontaneous arrangements of collage and automatic writing.

Cubism and Dada were to make of collage a vibrant and political medium, but in the hands of the Surrealists—Ernst, in particular—it became a delirious narrative form. The composition served as an enigmatic fable full of erotic innuendo. In Breton's second collection of poems, (*Clair de terre* (Earthlight; 1923), collage vied with a lyrical and narrative component that emerged from the hypothetical situation the poems set up and in the alliterative and anagrammatic play of words. "In the Eyes of the Gods" ("Au Regard des divinités"), for instance, which utilized a twelve-syllable mock Alexandrine and ended with "Eternity is looking for a wristwatch / Shortly before midnight near the landing stage" ("L'éternité recherche une montre-bracelet / Un peu avant minuit près du débarcadère"), depicted both "eternity" and earlier, the "azure," as metaphorical Cinderellas who had lost track of time and were about to undergo a transformation. This "about to" quality was particularly evident during the early phase of Surrealism, where it was attached to a feminine essence that triggered, as noted earlier, a kind of fugue in the poem, as space escaped into subject and subject escaped into space. Breton seemed in this poem to be trying to collapse subject and space into one entity. The images were reinforced by repetition of the mood of expectancy: "The child with the seashell, the one who was to be. . . ." ("L'enfant à la coquille, celui qui devait être . . .").

In the automatic works, *Les champs magnétiques* (The Magnetic Fields; 1919) in collaboration with Philippe Soupault, and *Poisson soluble* (Soluble Fish; 1924), what was particularly surprising were the references to the process of interiorization that automatic writing reflected, as self-entombment about to reverse itself into revelation. Like a darkened cinema, the mind, isolated from any aesthetic or external preoccupations, played host to its most compelling dramas. The longing for illumination permeated the imagery and the structural unfolding of the automatic texts, just as it did the poetry: "All we need do now is to open our hands and chests and then we'll be as open as this sunny day," wrote Breton and Soupault.

The *Manifeste du surréalisme* (Manifesto of Surrealism; 1924) and the *Second manifeste du surrealisme* (Second Manifesto of Surrealism; 1930) were followed by the shorter *Prolégomènes à un troisième manifeste du surréalisme ou non* (Prolegomena to a Third Surrealist Manifesto or Not; 1942) and *Surréalisme et ses œuvres vives* (Surrealism and Its Living Works; 1953). Together they reflected the trajectory of Breton's evolution and constituted the most widely disseminated and influential body of his work. The *Manifesto* of 1924, which was the defining document of Surrealism, was also one of the great manifestos of modern art and an impassioned defense of poetry, which Breton saw as bearing within itself "the perfect compensation for the miseries we endure."

Breton noticed the verve of automatic writing, despite the overconstruction of phrases. He observed how words that followed one another manifested the greatest solidarity and coherence. An illumined domain came suddenly into relief by the grace of chance, not as a result of labor but of recognition and receptivity. Breton's definition of the "marvelous" is based on the two paradoxical components of inspiration: surprise and foreknowledge, which comes about, as Plato noted in the *Phaedrus,* through "divine release from customary habit" or, as Breton would paraphrase Plato via Cornelius Agrippa in the *Second Manifesto,* "detach [your] mind completely from commonplace things."

Yet, there was something of the taxonomist as well in Breton. He created a movement constructed to break down the process of classification and logic, yet in the first *Manifesto* he also classified it as a philosophy, as a nonaesthetic approach, and listed the reasons why Surrealist images took so long to translate into practical language: (1) "seeming contradiction" or concealment of information; (2) anticlimax; (3) "ridiculous formal justification"; (4) hallucination; (5) giving "to the abstract the mask of the concrete or the opposite"; (6) "negation of some elementary physical property"; and (7) humor.

By the time Breton wrote the *Second Manifesto* (1930), his faith in shaping a political role for the movement vis-à-vis communism was replaced by a need to challenge the attacks on Surrealism from a variety of camps on the left and on the right. Although Breton lashed out at his enemies in the *Second Manifesto,* he also navigated Surrealism out of the line of political fire, proclaiming its "occultation" and making of alchemy the movement's avatar. He quoted Agrippa's citation of the four divine manias of Plato *(Phaedrus)* and asked for the return of this state of *furor.*

In *Prolegomena* (1942), as well as in *Surrealism and Its Living Works* (1953), Breton emphasized the importance of poetry as a means toward enlightenment: "It alone provides the thread that can put us back on the road to Gnosis as knowledge of suprasensible Reality. 'Invisibly visible in an eternal mystery.'" Breton came full circle in the evolution of his credo: the initial premise of deregulation led eventually to the discovery not of disorder but of a higher, hidden order.

Nadja (1928), *L'amour fou* (Mad Love; 1937), and *Arcane 17* (1944) reflected a genre created by Breton, the Surrealist version of the courtly tale. Breton paid homage to women whom he had loved and perceived as turning points in his life. These stories were distinguished by the author's insistence on their documentary authenticity, despite the fact that the "reality" they depicted seemed there only to be transformed into an "elsewhere," by the activation of desire. Nadja was the female version of Jacques Vaché, and like him reflected a desperate devil-may-care attitude toward life that Breton admired. He offered a book that was "ajar like a door" and invited the reader to look through him. He was an "open book": "Who am I. . . ?" he asked. What constituted his particular destiny? It was in *Nadja* that Breton stated, contrary to prior statements, that certain events and situations led him to believe that he was not at the helm alone and to proclaim "a beyond in this life."

In *Mad Love* and *Arcane 17,* on the other hand, Breton discovered an earthly paradise in the fusion of love and the landscapes of the Canary Islands and Quebec's Gaspé Peninsula. The hybrid style reflected a use of autobiography, philosophical meditation, polemic, romantic address, photographs, reproductions of art, art criticism, held together by a spirit of intense rambling and the adventure of moments being written about almost as soon as they were lived.

Breton's essays, first published in periodicals and/or as pamphlets, and finally collected in anthologies such as *Les pas perdus* (The Lost Steps; 1924), *Le surréalisme et la peinture* (Surrealism and Painting; 1928), *Point du jour* (Break of Day; 1934), *La clé de champs* (Key to the Fields; 1953), like his other works, intended to convey a vital rather than retrospective process of thought. They reflected his evolution in thinking from his early enthusiasms to his disenchantment with political solutions in the aftermath of World War II, to the reconstruction of faith based on his continued commitment and activity on behalf of Surrealist principles. The essays on art, in particular, serve as a model of how Breton approached the problem of artistic style, by viewing forms as bipolar structures fusing particularity and generality. As he wrote of Jean Arp's reliefs in *Surrealism and Painting* (1928), "an upsurge of anger" governed their form, and added, "these hard or tender loops represent for me the most effective summing up of the degree to which particular things can achieve generality."

In assessing Breton's work, one is forced to consider the "nonaesthetic" elements: the uneven composition, his reversals of thought and contradictory statements, his diatribes. The reader accepts the skips and breaks of his thought or his irrational fits (recorded for posterity) because the works are full of the vitality of Breton's thought process; that is, no attempt was made to hide the seams of thought; on the contrary, every possible attempt was made to indicate that they were part of its dynamic structure.

In the poem "They Tell Me over There," from *L'air de l'eau* (The Air of Water; 1934), the poet presented a tense paradise of interacting forms: "They tell me that over there the beaches are black / With lava gone down to the sea / And unfold at the foot of a huge peak smoking with snow / Beneath a second sun of wild canaries" ("On me dit que là-bas les plages son noires / De la lave allée à la mer / Et se déroulent au pied d'un immense pic fumant de neige / Sous un second soleil de serins sauvages").

The crevices, cracks, and seams that constituted the "grain" of Surrealist works always revealed slats or openings to an "over there" *(là-bas).* One of Breton's last, thematically unified poetic works, *Constellations,* illustrated by Joan Miró, 1949) was a series of prose poems that fused interior dream images with images of the stars and "profound caves of the sea." The weaving and plaiting, threads, wires, bobbins, and filaments incorporated in these poems, combined with Miró's expanding and contracting universe of constellatory abstract forms, indicated a kind of parallelism between poetic and scientific experimentation. Albert Einstein's discovery of relativity gave way to his "unified field theory," which he hoped would disprove that "God played dice with the universe." An underlying unifying principle would connect the process of the largest star to the domain of atomic and subatomic particles and waves. Breton, too, began with "chance" *(le hasard),* welcomed it as a liberating idea, only to arrive at a more inexorable principle of the cosmos. Breton's aesthetics was based on incorporating a metamorphosis of images that would convey a movement toward enlightenment and pristineness. Neo-Romantic in his emphasis on process, Breton easily proclaimed his Romantic ancestry. Yet, there was a classical streak in him that was more concealed and less acknowledged. It emerged via the Symbolist admiration of forms that were hard, durable, and pattern-ridden, such as fossils, resinous substances such as amber, minerals, phosphorescent rocks, precious stones, and crystalline substances, symbols of a type of universal poetic striving toward crystallization.

[*See also* Surrealism.]

BIBLIOGRAPHY

Works by Breton

Nadja (1928). Translated by Richard Howard. New York, 1960.
Arcanum 17 (1944). Translated by Zack Rogow. Los Angeles, 1994.
Young Cherry Trees Secured against Hares. Translated by Édouard Roditi (1946). Ann Arbor, 1969.
Conversations: The Autobiography of Surrealism (1952). Translated by Mark Polizzotti. New York, 1993.
Manifestoes of Surrealism (1962). Translated by Richard Seaver and Helen R. Lane. Ann Arbor, 1969.
Surrealism and Painting (1965). Translated by Simon Watson Taylor. New York, 1972. [First published in 1928 and expanded in a 1945, then a 1965 edition].
Poems of André Breton. Translated by Jean-Pierre Cauvin and Mary Ann Caws. Austin, Tex., 1982.
Œuvres complètes. 2 vols. Edited by Marguerite Bonnet et al. Paris, 1988–1992.

Other Sources

Balakian, Anna. *André Breton: Magus of Surrealism.* New York and Oxford, 1971.
Balakian, Anna, and Rudolf E. Kuenzli, eds. *André Breton Today.* New York, 1989. Includes selective bibliography, 1971–1988.
Behar, Henri. *André Breton: Le grand indésirable.* Paris, 1990.
Gershman, Herbert S. *A Bibliography of the Surrealist Revolution in France.* Ann Arbor, 1969.
Pierre, José. *A Dictionary of Surrealism.* Translated by W. J. Strachan. London, 1974.
Polizzotti, Mark. *Revolution of the Mind: The Life of André Breton.* New York, 1995.

BARBARA LEKATSAS

BRITISH AESTHETICS. *For discussions of British aesthetics from the eighteenth century to the present, see* Addison; Alison; Arnold; Bell; Berkeley; Blair; Bullough; Burke; Coleridge; Collingwood; Cooper; Dryden; Gerard; Home; Hume; Hutcheson; Knight; Morris; Pater; Price; Priestley;

Reid; Reynolds; Ruskin; Sidney; Smith; Stokes; Wilde; Williams; Wollheim; *and* Wordsworth.

BROOKS, CLEANTH. *See* New Criticism.

BRUT, ART. *See* Insane, Art of the; Outsider Art.

BUDDHIST AESTHETICS. *See* Chinese Aesthetics, *historical overview article;* Japanese Aesthetics, *historical overview article.*

BULLOUGH, EDWARD (1880–1934), British author of essays in aesthetics and empirical studies of aesthetic perception. Bullough taught modern languages and aesthetics at Cambridge until his death in 1934. Today, his reputation rests primarily on his 1912 essay "'Psychical Distance' as a Factor in Art and as an Aesthetic Principle," in which he brings to fruition his project of clarifying, grounding, and unifying discussions of art and aesthetic response without insisting on the centrality of beauty or any other quality common to all works of art. In his earlier essay "The Modern Conception of Aesthetics," Bullough argues that such analyses fail not only because they underestimate the variety of artworks and beautiful objects generally, but also because they seek to ground aesthetics on the objective world and thereby betray an unjustifiable prejudice against the subjective one. It is in the subjective experience of aesthetic response, then, that Bullough finds the unifying conception he seeks.

In his widely anthologized and still influential essay "'Psychical Distance' as a Factor in Art and as an Aesthetic Principle," Bullough develops an account of aesthetic response centered on the notion of psychical distance. "Imagine a fog at sea: for most people it is an experience of acute unpleasantness," producing annoyance, fear, discomfort, and feelings "of peculiar anxiety." And yet, one may direct one's attention "to the features objectively constituting the phenomenon": the opaque, milky veil, blurring outlines and distorting shapes; the creamy smoothness of the water belying any danger; the solitude and remoteness from the world. Indeed, the experience then may acquire, "in its uncanny mingling of repose and terror, a flavor of such concentrated poignancy and delight as to contrast sharply with the blind and distempered anxiety of its other aspects." We sometimes experience this sort of contrast, according to Bullough, in instants of direst extremity, when our "practical interest snaps like a wire from sheer over-tension, and we watch the consummation of some impending catastrophe with the marvelling unconcern of a mere spectator." Then, by putting the phenomenon "out of gear with our practical,

actual self," and by allowing it to stand outside the context of our personal needs and ends, we are able to view it "objectively."

It is telling that although this article discusses the nature of art, Bullough presents as the paradigmatic case of aesthetic experience a response to an extra-artistic situation, indeed, a situation in which the appreciator faces a kind of danger rarely encountered in the art gallery or concert hall. Bullough stops short of prescribing that one take the aesthetic point of view in such dangerous situations, although he at least implies, here and in earlier essays, that the shipwrecked aesthete's last moments will not have been wasted. In responding to art, however, aesthetic response should always prevail. Bullough acknowledges that particular artworks and, indeed, art generally may serve many important purposes (especially in "primitive" societies); nevertheless, "any interpretation of the function and value of Art is inadequate which does not lay primary stress on the *aesthetic* aspect." In fact, this aesthetic aspect (understood in terms of psychical distance) looms so large in Bullough's account of art that he reduces the fictional character of some art to it: If we do not leap from our theater seats onto the stage to aid our favorite characters, this is because "distance" has rendered the characters and their situation seemingly fictitious, not because "the fictitiousness of the characters alters our feelings toward them." After all, Bullough argues, "the same filtration of our sentiments and the same seeming 'unreality' of *actual* men and things occur, when at times, by a sudden change of inward perspective, we are overcome by the feeling that 'all the world's a stage.'" The important distinction for Bullough, then, is between aesthetic and nonaesthetic attitudes, not between art and life, realms that he seems to regard as not so very different after all.

Bullough's notion of distance is suggestive, but it raises a host of questions. Is the object one distances also the object one appreciates aesthetically? In the case of the fog at sea, for example, one separates "the object and its appeal from one's own self, by putting it out of gear with practical needs and ends." Here the object distanced seems to be the fog. But fear, he claims, changes to aesthetic appreciation only with the "insertion of Distance, which appears to lie between our own self and its affections, using the latter term in its broadest sense as anything which affects our being, bodily or spiritually, e.g., as sensation, perception, emotional state or idea." He speaks as well of "the self which has been distanced out of the field of the inner vision of the experiencer," and of the artist's capacity to distance feelings and sensations that others may find overwhelming. Thus, his analysis seems to involve two complementary objects of distance: on the one hand, external objects or situations, and on the other, internal psychological states, which, if not properly distanced, may threaten contemplation. Properly distancing the first, external sort of object, moreover, may well depend on properly distancing the second, internal sort; and in the end both objects may merge, as we project our subjective states onto some external object and come to interpret "even our 'subjective' affections not as modes of *our* being but rather as characteristics of the [appreciated] phenomenon."

Indeed, the very sorts of nonaesthetic interests and reactions that may disrupt aesthetic response also seem to contribute to it. According to Bullough, aesthetic appreciation fails when the appreciator either "underdistances" (that is, has too little distance) or "overdistances" (has too much). The inexperienced, terrified sailor may be underdistanced; the jaded old hand may have the opposite problem. But this contrast between over- and underdistancing is complicated by another example that Bullough gives. A jealous husband, he explains, may be so overcome by emotion while watching *Othello* that he loses distance. Bullough also admits, however, that the "jealous spectator of *Othello* will indeed appreciate and enter into the play the more keenly, the greater the resemblance with his own experience—*provided* that he succeeds in keeping the Distance between the action of the play and his personal feelings." Thus, again, it seems that the very feelings that must be distanced in order to safeguard aesthetic response are, once distanced, crucial to it.

The centrality of Bullough's notion of aesthetic distance has implications for his views on the evaluation of particular works of art. Like the later apostles of aesthetic experience John Cage or Stuart Hampshire, Bullough disparages (in his "The Modern Conception of Aesthetics") the "mania for preference-judgements" that requires everything "to be pigeon-holed in a hierarchy of value before one dares to admit one likes it." The character that emerges with aesthetic distance is unique in a way that frustrates evaluative comparisons with other works; appreciation should be "elative, not superlative." Of course, one may legitimately judge a work's quality, but such a judgment ought to measure a work of art only against one's cumulative experience of works of art. Indeed, one goal of the wide aesthetic experience and education that Bullough favors is the development of a catholic taste "so sure and refined" that one knows "intuitively the worth of a work." Bullough, then, is interested in giving standards less for art than for aesthetic response.

Bullough's emphasis on aesthetic distance also leads to a liberality about the proper subject matter for art; at least in theory, anything can be a candidate for aesthetic appreciation. On the other hand, the artistic endeavor requires that challenging content be contemplated aesthetically, and the capacity for aesthetic response, "partly innate and partly acquired," varies widely. Some spectacles, in art as in life, tempt the aesthetically irresolute into a loss of distance. "Explicit references to organic affections, to the material existence of the body, especially to sexual matters, lie normally below the Distance-limit, and can be touched upon by Art only with special precautions," causing many an artist to see "his work condemned and himself ostracised

for the sake of so-called 'immoralities' which to him were bona fide aesthetic objects." Art dealing with politics and morality, especially when it questions widely accepted doctrines or treats of "topical subjects occupying public attention at the moment" are also "dangerously near" the limit of most people's aesthetic capacities. In the latter case, at least, Bullough suggests that posterity will fare better, as time imposes a distance that the psyche cannot quite manage on its own. As for art treating of "the material existence of the body," perhaps only the aesthetic elite will be able to respond appropriately, just as, indeed, only a few passengers will appreciate the fog aesthetically when disaster threatens.

Bullough's emphasis on a disinterested, contemplative aesthetic experience and its primacy to art looks backward to Immanuel Kant and forward to what has become received doctrine, expressed, among other places, in the theories of Anglo-American philosophers Eliseo Vivas, Jerome Stolnitz, and Allan Casebier, all of whom have proposed interesting analyses of aesthetic response that share the spirit of Bullough's account even as they challenge its letter. J. O. Urmson (1957), objecting to the psychologistic cast of Bullough's view, has insisted instead that the criterion for aesthetic response be sought in "the explanation of the reaction or the grounds of the judgment" rather than in a psychological state; but even he has simply brought Bullough's view in line with the logical behaviorism fashionable among Anglo-American philosophers in the middle years of this century. In any case, for the most part, these analyses accept Bullough's contention that aesthetic character involves contemplative response, that it is in some important sense autonomous from other human activities or interests, and that it is essential to artistic activity.

Perhaps a more radical criticism comes from those who resist understanding the aesthetic as a quality of responses rather than of objects. Such criticism may focus instead on beauty, but it need not. George Dickie (1974), for example, argues that aesthetic response is nothing more than response to those qualities of artworks recognized as aesthetic by art-world conventions, and that any talk of special reasons, motivations, or states of mind is irrelevant or unintelligible. [*See* Dickie.] Dickie's criticism is motivated in part by the tendency of aesthetic response theories like Bullough's to dismiss politically or ethically engaged responses to artworks. But whereas Dickie's analysis may have its appeal as a normative proposal about what *should* be important in responding to art, it fails as a descriptive theory of such response by gravely underestimating the degree to which aestheticism pervades dominant understandings of and responses to art. Bullough's analysis may reflect and even celebrate this aestheticism uncritically, but Dickie's critique tries unsuccessfully to explain it away.

Admitting the centrality of something like Bullough's category of aesthetic experience, however, need not necessarily involve prescribing it as an ideal for response to art or anything else. Working mostly outside of the Anglo-American aesthetic tradition, some recent aesthetic theorists (for example, the French sociologist Pierre Bourdieu) have understood aesthetic response as a phenomenon that, for all of its claims to transcendence, is socially situated, tied not only to the rise of the modern practice of art in the eighteenth century, but also to the broader social and historical developments to which the practice of art itself is related: for example, urbanization, industrialization, the formation of modern classes, and the consolidation of modern categories of race and gender. For Bullough, of course, the history of art and aesthetic response will be nothing more than the story of how a rudimentary but unmistakably aesthetic impulse gathers force and, breaking free from its servitude to politics, the church, and moralism, finally emerges triumphant and autonomous with the modern practice of art. A more thoroughgoing historical and antiessentialist perspective, however, will understand the category of the aesthetic and the practice of art, for all of their seeming autonomy, to be deeply embedded, if in hidden ways, in various nonaesthetic dimensions of social life. Viewed from this perspective, the aesthetic attitude that Bullough describes seems less an explanation of what unifies art and aesthetics than the very phenomenon to be explained.

[*See also* Attitude, *article on* Aesthetic Attitude; *and* Disinterestedness.]

BIBLIOGRAPHY

Works by Bullough

"On the Apparent Heaviness of Colours." *British Journal of Psychology* 2 (1907): 111–152.
"The 'Perceptive Problem' in the Aesthetic Appreciation of Single Colours." *British Journal of Psychology* 3.4 (1910): 409–463.
"Mind and Medium in Art." In *Aesthetics: Lectures and Essays,* edited by Elizabeth M. Wilkinson. Stanford, Calif., 1957.
"The Modern Conception of Aesthetics." In *Aesthetics: Lectures and Essays,* edited by Elizabeth M. Wilkinson. Stanford, Calif., 1957.
" 'Psychical Distance' as a Factor in Art and as an Aesthetic Principle." In *Aesthetics: Lectures and Essays,* edited by Elizabeth M. Wilkinson. Stanford, Calif., 1957.

Other Sources

Bourdieu, Pierre. *Distinction: A Social Critique of the Judgement of Taste.* Translated by Richard Nice. Cambridge, Mass., 1984.
Brand, Peggy Zeglin, and Carolyn Korsmeyer, eds. *Feminism and Tradition in Aesthetics.* University Park, Pa., 1995.
Casebier, Alan. "The Concept of Aesthetic Distance." *Personalist* (Winter 1971): 70–91.
Dickie, George. *Art and the Aesthetic: An Institutional Analysis* Ithaca, N.Y., 1974.
Hampshire, Stuart. "Logic and Appreciation." In *Art and Philosophy,* 2d ed., edited by W. E. Kennick. New York, 1979.
Kant, Immanuel. *Critique of Judgment.* Translated by J. H. Bernard. New York, 1951.
Kostelanetz, Richard, ed. *John Cage.* Documentary Monographs in Modern Art. New York, 1970.
Mattick, Paul, Jr., ed. *Eighteenth-Century Aesthetics and the Reconstruction of Art.* Cambridge and New York, 1993.
Urmson, J. O. "What Makes a Situation Aesthetic?" *Proceedings of the Aristotelian Society* sup. vol. 31 (1957).
Vivas, Eliseo. "Contextualism Reconsidered." *Journal of Aesthetics and Art Criticism* (December 1959): 222–240.

SALLY MARKOWITZ

BURKE, EDMUND (1729–1797), British theorist of taste and of the sublime. Burke's *A Philosophical Enquiry into the Origin of Our Ideas of the Sublime and Beautiful,* which he undertook in 1747 at the age of eighteen and published in 1757, addressed the question of whether or not taste had any significant regularity and uniformity, and, thus, he maintained, the question of whether matters of taste were of any substantial interest. Whereas David Hume had, in his essay "On the Standard of Taste," argued that we acknowledge expertise in taste in the process of crediting some people with having better taste than others, his argument had extended only so far as the claim that taste was not wholly subjective or completely individualistic; the distinctions we regularly draw between one person's judgment and another's constituted a prima facie argument that people acknowledged the capacity to make distinctions between one object of taste and another, even when they could not explain what the criteria for their evaluations were. In the *Enquiry,* by contrast, Burke argued for a much stronger view. If Hume had made the negative argument that our recognition of expertise demonstrates that taste is not simply a personal matter, Burke sought "to find whether there are any principles, on which the imagination is affected, so common to all, so grounded and certain, as to supply the means of reasoning satisfactorily about them." Immediately proceeding from this announcement of his purposes to a statement of his position, Burke announced his positive account of the regularity and uniformity of taste: "And such principles of Taste, I fancy there are; however paradoxical it may seem to those, who on a superficial view imagine, that there is so great a diversity of Tastes both in kind and degree, that nothing can be more indeterminate" (Burke, 1968).

Burke's account revolved around a resolute commitment to the primacy of sensory experience, and he sought evidence of agreement in both examples of sensation and the language that people use to describe it. He argued first that, insofar as human organs of perception are "nearly, or altogether the same in all men, so the manner of perceiving external objects is in all men the same, or with little difference." Concluding that the "sceptical proceeding" of imagining that the senses "present to different men different images of things" was unacceptable because it would render "every sort of reasoning on every subject vain and frivolous," Burke proceeded to anatomize the operations of the senses and "the pleasures and the pains which every object excites in one man . . . and in all mankind" alike. Thus, whereas Burke joined a host of other writers in recognizing how loose a figurative term like *taste* was in describing people's responses to objects, he aimed to do more than to accept such vagueness; he aimed to introduce substance to the notion by cataloging the various kinds of sensory objects and the various pleasures and pains that they excited.

The most striking aspect of Burke's position lay in his claim that, "as there will be very little doubt that bodies present similar images to the whole species, it must necessarily be allowed, that the pleasures and the pains which every object excites in one man, it must raise in all mankind, whilst it operates naturally, simply, and by its proper powers only" (ibid.). With this move, Burke essentially treated pleasure and pain less as judgments on objects than as aspects of the sensory perception of those objects. Whereas other writers had imagined that sourness, for instance, might be recognized as sourness by many but that it would produce varying degrees of pleasure and pain, Burke was basically maintaining that the reactions of pleasure and pain were, at bottom, as unvarying as the recognition of sourness itself. In his account, it came to seem plausible to argue that smooth objects, for instance, are pleasing to humans because they produce pleasurable effects on the body. One did not need to examine one's cultural presuppositions or one's personal psychology in advancing the claim that smoothness was beautiful; to say that a smooth object was beautiful was simply to produce testimony from one's own body. It became the simple equivalent of saying that one had perceived it. In this tautologous account of the pleasurableness of certain kinds of sensations and the painfulness of others, Burke would thus insist that "the sense of feeling is highly gratified with smooth bodies," and would go on to suggest that the luxury of such things as "a bed smoothly laid and soft" is by no means a merely acquired taste but one that acknowledges the universal appeal of the feelings of overcoming "resistance" and perceiving anything "disposing to an universal relaxation" (IV, xx).

For Burke, then, the crucial aesthetic division was not between natural objects and artifacts but between objects that occasioned pleasure and those that occasioned pain. Yet, perhaps the most interesting aspect of the *Enquiry* was that Burke did not merely distinguish between objects that occasioned pleasurable sensations and those that produced painful sensations and did not stop with insisting that the preferences that people demonstrate are universal and transhistorical. He also showed a particular interest in the positive uses that both pleasure and pain had to play in human activity.

He distinguished sharply between the sublime and the beautiful, associating the sublime with the kind of awe we feel when confronted with objects that exceed our control and the beautiful with all the things that we take to be pleas-

ant because they submit to us. His scheme explicitly treated the pleasure and pain of the judgment as a comparative matter, in which an individual does not so much compare alternative experiences as compare the objects of experience with herself. In being confronted with a sublime object, "the mind is so entirely filled with its object, that it cannot entertain any other," and the sublime object "anticipates our reasons, and hurries us on by an irresistible force" (II, i). The beautiful, by contrast, is beautiful insofar as it continually presents occasions in which persons may feel satisfied with the adequacy of their sensations and their thinking about them. It is the domain of all that "submits to us," an external complement to the human faculties of perception that functions as a tribute to them. Indeed, Burke's insistence on the importance of the comparison between individuals and the objects of their perceptions leads him to argue against the view that proportion is a cause of beauty, and that the internal harmony of an object is what we respond to in calling it beautiful. His affectivist account stresses impact as opposed to the comparatively intellectual operation of perceiving such internal relationships as harmony. Most strikingly, he insists that judgments of taste are, at base, statements about the relative power between a perceiver and an object of perception. Thus, we seem not only to judge objects but also to be judged by them, and Burke specifically connects this competitive relationship between objects and their beholders with the feelings of contentment and ambition. He summarized his position with particular lucidity when he observed that "there is a wide difference between admiration and love. The sublime, which is the cause of the former, always dwells on great objects, and terrible; the latter on small ones, and pleasing; we submit to what we admire, but we love what submits to us; in one case we are forced, in the other we are flattered into compliance" (III, xiii).

For Burke, moreover, judgments of taste provide the elements for a psychological analysis that moves in the direction of a political psychology. Our feelings about beauty—whether they concern objects such as swans or roses or whether they concern the affection that one might feel toward a mother or a grandfather—operate to reinforce all the domestic, companionable feelings that tend toward the preservation of the human species. Our feelings about sublime objects—whether they be an ocean stretching to infinity, a father who arouses feelings of awe, or a hero like Achilles who has the remarkable capacity to count his own death as comparatively insignificant—spring from the same source as our instincts of self-preservation. Indeed, one of the most ingenious aspects of Burke's discussion is that he manages to contrast the sublime and the beautiful in virtually everything except their positive efficacy for human society. The beautiful obviously serves the purposes of society by making persons attractive to one another and thus by fostering what he calls the "passions of society," both that "of the sexes, which answers the purposes of propagation," and desire for "that more general society, which we have with men and with other animals, and which we may in some sort be said to have even with the inanimate world" (I, viii). Yet, the sublime, although it might remove us from the companionable charms of the beautiful, is likewise socially productive. Strength or might was "only useful," Burke maintained, it was "never sublime" (II, v). Anything that represented force beyond our control might produce sublime awe, which was itself useful to society insofar as the consciousness of the littleness of our own powers did not press too near, and did not thus conduce simply to fear; for in the experience of realizing that one could contemplate a potentially painful and dangerous might without being immediately affected by it, Burke saw a "delight" that revolved around having "an idea of pain and danger, without being actually in such circumstances" (II, xviii). Anything that produced such delight, he called sublime. And he found it emblematic of the ambition and exertion that animate heroes, persons who may not directly participate in the companionable virtues of society but who importantly advance its aims with their ambition and exertion.

Thus, Burke presents an account of the judgment of beauty and sublimity that is essentially oriented to the question of its usefulness. The notion of an object being pleasing or terrifying in itself thus never really makes an appearance in the *Enquiry;* and aesthetic experience is completely continuous with all other sensory experience, as befits what Immanuel Kant will later call Burke's "transcendental exposition of aesthetical judgments with the physiological"; that is to say that Burke's analysis of aesthetic experience operates to bring to explicitness the significance that people are attaching to messages that might previously have seemed random or at least implicit. Yet, perhaps the most intriguing aspect of Burke's discussion lies in his suggestions about how to harness the energies of the judgment. His remarks, steeped as they are in Adam Smith's description of sympathy as a chief moral force, stress the importance of identification in forming "our manners, our opinions, our lives" (I, xvi). Yet, it is perhaps the limits on identificatory sympathy that come to occupy Burke's attention most completely, and he repeatedly adverts to the gratifications of "flattery," which for him regularly involves recognizing an implicit comparison within what might appear to be the simple agreement of sympathetic identification. Imitation can be "one of the strongest links of society," he writes, because "it is a special relation of mutual compliance which all men yield to each other, without constraint to themselves, and which is extremely flattering to all" (I, xvi). Thus, Burke appropriates a classic problem of eighteenth-century discussions—why tragedy might be pleasurable, and why people seek to entertain themselves by watching the theatrical representation of other people's miseries—to get at a pleasure of representation that extends beyond the identification with the actors in it. The capacity to contemplate representations of what has happened—in actuality or in imagination—does not, he argues, involve our feeling satisfaction in the superiority of our situations to those of the actors who suffer them. Rather, it makes fictitious representations seem important for promoting the faculty of comparison itself, for prompting us to dwell on the incidents of the past or of others as if they had significance for us. Burke had begun the *Enquiry* by suggesting that we could produce widespread agreement among persons by asking them to compare a flower with an idea such as that of divine might, and by asking them to categorize each as beautiful or sublime. Yet, his examples proceed through such unequivocal experiments to an emphasis on objects that he sees in different aspects: "The horse in the light of an useful beast, fit for the plough, the road, the draft, in every social useful light the horse has nothing of the sublime; but is it thus that we are affected with him, *whose neck is cloathed with thunder, the glory of whose nostrils is terrible, who swalloweth the ground with fierceness and rage, neither believeth that it is the sound of the trumpet?*" (II. v). It thus becomes apparent that the force of his remarks is not so much to use the judgment to get at a scientific understanding of the properties of objects through sensory experimentation. Rather, he provides a real, if sketchy, argument for the importance of the judgment as a way of insisting on the variability of the value and significance of objects as an individual's relationship to them changes. His account of the judgment ends by neither promoting agreement about objects nor causing people to identify with one another's situations but by emphasizing the way in which aesthetic experience comes to mark individuals' consciousness of their changing relationship to unchanging objects. It was ultimately this interest in using aesthetic objects to talk about psychological interiority that made him particularly compelling to Romantic writers such as William Wordsworth and Samuel Taylor Coleridge; his claim on behalf of the possibility of generalizing about the regularity of human experiences of objects ultimately laid stress on the changeability of individual consciousness itself, on the difference between our mature judgments and the perceptions we had "in the morning of our days, when the senses are unworn and tender, when the whole man is awake in every part, and the gloss of novelty fresh upon all the objects that surround us."

[*See also* Beauty; Sublime; *and* Taste.]

BIBLIOGRAPHY

Work by Burke

Burke, Edmund. *A Philosophical Enquiry into the Origin of Our Ideas of the Sublime and Beautiful.* 2d ed. Edited by James T. Boulton. Notre Dame, Ind., 1968.

Other Sources

Caygill, Howard. *Art of Judgement.* Oxford and Cambridge, Mass., 1989.

de Bolla, Peter. *The Discourse of the Sublime: Readings in History, Aesthetics, and the Subject.* Oxford and New York, 1989.

Ferguson, Frances. *Solitude and the Sublime: Romanticism and the Aesthetics of Individuation.* New York and London, 1992.

Hertz, Neil. *The End of the Line: Essays on Psychoanalysis and the Sublime.* New York, 1985.

Hipple, Walter John. *The Beautiful, the Sublime, and the Picturesque in Eighteenth-Century British Aesthetic Theory.* Carbondale, Ill., 1957.

Knapp, Steven. *Personification and the Sublime: Milton to Coleridge.* Cambridge, Mass., 1985.

Monk, Samuel Holt. *The Sublime: A Study of Critical Theories in Eighteenth-Century England.* Reprint, Ann Arbor, 1960.

Morris, David B. *The Religious Sublime: Christian Poetry and Critical Tradition in Eighteenth-Century England.* Lexington, Ky., 1972.

Paulson, Ronald. *Representations of Revolution, 1789–1820.* New Haven, 1983.

Price, Martin. *To the Palace of Wisdom: Studies in Order and Energy from Dryden to Blake.* Garden City, N.Y., 1964.

Weiskel, Thomas. *The Romantic Sublime: Studies in the Structure and Psychology of Transcendence.* Baltimore, 1976.

FRANCES FERGUSON

BYZANTINE AESTHETICS. One of the trends in medieval aesthetics within the Greek-speaking culture of Byzantium (fourth to fifteenth century), Byzantine aesthetics was based on the aesthetic ideas of antiquity (first of all, Neoplatonism) and early patristics. Early patristics, in fact, rejects the majority of aesthetic values of the ancient (pagan) world—the "aesthetics of negation"—and focuses on spiritual beauty and the ideas of Christian symbolism which had just started to take root at that time. Byzantine aesthetics develops in several directions.

Patristic aesthetics, which is the main theoretical trend in Byzantine aesthetics, began in the pre-Byzantine period (the second- to third-century) within the new Christian ideology on the basis of Greco-Roman and old Hebrew aesthetics, a process that was mainly completed around the sixth century. Substantial contributions to the development of Patristic aesthetics were made by Athanasios of Alexandria, Basil the Great, Gregory of Nyssa, John Chrysostom, and pseudo-Dionysius the Areopagite. The most significant categories of patristic aesthetics were the beautiful, light, image, symbol, allegory, sign, name, and art. The transcendent ideal of Byzantine aesthetics was the incomprehensible and indescribable God in the antinomic unity of his three *hypostaseis.* He is the source of beauty that surpasses all beautiful things. All the universe (material as well as spiritual) is a system of images *(eikon),* symbols *(symbolon),* and signs *(semeion)* that point to him. In particular, all the beautiful things of the material world, including the handmade—light, color, and the innumerable images of literary, musical, and (Christian) representational arts—bring spiritual joy to the perceiver and are, ultimately, the images, symbols, and signs of God and the heavenly spheres, that is, the nonconceptual forms of expression of spiritual essences.

The anonymous Christian Neoplatonist, who was active sometime around 500 CE and entered the history of culture under the name pseudo-Dionysius the Areopagite, developed most fully the concept of the symbol in Byzantine aesthetics in its most general form. He saw the universe (including social formations) as a hierarchical system of the ascent (uplifting) of man to God and the conveyance of supreme knowledge from God to man through the steps of this hierarchy of celestial and terrestrial orders, or *taxeis.* According to pseudo-Dionysius, aesthetic elements have an important role in both processes. The spiritual "uplifting" *(anagoge)* is accomplished by means of antinomical "likening" to *(homoiosis),* and "imitation" of *(mimēsis),* God. As for the transfer of "knowledge" downward from above, it happens in the form of "illuminations," or progressive "light giving" *(photodosia).* Symbols, images, signs, and representations perceived by the senses—including the sphere of art almost in its entirety—are the forms of conveyance of spiritual light to a human person.

Psuedo-Dionysins's treatise *Symbolic Theology* has not survived, but he gave a rather detailed account of this theory in other works and letters. Symbols, both natural and artificial, at the same time serve the purpose of concealing (from the noninitiated) and revealing truth. Humans must learn to "see" and correctly decipher symbols. Pseudo-Dionysius distinguished between the two main categories of symbols: the "like," which have a certain likeness with the ptototype, and the "unlike," or "unlike likenesses" *(anomoia homoiotes).* It is the latter that he esteemed most highly, for it is with their help that the ascent to the spiritual essences is accomplished with greater ease. The human spirit that perceives the "unlike likenesses" does not stop at their external form—as the one that clearly has nothing in common with the object it designates—but goes on to search for the true prototype. Their main goal is to stir the soul by the "dissimilarity of representation" as such and direct it toward the perception of something quite removed from any representation, that is, supreme spiritual values. Thus, according to pseudo-Dionysius, who developed the ideas of Philo, Origen, and Gregory of Nyssa—his predecessors in the field of allegorical exegesis—many sensible and even ugly and obscene phenomena and objects can serve as symbols of high spirituality. By their own nature, symbols are polysemantic. A complete comprehension of a symbol causes ineffable pleasure. Pseudo-Dionysius understood the beautiful in the material world as the symbol of absolute transcendent Beauty, which, in its turn, is the "cause of consonance and lustre in all that exists." The ideas of pseudo-Dionysius had a significant impact on medieval Christian aesthetics, in both the East and the West.

It is the period of iconoclasm (eighth to ninth century) that saw further development of patristic aesthetics: the theory of the image in representational arts (or the theory of the icon) was being elaborated in detail, together with several other related questions on art. John of Damascus, Theodore of Stoudios, Nikephoros, patriarch of Constantinople, and the fathers of the Seventh Ecumenical Council assigned a number of functions to the icon. (Their ideas later formed the foundation of Orthodox aesthetics, including the theories of Russian religious thinkers of the beginning of the twentieth century.) In particular, the icon was understood as a representation of the ideal visible appearance (the "inner eidos," according to Plotinian terminology) of the prototype. The process of active formation of patristic aesthetics, which became a certain norm for the Byzantine—and even broader Orthodox (including Russian religious aesthetics)—culture, came to its completion around 850–900 CE. In the following period (tenth to fourteenth century), only the theory of light received further development (by Symeon the New Theologian and Gregory Palamas). The discussion of the problem of "Taboric light" (Christ's transfiguration, or shining, on mount Tabor; cf. Matt. 17.2, Luke 9.29) led Gregory Palamas and his followers to assert the possibility, in a certain situation, of sensible perception of noncreated divine light.

The aesthetics of asceticism, an interior and implicit rigoristic aesthetics formed in the milieu of Byzantine monasticism on the basis of the "aesthetics of negation" of the early Christians, influenced the development of many aspects of Byzantine culture and church art. The main themes of the aesthetics of asceticism, which saw its aesthetic object, as a rule, in the inner world of the aesthetic subject, were a total rejection of sensual pleasures in favor of spirituality; the ideal of poverty; the system of special spiritual psychophysical exercises in combination with prayer ("intelligent making") that lead to the contemplation of various visions—mainly of a lustrous character—and to the state of highest spiritual delight. The main theorists and practitioners of this aesthetics were the monks Makarios the Egyptian, Neilos of Ankyra, John Klimax, Isaac of Nineveh (Syros), and Symeon the New Theologian. The aesthetics of asceticism had a clearly expressed ethical, as well as mystical, orientation.

Liturgical aesthetics was a trend in late-patristic aesthetics that was mainly aimed at the comprehension of liturgical action as a mystical wholeness that unites the believers with God and spiritual orders in the process of liturgy. In particular, much attention was paid to the elaboration and understanding of the symbolic character of the ritual, including all artistic elements of church arts. In this context, the symbol (or liturgical image—*typos*) was understood by the late church fathers (with particular consistency by Symeon, archbishop of Thessaloníki in the fifteenth century) as a "real" (more precisely, sacred) carrier of divine energy, or the spiritual power of the prototype. The symbol was seen not only as a semiotic unit, but also as a sacred and ontological phenomenon that "manifests" in reality its spiritual prototype to the participants of liturgical action.

Numerous descriptions of works of art—*ekphrasis*—occupied a distinct place in Byzantine aesthetics. Their authors (Eusebius of Caesarea [Pamphilos], Prokopios of Caesarea, Romanos the Melode, Asterios of Amaseia, Chorikios of Gaza, Nicholas Mesarites, and others) gave a very clear notion of medieval understanding of art, thus contributing to the foundations of European art criticism. The most common view among them was the mimetic understanding of representational art, that is, considering it a naturalistic copy of the original that produces a strong impression on the beholder precisely through its likeness to the material reality (here they continued the ancient traditions of the interpretation of art). To them, the symbolic understanding of art was of only secondary importance.

The trend that aimed at imitating antiquity preserves, throughout the whole history of Byzantium, the traditions and main notions of Hellenistic and Roman aesthetics, with its particular taste for luxury, artistic elaboration, increased ornamentation, illusionism, and clearly manifested sensuality. This trend was especially favored at the emperor's court, and, beginning 850–900 CE, found supporters among Byzantine historians, philosophers, philologists, novelists, secular poets, and even well-educated urban clergy. The main representatives of this trend were patriarch Photios (ninth century), who started to collect, and comment on, ancient texts systematically, Symeon Metaphrastes, Michael Psellos, Theodore Prodromos, and Theodore Metochites. It is to this trend that European culture owes the preservation of many ancient texts and their primary textual and philological analysis.

[*See also* Icon; Iconoclasm and Iconophobia; Religion and Aesthetics; *and* Russian Aesthetics.]

BIBLIOGRAPHY

Bychkov, Victor V. *L'estetica bizantina: Problemi teorici*. Bari, 1983.
Bychkov, Victor V. "Die ästhetischen Anschauungen des Patriarchen Nikephoros." *Byzantinoslavica* T. L. Fasc. 2 (1989): 181–192.
Bychkov, Victor V. "Das Licht geistiger Verklärung, Einblick in die Lehre Hesychasten." *Stimme der Orthodoxie* (May–June 1991): 42–46.
Bychkov, Victor V. *Malaya istoriya vizantiyskoy estetiki* (A Concise History of Byzantine Aesthetics). Kiev, 1991.

Bychkov, Victor V. *Aesthetica Patrum: Estetika ottsov tserkvi,* vol. 1, *Apologety, Blazhenny Augustin* (The Aesthetics of Church Fathers). Moscow, 1995.

Grabar, André. *Plotin et les origines de l'esthétique médiévale.* Paris, 1945.

Hertzman, Evgenij. *Vizantijskoe muzykoznanie* (Byzantine Musicology). Leningrad, 1988.

Hunger, Herbert. *Aspekte der griechischen Rhetorik von Gorgias bis zum Untergang von Byzanz.* Vienna, 1972.

Hunger, Herbert. *Die hochsprachliche profane Literatur der Byzantiner.* 2 vols. Munich, 1978.

Kitzinger, Ernst. "The Cult of Images in the Age before Iconoclasm." *Dumbarton Oaks Papers* 8 (1954): 83–150.

Ladner, G. "The Concept of the Image in the Greek Fathers and the Byzantine Iconoclastic Controversy." *Dumbarton Oaks Papers* 7 (1953): 1–34.

Mango, Cyril A. *The Art of the Byzantine Empire, 312–1453: Sources and Documents.* Toronto, 1986.

Mathew, Gervase. *Byzantine Aesthetics.* London, 1963.

Micheles, P. A. *An Aesthetic Approach to Byzantine Art.* London, 1955.

Thümmel, Hans Geory. *Bilderlehre und Bilderstreit: Arbeiten zur Auseinandersetzung über die Ikone und ihre Begründung, vornehmlich im 8. und 9. Jahrhundert.* Würzburg, 1991.

VICTOR V. BYCHKOV
Translated from Russian by Oleg V. Bychkov

C

CAGE, JOHN (1912–1992), American composer, writer, poet, and performance artist. Cage has in many ways defined what the musical avant-garde is in the twentieth century. His contributions to music have included the extension of percussive means (most notably the invention of the prepared piano), the development of new rhythmic configurations in composition, the early use of electronically processed sounds, and the early use of "aleatoric" or "chance" elements. He reworked the Dadaist event into an occasion specifically for and about music, which produced the musical happening and was a progenitor of performance art. His relentless interrogations of musical concepts and practices, his utopian proclamations about new ways of hearing sounds and the new and improved people who would inhabit those ears, his multimedia experiments with dance, theater, and electronics, his experiments with houses full of music, rooms full of disparate events, and operas full of television have been unbridled. He has influenced generations of artists, composers, dancers, poets, and performance artists—from Robert Rauschenberg and Jasper Johns in the 1940s, to Pierre Boulez in the 1950s and the Fluxus group of performance artists in the 1960s, and finally to a whole generation of postmodern artists and philosophers in the 1980s and 1990s. He is the inventor of the mesostic music/poem, a form that at its best can be compared to the literature of James Joyce and Ezra Pound. His writings combine everything from technical discussions of electronic instruments to disquisitions on Arnold Schoenberg and Erik Satie, Indian philosophy, mushrooms, abstract painters, Zen monks, and southern California.

Cage grew up primarily in Santa Monica, California, far from the grip of Europe. His father was an inventor, something Schoenberg famously attributed to Cage himself. After dropping out of Pomona College and studying architecture for one year in Paris, Cage decided in the 1930s to become a composer, first studying piano and composition with Adolph Weiss (a pupil of Schoenberg's) in New York City, and then studying music theory with Schoenberg himself. Schoenberg's exasperation (and fascination) with Cage was countered by Cage's lifelong admiration and condemnation of Schoenbergian high modernist principles of musical structure, expression, and compositional control.

Cage's music and poetry are an extreme example of that tendency in the avant-garde that aims for disturbance, dislocation, and the breakdown of structure. It is conceptual because it represents a game played with music and language that perforce stimulates thought about what music, language, and life are. In this, Cage's work takes after that of his mentor, Marcel Duchamp. But Cage's work is, unlike Duchamp's, utopian. It aims to remake the quality of life by remaking the quality and character of our relations to sounds and to words, as if changes wrought in these relations would stimulate overall changes in how we view ourselves, treat one another, and inhabit the world generally. Cage's art has as its goal liberation from compositional structure, expressiveness, and control in music, rather than construction of new and pristine structure. Its goal is freshness, or the natural, not the composed and the designed. Like the rest of the avant-garde, Cage's writings and music aim to clear away the rubble of past music; his practice aims to get one's ears to hear from scratch. Cage does not aim to *construct* a new way of hearing but to so totally destroy the old that our ears will be reborn anew. Thus reborn, our ears will interact with sound without any mediation of structure and interpretation whatsoever, thus being open to, in Cage's favorite formulation, "whatever happens to happen."

Cage's earliest published musical compositions from the mid-1940s exhibit the influence of Anton Webern in their rhythmic organization, density of phrasing, and obsessive use of variations, but by the late 1940s and early 1950s he had already introduced chance operations into his music. Based in the *Yi jing*, these operations allow for a compositional freedom that loosens (while not eradicating) the intentions of the performer, for insofar as the elements of music are composed "by chance," they are freed from the immediate authority of the composer and allowed to happen as they might happen. By blocking the full authority of the composer, Cage's intent is to cultivate in himself and others an openness to the free play of the world's sound events. This silencing of the composer, performer, and listener (again always partial, as Cage's presence, taste, and preferences for certain sounds over others were never wholly eradicated, nor could they be) was replaced by a training in finding a kind of beauty and interest in the most unlikely places, which comes from noninterfering, nonjudgmental attentiveness. Cage trained himself—very much in the manner of his Protestant minister grandfather—to come to terms with, if not "enjoy," many sounds that were initially distasteful to him.

The aesthetics residing in this activity is in many ways derived from Japan and India. Cage's sense of himself was of a Zen monk for whom the dropping of the urge to find and project meaning and hierarchy in life is intended to produce a special and wondrous state of being in the world, a state that Cage also liked to refer to as that of "Moksha." Moksha is the state of enlightenment described by the Indian philosopher Sankara, a state in which everything goes on as it normally would, but one's own relation to reality is that having one's "feet a little off the ground." Always searching for new perspectives on reality, Cage's works are meant to undercut fixed positions on reality (while also retaining those positions, since the extraordinary is ultimately dependent on the continuity of ordinary habits of mind and action). By silencing what Cage believed was the omnipotent claim of the philosopher and the composer to know and control reality, Cage wished not only to open that person up to the special state of being dependent on the raising of questions that have no answer; he also wished to raise questions about the possibility of alternative positions to be taken on reality. Like the classical skeptics of ancient Greece, Cage aimed through his inscrutable writings, musical performances, and poems to defeat the urge to know and control reality and to thereby open the mind and the ear to its vale of immersion. He considered his music a training in this, its most famous example being his "silent piece," *4′33″*.

First performed by David Tudor in Woodstock, New York in 1952, *4′33″* was inspired by an "artwork" by Robert Rauschenberg, who erased a fine drawing by Willem de Kooning (de Kooning agreed to this erasure on condition that it be a first-class work of his that would be erased). Similarly, *4′33″* "erases" music (or, as the French would say, places it sous-rature): it consists of four minutes and thirty-three seconds of silence. Its tripartite score simply blocks out three consecutive units of time, which are meant to be filled in by whatever happened to happen in the world of the audience at the time of the work's performance. A gesture of silencing the performer (who does nothing but turn the pages of the score), it is important that the performer be a pianist, that he or she be very good at playing musical notes; for then, like a good de Kooning drawing, the musician's gesture is truly one of dropping a practice that he or she has already mastered—of dropping it in the name of entering into a new relation to music and sound. In this breaking down of the very distinction between sound and music, what is at stake is the capacity to hear in a way that is open to the unexpected, the ordinary, the not so fancy.

What does this dropping of a practice "preach"? What is it meant to do? At its most radical, Cage's idea of dropping practices of musical performance in the name of openness to all sounds proposes that the ear no longer hear sounds according to principles that cause it to group sounds into music versus noise. Calling for a total dissolution of "fixations" on hearing structure, expression, and hierarchy in sounds, he wishes to free the ear from its mode of perceptual projection. In a set of inflammatory essays written in the 1950s and early 1960s, Cage proposed that we drop our entire mode of hearing. Needless to say, this radical proposal may be less than coherent, yet behind it is a rigorous examination of what the ear in fact does when it groups sounds into structural hierarchies, seeking expression in these and, in the right circumstances, interpreting them as musical works. In short, in calling for the liberation of the ear from music as we know it, Cage produced a philosophical analysis of musical perceptions and practices. By calling for their replacement, he raised the possibility of alternative ways to seek and inhabit: in this he is an avant-garde modernist. Perhaps the best way to take this questioning of musical possibilities is as a rhetorical call for the human ear to engage in a kind of training in nonhierarchical, nonstructural forms of musical attention in which all sounds are found of interest "as they are": a call that, in the best modernist sense, will see just how far the ear can go in this direction.

After his experiments of the 1950s, Cage's work gradually became more politicized. No longer satisfied to wage battles with Western music alone, no longer content to believe in the avant-garde dream that changes in our ears would bring changes in life overall, deeply moved by the political naturalism and anarchism of Henry David Thoreau, and believing Thoreau's adage that "the best communication between men happens in silence," Cage began to compose poems in a Thoreauvian vein. Again, his invention of new poetic forms was unbridled.

As in his musical works, the formal key to Cage's mesostics resides in his use of chance operations. In these poetic compositions, Cage operated on tones, producing highly arbitrary strings of words that occupy a given time segment. A computer program (designed by Andrew Culver and Jim Rosenberg) churned out from "source texts" (carefully chosen for their poetic and political character) vertical strings of words in capital letters. The actual compositions proceed horizontally across the page, where Cage himself composed the "wing words" from a pre-given stock. Cage then subjected himself to the following procedure: in a full mesostic, using the vertical string as a central axis of the horizontal composition, he disallows the repetition of the second capital letter in the intervening horizontal lowercase letters between any two successive capital letters.

The technique, again antihierarchical with respect to form, makes music by imposing rhythmical continuity much in the manner of twelve-tone composition, through restrictions on the stock of words (confined to the source texts) and on which letters can be used when. These works are theater pieces, meant to be heard in the mind's ear, or better, in performance. Their repetitions of words from his sources at odd, fortuitous places, combined with the continuity imposed by his compositional form, gradually serve to calm one's ears and open them to the play of conceptual suggestions that wind in and out of each other in a diffuse, amniotic ambience. The feeling is one of a forest of signs in a montage without master editing that cuts between world events, information circuits, philosophical snippets, modernist jokes, the blooming, buzzing eclogues of Joyce, and the ecologies of philosopher/naturalists. We do not fear this apparent defeat of perceptual knowledge, but rather welcome it.

Cage's mesostics are Thoreauvian in that they are meant to represent a kind of passive resistance to the domain of meaning, interventionist desire, and control. By producing a poetic ambience in which the listener must drop his or her desire to grasp overall meaning, Cage defeats the listener's desire for control. Instead, the listener is presented with a beautifully homogenized world of disparate events—events juxtaposed partly by chance and partly by Cage's own (highly tasteful) sense of rhythm, flow, and association. These events represent a world in which the listener's grandiosity is silenced, thus opening him up to its play. This noninterfering relation to a disparate world of events is in Cage's mind the symbol of relation to people that his texts (often from Thoreau and others) propose: a relation that respectfully noninterferes with a humanity of persons composed by their differences from one another, differences that cannot be ranked according to moral or conceptual hierarchies. Cage's refusal to impose musical hierarchies onto these events (unless one believes that his own rules are hierarchical) becomes the symbol of a refusal of the law generally—in short, of anarchism.

Indeed, Cage was a utopian anarchist in the best Thoreauvian sense: one who hated the imposition of governmental laws and believed in the self-generated hard work of becoming natural to oneself and open to the free play of others. Cage's goal, exemplified by his own serious yet open engagement with life, is to propose a world without overall hierarchies, yet one that also contains powerful values: "Permission granted, but not to do whatever you like." This would be a world in which differences are respected rather than legislated, yet no one gives in to a mindless pluralism that says that everything is as "good" as everything else. All must work to become themselves and attend to the intricacies of others.

Thus, Cage's ethics is closely connected to his aesthetics. One may well raise questions about his collapsing of attitudes of respect into attitudes of noninterference, and about his view that hierarchies should never obtain. His challenge to the hierarchical, however, wherever it may be found, and his beliefs in the blossoming of human difference and in an openness to multiperspectival positions on reality, have made him an important figure for postmodern art and

thought. Indeed, Cage shares with a number of poststructuralists a mentality that identifies conceptual determinations of all kinds (be they constitutional laws, moral rules, linguistic rules, social codes, or musical hierarchies) with processes of domination and constriction, a mentality that conversely celebrates indeterminacy, opacity, and the aesthetics of the sublime. Cage's avant-garde politics of resistance to determinate knowledge, social control, and human grandiosity through the opacities of art is widely admired by poststructuralist and postmodern thinkers alike—illustrating how widely held is the paradigmatically avant-garde belief in the political force of experimentalist art practice.

At its deepest level, Cage's notion of silence is spiritual: it represents Cage's own way of coming to terms with (his) human mortality. In describing his *4'33"*, John Cage said: "Life goes on very well without me, and that will explain to you my silent piece, *4'33"*". From the ethical standpoint, Cage's *4'33"* is a training in the fact that sounds, people, and events have a life independent of the self and will continue without one. The overcoming of a grandiose and frenetic desire for immortality manifested as control becomes the kingpin to opening the self to others—others who must now be found independent of the self, because the self can no longer treat the world as its mirror of eternity. Cage's ethics are thus both Buddhist and postmodern, befitting a man for whom the whole world is in play in his work.

[*See also* Aleatoric Processes; Modernism, *article on* Modern Music; Music, *historical overview article; and* Performance Art, *historical overview article.*]

BIBLIOGRAPHY

Works by Cage

Silence: Lectures and Writings. Middletown, Conn., 1961.
A Year from Monday. Middletown, Conn., 1967.
Empty Words: Writings, 1973–1978. Middletown, Conn., 1979.
X: Writings, 1979–1982. Middletown, Conn., 1983.
I/VI: Charles Eliot Norton Lectures. Cambridge, Mass., 1990.

Other Sources

Gena, Peter, and Jonathan Brent, eds. *A John Cage Reader.* New York, 1982.
Herwitz, Daniel. *Making Theory/Constructing Art: On the Authority of the Avant-Garde.* Chicago, 1993.
Perloff, Marjorie, and Charles Junkerman, eds. *John Cage: Composed in America.* Chicago, 1994.
Tomkins, Calvin. *The Bride and the Bachelors: Five Masters of the Avant-Garde.* Exp. ed. New York, 1976.

DANIEL HERWITZ

CAMP. Camp may look simple in comparison to other artistic and cultural forms because its materials come from the everyday world—the images, wigs, cosmetics, clothes, shoes, mascara, nail polish, labels, songs, fabrics, textures, and shapes of popular and high culture. But all of these have to be reworked and filtered through the camp sensibility so that the quality of camp in them can be discovered and seen. Indeed, the distinctively camp sensibility through which such forms are transmuted could only have emerged out of a complex history often glossed under the name of modernity. Camp is an artifact of that modernity, the doppelgänger of modernist high seriousness, responding to that earnestness by resurrecting artifice in place of art, and style in place of content. Historically specific, what this concept reveals is the essential historicity of aesthetic forms. The "conditions for the possibility" of camp are in essence as complex as those of modernity itself, requiring a fourth critique in the post-Kantian vein of this most un-Kantian sensibility. Let us call it the *Critique of Pure Camp*, or, more succinctly, the *Critique of Upper New York* as the territory of camp par excellence, and, appropriately, the place just below which camp received its first "serious" description in 1961 by Susan Sontag.

Camp is a way of life, a mode of embodiment in the modern world of consumeristic societies, a mode of arranging preferences, deploying tastes, making judgments, attaching oneself—or failing to—to others, perhaps a politics but certainly an aesthetics in the fullest sense of this word. Indeed, as a form of *Lebenskunsterism* propelled by an indifference to all norms of quality, in its love of the déclassé, the *ordinaire*, the exaggerated, and the awful, it matches the free thinking and free living spirit of a Don Giovanni, although, at the same time resolutely refusing his machismo in favor of a more "feminized" relation to shopping, tasting, sampling, and trying on. The proof of life, one might say, resides in the fact of *probare*: of trying things on—the wigs, dark glasses, and Mae West gestures, the bad movies, old costumes, and décolletage of an Andy Warhol turned aging French chanteuse (heard, of course, over the radio on dark nights in the cellars of New York). It is this transposition of the deep emotionality of the chanteuse into the pleasure of her voice, her dress, and her sagging face that converts the high seriousness of art into the pleasures of its camping double, just as Kantian morality becomes replaced in the world of camp by the taste for drag queens, overweight rock stars, and outrageous clothes purchased at outrageously discount—or, conversely, outrageously over-the-top—prices.

What is common to all these acts, things, and behaviors, what makes them camp in the first instance is the eradication of any traces of the "natural" in its broadest sense. Camp occludes those norms of the social world that have through time, training, and custom become "naturalized," the fetishization of capital that has taken on the appearance of the natural, and the inner instincts of love, work, and attachment that spontaneously arise in those who fall under the name of the human. These norms and instincts become for the camp sensibility the objects of displacement, the occasion for theatrical games that place them under suspension and replace them with a love of the low, the florid, and the playful. In a pre-postmodern vein, camp celebrates the simulacrum, runs riot with the fetish of capital by harping on its essential unnaturalness—exploiting the commodification of life in a Disneyland of the imagination. It turns its back on the very idea of authenticity, turning the avant-garde into an occasion for an all-night party where the "camper" can enjoy his or her private form of outrageousness. Instead of mourning the loss of reality, decrying the instrumentalism of consumer society, and lamenting the commodification of the subject, camp pushes these "evils" to their limits, embracing the idea of artifice and artificiality. I am only as good as my dye job, my liposuction, my manicure, my designer body, my plastic surgeon, my bank balance, and that's just fine. This is all that is worth seeing of me: the rest I consign to silence and the graveyard of gravity. Camp is a protection against the loss of a real life, a real family, real feelings, real community. Because these are also the losses that arise out of the process of urbanization, that are associated with big-city life and all its concomitant evils and pleasures, camp is essentially a first-world, big-city phenomenon. It is difficult to imagine a camp sensibility existing in the developing world, although many of its products—especially those produced for the tourist market—appear camp to first-world travelers. Camp is the silver lining in the cloud of modernity, the recipe for commuting modern disenchantment into fun and games. It is thus unthinkable apart from the fact of modernity.

The etymology of the term dates from the sixteenth-century English theater, where young men who wore the costumes of women in performance were described as "camping," and possibly also from the French word *campagne*, where theatrical troupes turning life on its head often performed. The term's subsequent history is obscure. What is clear is that by the early 1960s, when Susan Sontag's locus classicus "Notes on Camp" was written, it was already a term enjoying a certain urban vogue. In deference to the ephemeral quality of the concept (what Charles Baudelaire might see as one-half of its modern character), Sontag eschews the linear essay form in favor of fifty-eight remarks or "jottings" that attempt to outline camp as an aesthetic, a vision, a quality projected onto objects and characteristic of certain people, a behavior ("to camp" as verb), and a pattern of tastes. She outlines three aesthetic attitudes and places camp third, following on the sensibility of seriousness (which dominates traditional high culture) and that of "anguish, cruelty, derangement," which, according to her somewhat Ingmar Bergmanesque view, dominates modernism. The first sensibility offers for our enjoyment the successful fulfillment of its aims, which Sontag outlines as truth, beauty, and seriousness. On such a basis, we appraise and declare valuable such works as the paintings of Rembrandt van Rijn, the music of Wolfgang Amadeus Mozart, the sonnets of William Shakespeare, and all the great works of the classical canon that we cherish and adore and that are so difficult to turn into the objects of camping. The avant-garde, according to Sontag's (somewhat questionable) idea, rejects truth and beauty, but is valued for its very fragmentation of those ideals, and indeed for its violence, emotionality, and extremism (again, according to the Sontag of 1961). These two sensibilities—classical and avant-garde—are the stylistic conditions for the possibility for the emergence of camp. Camp does not engage in oppositional polemics against these other sensibilities (that would be an avant-garde stance) inasmuch as it offers an alternative of divine indifference to them: ignoring "both the harmonies of traditional seriousness, and the risks of fully identifying with extreme states of feeling" in favor of style and aestheticization (Sontag, 1966, p. 287). One could not understand the concept and phenomenon of camp without first having the former sensibilities in place.

The hallmarks of camp taste are those already touched on—a love of artifice, decoration, style, the objects of the visual world, exaggeration, role playing, the cult of the personality, and extravagance. The motivations for camp are as complex and overdetermined as are the societies that provide its mise-en-scène. For Sontag, "the relation between boredom and Camp taste cannot be overestimated" (ibid.). In a penetrating and original display of modernist sensibility directed toward the play that is camp, she describes camp as a "feat goaded on, in the last analysis, by the threat of boredom" (ibid.). Because to be bored implies a certain leisure and hence a certain degree of wealth, she concludes that camp only occurs in "societies or circles capable of experiencing the psychopathology of affluence" (ibid.). Writing years ahead of her time, she also recognizes in camp the implicit fact of an identity politics as yet unable to voice its name and speaks of camp's tendency to reverse classical and avant-garde norms and its excessive attachment to stylization as encoding the desire of certain groups for self-legitimization. A sensibility, Sontag notes, often performs this function (it is for this reason that one may speak of it as expressive). With its sense of theatricalization and play, camp is often seen as a gay (Sontag uses the term *homosexual*) sensibility—one that, in thumbing its nose at conventional morality, seeks to overcome the barriers of "the norm" and one that contains more than a hint of gender reversal and cross-dressing. Yet, despite its strong association with gay men, camp taste, she notes, is not equivalent to "gay taste" (first because there is no essentializable quantity, and second because the domain of the happy camper is a straight as well as a gay domain, just as it is both a male and a female one). Sontag also finds a surprising kind of humanity in the camp sensibility, a generosity and kindness toward the human condition that comes from its refusal of established hierarchies of taste and its love of the overlooked, the idiosyncratic, and the *ordinaire*. Indeed, Sontag insists that camp's nastiness (perhaps *bitchiness* is a more appropriate word) is

its mode of identification rather than high-handed (i.e., modernist) judgment: (people who share this sensibility are not laughing at the thing they label as "a camp," they are enjoying it. "Camp is a *tender* feeling" (Sontag, 1961, p. 292; emphasis in original). Here lies the difference between being camp and being dandyfied—a difference that Sontag begins briefly to outline ("the dandy was overbred. His posture was disdain or ennui") and that will be explored here in more detail.

The historical conditions that conspire to make camp possible, namely, those of modernity itself, must be taken more seriously than Sontag did. To glean this point, one should turn to the prefiguration of the camp sensibility in that artifact of nineteenth-century bourgeois consumerism—the dandy. Sontag describes camp as modernity's answer to the dandy. As prêt-à-porter clothing is the answer for the masses to the designer outfit, so the camp personality is a way to be a dandy in the "age of mass culture." In contrast, the dandy of the nineteenth century was a product of the elite, a man who, in Baudelaire's words, "has been brought up amid luxury and has been accustomed since his earliest days to the obedience of others" (Baudelaire, 1964). In this case, the use of the masculine pronoun to describe dandyism is intentional because the concept is strictly limited to men only; for, despite its emphasis on grooming and the toilette, on clothes, etiquette, self-presentation, the collection of beautiful objects, and the dedication to pleasure, leisure, and affairs of the heart, dandyism was for the hypermasculine, analogous to, in the words of Baudelaire, "the strictest monastic order" (ibid.). Despite attention to what might be considered the trivia of life, Baudelaire insists that dandyism was impelled by a need to fight and eradicate triviality. From this need, he argues, sprang the dandy's haughtiness, his rejection of the ordinary and the base, his love of the heroic gesture, and above all, his coldness: "Dandyism is a sunset: like the declining daystar it is without heat and full of melancholy" (ibid.).

In his contempt for the "vulgarity" of contemporary life, engendered by the Paris of the nineteenth century with its rising bourgeois class, its democratization of taste, and its creation of the spectacle of Parisian shopping and Parisian display, the dandy looked back to the past, even as far back as to the antique past of Julius Caesar, in order to invent a "new" aristocracy and lineage for himself. In its coldness, its love of a romantic invented past, its refusal to be defiled by the ordinary present, its exclusivity and dedication to privilege and the "duties" that attend such a station—in other words, in its absolute seriousness of purpose and refusal of astonishment—dandyism is the opposite of that camp sensibility so attuned to the contemporary world.

Whereas that other, more famous artifact of the Parisian boulevards, the flaneur, took pleasure in the forms of modern life by shopping, sampling, tasting, and enjoying the impressionist stream of modern humanity, while also poised to offer autonomous critique, the dandy retreated from this historically modern form of the deployment of taste and thought back to older, aristocratic forms of private collecting. No more perfect example of ressentiment toward this spectacle of democratized and commodified life offered by vulgarized (modern) Paris can be found than that of the brothers Edmond and Jules de Goncourt. Hybrid products of both the aristocracy and the bourgeoisie—a mother in one camp, a father in the other—Edmond and Jules took nostalgia to new heights with their desire to return to the "good old days" of Louis XV (1715–1774). The historian Deborah Silverman describes the brothers as "resentful and bitter children of the nineteenth century" who "considered themselves born too late to enjoy the effervescent leisure and langorous sensuality that noble elites had enjoyed during the era of the *fêtes galantes*" (Silverman, 1989). Determined to escape their historical fate, the Goncourts devoted themselves to collecting not only the art of the *fêtes galantes,* but also the minutiae of the period, so as to entirely surround themselves in its latent ambience and make their retreat to aristocratic private fantasy as complete as possible. They housed themselves and their memorabilia in a vast Parisian mansion, creating an eighteenth-century "world" where they could live "completely surrounded by vestiges of a lost aristocratic culture" (ibid.), like Elvis fans on the path to re-create the state of grace in Graceland. Here, as Edmond noted, he could "open his eyes not on the era I abhor, but on the era that is the object of my studies and the love of my life" (ibid.).

Although the Goncourts clearly would appear camp to anyone with a camp sensibility (as does Marcel Proust's Baron de Charlus with his aristocratic fragrance and personal flagrance), in their refusal of the ordinary, their cold aestheticism, and their contempt for the crowd (again, Charlus), the Goncourts sought to be the opposite of what after them became camp. Indeed, the camp sensibility, most clearly conceptualized vis-a-vis a family of interrelated yet distinctive concepts, might be called dandyism remade under the sign of middle-class consumerism, which permits the camper to sample, look, buy, and return, as well as to find, invent, and collect. Camp allies itself with vulgarity and hence with democracy and mass production commuted into style and the idosyncratic. In its fascination with the world of products, it allies itself with the flaneur, but in its refusal to be astonished by the values of the age and to submit to the flow of what is considered natural, it allies itself with the dandy. Indeed, the camper is a hybrid of these two historically given types and it is not fortuitous that although the origin of camp resides in the Parisian dandy, the apotheosis of the type is found in America, land of shopping and of the love of the low par excellence. Camp aims for reversal: the reversal of the values of high and low, straight and gay, male and female, sacred and profane,

beautiful and vulgar, eternal and momentary, and Parisians with a taste for reversal (if not for cross-dressing) tend either to remain dandies (of the Charlus type) or to fixate on the uncanniness of the *ordinaire* and become Surrealists. In its reversal of values, camp also has its cognate in the phenomenon of kitsch. Yet kitsch contains the message of genuine valuation, although through the medium of the tacky, the simulated, and the tasteless, whereas camp revels in precisely that tastelessness through which kitsch voices its genuine aspirations.

As Susan Sontag says, "the ultimate Camp statement: it's good because it's awful" (Sontag, 1961). For camp, culture is wonderful precisely because it can be regarded apart from all serious intention: as a world of products, detritus, and the florid. We are singing in the wasteland, and it is no accident that camp is deeply connected to certain regions of Pop Art as well as postmodernism, finding its apotheosis in the Andy Warhol persona for whom the museum was a mere prototype for the shopping center. As Bloomingdale's would replace the Museum of Modern Art, and the cult of the celebrity that of the artist, so Warhol would replace Proust, and camp, the dandy.

Essential to camp is pleasure taken in displacement: the displacement of good works into mere product values or floridated styles, of instincts into symptoms, of the erotic into the childlike, of the gay into the closet; for, if essential to camp is its refusal of the attitudes of seriousness and passion, it is natural that this refusal be overdetermined in Sigmund Freud's sense and the happy camper may be the one who is uncomfortable in his instincts, just as his predecessor the dandy was uncomfortable with being astonished by the spontaneity of the modern world. It is here, perhaps, that Sontag's combination of attraction and repulsion to camp ("I am strongly drawn to Camp, and almost as strongly offended by it") finds its origin. The dandy's prideful refusal or inability to abandon himself to the reception of life is met by the refusal or inability of the camp personality to submit to the flow of his own instincts. In his enjoyment of denigration can perhaps be seen either the traces of unconscious masochism or the projection of a debased self-image onto the world. The aesthetics of camp pleasure, therefore, contain a kernel of (perhaps unconscious) pain. From the point of view of commodities, the "Lebenscamper" no doubt exercises his or her free capacity for autonomy by taking pleasure in the fetish of capital. But this fetishization also has its roots in the camper's own fear of the world of real human identity residing below that of commodity. It is inevitable that the American camper of genius, Andy Warhol, remained aloof from sex and commitment behind the dark glasses of his camp-creative genius. One might ask: What kind of freedom is this? Put another way, one might ask whether, at the basis of camp, is not an underlying melodrama of the unexpressed person who cannot or will not allow "instincts" spontaneous flow or working through. Perhaps there is something in the contemporary thought that camp has been the vehicle for the expression of an otherness (in taste, sexual proclivity, or personal identity generally) that has been historically unable to speak its name. Although certain postmodern theorists of resistance have attempted to find in the camp sensibility a germ of resistance politics, it is evident that the pleasure camp takes in indifference to serious self-assertion precludes one's making too much of this thought. It is expressive, yet veiled. One might ask what kind of freedom there is even in that form of indirect self-gesturing. Enough to build a life on? That is a question on which a truly "post-Kantian" critique of campian freedom can be founded. What, in the end, is the aesthetics of freedom? Under what circumstances does style occlude rather than foster freedom, or the florid efface the spontaneous? Of course, in a high falsetto, or in a blond wig, or with an impatient flap of manicured nails, camp would consign this question to the dustbin of high seriousness.

[*See also* Kitsch.]

BIBLIOGRAPHY

Baudelaire, Charles. *The Painter of Modern Life and Other Essays.* Translated and edited by Jonathan Mayne. London, 1964.
Ross, Andrew. *No Respect: Intellectuals and Popular Culture.* New York and London, 1989.
Silverman, Deborah L. *Art Nouveau in Fin-de-Siècle France: Politics, Psychology, and Style.* Berkeley, 1989.
Sontag, Susan. *Against Interpretation and Other Essays.* New York, 1966.
Warhol, Andy. *The Philosophy of Andy Warhol: From A to B and Back Again.* New York, 1975.

LUCIA SAKS and DANIEL HERWITZ

CANON. [*To clarify the debate about canon formation (that is, the process of deciding which ideas and persons are central in the history of a particular discipline) and its critique in literary theory, aesthetics, and art history, this entry comprises three essays:*

Historical and Conceptual Overview
The Canon in Aesthetics
Politicizing the Canon in Art History

The first of these essays is an overview of the meaning and history of the concepts of "canon" and "canonicity" in Western culture; it also discusses canon formation in Western literature. The second essay examines the historical meaning and philosophical development of canon formation in aesthetics. The third essay critically analyzes the politics of canons, specifically in the context of art history. For related discussion, see Appreciation; Evaluation; *and* Feminism.]

Historical and Conceptual Overview

As applied to books, the word *canon* originates in patristic theology. It is nowadays most familiar as a critical and faintly polemical expression for the established literary classics, but that is a recent appropriation. The Greek *kanon* simply denotes the stem of a cane, hence a measuring stick. Its metaphoric application to ethics and religion antedates its use in aesthetics: canons of conduct precede canons of taste. In fact, its first literary application has nothing to do with literary judgment at all, but with the conviction that certain books supply infallible instruction in doctrine and deportment: they calibrate canons of orthodoxy. The Alexandrian theologian Origen used the word in the third century, and the maker of the Vulgate Bible, Jerome (finding it already latinized for other uses), adopted it in the fourth to designate that body of texts, uniquely authoritative in the community of Christian readers, that had come to be known as *ta Biblia*, a plural noun in Greek that, in response to the forces of canonicity itself, became singular and remained so in the modern languages, the Bible.

Strict Canons. The early employers of the word would have maintained that the "canonical" character of the biblical texts lay more in the visible reliability of their faith and morals than in some separate mystery or prestige deriving from their putative origin. But every reader of the Bible is aware that its obscurities and ambiguities make a certain amount of readerly goodwill compulsory. Hence, whatever the official, commonsense limitation of the idea of the "canonic" among patristic writers, it probably possessed, and was at any rate bound to acquire, the metaphysical associations that would convert it into a full-fledged concept of scripture—the concept, that is, of a limited inventory of texts, forever immune to alteration and enlargement, but inexhaustible in their aptness to their readers' lives. Obviously, the attribution of such authority, such a priori relevance, to any work of literature is not the legacy of common sense alone.

If the word *canonic* underwent an effortless semantic shift in the minds of the early Christian apologists, denoting first the substance and then the stature of the works it designated, with the noun *canon* in its literary sense naturally following, this was largely because a concept of established and exclusive scripture was already awaiting them in the deliberations of "the men of the Great Synagogue" (as they are called in early tractates of the Talmud), the Roman-age rabbinic arbiters of tradition who appraised the texts of Jewish history and wisdom to determine which could be said to "defile the hands"—their extraordinary phrase for characterizing a book sacred enough to be admitted into the canon of Torah. (This well-known Hebrew word, *Torah*, corresponds, though imperfectly, to the Greek word *nomos* and our word *law*, and there is certainly a link between the impulse to canonize the written word and legalism.)

In this pious milieu, the canonizing spirit was bred on a logocentrism well established in the Old Testament itself, in which hearing is the principal mode of cognition and iteration the formal, almost ritual, precursor of interpretation:

"And these words . . . shall be in thine heart: And thou shalt teach them diligently unto thy children, and shalt talk of them when thou sittest in thine house, and when thou walkest by the way, and when thou liest down, and when thou risest up. And thou shalt bind them for a sign upon thine hand, and they shall be as frontlets between thine eyes. And thou shalt write them upon the posts of thy house, and on thy gates" (Deut. 6.6-9). There seems to have been no question of pitting human judgment against divine, of delving skeptically into texts already widely venerated. The very first maxim of the *Pirke Abboth,* a tractate of the Mishnah (the great compendium of rabbinic jurisprudence and anecdote) that purports to record the sayings of the first postbiblical sages, counsels the interpreter to "build a fence around the Law." The rabbinic debates, of course, entailed the rejection of many candidates for sacred stature, but, insofar as one can eavesdrop on them, they are more striking for their gingerliness than their ferocity. What looks to us like a process of selection appeared to those engaged in it as one merely of confirmation. As in all legalisms, the decisions of the judges were represented as findings, that is, ratifications of incontrovertible precedents, and not as acts of inspiration in their own right.

The truly canonical tendency in any case does not wait for proof of plausibility from within the substance of a text: tests of consistency, relevance, even harmony with already accepted writings simply are not applied. The rabbis seem to have sought only the most outward signs of quality, that is, of divine complicity, in the texts handed down to them. Pedigree was assurance of character: here was the (supposed) work of Moses, easily admitted, and of David, whom God loved. Whatever they say, whatever their vagrancies and inconsistencies, they surely defile the hands. Here is the work of Solomon, another of the elect; it is a collection of love songs, apparently bare of religion and perhaps a bit profane, but its authorship is its security—and it defiles the hands.

Its very obsession with authority paradoxically leaves canonical intelligence with few means and little will to determine authenticity; and, as the passage cited earlier from Deuteronomy perhaps suggests, true canonicity more or less suppresses the distinction between the pure, devout rehearsal of a text and its interminable elucidation. Interpretation often entails heroic (skeptics would say delusional) feats of hearing. Every even faintly audible meaning is acknowledged to be fully there in the divinely inspired words themselves, so that, as the Talmud asserts, "Even the most newfangled interpretation uttered this very day by a gifted student in the presence of his teacher, even this was already confided to Moses on Mount Sinai."

The rabbis are circumspect about acknowledging the existence of so much as a debating point concerning the merits of a sacred text. At most, there is a dispute about whether any of their forebears harbored doubts. Thus Rabbi Aqiba

(later first, early second century) on the illuminating, limiting case of the Song of Songs:

> No man of Israel ever doubted that the Song of Songs defiles the hands. The whole world is not worth the day on which the Song of Songs was given to Israel, for all the scriptures are holy, but the Song of Songs is the Holy of Holies. . . .
> If the rest of the Torah [Aqiba said elsewhere] were to vanish, the Song of Songs alone would be sufficient to assure the salvation of Israel.   (Pope, 1977, pp. 19 and 92, adapted)

Aqiba's hyperbole is instructive: it is not enough to say that the confirmation of canonical judgments is not perfectly rational. It can be exultantly irrational, or, more exactly, perverse. The erotic and connubial poetry of the Song of Songs requires strenuous exegetical alignment with themes more suitable to scripture, yet the task of achieving this is not taken on grudgingly but as an exhilarating venture in its own right, an enthusiastic mission promising arcane rewards. The Song of Songs has always been the text of choice for Judeo-Christian mystics.

The net result of this process of canon formation (or confirmation) is always an austerely closed system, not airtight in reality, perhaps, given the wear and tear of history, but perceived to be that by its adherents. For the cosmopolitan Jews of later antiquity, acquainted with two cultures, that of Hebraic orthodoxy and that of Hellenic humanism, the seal around tradition that locks out the very idea of individual talent also accounts for the conviction of sacredness surrounding the words of scripture:

> [Unlike the Greeks, we Jews] have not an innumerable multitude of books among us, disagreeing from and contradicting one another, but only twenty-two books, which contain the records of all past times [and] which are justly believed to be divine. . . . during so many ages as have already passed, no one has been so bold as either to add anything to them or take anything from them, or to make any change in them; but it becomes natural to all Jews, immediately and from their very birth, to esteem those books to contain divine doctrines, and to persist in them, and, if occasion be, willingly to die for them. For it is no new thing for our captives, many of them in number, and frequently in time, to be seen to endure racks and deaths of all kinds upon the theatres, that they may not be obliged to say one word against our laws, and the records that contain them; whereas, there are none among the Greeks who would undergo the least harm on that account, no, nor in case all the writings that are among them were to be destroyed; for they take them to be such discourses as are framed agreeably to the inclinations of those that write them.
> (Flavius Josephus, *Against Apion,* 1.38ff., from the often reprinted William Wiston translation)

Josephus (a first-century Palestinian Jew writing in Rome) perhaps unwittingly identifies the pressure that canonicity places on an austerely finite body of texts to remain relevant through all the vicissitudes of history—through conquests, captivities, and dispersions—with their perceived divinity. This pressure is inherent in canonicity. It leads, first of all, to a reversal of the logic of relevance in which the contemporary comes to be associated with obscurity and drift, and antiquated words with intelligence and truth. (The habit of identifying chronological with intellectual priority eventually extends to traditions involving the rabbis themselves, so that greater inspiration is attributed to earlier Talmudic masters than to later.) Where the determination of relevance is less a matter of intuition than of authority, the density and semantic reach of scripture become impenetrable and impossible to traverse. Translation becomes not only treachery but sacrilege. Hence, those apologetic fables that mean to win safe passage for translations of scripture by suggesting that they too were made in heaven, like that which has the seventy sages who produced the Septuagint, the Greek Old Testament, arriving without collaboration at identical texts. (Nonetheless, at least one passage of Talmud does denounce the day on which the Septuagint was written as comparable to "the day on which the golden calf was made.") It is to be noted that translations of the Qur'ān that revere Islamic tradition are not normally offered as translations, but as "interpretations" or "explanations." The doctrine of the "inimitableness of the Qur'ān" demands such locutions.

Ultimately, canonicity is kabbalism (to name it after its most extravagant manifestation in medieval Judaism), the tendency to bestow authoritative meaning on every feature of the text, not only its intelligible substance but also (and perhaps especially) its physical accidents, its grammatology, its orthography, even its layout and calligraphy. In radical contrast to the mimetic idea of the poem or book that (the medieval recess excepted) has figured into every Western variant of canonicity since classical times, in which the priority of an object to its representation assures a certain metaphysical modesty in the latter, the kabbalistic book dominates and even engenders its own objects of representation. The rabbis maintained that the Torah was assembled before the world itself was made and provided God with a kind of memorandum for executing his creation—which therefore could not exhaust the connotations of that text. (Cf. the concluding image in the Gospel of John of a book too large for the world to hold.) In early Islam, the view that the Qur'ān was "uncreated" extended even to individual copies of the scripture, although, under these circumstances, "copies" is a misleading designation for what they are.

Western Canons. It is possible to read the main line of literary argument and apology in the West from Plato on as an attempt to preserve the idea of privileged or authoritative texts without succumbing to the legalism, not to say the misplaced, superstitious concreteness, of full-fledged canonicity. Nor would it be mere ingenuity or anachronism to see the origins and history of the idea of the literary classic this way. The point of examining strict, "religious" canonicity, in the context of literary theory, is to identify the characteristic forms that reverence for texts is bound to take, whether or not this reverence belongs to a larger system of orthodoxy.

Kabbalism precedes the actual establishment of scripture as an institution and readily exists in its absence: any text esteemed long enough—in any milieu—will acquire among its reverent readers a kind of surplus value that common-sense considerations of its wisdom or beauty cannot explain. Plato's numerous allusions to the baleful hold over the thinking of his contemporaries exerted by written, or by merely reified, language—such as the apothegms of sages and the unparsable formulaic compounds of heroic poetry—suggest his recognition of the kabbalizing process. Poetry is for Plato the model of all such overestimated language. But his famous insistence that the "the quarrel between poetry and philosophy is inveterate" (so that it is a great error, for instance, to attribute either general sagacity or specific nonliterary skills to Homer) belongs to a more comprehensive conviction in the philosopher that no "truth," once captive in a text, retains the *force* of truth.

For Plato, the poem does its mischief image by image, so to speak, strophe by strophe. As in the strictest canonicities, the energy of the part is in no way subdued to the consistency of the whole. This unliterary, nonaesthetic way of seeing the (albeit regrettable) efficacy of the poem in its vivid elements rather than in its intelligible totality makes Plato's entire account of poetry puzzling to readers used to thinking of poems as works of art, entities with a specifically aesthetic mode of being. That mode of being is essentially depicted by Aristotle in his *Poetics*, generally taken as a rejoinder to Plato. It was Aristotle who first thought it worth mentioning that "poems have beginnings, middles and ends" (1450b); for the meaning of a literary work resides in its limited wholeness, in the sequence of its episodes and the integrity of its manner, and it is this wholeness that assures that the *mimēsis* of poetry will be "more philosophic than history."

Where the phenomena of canonicity are concerned, this conception of the poem as a well-ordered and harmonious artifact simultaneously consolidates its sovereignty and narrows it, limiting but at the same time complicating its way of making sense and turning the test of consistency (to which strict canonicity is utterly indifferent) into the first principle of "proper" reading. The despotic authority of the strictly canonical text is transformed into the more tractable rule of a constitutional monarch. (Nonetheless, just because of its newfound semantic plenitude, the classical text remains almost as untranslatable as the canonic.) In classical criticism from Aristotle through Horace, and ever after where classical ideas of the literary work of art prevail, this treaty that reduces both a text's authority and a reader's liberty expresses the latter's reward for his restraint under the term "pleasure." Poetry, according to Horace, has the twofold function of edifying and delighting (*prodesse et delectare*).

But the relationship between these two is not adventitious. Early in his *Poetics* (1448b), Aristotle draws a connection between a natural human delight in *mimēsis*, "representation," and its role in the process of understanding. As Samuel Johnson renders the idea in the eighteenth century, poetry instructs *by* pleasing. It is possible to understand this formula as a repudiation of legalism without a corollary repudiation of textual authority itself.

In theory, then, the literary classic system of Western humanism is a highly attenuated canonicity at best. Individual talent contends more or less freely with tradition in an effort to wedge its way in, and tradition, though dilatory, makes a place for it. The finite semiotic domain of the work of art humanizes it: humans may be ironic and ambiguous but (unlike the deity) they are not infinitely polysemous. Yet the human "author" possesses scant authority: in strict canonicity, discovering authorial (i.e., divine) intention is the final object of all exegesis, and it is to be found everywhere, even where common sense does not detect it. In the classic system, there has always been some version of the doctrine of "intentional fallacy," a caution against being guided by an author's own account of his meaning and a license, where the momentum of interpretation requires it, to reject intention blithely.

But, in reality, any system of literature, however dynamic its checks and balances, will always be devolving toward simple canonicity. The mere act of viewing texts as meritorious pretty much assures this, even if every provision is made to moderate their glamour. Authority is normally greater than the sum of its justifying merits, a commonplace fact that the finiteness of our power of attention perhaps makes inevitable. We see a little and we credit more; and sometimes (because there is an educational function at work here) we see nothing, being not yet trained to see, but do not turn away. For every canonicity, believing is at least as important as seeing. The limiting case that proves this truth is to be found in the canon of some secular savant— Karl Marx, say, or Sigmund Freud—which presumably attains its stature as a result of demonstrable intellectual merit but can also end up the scripture of an orthodoxy, with the master's words hearkened with prosthetic keenness. It is then assumed that, for any present question, these words set down in the receding past will divulge an almost preternatural freshness—if only one pores over them and patiently canvasses their intention. This intention, in turn, takes a privileged place among the answers pondered, so that the question itself is more likely to be revised than the canonical answer repudiated. Such an interpreter is perfectly able to acknowledge that he is following a fallible human author whose conclusions may demand revision, but he will all the same extend him the surplus of attention we observers of strict canonicities recognize as religious, permitting revision only when more devout measures undeniably fail.

This is not to say that the election of texts to a given canon is philosophically or aesthetically capricious: what we have learned to call the great books mostly are great books, and, for that matter, the books included in the biblical canon tend to be finer and deeper poetry than the myriad pseudepigrapha left out. But, whatever the actual intelligence and witting or unwitting taste of those who establish canons, the newcomer to these texts first experiences the arbitrariness of their choice, and one's progress in reading consists essentially in learning to justify what one has already more or less faithfully accepted. In many circles of contemporary literary thought, the subtle element of coercion in this process has come to overshadow its potential for edification or pleasure.

[*See also* Literature, *article on* Literary Aesthetics.]

BIBLIOGRAPHY

Ackroyd, P. R., and C. F. Evans, eds. *The Cambridge History of the Bible*, vol. 1, *From the Beginnings to Jerome*. Cambridge, 1970.

Auerbach, Erich. *Literary Language and Its Public in Late Latin Antiquity and the Early Middle Ages*. Translated by Ralph Manheim. Reprint, Princeton, N.J., 1993.

Barthes, Roland. *The Rustle of Language*. Translated by Richard Howard. New York, 1986.

Bloom, Harold. *The Western Canon: The Books and School of the Ages*. New York, 1994.

Bourdieu, Pierre. *The Field of Cultural Production: Essays on Art and Literature*. Edited by Randal Johnson. New York, 1993.

Fishbane, Michael. *Biblical Interpretation in Ancient Israel*. Oxford, 1985.

Kermode, Frank. *The Classic: Literary Images of Permanence and Change*. New York, 1975.

Pope, Marvin H. *The Anchor Bible: Song of Songs*. Garden City, N.Y., 1977.

Russell, D. A., and M. Winterbottom, eds. *Ancient Literary Criticism: The Principal Texts in New Translations*. Oxford, 1972.

Smith, Barbara Herrnstein. *Contingencies of Value: Alternative Perspectives for Critical Theory*. Cambridge, Mass., 1988.

Thomas, Rosalind. *Literacy and Orality in Ancient Greece*. Cambridge and New York, 1992.

Urbach, Ephraim E. *The Sages: Their Concepts and Beliefs*. Translated by Israel Abrahams. Reprint, Cambridge, Mass., 1987.

von Grunebaum, Gustave E. *Medieval Islam*. 2d ed. Chicago, 1953.

Weber, Max. "The Chinese Literati." In *From Max Weber: Essays in Sociology,* translated and edited by Hans H. Gerth and C. Wright Mills, pp. 416–444. New York and Oxford, 1946.

Wimsatt, William K., and Cleanth Brooks. *Literary Criticism: A Short History*. New York, 1957; reprint, Chicago, 1978.

RICHARD TRISTMAN

The Canon in Aesthetics

When one speaks of "the canon," one refers to a group or set of works—either objects or performances—that function canonically for an art (or other field of endeavor). Things must be something more than models to function canonically; they must not just set but be the standard; that is, canonical works are celebrated not just for satisfying standards that are abstracted from particular objects, but for their particular embodiment of the kind of value quintessentially achievable in their art.

Why a Canon? Why such individualized standards? The necessity that some objects function canonically emerges from the conception of aesthetic value as it has been understood since the eighteenth century. The idea—which pervades thinking about art—is that aesthetic evaluation resists being abstracted from particularized responses to exceptional works because each such work uniquely originates its aesthetic goodness. Evidently, when rules of artistic production are generalized from canonical works of art, they never enjoy the stature and influence that pertain to their source.

Over the past three hundred years, the conviction has grown that one cannot effectively derive informative rules or principles of aesthetic value, nor generalize instructively, even from exemplary art. In this regard, the influence of the eighteenth-century philosophers David Hume and Immanuel Kant remains strong. Hume's account of how we standards for taste are established identifies the approbation of certain individual works, such as those by Homer, as the locus of the most stable agreements in taste. Although Kant insists that a beautiful work of art, the product of genius, must be regarded as the instantiation of a rule, he warns that this kind of rule cannot be stated.

On this conception of aesthetic value, ostension is more effective than abstraction in conveying aesthetic standards. Consequently, works so celebrated they are canonical command the attention of much analytic and appreciative scholarship about the arts. For even if no generalized description of aesthetic goodness can be made convincing, by conversing about the singular works in the canon we at least come to see what makes for goodness in particular objects.

Canonical objects accomplish this not by modeling how other works should look (each should be unique) but instead by modeling how we should look at other works; that is, the eye or ear or sensibility of the prospective connoisseur is cultivated by exposure to art that the admiration of previous generations of connoisseurs has marked as canonical. But even if the epistemic structure of aesthetic valuation calls for a canon and thereby justifies there being one, this kind of consideration may not extend to justifying the selection of canonical objects. Thus, we should ask both what the canon is and what we would do without it.

What Is a Canon? At most times and places in the history of almost all the arts, and of some other disciplines as well, a canon exists and is cherished for representing the solid core of work that centers activity in the field. For example, the philosophical canon is the set of works accepted as establishing the core questions with which philosophers engage. As such, the philosophical canon demarcates the boundaries within which that pursuit may be conducted. Indeed, the definitiveness of canonical works is evidenced by how tenaciously they are positioned, for changing interests in any field dominated by a canon usually are accommodated by reinterpreting rather than replacing the canon's core works.

The canon also can be the list of books or objects accepted as genuine. An often-cited pre-eighteenth-century canon is the writings the church recognizes as the books of the Bible and the inscriptions of saints. These texts bear the power of the spirits of their authors. Later, the genuine products of any artist came to be regarded as that person's canon. In this usage, canonical objects must reach beyond themselves to their originators for their authority. Nevertheless, how the object itself is configured mainly establishes its connection to its external source.

Although the object may need to be the authentic expression of an admired individual to qualify as canonical, its authenticity is recognized by scrutinizing its internal features. In the mid-nineteenth century, for example, works were assigned to the African-American canon in virtue of being the artistic products of African Americans; yet, throughout this period it has been analyses of these works themselves—for instance, the detection of exalted characters ennobled through suffering—that has authenticated them. Subsequently, diction—the transliteration of African-American dialect—became the mark expected in works that authentically expressed the black perspective.

The canon is emblematic not merely of authority but of the authoritative weight of the past. Infused by tradition, the canon often shapes norms and so becomes the vehicle for shared culture. In its more prominent manifestations, the canon does not merely inspire attention. Rather, it comes to command where attention is directed.

To illustrate, a painting expelled from the canon of Rembrandt van Rijn's work no longer will be included in studies of his art; and objects that diverge too extremely from those that form the artistic canons are not perceived to be art at all. This result obtains because the canon is a collective that is more than a casual or serendipitous batch of exemplary items, so the members of a canon must somehow be linked.

Building a Canon. That the canon is conceived as an intelligibly coherent collection of singular objects presses the question of what bonds or links its constituents one to another. Artists undoubtedly energize the canon by taking the esteemed works of earlier ages for their models. How canon formation unfolds thus is influenced by how artists choose the models they emulate. But the canon's components are not determined solely by them. As often as recognition by successors propels an artist's oeuvre into the canon, equally often successors are stimulated to surpassing work as a response to the work of already established canonical predecessors.

This is the case in the great art traditions of both the East and the West, where aesthetic evaluation is mediated through histories structured by the dynamic links between canonical predecessors and innovative successors (Silvers, 1991). The most familiar approach to canon formation thus is to embed canonical works within a theoretical frame of dynamic artistic development and attempt to explain how the accomplishments of each canonical work enable or stimulate the achievements of its successors.

From the requirements of coherent collectivity emerges a constraint on the degree of distinctiveness compatible with canonicity. Innovative objects tend toward incongruity and so are disruptive of developmental progressions and of other devices that make collections cohere. Objects so singular as to be idiosyncratic thereby resist being incorporated into the canon. The very logic of canon formation consequently denies whatever does not correlate or otherwise link in some evident way with the preexisting constituents of the canon. (Works that explicitly repudiate their predecessors cannot help but refer to them; in so doing, they sometimes connect themselves to securely canonical works importantly enough to be embraced by the canon themselves.)

Self-Defeating Canons. Hence, two competing notions struggling for dominance infuse canon formation. One is an emphasis on the singularity attained by each canonical work as it uniquely composes its own aesthetic value. But the other casts the canon as a collective. Under this second aspect, the canon may bar objects too much unlike their predecessors precisely because of their singularity.

The benefits of the canon thus are volatile. The canon stabilizes discourses that otherwise might be fragmented by how significantly their singular subjects diverge from one another. But the canon also has the potential to immobilize discourse. If the stability of the canon becomes an end in itself rather than merely a means for securing common reference, canonical models are apt to be used to homogenize the objects that the discourse addresses and thus to stifle innovation.

In this event, canonical force may devolve from sustaining aesthetic perception to controlling it. There are circumstances in which the canon's substance undoubtedly comes to be felt to weigh in as oppressively heavy. If the set of canonical works becomes too fixed, offering no room for originality or growth, the canon becomes self-defeating because it no longer effectively facilitates discourse about objects that are original in their achievement of value.

Within any discourse addressing an art, the positive contributions of appeals to canons tend to wax and wane cyclically. A discourse too fluid to be conclusive likely improves as it is secured by an enduring canon. So too has the growing accord in regard to the African-American canon advanced the level of dialogue in African-American criticism. Yet, a discourse so static that most questions are closed likely suffers from the domination of an immutable canon, like the neo-Aristotelian criticism that is fused to antique models.

Dysfunctional Canons. But there are other ways that a canon's functionality can deteriorate. The most important, because most familiar, is that it comes to be regarded as primarily ideological and as securing references that are partial or biased or obscure rather than equitably common and accessible. For instance, Elaine Showalter writes (1990): "Canon-formation . . . is now understood as a historically grounded process, rather than an assertion of aesthetic value. . . . Canon-formation is an aspect of the power of critical discourses and institutions. . . . We cannot expect that women's writing will make an impact on the canon on its own." Showalter holds that canons emerge and change through the exercise of competing groups' interests. "We will never abolish canons," she says, but we can demystify "their pretenses to be absolute and permanent monuments of greatness." We can reveal "their material contexts and circumstances, and the 'social and historical relativity of aesthetic standards.'"

Similarly, Linda Nochlin argues (1988) that how women must be represented for a painting to be canonical is the consequence of patriarchal ideology. Laura Mulvey (1975) believes that because prevailing social ideologies construct the standpoints that cinema imposes on its viewers, female viewers of canonical films are forced into watching them with the gazes of men.

Now no doubt the canon will for the most part be found to be aligned in some way with whatever constitutes the dominant social and political ideology. This may reflect nothing more than that the works that it comprises are suffused with the cultural climate in which they originated. That most works acknowledge moral or social values acknowledged to some degree is to be expected because art cannot be totally divorced from the conditions of its creation, but this does not entail the social determinism that sees art as always promoting the values of its originating culture.

Framing this debate is the question of how canons are formed. Is it for aesthetic or for ideological reasons that works collect into a canon? Do works become canonical because they support certain social and political values, or instead are those social and political values elevated by being read into previously canonized works?

Robert Lecker's (1990) analysis of the creation of the Canadian literary canon is typical of accounts that view the canon as determined by nonaesthetic self-interests. Describing the Canadian canon that has evolved over the past four decades as "the product of academics who have worked with publishers to create the Canadian literature industry," Lecker portrays it as a concept that

has been transmitted in works of Canadian criticism that promote the idea of coherence by arguing the validity of tradition, influence, pattern, or literary solidarity among authors of different eras. Such criticism imagines a unified view of Canadian literature as the reflection of a unified country. . . . the dream of national unity remains the driving force behind the literary and critical values we . . . support. . . . We create the canon in order to embody a vision of something larger we want to sustain.

In contrast, David Perkins (1992) argues that aesthetic value must be prior to ideology in canon formation because works that equally express the ideas common to their shared cultural venue nevertheless are not uniformly canonical. Perkins observes: "Goethe was ideologically appropriated by different groups, but he was already canonical in the first important history of German literature by Gervinus. . . . Hohendahl explains the ideological functions Gervinus made Goethe serve. He does not have to explain why Gervinus cast Goethe, rather than some other writer, in the important role" (1992).

How There Can Be Canons. The question, then, is not whether canonical art is ideological, but whether it is nothing more than ideological; for, if there is some respect in which canon formation remains independent of nonaesthetic interests, then the constituents of the canon need not be creatures of ideology, however much they serve as vehicles for it. Hume is perhaps the best-known proponent of the philosophical view that casts the canon as a tool for enabling a natural process of valuation that transcends ideological differences.

Writing in the eighteenth century, in an age that relativized the value of art to the diverse responses of observers, Hume appeals to "the relation, which nature has placed between the form and the sentiment" and famously comments:

> We shall be able to ascertain its influence not so much from the operation of each particular beauty, as from the durable admiration which attends these works, that have survived all the caprices of mode and fashion, all the mistakes of ignorance and envy. The same HOMER, who pleased at ATHENS and ROME two thousand years ago, is still admired at PARIS and LONDON. All the changes of climate, government, religion, and language, have not been able to obscure his glory. Authority or prejudice may give a temporary vogue to a bad poet . . . but his reputation will never be durable or general. . . . On the contrary, a real genius, the longer his works endure, and the more wide they are spread, the more sincere is the admiration which he meets with.   (1994)

Hume here voices the theme with which the eighteenth century marked aesthetics. An artwork becomes canonical in recognition of the cumulative evidence of its broad innate ability to elicit approbation across time and different cultural venues. It is a natural attractiveness sufficiently compelling to defy the vagaries of social custom that qualifies objects as canonical.

But to naturalize the process of selecting canonical objects is not to naturalize the canon itself. What determines that

there is a canon is not what determines the content of the canon. Hume did not confuse these issues, nor should we.

Ours is by no means the first age to be destabilized by the increasing prominence of multicultural diversity. In the eighteenth century, a similar phenomenon—a flourishing engagement with non-European art—accentuated the fragility of the familiar idea of beauty. (It is at this time that the idea of Western culture as a distinct type appears.) To bolster the stability of a public sphere engaged with aesthetic value, eighteenth-century convention fashioned an instructive set of models drawn from antiquity, namely, a classical Western canon.

Hume thought that time's test was evidence that the models that constitute this canon surface as a result of a natural, and thereby culturally neutral, process. He saw the canon as an artifact, but as one that can underwrite the possibility of aesthetic discourse because it is powered by the natural operation of taste. But Hume did not imagine that art could level all personal and cultural difference. Disparities in the life experiences of audience members, and in their religious and moral allegiances, result in some insuperable differences in the art that appeals to different types of people, he thinks.

Can There Be No Canons? We are left to weigh whether to follow Hume in conducting discussions about art as if some works at least possess the broad appeal to level social differences. Crucial to Hume's strategy is his depiction of canonical works as empowered by taste to prevail over cultural division. Unlike Hume, E. D. Hirsch (1987) does not suppose the objects that have commanded the most enduring attention to be intrinsically deserving of it. They are merely the random beneficiaries of indiscriminate historical processes.

Hirsch has proposed fortifying the public sphere by compiling a list of familiar artifacts that are to be studied in all schools in order to anchor cultural literacy and advance social solidarity. He takes the objects he selects to have come into prominence as objects of cultural veneration almost accidentally and for nonaesthetic reasons. But absent a coherent appeal to some principle that linked these one to another, Hirsch's choices have had little impact.

Robert von Hallberg (1983) warns: "There is a danger of academic critics overestimating their own importance . . . in the process of canon-formation and wrongly thinking they can dispense with canons. . . . The prospect of teaching art without canons—quite different from that of teaching a critical approach to canons— . . . is not altogether encouraging." Von Hallberg reminds us that a matter of art—namely, artists' choices of those predecessors they strive to surpass—creates the traditions that inform canons: "that the emulation of Callimachus by Virgil and Horace can be fully explicated by social analysis or that Manet's allusions to Velasquez were politically motivated."

It is in the nature of canons to invite one to attend to some objects rather than to others. If one comes to regard this selection as inescapably privileging some group's interests over others rather than as transcending these, chasms appear in the ground canons afford aesthetic discourse. It is no longer common and accessible, and so canons become dysfunctional. Believing that canons cannot help but represent divisive and repressive practice, some commentators—notably, Showalter in literary theory and Griselda Pollock in art history—urge abandoning them altogether.

Lucian Krukowski (1991) sees the choice as follows: "An autonomist aesthetic, . . . that sees much of its task as the culling out of masterpieces from the commonality of artworks, could come to be regarded as atavistic, unworkable, and—even—undemocratic. A contextualist might argue that when artworks lose their individual ambitions for immortality, they have more of a collective chance at being noticed in the present."

In this event, the discourse becomes infused by political concerns, both those seen as controlling it and those seen as repressed by it. Critical discourse then replaces art as the object of its own attention and, in doing so, jettisons more than just canons; for the very notion that artworks originate their own value must also be abandoned, to be replaced by a view of art as aggregate rather than individualized, and by an aesthetic discourse standardized by general principles rather than centered by singular models. Ironically, it is precisely to avoid this tyranny of abstraction that canons rather than rules have been adopted as the embodiment of aesthetic standards.

Also ironically, exploding canons may not liberate even those thought to have been most victimized by the prevailing system. Speaking in defense of attempts to define a black American canon, Henry Louis Gates, Jr. (1992) observes: "we can and must cite (a black text) within its own tradition. . . . For anyone to deny us the right to engage in attempts to constitute ourselves as discursive subjects is for them to engage in the double privileging of categories that happen to be preconstituted." This suggests that to be inclusive of diverse cultural traditions, it is more effective to forge canons than to flee from them.

[*See also* Hume; *and* Kant.]

BIBLIOGRAPHY

Gates, Henry Louis, Jr. *Loose Canons: Notes on the Culture Wars.* New York and Oxford, 1992.

Hirsch, E.D., Jr. *Cultural Literacy: What Every American Needs to Know.* New York, 1987.

Hohendahl, Peter Uwe. *Building a National Literature: The Case of Germany, 1830–1870.* Translated by Renate Baron Franciscono. Ithaca, N.Y., 1989.

Hume, David "Of the Standard of Taste." In *Art and Its Significance: An Anthology of Aesthetic Theory,* edited by Stephen David Ross. Albany, N.Y., 1994.

Krukowski, Lucian. "Contextualism and Autonomy in Aesthetics." In *Cultural Literacy and Arts Education,* edited by Ralph A. Smith, Urbana, Ill., 1991.

Lecker, Robert. "The Canonization of Canadian Literature: An Inquiry into Value. Response to Frank Davey." *Critical Inquiry* 16.3 (Spring 1990): 656–689.

Mulvey, Laura. "Visual Pleasure and Narrative Cinema." *Screen* 16.3 (Autumn 1975): 6–18.

Nochlin, Linda. *Women, Art, and Power and Other Essays.* New York, 1988.

Parker, Rozika, and Griselda Pollock. *Old Mistresses: Women, Art, and Ideology.* New York, 1981.

Perkins, David. *Is Literary History Possible?* Baltimore, 1992.

Showalter, Elaine. "Feminism and Literature." In *Literary Theory Today,* edited by Peter Collier and Helga Geyer-Ryan. Ithaca, N.Y., 1990.

Silvers, Anita. "The Story of Art Is the Test of Time." *Journal of Aesthetics and Art Criticism* 49.3 (Summer 1991): 211–224.

von Hallberg, Robert. Introduction to issue on the topic "Canons." *Critical Inquiry* 10.1 (September 1983). See also the essays in this issue.

ANITA SILVERS

Politicizing the Canon in Art History

The canon of artists and works around which the history of art is organized could be said to represent some of the discipline's most deeply naturalized assumptions. Questions regarding the purpose and function of privileging certain artists and works are rarely raised. Others concerning the esteem in which the canon is held are not regarded as belonging to art history but rather to aesthetics, a branch of philosophy, or to the criticism of contemporary art. For the most part, art history's disciplinary work is carried on as if there were no need to articulate the social function it is supposed to serve. The discipline's promotion and support of the canon is all too often taken for granted. It is as if a consensus had been arrived at sometime in the past so that there is no further need for discussion. The problem, it seems, is that somehow the notion of "quality," that most subjective of judgments, is thought to be self-evident and unquestionable. As it stands now, the history of art could be described as an unacknowledged paean of praise addressed to the canon, and the intensity of this devotion can, perhaps, be measured by the sobriety of the professorial demeanor with which this task is accomplished.

The conviction underlying these attitudes is a commitment to tradition. The canon of artists and works discussed in art-history courses are those that were found meritorious by previous generations of scholars responding to historical situations very different from those of the present. Like Mount Everest, the works, the artists, and even the methodologies for interpreting them are simply there, and like mountain climbers, it is the mandate of art historians to climb their peaks and sing their praises to future generations. In doing so, they are often unwittingly engaged in the unthinking reproduction of culture: reproducing knowledge, but not necessarily producing it. As a consequence,

CANON: Politicizing the Canon in Art History　**339**

the discipline as a whole becomes a powerful conservative force in a rapidly changing society.

One way to speculate about how this disciplinary moment was reached might be to recall the values that inform the work of two of the most influential art historians of this century, Erwin Panofsky and Ernst Gombrich. Both of them advise the historian to steer clear of a consideration of the historian's role in the promotion and perpetuation of the received canon of Western art. Panofsky's reticence about the larger cultural function of history, his reluctance to articulate the concerns that animate his scholarly work, as well as his conception of history as a positivistic discipline, find their theoretical justification in "The History of Art as a Humanistic Discipline" of 1940. In this reflective essay, Panofsky suggests that the historian is involved in two very different types of activity. In responding to the work of art (which is defined as a "man-made object demanding to be experienced aesthetically"), the art historian must both "re-create" the work by attempting to intuit the artistic "intentions" that went into its creation and then submit it to archaeological investigation. The aesthetic re-creation of the work is deemed to depend "not only on the natural sensitivity and visual training of the spectator, but also on his cultural equipment." The difference between a naive beholder and an art historian is the fact that the latter is aware of his cultural predispositions; that is, he is aware of the contemporary perspective he brings to the work of interpretation as a consequence of belonging to a culture different from the one under investigation, whereas the naive beholder is not. The point of the historian's awareness of his own cultural values is not to acknowledge them as part of the historical narrative that will result as a consequence of his engagement with the past, not to understand that whatever he comes up with will inevitably be filtered through the peculiar configuration of his own subjectivity, but rather to suppress or eliminate all aspects of his approach to the study of the past that might result from his participation in the historical horizon to which he belongs. It is by means of his knowledge of the past that the historian is to control, if not to extirpate altogether, the affective and valuational baggage he brought to the enterprise in the first place. The goal is to be as "objective" as possible.

Panofsky's equation of canonical value with traditional value was espoused and supported by Ernst Gombrich, arguably the other most influential art historian of this century. It is because art historians are the custodians of this tradition that they can be distinguished from social scientists, who approach works of art as part of the material of culture. In a lecture titled "Art History and the Social Sciences" of 1973, Gombrich took it upon himself to defend art history's preoccupation with a canon of works that had been recognized as "great" against those who advocated the study of works of art as cultural artifacts. He argued that

whereas the study of historical circumstance would significantly affect our appreciation of the art of the past, it was no substitute for the connoisseur's capacity to discern "quality." For Gombrich, the canon

> offers points of reference, standards of excellence which we cannot level down without losing direction. Which particular peaks, or which individual achievements we select for this role may be a matter of choice, but we could not make such a choice if there really were no peaks but only shifting dunes. . . . the values of the canon are too deeply embedded in the totality of our civilization for them to be discussed in isolation. (1975)

What was it that led art historians such as Panofsky and Gombrich to dismiss any discussion of the cultural qualities of exceptional works of art on the basis that they were self-evident? What supported their belief that artistic merit was universally discernible? The unstated assumption underlying their position regarding what constitutes the canonical status of a work of art would appear to be a universalist theory of aesthetics.

According to the theory of aesthetics formulated by Immanuel Kant in the late eighteenth century, certain works of art had the capacity to provoke a universal recognition of their extraordinary quality. The existence of the beautiful was thus something located in the human response to objects rather than in the objects themselves. By making the capacity to recognize artistic quality part of the definition of "human nature," Kant's theory offered a basis for the identification of canonical status with the judgment of tradition. Both Panofsky and Gombrich belong to the humanist tradition of which Kant's theory is a part; that is, they share the faith that "human nature" affords human beings an adequate epistemological foundation on which to understand both the world and "man's" place within it. It is for this reason that it is possible for them to reassert that the artistic quality of certain cultural artifacts is "self-evident."

The humanist conception of human subjectivity as something stable, continuous, autonomous, and not liable to modulation according to circumstances of time and place has undergone devastating criticism in this century. Psychoanalysis, for example, has tended to emphasize the contingency of the subject. According to Jacques Lacan, the subject is split on the acquisition of language into that which represents the desires and drives of a preconscious (the unconscious) and that which represents the codes and conventions that govern social life (the symbolic). On this account, subjectivity is shifting and unstable, constantly under revision as the relation between the unconscious and the social is renegotiated in the light of the ever-changing circumstances of everyday life. This view of the subject clearly militates against the concept of "human nature," against the assumption that all human beings could ever react in the same way toward anything, let alone works of art. One of the most powerful critiques of Kant's aesthetic theory has been mounted by the Marxist sociologist Pierre Bourdieu, who used the concept of class to show that the location of individuals in the social hierarchy is crucial in determining their response to works of art.

Panofsky's attempt to naturalize the concept of artistic quality and Gombrich's claim that quality is one of the implicit value judgments that make up our civilization were never completely convincing. Not only is the validity of such positions questionable in the light of contemporary theory, but they were also challenged within the historical horizon in which they were enunciated. It was not until the advent of feminism, however, that the equation of the art-historical canon with tradition received a lasting challenge. More than any other historian or critic, it was Linda Nochlin in her famous piece "Why Have There Been No Great Women Artists?" (1971) who placed the issue of artistic merit squarely in the foreground of the discipline's attention. She showed just how unsatisfactory the concept of tradition was to a definition of the canonical status of a work of art, by underscoring the extent to which a putative *master*piece serves to articulate and support a hierarchy between the sexes. The equation of artistic merit with tradition honored the cultural achievements of men because social forces prevented women from participating fully in the processes of artistic production. Rather than attempt to insert women into a canon that had been constructed on the basis of their exclusion, subsequent feminist critics demanded its complete destruction. Writing in the context of poststructuralism, Griselda Pollock (1988) used semiotics and the work of Michel Foucault to argue that art history was a discursive practice, a form of making meaning that was imbued with the attitudes of those—namely, men—who as the dominant gender had inaugurated and supported it as a cultural institution. Her conclusion was that feminist scholarship no longer had a place within art history as it had traditionally been defined.

The consequences of poststructuralist theory for the art-historical canon, in particular the necessity of recognizing that the work of the historian—the historical text—is inevitably colored by the writer's position in history and culture, has also been recognized by many. If art history is regarded as a discursive practice, a socially sanctioned form of making cultural meaning, then it is susceptible to the type of textual analysis known as deconstruction. Jacques Derrida has shown that language is involved in a game of absent presence, that it serves to confer ontological status on what is otherwise only an unstable and shifting system of signs that draw their meaning not from their capacity to refer to objects in the world, but rather from the cultural attitudes with which they are invested by their users. The cultural category "art" and the discursive practice "art history" are social constructs rather than eternal constants in the history of civilization.

Once the concept of tradition has been shown to be historically compromised, laden with the cultural attitudes of a particular historical moment, as feminist critics have shown, and once every attempt to make textual meaning has been shown to be less about the world and more about the projection of authorial bias and prejudice as well as insight and understanding, then it seems clear that art historians must address the question of why they believe that the works they discuss are worth talking about. Once there is no longer anything self-evident about the status of the works that are the focus of art-historical attention, it is necessary to argue for the choice of certain works rather than others. The subjective attitudes and cultural aspirations of the art historian become just as important an aspect of the narrative as the works that are its object. Instead of history used to buttress the existence of a traditional canon, instead of the historical imagination made to serve the status quo, a politicized canon can be used to destabilize and call into question the assumptions and prejudices of that culture by insisting on their contingency and relativity.

Rather than legitimating a preestablished canon of artists and works following the principle of "objectivity," historians might pursue their own agendas and articulate their own motives for engaging in the process of finding cultural meaning in the art of the past. Instead of regarding the subject of art history as fixed and unchanging, scholars have an opportunity to define what that subject might be. In doing so, they can display rather than conceal the cultural issues that preoccupy them. The subject of art history thus becomes manifestly an allegory of the historical circumstances that have both shaped and empowered the subjectivity of the author. Because the cultural codes and conventions that serve to define individual subjectivity also enable it to participate in social life, because the subject is both constituted by and constituting of the circumstances in which he or she exists, the historian can play an active role in the creation and transformation of culture. The recognition that the canon is politicized does not assume that the historian's motives are transparently accessible, but rather, within the context of psychological and ideological determination, it insists on the author's powers of agency to articulate and promote political agendas that are relevant to the cultural circumstances in which he or she is located.

[*See also* Politics and Aesthetics.]

BIBLIOGRAPHY

Alpers, Svetlana. "Is Art History?" *Daedalus* 106.1 (Winter 1977): 1–13.

Barzman, Karen-Edis. "Beyond the Canon: Feminists, Post-modernism, and the History of Art." *Journal of Aesthetics and Art Criticism* 52.3 (Summer 1994): 327–339.

Bourdieu, Pierre. *Distinction: A Social Critique of the Judgement of Taste.* Translated by Richard Nice. Cambridge, Mass., 1984.

Gombrich, E. H. *Art History and the Social Sciences: The Romanes Lecture for 1973.* Oxford, 1975.

Kant, Immanuel. *Critique of Judgement.* Translated by James Creed Meredith. Oxford, 1952.

Lacan, Jacques. "The Agency of the Better in the Unconscious, or Reason since Freud" In *Écrits: A Selection,* translated by Alan Sheridan, pp. 146–178. New York, 1977.

Lacan, Jacques. "The Mirror Stage as Formative of the Function of the I." In *Écrits: A Selection,* translated by Alan Sheridan, pp. 1–7. New York, 1977.

Nochlin, Linda. "Why Have There Been No Great Women Artists?" *Art News* 59 (1971): 23–39, 67–69.

Panofsky, Erwin. "The History of Art as a Humanistic Discipline" (1940). In *Meaning in the Visual Arts,* pp. 1–25. Garden City, N.Y., 1955; reprint, Chicago, 1982.

Pollock, Griselda. "Feminist Interventions in the Histories of Art: An Introduction." In *Vision and Difference: Femininity, Feminism, and Histories of Art,* pp. 1–17. London and New York, 1988.

Preziosi, Donald. *Rethinking Art History: Meditations on a Coy Science.* New Haven, 1989.

Rifkin, Adrian. "Art's Histories." In *The New Art History,* edited by A. L. Rees and Frances Borzello, pp. 157–163. London, 1986.

Steinberg, Leo. "Objectivity and the Shrinking Self." *Daedalus* 98.3 (Summer 1969): 824–826.

KEITH MOXEY

CARIBBEAN AESTHETICS. Defining concepts such as "aesthetics," "aesthetic expression," "artist," and "work of art" within the socioeconomic contexts of the Caribbean is extremely problematic for several reasons. First, owing to the fact that efforts to distinguish the area from the rest of the world have been quite recent, these concepts, which traditionally suggest a universality consistent with eighteenth- and nineteenth-century philosophy, are infrequent in Caribbean discourse. Caribbean discourse, not organized until well into the twentieth century, tends to refer more to politically and socially committed terms, such as "culture," "cultural expression," "cultural identity," "sociocultural system," and, more recently, even "Caribbeanness," a concept with nationalistic aspirations that claims for the area a cultural identity and a socioeconomic matrix—the slave plantation—that are more or less shared. Second, one must bear in mind that whatever method is used to study the area as a whole, the end results will always be subject to dispute, because it is impossible to delineate exactly the boundaries of the Caribbean.

If one takes into account physical geography, the area would be composed of the territories bordering the Caribbean Sea, excluding those regions facing the Gulf of Mexico, as well as the Bahamas, Barbados, Guyana, Cayenne, and Surinam, nations that are customarily considered Caribbean; on the other hand, Honduras, Nicaragua, Costa Rica, and Panama, which are usually seen as Central American nations, would be included. Under a socioeconomic criterion, the Caribbean could be studied in terms of Plantation America, namely, the parts of the American continent where a slave plantation economy was developed. If one were to follow this criterion strictly, the Caribbean would include, apart from the Antilles, a large portion of the United States and Brazil, as well as the coastal regions of the north of South America and the west of the former viceroyalty of Peru.

Even if this criterion were discarded and the Caribbean were reduced to a more manageable area—for example, the Antilles—other problems would always remain. For instance, were one to opt for identifying the territories of the archipelago starting from the presence of a common nationalism, it would be shown straightaway that the population lacks a Caribbean national conscience. For most Caribbeans, the region appears fragmented in linguistic blocs that reflect the different colonial powers that imposed their rule in the area: Spain, England, France, and Holland, among others. Neither is it feasible to find an ethnological pattern common to all the territories. Although Amerindians, Europeans, Africans, and Asians converged in the region, their territorial distribution was uneven. Thus, granting the difficulty in establishing precisely the geographic, national, socioeconomic, and ethnological borders of the area, one must see concepts such as "Caribbean culture" and "Caribbeanness" as being in perpetual oscillation and shift. Thus, the complexity of the Caribbean sociocultural system presents an enormous challenge for the researcher, because its dynamics are interconnected with macrofactors such as the Conquest and European colonization, the history of the Atlantic economy, the implementation of the plantation system, the importing of African slaves, the hiring of Asian labor, resistance to assimilation, armed and civil struggles for independence, the cultural influence of the United States, and others. This complexity accounts for the fact that the development process of Caribbean culture has been studied through different perspectives, each of them emphasizing terms such as criollization, indigenization, transculturation, *mestizaje, marronage,* fusion, resistance, deculturation, assimilation, acculturation, shock, confrontation, encounter, penetration, interaction, dialectic, symbiosis, osmosis, miscegenation, and interplay. Naturally, many of these concepts are usually used for the purpose of caricaturing the culture of the area.

History of Ideas of Caribbean Culture. The earliest relevant attempts to define a West Indian culture occurred in the 1930s and 1940s, and all shared the desire to underscore the importance that the African cultural legacy assumed in the area. These efforts were influenced by events that transpired in large part out of the region: among them, the upsurge of popularity of African art in Europe, the ideas of Leo Frobenius and Oswald Spengler, the emergence of black nationalism in the United States, the works of the Harlem Renaissance authors, the Africanist agenda of the Jamaican Marcus Garvey (which was also promoted from New York's Harlem), and the impact of Surrealism.

In the Caribbean, where the predominant population has always been black and mulatto, looking to Africa served practical ends: first, it helped liberate blacks from the feeling of uprootedness and cultural inferiority with which slavery marked them, and provided them with an ethnological fatherland abroad (following the "Back to Africa" doctrine espoused by Garvey); second, the feeling of cultural pride helped the black masses to extricate themselves from political and social passivity demanded by colonial rule (the negritude movement organized by the Martinican Aimé Césaire); or rather, in the case of Haiti, it contributed to the reinterpretation of the national culture by exalting the old African traditions preserved by the peasantry (Jean Price-Mars). Moreover, in Hispanic nations such as Cuba, the Dominican Republic, and Puerto Rico, where blacks were a minority subjected to discrimination, Africanist consciousness led to the development of a new strain of nationalism that sought to place whites, blacks, and mulattos on equal footing under the symbols of the nation (the *afrocubanismo* of Fernando Ortiz; the *negrista* poetry of Luis Palés Matos, Nicolás Guillén, Manuel del Cabral, and others). The fact that the cultural discourse of the Caribbean has been founded on such strategies has had crucial importance. Although nowadays the identity of the Caribbean peoples is defined as the product of a violent and problematic encounter of cultural components from Europe, Africa, Asia, and Indoamerica, the cultural presence of Africa in the region is considered decisive (C. L. R. James, Edward [Kamau] Brathwaite, Rex Nettleford, George Lamming).

It would be well to add that, seen from the present-day perspective, these early attempts to define the culture of the region, although useful in manifesting a Caribbean discourse, started from more or less reductionist criteria. In general, such efforts resulted in one or several of the following: disparagement of the contributions of Indoamerica and Asia (India, China, Java, etc.); a tendency to define the different cultures of Africa and Europe in terms of unity; predictions about the upsurge of "African civilization" and the decline of "Western civilization" (Oswald Spengler); description of the Caribbean culture as neo-African (Janheinz Jahn, 1961); from the most radical stances of negritude, manipulation of the notions of culture, race, and power; the argument that the "European culture" and the "African culture," through the process of criollization or *mestizaje,* had crystallized into a stable synthesis, or were on the verge of achieving it (the idea of a mulatto culture, espoused by Guillén); as a means of departing from negritude, embracing of Afro-Caribbean beliefs as a foundation on which to build the so-called *realismo maravilloso* or magic realism (Alejo Carpentier, Jacques Stéphen Alexis). Subsequently, as anthropological discourse passed through the age of decolonization and structural analysis, it became fairly common to define the cultural field of the area in terms of binary oppositions, such as dominant culture/dominated culture, popular culture/elitist culture, culture of the colonizer/culture of the colonized, dependent culture/sovereign culture, and so forth (Frantz Fanon). Moreover, the systemic method of analysis, adopted with nationalistic goals, defined the culture of the Caribbean as "new," granted that, given the rapid disappearance of the aborigine, the men and women who arrived on these islands and produced, through the process of criollization, the national cultures of the countries in the area, were "new."

In the last two decades, Caribbean discourse, influenced by postmodernity, has turned less Manichaean and more self-conscious as a discourse (Wilson Harris, Edouard Glissant, Antonio Benítez-Rojo). The matter of identifying a priori the boundaries of the area would not constitute a serious problem today. From the new perspective, Caribbean culture would transcend the boundaries of both the Caribbean Sea and Plantation America. Rather, it would constitute a permanently open macrosystem whose origins would be irrecoverable, for they are wide-ranging, scattered spatially and temporally throughout Europe, America, Africa, and Asia. Thus, postmodern researchers will tend to study Caribbean culture by starting from the observation of certain correlations or patterns that repeat here and there, preferably in popular culture, in a assemblage of cases whose universe from the start they consider unknown. Additionally, they will have to discard certain models, methods, or interpretations that took their cue from Western historicism (those of G. W. F. Hegel, or Karl Marx), replacing them with narratives such as myth and the novel (Harris, Glissant), thereby compensating for the loss of the past suffered by the collective memory of the region's peoples. Postmodern researchers would likewise reject the ideas of "unity," "center," "homogeneity," "synthesis," "stability," "coherence," and so on. For postmodern researchers, the cultural system of the Caribbean would be acentric, heteroclite, unstable, ambivalent when not paradoxical, and in a constant state of flux and transformation; it would be, above all, carnivalesque. Such researchers would naturally reject the probability that the sociocultural system has ever achieved synthesis or that it is headed toward attaining it; in sum, they would be inclined to see the system as a turbulent interplay of coexistent differences (Glissant, Benítez-Rojo).

Nevertheless, although the postmodern perspective is serviceable for the purpose of dismantling the old absolutes, binary dialectics, and other devices through which Caribbean culture could not reveal its ambiguities and complexities, this perspective in turn imposes limits. For instance, the discourse of postmodernity and that of modernity both intend to be scientific (ethnocentric), excluding beliefs, myths, and other folk traditions from their respective systems of thought, an exclusion that disclaims the authority of "narrative" knowledge (Jean-François Lyotard) on which certain Caribbean societies depend to a great extent. In any case, although the most important researchers and writers set out to cease echoing in their works the victor/victim paradigm characteristic of negritude, they endeavor to construct a kind of local postmodernity whose discourse refers more to the differences of the collective Caribbean entity than to its similarities, more to the future than to the past, more to experimental creation and performance than to the Idea and the work of art consecrated by Western tradition.

Cultural Expressions in Caribbean Culture. The most important cultural expressions in the Caribbean belong to the performing arts. Creole music and dances, formed from an interplay of European and African elements, reached Spain as early as the latter half of the sixteenth century, and were commented on by Lope de Vega, Miguel de Cervantes, and other writers. The Inquisition denounced these popular dances, and the latter wound up being prohibited in that they were seen as indecent—particularly the *zarabanda*—and instigative of public disorder. Subsequently, creole dances and songs were described by Jean-Baptiste Labat and M. L. E. Moreau de Saint-Méry, as well as other travelers from the seventeenth, eighteenth, and nineteenth centuries. In their observations, all agreed on several points: the importance of percussion, the great variety of drums, the complexity of rhythms, the sensuality of the dances, the antiphonal song, the participation of blacks and whites of different social classes, and the collective and public nature of said expressions. Given that these observations still maintain their validity, especially during carnival, we can take them as constants for defining Caribbean performing arts. In any event, the variety of creole musical forms is striking. Some musical genres of today already existed in old forms three hundred years ago. Labat spoke of the *merengue* in Saint Domingue, the *beguine* in Martinique, and celebrates the *calypso*s of Trinidad, Jamaica, Saint Lucia, Antigua, Dominica, and Guyana. In the last fifty years, Cuba alone has produced the *danza cubana*, the *habanera*, three kinds of *rumba*, the *danzón*, the *son*, the *guaracha*, the *guajira*, several types of *bolero*, the *conga*, the *mambo*, the *cha-cha-cha*, and the groundwork for *salsa* and so-called Latin jazz. Other genres enjoying great popularity are *reggae* (Jamaica), the *plena* (Puerto Rico), the *cumbia* (Colombia), the *joropo* (Venezuela), and the Dominican *merengue*.

The literary arts also have great importance in the region. Afro-Caribbean oral literature includes myths, folktales, proverbs, jokes, and spells. Among the most often mentioned folktales are the stories of Anancy (a spider man) and Jicotea (a turtle man), which find their respective referents in West African cultures. Written literature embraces all genres and has attained unique forms in the *marvelous realism*, or *magic realism* novel, and in Afro-Caribbean rhythm poetry. Despite its being a new literature, taken as a whole it is one of the most notable in the world today; the works of Gabriel García Márquez and Dereck Walcott have earned the Nobel prize. In the visual arts, the Caribbean has been typified by the production of popular painting (Haiti), wood carvings (Jamaica), and by the sculpture, painting, and engraving of Caribbean themes (Cuba, Colombia, Venezuela, Puerto Rico).

Since the 1930s, the extraordinary importance of rhythm in Caribbean music—and by extension, in dance, song, and poetry—has been stressed time and again. Thus, within Caribbean discourse, the aesthetic experience would derive mainly from rhythm as an aesthetic object. Although in past decades it was usually said that the rhythmic complexity of Caribbean music descended from Africa, this is a mere simplification. Certainly, one might state that the polymetrics and polyrhythm in African music passed to the Caribbean, but one could also assert that many of the characteristics of Caribbean rhythms—their combinations and permutations, their percussive timbre, their proclivity for improvisation, their integration into melodic and harmonic patterns, and their interrelationship with dance—are not mere copies of African models. Actually, the rhythmic system of the Caribbean is the fruit of a never-ending process of criollization involving the interaction of elements from Africa, Europe, and most recently, the Far East, the Middle East, South America, and the United States. Regardless, in the Caribbean it is useful not to separate entirely the profane rhythms and dances from the sacred ones, the latter meaning those ritual rhythms and dances observing Afro-Caribbean beliefs such as voodoo and *petro* (Haiti), *santería*, the *palo mayombe* and *aradá* cults (Cuba), *pocomania* and the *rastafari* cult (Jamaica), the *María Lionza* cult (Venezuela), and others. In these rhythms, generally played by sacred drums, the cultural presence of Africa is much greater than those of profane music. Their aesthetic value would lie in creating in the dancers a particular state of mind (ecstasy) from which one makes contact with the gods (possession). Bearing in mind that in certain Caribbean societies there is a connection between the sacred and the profane—a link observed by researchers such as Fernando Ortiz, Alfred Métraux, Janheinz Jahn, Katherine Dunham, and others—one must not rule out the possibility that the spiritual uplift that the Caribbean peoples experience when dancing to profane music has some roots in the ecstasy induced by sacred rhythms. Dunham, after dancing the Haitian *yambalou*, states: "We danced, not as people dance in the *houngfor*—voodoo temple—with the stress of possession or the escapism of hypnosis or for catharsis, but as I imagine dance must have been executed when body and being were more united, when form and flow and personal ecstasy became an exaltation of a superior state of thing, not necessarily a ritual to any one superior being" (1983). This author is of the opinion that the Caribbean aesthetic experience derives not only from the relationship of dance with the rhythmic play of percussion; underlying both would be a type of metarhythm to which all things Caribbean would point; that is, music, dance, theater, literature, the visual arts, cuisine, speech, belief, manner of walking, and even the Caribbean body and psyche themselves as a collective being. This metarhythm—the fluid rhythm of Caribbeanness in continual transformation— would emanate from the interplay of ethnological, economic, social, and political dynamics that converged and continue to converge in the region.

[*See also* African Aesthetics; Comparative Aesthetics; Cultural Studies; Latin American Aesthetics; *and* Postcolonialism.]

BIBLIOGRAPHY

Alexis, Jacques Stéphen. "Du réalisme merveilleux des Haïtiens." *Présence Africaine* 8 (1956).

Ballagas, Emilio, ed. "Situación de la poesía Afro-Americana." *Revista Cubana* 21 (1946).

Benítez-Rojo, Antonio. *The Repeating Island: The Caribbean and the Postmodern Perspective*. Durham, N.C., 1992.

Bernabé, Jean, Patrick Chamoiseau, and Raphael Confiant. "In Praise of Creoleness." *Callaloo* 13 (1990).

Brathwaite, Edward Kamau. *Contradictory Omens: Cultural Diversity and Integration in the Caribbean*. Mona, Jamaica, 1974.

Brathwaite, Edward Kamau. *History of the Voice: The Development of Nation Language in Anglophone Caribbean Poetry*. London, 1984.

Cabrera, Lydia. *El monte*. 4th ed. Miami, 1975.

Carpentier, Alejo. "Prólogo." In *El reino de este mundo*. Mexico City, 1949.

Césaire, Aimé. *Discours sur le colonialisme*. 4th ed. Paris, 1955.

Coulthart, G. R. *Race and Colour in Caribbean Literature*. New York and Oxford, 1962.

Crahan, Margaret E., and Franklin W. Knight, eds. *Africa and the Caribbean: The Legacies of a Link*. Baltimore, 1979.

Dash, Michael. "Marvelous Realism: The Way Out of Negritude." *Black Images* 3.1 (1974).

Depestre, René. *Bonjour et adieu à la négritude*. Paris, 1980.

Dunham, Katherine. *Dances of Haiti*. Los Angeles, 1983.

Fanon, Frantz. *The Wretched of the Earth*. Translated by Constance Farrington. New York, 1963.

Fanon, Frantz. *Black Skin, White Masks*. Translated by Charles Lam Markmann. New York, 1967.

Glissant, Edouard. *Caribbean Discourse: Selected Essays*. Translated by J. Michael Dash. Charlottesville, Va., 1989.

Glissant, Edouard. *Poétique de la relation*. Paris, 1990.

Guillén, Nicolás. *Songoro cosongo: Poemas mulatos*. Havana, 1931.

Harris, Wilson. *Tradition, the Writer, and Society*. London, 1967.

Harris, Wilson. *Explorations: A Selection of Talks and Interviews, 1966–1981*. Edited by Hena Maes-Jelinek. Aarhus, Denmark, 1981.

Harris, Wilson. *The Womb of Space: The Cross-Cultural Imagination*. Wesport, Conn., 1983.

Horowitz, Michael M., ed. *Peoples and Cultures of the Caribbean*. Garden City, N.Y., 1971.

Jahn, Janheinz. *Muntu: An Outline of the New African Culture*. Translated by Marjorie Grene. New York, 1961.

James, C. L. R. *Beyond a Boundary*. London, 1963.

Knight, Franklin W. *The Caribbean: The Genesis of a Fragmented Nationalism*. New York and Oxford, 1978.

Lamming, George. "The Role of the Intellectual in the Caribbean." *Cimarrón* 1 (1985).

Mintz, Sidney W. "The Caribbean as a Socio-Cultural Area." *Cahiers d'histoire mondiale* 4 (1966).

Métraux, Alfred. *Voodoo in Haiti*. Translated by Hugo Charteris. Reprint, London, 1972.

Nettleford, Rex. *Caribbean Cultural Identity: The Case of Jamaica*. Los Angeles, 1979.

Ortiz, Fernando. *Contrapunteo cubano del tabaco y el azúcar*. Havana, 1940.

Ortiz, Fernando. *La africania de la música folklórica de Cuba*. Havana, 1950.

Ortiz, Fernando. *Los bailes y el teatro de los negros en el folklore de Cuba*. Havana, 1951.

Price-Mars, Jean. *Ainsi parla l'oncle*. Port-au-Prince, 1928.

Ramchand, Kenneth. *Introduction to the Study of West Indian Literature*. London, 1976.

Williams, Eric. *From Columbus to Castro: The History of the Caribbean, 1492–1969*. New York, 1970.

ANTONIO BENÍTEZ-ROJO
Translated from Spanish by R. Kelly Washbourne

CARICATURE. Caricature is as old as art itself, but was theorized as an aesthetic category from the eighteenth century onward, with the advent of the philosophical and artistic interest in physiognomy, character types, and theories of the passions. First defined as the exaggeration of physical or moral traits for comic, especially satirical, effect (the term, from the Italian *caricare,* to charge or load, dates from the late sixteenth century), it was viewed as a category of the genres and styles it violated, notably portraiture (see, for example, William Hogarth's 1743 engraving *Characters and Caricaturas*). This ambiguous relation with the norm it seeks to surpass accounts for the extraordinary influence of caricature on the development of modern art, and for the central role it came to play as a theoretical model for art in general. Maintaining a likeness while simultaneously deforming it, preserving in its distortion the very object it attacks, caricature occupies a special place in the vanguard of artistic change, providing in a single image both the dominant standard and the means by which that standard is questioned, transgressed, and reformed (compare the role of parody in literary history). It is a revolutionary art, necessarily bound to the system it overthrows, and regenerating it from within, providing viewers with the conceptual means by which to discern and interpret the new.

In social and political terms, caricature responded to the same circumstances that favored the development, during the same period, of that other quintessentially modern genre, the realist novel, and, like this, first flourished in England: an educated middle class, independent of the nobility and the monarchy alike, committed to the concept of the individual, enjoying relative political freedom and economic autonomy, and interested in the representation, here in the satirical mode, of its own experience—political personalities, topical events, and contemporary social types and practices.

In philosophical terms, the theorization and defense of irony and the grotesque carried out in the German Romantic tradition (Karl Friedrich Flögel, Christoph Wieland, Friedrich Schlegel, Jean-Paul Richter) as part of the larger discussion of the sublime (Immanuel Kant, Friedrich von

CARICATURE.   Grandville [Jean-Ignace-Isidore Gérard], *"A quoi bon la personne?"* (*"Why do we need a human person?"*), lithograph from the series "Une Autre Monde" (1844). (Courtesy of Michele Hannoosh.)

Schiller), and in response to the aesthetics of neoclassicism, included caricature in its sphere. In particular, German philosophy brought out (1) the social equalization that caricature effects (in ridiculing the powerful, for example), (2) its moral utility (in presenting an image of our own potential ugliness), and (3) the subjectivity of the laughter it provokes, dependent on the disposition of the laughter. In France, the association of Romanticism with revolution (social, political, and aesthetic) extended to caricature too, investing it with a subversive and transformative power. An art that, in its very form, takes liberties with authority, caricature had indeed played a major part in the French Revolution; this role would increase in the nineteenth century, with the easy availability of inexpensive prints and the widespread distribution of illustrated periodicals. Political caricature was one of the fundamental issues of the 1830 revolution, and became, during the early years of the July Monarchy, the main expression of opposition, with the brilliant productions of Honoré Daumier, Jean Ignace Grandville, Charles Joseph Traviès, and others in the weekly pages of *La caricature*.

The most important formulation of the specific link between caricature and modernity came from the poet and critic Charles Baudelaire. In his three essays on the subject—*De l'essence du rire et généralement du comique dans les arts plastiques* (1855), *Quelques caricaturistes français,* and *Quelques caricaturistes éstrangers* (1857)—he offered the first sustained defense of the value of caricature as a serious art, worthy of study in its own right, at a time when it was considered a minor genre, as impermanent as the events it chronicled. In so doing, he developed not only an aesthetic of caricature, but also a "caricatural" aesthetic—of beauty in "ugliness," the monstrous, satanic, violent, and grotesque, the ironical, farcical, and sinister—which defined his conception of modernity and of an art of modern life, the special beauty, sublimity, and heroism of contemporary experience.

For Baudelaire, caricature, like the laughter it inspires, is dual and contradictory, a sign of both superiority and inferiority: superior to the object it satirizes, inferior in its ugliness and deformity; a mirror that distorts, sending back an image at once laughable and troublingly recognizable, through which we come to know ourselves as *other,* as both "superior," confident subject and "inferior," ridiculous object; an image of vice and folly that produces pleasure and delight, an image of beauty in ugliness, a true *fleur du mal.* From the tension, the "clash" or *choc* of the two, springs the ambiguous convulsion that is laughter, expressing both pleasure and unease, an affirmation of the self and an apprehension of a threat to the self—an idea developed later, in a different context, by Sigmund Freud.

The dualism of caricature thus ensures a reversal in its effect, converting, in Baudelaire's theological metaphor, the products of the Fall (laughter, caricature, the comic) into the means of redemption, ugliness into beauty, the ephemeral into the eternal, the particular into the universal, the phenomenal into the ideal. The dualism, division, and isolation of the self can be transcended precisely through self-conscious, "comic" *doubling,* by knowingly creating an image of ignorance to bring others to a consciousness of dualism too. Moreover, the experience of caricature inescapably entails reflexivity and reciprocity, the implication of those who laugh in their own laughter.

Inspired by the work of Daumier, Baudelaire associates caricature specifically with the modern city, "terrifying, grotesque, sinister, and farcical," in all its "fantastic and gripping reality." The Baudelairean city is indeed the space of the comic and caricatural, demonic and infernal, the degradation of a mythical eternal paradise into a place of filth, stench, and noise, in incessant flux, a place of disorder and incongruity, inhabited by eccentric, freakish figures. Like caricature, the city is dual and contradictory, inspiring in the *flâneur,* the emblematic urban stroller who roams its streets, a sense of both isolation from, and communion with, the crowd, both anxiety and pleasure, confusion and limitless meaning. Moreover, Baudelaire's notion of the reversible, reciprocal effect of caricature applies to the *flâneur* as well: moving through the city, imaginatively becoming each person and object encountered, the *flâneur* is at once self and other, spectator and spectacle, gazing out onto the world and reflecting it back, an image of and for the crowd. The "caricatural" city performs the function of caricature itself, presenting the *flâneur* with an image of "inferiority," of one's status as an object, implicated in the same experience one might seem to control.

For Baudelaire, the *flâneur* represents the experience of the modern individual, and the caricatural city the poetics of modernity. The aesthetic of modernity formulated in *Le peintre de la vie moderne* (1863)—extracting beauty from ugliness, poetic from historical, eternal from transitory, fantastic from real, epic from trivial—restates the aesthetic of caricature: the beauty found in works representing moral and physical ugliness, the pleasure taken in such a "lamentable spectacle," the enduring power of works "hanging on events," the epic created from the fleeting and prosaic experience of contemporary history. The art of modern life testifies to the same dualism as caricature, discovering the ideal in and through the real, finding the timeless and universal in and through the phenomena of a particular age and culture, an art by which the ephemeral may endure, the historical enter the eternal, and conversely, the mysterious provoke recognition and knowledge of the real. Modern art, like caricature, presents, on the one hand, an image of dualism and exile, and, on the other, the possibilities of overcoming this through the doubling of the comic artist, and the corresponding "cosmopolitanism" by which the *flâneur* willfully empties the self to adopt the multiple forms of the crowd, thereby becoming a "kaleidoscopic" mirror to the world,

and sending back an image of its multiple and ever-changing meanings.

It was this aspect of Baudelaire's theory that most inspired Walter Benjamin's analysis of the origins of modernity, particularly in his unfinished "Arcades Project." The dualism by which Baudelaire defines caricature and modern art was for Benjamin both a symptom and a result of modern alienation, reflecting and exposing the illusions of contemporary culture, specifically the myths constructed by capitalism to hide the dehumanization of experience in a world of mechanized technology and merchandise. Benjamin's *flâneur* is a product of modern culture, a fantasized image of endless consumerism, bombarded by the sights, sounds, and smells of the city as a shopper is by the endless display of goods in the urban arcades of the period. But just as caricature, in deforming an object while keeping it identifiable, breaks down the object's external appearance of unity, rationality, order, and intelligibility, to reveal it as other than it may seem, so the figure of the *flâneur* represents and uncovers, for readers and viewers, the fantasies of that culture, rends the veil of illusion, calls attention to the "phantasmagoria" as such, illuminates the ideological myths that dominate contemporary experience and that attempt to prevent access to a genuine experience. Caricature is a radical art, provoking a crisis in the aura that for Benjamin surrounded a unique work of art or any similarly "sacred" image, showing it to be a mere object; the disfiguration lays bare the transfiguration.

Specific features of Baudelaire's aesthetic also recur in Mikhail Bakhtin's influential theory of the grotesque: the reflexivity of laughter, which implicates the one who laughs as well as the object of laughter; the ambivalent and contradictory nature of grotesque images, which incorporate old and new, death and rebirth, ugliness and fullness of life; the overcoming of isolation that they effect, integrating the grotesque body with the world and with others. Moreover, Bakhtin saw in the grotesque image—protean, unstable, and regenerative—an awareness of history and historic change, which made it a feature of periods of crisis and transformation: notably the Renaissance, in his study of Rabelais where he develops the theory, but the nineteenth century as well. Apart from Rabelais, the other main object of Bakhtin's thought was a writer from Baudelaire's own time, imbued with the literature and culture of the modern city, and with the grotesque and caricatural: Fyodor Dostoyevsky.

The relation between comic art and modern art that Baudelaire's essays established subsequently became a fundamental principle of aesthetic theory and practice. Caricature, so much a product of the age of revolution, became in the postrevolutionary modern world a model for artistic expression generally. From the radically caricatural methods of Gustave Courbet, Édouard Manet, and Edgar Degas— abbreviated and exaggerated forms, strong outline, bold coloring, summary backgrounds, effects of improvisation, even the progressive flattening of the picture plane associated with pictorial modernism—to the Cubist play with representation, and the distortion, irreverent humor, uncanniness and license characteristic of twentieth-century art forms, modern art has been dominated by the caricatural. Caricature provided not only a means of overthrowing established standards but also of defining them, locating, from Freud to Bakhtin, general principles and models of individual, social, and cultural behavior, within the distortion of the same. More recently, the postmodern emphasis on the parodic has extended the aesthetic of caricature further, defining creation as a deformation and reformation, revising the old to call into question the values and standards it represents and to interpret them differently, in keeping with the vision of a new age; moreover, as a metadiscursive form, caricature, like parody, offers a commentary on representation generally. A constantly changing art, ever bound to the now, as both Baudelaire and Benjamin saw, caricature not only derides (and thereby preserves) its object, but offers an image of the multiple possibilities of interpretation and creation in a single set of materials: a creative formula as yet unexhausted, and perhaps, by its very nature, inexhaustible.

[*See also* Bakhtin; Baudelaire; Benjamin; *and* Grotesque.]

BIBLIOGRAPHY

Bakhtin, Mikhail. *Rabelais and His World.* Translated by Helene Iswolsky. Cambridge, Mass., 1968; reprint, Bloomington, Ind., 1984.
Baudelaire, Charles. *Œuvres complètes.* 2 vols. Edited by Claude Pichois. Paris, 1975–1976.
Benjamin, Walter. *Das Passagen-Werk.* In *Gesammelte Schriften,* edited by Rolf Tiedemann, vol. 5. Frankfurt am Main, 1982.
French Caricature and the French Revolution, 1789–1799. Chicago, 1988. Exhibition catalog, Grunwald Center for the Graphic Arts, University of California, Los Angeles.
Freud, Sigmund. "The Uncanny." In *The Standard Edition of the Complete Psychological Works of Sigmund Freud,* edited by James Strachey, vol. 17, pp. 217–252. London, 1955.
Freud, Sigmund. *Jokes and Their Relation to the Unconscious.* In *The Standard Edition of the Complete Psychological Works of Sigmund Freud,* edited by James Strachey, vol. 8. London, 1960.
Hannoosh, Michele. *Baudelaire and Caricature: From the Comic to an Art of Modernity.* University Park, Pa., 1992.
Hofmann, Werner. *Caricature from Leonardo to Picasso.* New York, 1957.
Kayser, Wolfgang. *The Grotesque in Art and Literature.* Translated by Ulrich Weisstein. Bloomington, Ind., 1963; reprint, New York, 1981.
Kris, Ernst, and E. H. Gombrich. "Principles of Caricature." In *Psychoanalytic Explorations in Art,* by Ernst Kris, pp. 189–203. New York, 1952.
Wechsler, Judith. *A Human Comedy: Physiognomy and Caricature in Nineteenth-Century Paris.* London, 1982.
Wechsler, Judith, ed. *The Issue of Caricature.* Special issue of *Art Journal* 43.4 (Winter 1983): 317–385.

MICHELE HANNOOSH

CASSIRER, ERNST (1874–1945), German philosopher and essayist whose work focused on Immanuel Kant and "symbolic forms." Cassirer was born in the German city of Breslau in Silesia (today Wrocław, Poland). His inaugural dissertation, done under the direction of Hermann Cohen, the leader of the Marburg school of Neo-Kantianism, was on René Descartes's critique of mathematical and natural scientific knowledge. Cassirer lectured as *Privatdozent* at the University of Berlin from 1906 to 1919, when he was named professor at the newly founded University of Hamburg, where he also served a term as rector (1929–1930). With the rise of Nazism, Cassirer, a Jew, left Germany in the Spring of 1933. He went first for two years to All Souls' College in Oxford, then taught for six years at the University of Göteborg, Sweden. In the Summer of 1941 he came to the United States, where he taught at Yale until 1944. He began to teach at Columbia University in the Fall of 1944. He died suddenly, of a heart attack, on the Columbia campus on 13 April 1945. Cassirer considered his career an "intellectual odyssey," during which he published more than 125 books, essays, and reviews.

Cassirer's writings fall into two main categories: those of his systematic philosophy and those in the history of philosophy and ideas. The central work of his systematic philosophy is *The Philosophy of Symbolic Forms* (vol. 1, *Language;* vol. 2, *Mythical Thought;* vol. 3, *The Phenomenology of Knowledge*), published in the 1920s. A fourth volume of *The Philosophy of Symbolic Forms,* titled *The Metaphysics of Symbolic Forms,* was begun in 1928 but left unpublished at his death (published 1996). Cassirer summarized and revised his philosophy in *An Essay on Man: An Introduction to a Philosophy of Human Culture* (1944), which was followed by a work on political philosophy, *The Myth of the State* (1946), that appeared the year after his death. Cassirer first projected his conception of a system of symbolic forms in an early work on the philosophy of science, *Substance and Function* (1910).

The largest work of Cassirer's historical studies is his *Das Erkenntnisproblem in der Philosophie und Wissenschaft der neueren Zeit* (1907) (The Problem of Knowledge in Philosophy and Science in the Modern Age). He traces the development of the problem from Nicolas Cusanus to Immanuel Kant (vols. 1 and 2, 1906–1907), then to Georg Wilhelm Friedrich Hegel (vol. 3, 1920), and finally from Hegel up to the contemporary sciences in the 1930s (vol. 4, 1950). This large work is supplemented by Cassirer's studies on Renaissance philosophy, the Platonic Renaissance in England, and the Enlightenment, which he regarded as presenting a "phenomenology of the philosophic spirit." Among his studies of individual philosophers is his *Kant's Life and Thought* (1916).

Cassirer also wrote a number of essays on various literary figures, especially Johann Wolfgang von Goethe, whom he treats in relation to the history of literature and the ideas of Western culture. Cassirer's encyclopedic writings range throughout most fields of contemporary thought, from mathematics to linguistics, from history to psychology.

Despite the enormous range of his work, Cassirer never produced a separate volume on art or aesthetics. In various works, when he mentions a list of symbolic forms he often includes art among them, and in a letter of 13 May 1942, to Paul Arthur Schilpp in connection with the preparation of the Library of Living Philosophers' volume on his work, Cassirer says that he intended to write a volume on art, that it was part of his original plan for *The Philosophy of Symbolic Forms,* but that the *Ungust,* the "disfavor" of the times (referring to his years of exile), had made him postpone it again and again. Throughout the three volumes of *The Philosophy of Symbolic Forms,* Cassirer often mentions art along with myth and religion, as a triad, but he says little about art in these places. The understanding of his conception of art as a symbolic form depends on his chapter on art in *An Essay on Man,* on two papers on the topic "Language and Art" left unpublished at his death (published in *Symbol, Myth, and Culture,* 1979), and on a paper, "Mythic, Aesthetic, and Theoretical Space," which he presented at an aesthetics congress in 1931.

The term *symbolic form (symbolische Form)* itself (of which art is one major example) has its origin, or at least a great part of its origin, in aesthetic theory. In an essay, "Der Begriff der symbolischen Form im Aufbau der Geisteswissenschaften" (The Concept of Symbolic Form in the Structure of the Humanities; 1956), Cassirer uses the term *symbolic,* and explains that this concept had its origin in Goethe's interest in the symbolic, which passed into aesthetic theory through the philosophies of Friedrich Wilhelm Joseph von Schelling and Hegel. From this basis, the Hegelian aesthetician Friedrich Theodor Vischer claims that the *Symbolbegriff* is the foundation of the aesthetic itself. Cassirer claims to derive the conception of symbolic form from a well-known essay by Vischer, "Das Symbol" (1887), although Vischer does not use the term *symbolische Form* as such. Cassirer says that he wishes to expand this conception of symbolic form from an aesthetic conception to a notion that can cover each form of the human spirit, including not only art but also language, myth, and religion.

In an earlier work, *Freiheit und Form: Studien zur deutschen Geistesgeschichte* (Freedom and Form: Studies in German Cultural History; 1916), written in reaction to the political conditions that followed World War I, Cassirer connects the problem of freedom to that of form in German classical aesthetics, with Friedrich von Schiller, Kant, and Goethe. He brings out an essential feature of his concept of form, one that he later incorporates into his philosophy of symbolic forms: that the ability to form experience through the power of art and language is at the basis of human freedom. The power of human beings to form their world in terms of symbols frees them from the bonds of the immediacy of pure sense experience.

In *An Essay on Man,* Cassirer connects the world of symbolic forms of culture with the ancient philosophical project of self-knowledge. Each symbolic form is a kind of concrete universal, in which particular elements are held together in a whole. Cassirer's conception of symbolic form has roots in the German idealist aesthetics of art as a particularized universal, in which the artwork is a unique particular, but one that carries a universal meaning.

The standard list of symbolic forms in Cassirer's philosophy follows the chapter titles of the second part of *An Essay on Man:* "myth and religion," "language," "art," "history," "science." For Cassirer, a symbolic form is both a form of knowledge and a form of human culture. Each symbolic form has its own logic, that is, its own way in which the general categories of experience are employed to order sensation. Within each symbolic form is established a particular relationship between subject and object, causality, spatial and temporal form.

Cassirer grounds his conception of symbolic form in his conception of "symbolic pregnance" *(symbolische Prägnanz).* Any act of perception is symbolically pregnant in the sense that any sensory experience contains at the same time a nonsensory meaning that is embodied in it. A perceptual here and now is experienced only in its interrelation to some broader formation of experience that can be found writ large in the various systems of symbols that comprise human culture. Cassirer's example is to consider a *Linienzug* (a line drawing such as a curve in a graph) that can be variously experienced. One may apprehend it simply as an expressive object, having contrasts of light and dark and suggesting a certain mood, or as representing a geometrical law; further, one's perspective may be shifted again, and it appears as a mythical object or an aesthetic form.

Cassirer defines the human species as *animal symbolicum.* Humans make the world of culture in which they live. Cassirer claims that art, like other symbolic forms, is not the reproduction of a given reality; it is one of the ways that humans are led to have an objective view of things and of human life. Language and science are ways in which we produce our concepts of the external world. Art does not imitate reality but is one of the ways that we give form to reality. Any given artist discovers reality in a particular way. This means that the artist gives form to things in a certain way, and once we understand the aesthetic perspective of a given artist we can continue to comprehend things in that way. Language and science give us abbreviations of the real, but art gives us an intensification of the real. Although art produces the world of the subjective—as opposed to science, which attempts to exclude the subjective from all of its conceptual formulations—art is not simply subjective. The artist creates a work of art that has its own sense of objective form. The artist does not arbitrarily invent things but reveals forms that are actually there. Through the work of the artist, these forms become visible and recognizable.

Cassirer claims that all controversies between schools of aesthetics have one point in common: all schools of aesthetics admit that art is an independent "universe of discourse." Cassirer stands against any form of reductionism of art to some feature of mental life, such as the expression of emotions, the pursuit of pleasure, or morality. Art has its own "inner form." For Cassirer, to account for art in psychological or political terms is to miss the point of art. Cassirer claims that art is an original direction of the human spirit in its effort to create its world of human culture. In this drive toward aesthetic form, the artist has the power to give shape to our most obscure feelings.

Cassirer holds that art is not a "language," as is so often said of art. Both art and language are representations, not imitations, of things or actions. But the medium of sensuous forms differs from verbal and conceptual representations. Cassirer can avoid the confusions inherent in calling art a "language" because of his conception of calling both of them symbolic forms. Symbols are used in each of these areas, but they are used in different ways and have different inner forms, different ways in which an object is apprehended.

Cassirer holds that art may be described as knowledge, but knowledge of a peculiar and specific kind. One can speak of a "truth of art," Cassirer says, but it is different from that truth arrived at in science. He claims that art and science operate on completely different planes and do not contradict each other; each has its own "angle of refraction."

From the standpoint of his philosophy of symbolic forms, Cassirer can make an important distinction between myth and a work of art. From the perspective of myth, what is said in the myth is categorically true. On the level of mythical thinking, what is said in the myth is a complete comprehension of the subject matter of the myth—for example, the relationship between man and nature or between the human and the divine order. A work of art that treats these subjects, even a work of great wholeness and breadth such as Dante Alighieri's *Divina commedia* or Goethe's *Faust*, does not claim to be categorical in the truth it states. The great truths of the aesthetic imagination are "hypothetical"; they show one aspect, even if a very inclusive one, of their subjects. The myth absorbs the audience in the immediacy of its object and claims a final and "categorical" truth. The work of art is always something mediated, because, from Cassirer's standpoint, the consciousness capable of aesthetic representation is also capable of scientific representation. It is capable of both imaginative truths and those cognitively formed.

In regard to twentieth-century aesthetics, Cassirer devotes several pages of the last chapter of *The Logic of the Humanities* (*Logik der Kulturwissenschaften;* 1942) to a criticism of Benedetto Croce's view that art is essentially the expression of emotions and that anything that attempts a classification of the arts by their various forms or genres has no basis whatsoever. Cassirer agrees with Croce's motive, to put a stop to the error that runs throughout the history of aesthetics of attempting to determine which genre attains the highest level of art—for example, which contains the highest aim of poetry, the ode, idyll, or tragedy, and so on. In accordance with his general interest in the importance of form, Cassirer holds that any artwork must be understood both in terms of its particular form and in relation to what it expresses. There is no ready-made world of "forms" of art. Any work of art may modify an existing form or even create a new form of artistic expression.

Susanne Langer is the single thinker in aesthetics with whom Cassirer's views are most identified. Langer translated Cassirer's *Language and Myth,* and dedicated her major work of aesthetics, *Feeling and Form* (1953), to him. Contrary to common opinion, Langer was not Cassirer's student; she met him after he arrived in the United States. Her own work on symbolism was going in a direction similar to Cassirer's and was influenced by his work. In *Philosophy in a New Key* (1951), Langer makes explicit a distinction between presentational and discursive symbolism, which is implicit but not fully made in Cassirer's conception of symbols, and in *Feeling and Form,* which also shows the influence on Langer of Alfred North Whitehead's concept of feeling, can be seen Cassirer's conception of "expression" *(Ausdruck)* and his conception of form. Langer may be said to have taken her own step toward producing the book on art that Cassirer did not live to write.

BIBLIOGRAPHY

Works by Cassirer

Kant's Life and Thought (1916). Translated by James Haden. New Haven, 1981.

The Philosophy of Symbolic Forms (1923–1929). 3 vols. Translated by Ralph Manheim. New Haven, 1953–1957. Consists of vol. 1, *Language;* vol. 2, *Mythical Thought;* vol. 3, *The Phenomenology of Knowledge; The Philosophy of Symbolic Forms,* vol. 4; *The Metaphysics of Symbolic Forms* (posthumous, 1995). Translated and edited by John Michael Krois and Donald Phillip Verene. New Haven, 1996.

Language and Myth (1925). Translated by Susanne K. Langer. New York, 1946.

"Mythic, Aesthetic, and Theoretical Space" (1931). Translated by Donald Phillip Verene and Lerke Holzwarth Foster. *Man and World: An International Philosophical Review* 2 (1969): 3–17.

The Logic of the Humanities (1942). Translated by Clarence Smith Howe. New Haven, 1961.

An Essay on Man: An Introduction to a Philosophy of Human Culture. New Haven, 1944.

"Der Begriff der symbolischen Form im Aufbau der Geisteswissenschaften." In *Wesen und Wirkung des Symbolbegriffs.* Darmstadt, 1956.

Symbol, Myth, and Culture: Essays and Lectures of Ernst Cassirer, 1935–1945. Edited by Donald Phillip Verene. New Haven, 1979.

Other Sources

Ferretti, Silvia. *Cassirer, Panofsky, and Warburg: Symbol, Art, and History.* Translated by Richard Pierce. New Haven, 1989.

Krois, John Michael. *Cassirer: Symbolic Forms and History.* New Haven, 1987.

Schilpp, Paul Arthur, ed. *The Philosophy of Ernst Cassirer.* Evanston, Ill., 1949.

Verene, Donald Phillip. "Cassirer's View of Myth and Symbol." *Monist* 50.4 (October 1966): 553–564.

Verene, Donald Phillip. "Kant, Hegel, and Cassirer: The Origins of the Philosophy of Symbolic Forms." *Journal of the History of Ideas* 30.1 (January–March 1969): 33–46.

DONALD VERENE

CATHARSIS. *See* Katharsis.

CAVELL, STANLEY. [*To explore the thought of contemporary American philosopher Stanley Cavell, this entry comprises two essays:*

Survey of Thought
Cavell and Film

The first essay analyzes his philosophy in general and the role of aesthetics therein; the second essay explains the particular importance of film in both his aesthetics and his philosophy. For related discussion, see Metaphor; *and* Wittgenstein.]

Survey of Thought

Stanley Cavell (b. 1926) is an American philosopher and critic whose contributions to aesthetics must be assessed both within his relation to specific arts of literature, drama, music, and film and against the central visions of his writing. Cavell's books are, without exception, anchored in what he painstakingly characterizes as "readings" of particular works. He is a practicing critic, whose books have addressed William Shakespeare, film comedy and melodrama, Romantic and modernist poetry, Ludwig van Beethoven, opera, Edgar Allen Poe, Henry David Thoreau, and Samuel Beckett. This critical labor is continuous, or intimately discontinuous, with his readings of Ludwig Wittgenstein, J. L. Austin, René Descartes, Ralph Waldo Emerson, Friedrich Nietzsche, John Rawls, and Saul Kripke.

The practices involved in "reading a text" are not easy to delineate accurately, and the demands of critical attentiveness draw Cavell's work toward an inveterate particularity of detail and example. This makes his work nearly impossible to summarize usefully. But his writing also contains a series of unifying poles of investigation, around which his work is constantly circulating and from which he recurrently takes his bearings. The two most central of these investigations have been his efforts to diagnose and to undermine skepticism, and his efforts to delineate a dimension of existence that he calls moral (or Emersonian) perfectionism. These investigations require a recovery of the voice, both literally and allegorically, from philosophical or human suppression. *Voice* accordingly becomes a third fundamental term in Cavell's work, bridging the investigations of per-

fectionism and of skepticism. This idea of "voice," consistently correlated with his practices of reading, is especially suggestive for contemporary aesthetics. At the same time, the interplay of reading and voice invites comparison with Jacques Derrida's early depiction of the suppression of writing by the metaphysical idea of the voice.

Skepticism here refers less to an intellectual position concerning the impossibility of knowledge and more to the condition that Cavell diagnoses as underlying that position. For Cavell, skepticism is a contemporary version of the ancient human effort to escape the limitations of the human. Cavell characterizes the wish underlying the theoretical problems of skepticism as intellectual refinements of a wish to repudiate the world. Descartes's withdrawal from the world of everyday cares and transactions is an emblem for Cavell of the philosopher's determination to remove himself from ordinary links to the world. Cavell reads the skeptic's sense of the insufficiency of those links as first of all a sense of the catastrophic inadequacy of the ordinary world as a scene of knowledge and the inadequacy of our position within that world. The skeptic, then, characterizes his sense of the inadequacy of our position in the ordinary world as a failure of our knowledge of that world.

Cavell depicts skepticism not as a false theory but as a belated interpretation of the situation of human beings as knowers of the world. Skepticism covers over a deeper anxiety about our place in the world. Such anxiety reveals something about the fateful precariousness of our knowledge, which the epistemic constructions of skepticism can never catch up with or domesticate. What philosophy takes as the theoretical problems of establishing the existence of what it calls the "external world" or of "other minds" are further characterized by Cavell as maintained within the grip of the very wishes and fears they purport to overcome. The wish to refine the terms in which we ordinarily conceive of and grasp the world is revealed as a wish to repudiate our ordinary grasp of that world. And this wish, in turn, is revealed as a wish to repudiate the world as such.

Cavell relates his diagnosis of skepticism to Wittgenstein's sense of our craving for a totality outside of our forms of life; to Emerson's chagrin at our shamefaced withdrawal of words from their indebtedness to the world; and to Nietzsche's diagnoses of nihilism, nostalgia, and other less nameable revenges against time. The problem is therefore not one of refuting skepticism by, for instance, establishing the mind's capacity to secure a true representation of a world external to us or of other minds. This way of putting the problem already accepts too much of skepticism's self-interpretation. Skepticism believes that it has found a previously overlooked problem for the mind, a gap in our knowledge of what we had all been inclined to take for granted. For Cavell, the task of overcoming skepticism is not to prove the skeptic wrong, but rather to undo the ways in which the mind has suppressed its ordinary connections to the world. We are thereby to undo the distortion of the criteria and conditions of a knowledge of objects, events, and people that is otherwise unavoidable, or avoidable only at more obvious costs of isolation and madness. The skeptic accepts the problem of the mind working itself out of a theoretical isolation as a cover—and perhaps as a consolation—for the deeper and less manageable separateness of human beings.

In Cavell's reading, Shakespearean tragedy measures the cost of our extraordinary efforts at once to know and not to know. The connection between the drive to knowledge and the refusal of acknowledgment is already in place in Cavell's "The Avoidance of Love: A Reading of *King Lear*" (1969, pp. 282–285). Although the links between skepticism and tragedy are only implicit in this essay, and in its predecessor, "Knowing and Acknowledging," the drawing out of these links occupies the next two decades of his work. The further effects of this connection of skepticism to its various enactments form the ground of every approach he makes to a work of drama, including film and opera.

The point and scope of these connections have often been misunderstood. Not every tragic denial is analogized in the skeptic's renunciations, and not every skeptical collapse can be tracked in the precipitousness of a tragic fall. The denial and banishment of another in order to prevent the exposure of one's love for that other does not possess a ready-made analogy to the skeptic's renunciations of the world. Before such denials become the stuff of skepticism, they must have allowed the other to represent not only the effects of vulnerability to pain and rejection but also of our liability to losing the world and the world's intelligibility. The tragic protagonist is seen to be preparing for—and thus to be precipitating—the return of some quite particular forms of chaos, comprehensible in terms of the destruction of that intelligibility.

Cavell's study of perfectionism is a further nodal point of the problematic of the self and its various capacities for transformation and retrogression. Perfectionism is meant to provoke us to a transformation according to an ideal internal to the self's constitution, not one imposed from without. Cavell links the dimension of human self-transformation to Aristotle and to Plato's notion (in his *Apology*) of the "care of the mind." In the modern era, he tracks its primary forms in Emerson and in what Nietzsche made of Emerson. Hence, perfectionism is not merely an upward path, out of the Platonic cave of imprisonment to a brighter region of more perfect being or to some Arnoldian or Eliotic realm of the cultured. Perfectionism is always equally the demand for the relinquishment of false perfections, including the falseness or constriction of those virtues that have outlived themselves. Conformity to a false sense of completion is as much what Emerson averts us from as conformity to the false standards of our neighbors. Showing these conformities to be, or to stem from, the same state would be a task of

Emersonian epistemology, one that Cavell attempts in *Conditions Handsome and Unhandsome* (1990).

As with skepticism, the philosophy of perfection is not so much illustrated in works of literature as contested by them. This contest is essential to Cavell's understanding of the relation of literature to philosophy, where both fields undertake to form themselves from a more primitive and somewhat mythological state of voicelessness and self-stupefaction. The "ancient quarrel" of philosophy and poetry is not over who gets to voice the claims of reason. The quarrel is over which field, at a given moment, is capable of undoing the self-constriction of those claims and of permitting the formation of those voices. The common reliance on voice is as much a cause of the tension as it is of the reciprocity between philosophy and literature.

Such tensions between the voices of philosophy and literature are part of the risks that the perfectionist vision must run. As one risk in the Wittgensteinian response to skepticism is a kind of banal rejoicing in the completeness of the ordinary, so a risk of Emersonian perfectionism is the willingness to accept aesthetic achievement in the place of inner change. It is hard to articulate the relation between perfectionism's exaltation of the voice and skepticism's suppression of it, without slipping into a kind of melodramatic aestheticism. One must do more than measure the philosopher's self-stultification against the thrill of Greta Garbo's looks or the sublimity of an aria.

A principal problem for those who would investigate Cavell's work goes like this: the voice that is suppressed by the skeptic relies on and expresses something like Wittgensteinian criteria and hence the ordinary transactions of our daily lives. The recovery of the voice here signifies the return of just this ordinary world, which is at first the only way the world as such can return to us. What is affirmed in the perfectionist ecstasy of the voice is, among other things, something like the possibility of rising above the second-rateness of this world. These possibilities may or, indeed, must coexist in a single self, but it is not always easy to see how. The voice recovered from the skeptical denials can only coincide for a passing moment or in the space of a breath with the voice that is achieved and memorialized in a perfectionist affirmation.

A crucial corollary follows from the transience of these solutions: in perfectionism, the voice is not figured as an icon of some actual self, glorying in its self-sufficient presence to itself. That may be a reasonable way of characterizing either Hollywood's self-image of its repetitious glamour or reconstruction's vision of the metaphysics of "presence." In Cavell's work, the voice betokens not the self-presence of the actual self but the terrifying proximity of what he calls the *next* self. Hence, the very expressive success of the voice (whether in the soprano's melisma or in the banter of Spencer Tracy and Katharine Hepburn) alludes to the current self as but "half-expressed" (in Emerson's phrase) and as otherwise suffocated and isolated. That the achievements of perfectionism are temporary is hardly surprising in a vision that emerges from the temporal character of our existence, in particular, from the fact of our having begun as children.

Like other philosophers who delineate a field of struggle between philosophy and the specific arts, Cavell's work tends to subvert the very idea of a study of the arts that is essentially separable from the burden of philosophy as a whole. But the study of aesthetics reemerges as an essential dimension of philosophy's knowledge of its own conditions. Cavell isolates a kind of analogy between the conditions of our judgment of a work of art and the conditions under which philosophy seeks to formulate and to communicate its own results. In an early essay, "Aesthetic Problems of Modern Philosophy," he notes Kant's invocation of the idea of a "universal voice" as a means of characterizing the subjective necessity in an aesthetic judgment. He goes on to draw an analogy between such a judgment and the expression of a claim to know what "we ordinarily say" in a given situation.

It is no longer easy to imagine the audience for a comparison between the claim that "The *Hammerklavier* sonata is a perverse work" and the claim that "When we ask 'Do you dress like that voluntarily?' we must be implying that there is something untoward about the way you are dressed." Both remarks can seem to be merely matters of empirical psychology, or perhaps effects of some well-known rhetorical quantities. Moreover, both the aesthetic and the philosophical claim are likely to be taken as *demands* for agreement, whereas Cavell is arguing that it is truer to the spirit of such claims that they are rather (1) invitations to investigate whether such an agreement in our responses already exists; or (2) part of an effort to make sense of the fact that we go on making such judgments in the likelihood precisely of *disagreement*.

In the case of the philosophical claim (e.g., that there is something fishy about an action), Cavell argues that disagreement is still the beginning of philosophy, not the end of it: it is a datum for investigation. In the case of aesthetics, the controversy in the claim is an invitation to further experience, on the part of those to whom the claim is directed but also on the part of the one who makes the claim. The practice of making aesthetic claims is absorbed into the practices of reading and into the (self-)critical efforts to disable the mechanisms by which we keep our reading and our experience at arm's length.

Cavell's appeal to experience and to the practices of reading and criticism imply a rigor of attentiveness that is difficult to capture in (further) words. Apart from his ability to evoke a corresponding power of attentiveness and absorption on the side of his reader, his appeals will seem empty. In the absence of such an absorption and such a willingness

to follow the movements of his text, Cavell's writing will tend to be seen merely as a series of critical impressions. And his efforts to describe the path of his words and argument will seem to be the expression of a merely personal sensibility, at once refined and extravagant. Such exaggerations have become part of the reception of his work, and the tendency to such exaggeration seems to be independent of whether the reception is hostile or sympathetic.

Perhaps partly in response to this situation, Cavell's writing increasingly formulates the explicit wish to create the understanding by which the precise angle of a thought is to be calibrated and the ear by which his tone is to be apprehended. The wish to intervene directly in the formation of the audience for his words—and hence in the reciprocal formation of himself as the "author" of the words—puts his writing in a line of descent from the Romantic responses to Kant. Cavell insists on the capacity of a philosophical text to intervene in the education of a reader's responses, and this education must not be parcelled out in advance among the various disciplinary structures that we inhabit. Along with this insistence, Cavell refuses to grant philosophers the possibility that their discourse might be, in principle, both separable from the work it addresses and unmystified in its self-conception as aesthetics.

Nevertheless, one can still say something about Cavell's relation to the subject of aesthetics, more traditionally construed. Cavell's early work in aesthetics shows both his debts to Kant and his departures from a traditional Kantian orientation. In "Music Discomposed" (1969), he puts his finger on the sorest point of Kant's avowals of formalism, namely, his apparent reliance on characterizing the state of mind of the beholder as "disinterested." Rather than abandoning the double bind of a formalism that tends to psychologize the audience of fine art, Cavell's work tries to get underneath both sides of the dichotomy. He insists that the "psychology" of the spectator cannot be understood as prior to the formal considerations of the critic or as known apart from the workings of the work in question, and he advances arguments against any consideration of form as existing apart from an audience, evolving as a mere end in itself.

Cavell has presented treatments of such topics as intention (1969), expression (1979) metaphor, and representation (1969). He has consistently monitored the shifting ground between criticism and its objects. More recently, his work on Shakespeare, film, and opera has led him back to a further consideration of the notion of form. As early as his essay "Music Discomposed," Cavell's work mounts a relentless assault on any comfortable isolation of form from content or of "the work itself" from the terms of its address to an audience. Conversely, he insists that one cannot understand the "psychology" of the audience apart from understanding the spirit in which the audience receives a given work. It is an open question how far understanding this spirit entails that one share in it.

Cavell gradually displaces the idea of the "content" as some sort of passive subject matter or neutral fund of material. At the same time, he dismantles the idea of form as the more or less attractive "container" or conduit by which the content is delivered to the appropriate audience. Cavell therefore rejects those accounts that give the highest aesthetic ranking to achievements of form, at the price of insulating the form from the pressure of the realities of history and of everyday life. More generally, Cavell objects to whatever renders the work inert in relation to the audience and the audience passive in relation to the work.

Cavell replaces the idea of form as a kind of envelope or container with an idea of form as a kind of medium of knowledge and power. The form of the work is what presents itself as *active* in that work: active in the work's claim on an audience; active in its working out of the implications of a particular "content" or element; and active in its relations with other members of a genre or medium of an art. Thus, the concern with the state of mind of the beholder is, in part, transposed toward questions about the implications of form, and of how these implications are to be received by a representative member of the audience. "Form" and the representative apprehender of form must be defined in relation to each other.

Especially beginning in his work on "the comedy of remarriage" (1981), Cavell explores this developing idea of form as a kind of conversation with other members of a genre. Cavell follows Northrop Frye in resisting the intellectual's typical condescension to popular comedy. Both critics resist the idea of the conventions of a genre as constituting a static formula, whose instances are therefore easy to absorb and in that sense "popular." Cavell's essay "Hamlet's Burden of Proof" (1987) explores an idea of form as working out the conditions under which a Shakespearean drama allows us to know a specific content, construed as a scene of knowing, and he explores some related problems about form and significance in music, most recently turning to questions about opera (1994).

Well before the supposed postmodern promotion of critic to performance artist, Cavell characterized the critical responsiveness of the artist as part of the constitution of a work. Accordingly, in the modern period, the experience of criticism may become "internal to the experience of art" ("Music Discomposed" [1969]). By the same token, a given work might seek to undo the terms of criticism and reception that it anticipates from a given audience. Cavell thus also resists the relegation of the category of "intention" to some place safely within the artist's "psychology." As with the situation of a human being learning to speak, Cavell thinks of the working out of art's significance as produced in the realm where the individual's capacity for meaningful-

ness meets the resources of a given culture. Each may find the other wanting, and each might try to suppress what the other is seeking to say. But each is made for—and by—the other.

[*See also* Kant; *and* Opera.]

BIBLIOGRAPHY

Works by Cavell

Must We Mean What We Say? New York, 1969; reprint, Cambridge and New York, 1976.

The World Viewed: Reflections on the Ontology of Film. New York, 1971; enl. ed., Cambridge, Mass., 1979.

The Senses of Walden. New York, 1972; exp. ed., San Francisco, 1981; reprint, Chicago, 1992.

The Claim of Reason: Wittgenstein, Skepticism, Morality and Tragedy. Oxford, 1979.

Pursuits of Happiness: The Hollywood Comedy of Remarriage. Cambridge, Mass., 1981.

Themes Out of School: Effects and Causes. San Francisco, 1984; reprint, Chicago, 1988.

Disowning Knowledge: In Six Plays of Shakespeare. Cambridge and New York, 1987.

In Quest of the Ordinary: Lines of Skepticism and Romanticism. Chicago, 1988.

This New Yet Unapproachable America: Lectures after Emerson after Wittgenstein. Albuquerque, N.Mex., 1989; reprint, Chicago, 1989.

Conditions Handsome and Unhandsome: The Constitution of Emersonian Perfectionism. The Carus Lectures, 19th series. LaSalle, Ill., 1990; reprint, Chicago, 1990.

A Pitch of Philosophy: Autobiographical Exercises. Cambridge, Mass., 1994.

Philosophical Passages: Wittgenstein, Emerson, Austin, Derrida. Oxford and Cambridge, Mass., 1995. Contains comprehensive bibliography of Cavell's writing.

The Cavell Reader. Edited by Stephen Mulhall. Oxford and Cambridge, Mass., 1996.

Contesting Tears: The Hollywood Melodrama of the Unknown Woman. Chicago, 1996.

Other Sources

Cohen, Ted, Paul Guyer, and Hilary Putnam, eds. *Pursuits of Reason: Essays in Honor of Stanley Cavell.* Lubbock, Tex., 1993.

Fischer, Michael. *Stanley Cavell and Literary Skepticism.* Chicago, 1989.

Fleming, Richard, and Michael Payne, eds. *The Senses of Stanley Cavell.* Lewisburg, Pa., 1989.

Fleming, Richard. *The State of Philosophy: An Invitation to a Reading in Three Parts of Stanley Cavell's The Claim of Reason.* Lewisburg, Pa., 1993.

Mulhall, Stephen. *Stanley Cavell: Philosophy's Recounting of the Ordinary.* Oxford, 1994.

Smith, Joseph H., and William Kerrigan, eds. *Images in Our Souls: Cavell, Psychoanalysis, and Cinema.* Baltimore, 1987.

TIMOTHY GOULD

Cavell and Film

Stanley Cavell's *The World Viewed* (1971) opens with the words, "Memories of movies are strand over strand with memories of my life." Writing about movies has been strand over strand with Cavell's philosophical life from this early book, published between *Must We Mean What We Say?* (1969) and *The Senses of Walden* (1972), to *Pursuits of Happiness: The Hollywood Comedy of Remarriage* (1981; a companion piece to *The Claim of Reason*, 1979), to *Contesting Tears: Hollywood Melodramas of the Unknown Woman* (1996), his latest book, which shares the profound philosophical concerns of his work of the past decade.

As Timothy Gould notes in his article on Cavell in this volume, Stanley Cavell is a practicing critic as well as a philosopher. All his books are anchored in "readings," whether of plays by William Shakespeare or Samuel Beckett; operas; Hollywood romantic comedies or melodramas; or philosophical works by Immanuel Kant, Ralph Waldo Emerson, Martin Heidegger, Ludwig Wittgenstein, or J. L. Austin. In reflecting on Cavell's writing about film, however, several points must be noted about the relationship, as he understands it, between criticism and philosophy.

First, it is one of Cavell's guiding insights that criticism is internal to philosophy; the history of Western philosophy cannot be separated from the shifting terms of criticism that philosophers have brought to bear against competing views. Second, in Cavell's writing, the criticism is always philosophically motivated, and the philosophy is always motivated by a critical impulse to make sense of—to attach meaningful words to—particular objects as they are experienced. As Gould notes, criticism and philosophy are as capable of contesting as of supporting each other. Hence, it is an *achievement* of Cavell's writing that within it there is no conflict or tension between criticism and philosophy, or, rather, none that the writing does not overcome or transcend by acknowledging it critically and also investigating it philosophically. Third, Cavell understands his "readings" to be no less philosophy when their objects are operas, plays, or movies than when they are works of philosophy. Unlike operas or Shakespearean tragedies, which are acknowledged high points of Western culture, movies might seem surprisingly "low" cultural objects to call for philosophical analysis. Yet, in Cavell's writing an intimate kinship or affinity emerges between philosophy, as he understands and practices it, and the movies in his experience. He likes to cite, as an instance, the link between the source of Buster Keaton's comedy in the discovery that objects on film have inner and fixed lives and the mode of perception or consciousness of the world that Heidegger characterizes as "the worldhood of the world announcing itself." (To say that there is an intimate kinship or affinity between philosophy and film is not to deny that philosophy may have an equally intimate bond with opera, theater, or any of the other arts that Cavell has written about.)

Embracing Wittgenstein's and Austin's methodological principle that one can find out what kind of object something is (grammatically) by investigating expressions that show the kinds of things that can be said about it, *Must We Mean What We Say?* undertakes philosophical investigations of many subjects, including the procedures of ordinary language philosophy that Cavell adopts but also transforms by raising to an explicit self-consciousness.

In *The World Viewed*, the subject Cavell investigates, philosophically, is film. The book contains reflections on an astonishing diversity of matters pertaining to film's origins; its historical development; its characteristic forms and genres; the myths and the human types around which those genres revolve; the medium's ability, until recently, to stave off modernism, to continue to employ unself-consciously traditional techniques that tap naturally into the medium's powers; and so on. And in reflecting on such matters, *The World Viewed* incorporates critical remarks about an equally astonishing diversity of particular films, particular genres, particular stars, particular cinematic techniques.

In *The World Viewed*, film is not part of the subject, not one subject among many, not a subject addressed by some remarks but not others; film *is* the subject, is *the* subject, of the book. It is a corollary of this that in *The World Viewed* there is an almost complete absence of the kinds of remarks about philosophy in general, and about Cavell's own philosophical procedures in particular, that are everywhere to be found in *Must We Mean What We Say?* This does not mean that in Cavell's little book about film the subject of philosophy plays a less central role, however. In *The World Viewed*, it can be said of philosophy, as surely as it can be said of film, that it is not part of the subject, not one subject among many, not a subject addressed by some remarks but not others; no less than film, philosophy *is* the subject, is *the* subject, of the book. What makes this possible is the fact that in *The World Viewed*, as in the movies that motivate its writing, philosophy and film are not separate subjects; they are joined in a conversation so intimate as to constitute a kind of marriage (the kind of marriage of equals envisioned by the Hollywood "remarriage comedies" that *Pursuits of Happiness* goes on to study).

Like Wittgenstein and Austin, Cavell proceeds, in all of his writing, by appealing philosophically to what we ordinarily say and mean. To ask someone who has mastered the language—oneself, for example—such questions as "What should we say if . . . ?" or "In what circumstances would we call . . . ?" is to ask that person to say something about himself or herself. Hence, Cavell's appeals to what we ordinarily say and mean (like Sigmund Freud's procedures of free association, dream analysis, investigation of verbal and behavior slips, noting and analyzing "transferred" feeling, and so on) are procedures for acquiring self-knowledge. They are appeals to facts—about language, the world, ourselves—so obvious that we cannot simply fail to know them. When what we fail to know is so obvious we cannot simply fail to know it, our ignorance cannot be cured by additional information, or by defining words or introducing new ones;

it is a refusal to know. Knowing something we can fail to know only by refusing to know it reveals a special region of the concept of knowledge, one that is not a function of certainty but of acknowledgment. In investigating the kind of knowledge of which self-knowledge is a paradigm, Cavell employs philosophical procedures that enable one to acquire self-knowledge. Without knowing oneself, one cannot know what self-knowledge is.

The World Viewed begins with an acknowledgment that what Cavell calls his "natural relation" to movies has been broken. He calls on us to acknowledge that we, too, are no longer possessed by the world of movies the ways we once were, that we no longer possess the world of movies the ways we once did. In giving thought to our new sense that the world of movies has become lost to us, Cavell proceeds by investigating, philosophically, what we say, what we are inclined to say, about movies. By investigating an experience of movies that has been ours as well, *The World Viewed* calls on us to make that experience present to us. The goal is not to restore the relation to movies that once came naturally, but to achieve a new philosophical relation to movies, to others, to ourselves.

One way *The World Viewed* embraces the principle that one can find out what kind of object a thing is by investigating expressions that show the kinds of things that can be said about it is by taking its own writing to be such an expression. *The World Viewed* is one kind of thing that can be said about movies. By investigating this expression philosophically, by taking its own philosophical motivation to be internal to what this writing is about, *The World Viewed* enables one to know something about what film is (and something about what philosophy is as well). *The World Viewed* declares that its marriage of philosophy and film is not only possible but necessary, that philosophy can no longer deny or avoid the subject of film, and that it is not possible to begin thinking seriously about film apart from the perspective of self-reflection that only philosophy can provide.

If we stop to think about it, the fact that when we look at a photograph we see things not present remains as puzzling to us as it was when we first learned what photographs were. That ordinarily we do not stop to think about photographs, that we forget our original puzzlement, is itself a puzzling fact about photographs and about ourselves. "It may be felt that I make too great a mystery of these objects," Cavell writes. "My feeling is rather that we have forgotten how mysterious these things are, and in general how *different* different things are from one another, as though we had forgotten how to value them" (1979, p. 19). When we forget how different photographs are from other kinds of things, we also forget how different human beings are from other kinds of beings, how different we are from each other. We forget how to value our own lives, our own experience. We forget something mysterious, something of value, about being human.

On film, reality is not merely described or merely represented, *The World Viewed* reminds us. Movies project and screen reality rather than describing it, as (some) novels do, or representing it, as (some) paintings do. Insofar as movies represent reality, they do so by way of projections, not representations, of reality. The ontological difference between film and painting—what their difference comes to, what it makes possible, and what it makes necessary, for each—is a central theme of *The World Viewed*, which develops that theme, in part, by addressing the mysterious relationship between a photograph and the thing(s) and/or person(s) in that photograph.

The mystery of photographs resides, Cavell suggests, in their capacity to allow persons and things in the world to reveal themselves, without human intervention. Yet, it is misleading to claim, as does the influential French film critic/theorist André Bazin, that the inescapable fact of automatism in the making of photographs enables them to satisfy, once and for all, our obsession with realism. This is so, first, because our obsession was never with realism but with reality. So far as photography satisfied a wish, in Cavell's view, it satisfied the human wish—intensifying in the West since the Reformation—to reach this world, to achieve selfhood, by escaping the metaphysical isolation to which we have become condemned by virtue of our subjectivity. One of Cavell's most powerful and original philosophical intuitions is that selfhood cannot be achieved apart from the acknowledgment of others (their acknowledgment of us, and ours of them). "Apart from the wish for selfhood (hence the always simultaneous granting of otherness as well), I do not understand the value of art," Cavell writes. "Apart from this wish and its achievement, art is exhibition" (ibid., p. 22). Second, photographs are not more realistic than paintings. Indeed, it makes no more sense to speak of photographs as realistic than to speak of reality as realistic. Realistic as opposed to what? Fantastic? What could be more fantastic than reality? (Reality is precisely what fantasy may be confused with.) When objects and persons are projected and screened, they are displaced from their natural sequences and locales. This displacement, which enables movies to depict the fantastic as readily as the natural, is itself an acknowledgment of physical reality. Only what exists in the world can be subject to photography's ways of displacing things and people; and what exists in the world already bears the stamp of our fantasies.

While agreeing that movies, being photographic, communicate only by way of what is real, Cavell rejects the unabashed appeals to reality inherent in Bazin's view that cinema is essentially a dramaturgy of Nature or Erwin Panofsky's view that the medium of movies is physical reality as such. Panofsky and Bazin do not ask Cavell's question: What *becomes* of reality when it is projected and screened, when film displaces objects and persons from their natural sequences and locales?

There are no particular features by which the world on film can be distinguished from reality. The objects and persons projected on the movie screen appear real in every respect for the simple reason that they *are* real. Yet, these objects and persons do not exist (now), are not really (now) in our presence. The role that reality plays in movies makes the world on film a moving image of skepticism, as "More of *The World Viewed*" (1974) evocatively puts it. But for Cavell it is also a fundamental philosophical principle that the possibility of skepticism is internal to the conditions of human knowledge. That we do not know reality with absolute certainty is a fact about human knowledge, a fact about what knowledge, for human beings, is; it does not follow from this fact that we cannot really know the world, or ourselves in it. The theoretical frameworks that dominate contemporary film study assure us either that we have nothing to lose by embracing skepticism or that they provide systems of thought that enable us to know films with a certainty unattainable by acts of criticism accountable to our experience. Denying us both these assurances, *The World Viewed*—like all of Cavell's writing—continually turns in on itself, turns us to ourselves, calls on us to go forward, to reach this world and achieve selfhood. In returning us to our own experience, it reminds us of the importance of turning to conversation, the importance of expressing ourselves with conviction, and the equal importance of acknowledging each other's words and voices.

In raising Wittgenstein's and Austin's philosophical procedures to an explicit self-consciousness, Cavell participates in transforming the tradition of analytic philosophy from within. In terms of his professional training, Cavell is to be located—he locates himself—on the English-speaking side of the Continental divide between philosophy as understood and practiced in England and the United States (where analytic philosophy has long prevailed) and on the continent of Europe (where philosophy has long edged closer to literature than to science, mathematics, or logic). Between these divergent philosophical traditions, there has been a history of mutual ignorance, neglect, incomprehension, and distrust. But in making this rift within Western philosophy a subject for philosophy, Cavell aspires to bring the two traditions into closer alignment, or to reveal how intimately they have always been aligned. In this spirit, Cavell's writing repeatedly returns to the affinities he finds between Wittgenstein and Heidegger.

The question of the beginning of philosophy, for example, is for Cavell, as for Wittgenstein, a question about the ways philosophy directs itself, motivates itself, in every given instant in which it has its origination. But Cavell also understands, as Heidegger does, the beginning of philosophy to be a historical event at least in principle datable, as are such events as the beginning of skepticism, the emergence of the modern in philosophy, and the splitting of the philosophical spirit between the Anglo-American and the continental traditions itself. This last, for Cavell, is an event that occurred in the nineteenth century. Yet, he also finds this "splitting" to be playing itself out whenever he engages in philosophy. But, if Cavell's professional training places him on the "analytic" side of the gulf, how is it possible for both halves of the divided philosophical spirit to be internal to his philosophical ways of thinking?

The solution to this conundrum, Cavell increasingly comes to recognize, resides in his inheritance of the American transcendentalism of Emerson and Henry David Thoreau. In an illuminating interview, Cavell remarks:

> In their attention to the intimacy of words with the world, and in their inheritance of the transcendental strain in philosophy, Emerson and Thoreau underlie . . . the idea of ordinariness as that surfaces in ordinary language philosophy. At the same time, Emerson underlies in a direct historical way exactly what seems to be the opposite force in contemporary philosophy, so-called Continental philosophy, because through Nietzsche, who loved Emerson's writing, Emerson is at play in the work of Heidegger. . . . I might take 'Emerson' as a name for the fact about the splitting of the philosophical spirit that neither ordinary language philosophy nor Continental philosophy is prepared to acknowledge an apparently opposite form of thinking as an ancestor, much less as a common ancestor.
>
> (Quoted in Fleming and Payne, 1989, p. 52)

The fact that Emerson underlies the new French thought, conjoined with the fact that both the Continental and analytic traditions have forgotten their common ancestor and thus their kinship, intensifies the irony that American literary and film criticism turned to France to receive a philosophy that was American to begin with. This descendant of Emerson's philosophy, received back in America, is no longer something Emerson would simply call philosophy. For Emerson, philosophy is not a gospel that *can be* received; philosophy is always *to be* received.

To read Cavell's writing in a way that acknowledges his philosophical procedures, one must free oneself from prejudicial theories as to how serious philosophy has to *look:*

> If you give up something like formal argumentation as the route to conviction in philosophy, and you give up the idea that either scientific evidence or poetic persuasion is the way to philosophical conviction, then the question of what achieves philosophical conviction must at all times be on your mind. The obvious answer for me is that it must lie in the writing itself. But in *what* about the writing? . . . The sense that nothing other than this prose just here, as it's passing before our eyes, can carry conviction, is one of the thoughts that drives . . . what I do. Together with, I suppose, one other feature . . . I wish to radicalize, if I may say it, the sense that philosophy is at all moments answerable to itself, that if there is any place at which the human spirit allows itself to be under its own question, it is in philosophy; that anything, indeed, that allows that questioning to happen *is* philosophy.
>
> (Ibid., p. 59)

A further key to Cavell's writing may be found in the introduction to *Disowning Knowledge* (1987), where he observes that the ensuing readings of Shakespeare plays work out what he calls his "intuition" that Shakespeare's plays interpret and reinterpret the skeptical problematic:

> In calling my guiding theme an intuition I am distinguishing it from a hypothesis. . . . A hypothesis requires evidence and it must say what constitutes its evidence. . . . An intuition, say that God is expressed in the world, does not require, or tolerate, evidence but rather, let us say, understanding of a particular sort. . . . Emerson says in "Self-Reliance": "Primary wisdom [is] intuition, whilst all later teachings are tuitions." He is accordingly called, not incorrectly, a philosopher of intuition. For some reason it is not typically noticed that he is at the same time a teacher of tuition. I read him as teaching that the occurrence to us of intuition places a demand upon us, namely for tuition; call this wording, the willingness to subject oneself to words, to make oneself intelligible. (Tuition so conceived is what I understand criticism to be.) (1987, p. 3)

Like Emerson, Cavell is at once a philosopher of intuition and a teacher of "tuition." Once an intuition occurs to Cavell, he takes it upon himself to find words of common language to make his intuition—to make himself—intelligible. From the earliest essays of *Must We Mean What We Say?* to his latest writing on Hollywood melodramas, Cavell's prose always seeks at once to exemplify the importance of intuition and to teach the discipline of finding words that achieve a perspective enabling a certain kind of understanding to take place.

The potential importance of *The World Viewed* to the serious study of film is a function of the exemplary scrupulousness by which its prose—chapter by chapter, paragraph by paragraph, sentence by sentence, word by word—"follows out in each case the complete tuition for a given intuition" so that "this prose just here, as it's passing before our eyes," achieves conviction. But the book's potential importance to the serious study of film is no less a function of the fruitfulness of its guiding intuitions.

For example, it is one of the guiding intuitions of *The World Viewed*, as "More of *The World Viewed*" points out, that American westerns, musicals, romantic comedies, and melodramas of the thirties and forties, no less than European masterpieces of the period like Jean Vigo's *L'Atalante* or Jean Renoir's *Grand Illusion* and *The Rules of the Game*, are about the human need for society and the equal human need to escape it, about human privacy and unknownness, about the search for society or community outside or within society at large.

A closely related intuition, which pertains to the morals of movies, underlies Cavell's observation that in films such as *Now, Voyager, Intermezzo*, or *The Man in the Gray Flannel Suit* the man understands himself to have an obligation to return to his wife, rejecting the possibility of staying with the woman of intelligence, depth, and independence whom he really loves, but that these movies understand him also to have an obligation, perhaps an overriding one, to remain with the "woman outside," to create with her a more fulfilling marriage, albeit one that requires that he acknowledge his own outsideness. In movies, it is a virtue—indeed, a moral imperative—to quest for human fulfillment.

What Cavell has discovered about film, in discovering this fact about the morals of movies, is the depth of the medium's commitment to the moral outlook or dimension of thought about morality that in later writings he will call "moral perfectionism." Moral perfectionism, as Cavell goes on to develop it, reformulates the terms of moral philosophy by locating the emergence of what Matthew Arnold calls "the best self" as being at the heart of morality. For Cavell, moral perfectionism is not a theory of morality, however. It is "something like a dimension or tradition of the moral life that spans the course of Western thought and concerns what used to be called the state of one's soul, a dimension that places tremendous burdens on personal relationships and on the possibility or necessity of the transforming of oneself and of one's society" (Cavell, *Conditions Handsome and Unhandsome*, 1990, p. 3). Because moral perfectionism is "an outlook or dimension of thought embodied in a set of texts spanning the range of Western culture," Cavell conceives of his project as developing, through textual readings and theorization motivated by those readings, what he calls an "open-ended thematics" of perfectionism, not as trying to arrive at "some imaginary, essential definition of the idea" (ibid., p. 4).

One such text—*Pursuits of Happiness* cites it as an important historical source of the "remarriage comedy"—is Henrik Ibsen's *A Doll's House*. Cavell's reading of the play in *Conditions Handsome and Unhandsome* focuses on Nora's outrage that hers is not a true marriage. "[Her] imagination of her future, in leaving," in rejecting her marriage in a way that makes her a prototype for film's "woman outside," turns on "her sense of her need for education whose power of transformation presents itself to her as the chance to become human. In Emerson's terms, this is moving to claim one's humanness . . . , to follow the unattained" (ibid., p. 118).

Although Cavell does not use the term in *Pursuits of Happiness*, moral perfectionism is as internal to the "remarriage comedies" the book addresses as it is to *A Doll's House*. In *It Happened One Night, The Awful Truth, Bringing Up Baby, His Girl Friday, The Philadelphia Story, The Lady Eve*, and *Adam's Rib*, the woman—like the figure of the author in *Walden*, or like Emerson in his journals—is on a quest to become fully human. She is fortunate to be married to a man prepared to embrace her quest and preside over her education.

The theme of a woman rejecting a conventional or traditional marriage in order to "follow the unattained" is most fully explored in *Contesting Tears,* Cavell's book about the genre he calls "the melodrama of the unknown woman." In such films as *Stella Dallas, Now, Voyager, Gaslight,* and *Letter from an Unknown Woman,* the woman does not have the luck to be married to Cary Grant or Spencer Tracy, and must seek fulfillment beyond marriage. In the essays that comprise this book, Cavell explicates different paths that the woman takes in these melodramas. At the end of *Now, Voyager,* for example, the woman follows the unattained by walking away from the man and the world generally. *Stella Dallas* ends with the woman walking not away but toward and then past the camera, declaring that she has embarked on a transcendental path of self-discovery.

Already in *The World Viewed,* it is a guiding intuition that there is a serious moral philosophy, or way of thinking about the claims of morality, that was not imposed on movies from the outside, like the Production Code, but is internal to the stories that movies are forever telling. But there are a number of intuitions crucial to *Pursuits of Happiness* and *Contesting Tears* that had not yet occurred to Cavell during the period when he was writing *The World Viewed.* It had not yet fully dawned on him, for example, that the unique combination of popularity and artistic seriousness of American movies of the thirties and forties was in part a function of their inheritance of focal concerns of American transcendentalism—concerns for society, for human relationship generally—exhibited in the work of Emerson and Thoreau. Nor had it yet fully dawned on him that his own philosophical procedures constitute an inheritance of Emerson's and Thoreau's practice of philosophy, too. No less than the movies he finds himself continually thinking about, Cavell's writings are texts that embody moral perfectionism.

These intuitions help motivate, and are motivated by, the significant deepening of Cavell's work that coincides with the publication (all in 1979) of his first essay on Emerson ("Thinking of Emerson"); his reading of *The Lady Eve,* a cornerstone of *Pursuits of Happiness;* and the monumental *The Claim of Reason.* In *Pursuits of Happiness* and *Contesting Tears,* his intuition that Hollywood movies have inherited the concerns of American transcendentalism, conjoined with his intuition that he, too, has inherited these concerns leads Cavell to the astonishing further intuition that his own philosophical procedures are underwritten by the ways American movies "think" about society, human relationships, and their own condition as films. It is in the very movies that were for so many years a normal part of Cavell's week that Emerson's ways of thinking remained alive within American culture, available as an inheritance. Apart from the essential role that Hollywood movies played in Cavell's philosophical education, it would not have been possible for a philosopher who received his professional training within an analytic tradition that—like its Continental counterpart—has never acknowledged Emerson's writ-

ing as (simply) philosophy to have "inherited" Emerson's ways of thinking at all.

"Emerson and Thoreau write comprehensively, brilliantly, with full literary and philosophical achievement, at a moment before the split between the traditions of philosophy is set," Cavell remarks. "If American movies for two decades continued their concerns, then perhaps American movies of that period were accomplishing a feat of philosophical imagination that neither tradition of philosophy could accomplish on its own" ("An Interview with Stanley Cavell," 1989, p. 52). In part from these movies, Cavell learned the ways of thinking that enabled him to accomplish those "feats of philosophical imagination" called *The World Viewed, Pursuits of Happiness, Contesting Tears,* and, for that matter, *Must We Mean What We Say?, The Claim of Reason,* and all the other writings that comprise this American philosopher's singularly ambitious oeuvre.

[*See also* Film.]

BIBLIOGRAPHY

Works by Cavell

The World Viewed: Reflections on the Ontology of Film. New York, 1971; enl. ed., Cambridge, Mass., 1979.

"More of *The World Viewed.*" *Georgia Review* (Winter 1974): 571–631. Reprinted in the enlarged edition of *The World Viewed* (Cambridge, Mass., 1979).

"Leopards in Connecticut." *Georgia Review* (Summer 1976): 233–262. Revised and reprinted in *Pursuits of Happiness* (Cambridge, Mass., 1981), pp. 111–132.

"What Becomes of Things on Film?" *Philosophy and Literature* (Fall 1978). Reprinted in *Themes Out of School: Effects and Causes* (San Francisco, 1984; reprint, Chicago, 1988), pp. 173–183.

"On Makavejev on Bergman." *Critical Inquiry* (Winter 1979): 305–330. Reprinted in *Themes Out of School* (San Francisco, 1984), pp. 106–140.

"Pursuits of Happiness: A Reading of *The Lady Eve.*" *New Literary History* (Spring 1979): 581–601. Revised and reprinted in *Pursuits of Happiness* (Cambridge, Mass., 1981), pp. 45–70.

"Knowledge as Transgression: Mostly a Reading of *It Happened One Night.*" *Daedalus* (Spring 1980): 147–175. Revised and reprinted in *Pursuits of Happiness* (Cambridge, Mass., 1981).

"North By Northwest." *Critical Inquiry* (Summer 1981). Reprinted in *Themes Out of School* (San Francisco, 1984), pp. 152–172, and in *A Hitchcock Reader,* edited by Marshall Deutelbaum and Leland Poague (Ames, Iowa, 1984), pp. 249–264.

Pursuits of Happiness: The Hollywood Comedy of Remarriage. Cambridge, Mass., 1981.

"The Fact of Television." *Daedalus* (Fall 1982): 75–96. Reprinted in *Themes Out of School* (San Francisco, 1984), pp. 235–268.

"The Thought of Movies." *Yale Review* (Winter 1983): 181–200. Reprinted in *Themes Out of School* (San Francisco, 1984), pp. 3–26.

"A Capra Moment." *Humanities* (August 1985): 3–7.

"What Photography Calls Thinking." *Raritan* (Spring 1985): 1–21. Reprinted in *Raritan Reading* (New Brunswick, N.J., 1990), pp. 47–65.

Disowning Knowledge: In Six Plays of Shakespeare. Cambridge and New York, 1987.

"Psychoanalysis and Cinema: The Melodrama of the Unknown Woman." In *Images in Our Souls: Cavell, Psychoanalysis and Cinema,* edited by Joseph H. Smith and William Kerrigan, pp. 11–43. Baltimore, 1987. Expanded version in *The Trial(s) of Psychoanalysis,* edited by Françoise Meltzer (Chicago, 1988), pp. 227–258; revised and reprinted in *Contesting Tears* (Chicago, 1996).

"The Advent of Video." *Artspace* (May–June 1988): 67–69.

"An Interview with Stanley Cavell" (conducted by James Conant). In *The Senses of Stanley Cavell, Bucknell Review,* edited by Richard Fleming and Michael Payne (Lewisburg, Pa., 1989).

"Naughty Orators: Negation of Voice in *Gaslight.*" In *Languages of the Unsayable: The Play of Negativity in Literature and Literary Theory,* edited by Sanford Budick and Wolfgang Iser, pp. 340–377. New York, 1989. Revised and reprinted in *Contesting Tears* (Chicago, 1996).

Conditions Handsome and Unhandsome: The Constitution of Emersonian Perfectionism. The Carus Lectures, 19th series. LaSalle, Ill., 1990; reprint, Chicago, 1990.

"Letter to the Editors: Reply to Tania Modleski." *Critical Inquiry* (Fall 1990): 238–244.

"Postscript (1989): To Whom It May Concern." *Critical Inquiry* (Winter 1990): 248–289. Revised and reprinted in *Contesting Tears* (Chicago, 1996).

"Ugly Duckling, Funny Butterfly: Bette Davis and *Now, Voyager.*" *Critical Inquiry* (Winter 1990): 213–247. Revised and reprinted in *Contesting Tears* (Chicago, 1996).

"Stella's Taste, on *Stella Dallas.*" In *Working Papers in Cultural Studies,* vol. 8. Cambridge, Mass., 1991. Revised and reprinted in *Contesting Tears* (Chicago, 1996).

"Nothing Goes without Saying, Reading the Marx Brothers." *London Review of Books* (6 January 1994): 3–5.

Contesting Tears: Hollywood Melodramas of the Unknown Woman. Chicago, 1996.

WILLIAM ROTHMAN

CENSORSHIP. *See* Law and Art; *and* Obscenity.

CHANCE. *See* Aleatoric Processes.

CHILDREN'S ART. For some, the idea of visual art created by children is a contradiction in terms. For others, it is an obvious given. Whatever one's perspective on this matter, it is undoubtedly the case that children engage in creative activities that utilize media similar in relevant respects to those used by adults and produce objects that are also similar in many respects to the work of adults who are readily identified as artists and whose work is unreservedly called art. Even such well-known artists as Paul Klee and Pablo Picasso have made pronouncements on the matter. It is, thus, reasonable to consider the art or artlike products of children and the conditions of child development that lead to their possibility, as well as an aesthetic understanding of the interest of adult artists to emulate the child in graphic production.

Artistic Production by Children. Can children create art? To evaluate the possibility, several factors must be examined: (1) Is "art" to be understood descriptively, evaluatively, or perhaps even metaphorically when it is applied to children? Is art merely the rendering of visual patterns and pattern combinations, or does art necessarily include the expression of concepts or emotional states in the graphic medium? (2) Is the attitude or intention of a child relevant in determining whether his or her work is art? If so, what sorts of attitudes or intentions will be relevant, and to what extent is the success of the child in realizing his or her particular intentions relevant? Must a child intend to make art for the product to be art? Or, must a child's rendering of a house, for example, meet his or her intentions as to how the house should look in order for the picture of the house to be art? (3) To what extent are the skills of the child relevant in identifying his or her work as art? In other words, to what extent must a child have had specialized art training, exercise and exposure to art to qualify as an artist? (4) To what extent is the artistry of the child to be found in the eye of the adult beholder? Aside from whatever the child understood himself or herself to be doing, if appropriately disposed adults regard the works produced as art, do they then merit that appellation? It is on the basis of answers to these questions that one assents to or rejects the possibility of child artists, and thus of child art.

Whatever their particular views are on these issues, most developmental psychologists and arts educators agree that there are certain stages of artistic activity that are sequential and fairly fixed that each child will go through, so long as the child continues to pursue and cultivate graphic skills. Often children who possess talent as well will go through the stages more quickly and earlier than others. Other factors such as availability of materials and frequent opportunity to engage in their use, as well as adult encouragement, can play a role in the development of a child's artistic capabilities. The general developmental stages of a child's graphic capacities are as follows (not all authors on the subject agree on nomenclature or number of the stages, so the list given is to be understood as a descriptive compilation of those discussed by the many who have written on the subject): (1) scribbles, (2) formation of rough geometric shapes (sometimes described as mandalas), (3) rendering of tadpole-like objects, including human forms, (4) individualistic representation of particular objects, (5) realistic representation of objects, (6) use of simple perspective in representation of objects, (7) expressive representation with skilled perspective, (8) expressive problem solving, representational or abstract, by means of the graphic medium.

It is also clear to observers that what a child does while drawing or painting often involves more than merely setting pencil to paper. The child may tell a story, engage in fantasy play, work through possible outcomes of matters of personal importance, and so on. The graphic medium may function as a means of obtaining access to thoughts and reflections of deep significance or satisfaction to the child. It is said that the work of a child is play, and graphic activity can be one such path of deep engagement for a child. These accomplishments remain available to the child throughout all levels of development.

Typically, there are two points in the artistic development of children that allow for the production of recognizably artlike works, the individualistic representation of particular objects, and expressive problem solving by means of the graphic medium. The former stage is characteristically one of unself-conscious rendering of feelings and thoughts carried out by drawing creatures and characters from favorite stories or taken from other interests embraced by the child. Because the child at this stage is uninhibited by social or self-imposed rules or other constraints, his or her productions are often compelling, striking, and fresh.

With the beginning of first grade, the characteristic unself-consciousness of this stage is overcome by the child's growing need to conform and act according to the rules, even in the area of graphic activity. The child's expressive capacities seem to go underground while mastery of certain skills becomes preeminent, along with the aim to draw or paint "realistically," and usually very predictably. Although children seem to go through the mastery of skills stage during the time (school age) that they would typically become more aware of what traditionally counts as successful art from an art-historical perspective, there seems to be no causal link between such exposure and a child's movement toward or away from mimicry and "realism." Such exposure, however, seems to be significant and beneficial for those children who progress toward the final developmental stage.

That stage, expressive problem solving by means of the graphic medium, is not achieved by all children, and is realized only by some of those young people who persist in their engagement with graphic activity. This stage exemplifies a young person's use of graphic activity as a means of exploring and discovering his or her own understanding of personal issues of significance. It is at this stage that recognizably artlike works again are manifested and may lead to adult artistic activity. Such work is often complex, demonstrates cultivated skill and distinctive technique, and offers content for reflection and contemplation.

The earliest stages of graphic development are often less likely to yield artlike products because they are primitive and unformed, and intermediate stages are often so dedicated to conventional mastery of certain skills, particularly the ability to draw or paint objects realistically, that these stages less frequently allow for noteworthy work. Nonetheless, many would willingly include works from all stages in the realm of art, whereas others would allow none.

Although there is much disagreement over what a child is doing when he or she puts crayon to paper, the focus of attention in considering the works of the theorists discussed here is whether or not children can create art, and what is meant in referring to the works of children as art. Although much has been written about children's graphic activities, the scholarly focus is usually on whether or not children draw what they do because they are cognitively or physically immature and thus deficient, or because the child's ability to solve graphic problems is different from his or her ability to solve other cognitive problems. Another concern has been with the significance of graphic activity on the part of the child as a means of exhibiting feelings or emotional concerns. The concerns of these approaches are cognitive, or physical or emotional. These approaches specifically do not address the aesthetic issue of whether or not children's productions are art. Although it is obvious that children make sketches and paintings and other visual works in various media, the question remains if these productions can be reasonably called art. What conditions must hold for a painting by a child to be called art? In only a few instances do researchers in the field treat this question. The two discussed here specifically address the issue.

Many arts educators identify Rhoda Kellogg (1969) as the authority on art by children. Over the course of her professional life as a nursery school educator, she amassed a collection of more than five hundred thousand children's drawings, made by toddlers to teens, which include works by children from all over the world. Her approach was to classify children's works in terms of the patterns and pattern combinations she found in them. She also developed classifications for pattern sequences from the most simple scribbles to more complex renderings of identifiable objects. Her view is that children create art, and by art she means the visual rendering of patterns and pattern combinations, either with or without the incorporation of conventional cultural formulas and developed technique. Adult artists, as well as older children, typically incorporate cultural formulas and technique, with greater or lesser degrees of success. The relevant component for Kellogg, which makes the work of all of them (including the scribbles of the young toddler) art, is the rendering of basic patterns, both abstractly and in representational images. She maintains that a person's intention and ability to conceptualize are not relevant in the identification of graphic work as art, and evaluation of the graphic works is a matter separate from their identification as art. She also suggests that certain prejudices constrain adult recognition of children's productions as art, moving adults to judge the work of children to be inferior because it is unconventional and self-taught.

Specialists in child development and psychology, however, approach the issue from a variety of perspectives. Most are concerned with cognition and emotion, and their manifestations in children's graphic activities. The work of Rudolf Arnheim (1977) is among the earliest to suggest important developmental reasons to consider the graphic activities of children as significant in themselves, not deficient from an adult measure of competency and understanding (for example, Piaget and Inhelder, 1956, 1971). Most psychologists do not, however, specifically address the artistic status of a child's drawing. All such work is typically identified as "child art," simply assuming the appelation applies, or not wishing to become involved in the ultimate question implied, namely, what is art? Howard Gardner (1980), however, does offer a view on the matter. Gardner's developmental view asserts that although children's work may be artful, it is not art. On this view, to paraphrase Gardner, art is the expression of significant intellectual or emotional insights imparted with an organic sense of form or composition, by a developed and reflective personality, with a certain measure of technical accomplishment. The works of children may engage adult viewers because they are unconventional and fresh, and may provoke in adults reflective considerations because of their spontaneity and lack of self-consciousness, but their work is undeveloped and often unpredictable, and hence, for Gardner, it lacks the necessary depth and complexity of work properly called art. This is not to suggest that Gardner disparages the graphic productions of children; quite the contrary. Rather, his view is that continued engagement with work in the graphic medium may lead to art, given the proper cultivation and encouragement of the child.

Childlikeness in Adult Art. An intriguing and related subject is that of childlikeness expressed in the works of adult artists. This can be understood in two ways: the ways in which the artistic productions of adult artists are like the productions of children, and the ways in which adult artists were influenced by their childhood experiences in a broader sense, and thus produce works that have developed from those experiences. The latter is a topic broad and deep, and is as individualized as each unique person. Many artists' biographies address these childhood influences, and although they contribute to the development of adult artists' interests and approaches to art, they are not specifically the stuff of aesthetic theory. The former topic, however, offers some food for aesthetic thought.

Howard Gardner suggests that in those instances when adult artists successfully achieve childlikeness in their artistic endeavors, it is because they have been able to reduce their artwork to simple forms and combine them for expressive ends. The adult artist suppresses his or her sophistication to arrive at the freshness of childlike simplicity. He or she consciously strives to create works that express innocence despite his or her actual maturity and highly developed skills. But it is Arnheim (1977) who has articulated just what such a cultivation of childlikeness by the adult artist could entail. Contrary to what had been commonly thought by earlier developmental theorists, Arnheim demonstrates that children produce the graphic images they do, not because they are unskilled at the conventions of "realistic" perspectival drawing, nor because they are not observant, nor because they draw what is easier rather than what is more difficult, but because the child very carefully does draw an economical, simplified representation of what he or she sees.

Arnheim argues that the child creates logically, on the basis of his or her actual perceptions, not from conventional-ized, learned ways of adapting what is seen. He shows that perception begins with generalities (triangularity, roundness, etc.) and develops into distinctions among particulars later. Thus, a human head is drawn by the child as a circle, because the child invents a shape that will satisfy the visual generality of roundness perceived by the child. The child spontaneously arrives at the understanding that a certain visual image on paper may stand for something dramatically different in nature so long as its equivalent is constructed or developed in a given medium. What seems obvious to the ordinary adult observer in the Western tradition—namely, that a painting is supposed to imitate both the object and the object as it is in physical space—is really only one specific view from a particular civilization that merely happens to have been around for some time.

According to Arnheim, the hand gives specific form, by means of the various media available, to what the eye perceives. The relationships of the hand and eye begin by using available media (pencils, crayons, etc.), which most typically form lines (a highly abstract choice of representation) that yield simple shapes (circles, curves). Over time, the circles are differentiated by additions and variations. Straight lines are developmentally complex, because of the effort required to create them. They are also the means for establishing boundaries on a work surface and thus defining graphic space. Use of diagonals allows for expression of movement, direction, and other relationships, eventually leading to complex patterns by the use of a number of simple ones. The child perceives the world and invents a means of forming those perceptions within the constraints of the media available, characteristically operating logically and economically in his or her rendering. The contemporary adult artist must select from his or her treasury of technique and skill to recover the simplicity and economy of the child, and consciously set aside the conventions that dominate in the Western tradition. Picasso was a master of such linear ability. By means of curved lines and simple strokes, he was able to capture many details of the human physiognomy.

Relative size of objects pictured can be understood as similar to the transposition of a piece of music from one key to another, that is, not crucial to understanding the overall work, according to Arnheim. It is typical of the work of artists in many cultures to alter size of objects in relation to other objects for many ends other than Western realism. For example, certain figures may be larger than others because of their importance; this may be true of persons as well as objects. Three-dimensionality, however, is a challenge to artistic inventiveness. The child must solve the problem of showing only two of three dimensions in the picture plane. Many solutions have been generated in response to this challenge.

Early on, the child may use a variety of perspectives in the same picture plane to exhibit three-dimensionality. By this time, the child draws what he or she knows is present as well as what he or she sees. For instance, people in a house around a dinner table may be rendered by drawing a table from an aerial view, with full-length figures drawn as if lying on the four sides of the table (with feet facing the sides), inside of a house drawn as a rectangle with a triangle roof. Later, the sides of the house may be added on as additional rectangles on either side of the central one. Additional solutions to three-dimensionality can include depicting the side walls as parallelograms placed at opposite oblique angles to the central rectangle, with the part of the figure farthest away from the viewer widened rather than narrowed. This so-called inverted perspective is not uncommon; one may find it in medieval manuscript illumination, or in Chinese or Persian paintings. It is one of the series of logical solutions to the visual problem being solved. Arnheim is careful to note that the various solutions emerge in a sequence; as the mind masters one solution, the way is made for the next, more complex possibility. Hence, the history of art exemplifies many of these solutions, according to Arnheim. Similar incisive simplifications can be understood to be made in the use of color, or in rendering forms sculpturally in three dimensions. In contemporary Western contexts, Cubism may be seen as exemplifying a rediscovery of some of these solutions to the problem of three-dimensionality.

If a child is taught to mimic some advanced stage of graphic rendering before he or she has experimentally arrived at that point, Arnheim believes that the child will have thus lost the intuitive sense of perceptual mastery and instead will proceed in a merely imitative way. According to Arnheim, the child and the successful artist both are able to give the simplest shape to a visual rendering because they do not engage in imitation.

Klee expressed a similar view decades before Arnheim; he believed that children are preoccupied with and discover how to find a formal structure appropriate to content. Klee strove in a disciplined way to so reduce everything he drew in accordance with such simple visual economy. The successful artist differs from the child in that he or she consciously returns to the convention-free ways of perceiving and is able to render them with the skill and dexterity of the graphically cultivated adult. Picasso has been quoted as saying that in his young manhood he drew like Raphael, but in his maturity he was able to draw like a child, that is to say, recapturing the perceptual freshness of the child.

Aesthetic Theory and Children's Art. What might one learn from considering the writings of art theorists who have not written on children's art specifically, but who have written major documents on the nature of art? To consider a brief sampling of them and their views from the late nineteenth into the recent twentieth century will provide some insight into the issue. Clive Bell maintained that for an object to be art it was sufficient that one be able to observe something he called significant form. For Benedetto Croce, Curt Ducasse, and even Leo Tolstoy, a necessary condition

for art was that it be expressive of the artist and that it communicate that expressiveness to observers. More recently, for George Dickie and Arthur C. Danto, a work is art only if it is admitted to be so by the art world, that is, those who are in authoritative positions in the realm of professional art.

In juxtaposition to these aesthetic theorists, the psychologist Howard Gardner requires that fairly extensive conditions be met by an artist, hence, more demanding conditions are necessary for an object to be considered art by him. For Gardner, it is virtually impossible for a child to produce art because a child is an incompletely developed personality, and may also lack some of the other qualifications he has stipulated. Because the child lacks some or most of the necessary components required for artists, the child cannot be an artist, and thus cannot produce art. Gardner's view makes the meaning of art evaluative, as is the case with most art theorists, but his requirements are perhaps more demanding than most.

Art educator Rhoda Kellogg and those who follow or are sympathetic to her view require less than any of the art theorists mentioned above, and far less than would be required by Gardner. For her, instances of the various categories of patterns she has identified to be exhibited graphically are sufficient for a work to be art. One might argue that, for her, art is merely the making of patterns, designs, or images. The quality of the works produced do not weigh for or against their being art. Thus, children are artists, and they produce art, because they can produce the full complement of patterns and pattern combinations that she has identified, as can virtually any other human being. (Other primates are left out because they cannot produce all the pattern possibilities, according to her research.) Her view makes the meaning of art not only simply descriptive, but perhaps even metaphorical, compared to more mainstream accounts of the nature of art.

In some sense, the graphic productions of children fare most reasonably when evaluated in terms of mainstream aesthetic or theoretical explanations of what art is. Certainly, there have been no difficulties in accepting childlikeness when exhibited by adult artists, because, in a contemporary context, unconventionality is usually considered creative and thus is positively valued. Under most explanations, some children's work will be designatable as art because it is expressive, or well formed, or recognized by noteworthy members of the art world and treated accordingly. There have been gallery showings of children's artistic productions for decades. Perhaps one of the reasons the views of Kellogg and Gardner result in extreme consequences for the artistic productions of children is that they neglect a relevant component in considering what makes a work art, and that is the role of the observer. In most art-theoretical accounts, the observer is relevant to the designation of a work as art, typically because of some sort of noteworthy response—behavioral, cognitive, or emotional—occurring in the observer. This in part explains why many adults are willing to identify some of the productions of children as art: children's works can evoke noteworthy responses of the kind that recognized artworks by adults do.

The philosopher Gareth Matthews (1994) specifically considers some of these matters in discussing how to regard child art. He readily admits the graphic productions of children to the realm of art, because they may well evoke appropriate responses in observers, but he laments their exclusion from most reputable contexts for viewing art. Although he notes the existence of the International Museum of Children's Art in Oslo, Norway, he offers an explanation for the rarity of serious recognition of children's art. Matthews points out that maturity is positively valued in most societies and immaturity is negatively valued. Thus, the works of immature persons, that is, children, are considered inappropriate for inclusion with the most mature achievements in art, those worthy of being collected and preserved in museums. In contrast, Matthews argues that just as children are not "proto-people," neither are their graphic productions proto-art. For some, their childhood graphic productions are not equaled nor surpassed by their adult graphic productions. Matthews wonders why this child work should not be regarded seriously, and included in museums and galleries as adult work is.

Ultimately, it is one's requisite conditions on artists, artworks, and observers that will determine one's view on the possibility of art by children, and the aesthetic significance of childlikeness in artistic production. So long as multiple views remain alive on these matters, so too will varying views be actively considered among those interested in the subject.

[*See also* Education, Aesthetic; *and* Psychology of Art.]

BIBLIOGRAPHY

Arnheim, Rudolf. *Art and Visual Perception: A Psychology of the Creative Eye.* New exp. rev. ed. Berkeley, 1974.
Britsch, Gustaf. *Theorie der bildenden Kunst.* Munich, 1926.
Chapman, Laura H. *Approaches to Art in Education.* New York, 1978.
Coles, Robert. *Their Eyes Meeting the World: The Drawings and Paintings of Children.* Edited by Margaret Sartor. Boston, 1992.
Gardner, Howard. *Artful Scribbles: The Significance of Children's Drawings.* New York, 1980.
Geist, Hans Friedrich. "Paul Klee and the World of the Child." *Werk* (June 1950).
Gesell, Arnold, ed. *The First Five Years of Life.* New York, 1940.
Golomb, Claire. *Young Children's Sculpture and Drawing: A Study in Representational Development.* Cambridge, Mass., 1974.
Golomb, Claire. *The Child's Creation of a Pictorial World.* Berkeley, 1992.
Grozinger, Wolfgang. *Scribbling, Drawing, Painting: The Early Forms of the Child's Pictorial Creativeness.* New York, 1955.
Kellogg, Rhoda. *Analyzing Children's Art.* Palo Alto, Calif., 1969.
Matthews, Gareth B. *The Philosophy of Childhood.* Cambridge, Mass., 1994.
Piaget, Jean, and Barbel Inhelder. *The Child's Conception of Space.* Translated by F. J. Langdon and J. L. Lunzer. London, 1956.
Piaget, Jean, and Barbel Inhelder. *Mental Imagery in the Child.* Translated by P. A. Chilton. New York, 1971.
Rank, Otto. *Art and Artist: Creative Urge and Personality Development.* New York, 1932.
Read, Herbert. *Education through Art.* 2d ed. New York, 1945.
Schaefer-Simmern, Henry. *The Unfolding of Artistic Activity.* Berkeley, 1948.

CYNTHIA ROSTANKOWSKI

CHINESE AESTHETICS. [*This entry comprises two essays on the artistic and aesthetic traditions of China:*
 Historical Overview
 Painting Theory and Criticism
The first essay traces the history of Chinese aesthetics and, in particular, the shifts in theoretical and critical focus within the discussions of the arts; contrasts are also made at times with Western aesthetics. The second essay examines in detail the history of the theory and criticism of Chinese painting, which provides a good basis for a comparison to Western aesthetics, where painting has been central. See also Comparative Aesthetics; Criticism; Daoist Aesthetics; *and* Japanese Aesthetics.]

Historical Overview

For the purposes of surveying the history of aesthetic doctrines in China and comparing that history with parallel developments in other cultures, two themes stand out: one is the alternation of different artistic media as the dominant source of models for aesthetic theorizing; the other is shifts in the philosophical orientation of the theories themselves.

The Archaic Period: Music as the Measure (c.1000 BCE–300 CE). The Chinese Bronze Age has bequeathed us impressive works of art—bronze vessels, poems, narratives—and some persistent patterns of interpretation. The first aesthetic theories to develop in China took courtly ritual as their reference and end value, and music as their leading model. "The way of music and the way of governing are one." "When the Eight Sounds harmonize, men and Spirits rejoice" (*Li ji* [Records of Ritual], c.200 BCE). Musical performance was, of course, only one element in a complex of ritual activities including tribute, hunting, investitures, communal feasting, archery demonstrations, weddings, funerals, and ancestral sacrifice; but the theory of music possessed a formal language apt to elucidate the patterns common to all these endeavors. In musical performance, elements that are simply diverse (such as sounds and dances, or bells and pipes) or that are similar in kind but distinctively graded (such as notes and modes) come together for a common end. This unity in diversity struck ancient writers as the very pattern of a well-organized society:

> When unlike is joined to unlike, the result is called harmony [*he*]. . . . But if sameness is added to sameness, exhaustion is reached and matters are at an end. . . . Where there is but one

sound, hearing ceases; where there is but one kind of material, pattern is absent; where there is but one kind of taste, there is no sweetness; where there is but one kind of example, there is no persuasion.

(Discussions of the States [Guo yu]; from a speech purportedly delivered in 779 BCE)

The "Record of Music" section of the *Li ji* elaborates on such analogies, assigning each note of the five-note scale a social correlate, with the lowest or foundational note standing for the ruler, the next lowest his chief ministers, and so forth. Music with one or more notes "out of place" betokened political disaster. Although music is, in the thinking of early authors, ultimately subordinate to ritual norms, it is occasionally said to counterbalance the excesses of ritual, for whereas "ritual distinguishes [people] insofar as they are unlike, music unifies [them] insofar as they are similar" *(Li ji)*. If beauty is (to borrow the Kantian phrase) a "symbol of morality" for the early Chinese, the likeness rests on the properties of distinction, inclusiveness, integration, and compensatory balancing (the chief elements of the idea of *he* or harmony as expounded in ancient texts). The gentleman practices the art of music and recites the Odes in order to deepen his moral training; the king surrounds himself with the symbols of order and balance (bells, drums, patterned bronze vessels, many-colored embroideries, and so forth) in order to have always before him reminders of the standards of wise rule. Only Mozi (fl. 479–438 BCE) condemned music as a waste of resources and time with no ethical benefit.

The aesthetic of musical and ritual values is bound up with the historical vision common to the Confucian thinkers of the preimperial age (sixth to third centuries BCE). These thinkers looked back to a legendary period of political and cultural unity as their utopia, when sage-kings created institutions for the general good of later generations. Accordingly, late-classical texts of musical theory present a defense of the sacred tradition against the encroachment of mere entertainment music. A distrust of aesthetic pleasure thus enters the tradition. Confucius (551–479 BCE) said: "I detest purple for displacing vermilion. I detest the tunes of Zheng for corrupting classical music" *(Analects [Lun yu]*, translated by D. C. Lau). The argumentative structure of Confucius's comment on colors and tones—a standard of propriety (or purity) set against examples of depravity (or admixture)—informs the oldest surviving document of literary interpretation, the *Prefaces* and *Commentary* (c.140 BCE) attached to the classic *Book of Odes* (*Shi jing*, c.800–500 BCE). These exegeses, which to modern eyes seem far-fetched and exaggeratedly moralistic, present the words of each Ode as symptomatic of tendencies in the government of its time. Such interpretation indicates that poetry has to render accounts to political authority, that the final standards of aesthetic judgment are utilitarian or moralistic. The moral-political understanding of art has persisted down to the present. The merciless demand for conformity with an elusive (because inconsistent) party line in art during the Great Proletarian Cultural Revolution (1965–1973) has, however, somewhat discredited such attitudes. The recent popularity of autotelic art and "misty" poetry is largely a compensatory reaction against the aesthetic criticism of ignorant official censors.

Once the Qin (221–207 BCE) and Han (206 BCE–220 CE) dynasties had realized the political dream of the unified empire, a period of consolidation set in. Court styles of music and poetry attracted practitioners and regional imitators. A new genre of expository "rhapsodies" *(fu)*, uniting description, allusion, mythology, and instruction, spread forth in endless detail the marvels of the Han world. "Music Bureau poetry" *(yuefu shi)* recorded folk songs and ballads in a style consonant with court literary decorum. History writing took on drama and pathos with the vigorous, dense writing of Sima Qian (*Records of the Historian [Shi ji]*, completed c.86 BCE). Forms of pictorial art with fixed political and ethical connotations were elaborated and widely diffused (see Powers [1991] on the "classicism" of tomb reliefs of the late Han). No less a part of this cultural ingathering was the compilation of great syncretic works in which philosophical, aesthetic, political, and scientific issues are tightly interwoven: examples are the *Springs and Autumns of Lü Buwei* (*Lüshi chunqiu*), the *Huainan zi* compiled under the supervision of Liu An, the *Copious Dew of the Spring and Autumn Chronicles* (*Chunqiu fanlu*) of Dong Zhongshu. All speak of a cosmic order in which symmetries and patterns play an integrative role.

Han cosmologies are often described as "associative" or "correlative." They build up cycles of opposed qualities and map cycles on one another in an indefinite system of correlations. Thus the five directions (West, East, North, South, and Center) are matched with the Five Phases of matter (metal, wood, water, fire, earth), with the five flavors, the five musical notes, and so forth. The system in all its refinements appears in calendrical and divinatory manuals (among them the later strata of the *Yi jing* or *Book of Changes* and the *Canon of Supreme Mystery* (*Tai xuan jing*) of Yang Xiong (53 BCE–18 CE). Here one may recognize a reappearance of the differentiated sets of elements first put into circulation by theorists of music and ritual. Students of comparative philosophy are bound to take an interest in these models, because their lingering influence has often been blamed for the neglect of the cause-and-effect paradigms preferred by the Greek and Arab philosophers (see Needham, 1956–). Whether the correlative mannerism is deemed to have ensured the stability of traditional Chinese thinking or to have foreclosed the possibility of scientific investigation, a ritual aesthetic seeking order, balance, and symmetry is certainly among its predisposing conditions. The shadow cast by the early theorists of music is accordingly long.

From "Pure Conversations" to a Renewed Classicism (c.300–1400). The dissolution of the Han empire in the third century left the ritual aesthetic unsupported by a public framework, even a nostalgic one. The next four centuries of political fragmentation proved more congenial to individualist programs. A fifth-century collection of anecdotes, the *Shi shuo xinyu* (A New Account of Tales of the World) of Liu Yiqing, contains many vivid stories about scholars who, in retreat from a chaotic public world, take their bearings from art, wine, and fellowship with nature. By abandoning his official career and retiring to the countryside, not out of any sense of aggrieved merit but simply because he was no longer willing "to bow and scrape for five monthly pecks of rice," the poet Tao Qian (Tao Yuanming, 365–427) inaugurated a new model of the literary life, one that, in Tao's words, "cherished rusticity" rather than fame or influence and "returned to things as they are" ("Gui yuantian ju" [On Returning to Gardens and Fields], poem 1 of 5). In this period of disunity, the writings of the early Daoist author Zhuangzi (Zhuang Zhou, c.370–290 BCE), with their insistence on the incommensurability of subjective experiences, the futility of normative judgments, and the triviality of worldly concerns, enjoyed a new popularity. In the debating sessions known as "Pure Conversations" [*qingtan*], scholars, officials, and monks discussed themes such as "Music has no grief or joy." Now, if ever, aesthetics could compete with ethics in determining the content of the well-lived life.

By this time, too, Buddhism had taken root among the literate classes, bringing its conceptions of the illusory character of perceived reality. The influence of Buddhist speculation on the nature of knowledge and perception is to be seen in the vocabulary that came to take the place of the earlier language of ritual norms and measures: now the problem of art was seen as one with the problem of perception. Writing on art now comes to speak of adequation as the goal of the well-made work. But this adequation does not propose to reproduce objects or actions; rather, the artist's or writer's task is to cause the viewer to experience the very state that had triggered the composition:

> If response by the eye and accord by the mind [to nature] is considered a universal law, when similitude is successfully achieved, eyes will also respond completely and the mind be entirely in accord. This response and accord will affect the spirit [*shen*] and, as the spirit soars, the truth [*li*] will be attained. . . . Furthermore the spirit, which is essentially limitless, resides in forms and stimulates all kinds of life, and truth enters into reflections and traces. . . . I rejoice in my spirit, and that is all. What could be placed above that which rejoices the spirit?
>
> (Zong Bing [375–443], cited in Bush and Shih, 1985, pp. 36–38)

The arguments of the most comprehensive Chinese work of literary theory, Liu Xie's *Wenxin diaolong* (The Mind of Letters and the Carving of Dragons, c.520), display both a Confucian concern with public decorum and the Daoist-Buddhist fascination with insights beyond words and forms. Consonant with the primarily social focus of early Chinese philosophy, literary theorists considered that the writer's aim was to evoke a vivid, identificatory response from the reader: images in verse or likeness in painting were to be judged according to that purpose, and not primarily as representations of things.

The Chinese creation of Chan or meditative Buddhism (better known in the West under its Japanese name of Zen) combined with the traditional literati values of sincerity and intelligent amateurism to generate a classical stylistic sense whose values survived as long as the imperial system flourished, although their realizations might change. Yan Yu (fl. c.1250), in his *Canglang shihua* (Canglang's Remarks on Poetry) singled out for supreme honor those poets who "were antelopes that hang by their horns, leaving no tracks to be followed" by the reader of their works. True poetry, for Yan, possessed "a limpid and sparkling quality that can never be quite fixed and determined—like tones in the empty air, or color in a face, or moonlight in the water, or an image in a mirror: the words [of the poem] are finite, but the meaning is never exhausted" (translated by Stephen Owen [1992], modified). Each clause in the passage just quoted evokes a traditional Chan parable for the unreality of appearances. Also favoring a reinterpretation of art in the language of Zen was the brevity of the major Chinese art genres, which may have predisposed thinkers to form an aesthetic of intensity rather than of systematicity, of implication rather than of exhaustive presentation. The four- or eight-line poem, the calligraphic inscription, and the ink landscape on white paper express the elegant frugality of literati taste, a taste that prized, in fact, the "insipid" [*dan*] over all other flavors. Books of "poetry-talk" [*shihua*] and colophons added to paintings are valuable records of responses to artworks experienced under these norms. The reader of a poetry collection and the viewer of a picture took in, alongside the artwork itself, the responses of earlier observers, recorded as commentary or inscription. Taste became a mode of self-definition; readers defined themselves against other readers whose annotations became part of the history of the poets they read. Such competition and emulation links the reception of works of art to such nodal points of public culture as the civil-service examinations; it also forms an area of interchange with the rising commercial classes of the later empire (see Clunas, 1991).

The Reevaluation of the Familiar (c.1400–1911). Poetry and painting, the chosen arts of the scholar-gentry, were the focus of most express aesthetic theorizing. Drama, narrative fiction, music, dance, and sculpture, considered decorative or entertainment genres, were in principle left to the care of professionals; commentary on these forms was generally unambitious, technical, or connoisseurly. But as social cataclysms (such as the Mongol domination of China

[1260–1368], the educational and bureaucratic stagnation of the last years of the Ming dynasty [1368–1644], or the bloody transition from Ming to Qing [1644–1911]) dislodged former members of the scholar-official class from their positions, and as printed books became more readily available, the subordinate genres increasingly became vehicles (and transforming catalysts) of literati taste. The new prominence of popular drama and the novel brought new aesthetic concerns, notably an attention to the imitative properties of art. In this regard, practitioners led theoreticians. The theater of the late Ming often stages reader response as dramatic action. In Tang Xianzu's (1550–1617) *Mudan ting* (The Peony Pavilion), for example, a young woman is resurrected from the dead by the devotion of a young man who knows her mainly from gazing on her portrait and reading her scraps of verse. The two are married after a special audience before the emperor clears the young man of the charge of grave robbing. The moral of the play, according to a brief introduction by its author, is that passion *(qing)* is strong enough to conquer anything. The cult of *qing* provoked by Tang's drama stimulated a poetics and ethics of spontaneity, at odds with the increasingly stiff and moralistic official culture of the Ming and Qing periods. In addition, the repression of political activism among the gentry in the seventeenth and eighteenth centuries forced artists and writers to give their frustrations the form of personal manias and nostalgias: see, for example, the extraordinary paintings of the refugee Ming prince and Zen monk Bada Shanren (personal name Zhu Da), combining quirky observation of nature with the bite of allegory and satire. The artistic complexity of works produced under these conditions surely derives in part from the fact that their authors were unable to adopt positions of cultural authority or the corresponding reflexes of moral dogmatism.

Generally admitted to be allegorical (but allegorical of what?), the immense novel *Hong lou meng* (Dream of the Red Chamber) by Cao Xueqin (?1715–1764) displays both an encyclopedic awareness of the many kinds of art and a chameleon-like gift of imitation. Sermons, mantras, social verse, examination essays, opera scenes, drinking games, riddles, medical prescriptions, philosophical parody, and epitaphs all find their place in the novel, cleverly subordinated to the novelist's concern with story and character. Cao's fusion of different art forms and his integration of "high" artistic values into "low" genres remain, for most readers, an unsurpassable summa.

CHINESE AESTHETICS. Wang Fu, *Remembering Ni Zan's "Wutong Tree and Bamboo by a Thatched Pavillion"* (1408), hanging scroll, ink on paper, 104.0 × 30.2 cm; Art Museum, Princeton University (Gift of Professor Wen Fong, class of 1951, and Mrs. Fong, in honor of John B. Elliot, class of 1951). (Photograph copyright 1998 by the Trustees of Princeton University; used by permission.)

Commentaries on novels, attentive to technique and implication, had circulated since the early Ming period; but it was not until the last days of imperial China that a philosophically ambitious theory of aesthetic experience based itself primarily on drama and fiction. (The renegade philosoper Li Zhi [1527–1602] had written in praise of the bandit novel *Shui hu zhuan,* but that was still a gesture of defiance.) This theory was the work of the great critic, antiquary, and poet Wang Guowei (1877–1927). Guided by Arthur Schopenhauer's philosophy and by Buddhist epistemology, Wang proclaimed the *Dream of the Red Chamber* and the popular theater of the Mongol period the privileged exhibits of an aesthetic that saw the business of art as the creation of simulacra, *jingjie* (literally, "domains" or "spheres"), worlds within the world that can be contemplated without interest or passion (*Hong lou meng pinglun* [On the *Hong lou meng*], 1904; *Renjian cihua* [Poetry-Talk in the Human World], 1910, 1928; *Song Yuan xiqu kao* [An Examination of Song and Yuan Drama], 1912). The Aristotelian resonance is plain; but the mimetic leanings of Wang's theory were balanced by a reinterpretation of the evocation-and-response aesthetics traditional to Chinese poetry-talk. A terminological innovation reveals the hybridity of Wang's aesthetic. Poetry that seems to afford direct access to the poet's perceptions and emotions wins from him the description *bu ge,* "without a veil," while poetry that impresses its stylistic refinements on the reader is qualified as *ge,* "veiled." As in certain epochs of Western aesthetic thinking, transparent language is valued above language that calls attention to itself; but that on which transparent language opens is not represented by things but states of mind.

Colloquial, Mass, and Market Art (1911–1990s). Behind Wang Guowei's theory of art one sees the suggestive power of imported theory and examples. Around the turn of the twentieth century, European literature was represented in translation mainly by contemporary novels and drama, which drew the attention of Chinese readers by their insistent claims of realistic depiction. Aristotle, it might be said, entered China on the coattails of Charles Dickens, Émile Zola, and Henrik Ibsen. (The definition of the "realism" particular to late-imperial Chinese fiction is still a matter of debate; surely it is not identical to that of nineteenth-century Europe; but it is significant that Chinese practitioners of journalism and memoir fiction thought that they saw justification for their work in translated European authors.) With the demise of the imperial educational system, the classical language of poetry and belletristic prose lost its forum. The new literature of Republican China, as a 1917 manifesto of Hu Shi (1891–1962) and Chen Duxiu (1879–1942) put it, would depict contemporary reality in colloquial language: a doubly mimetic program. From the 1920s forward, leftist intellectuals called for (and critiqued each other for not providing) art of, by, and for the masses.

One result was the cultivation of folk art and of folk-derived art forms (e.g., ballads and woodblock prints), but shorn of their "feudal" values. Mao Zedong's "Yanan Talks on Literature and Art" (1942) consolidated the Communist Party's position that literary and artistic workers were to be "cogs and wheels" in the revolutionary cause. Just how demanding this requirement could be was seen in the Cultural Revolution—an epidemic of denunciations and purges touched off, and surely not accidentally, by literary criticism: a series of articles attacking Wu Han's historical drama *Hai Rui baguan* (Hai Rui Dismissed from Office).

Since around 1980, the opening of the art market to foreign buyers and Chinese writers' ready access to publishers and audiences outside the People's Republic have encouraged borrowing and experiment. The academic study of aesthetics, no longer bound to display orthodoxy, has rediscovered the works of Zhu Guangqian. (A brilliant analyst of Sigmund Freud and Benedetto Croce, Zhu was condemned for "idealism" in the 1950s and for many years published translations only—but translations of G. W. F. Hegel's *Aesthetics* and Giambattista Vico's *New Science,* no less!) Li Zehou has worked the Kantian themes of sublimity, teleology, and the free play of the faculties into a Marxian anthropology. Li's work has been the subject of broad public debate in China, where aesthetics is considered an essential philosophical field. But readers trained in Western methods may find more stimulation in the reexamination of the texts of the Chinese tradition, as carried out in Zhu's *Tan mei* (Speaking of the Beautiful) and Li's *Huaxia meixue* (The Chinese Aesthetic).

BIBLIOGRAPHY

Bush, Susan, and Christian Murck, eds. *Theories of the Arts in China.* Princeton, N.J., 1983.

Bush, Susan, and Hsio-yen Shih, eds. *Early Chinese Texts on Painting.* Cambridge, Mass., 1985.

Clunas, Craig. *Superfluous Things: Material Culture and Social Status in Early Modern China.* Cambridge, 1991.

Denton, Kirk A., ed. *Modern Chinese Literary Thought: Writings on Literature, 1893–1945.* Stanford, Calif., 1996.

Falkenhausen, Lothar von. *Suspended Music: Chime-Bells in the Culture of Bronze-Age China.* Berkeley, 1993.

Li Zehou. *Huaxia meixue* (The Chinese Aesthetic). Hong Kong, 1988.

Li Zehou and Liu Guangji. *Zhongguo meixue shi* (A History of Chinese Aesthetics). Beijing, 1984–1987.

Liu I-ch'ing (Liu Yiqing). *Shih-shuo Hsin-yü: A New Account of Tales of the World.* Translated by Richard B. Mather. Minneapolis, 1976.

Needham, Joseph, ed. *Science and Civilisation in China.* Cambridge, 1956–.

Owen, Stephen, ed. *Readings in Chinese Literary Thought.* Cambridge, Mass., 1992.

Plaks, Andrew H. *The Four Masterworks of the Ming Novel.* Princeton, N.J., 1987.

Powers, Martin J. *Art and Political Expression in Early China.* New Haven, 1991.

Rolston, David L. *Traditional Chinese Fiction and Fiction Commentary: Reading and Writing between the Lines.* Stanford, Calif., 1997.

Saussy, Haun. *The Problem of a Chinese Aesthetic.* Stanford, Calif., 1993.

Wang Fang-yu and Richard Barnhart. *Master of the Lotus Garden: The Life and Art of Bada Shanren, 1626–1705.* Edited by Judith G. Smith. New Haven, 1990.

Wang Kuo-wei (Wang Guowei). *Jen-chien Tz'u-hua: A Study in Chinese Literary Criticism.* Translated by Adele Austin Rickett. Hong Kong, 1977.

Zhu Guangqian. *Tan mei* (Speaking of the Beautiful). Taipei, 1967.

HAUN SAUSSY

Painting Theory and Criticism

Aesthetics, if it is narrowly defined as a philosophical discipline concerned with the study of beauty, was only imported into China in recent times when Western philosophy began to be read in translation. Still, in dynastic China, as in the Greco-Roman world and in postmedieval Europe, the appreciation and collecting of painting flourished, and famous artists were recorded in collections of biographies. A few references to painting occur in early Chinese texts, and essays on Chinese art theory and criticism are extant from the fifth century CE. That being the case, it is of interest that different attitudes toward nature and art are embodied by culture heroes in Chinese and Greek mythology. Prometheus, the fire stealer, who was punished by Zeus for this gift to mankind, and Icarus, the first astronaut, who did not heed the warnings of his craftsman-father Daedalus, exemplify overreachers who transgress patriarchal authority in an attempt to master the secrets of nature. By contrast, the early sage-rulers of China, often part beast or dragon, benevolently deliver their cultural inventions by discerning natural laws with their special insight. One can think of the Yu, the first engineer to dam a great river, whose irrigation projects depended, as it were, in going with the flow. The four-eyed Cang Jie created writing, and hence calligraphy and painting, when he traced written ideographs suggested by the prints of birds' claws or the markings on tortoise shells. Evil spirits were said to howl at the time of Cang's invention, recognizing its magical power. The sage's role was to civilize by interpreting the natural order, and it is noteworthy that Chinese creation myths lack a strong creator god or father figure.

In historical times, Chinese philosophy of the Warring States Period was the source for two valuable perspectives, Daoist and Confucian, that were to serve as framing polarities in later art theory. The *Zhuangzi* text (fourth to third centuries BCE) contained stories of master craftsmen whose arts of butchering or carving were perfected by practice to the extent that they were guided by spirit alone. On the other hand, a few well-known statements contrasting substance and decoration, and truth and beauty, occurred in the Confucian *Analects,* traditionally dated somewhat earlier. The *Lidai minghua ji* of 847 CE begins by stating two views in two sentences: "Now painting is a thing which perfects civilized teachings and helps social relationships. It penetrates completely the divine permutations of nature and fathoms recondite and subtle things."

Painting's educational aspect came to the fore in the later Han dynasty (25–220 CE) when portraits of historical figures and Confucian officials were done on palace walls. Then it was thought that a shared capacity for stimulus and response ensured that paragons would be admired and villains abhorred. However, there was some debate about whether a famous man was best known through his words rather than through portraiture. The names of several court muralists have been recorded, indicating that by Han times painting was considered more than mere decoration.

Confucian influence waned with the breakdown of imperial bureaucracy in the Six (or Southern and Northern) Dynasties (220–589). Then barbarian invasions overran northern China causing massive emigrations of Chinese to the south, where an aristocratic émigré elite held power in a series of unstable kingdoms (the Southern Dynasties), and proved receptive to a reinterpreted philosophical or religious Daoism. Their cultural ideal was the writer, poet, or debater rather than the warrior-official of pre-Han lore, and literary figures in landscape settings began to be portrayed in palaces and tombs. Aesthetic appreciation of scenery was celebrated in poetic competitions, and the resulting landscape poetry inspired the earliest landscape painting. The best-known artist of the period is Gu Kaizhi (c.345–c.406). Labeled a wit, half-genius, and half-fool, he managed to paint for the several competing strongmen of his era and to survive, whether by subtle flattery or by true simpleness is hard to say. In any case, he served as a prototype for later individualist artists who acted, or were, mad, often at times of dynastic change. Gu himself was a literary figure, the author of extant poetic fragments and the subject of an official biography and several contemporary anecdotes. Hence, paintings in Southern Dynasties style were attributed to him by later connoisseurs, and several early painting texts that illustrate poems or poetic prose also go under his name.

These texts consist of the earliest treatise on the technique of painting, mislabeled and mixed up with collected critical appreciations of specific scrolls, *Lun hua* (Essay on Painting), and the first description of how to paint a landscape, *Hua Yuntaishan ji* (Record on Painting the Cloud Terrace Mountain). The latter depicted the leaders of a religious Daoist sect, and Gu's family evidently had Daoist affiliations. Although Gu is known to have appreciated landscape scenery and to have placed his subjects in natural settings, his forte was figure painting and portraiture. He prescribed capturing the vitality of a sitter, *chuan shen* (transmitting the spirit), by dotting in eye pupils or adding chin hairs, or directing a gaze toward an object of interest, and he stressed the importance of *gu* (bone, or structure) in figures and *shi* (structural force) in dynamic landscape forms. His interests foreshadow much later Chinese painting.

Two Southern Dynasties texts are often paired under the labels of "landscape Daoism" or "landscape Buddhism." *Xu hua* (Discussion of Painting) by the young aristocrat Wang Wei (415–443) defends painting in neo-Daoist terms as an art comparable to calligraphy with the conceptual scope of the *Yi jing* images. Forms are infused with *ling* (soul), but it is *Xin* (mind) that is the catalyst for movement. Painting's achievement is to depict all things in the universe according to kind and shape, but its true experience is the response to natural scenery stimulated in the viewer. Similarly, the *Hua shanshui xu* (Introduction to Painting Landscape) stresses that even large mountains can be represented in proportion on a small scale and that similitude will trigger the viewer's response to depicted scenery. Its author, the Buddhist layman Zong Bing (375–443), was both an avid mountain climber and an artist. In his old age, possibly influenced by Buddhist meditation practices, he made use of paintings to travel in his mind's eye and strengthen his *shen* (immortal spirit). It is of interest that both texts end with a lyrical appreciation of nature as seen in the viewer's imaginative response. One might note that the landscape style of the period was relatively primitive and conceptual, and that poetic appreciations were the hallmark of Southern Dynasties writing.

These last points should be kept in mind when one assesses the critical biographies of artists collected by the early sixth-century portraitist Xie He in the *Gu huapin lu* (Classification of Painters). Unlike Gu K'ai-chih, most well-known artists did not merit official biographies, hence the reason for Xie's text. Contemporary practices of rating officials in grades and of characterizing personalities in atmospheric phraseology influenced the ranking of artists and descriptions of styles. Binomial terms beginning with *feng* (wind) and *qi* (breath, vapor, spirit, or energy) abound, and their references to painters or styles or subjects can seem ambiguous at times. The most famous term, *qiyun*, is usually translated as "spirit resonance" or "spirit consonance" (one recent rendering is "resonant spirit"). It occurs as the first part of the First Law (or Canon), one of the six laws of painting recorded in Xie's preface that were to be interpreted in various ways down to modern times. Reading in reverse from least to most important, the sixth law seems to refer to copying old works, a matter of details and training. The fifth describes composition as placing and arranging, no doubt initially of figures and props rather than of the surface area of scroll, screen, or mural. The third and fourth are usually taken as referring to correct kind and shape and to appropriate coloring or surface, in other words to what is later thought of as technique. The second, *gufa yong bi*, "bone-means/structural method, (by/in) using the brush," may conceivably indicate the importance of structure in figures as given by brush outlines but comes to mean brushwork with inner strength. The first law is the most controversial and most quoted, and may have been used to

describe liveliness or a sense of energy in an artist's subjects. In it, *qiyun* is paired (or explained) with *shengdong* (life-motion, or vitality), a term applied to all living things in Tang paintings. In later interpretations, the *qi* of "spirit resonance" is found in landscape or brushwork and the first law is used to praise paintings imbued with an artist's energy or personality. The legacy of the first and second laws can be seen in modern connoisseurs' appreciation of vitality and brushwork. Note that a "still life" is more than an oxymoron in Chinese terms: a painting that merely depicts objects' mass and volume can seem dead to Chinese eyes.

Xie He's text is the first in a series of collected biographies of artists. Imperial patronage sponsored innumerable palace screens and temple murals during the Tang dynasty (618–906), and religious and secular figure painting reached a height. Wars and Buddhist persecutions, however, had destroyed many important works of art by 847, inspiring Zhang Yanyuan to write the *Lidai minghua ji* (Record of Famous Painters of All the Dynasties). His compendium contained various essays on painting history, schools, connoisseurship, and technique, and is an invaluable source for the pre-Tang painting texts that he included in the biographies and for the definitions and critiques that he cited in his arguments. The best candidate to stand as the Chinese Vasari, Zhang came from a family of officials who had practiced calligraphy and collected painting for several generations, and he later edited essays on examples of calligraphy. When considering the styles of important masters, he stressed the calligraphic technique of their brush lines, a Tang insight, and admired the bravura performance of Wu Daozi, whose Buddhist and Daoist images seemed to turn and move off the wall.

Another extant text of the 840s is Zhu Jingxuan's *Tangchao minghua lu* (Record of Famous Painters of the Tang Dynasty). Literary in tone but more limited in scope, it is chiefly known for its modification of the official ninefold grading system to list at the end a separate *yipin*, or "Untrammeled Class," for unorthodox masters who worked outside the system. On the fall of Tang, many court painters fled southwest to Shu, modern Sichuan, and by 1006 a regional classification of painters, the *Yizhou minghua lu*, placed the *yi* class at the head of its listings to contain the exceptional muralist Sun Wei, who specialized in large-scale temple murals bristling with swiftly rendered images. In later scholarly texts, painters with Buddhist or Daoist affiliations who aspired to "untrammeled" styles were to be characterized as wild and reckless. And after the fourteenth century, when the term *i* was applied to certain literati landscape styles, its "untrammeled" aspect was minimalized to accommodate a more genteel approach to art then in favor. In this instance, varying interpretations of a term can mirror a significant shift in taste and subject matter.

The Northern Song dynasty (960–1126) was a watershed for art theory and criticism. Different genres of painting reached their peak then, and a variety of techniques were developed. Mid-eleventh-century biographies of painters by Liu Daochun graded them by their separate abilities in different subject categories. By 1120, the imperial catalog of the Xuanhe collection listed information about artists and titles of their works under ten genre headings, organized in a sequence reflecting their relevance to the emperor: Daoist and Buddhist subjects, secular figures, architecture, barbarians, dragons and fishes, landscape, domestic and wild animals, flowers and birds, ink bamboo, and vegetables and fruit. Slightly earlier, genre diversification enabled Guo Ruoxu to achieve a historical perspective on the development of painting from 847 up to the 1080s. Taking Zhang Yanyuan as his model, Guo included essays on a variety of topics in his *Tuhua jianwen zhi* (An Account of My Experiences in Painting). He noted that whereas figure painting had achieved perfection in Tang times with Wu Daozi, great advances had been made in flowers and birds and landscapes from the tenth century onward. His descriptions of rock and tree motifs were to be used as clues for identifications by later connoisseurs, as were his vivid characterizations of a rich assortment of brush techniques. Traditional Chinese connoisseurship continues to focus on such motifs and brushwork. Different types of *cun,* or "texture strokes," that gave substance to rocks now appeared in the vocabulary of landscape art. For example, mountain faces, done in the granitic style of the north, were described as like "alum (crystal) lumps," a term that would later indicate rounded outcroppings on the grassy hills of southern landscapes. Guo's discussion of brushwork focused on a balance between strength and flexibility, and his interpretation of the first law stressed that *qiyun* in painting was like a signature, a "mind print" that reflected the artist's character.

Guo's text was seminal in several ways, even though its standard of excellence was not equaled. His practice of listing Song nobles or scholars separately at the head of the Song biographies was developed and expanded in later works. The shift to classification by status follows the social ranking found in official histories, and indicates the influence of the scholar-officials. As their interests radically limited the range of subject matter in painting, classification by genres dropped out of favor.

By Song times, the only appropriate career for an ambitious man was that of a scholar-official. Those who achieved this position through literary talent alone formed an elite. In proper Confucian fashion, after drafting imperial documents they sought amusement in the arts, and they disparaged the nobles' expensive pursuits of horses and women. The scholarly arts in which character and talent could be exhibited were prose, poetry, calligraphy, and painting, listed in order of importance, and the fact that painting made the list meant that it was accepted as a fine art. The writer who formulated this sequence was the "gay genius" Su Shi (1037–1101), a famous poet, calligrapher, and critic,

and an amateur painter. His temperament, talents, and wit made him the center of an influential circle that included his family, his literary models, and his followers. The painting practiced by the literati was a social art comparable at times to poetry games played at banquets in response to set lines, and the brush, ink, and paper used for sketching were those employed to transcribe poems in calligraphy; hence, the close ties between these several arts, which formed the literati credo. Su Shi did serve as a provincial governor and briefly as prime minister, so one might consider comparing him to Western politician-artists like Churchill or even Eisenhower. But he gained his place in history through works written in periods of banishment and persecution as (Su) Dongpo, the poet of the Eastern Bank. Thus, like his calligraphy, his painting was a historical relic to be treasured and appreciated in colophons attached by scholar-officials. It is no exaggeration to say that Su Shi shaped the course of later Chinese painting. His art provided a model for all scholar-artists, who were writers first, then calligraphers and painters, and whose training consisted of classical studies rather than technical apprenticeship. Down to recent times, a mother might still advise her son to read books, travel widely, and form his character if he wanted to become a successful professional artist.

Like literati painting, literati art criticism was jotted down in a deceptively casual fashion, in poetic couplets or colophons and letters addressed to friends. Its underpinnings can be found in the practices and tastes of the Southern Dynasties poets, and its content also reflected Daoist and Buddhist concepts blended with contemporary Confucianism, now called Neo-Confucianism. As a literary figure, Su himself was a practicing Confucian humanist; still, he associated and debated with Buddhist monks and also engaged in life-prolonging Daoist exercises. Unlike Guo Ruoxu, Su did not refer to earlier painting histories or the much-interpreted "Six Laws." Instead, secure in his classical learning, he defined "scholars' painting" as such and distinguished it from the work of artisan painters. He also cited Wang Wei (701–761), the Tang poet-painter and Buddhist layman, as a model of spirituality. In Su's most famous poetic critique, he disparaged formal likeness and also stated that the one rule in painting was naturalness and originality. According to Su, true naturalness arose spontaneously when his cousin Wen Tong did ink bamboo, and Wen's character and personality were clearly discernible in his painting. Natural simplicity and spontaneity are Daoist concepts and Su quoted *Zhuangzi* when discussing artistic creation or appreciation as a fusion of subject and object. On the other hand, there was always a moral dimension to seeing the artist in his work, and Su once distinguished constant principle from constant form, indicating that *li* (principle), a Neo-Confucian term, could only be understood and re-created in images by a superior man. His comments on connoisseurship recommend a balancing act between sensual entanglement and disengagement: a gentleman should merely rest his thoughts on objects and not be obsessed with them. In eighteenth-century England, Joshua Reynolds, who associated with well-known writers, also subscribed to a literary view of painting.

"Art and the Gentleman" was a heading once applied to Southern Dynasties comments on the danger of being taken for an artisan painter. This theme reoccurs from Tang times onward, along with the idea that an artist must be a superior man. Thus, some of the ideas put forth by Su Shi and his friends were not unique to their period or their circle. But what sources are available that express the concerns of professional masters? For Song, there are the landscape texts, forerunners of later painting manuals.

By the eleventh century, monumental landscapes were painted on silk hanging scrolls in monochrome ink techniques: one such work is *Early Spring,* signed and dated to 1072 by Guo Xi, the favorite court artist of the period. Also extant are his comments on painting, *Linquan gaozhi* (The Message of Forests and Streams). This text was edited around 1110–1117 by Guo's son Si, a scholar-official who presumably was responsible for the quality of the writing. Guo Xi, the first in his family to paint, had a Daoist education and traveled when young. Still, Guo shared a certain amount of Su Shi's culture: he cited *Zhuangzi* stories of concentration to illustrate spontaneous artistic creativity, and he prepared to paint by reciting couplets, believing that poetry was formless painting and painting, poetry with form. Guo's work, however, imparts the techniques of landscape painting, as do various short pieces attributed either to the Tang poet Wang Wei or to the landscapists Jing Hao and Li Cheng. Often rhymed like earlier oral transmissions from master to pupil, these technical secrets include a listing of mountain formations and tree and rock types, a concern for proportion, from large to small or near to far, and for seasonal atmospheric mood. For Guo Xi, composition consists of balancing portions for heaven and earth, and positioning major peaks and pines is here likened to emperors and chief officials. His section on "the secrets of painting" describes different brush techniques and color tintings more specifically than in previous works, and this trend will be further developed later.

Guo's text remains unique in in its ability to convey a sense of landscape as a living organism and prototype of change. Essentially, the cosmic opposition of *yang* and *yin* forces is evident in his treatment of mountain and water, the components of the term "landscape," *shanshui* (mountain water). Like Zong Bing, Guo loved to roam in mountain scenery, and his paintings are meant to evoke the experience of nature and provide a release for the confined city dweller. As he explained, and as can be seen in his work of 1072, the bottom of a scroll should be filled with interesting detail, while empty areas to the sides should lead the eye into the distance. Mountains and rivers should twist and turn to show their various aspects, and be partially concealed by atmosphere to emphasize height and distance. Different regional landscape schools are acknowledged, but it is assumed that a great master, like a true scholar, will not be restricted to one alone.

A spiritual approach to nature is also combined with technical advice in the earlier *Bifa ji* (A Note on the Art of the Brush). Couched in the form of a Daoist fable, it was written by a Confucian scholar, Jing Hao (c.870–c.930), who painted landscapes and pines and rocks. He underlined the Confucian polarities of inner substance versus outer ornament and stressed the importance of a moral education to enable an artist to grasp the essential character or resonance of the pine tree. His technical secrets consisted of a revision of the Six Laws in terms of monochrome landscape painting along with a short list of landscape elements and models for brushwork. In a concluding poem, the evergreen pine was compared to the superior man or scholar, in one of the earliest definitions of a scholarly subject. Bamboo, celebrated by Su Shi, could also stand for the unbiased scholar, flexible but upright, and, when painted in ink, a reflection of his cousin's character. In association with ink plum or prunus, bamboo and pine belonged to the "three friends" of wintertime, symbolizing endurance. The prunus that bloomed in late winter and old age might also stand for resistance to Mongol oppression. Grouped as four along with the ink orchid emblematic of the loyal official, these trees and plants could be associated with the changing seasons. In the fourteenth century, specialized painting manuals were extant for bamboo and prunus as well as landscape. By the early eighteenth century, *Jieziyuan huazhuan* (The Mustard Seed Garden Manual of Painting) had separate sections for landscape, figures, and ink flowers and trees. Scholarly taste, as voiced by Su Shi and later critics, helped to limit the scope of subject matter and channel motifs and techniques into set formulas. Professional artists now painted in literati styles for profit.

As far as painting theory goes, the most influential later figure was Dong Qichang (1555–1636), a scholar-official, calligrapher, and painter responsible for defining the correct models in painting, the so-called Northern and Southern Schools named after the schools of Chan Buddhism. In general, painters listed in the Northern School worked in detailed or highly colored styles, whereas the Southern School amateur geniuses did lighter ink sketching. This line-up mirrors the earlier opposition between the Zhe School professionals of the fifteenth century and the Wu School literati of the sixteenth. It was Dong Qichang who coined the phrase *wenren hua* (literati painting), and whose emphasis on style and composition transformed later Chinese painting. Although he preferred the motifs and brushwork of the fourteenth-century masters, he organized his landscapes in large divisions after the earlier Song landscapists. He aimed for *shi* (structural force) in dynamic mountain forms, and his followers, the Traditionalists, stressed the need for *long mo* (dragon veins), comparable to currents of energy in mountain ranges, to fuse their close-knit constructions. By this time, compositions were definitely conceived of as on the surface in rhythmic segments, but landscape elements might be considered to extend beyond the unframed format of the scroll. *The Mustard Seed Garden Manual of Painting* contains illustrations of careful outlining and texturing of peaks in the Traditionalists' manner.

Just when literati painting became an academic art, packaged in a teachable form and practiced by court artists and professionals alike, more experimental masters invented abbreviated manners that prefigured modern Chinese ink painting. The most important of the Individualists was Shitao or Yuanji (1642–c.1707), a Chan monk descended from the Ming imperial family who wrote the *Huayu lu* (Enlightening Remarks on Painting) late in his life under Daoist influence. His credo was *yibi hua* (one-stroke painting), and his "Holistic Brushstroke" served to unify and transform unstable entities. He wrote that oceans were like mountains and mountains like oceans, and painted in large-scale rhythmic contrasts illustrative of his name, Stone Waves. Even when doing landscapes loosely after earlier masters, he disavowed their influence in striking terms. It is understandable from a contemporary Communist perspective that the disinherited Shitao should be a better model than the unpopular landlord and official Dong Qichang. Hence, it is historically appropriate that the individualist outlook and manner can be discerned in contemporary Chinese art, even when filtered through various strands of Western influence.

Modern landscapes can still have traditional literary interpretations. Hence, more mountain peaks could be added to an oil painting hanging in a museum to indicate yet loftier aspirations, and depictions of various sites associated with Mao Zedong could decorate hotel rooms (the spirit of the place equals the man). Chinese art is often said to be influenced by Daoism. This implies more than the often-cited *Zhuangzi* stories of subject and object fused in the process of creation. Relevant here are underlying magical beliefs that helped to form aesthetic tastes. In an adept's search for longevity, certain types of peaks or rock formations were gateways to the realm of the immortals, and strange-shaped old trees and rocks were thought to have indwelling spirit. Even the rockeries of imperial gardens were initially conceived to promote male heirs and the continuation of the dynasty. Thus, the appropriate Chinese preference came to be for age over beauty, for evergreens over flowering plants, for sparseness over luxuriance in rock forms, shrubbery, calligraphy, and eventually painting. Garden arts do tie in to painting and the influence flows both ways; and, just as no scenic spot or garden setting is considered complete without engraved calligraphic appreciations, so seals, inscrip-

tions, and colophons on scrolls are a part of an ongoing artistic work. Ultimately, in the characteristic Chinese focus on the word, *wen* (pattern, literature, culture), Confucius does indeed have the last say.

Here modern Chinese aesthetics can only be covered in a brief epilogue. It stands apart from traditional art theory and criticism as a "mixed mode" of assimilation and redefinition of or in terms of Western philosophy. After the founding of the Republic of China in 1912, the most influential aesthetician was Cai Yuanpei (1868–1940). He studied philosophy in Germany before becoming minister of culture and chancellor of Beijing University. An idealist who believed in universal artistic values and saw culture and art as substitutes for religion in education, Cai was able to place important painters as heads of regional art schools and hence his influence was felt until the period of World War II. When the Communists took over in 1949, Soviet Socialist Realism peaked in art and theory and the dictums of Mao Zedong were expressed as imperial dictates. The role of art was to serve the people, and the artist's task was to make the past serve the present and foreign things serve China. In more recent times, writers in mainland China, well schooled in Western philosophy in translation, could consider such topics as beauty, art appreciation, and the aesthetic experience. In Ye Lang's formulation of the 1980s, they might aspire to a thorough grounding in traditional and contemporary aesthetics, and hope to merge Eastern and Western aesthetics, to incorporate a knowledge of other relevant disciplines, and to develop both theoretical and practical aesthetics. Of course, Chinese in Taiwan, Hong Kong, and elsewhere had been able to engage in this process for a longer period of time. As the newest development in the field, mainland Chinese trained and practicing in Western disciplines in the West may now seek to define traditional art theory in their own terms. Intellectual freedom of this sort will presumably lead to new insights on the past.

BIBLIOGRAPHY

Acker, William Reynolds Beal, ed. *Some T'ang and Pre-T'ang Texts on Chinese Painting*. 2 vols. Leiden, 1954–1974.

Bush, Susan. *The Chinese Literati on Painting: Su Shih, 1037–1101, to Tung Ch'i-ch'ang, 1555–1636*. 2d ed. Cambridge, Mass., 1978.

Bush, Susan, and Christian Murck, eds. *Theories of the Arts in China*. Princeton, N.J., 1983.

Bush, Susan, and Hsio-yen Shih, eds. *Early Chinese Texts on Painting*. Cambridge, Mass., 1985.

Cahill, James. "Confucian Elements in the Theory of Painting." In *The Confucian Persuasion*, edited by Arthur F. Wright, pp. 33–63. Stanford, Calif., 1960.

Cahill, James. "The Six Laws and How to Read Them." *Ars Orientalis* 4 (1961): 372–381.

Cahill, James. "Tung Ch'i-ch'ang's 'Southern and Northern Schools' in the History and Theory of Painting: A Reconsideration." In *Sudden and Gradual: Approaches to Enlightenment in Chinese Thought*, edited by Peter N. Gregory, pp. 429–446. Honolulu, 1987.

Fong, Wen C. "Ch'i-yün-sheng-tung: 'Vitality, Harmonious Manner and Aliveness'." *Oriental Art* n.s. 12 (1966): 159–164.

Gao, Jianping. *The Expressive Act in Chinese Art: From Calligraphy to Painting. Aesthetica Upsaliensa* 7. Upsala, 1996.

Sirén, Osvald, ed. *The Chinese on the Art of Painting: Translations and Comments.* Reprint of 2d ed. New York, 1963.

Soper, Alexander Coburn. "The First Two Laws of Hsieh Ho." *Far Eastern Quarterly* 8 (1949): 412–423.

Soper, Alexander Coburn, ed. *Kuo Jo-hsü's Experiences in Painting (T'u-hua chien-wen chih): An Eleventh Century History of Painting.* Washington, D.C., 1951.

Soper, Alexander Coburn. "*T'ang ch'ao ming hua lu:* Celebrated Painters of the T'ang Dynasty by Chu Ching-hsüan of T'ang." *Artibus Asiae* 31 (1958): 204–230.

Strassberg, Richard E. *Inscribed Landscapes: Travel Writing from Imperial China.* Berkeley, 1994.

Strassberg, Richard E., ed. *Enlightening Remarks on Painting by Shih-t'ao.* Pasadena, Calif., 1989.

Zhu Liyuan and H. Gene Blocker. *Contemporary Chinese Aesthetics. Asian Thought and Culture,* vol. 17. New York, 1995.

Zurcher, Erik. "Recent Studies on Chinese Painting, I." *T'oung Pao* 51 (1964): 377–422.

SUSAN BUSH

CICERO, MARCUS TULLIUS. *See* Rhetoric; *and* Roman Aesthetics.

CINEMA. *See* Film.

CLASSICISM. In contrast with modern artistic terms such as Romanticism, Futurism, or Surrealism, which were invented by artists eager to proclaim the novelty of their practice, Classicism has rarely been used as a self-designating label. When it describes an aesthetic program, the appellation *Classicism* is applied retroactively by sympathizers, adversaries, or historians. It follows that, in order to grasp the content of the term, one must examine the contexts in which it has acquired its meaning. Set off against the art of the moderns, Classicism designates an atemporal, universalist artistic project, impervious to chronology and local particularities; in contrast with Romantic art, Classicism embodies an objective, rule-governed aesthetics that minimizes the subjective freedom of the artist; finally, in opposition to the exuberance of the Baroque, classicist art displays balance, poise, and restraint.

Ancient versus Modern. The earliest occurrence of the designation "classic" is found in Aulus Gellius (second century), who, in *Noctes Atticae* (book 19, chap. 8, par. 15), calls the writers of the highest order *scriptores classici,* a metaphoric use based on the expression *cives classici* ("citizens belonging to the highest class"). A later meaning of *classicus* was "student who attends classes" (sixth century), and in the Renaissance the term referred to literary authors who were studied in school and served as models of moral and rhetorical excellence. Thus, *classical* came to designate the great works and authors belonging to a stable literary

heritage. In contemporary French, *classique* still refers to the most important authors who are objects of study in school.

Because, until the end of the seventeenth century, Greek and Latin authors were deemed to have produced the highest achievements of literature and, as a consequence, their works were assiduously read in school, the ancients became known as the classics, a term that in English continues to designate the study of Greek and Roman history and culture. In a related usage, the literary language of imperial Rome, a somewhat artificial dialect distinct from spoken Latin, was described by philologists as Classical Latin (as opposed to the spoken Vulgar Latin), a designation that served as model for terms such as Classical Arabic and Classical Chinese, which refer to highly codified idioms devised by the literati during the golden ages of these cultures and subsequently kept unchanged by later generations of writers and scholars.

Greek and Latin arts and letters, considered as paradigms of perfection, were the models of Renaissance and early modern artists and writers. The Italian Renaissance rediscovered the elegant complexity of Classical Latin, the illusionist appearance of Roman frescoes and mosaics, and the monumentality and decorum of Roman architecture. Building on Plato's and Plotinus's philosophy of the beautiful, on Aristotle's poetics, and on Cicero's and Quintilian's rhetoric, Renaissance theoreticians of art and literature (Leon Battista Alberti, Luigi Castelvetro, Julius Caesar Scaliger, and Torquatto Tasso) developed an aesthetics that praised mastery of illusionist skills, but only insofar as it allows artists to reveal the Idea or nature of things: art, these theoreticians believed, should aspire to represent ideal beauty, which emerges from fragments of terrestrial beauty unified by the mind of the artist. Although Italian theoreticians admired ancient authors for their ability to represent an idealized nature, they sometimes argued that more recent, or modern, artists and poets can equal or even surpass their predecessors.

Sixteenth- and seventeenth-century France inherited the Italian admiration for classical antiquity, as well as the debates on the respective merits of ancient and modern artists. The Partisans of the Ancients, an important group of French writers led by the critic Nicolas Boileau (*Art poétique,* 1674), forcefully argued that the imitation of the Greeks and Romans was the only key to artistic success. They polemicized with the Partisans of the Moderns led by Charles Perrault (*Parallèles des Anciens et des Modernes,* 1688–1997), who were convinced that modern achievements represent a progress in comparison with Greek and Roman art. The exchange emphasized the atemporal character of artistic taste and genius, the dependence of art on the nature (or essence) of things, and the connection between political and artistic greatness. According to the Partisans of the Ancients, Greek and Roman art, in particular the art produced in Pericles' Athens and Augustus's Rome, remained attractive over the centuries because it had discovered and represented the nature of things faithfully. The Partisans of the Moderns answered that if indeed genius is independent of time, nothing prevents modern artists from being as gifted as their predecessors; moreover, if the task of art is to imitate the nature of things, modern art can do better than the ancients, because, thanks to Christianity and Cartesian science, moderns know nature better; if, finally, artistic greatness is linked with political success, Louis XIV's France, having surpassed the political glory of Athens and Rome, can as well surpass the art of the ancients. Although the arguments of the Partisans of the Moderns had a long-term influence on the artists and critics of the Enlightenment, in the short term the moderns lost their battle because the better, more enduring, seventeenth-century works of art and literature were produced by the opposite camp, as pointed out by Jean-François Marmontel's article "Anciens" published in his *Éléments de littérature* (1787). An earlier conciliatory view was expressed by Abbé du Bos (*Réflexions critiques sur la poésie et la peinture,* 1719), who, while agreeing that in poetry the ancients were the stronger, argued that modern painters (Raphael, Peter Paul Rubens, Paolo Veronese) handled color and composition more competently than the ancients. Du Bos's point was that those artists who imitate nature better are the greater, be they ancient or modern. The admiration for the ancients, combined with the sense that their achievements could be reenacted and paralleled in modern times, spread beyond Italy and France to England, where John Dryden (*An Essay on Dramatic Poesy,* 1688) and later Alexander Pope (*Essay on Criticism,* 1711) took a moderate classicist stand.

By encouraging comparisons between artists who lived in vastly different historical periods, the participants in the debate assumed that great art transcended time by excelling in the idealized imitation of nature. They believed that such excellence is achieved in privileged periods during which a group of unusually talented artists discovers and codifies the best means for representing ideal beauty. Both the Partisans of the Ancients and the Partisans of the Moderns assumed that the province of great art includes modern successes, either because they emulate the great example of the ancients formally and thematically (e.g., Italian architecture of the fifteenth century, French tragedy of the seventeenth century) or because they belong to a domain of art in which perfect imitation of nature has been achieved only recently (e.g., oil painting). Political grandeur, they believed, was the necessary background of great art, but because humanity has managed to rise to such heights on only a few occasions, the great political and artistic ages were limited to four golden ages, which include Athens under Pericles, Rome under Augustus, Florence under the Medici, and France under Louis XIV (Voltaire, *Le siècle de Louis XIV,* 1751). The masterpieces produced during the last two golden ages, they thought, do not differ essentially from the

achievements of the ancients, because all art follows the same immutable standards of perfection.

In time, these assumptions incited other nations, in particular England, Germany, and Spain, to exalt their own political and artistic grandeur, either in the name of a better, more faithful reenactment of ancient perfection or of the idea that art must express national genius and the spirit of the time rather than imitate universal human nature. Both aspirations were explicitly formulated by Romanticism.

Classic versus Romantic. Although Romanticism strongly opposed seventeenth- and early eighteenth-century aesthetics, it admired the ancients and often attempted to emulate them. Therefore, one must distinguish between the classicist and the anticlassicist strands in Romantic art and literature. Among the ancients, German Romantics preferred the Greeks, in whose art they found, in the wake of Johann Joachim Winckelmann and Gotthold Ephraim Lessing, the representation of harmonious perfection as well as of human failure and suffering. Lessing's *Hamburgische Dramaturgie* (1767–1769) praised the affective power of Greek tragedy and its description in Aristotle's *Poetics* rather than the formal rules of composition prescribed by the Italian and French poeticians of the Renaissance and the seventeenth century. In a more polemical mode, Friedrich von Schiller's *Naive and Sentimental Poetry* (1795) asserted the reflective mode of recent poetry, in opposition to the spontaneity of classical art. According to Friedrich Schlegel, Romantic poetry is an inexhaustible becoming, a living, free infinity that cannot be fully captured by any criticism; as such it is opposed to the poetic approach of the ancients, who aimed at finding a finite form for infinite feelings (Fragments in *Athenaeum,* 1798).

Unlike the older Partisans of the Moderns, whose artistic standards were essentially the same as those of the Partisans of the Ancients, the Romantics, whether or not they worshiped classical antiquity (as did Johann Wolfgang von Goethe, Schiller, Friedrich Hölderlin, and John Keats), brought about a dramatic change in the criteria for artistic achievement. Instead of obeying perennial norms and rules, like the classics, they advocated artistic freedom; rather than revering tradition, they sought novelty; and instead of the abstract representation of universal human passions, they appreciated singularity, expressivity, and local color. They were convinced that artists find truth less in the imitation of appearances than in the depth of their own soul; accordingly, unlike the classics, who searched for a common language and clarity of expression, the Romantics considered artistic truth as bordering on inexpressibility and hence inaccessible to common mortals.

Most important, they replaced the older transhistorical and universalist view of art with a historicist awareness of each period's uniqueness. Whereas seventeenth- and eighteenth-century artists and critics felt that they were essentially living in the same world as the ancients, the Romantics were haunted by the realization that the past was irretrievably gone. Therefore, the nineteenth-century writers, artists, and philosophers who admired Greek or Roman art (e.g., Hölderlin, Gottfried Semper, Friedrich Nietzsche) were intensely aware of the historical distance that separated them from the happy youth of humanity. Although Goethe could still give the term *Classicism* an atemporal meaning, for nineteenth-century Romantics, Classicism had a definite historical reference: Ancient Greece for German Romantics and seventeenth-century art and literature for the French. In order to emphasize the nostalgic nature of late eighteenth- and nineteenth-century art and architecture inspired by Greek, Roman, and Renaissance models, this art is sometimes called neoclassical.

In France, Mme de Staël (*De l'Allemagne*, 1813) distinguished between the Classicism of Mediterranean cultures and the Romanticism of the north, while Stendhal (*Racine et Shakespeare*, 1823–1825) and Victor Hugo (Preface to *Cromwell*, 1828), who were irritated by the survival of the seventeenth- and eighteenth-century classicist tradition in their own literature, created the polemical notion of a conservative Classicism, punctiliously observing rules and conventions, oppressive of genius, devoted to banality, repetitious, captive to empty universality and superficial rhetoric. The French Romantics disseminated the image of Classicism as an intellectualist, deliberate method of artistic creation. In their eyes, Classicism was a formalist trend, suspicious of innovation, insensitive to historical and ethnic particularity, and deaf to the depths of the human soul.

Although the Romantic characterization of Classicism aptly captured its objectivist and intellectualist biases, many of the accusations leveled against early modern European Classicism were unfair. Classicist rules for composition (perspective in painting discovered by Leon Battista Alberti, the rules of unity of place, time, and action in dramatic poetry elaborated by Luigi Castelvetro [*Poetica d'Aristotele vulgarizzata e sposta*, 1570] and adopted in France by the Abbé d'Aubignac [*La pratique du théâtre*, 1657] and by Pierre Corneille [*Discours sur le poème dramatique*, 1660]) were intended less as constraints on artistic freedom than as procedures for facilitating the public's understanding of the artistic representation. Perspective saves the viewer the effort, required by Byzantine art, of calculating distance and proportion several times for each painting; similarly, the rules of unity in drama bring the time and space of representation closer to the represented time and space, thus making the play's reception easier. The same courtesy toward the viewer explains the classicist preference for an idealized representation of human passions that uses concrete details, local color, and historical precision only sparingly. The aim of classical idealization is ease of recognition: the audience can identify and appropriate passions faster and easier when they are described in universal terms rather than in exotic detail. Whereas the freedom of the Romantic artist encourages the production of difficult, idiosyncratic works of art whose reception is often painstaking, classicist art restrains the artist in order to put the public at ease.

Classic versus Baroque. The rise of historicism in the nineteenth century made possible a more detached examination of Classicism, freed from Romantic polemics. Historians of art and literature played down the normative aspects of the term and attempted to demonstrate the links between classicist aesthetics and its surrounding political and cultural environment. In Désiré Nisard's *Histoire de la littérature française* (1844), French literature and culture of the seventeenth century, in particular of the years 1660–1700, are explicitly linked with the triumph of royal absolutism. Nisard shows that the canonical writers belonging to this period (Jean Racine, Blaise Pascal, Molière, Mme de La Fayette, Boileau, Jacques-Bénigne Bossuet, and Fénelon) were in most cases Partisans of the Ancients, whose impeccable artistic taste and self-restraint made their works impervious to the Romantic critique. Their artistic efforts seemed to fit the historical context unusually well, he argues, because their ostensibly conservative aesthetic of idealization and restraint appeared to echo the monarchic desire to impose a strict control over the country. It looked as though seventeenth-century French Classicism was inextricably linked with the political culture of the period.

Yet, such links were not always evident. German literary Classicism, that is, the period of Goethe and Schiller's emulation of Greek models (1770–1800), did not coincide with a historical glorious age. In seventeenth- and eighteenth-century England, imitation of the ancients was most often an imitation of Italian and French Partisans of the Ancients. John Milton, meanwhile, who was a true emulator of Latin verse, qualified nevertheless as a Partisan of the Moderns, because his epic poetry treated a biblical, rather than a Greek or Latin, subject. The historicist definition of classicist periods becomes even fuzzier when one attempts to coordinate classicist literature with classicist visual art. French architecture, for instance, borrowed classicist standards from Italy long before French literature reached its classicist apex.

Some art historians attempted to avoid such difficulties by defining Classicism as a recurring historical style. Heinrich Wölfflin (1915) proposed a synthesis between the understanding of Classicism as an artistic ideal that transcends history and the historicist description of the term. Discounting influence and imitation (that is, the reverence for the ancients), Wölfflin examined the shift from High Renaissance to seventeenth-century Italian painting, distinguishing between an earlier classicist style and a later, more sophisticated, Baroque style. In his view, Classicist art is characterized by linearity (i.e., clarity of spatial relations), planimetry or division of the represented space in parallel planes, closed form (with respect to the edges of the painting), relative unity of composition, and absolute clarity of the subject matter, whereas Baroque art is painterly (i.e., represents fuzzy spatial relations), recessional (the space is not divided carefully), open in relation to the edges of the picture, fully unified, and only partly clear in the presentation of its subject matter. Pictorial Classicism is therefore conceived as an art of simplicity, restraint, and intellectual clarity, whereas the Baroque style is seen as a refinement of classical forms, to which it adds movement, energy, and drama. Wölfflin's distinctions had an immense influence and were soon applied to the study of literary style by Oskar Walzel (1929), who called the construction of classicist drama well balanced or "tectonic," as opposed to the "nontectonic" structure of Baroque plots. Along the same lines, Leo Spitzer (1931) described in great detail the stylistic restraint of Racine's classicist language.

The difficulty with the stylistic definition of Classicism and Baroque is the inescapable vagueness of the terms involved. Simplicity and complication, restraint and exuberance, intellectual clarity and affective impulse can be found in various proportions in most works of art, and it is not an accident that virtually each French classicist writer was at one point in the twentieth century described as Baroque. Moreover, because, in France and Germany, the Baroque era preceded Classicism rather than developed from it, Wölfflin's claim that Baroque complexity emerged from classicist forms is historically incomplete.

Music provides another example of a Baroque–classical stylistic sequence. The style called Baroque by musicologists flourished between 1580 and 1750, before the rise of the sonata form, the classical orchestra, and the careers of Franz Joseph Haydn, Wolfgang Amadeus Mozart, and the early Ludwig van Beethoven. These composers had already been called "classic" by late eighteenth-century musical critics, under the influence of the classicist revival in German art and literature. As early as 1798, Franz Niemetschek, Mozart's biographer, compared his works to the masterpieces of Greek and Roman art. Some twentieth-century musicologists (Charles Rosen, 1971) concur: not unlike classical art and literature, classical music owes its universal appeal to the use of simple, well-articulated themes, the abstractness of developments, the firmness of structure, and the overall sense of balance. Others (Blume, 1970) describe German music in the late eighteenth and early nineteenth century as a synthesis between Classicism and Romanticism.

In the twentieth century, Classicism ceased to be a central topic in artistic debates and the massive return of Classicism prophesied in 1913 by T. E. Hulme never materialized. But hostility to Romanticism, modernism, or both occasionally led some writers, musicians, painters, architects, and critics to express interest in classicist ideals. Notably, most twentieth-century literary critics who defended an impersonal, antisubjective aesthetics (Paul Valéry, T. S. Eliot,

the Russian Formalists, the American New Critics, the School of Chicago, and the French structuralists) felt close to classicist poetics.

[*See also* Baroque Aesthetics; Hellenistic Aesthetics; Poussin; Roman Aesthetics; Romanticism; *and* Winckelmann.]

BIBLIOGRAPHY

Blume, Friedrich. *Classic and Romantic Music: A Comprehensive Survey.* Translated by M. D. Herter Norton. New York, 1970.

Blunt, Anthony. *Artistic Theory in Italy, 1450–1600.* Oxford, 1940.

Blunt, Anthony. *Art and Architecture in France, 1500–1700.* Harmondsworth, England, 1953.

Bray, René. *La formation de la doctrine classique en France* (1927). Paris, 1967.

Colquhoun, Alan. *Modernity and the Classical Tradition: Architectural Essays, 1980–1987.* Cambridge, Mass., 1989.

Fumaroli, Marc. *L'école du silence: Le sentiment des images au XVIIᵉ siècle.* Paris, 1994.

Hazard, Paul. *The European Mind: The Critical Years, 1680–1715* (1935). New Haven, 1953.

Honour, Hugh. *Neo-Classicism.* Harmondsworth, England, 1968.

Hulme, T. E. "Romanticism and Classicism" (1913–1914). In *Critical Theory since Plato*, rev. ed., edited by Hazard Adams, pp. 728–734. New York, 1992.

Kermode, Frank. *The Classic: Literary Images of Permanence and Change.* Corr. ed. Cambridge, Mass., 1983.

Lacoste, Jean. *L'idée de beau.* Paris, 1986.

Levey, Michael. *Early Renaissance.* Harmondsworth, England, 1967.

Levey, Michael. *High Renaissance.* Harmondsworth, England, 1975.

Lichtenstein, Jacqueline. *The Eloquence of Color: Rhetoric and Painting in the French Classical Age* (1989). Translated by Emily McVarish. Berkeley, 1993.

Murray, Gilbert. *The Classical Tradition in Poetry.* Cambridge, Mass., 1927.

Panofsky, Erwin. *Idea: A Concept in Art Theory* (1924). Translated by Joseph J. S. Peake. Columbia, S.C., 1968.

Pauly, Reinhard G. *Music in the Classic Period* (1965). 3d ed. Englewood Cliffs, N.J., 1988.

Pavel, Thomas. *L'art de l'éloignement: Essai sur l'imagination classique.* Paris, 1996.

Peyre, Henri. "Le classicisme." In *Histoire des littératures*, edited by Raymond Queneau, new ed., vol. 2, pp. 111–139. Paris, 1968.

Podro, Michael. *The Critical Historians of Art.* New Haven, 1982.

Rosen, Charles. *The Classical Style: Haydn, Mozart, Beethoven.* New York, 1971.

Scherringham, Marc. *Introduction à la philosophie esthétique.* Paris, 1992.

Spitzer, Leo. "Racine's Classical *Piano*" (1931). In *Essays in Seventeenth-Century French Literature*, translated and edited by David Bellos, pp. 3–113. Cambridge and New York, 1983.

Strich, Fritz. *Deutsche Klassik und Romantik oder Vollendung und Unendlichkeit: Ein Vergleich.* Munich, 1928.

Turner, Frederick. *Natural Classicism: Essays on Literature and Science.* New York, 1985.

Walzel, Oskar F. *Gehalt und Gestalt im Kunstwerk des Dichters* (1929). Darmstadt, 1957.

Weinberg, Bernard. *A History of Literary Criticism in the Italian Renaissance.* Chicago, 1961.

Wellek, René. "The Concept of Classic and Classicism in Literary Scholarship" (1965). In *Discriminations: Further Concepts of Criticism*, pp. 55–89. New Haven, 1970.

Wimsatt, William K., Jr., and Cleanth Brooks. *Literary Criticism: A Short History* (1957). Chicago, 1978.

Wittkower, Rudolf. *Architectural Principles in the Age of Humanism* (1949). New York, 1971.

Wölfflin, Heinrich. *Principles of Art History: The Problem of the Development of Style in Later Art* (1915). Translated by M. D. Hottinger. London, 1932.

THOMAS PAVEL

CLOTHES. *See* Fashion.

COCHIN, CHARLES-NICOLAS (1715–1790), French designer, engraver, and writer. Cochin is one of the few artists to take part in debates over the nature and function of the work of art in Enlightenment France, but the scattered nature of his writings, which often appeared anonymously and are more practical than speculative, scarcely assured him the interest of future generations. Only his works on antique painting and Italian art were deemed worthy of criticism after his death; the others were quickly forgotten. Cochin remains a somewhat marginal figure in the field of artistic theory despite the importance ascribed him during his lifetime.

Cochin never published anything resembling a real treatise, preferring to make his views known in brief press articles, lectures, and pamphlets. He did not limit himself to occasional texts, however, for he published two anthologies in 1757 and 1770, under the title *Recueil de quelques pièces concernant les arts* (Collection of a Few Pieces concerning the Arts), most of which reappeared in a simple publication in 1771, *Œuvres diverses de M. Cochin* (Various Works of M. Cochin). Consequently, his thought must be reconstituted from dispersed texts, a task all the more difficult because Cochin was not a speculative thinker; principles interested him only to the extent that they could be put into practice and thus serve artistic creation.

His approach was essentially pragmatic. He drew on his own experience in developing his ideas, many of which were original. Since his youth as an engraver, he had pondered this art, in which formal qualities, not imagination, provide the sole basis for distinguishing one work from another. His friendship with Jean-Baptiste Siméon Chardin and Joseph Vernet also led him to reflect on their paintings, whose quality is a function not of their inventive subjects but of a certain sensibility evident in their transpositions of nature. His artistic horizons were not limited to works visible in Paris, however, but were expanded by a twenty-month sojourn in Italy as well as by a two-month trip to Flanders and Holland. He had, then, to account for works as varied as those of Michelangelo and François Boucher, of Rembrandt van Rijn and Jean-Baptiste Siméon Chardin. Accordingly, he came up with a new definition of painting as "the art of rendering nature with truth and feeling, on whatever premise" ("l'art de rendre la nature avec vérité et sentiment, dans une supposition quelconque").

Cochin's naturalism follows from his adherence to the empiricism of John Locke, whose *Essay concerning Human Understanding* he read at a very young age. He rejected the theory of innate ideas and considered all knowledge to stem from experience; thus, he thought it impossible for artists to form any idea of beauty exceeding sensible nature. He maintained that one could come to know it only by comparing visible forms, a position that led him to deny even the possibility of *le beau idéal* or ideal beauty. Even so, an artist's personality appears in his work through his choices of what to represent and the "premises" with which he informs his subjects, namely, the feelings that he experiences before nature and his stylistic translation of such feelings into painting or sculpture, an activity Cochin called *le faire* (literally, "the doing," usually translated as "handling"). In his eyes, *le faire*, defined as "the effect of feelings affecting the artist as he proceeds," ("l'effet du sentiment qui meut l'artiste en opèrant"), is the touchstone for judging works of art. On the whole, Cochin was more sympathetic to productions in which the artist's labor remained apparent, tending to denigrate overfinished paintings and statues. The personality of the artist is fundamental; despite all efforts, a mediocre artist will never be able to move beyond mediocrity in his works and should abide by established rules because any liberties he might take would be contrary to taste (this was the basis of Cochin's criticism of Rococo architects and designers). On the other hand, a great artist should be accorded complete freedom from regulatory norms. For him, "that which makes real beauty is not the absence of flaws but the presence of compensatory beauties" ("ce qui fait le vrai beau n'est pas d n'avoir point de défauts, mais d'avoir des beautés capables de les compenser"). Nevertheless, the imitation of nature remains primordial for Cochin and, although he denies the possibility of illusion in painting and sculpture, he condemns all works that he finds mannered and based on conventions as opposed to observation of the effects of nature.

Thus, the literary or expressive interest of a painting is secondary to its formal qualities; fidelity to literary sources and respect for custom are irrelevant to the essence of artistic creation; it is necessary only to avoid any inaccuracies that might disturb the average spectator. The most important thing about a work of art is not what it represents, but the way it is painted or sculpted. On this point, Cochin is fundamentally at odds with most contemporary men of letters and art critics who judge works exhibited at salons on the basis of subject matter and expressive qualities.

Most of Cochin's writings are unabashedly polemical; they were meant to enable contemporary artists to resist pressures that he felt would lead art to its demise. Giving his thought a social dimension, he attributed the inadequacies of contemporary art to exterior pressures affecting artists. He found fault with collectors whose ignorance of natural effects led them to favor conventional uses of color; with patrons who constrained artists to follow even the most irrational modes; with men of letters attached to ideal beauty and expression; and with critics who looked only for inadequacies in paintings and condemned painters to an eclectic mediocrity rather than allow them to develop qualities of their own capable of counterbalancing the flaws in their works.

Thus, Cochin's writings were intended both to convince artists to return to the imitation of nature and to shape public opinion in hopes of reducing constraints detrimental to both art and artists. They articulate views pervasive in advanced academic circles for a period of about twenty years, and they exercised considerable influence on a number of critics, most notably Denis Diderot.

BIBLIOGRAPHY

Works by Cochin

Observations sur les antiquités d'herculanum. Collaboration with Jérome Charles Bellicart. Paris, 1754.
Voyage d'Italie, ou recueil de notes sur les ouvrages de peinture et de sculpture qu'on voit dans les principales villes d'Italie. Paris, 1758. Critical edition edited by Christian Michel in 3 vols. (Rome, 1991).
Œuvres diverses de M. Cochin, Secrétaire de l'Académie royale de Peinture et de Sculpture, ou recueil de quelques pièces concernant les Arts. 3 vols. Paris, 1771.
Lettres à un jeune artiste peintre pensionnaire à l'Académie royale de France à Rome. Paris, 1774.
Discours sur l'enseignement des Beaux-Arts prononcés à la séance publique de l'Académie de Rouen. Paris, 1779.
Recueil de quelques pièces concernant les arts. Geneva, 1972. Reprint of the two volumes *Œuvres diverses . . .* (1771) and *Discours sur l'enseignement . . .* (1779).

Other Sources

Michel, Christian. *Charles-Nicolas Cochin et le livre illustré au XVIIIᵉ siècle.* Geneva, 1987.
Michel, Christian. *Charles-Nicolas Cochin et l'art des lumières.* Rome, 1993.
Tavernier, Ludwig. *Das Problem der Naturnachahmung in den Kunstkritischen Schriften Charles-Nicolas Cochin d.J.* Hildesheim and New York, 1983.

CHRISTIAN MICHEL
Translated from French by Terri Gordon and John Goodman

COGNITION. *See* Literature, *article on* Literature and Cognition.

COGNITIVE SCIENCE. *See* Artificial Intelligence and Aesthetics; Attitude, *article on* Pictorial Attitude; *and* Imagery, *article on* Visual Imagery in Reading.

COLERIDGE, SAMUEL TAYLOR (1772–1834), English poet and exponent of Romantic aesthetics and criticism. As the major edition of Coleridge's works, the *Collected Coleridge,* has gradually appeared since 1969, he has come to be recognized as the most distinguished poet-critic in the history of English letters, and has a place also in the annals of European aesthetics. He developed in his own way the post-Kantian aesthetics of the first Romantic generation, and excelled in exemplifying it in his own writings and in his interpretative readings of others. Whereas his most influential work in the nineteenth century was *Aids to Reflection* (1825), which reinterpreted religion in the light of the new philosophy in order to reanimate it imaginatively and create a viable belief for modern times, in the twentieth century his most influential work has been *Biographia Literaria* (1817), which sets out his aesthetic philosophy and theory of the imagination and applies them in the critical context of his own early collaboration with the poet William Wordsworth.

As a student at Jesus College, Cambridge, and then in Bristol, in the early 1790s, he moved in radical dissenting circles, and became aware of important new movements in philosophy and biblical criticism on the Continent and their possible implications for literature. He planned a journey to Germany to gather materials for a Life of Gotthold Ephraim Lessing, and, setting off with Wordsworth, spent a year in Germany in 1798–1799. Coleridge became closely engaged with the intellectual life at the University of Göttingen, then the best German university, applied himself to learning German well enough to follow the demanding new lines of thought, and heard lectures by leading thinkers in several fields: J. G. Eichhorn, the biblical critic, whose critical challenge to the traditional dating and authorship of the Hebrew Scriptures (Old Testament) was just then being carried into the New Testament, placing the writers of the Gospels at considerable distance from the events described; J. F. Blumenbach, the physiologist; and, perhaps most seminal, Christian Gottlob Heyne, the Greek scholar and theorist of mythology, with whom other leading Romantic writers also studied, including Friedrich Schlegel.

Coleridge carried home with him not only a headful of new ideas but a library of German philosophy and literature. During the next decade he studied in more depth and detail the major writings of Immanuel Kant, Friedrich Wilhelm von Schelling, Johann Gottlieb Fichte, Friedrich Heinrich Jacobi (whose attacks on Lessing had been one of his earliest points of interest), and a host of others. They encountered a mind already well stocked with the major works of epistemology, political philosophy, theology, and of course literature of the previous two centuries as well as the classics. Coleridge's prodigious and attentive reading, at once imaginative and critical, has now been traced in great detail through the publication of his marginalia. The exact dating cannot always be established, and he often returned to give certain books and authors a fresh reading; but in general the early years of the nineteenth century were the time of his first encounter with the "giant hand" of Kant, and in 1807–1808 he was immersed in Schelling.

A number of contemporary critics (Thomas DeQuincey, Henry Crabb Robinson, J. C. Ferrier) questioned how many of Coleridge's writings were original, how much borrowed from these still relatively little known sources. This theme has run through Coleridge criticism ever since, leading his detractors to belittle his originality, and his defenders to conceal and to palliate his borrowings. The terms were restated by René Wellek in *Immanuel Kant in England* (1931), an important work on Kant's reception, minimizing Coleridge's own contribution, a view combated over a lifetime by Kathleen Coburn, who pursued her faith in the value of his work, first with her publication of the lost *Philosophical Lectures* and his *Notebooks,* and then by overseeing the massive task of editing Coleridge's complete works (1969–), which is only now drawing to a close.

The documentation of his borrowings is now so full and so detailed that his indebtedness can no longer be denied. Instead, it is now acknowledged that Coleridge deserves credit rather than blame for having recognized the leading international philosophical movement of the time and having done more than any other single figure to acclimatize it in Britain. Once placed where he belongs, within the movement of transcendental idealism, his original contributions stand out more clearly.

The extensive documentation of specific borrowings, felicitous translations and adaptations, and brilliant coinages, enriching the language with new concepts (for example, the "unconscious") has shown Coleridge not as a "plagiarist" but as an intellectual collaborator with those from whom he borrowed. His own phrase for this was "genial affinity," itself an aspect of the hermeneutic program he shared with other Romantics, especially Friedrich Schleiermacher.

Related to the charges of specific "borrowings" was the more general assumption that, as Wellek put it, "these adaptations of other thought are heterogeneous, incoherent and even contradictory" and so render the study of Coleridge's philosophy "ultimately futile" (Wellek, 1965, pp. 67–68). Elsewhere he directed his charges specifically at Coleridge's aesthetics as "fragmentary and derivative." Today, with the works of Coleridge available to us, it can be seen that his struggle to master and assess a new and challenging mode of thought is in itself a salutary study, and that he finds a route through it which permits him to formulate an aesthetics, a theory of literature, and an exemplary practical criticism.

Kant above all made aesthetics central to philosophy, and assigned a role to art that conferred a function of great significance on it. For Coleridge as for the other post-Kantians, the most important text was the *Critique of Judgment* (1790). In effect, important concepts of religion and philosophy had been shown to be unprovable by the *Critique of Pure Reason* and the *Critique of Practical Reason* (God, the soul, freedom, and immortality); but they still retained a special status, that of reflective ideas, essential to human thought. The *Critique of Judgment* showed they could be deployed in the production of works of art that would serve as bearers of these ideas. God, the soul, and freedom could no longer be regarded as belonging to the proven or the demonstrable; they could be lent an existence only in the realm of art. But so vital were they that their status was not that of mere fictions; the new and important function that art had taken on within philosophy had to be secured by a new aesthetics and a new poetics operating in the traditional sphere of art and the community of artists. Thus, the challenge to traditional theology brought with it a new opportunity for serious art; or rather, the crisis of faith could be partially answered by a reformulation of the nature of art. Art and Christian faith were always to have a close relationship for Coleridge; but art and religion were so closely related precisely because of the skeptical inroads into traditional proofs of the existence of God, on the one hand, and the doubt attaching to the so-called Christian evidences, or historical evidence for the miraculous events of the Bible, on the other. His keen interest in Lessing was grounded in Lessing's denial of the validity of historical evidences, just as his interest in Kant was based on the latter's attack on philosophical evidences. Kant delivered a series of blows to the intellectual respectability of religious argument even while opening the way for a partial rehabilitation of some of its crucial ideas in a new aesthetic location (although stripped of any direct rational underpinning).

The reception of Kant by the literary community in Germany was already well advanced when Coleridge traveled to Germany. The key figure was Friedrich von Schiller, whose series of critical essays on the aesthetic categories of the beautiful and the sublime, and the "spontaneous and reflective" in poetry (with its important claims for Shakespeare as the quintessential modern writer), and his *Aesthetic Education of Mankind* (1794) had absorbed and in certain respects resisted Kant while giving him wider currency. He made Kant's "free play of the faculties" in art a hallmark of humanity.

Coleridge's own account in the *Biographia Literaria* (1817) of the development of his thought, his aesthetic position, and his theory of the imagination is followed by his account of his collaboration with Wordsworth on their joint volume of poetry *Lyrical Ballads* (1798), often considered the inaugural work of the Romantic movement in England, and containing his own major poem, *The Ancient Mariner.* His analysis of the divergence of their views since that time underpins his critical appraisal of Wordsworth's poetry. The genre of this work is that of the biographical exposition of the growth of a mind, the mind of a philosopher-poet, now in a position to turn back to reconsider the foundations of their own achievement. As Coleridge describes it, in the developmental and organic mode that characterizes the period, "the [transcendental] philosopher contemplates intelligence in its growth, and as it were represents its history to the mind from its birth to its maturity" (*Biographia Literaria*, 1907, vol. 1, p. 297). Behind this "master thought" lies the actual collapse of the partnership and the decay of the friendship between the two poets, one of whom, Wordsworth, has gone on to become (as Coleridge argues) the greatest poet of the age, whereas he himself has outgrown his poetic talent and turned to philosophical criticism. Yet, in the *Biographia* the two poets are returned to their moment of creative collaboration, and their diverging ways as poet and as philosopher together form the Romantic model of the philosopher-poet. The great poet must also be a philosopher if he is to carry out the high purpose of poetry. This work of appraisal of Wordsworth is considered one of the finest pieces of criticism in the language; it sets out justly from the aesthetic high ground both his greatness and his frailties as a poet. Thus, Coleridge himself fulfills one of the main criteria for Romantic criticism: the poetic exemplification is the projection of the aim set out for poetry by the philosophical premises. Critical prose of this kind is itself literature: the aesthetics is fulfilled by the interpretation of the work of art. Coleridge here wrote his own "philosophical poem."

He lays out first the main heads of his own education as a poet, and tells the story of his philosophical conversion from the association theory of David Hartley, author of *Observations on Man* (1750), to the transcendentalism of Kant, that is, from the empiricist theory of the mind as a tabula rasa "written on" by successive impressions from outside it and organized simply by elementary rules of association, to the transcendental theory of mind, which infers a complex internal structure of the mind that alone, according to Kant, can account for the characteristic modes of cognition of the human being.

One of the modes of cognition is the aesthetic mode, which does not yield rational (scientific) understanding of the world, but renders up through the medium of the art object an awareness of the characteristic activities and values of human makers. As there can be no proof, so there can be no rational understanding of such ideas as God, the soul, or freedom; but in the work of art the mind is strengthened in its consciousness of the possibility of the realization of such ideas, or simply in its consciousness of possessing the capacity to be moved by such ideas.

Coleridge employed the pattern laid out in the major post-Kantian work of Schelling, the *System of Transcendental Idealism* (1800), which he set out in a series of ten theses, to show that an analysis from the side of the "object" in the world would confirm an analysis from the side of the "subject" or world-building consciousness. This two-pronged structure appealed to Coleridge precisely because he never accepted the full idealist case of Fichte in which originating power is attributed only to the self or subject of which the world is a reflection. The dual approach also suggested a modified form of dialectical movement. Schelling's construction, moreover, had the advantage that it offered two modes of insight, one the purely philosophical (the absolute intuition [*intellektuelle Anschauung*] denied by Kant), the other the aesthetic insight accessible through the projection of the work of art as a wholly human object into the world. Although Coleridge like Schelling was interested in claims to absolute insight or direct visionary power, and both men in later works explored them further, under the restraining power of Kant they opt for the aesthetic solution.

The capacity of the mind to project its ideas into objects resides in the faculty of imagination (which in Kant's "reproductive" imagination is no more than a technical capacity to recall and carry over items in the memory, what Coleridge called the mere "image-forming or re-forming power, the imagination in its passive sense"). Coleridge's much-quoted definition (often severed from its enabling philosophical framework) of the poetic imagination in *Biographia* chapter 13 is as follows:

> The IMAGINATION then I consider either as primary, or secondary. The primary IMAGINATION I hold to be the living Power and prime Agent of all human Perception, and as a repetition in the finite mind of the eternal act of creation in the infinite I AM. The secondary I consider as an echo of the former, co-existing with the conscious will, yet still as identical with the primary in the *kind* of its agency, and differing only in *degree,* and in the *mode* of its operation. It dissolves, diffuses, dissipates, in order to re-create; or where this process is rendered impossible, yet still at all events it struggles to idealize and to unify. It is essentially *vital,* even as all objects (*as* objects) are essentially fixed and dead.
> (*Biographia Literaria,* 1907, vol. 1, p. 304)

He goes on to distinguish the secondary or poetic Imagination from "Fancy, a mode of Memory" that "must receive all its materials ready made from the law of association" (ibid., p. 305). The distinction between Imagination and Fancy had been made before in many forms; for Coleridge, it serves to supply a grounding for the new literature of Romanticism and to relegate the philosophy of associationism together with the concomitant literature of the Augustan age to a lower rank. Here, as more fully in the *Philosophical Lectures* (1818–1819), he suggested a revisionary cultural and literary history.

Imaginative literature is thus rooted in the transcendental analysis of the human faculties. The poetics that follows from this aesthetic idealist position is characterized by a concern with the role that aesthetic ideas may play in the functioning of human cognition, and with the role that the work of art may have in reminding the reader of these ideas. As in other Romantic interpretations of Kant's *Critique of Judgment,* and their existentialist and phenomenological heirs, the stress is on "creation." The process of creation takes place both through the imagination ("a dim Analogue of Creation"), exemplified by poetic genius, for Coleridge preeminently Shakespeare (*Biographia Literaria* chap. 15, and his *Lectures on Shakespeare* [1808–1819]), and through the reflective idea of teleology or "destination" of life (the idea by which humankind interprets the significance of nature), and that of human "freedom" (the idea that makes moral action possible). It is through this oblique capacity for reminiscence of reflective (noncognitive) ideas that the work of art plays a role in morality, not through any direct didactic or moral message. The aesthetic judgment that was most productive in this respect was that of the sublime, redeveloped from Longinus by Edmund Burke, Kant, and others in the eighteenth century. The figure that best expressed the creative power of the Imagination was metaphor; that which best conveyed the reminiscence of reflective ideas was the symbol, or, as Coleridge put it, the "translucence of the eternal through and in the temporal" (*The Statesman's Manual* [1816, 1972], p. 450). Coleridge also applied his thinking to art and music, and he perspicaciously singled out his contemporary Washington Allston, now considered the major American Romantic painter, as he had Wordsworth in poetry.

The question "What is poetry?" is answered through a description of the poet's work:

[He] brings the whole soul of man into activity, with the subordination of its faculties to each other, according to their relative worth and dignity. He diffuses a tone and spirit of unity, that blends, and (as it were) *fuses,* each into each, by that synthetic and magical power, to which we have exclusively appropriated the name of imagination. This power, first put in action by the will and understanding, and retained under their irremissive, though gentle and unnoticed, control . . . reveals itself in the balance or reconciliation of opposite or discordant qualities: of sameness, with difference; of the general, with the concrete; the idea, with the image; the individual, with the representative; the sense of novelty and freshness, with old and familiar objects; a more than usual state of emotion, with more than usual order; judgement ever awake and steady self-possession, with enthusiasm and feeling profound or vehement; and while it blends and harmonizes the natural and the artificial, still subordinates art to nature; the manner to the matter and our admiration of the poet to our sympathy with the poetry.

(*Biographia Literaria,* 1907, vol. 1)

In his work after 1819, Coleridge developed the reflective idea in the sphere of religion, in *Aids to Reflection* carefully scrutinizing Kant's treatment of the "aid to reflection" in *Religion within the Limits of Reason Alone* and extending it to some areas and practices that Kant ruled out. Just as he could not accept the full Kantian case for "disinterested-

ness" in art, stressing the legitimate role of emotion both at the source and as a consequence of the aesthetic experience, he perceived the need for aids to the reflective ideas to persuade the will to opt for a form of community rather than for its own radical apartness. Religious experience received a new lease of life within the aesthetic realm, a solution that was to evoke a strong affirmative response in the ensuing century, as increasing numbers of people became aware of the untenability of direct "proofs" of religious claims, whether theoretical or historical. In the *"Opus Maximum,"* he attempted a large-scale systematic framework for all his thinking, and although he was never satisfied with it and left it unpublished at his death, it includes some of his finest Shakespeare criticism, as Shakespeare is accorded the mantle of the philosopher-poet that Coleridge had aspired to be.

[*See also* Kant; Literature, *article on* Literary Aesthetics; Poetics; Romanticism, *article on* Philosophy and Literature; *and* Wordsworth.]

BIBLIOGRAPHY

Works by Coleridge

The Collected Works of Samuel Taylor Coleridge. 16 vols. Edited by Kathleen Coburn. Princeton, N.J., 1969–.
Philosophical Lectures of Samuel Taylor Coleridge. Edited by Kathleen Coburn. London and New York, 1949. Reedited by J. R. de J. Jackson as *Collected Works of Samuel Taylor Coleridge,* vol. 8, *Lectures, 1818–19: On the History of Philosophy* (Princeton, N.J. 1997).
"Shorter Aesthetical Essays." In *Biographia Literaria,* vol. 2, edited by J. Shawcross. Oxford, 1907. Compare modern editing in *Collected Works of Samuel Taylor Coleridge,* vol. 7, *Biographia Literaria,* edited by James Engell and W. Jackson Bate (Princeton, N.J., 1983); and for the "shorter aesthetical essays" ("On Poesy or Art"; "On the Principles of Genial Criticism concerning the Fine Arts"; "On Taste" and other fragments) compare *Collected Works of Samuel Taylor Coleridge,* vol. II, 1–2, *Shorter Works and Fragments,* edited by H. T. Jackson and J. R. de J. Jackson (Princeton, N.J., 1996).
The Statesman's Manual [on symbolism]. In *Collected Works of Samuel Taylor Coleridge,* vol. 6, *Lay Sermons,* edited by R. J. White. Princeton, N.J., 1972.

Other Sources

Abrams, M. H. *The Mirror and the Lamp: Romantic Theory and the Critical Tradition.* New York and Oxford, 1953.
Abrams, M. H. "Coleridge, Baudelaire and Modernist Poetics." In *Immanente Ästhetik, Ästhetische Reflexion: Lyrik als Paradigma der Moderne,* edited by W. Iser. Munich, 1966.
Abrams, M. H. *Natural Supernaturalism: Tradition and Revolution in Romantic Literature.* New York, 1971.
Engell, James. *The Creative Imagination: Enlightenment to Romanticism.* Cambridge, Mass., 1981.
McFarland, Thomas. *Coleridge and the Pantheist Tradition.* Oxford, 1969.
Monk, Samuel. *The Sublime: A Study in Critical Theories in Eighteenth-Century England.* New York, 1935; reprint, Ann Arbor, 1960.
Muirhead, John H. *Coleridge as Philosopher.* London, 1930.
Orsini, G. N. G. *Coleridge and German Idealism: A Study in the History of Philosophy with Unpublished Materials from Coleridge's Manuscripts.* Carbondale, Ill., 1969.

Shaffer, E. S. "Coleridge's Theory of Aesthetic Interest." *Journal of Aesthetics and Art Criticism* 27.4 (Summer 1969): 399–408.

Shaffer, E. S. *"Kubla Khan" and the Fall of Jerusalem: The Mythological School in Biblical Criticism and Secular Literature, 1770–1880.* Cambridge and New York, 1975.

Shaffer, E. S. "'Infernal Dreams' and Romantic Art Criticism: Coleridge on the Camposanto, Pisa." *Wordsworth Circle* 20 (1989): 9–19.

Shaffer, E. S. *Coleridge's Literary Theory.* Cambridge and New York, 1998.

Swiatecka, M. Jadwiga. "'Symbol' and Its Cognates in the Thought of Coleridge." In *The Idea of the Symbol: Some Nineteenth-Century Comparisons with Coleridge,* pp. 31–67. Cambridge and New York, 1980.

Wellek, René. *Immanuel Kant in England, 1793–1838.* Princeton, N.J., 1931.

Wellek, René. *Confrontations: Studies in the Intellectual and Literary Relations between Germany, England, and the United States during the Nineteenth Century.* Princeton, N.J., 1965.

Winkelmann, Elisabeth. *Coleridge und die Kantische Philosophie. Palaestra,* 184. Leipzig, 1933.

ELINOR SHAFFER

COLLAGE. [*To explain the meaning and historical significance of the artistic technique of collage, which is sometimes also understood as a metaphor for the distinct artistic practices of modernism, this entry comprises three essays:*

    Conceptual and Historical Overview
    Collage and Poetry
    "The Pasted-Paper Revolution" Revisited

The first essay clarifies the theory and practice of collage, the second explores the place of collage in poetry, and the third discusses collage as it has been used and understood in the visual arts, where it has been most prominent. For related discussion, see Appropriation; Film; Modernism, *overview article; and* Pastiche.]

Conceptual and Historical Overview

Within the visual arts, collage is usually associated with Cubism (particularly the work of Pablo Picasso, Georges Braque, and Juan Gris), Dada (including quasi-abstract and politicized works), and Surrealism (in a variety of products and manifestations). Collage has also been a central element in many practices since World War II, ranging from the Independent Group in the United Kingdom to Pop artists in the United States of America; from activist art in the 1960s (such as *The Collage of Indignation,* 1967) to feminist work produced since the late 1960s (such as by Nancy Spero, Martha Rosler, the *Heresies* collective, and Barbara Kruger). Clearly, from these examples, the term *collage* relates directly to what is called photomontage and montage. Both of the latter have been major elements in representations of modernity: photomontage in, for example, highly politicized posters and journals, most notably during the 1930s and, again, in anti–Vietnam War imagery; montage in

the development of film, as in Fernand Léger's *Ballet Mécanique* (1924). Recently, *collage* and *montage* have described processes and effects within television, video, and varieties of products resulting from digital image manipulation: selecting, cutting, editing, piecing together, and thereby producing a particular combination.

Significantly, collage has also been related to texts and analyses within the areas of semiotics and structural linguistics. These have ranged from Roman Jakobson recalling that the example of Cubism was an impetus for the linguistic and literary investigations resulting in the theories known as Russian Formalism, to the use of versions of Saussurean semiotics to account for collage as central to modernism and/or postmodernism.

The French word *collage* has various meanings. Literally, it means sticking or gluing. In particular contexts, uses of the word can also imply pasting or paperhanging with connotations of advertising, billboards, public notices, and decorating. Colloquially, *collage* also means having an affair, or an unmarried couple "living in sin." The colloquial usage is apt in the context of visual and verbal conventions and traditions. For example, in Cubist collages, from 1912 onward, words and images cohabit, producing novel combinations and contexts. Here, conventions, genres, and expectations of high art and the supposedly incompatible materials of, and references to, popular and mass culture are found in intimate, even transgressive, embrace.

Such transgressions have been read differently. To some, such as Alfred H. Barr, Jr., collage is part of a Cubist confirmation of modern artists, "bored with painting facts," pursuing an art of immanent critique, within which formal and technical criteria are paramount. In elaborations of such accounts, collages are regarded as specialist examples satisfying the bourgeois love of radical artistic objects processed and legitimated by the modern entrepreneurial dealer: Daniel-Henri Kahnweiler as the émigré radical in Paris providing a cultural site, the private "gallery," for viewing and purchasing novel examples of visual excitement, or of contemplation, or of salvation. The "love of art" for modern collectors or museum trustees can even encompass the veneration of objects made, as with collage, from the debris of everyday life.

On the other hand, collage is regarded, by others, as the manifestation of a specific historical moment, a moment of crisis in consciousness, bourgeois and its alternatives, "readable," however problematically, in representations where the structure of a visual "language" became foregrounded. Such a view has been variously emphasized. Meyer Schapiro's "Nature of Abstract Art" (1937), a famous critique of Barr's *Cubism and Abstract Art* (1936), argued for a social and political analysis of transformations in visual representations in the late nineteenth and early twentieth centuries. Schapiro's arguments were indebted to Karl Marx, Leon Trotsky, and Max Weber, and paralleled debates raised by Walter Benjamin and Theodor W. Adorno in the 1930s. Thomas Crow's "Modernism and Mass Culture in the Visual Arts" (1983) expands on Schapiro's and Adorno's analyses, drawing attention to a relationship between claims for the elevated autonomy of high art and those for the debased conformity of mass culture. Collage is a prime example of how representation can be the site of struggle and critique in these areas. In 1936, Adorno took issue with what he regarded as an unwarranted optimism or romanticism in Benjamin's "The Work of Art in the Age of Mechanical Reproduction" (1936), an essay that could not have been written without the existence of collage and the variety of visual practices indebted to its examples, such as calligrams, montage, and photomontage. In his famous letter to Benjamin, in March 1936, Adorno argued that both "autonomous" high art and the products of so-called mass culture "bear the stigmata of capitalism. . . . Both are torn halves of an integral freedom, to which, however, they do not add up. (Adorno, *Aesthetic Theory*, 1997). Collage exemplifies the "torn halves," literally and metaphorically.

The echoes in Adorno's letter, and in collage's materials and references, are to the two "halves" of Baudelairean "modernity": "the transitory, the fugitive, the contingent, the half of art whose other half is the eternal and immutable" (Baudelaire, "The Painter of Modern Life," 1863). For Baudelaire, the contradictions of modern life are so profound that social consciousness can only be represented in "art," by means of metaphors, puns, novel contexts, and juxtapositions. These can engender what came to be called, in the 1920s, "defamiliarization." What may transpire for the viewing subject, from the experience of expressions of "modern life," is a critical consciousness of the processes of capitalist transformations, in which "all that is solid melts into air."

Analyses that consider aspects of what we might call moments and examples of Adorno's "torn halves of an integral freedom," and of Baudelaire's "modernity," can be found in the work of historians of collage such as Patricia Leighten (1989) and Christine Poggi (1992). From differing perspectives, each reminds a late-twentieth-century audience, saturated in theory, that historical analyses, theoretically informed, can recover the specific moments of collage's intervention in bourgeois notions of high culture. For example, in some of Picasso's Cubist collages, the transitory materials of demotic life (newspaper, labels, advertisements, wallpaper, and so on) and the immutable signifiers of mortality in reports of Balkan slaughter, selected from a compromised Western press, are in transgressive juxtaposition. So, too, in other collages, signs for the world of the department store, with all its mythologies of gender and commodification, are combined with high art references to Stéphane Mallarmé and Guillaume Apollinaire. In the light of such instances of modernist complexity, Raymond Williams has asked: "When was Modernism?" In reply, one might begin by considering collages as significant expressions of metropolitan "modernity."

Within criticism, collage has held a central place in debates about the significance of the "modern" and of the problems of representation in developed capitalism. In the 1950s, the American critic Clement Greenberg claimed "collage" for a particular reading of Cubism as prefiguring the supposed autonomous concerns of the Abstract Expressionists. His emphases in "The Pasted-Paper Revolution" (1958) on "literal" and "depicted flatness," "opticality," shallow space, and other formal characterizations of the work of Picasso, Braque, and Gris were rooted in a tradition that connects Heinrich Wölfflin, Clive Bell, Roger Fry, and Barr. His neglect of the sociological and dialectical meanings of collage can be indexed to cold-war assumptions about the relationships between specialized readings, creative individualism, and a censorial distaste for the artist as political. The immediate possibilities for contemporary critique in collage, and its variants, have often been denigrated by those concerned with the supposed transcendental qualities of high art. Thus, for instance, the works of Hannah Hoch and John Heartfield have been marginalized as too sociological or as too historically specific. One reason for this marginalization is that because such works include a critique of the category "Art," are tendentious, and take a critical position within the systems of production, consumption, distribution, exchange, and circulation, they do not fit comfortably within dominant accounts for the role of visual art in modern high culture. Such accounts include various versions of postmodernism. In one influential example, Rosalind Krauss claims that a systematic understanding of collage confirms that we are "standing on the threshold of a postmodernist art, an art of a fully problematized view of representation, in which to name (represent) an object may not necessarily be to call it forth, for there may be no (original) object" (Krauss, 1981). The "protohistory" of the "structure of postmodernism" is, for Krauss, exemplified by "the opening of the rift between collage as system and modernism proper" (ibid.). Here we have a return to Greenberg's 1958 emphases but with Wölfflin's formalist polarities retheorized by a particular Saussurean tradition.

The relationship between collage and traditions of semiotics indebted to Ferdinand de Saussure's theories go back to Jakobson and V. N. Voloshinov. Debates have raged about semiotics as "mainstream," and potentially formalist, or as "social," with specific "utterances" potentially eruptive and transgressive. An attempt to recover Voloshinov's critique of Saussure can be found, for example, in Jo Spence's "The Sign as a Site of Class Struggle: Reflections on Works by John Heartfield" (1981). Here, Voloshinov's semiotics, which emphasize that both *langue* and *parole* are social, enable differentiation between "uniaccentual" and "multiaccentual" signs. By the latter, Voloshinov meant instances where "differently oriented [social] accents intersect"; the sign (for, e.g., a specific collage or photomontage) thus becomes "an arena of class struggle" (Voloshinov, 1986). Signs that do not have social potential are "uniaccentual," conforming to a systematic meaning socially and politically valued by dominant groups or classes. For Spence, Voloshinov's distinctions relocate the position of Heartfield's photomontages, indebted as they are to collage. Heartfield's processes of selection and combination resulted in "utterances" that kept alive what Voloshinov calls the "*inner dialectical quality* of the sign," kept alive in circumstances in which a dominant group tries to make the sign "uniaccentual," in order to stabilize social struggles and contradictions for their own ideological purposes. With Heartfield, it was the propaganda effects of National Socialism; with other practitioners it is, for example, the role of patriarchal and medical discourses on the gendered body, or the role of institutions and corporations in defining culture within capitalism.

Such distinctions do not mean that the media of collage or photomontage are inherently or essentially transgressive or somehow "democratic." Photomontages by Gustav Klutsis in the Stalinist USSR or Leni Riefenstahl's imagery in Nazi Germany demonstrate that the specific "utterance" of the collage or photomontage as sign is crucial. Many artists in the United States during the 1960s and early 1970s recognized this lesson. *The Collage of Indignation* (1967) in New York was a collective and specific "installation" of the "artist" as, in Leon Golub's words, "an angry artist." Works by those in the Art Workers Coalition, Artists and Writers Protest, and the early feminist groups were produced in conditions of cultural and political dominance. Reusing past strategies and media, such as collage, photomontage, and Dada "performance," was one way of producing transgressive possibilities.

From the earliest examples of collage, the role of humor and irony, notably through the uses of visual and verbal puns, has been an important element. In both the realm of "puns" (historical relations between signs from different periods) and the realm of etymology (historical relations between signs from different periods), two similar but distinct signifiers are brought together and the "surface" relationship between them invested with meaning through the inventiveness and rhetorical skill of the practitioner. Such possibilities, most evident in Cubist and Surrealist collages (for example, by Max Ernst), can act to destabilize notions of "fixed" meanings or dominant distinctions between "real" and "false" connections. Collage (including photomontage and montage) is a resource on which to draw, whether by Dadaists, thirties political activists, anti–Vietnam War protesters (as in Martha Rosler's series *Bringing the War Home: House Beautiful,* 1969–1971), or feminists in the 1970s and 1980s.

[*See also* Futurism.]

BIBLIOGRAPHY

Barr, Alfred H., Jr. *Cubism and Abstract Art.* New York, 1936; reprint, Cambridge, Mass., 1986.

Crow, Thomas. "Modernism and Mass Culture in the Visual Arts." In *Modernism and Modernity: The Vancouver Conference Papers,* edited by Benjamin H. D. Buchloh, Serge Guilbaut, and David Solkin, pp. 215–264. Halifax, Nova Scotia, 1983.

Drucker, Johanna. *The Visible Word: Experimental Typography and Modern Art, 1909–1923.* Chicago, 1994.

Frascina, Francis. "Realism and Ideology: An Introduction to Semiotics and Cubism." In *Primitivism, Cubism, Abstraction,* by Charles Harrison, Francis Frascina, and Gill Perry, pp. 87–183. New Haven, 1993.

Greenberg, Clement. "The Pasted-Paper Revolution." *Art News* 58 (September 1958): 46–49. Revised and expanded as "Collage" in *Art and Culture* (Boston, 1961).

Krauss, Rosalind. "In the Name of Picasso." *October* 16 (1981): 5–22.

Lavin, Maud. *Cut with the Kitchen Knife: The Weimar Photomontages of Hannah Hoch.* New Haven, 1993.

Leighten, Patricia. *Re-ordering the Universe: Picasso and Anarchism, 1897–1914.* Princeton, N.J., 1989.

Poggi, Christine. *In Defiance of Painting: Cubism, Futurism, and the Invention of Collage.* New Haven, 1992.

Rosler, Martha. "War in My Work." *Camera Austria* 47–48 (1994): 69–78.

Schapiro, Meyer. "Nature of Abstract Art." *Marxist Quarterly* 1.1 (1937): 77–98.

Spence, Jo. "The Sign as a Site of Class Struggle: Reflections on Works by John Heartfield." *Block* 5 (1981): 2–13.

Teitelbaum, Matthew, ed. *Montage and Modern Life, 1919–1942.* Cambridge, Mass., 1992.

Voloshinov, V. N. *Marxism and the Philosophy of Language* (1929). Translated by Ladislav Matejka and I. R. Titunik. Reprint, Cambridge, Mass., 1986.

FRANCIS FRASCINA

Collage and Poetry

The word *collage* comes from the French verb *coller* and refers literally to "pasting, sticking, or gluing," as in the application of wallpaper. In French, *collage* is also idiomatic for an "illicit" sexual union, two unrelated "items" being pasted or stuck together. This undertone of illicitness is actually germane to the meaning of the word, for *collage* does not just apply to any pasteup. "Si ce sont les plumes qui font le plumage," as Max Ernst wittily put it, "ce n'est pas la colle qui fait le collage" ("If it is the feathers that makes the plumage, it is not the clue that makes the collage."). In her monumental study of the subject (1968), Herta Wescher made clear that although, strictly speaking, collaging diverse elements is hardly a new idea, such familiar items as lace and paper valentines, or the trompe l'oeil pictures of vases made from tiny postage stamps, popular in nineteenth-century America, or, say, the feather mosaic pictures made by the Aztecs of Mexico, are not quite *collages* in our sense of the word, for collage always involves the *transfer* of materials from one context to another. As the authors of the 1978 Group *Mu* manifesto put it: "Each cited element breaks the continuity or the linearity of the discourse and leads necessarily to a double reading: that of the fragment perceived in relation to its text of origin; that of the same fragment as incorporated into a new whole, a different totality. The trick of collage consists also of never entirely suppressing the alterity of these elements reunited in a temporary composition" (Group *Mu,* 1978).

It is this oscillation or doubleness that makes collage such a distinctive modernist invention—perhaps, as Gregory L. Ulmer suggests, "the single most revolutionary formal innovation in artistic representation to occur in our century" (1983). When, in the Spring of 1912, Pablo Picasso pasted a piece of oilcloth printed with a trompe l'oeil chair-caning pattern to the surface of a small, oval canvas representing a still life on a café table, and then "framed" the composition with a piece of coarse rope, he was challenging the fundamental principle of Western painting from the early Renaissance to the late nineteenth century—namely, that a picture is a window on reality, an imaginary transparency through which an illusion is discerned. Collage typically juxtaposes "real" items—pages torn from newspapers, color illustrations taken from picture books, letters of the alphabet, numbers, nails—with painted or drawn images so as to create a curiously contradictory pictorial surface. Each element in the collage has a kind of double function: it refers to an external reality even as its compositional thrust is to undercut the very referentiality it seems to assert. And further: collage subverts all conventional figure-ground relationships, it generally being unclear whether item A is on top of item B or behind it or whether the two coexist in the shallow space that is the "picture."

It is customary to distinguish between *collage* and *montage:* the former refers, of course, to spatial relationships, the latter to temporal; the former to static objects, the latter, originally a film term, to things in motion. But it may be more useful to regard collage and montage as two sides of the same coin, in view of the fact that the mode of construction involved—the metonymic juxtaposition of objects (as in collage) or of narrative fragments (as in montage)—is essentially the same. Both, moreover, are inconceivable without the technological revolution of the late nineteenth century: the mass production of paper and textile products, with the attendant possibilities for splicing film, photographs, and printed materials.

Given its origins in the Cubist collage of Picasso and Georges Braque of 1912–1913, collage is a term primarily used with reference to visual composition. There are (as the author has argued in *The Futurist Moment* [1992]), significant family resemblances between Cubist and Futurist (both Italian and Russian) collage. In Cubist collage, the objects, though disparate, are drawn from the same radius of discourse: usually domestic or everyday items like wineglasses, bottles, apples, calling cards, newspaper bits, vases of flowers, guitars, and so on; and the larger scheme

into which these fragments are drawn is still that of a unified pictorial composition. Futurist collage—for example, Carlo Carrà's great *Interventionist Manifesto* of 1914— is similar, although it tends to have a more overtly polemical thrust, relying on the juxtaposition of words and phrases as well as bold color planes to create an "agitprop" effect.

Dada and Surrealist collage deviates significantly from this paradigm. In Dada collage, pictorial composition gives way to a new emphasis on the materials assembled themselves. Kurt Schwitters, one of the greatest collagists, uses banal items like ticket stubs, buttons, advertising flyers, playing cards, bits of cloth, and pieces of metal, and juxtaposes these so as to create subtle formal and material as well as semantic tensions. In his *Merzbilder* (the title alludes to *Kommerz* as well as to *merde* [shit]), the fragments are not absorbed into the larger composition as they are in Picasso or Braque or Juan Gris; they retain their separate identity. Surrealist collage is different again: here cutups from different sources are most frequently used to produce a fragmented narrative, rich in sexual puns and double entendre, as in Max Ernst's *La femme 100 têtes.*

All these variants on early modernist collage have been documented frequently, as have such verbal variants of Futurist collage as Filippo Tommaso Marinetti's *Parole in Libertà* (those innovative free-word compositions of the late 1910s in which giant letters, mathematical symbols, onomatopoeic verbal representations, and schematic visual forms produce dynamic depictions of warfare, violent action, and so on). But what is less well understood is that collage aesthetic plays a major role in all the modernist art forms, perhaps most notably in poetry.

David Antin has observed that, as a mode of juxtaposition, "collage involves suppression of the ordering signs that would specify the 'stronger logical relations' among the presented elements. By 'stronger logical relations' I mean relations of implication, entailment, negation, subordination and so on. Among logical relations that may still be present are relations of similarity, equivalence, identity, their negative forms, dissimilarity, nonequivalence, nonidentity, and some kind of image of concatenation, grouping or association" (1974). This is an important point. Take the famous conclusion to T. S. Eliot's *The Waste Land:*

> I sat upon the shore
> Fishing, with the arid plain behind me
> Shall I at least set my lands in order?
> London Bridge is falling down falling down falling down
> *Poi s'ascose nel foco che gli affina*
> *Quando fiam uti chelidon*—O swallow swallow
> *Le Prince d'Aquitaine à la tour abolie*
> These fragments I have shored against my ruins
> Why then Ile fit you. Hieronymo's mad againe.
> Dadda. Dayadhvam. Damyata.
>   Shantih   shantih   shantih

The first two lines might have appeared in a nineteenth-century dramatic monologue: the speaker has evidently found the resolve to begin a new life, to turn his back on his stultifying, arid past, which the poem has so graphically presented, and prepare to "set [his] lands in order." But whereas Robert Browning would have had his protagonist continue logically, or at least sequentially, in this vein, in *The Waste Land*, the protagonist's question is followed by a series of seemingly unrelated fragments—from nursery rhyme ("London Bridge is falling down . . ."), to Dante's account in the *Purgatorio* of Arnaud Daniel's entrance into the purgatorial fire, to the plaintive song of the anonymous Latin poet of the *Pervigilium Veneris*, who wonders when spring will return ("O swallow swallow"), which here comes together with the cry of Philomela, raped by Tereus, and longing for the transformation her sister Procne has already undergone, to Gérard de Nerval's Romantic lyric of dispossession *("Le Prince d'Aquitaine à la tour abolie"),* and Hieronymo's decision, in *The Spanish Tragedy*, to participate in a grisly revenge plot to kill his enemies. When the words of redemption ("Give. Sympathize. Control") finally come, they are in the most esoteric and remote of languages—Sanskrit—as is the final "Shantih," the "Peace that passeth understanding" from the *Upanishads.*

What hope, then, for the Wastelanders? Much ink has been expended on this question. Take the London Bridge line. It sounds very negative, especially in conjunction with the "Unreal City" passage in part 1: "A crowd flowed over London Bridge, so many, / I had not thought death had undone so many." On the other hand, the destruction of the bridge (the song actually refers to the Gunpowder Plot) may lead to rebirth. In the same vein, Arnaud Daniel is purged of the sin of lust, and Philomela will be reborn as a nightingale. But Hieronymo's "Why then Ile fit you" leads to nothing but the grisly death of all concerned, and Nerval's Prince of Aquitaine is cut off from his birthright as well as from possible transcendence. It is never clear, then, what the "fragments I have shored against my ruins" add up to. And no doubt Eliot wanted it that way. Coordination rather than subordination, likeness and difference rather than logic or sequence or even qualification—here are the elements of verbal collage. The things described *exist:* the poet puts them before us without explicit comment or explanation.

Ezra Pound's *Cantos* carry this collage principle even further. Here is a typical sequence from the Pisan Cantos:

"Such hatred"

        wrote Bowers,

            and la Spagnuola saying:

"We are perfectly useless, on top,

            but they killed the baker and cobbler."

"Don't write me any more things to tell him

            (scripsit Woodward, W. E.)

"on these occasions

                        HE

TALKS." (End quote)

"What" (Cato speaking) "do you think of

                murder?" (Canto LXXXVI)

In what Pound himself referred to as the "ply over ply" method, he collages the words of Claude Gernade Bowers, the ambassador to Spain between 1933–1939, who wrote Pound a letter about "the atmosphere of incredible hate" in Spain, with the comments of an unidentified Spanish woman, with the historian William E. Woodward's wry reference to Franklin Delano Roosevelt's response to Pound's economic "advice" from abroad, and then with an allusion to Cato's equation (according to Cicero's *De Officilis*) of moneylending to murder. In the space of twelve lines, the poem uses lineation, spacing, typeface, and font (note the giant "HE," which gets a line to itself) to convey the economic anarchy and decay of the Spanish civil war and the pre–World War II years. But rather than providing an actual analysis of this historical vector, the poem works by comparison and contrast: the deprecating reference to Roosevelt ("HE / TALKS") contrasted to the wisdom of Cato, and so on. Notice that Pound's effect depends on ellipsis and the denial of disclosure of key information. "'What' (Cato speaking) 'do you think of / murder?'" belongs at the end of a sequence where Cato is asked what he thinks the most profitable feature of an estate and replies that it is raising cattle. After a few such questions, he is asked, "What do you think of money-lending?" And it is then that the cited response comes. In omitting the context, Pound both arouses the reader's curiosity and heightens the Roosevelt/Cato contrast. Then, too—and this is how collage works—juxtaposition replaces exposition, a convenience given that a reasoned account of Roosevelt's economic decisions might not produce the conclusions that Pound wants.

In its refusal of unity and coherence, of what Eliot himself called "the aura around a bright clear centre," collage has been open to criticism, both from the right and from the left. For his fellow poets as for the New Critics of the 1940s and 1950s, Pound's *Cantos* were simply incoherent. "He has not," Yeats declared, "got all the wine into the bowl." For a Marxist critic such as Fredric Jameson, on the other hand, the collage-composition of Wyndham Lewis (and, by implication, of Pound as well) "draws heavily and centrally on the warehouse of cultural and mass cultural cliché, on the junk materials of industrial capitalism, with its degraded commodity art, its mechanical reproduceability, its serial alienation of language" (Jameson, 1979). Collage, in this scheme of things, is a "degraded" or "alienated" version of earlier (and presumably superior) genres, an index to to the aporias of capitalism.

Whether or not this is the case, one thing that does seem certain is that the mode of detachment and readherence, of graft and citation, that is collage is a way of undermining the authority of the individual self, of the "transcendental signified." As such, it has become, in the late twentieth century, an important mode of theorizing and model building as well as art making: witness Jacques Derrida's *Glas* or Roland Barthes's *Empire of Signs*, or, in a different vein, John Cage's change-generated mesostic compositions such as *Duchamp. Satie. Joyce* or Jackson Mac Low's *The Pronouns*. Whole "textbooks"—for example, bp nichol and Steve McCaffery's *Rational Geomancy* (1992)—have taken on a collage form.

Ironically, however, even as collage has entered the critical-theoretical domain, it is beginning to withdraw from the aesthetic realm. What was once a revolutionary technique is now the staple of advertising and greeting cards. At the same time, postmodern artworks tend to be at once less "cut up" and yet, paradoxically, more equivocal than their modernist counterparts. In the poetry of John Ashbery, for example, the technique of juxtaposing citations or fragments of conversations has given way to what looks like a more seamless and continuous discourse—often a narrative—but which, on inspection, cannot be decoded as yielding any sort of coherent meaning. It is as if the individual units are "always already" collaged to begin with. Similarly, Jasper Johns's number or alphabet series operate not by collage principles (each canvas will have one letter or number, the textures of the encaustic itself producing the complexity and indeterminacy of meaning), but by the disruption of the "normal" contract between artist and viewer. Even in Robert Rauschenberg's famed "combine" paintings, the separate object layers remain starkly separate: they do not undergo the sort of transfer from one context to another that one finds in Picasso or Schwitters.

The shift in such "postcollage" works is from the juxtaposition of carefully chosen citations or statements (as in the shift in *The Waste Land* from "O swallow swallow" to *"Le Prince d'Aquitaine à la tour abolie"*) to a focus on the inherent poetic and artistic possibilities of the "ordinary," the "everyday," as in the contemporary poetry and fiction deriving from Gertrude Stein, herself by no means a collagist. But for the better part of the century—in James Joyce's *Ulysses* as in Pound's *Cantos*, in Joseph Cornell's boxes as in Kazimir Malevich's *Girl at Poster Column*, in Erik Satie's "furniture music" as in Cage's *Europeras*, collage has been the most important mode for representing a "reality" no longer quite believed in and therefore all the more challenging.

[*See also* Poetics.]

BIBLIOGRAPHY

Antin, David. "Some Questions about Modernism." *Occident* 8 (Spring 1974): 7–38.
Aragon, Louis. *Les collages*. Paris, 1965.
Group *Mu*, eds. *Collages*. Revue d'esthétique, nos. 3–4. Paris, 1978.
Jameson, Fredric. *Fables of Aggression: Wyndham Lewis, the Modernist as Fascist*. Berkeley, 1979.
Krauss, Rosalind E. *The Originality of the Avant-Garde and Other Modernist Myths*. Cambridge, Mass., 1985.
Perloff, Marjorie. *The Futurist Moment: Avant-Garde, Avant Guerre, and the Language of Rupture*. Chicago, 1986.
Poggi, Christine. *In Defiance of Painting: Cubism, Futurism, and the Invention of Collage*. New Haven, 1992.
Seitz, William C. *The Art of Assemblage*. New York, 1961.
Ulmer, Gregory L. "The Object of Post-Criticism." In *The Anti-Aesthetic: Essays on Postmodern Culture*, edited by Hal Foster, pp. 83–110. Port Townsend, Wash., 1983.
Wescher, Herta. *Collage*. Translated by Robert E. Wolf. New York, 1968.

MARJORIE PERLOFF

"The Pasted-Paper Revolution" Revisited

In the spring of 1912, Pablo Picasso glued a piece of oilcloth printed with imitation chair-caning to a painting of a café still life, thereby inaugurating the aesthetically revolutionary practice of collage. The *Still Life with Chair Caning*, which the artist also framed with a coarse mariner's rope, is a small, oval, seemingly modest work, yet its effects on twentieth-century art have been profound. The intrusion of everyday, nonartistic materials into the domain of high art challenged some of the most fundamental assumptions about painting inherited from both the classical and the more recent avant-garde traditions. The invention of collage put into question prevailing notions of what and how works of art signify, what materials artists may use, and what constitutes unity in a work of art. It also challenged the value of craft and of the handmade, the definition of originality as unmediated self-expression, and belief in the a priori partitioning of the aesthetic field into separate media such as painting, sculpture, and writing. By bringing into a relation of proximity and exchange the quintessential forms of high and low culture (through the juxtaposition of oil paint and oilcloth, the hand-painted and the machine-printed, the abstracted and the illusionistic, the hermetic and the popular), collage undermined some of the founding principles of the formalist impulse within modernism. In so doing, it further subverted the exclusively visual and presumably "disinterested" approach to modern art, which emphasized purity of medium and artistic sincerity in the manipulation of materials. Picasso's collages issue instead from a more conceptual approach to making art, in which wit and the ironic negation of norms and of the distinctive properties of media and materials prevail. In Picasso's collages and in the constructed sculptures that are related to them, pictorial and sculptural, visual and verbal, high and low forms of representation collide in chiasmic exchange. The result is an art of fragmentation and rupture, a hybrid art that resists equally the drives to purity, to the motivated sign, and to the full disclosure of stable meanings.

Can so much have been implied in *Still Life with Chair Caning?* Did this work arrive somehow without precedent to announce a decisive break with the past? During the previous four years, Picasso and Georges Braque had been engaged in the elaboration of Cubism, a seemingly new language of representation, but one in fact based on the subversion and recombination of the techniques of traditional illusion, especially perspective, chiaroscuro (modeling from light to dark), and the figure/ground relation. Early Cubist paintings such as Braque's *Houses at L'Estaque* of 1908 (Kunstmuseum Bern) or Picasso's *Houses on the Hill* of 1909 (Museum of Modern Art, New York) demonstrate a joint effort to put on display the classical systems of perspective and modeling, but here gone awry and rendered the subject of self-reflexive representation. As the Russian Formalists put it, they "lay bare the technique" through a process of estrangement, divorcing each device from its expected function, so that it becomes visible as technique.

Cubist works executed between 1909 and 1912 are remarkable for the logic and consistency of their development of a disjunctive, fragmentary style characterized by the principle of spatial indeterminacy. The subdued palette, the increasingly gridlike organization of lines and flickering planes, and the near reconciliation of figure and ground nevertheless create a strong sense of pictorial unity. But Picasso and Braque also worked against the imposition of coherence on all aspects of a work. Braque is known for having introduced a projecting trompe l'oeil nail in two paintings of winter 1908–1909, as well as lettering, sand, and imitation wood grain in a series of innovations in 1911 and 1912. Yet, these remained fairly minor tokens within otherwise highly unified works. Picasso, however, had long been drawn to the principle of stylistic heterogeneity within a single painting. As Leo Steinberg has observed, the deliberate juxtaposition of divergent styles occurs already in *At the Lapin Agile* of 1905 and in the famous *Demoiselles d'Avignon* (Museum of Modern Art, New York) of 1907. William Rubin (1989) has analyzed a similar heterogeneity in *Bread and Fruitdish on a Table* (Kunstmuseum Basel) of Winter 1908–1909. In these paintings, Picasso severs the seemingly transparent and organic relation of the artist's inner self to an expressive manner or technique. Instead, he displays the virtuoso ability to imitate the styles of others, from Henri de Toulouse-Lautrec and Édouard Manet to Paul Cézanne and the Douanier Rousseau, from Iberian sculpture to that of Africa.

By quoting the signature styles of others, so that they remain identifiable while also taking on new significance, Picasso adopted what today might be called an "allegorical" approach to making art. Allegory, that is, a manner of speaking as if with two or more voices (*allos* = other + *agoreuei* = to speak), is both a method and a mode of perception. Acting as an allegorist, Picasso appropriated the styles and images of others, in order to superimpose upon them a new, second-order meaning. He thereby drove a wedge between the ideal unity of form and meaning that characterizes the symbol, allegories' opposing term.

With the invention of collage, the principle of stylistic heterogeneity is extended to materials and in particular, to materials drawn from the world of mass production. The oilcloth in *Still Life with Chair Caning* is a cheap, machine-made, synthetic material, rather than genuine chair-caning. In Picasso's collage, its trompe l'oeil pattern counterfeits not only actual chair-caning, but the act of illusionistic painting as well. By simply appropriating this ready-made material, Picasso refuses the task of imitation, consigning it to the realm of facile effects more adequately achieved through mechanical means. His own more conceptual and inventive art will be defined in opposition to the popular taste for demonstrations of manual skill and perfected illusionism. Yet, paradoxically, he will interpolate popular cultural materials into his collages, thereby also challenging the purity of fine art and its distance or difference from kitsch. The rope frame in *Still Life with Chair Caning* may have been inspired by the ropes used to frame mirrors in port towns, as Robert Rosenblum (1973) has speculated, or by the use of rope or hemp frames in popular chromolithographs. Like oilcloth, it is a ready-made, mass-produced material that stands in for a handcrafted object; and just as the inclusion of oilcloth parodies the value accorded the medium of oil painting, the rope frame parodies the elaborate carved frames that mark the presentation of high art.

Picasso's rope frame serves a further paradoxical function, however. Picasso had already used fragments of twisted rope, sometimes accompanied by fringe, as a sign for the decorative edge of a tablecloth in several still lifes of 1911. Indeed, photographs of Picasso's studio in 1909 reveal that he owned a small round table covered with a fringed tablecloth, including a ropelike border. In making the rope signify both a picture frame and the edge of a table, Picasso sought to conflate his oval canvas with the very café table it represents. As Rosenblum was the first to observe, the *Still Life with Chair Caning* can be read as the horizontal plane of a literal table, uprighted to hang on the wall as a picture. Yet, Picasso, in characteristically ironic fashion, also subverts the possibility of seeing the canvas as synonymous with its referent—of reading it, that is, as a perfect symbol. The ambiguous oval shape may be interpreted as a round table viewed from an oblique angle, somewhat as a person seated before it might see it. Picasso has further complicated matters by depicting a straight-edged table receding into space at the lower right within the border of the oval table. This alternate rectangular table renders impossible any univocal interpretation of the *Still Life with Chair Caning* by causing the divergence of a depicted horizontal plane from the literal vertical of the canvas. The oscillation of literal and depicted, vertical and horizontal planes will continue to establish conflicting, doubled

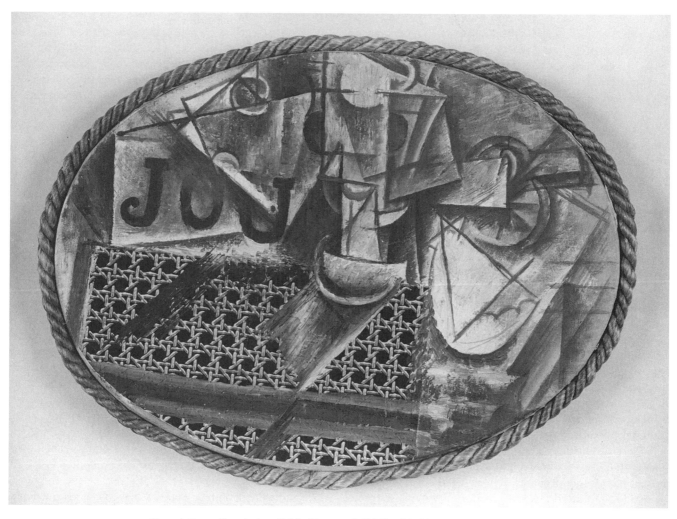

COLLAGE: Pasted-Paper Revolution. Pablo Picasso, *Still Life with Chair Caning* (1912), oil on canvas collage with chair caning, 27 × 35 cm; Musée Picasso, Paris. (Copyright 1998 by the Estate of Pablo Picasso/Artists Rights Society, New York; photograph courtesy of Lauros/Giraudon/Art Resource, New York; used by permission.)

grounds in many of Picasso's subsequent collages and constructed sculptures. Similarly, the simultaneous assertion of curved and straight-edged profiles in the tables, bottles, pipes, and glasses that populate his still lifes will destabilize any reading of these objects as iconic analogues of nature. The consistent opposition of these diacritical terms reveals the principle guiding Picasso's artistic practice from 1912 (and perhaps even earlier)—that every descriptive assertion about an object encounter its negation, so that reference is suspended in a play of multiple but contradictory possibilities.

A similar undecidability determines the structure of Picasso's contemporary constructed sculptures, which are closely related to the collages. Picasso executed his first construction, the *Guitar*, in paper during the Fall of 1912 and only translated it into the more famous sheet-metal version

sometime later, probably in 1914. The *Guitar*'s most interesting and revealing appearance, however, occurred as part of a larger construction, which is preserved only in the form of the photograph published in *Les Soirées de Paris* in November 1913. Like the *Still Life with Chair Caning*, the *Guitar* is an inaugural work that in this instance breaks with the centuries-old tradition of monolithic, carved, or modeled sculpture. Inspired by an analysis of the material and formal strategies of African Grebo masks, Picasso created this three-dimensional work by assembling a series of planes that define profiles and spatial relationships without embodying them as mass. Most significant is the way the central portion of the *Guitar*'s body is figured as a void or absence, and the way the sound hole thrusts forward from this "negative" space. The reversal of solid and void, near and far at work here is a transposition of the Grebo sculptor's disjunctive and at times arbitrary treatment of spatial relations, forms, and materials. As Picasso later recounted to William Rubin, he was struck by the fact that the eyes in Grebo masks project forward from the recessed plane of the face, whereas in his own prior sculptures, Picasso had always conceived the eye in terms of the socket—that is as a depression in its surface.

For Picasso, the projecting cylindrical eyes of the Grebo mask exemplified the "reasonable" view that art is a kind of conceptual language that re-presents nature rather than merely imitates it. In depicting the eyes as salient, the Grebo sculptor had reversed the natural relation of depth to surface. This reversal, however, had retained the spatial difference between the planes of the eyes and face, and given their placement within the figurative context of the mask, this difference proved sufficient for the cylinders to be interpreted as eyes. What was crucial, then, was not the resemblance of any form to its referent in nature, but its relational value (derived from its position as if it were a chess piece) within a particular context. The projecting cylinder in Picasso's *Guitar* functions similarly; if we interpret it as a sound hole or spatial recession, it is due to the principle that opposing terms (projection/depression) can become interchangeable since their meaning derives from mutual difference.

Picasso's *Construction with Guitar* further confounds near and far by reversing the expected difference in scale in the depiction of profiles. The double curve at the right is smaller than its counterpart at the left, although the latter is farther back (and probably represents the guitar's distal plane). Picasso heightened this incongruity by twisting the guitar spatially, so that its frontmost plane recedes sharply to the left, while the sound hole thrusts out to the right—each orientation applying pressure on the other. The guitar is also doubly situated; it both hangs from the wall, whose articulation includes a decorative border, and rests on a tilted table, complete with a bit of fringe. It is no doubt significant that *all* of Picasso's three-dimensional constructions are meant to be hung like pictures on a wall, so that they defy easy categorization as painting or freestanding sculpture.

In many of Picasso's constructions, the clear opposition of vertical and horizontal planes, and their associations with the pictorial and the sculptural, the illusory and the real, is undermined. The table in *Construction with Guitar* is tilted upward, like the tables in so many modernist paintings from Cézanne to Henri Matisse and including many of Picasso's own, so that its surface might more closely cohere to the vertical plane of the pictorial field. Moreover, Picasso has pinned a folded supporting structure beneath this table, but so that it just misses resting on the floor. On close examination, then, the table itself proves to be hung from the wall, like a picture, while the plastic treatment of the wall gives it an unusual three-dimensional presence.

This play of formal oppositions subverts the conventional meaning of each term (table/tableau, vertical/horizontal, near/far, presence/absence, pictorial/sculptural, straight-edged/curved, figure/ground, and so forth), while retaining the notion of difference. Figure continues to be defined in relation to ground, for example, even while the stability of their relation is questioned. Picasso's understanding of the diacritical character of these terms seems to derive from a perception of their arbitrariness vis-à-vis the world of nature, of the nonidentity of art with what it represents. As he stated in an interview of 1923, "They speak of naturalism in opposition to modern painting. I would like to know if anyone has ever seen a natural work of art. Nature and art, being two different things, cannot be the same thing. Through art we express our conception of what nature is not."

Picasso's awareness of the difference between art and nature, and therefore between the conventional or arbitrary nature of the codes of representation, seems to have led him to conceive Cubism as a kind of language. For this reason, structural linguistics and semiotics have provided valuable heuristic models for its interpretation. The contemporary linguistic theory of Ferdinand de Saussure, who argued that languages were based not on the substantive or motivated relation of sounds to things, but on the arbitrary link of signifier (form, sound) and signified (meaning), has proved especially illuminating. My own analysis is indebted to the analyses of Leo Steinberg, Rosalind Krauss, and Yve-Alain Bois, for whom Picasso's Cubists works, and particularly his collages and constructions, put into circulation pictorial and sculptural devices that reveal their arbitrariness, and hence their mutually defining, relational value vis-à-vis the depiction of objects, and their spatial disposition. If, in Picasso's collages and constructions, visual signifiers are always deployed simultaneously with their opposing terms, so that they frequently cancel each other out, or exchange properties and function, it is because no essential meanings inhere in any given form or material element. Hence, the remarkable mutability of the formal devices at play in Cubism, a mutability that gave Picasso the freedom to reimagine the language of representation while retaining its vocabulary.

As a corollary, Picasso's use of materials will frequently be arbitrary and inventive, like that of a primitive *bricoleur* who must make do with whatever materials and tools are at hand to accomplish his or her goals. As early as 1914, the Russian critic Vladimir Markov praised the materials and technical heterogeneity of African art as evidence of an imaginative freedom that Westerners could only envy. Picasso, who acknowledged the liberating effect of a Grebo mask on his thinking about form, must also have been struck by the diversity of its materials. Indeed, African masks frequently comprise a number of materials, many of them ephemeral: wood, paint, feathers, fibers, beads, shells, and so on. Constructed out of both carved and found elements but also painted, meant to be worn, yet hung on the walls of Parisian studios, these objects defied Western aesthetic classification. Picasso's first *Guitar,* constructed out of paper, and its later sheet-metal-and-wire version, still preserved a classic unity of material. In subsequent constructions and collages, Picasso deployed a variety of materials, whose nonaesthetic qualities made them seem unlikely candidates for inclusion in works of art: sheet metal and wire, milk tins, rope, sand, bits of upholstery fringe, scraps of wallpaper and newspaper, fragments of wall molding, playing cards, liquor and tobacco labels, musical scores, and even, in one case, a gingerbread heart. But it was the inappropriateness of such materials and the difficulties they presented the artist that interested Picasso. As he told Jaime Sabartes, "We sought to express reality with materials that we did not know how to handle and which we prized precisely because we knew that their help was not indispensable to us, and that they were neither the best nor the most adequate."

That most of these materials were drawn from the world of popular and commercial culture, and that they were mass-produced, gives a sense of the attraction they held for Picasso. Rather than describe these materials as "bits of reality," as has sometimes been done, one might more accurately describe them as already circulating cultural signs, confiscated by Picasso in order to be redeployed in the world of high art. Within their new context, the prior meanings of these elements is partly effaced and new meanings are superimposed. A single milk tin may be cut and twisted into a still life, newspaper may serve as the fringe of a tablecloth, as the body of a glass, or as the label on a bottle, while a wallpaper border may represent alternately (or simultaneously) the molding on a wall, a table edge, and a picture frame. Consistently, one sees the cheaper, mass-produced object or material substituting for and ultimately displacing the singular, handmade object, as well as the expressive marks of the artist's hand. One can point, for example, to Picasso's ironic use of spotted wallpaper as a reference to the pointillism of the Neo-Impressionists and their followers in *Pipe and Musical Score* (Museum of Fine Arts, Houston). In this collage, the mechanically produced, repetitive, and monochromatic dots negate the meaning of pointillist technique—to register the sensation of light by means of regularly applied touches of pure, complementary colors. The uncanny resemblance of this wallpaper to a fine-art technique allows the latter to be seen in new terms, as a style with its own conventions, now often repeated and transformed into merely decorative pattern. From this perspective, even the hand-painted, colored dots that stream like rays of light across the center of the collage appear secondhand. Picasso also framed *Pipe and Musical Score* with a wallpaper border, to which he affixed a paper nameplate. Hand-printed in imitation of stenciling, this "PiCASSO" [*sic*] functions to parody the bronze or gilded plaques that, along with elaborate frames, serve to signify high art in mu-

seums or in bourgeois homes. The mock nameplate also parodies the artist's signature, valued as the inimitable trace of his presence and guarantee of the work's authenticity. Given the use of so many counterfeit and mass-produced materials in this collage, the ability of the signature/nameplate to proclaim it a masterpiece worthy of museum presentation seems in doubt. If one recognizes Picasso at work here, it is due not to the uniquely expressive marks of his hand, but to the ironic humor and subversive formal wit everywhere in evidence.

As *Pipe and Musical Score* demonstrates, for Picasso the making of collages and constructions was never a process that implied creation ex nihilo, but the recombination of the separable, semantic elements of preexisting cultural codes—whether they be bits of chiaroscuro and perspective orthogonals or recycled fragments of newspaper, oilcloth, wallpaper, and commercial typography. That these elements appear as the remnants of a prior discourse, quoted out of context, allows for the partial depletion of their everyday meanings or uses, and opens them to a dialectical process of recognition and critical reinterpretation. The speckled wallpaper in *Pipe and Musical Score* refers at once to pointillism, to its decorative descendants, and to the proliferation of mechanically produced substitutes for handcrafted objects, just as it functions as both figure (of a wall or pointillist painting) and ground (for the painting that is depicted on it).

At a distance of more than seventy-five years, one can now perhaps begin to measure the revolution set in motion by the invention of collage. When in 1958 Clement Greenberg sought to understand collage in "The Pasted-Paper Revolution," it appeared to him as the solution to the central formal problem confronted by modernist artists: the reconciliation of depicted three-dimensional space with the literal flatness of the pictorial surface. As Greenberg put it: "Painting had to spell out, rather than pretend to deny, the physical fact that it was flat, even though at the same time it had to overcome this proclaimed flatness as an aesthetic fact and continue to report nature." In Picasso and Braque's effort to call attention to the flatness of the picture plane, they eventually began to affix flat pieces of paper to it—both in order to embody that flatness literally and to establish a contrast with the depicted planes that still flickered in a shallow simulacrum of depth both behind and before the pasted element. Yet, the opposition of the literal and the depicted proved to be unstable, subject to fluctuation and reversal. According to Greenberg, "Thus every part and plane of the picture keeps changing place in relative depth with every other part and plane; and it is as if the only stable relation left among the different parts of the picture is the ambivalent and ambiguous one that each has with the surface" (1961). But even this surface could not be simply stated or presented; it had to be "depicted" and "re-created." "Flatness may now monopolize everything, but it is a flatness become so ambiguous and expanded as to turn into illusion itself—at least an optical if not, properly speaking, a pictorial illusion. Depicted, Cubist flatness is now almost completely assimilated to the literal, undepicted kind, but at the same time it reacts upon and largely transforms the undepicted kind—and it does so, moreover, without depriving the latter of its literalness; rather, it underpins and reinforces that literalness, re-creates it" (ibid.).

Although he was an astute observer of the relational, ever-shifting value of surface and volume in Cubist works, Greenberg continued to assume that the pictorial ground was an a priori fact whose integrity must be affirmed. Without this stable reference point, the modernist impulse toward purity of medium through the progressive elimination of illusion and literary narrative would appear merely arbitrary. Nor would there be a firm basis for distinguishing the products of high culture—whose quality is guaranteed by truth to medium—from the facile products of a commercially driven, lowbrow culture.

Picasso's collages and constructions share the self-critical enterprise associated with Greenbergian modernism, but they do so in order to subvert rather than affirm the autonomy and purity of the media of painting and sculpture. By introducing a variety of materials and techniques, including those drawn from the world of kitsch and mass culture, by refusing to respect the "nature" of the materials he employed, and by confounding pictorial and sculptural conventions, Picasso created a series of hybrid works that challenge the mythology of purity, as well as belief in the perfect, "symbolic" coherence of form and meaning. For Picasso, the Symbolist ideal (inherited by a certain strain of modernism), of an art of presence in which the relation of signifier to signified would be fully motivated, was impossible, because all representation depended on convention. Nor did Picasso seek to emphasize the exclusively visual and therefore immediate character of the plastic arts, as opposed to the temporal arts (music, theater, or literature). By including fragments of typography, newsprint, and advertising, as well as musical scores, in his collages, Picasso suggests that looking, based on a recognition of the use and misuse of conventions, may be an allegorical form of reading.

As interpreted here, Picasso's attitude toward the making of his collages and constructions is analogous to that of the Baroque allegorist as described by Walter Benjamin. Precisely because in allegory meanings can only be assigned belatedly to objects or images, after they have fallen into ruin or otherwise been removed from their prior context, the temporal distance between the signifier and signified remains in evidence. Superimposed onto existing but partially depleted signs, allegorical meaning is always arbitrary and multiple, and calls for decoding rather than empathetic response. Yet, it was this very quality of allegory that Benjamin saw as politically significant. Similarly, in Bertolt Brecht's epic theater and in photomontage, according to Benjamin, the goal was to negate the unity of the illusion, to prevent the possibility of audience identification or absorption, in order to shock it into a fresh perception and evaluation of familiar situations and attitudes. Although not overtly political in themselves, Picasso's collages share in the critical, distancing, nonempathetic approach to aesthetic production evident in allegory, Brechtian theater, and montage. Among the many legacies of the invention of Cubist collage are the political montages of the twenties, executed primarily in Germany and in the Soviet Union, and more recent multimedia works sometimes characterized as postmodern, in which the arbitrary and allegorical properties of representation are both acknowledged and deployed to critical purpose.

[*See also* Cubism; *and* Picasso.]

BIBLIOGRAPHY

Benjamin, Walter. "The Work of Art in the Age of Mechanical Reproduction" (1936). In *Illuminations,* edited by Hannah Arendt, translated by Harry Zohn. New York, 1969.

Benjamin, Walter. *Understanding Brecht.* Translated by Anna Bostock. London, 1973.

Benjamin, Walter. *The Origin of German Tragic Drama.* Translated by John Osborne. London, 1977.

Bois, Yve-Alain. "The Semiology of Cubism." In *Picasso and Braque: A Symposium,* organized by William Rubin, proceedings edited by Lynn Zelevansky. New York, 1992.

Crow, Thomas. "Modernism and Mass Culture in the Visual Arts." In *Modernism and Modernity: The Vancouver Conference Papers,* edited by Benjamin H. D. Buchloh et al., pp. 215–264. Halifax, Nova Scotia, 1983.

Greenberg, Clement. "The Pasted-Paper Revolution." *Art News* 57.5 (September 1958): 46–49ff. A revised version was published as "Collage," in *Art and Culture: Critical Essays* (Boston, 1961).

Greenberg, Clement. "Avant-Garde and Kitsch" (1939). In *Art and Culture: Critical Essays,* Boston, 1961.

Krauss, Rosalind. "Re-Presenting Picasso." *Art in America* 68.10 (December 1980): 90–96.

Markov, Vladimir. "L'art des nègres." *Cahiers du Musée national d'art moderne* 2 (1979): 319–327. Translation by Louis Paudrat and Jacqueline Paudrat of *Iskusstvo negrov,* written in 1913–1914 and posthumously published in 1919.

Owens, Craig. "The Allegorical Impulse: Toward a Theory of Postmodernism," parts 1 and 2. *October* 12 (Spring 1980): 67–86; 13 (Summer 1980): 58–80. Reprinted in *Beyond Recognition: Representation, Power, and Culture,* edited by Scott Bryson et al. (Berkeley, 1992), pp. 52–87.

Poggi, Christine. *In Defiance of Painting: Cubism, Futurism, and the Invention of Collage.* New Haven, 1992.

Rosenblum, Robert. "Picasso and the Typography of Cubism." In *Picasso in Retrospect,* edited by Roland Penrose and John Golding. New York, 1973.

Rubin, William. *Picasso and Braque: Pioneering Cubism.* New York, 1989. Exhibition catalog, Museum of Modern Art.

Shklovsky, Victor. "Art as Technique." In *Russian Formalist Criticism: Four Essays,* translated by Lee T. Lemon and Marion J. Reis, pp. 3–24. Lincoln, Nebr., 1965.

CHRISTINE POGGI

COLLINGWOOD, ROBIN GEORGE (1889–1943), professor of metaphysics at The University of Oxford and philosopher best known for his close linking of art with expression, imagination, and language. Collingwood worked in both history and philosophy, and his interests in the latter were wide-ranging. The primary philosophical influences on his thinking were G. W. F. Hegel, Giambattista Vico, and especially Benedetto Croce. He also worked under the personal influence of his father, who, as friend and biographer of John Ruskin, brought Ruskin's work to bear on Collingwood's way of thinking. Collingwood's aesthetics must be understood in light of his fuller philosophical project: to disclose the modes of human experience and their functions. Within this project, his aesthetics is an attempt to discover art's role in life and culture. For Collingwood, the "philosophy of art is the attempt to discover what art is; and this involves not an examination of the world around us in order to discover and analyse instances of it, as if it were a chemical substance, but a reflection upon our own activities, among which art has its place" (1964, p. 48).

There are two schools of interpretation concerning Collingwood's work. The first argues that he made a radical change from his early work to his late work, and the second argues for a strong continuity between the two. Despite Collingwood's dismissal of some elements of his early work as unsatisfactory, the second interpretation seems the more sound, especially where his aesthetics is concerned. In his first important book, *Speculum Mentis* (1924), art found its general role as prefatory to religion, science, history, and philosophy. With modifications, this role was developed by Collingwood in 1925 in *Outlines of the Philosophy of Art*. Here he argued that aesthetics should focus not on artifacts but on the activities of persons deemed artists. This focus led to Collingwood's emphases on expression and imagination as the key to understanding art. In *Outlines,* he attempted to describe the activity of imagination in terms of beauty, using the term in a novel, transactional way. He maintained that

> real beauty is neither "objective" nor "subjective" in any sense that excludes the other. It is an experience in which the mind finds itself in the object, the mind rising to the level of the object and the object being, as it were, preadapted to evoke the fullest expression of the mind's powers.   (1964, p. 87)

Despite his caution, Collingwood found that his employment of *beauty* seemed to lead inevitably in the direction either of a realism invoking a real quality of artifacts or of a thoroughgoing subjectivism of taste. In light of this tendency, he abandoned his reconstruction of "beauty" in favor of his reconstruction of "imagination" as that human activity "that thought presupposes" (ibid., p. 55) and that initiates the process of self-knowledge. Thus, in 1926 in "The Place of Art in Education," Collingwood further foreshadowed his full theory of art that later appeared in *The*

Principles of Art (1938). Here he emphasized art's role in initiating self-knowledge: "To be an artist is to create for oneself a world of imaginary objects whose function is to express to oneself one's own mind" (1964, p. 195). He also introduced the connection between imagination and language that played a central role in his final conception of art: "Thus the act of imagining, which is the act of uttering language, is not an embroidering of a pre-existent thought; it is the birth of thought itself" (ibid., p. 196).

Collingwood's work in aesthetics reached its final form with the publication in 1938 of *Principles,* a text both widely read and widely criticized. *Principles* is divided into three books, and following the foci of these books provides a way of drawing an overview of Collingwood's theory of art.

Book 1 is essentially negative in purpose; it distinguishes what Collingwood called "art proper" from "art falsely so called." Here Collingwood attacked the "technical theory of art" that he believed to be dominant in the early part of the century. The technical theory treats "works of art" as artifacts and takes the activity of artists to be employing these artifacts to achieve some preconceived end. In doing so, it confuses "art" with "craft," which he identified as "the power to produce a preconceived result by means of consciously controlled and directed action" (1938, p. 13). Craft, for Collingwood, encompassed a range of ends such as amusement, propaganda, exhortation, instruction, and practical value (which Collingwood termed "magic"). Thus, he saw the identification of works of art with artifacts as in league with a variety of theories of art that either openly or surreptitiously make artistic activity subservient to some nonartistic end, thus making it "technical." This he took to be "the main error against which a modern aesthetic theory must fight" (ibid., p. 26).

In developing his case against identifying art and craft, Collingwood made some initial claims about what art is: (1) art is not an artifact but an activity, and (2) art is creative, the making of art is a controlled making but one that does not have a preconceived end. More provokingly, he argued in book 1 that "a work of art may be completely created when it has been created as a thing whose only place is in the artist's mind" (ibid., p. 130). This Crocean claim has led many readers to consider Collingwood to be an idealist narrowly construed, especially when it is read from the perspective of some version of the technical theory that sees the claim as eliminating the importance of the artifact or art object. Collingwood's point, however, is precisely to force the reader to consider the work of art not as an artifact but as a particular kind of activity or experience: "a work of art proper is a total activity which the person enjoying apprehends, or is conscious of, by the use of his imagination" (ibid., p. 151). To accomplish his reconception of art, Collingwood turned in book 2 of *Principles* to an exposition of expression and imagination.

Book 2 returns to Collingwood's ongoing project to locate art as a dimension of human experience. He made art dependent on imagination and maintained that "imagination is a distinct level of experience between sensation and intellect, the point at which the life of thought makes contact with the life of purely psychical experience" (ibid., p. 215). Thus, art functions as the initial level of thought. The key to following Collingwood at this juncture is to avoid equating "imagining" and "making believe"; imagining is rather the active making of a world for consciousness. In standing between sensation and intellect, imagination, and therefore art, plays a central role in the life of the mind. It is the activity of bringing feelings—sensa together with attendant emotions—to consciousness. Collingwood, like Charles Peirce and John Dewey, challenged the traditional empiricist conception of sensa as fixed data. Indeed, he argued that it is precisely such a static view of feelings that underlies the technical theory of art and the identification of art with artifacts. For Collingwood, art is the activity of expressing feelings that are inherently dynamic, transforming them from a psychic level of experience to an imaginative level. In this way, as he had suggested earlier in his career, art plays a crucial role in self-knowledge and, ultimately, in knowledge of the world. In the total imaginative experience that occurs when we express our emotions, we in effect solve a problem with which we have been wrestling. Furthermore, the expression of emotion creates language, so that art, for Collingwood, is pragmatically the same as the initial level of language, which is itself "an imaginative activity whose function is to express emotion" (ibid., p. 225).

Collingwood addressed some more traditional aesthetic questions in the third and final book of *Principles*. He inquired, for example, into the distinction between good and bad art in light of his own new conception of art proper:

> The aesthetic experience, or artistic activity, is the experience of expressing one's emotions; and that which expresses them is the total imaginative activity called indifferently language or art. This is art proper.　　　　　　　　　　　(Ibid., p. 275)

Because art proper is distinct from craft or art falsely so called, it is a mistake to maintain that examples of craft are "bad art." They are simply other than art. Furthermore, because art is a conscious activity of trying to express emotions, "bad art" is for Collingwood the result of a failure to express when one is trying to: "A bad work of art is the unsuccessful attempt to become conscious of a given emotion" (ibid., p. 282). As many commentators have noted, this leaves critics little room for criticism except in a technical, nonaesthetic sense. On Collingwood's theory, the sole cause of bad art is not lack of technique or experience but a "corrupt consciousness" that is unable to face its own emotions.

In identifying art as language, Collingwood also reintroduced the question of the status of a work of art. His claim in book 1 that a work can take place in the mind of the artist suggests a thoroughgoing idealism. If one recalls, however, that for him the work of art is itself an activity, one can see that it may include physical gestures and the production of artifacts. Creating language is, for Collingwood, an extremely diverse activity. Thus, although a work of art need not be physical or external, in many cases, Collingwood argued, physical production is crucial to the full expression of an emotion. With a painting, for example, the "production is somehow necessarily connected with the aesthetic activity, that is, with the creation of the imaginative experience which is the work of art" (ibid., p. 305). To see his point, one must avoid confusing his assertion that a work of art is an activity with the claim that it is a product or artifact in the mind. Collingwood's description of art proper as an activity has been perhaps the most frustrating element of his aesthetics for those who follow twentieth-century common sense in identifying works of art as artifacts. Again, his assertion is tied to his general opposition to traditional empiricism's mechanical conception of perception and its notion of static sense data.

The final question that Collingwood addressed has to do with the relationship of an artist to her or his community. As he saw it, nineteenth-century artists and aestheticians had so isolated art from the rest of culture that art had come to be seen as a private affair of the artist. Such a habit had led, he believed, both to an increase in craft masquerading as art and to an increase in bad art through failed expression. Collingwood sought to counter this trend by examining, within the confines of his theory of art as language, an artist's relationship to an audience. He maintained that art proper involves the silent collaboration of an audience and he rested his argument on an appeal to experience. Artists, he said, have always seemed to be concerned with an audience's response to their work. Furthermore, if an artist "attaches any importance to the judgment of his audience, it can only be because he thinks that the emotions he has tried to express are emotions not peculiar to himself, but shared by his audience, and that the expression of them he has achieved (if indeed he has achieved it) is as valid for the audience as it is for himself" (ibid., p. 315). Artists, on Collingwood's view, often collaborate with those who have influenced them, as well as, in some arts, with those who execute elements in an artistic activity. Thus, for example, Paul Cézanne can be said to have collaborated with Impressionists and any playwright can be said to collaborate with actors. He further claimed, however, that artists *always* collaborate imaginatively with an audience, a community for whom the artist expresses emotions. Members of an audience, then, can actually judge an artist's success by re-creating the work of art, that is, by expressing the same emotion that the artist has brought to consciousness. Dewey made a strikingly similar proposal in *Art as Experience* (1934). As a result of their claims that audiences can re-create an artist's work, both Collingwood and Dewey repeatedly have been challenged to show how one might know that the same expression is repeated. For Collingwood, the question was an experiential one, not a strictly logical one, and his response was to claim that experientially, just as in ordinary linguistic communication, one has "an empirical and relative assurance" that one can repeat a work of art as an imaginative activity (ibid., p. 309).

This last element of Collingwood's aesthetics has been the most consistently criticized. It seems, to many commentators, to create two fundamental inconsistencies in Collingwood's theory. First, the act of collaboration seems to *require* some external artifact of language for an audience to behold, a requirement that Collingwood repeatedly denied for art proper. Second, the artist's active consideration of an audience's response seems to aim his or her activity toward a nonaesthetic end, thus making the activity an instance of craft. Collingwood addressed the first concern by retreating to his claim that the audience is always imaginatively, not existentially, present for the artist in a total imaginative experience. The latter case, he admitted, is possible in particular instances, but it is not necessary because the audience may function imaginatively only as a check against a corrupt consciousness. In any case, the importance for Collingwood of this collaborative dimension of art proper is that it discloses the artist's dependence on a community: "a man, in his art as in everything else, is a finite being. Everything that he does is done in relation to others like himself" (ibid., p. 316). On the positive side, collaboration points to the historical and cultural public nature of art, to its role in bringing not only individuals but human communities to awareness of themselves and their world.

Collingwood openly worked against the grain of his own philosophical community. He retained a strand of idealism, though, as with the American pragmatists, it was a strand that recognized the transactional nature of perception, imagination, and experience as a whole. In keeping with his initial aim, Collingwood found art to function as a link between merely psychic and fully intellectual modes of experience. Art, as language, brings to consciousness for both individuals and communities that which was previously felt but not articulated. Collingwood's work remains an important alternative to present theories. On the one hand, it challenges the many contemporary thinkers who continue to adopt some version of the technical theory of art. On the other hand, its dialectical relating of art to intellectual activity resists the various postmodern and neopragmatic philosophies that seek to conflate art and philosophy.

[*See also* Expression Theory of Art.]

BIBLIOGRAPHY

Works by Collingwood

Speculum Mentis: or, The Map of Knowledge. Oxford, 1924.
The Principles of Art. Oxford, 1938; reprint, New York and Oxford, 1958.
The Idea of History. Edited by T. M. Knox. Oxford, 1946. Revised by Jan van der Dussen (Oxford, 1993).
Essays in the Philosophy of Art. Edited by Alan Donagan. Bloomington, Ind., 1964.

Other Sources

Donagan, Alan. *The Later Philosophy of R. G. Collingwood.* Oxford, 1952.
Krausz, Michael, ed. *Critical Essays on the Philosophy of R. G. Collingwood.* Oxford, 1972.
Mink, Louis O. *Mind, History, and Dialectic: The Philosophy of R. G. Collingwood.* Bloomington, Ind., 1969.
Rubinoff, Lionel. *Collingwood and the Reform of Metaphysics.* Toronto, 1970.

DOUGLAS R. ANDERSON

COLOR. [*This entry comprises two essays on the concept of color in the history of aesthetics:*

Color in the Arts
Color Science

The first essay demonstrates the central role of color in the history of the various arts, especially architecture, literature, music, and painting. The second essay provides a closer look at how scientists and philosophers have understood color, both in the past and today. For further discussion, see Abstract Expressionism; Kandinsky; Perception, *article on* Psychology of Perception; Psychology of Art; Science and Aesthetics; *and* Synaesthesia.]

Color in the Arts

The symbolic and iconographic range of associations between colors and ideas, emotions or beliefs is one of the first aspects of color to come to mind, and one of its most potent dimensions. Much of the current and historic thinking on color involves the reading of a symbolic language in which colors are ciphers. From medieval alchemy to the works of Carl Gustav Jung, the four basic colors of the humors are usually identified as yellow (gold, the sun), red (blood, fire or affectivity) green (bile, sensation), and blue (for the spiritual process, nous or mind as well as heaven, although in Tibet, blue is replaced by white). The connotations of green in the Islamic world, for example, are entirely different from those of the green used by Edgar Degas or Ellsworth Kelly. One of the areas in which this is particularly meaningful is heraldry, which conveys the narratives of genealogy and political allegiance through a language of color.

Color Codes: The Symbolic and Psychological Schemata. Color theorists are confronted with the difficulty of making color behavior—the interaction of colors—fit the elaborate charts and diagrams devised through optics as well as design. Tables and other schemata are by nature linear and, it seems, almost by nature unable to adequately represent color as a vital force. There exist color wheels, stepped scales, rectangular charts and atlases, pyramids and spheres, and all sorts of convoluted geometric configurations. Some have astrological or numerological connotations, others are based on the quantitative rules of physics and chemistry. Each ventures its formula for primaries, complementaries, harmonies, and dissonances. None is exhaustive or even accurate. The aim of color schemata is the planar, spatial representation of interaction, vibration, movement toward and from the viewer, and afterimages—all temporal, changing, moving, and shifting phenomena. In other words, static schemata are asked to capture dynamic effects on the eye in its most active state. Moreover, the characterization of color relationships is made all the more enigmatic by the strong emotional responses involved, and although it always sounds vague, what "works" aesthetically or psychologically is not always what is supposed to work according to even the most advanced and logically sound system. This leads to the ever-elusive notion of the "color sense," the enviable instinct of certain painters, writers, designers, and musicians for whom color practice is a law unto itself.

The schemata are symptoms of a human impulse that might be called the tendency to tabular thinking. Just as scientific tables—the periodic table of elements is a paradigm—simultaneously summarize a panoply of phenomena, so a color chart is meant to be the orderly arrangement of a universe of sensations. Tabular thinking strives to establish a regular order, relies on symmetry and periodicity, and places every element or set of data in a predetermined space according to ground rules. In the case of color, the tabular approach is often hierarchical and prescriptive, governing the way colors are matched, balancing color families, prescribing dissonant and harmonic combinations, and suggesting compositional patterns. Are the charts reliable? Only to a limited extent, aesthetic history suggests. Although color wheels and atlases traditionally used by painters come to mind, there are also color-based tables in music (like the pitch tables of Alban Berg and Milton Babbitt or the "spectral envelopes" of Wayne Slawson); the truth tables of philosophy and broad historical tables of Oswald Spengler; the "map of misreading" offered to students of literature by Harold Bloom as a guide to hidden lyric and psychological structures, as well as James Joyce's table of correspondence (including a column of colors) for Ulysses; and the various schemata of psychological inquiries into behavior related to color such as those devised by Leo Hurvich and Dorothea Jameson and by scientists working on the neurophysiological, optical, and chemical causes of color phenomena. When one opens most color manuals, one is likely to encounter charts, grids, graphs, and tables that are based on quantitative data. Their accuracy is not in question, but their broader applicability to the way in which color is really used and experienced in the arts is dubious.

Painting and Architecture. In most artists' studios, the practical arrangement of colors on a palette is more important than the more systematic or mathematical arrangement according to a table, or the natural spectrum. Rather than codify color relationships according to a system of objective rules, the palette allows for an individualized array of tones and their mixtures, which changes with each painting and from one phase in a career to the next (e.g., the blue period of Pablo Picasso yields to rose). Beyond the subjectivity of color choice, every medium exacts its own practical demands on hue, value, chroma, opacity, and translucency. The powerful effect of gold leaf in medieval illuminated manuscripts and of golden backgrounds in Byzantine mosaics is just one example of the effect that the choice of medium can exert. A palette for oils will not translate well into a guide for watercolors, acrylics, or the eccentric concoctions of paint and solvents used by various Abstract Expressionists (particularly Mark Rothko) and contemporary artists (such as the Day-Glo pigments of Peter Halley, the neon lights of Dan Flavin, or the richly colored glass of the cathedral at Chartres, or a vessel by contemporary glassblower Dale Chihuly).

Dividing painters into two groups according to their devotion to color (Matthias Grünewald, Titian, Veronese, Peter Paul Rubens, Eugène Delacroix, Vincent van Gogh, Robert and Sonia Delaunay, Wassily Kandinsky, Henri Matisse, Hans Hoffman, and Frank Stella) or line (Michelangelo, Raphael, Dominique Ingres, Edgar Degas, Pablo Picasso, Jasper Johns) is a great pastime among critics. The old tenet that color is a secondary quality and that drawing must precede painting, whether in the genesis of a work or in the training of the artist, reflects this division. Habits of association persist in equating line with the rational, the structured, the formal, the honest, the reliable frame of mind, even moral rectitude. Color is identified with the emotional, rhapsodic, emancipated, formless, and even decadent or deceitful in art. Many artists express great anxiety at its powers, including the magisterial painter and theorist Josef Albers, whose seminal course and text on the "interaction of color" began with the simple dictum: "Color deceives continually."

Perhaps because of its elusive character, the great bursts of colorism in art have been explosive but brief, including the sixteenth-century Venetians, the early twentieth-century Fauves, and the "hard-edge" or Color Field painters of the 1960s and 1970s. Colorism in art has relied heavily on eccentric rule-breakers, such as Vincent van Gogh, whose bold use of such forceful tones induced complementary echoes, the analytic "divisionism" of Georges Seurat, or the "simultaneity" of the spectral work of Robert and Sonia Delaunay. Among the first to lay a chromatic foundation for abstraction was Paul Cézanne, who took a relational approach to color, anticipating not only Matisse, who found a way to "construct by relations of color," but Albers on "interaction" and later generations who have made the monochrome the autonomous basis for entire works. According to Cézanne, "Contrasts and relations of color—that is the whole secret of drawing modeled forms. . . . One can therefore say that to paint is to contrast" (as quoted in Riley, 1995).

After Cézanne, the progress of color toward abstraction may be tracked through the liberation of color from line in the work of Matisse, to the strongly psychological as well as synaesthetic color correspondences posed by Kandinsky in his teaching and lyrical manifesto, *Concerning the Spiritual in Art* (1977), as well as in his dynamically balanced compositions. The kinetic dimension was added by the "push and pull" of Hoffmann's heavily textured "slab" paintings, while the transparency of great Cézanne and Matisse was extended by the "veils" of Morris Louis as well as the sfumato effects achieved by Mark Rothko, Barnett Newman, and Milton Avery. In our time, the painterly approach to exuberant colorism has been pursued by Willem de Kooning, who dreamed of how "to get all the colors in the world into one brush stroke," as well as Gerhard Richter, Sandro Chia, and Charles Clough, while a more rationalistic, as well as geometric, avenue has been taken by Frank Stella, Ellsworth Kelly, Peter Halley, and others. The daring use of bright hues should not be the sole criterion of great colorism, however, and it is important to recall the powerful effects achieved within a distinctly limited palette as, for example, when artists such as Andrea Mantegna, Camille Corot, Édouard Manet, Jasper Johns, Brice Marden, and Nancy Haynes delve into the radiance of gray, or in the virtuoso handling of the spectral possibilities of white by J. M. W. Turner, Degas, Cy Twombly, Robert Ryman, and Mark Milloff. One of the most dramatic examples of the war between color and line in the work of a single artist can be found in the paintings of Chuck Close, who scores the canvas in a grid across which he uses tiny expressionist, highly toned paintings that break down the measured, linear matrix of the grid and conquer it with color. Viewed from a distance, Close's pixillation of a photographic image pulls back into focus from an abstract image.

Manipulating the spatial illusions induced by color is one of the great challenges of architecture. No restoration has had as great an impact on our impression of the interior of a building as the restored vibrancy of the Sistine Chapel, and the immense difference in the sense of the volume is entirely attributable to the alteration in the colors. The great Baroque interiors, particularly the illusionistic ceilings of the dome of Saint Andrea della Valle or Pietro da Cortona's Barberini ceiling, offered virtuoso examples not only of the handling of light and shadow, but of the use of the value scale of coloring, linking one part of the interior to the next through not only structural means, such as repetition, but chromatically, part to part.

As painting has the war between line and color, there is a distinction in modern and postmodern architecture between the proponents of the "white cube" and the champi-ons of polychromy. The powerful (to the point of being offensive) chromatic statements of the Miami-based Arquitectonica, or the late Scottish architect James Stirling in his design for the Staatsgalerie in Stuttgart, stand at one end of the spectrum. The subtly harmonized range of blues and greens in Caesar Pelli's tower addition to the Museum of Modern Art in New York, the powerful pinks and oranges of Louis Kahn's pastel studies, or the color coding in blue and red of Renzo Piano's Pompidou Center in Paris are examples of independent approaches to chromaticism. In the work of Michael Graves, stemming in part from his designs for murals, there is a tendency to mimetically echo the blues of the sky in the top part of the building or the green of surrounding trees in the lower part (to use the famous example of his Portland Building). Frank Stella has recently joined the ranks of the extravagant colorists with his own architectural and mural designs, and innovations in lighting as well as materials promise still more bold and unusual color strategies to come.

Color in Music and Literature. Even in music, color must accept secondary status, both as a matter of historical record and in the consensus regarding the primary importance of structure and clarity. The so-called chromatic scale was developed in Greece in the fourth century BCE, after the diatonic and enharmonic scales, and even today the nuances of chromaticism are attained only at a later moment in a musician's development (those who recall their first piano lessons know that the black keys are learned later). The tight relationship between musical and visual color even in ancient Greece gave rise to the adoption in painting of musical terms such as tone and harmony. In medieval and Renaissance notation, the synaesthetic aspect of color thinking in music was reflected in the use of different colors of ink for the Greek modes (in one eleventh-century example, the Dorian was to be written in red, the Lydian in yellow, the Phrygian in green, and the Myxolydian in purple). By the end of the sixteenth century, composers were using a kind of color mixing, analogous to the mixed tones on the painter's palette, and the schematic interrelationships between visual and aural color had become the basis for compositions and treatises by Gloseffo Zarlino as well as by the painters Leonardo da Vinci and Giuseppe Arcimboldo and others.

The impact on music of Isaac Newton's work on optics (Newton himself wrote extensively about musical harmony) included the creation of instruments such as Louis-Bertrand Castel's "ocular harpsichord," for which Jean-Philippe Rameau wrote compositions, as well as similar instruments used in the music of Georg Philipp Telemann.

In Romantic and modern musical literature, color takes on a more powerful, yet enigmatic, importance. Because chromaticism is such an important (and slippery) term in music, the synaesthetic association of Richard Wagner and Hector Berlioz with the visual impression of bright and varied colors was part of their own theoretical approaches to composition. With Claude Debussy, Camille Saint-Saëns, and Maurice Ravel, the rethinking of orchestration through the amplification of the available palette of timbres transformed the prevailing thinking on dynamics, harmony, and balance. After them, the most important figure in the exploration of sound and color is Arnold Schoenberg, who collaborated with the painter Kandinsky in formulating "pantonal" musical compositions that were composed in part with visual color intervals or relationships in mind. The expansion of the role of electronic synthesizers has multiplied the diversity of possible chromatic effects and in effect changed the musical meaning of chromaticism during the past two decades; some composers, among them Wayne Slawson, use "color sounds" as the elemental units of their work.

Part of the confusion about what color means to music results from the overlap with two similar terms, *timbre* and *orchestration,* which refer to an impurity of tone that predates the use of electronic synthesizers, relying on the "rough" secondary characteristics by which individual voices can be sorted out. Much of what is new in today's concert halls is directly attributable to color. Although some of the changes have to do with recent literature based on color tables and innovations in sound color, a great deal of the new color comes from the reinterpretation of familiar works through unconventional orchestral settings that produce a change of timbre and coloring, such as the "early music" or "original instruments" movement, which has brought major work by Ludwig van Beethoven, George Frideric Handel, Johann Sebastian Bach, Antonio Vivaldi, Wolfgang Amadeus Mozart and even later composers such as Hector Berlioz to be played on period instruments, with an orchestra reconfigured in terms of seating. Finally, there are visual complements to timbral effects, such as Aleksandr Scriabin's scheme for a light show to accompany the Prometheus Symphony (using a table of correspondences between key and color), the high-tech lighting effects created by David Hockney for the staging of *Tristan and Isolde,* or the lighting effects used by the Kronos Quartet in conjunction with a work by the Minimalist composer Sofia Gubaidulina.

In literature, the most prevalent role of color is its deployment as part of a symbolic code, as in the work of Dante or Thomas Hardy (among many others). There is another level of chromaticism in fiction and poetry, however, involving a more elemental sense of color and its relation to language, principally through synaesthesia. The pioneer of this immersion in color was Charles Baudelaire, and it can also be traced in Marcel Proust's attentiveness not just to familiar reflected colors but to the ultraviolet that lies beyond the threshold of visibility, or to James Joyce's nocturnal colors in *Finnegans Wake* and the incorporation of color into the table of correspondences that is the key to *Ulysses.* Certain poets

can be associated with the particular colors that become emblems of their work, as with the blue of Georg Trakl, the white of Stéphane Mallarmé or Hart Crane, or the green of Wallace Stevens. When color becomes the argument of the work of literature, as in John Hollander's lyric sequence "Spectral Emanations," William Gass's *On Being Blue,* or Thomas Pynchon's *Gravity's Rainbow,* which explores the invisible infrared and ultraviolet ends of the spectrum (as Proust did) as well as the gamut of tones between, then it can be considered a fundamental stimulus and guiding principle in the composition of the work.

Conclusion. It is important to realize that color has an uncanny ability to evade all attempts to codify it systematically in the artistic realm. The sheer multiplicity of codes attests to the profound subjectivity of the color sense and its resistance to categorical thought. Color behavior does not conform to one paradigm, chart, or episteme. The topic has become a watershed for thinking about models and about art that is created by systems, simply because it is such a devourer of models and systems. It has attracted and ultimately confounded systematic innovators in the arts and psychology, including painters, sculptors, architects, writers, and composers who attempt to use precompositional systems. This is why the multidisciplinary approach to the role of color in aesthetics and social sciences is imperative. Despite this apparent fragmentation, color can also be the aesthetic dimension that holds formal and psychological elements together, whether within a work or as an approach to a work of art. If "color is the type of love," as John Ruskin wrote, its great erotic task is one of holding a world in relation. For art's great colorists—Titian, Delacroix, Pierre-Auguste Renoir, Kandinsky, Jung, Wagner, Berlioz, Schoenberg, Goethe, Joyce, and others—the color sense is a third Promethean gift, along with language and fire. Completely mastering it is impossible, but the power it imparts to those who dare to handle it is as profound as that of light itself.

BIBLIOGRAPHY

Albers, Josef. *Interaction of Color.* New Haven, 1963.

Cheetham, Mark A. *The Rhetoric of Purity: Essentialist Theory and the Advent of Abstract Painting.* Cambridge and New York, 1991.

Delaunay, Robert, and Sonia Delaunay. *The New Art of Color: The Writings of Robert and Sonia Delaunay.* Edited by Arthur A. Cohen, translated by David Shapiro and Arthur A. Cohen. New York, 1978.

Gage, John. *Color and Culture: Practice and Meaning from Antiquity to Abstraction.* Boston, 1993.

Gass, William. *On Being Blue: A Philosophical Inquiry.* Boston, 1976.

Goethe, Johann Wolfgang von. *Theory of Colours.* Translated by Charles Lock Eastlake. Reprint, Cambridge, Mass., 1970.

Kandinsky, Wassily. *Concerning the Spiritual in Art.* Translated by M. T. H. Sadler. Reprint, New York, 1977.

Kemp, Martin. *The Science of Art: Optical Themes in Western Art from Brunelleschi to Seurat.* New Haven, 1990.

Matisse, Henri. *Matisse on Art.* Edited by Jack D. Flam. Rev. ed. Berkeley, 1995.

Newman, Barnett. *Barnett Newman: Selected Writings and Interviews.* Edited by John P. O'Neill. New York, 1990.

Pleynet, Marcelin. *Painting and System*. Translated by Sima Godfrey. Chicago, 1984.

Riley, Charles A. *Color Codes: Modern Theories of Color in Philosophy, Painting and Architecture, Literature, Music, and Psychology*. Hanover, N. H., 1995.

Schoenberg, Arnold. *Theory of Harmony*. Translated by Roy E. Carter. Berkeley, 1978.

Slawson, Wayne. *Sound Color*. Berkeley, 1985.

Stella, Frank. *Working Space*. Cambridge, Mass., 1986.

Westphal, Jonathan. *Colour: Some Philosophical Problems from Wittgenstein*. Oxford and New York, 1987.

Wittgenstein, Ludwig. *Remarks on Colour*. Translated by Linda L. McAlister and Margarete Schattle, edited by G. E. M. Anscombe. Berkeley, 1977.

CHARLES A. RILEY II

Color Science

The chromatic or hued colors include red, yellow, green, and blue. The achromatic or hueless colors are black, white, and the grays. All other colors may be described as perceptual combinations of these. Thus, orange is a red-yellow, brown a blackish orange, and lime a yellowish green. Colors may be ordered three-dimensionally by their hue, their lightness (for reflective surfaces) or brightness (for lights), and their saturation, or percentage of hue.

Earlier color theories were beset with confused disputes about which chromatic colors are to be understood as primary. It is now understood that what is primary depends on the task at hand. To mix pigments or inks to match the color of any reflective sample, one requires only magenta (bluish red), yellow, and cyan (greenish blue). These are the subtractive primaries of painters and printers. To match any colored light, it suffices to combine lights that look, respectively, red, green, and violet. These are the additive primaries of video engineers. If the task is to find colors that are perceptually pure, that is, display no visible trace of other colors in them, there are exactly four: red, yellow, green, and blue. These are the perceptual primaries of psychologists. Painters commonly object that green is not "truly" primary, but is a mixture of yellow and blue. The response is of course that a pure green does not look yellowish blue (what does?), whereas a purple looks reddish blue.

Color and the Visual System. Our experience of color significantly depends on the spectral composition of the light that meets our eyes, but perhaps even more on the functional organization of our visual systems. By gaining a rough understanding of how the color vision system works, we can come to understand the basis for many of the principles of managing color that were wrested so laboriously from the experiences of painters. We are also able to avoid many of the confusions and mistakes that burdened color theories of the past.

Unlike the camera film to which it has so often been compared, the eye's retina is a highly active piece of extruded brain tissue that performs elaborate computations. It processes color in two distinct stages. At the first, receptoral, stage, the light that enters the eye is absorbed by three types of cone in the retina, each responding to a portion of the visible spectrum. All of the wavelength information that the brain uses is at the outset coded as ratios of the responses of these cones. Consequently, if two patches of paint reflect light to the eye in such a way as to excite identical ratios of cone responses, the eye will see them as having the same hue, even though their overall reflection spectra are dissimilar. Because of this phenomenon, known as metamerism, three well-chosen primaries can match any color. This is what makes color television and four-color printing possible. It is also responsible for the fact, so vexing to restorers of old paintings, that two samples that look to have the same color under one set of lighting conditions may fail to match under another.

In the second stage of color processing within the eye, the outputs of the three cone types are cross-connected to yield three channels of color information. Two are antagonistically coded chromatic channels, one for red/green, the other for yellow/blue. It is convenient to think of red and yellow as signaled by positive neural activity, and green and blue as signaled by negative neural activity, with the neutral state conveying an achromatic signal. Thus, when blue and yellow signals are of equal strength, the perceptual result is achromatic, but when the blue/yellow channel has a net negative value (tokening blueness), and the red/green channel has a net positive value (tokening redness), then a reddish blue or bluish red—that is, purple—will be seen. The third kind of channel is an achromatic black/white channel, with levels of gray corresponding to the overall balance of activity. These neural arrangements are responsible for there being four perceptual chromatic primaries, as well as dictating the structure of color complementaries.

The antagonistic, or opponent, processes within the three color channels have their spatial and temporal counterparts. Activity in one region of the retina and associated brain areas will tend to suppress activity in neighboring regions, and a receptor cell that is excited will rapidly lose its sensitivity. The first of these phenomena is the basis for simultaneous contrast, or color induction, in which a region of color will drive its neighbors to take on the complementary color. This contrast can involve hue as well as lightness, with the latter typically the stronger of the two. The second phenomenon causes successive contrast, or afterimaging, whereby intense exposure to one color will generate a sensation of its complement. The antagonistic processes that underlie complementation and contrast provide the means to resolving a number of misunderstandings, which typically rest on a failure to distinguish the physical stimuli of color perceptions from the perceptions themselves. For example, one often hears that "White is all colors blended together, and black is the absence of color." But, of course, white does not look like a blend of colors, and black is a very pronounced visual quality. Ordinary "white" light is indeed composed of a very large number of wavelengths, but this is not to say that it is composed of a large number of colors. As Isaac Newton (1642–1727) remarked, "For to speak properly, the rays are not colored. In them there is nothing else than a certain power and disposition to stir up a sensation of this or that color." Furthermore, any white light can be matched exactly in appearance by a mixture of two monochromatic lights, and in an indefinite number of ways. The relevant observation to be made about black is that what is perceived in the absence of light is a dark gray; a deep black arises only by simultaneous contrast with white. This effect is easily demonstrated in a dark room in which a gray scale is illuminated by a lamp equipped with a dimmer. When the light is dim, the gray scale is compressed. As the brightness increases, the scale expands in both directions: not only does the white becomes whiter, but the black becomes blacker.

Color Theories. The first known color theory comes from the school of Aristotle. There are, said the Aristotelians, two basic colors, black and white, and from these are derived yellow, red, purple, green, and blue, each of which is to be understood as a particular ratio of white to black. This one-dimensional ordering was no great boon to artistic practice, but it kept alive the hope that a set of mathematical principles of color ordering, mixing, and harmonious combination could be found. Predictably, this gave rise to a variety of Pythagorean speculations of the sort of which Renaissance writers were notoriously fond. The Renaissance did, however, see the codification of a substantial amount of painterly lore by Leonardo da Vinci and others on the use of color to represent illumination, shadows, depth, and the like. Modern color theory begins with Isaac Newton's analysis of the spectrum in his *Opticks,* and his construction of a hue circle that gave a rough sense of how colored lights could be mixed to produce white. His division of the spectrum into seven parts was dictated more by musical analogies than by perceptual salience; just what he intended by "indigo" is still disputed. Johann Wolfgang von Goethe's (1749–1832) *Theory of Colours* is a curious mixture of regressive physics and perceptive discussions of color phenomenology, especially concerning complementaries, simultaneous contrast, and colored shadows. During the subsequent course of the nineteenth century, there emerged a scientifically based color theory that could be of genuine use to painters. The chemist Michel-Eugène Chevreul (1786–1889) systematically analyzed simultaneous contrast effects. Thomas Young (1773–1829), pioneer of the wave theory of light and co-decipherer of the Rosetta stone, proposed that some basic facts of color mixture could be understood if we suppose that the eye contains just three kinds of receptors. Through the efforts of physicists James Clerk Maxwell (1831–1879) and Hermann von Helmholtz (1821–1894), the understanding of light mixtures and their effects on the eye—in what is now understood to be the first stage in color vision—was put on a firm scientific footing. We owe our present understanding of the second, opponent, stage of color vision to the physiologist Ewald Hering (1834–1918), whose ideas were not widely accepted until the late 1950s.

Color Ordering Systems. Orderly arrangements of colors have been devised to provide unambiguous color designations, to display the significant relationships that colors bear to each other, and to provide a systematic basis for combining colors so as to please the eye. The first successful three-dimensional representation of color relationships—a color sphere—was the work of the Romantic painter Otto Runge (1777–1810). Since then, a variety of other arrangements have been proposed. The plurality is unavoidable, because the character of the configuration is governed by the relationships that one wishes to exhibit. For example, a hue circle intended to serve the interests of pigment mixture will inevitably differ from one that is meant to show how lights might be combined. Two ordering systems in current use that are based on color appearance are the Munsell System, originally developed by the painter Albert Munsell (1858–1918), and the Natural Color System (NCS), the Swedish standard. The former is defined by the samples in an atlas, and employs a hue circle of five equally spaced primaries—red, yellow, green, blue, and purple—surrounding a perpendicular achromatic axis. It uses as its dimensions Hue, Value, and Chroma, with perceptually equal spacing of the samples along each dimension. The Natural Color System proceeds on the assumption that we all carry around in our heads mental representations of the Hering primaries: black, white, red, yellow, green, and blue. It was designed to permit direct estimations of colors according to their degree of resemblance to the six ideal colors without referring to an atlas of colored samples, though an atlas was prepared to illustrate the system. The NCS dimensions are Hue, Blackness, and Chromaticness.

Human Response to Color. "The union of design and color is necessary to beget painting just as is the union of man and woman to beget mankind, but design must maintain its preponderance over color. Otherwise painting speeds to its ruin: it will fall through color just as mankind fell through Eve" as quoted in Riley, 1995. These words penned by Charles Blanc in 1870, reminiscent of Immanuel Kant's remarks about color and form in the *Critique of Judgment,* express both deeply rooted prejudices and the fundamental tensions that came to a flash point in French art of the late nineteenth century. They bear testament to the emotional power of color as well as anxieties about how that power is to be controlled. Every sighted person is aware of this power, but most attempts to characterize the meanings that colors have for us, or describe just how they move us, are less than convincing. "Blue is the color to be associated with schizophrenia" (Faber Birren). "Yellow . . . can never have profound meaning" (Wassily Kandinsky). "Red excites, but blue calms" (just about everybody). The assurance with which such pronouncements are made seems inversely proportional to the evidence for them. Two considerations render this and similar color lore problematic. The first is that the meaning and effect of colors always depend on their context: the illumination, the size, shape, and nature of the colored object, the surrounding colors, cultural significance, and individual experiences, to name just a few of the relevant factors. The second is that there are few careful empirical studies of human response to colors, either individually or, more realistically, in combination. Most studies, though frequently cited, are marred by underspecified stimuli, inadequate samplings of subjects, and uncontrolled conditions. Here is fertile ground for a series of exercises in experimental aesthetics.

[*See also* Goethe; *and* Helmholtz.]

BIBLIOGRAPHY

Agoston, George A. *Color Theory and Its Application in Art and Design.* 2d rev. ed. Berlin and New York, 1987.

Albers, Josef. *Interaction of Color.* New Haven, 1963.

Arnheim, Rudolf. *Art and Visual Perception: A Psychology of the Creative Eye.* New exp. rev. ed. Berkeley, 1974. See chap. 7, "Color."

Goethe, Johann Wolfgang von. *Theory of Colours.* Translated by Charles Lock Eastlake. Reprint, Cambridge, Mass., 1970.

Hardin, C. L. *Color for Philosophers: Unweaving the Rainbow.* Exp. ed. Indianapolis, 1993.

Hering, Ewald. *Outlines of a Theory of the Light Sense.* Translated by Leo M. Hurvich and Dorothea Jameson. Cambridge, Mass., 1964.

Hurvich, Leo M. *Color Vision.* Sunderland, Mass., 1981.

Kemp, Martin. *The Science of Art: Optical Themes in Western Art from Brunelleschi to Seurat.* New Haven, 1990. See part 3, "The Colour of Light."

MacAdam, David L., ed. *Sources of Color Science.* Cambridge, Mass., 1970. Excerpts by Aristotle, Newton, Young, Maxwell, von Helmholtz, and others.

Riley, Charles A. *Color Codes: Modern Theories of Color in Philosophy, Painting and Architecture, Literature, Music, and Psychology.* Hanover, N. H., 1995.

C. L. HARDIN

COMEDY. From its birth in ancient Greece, comedy has been associated with tragedy, and it is useful to consider them together. Comedy is more diverse and more complicated than tragedy. There is nothing in tragedy, for example, comparable to comedy's subdivision into farce, satire, parody, burlesque, comedy of manners, and so on. Whereas tragedies traditionally had one important character, from the upper class, comedies typically feature many kinds of characters from different social classes.

Aristotle offered the first systematic treatment of comedy and tragedy in his *Poetics.* Unfortunately, most of what he said about comedy was in the lost second book. In the surviving text, he says that tragedy is an imitation of people who are superior to the average, whereas comedy is an imitation of people worse than average. They are worse not in every way, but as regards "the Ridiculous, which is a species of the Ugly. The Ridiculous may be defined as a mistake or deformity not productive of pain or harm to others" (Aristotle, 1941).

Tragedy, along with epic, was part of the heroic tradition. Tragic heroes are noble beings capable of great thoughts, emotions, and actions. Aeschylus's Prometheus was divine, and other Greek tragic heroes were descended from the gods. Several of William Shakespeare's heroes seem like gods, and Christopher Marlowe's Dr. Faustus bargained for divine knowledge. August Wilhelm Schlegel said that it was the distinctive aim of tragedy to establish the claims of the mind to a divine origin.

Comedy, by contrast, is full of characters of low social and moral standing. Even when heroes, gods, and revered figures like Socrates appeared in Greek comedy, they were humiliated rather than honored. Throughout comedy, the emphasis is on human limitations rather than greatness. From its earliest days, it has highlighted deformity, ignorance, folly, failure, and vice; its stock characters have included the hunchback, the fool, the windbag, the drunkard, the lecher, the impostor, and the hypocrite.

Much of the enjoyment of comedy is laughing at these "comic butts," and much traditional theorizing about comedy is concerned with ridicule. But besides these characters we laugh *at*, there are also those we laugh *with*. Unlike tragic heroes, who strive for something great, these characters are typically trying merely to get along and have a good time. Even when they defeat an opponent, it is seldom through strength or courage, and often through trickery, which in comedy trumps raw power and even moral greatness. Many of these characters, indeed, are proud of being unheroic. Shakespeare's Sir John Falstaff, for example, is a cowardly liar who likes to overeat and get drunk. "Comic hero," the usual term for these characters we laugh with, is misleading; for want of a better term, they will be called "comic protagonists" in this article.

Comedy shares with tragedy a focus on the problematic side of life. In both, the world is a tangle of conflicting systems where human beings live in the shadow of failure, suffering, and death. Life is full of tension, danger, and struggle, and our success or failure often depends on chance factors that we do not understand. But comic characters—both butts and protagonists—deal with life's problems quite differently than tragic heroes, who face problems squarely, decide how they will act, and then stay the course, even though it leads to their downfall. Comic protagonists typically respond to problems not with heroic self-assertion and confrontation, but with clever, indirect methods. They do not lock themselves into a single way of thinking or acting. Rather than fight, protest, or bemoan their fate, they unemotionally use their wits to get out of trouble, and their mental flexibility succeeds. Tragic heroes nobly stick to their guns and die; comic protagonists finagle, compromise, even surrender, but live to tell the tale. As Søren Kierkegaard said, "comedy presents contradiction with a way out. Tragedy despairs of a way out" (1941).

The differences between the tragic hero and the comic protagonist make a difference in the audience's responses to them. Tragic heroes are passionate about their lives and about the human condition. Their emotions, such as courage, pride, and anger, reveal their tragic stature and elicit the audience's emotions. The emotions of the supporting characters toward heroes, such as admiration and pity, also reveal their tragic stature and cue us as to how we should feel toward the hero.

Beyond the drama itself, tragedy fosters a heroic attitude toward life. It recommends that we be emotionally engaged with problems, that we confront them head-on and single-mindedly, and that we protest when we fail; and through whatever struggles we face, we are to maintain our dignity and stick to our principles. In short, tragedy recommends that we take life seriously.

Comedy's attitude toward problems and toward life itself is as different from the tragic attitude as the laughing comic mask is from the serious tragic mask. Since the Greeks, laughter has been the characteristically comic response, and throughout history, theories of laughter have shaped theories of comedy.

The most general understanding of laughter is that it is an expression of pleasure: we laugh because we feel good. This idea is found today in what can be called the Celebration Theory of comedy. Critics such as Mikhail Bakhtin characterize comedy by its festivity, its carnivalesque spirit. The idea that laughter is an expression of pleasure, however, is seldom left that simple in theories of laughter, humor, and comedy. The two most important theories, the Superiority Theory and the Incongruity Theory, give it more detail by specifying the object of pleasure.

From Plato until the eighteenth century, the Superiority Theory of laughter was virtually the only theory. What we enjoy in laughing, according to this view, are feelings of superiority to another person, or to our former selves. Even wit, Aristotle said, is "educated insolence." Thomas Hobbes called the feeling in laughter "sudden glory." In this view, because comedy is designed to evoke laughter, it has an element of hostility to it. Al Capp, creator of the "Li'l Abner" comic strip, put it this way: "All comedy is based on man's delight in man's inhumanity to man."

The Superiority Theory of laughter influenced theories of comedy in at least three ways. First, it provided a ready explanation for the large number of physically, mentally, and morally inferior characters in comedy—they are there for our ridicule. Second, it prompted the moral criticism that comedy fosters scorn, disdain, and contempt in the audience toward one's fellow human beings, "pain in the soul," Plato called it. Aristotle wrote in his *Nicomachean*

Ethics (4.8) that "a joke is a kind of mockery, and lawgivers forbid some kinds of mockery—perhaps they should have forbidden some kinds of jokes." Roger Scruton (1983) has analyzed amusement as a kind of "attentive demolition" of a person or something associated with a person. Hobbes wrote that those who laugh the most at other people are those who have the least self-esteem and who maintain what little they have by comparing themselves with inferior people. Charles Baudelaire traced laughter to the fall of Adam and Eve, and said its source was "the idea of one's superiority. A satanic idea, if there ever was one" (1956). Percy Bysshe Shelley was convinced that there can be no entire regeneration of mankind until laughter is put down.

The third way the Superiority Theory influenced thinking about comedy is that it provided a reply to the traditional criticism of comedy that the vices of its characters could adversely affect the morality of the audience. Since the Renaissance, the standard defense of comedy against this charge has been that the drunk and the liar are not presented as role models, but as people to ridicule, and so not to emulate. Indeed, the idea that comedy is essentially satirical and didactic became part of the received wisdom about comedy. Gian Giorgio Trissino wrote in his *Poetica* in the early sixteenth century, "As tragedy teaches by means of pity and fear, comedy teaches by deriding things that are vice." Sir Philip Sidney in *The Defense of Poesie* (1595) saw comedy as "an imitation of the common errors of our life, which [the dramatist] representeth in the most ridiculous and scornful sort that may be, so as it is impossible that any beholder can be content to be such a one." Ben Jonson, Henry Fielding, and others agreed. Samuel Johnson even defined satire as "a poem in which wickedness or folly is censured."

In the nineteenth and early twentieth century, George Meredith and Henri Bergson further entrenched this satirical, didactic view of comedy. Meredith (1897) argued that comedy is essential to civilization, for it is an expression of critical common sense that brings the social group together to reject folly. Bergson's *Laughter* (1911) analyzes laughing as a social gesture of humiliation directed against a group member who is acting mechanically rather than humanly. We laugh at the miser, the pedant, and other comic types, he says, in order to wake them up from their "mechanical inelasticity" and bring them back into society.

Despite the popularity of the Superiority Theory for two millennia, and its usefulness in defending comedy against one moral criticism, however, we have already seen that by treating all laughter as ridicule, it opens comedy to another moral criticism—that cultivating a scornful attitude toward people is itself vicious.

In the eighteenth century, critics such as Francis Hutcheson showed that the Superiority Theory also had philosophical problems. If Hobbes were right, Hutcheson argues, two conclusions would follow. First, there could be no laughter where we do not compare ourselves with others or with some former state of ourselves. Second, whenever we feel sudden glory, we would laugh. But neither is true. First, there are cases where we laugh without engaging in self-evaluation: here Hutcheson offers some witty phrases from literature. What is funny in them, he argues, is the writer's verbal cleverness and not any inferiority in the writer or anyone else. The second conclusion above is also false. "If we observe an object in pain while we are at ease, we are in greater danger of weeping than laughing; and yet here is occasion for Hobbes's sudden joy." The basic mistake of the Superiority Theory, according to Hutcheson, is that it does not distinguish between laughter and ridicule.

Even in those cases where we are laughing at a person and that person shows some kind of inferiority, moreover, we can distinguish between two kinds of laughter, the laugh of scorn and the laugh of humorous amusement. If all that is going on in a particular instance of laughter is that I am feeling superior to someone—say, an opponent whom I have beaten—then no humor at all is involved. Of course, what often triggers laughter at an opponent is not simply that person's loss, but what we regard as an *awkward* move, a *stupid* error, or some other shortcoming that is *funny;* and then our laughter may express humorous amusement.

Before the late seventeenth century, it was difficult to see this distinction between the laugh of scorn and the laugh of humor because the word *humor* had not acquired its current meaning. But with the distinction, it is easy to see that comedy tries to evoke not just any laughter, but the laughter of humorous amusement. A play that evoked simple contempt and disdain for its characters would hardly be a comedy.

Once the Superiority Theory was in doubt, thinkers as diverse as James Beattie, Immanuel Kant, Kierkegaard, Arthur Schopenhauer, and William Hazlitt began offering new explanations for the laughter of humorous amusement, and hence for the proper response to comedy. Their explanations became the Incongruity Theory, which is today the most widely accepted account of humorous laughter in philosophy and psychology. In its most general form, this theory says that humorous laughter expresses our enjoyment of a discrepancy between what some thing or situation is and what we expect it to be.

Before the eighteenth century, there had been hints that laughter can be a response to something incongruous. Aristotle advised in his *Rhetoric* that one way to get a laugh is to set up an expectation in the audience and then surprise it with something different. In the late Renaissance, incongruity was important in Sidney's account of comedy as ridicule. John Dryden's *Of Dramatick Poesie* (1668) analyzed the comic effect in Aristophanes as based on "some odd conceit which had commonly somewhat of unnatural or obscene in it." In his critique of Hobbes, Hutcheson pointed out that the juxtaposition of opposites can be comic—such as dignity and baseness, or sanctity and profanity.

In the eighteenth and nineteenth centuries, ideas like these were developed into versions of the Incongruity Theory of laughter. According to Kant, "In everything that is to excite a lively convulsive laugh, there must be something absurd (in which the understanding, therefore, can find no satisfaction). Laughter is an affection arising from the sudden transformation of a strained expectation into nothing" (1892). Our pleasure at a joke, like our pleasure in music and in games of chance, is based on the "changing free play of sensations." In a game, what causes those sensations is our changing fortune; in music, it is sounds; and in amusement, it is our shifting thoughts. The violation of mental patterns and expectations in humor is not directly enjoyable to the understanding, Kant says, but it does cause pleasurable oscillations of our internal organs, and these movements are communicated to the diaphragm, leading to laughter.

In Schopenhauer's theory, "the cause of laughter in every case is simply the sudden perception of the incongruity between a concept and the real objects which have been thought through it." When we are struck by the difference between a concept and a perception of the same thing, and we enjoy that mental jolt, we laugh.

Kierkegaard wrote about contradiction rather than incongruity, but his account of laughter is similar to other versions of the Incongruity Theory. We laugh when we can take delight in some clash within our minds.

Each of these versions of the Incongruity Theory has been criticized, and in the twentieth century, refinements have been made in the theory. A major task here is to distinguish the enjoyment of incongruity in humor from the enjoyment of incongruity in other aesthetic categories such as the bizarre, the fantastic, the grotesque, the macabre, and the horrible. But, for our purposes, what is more important is the effect of the Incongruity Theory on ideas about comedy. If, as Hazlitt suggested, incongruity is "the essence of the laughable," then comedy looks quite different than it does under the Superiority Theory.

The Incongruity Theory offers a more comprehensive explanation of comedy. It accounts for not only satire, but also parody, burlesque, puns, and conceptual comedy such as that of Ernie Kovaks and Steven Wright, which are not plausibly explained as based on feelings of superiority. Parody often makes us laugh, for example, not by evoking emotions toward the characters, but by imitating scenes from other works so that we think of those works in a jarring way. In burlesque, similarly, we may laugh at the exalted way some trivial matter is treated, or the trivial way some exalted matter is treated, so that, again, our amusement is not an emotion toward characters but a higher-order response to the work.

If amusement in comedy were an emotion felt toward characters, then comedy would encounter the puzzle faced by tragedy of how we can feel emotions toward fictions. But it has never seemed puzzling that we find comedies funny knowing they are not real.

In general, our amusement at comedy seems to be a cognitively higher response than emotions, something Bergson hinted at in his claim that laughter requires a "momentary anesthesia of the heart." What is enjoyed is not some condition or action of a character itself, but, as Kant suggested, the shaking of our wits.

In comedy, of course, we do sometimes laugh at ugliness, stupidity, and vice. Here the Incongruity Theory can explain our amusement as the enjoyment of various ways in which characters do not match our concepts of human beings. It does not have to claim that we feel negative emotions toward the characters we are laughing at. In most people's experience of most comedy, after all, it is inaccurate to say that they feel scorn, disdain, or contempt.

Laughing *with* comic characters rather than *at* them is also easier to explain in the Incongruity Theory: we are enjoying some incongruity just as they are. We do not have to be laughing at anyone, as the Superiority Theory claims.

The Superiority Theory also has trouble explaining comic situations in which characters show levels of physical dexterity, intelligence, or skill superior to our own. How could we laugh out of feelings of inferiority? But in the Incongruity Theory, comic characters who are superior to us in some respect present no problem. If they surprise us with a clever physical or mental feat, we can take delight in it without comparing ourselves with them. Indeed, we can take delight in it even if we do compare ourselves negatively with them.

The last advantage of the Incongruity Theory is that it is not committed to the idea that comedy is a social corrective. Although some playwrights have defended themselves by claiming didactic value for their comedies, it is dubious that most of them really intended their work that way. It is just as dubious that comedies in fact motivate audiences to avoid vice. Consider comedy's treatment of drunkenness. Laughing at drunks is as old as comedy itself, but how many people have been motivated by comedies to cut down on their own drinking? The standard drunk in comedy is jovial, someone who gets into scrapes, to be sure, but has fun in the process. Of the millions of people who have watched Shakespeare's Falstaff, has a single one has left the theater musing, "Yes, I should definitely stop drinking"? More generally, do audiences leave comedies thinking, "Yes, I must be careful to avoid acting like *them*"? If audiences evaluate characters' actions and attitudes for their own adoption at all, one suspects that most of them find more to emulate in Falstaff than in, say, Hotspur or even Prince Hal.

Although the Superiority and Incongruity Theories have had the most influence on theories of comedy, a third traditional theory of laughter should be mentioned, the Relief Theory. Whereas the Superiority and Incongruity Theories try to explain laughter by characterizing the object of enjoyment, the Relief Theory tries to explain why laughter takes the physiological form it does—why we inhale and exhale spasmodically, shake our heads, and so on. The basic explanation is that laughter is the venting of nervous energy.

Early in the eighteenth century, Anthony Ashley Cooper, earl of Shaftesbury, hinted at the Relief Theory in a political essay on humor: "The natural free spirits of ingenious men, if imprisoned or controlled, will find out other ways of motion to relieve themselves in their constraint; and whether it be in burlesque, mimicry, or buffoonery, they will be glad at any rate to vent themselves, and be revenged on their constrainers" (1727). In the nineteenth century, Herbert Spencer developed a full-scale physiological theory of laughter, and in the twentieth century, Sigmund Freud made the release of nervous energy the basis of his theory of jokes, the comic, and humor. In all three laughter situations, Freud (1976) said, we summon a certain quantity of nervous energy for a mental task, but that task turns out to be unnecessary, and so the energy is superfluous. We release this excess energy by laughing. In listening to Mark Twain's story of his brother working on building a road, for example, we hear how a dynamite charge went off prematurely, blowing the man into the sky. At this point in the story, we have summoned pity, Freud says. But the end of the story is that when the man landed, he was docked half a day's pay for his time in the air "absent from his place of employment." As we listen to this twist, we realize that our pity is unnecessary, and we laugh it off.

There is not space here to examine the subtleties of Freud's account of laughter, but we can note a possible connection between the Relief Theory in general and comic theory. A common suggestion about the lost second book of Aristotle's *Poetics* is that he may have analyzed comedy as parallel in structure and function to tragedy. If he did, then he may have made the release of some emotions through laughter the proper effect of comedy, just as the catharsis of pity and fear is the proper effect of tragedy.

In the late twentieth century, as theories of all kinds come under scrutiny, it is not surprising that traditional comic theories have been reexamined. Some of the most promising lines of criticism are coming from feminists.

Comedy has power, both to change the status quo and to preserve it. Creating, criticizing, and theorizing about comedy are political acts. Men's humor has traditionally emphasized aggression. Racist and sexist jokes, sarcastic putdowns, and practical jokes have all been ways that men "score points" against others. Part of men's power agenda has been the assumption that only their kind of humor is really humor. Indeed, very soon after the word *humor* had acquired its modern meaning in the late seventeenth century, there were critics like William Congreve denying that women were capable of humor.

When men have theorized about laughter, humor, and comedy, it is not surprising that they have produced accounts like the Superiority Theory. But, however well men's theorizing fits their humor, feminist critics say, it does not explain women's humor. As Regina Barreca (1988) and other have pointed out, when women are laughing together, they are seldom competing for power; usually they are sharing feelings to establish intimacy and solidarity. Any informed discussion of comedy, therefore, cannot assume a male paradigm of laughter.

Feminists have also challenged the essentialism of traditional theories of laughter and comedy. Like sexuality, Frances Gray (1994) suggests, humor may not be a single stable phenomenon but a number of changing social constructs. Whether feminists will produce a comprehensive theory of comedy remains to be seen. But, because of humor's political dimensions, as Gray says, "if feminism is to change all that needs to be changed . . . it is essential for women to clarify their relationship to laughter" (1994).

[See also Comics; Jokes; and Parody.]

BIBLIOGRAPHY

Aristotle. *Poetics, Nicomachean Ethics, Rhetoric*. In *The Basic Works of Aristotle*, edited by Richard McKeon. New York, 1941.

Baudelaire, Charles. *The Essence of Laughter and Other Essays, Journals, and Letters*. Edited by Peter Quennell. New York, 1956.

Bakhtin, Mikhail. *Rabelais and His World*. Translated by Helene Iwolsky. Cambridge, Mass., 1968; reprint, Bloomington, Ind., 1984.

Barreca, Regina, ed. *Last Laughs: Perspectives on Women and Comedy*. New York, 1988.

Beattie, James. "An Essay on Laughter and Ludicrous Composition." In *Essays*, 3d ed. London, 1779.

Bergson, Henri. *Laughter: An Essay on the Meaning of the Comic*. Translated by Cloudesley Brereton and Fred Rothwell. New York, 1911.

Dryden, John. *Of Dramatick Poesie*. London, 1684.

Freud, Sigmund. *Jokes and Their Relation to the Unconscious*. Translated and edited by James Strachey, revised by Angela Richards. Harmondsworth, England, 1976.

Gray, Frances. *Women and Laughter*. Charlottesville, Va., 1994.

Gutwirth, Marcel. *Laughing Matter: An Essay on the Comic*. Ithaca, N.Y., 1993.

Hazlitt, William. *Lectures on the English Comic Writers*. London, 1819.

Hutcheson, Francis. *Reflections upon Laughter*. Glasgow, 1750.

Kant, Immanuel. *Critique of Judgment*. Translated by J. H. Bernard. London, 1892.

Kerr, Walter. *Tragedy and Comedy*. New York, 1967.

Kierkegaard, Søren. *Concluding Unscientific Postscript*. Translated by David F. Swenson and Walter Lowrie. Princeton, N.J., 1941.

McGhee, Paul E., and Jeffrey H. Goldstein, eds. *The Psychology of Humor: Theoretical Perspectives and Empirical Issues*. New York, 1972.

Meredith, George. *An Essay on Comedy and the Uses of the Comic Spirit*. Westminster, 1897.

Monro, D. H. *Argument of Laughter*. Melbourne, 1951.

Morreall, John, ed. *The Philosophy of Laughter and Humor*. Albany, N.Y., 1987.

Plato. *Philebus* 48–50, *Republic* 388e. In *The Collected Dialogues of Plato*, corr. ed., edited by Edith Hamilton and Huntington Cairns. Princeton, N.J., 1963.

Schopenhauer, Arthur. *The World as Will and Idea*. 6th ed. 3 vols. Translated by R. B. Haldane and J. Kemp. London, 1907–1909.

Scruton, Roger. "Laughter." *Proceedings of the Aristotelian Society* Supp. vol. 56 (1982): 197–212.

Scruton, Roger. *The Aesthetic Understanding: Essays in the Philosophy of Art and Culture*. Manchester, 1983. See ch. 12.

Shaftesbury. "The Freedom of Wit and Humour." In *Characteristicks*, 4th ed. London, 1727.

Spencer, Herbert. "On the Physiology of Laughter." In *Essays on Education and Kindred Subjects*. London, 1911.

JOHN MORREALL

COMICS.

As a popular art form, comics have been ignored for the most part by the scholarly establishment; most commentary has been restricted to the sort of sociological analysis befitting a medium perceived (erroneously) as essentially for children. Only recently have critics begun to treat comics as a category of aesthetic object worthy of study, a development reflecting larger trends in the widening scope of aesthetics and literary study and reflecting some changes in the field of comics itself. Loosely defined, a "comic" is a form of drawn sequential art, a fusion of words and images into a narrative; the "strip" or "book" distinction refers primarily to the length and format of the work. Comics are unavoidably associated with the most common examples of the medium in the form of superheroics, humorous talking animals, or slapstick gag strips, associated with certain characters that have become embedded parts of our collective cultural memory, but the medium encompasses as subject matter the full range of anything artists and writers can imagine and execute. Despite the English word, there is nothing necessarily "comic" about most comics, though "comic" does characterize a significant number of early American newspaper strips around which the term gained currency, and around which also arose the expression "the funnies." The difference should also be noted between a comic and a "cartoon," distinguished in the modern sense as a single drawing. Although many countries with distinguished traditions of drawn strips have their own terms for the medium (such as the French *bande dessinée*), "comics" has acquired the highest degree of international recognition and use.

More exacting definitions of comics have varied over the years depending on the source. Artists writing on comics, such as Scott McCloud, may want to keep open the avenues of formal experimentation, so that comics are juxtaposed sequential images, other issues being matters of style or artistic decision. Early accounts from advocates of the form have in a similar spirit tended to leave the category broad enough to incorporate works as diverse as Egyptian papyri or the Bayeux tapestry as early versions of comics, partly in the search for greater artistic respectability. Scholars and historians, given their jobs as classifiers of information, find comparisons to such narrative art forms taxonomically unrigorous (in that such works are graphic narration without text rather than the hybrid form of comics), and rather seek to narrow the boundaries to distinguish comics from related forms such as illustrated prose fiction. The favored definition of art historian David Kunzle contains the following key elements: comic strips are a sequence of separated images, with a preponderance of image over text, produced for a mass media, telling a moral or topical story. Comics historians such as Bill Blackbeard, Maurice Horn, and Thomas Inge (among others) have a different set of criteria: for them, a comic strip is a serially published, episodic, open-ended dramatic narrative about recurring characters, told in successive drawings, regularly enclosing ballooned dialogue or its equivalent, and utilizing minimal narrative text.

The difference between these two influential positions manifests two different emphases in the historical account of the development of the comic strip. The story favored by Kunzle begins with the fifteenth-century invention of printing in Europe, and covers a host of religious and political strips distributed for popular consumption, of two primary types: narrative strips (a series of images on a single sheet, often divided by frames) and picture stories (single images in series of pages, such as the prints of William Hogarth). With the introduction of caricature into the narrative strip in the 1780s, Kunzle finds the essential elements present to label the result the "comic strip"; indeed, the innovative work and insights of Rodolphe Töpffer's "picture novels" in the early 1800s led many (such as E. H. Gombrich) to call him "the father of the comic strip," while others have focused on the stylistic contributions of Wilhelm Busch as defining the paradigms of the form. The comic-strip form appeared in numerous European variations throughout the nineteenth century, distributed especially in numerous graphic humor magazines, appearing alongside more traditional humor illustrations and caricatures. Certain British critics (Denis Gifford, Roger Sabin) have gone on to assert that the first continuing comic character is Ally Sloper (first appeared in 1867, first given his own magazine in 1884); thus, for them England is the birthplace of comics.

The view of Blackbeard et al. is that the strips in question are picture stories but not really comic strips. By emphasizing the use of ballooned dialogue and recurrent characters as both essential constitutive elements, they place the birth date of the comic strip at 1896 in America with the appearance of R. F. Outcault's "The Yellow Kid and His New Phonograph." (The character had appeared before in cartoons by Outcault, leading some writers of a similar point of view to place the date at 1895, his first appearance in a newspaper cartoon, a choice that confuses the formal issues at stake.) The difference in the "Phonograph" was Outcault's use of a sequence of panels combined with dialogue balloons that have to be read to grasp the point of the sequence. Outcault did not systematically continue the formula, but other Americans such as Rudolf Dirks with the *Katzenjammer Kids* did, which has led some historians to give the credit to Dirks (who was in fact directly imitating

Busch's *Max und Moritz*). This was the birth of the American newspaper comics industry, which subsequently dominated the form; the result is that comics are claimed as an American innovation, and indeed, Inge has called the comic strip, along with jazz, America's indigenous contribution to world culture (1990).

This scholarly disagreement contains differences of a political and ideological nature and unfortunately the two sides have had little substantive exchange. (Indeed, Kunzle has barely addressed the American comic strip in any depth yet). A way around this impasse might be simply to refer to the particular manifestation of the comic strip in the 1890s and on as the modern comic strip, preserving some account of a substantive shift in the grammar and vocabulary of the strip, avoiding the stricter separation and its resulting intricacies. The desire for an artificial revolutionary moment that would give the American comic strip clear foundational importance creates unfortunate terminological wrangling. For instance, one difficulty with a strong version of the Americanist perspective is that by focusing so heavily on the balloon (which in fact appeared intermittently in European and American cartoons and strips for centuries, though it was never systematically adopted), post-1890s strips without balloons such as classic 1930s American adventure strips *Flash Gordon* (Alex Raymond), *Tarzan* (Hal Foster/Burne Hogarth), or *Prince Valiant* (Foster) are thus excluded from being true comic strips, despite these artists being prized by Americanists for their contributions to the comic art form.

On the other hand, there is also a truth to the importance placed on the balloon as a significant device and its prevalence in twentieth-century comics. A recurring notion in aesthetic accounts of particular comics (especially from Robert Harvey) is often of seeking a balance between the verbal and the visual realms; too great a verbal dependence results in a dissipation of the medium's access to a feeling of immediacy, whereas too great a focus on imagery results in a page without narrative flow. Three main types of verbal/textual usage with distinctive visual identities have evolved in the modern comic strip: narration, dialogue, and sound effects. The balloon's importance rests in its development as a visual signifier of speech, a vehicle to integrate the aural realm represented by the text into the frame of the pictorial image, as concurrent, connected with the depicted action. From a phenomenological standpoint, the ballooned strip simply reads differently from a captioned strip in its conveyance of this crucial temporal dimension; this sense of the present unfolding that comic art achieves (a quality some have called "timeless") is accomplished in great part through the balloon's integrated nature. Captions are most often today utilized as explicit indications of a past tense or the expression of an authority from outside of the time of the story. It is perhaps notable that hand-lettered balloons are still preferred today in comics, even to the point of creating computer fonts to simulate hand lettering; typeset lettering takes away from the sense of immediacy, the unity of the artwork and the balloon as simultaneous, originating from the same point, and it counteracts the irregular cadences of human speech that the handwritten text represents. Letterers vary their renderings of the text to signal readers to changes of tone, differing degrees of sound volume, the specific medium of the represented sound; the balloon itself can be modified—for example, to represent thought rather than spoken words.

Comic artists have developed an ever-expanding vocabulary of graphic techniques and visual icons, pictorial symbols for nonvisible elements such as sound, movement, interior states of characters, absorbing the lessons of caricaturists. The resulting codes vary from culture to culture and tradition to tradition (Japanese comics, which have arisen from a combination of different sources, regularly utilize many pictographic devices that American comics do not, for example). Any number of rendering styles have been used in comics, from the highly abstract to the hyper-realistic, and the specific signifying conventions might shift accordingly, but the need to render the nonvisible through visual codes remains constant. This representational dilemma is certainly not unique to comics, but the hybrid nature of comics, blending textual and pictorial elements to create graphic storytelling, has brought about unique solutions in attempting to overcome the static limits of the medium.

Whereas motion pictures can manipulate narrative time in a complicated dialectic that involves screen time and editing, in comics, narrative time is essentially a function of how visual space is utilized, in the placement and relationships of figures and environs within panels and in the relationships of the panels comparatively. In film editing, image replaces image in steady progression, whereas in comics, panels are side by side, page by page, and readers can dwell with leisure, going back from panel to panel. The frame is the important unit for this graphic montage, signaling a break in space and time: sometimes a panel represents a large passage of time with multiple events occurring in sequence within a single panel; sometimes a panel represents no perceptible passage of time at all. Time in comics does not mirror real-time dynamics and its peculiar constructions are sometimes charming and impossible to re-create in other forms (witness panels where lengthy, verbose dialogue occurs between combatants in the midst of actions of almost no real-time duration). The reader must piece together the visual and textual clues to create a sense of duration, the time of actions, bridging panels. McCloud (1993) has used the term *closure* to describe this process, breaking down the basic panel-to-panel transitions into six varieties of time-space jumps in order to elucidate the sorts of meaning production that readers are typically asked to make, creating time and duration through the layout of the panel, the lay-out of the page, and the rhythms of patterns. This panel-to-panel relationship is perhaps the key to comic artistry, the choice of shown and not-shown in telling the story being the dialectic that produces meaning. Some have characterized the reader as constructing a continuous fictive reality in a significantly more active way than a film spectator (in a parallel notion to film theory's "suture") from the ellipses in the visual narrative; indeed, Umberto Eco (1976, 1987) reports studies indicating that readers often misremember having seen actions that actually occurred in between panels (amusingly, comic artists such as Will Eisner have referred to this space between panels as "the gutter").

The differences and parallels with film are useful because the development of the modern comic strip parallels the birth of the technology that enabled the moving image and the two media have been intertwined in many respects ever since, both exchanging from their repository of images and storytelling techniques (films being referred to as having a "comic-book style," comics referred to as "cinematic," both terms used pejoratively on occasion). This interrelation is perhaps best seen in the works of Winsor McCay, with his fascination with carrying motion from panel to panel like stills from filmstrips, with his significant early innovations in animation, a significant meeting ground of the two forms. The development of both media mirrored the emergence in the nineteenth century of a modern conception of space and time, created by technological and economic changes that altered the everyday perceptions and understanding of people. Artists in both media grappled with the changing speeds of bodies under new pressures (from modernity's new urban and industrial landscape with its accompanying fragmentation of community and the individual) and granted new abilities to transcend biological limitations through mechanization. Comics in particular have demonstrated persistent interest in the abuse, abilities, and malleability of human bodies moving through space, an obsession with speed and the utopian/dystopian possibilities of technological power.

Despite responding to similar representational issues, comics have rarely been connected to historical modernism in fine art, except as an illustration of how various modernists of various movements engaged with popular culture (anecdotally with stories of how Pablo Picasso read comics, how the Surrealists and many other artists found George Herriman's *Krazy Kat* a kindred work, how Lyonel Feininger's early comic-strip work impacted his later paintings). In an attempt to reassess this relationship, Adam Gopnik (1990) has described early comics and modern painting as two movements, narrative and antinarrative, that stumbled across each other while sharing dreams of a new language for art. He sees a shifting relation as the energy of the early comic strips goes bankrupt and modernists begin to see the comic not as kindred mythmaking but as an object of kitsch, entering the Pop era. Most attention paid to comics from an art-historical standpoint has been focused on this appropriation by Pop artists (most famously in the work of Roy Lichtenstein and Andy Warhol) of comic iconography, using the resulting work as a starting point for speculations about the interplay of high art and low art and about the concepts of artist and originality. The Pop art–comics relationship is ambiguous and open to great debate concerning whether Pop closes that gap of high and low or restates the case for it, and, much less discussed, concerning how Pop has impacted on the modern comic. In such considerations of Pop, however, a persistent model exists of characterizing Pop artists' work as taking from the product of nameless, talentless commercial workers, which the real artist turns into art by an act of transforming in scale, medium, and thus content. Comics are relegated to mere source material for modern art, an image bank to be pilfered with no originals, only reproduced and reproducible imagery, thus no art. In the heroic modernist opposition of artistry versus mass culture, comics wind up on the wrong side of the equation, consumer art produced and distributed by commodity capitalism for mass consumption.

Viewed in this light, critics have concentrated on ideological critiques from all sides, concerned about the seductive power of the image over readers, in which the legibility and communicative abilities of the comic are viewed as dangerous. For many conservative critics, the true gems of the form are the comic strips that best exemplify American optimism and cultural spirit. Although the comic strip, carefully regulated by newspaper syndicates, has remained relatively uncontroversial, the comic book's recurrent emphasis on violence and often sensationalistic material, pushed to the extremes by the competition between independent publishers, led to the virtual destruction and censorship of the American industry during the McCarthy hysteria of the 1950s by crusading forces from the right and from a paternalistic liberal side as well (the comic in Europe has generally escaped such systematic persecution). The underground comic emerged to create far more explicit displays of sexuality, violence, and antiauthoritarianism in the exploratory atmosphere of the liberalized counterculture (the high point being the continuing work of Robert Crumb).

The most popular comics championed by progressive academics, such as the classic strips *Little Nemo* or *Krazy Kat*, the highly personal independent comics of the post-underground, or even the mainstream *Watchmen* comic books, are those that actively explore the nature of representation in explicit ways, ones that maintain a degree of critical awareness toward the form's paradigms, or a higher level of narrative difficulty rather than the direct, simple qualities that characterize many comics. Less self-reflective or outwardly experimental work is rarely interesting to critics except as material for political analysis of message. Most comics are produced by corporate merchandising machines and are thus dissected for propaganda content only: critics from a perspective of feminist or gender criticism have found much material misogynist, given that the medium is dominated for a variety of reasons by male producers for a predominantly male audience; from a literary-critical perspective, critics have found in the serial formulaic dimension of comics, the general divorce of continuous strips from contemporary events, an insidious disempowering effect, effacing history and human action. One of Kunzle's few discussions of the twentieth-century comic is an analysis of Carl Barks's Donald Duck/Uncle Scrooge comics that builds on writings by the Chilean Ariel Dorfman and Armand Mattelart (1975) attacking imported Disney comics and their reactionary content. Many of these sorts of criticisms are quite accurate; in the case of Carl Barks, for example, it is certainly true that a good many of the Duck stories are thinly veiled allegories from a pro-capitalist, pro-imperialist, pro-American viewpoint. It might be argued, though, that such multiple layers of meaning are precisely why many of Barks's adult readers consider him a great artist. Martin Barker (1989) has, from a left perspective, criticized the notion of ideology employed in most comics-related work of all political agendas as being too one-dimensional in presenting the reader as just absorbing meaning rather than producing it, failing to recognize the significantly active relationship of the comics reader to the text.

Given that the majority of comics are assembly-line commercial products created under deadlines and marketing pressures, it is perhaps remarkable that any artistically interesting work has been accomplished, but then some artists have found it liberating to work in a popular medium considered to be disposable. There have been many recent positive signs for the art form: the increasing international exchange of comics; the rise of the American "graphic novel" market in the 1980s for adults, inspired by European production standards using higher-quality printing and coloration techniques; the success of Art Spiegelman's *Maus* (winner of the Pulitzer prize); the inclusion of comics in museum shows and galleries along with the sale of comic collectibles by major art auction houses; and so on. There have been many negatives as well: in America, the quality of once-mighty newspaper comic strips has generally declined decade by decade, regulated and compacted into sameness by the syndicates, artistry squeezed out by strips continued long after ideas have run dry, while the comic-book industry has demonstrated an alarming tendency toward short-sighted gimmickry addressed to collectors and speculators, milking trends and encouraging homogeneity after a period of real artistic progress driven by the independents of the 1970s and 1980s. It remains to be seen whether the artistic possibilities of the form will continue to expand, whether the readership will expand or shrink, even as critical vocabulary and insight into the comic form advance.

[*See also* Cultural Studies; Pop Art, *overview article; and* Popular Culture.]

BIBLIOGRAPHY

Abbott, Lawrence L. "Comic Art: Characteristics and Potentialities of a Narrative Medium." *Journal of Popular Culture* 19 (Spring 1986): 155–176.

Barker, Martin. *Comics: Ideology, Power, and the Critics.* Manchester, 1989.

Blackbeard, Bill. "The Yellow Kid, the Yellow Decade." In *The Yellow Kid: A Centennial Celebration of the Kid Who Started the Comics,* pp. 16–136. Northampton, Mass., 1995.

Carlin, John, and Sheena Wagstaff, eds. *The Comic Art Show: Cartoons in Painting and Popular Culture.* New York, 1983.

Couperie, Pierre, et al. *A History of the Comic Strip.* Translated by Eileen B. Hennessy. New York, 1968.

Dorfman, Ariel, and Armand Mattelart. *How to Read Donald Duck: Imperialist Ideology in the Disney Comic.* Translated by David Kunzle. New York, 1975.

Eco, Umberto. "The Myth of Superman." In *The Role of the Reader,* pp. 107–124. Bloomington, Ind., 1979.

Eco, Umberto. "A Reading of Steve Canyon." In *Comic Iconoclasm,* edited by Sheena Wagstaff, pp. 21–25. London, 1987. Originally published in *Twentieth Century Studies* (December 1976).

Eisner, Will. *Comics and Sequential Art.* Exp. ed. Tamarac, Fla., 1991.

Gifford, Denis. *The International Book of Comics.* New York, 1984.

Gopnik, Adam. "Comics." In *High and Low: Modern Art and Popular Culture,* by Kirk Varnedoe and Adam Gopnik, pp. 153–229. New York, 1990.

Harvey, Robert C. *The Art of the Funnies: An Aesthetic History.* Jackson, Miss., 1994.

Harvey, Robert C. *The Art of the Comic Book: An Aesthetic History.* Jackson, Miss., 1996.

Herdeg, Werner, and David Pascal, eds. *The Art of the Comic Strip.* Zurich, 1972.

Horn, Maurice, ed. *The World Encyclopedia of Comics.* New York, 1976.

Horn, Maurice. "100 Years of Comics: An Introduction." In *100 Years of American Newspaper Comics: An Illustrated Encyclopedia,* edited by Maurice Horn, pp. 11–19. New York, 1996.

Inge, M. Thomas. *Comics as Culture.* Jackson, Miss., 1990.

Kunzle, David. *The Early Comic Strip: Narrative Strips and Picture Stories in the European Broadsheet from c. 1450 to 1825.* Berkeley, 1973.

Kunzle, David. "Dispossession by Ducks: The Imperialist Treasure Hunt in Southeast Asia (American Imperialist Ideology in the Walt Disney Duck Comics)." *Arts Journal* 49 (Summer 1990): 159–166.

Kunzle, David. *The History of the Comic Strip: The Nineteenth Century.* Berkeley, 1990.

McCloud, Scott. *Understanding Comics: The Invisible Art.* Northampton, Mass., 1993.

Sabin, Roger. *Comics, Comix, and Graphic Novels: A History of Comic Art.* London, 1996.

Schodt, Frederik L. *Manga! Manga! The World of Japanese Comics.* Rev. ed. Tokyo and New York, 1986.

Silbermann, Alphons, and H. D. Dyroff, eds. *Comics and Visual Culture: Research Studies from Ten Countries.* Munich and New York, 1986.

Wagstaff, Sheena, ed. *Comic Iconoclasm.* London, 1987.

JOHN SMYLIE

COMPARATIVE AESTHETICS. [*This article identifies and explains some of the philosophical issues that typically arise whenever two or more aesthetic traditions are compared. These hermeneutic or interpretive issues are important in this encyclopedia because there are many actual and potential comparisons in the various entries that concern either non-Western aesthetic traditions or earlier stages of Western aesthetics.*]

"Comparative aesthetics," as one might well anticipate, means different things to different "comparativists." For those at one end of the spectrum, the task of comparative aesthetics is to examine carefully the aesthetic thinking and artistic achievements of cultures different from one's own primarily for the sake of expanding one's basic knowledge of philosophy and art. For those at the other end, the enterprise of comparative aesthetics is to engage other traditions for the opportunity to learn from them in such a way as to bring about a reexamination of one's own cultural presuppositions and the development of new approaches and insights for aesthetics in general. In short, the spectrum runs from pure scholarship to creative philosophizing, with, as one might suspect, most comparatives—whether they are situated in Western or non-Western traditions—working somewhere in between, combining scholarship and creative thinking in varying ways.

On the scholarship side, apart from all the many difficulties involved in adequately translating complex texts and subtle concepts, the comparativist is faced with a number of hermeneutic or interpretive problems, the most important of which is how to engage the aesthetic thought and art of another culture in ways that do not, on the one hand, superficially assimilate it to one's own cultural experience and, on the other, alienate it in such a way as to make it only an exotic curiosity. Cultural anthropologists face this problem across the entire range of human activities, from the social patterns to the religious practices of other civilizations, with some, such as Clifford Geertz (see his *The Interpretation of Cultures*), carefully articulating the inadequacies in both "cultural imperialism" (the uninhibited imposition of the concepts and categories of one's own tradition onto the object of study, assuming thereby their universality and normative force), and "going native" (the naive attempt to suspend completely one's presuppositions and values in favor of substituting them for what is radically "other" to, and incommensurable with, one's own cultural background). Here again, in aesthetics at least, some middle ground is usually staked out, with the comparativist becoming sensitive to what is distinctive in other traditions and to the need to alter presuppositions (and methodologies) in the light of the give-and-take encounter with what might initially be seen as alien.

On the creative side, the comparativist is faced with the task—not altogether dissimilar to that of engaging the history of philosophy and art of one's own tradition—of *appropriating* what one learns from another culture and tradition in such a way as to allow it at once to deepen one's understanding of human aesthetic experience and to extend the ways in which that experience can be enriched and made intelligible.

In any event, for most comparativists, the study of other traditions, with respect to both their fundamental aesthetic concepts and their artistic expressions, does make evident to them that significant differences obtain regarding the understanding of what constitutes artistic creativity, of what counts as a work of art, of what demands are placed on a participant-viewer, of what is the appropriate relation between art and morality, and art and religion, and of what the broader cultural function is of aesthetic consciousness—and that these differences do indeed impact importantly on the questions and problems raised in diverse aesthetic analyses.

This essay briefly examines the nature of the relationship between art and morality and the nature of the creative process, and, in that context, outlines how the central concepts of "imitation" and "expression" in Western tradition might be reformulated and become more closely interrelated in the light of a cross-cultural encounter—in this instance, with selected traditions within Asian culture, with an emphasis on the Indian experience.

First, though, it should be remarked that there is no single Asian or Eastern tradition: the differences between the aesthetics of, say, classical India and that of China are as noteworthy as the differences between either of these and that the West (which, of course, has—as do the particular Asian traditions themselves—historically its own plurality). The very idea of philosophical aesthetics itself differs a great deal between East Asian (Chinese and Japanese) and South Asian (Indian) traditions, the latter being closer to Western traditions in the problems it raises and the manner in which it works them out. Aesthetics in the East Asian traditions tends to be embodied in a wide range of literary forms and handbooks with, as with the Japanese, remarkably few concepts (such as *yūgen, aware, sabi*) having to carry a good deal of weight.

One enduring issue or problem in aesthetics that exhibits a rather clear difference between the traditional thinking in Asian cultures from that of the contemporary West is that of the relationship between art and morality. Although many positions on this issue have been put forward in recent times (from *l'art pour l'art* stances that stress the absolute autonomy of the aesthetic to Marxist-like ones that insist on various social-political requirements that artworks must fulfill), the general consensus in the West today seems to favor strongly a sharp differentiation, if not outright opposition, between art and morality or aesthetic and ethical consciousness. The two represent, it is thought, different spheres of human experience and have accordingly different intentions, roles, and values. The general, but by no means unanimous, attitude seems to be that a work of art that is aesthetically right is simply "good" in virtue of that rightness, without moral remainder.

Guo Xi, an eleventh-century Chinese painter and writer, in his *An Essay on Landscape Painting (Lin quan gao zhi),* set forth what many scholars take to be a typical Chinese view:

> [If the artist] can develop a natural, sincere, gentle, and honest heart, then he will immediately be able to comprehend the aspect of tears and smiles and of objects . . . and they will be so clear in his mind that he will be able to put them down spontaneously with his paintbrush.

The quality of the state of being of the artist, Guo Xi maintains, is always reflected or embodied in his work. The kind of person one is as a moral, spiritual being will always show in one's work. It is not just that an artist may or may not present a moral viewpoint as a set of beliefs or claims in his work, or express through his characters or depictions a certain attitude toward social and political conditions, but rather that he will always be disclosed in his work as the kind of moral person he is and that this disclosure will contribute importantly to the aesthetic value of his work.

Also, within the Chinese tradition, one finds a noticeable absence of many motifs or subject matters (such as the representation of human-made horrors—massacres and the like) that have so often been important to Western art experience. It was perhaps because these horrors were understood to be *un-natural,* according to the profound sense that the *dao* had to the Chinese, that they were rejected by the artist.

Turning now to the creative process: artistic creativity is understood in East Asian experience primarily as a disciplined spontaneity that is carried out in obedience to nature, whether the latter is understood in the Daoist "ontological" terms of *dao* and *de* or the (Neo-)Confucian *li* (inherent principle or structure). This understanding is set forth by one Xie He in the fifth century in his famous primary canon, *qiyun shengdong* (translated by Laurence Binyon as "rhythmic vitality, or spiritual rhythm expressed in the movement of life"). The canon demands that the artist identify himself completely with a spiritual vitality or movement of life that is ubiquitous in nature and that this subtle natural-spiritual rhythm, by means of a highly disciplined spontaneous mastery of the medium, resound in his work. Unlike some contemporary Western thinking, it is believed here that the creative process is always made evident in the work in a manner that rules out the possibility that a work of art and some other kind of object could ever be perceptually indiscernible, in virtue of their apparently identical visual properties, to a knowing-sensitive observer. Such an observer would always *recognize* the creative process *in* the work.

For Indian aesthetics, on the other hand, creativity is seen in the more "expressionist" terms of the artist embodying a *depersonalized* emotion and religious insight in her work, aspiring thereby to the status of a *karmayogin,* one who acts without attachment to the fruits of her action in a manner of loving concern or devotion *(bhakti).* This "moral-religious" attitude must, it is said, be informed by knowledge *(jñāna)* of the self and reality, which knowledge enables one's creative action to become genuinely "skillful." A virtual world is brought forth that is informed throughout with joyful insight. As with the making of worlds generally, artistic creativity becomes an illusion making that is wholly conscious of itself.

The central concept in Indian aesthetics is that of *rasa*— "flavor" or that which is "tasted" in art. The theory allows that a number of basic life emotions can be distinguished (e.g., delight, humor, sadness, anger, fear) and that these are transformed in artworks into corresponding overall aesthetic qualities or *rasa*s (e.g., the erotic, the comic, the pathetic, the furious, the terrible) that are no longer "personal" as such.

According to the classical Indian view, art is a kind of mimesis, an "imitation" not of actual things, events, or happenings but of the potentiality of experience in its universal terms. It is an imitation that, albeit deeply grounded in life emotion, gives rise to what is imitated. The *rasa* theory suggests, then, that an adequate concept of imitation calls for artistic creativity to be "rooted in," to be "influenced by," to "partake of" the essential character of that which is the source of the influence. Conflating this with the typical Chinese view, "imitation" means to have one's creativity be in accord with, be derived from, a spiritual power and rhythm of being. "Imitation," then, is to be understood more as a *property* than as a *relation;* which is to say, as a quality that pervades the artwork rather than that which obtains (as does a copy or a representation) between the artwork and something external to it.

"Imitation," in this sense, thus may help us to understand better the assertion so often made in our own times that a work of art is its own meaning, that art is autonomous. A classical Indian aesthetician would not hold, as Clive Bell and others in the West have done, that art need not draw anything from life, that "to appreciate a work of art we need bring with us nothing but a sense of form and color and knowledge of three-dimensional space"; he would argue, rather, that the aesthetic content of an artwork, if it is to be meaningful, must bear the strength and confidence of its being influenced by reality so that it can present a genuinely new reality. How is this possible? [*See* Rasa.]

The Schopenhauerian-like answer given by the Indian aesthetician would be that artistic imagination is among the most *objective* forms of consciousness. In contrast to fantasy, which works from the wish-fulfilling needs of the ego, imagination discloses and proffers a direct presentation of some essential feature of experience and reality. Artistic creativity becomes, then, a kind of play (*līlā* in Sanskrit), a self-determining activity that is carried out for its own sake. Imagination, creative insight, does not, however, take place independent of its embodiment in form. Creativity in art has always to do with working with a particular medium, be it pigments, stones, or words, and this requires, once again, that the action be skillful, the result of arduous discipline.

Turning to the concept of "expression," the *rasa* theory opens up new possibilities for what it means to express emotion in art. As already indicated, *rasa* has nothing to do as such with the artist expressing (exhibiting, venting, articulating) his or her own private emotions; rather, it concentrates on a "depersonalized" emotionality that becomes the very aesthetic force of the work itself as experienced by a sensitive and knowing participant-viewer. Emotion in art is understood as a kind of performance, a presentation of its own unique affective qualities. It may be distinguished from life emotion in virtue of, among other things, its lack of belief-based cognition. Life emotions involve in a very central way judgments about that which occasions the emotion, and we look, in ourselves and to others, for a certain proportionality to obtain between the situation that gives rise to the emotion and the intensity of the belief-induced response to it. Art emotions—the *rasa*s—do not involve judgments about specific states of affairs; they stand, rather, in their own affective integrity, their "proportionality" being internal to the work and not a measure of some kind between the work and a situation external to it.

Again, *rasa*-theory emotionality becomes the very aesthetic force of the work itself as experienced by a sensitive and knowing participant-viewer. Although great works of art often have a compelling power that seems to reach out and take hold of the one who experiences them, the emotionality and the meaning associated with that power in art calls, according to the *rasa* theory, for a respondent who is equal, as it were, to the work. Indian aesthetics often refers to the ideal of the *sahṛdaya,* "one of similar heart." Emotionality in art is present aesthetically only to one who is able to attend, with knowing concentration, to that which is presented as the work. The participant-viewer must transform his own private concerns and attachments to achieve precisely the impersonality associated with the *rasa*. The ideal *sahṛdaya* does achieve, then, a certain "disinterestedness" or "psychical distance," but he is called on to achieve a great deal more than having a certain "aesthetic attitude," for he must in fact become part and parcel of the creative process itself. The participant-viewer is not regarded as being sundered or "detached" from the artwork, but rather is seen as essential for the work's completion.

The "expression of emotion" here clearly takes us in directions other than what we find in Western traditional, if not entirely contemporary, expressionist and related communication theories of art. Perhaps the Indian view enables us to reformulate some of our basic notions of emotionality in ways that allow us to understand art-emotion as *sui generis,* yet deeply grounded in life-emotion, and as that which is properly realized as such only when certain stringent requirements are fulfilled by a knowing participant-viewer.

In general, it seems that the philosophical explorer of other aesthetic traditions needs to perform a dual role, which are two sides of the same coin. The first is to *understand* as best one can the basic presuppositions, styles of argument, historical experience and the rest that are associated with other cultures, an understanding that does seek finally to locate what is truly distinctive in these traditions and to identify what can be contributory to enriched and enhanced aesthetic possibilities. This leads quite naturally to the second role or task which is the creative one of appropriating, in an unself-conscious way, those distinctive contributing elements so as to make them an inseparable part of one's own background of thought. The aim of comparative aesthetics, in the end, is simply that of becoming better aestheticians in the light of the engagement with other cultures.

[*See also* African Aesthetics; Anthropology and Aesthetics; Arab Aesthetics; Caribbean Aesthetics; Chinese Aesthetics, *historical overview article;* Hellenistic Aesthetics; Indian Aesthetics, *historical and conceptual overview article;* Islamic Aesthetics; Japanese Aesthetics, *historical overview article;* Latin American Aesthetics, *article on* Latin American Aesthetics and Modernity; Pre-Columbian Aesthetics; Roman Aesthetics; *and* Russian Aesthetics, *article on* Religious Aesthetics.]

BIBLIOGRAPHY

General Sources

Coomaraswamy, Ananda K. *Christian and Oriental Philosophy of Art.* New York, 1956.
Deutsch, Eliot. *Studies in Comparative Aesthetics.* Honolulu, 1975.
Deutsch, Eliot. *Essays on the Nature of Art.* Albany, N.Y., 1996.
Pandey, K. C. *Comparative Aesthetics.* 2d ed. 2 vols. Varanasi, India, 1959–1972.
Rowland, Benjamin, Jr. *Art in East and West: An Introduction through Comparisons.* Cambridge, Mass., 1954.

Indian Sources

Chari, V. K. *Sanskrit Criticism.* Honolulu, 1990.
Coomaraswamy, Ananda K. *The Transformation of Nature in Art.* Reprint, New York, 1956.
Coomaraswamy, Ananda K. *The Dance of Shiva.* Rev. ed. New York, 1957.
Dasgupta, S. N. *Fundamentals of Indian Art.* Bombay, 1960.
De, S. K. *Sanskrit Poetics as a Study of Aesthetic.* Berkeley, 1963.
Gerow, Edwin. *A Glossary of Indian Figures of Speech.* The Hague, 1971.
Gerow, Edwin. "The Persistence of Classical Esthetic Categories in Contemporary Indian Literature." In *The Literature of India: An Introduction.* Chicago, 1974.
Gnoli, Raniero, ed. *The Aesthetic Experience according to Abhinavagupta.* 2d rev. enl. ed. Varanasi, India, 1968.
Hiriyanna, M. *Art Experience.* Mysore, India, 1954.
Kane, P. V. *History of Sanskrit Poetics.* 3d rev. ed. Delhi, 1961.
Masson, J. L., and M. V. Patwardhan. *Śāntarasa and Abhinavagupta's Philosophy of Aesthetics.* Poona, India, 1969.
Zimmer, Heinrich. *The Art of Indian Asia: Its Mythology and Transformations.* Completed and edited by Joseph Campbell. 2 vols. New York, 1955; reprint, Princeton, N.J., 1968.

Chinese Sources

Binyon, Laurence, et al. *Chinese Art.* London, 1935.
Bush, Susan. *The Chinese Literati on Painting: Sushih, 1037–1101, to Tung ch'i-ch'ang, 1555–1636.* 2d ed. Cambridge, Mass., 1978.
Cahill, James. *Chinese Painting.* Geneva, 1960.
Chang, Chung-yuan. *Creativity and Taoism: A Study of Chinese Philosophy, Art, and Poetry.* New York, 1963.
Fong, Wen. "On Hsieh Ho's 'Liu-fa'." *Oriental Art* 9.4.
Gulik, R. H. van. *Chinese Pictorial Art as Viewed by the Connoisseur.* Rome, 1958; reprint, New York, 1981.
Li Zehou. *The Path of Beauty: A Study of Chinese Aesthetics.* Translated by Gong Lizeng. Reprint, Hong Kong, 1994.
Rowley, George. *Principles of Chinese Painting.* 2d ed. Princeton, N.J., 1959.
Sirén, Osvald. *Chinese Painting: Leading Masters and Principles.* 7 vols. New York, 1956–1958.
Sirén, Osvald, ed. *The Chinese on the Art of Painting: Translations and Comments.* Reprint, New York, 1963.

ELIOT DEUTSCH

COMPUTER ART. Originally built in the 1940s as a war machine, the computer has since become a powerful creative force in the arts. Only a few pioneering fine artists were adventuresome enough to experiment with these cumbersome contraptions in the early days. But by the beginning of the 1990s, most of the arts were computerized and some of them were revolutionized as a result. The appearance of affordable personal computers at the end of the 1970s consolidated a broad transformation in postindustrial societies from analog to digital methods of communication and record keeping. In the process, programmable machines transcended the humble servitude of mechanized implements to become agents of culture.

Small computers became increasingly accessible throughout the 1980s and commercial art was quickly dominated by computer-generated imagery. Television, cinema, graphic design, and photography each in turn found the machine indispensable as a production resource that was not only less expensive but safer than traditional materials and methods. Although initially motivated as much by economics as by aesthetics, these arts soon discovered the computer to be more than an improved version of their animation stands, T squares, and darkrooms. The intelligent machine began to assume the unprecedented role of creative partner. It turned out to be not only a dervish with details, but also a clever cynosure opening portals to unknown or unexplored creative opportunities. This fecundity has subsequently lured fine artists in growing numbers to use computers as a gateway to new vistas.

But, like the technologies that gave rise to the distinction between commercial art and fine art in the first place, computers are beginning to unravel and restructure regnant cultural concepts. The theories and institutions that shaped art in the nineteenth and twentieth centuries exalted the analog precipitates of creative activity that are exhibited as passive objects or performed as scripted events. Thus, many of the categories used to examine products of culture throughout the modern era are little help in navigating a globally networked discourse that embraces dynamic digital devices.

The Renaissance often crops up in discussions of computer art because of the wide embrace of science and aesthetics that that era shares with ours. Like Leonardo da Vinci, a computer artist often combines rational insight with artistic vision. With its potent breadth, the computer infuses and extends traditional art making as practiced since the quattrocento; but its impact extends much deeper than the revitalization of traditional genres. It appears to be bringing about a much more fundamental change in civilization than the one marked by the migration of pictures from stationary walls to portable frames. We are experiencing something more like a scary invasion of aliens than a comforting rebirth of ancestors.

Long before the Renaissance—indeed, long before recorded history—artists plied media with tools to form matter into concrete expressions of perceptions, memories, and dreams. By embodying their visions in physical material, they expanded the boundaries of space and time to communicate beyond their immediate spheres of influence. Artistic media, from pigment in caves to silver on celluloid, have served as material repositories for thoughts and aspirations wafting across the river of time. The arts have tended to be grouped in categories determined by the physical materials and events that serve as the substrates for presentation and performance. Paintings are pigment brushed onto canvas, music consists of sounds squeezed into the air, and literature is words stamped into books. For many centuries, tools and media have mated in the hands of artists to give birth to expressions of thoughts and feelings through formed matter.

Digital technology is changing this fundamental paradigm that has shaped the practice of art for so long. The computer is neither a medium nor a tool. It computes abstract numbers with mathematical algorithms rather than plying physical material with manual implements. Computer art of all types is more like literature than any other traditional art form by being inherently engaged with organized sets of symbols. But, unlike literature, the symbols it uses are not directly scrutable by human eyes and ears. Furthermore, digital symbols are intrinsically computable, which is what distinguishes writing with a word processor from writing with a quill or a typewriter. Even more remarkable, computer art is protean: its symbols can appear as words or sounds, as still images or animated sequences. Although the computer is not itself a medium, it can interface with nearly all the traditional media and is usually parasitic upon them since it needs them to reach us.

Literature tends to be printed in sometimes precious books and performed with distinctive verbal intonations, but the symbols used by a computer have no preordained physical outlet. A computer focuses on abstraction, and cares not whether a particular symbol is stored in a magnetic field or an optical plate. The contrast is even more marked when one compares computer art with plastic media. A sculptor manipulates pliable clay by hand to give shape to an object, whereas a computer artist manipulates a set of symbols with formulas to come up with another set of symbols. Media-based art focuses on concrete embodiments, whereas computer art focuses on abstract processes. Computers do affect perceivable objects and events, but they are interfaced with them rather than being embodied in them. When a medium-based art object is made, the goal is to fix form in matter as rigidly as possible; but an interface is designed for constant change as one set of symbols after another repeatedly drives a phantasmagoric display. This difference gets ramified for the audience by changing its role from passive spectator to active participant. Viewers are transformed into users. A museum visitor is forbidden from chipping stone out of a sculpture, but a computer user is invited to engage in the same interactive symbol manipulation practiced by the computer artist who conjured up the habitable scenario.

Instead of making things, the computer manipulates data. The import of this difference can be summed up with two related concepts: virtuality and interactivity.

The entities computer artists work with inhabit a "virtual reality," where properties are described numerically in a coordinate system rather than being embodied concretely in physical objects. By using numbers, symbols, and formulas, one can create a universe inside the computer that is manipulable through interfaces even though its existence is abstract. Computed worlds are much more ephemeral than their constructed counterparts in traditional art because they consist of entities whose existence is nonphysical. But they are also more like realities than representations because we can reach into them and change them. Simulation is superseding mimesis as the paradigm of representation because computers change the process of articulation from actual to virtual specification.

The second main feature of computer art is its interactivity. The raison d'être of the computer is to compute, so the numbers delineating virtual existence are eminently pliable. With the right interface, one can move virtual objects in virtual space and manipulate them in myriad ways, even metamorphosing them into their contraries. In cinema, the "morph" from one character to another has become a popular new kind of transition that expands the range of montage beyond the limits of photographically based effects. Artists are thrust into a new creative environment, a virtual studio filled with virtual tools that obey logical rather than physical laws. But the interactivity of virtual art can also be opened up to the audience, originating an art form dedicated to process rather than product. Instead of trying to embody a static vision that the audience can perceive and contemplate, the computer artist often creates a universe that the user can navigate. More freedom and power are put into the hands of the user, whose role extends beyond that of an audience. The purpose of interactive creations is not to lock down a medium to a confined expression, but to open up a virtual environment for extensive explorations. Physical tools operated with manual force are being supplanted by conceptual agency implemented through logical commands. Interaction is replacing automation as the fulcrum on which technology moves society.

Media, by contrast, are neither virtual nor interactive. Traditional art is manually constructed rather than conceptually computed. Paintings and concerts are resolutely lodged in physical objects and events, so that to experience them is to feast at the table of institutions organized to serve up gobbets of cultural substance. Due in part to the inertial mass of this physicality, media are also relatively passive. Their messages are frozen once embodied. Media do not hear us and they cannot speak back. This was especially pronounced when the medium became the message in modern art and in the mass media. There has always been a dialogue among traditional artists and their audiences through media; but these art forms cannot themselves engage in discourse. It takes the constant renewal of artistic creation to keep media alive, whereas computer art can perpetuate a dialogue without continuing creative sustenance. In computer art, the message is independent of the medium because its meaning resides in symbols rather than in things. This is why a computer can be a creative partner, sparring with the artist and supporting creative work more like an intelligent assistant than a pliant tool. It can also become an interlocutor in the gallery or on a network where the goal of artistic endeavor is to open possibilities of action rather than to focus perceptions of phenomena.

The digital nature of computer activity gives rise to a variety of profound developments, from telecommunications to multimedia. Because they have no intrinsic material form, digital creations are easily spirited around the globe to join together many people at remote locations, as well as to unite many forms of expression with diverse perceptible facets into a single experienced whole. Cultural expressions that used to be sorted into media displayed at remote locations are converging into multimedia delivered to ∩ne's doorstep. Communications are becoming more unified as text, sound, and images are integrated into a single environment, such as the Internet, that everyone can inhabit simultaneously without going anywhere. Because of this unifying effect, the computer may be making art more relevant to social intercourse in general. As communication becomes increasingly computer-mediated, the graphic design and navigational flow of interfaces are becoming more critical to clear and successful interactions. In the early days, companies were content to leave these matters to technicians, but it has now become evident that artistic talent is needed to achieve successful designs.

Computer art is a broad category that now encompasses virtually any artwork made with the assistance of a computer. It includes two-dimensional images manipulated with software into seamless collages that challenge our sense of photographic truth. It contains digitally composed music that knells previously unheard sounds, and also interactive telecommunications events that exist nowhere and everywhere while potentially gathering together the entire congregation of humankind. It is also an eclectic category grouping together diverse activities that range across the spectrum from painting to programming. The computer is neither a tool nor a medium that serves to define an art form. It is a polymorphous and omnipresent interlocutor ready to appear in surprising new guises as both a help and a hindrance.

The term *computer art* will undoubtedly be superseded. In the absence of an attractive alternative, it is fashioned after familiar taxonomies of art based on the medium of expression: a placeholder until digital culture gives birth to its own rubrics. The emergence of ubiquitous computing will make these thinking machines even less visible than they now are as they become more integrated into our daily lives and our quotidian environments.

[*See also* Artificial Intelligence and Aesthetics; Cyberspace; Digital Media; Hypertext; Multimedia; *and* Virtual Reality.]

BIBLIOGRAPHY

Binkley, Timothy. "The Quickening of Galatea: Virtual Creation without Media or Tools." *Art Journal* 49.3 (Fall 1990): 233–240.

Franke, Herbert W. *Computer Graphics, Computer Art* (1971). 2d rev. enl. ed. Translated by Gustav Metzger and Antje Schrack. Berlin and New York, 1985.

Gardiner, Jeremy. *Digital Photo Illustration*. New York, 1994.

Goodman, Cynthia. *Digital Visions: Computers and Art*. New York, 1987.

Schwartz, Lillian F., and Laurens R. Schwartz. *The Computer Artist's Handbook: Concepts, Techniques, and Applications*. New York, 1992.

TIMOTHY BINKLEY

CONCEPTS, AESTHETIC. *See* Attitude, *article on* Aesthetic Attitude; *and* Qualities, Aesthetic.

CONCEPTUAL ART. [*This entry comprises three essays on the history of conceptual art and its impact on aesthetics:*

Historical and Theoretical Overview
History of the Unformed
Conceptual Art and Philosophy

The first essay, written by an art historian, traces the multiple histories of conceptual art from the 1960s to the present. The second is an example of the self-representation of Conceptual Art by Art & Language, one of the earliest groups to engage in this art form. The final essay, the author of which is an artist as well as a philosopher, is an analysis of some of the philosophical and aesthetic issues distinctive of conceptual art; at the same time, this essay introduces conceptualism, a broader sense of conceptual art that is an integral part of contemporary art. See also Cage; Contemporary Art, article on Postmodern Transformation of Art; Duchamp, article on Survey of Art; Installation Art; Institutional Theory of Art; Performance Art, historical overview article; and Wittgenstein, article on Reception of Wittgenstein.]

Historical and Theoretical Overview

What precisely constituted the aesthetic theory of conceptual art in the mid to late 1960s is not yet readily apparent. Indeed, conceptualism during that period was a contested field of multiple and opposing practices, rather than a single, unified artistic discourse and theory. Although that field is too vast to do justice to its complexity here, this entry will single out four significant aesthetic models of conceptual art: linguistic conceptualism, antihumanism in art, an art that completes the project of participatory aesthetics, and an artistic project that aims for a communicative model of interaction. In the process, not only will the standard accounts of the aesthetic theories themselves be revised, but also the multiple implications of conceptualist art practice.

Linguistic Conceptualism. In textbook accounts of postwar art history, linguistic conceptualism has been cited as the dominant aesthetic theory of conceptualism. The work of Joseph Kosuth, Christine Kozlov, and the Art & Language group in the mid to late 1960s best exemplifies this theoretical model. Kosuth himself describes the distinguishing characteristics of this aesthetic theory in his 1969 essay "Art after Philosophy." In this three-part essay, he advances a very narrowly focused exposition of conceptualism undergirded by the tenets of logical positivism, in particular A. J. Ayer's *Language Truth and Logic* (1946). According to Kosuth, questioning the nature of art should be the main concern of artists. Remaining within categories of painting and sculpture, however, obstructs such inquiry because these artistic categories are conventional and their legitimacy is taken for granted, accepted a priori. Thus, these categories should be disavowed, regarded as anachronistic, useless, even detrimental, to artists.

This main line of argument leads Kosuth to reconsider the history of modern art as it is conventionally narrated, and to dismiss the relevance of artists such as Édouard Manet, Paul Cézanne, and the Cubists whose work as art is valid only on morphological grounds, that is, only insofar as they remained tied to the medium of painting. Instead, Kosuth champions an alternate canon of art—one that is characterized by the subversion of the old classifications—

represented by the legacy of Marcel Duchamp. "The 'value' of particular artists after Duchamp," he writes, can be weighed according to how much they rejected "the handed-down 'language' of traditional art" and thereby freed from morphological constrictions inquiry into the meaning of art (Kosuth, 1991). Given this formulation in which a work's importance is exclusively located in its meaning, the problem of referentiality arises. Presumably, prioritizing the conceptual content of art, its intelligibility, requires an account that is more than self-reflexive.

It is in this connection that Kosuth introduces Ayer's evaluation of Immanuel Kant's earlier distinction between analytic and synthetic propositions. Following Ayer, Kosuth argues that forms of art that depend for their validity on being verified by the world and "the 'infinite space' of the human condition" are synthetic propositions, whereas "forms of art most clearly finally referable only to art" are analytic propositions. Then, making the unlikely pairing of analytic proposition and meaning, on the one hand, and synthetic proposition and language, on the other, Kosuth brackets off and expels any questions of a referential dimension from his theoretical model, concluding that "art's only claim is for art. Art is the definition of art" (ibid.).

This last point bears elaborating, and perhaps can best be understood by comparing Kosuth's claims about his own work with the theoretical underpinnings of the work of his closest associates in the early 1970s, Terry Atkinson and Michael Baldwin of the Art & Language group. The main corpus of Atkinson and Baldwin in the late 1960s consists of numerous texts presented in an art context as analytic arguments about the nature of art objects and assertions about art. As early as 1967, these artists articulated a position that parallels the claims that Kosuth was to make in the next couple of years, for example, their shared repudiation of art legitimated on the basis of morphology, and their avowal of what Atkinson referred to as a "declarative methodology" whereby artworks are deemed to achieve their status as such by the nominal, metalinguistic act of asserting their "art-context." But whereas Kosuth's investigations, as noted earlier, interrogate the nature of art, Atkinson and Baldwin's work focuses on an analysis of the linguistic usage of both plastic art itself and its support languages, namely, "word-language."

If Kosuth's point of departure is his rejection of formalist art legitimated only by its morphological similarity to previous art, Atkinson and Baldwin's point of departure is the rejection of the simple materiality of minimal art; for, as Baldwin noted in an early expository article on his and Atkinson's prescient "Air Conditioning Show," even the site-specific work of Minimalism depends on the visual dimension for cognition. Indeed, Baldwin's comments in this article summon a range of issues that concerned the Art & Language group in the following years. First, Baldwin traces the development of reductivism that characterizes avant-garde practice in New York in the preceding years—from self-sufficient objects placed within a gallery, to site-specific artworks visible in the gallery space, to the invisible site-specific artwork—and places the notion of an "Air Conditioning Show" firmly within that trajectory. Second, the idea proposed by Baldwin of an invisible art shifts the cognitive emphasis of the artwork from material vehicle to conceptual content in a way that parallels Kosuth's arguments for the de-emphasis of language in favor of meaning. Finally, there is the issue of language. If the material employed in the "Air Conditioning Show" discussed by Baldwin is perceptually invisible, it is so only if one expects art to be solely a matter of "'looking at' objects" rather than "'reading from' objects," as Atkinson phrased it. But if one accepts written language—that is, "paper with ink lines upon it"—to be physically and visually perusable, then works such as the "Air Conditioning Show" not only become visible, but nothing prevents the idea of art broadening to include critical or theoretical speculations on art as an art material as well. Of course, once art language is considered "inside the framework of 'conceptual art,'" the distinction between work and text becomes blurred, leading to questions about the status of artworks such as the following posed by Atkinson in the first issue of *Art-Language: The Journal of Conceptual Art:* "Can this editorial," asks Atkinson rhetorically, "in itself an attempt to evince some outlines as to what 'conceptual art' is, come up for the count as a work of conceptual art?"

Similar to Atkinson and Baldwin, Kosuth's starting point, as suggested earlier, is also in the declarative act of deeming art objects (or, in Kosuth's terms, "art-propositions") meaningful as such. But that nominal act reaches its threshold much earlier in Kosuth's art practice than it does in Atkinson and Baldwin's. Whereas the latter are concerned primarily with the function of the metalanguage in which the physical art objects reside, Kosuth's exclusive concern is with the nature of the thing declared an art object. Put another way, unlike Atkinson and Baldwin's inquiry into the relationship between the specific artwork and the more general art discourse ("the language-use of the art society," as Atkinson once so pithily put it), Kosuth's project is concerned with the relation of the definition of art to art, which he locates exclusively in the completeness of the artist's idea of art.

Antihumanism in Art. Although the aesthetic model of conceptualism articulated and given form by Kosuth and the Art & Language group quickly became, and has remained, the dominant one, the conceptualist work of Sol LeWitt, Hanna Darboven, Dan Graham, and others in the mid- to late 1960s deals with different—even opposed—sets of interests than those of linguistic conceptualism. LeWitt, for example, argued that the elimination of the perceptual object in favor of an emphasis on the conceptual process was a way of dismantling myths of integrated subjectivity.

In what stands as the first manifesto of conceptual art, "Paragraphs on Conceptual Art" (1967), LeWitt sets up a binary between Expressionist art that requires rational decisions to be made throughout the process of an artwork's execution, and conceptual art in which all decisions about execution are made in advance. By extension, LeWitt differentiates between perceptual art that depends on visual forms, and conceptual art that "is made to engage the mind of the viewer rather than his eye." LeWitt's account of conceptual art, then, proposes that the concept determines what the artwork will look like. The idea, he writes, becomes "a machine that makes the art," a logical operation that "eliminates the arbitrary, capricious, and the subjective as much as possible." But, unlike Kosuth's aesthetic theory, which posits that the idea can itself be considered the art, for LeWitt the process of conception stands in a complementary relation to the process of realization, mutually supplying each other's lack, and thus they are of equal importance.

LeWitt's aesthetic theory is thus fundamentally opposed to Kosuth's. Whereas the latter's is characterized by a rational mode of artistic production that affirms the artist—centered, authorial, the presumed father and master of the work, the decision maker from beginning to end—LeWitt's theory proposes a mode of production that is opposed to rationalism; the work is produced following a logical sequence that does not require intuition, creativity, or rational thought. Thus, the work reads without the testimony of the father, the artist is no longer privileged, paternal; this process of production is fundamentally, in a word, *irrational*. Furthermore, consistent with his rational approach, Kosuth's aesthetic theory clearly restricts viewing experience to two possibilities: the viewer either comprehends the idea, or does not. It follows that the public for this model of conceptual art is relatively small, which was a situation that evidently did not concern Kosuth. "The public's not interested in art anyway," he said in a 1969 interview. "They're no more interested in art than they are with physics." In contrast, LeWitt's model of conceptualism posits an unlimited public. Artworks produced following this model are plural—which is not simply to say that they are located in public places, but that their content is more than the private history of the artist and allows a multiplicity of readings. In this respect, whereas Kosuth formulates an aesthetic theory based on the epitome of positivist thinking—the tautological model—LeWitt's aesthetic theory references positivism only to break out of it by introducing the subjective dimension of the beholder. "Once out of his hand," LeWitt writes, "the artist has no control over the way a viewer will perceive the work. Different people will understand the same thing in a different way" (1967).

It is in this context that the early work of artists such as Adrian Piper who steered conceptual art toward an increasing emphasis on social issues ought chiefly to be seen.

Piper's *Meat into Meat* of 1968, for instance, provides a concrete example of a type of work that integrates the decentering of the artist into its formal and constitutive elements while addressing social concerns. *Meat into Meat* is essentially an objectification of a certain temporal procedure. It systematically charts through time the process of change undergone by four hamburger patties as they were cooked and eaten by the artist's lover. At nine predetermined moments during this routine, Piper photographed the successive stages in the preparation and consumption of these objects. The detatched, methodical manner in which the work was produced made a point about the immorality of eating flesh. The transformation of the individual subject preparing and eating the meat into an aesthetic object sets up a confrontation between the vegetarian artist and the flesh-eating protagonist that establishes a connection between the personal, the political, and the aesthetically concrete.

In addition, relying on an a priori scheme that generates itself once the environment or person to be objectified as art is selected, Piper's *Meat into Meat* does not require the artist to make any choices. Snapping the shutter at predecided time intervals, decisions of time and space are out of the artist's hands, as it were, and he virtually disappears behind the system's self-generation. The work is thus reduced to a purely documentary account of the feeding episode, and all composition and interiority is negated. In what is now the inverse of a work that functions as "a working out, a thinking out, of all the implications of all aspects of the concept 'art,'" as Kosuth puts it (1991). With *Meat into Meat* there is little connection back to the artist through the work. Rather, it is the increasingly antagonistic experience of the person objectified by being photographed as part of an artwork that now becomes the focus, while the immoral practices and everyday conventions of the social structure that condones practices such as the consumption of relatively expensive forms of protein such as meat in the face of a global phenomenon of undernourished peoples becomes the context of the work.

Participatory Aesthetics. A third aesthetic theory of conceptual art can be discerned in the late 1960s work of Lawrence Weiner—one that integrates the decentering of the artist into its formal and constitutive elements in an attempt to democratize the production and reception of art. Weiner's art practice of this period is characterized by a radical dislocation of the notion of the sign. Rather than functioning as a general sign, presenting the physical art object and the conceptual information that supplements and closes the art object, Weiner most often presents the information of the work only in the form of a statement. These statements define linguistically the material structure of the work, presenting in the past participle facts about its materials and processes of production. A case in point is *One Hole in the Ground Approximately 1' × 1' × 1'. One Gallon Water Based White Paint Poured into this Hole.* The use of the

past participle is in itself significant insofar as it simultaneously allows for the conclusiveness of the description as well as the prospect of a future realization. Importantly, Weiner does not write, for example, "dig a hole in the ground, and take a gallon of water based white paint and pour it into this hole," but chooses the past tense exclusively because, as he put it, "To use the imperative would be for me fascistic. . . . The tone of command is the tone of tyranny." But one of the extraordinary features of Weiner's art is that it's equally valid whether communicated verbally or materially documented. In this sense, the hole into which a gallon of water based white paint was poured is not a discrete work, but one link in a chain of signifiers which summon and refer to one another. The work, like language, is structured but off-centered, without closure, equally present in a metonymic chain that includes the oral communication, the published statement, the process of carrying out the declaration, the residue of this act, the photographic documentation, and so on. In short, the work could take innumerable physical forms.

Even more unsettling, perhaps, is Weiner's assertion that the work does not even have to take form; for, at the time, Weiner also formulated the by now infamous "declaration of intent" that has been the criteria for the execution of his work since late 1968:

1. The artist may construct the piece
2. The piece may be fabricated
3. The piece need not be built
   Each being equal and consistent with the intent of the artist, the decision as to condition rests with the receiver upon the occasion of receivership.

In light of the interpretation of Weiner's art that has so far emerged, several aspects of this proclamation seem particularly significant. For one thing, it posits either the artist or somebody else fabricating or describing the piece as equal conditions for the production of his work, thereby abolishing the traditional notion of artist-centered production. For another, the proclamation indicates that the artwork requires that one try to diminish the distance between beholding and producing, joining the beholder and the work in a single signifying practice. Further, Weiner's instructions are for any interested body, collector or otherwise, and hence destabilize the myth of authority and authorship. In this sense, the work represents a radically egalitarian method of art production, distribution, and consumption.

The inversion of traditional practices of fabricating, exhibiting, and distributing works of art put into operation by Weiner's theoretical model of conceptualism clearly locates his work outside the parameters of LeWitt's aesthetic theory of conceptual art. Although LeWitt eliminated rational decision making from the manufacture stage of the work, thereby separating execution from artistic value, he maintained that the work should take physical form. Weiner's work of the late 1960s is set apart from LeWitt's because the participatory model is pushed to its logical conclusion. One of the explicit conditions of the work is that it need not be built, and the decision whether to actually give the piece physical form is left completely up to the viewer, or, in the terminology of Weiner at the time, the "recipient." The activation of the recipient is the direct result of the eclipse of the authorial figure of the artist.

Communicative Interaction. What makes Weiner's work of the late 1960s so suggestive is the introduction it provides for an analysis of an even more radical alternative to what later came to be the dominant theoretical model of conceptualism. In contrast to the other strands of conceptualism thus far examined, this one did not stop its interrogation of the underlying essence of an artwork at linguistic or economic conditions. Rather, artists such as Daniel Buren, Hans Haacke, and a few others deemed the ideological conditions of the institution of art to be fundamental to the validation of artworks. This development was part of a larger shift from the primacy of works that critiqued the idea of autonomous art and authoritative artists toward works that addressed the invisible institutional mechanisms that structure and define art in advanced capitalist society—more accurately, from work that decentered the artist to work that commented on the decentered artist. From this point of view, artistic production is considered to be overdetermined by the underlying system of rules of the institution of art. The individuality and creativity of artists capable of producing and exhibiting works—indeed, everything that had been attributed to artistic subjectivity—now come to be considered residual, alienated phenomena.

Haacke's model of conceptualism developed over the course of the 1960s. As the decade unfolded, however, the emphasis in his work shifted from a concern with natural and biological systems to social systems such as real estate, election returns, and questionnaires. Part and parcel of this shift was the diminished role of the artist, culminating in works that, once in place, virtually produce themselves, such as *MoMA-Poll* and *Gallery-Visitor's Profile,* which employ systemic methods for gathering data on social phenomena. In addition to the reduced role of the artist as producer, these works also problematize the networks of relationships through which power is exercised in the art world and expose the social, economic, and political bases of that power.

In this connection, it is revealing to look briefly at one of Haacke's earliest conceptualist works, the *Gallery-Visitor's Profile.* Haacke's schema reflects on the characteristics of the people who attend the site where it is exhibited. The work employs an empiricist method of accumulating information to compose a statistical breakdown of the gallery-goer: according to age, gender, religious belief, ethnicity, class, occupation, and so on. The result is a work that explicitly recognizes that the work of art's status as such arises

not from characteristics of its own inner logic, nor from the nominal act of the autonomous agent in absolute control of his creative impulses, but, in the first place, from the "relative ideological frame" of the privileged social group that constitutes the art audience and administers the discourse of art in our society, and second, from the gallery-museum power nexus that bestows value on a work of art.

In a similar way, Daniel Buren's late 1960s work integrates the framing conventions of not only the art object but also the art world in general into its formal and thematic content. At the same time, Buren's work unsettles myths of integrated subjectivity and the authorial role of the artist, thereby echoing the work of his U.S. counterparts such as LeWitt and Weiner. But whereas the latter maintained their investigations on the abstract level, Buren turned instead to submitting the constant of his stripe motif to an ever-changing variety of contexts. In the resulting dialectical relation between the aesthetic sign and its environment, not only the artistic traditions that artists locate themselves in, but also the effect that the institutional container of art— that is, the museum, gallery, or other display mechanisms— has upon the designation and design of artworks themselves, is problematized and subverted from within.

In his writings of the late 1960s, Buren argues that the interior space of the artwork, its "content," has been decimated by institutional mechanisms that regulate the exhibition and distribution of artworks in our society. Under these catastrophic conditions, Buren claims, art comes to buttress the existing order of things by offering proof that fine art is thriving and well. Furthermore, any form that art takes, however unconventional, is acceptable because the institutional network or structure of art has so thoroughly taken hold of the development of culture that any avant-garde gesture is immediately appropriated. Buren's response to these conditions is to de-emphasize the importance of the art object per se, focusing instead on the means by which the art system affirms the art object as significant, or as meaningful, avant-garde art.

Thus, Buren rejects the idea that the art object could have an inherent subject—a denial not unlike that proposed by the work of Kosuth or LeWitt. But the institution-critical dimension of the latter quickly reaches its limit insofar as the notion that the artwork could have a concrete relation to the problematic of display is excluded from both the operation of this work and the supplementary texts the artists produce to explain it. In contrast, the very inadequacy of the striped canvases (or posters) that Buren exhibits as art indexes his writings, which, as just noted, expound a theoretical position that critically analyzes the containment of art by institutional techniques and means, and thereby stimulates critical reflection on the part of the viewer.

In conclusion, then, rather than an aesthetic theory grounded in analytic philosophy that sought to pursue a more reduced, more "pure" form of art, conceptualism during the moment of its emergence was a heterogeneous field of artistic practices, the reverberations of which continue to be felt.

[*See also* Beuys; Contemporary Art.]

BIBLIOGRAPHY

Altshuler, Bruce J. *The Avant-Garde in Exhibition: New Art in the Twentieth Century.* New York, 1994.

Art-Language: The Journal of Conceptual Language 1.1 –5.3 (May 1969–March 1985).

Art-Language: The Journal of Conceptual Language n.s.1 (June 1994).

Avalanche 1–13 (Fall 1970–Summer 1976).

Battcock, Gregory, ed. *Idea Art: A Critical Anthology.* New York, 1973.

The British Avant-Garde. New York, 1971. Exhibition Catalog, New York Cultural Center.

Buchloh, Benjamin H. D. "Formalism and Historicity." In *Europe in the Seventies: Aspects of Recent Art,* pp. 83–123. Chicago, 1977. Exhibition catalog, Art Institute of Chicago.

Buren, Daniel. *Les écrits, 1965–1990.* 3 vols. Edited by Jean-Marc Poinsot. Bordeaux, 1991.

Burn, Ian. "The 'Sixties': Crisis and Aftermath (or Memoirs of an Ex-Conceptual Artist)." *Art & Text* 1.1 (Fall 1981): 49–65.

Celant, Germano. *Art Povera: Earthworks, Impossible Art, Actual Art, Conceptual Art.* New York, 1969.

Douglas Huebler. Eindhoven, 1979. Exhibition catalog, Stedelijk Van Abbemuseum.

The Fox 1–3 (1975–1976).

Goldstein, Anne, and Anne Rorimer, eds. *Reconsidering the Object of Art, 1965–1975.* Cambridge, Mass., 1996. Exhibition catalog, Los Angeles Museum of Contemporary Art.

Graham, Dan. *Rock My Religion: Writings and Art Projects, 1965–1990.* Edited by Brian Wallis. Cambridge, Mass., 1993.

Graham, Dan, ed. *Aspen* 8 (Fall–Winter 1970–1971).

Harrison, Charles. *Essays on Art & Language.* Oxford and Cambridge, Mass., 1991.

Harrison, Charles, and Fred Orton. *A Provisional History of Art & Language.* Paris, 1982.

Honnef, Klaus. *Concept Art.* Cologne, 1971.

Ian Burn: Minimal-Conceptual Work, 1965–1970. Perth, 1992. Exhibition catalog, Art Gallery of Western Australia.

Information. New York, 1970. Exhibition catalog, Museum of Modern Art.

Kelly, Mary. *Imaging Desire.* Cambridge, Mass., 1996.

Kosuth, Joseph. *Art after Philosophy and After: Collected Writings, 1966–1990.* Edited by Gabriele Guercio. Cambridge, Mass., 1991.

Kozloff, Max. "The Trouble with Art-as-Idea." *Artforum* 11.1 (September 1972): 33–37.

Krauss, Rosalind E. *The Originality of the Avant-Garde and Other Modernist Myths.* Cambridge, Mass., 1985.

Legg, Alicia, ed. *Sol LeWitt: The Museum of Modern Art, New York.* New York, 1978. Exhibition catalog.

LeWitt, Sol. "Paragraphs on Conceptual Art." *Artforum* 5.10 (Summer 1967): 79–83.

Lippard, Lucy R. *Changing: Essays in Art Criticism.* New York, 1971.

Lippard, Lucy R., ed. *Six Years: The Dematerialization of the Art Object from 1966 to 1972.* New York, 1973.

Mel Bochner: Thought Made Visible, 1966–1973. New Haven, 1995. Exhibition catalog, Yale University Art Gallery.

Meyer, Ursula. *Conceptual Art.* New York, 1972.

Millet, Catherine. "L'art conceptuel." *VH 101* 3 (Autumn 1970): 1–53.

Morris, Robert. *Continuous Project Altered Daily: The Writings of Robert Morris.* Cambridge, Mass., 1993.

O'Doherty, Brian, ed. *Aspen* 5–6 (Fall–Winter 1967).

Piper, Adrian. *Out of Order, Out of Sight.* 2 vols. Cambridge, Mass., 1996.

Ramsden, Mel. *Abstract Relations.* New York, 1968.

Robert Morris: The Mind/Body Problem. New York, 1994. Exhibition catalog, Solomon R. Guggenheim Museum.

"Roundtable: Conceptual Art and the Reception of Duchamp." *October* 70 (Fall 1994): 127–146.

Wall, Jeff. *Dan Graham's Kammerspiel.* Toronto, 1991.

Wallis, Brian, ed. *Hans Haacke: Unfinished Business.* Cambridge, Mass., 1986. Exhibition catalog, New Museum of Contemporary Art, New York.

Wilson, Ian. "Conceptual Art." *Artforum* 22.6 (February 1984): 60–61.

ALEXANDER ALBERRO

History of the Unformed

We have thought of conceptual art as modernism's nervous breakdown—a form of response to intolerable conditions on the part of individuals for one reason or another unable to act in accordance with the protocols of a dominant culture. The conceptual art we have in mind was resistant to the entrenched competences of modernism, a resistance that was in part an objection to the entrenchment of painting and sculpture as artistic categories. It was also resistant to the constitutiveness of modernist criticism and to the curatorial and entrepreneurial instruments of modernist culture—a resistance that recognized the efficiency of the criticism and the power of the distributive instruments to co-opt resistance itself.

Locally, this resistance developed during the late 1960s both in face of the new modernist professionalism of the Minimalists and as an extension—or reductio ad absurdum—of the Minimalists' concern with conditions of display. In general, the post-Minimalist framing of paradoxical or "dematerialized" types of object required the use of language. There was a consequent need for new competences—or rather, for competence-like capacities and self-descriptions. These involved writing and reading (of kinds often unduly dignified in retrospective accounts). There was a tendency for the resultant work to take a conversational and collaborative form, as it did within Art & Language. The journal *Art-Language* was first published in England in the spring of 1969 and served at once as an outlet for such work and as a form of "home" for an argumentative practice without a studio.

Viewed from a larger perspective, the development of conceptual art was driven by a negative concept of artiness, and by the hostile intents of those whose self-image and sense of class politics ruled out any easy familiarity with high culture. Although much of what was called conceptual art was produced by artists who impersonated executive forms of professionalism, or by obsessives, the "strong poets" of conceptual art were people in process—mostly young and concerned to extricate themselves from unwanted material and cultural conditions. For such people there is relatively little pressure to identify with a consistent range of products. What follows from this is that no real historical probity can be associated with a conceptual art that is conceived of as a style that could even possibly be pure or consistent. Indeed, the clean black-and-white manner that rapidly became conceptual art's curatorial identity may be thought of as a form of loss or betrayal of that aggressive critical effect that was the promise of the moment. For us, putting the writing on the wall was not primarily the adoption of an avant-garde medium. It was a means both to show and to transform the power of the criticism that "made" modernist art.

The politics of conceptual art was informal and undisciplined, but it was vigorous. The discursive tools employed were not those normally found in the hands of artists at the time. Conceptual art was homeless practice—an art without studios, and with galleries and exhibitions only insofar as these could be exploited to air the proceedings of anomalous researches. Conceptual art did not simply involve the taking of a linguistic turn, however, nor did it entail a reduction of the pictorial to the linguistic. The point is, rather, that the possibility of cultural aggravation is to be found in the interstices between the pictorial and the textual. In this sense, the eruption of the text into the cultural and historical space of the picture was an exemplary moment, bringing the nature of artistic practice itself into question. This interrogative and negative virtue of conceptual art was a function of the youthfulness of those who practiced it—and of their youthful ability to spend without counting costs. Conceptual artists need to grow up like everyone else. A continuing morale, however, may be identified with the tendency to interrogate those practices and competences by which artistic culture is defined.

Art & Language's Documenta Index of 1972 was the pivot between early and later Art & Language work. As installed in Kassel, it comprised eight filing cabinets containing the entire contents of the journal *Art-Language,* together with other writings by those involved. Around the cabinets, the four walls of the room were papered with a form of index, photographically enlarged from an original typescript so as to cover the entire surface available. The index provided an individual listing for each text included. Under each of some 350 separate citations, the various other texts were designated under one or another of three possible relations to the text cited. These relations were symbolized as "+," signifying a relationship of compatibility between a given pair of texts; "−," signifying a relationship of incompatibility; and "T," signifying that the relevant documents belonged in different logical/ethical spaces and were therefore not to be compared in advance of some notional transformation of those spaces. The names listed at the entrance to the installation were those of the *Art-Language* editorial board as then composed: Terry Atkinson, David Bainbridge, Michael Baldwin, Charles Harrison, Harold Hurrell,

Joseph Kosuth, Ian Burn, Mel Ramsden, Philip Pilkington, and David Rushton.

Within five years, the contributors to Art & Language projects had been reduced to the three present signatories, with whose collaborative work the name has been associated since then. At the time, however, the index seemed to many others to represent a new place of work, offering the glimpse of people in a cooperation that could be nonaccidental without being professionalized. In that sense, it stood at a considerable distance from those forms of conceptual art that were attenuations of the Duchampian ready-made into the realm of fictional and theoretical entities. Art & Language's indexes might be thought of as practical forms of internal exile within the international culture of modern art—a culture within which the ready-made had become a standard means to professional advancement.

Through a form of continuation of the indexing project, an extended Art & Language community developed in New York between 1972 and 1975. But this considerable growth of Art & Language at once entailed and coincided with a tendency for conceptual art, as it attracted notice, to become itself a form of cultural administration. By the latter year, when Art & Language published *The Fox* in New York, the continuation of text-based work seemed possible only as radical university art or as a form of knowing journalism. By neither route would conceptual art's critical homelessness be maintained.

This analysis receives confirmation from the fate of more recent "neoconceptual art," caught as the latter is in the desert between cultural studies and the media. The proliferation of such work testifies to a recurrent anxiety about the need for significant content. In the mid-1970s, in face of similar anxieties about conceptual art's distinctiveness and effectiveness, pictures and graphic devices of various kinds started to look potentially radical again. Once conceptual art had become standard culture, that is to say, the possibility of critical distance resided in that which conceptual art itself was wont to disparage. Indeed, exile is conceivably the only vivid and continuing legacy of conceptual art. If there is a history of conceptual art, it needs to be not the cultural form of paranoid imperialism but a story of some artists and of how they tried to account for themselves under conditions that remain open to inquiry.

This view of conceptual art and of its representatives is admittedly at odds with the kind of valuation that allows Benjamin Buchloh, for instance, to single out Marcel Broodthaers and to accord a form of "maturity" to the objects he produced. It is also at odds with those accounts of conceptual art that would see a "pure" form of "language art" as distinguished from other types of post-Minimalism by virtue of some special engagement with "meaning." In accounts of this latter form, conceptual art tends to be idealized as an epochal break, while the requirement made of subsequent developments is that they be seen to keep the faith.

The effect is to polarize historical interpretations, so that the self-image of the purist and the skepticism of the hostile critic alike receive confirmation. Under these conditions, debate is rendered automatic and fraudulent. One matter that then goes unquestioned is the assumption of justified and continuous property values on which the purist bases the worth of his oeuvre. Mercantile status and originary value become reciprocal. "Early works" are dignified as the building blocks of a designer's art-historical edifice, ceasing in the process to be what they are—callow adolescent endeavors that get their moment in the spotlight, if they do, by virtue of some unforeseen historical and mercantile accident.

This present account is also inconsistent with those principally American narratives of conceptual art in which a direct lineage is traced from Marcel Duchamp, through Jasper Johns, with Ad Reinhardt as an optional supplement. In such accounts, conceptual art needs to be made to be that which is derivable from Duchamp, Johns, or whomever. This historicizing process necessarily misrepresents both conceptual art's actual historical and cultural contingency and the diffuseness of reasons according to which conceptual art was produced.

We turn to the question of what it is that the category "conceptual art" serves usefully to distinguish? Our answer is that it serves to invoke some anomalous and unstable activity, or form of morale, in which subversiveness and incompetence are combined in undecidable proportions. It is a truism of modern art history that the affronted viewer of early avant-garde art had publicly to assert the incompetence of that which he actually felt to be subversive. Under the regime of late modernism, however, the recognition of competence came to be identified with what Clement Greenberg called the "challenge to taste." The capacity for a kind of sophisticated self-criticism thus became part of the spectator's normal baggage. It was left to conceptual art to render this sophistication nugatory.

We have in mind a recent work by Art & Language, in which an actual painting is largely obscured by a printed text promising an amateurish landscape to be painted in the future. The amateurism in question, like the "amateurism" of conceptual art, is not merely involuntary incompetence—or is it? In either case, in face of manipulative or coercive professional culture, it represents a form of critical displacement or exile.

Self-displacement cannot be represented as occupation of historical territory. According to our understanding of the morale of Conceptual Art, talk of "classical conceptual art" effectively denies the work in question any significant difference from artistic norms. This is not to say that conceptual art is immune from retrospective accounts, but rather that it is its radical incompleteness that renders conceptual art interesting. It does not follow that "conceptual art" is subject to practical revival. Conceptual art had better not look to conceptual art for its future.

BIBLIOGRAPHY

Art-Language 1–5 (1969–1985); new series, 1 (June 1994).
Art & Language. Paris, 1993. Museé du Jeu de Paume, catalog.
Art & Language: The Paintings. Brussels, 1987. Palais des Beaux-Arts, catalog.
Harrison, Charles. *Essays on Art & Language.* Oxford and Cambridge, Mass., 1991.
Harrison, Charles, and Paul Wood, eds. *Art in Theory, 1900–1990.* Oxford and Cambridge, Mass., 1992. See section 7.

ART & LANGUAGE (MICHAEL BALDWIN,
CHARLES HARRISON, and MEL RAMSDEN)

Conceptual Art and Philosophy

The term *conceptual art* (and the variants *concept art* and *conceptualism*) are used in two different ways. According to a narrower use of the term, conceptual art refers to an art movement that existed from the late 1960s to the early 1970s. The original group of conceptualists included Joseph Kosuth, Lawrence Weiner, Robert Barry, Douglas Huebler, Dan Graham, and the British group Art & Language. There was also a considerably larger group of artists whose activities were considered, at the time, to be related to those of the American and British members. This group included, among others, John Baldessari, Daniel Buren, Jan Dibbets, and Ian Burn.

According to the second, broader, use of the term, conceptual art stands for an artistic undercurrent or sensibility that existed continuously from the early 1960s to the present. Those who partake in this undercurrent believe that artists should examine all preconceived notions and presuppositions and attempt to expand the range of artistic activities. Consequently, their art does not always fit neatly within the existing categories of painting and sculpture. On a more abstract level, conceptual artists share an opposition to the "formalist" outlook on art, and they emphasize the continuity between their artistic activities and various philosophical, political, and sociological activities. According to this definition, artists as diverse as John Cage, Pietro Manzoni, Joseph Beuys, Chris Burden, Jenny Holzer, Clegg & Guttmann, and Andrea Frazer can be called conceptual artists.

To try to present the ideas that the original conceptualists developed at the time, it is helpful to follow the method of intellectual history. This method is recommended because of the lively intellectual exchanges that accompanied the formation of the conceptualist movement. The members of the original group wrote explanatory articles and they participated in numerous interviews that were transcribed and published. This was not an incidental but a most important point. One of the beliefs shared by most of the original conceptualists was that theorizing about art was continuous with making art. Nevertheless, one should be forewarned that the method of intellectual history is fraught with difficulties. First, an undue importance is invariably given to published materials. Second, one always tries to capture "commonly held" beliefs and that kind of investigation is always conducted at the expense of the articulation of the thoughts and practices of the participating individuals. Third, anachronism is difficult to avoid. One cannot help being influenced by later ideas and accounts. These difficulties are serious, maybe even insuperable. Without such attempts, however, we are in danger of forgetting the specific intellectual flavor of one of the most ambitious and interesting artistic movements of the twentieth century.

In many ways, the conceptual art movement followed the ambitious antiformalist paradigm that was developed by minimalists. This new paradigm resonated greatly and was applied even in other fields, notably in dance and music. The grand strategy was to resist the attempts to sever the art object from its context. The tactic, more often than not, was to present objects that did not appear as art objects in a manner in which art objects are not usually presented. Scores of young artists in the late 1960s and early 1970s investigated both the possibility of making art from "poor" and nondurable materials not usually associated with art and the possibilities of exhibiting artworks in a variety of indoor and outdoors locations not usually associated with the presentation of art. Some works produced in this manner were interesting and they genuinely expanded the original minimalist paradigm. This was the case, for example, with Robert Smithson's projects, which involved the presentation of monumental manipulation of the natural landscape as artworks. Nevertheless, it also became evident that the "minimalist revolution" was in danger of being degraded into a mere stylistic preoccupation, into art that celebrates change for its own sake. This realization was, in a way, the point of departure of the conceptualists. They realized that, first, the methodological basis of antiformalism had to be better articulated and, second, that they had to prevent the art of their time from sliding back into the preoccupation with novel materials and forms, which is how formalism threatened to reappear.

In certain respects, conceptual art may be regarded as a continuation of the minimalist paradigm. The art of the conceptualist was, without exception, "impersonal" and de-aestheticized, attention was paid to the mode in which the work was installed, and many of the works were produced using transparent and predetermined procedures. Nevertheless, there were novel elements that were clearly absent from the work of the minimalists. The most important of these was the attempt by conceptual artists to create conditions that would make it possible to see works of art as an embodiment of a philosophical investigation. More specifically, they made it possible to view art as a tool for investigating the concept of art. The conceptual artists emphasized the continuity between artistic action and self-reflection. They sought to determine the "grammar" of art.

All these features did not exist in the same way in the pre-conceptual period.

The starting point of the conceptualists was the new interpretation they offered to Marcel Duchamp's readymades. For the conceptualists, the aim of Duchamp's readymade was an investigation of the conditions that make art possible. According to this interpretation, Duchamp asked the following question: Let us take an arbitrary object with no particular aesthetic qualities. Under which conditions can this object be presented as an art object? If a set of such conditions can be found, it can teach us a great deal about the concept of art. Duchamp's readymades are partial answers to this question. In each case, he presented an object in a peculiar manner, using various devices to convey the impression that the object was believed to have a certain significance for a fictitious person who "authored" it, without having, literally, produced it. The various devices (renaming the object, slightly altering it, inscribing on it, etc.) define a set of conditions. In each case, the viewer has to ask himself or herself whether the conditions are sufficient for making the object into the center of his or her aesthetic attention. If the answer is positive, and it usually is, the viewer has obtained a concrete example of an extreme case of aesthetic appreciation. Such cases, together, constitute invaluable information for those who wish to understand the concept of art.

In some sense, the issue presented by the readymades is familiar. Every person who ever used a frame or a pedestal knows the power of these devices to make objects into the subjects of aesthetic appreciation. The question that Duchamp asked, however, concerned the proper generalization of these devices. Because the Cubists used newspaper in their artworks, it became obvious that the artist does not have to literally produce the art object for it to be regarded as his or her artwork. The newspaper in the Cubist collage continues to be a newspaper; but the collage is still regarded as a work of art. In other words, the Cubists introduced the possibility for an artwork to have parts whose identity is not completely subordinated to the whole. From this point of view, the readymade is a more extreme and consequential exercise in art that lacks organic unity. This time the whole object, and not just a part, retains its nonartistic identity. Such art raises a general question: How do such objects become art? Obviously, the answer has to do with the mode in which the object is presented. Duchamp's work clears many of the issues surrounding the notion that what makes objects into art are not the properties that determine their identity but the mode of their presentation. The conceptual artists continued in this vein.

The conceptualists maintained that the presentation of artworks required a "support language." By that they meant a system of external devices, lacking any aesthetic dimension, that determine our aesthetic disposition. These devices act like signs that point at an object and say THIS IS ART! The broader thesis that the conceptualists presented was that as long as there is no reason to doubt the credibility of the signs, we will be willing to give them the benefit of the doubt and regard the objects to which they point as artworks. The controversial part of the thesis was that we shall continue doing so even when the objects do not have any obvious aesthetic qualities.

In reality, what constitute the support language for art are plaques, labels, wall inscriptions, and, of course, frames, pedestals, and velvet ropes. Therefore, the interest in support language led to a large body of conceptual artworks that were concerned, literally, with these objects and devices. The notion of support language, though, is not exhausted by the use of plaques and labels. A profound point made by the conceptualists was that the typical modernist exhibition space, the "white cube," itself functioned as a frame or pedestal. In other words, any object presented in the modernist exhibition space could be perceived as an artwork. (Many a viewer found himself or herself momentarily looking at a fire extinguisher located at a museum as an artwork.) This realization led to a large body of work by conceptual artists who presented alterations of the exhibition space as artworks. (Weiner, for example, presented a wet wall as an artwork, and Bruce Nauman constructed narrow corridors that literally enclosed the viewer.) Again, the purpose of such projects was to present extreme and problematic cases of artworks that necessitated a revision of the viewer's preconceived ideas on the nature of art.

Many other early works by the conceptualists were conceived of as attempts to generalize the notion of the readymades. This was clearly the aim of many of the early works of Art & Language, a group of British artists who produced their art collectively. The members of the group tried to examine the possibility of generalizing Duchamp's methods further, that is, beyond the presentation of an arbitrary middle-size object in a well-recognized exhibition space. Among their variations on the theme of the readymade was the presentation of an electric field that reacted to the presence of viewers, a presentation of the air-conditioning system as an artwork, and the presentation of the transcripts of the artists' conversations in an art gallery. In one work, they designated the county of Oxfordshire as an artwork and formulated their intentions in a text that they wrote on this occasion. This highly experimental work was characteristic of the investigative spirit of the conceptualists.

The conceptualists, then, attempted to expand Duchamp's method of investigating the concept of art. What was different in the conceptualist project, however, was that the idea that art should investigate itself was given a fundamental status: it was elevated to the very purpose of avant-gardist art. This thesis was clearly articulated by Kosuth. Art, according to Kosuth, should be differentiated from the particular forms that it took. In particular, art should not necessarily be identified with painting or sculpture. On the contrary, artists who do not question the traditional artistic techniques lose the very center of their vocation, namely, the critical task of continuously redefining their activities. Art, according to this conception, is an ever-changing sphere of cultural activities that resists closure. In that sense, art is essentially self-reflective, philosophical, investigative. It is a meditation on the manner in which human beings can reshape their reality by using their creativity and their sense of form. When art loses this quality, it is reduced to a mere craft. Kosuth's early works thematized the idea that it is the essence of art to redefine itself. In a series of works that he called "art as an idea as an idea," he presented the definitions of various concepts. These definitions were presented as a background in the presence of which one was supposed to contemplate the art objects that Kosuth presented.

In later years, the preoccupation with the support language led many conceptual artists beyond issues directly related to signs or architectural details to an interest in the institutions that produced the signs and designed the exhibition spaces. Buren was one artist who systematically investigated the relations between art and its institutional setting. He created a "module," a pattern of blue and white stripes, which he used like a constant quantity in a controlled experiment. The object of the experiment was the effect of the changing context on the reception and the meaning of a given object. Buren initiated a series of investigations in which the pattern was placed in a variety of different institutional settings. The artworks of Hans Haacke, too, systematically shifted the attention from the manner in which the art institutions provide a context that defines objects as art, to the art institutions themselves. Applying a system-theoretical approach, Haacke argued that one should always investigate, simultaneously, the context, the object, and the symbiotic relations between the two. This approach prompted Haacke to pose a new set of questions: Why is art promoted in the first place? What type of benefits does art provide to its institutional setting? Haacke attempted to answer these questions by investigating the contexts in which art is presented and proposed that art provides a public-relations function for these institutions. In a project designed for the Guggenheim Museum, Haacke investigated the real-estate holdings of the members of the board of directors of the museum. In another project, he turned his attention to the visitors to the museum, another aspect of the institutional context, and initiated a sociological study of this group of people.

To sum up, there is a strong link between the aims of the conceptual artist and the critique of art institutions. The former attempts to question the existing artistic conventions and, by doing so, to expand the boundaries of art. The latter attempts to provide an insight into the workings of the art institutions by subjecting them to a historical-genealogical analysis. Viewed from the point of view of the theory of social institutions, both types of critiques are extremely useful: they help us to see whether the institutions still fulfill their intended function; they point to areas in which stagnation set in and to ways to improve them.

There is a distinction between the narrow definition of conceptual art, which refers only to the group of artists who originated the conceptual movement, and a much larger group of people whose sensibilities are considered conceptual in a wider sense of the term. The understanding of the legacy of the conceptual movement may very well be more important than the historical investigation of a particular group of people in a narrow interval of time. Conceptual art has became synonymous with openness, invasiveness, responsiveness to the social and political context, and the possession of a critical edge; thus, the investigation of conceptual art in the wider sense of the term is nothing short of what lies behind the attempts to preserve and expand a concept of art making that allows for an ambitious, responsible, and critical art. The present context, however, focuses on the ideas of the originators of conceptual art; therefore, we shall now present some ideas that became associated with conceptual art and ask whether they did, indeed, feature in the discussions of the original conceptualists in the formative years of their movement.

The first and most difficult issue is the concept of the dematerialization of art. Many writers on the subject take it as a given that the conceptualists tried to dematerialize art. Nevertheless, the very notion, as we shall see, is far from being clear and neither is the extent to which it played a part in the original discussions. The first point to be made concerning the notion of dematerialized art is that since the late 1950s, many artists who were influenced by Cage began to view art as aiming at a state of mind of complete openness to the environment. Their aim was to make art that helps people to "take the world in" without being disturbed by preconceived ideas or by emotions or needs. Art objects, according to this conception, are merely material instruments for achieving this state of mind; in and of themselves they are unimportant. This approach offers an interpretation and a raison d'être of dematerialized art. These ideas were articulated by artists who were associated with the Fluxus movement. (The works of Yoko Ono are a good example of this approach; in her work she gave the viewer instructions to think thoughts of a certain kind.)

There is no doubt that Cage's conception of art was important and that any historian of the period should come to terms with it. There is also no doubt that Cage influenced the conceptual movement rather deeply. (He influenced the entire generation of the conceptualists!) Nevertheless, the logic of Cage's conception of art stems from the belief in the spiritual value of complete openness. (Only a strong belief of this kind may justify the idea that the value of art is predicated on its ability to produce such openness.) The artists who formed the conceptual movement did not share this belief. Therefore, one should not confuse Cage's poetics of the dematerialization of art with the aims and methods of the conceptual artists.

A second sense of the dematerialization of art, which has more to do with the ideas of the conceptualists is, simply, the belief that art is primarily an intellectual endeavor. Artworks are cultural and not only material products. Therefore, artists should be accorded the status of intellectuals and not treated as elevated craftsmen. This issue, which concerns the social status of the artistic profession, was not discussed explicitly. But behind many of the arguments of the conceptualists, there was a thinly veiled complaint that artists were not taken sufficiently seriously as intellectuals. These types of arguments, it should be remarked, are not uncommon in the history of art. (The hierarchy of the genres was created in order to differentiate between artists of different cultural and intellectual levels.) It should also be remarked that artists usually appeal to their proficiency in philosophy and to their general learnedness to substantiate the claim that their art contains philosophical insights that should be taken seriously. In this sense, conceptualism may be seen as a movement aspiring to elevate the status of art and place it on a footing equal to that of other intellectual disciplines.

A somewhat deeper sense of the notion of dematerialized art has to do with the idea of art whose formal and material facets are all determined by a preset procedure, by a concept. The subordination of the form that the art object takes to its concept is sometimes referred to, somewhat misleadingly, as the dematerialization of art. The notion of art that is produced according to an aesthetically indifferent and preset concept or procedure was formulated by Sol LeWitt. In fact, he coined the term *conceptual art* in an article he wrote on the topic. Indeed, there is no doubt that LeWitt was an important link between minimalism and conceptual art. Originally, LeWitt's ideas were probably meant as means for frustrating formalist interpretations. The use of aesthetically neutral preset procedures preempted attempts to read into the work and think of it as a composition. The conceptual artists extended the notion of procedure or concept and used it for more positive ends. Instead of using a set of combinatorial rules, as LeWitt did, they used various methods of research and observation as their preset procedures. Even while one looks at conceptual works of art, one is made aware of the fact that many, perhaps most, of those formal aspects of the work, including those the viewer finds striking, are contingent and incidental. Like LeWitt's drawings, the form the work takes depends in crucial ways on the measure and the proportion of the rooms where it is presented, as well as on various architectural details. Thus, even when aspects of the work are aesthetically pleasing, one cannot ascibe them to the artwork but must regard them as incidental features. A good example are Weiner's sentences. The same sentence may be drawn on an internal wall, on the side of a building, on a highway, or on a river raft. From Weiner's point of view, all these possibilities are different ways of presenting the same work of art. Hence, any formal analysis of his work will necessarily fail: any aspect of the work that is not related to the concatenation of the letter is incidental. This strategy, then, constitutes a new conceptualist version of antiformalism. The content of the conceptual work is given in linguistic or ideational terms; hence, no visual or formal aspect of the work is stable enough to be regarded as an internal part of the work of art itself.

The same method was later used by many other artists who initiated various forms of research and presented their results as artwork. Huebler, for instance, watched a boxing match and documented "the most Baroque" composition on the TV screen. The result was a work of art whose formal properties cannot be ascribed to the artist; they are determined by factors that are not aesthetically relevant. The experimental branch of conceptualism was developed and articulated by many California-based artists. Burden's performances, for example, were conceived of as prearranged experimental scenarios that used the artist himself as a medium. The artworks that remained were the documentations of the experiments.

Another interpretation of the aim of the conceptualists is that they wished to dematerialize art because they wanted to undermine and destabilize the commodity status of art objects. According to this view, this basic objective inspired the use of two types of strategies. On the one hand, it inspired the use of nontraditional media and "poor" materials; such techniques and materials, it is often argued, cannot be used to make "marketable" art. On the other hand, the motivation behind the use of concepts and preset procedures was also related to the aim of making unmarketable art; such procedures, one might argue, produce decidedly deaestheticized artworks that cannot fulfill the function of conventional paintings and sculpture.

Note that the argument, as it stands, assumes that one's conception of art cannot be genuinely expanded beyond the traditional media; those who believe that it might will not be so categorical in their view that only art made according to traditional taste can fulfill the functions of art. In fact, there is a great deal to suggest that the contrary is true. After almost a century of experiments in nontraditional techniques, it is clear that the notion of art was expanded beyond the traditional categories and that the "poor" art of today is the cherished and sought-after art of tomorrow. The same is true for art that uses preset rules and procedures. One should distinguish between the serious and ambitious attempt to produce art that is not susceptible to a formalist interpretation from the more pedestrian idea of working against conventions. The former aims at transforming our notion of the aesthetic; the latter is merely an attempt to change the prevailing taste. The difference between the two was certainly appreciated by the conceptualists.

The next issue, which is directly related to the preceding discussion, concerns the place of nontraditional media within the conceptualist framework. In its colloquial use, the term *conceptual art* is nearly synonymous with art that uses photography, video, film, or performance. This identification is not entirely justified even relative to the broader use of the term *conceptual art*. Most conceptual artists, to be sure, use nontraditional media; but not every performance artist or artist who uses photography or video should be regarded as a conceptual artist. A better grasp of the distinction can be obtained by looking at the reason for the use of new media by the members of the original conceptualist group.

The most important reason for the introduction of new materials, techniques, and media into art is the investigation of the possibilities of extending the notion of art. The investigation of the concept of art is not meant to be justified only as an intellectual endeavor. Art is an institution and the possibility of transforming it, extending it to its full potential, demonstrates how one should approach every institution. Nothing should be taken for granted; every traditional or arbitrary facet should be examined and debated. The best way of doing so is, of course, by suggesting alternative arrangements. In the sphere of art, the use of novelties is justified primarily when it is part of a discussion about the possibilities of transforming the institution of art. One of the first projects of the conceptualist group was an exhibition of various works of art in a photocopied book. This experiment clearly presented the limitation of the ordinary conventions of art exhibitions. Why, indeed, can a book not be conceived as being, literally, an exhibition space? This example demonstrates how the very formulation of alternatives forces the issue of the justification of the conventional mode of exhibiting art.

A second reason for the use of new media is that some instances of it can be justified as attempts to "break down the boundaries between art and life" and thereby to reject the notion that art should function as an escape from the brutalities of the real world. According to this conception, any device should be used that makes the viewer aware of his or her environment. This conception applies to works by Nauman and Graham. Nauman installed a closed TV circuit that made it possible for each viewer to see himself or herself approaching from behind. Graham created environments where the viewers could see themselves, en masse, and become aware of their presence in the exhibition space. The result was, literally, a heightened awareness of the experience of spectatorship.

Another reason why the conceptualists chose nontraditional media was their wish to do justice to their investigations by presenting them in discursive and openly intellectual forms. The efforts in this direction led the artists to write essays and participate in interviews that were not perceived, in and of themselves, as artworks. But, more important, the conceptualists consistently looked for ways for emphasizing the ideational and intellectual content of their work. This emphasis led to the use of a whole variety of means, from the use of photography by Huebler, Graham, and Kosuth to the use of video by Nauman and Graham. One may also regard the use of printed sentences by Kosuth and Weiner as an instance of this trend. At least in the case of Kosuth, however, the use of language was meant to bring up another point, namely, the continuity that exists between art and the discourse on art. We shall return to this issue shortly.

It is important to clarify the notion that conceptual art is concerned with language, that it is a philosophical art, and that the sources of conceptual art are to be found with the philosophy of language in general and with Ludwig Wittgenstein in particular. To be sure, there is no doubt that there was a keen interest in linguistic philosophy among the conceptualists. Nevertheless, there is considerable lack of clarity on the particular manner in which this interest was related to the more basic aims of conceptual art.

Let us begin with a historical remark. After World War II, there was a lively debate among American philosophers about the aims and methods of philosophy. The more aggressive participants in the debate were the analytic philosophers. These philosophers emphasized the importance of the sciences and viewed their philosophy as a service to the sciences; they warned against the danger that pseudoquestions posed to philosophy and advocated the use of logical and linguistic analysis to guard against it. The followers of the analytic school actively campaigned against other approaches to philosophy and blamed them for fostering various irrational beliefs that manifest themselves in nondemocratic practices. The analytic school was very successful in creating for itself a hegemonic position in American philosophy departments and it exerted a considerable influence over other academic disciplines as well.

In retrospect, the fascination of the conceptual artists with the relatively difficult and technical writing of the analytic philosophers might seem strange and misplaced. (At least in the case of Kosuth and the Art & Language group, there is no doubt that the interest was genuine.) In fact, in later periods, the conceptualists too distanced themselves from their earlier interest in analytic philosophy. Nevertheless, the manner in which they supported the claim that conceptual art constituted a philosophical discourse on the conditions of the possibility of art greatly benefited from their interest in the philosophy of language.

The conceptual artists formulated their activities as an investigation into the language and grammar of art. This formulation reflected a broader attitude that bore the influence of the philosophy of language. According to this attitude, every sphere of cultural activity can be described as a set of rules, akin to the rules of grammar, which select among all the possible practices those that will be considered legiti-

mate and those that will be considered ill-formed and meaningless. The same is true in the case of art. In order to understand the notion of art, one must understand the "grammar" of art, the conditions that are necessary for making an object into the focus of aesthetic attention.

The second influence from analytic philosophy is a direct continuation of the first. Many philosophers of language remarked on the fact that the discourse on language is itself always conducted in a metalanguage. Therefore, they concluded, there is no escape from the use of language. The conceptual artist argued that, since Duchamp, the same was true of art. The investigation into the nature of art was conducted by artistic means. The results of the investigation were artworks. The content of these artworks was the demonstration that the concept of art could be expanded in various directions. This view of art brings to mind some of Wittgenstein's remarks on the evolution of language. Wittgenstein argued that many of our notions are in a state of constant evolution. In one of his examples, he claimed that we constantly revise our conception of measurement by introducing new practices as "measurement practices." New measurement tools are introduced in order to measure what was previously unmeasurable, and new conventions are devised to define the relationship between the old and the new methods. According to the conceptualists, new artworks should expand the notion of art in a similar manner. New practices that were not part of the notion of art in previous periods become part of an extended notion of art and, in the process, the very notion of art evolves. This evolutionary process is open-ended and creative but not entirely arbitrary. Typically, the new practices conform to the tradition in some ways, while breaking it in others. The expectation is that the new practices will shed new light on the notion of art as a whole.

The notion of a practice in not a purely linguistic notion. Any attempt to understand how new practices are instituted must include references to the social mechanisms that make the institution of such practices possible. This general remark applies to the evolution of the concept of art as well. The expansion of the notion of art is a social process and, typically, those who initiate it have to overcome resistance. Therefore, the investigation into the evolution of art contributes to our understanding of the conditions that make social change possible.

It is now possible to discuss, briefly, the notion of conceptual art in the extended sense of the term. The discussion will take the form of an epilogue centered on the question of the subsequent development of the sensibilities of the conceptualists. The reason such a discussion is needed is that the art of the conceptualists created a new paradigm that is not perceived today merely as a specific movement. This paradigm, which is followed by contemporary artists, is what can be referred to as conceptual art in the extended sense of the term. What follows are some of the directions taken by artists belonging to this new paradigm. They are examples only and thus do not cover the whole field or even represent all its most important aspects.

A most enduring and interesting tradition associated with the notion of conceptual art in the extended sense of the term is the idea of art that is preoccupied with "institutional critique." The idea was to produce artworks that formulated and reflected their own relations with their context. As noted earlier, some aspects of this idea can clearly be seen in the work of Buren and Haacke. But the issue became more widely discussed in the 1970s when a group of artists, which included Michael Asher and John Knight, made work that consisted of slight interventions with the routine of various art institutions. The idea was to create work that highlights the nature of the art context, forcing the institutions where the art was presented to reveal their identity. This type of approach was reformulated in the 1980s to include the private sector of art collectors, the collections acquired by various financial institutions, and the educational and other auxiliary departments of art museums. Louise Lawler, for example, documented the way that art was re-contextualized, together with furniture and objects d'art, in various art collections. Clegg & Guttmann made group portraits of the governing boards of various institutions. Frazer presented fictional guided tours in museums as her artwork.

Another enduring idea was to conceive of art as an activity whose objective is to analyze its own language, the language of art. This idea was present in the work of Kosuth and the work of Art & Language. But it was transformed and invigorated by Baldessari's "semiotic" interpretation of this conception of art. Baldessari's artworks investigated the language of images in general, and the language of cinema in particular. The idea of art that researches the visual language was given a more political reading by Victor Burgin, Barbara Kruger, Richard Prince, and Cindy Sherman. They made artworks that "decoded" the language of advertising and researched the way advertisers disseminated conservative ideology.

There are, of course, many other reasons for using language in art. Jenny Holzer, for example, used language to articulate how sentences from the news or from advertisements become subconsciously held beliefs, and how the political and ethical ideas that these sentences express gain a hold on our thoughts and actions, without being subjected to our critical faculties. In many ways, this work continues the ideas of Weiner. In both cases, the artist strongly distinguishes between the ideational content of the sentences and the mode in which they are conveyed (e.g., the use of the electronic screens).

Another group of artists whose work bears relation to the conceptualists forms what can be called conceptual performance art. These artists create work based on the idea of using preset procedures involving themselves to create work that is at once conceptual and very personal. The original force behind this group is clearly Nauman and Graham. Many of the ideas belonging to this tradition, however, were developed by other artists—for example, by On Kawara. In Kawara's case, the work was based on actions that were performed each day (e.g., every day he sent postcards stating the fact that he was still alive). Many of Hana Darboven's works, too, were based on the daily iterations of various routines. Adrian Piper's performances should also be included in this category. Many of the performance and video artists who work on the West Coast continue this tradition.

Finally, those artists who continue the tradition of Duchamp and investigate the nature of the art object should be mentioned. In this tradition belongs Sherrie Levine's work, for example, which involves the idea of regarding the reproduction of existing works of art as themselves being works of art. [See Appropriation.]

The activities referred to as Conceptual Art in the extended sense of the term may be continuations of various paradigms introduced by the original conceptualists, but the connecting tissues are not always very strong. The art of the conceptualists of today is, in large measure, independent of its historical point of origin. Because the ideational content is emphasized by all the artists mentioned, however, the lines of continuity between the original conceptualists and their heirs are clearly visible and accorded considerable importance. In this sense, the tradition of conceptual art depends on the extent to which the work is perceived through intellectual and political categories rather than in formal or aesthetic terms. This shift may be the most important and enduring feature of conceptual art.

YAIR GUTTMAN

CONDILLAC, ÉTIENNE BONNOT DE (1715–1780), French philosopher.

Born in Grenoble and ordained a priest in 1740, the Abbé de Condillac was a central but somewhat atypical figure of the French Enlightenment. Although greatly admired by his contemporaries, he was a discreet and retiring man who had little taste for the Parisian salons in which the philosophes flourished. As a self-styled disciple of John Locke, Condillac did much to disseminate the doctrine of sensationalism with his treatises *Essai sur l'origine des connaissances humaines* (1746) and *Traité des sensations* (1754). In the *Essai* (conceived as a more orderly version of Locke's *Essay*), Condillac examined the primitive origins of human knowledge, including the inception of language and art. In the *Traité des sensations,* he proposed to explain the workings of the mind through an epistemological fable centered on a statue-man who acquires all of his mental and emotional faculties, save speech, via the successive activation of his senses. Condillac never wavered in his empiricist philosophy of the mind, yet he was not a pure sensationalist: despite the mechanistic tone of his epistemology, he insisted on the noncorporeal existence of the soul, and accorded a special status to creative genius in the development of each society's distinct culture. Moreover, although the notion of signs is absent from his statue-man fable, Condillac assigned a central role to language in the operations of perception and reflection. Language thus constitutes a major axis of his writings, which touched on fields that include psychology, history, political economy, the philosophy of language and science, and aesthetics.

Condillac began his career as a close friend of Denis Diderot and Jean-Jacques Rousseau, who were influenced by his views on the origins of the intellect and language; yet, he withdrew from worldly intellectual society soon after entering it. From 1758 to 1767, Condillac served as tutor to the young Prince of Parma, for whom he composed a *Cours d'études* (1775) that included treatises on grammar, history, and the arts of thinking and writing. He also wrote *La logique* (1780), a textbook on elementary logic that remained popular among French educators and philosophers until the 1830s (Albury, 1980). *La logique* is the most mature expression of Condillac's lifelong quest to devise a universal method of analytic thinking, and to remodel modern languages according to the principles of algebra, which he viewed as the only semiotic system to have attained the status of a truly "well-made" language (Aarsleff, 1982; Auroux, 1982).

Although Condillac's comments on aesthetics proper were indirect, he did include certain ideas on the origins and function of art in his theory of the mind. His most sustained discussion of this subject is found in part 2 of his *Essai sur les origines des connaissances humaines,* where he used his characteristically abstract, "genetic" method of analysis to explain the importance of language and art in the primitive development of the mental faculties. With his emphasis on social utility as the primary impetus for the evolution of the arts, his insistence that sentiment plays a greater role than reason in aesthetic experience, and his belief that every people has a unique "genius" that dictates the character of its language and art forms, Condillac can be said to have contributed to the demise of classical aesthetics (Knight, 1968). He was nonetheless highly conservative, if not elitist, on the question of taste: taste, as he defined it in the *Essai,* "is a manner of feeling so felicitous that one perceives the value of things without the aid of reflection. . . . It is the effect of an imagination that, having been exercised early on choice subjects, preserves their memory and naturally makes them models for comparison. It is for that reason that good taste is ordinarily restricted to high society."

Condillac was elected to the Académie française in 1768, and died in 1780, leaving behind two unfinished manuscripts, the *Langue des calculs* and the *Dictionnaire des syn-*

onymes. His philosophy remained influential for another fifty years: his method of analysis was widely applied by the scientists of the revolutionary and Napoleonic periods, and his philosophy was elevated to official academic status by the *idéologues* who controlled the French schools at the time. Condillac's influence as a philosopher was already waning by 1815, however, in part because of the spiritualist reaction against sensationalism led by Pierre Maine de Biran. Since the late 1960s, Condillac's theories have enjoyed renewed interest among both scholars of the Enlightenment and specialists in the history of linguistics.

[*See also* Diderot.]

BIBLIOGRAPHY

Work by Condillac

Œuvres philosophiques de Condillac. 3 vols. Paris, 1947–1951.

Other Sources

Aarsleff, Hans. *From Locke to Saussure: Essays on the Study of Language and Intellectual History.* Minneapolis, 1982. See pp. 146–207.
Albury, W. R. Translator's Introduction. In Condillac, *La logique/Logic,* pp. 7–34. New York, 1980.
Auroux, Sylvain. "Empirisme et théorie linguistique chez Condillac." In *Condillac et les problèmes du langage.* Geneva, 1982.
Cassirer, Ernst. *The Philosophy of the Enlightenment.* Translated by Fritz C. A. Koelln and James P. Pettegrove. Princeton, N.J., 1951; reprint, Boston, 1955.
Derrida, Jacques. "L'archéologie du frivole." Preface to Condillac, *Essai sur l'origine des connaissances humaines,* pp. 15–57. Paris, 1973.
Diderot, Denis. *Lettre sur les aveugles à l'usage de ceux qui voient* (1749).
Knight, Isabel F. *The Geometric Spirit: The Abbé de Condillac and the French Enlightenment.* New Haven, 1968.
Le Roy, Georges. "Introduction à l'œuvre philosophique de Condillac." In *Œuvres philosophiques de Condillac,* vol. 1, pp. vii–xxxi. Paris, 1947.
Maine de Biran, Pierre. *Mémoire sur la décomposition de la pensée* (1805). In *Œuvres,* vol. 3. Paris, 1984.
Rousseau, Jean-Jacques. *Discours sur l'origine de l'inégalité parmi les hommes* (1754).
Sgard, Jean, ed. *Condillac et les problèmes du langage.* Geneva, 1982.
Thomas, Downing A. *Music and the Origins of Language: Theories from the French Enlightenment.* Cambridge, 1995.

ANNE VILA

CONNOISSEURSHIP. *See* Berenson; Stokes; *and* Wordsworth.

CONSTRUCTIVISM. From its Russian and revolutionary beginnings in 1915, through its relations with the Bauhaus, to its incarnations in England, Italy, and Latin America, the Constructivist project of art and design has been of central importance to twentieth-century culture. Its emphasis on art as a process of abstract construction from basic design materials and forms has engendered major stylistic achievements, including some of the first composed sculptures, abstract paintings, and uses of new technologies (the photogram, kinetic sculpture). Its approach has set an example of clarity of vision and formal purity in art; Constructivist writers and teachers from Vladimir Tatlin, El Lissitzky, and Naum Gabo to László Moholy-Nagy and Jesús Soto have taught generations to appreciate the aim of exploring how far and with what degree of lucidity a plastic medium can be articulated. These internal commitments in art have been matched by the scope of Constructivism's utopian aspirations for art in the larger social world. If its utopian aspirations have not been fulfilled, its design legacy has extended to the fabric of the present world, from our concepts to our doorknobs, teapots, Op art murals, buildings, and cities.

Central to Constructivism is the idea that artworks are designed to actively and explicitly exhibit their mode of construction from simple geometrical elements, materials, or colors. No doubt all art to some degree exhibits its mode of (formal) composition—be it the perspectival lucidity of Piero della Francesca's compositions or the fragmented angularities of late Cubist work. Constructivism, however, makes the exhibition of the object's mode of construction the central point of its work. Moreover, Constructivism dynamizes form, presents it as an active compositional agent, as if what is at stake is the thrusting of new and experimental modes of construction onto the world that would abolish the old and create the radically new. The utopianism residing at the basis of Constructivist art derives from the rhetoric in this process of laying bare the work's internal structure, of designing it so that it gives the impression of a world under transparent construction. Gabo, theorist of Constructivism and chief writer of the *Constructivist Manifesto* (1924), speaks of the art object as a "demonstration" of its own construction from simple and indubitable parts, thus extending René Descartes's language of proof to the domain of art and, by extension, historical reality. He illustrates this principle by means of a cross-sectional representation of a simple cube whose inner geometry is thereby made transparent to perception—as if Constructivist sculptures could and did measure up to the clarity of this geometrical form's construction from its "Euclidean" parts.

For Gabo, what matters is simply complete transparency of form, not the discovery of scientific facts or principles. Needless to say, Gabo never achieves such "complete transparency": his sculptures are not conceptually "simple" in the way mere geometrical cubes are. What Gabo's sculptures provide is the *feel* of transparency rather than transparency taken as a geometrical criterion of construction. They feel transparent in roughly the same way that a Miesian office building or Bauhaus factory feels cleanly functional. For both, the art is to make the building look functional, to make it celebrate the functional with complete modernist audacity, as if the functional were an expressive requirement. The most crystalline of the Constructivists

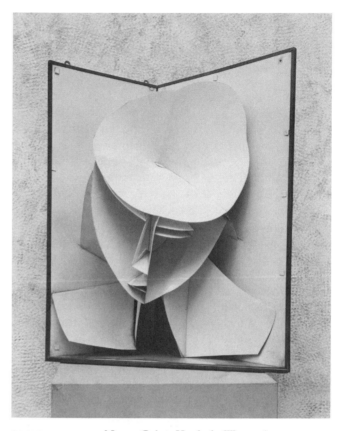

CONSTRUCTIVISM. Naum Gabo, *Head of a Woman* (c.1917–1929, after a work of 1916), construction in celluloid and metal, 24 1/2 × 19 1/4 × 14 inches (62.2 × 48.9 × 35.4 cm); Museum of Modern Art, New York (Purchase). (Photograph copyright 1998 by the Museum of Modern Art; used by permission.)

and possibly the most articulate, his innovations lay in making sculpture abstract, in freeing it from depiction and reliance on weight of materials as a basis of sculptural expression—something he commenced to do around 1920.

By 1915, Vladimir Tatlin, the first of the Constructivists, had already removed sculpture from the realm of depiction. Tatlin's wood constructions (under the influence of Pablo Picasso's pictorial collages from 1912 and 1913) bring a range of found materials to the sculptural arena, but for Tatlin this is not to enlarge the possible depictive resonances of such materials. Rather, Tatlin aims in his wood constructions for an abstract organization of elements in which an architecture is felt to evolve that derives from the densities and sizes of the materials. Tatlin constructs his complex shapes like an engineer, integrating the specific gravities and stresses of his materials into an overall plan.

Tatlin's sculptural constructions fundamentally rely on the strong downward gravitational pull in their heavy materials for their power and force. His wood constructions, stuck in the corners of rooms with large pieces of metal and wood horizontally emergent from them, seem at once to acknowledge and to actively defy the force of gravity, as if they are hard at work in their fight with that determining force. The Tatlin artwork seems to force its own labor of existence onto one. One feels its labor—a difficult, exuberant, and determined labor—just as one feels its pictorial clarity, as if it is a painting that has arrived three-dimensionally off the wall.

Gabo's use of materials is quite different. He chooses materials for their potential transparency rather than for their gravity or resistance to gravity, thus dispensing with a sculptural tradition as old as Archaic bronzes (and as famous as Michelangelo Buonarotti) that forges sculptural expression from the musical and dramatic interplay between sculptural materials and the downward-pulling force of gravity. Gabo favors plastic, Perspex, and metals that can be employed with the lightness of a Miesian steel-and-glass curtain wall. (In this, Gabo is closer to Moholy-Nagy, who uses glass in a series of constructions done in the 1920s.) Gabo aims for a kind of floating transparency of form that negates all role for the pull of gravity in sculptural expression.

Gabo conceives of the rhythmic, kinetic element in his art as the bearer of time. When Gabo announces in the "Realist Manifesto" that "space and time are re-born in us today," he means that his artwork exemplifies the construction of life both in space and in time. In their radiant, lucid pas de deux with space, Gabo's sculptural forms mirror change, growth, action, and reaction. What is remarkable about a Gabo sculpture is its capacity to at once claim a dynamic or musical relation with the space it inhabits and at the same time to seem as self-transparent as a nineteenth-century bridge or a geodesic dome.

This celebration of the complexity of immersion, the convergence of avant-garde excitement and spirituality, can also be found in the sparkling, abstract paintings of Liubov Popova.

The metaphysical principle by which Constructivism announces fully transparent self-construction as the route by which the revolutionary future will be brought about is Cartesian: it claims that the historical future of humanity can be similarly planned from scratch (from the bottom up, from simple elements according to clear formation rules) in a way that would allow its inner design to be perfectly manifest in historical reality. Constructivism thus believed (at least in its more optimistic moods) that its artworks were the proof to the world that the new historical reality could be brought about with equivalent visual, and hence conceptual, control. The Constructivist "laboratory" was meant to stand in the forefront of history as an avant-garde exemplar to the world that it too could jump on the bandwagon and experimentally create cities, societies, and global systems out of the "raw materials" of history.

Yet, the Constructivist object is also an "acid that bites into everything it touches" (Lissitzky), a "sermon in metal"

(Vladimir Mayakovsky), preached in the clanging, ebullient currency of hard historical construction about the labor of art and of historical change. It is an act of profound experimentation, an attempt to stretch the human sensorium in new directions and to appropriate new technologies (almost every Constructivist—with the exception of Liubov Popova—gave up painting as an art too tied to the bourgeois excrescences of past art in favor of such new technologies and materials as the photogram, metallic sculpture, work in graphic media, and the like).

The claim to abandon art to the clanging of experimentation and at the same time to preserve total transparency in the art world translated into a utopian belief that the revolutionary (whether an artist or an activist) could ride the whirl of sublime historical change yet remain in control of the underlying historical plan. In this, Constructivism was in accord with the utopianism of Karl Marx; for although Marx believed that the revolutionary path to the future classless society was a historical plan rationally determined by the forces of history, when it came time for him to speak in detail about how history would approach and "construct" its apogee, he found himself at a loss. Marx referred to the transition to a classless society as a "vague immensity," an event of enormous proportions that he could not envision. Nobody could have envisioned it, granted its radical character, granted how much of ordinary life would have had to have changed in order for the revamped world of the revolution to happen. Imagination is essentially constrained by the here and now, and the radically new (the utopian) must therefore remain a dimly felt, if historically "inevitable," dream.

This conceptual point about the position of the utopian dreamer allows one to understand why the laboratory in which Constructivism created and theorized its art objects was, like the Bauhaus (1919–1933), a laboratory of constantly shifting strategies for design and constantly new theoretical approaches; for the utopian must approach a future that demands to be imagined (for it must be planned in practice and exemplified in images), yet that cannot be imagined but is at best felt like the luminous light of a distant planet. Thus, the utopian must experiment with a variety of images of it, including theoretical images, in order to make it, and the route to it, comprehensible. Utopia brings forth the aesthetics of the sublime, the question of finding ways to present, exemplify, plan, and bring about the as yet unpresentable (unimaginable, conceptualized in detail). The relentless search for new theoretical as well as design images became central to art practice in the context of the avant-garde laboratory. These terms of art practice are still fundamental to postmodernism, proving it to be a direct legacy of avant-garde art in this respect.

The work of the Hungarian artist Moholy-Nagy most clearly exemplifies this aesthetic. Moholy-Nagy, a member of both the Constructivist movement and the Bauhaus (and the founding director of New Bauhaus in Chicago), held two somewhat contradictory theories of the role of art in the construction of the new world. First, according to his biologically based conception of the human, a person is a conglomeration of "functional apparatuses" whose extension and satisfaction are the goals of art and life. Art trains the mind by stretching it to embrace new configurations and connections. Moholy-Nagy's theory is offered as a defense of modernism, a rationale for the new and experimental in art. It is nowhere better exemplified than in his photographs, which, like those of Aleksandr Rodchenko, picture cities at oblique angles and often from above. Their tilted, vertiginous perspective renders everything in motion by dynamizing the viewer, for the viewer feels as if he or she is seeing the shape while momentarily twisting to the side or falling toward it from a curved height. Moholy-Nagy's synoptic, wide-angle perspective is most explicit in his photographs of people, squares, and buildings. These masterful executions from above and from oblique angles dynamize the scene by presenting it from an angle that the viewer can take up only by feeling himself or herself move toward or away from what is shown. The kinesthetic relation one must assume toward his photographed event makes one intensely aware that one *has* a position, which could change—indeed, must change— were one to follow it through, for one could no more remain in the position of falling toward what is shown than one could remain suspended in the middle of a cathedral of light after jumping from its flying buttresses. The viewer is then taught the lesson that perception exists in the process of continuous construction and reformulation.

But second, Moholy-Nagy believes that art should play a role in the search for principles on which to build a (better) world. Art experiments should not only stretch the mind's capacities but also serve in the discovery of the "biological universals of human needs and human social organization": principles that may be used to improve life. This search for universals (a central Bauhaus preoccupation) turns art into a branch of experimental, biological science. Art (especially architecture and design) is meant at once to discover these laws and to design its objects, office spaces, and houses in accord with them. From this perspective, Moholy-Nagy's goal is not to create new forms of vision in us but to scientifically discover universal and stable laws of vision and visual aesthetics to which we all, as human beings, conform. His former conception points the way toward the creation of what the modernist will call, in his gendered way, the "new man," by extending his biological apparatuses and changing his life. His other conception points the way not toward the creation of a new person but toward the discovery of stable laws about the old and conservative person whose discovery and implementation in good aesthetics will help that person to live better.

We can see that Moholy-Nagy's commitment both to a stable conception of the person that makes her the object of visual science and to a conception of the person that views her as experimentally malleable derives from the requirements of avant-garde, utopian art. His commitment to constructing a new world order according to a utopian plan of construction required him to believe that the human being exhibits universal and stable laws that would make such planning possible. This commitment to the design of the future pushed the Bauhaus generally in the direction of a scientific theory of design. On the other hand, Moholy-Nagy's position as an artist who desired to bring about a utopian future that was as yet unimaginable to him in any detail pushed him, as it had to push any such artist, in the direction of wishing to create a new and as yet unenvisioned person: the new man who would inhabit this dreamlike, dimly felt utopian world. Hence, Moholy-Nagy was required to trust in a conception of vision that stressed the malleability of vision and the capacity of a new person and a new world to arise through cultural experimentation itself.

It is in the rhetoric of El Lissitzky's *Prouns* (literally, projects for the construction of the new) where the full acidity of Constructivist rhetoric and the full throttle of Constructivist force can be found. For Lissitzky, the very existence of art is justified because and only because art is a form of work. According to Lissitzky, art as a concept is fundamentally in doubt; art must be pressed to justify its existence as labor or die. If it cannot produce sermons in metal that will stimulate the future, if it cannot speak in the name of Marxist science and human social requirement, if it cannot pose its own construction with such Cartesian clarity that it will serve as a utopian model for how the future might be similarly constructed, it will be expelled from the pantheon of culture as a late-bourgeois excrescence better suited to the mausoleum of European history. Thus, one can find in certain regions of Constructivism the seeds of political correctness, which demands that art legitimate itself through its political/utopian roles. Indeed, this demand for art to be of "immediate use" caused a whole element within the Constructivist movement, led by as great a painter and sculptor as Tatlin, not only to give up painting (which just about every Constructivist did), but to give up much of what one thinks of as art generally, in favor of directly utilitarian furniture, clothing, and theater design. In 1924, Tatlin turned exclusively to graphic design, architecture, and engineering, and he designed a stove—endeavors that he thought had more social utility than painting or sculpture. In effect, Tatlin retained the old eighteenth-century distinction between the fine arts and the useful or functional arts, but reversed the evaluation of the pair: useful arts were to be the more valued of the two. Lissitzky, Gabo, Antoine Pevsner, and others did not follow this low road with Tatlin; however, they felt the need to stress a thousand ways in which plastic arts (painting, sculpture, and design) could satisfy the mandate of revolutionary work. Their aim was to make the unfolding of a Constructivist work more labor-intensive, labor-explicit, and labor-celebratory than any art of the past.

There is always a vast space between an art movement's own vision of its role in history, that is, its vision of its power to effect historical change, and what is really the case. In fact, Vladimir Lenin had tolerated Constructivism without having much enthusiasm for it. But Joseph Stalin actively despised it (and all productions that inculcated the free play of the revolutionary imagination). By the mid-1930s, the movement (along with similar movements in cinema and literature) was decimated, its vision of the historical sublime replaced by the constricted, politically correct, and nationalist art of Socialist Realism, its inernational dreams of a transformed world indefinitely deferred by the Stalinist ideology of "socialism in one country." Gabo emigrated to England; others, such as Tatlin and Lissitzky, were cast into obscurity. Popova died. Kasimir Malevich, the great Minimalist painter of iconic spirituality and the inventor of abstract painting (simultaneously produced by the American Georgia O'Keefe), ended his career by painting enormous figures with visages as empty as machines, a paean to the existential anhedonia of the "new man." The history of Constructivism was transposed to Italy, Spain, American, England, and especially Latin America, where it was recast in the form of the desire to turn the local color of Latin culture into the professionalized and modernized space of the International Style.

According to the Venezuelan painter Soto (1974), what Latin America needed to be taught by its Constructivist painters was how to become part of the modern, rational world in one fell swoop that would eliminate and overcome its tendency toward magical (read: irrational) realism. Soto's Optical art is complex and original and his theory utopian. But it is another of the Venezuelan constructivists, Carlos Cruz-Diez, who succeeds in being both a utopian and a practical artist with pragmatic ideas about the way that art and aesthetic theory can help improve the barrios of Caracas, Venezuela. Cruz-Diez's studio is at the edge of such a barrio in the center of Caracas, and there he is known as "the painter" because of his frequent forays into that community. Cruz-Diez works with people to make their houses better organized and more aesthetic, to make street signs more legible and colorful, to make playgrounds more playable and fun, to construct things that are simple, safe, and beautiful. He is among the few in the history of Constructivism who have taken the practical value of Constructivist design off its messianic horse and into the local streets in a way that works with people rather than imposing utopian form onto their environment. Tatlin had already tried to produce useful products for the masses but had directed his inventiveness to the field of the creation of "universal prototypes" like the Bauhaus. When Russian Constructivists worked contextually, they did so in the theater and the world of the artistic typeface, not in the streets. By

contrast, Cruz-Diez's appreciation for the local context in which "social construction" ought to take place and his sense of the contextual character of design brand him as an early postmodernist in the field of design, one whose theoretical utopianism and commitments to artistic transparency are moderated by a pragmatic contextualism that addresses not "man" as a universal, theoretical (and gendered) item, but instead, actual people. Cruz-Diez does not sermonize; he looks, listens, and responds.

[*See also* Avant-Garde; Bauhaus; Design; Modernism, *overview article;* Russian Aesthetics; Sculpture; *and* Suprematism.]

BIBLIOGRAPHY

Bann, Stephen, ed. *The Tradition of Constructivism.* New York, 1974; reprint, New York, 1990.
Bowlt, John E., ed. *Russian Art of the Avant-Garde: Theory and Criticism, 1902–1934.* Rev. enl. ed. London, 1988.
Bürger, Peter. *The Theory of the Avant-Garde.* Translated by Michael Shaw. Minneapolis, 1984.
El Lissitzky, 1890–1941. Cambridge, Mass., 1987. Exhibition catalog, Busch-Resinger Museum.
Herwitz, Daniel. *Making Theory/Constructing Art: On the Authority of the Avant-Garde.* Chicago, 1993.
Krauss, Rosalind E. *Passages in Modern Sculpture.* New York, 1977; reprint, Cambridge, Mass., 1988.
Lewison, Jeremy, ed. *Circle: Constructive Art in Britain, 1934–1940.* Cambridge, 1982. Catalog of the exhibition Circles: International Survey of Constructive Art, held at Kettle's Yard Gallery, 20 February–24 March 1982. See "Constructive Art" by Naum Gabo, pp. 59–61.
Milner, John. *Vladimir Tatlin and the Russian Avant-Garde.* New Haven, 1983.
Passuth, Kriztina. *Moholy-Nagy.* Translated by E. Grusz et al. New York, 1985.
Perloff, Marjorie. *The Futurist Moment: Avant-Garde, Avant-Guerre, and the Language of Rupture.* Chicago, 1986.
Soto, Jesús. *Soto: A Retrospective Exhibition.* New York, 1974. Exhibition catalog, Solomon R. Guggenheim Museum.

DANIEL HERWITZ

CONTEMPORARY ART.

[*This entry comprises three essays on contemporary developments in the aesthetics of art.*

Postmodern Transformation of Art
Aesthetics of Contemporary Art
Images and Desire

The first essay explains the historical and conceptual background of contemporary art, namely, modernism and the transition to postmodernism. The second essay explores the aesthetics of contemporary art, emphasizing many of its defining theoretical influences and concrete cases. The third essay, written by an artist, explores the prominent issues of desire, the body, and feminism that are prominent in contemporary art. For further discussion, see Appropriation; Computer Art; Conceptual Art; Digital Media; Installation Art; *and* Performance Art.]

Postmodern Transformation of Art

In the Western world, the art history of the generation that followed World War II was dominated by the achievements of the New York school, especially Abstract Expressionist painting. This period—roughly 1945 to 1965 or 1970—is, art-historically, late modernism. It is almost exactly coterminous with the chronology of its crowning manifestation, Abstract Expressionism. That movement may be said to begin in 1947–1948, when both Jackson Pollock, with *Cathedral* and *Full Fathom Five*, and Barnett Newman, with *Onement I*, made their major breakthroughs into their signature styles and formats. It may be conceived as ending in the late 1960s, with the Rothko Chapel paintings, which may be regarded as the movement's cenotaph.

Kant and Late Modernism. Abstract Expressionism was the culminating moment of what many would regard as the central thread of Western art in the twentieth century: the abstract sublime. Visually, this tradition had dim roots going back to J. M. W. Turner's paintings of the 1840s, but it began with all possible clarity with Kasimir Malevich's *Black Square,* often dated to 1915, and continued through the eras of Suprematism, Neoplasticism, and the mid-century metaphysical monochrome, to culminate in Abstract Expressionism, especially the work of Newman, Pollock, Mark Rothko, Willem de Kooning, Franz Kline, and Adolph Gottlieb.

Modernist abstraction, with the sublime at its center, has been theorized in various ways since the end of the epoch itself. (More recent neo-abstractionist revivals, such as Simulationism or Neo-geo, do not appear to be continuations of the age so much as reprisals of or responses to it.) In the catalogs of major exhibitions in the 1980s, attempts were made to derive abstract metaphysical art from the coming of the machine age, from the tradition of alchemy, and from the varied European tradition of occult societies in general. In each case, an argument was presented to the effect that the work had a referent and that it was such and such. There may be a grain of truth to each of these claims, but during the actual era of Abstract Expressionism they were not heard.

In its own day, the work was theorized primarily either through the metaphysical approach articulated by Harold Rosenberg or the formalist approach of Clement Greenberg. Greenberg's view, for better or for worse, clearly became dominant, and has continued to exercise an amazing dominance in certain contexts. In this view, Abstract Expressionism was "pure painting," meaning that it lacked any external referent whatever. It was form without content. It is clear that some of the artists involved felt misrepresented by this claim, but nevertheless that is how the work was widely understood in its day.

Greenberg's approach to art was based on the theory articulated by Immanuel Kant in the *Critique of Judgment* (1790). This theory had older—indeed, ancient—roots, representing what Richard Rorty has called "the Plato to Kant axis," but Kant's articulation of it was the most influential for the nineteenth and twentieth centuries. Kant argued in general that the human personality is made up of three faculties—each of which he treated in one of his *Critiques:* a cognitive faculty (treated in the *Critique of Pure Reason*); a social or ethical faculty (the *Critique of Practical Reason*); and an aesthetic faculty (the *Critique of Judgment,* or the *Critique of Taste*). [*See* Kant.]

This trichotomy was actually quite ancient; Kant may have encountered it first in Aristotle's *Nicomachean Ethics.* But Kant was distinctive in shifting emphasis from the faculties themselves to the relationship among the faculties, which he argued was one of separateness or isolation, conceiving the three faculties on the model of the senses. Just as one cannot use the hearing or touch senses to confirm or disconfirm the visual sense's impression that it is seeing red, so one cannot use either the cognitive or ethical faculties to confirm or disconfirm a judgment of quality that the aesthetic sense has made. The faculties, like the senses, deal with radically separate domains and can have nothing to say about one another.

Greenberg's distinction, in turn, was to pursue this doctrine of the isolation of the faculties to an extreme conclusion that gained a powerful hold on the art consciousness of his time. If, he argued, the aesthetic faculty is completely isolated from the cognitive and ethical ones, then the artwork should exclude all cognitive and social references. There should be nothing in the work that needs to be grasped by the cognitive faculty (no language, no ideas, no representations of recognizable objects, no element of narrativity or iconography) nor anything that needs to be grasped by the ethical faculty (no social distress, pleas for compassion, conundrums of love). Nothing was to be allowed into the pure painting but the abstract working of color and line, whose appeal would bypass the other faculties and target the aesthetic bull's-eye exclusively. [*See* Greenberg.]

From this premise other ramifications followed. The artist himself (late modernism did not really recognize women artists) was expected to be noncognitive, as his work was. The artist was not supposed to be able to give a linguistic account of what he was doing; if he could do so, then something was wrong. Pollock, inarticulate almost to the point of speaking in grunts, became the paradigm of the artist—a creature of pure intuition whose sensibility channeled directly into the personal and collective unconsciousnesses, dredging up configurations of line and color that were and remained unaccountable. Their unaccountability was in fact the warranty of their authenticity.

Antimodernism. This intensified mode of the Kantian theory held sway in the United States, under the name "Formalism," for at least twenty years—from, say, 1945 to

1965. It still dominates many American university departments of art and art history, but it is no longer dominant among artists and critics who are engaged in the foreground discourse of contemporary art—that is, the discourse that will eventuate in the art-history texts used in the universities of the next generation.

The transition from the Formalist discourse to another was slow, and proceeded at first through an age of pluralism in which the somewhat enforced critical consensus that had maintained the hegemony of Formalism came apart. Already in the 1950s there were counterstatements. When Robert Rauschenberg, for example, stated his intention to work in the gap between art and life, and when Jasper Johns, in the same decade, used everyday objects and representations of them in his paintings, they were implicitly combating the Greenbergian doctrine of the extreme *sui causa* isolation of the artwork from the rest of the world.

In the 1960s, criticism of the doctrine of the pure painting became more widespread and strident, especially as the United States' involvement in the war in Vietnam accelerated. As the whole society went into crisis, with the civil rights and Black Power and women's movements fueling the intensity of the antiwar movement, pure aesthetic abstraction came to seem a useless and arid preoccupation. Many artists began to wonder what good this mode of communication was if it did not allow one to communicate about the most pressing issues of society. To many it came to seem not merely an asocial doctrine but actually an antisocial one, in that it eliminated art as a force for social change and relegated the artist to the periphery. Carolee Schneemann once remarked, about that period, that it was as if the artists were children who were sent to the nursery to play with their crayons while the grown-ups, in another room, dealt with the real issues of life.

Many artists who had received formalist training in art schools, and began in good faith to continue the directions they were trained in there, felt betrayed: they had been trained in an archaic mode that had already been denounced by the leading artists of their time. John Baldessari's act, in 1968, of burning all his paintings, then giving an exhibition of the ashes, was an anti-formalist gesture characteristic of the time; it was also characteristic of the time that Formalism was more or less equated with the tradition of painting, and for a time the anti-formalist stance expressed itself primarily through attacks on painting.

Vito Acconci summed up this attitude when, being asked in a discussion in Los Angeles what he thought was the most dangerous word in the English language, he replied, "Beauty." The hierarchy of values was completely reversed: whereas the artist had once been told that he should act only on the mandate of pure beauty, he now was to gird himself to do battle *against* beauty on the grounds that it was a false face or pretty cover-up for the dismal problems of society.

This polar reversal of the artist's mandate was the first stage of what has come to be called postmodernism in the visual arts; that first stage could be called antimodernism, since its task was the undermining and subversion of the foundational ideas of modernism, a clearing of the field, as it were, so that something else could take place upon it.

Hegel and Late Modernism. These foundational ideas extended far beyond the milieu of art, dominating the conceptualization of international history for several centuries. They include the idea of progress, which served as a justification for colonialism and imperialism. G. W. F. Hegel, the most influential Western philosopher of this subject, viewed history as the incarnation of the force of progress; that is, history has, built into it, a certain trajectory; it is going toward a certain end or goal, and that is why Western (capitalist, democratic) societies revere the dynamic of change—because the imperative of change shows that a society is on its way toward the goal of history; a static society, on the contrary, has gotten stuck somewhere along the path. [*See* Hegel.] On this reasoning Hegel stated, in *The Philosophy of History*, based on a series of lectures given in 1822, that "World history happens in Europe," and that Africa, China, and so on, were "ahistorical." The self-proclaimed "advanced" nations of Europe had to take the rest of the world in hand and drag it into history. Empire was "the white man's burden," as Rudyard Kipling put it.

The idea of progress was buttressed by the idea of the hierarchization of cultures: if all societies are innately going toward the same end, yet there are great differences among them, then one way to account for those differences is to assert that some societies are farther along toward the goal than others. The idea of hierarchization was buttressed in turn by the positing of transcultural universals that alone could justify the assertion that one society was more advanced than another. Western society, supposedly, was plugged directly into the universals, which other societies had missed.

The Romantic doctrine of aesthetics, which was more or less the high- and late-modernist one, consisted of the Kantian doctrine of sensibility with an added historical aspect supplied by Hegel and the so-called analytic art historians, especially Karl Schnaase. It was Schnaase who explicitly transposed the global doctrine of Hegel to the small specialized realm of visual art. As he wrote in *Niederländische Briefe* (1834), the onward-rushing advance of history could be seen most purely and clearly in the development, from generation to generation, of linked series of formal problems and solutions in the visual arts. As this view developed in the Romantic era, the doctrine of genius presented an individual form of the global process. The imperative of originality and innovation in art reflected the force of progress. The (claimed) art-historical leadership of the West reflected the hierarchization of cultures; and the belief that pure painting can ascend beyond the world, to bring back glimpses of a timeless beyond, reflected the posited universals.

Whether educated in philosophy or not—whether familiar with the names Kant and Hegel or not—everyone engaged in the art activity in the West in the late-modernist period was permeated with this ideology, which had become so universal as to seem natural or given. In fact, when it began to become clear, in the early 1960s, that this ideology was losing credibility, the fact seemed astounding. But modernism was rooted above all in the myth of progress, and by the 1950s and 1960s the myth of European culture leading the rest of the world to the culmination of history had taken an ironic and painful turn. Two world wars, the Holocaust, the development (and actual *use* against a nonwhite culture) of nuclear endgame weaponry, the dizzying proliferation of ecological disasters—these and other factors had revealed the dark side of the Hegelian myth: the end of history that we were supposedly advancing toward was not to be a happy ending; it would be nothing less than the destruction, or self-destruction, of our world. Malevich's *Black Square* was simply the abyss of darkness and oblivion following this destruction.

The Transformation of Painting. John Barth remarked, at a panel on postmodernism in Denton, Texas, in 1986, that postmodernism in America began on 22 November 1963 with the assassination of John F. Kennedy. He seems to have meant that at that moment many Americans began to realize, with an uneasy feeling of surprise, that history seemed to be taking us in some monstrous direction we did not want to go.

In terms of the arts, the postmodern realization became increasingly unavoidable in the postwar period; it began to sprout almost unnoticed within the rich garden of Abstract Expressionism. In the late 1950s, performance art began with works such as Claes Oldenburg's *Happenings*. In 1963, Henry Flynt invented the term *concept art,* which Sol LeWitt, in 1967, altered to *conceptual art,* the term that became entrenched. Both these developments need to be seen as reactions against the Kantian legacy (although most Americans thought of it as Greenbergian). [*See* Conceptual Art.]

The Kantian trichotomy of faculties was one of the central targets. Formalism had excluded the cognitive aspect from the art experience, so conceptual art brought cognition into the center. Artists such as Joseph Kosuth, Lawrence Weiner, William Anastasi, and Robert Barry made cognition the very material of the artwork, shaping it as artists had once shaped clay or paint. Similarly, formalism had excluded the social or ethical from art, so performance artists brought the social or ethical to the center. This was especially true of the early period known as body art, in which Hermann Nitsch, Chris Burden, Schneemann, and others made their own bodies the site of the artwork, often involving themselves in real physical danger. Because it involves the artist's actual body, and because the artist of-

ten lays his or her body on the line, performance art is innately ethicist in its goals; its relationship to ancient ritual and its confrontational approach to social authority made it innately social as well. [*See* Performance Art.]

In the antimodernist, or early postmodernist, period, the 1960s and early 1970s, both these movements persisted in inverting the Greenbergian hierarchy: cognition and ethicism, previously excluded, were now at the center; the aesthetic aspect, previously at the center, was now on the periphery and neutralized. Of course, as long as the artist was making a physical object, design decisions could not be avoided except through the use of randomness or chance. Classical conceptualists of the 1970s actually tried to eliminate the aesthetic aspect from their work altogether, but always there remained design decisions, and always the design decisions impinged on sensibility. The point became to acknowledge but minimalize, or somehow neutralize, the shameful aspect of aesthetic sensibility. This was the root of many conceptualist strategies worked out with surgeonly precision with the critical scalpel. In Kosuth's use of reversed photostats of dictionary definitions, for example, the size of the piece, the reversing of the black and white, the framing and hanging were all design decisions, but minimal ones that tended to disappear or efface themselves in the viewer's experience. Similarly, Weiner's classic works with words and phrases painted on the wall involved decisions of typeface (serif or sans serif), size, and placement on the wall—again, relatively minimal recourse to sensibility.

Meanwhile, painting—because it above all genres had virtually deified sensibility, and had been deeply complicit in the modernist project of prettifying reality and positing an imminent sublime—was reviled. The claim that painting was dead had been heard before, but never with such intensity or widespread credibility. Abstract painting above all seemed outlandishly alien suddenly, like an evil force that one had luckily driven out in the nick of time. In the museums of Europe and the United States, the 1970s are almost invisible, because of their characteristic avoidance of the aesthetic object.

Then, in the late 1970s, painting began to come back from the dead. It seemed bizarre and almost frightening, as if the corpse of Formalism had risen like a zombie from the grave. But in fact that was not the case. Young artists who chose the medium of paint on canvas again in the late 1970s and early 1980s had been raised and educated in the era of conceptual and performance art. They could not ignore it; it had been one of the forces shaping them. To go into denial about it would be to betray a part of themselves. Thus, what ensued was not a return of pure painting in the late-modernist sense, but a practice of painting that had been deeply revised by the conceptualist and performative critiques of formalism. It was, in a sense, not painting per se at all but a new genre that could be called conceptual painting—or, even, conceptual art that uses painting as its means. In a way, this was the most telling moment of the postmodern revision, because it was painting itself, once the cherished vehicle of modernism, that now was carrying forward its critique. This was the end of the first, or antimodernist, phase of postmodernism.

Quotational Painting. In the 1980s, conceptual painters, often self-consciously postmodernist, carried out a clear and detailed deconstruction of the ideology of pure painting. Most focused their efforts, with quasi-scientific precision, on one limb or another of the ideology. One of the favored strategies was appropriation or quotation.

Since the 1950s there had been occasional artists whose method had involved the undisguised appropriation or quotation of famous works by earlier artists. Pop artists also appropriated—or "quoted"—images, usually from popular cultural sources such as comic books and advertising; this too was an early manifestation of the postmodernist spirit, intended to deflate the bubble of metaphysical self-importance with which Abstract Expressionism had surrounded itself. But it was not until the early 1980s that this practice found a moment that could supply a compelling theoretical justification for it. For postmodernist artists of the early and mid-1980s, repetition of images, styles, or motifs from earlier ages, openly flaunting the imitative nature of the practice and mocking the idea of genius or innovation, was understood as a deliberate confounding of the idea of history as progress, and of the idea of the originality of the artist as the embodiment or instrument of progress.

Around 1982, artists such as Sherry Levine and Mike Bidlo began making and exhibiting quotational works. [*See* Appropriation.] Levine copied works by canonical male artists—Fernand Léger, Paul Klee, and others—but altered the medium, employing, instead of oil and canvas, watercolor and paper in a reduced size. She had transposed the icons of male innovation into smaller, delicate, and less declarative feminine modes. Bidlo, by contrast, performing homage to the supposedly masculine force of Genius, copied classical modernist works in their original materials and sizes. There was something simultaneously comical and profound in this sight of young artists abrogating the Romantic mandate of innovation—the cult of the future—by turning cultically to the past. But there was a mischief to the cult. Historical sequences—such as, say, the transition from Geometric to Archaic, or from Mannerism to Baroque—that had seemed sacrosanct and inevitable within the modernist cult of history now were tauntingly discombobulated and naughtily tossed up into the air to fall where they might.

The project of tangling up historical linearity, and with it the idea of progress, was taken to another limit by Pat Steir in her *Brueghel Series: A Vanitas of Style* (1982–1984), in which she included sixty-four panels, each quoting a specific painterly style from the Renaissance to the 1980s. Together, these sixty-four panels made up a greater image of a vase of flowers painted by Jan Brueghel the Elder in 1599.

The various artists and their styles seemed not linear and transcendent but simultaneous and relative. She had engorged herself with all of them in one huge attack of appetite; by becoming them all, she made them all simultaneous. The linear onrush of history had smashed into a wall and flattened out.

The quotational practice attacked modernist purism from another direction in its flaunting of the idea of commitment to a style. A late-modernist artist such as Pollock or Newman was constrained by a signature style and, because this was supposedly based on unchanging universals, could not change it without betraying its claim. If it changed, then either the old style had not, in fact, been universal, or the new one would not—could not—be. The late-modernist worship of style as signature, as sign of selfhood, as fingerprint, of style as an embodiment of truth, was openly mocked by the quotational practice, in which styles became simply pieces to be moved about in a metagame or metastyle in which all particular styles are merely relative and it would be absurd to commit passionately to any.

Incorporation of Language. Late-modernist art, with its conviction about the separateness of the faculties, had for the most part excluded language from the artwork as irrelevantly cognitive. Conceptual art, in the early phase of postmodernism, had brought language into the very center of the work. In the 1980s, when painting came back from exile and these two approaches were sublated somewhat, language was reintegrated with the image in various ways.

Some artists, many of them women, such as Barbara Kruger and Jenny Holzer, viewed themselves as the inheritors of the conceptual tradition and integrated linguistic elements, often involving social protest (hence both the cognitive and the ethical faculties), with visual presences based on nonexpressionistic, technology-based media. For Holzer, it was the light sign; for Kruger, the found photograph, usually from magazine advertising.

Those artists, most of them men, who were called neo-Expressionist painters—such as Julian Schnabel and David Salle—began the decade of the 1980s with a tendency to reject language and revert to an ideology of pure form. But by the late 1980s, the gap had narrowed. In the early 1980s, Schnabel had been the most reviled by those perpetuating the saintly lineage of conceptualism; but, beginning in 1985, his paintings became increasingly conceptual, regularly incorporating language, sometimes using *only* a linguistic element presented in a painterly style.

A New Conception of the Artwork. By the late 1980s, a kind of Hegelian synthesis, or sublation, of these opposed forces had emerged. For the first time since the eighteenth century, a new conception of the artwork had established itself. Viewed in terms of the Aristotelian-Kantian trichotomy, it was an enlarged mandate: that the artwork should involve all three of the faculties in some way or proportion or other. This was felt as a recognition or acknowledgment of the wholeness of human experience, a wholeness achieved, paradoxically, through the multiplicity and contradictory nature of the various forces working together to drive a human self.

By the late 1980s, in the works of, say, Kruger and Schnabel, the aesthetic faculty was openly acknowledged, while the cognitive faculty was present in the linguistic element, as well as in other, mostly language-like, iconographic ways, and the ethical faculty was acknowledged through a tendency to link the work always with some social issue. In Kruger's case, this was often a feminist critique of the patriarchy mediated by ironic side-glances; in Schnabel's, it might be a lament about AIDS or a general profound nostalgia for the snows of yesteryear. Content and intelligence had come openly back into art.

The proportion among these three aspects varied with the artist's sensibility. Some focused fiercely on the ethical issue, making it the center of the work. Leon Golub's and Nancy Spero's works of political protest, from the late 1950s to the present, suddenly came to the forefront of attention at this time and seemed rivetingly new and unforeseen. Sue Williams concentrated on violence against women, as, sometimes, did Ida Apfelbroog and Nicholas Africano. Each of the three faculties was aggressively promoted by its group of artists; the general effect was that all were acknowledged and the interactions among them became a new focus of attention in the contemplation of the artwork.

Humor: The Sublime of the Ridiculous. The Surrealists, early in this century, sought to gain a kind of sublime by juxtaposing objects felt as alien to one another—by emphasizing (in terms of Plato's *Philebus*) difference over sameness. As the quotational art of the 1980s developed, various artists, rather than quoting a single iconic image, took to combining contradictory visual languages, often in ways that were perceived as provocative and humorous. Initially, as in the work of Malcolm Morley, Gerhard Richter, and Salle, contradictory visual languages from the same tradition were mixed—say, Abstract Expressionist painterliness combined with Neoplasticist geometry or naive representation. Subsequently, the contradictions involved were intercultural.

In the 1980s, Alexander Kosalopov, a Russian émigré living in New York, made multiculturalist quotational paintings that usually combined an image from American popular culture with an image from Soviet Marxist culture—say, the Coca-Cola logo with the official profile of Lenin, over the message: "It's the real thing." T. F. Chen, a Taiwanese by birth but now a resident of New York, combined images from the Western canon with those from the Eastern—say, Shinto warriors from medieval Japanese culture peering in a window at a reclining female figure based on Titian's *Venus of Urbino*. Masami Teraoka, Japanese-born, currently living in Hawaii, combined, in a very different spirit, images from

traditional Japanese culture with images from contemporary American popular culture—say, McDonald's hamburgers and foil-wrapped condoms.

By the mid- to late 1980s, the proliferation of such works in many nations suggested that the early phases of postmodernism, in which the West would deconstruct its own tradition, had given way to a larger and more mature phase in which the openness momentarily created by this deconstruction would be filled by the inrushing force of other cultures.

Postmodernism and Postcolonialism. Like Modernism, Postmodernism has been defined in various ways. Some who have contemplated it have stressed communications technology, which has brought cultures from around the globe into one another's homes, inevitably relativizing mores. Others have experienced it, in a crypto-Hegelian reverie, as an epiphenomenon of the onrush of the inevitable, the appearance of ambiguity being only a flourish or trick. To yet others it appears as a tentative liberation from history, the "nightmare from which I am trying to awaken," as Stephen Daedalus put it in *Ulysses*. Perhaps the most down-to-earth view, the view most rooted in the plain facts of history, sees the issue in terms of the passing of colonialism.

Trying to reduce things to the kernel, one might say that modernism was the ideology of colonialism, postmodernism the ideology of the postcolonial situation. When Michel Foucault talks about decentering, when Gilles Deleuze and Félix Guattari focus on nomadism, when Homi Bhabha applies the concept of hybridity, and so on, they are all talking about the ultimate bottom line: that in 1950 there were about fifty nations in the United Nations, and now there are some 180. The "freeing" of colonies began with the British withdrawal from India in 1947 and increased in pace throughout the 1950s and into the 1960s, being more or less complete by about 1967.

With the end of colonialism, the number of voices in the world community multiplied. Many of these newly heard voices insisted angrily on expressing points of view that differed prominently from those of the Western colonizers. With the multiplication of points of view, a general relativism and skepticism set in; the universals posited by modernism were denied, as was the hierarchization of cultures.

Western artists, often keenly aware of this radical change in the global community, gestured in their work toward the reality of non-Western societies. Joseph Beuys and Sigmar Polke both made works about Native American culture that seemed to heroize it somewhat. In the United States, Mel Chin, Mark Dion, Maura Sheehan, Renee Greene, Elaine Reichek, and others have made colonialism and its demise the subject of complex installation pieces. [*See* Postcolonialism.]

Curatorial Strategies. Meanwhile, curatorial strategies began to shift in ways that reflected this expanded world theater. In fact, as postmodernism came increasingly to know itself, it was discovered that the role of the curator was to be of expanded and intensified importance. It was the curator, even more than the artist perhaps, who aimed artworks at a particular agenda and who could, by changing strategies, contribute toward changing the agendas.

In 1984, the exhibition "'Primitivism' in Twentieth-Century Art: Affinity of the Tribal and the Modern" was mounted at the Museum of Modern Art in New York; it was widely received as anachronistically modernist, a relic of colonialist attitudes, relegating nonwhite cultures to the status of footnotes, or perhaps mascots, to Western art history. Five years later, the exhibition "Les magiciens de la terre," at the Centre Pompidou in Paris, attempted to reshape this strategy for the postcolonial era. Contemporary works of artists from the so-called third world, that is, from previously colonized cultures, were shown with Western contemporary art without any implications of influence or hierarchy. The arts of, say, Africa and Oceania had previously been viewed as primitive or tribal arts; to turn away from such work and look instead at contemporary art by living artists from the former third world—individuals with names and stories—was a clear acknowledgment of the postcolonial situation, of the reality of the present over the past. That, however, was still the West exhibiting the rest. The next step occurred when previously colonized cultures began to exhibit themselves on their own terms, in a new series of international exhibitions of contemporary art in third-world capitals.

The Venice Biennale, founded in 1895, had maintained the idea of an artistic and cultural mainstream located in the West. It was identified with late nineteenth-century imperialism and more or less limited to the Western imperial powers. As colonialism passed and previously colonized cultures began to speak in their own voices, they also wanted a visual language that was imprinted with their sense of their own identity. In the postcolonial situation, the image of a culture's self or consciousness, and the art activity that leads to it, can contribute to the emergence of new intercultural relationships. A culture's visual tradition, when exported, serves as a kind of ambassador, and visual borrowings and mergings constitute a sub-rosa level of foreign policy.

One way to enter into the international discourse was through the institution of the regularly recurring (usually biennial) international exhibition of contemporary art. Starting in the 1960s, such exhibitions were founded in New Delhi, São Paulo, Cairo, Kinshasa, Dakar, Istanbul, Johannesburg, Saarema, and elsewhere. In some cases, such exhibitions were seen as a way to enter modernism. Although entering modernism today may seem an archaic desire in the West, to much of the world it still seems the way to wealth and respectability. At Cairo, for example, it is primarily the Arab world that is represented (though there are

Western exhibits, including an American one) and it is somewhat old-style modernist abstract paintings that are the vehicle of choice. The exhibitions at Istanbul, in contrast, tend to be aggressively postmodernist in their mixture of works. The First Estonian Biennale, at Saarema in 1995, was rooted in the antimodernist moment, containing no paintings at all. Regardless of where they seek entry, the nations that have instituted such exhibitions have declared that they are their own centers, and have taken their culture's imagery into their own hands.

Tidying Up the Record. The high- and late-modernist view of the meaning of human life was neat: a linear Hegelian flow of thesis, antithesis, synthesis, new antithesis, new synthesis, endlessly uncoiling with meaning and logic as somewhat occult driving forces. The meaning and logic might blur out around the edges, but they seemed to hold true, like a spotlight, at the center.

Postmodernism tried to rattle this structure, but then came to wonder if its rattling was not just the next step, just a slight revision of that structure. A new periodization arose, a periodization, one might say, of the advancing denial of periods (and of advance).

The first stage was antimodernism—the violent polar reaction, in the late 1960s and most of the 1970s, against the tradition of pure painting, the Kantian-Greenbergian ideology of the autonomy of art, and the Hegelian myth of history as progress. Conceptual and performance art in this era were carried out puristically, with a severe rejection of any vestigial modernism that could be recognized as such.

The second stage involved the return of painting around 1980, but in a new modality: quotational painting, especially, was used to deconstruct the authority of the Western tradition and its canon, using the iconic moments and motifs of Western art history in ways that contradicted one another and, to a degree, held them up to mockery. Related strategies, such as the mixing of visual languages that would have been kept rigorously apart in the period of modernist purism, were developed with patient focus throughout the 1980s.

The third stage was the expansion of quotationalist practice from the critique of Western culture to a sardonic multicultural pastiche involving combinations of elements from different cultures, combinations that would once have seemed glaringly inappropriate. The visual languages that were being mixed were no longer different visual signatures from one culture, but elements from different cultures thrown as if wantonly together.

The fourth stage was the aggressive confrontation with postcolonial issues by Western artists, mostly in installation art of the mid- to late 1980s. These artists directed the viewer toward the products of other cultures, despite the fact that they themselves were Westerners.

The fifth stage sees the emphasis shift from Western artists' gestures toward non-Western cultures to the contemporary products of non-Western cultures themselves. This process began in the 1960s but peaked (if indeed it has yet peaked) in the early 1990s. It involves the increasing awareness, on the part of previously colonized cultures, that they are now their own centers; the multiplication of biennial exhibitions is a key sign of this development.

Postmodern Cynicism. Underlying a lot of skepticism about postmodernism around the third world is what Cuban art critic Gerardo Mosquero, at an art critics' conference in Stockholm in 1995, called "postmodern cynicism." The cultural discourse among nations, Mosquero noted, has indeed loosened up in a refreshing way, and previously marginalized viewpoints such as the Cuban have begun to assume again voices they feel to be their own. Still, he admonishes, this cultural discursive shift is not reflected on the economic level; wealth and privilege remain in the north, poverty and disenfranchisement in the south. The whole value of cultural discourse is thrown into question by this observation.

Are the cultural and discursive shifts known as postmodernism simply a superstructural sleight of hand that has nothing to do with the reality of the economic base? Could they even be just a new form of cover-up for the economic reality—as if the Western hegemon were thinking, We'll let them write and paint now, and pay interested attention to their books and pictures, if that will keep them happy while we continue to rob them blind in the ways that matter on the bottom line? Or is the artist acting, as Ezra Pound once said, as a kind of antenna sensing the reality that is about to dawn? Can the superstructure intuitively divine the next slow massive gearshift of the base?

There are those—often in the United States, including feminists, African Americans, and Marxists—who argue that postmodernism cannot truly be a social force, that it must be a cover-up for yet another hegemonic move, because it is primarily a discourse of white Western males endlessly playing their sub-Hegelian and sub-sub-Hegelian games. Yet, on the level of discourse, at least, including the image-discourse of the visual arts, postmodernism has already effected a major shift. Around the world one finds artists, critics, and theorists who are consciously working on the multicultural project of sameness-in-difference. Artists such as Gieve Patel, Nalini Malani, and Gulam Sheikh in India, Tamsir Dia and Moustapha Dime in West Africa, Maria-Fernanda Cardozo and Fabian Marcaccio in South America are actively engaged in the visual diplomacy of remaining rooted in their individual heritages while finding ways to inject them meaningfully into a pluralistic global discourse.

The focus of art has shifted from the search for aesthetic universals to the search for images that will convey cultural identity, simultaneously reflecting and guiding its shifts. In a changing world, art does not simply define the present moment; it both prods it to shift and redefines it as it does so, in a new dynamic relationship among image, self, history, and the world.

[*See also* Postmodernism.]

BIBLIOGRAPHY

Ferguson, Russell, et al., eds. *Discourses: Conversations in Postmodern Art and Culture.* Cambridge, Mass., 1990.

Foster, Hal, ed. *The Anti-Aesthetic: Essays on Postmodern Culture.* Port Townsend, Wash., 1983.

Frascina, Francis, ed. *Pollock and After: The Critical Debate.* New York, 1985.

Lippard, Lucy R., ed. *Six Years: The Dematerialization of the Art Object from 1966 to 1972.* New York, 1973.

McEvilley, Thomas. *Art and Otherness: Crisis in Cultural Identity.* Kingston, N.Y., 1992.

McEvilley, Thomas. *The Exile's Return: Towards a Redefinition of Painting for the Post-modern Era.* Cambridge and New York, 1993.

McEvilley, Thomas. *Fusion: West African Artists at the Venice Biennale.* Munich and New York, 1993.

McEvilley, Thomas. *Capacity: History, the World, and the Self in Contemporary Art and Criticism.* Commentary by Roger Denson. New York, 1996.

Vogel, Susan, ed. *Africa Explores: Twentieth-Century African Art.* Munich and New York, 1991.

Wallis, Brian, ed. *Art after Modernism: Rethinking Representation.* Boston, 1984.

THOMAS MCEVILLEY

Aesthetics of Contemporary Art

While seeking to be something else, contemporary art depends as much if not more than Modernist art on the gallery system—to some the modern's defining characteristic—and on the equally modern idea of the museum as an institution able to locate works of art in art history, and in so doing to present them as its culmination, so that one may say that the gallery and museum systems have stayed the same even as they have expanded in popularity and ubiquity, but what they contain has changed. For many, art has become less concerned with the aesthetic than the historicocultural, coinciding in this with developments in the academy, where over the past two decades art history has to an extent given way to cultural studies, and philosophical aesthetics to comparative literature—the ontological to the ideological, the essential to the relative.

There can be little doubt that this change reflects the part played in contemporary art's (and the contemporary academy's) development by theory imported from France—Donald Keefer has observed that an anthology compiled by Brian Wallis in 1984 "contains more attention to Barthes' writings, and particularly the 'Death of the Author', than any other author or artist" (Keefer, 1995)—and by a revived interest in Walter Benjamin and the Frankfurt Institute, which got under way just before the art world rediscovered the French in or about the mid-1970s. In a manner not without precedent, contemporary artists and critics often attribute a reductivism and lack of complexity to modernism and its interests that were not necessarily attendant on them when they were fashionable. Chief among these are the ideas of the essential, the autonomous, and originality, this last seen as a value derived from Romanticism but in modernist art combined with the equally outmoded idea of historical progress.

Modernism is also felt to be generally less ideologically aware than the contemporary, despite Bertolt Brecht's being both a model for a great deal of contemporary art and indisputably a modernist. Thus, although contemporary art's rejection of essentialism is indebted to Jacques Derrida (who has, however, not had much direct affect on contemporary art and its criticism—his *The Truth in Painting* [1987] lies unread in many a studio or study littered with well-thumbed books by Roland Barthes and Michel Foucault), in the anglophone world at least, its conception of itself as more ideologically aware than the modern is for the most part derived from the Frankfurt Institute, albeit a reconceived Frankfurt where Karl Marx has been reconciled with Foucault and Sigmund Freud revised by Jacques Lacan. In the 1970s, the German art theorist Peter Bürger put forward a Habermasian reconciliation of Marcel Duchamp's readymade with Brecht's alienation effect that allows one to see the work and the artist as engaged in an "exemplary practice" that facilitates one's reconsideration of social contradictions, and which is the (in the United States, generally unacknowledged) basis of a great deal of contemporary art and theory. That a lot of contemporary artists wish to infuse art with a social-activist emphasis would require their work to be Brechtian—or post-Brechtian, in that its conversion of the modernist theme of defamiliarization into a demystification of (the) culture as a whole implicitly promises to replace history with a goal with historicism without end—but one notes that it is difficult to reconcile the concept of "exemplary practice" with the Nietzscheanism of French theory. An argument developed from Jean Baudrillard, for instance, might suggest that having the socially conscious artist Jenny Holzer represent Ronald Reagan's America at the Venice Biennale means that an accommodation has been reached between the right's silent majority and the left's marginalized minority, and that her using slogans and one-liners like advertisers and right-wing politicians suggests not an alternative language or attitude but a complementary version of the dominant one, the museum or gallery becoming in this the institution that houses the anti-institutional.

Often, in wanting to sum things up but move beyond them (through what can only be called a heightened self-consciousness, presumably conscious of itself as not a unified self or something like that, singular in a multiplicitous sort of way), contemporary art seems to mirror that which it seeks to escape, recalling in other terms the ambition attributed to Piet Mondrian by Mark Cheetham, of "maintain[ing] the past in . . . art, and the history of art by including it in purified form within the new" and in that approaching "the Hegelian *Aufhebung,* that dialectical process of abrogation in which the negation or cancellation of an element within the dialectic is at the same time a preservation of that element within a higher unity" (1991, p. 55). It may want to be seen as materialist where the modern was idealist, relativist where the latter was absolutist, but contemporary art remains Hegelian precisely in its desire to separate itself from its (Hegelian) past while being recognized as that past's legitimate (or better, illegitimate) heir.

Jean-François Lyotard has suggested that one might think of modernist works themselves as having been postmodern before they were modern—the artist strove to get outside of the modern, but once made and out in the world, the work inevitably became part of that historical project that was modernism. In addition to reflecting the difficulty inherent in trying to formulate an implicitly historical project when one is explicitly attempting to distance oneself from the idea of historical projects, contemporary art would have to begin with the modern as ghost. The task of getting out of the modern having been done for it by modernism—the modern is over, it is not there to be in so one cannot work at getting out—the contemporary would be the first postmodernism to be outside of the modern historically as well as in every other way. The modern being now only retrospectively with us, the contemporary is in no danger of being placed within it, although it can never be free *of* it, because it is itself concerned with what constitutes art practice—if not in the sense of what constitutes a painting, then in that of what can (only) be shown in a gallery (and therefore, inversely, of what happens when things that are found everywhere or anywhere else are shown in an art gallery). It may have divorced itself from the modernist historical project, but it is founded in the history of modernism, the end of which contemporary art discourse usually presents as the triumph of the margin over the center—the Brechtian version of modernist art history being in its revisionism an allegorical longing for what should have happened in history at large. Where a modernist such as Viktor Shklovsky had art developing through one generation paying attention to what the previous one neglected, the Brechtian contemporary would be one in which the oppressed and neglected gain access to that from which they had been excluded, not merely occupying the center but depriving it of its centrality by collapsing it and its marginalia into one another.

It is in the light of this possibly mythical struggle between the official tradition and all that it excluded—or continues to exclude, depending on one's point of view—that contemporary art is often seen as the product of a struggle between Henri Matisse and Duchamp that the latter has won. This version of twentieth-century art history would have the war waged twice: once when Duchamp demolished "the retinal"—to some an inherently conservative rejection of Impressionism and its consequences that sought to return the visual to the role of a passive vehicle for an idea, to others a new way of activating the (historicized, psychologized, industrial, and technological) cultural sign, in practice always both—with the help of the readymade (a procedure that defers and displaces the notion of a kind of biologically induced originality); and again when the New York school reasserted the hegemony of painting, only for it to be displaced by a reborn Duchampianism that was, in its reincarnated form, Janus-faced, manifesting itself as both Pop art and conceptualism, the final triumph of, respectively, the readymade over putatively implausible notions of creativity and of the Idea over the sensory, reason over the retinal, the concept over the percept.

As Amelia Jones (1994) and others have demonstrated, Duchamp provides, in particular in his collaborative engagement with Man Ray on the production of the fictional Rrose Sélavy, a beginning for the explicit concern with gender that provides a basis for a lot of art made since the 1970s. John Welchman (1995) has shown how, from a Duchampian perspective, contemporary art may be seen as an array of investigations and reconsiderations of the limits of the Western cultural object and its capacity to interact with others and to articulate its (and by extension its own culture's) interaction with others. Welchman, although not directly indebted to him, could be described as an art historian who takes Bürger's project of redeeming a modernism that had lost its way for granted.

At the same time, as Matei Calinescu (1987) pointed out in the postmodern debate, once one has Andy Warhol, one does not need Duchamp as far as the industrially produced image is concerned, and Welchman implies something similar vis-à-vis Duchamp and Joseph Kosuth, whose approach to philosophy—ready-made systems of thought—is comparable to Warhol's use of Campbell's soup can labels, and this seems to be confirmed by those contemporary art practices indebted to Pop and conceptualism.

One tendency on the Pop side of things involves the constant retrieval of the banal from more and more nooks and crannies. It would be a fundamental principle of either Brechtian (or any other) realism or of any interpretation of the readymade that the banal was not banal, and this lies at the heart of the contemporary project of symbolically leveling the disparity between the high and the low. This approach, which makes it possible for the work of art in question to be engaged in issues of ethnicity, class, and gender, has exfoliated into an aesthetic that can include, for example, Jim Shaw's exhibitions of paintings bought at garage sales (suburban culture as both readymade and revelation, symbolically redeemed by its redisposition into the space of official art, the latter itself redeemed by accommodating the redisposition) and—which is bound to be seen as in part a response to women's art—what might be called a Rousseauism of the adolescent male as noble savage (alienated and with acne, not trapped in sophistication but constituted of and by an elaborate sign system). Along with interests in the social such as these one finds an elaboration of the private, which also finds itself through the iconography of a youth culture and through a valorization of disjunction, if not the dysfunctional, as in the work of Matthew Barney, which might suggest that after a long period in which art historians have found modernism's (if not art's) great achievements to be involuntarily founded in idiosyncrasy—as in Meyer Schapiro's speculation that Paul Cézanne achieved so much through still life because he was more comfortable in the presence of bowls of fruit than of naked women—artists now begin with the idiosyncratic and apparently unconnected consciously and by choice.

The other (conceptualist) post-Duchampian tendency is less readily assimilable to any kind of social practice, involving instead a kind of *poesis* of convention and the institution. One could speak of it in terms of two generations. The first would include Daniel Buren, whose work is said to deconstruct the institution through "intervening" in it, Gerhard Richter, whose career is predicated on an ability to move from one type of painting to another, which is read as a demystification of traditional ideas about style (an instance of the postmodern preserving the modernist ghost of its choice), the aforementioned Joseph Kosuth, and Lawrence Weiner, while the second generation would be represented by a work such as Stephen Prina's *Monochrome Painting*, a group of monochrome paintings not fabricated by the artist and that reproduce the dimensions of monochrome paintings by members of the New York school and its immediate successors, thus referring in one swoop both to the modernist ghost and to aestheticizings of institutional critique such as Buren's.

Although either the Pop or conceptual varieties of contemporary art could be shown to have moved beyond the readymade as first conceived, or even beyond Bürger's notion of "exemplary practice," both remain similarly committed to an irreducibly historicist view of meaning production in art and what surrounds it. Elsewhere, however, one sees signs that Duchamp's victory over Matisse (of the conceptual and irreversible over the affective and nondialectical) may be less than complete. In painting, historically the most historicist art of all (excepting, possibly, architecture), one finds attempts at getting the work of art to do something that begins elsewhere than with Duchamp or in Frankfurt. Precisely as a result of its commitment to avoid representing, nonrepresentational painting in particular has been led further and further into an engagement with French thought and away from an overt historicism of either the convention or the context.

Gilles Deleuze has emerged as an important influence—becoming as much a feature of writing about nonrepresentation as Barthes once was of that about representation—for his articulation of multiplicity, which allows painting to escape the question of style without becoming merely referential, his version of the differential relationship between similarity and difference, his suggestion that flow and the rhizomic might replace the models of inside and outside and of the tree, and his definition of the event as that which, in happening, is irreducible to its causes and effects. [*See* Deleuze.] Among many whose works invite some sort of Deleuzian reading one could point to David Reed, whose paintings involve movement without interiority, and Fandra Chang, whose work does not so much contain external references as it plays with the look of the referential. Nick Millet (1995) and David Moos (1995) have discussed the practice and condition of nonrepresentational painting through terms provided by Deleuze, who also seems to offer a way of talking about painting's relationship to other media (especially video and film) that need not become a determinist comparison of apparatuses. It may be that through such a reading, which would require that concepts of demystication themselves be demystified, art and its discourse might be led to a reconsideration of that from which modernism shrank and its successors recoil, namely, the possibility of the beautiful (but that is a subject for a discussion not limited, as this has been, to what has occurred). It is also unclear whether Deleuzianism could flourish in the Hegelian world of the gallery system, which has never had difficulty in accommodating (dare one say "appropriating"?) Marx but which has a sound commercial interest in retaining historical change as a selling point.

To conclude, the contemporary is itself an event not so much irreducible to its causes and effects as made up of differences of opinion about them and their relationship to one another. Contemporary art is not one art or kind of art, but simultaneously it and its theories seem to proceed from the assumption that there are no substantive differences between the arts, art having instead become something defined as much as anything by where it takes place. In this it may have found a way to evade metaphysics—not the fractured subject but the symbolic order of the Other, not essence but deferral, not the Grand Tradition but the authenticity of the folk tradition rediscovered in lumpenbourgeois kitsch, not the Romantic genius but the dysfunctional adolescent—but evasion is a way of relating reactively, inasmuch as decentering requires a center to displace, is dependent on the memory of one, and cannot leave what it recalls. It may be that the most successful contemporary art, and the (counter)theory that serves it best,

will be not couched in that language of disjuncture, opposition, and critique that unites the modern with what preceded and succeeds it, thereby precluding the contemporary from separating itself from anything. Success would mean that, in being contemporary, art had become something other than the not-modern.

[*See also* Duchamp; *and* Pop Art.]

BIBLIOGRAPHY

Bürger, Peter. *Theory of the Avant-Garde.* Translated by Michael Shaw. Minneapolis, 1984.

Calinescu, Matei. *Five Faces of Modernity: Modernism, Avant-Garde, Decadence, Kitsch, Postmodernism.* Bloomington, Ind., 1987.

Cheetham, Mark A. *The Rhetoric of Purity: Essentialist Theory and the Advent of Abstract Painting.* Cambridge and New York, 1991.

Derrida, Jacques. *The Truth in Painting.* Translated by Geoff Bennington and Ian McLeod. Chicago, 1987.

Jones, Amelia. *Postmodernism and the En-Gendering of Marcel Duchamp.* Cambridge and New York, 1994.

Keefer, Donald. "Reports on the Death of the Author." *Philosophy and Literature* 19.1 (April 1995): 78–84.

Millett, Nick. "The Third Eye." In *Abstraction: Journal of Philosophy and the Visual Arts,* no. 5, pp. 36–42. London, 1995.

Moos, David. "Lydia Dona: Architecture of Anxiety." In *Abstraction: Journal of Philosophy and the Visual Arts,* no. 5, pp. 43–51. London, 1995.

Wallis, Brian ed. *Art after Modernism: Rethinking Representation.* Boston, 1984.

Welchman, John. *Modernism Relocated: Towards a Cultural Studies of Visual Modernity.* London, 1995.

JEREMY GILBERT-ROLFE

Images and Desire

"In this matter of the visible," writes Jacques Lacan, "everything is a trap" (1978b) The field of vision is ordered by the function of images, at one level, quite simply by linking a surface to a geometric point by means of a path of light; but, at another level, this function seems more like a labyrinth. Because the fascination in looking is founded on separation from what is seen, the field of vision is also, and most appropriately, the field of desire. Here the viewer enters the realm of lost objects, of vanishing points determined not by geometry, but by what is real for the subject, points linked not to a surface, but to a place—the unconscious—and not by means of light, but by the laws of primary process.

In the matter of images of women, then, it would seem that everything is doubly labyrinthine. Desire is embodied in the image that is equated with the woman, who is reduced to the body, which in turn is seen as the site of sexuality and the locus of desire—a familiar elision, almost irresistible, it would seem, judging from the outcome of so many conference panels and special issues devoted to this theme. Nevertheless, it is a dangerous and circuitous logic that obscures a certain progress, a progression of strategies, of definitions made possible within feminist theory by the pressure of political imperatives to formulate the problem of images of women as a question: how to change them? The legacy is not a through route but a disentangling of paths that shows more clearly their points of intersection and draws attention to the fact that it is not obligatory to start over again at the beginning.

Discourses on the body and on sexuality, for instance, do not necessarily coincide. Within the modernist paradigm, it is not the sexual body, but the phenomenological (Husserlian) body that takes precedence, what belongs to me, my body, the body of the self-possessing subject whose guarantee of artistic truth is grounded in actual experience, often deploying the painful state as a signature for that ephemeral object. Thus, the contribution of feminists in the field of performance has been, exactly, to pose the question of sexuality across the body in a way that focuses on the construction of the sexed subject and at the same time problematizes the notion of the artist/auteur. The body is decentered, radically split, positioned—not simply my body, but his body, her body. Here, no third term emerges to salvage a transcendental sameness for aesthetic reflection. Yet, these artists continue to counterpose a visible form and a hidden content, excavating a different order of truth—the truth of the woman, her original feminine identity. Although the body is not perceived as the repository of this truth, it is seen as a hermeneutic image; the enigma of femininity is formulated as a problem of imagistic misrepresentation that is subsequently resolved by discovering a true identity behind the patriarchal facade.

The enigma, however, only seems to encapsulate the difficulty of sexuality itself and what emerges is more in the order of an underlying contradiction than an essential content. The woman artist sees her experience as a woman particularly in terms of the feminine position, that is, as the object of the look. But she must also account for the feeling she experiences as the artist, occupying what could be called the masculine position, as the subject of the look. The former she defines as the socially prescribed position of the woman, one to be questioned, exorcized, or overthrown, while the implication of the latter—that there can be only one position with regard to active looking, a masculine one—cannot be acknowledged. It is construed instead as a kind of psychic truth, a natural, instinctual, preexistent, and possibly unrepresentable, femininity. Often the ambivalence of the feminist text seems to repudiate its claims to essentialism; it testifies instead to what extent masculine and feminine identities are never finally fixed, but are continually negotiated through representations. This crisis of positionality, this instability of meaning, revolves around the phallus as the term that marks the sexual division of the subject in language. Significantly, Lacan (1958) describes the woman's relation to the phallic term as a disguise, a masquerade. In being the phallus for the other, she actively

takes up a passive aim, becomes a picture of herself, erects a facade. Behind the facade, finally, there is no true woman to be discovered. Yet, there is a dilemma: the impossibility of being at once both subject and object of desire.

Clearly, one (so-called postfeminist) response to this impasse has been to adopt a strategy of disavowal. It appears in the guise of a familiar visual metaphor: the androgyne. She *is* a picture, an expressionistic composite of looks and gestures that flaunts the uncertainty of sexual positioning. She refuses the lack, but remains the object of the look. In a sense, the fetishistic implications of not knowing merely enhance the lure of the picture, effectively taming the gaze, rather than provoking a deconstruction. Another (and perhaps more politically motivated) tactic has been to assume self-consciously the patriarchal facade, to make it an almost abrasive and cynical act of affirmation. By producing a representation of femininity in excess of conventional codes, it shatters the narcissistic structure that would return the woman's image to her as a moment of completion. This can induce the alienating effect of a misrecognition, but the question persists: how can she represent herself as a subject of desire?

The (neo)feminist alternative has been to refuse the literal figuration of the woman's body, creating significance out of its absence. But this does not signal a new form of iconoclasm. The artist does not protest against the lure of the picture. In another way, however, her practice could be said to be blasphemous insofar as she seeks to appropriate the gaze behind it (the place of gods, of auteurs, and evil Eves). In her field of vision, femininity is not seen as a pregiven entity, but as the mapping out of sexual difference within a definite terrain, a moment of discourse, a fragment of history. With regard to the spectator, it is a tactic of reversal that attempts to produce the woman, through a different form of identification with the image, as the subject of the look.

A further consequence of this reversal is that it queries the tendency of psychoanalytic theory to complement the division of the visual field into sexually prescribed positions by rhyming repression/perversion, hysteria/obsession, body/word with the heterosexual couplet seer/seen. Yet, this division does not seem to be sustained in Sigmund Freud's work itself. According to Freud (1924), sexual identity is said to be an outcome of the precarious passage called the Oedipus complex, a passage that is in a certain sense completed by the acceptance of symbolic castration. But castration is also inscribed at the level of the imaginary, that is, in fantasy, and this is where the fetishistic scenario originates and is continually replayed. The child's recognition of difference between the mother and the father is above all an admission that the mother does not have the phallus. In this case, seeing is not necessarily believing, for what is at stake for the child is really the question of his or her own relation to having or being. Hence, the fetishist, conventionally assumed to be male, postpones that moment of recognition, although certainly he has made the passage—he knows the difference, but denies it. In terms of representation, this denial is associated with a definite iconography of pornographic images where the man is reassured by the woman's possession of some form of phallic substitute or, alternatively, by the shape, the complete arrangement, of her body.

The question of masculine perversions is an important one. But it would be a mistake to confine women to the realm of repression, excluding the possibility, for example, of female fetishism. For the woman, insofar as the outcome of the Oedipal moment has involved at some point a heterosexual object choice (that is, she has identified with her mother and has taken her father as a love object), it will also postpone the recognition of lack in view of the promise of having the child. In having the child, in a sense she has the phallus. Thus, the loss of the child is the loss of that symbolic plenitude—more exactly, the ability to represent lack.

When Freud describes castration fears for the woman, this imaginary scenario takes the form of losing her loved objects, especially her children; the child is going to grow up, leave her, reject her, perhaps die. In order to delay, disavow, the separation that she has already in a way acknowledged, the woman tends to fetishize the child by dressing him up, by continuing to feed him no matter how old he gets, or simply by having another little one. Therefore, perhaps in place of the more familiar notion of pornography it is possible to talk about the mother's memorabilia—the way she saves things: the first shoes, photographs, locks of hair, or school reports. A trace, a gift, a fragment of narrative, all of these can be seen as transitional objects, not in Donald Woods Winnicott's sense, as surrogates, but in Lacan's terms, as emblems of desire. The feminist text proceeds from this site, not in order to valorize the potential fetishism of the woman, but to create a critical distance from it, something that has not been possible until now because it has not been generally acknowledged. Here the problem of images of women can be reformulated as a different question: how is a radical, critical, *and* pleasurable positioning of the woman as spectator to be done?

Desire is caused not by objects but in the unconscious, according to the peculiar structure of fantasy. Desire is repetitious; it resists normalization, ignores biology, disperses the body. Certainly, desire is not synonymous with images of desirable women, yet what does it mean, exactly, to say that feminists have refused the image of the woman? First, this implies a refusal to reduce the concept of the image to one of resemblance, to figuration, or even to the general category of the iconic sign. It suggests that the image, as it is organized in the space called the picture, can refer to a heterogeneous system of signs—indexical, iconic, and symbolic—and thus, that it is possible to invoke the nonspecular, the sensory, the somatic, in the visual field, to invoke, especially, the register of the invocatory drives (which, ac-

cording to Lacan, are on the same level as the scopic drives, but closer to the experience of the unconscious), through *writing*. Second, it should be said that this is not a hybrid version of the hieroglyph masquerading as a heterogeneity of signs. The object is not to return the feminine to a domain of prelinguistic utterance, but rather to mobilize a system of imaged discourse capable of refuting a certain form of culturally overdetermined scopophilia. But why? Would this release the female spectator from her hysterical identification with the male voyeur?

Again, the implications of suggesting that women have a privileged relation to narcissism or that fetishism is an exclusively male perversion should be reconsidered. Surely, the link between narcissism and fetishism is castration. For both the man and the woman, this is the condition for access to the symbolic, to language, to culture; there can be no privileged relation to madness. Yet there *is* difference. There is still that irritating asymmetry of the Oedipal moment. There is Freud's continual emphasis on the importance of the girl's attachment to her mother. And there is Dora. What did she find so fascinating in the picture of the Sistine Madonna? Perhaps, above all, it was the possibility of seeing the woman as subject of desire without transgressing the socially acceptable definition of her as the mother: to have the child as phallus; to be the phallic mother; to have the pleasure of the child's body; to have the pleasure of the maternal body experienced through it. Perhaps, in the figure of the Madonna, there was a duplication of identification and desire that only the body of another woman could sustain.

For both the man and the woman, the maternal body lines the seductive surface of the image, but the body he sees is not the same one she is looking at. The woman's relation to the mother's body is a constant source of anxiety. Michele Montrelay (1978) claims that this relation is often only censored rather than repressed. Consequently, the woman clings to a precocious femininity, an archaic oral-anal organization of the drives, which bars her access to sublimated pleasure (phallic *jouissance*). Similarly, with regard to the artistic text, and if pleasure is understood in Roland Barthes's sense of the term as a loss of preconceived identity, rather than an instance of repletion, then it is possible to produce a different form of pleasure for the woman by representing a specific loss—the loss of her imagined closeness to the mother's body. A critical, perhaps disturbing sense of separation is effected through the visualization of exactly that which was assumed to be outside of seeing: precocious, unspeakable, unrepresentable. In the scopic register, she is no longer at the level of concentricity, of repetitious demand, but of desire. As Lacan points out, even the eye itself belongs to this archaic structure, because it functions in the field of vision as a lost object. Thus, the same movement that determines the subject's appearance in language, that is, symbolic castration, also introduces the gaze—and the domain of imaged discourse.

Until now, the woman as spectator has been pinned to the surface of the picture, trapped in the path of light that leads her back to the features of the veiled face. It is important to acknowledge that the masquerade has always been internalized, linked to a particular organization of the drives, represented through a diversity of aims and objects; but, at the same time, it is important to avoid being lured into looking for a psychic truth beneath the veil. To see this picture critically, the viewer should be neither too close nor too far away.

[*See also* Feminism; Freud; Lacan *and* Sexuality.]

BIBLIOGRAPHY

Freud, Sigmund. "Fragment of an Analysis of a Case of Hysteria" (1901). In *The Standard Edition of the Complete PsychologicalWorks of Sigmund Freud,* edited by James Strachey, vol. 7, pp. 3–122. London, 1953.
Freud, Sigmund. "The Dissolution of the Oedipus Complex" (1924). In *The Standard Edition of the Complete Psychological Works of Sigmund Freud,* edited by James Strachey, vol. 19, pp. 173–179. London, 1961.
Lacan, Jacques. "The Meaning of the Phallus" (1958). In *Feminine Sexuality,* edited by Juliet Mitchell and Jacqueline Rose, translated by Jacqueline Rose, pp. 74–85. New York, 1982.
Lacan, Jacques. "The Line and Light" (1964–1965). In *The Four Fundamental Concepts of Psychoanalysis,* edited by Jacques-Alain Miller, translated by Alan Sheridan, pp. 91–104. New York, 1978a.
Lacan, Jacques. "What Is a Picture" (1964–1965). In *The Four Fundamental Concepts of Psychoanalysis,* edited by Jacques-Alain Miller, translated by Alan Sheridan, pp. 105–118. New York, 1978b.
Montrelay, Michele. "Inquiry into Femininity." *m/f* 1 (1978): 86–99.

Mary Kelly

CONTINENTAL AESTHETICS. *For examples of essays characteristic of Continental Aesthetics (derived from nineteenth- and twentieth-century European philosophy of the Continent, exclusive of Great Britain), which is often contrasted with Analytic Aesthetics (derived from twentieth-century Anglo-American philosophy),* see Alienation, Aesthetic; Avant-Garde; Difficulty, Aesthetics of; Essentialism, *article on* Anti-Essentialism; Imagination, *article on* The Imaginary; Gaze; Imagination; Metaphor, *article on* Derrida and de Man on Metaphor; Metonymy; Semiotics, *article on* Semiotics as a Theory of Art; *and* Text.

COOPER, ANTHONY ASHLEY (1671–1713), third earl of Shaftesbury, English philosopher whose main contributions were on the topics of morality and art, specifically beauty and taste. Shaftesbury was raised and educated by his grandfather, the first earl, who was a controversial political figure during the Restoration and actively promoted the Protestant succession of William and Mary. John Locke was his personal physician and adviser. Shaftesbury privately expressed his disagreement with Locke's modernism and

his empirical rejection of innate ideas, but Locke's influence can be detected nevertheless. Shaftesbury served in Parliament before succeeding to the earldom and taking his seat in the House of Lords. For a time, he played an active role in Whig political circles. He was by temperament more suited to the life of an intellectual and connoisseur, however, and when his health failed, he withdrew first to Holland and then to Italy, where he died.

Shaftesbury's first published work, in 1698, was a preface to a collection of sermons of Dr. Benjamin Whichcot. Whichcot was a part of the Cambridge Platonist movement, and Shaftesbury's preface includes an attack on the moral doctrines of Thomas Hobbes. In 1699, the radical deist and political pamphleteer, John Toland, who had received support from Shaftesbury, published an unauthorized version of Shaftesbury's *Inquiry concerning Virtue or Merit.* According to his son, Shaftesbury disapproved and bought up virtually all of the copies to destroy them. After his health forced him to give up his political career, he published several treatises on morality and art that were drawn together with a corrected version of the *Inquiry concerning Virtue* in *Characteristics of Men, Manners, Opinions, Times,* published in 1711. Shaftesbury was making corrections to these essays at the time of his death and had written additional treatises on art that he intended to publish as *Second Characters: or, the Language of Forms.* This material was finally published by Benjamin Rand in 1914.

Shaftesbury's work centers on moral philosophy. He opposed the egoism of Hobbes and sought to found public benevolence on a moral sense that responded to the good of the system or society to which it belonged. Two competing and seemingly inconsistent elements guide Shaftesbury's moral philosophy. On the one hand, he is a Platonist who holds that the good and beautiful are forms embedded in the human mind. On the other hand, he relies on a moral sense to which each individual may appeal. This sense informs one of the good not only of the self (self-interest) but the good of the whole system to which one belongs. Thus the single-minded empiricism of Hobbes is seen as empirically as well as morally deficient. The tension between Shaftesbury's Platonism and his empiricism leads him to advocate a form of reliance on sentiment or feeling that can be tested by self-examination and critical assessment, including "raillery" and satire. Shaftesbury is at once the advocate of moral sentiment, therefore, and the opponent of enthusiasm when it takes the form of unexamined and unbridled expression. Shaftesbury is, above all else, an aristocratic and neoclassical advocate of public obligation and virtue.

For Shaftesbury, response to the arts is never independent of morality. The independence of aesthetic sensibility that developed later in the eighteenth century has no place in Shaftesbury's thought. Sensibility and emotional response to art are indicative of the moral and social character of the respondent. Thus, Shaftesbury is concerned not with sensibility for its own sake but with its development as an integral part of character. Sense, by itself, is not to be trusted, and self-indulgence is not only a moral but an aesthetic failure. A basic problem for Shaftesbury is that pleasure and passion are changeable, whereas character needs to be stable. He cannot completely reconcile his acknowledgment that passion governs us with his demand that our self be formed on some stable basis. Instead of proposing some alternative to sentiment, Shaftesbury looks for some sentiment that is lasting and stable. He finds it in the moral and social pleasures. He acknowledges that one cannot escape one's humors and fancies; what one can do is train them so that they are not capricious. His opponents were offended at the lack of authority and the acquiescence to merely human control that that implied, but they did not give sufficient credence to his stoic virtues of self-examination and self-control. The lurking contradiction is that only by feeling the moral virtues can one oppose and control fancy, and that seems no more than fancy itself. Shaftesbury answers that one is not convinced by arguments but by being shown a moral alternative that is itself felt as a more stable pleasure, a measure of a happy life. Art is enlisted in this showing: "Thus we retain on virtue's side the noblest party of the Muses. Whatever is august among those sisters, appears readily in our behalf. Nor are the more jocund ladies wanting in their assistance when they act in the perfection of their art, and inspire some better geniuses in this kind of poetry" (1964, vol. 1, p. 204).

In the areas of what came to be called aesthetic response, Shaftesbury is led to make use of an internal sense, an idea that is developed by Francis Hutcheson in his *Inquiry into the Original of Our Ideas of Beauty and Virtue* (1725) into a full-fledged theory of aesthetic response. Shaftesbury's use of an internal sense is more ambiguous than Hutcheson's, however. Both because he continues to think very much in classical terms and because he is unsystematic in his presentation, Shaftesbury continues to use *internal sense* in ways that recall its role in Aristotle and Augustine. There, an internal sense is not an additional sense but an internal unification of sense perception into coherent ideas. In classical theory, sight and touch perceive independently, and they must then be united into a single idea of an object by an internal sense. In Augustine, the internal sense is also the judge of the external senses, correcting the misperception resulting from illusion and ambiguity. That usage is consistent with Shaftesbury's distrust of "mere sense" and his emphasis on the control over sensibility exercised by a good moral character.

At the same time, Shaftesbury appeals to a sense that is much more direct and immediate than the classical internal sense:

> The mind, which is spectator or auditor of other minds, cannot be without its eye and ear, so as to discern proportion, distin-

guish sound, and scan each sentiment or thought which comes before it. . . . It feels the soft and harsh, the agreeable and disagreeable in the affections; and finds a foul and fair, a harmonious and a dissonant, as really and truly here as in any musical numbers or in the outward forms or representations of sensible things. . . . So that to deny the common and natural sense of a sublime and beautiful in things, will appear an affectation merely, to any one who considers duly of this affair.

(Ibid., pp. 251–252)

The spectator mind is, of course, consistent with Locke's view. Only reflectively does one have this immediate sense, and the extent to which it is a sense is obviously metaphoric. Shaftesbury's argument here is that to deny the affections is impossible. What cannot be denied must be the case. Their source must be a sense, therefore. His "internal sense" is much more qualified than what it will become in Hutcheson, however.

Shaftesbury relies heavily on the development of good taste. His theory of taste is judgmental, and it is itself subject to judgment in terms of what it contributes to the character of the individual. In this respect, Shaftesbury is following the main line of development of taste in the arts as a combination of the Renaissance and seventeenth-century concepts of judgment and manner. Taste is a manner that distinguishes the character of an individual. The function of a philosopher is to study and perfect that taste. Speaking of himself in the third person, Shaftesbury writes:

> According to our author, the taste of beauty and the relish of what is decent, just, and amiable perfects the character of the gentleman and the philosopher. And the study of such a taste or relish will, as we suppose, be ever the great employment and concern of him who covets as well to be wise and good as agreeable and polite.   (Ibid., vol. 2, pp. 255–256)

Taste is bringing one's own response into line with that which will be approved by the best judges, and those judges are known by their social superiority and their ultimate success in approving that which independently emerges as the good and beautiful. The final judgment in such matters remains the good of a system to which the individual belongs. Shaftesbury does not probe more deeply into the potential conflicts that his reliance on system might produce. His opponent is Hobbes, on the one hand, and traditional religious and Tory authority on the other. Hobbes's appeal to self-interest is rejected because taste and sense respond to more than one's own self-interest. They include a larger whole. But that whole or system cannot be rational or religious authority because, as Locke taught, we can have no other appeal than to our own experience and ideas, so only a sense can be authoritative. Later empiricists, including George Berkeley in his anti-Shaftesburian dialogue *Alciphron or the Minute Philosopher,* and David Hume throughout his work, recognize that one is led to a potential skepticism or relativism by Shaftesbury's reliance on sense as sentiment, but

Shaftesbury himself is optimistic enough to believe that the good and beautiful alone will provide true satisfaction. In this, he is true to Platonic beliefs that identify a lack of goodness and virtue as a form of nonbeing that must ultimately fail.

Shaftesbury remains confident that in disinterested cases, one can rely on sentiment to disclose the true beauty that is also moral:

> In these vagrant characters or pictures of manners, which the mind of necessity figures to itself and carries still about with it, the heart cannot possibly remain neutral; but constantly takes part one way or other. However false or corrupt it be within itself, it finds the difference, as to beauty and comeliness, between one heart and another, one turn of affection, one behaviour, one sentiment and another; accordingly, in all disinterested cases, must approve in some measure of what is natural and honest, and disapprove what is dishonest and corrupt.
>
> (Ibid., vol. 1, p. 252)

Clearly, such disinterestedness is a long way from the later aesthetic disinterestedness of intuition or attitude that separates aesthetic experience from moral and practical interests. On the contrary, for Shaftesbury, disinterestedness is only one more element in the morality of true sentiment. It arises from the coincidence of self-interest and the interest of the whole that is true virtue. Self-interest by itself will provide only a constantly changing pleasure that contradicts its own responses. What pleases at one moment will not please at a later moment. In that situation, the continuing self cannot know its own interest. Thus, self-interest alone is forced into a form of *reductio:* if anything can be my interest, then nothing is. Disinterestedness in that context is a way to discover what will truly and lastingly please.

Shaftesbury's theory of sense also commits him to defend the role of critics. In contrast to later aesthetics that distrusts criticism as an intellectual intrusion into the realm of pure aesthetic pleasure, Shaftesbury understands criticism as a way of testing sense to see that it is indeed truly in one's self-interest and thus that it will withstand the test of continued experience. In fact, the critic is for Shaftesbury very close to a moral instructor. Again, this is consistent with the view of taste found in Balthasar Gratian (1945), where taste is identified as a quality that indicates a cultivated judgment. It is also, as it is for Gratian, a matter of public standing and agreement. For Shaftesbury, lack of criticism leads to a subjective version of taste that is not prepared to defend its judgment. Shaftesbury does not approve of all taste. The question must be how one knows which taste is venal and which produces a good character. The answer is that what is approved by affection, under the tests to which affection is subjected, distinguishes taste. It is a form of judgment as well as a form of sense.

> For this reason we presume not only to defend the cause of critics, but to declare open war against those indolent supine au-

thors, performers, readers, auditors, actors or spectators who, making their humour alone the rule of what is beautiful and agreeable, and having no account to give of such their humour or odd fancy, reject the criticizing or examining art, by which alone they are able to discover the true beauty and worth of every object.
>
> (1964, vol. 2, p. 257)

The critic's role is both to test response by holding it up to the standard supplied by benevolence and a socially responsible sensibility and to educate that sensibility at the same time. Here too Shaftesbury's relatively unsystematic presentation allows him to ignore the implicit circularity in making the critic the educator and simultaneously identifying true taste by what the critic teaches us. In the chaotic and rapidly changing art world of the late seventeenth century, the danger of mistaking taste appears to arise from the mechanical, neoclassical application of rules and not from the competing tastes of the new critical journals, poems, and coffeehouse discussions. Thus, Shaftesbury defends not only critical writing but what he calls "raillery," a subjecting of rules and authoritative pronouncements to ridicule and satire. Once again, Shaftesbury's practice calls for a kind of empirical testing, while his faith in the essentially eternal nature of the good and beautiful makes him confident that such testing cannot be misled or destructive over the long term, no matter how disrespectful it seems of established verities in the immediate present.

Shaftesbury's theory of beauty, which is at the heart of his confidence in sentiment, remains essentially Platonic. There is, he holds, a real harmony and proportion within music, painting, and architecture, and no matter how eccentric the ear or the eye of the beholder, it cannot change that reality. To the extent that Locke would subject that reality to individual experience and subjective judgment, Shaftesbury condemns him. Yet, for Shaftesbury, the only way that one perceives that beauty is through the senses. Thus, sentiment must be acknowledged as the sense by means of which we come to whatever experience we have of beauty. As Shaftesbury says in a letter written in 1709, there is a Gothic (which is to Shaftesbury a synonym for barbarousness) in architecture that would remain Gothic even if we were all Goths (1900, pp. 416–417), but he also believes, as he says in an allegory on a pictures of Cebes, that if one understands what one sees and hears, one will be saved (1914, p. 74). At the same time that he condemns the taste of his age because it follows every fashion, he believes that true taste is the moral as well as the aesthetic foundation of character. Everyone can discover beauty. Reason is an inward capacity, not a deduction or a transcendent perfection: " 'Tis we ourselves create and form our taste. If we resolve to have it just, 'tis in our power. We may esteem and resolve, approve and disapprove, as we would wish" (1964, vol. 2, pp. 271–272).

Shaftesbury's influence in moral philosophy continued through the eighteenth and nineteenth centuries on the

Continent, but the empiricism of Hume and the Scottish commonsense philosophers found his florid style and Platonism uncongenial. Hutcheson specifically acknowledges a debt to Shaftesbury, however, and Hume's reliance on sentiment as opposed to rationalist formulations in aesthetics also owes a great deal to Shaftesbury. Shaftesbury's ideal critic anticipates Hume's description in "Of the Standard of Taste." As much as anything else, Shaftesbury's influence wanes because the situation necessary for his combination of aristocratic taste and moral education is replaced by the more middle-class virtues of popularity and industry. Shaftesbury's aesthetic is an aristocratic, country-Whiggish combination of virtue and taste. It applies to the young gentleman and the country squire. But it cannot retain the union of virtue and aesthetic sensibility when applied to an entrepreneurial capitalism that separates labor and consumption. For that, aesthetics must be distanced not only from the practical consequences of its objects but from the moral values of those objects as well. Only in that way can aesthetic objects be saved from the paradox implied by a value system that places its central value on industriousness and work but seeks to retain an essentially contemplative, leisured art.

[*See also* Beauty; Disinterestedness; Hume; Hutcheson; *and* Taste, *article on* Modern and Recent History.]

BIBLIOGRAPHY

Works by Shaftesbury

Characteristics of Men, Manners, Opinions, Times, 2 vols. in 1. Edited by John M. Robertson. Indianapolis, 1964.
The Life, Unpublished Letters, and Philosophical Regimen of Anthony, Earl of Shaftesbury. Edited by Benjamin Rand. London, 1900.
Second Characters: or, The Language of Forms. Edited by Benjamin Rand. Cambridge, 1914.

Other Sources

Dussinger, John A. "The Lovely System of Lord Shaftesbury." *Journal of the History of Ideas* 42.1 (January–March 1981): 151–158.
Gratian, Balthasar. *The Art of Worldly Wisdom.* Translated by Joseph Jacobs. New York, 1945.
Hutcheson, Francis. *An Inquiry into the Original of Our Ideas of Beauty and Virtue.* London, 1725.
Rogers, Pat. "Shaftesbury and the Aesthetics of Rhapsody." *British Journal of Aesthetics* 12.3 (Summer 1972): 244–257.
Townsend, Dabney. "Shaftesbury's Aesthetic Theory." *Journal of Aesthetics and Art Criticism* 41.2 (Winter 1982): 205–213.
Uphaus, Robert W. "Shaftesbury on Art: The Rhapsodic Aesthetics." *Journal of Aesthetics and Art Criticism* 27.3 (Spring 1969): 341–348.
Voitle, Robert. *The Third Earl of Shaftesbury.* Baton Rouge, La., 1984.
White, David A. "The Metaphysics of Disinterestedness: Shaftesbury and Kant." *Journal of Aesthetics and Art Criticism* 32.2 (Winter 1973): 239–248.
Woodfield, Richard. "The Freedom of Shaftesbury's Classicism." *British Journal of Aesthetics* 15.3 (Summer 1975): 254–266.

DABNEY TOWNSEND

CORBUSIER. *See* Le Corbusier.

COUSIN, VICTOR (1792–1867), French philosopher and educator. No French philosopher was as well placed as Cousin to exploit the particular conditions of intellectual and political life in the three decades following the fall of the Napoleonic empire. The son of a laundrywoman and a jeweler, he rapidly ascended the ladder of the educational system installed as a result of the Revolution, first attending the Lycée Charlemagne and later being one of the earliest and most brilliant students of the École normale. With the patronage of the politician Pierre Paul Royer-Collard, who temporarily abandoned his teaching of philosophy at the Sorbonne in 1815 to take up an influential political career, Cousin rapidly became the most prominent philosopher in Paris. Although his professed liberalism caused him to leave his teaching post at the Sorbonne in 1820, he returned with a vengeance before the end of the decade, and prospered throughout the July Monarchy. During the ten years between 1830 and 1840, he was successively professor at the Sorbonne, director of the École normale, conseiller d'État, pair de France, and finally minister of public instruction.

Cousin's unique combination of prestige as a teacher and influence as a politician enabled him to set his mark on the French educational system. More than anyone else, he was responsible for entrenching the study of philosophy in French secondary education. He paid for his meteoric career, however, with a considerable loss of prestige after the Revolution of 1848. By 1857, Hippolyte Taine was able to present him as "a mere rhetorician who employed political opportunism to impose an unoriginal spiritualism." This verdict has not been significantly revised. By being so closely identified with the French experiment with liberalism, under a constitutional monarchy, Cousin has been relegated as irrelevant to the modern republican tradition. Nevertheless, his philosophical teaching permeated the intellectual climate in which French Romanticism, and ultimately modernism, were engendered. His views on aesthetics, though based in the traditions of neoclassicism, offered new concepts to artists of the generation immediately following him. His knowledge of the history of French art, though sometimes dismissed as superficial, was in fact considerable and demonstrates a critical awareness that was unusual among the philosophers of his time.

Cousin's accelerated career inevitably meant that he was running before he could walk. As early as 1817, he traveled to Germany and met G. W. F. Hegel for the first time. He returned in 1824, for a third time, and when he was arrested in Dresden under suspicion of being a liberal agitator, it was Hegel who intervened to secure his release. Cousin's knowledge of the development of modern German philosophy was probably unequaled among his French contemporaries, and a considerable advance over the schematic presentation of Immanuel Kant's ideas undertaken earlier by the French émigré Charles de Villers. Nonetheless, he was often accused of being insufficiently familiar with the German language to do justice to the complexities of Kant's ideas. Equally, he was no expert in Greek when he first began to teach the subject at the École normale and, although he spent much of his enforced leisure during the 1820s on a translation of the complete works of Plato, his knowledge of the language was questioned by a later generation of less hastily formed scholars.

Cousin's overall philosophical doctrine, which he termed Eclecticism, cannot but seem a reaction to the turbulent historical circumstances of his early life. Yet, in that respect, it also suited the needs of his contemporaries, whose experience was inevitably comparable. His strategy was to pitch philosophical systems against one another: initially the sensualism of the French and English tradition (John Locke, Claude Adrien Helvétius, Étienne Bonnot de Condillac) against the idealism of George Berkeley and the German school; at a later stage, the skepticism of Voltaire and David Hume against the mysticism of Emanuel Swedenborg and Louis Claude de Saint-Martin. He saw this fourfold structure as being the manifestation of the human spirit working through history. Its progress was, however, not dialectical but the progressive discovery of an equilibrium, in which the pretense of any one system to constitute the entire truth was revealed as illusory. In this respect, Cousin's approach cohered with the historicist tendencies of the Romantic generation, and helped to foster them. He is known to have introduced the almost unknown writings of Giambattista Vico to the young Jules Michelet.

In the sphere of aesthetics, Cousin recognized the exceptionally important contribution of Kant, yet he did not relinquish the possibility of harmonizing Kant's ideas with the traditional philosophical bases of neoclassicism. In the words of Frederic Will, "[his] aesthetic, being basically Platonic, accepted only influences which could be harmonized with that basis" (1965). In many respects, his emphasis on ideal beauty, as opposed to the beauty to be derived from the copying of natural form, endorsed the contemporary approach of such paragons of neoclassicism as Antoine Quatremère de Quincy, while finding additional inspiration in the German writings of Johann Joachim Winckelmann. He particularly admired Winckelmann's celebrated passage on the Apollo Belvedere, acknowledging the rhetorical cogency of this new style of ekphrastic writing with the comment: "The tone of the learned antiquarian rises little by little to enthusiasm, and his analysis becomes a hymn to spiritual beauty."

If Cousin's own language often fails to make this leap, it is nonetheless true that his aesthetic concepts were acknowledged as having vital significance in the period when Jacques-Louis David and his school were yielding to the onslaught of the Romantic generation. Writing in the late 1850s, the secretary of the Académie des beaux-arts, the composer Fromental Halévy, adduced Cousin's concept of "moral beauty" as a key to the evolving style of the most popularly acclaimed French painter of his age, Paul Delaroche.

Yet, if Cousin's ideas can be held as one of the causative factors that led Delaroche in the direction of historical, and finally religious, themes, it should not be assumed that he stood for a mere dogmatic moralism. Indeed, he has a proven claim to have formulated for the first time the doctrine that would later be formulated as "art for art's sake." His knowledge of Kant's aesthetic writings led him to insist on the subjective disinterestedness of aesthetic judgment, and to put the issue forward in a fashion that could be taken as highly provocative: "There must be religion for religion's sake, morality for morality's sake, as there is art for art's sake [*l'art pour l'art*]." Cousin published this sentence in the edition of *Du vrai, du beau, et du bien* which dates from 1836, the year after Théophile Gautier promoted the ideology of aestheticism as being divorced from all utilitarian purposes in the Preface to *Mademoiselle de Maupin*. But his lectures had expounded the notion to what the philosopher and statesman Charles de Rémusat calls "enthusiastic youth" from 1818 onward, and there can be little doubt that Gautier was acquainted with his approach to aesthetics.

Cousin's own most perceptive comments on the visual arts were, however, reserved for the great tradition of French painting, up to but not including the innovators of his own day. In reviewing this tradition, he managed to highlight aspects that were of particular relevance to his own contemporaries. Among his heroes, Nicolas Poussin occupied a major place, and his withering denunciation of the French for allowing so many of Poussin's masterpieces to cross the Channel to England implies a remarkable firsthand knowledge of the work. His choice of Eustache Le Sueur as the other exemplary French painter, as opposed to Charles Le Brun, who founded the French academic tradition, is a calculated move in the promotion of of the idea of a national art, not unduly in thrall to the Italian schools, and had its effect in stimulating the self-confidence of the young Romantic painters. Invariably, Cousin's specific comments on paintings in the section on French art that constitutes the "sixth lesson" of *Du vrai, du beau, et du bien*, are original and illuminating. His remarks on David's *Death of Socrates*, which contrast the "theatrical genre" of the work with what Michael Fried might term the "absorptive" effect of Plato "deep in the contemplation of the intelligible world," provide yet another indication of his success in using aesthetic concepts to promote new readings of the visual heritage.

[*See also* French Aesthetics; *and* Poussin.]

BIBLIOGRAPHY

Work by Cousin

Cours de philosophie professé à la Faculté des lettres pendant l'année 1818 . . . sur le fondement des idées absolues du vrai, du beau et du bien. Paris, 1836.

Other Sources

Faguet, Émile. *Politiques et moralistes du dix-neuvième siècle,* 2d series. Paris, 1898. *See* pp. 229–280

Fried, Michael. *Absorption and Theatricality: Painting and Beholder in the Age of Diderot.* Berkeley, 1980.

Goldstein, Jan. "Saying 'I': Victor Cousin, Caroline Angebert, and the Politics of Selfhood in Nineteenth-Century France." In *Rediscovering History: Culture, Politics, and the Psyche,* edited by Michael S. Roth, pp. 321–335. Stanford, Calif., 1994.

Lefranc, Jean. "Victor Cousin." In *Dictionnaire des philosophes,* edited by Denis Huisman, pp. 630–634. Paris, 1984.

Leguay, P. "Victor Cousin." In *Dictionnaire de biographie française.* vol. 9, pp. 1069–1073. Paris, 1961.

Will, Frederic. *Flumen Historicum: Victor Cousin's Aesthetic and Its Sources.* Chapel Hill, N.C., 1965.

STEPHEN BANN

CRAFT. Craft has developed two related meanings within modern aesthetics. Craft signifies human ability in production or performance, a meaning identical with that of "art" from the time of the Greek *technē* and Roman *ars* down to the eighteenth century. Craft also signifies a class of activities or objects that result from such abilities. When the "fine arts" were split off from the arts in general around 1750, "craft" remained synonymous with art in the older sense of skilled performance and its products. As a result, when nineteenth-century usage dropped the *fine* from *fine art,* the contrast between fine art and art in general began to be expressed as one between art and craft (although other terms might be used: *useful arts, decorative arts, industrial arts*). By the mid-nineteenth century, the old contrast of "art versus nature" had been largely replaced by the new polarity, "art versus craft." Paradoxically, the "art" in the new pair art versus craft was now itself conceived on the model of nature as spontaneous creation, whereas "craft" took on the older meaning of art as a product of human skill. In the context of the new polarity, four elements became associated with the idea of craft: (1) the primacy of function, (2) the predominance of manual skill and traditional forms, (3) an engagement with the demands of the market, and (4) the use of media considered beneath the dignity of fine art (clay, metal, fiber, wood in the visual arts and popular song, dance, and story forms in music and literature).

Prior to the eighteenth century, however, there was a division *within* art in general that foreshadowed the modern fine art/craft polarity: the schema of liberal versus mechanical arts. From late antiquity to the seventeenth century, the liberal arts included grammar, rhetoric, dialectic, arithmetic, geometry, astronomy, and music; the mechanical arts comprised everything else, from making shoes and carving statues to cooking, painting, and horse breaking. None of what would later be considered the fine arts was originally included among the liberal arts except, indirectly, poetry ("music" meant primarily music theory because performance was a manual activity). An often-repeated commonplace of art and music history is that fine art and craft were separated during the Renaissance, but this claim applies primarily to a small number of court painters, sculptors, composers, and writers. Claims for the "liberal" rather than "mechanical" status of painting and sculpture, for example, were still contested in most of Europe down to the end of the seventeenth century. And even many of the elite on whom art history has traditionally concentrated worked under restrictive contracts and produced works intended for a specific purpose and place; Leonardo da Vinci's contract for *Virgin of the Rocks,* for example, specifies content, colors, delivery date, and a repair guarantee. Although one can trace a gradual rise in the prestige of painting and sculpture from the Renaissance to the seventeenth century, most painters or sculptors continued to belong to craft guilds and to turn out functional products from workshops on commission, and most composers labored in great houses or religious establishments under restrictive contracts that often made them little better than servants. This lack of a sharp practical differentiation between artists and craftspeople was reflected semantically in the fact that the primary reference of the term *artist* down to the mid-seventeenth century was not to painters, sculptors, and architects as a group but to either liberal arts students or alchemists and that the terms *artist* and *artisan* continued to be used interchangeably well into the eighteenth century.

When the Abbé Batteux provided one of the first systematic statements of a generalized category of beaux arts in 1746, he separated the fine arts from the mechanical on the basis of pleasure versus utility. The new terminology and criteria spread rapidly over Europe and soon a core of five fine arts was recognized (poetry, music, painting, sculpture, architecture), to which a sixth or seventh might be added from among rhetoric, dance, engraving, and landscape gardening. Everything else remained part of the mechanical arts or handicrafts. (*Handwerk* in German, *métier* or *artisanat* in French, *mestiere* in Italian). The art versus craft schema not only distinguished the fine arts as a group from the realm of instrumental crafts such as pottery, weaving, and embroidery, but began to applied within each of the fine arts; for example, easel painting was now sharply separated from most decorative painting, operatic and symphonic music in concerts from music to accompany dining or dancing. Even within the kinds of art deemed "fine" there were gradations, for example, from history painting down through landscape, portrait, and genre to flower painting, with the lowest-ranked genres coming near the realm of craft, just as the rare piece of silver work or furniture, such as Louis XV's cylinder desk, might approach fine-art status.

At the same time that the older idea of art was being split into fine art versus craft, the older, integrated idea of the artisan/artist was also definitively split into artist versus artisan, creative genius versus skilled craftsperson. By the end of the eighteenth century, the term *artist* had finally taken on its modern meanings, becoming a general term for makers in all the fine arts, including music and literature, and gathering to itself the ideals of independence, creativity, and imagination. *Artisan* or *craftsman,* on the other hand, was now reserved exclusively for the makers of useful crafts and explicitly defined in contrasts to *artist,* using such ideas as skill, imitation, subservience, and trade. The ideal artist was increasingly seen as the individual genius driven to create by an inner fire and oblivious of money or opinion; the artisan or craftsperson, by contrast, was envisaged as producing in a workshop atmosphere, make things to order with a concern for profit as in any other business.

Near the end of the eighteenth century, Immanuel Kant sought to ground these now regulative art/craft and artist/artisan polarities philosophically. He distinguished craft as "paid art" from "free," art which aims only at pleasure, and then distinguished sensual pleasure from aesthetic pleasure in the fine arts, which is based on the disinterested play of imagination and understanding responding to form. The craft work, by contrast, is something appreciated on the basis of an interest or purpose. Kant also distinguished fine art from craft by the way each is made. Fine art is the product of genius and imagination, rich in attributes that become a source of inexhaustible play for the mind. The work of craft, by contrast, is the result of a specific intention carried out according to routine procedures. Although craft makers often give works such as tableware a tasteful form, Kant observes, that does not make them fine art unless they are contemplated aesthetically apart from purpose.

The main contribution of the Romantic theorists and idealist philosophers to the fine-art/craft opposition was to increase the distance between art and craft by elevating the idea of fine art to the status of a metaphysical absolute and the ideal of the artist to that of a spiritual vocation. Meanwhile, as the flood of cheap goods from the industrial revolution forced thousands of weavers, potters, and others to give up their workshops and enter the factories as laborers, many crafts began to disappear along with craft skills. The brutal conditions of many English factories and the mediocre design of their products led John Ruskin and William Morris to attack both the industrial system and the polarity of fine art and craft. They called for a free work environment where artisans could design and execute their own works with hand tools. Despite Ruskin's and Morris's call for reuniting the fine arts with the crafts, both writers accepted the established hierarchy of the arts, viewing them as a pyramid, with the many crafts at the base and the fine arts of painting, sculpture, poetry, and music at the apex.

The utopian experiments of the Arts and Crafts movement that grew out of these ideas soon disappeared, but left two legacies: the idea of total design, closely linking the decorative arts to architecture and industry, and the studio craft movement with its small production potteries and individual weaving, jewelry, and furniture studios. The design movement, however, contravened the central principle of Ruskin and Morris by separating the designer (artist) and the maker (artisan). The studio craft movement also failed to liberate the craft worker, remaining a middle-class affair, tinged by nostalgia for the simple life. Yet, the studio craft movement did give the term *crafts* an additional meaning—the handmade item of decorative art in clay, fiber, wood, glass, or metal sold as an alternative to machine products. Art museums generally preferred the term *decorative arts,* which embraced both the handcrafted work for everyday use and the industrial products of modernist design. Moreover, the term *craft* had by now come to be associated with three other types of activity, also of lower cultural status: the "craft unions" (carpentry, plumbing, masonry), the fast-disappearing "country crafts" (blacksmithing, chair making, quilting), and the "home," "hobby," "school," and "camp" crafts (woodworking, sewing, model building).

Most twentieth-century philosophers have concerned themselves with problems within the fine arts, giving scant attention to the crafts as product and not much more to craft as skill. Among the few who have explored the general idea of craft, R. G. Collingwood (1938) made the art/craft polarity a driving motif of his aesthetics. [*See* Collingwood.] Collingwood attacked the confusion between "art proper" and craft, defining craft as the attempt to achieve a preconceived result through a series of means-ends relations—planning and execution, raw material and product, matter and form. Art proper, for Collingwood, is a matter of imagination and expression in which the artist does not know in advance what the outcome will be. Like Kant, Collingwood sought a philosophical distinction that would separate art and craft on grounds of principle rather than genre or medium. Thus, music created as a means to arouse emotion, such as hymns or patriotic marches, is craft, whereas music that expresses emotion in a way that demands an act of interpretation is art. Although many philosophers have criticized Collingwood's version of the art/craft polarity as too severe, especially his idealist view of art, few have rejected the art/craft distinction outright. On the contrary, the art/craft distinction has been taken for granted in most aesthetics, art criticism, and art history. H. W. Janson's (1962) art-history text, which was widely used between 1962 and the early 1990s, opens with an essay that makes the distinction between art and craft the presupposition of doing art history at all.

John Dewey was among the few philosophers to reject the separation between art and craft. By making aesthetic experience an aspect of experience in general, he hoped to reconnect fine art with everyday life and the useful arts. Affirming a continuum from the lowliest peasant bowl to the finest Renaissance painting, Dewey insisted that the utility of an object does not prevent the kind of intense consummatory experience he calls aesthetic. Despite his criticism of the prevailing dualism between fine art and craft, however, Dewey believed that only an object's metaphorical "use" for integrative life experiences counts aesthetically. He also emphatically placed craft skill in a secondary status, dismissing works in which technique is prominent as merely "mechanical." [See Dewey.]

One might expect that some of the self-conscious "anti-art" proponents of the twentieth century would revalue craft vis-à-vis fine art. With the exception of Russian Constructivists such as Aleksandr Rodchenko and Varvara Stepanova, however, most of those who have attacked the cult of fine art have had little time for craft or craftspeople. Marcel Duchamp disdained the remaining elements of craft skill in painting, rejecting what he called the "merely retinal," whether in its Post-Impressionist or abstract versions. Nor did Duchamp's "readymades"—ordinary manufactured items such as a snow shovel, bottle rack, or urinal—reflect an affirmation of craft values. As industrial goods, they were not chosen for their skilled making and Duchamp's exhibiting them as signed works of art denied their functionality. Paradoxically, Duchamp, like later conceptual art theorists, demoted art only to elevate the artist as intellectual. What counts are the artist's ideas, not skill; the artist's independence, not ordinary needs; the artist's creative gesture, not the object—whether the autonomous piece of fine art or the useful piece of handicraft.

Over the last two decades, an increasing number of critics and art historians have claimed that fine-art and certain kinds of studio craft objects have become so alike that the line separating art and craft has disappeared. The convergence of fine art and studio craft began in the late 1950s when artists started using craft media such as metal, wood, or plastics in "mixed media" works and a few craftspeople adopted the latest art-world styles to make nonfunctional objects in clay or fiber. Critics, galleries, and art museums responded enthusiastically and by the 1970s potters were being called "ceramic sculptors," weavers were renamed "fiber artists," and the new kind of craft was collectively designated "art in craft media" or "crafts-as-art." At the same time, feminists were attacking the exclusion of domestic crafts such as quilts and embroidery from fine art and soon quilts were promoted to art status and fiber artists began turning out "art quilts." In the 1990s, the Smithsonian's Renwick Gallery made "aesthetics not function or design . . . the essential criteria" for its permanent collection of American crafts. Most of the crafts-as-art objects in the Renwick could as easily be exhibited in a museum of contemporary art as in one dedicated to craft. The only connection between many of these objects and traditional crafts is their being made of clay, wood, fiber, metal, or glass and a lingering evidence of technical virtuosity. Yet, compared to a great deal of what passes for cutting-edge fine art, many craft-as-art works are still too beautifully made and insufficiently cerebral or political to claim wider art-world interest.

By the late twentieth century, the range of objects and activities that can be included under fine art has become so broad that the art/craft polarity has indeed been partially effaced, at least with respect to two of the four traditional characteristics of craft. Art-world practice has long since assimilated the media historically associated with craft, whether clay and fiber or popular song and dance. Aestheticians from Dewey to Ted Cohen and Arthur C. Danto have declared that practical function per se is no impediment to art status. The only aspects of craft that remain a handicap to art status are an overt concern for the market and an emphasis on skill and established forms. Because traditional craftspeople make items of use, they have never tried to hide their relation to economic transactions or client demands. This makes them vulnerable to the snobbery of a fine-art world that has covered its own market practices with ideals of creative genius, the self-sufficient work, and aesthetic contemplation. As for skill, there is a long tradition going back to the Renaissance of subordinating technique to idea and inspiration, but only in the twentieth century has clumsiness become for some a mark of advanced art status. Not only is craft in the sense of skill devalued by the contemporary art world, but since the eighteenth century, technique in general has been regularly disparaged by most aestheticians, something on which Kant, Collingwood, and Dewey were agreed. Among contemporary philosophers, V. A. Howard (1982) is one of the few to have given craft skill a sympathetic and extended analysis.

Yet, many craftspeople continue to make functional objects that reflect traditional techniques and forms in the belief that the integration of form with function gives the craft work a depth lacking in contemporary fine art. Many traditional craft makers believe that their work connects them not only to a millennial European craft tradition but to a worldwide multicultural practice, whereas their colleagues who have become part of the "art world" have narrowed their horizons. From the traditionalist's perspective, the crafts-as-art people have not overcome the art/craft polarity, but simply surrendered to the fine-art world on fine art's terms. Naturally, European and American craft makers are not neatly divided into two camps; many craftspeople hold intermediate positions between crafts-as-art and traditionalism, such as the makers of "art furniture" or "art quilts" who adopt innovative forms and techniques but still intend their works to be used. Yet, the persistence of the debate over how far craft makers should go in embracing the values of the contemporary art world suggests that there is matter here for aesthetic reflection.

The great value of the traditional craft object, a value that links it to the old idea of art before it was split into fine art and craft, is the craft work's relation to touch, use, and the body. A functional craft work is not something to be merely contemplated but to be touched and enjoyed in being used, whereas the preferred destination of the craft-as-art object, like the autonomous fine-art work, is the gallery or museum, the "do not touch" venues par excellence. One reason the traditional craft object has been ranked so low is that it is connected to bodily functions such as eating, drinking, sitting, sleeping, and dressing and that women have been among the principle craft makers. Some feminists have recognized that besides getting more women artists or women-identified genres into fine art, we ought to rethink our ideas of art and the aesthetic from the point of view of craft and everyday use.

Where would one turn in the history of aesthetics to get a start on an aesthetics of craft that was neither Ruskinian nostalgia nor vulgar Marxist utility? Certainly, there are still resources in the writings of Morris and Dewey and further back in William Hogarth's sensuous and functional idea of beauty or in Johann Gottfried von Herder's championing of "touch" against the assumed superiority of eye and ear. One might also look to women's reflections on the importance of the everyday, to writers such as Emily Dickinson, Sarah Orne Jewett, or Virginia Woolf, or to the many women painters who were pushed toward domestic portraiture, still life, and flowers. Moreover, recent feminist explorations of the place of the body or of the importance of detail in women's work would play a part. Just as some contemporary moralists such as Todorov have meditated the difference between a "heroic" and an "ordinary" morality, one needs to explore what an aesthetics would look like that finally laid to rest the ideals of disinterested contemplation, the self-sufficient artwork, and the sublime artist-genius. The danger in conceiving such a program in terms of an "aesthetics of craft" is that one could easily fall back into subsuming craft under existing ideas of the aesthetic as if that were a promotion. What is needed is not so much an aesthetics of the ordinary as an ordinary aesthetic.

[See also Anthropology and Aesthetics; Artifact; Feminism; Folk Art; Food; and Glass.]

BIBLIOGRAPHY

Cohen, Ted. "Clay for Contemplation." *Crafts* 99 (November–December 1990): 17–19.
Cole, Bruce. *The Renaissance Artist at Work: From Pisano to Titian.* New York, 1983.
Collingwood, R. G. *The Principles of Art.* Oxford, 1938.
Danto, Arthur C. "Fine Art and the Functional Object." *Glass* 51 (Spring 1993): 24–29.
Dewey, John. *Art as Experience.* New York, 1934.
Diamonstein, Barbaralee. *Handmade in America: Conversations with Fourteen Craftmasters.* New York, 1983.
Donovan, Josephine. "Everyday Use and Moments of Being: Toward a Nondominative Aesthetic." In *Aesthetics in Feminist Perspective*, edited by Hilde Hein and Carolyn Korsmeyer, pp. 53–67. Bloomington, Ind., 1993.
Guthrie, Derek. "The Eloquent Object Gagged by Kitsch." *New Art Examiner* 16.1 (September 1988): 26–29.
Haskell, Francis. *Patrons and Painters: A Study in the Relations between Italian Art and Society in the Age of the Baroque.* Rev. enl. ed. New Haven, 1980.
Howard, V. A. *Artistry: The Work of Artists.* Indianapolis, 1982.
Janaway, Christopher. "Arts and Crafts in Plato and Collingwood." *Journal of Aesthetics and Art Criticism* 50.1 (Winter 1992): 45–54.
Janson, H. W. *History of Art* (1962). 5th ed. Revised and expanded by Anthony F. Janson. New York, 1995.
Kant, Immanuel. *The Critique of Judgment.* Translated by Werner S. Pluhar. Indianapolis, 1987.
Kristeller, Paul Oskar. *Renaissance Thought and the Arts.* Exp. ed. Princeton, N.J., 1990.
Lucie-Smith, Edward. *The Story of Craft: The Craftsman's Role in Society.* Reprint, New York, 1984.
Manhart, Marcia, and Tom Manhart, eds. *The Eloquent Object: The Evolution of American Art in Craft Media since 1945.* Tulsa, Okla., 1987.
McMorris, Penny, and Michael Kile. *The Art Quilt.* San Francisco, 1986.
Todorov, Tzvetan. *Facing the Extreme: Moral Life in the Concentration Camps.* Translated by Arthur Demer and Abigail Pollak. New York, 1996.

LARRY SHINER

CREATIVITY. [*To treat the aesthetics and psychology of creativity, this entry comprises three essays:*
Conceptual and Historical Overview
Explaining Creativity
Creativity and Psychology
The first essay is an overview of the topic of creativity in the history of aesthetics from Plato to the present. The second and third essays are reflections on, first, the question whether creativity can be explained and, second, the treatment of creativity in psychology. For related discussion, see Appropriation; Artificial Intelligence; Artist, *article on* History of the Concept; Genius; *and* Originality.]

Conceptual and Historical Overview

Studies of creativity have been extraordinarily varied in scope and purpose. They are found in inquiries about artificial intelligence, hemispherical brain theory, psychoanalysis, literary criticism, experimental and cognitive psychology, and philosophy, among others. Although philosophical and psychological studies of the topic are typically interdependent, it is the former that will be of chief concern in this survey. Within philosophical approaches, there are also varied kinds of study, the most noteworthy of which are represented by interests in creativity in science and in art. Contemporary ideas of creativity in science and, indeed, in all forms of activity have origins in conceptions of artistic creative achievement. In what follows, this origin, its evolution, and the general kinds of questions that are asked about creativity will be central.

Assumptions about the features that mark off creative acts undergird creativity studies, guiding their approaches and the directions these approaches take, and these should be brought to the fore. In both informal or everyday conversations and in formal, scientific, and philosophical discussions, creative persons and creative acts are referred to as if most, if not all, of us knew the difference between creative and noncreative persons and activities. If asked which persons and activities serve as examples, our answers should suggest what features prompt the designation "creative." One most general expectation is that creative persons have a disposition or condition (a "capacity") for bringing something into being. Not just anything brought into being invites us to call it a creation, however. There is a stronger or radical and normative expectation that what is brought into being be regarded as having *newness* and (at least for the creator) *value*. The newness of the outcome of such a radical creative act is a characteristic not simply of another instance of a known class—a numerical newness, such as may be attributed to a freshly stamped penny or a blade of grass that has just matured—but is an instance of some new kind. It is a thing that is one of its kind that occurs for the first time, and being thus newly intelligible, is valuable.

In addition to the value of intelligibility, one expects the value of the outcome of a creative act to be beautiful, or more generally, excellent—that is, appreciated for its own sake. One test of a creation's being valuable for its own sake is its capacity for sustaining appreciation and the likelihood that it inspires future achievements. Creations, then, usually are expected to have an "instrumental" or extrinsic value, influencing the future evolution of styles. If these features of the product are unprecedented and unpredictable, the act that leads to them may be thought of as a creation ex nihilo—having intelligibility and value that are not exhaustively reducible to antecedents. Whether one accepts or rejects this radical conception of creativity in part depends on whether one assumes some form of metaphysical determinism. In any case, the two senses of "creativity," the weaker and the stronger, underlie the ways that creativity has been approached.

The earliest written discussion of appreciable length concerning what have become the major questions about creative activity in art is found in Plato's little dialogue, the *Ion*. Plato here proposed one of the key hypotheses found in later literature: creative persons—in this case, the rhapsodist, Ion—are dependent on a source beyond their rational powers. The conclusion is that performers and their sources (creative persons) are "out of their minds" and the source of excellence in creative work is a muse or a divine power that inspires the creator. Plato thus set the stage for the approach to creativity that does not rely on trying to find an explanation that makes creations humanly predictable. [*See* Plato.]

In contrast to the idea of inspiration, Aristotle set forth an explanation of art as craft, according to which creating is a straightforward and productive process of imposing a preconceived plan on some material—a bronze sphere is produced when brass is shaped by an agent, the artisan, who works according to an envisaged form of a sphere. This view exemplifies the weaker sense of "creativity" according to which creative acts simply bring something into being, even if what is brought into being is not a new form, or new kind of thing, but simply a different instantiation of an antecedent form. Aristotle's conception of creating as a natural process serves as a source for the second major approach to the topic, the approach that treats creative activity as a kind of event that can be explained with reference to conditions and laws or regularities common to psychological phenomena and natural processes in general. [*See* Aristotle.] Plato's and Aristotle's conceptions underlie the approaches that can be identified in the later writers of the nineteenth and twentieth centuries.

The third major conception of creativity is suggested by Immanuel Kant, who offered an option that was an important, if not the primary, impetus to creativity studies as they are known today. Kant's contribution is found in his discussion of genius in *The Critique of Judgment*. Genius is the condition by which new rules are given to art. New rules are the new ways artworks are formed so that they initiate new styles. These rules or ways of forming works of art are prompted by ideas ("aesthetical ideas") that express or mean more than can be understood conceptually. Neither these aesthetic ideas nor the rules are concepts; they cannot be conceptualized. They cannot serve as principles by which future works of new greatness and beauty can be produced (although they may be used by imitators or mannerists). Yet, they are exemplary in works of art that inspire future genius—that is, other creations of new rules—and thus the evolution of new styles. [*See* Kant.]

The general conception of the mind as creative evolved in nineteenth-century idealism and was influential in views of creativity in the arts proposed by literary scholars and poets such as Samuel Taylor Coleridge and William Wordsworth and by aestheticians such as Benedetto Croce and R. G. Collingwood. Croce's and Collingwood's aesthetic theories stressed the crucial role of imagination (which must be distinguished from conceptual thought) as creative and integral to expressive activity in the creator's experiences.

The idea that creative activity can be traced neither to a source beyond human and natural activity nor to established regularities suggests that special attention should be given to the creative agent and the productive process. As a result, most studies in this century have been focused on three distinct kinds of interests: (1) the person (the agent who works creatively), (2) the process itself, and (3) the product (the outcome of the process, which is what alerts us to something noteworthy about the character of the process that leads to a created product).

These foci of interest are the basis for a set of primary but overlapping questions according to which creativity studies can be organized: Who? Why? What? and How? Each question represents a set of concerns present when inquirers from diverse disciplines offer accounts of creativity.

The questions Who? and Why? are directed toward the personality traits and the motivations that may be distinctive to creative persons. The inquiries that fit these questions usually fall under the province of psychologists and, more generally, social and humanist scientists, although philosophical discussions can hardly avoid including some, if not fairly extensive, consideration of the characteristics and motives of creative persons. For instance, Croce's, Collingwood's, and John Dewey's views of creative activity embrace implied as well as explicit characterizations of the artistic motives and traits of those they regard as creative in the arts. Moreover, psychological studies sometimes become speculative and appear to be loosely undertaken excursions into philosophical territory. Psychoanalytic theorizing by Otto Rank and Carl Jung, for example, includes what may be regarded as philosophical speculation.

The question What? applies to attempts to describe the distinctive features, if any, and characteristic stages or phases of creative processes. Graham Wallas's (1954) classic description, which has been influential on both philosophical and psychological studies, identifies four stages: preparation, incubation, illumination or insight, and (in science) verification or (in the arts) elaboration. Preparation consists of the initial groping and systematic exploration of the problem or envisaged task. Incubation occurs when conscious work on the task is temporarily stopped; this stage is supposed to take place in a nonconscious or subconscious level of activity, which is presupposed, although of course not directly observed. Illumination or insight is the crucial stage when a solution is realized or when divergent ideas and qualities and materials fall into place and the "aha" experience is reached. From the creator's point of view, the new ideas seem to be discoveries. From the observer's or appreciator's view, the new idea is a creation. Illumination may occur in a moment, as it may have occurred for Amadeus Mozart, who is supposed to have said that he envisaged whole compositions and only needed to transcribe these as written scores. Or illumination may take place gradually over a relatively long period of time, as seems to be the case for Ludwig van Beethoven, who subjected his compositions to numerous revisions. The final stage, verification or elaboration, consists in refining what appeared to be discovered or created in the stage of illumination, and, as in the case of Beethoven, it may have occurred as incremental moments of the third, crucial stage.

The general problem of description has fallen into the province of psychologists such as Wallas, but it also is included in philosophical discussions such as those of Dewey, Collingwood, and more recent writers of articles who have been influenced by philosophers in the traditions initiated by Plato and Aristotle.

The final question, How? concerns explaining the way creative agents bring something new into being. This question has been addressed by psychologists, social scientists in general, and, as indicated earlier, philosophical inquirers—such as Plato, Aristotle, and Kant. In this century, such accounts have been offered from quite different philosophical frameworks by Jacques Maritain (1953), Monroe Beardsley (1965), and Paul Weiss (1992), and, in interdisciplinary work, for instance, by Arthur Koestler (1964). The hope of fostering creativity, a hope that underlies much contemporary interest in the topic, presupposes some form of explanation. The question How? also raises the issue of what can be expected of an explanation when sought for in the case of creativity. This aspect of the topic has been addressed explicitly by, among others, Carl Hausman (1984), John Hospers (1985), Douglas Morgan (1953), Vincent Tomas (1958), and Eliseo Vivas (1955). These writers question the idea that specific explanations could enable us to make confident predictions about creative persons or creative acts. They ask about the possibility and the meaning of explaining creativity.

An attempt to address the latter dimension of the problem raises an issue that is not always recognized or admitted by inquirers who address the other main problems. This issue brings into focus the distinctive features of the product or outcome of creative processes. It also returns us to the point that our topic may be divided according to two most general interests: (1) the person and process and (2) the product or outcome. One interest may be given priority over the other, for, on the one hand, it may be maintained that if one is to understand what created products are, one must understand what kind of process is creative and what kind of agent is capable of and responsible for bringing forth a new and valuable outcome—that is, who is responsible for the process. On the other hand, it may be insisted that one cannot identify and understand persons and processes thought to be creative if one does not first determine what distinguishes products as created. Disputes over which approach is the more appropriate are, in one way, pointless, for each proponent of one of the perspectives grants the relevance of the other. Even those such as Eric Fromm and Carl Rogers, who think that all humans are or in some degree can be creative—in flower arranging or in everyday activity as well as in science and art—can hardly avoid acknowledging as models the dramatic cases, such as Michelangelo, Mozart, Beethoven, Paul Cézanne, and Pablo Picasso, and that these artists are considered to be creative because of their achievements that were new and valuable.

If we then ask the question How? as it applies to what leads to products that are valuable and new in the strong sense mentioned earlier, we raise the issue of what we expect of an answer. Can we discover how to predict specific creative acts and the new and valuable properties of their created outcomes? If so, we seem to imply that such predictable outcomes are, after all, not new in the strong sense but either were created in the prediction itself or were potentialities functioning in antecedent conditions, so that creativity is subject to established laws or regularities. The first alternative simply shifts what is to be explained from the creation to the explanation itself. The second alternative implies a determinism of some kind, even if only that of a presupposition that the cosmos is in principle explainable in terms of scientific theories that meet the test of predictability. J. P. Guilford's and B. F. Skinner's experimental and behavioral approaches serve as examples in psychology, and, in philosophy, Brand Blanshard (1964) argued that creative acts have their basis in a fundamental teleological system that pervades the world and human thought. In contrast, Henri Bergson (1911, 1946) and Charles Peirce (1982) answered the question by arguing against the determinist assumption.

These issues have implications in aesthetics especially with respect to considerations of what is appropriate for critics' and art historians' interests in tracing works of art to their sources. The relevance of political and social conditions, artists' personalities, biography, and so on, for the task of analyzing and appraising works of art can be viewed in light of the extent to which such considerations show us how to understand what may not have been predictable or what may not have been exhaustively traceable to these factors. Further, and most obviously, if newness is an ingredient in created products, we face the question, How is what is new in an artwork to be characterized and interpreted in a way that avoids reducing the qualities of the outcome to aesthetic values that were accepted in the past?

[*See also* Bergson.]

BIBLIOGRAPHY

Seminal Works: The Origin of Philosophical Approaches

Aristotle. *Physics* and *Poetics*. In *The Basic Works of Aristotle*, edited by Richard McKeon. New York, 1941. See *Physics*, bk. 2, chs. 5–6, pp. 244–247.

Kant, Immanuel. *The Critique of Judgement*. Translated by J. C. Meredith. Oxford, 1952, See sections 46–50.

Plato. *The Ion*. Translated by Lane Cooper. In *The Collected Dialogues of Plato*, corr. ed., edited by Edith Hamilton and Huntington Cairns. Princeton, N.J., 1963.

Plato. *Phaedrus* and *Symposium*. In *The Dialogues of Plato*, translated by Benjamin Jowett. Oxford, 1889.

Representative Philosophical Perspectives

Bailin, Sharon. *Achieving Extraordinary Ends: An Essay on Creativity*. Dordrecht and Boston, 1988.

Beardsley, Monroe. "On the Creation of Art." *Journal of Aesthetics and Art Criticism* 23 (Spring 1965).

Bergson, Henri. "The Possible and the Real." In *Creative Evolution*, translated by Arthur Mitchell. New York, 1911.

Bergson, Henri. *The Creative Mind*. Translated by Mabelle L. Andison. New York, 1946.

Blanshard, Brand. *The Nature of Thought*. 2 vols. Reprint, New York, 1964. See vol. 2, chs. 22–24.

Dewey, John. *Art as Experience*. New York, 1934.

Dutton, Dennis, and Michael Krausz, eds. *The Concept of Creativity in Science and Art*. The Hague and Boston, 1981.

Freud, Sigmund. *Creative Writers and Day-Dreaming*. In *The Standard Edition of the Complete Psychological Works of Sigmund Freud*, edited by James Strachey, vol. 9. London, 1959.

Guilford, J. P. "Creativity." *American Psychologist* 5 (1950): 444–454.

Hausman, Carl R. *A Discourse on Novelty and Creation*. Reprint, Albany, N.Y., 1984.

Hospers, John. "Artistic Creativity." *Journal of Aesthetics and Art Criticism* 43.3 (Spring 1985): 243–255.

Jung, Carl G. "General Description of Types." In *Psychological Types*, translated by H. Godwin Baynes, pp. 412–517. New York, 1923.

Jung, Carl G. "Psychology and Literature." In *Modern Man in Search of a Soul*, translated by W. S. Dell and Cary F. Baynes, pp. 175–199. New York, 1933.

Koestler, Arthur. *The Act of Creation*. New York, 1964.

Langer, Susanne K. *Feeling and Form*. New York, 1953.

Maritain, Jacques. *Creative Intuition in Art and Poetry*. New York, 1953.

Morgan, Douglas. "Creativity Today." *Journal of Aesthetics and Art Criticism* 12 (1953): 1–24.

Peirce, Charles S. "The Doctrine of Necessity Examined." *Monist* 2 (1892).

Rank, Otto. *Art and Artist: Creative Urge and Personality Development*. Translated by Charles Francis Atkinson. New York, 1932.

Rothenberg, Albert, and Carl R. Hausman, eds. *The Creativity Question*. Durham, N.C., 1976.

Skinner, B. F. "A Lecture on 'Having' a Poem." In *Cumulative Record: A Selection of Papers*, 3d ed. New York, 1972.

Tomas, Vincent. "Creativity in Art." *Philosophical Review* 67.1 (January 1958): 1–15.

Vivas, Eliseo. *Creation and Discovery: Essays in Criticism and Aesthetics*. New York, 1955.

Wallas, Graham. "Stages of Control." In *The Art of Thought*. Reprint, New York, 1954.

Weiss, Paul. *Creative Ventures*. Carbondale, Ill., 1992.

CARL R. HAUSMAN

Explaining Creativity

Several arguments suggest the conclusion that creativity cannot be explained. Yet, aspects of it can be rationally discussed. What part of it is inexplicable? This part turns out to be rather small.

Creativity and its cognates mean the ability to produce something original (in the sense of new rather than authentic) in the arts, in the sciences, and in any other endeavor. Attempts to explain this ability result in paradox. The paradox cannot be dispelled at the individual level, only at the social level of tradition. An ascription of creativity to an object, and by extension to its creator, is a social matter, rather than disclosure of an inherent property of thing or person.

The Greek myth of the Muses as found in Homer and Hesiod illustrates the ancient view that creativity requires supernatural explanation (see also Plato, *Apology* 22c and *Phaedrus* 245a).

Say, Virgins, seated round the throne divine,
All-knowing goddesses! Immortal nine!
. . . Daughters of Jove, assist! Inspired by you,
The mighty labour dauntless I pursue.
(Homer, *Iliad,* book 2, 572ff., translated by Alexander Pope)

So spoke the fresh-voiced daughters of great Zeus
And plucked and gave a staff to me, a shoot
Of blooming laurel, wonderful to see,
And breathed a sacred voice into my mouth
With which to celebrate the things to come
And things which were before. They ordered me
To sing the race of blessed ones who live
Forever, and to hymn the Muses first
And at the end.
(Hesiod, *Theogony* 30ff., translated by Dorothea Wender)

This ancient theory that creativity is a gift of the gods remains influential in our culture (laminated into the etymology of "inspiration"), especially as far as the arts are concerned; it was eliminated from science thanks to Sir Francis Bacon's intervention (at the dawn of the scientific era), in an attempt to naturalize and foster creativity, relying on purely secular and even mechanical means, that is, research techniques. Although a great writer, Bacon focused on creativity in scientific research, not in the arts. His model was the change of draftsmanship from a knack to a reliable technique available to all and sundry with the invention of the ruler and the compass. He sought the analogue of these draftsman's tools in a methodology for scientific research, hoping that this would eliminate much that passed for knowledge but that seemed to him mere imaginative fiction (his famous idols of the tribe, the cave, the marketplace, and the theater [Bacon, 1620]). Because knowledge was for use, he said that fact should replace fiction. Bacon was hostile to inspiration and imagination as tools for those who would understand the natural world, "Nature." Researchers attempting to comprehend nature should prepare their minds by humbly emptying them of prejudices, so as to be able to observe natural facts as they are, undistorted, while resisting the temptation to jump to conclusions. This is Bacon's theory of science as inductive. Despite latter-day objections by such great scientists as Albert Einstein (1949) and such great philosophers as Karl Popper (1959), it remains immensely influential, not least in the arts, where rejection of science usually amounts to rejecting the unimaginative-pedestrian-observational, that is, an oversimplified Baconian view of science. Contra Bacon, scientific research is imaginative, and bears little resemblance to Baconian induction. Yet, Bacons's views prevail among the supporters and the opponents of science.

At the dawn of science, artists were not hostile to what was emerging. Many artists considered themselves students of nature, so in the wake of the Renaissance masters and in accord with the scientific revolution, they sought to approach it through the study of perspective, optics, color,

and so on, looking for the secrets of representing it truly, that is, without prejudice, and with the personal creative equation minimized. This attitude survived into the nineteenth century: " 'Painting is a science', Constable said, 'and should be pursued as an inquiry into the laws of nature. Why, then, may not landscape painting be considered as a branch of natural philosophy, of which pictures are but the experiments' " (Gombrich, 1960, p. 33).

Similarly, countless novelists, and even poets, have declared the supremacy of a scientific attitude (as described by Bacon) over free inspiration. This obedience to science and minimizing of the personal equation aroused the scorn of William Blake and the Romantics, who, in a powerful but not wholly coherent critique, linked creativity to the life force and science to the hubristic death wish (Mary Shelley, *Frankenstein,* 1818). The Romantic critique of science attacked it as dehumanizing, concluding that life-affirming art was superior to science. In the twentieth century, the Romantic polarizing of art and science became the dominant or established view.

We are today surrounded by echoes of these past ideas and debates over the Muses and induction, over science and art, over enlightenment and Romanticism. Science counterattacked the Romantic remystification of creativity. The rise of scientific psychology and sociology in the nineteenth century gave impetus to (Baconian) attempts to provide a scientific account of creativity, hoping thereby not only to explain it but to tame it, to shift it from an independent variable to a dependent variable, from the supernatural and irrational to the rational. Under such scientific control, it might then even be possible to foster creativity. These attempts cover a range from the purely psychological (psychoanalytic, behavioristic [Subotnik and Arnold, 1994], neuropsychological [Bunge, 1993], and all points in between [Hershman and Lieb, 1988; Leddy, 1990; Isaksen et al., 1993]) to the social (including Marxism and its derivative the sociology of knowledge). Much creativity, perhaps more poetic than scientific, went into these attempts to find a causal variable that would account for creativity in the arts as well as in the sciences.

Yet, a paradox lurks in the vicinity of all attempts at explaining creativity. It is a special case of Plato's paradox of knowledge *(Meno).* An explanation is nowadays standardly taken to consist in the deduction of the statement describing what is to be explained from a set of other statements, including some of a (putative) universal character (laws). Logically, any such explanation can also be used to predict future creative acts. But predicting a future act of creation is paradoxical: predicted, it is already known (Tomas, 1958; pace Henze, 1966). The result of an act of creation is original, and so it is unpredictable. If it could be anticipated or predicted, then it would not be original, but rather, "predictable." Indeed, a major overtone of *creativity* is *unique.* The soaring achievements of great artists such as Homer,

William Shakespeare, Leonardo da Vinci, Rembrandt van Rijn, Johann Wolfgang Goethe—or, for that matter, of great scientists such as Galileo Galilei, Isaac Newton, and Einstein—are hardly repeatable events in the sense required by scientific explanation. Unique events are the domain of history, and they invite *historical* explanation, where the explaining laws are of the most obvious kind, possibly even trivial. Historical explanation will not discover a new causal variable, least of all a magic bullet of creativity.

What is the situation created by this paradox? Uncertainty as to whether there is such a thing as a faculty or condition of creativity or whether there are only unique, inexplicable talents and "gifts." In our egalitarian era, all natural talents create social and hence intellectual tension, ambivalence. Accomplishments in the arts, in performance, in science, and in sports require a certain amount of training, practice, encouragement, and other routinized attentions. Thomas Alva Edison said that genius is 1 percent inspiration and 99 percent perspiration, pithily summarizing the view of many artists as well as scientists. But egalitarianism does not and cannot mean that training is a sufficient cause for creativity, that with enough of it *anyone* can become an innovative scientist, author of literature, or artist of the zeitgeist. Only inductivists think that enough perspiration (of the right kind) undergoes a qualitative change into inspiration.

The Romantics (creativity is mysterious) and the scientific investigators of creativity (creativity is explicable, hence not mysterious) share a common assumption: that creativity is a mental faculty, an internal state that can be brought out, or cultivated, or encouraged. Perhaps this assumption should be challenged (Briskman, 1980; Becker, 1982; Hospers, 1985). Few are creative or gifted, fewer still are able to sustain creativity over a career, and still fewer shine in more than one field. (The physicists Einstein and Richard Feynman, interestingly, were, in their different ways, masters of the short literary form, the essay.) Children, even young adults, can seem bright and gifted, but then achieve little later on, despite recognition and encouragement. How did the mental faculty fail?

If treating creativity as a faculty is common sense, so also is the idea that there is an impersonal and objective side to creativity: it is an ascription more than it is an achievement. In commonsense usage, *creativity* is a comparison word: its use presupposes that there are other works that are not creative—routine, stale, formulaic, unoriginal. Such lesser works constitute the background against which the judgment of creativity is made; and so by common sense, creativity is a judgment about works rather than a faculty of minds. In much the same way, when a work is judged great, it is compared to its competitors, not claimed to possess some attribute—greatness—that its competitors lack. By common sense, creativity, like greatness, is ascribed, not

achieved. Common sense, we see, is conflicted between hypostatizing creativity as a mental faculty of persons or a property of works, and construing it instead as a judgment, an ascription.

If we press further the account of creativity as judgment, we will find that only a small element continues to elude rational discussion. Judgments as to creativity (like greatness) invariably appear first as individual judgments. Later on, some of these judgments gain wide acceptance and thus become part of the tradition of artistic assessment, which is part of the artistic tradition as a whole. This account of matters need not postulate that there is some property of creativity to be found in works of art or in their creators. Assessing creativity requires viewing the tradition as a whole, locating the work (and the artist) within it, and then making a judgment (of creativity).

The arts (and the sciences) are historical traditions in which a work is judged creative because of the relative value ascribed to it *in the tradition*. A plausible model of this aspect of artistic traditions is that put forward by E. H. Gombrich (1960). According to Gombrich an artistic tradition is a series of problem situations, to do with such matters as the representation of nature or the evolution of style. Ingenious new works, with no bearing on any problem situation, will not "register," that is, not strike anyone as new or ingenious, and hence will not be embraced by the tradition, or enrich it, or reshape it. Gombrich's model specifies the kind of comparison that is made between works when some are judged creative. Accounts of creativity that treat it as a mental faculty or property cannot explain the difference between work that influences all subsequent art and work that is ignored. Those matters are judgments delivered within the tradition (Bailin, 1988). No single individual controls the tradition, but each is subject to and may influence its collective judgments (which may, of course, be revised: consider the nineteenth-century revaluations of Johann Sebastian Bach and of Wolfgang Amadeus Mozart). Creativity only shows itself against this background of tradition, a social production involving many individuals who ascribe creativity to work that subsequently the tradition treats accordingly. Above all, such judgments of creativity are post hoc and thus neither offer any formula for fostering creativity nor are in any danger from the paradox of predicting future creations.

The scientific project of demystifying creativity as far as possible is an attractive one. The Muses and the inchoate Romantic forces of personality are neither necessary nor sufficient for art nor for science. If creativity is a post hoc judgment, is there anything left of that mysterious moment of inspiration, of that mysterious talent or gift given (by the gods) to some but not to all? Should one try to specify further the factor that is lacking in the run-of-the-mill efforts within a preexisting tradition and present in a lucky few that alter, even transcend, it? Hardly, but in some measure of compensation for this lack, perhaps the following observation could be added: In science, most bright ideas turn out to be false and are quickly discarded by their originators; perhaps the same is true in art. The original and the new are not in short supply. What is in short supply is the judgment and the persistence necessary to take a momentary flash, or fortunate gift, and turn it into something more permanent, into something that will signify in the whole tradition. This is where we may be able to train, to challenge, to encourage, and even to foster the work that may eventually have creativity ascribed to it and its creator.

[*See also* Nature, *article on* Nature and Artistic Creation.]

BIBLIOGRAPHY

Bacon, Francis. *Novum Organum* (1620). In *The Works of Francis Bacon,* edited by James Spedding, Robert Leslie Ellis, and Douglas Devon Heath, vol. 1. London, 1857.

Bailin, Sharon. *Achieving Extraordinary Ends: An Essay on Creativity.* Dordrecht and Boston, 1988.

Becker, Howard S. *Art Worlds.* Berkeley, 1982.

Briskman, Larry. "Creative Product and Creative Process in Science and Art." *Inquiry* 23 (1980): 83–106.

Bunge, Mario. "Explaining Creativity." In *Creativity and Consciousness: Philosophical and Psychological Dimensions,* edited by Jerzy Brzezinksi, Santo Di Nuovo, Tadeusz Marek, and Tomasz Maruszewski, pp. 299–304. Amsterdam and Atlanta, 1993.

Einstein, Albert. "Autobiographical Notes" (1949). In *Albert Einstein: Philosopher-Scientist,* 2d ed., edited by Paul Arthur Schilpp. New York, 1951.

Feyerabend, Paul. "On the Improvement of the Sciences and the Arts, and the Possible Identity of the Two." In *Proceedings of the Boston Colloquium for the Philosophy of Science 1964–1966, in Memory of Norwood Russell Hanson,* edited by Robert S. Cohen and Marx W. Wartofsky, Boston Studies in the Philosophy of Science, vol. 3, pp. 387–415. Dordrecht and Boston, 1967.

Feynman, Richard P. *Surely You're Joking, Mr. Feynman: Adventures of a Curious Character.* As told to Ralph Leighton, edited by Edward Hutchings. New York, 1985.

Gombrich, E. H. *Art and Illusion: A Study in the Psychology of Pictorial Representation* (1960). 2d rev. ed. Reprint, Princeton, N.J., 1969.

Henze, Donald F. "Creativity and Prediction." *British Journal of Aesthetics* 6 (1966): 230–245.

Hershman, D. Jablow, and Julian Lieb. *The Key to Genius.* Buffalo, N.Y., 1988.

Hospers, John. "Artistic Creativity." *Journal of Aesthetics and Art Criticism,* 43.3 (Spring 1985): 243–255.

Isaksen, Scott G., Mary C. Murdock, Roger L. Firestien, and Donald J. Treffinger, eds. *Understanding and Recognizing Creativity: The Emergence of a Discipline.* Norwood, N.J., 1993.

Jarvie, I. C. "The Objectivity of Criticism of the Arts." *Ratio* 9.1 (June 1967): 67–83.

Jarvie, I. C. "The Rationality of Creativity." In *The Concept of Creativity in Science and Art,* edited by Denis Dutton and Michael Krausz, pp. 109–128. The Hague and Boston, 1981.

Leddy, Thomas. "Is the Creative Process in Art a Form of Puzzle Solving?" *Journal of Aesthetic Education* 24.3 (1990): 83–97.

Ludwig, Arnold M. *The Price of Greatness: Resolving the Creativity and Madness Controversy.* New York, 1995.

Shelley, Mary. *Frankenstein or the Modern Prometheus* (1818). Edited by D. L. Macdonald and Kathleen Scherf. Peterborough, Ontario, 1994.

Subotnik, Rena F., and Karen D. Arnold. *Beyond Terman: Contemporary Longitudinal Studies of Giftedness and Talent.* Norwood, N.J., 1994.

Tomas, Vincent. "Creativity in Art." *Philosophical Review* 67.1 (January 1958): 1–15.

I. C. Jarvie

Creativity and Psychology

The notion of creativity is relatively recent in Western history. Although there were surely artists and possibly even musicians in early prehistoric times and all forms of art flourished to some degree thereafter, the modern conception of creation by an individual or group arose during the period of the Renaissance in Europe. The advent of Romanticism in the last century was accompanied by increased interest in and valuation of creativity as a special individual capacity in literature, art, and music. Toward the end of that century, creativity became a subject of analysis and study among diverse disciplinary groups and the focus has continued to the present day.

Despite a large amount of literature on the topic, the conceptual status of creativity is largely unsettled. Many writers treat creativity as synonymous with making of any type without restrictions such as innovation, tangibility, value, or even appropriateness. Others follow restrictions carefully and limit usage to high-level achievement in the arts, technological invention, and inspiratory and theoretical thinking in intellectual disciplines. Sometimes connected with a focus on high-level achievement are metaphysical speculations about the possibility of creation ex nihilo. Cultural factors influence these points of view; there is a tension between Western egalitarian perspectives emphasizing creative activity in everyday pursuits or creative potential in everyone and what some consider an elitist focus on the highest levels of capacity and achievement. In Eastern cultures, where ideas related to creativity were propounded far earlier than in the West, even though the specific term *creativity* may only recently have come into general use there, emphasis is on a nonindividualized inner experience or inner mental state where no tangible product results.

The common factor underlying all viewpoints about the concept is that creativity is positively valued; often it is considered the highest capacity that human beings possess. Recognizing the universal valuation placed on the concept, together with the most commonsense considerations regarding making, that is, making or bringing into being something new, the most consistent and appropriate definition of creativity is the capacity or state of bringing forth something *both valuable and new.* This value may consist of pragmatic and extrinsic usefulness as found in such fields as science and technology or it may consist of intrinsic and sometimes intangible positive worth as in art and theology.

Aesthetic approaches to creativity have by and large considered features of the aesthetic object and attempted to determine or deduce necessary factors in its production. Or, creativity and the creative process have been viewed in their broad overall manifestations or characteristics and conclusions about these applied to aesthetics as a particular case. Consequently, there are theories such as Benedetto Croce's that, as art is autonomous, the work of art is created in the artist's mind.

The scientific approach to creativity has largely been concerned with attempting to make it explainable in physical or psychological terms, to render it predictable or otherwise comprehensible and analyzed. Psychologists, as well as other social scientists, have hoped to identify particular cognitive, affective, motivational, and social factors that account for creative capacity and achievement. To do so, they have employed personality and intelligence tests with creative people and reported correlations with general factors such as a high proportion of movement responses and adaptive control of psychological regression on Rorschach tests, high degrees of psychopathology together with ego strength on the Minnesota Multiphasic Inventory, and a variety of general personality characteristics such as courage, autonomy, internal locus of control, and introversion, as well as its contrary, extraversion. Other approaches have consisted of demographic and historical surveys, direct and indirect observations of creative work in progress, and experiments involving creative activity such as producing metaphors, or else presumed simulations of creative thinking such as producing unusual associations or unusual ideas, producing large numbers of associations, or responding effectively to open-ended questions and tasks. In addition to the difficulty in establishing whether particular correlational factors are either necessary or sufficient to account for creative outcomes, serious questions must in particular be raised about whether the simulated tasks used so far have involved meaningful or valid aspects of creative activity.

From the point of view of those conceptualizing creativity as the production of elements ex nihilo, that is, the production of a thing or things distinguished as unprecedented and without any connections (or at least, without any clear connections) to antecedent factors or elements, the attempt to make predictions about creativity—about who will create, what or when created elements will occur—is fruitless and contradictory. Without direct or discernible connections to past factors, creative events are intrinsically unpredictable. Restricting creativity and creative production to an ex nihilo condition seems to put limits on human agency, however, and some adherents of this position adopt theological or supernatural explanations, deity being the only agent conceived as capable of bringing something out of nothing. Other adherents of this position usually adopt a view that creativity is intelligible in terms of component factors such as spontaneity but an indeterminate element is involved.

Social-science explications and perspectives regarding creativity fall into four categories: individual differences; endowment; functional; conflict. Although these categories overlap to a certain extent, they characterize essential features of findings, theories, and approaches. The individual differences perspective is the most prevalent one among psychologists. Creativity is considered to be the resultant of a special trait or collection of intercorrelated traits in particular individuals. Tests are constructed to identify the creativity trait and other intercorrelated traits derived from experiments, biographies, or other descriptions of creative production or orientation. One finding is that intelligence, as measured by current intelligence tests, does not correlate directly with such identified creativity. A certain level of intelligence—average to slightly above average—is required for most types of creativity, but higher levels of intelligence do not correlate with higher levels of creativity (except possibly in the sciences). Other defined traits identified with some frequency in numerous studies that have been carried out are preference for asymmetry, associational fluency, field independence, and tolerance for ambiguity. Various forms of psychological imbalance, including what one investigator terms "psychoticism" (Eysenck, 1993), have also been reported, but ratings of such traits have often been inappropriately based primarily on the unusual and sometimes deviant ways of thinking used by creative people. Although psychological imbalance and creativity are both deviations from the norm, they are not therefore equivalent.

Other correlations have been sought between creative traits and capacities and factors that facilitate or inhibit their expression. An age factor operates particularly in the fields of physics and mathematics where creative achievement peaks much earlier than in other fields. Education facilitates creativity in most fields according to the degrees represented on an inverted U-shaped curve, where neither small nor large amounts of education correlate with creative achievement. With respect to gender, aggressive personality features in women have been associated with creative achievement in mathematics; however, historical lack of opportunity for expression of tangible creativity by females has been so extensive that all such findings have to be assessed in a sociological context. Particular skills are clearly found to correlate with creative success in a number of fields, the most notable being auditory skills in music, drawing skills in visual arts, verbal skills in literary and conceptual fields. In addition to high conceptual capacities, broad interests and use of visual imagery have also been identified in groups of successful scientists.

Followers of the individual differences perspective tend not to take any position on whether traits measured are inborn or produced during the course of growth and development. For the endowment perspective, the distinguishing feature is an assumption, usually implicit but sometimes explicitly stated, that creativity is an inborn or endowed capacity. Biographical analyses, psychoanalytic studies, and so-called pathographical studies that trace pathological, particularly psychopathological, factors in well-known creative people are all of this type insofar as they describe influences on a person's creative gift. Similarly, when such studies assert that creative persons transform or otherwise alter their experiences, personal conflicts, and social or other influences by means of an undefined creative gift, capacity, or genius, they adopt the endowment position. Because the gift is considered to be present prior to any of the other phenomena described, it must either be inborn or be endowed in a metaphysical fashion. Endowment types of studies have proposed that persons possessing such assumed capacities have been motivated to be creative because of both positive and negative factors and experiences, that the subject matter and style of creative works, especially artworks, often derive from particular constellations of intrapsychic or interpersonal events, that various types of pathology are overcome in producing creative work, and that having inborn creative capacities influences overall psychological development.

Both the endowment and the individual differences perspectives are concerned with qualities of the creative person or agent, whereas the functional and conflict perspectives focus more directly on creative processes and products. The functional perspective accounts for creative activities and events on the basis of the needs and purposes fulfilled. Describing creativity as a special form of problem solving is a clear example. Followers of this position are often cognitive scientists who describe computer programs—such as one named "Bacon" (Langley et al., 1987) and others based on associational thought models known as parallel-processing operations—that are capable of replicating important scientific discoveries and other types of high-level problem solving. Others have described problem finding and concern for discovery as creative strategies as well as an exploratory creative problem-solving approach rather than a restricted conventional one. The concept "divergent production" (Guilford, 1967) is another type of functional operation. In distinction to "convergent production," which is the designated way of solving problems with only one correct solution, divergent production solves open-ended problems having several different types of adequate solutions. Many psychological tests for creativity have been based on the concept of divergent production. Factors such as fluency, flexibility, originality, and elaboration are assessed in such measures.

Quite a different type of functional perspective is manifest in the psychoanalytic description of the creative process as a "regression in the service of the ego" (Kris, 1952). Here, the creative process functions both to enhance an intrapsychic structure, the ego, and to bring intrapsychic unconscious material into consciousness. Unlike psychopathological conditions where regression produces earlier manifestations of psychological functioning—for example, dependent behavior representative of the oral phase—in creativity, regression is controlled by the ego. Emotions and thoughts from the earlier phases of functioning, both conscious and unconscious, are thereby available to the ego as inspirations and other bases for creative work.

Functional perspectives base their formulations about creativity on the purposes and functions, psychological, sociological, or aesthetic, served by creative production. Conflict views of creativity attempt to account to some degree for the production of new as well as valuable features in creations. According to these views, elements that were previously unrelated, remote, or antagonistic are brought together to produce new entities. Or, if these entities cannot be considered truly new in a nondetermined sense, they are at least perceived as being new. Resolution or else incorporation into a creation of elements in conflict is perceived or experienced as either intrinsically or practically valuable.

The Jungian conception of autonomous complexes is clusters of conflictual psychological factors that operate to produce autonomous and therefore new creations. Other psychoanalytic conceptions emphasize the generating effects of internal intrapsychic conflicts; they claim that such conflicts become incorporated and impart value to a work of art by allowing viewers or readers to experience their own conflicts in objectified or externalized form. Dialectical formulations, as well as some associative conceptions of creativity such as "bisociation" (Koestler, 1964) and the "remote associations theory" (Mednick, 1962), postulate the bringing together of conflictual elements through combination or other types of resolutions. Dialectical theories postulate that opposing positions of thesis and antithesis are resolved through synthesis, that is, making, combining, or unifying, and thereby produce apparently new as well as valuable solutions. The bisociation theory postulates that two elements or factors that have been habitually unrelated are associated or combined to produce creations of all types and the remote associations theory proposes that, in creative thinking, two or more uncommonly related words or ideas are brought into contiguity with each other and combined.

Rather than resolution of conflict or the combining of conflictual elements, two quite different types of formulations propose that conflict leads directly to novelty as well as value. Gestalt theory describes the breaking of gestalts or of organized wholes and structures as the key factor in productive thinking and creative production. According to this, the mental breaking of existing organized conceptions and perceptions leads to the production of new wholes or gestalts in the form of new ideas, new scientific theories, or new works of art. The newly achieved gestalt structure of these entities imparts positive value to them.

The other type of conflict formulation describes two specific types of mental processes, designated janusian and homospatial (Rothenberg, 1979) that function to produce creations. The janusian process consists of actively conceiving multiple opposites or antitheses simultaneously, and the homospatial process consists of actively conceiving two or more discrete entities or images as occupying the same mental space. Because opposites or antitheses are conceived simultaneously and mentally held in apposition or juxtaposition with each other in the janusian process, they generate conflict, tension, and novelty. In the homospatial process, the discrete entities or sensory images are in conflictual competition for occupancy of the same space. For the creative thinker, conflicting factors in both processes are in an oscillatory state until they are modified or elaborated further into new, integrated products or creations.

In addition to the importance for aesthetics and aesthetic theory, understanding and delineation of creativity and creative processes have been considered to have wide application to a number of intellectual and social fields including health, business, and politics.

[*See also* Psychology of Art.]

BIBLIOGRAPHY

Individual Differences

Barron, Frank. *Creative Person and Creative Process.* New York, 1969.
Eysenck, Hans J. "Creativity and Personality: Suggestions for a Theory." *Psychological Inquiry* 4 (1993): 147–178.
MacKinnon, Donald W. "Personality and the Realization of Creative Potential." *American Psychologist* 20 (1965): 273–281.
Roe, Anna. *The Making of a Scientist.* New York, 1952.
Wallach, Michael A., and Nathan Cogan. "A New Look at the Creativity-Intelligence Distinction." *Journal of Personality* 33 (1965): 348–369.

Endowment

Bonaparte, Marie. *The Life and Works of Edgar Allan Poe: A Psycho-Analytic Interpretation.* Translated by John Rodker. London, 1949.
Gedo, John E. *Portraits of the Artist: Psychoanalysis of Creativity and Its Vicissitudes.* New York, 1983.
Greenacre, Phyllis. "The Childhood of the Artist." *Psychoanalytic Study of the Child* 12 (1959): 47–72.
Meyer, Bernard C. *Joseph Conrad: A Psychoanalytic Biography.* Princeton, N.J., 1967.
Terman, Lewis M. ed. *Genetic Studies of Genius.* 5 vols. Stanford, Calif., 1925–1959.

Functional

Amabile, Teresa M. *The Social Psychology of Creativity.* New York, 1983.
Getzels, Jacob W., and Mihalyi Csikszentmihalyi. *Creative Thinking in Art Students: An Exploratory Study.* Chicago, 1964.
Gruber, Howard E. *Darwin on Man: A Psychological Study of Scientific Creativity.* New York, 1974.
Guilford, Joy P. *The Nature of Human Intelligence.* New York, 1967.
Kris, Ernst. *Psychoanalytic Explorations in Art.* New York, 1952.
Langley, Pat, Herbert A. Simon, Gary L. Bradshaw, and Jan M. Zytkow. *Scientific Discovery: Computational Explorations of the Creative Processes.* Cambridge, Mass., 1987.
Rank, Otto. *Art and Artist: Creative Urge and Personality Development.* Translated by Charles Francis Atkinson. New York, 1932.

Simonton, Dean Keith. *Genius, Creativity, and Leadership.* Cambridge, Mass., 1984.
Torrance, E. Paul. *Education and the Creative Potential.* Minneapolis, 1963.

Conflict

Ehrenzweig, Anton. *The Hidden Order of Art: A Study in the Psychology of Artistic Imagination.* Berkeley, 1967.
Jung, Carl G. "On the Relation of Analytic Psychology to Poetic Art." In *Contributions to Analytical Psychology.* Translated by H. G. Baynes and Cary F. Baynes, pp. 412–517. London, 1928.
Koestler, Arthur. *The Act of Creation.* New York, 1964.
Mednick, Sarnoff. "The Associative Basis of the Creative Process." *Psychologic Review* 69 (1962): 220–232.
Rothenberg, Albert. *The Emerging Goddess: The Creative Process in Art, Science, and Other Fields.* Chicago, 1979.
Wertheimer, Max. *Productive Thinking.* New York, 1945.

ALBERT ROTHENBERG

CRITICAL THEORY. *See* Adorno; Barthes; Benjamin; Criticism; Derrida; Feminism; Foucault; Habermas; Marcuse; Postcolonialism; *and* Poststructuralism.

CRITICISM. [*This entry comprises four essays on the forms of criticism specific to different artistic or cultural spheres:*

Art Criticism
Cultural Criticism
Dance Criticism
Music Criticism

Because criticism is where aesthetics is put into practice, one could also say it is where philosophy and art meet. The results are different in the various arts, several of which are discussed in depth here. For the discussion of literary criticism, see Literature, *article on* Literary Aesthetics; *and for criticism in the other arts not discussed here, see their respective entries. For related discussion, see* Appreciation; Beardsley; Chinese Aesthetics, *article on* Painting Theory and Criticism; Evaluation; Home; Interpretation; *and* New Criticism.]

Art Criticism

To anyone in the habit of thinking dialectically, the term *art criticism* must raise familiar questions. That the term itself suggests both the mutual dependence and the relative autonomy of two very distinct kinds of activity has generally been overlooked by most scholars who cling to the idea of criticism as simply a "response" to art. Framed in this manner, art criticism has been interpreted in two ways: on the one hand, as a particular literary genre whose emergence in mid-eighteenth-century France corresponded to the reorganization and expansion of public and private exhibitions, of which Denis Diderot's salons are taken as the paradigmatic example; on the other hand, defined more broadly, the term also denotes any commentary on a work of art, contemporary or past. In the latter sense, it can include genres as diverse as exhibition reviews, museum guides, monographs, historical studies, dictionary entries, travel accounts, caricatures, essays, poetry, biography, fiction, and personal correspondence, all of which draw, in varying degrees, on the disciplines of aesthetics, art theory, art history, and literature. While the boundaries that separate art criticism from these discourses (which make up what Julius von Schlosser [1924] termed *Kunstliteratur*) are extremely elastic, criticism is generally differentiated from the fields of aesthetics and art history by virtue of the values (explicit or not) that art-critical judgment seeks to mobilize, and the defined position from which the critic speaks. It is precisely its mobilization of judgments of value concerning works of art that constitutes the specificity of the art-critical text. In this regard, one might equally consider acts of valuation such as vandalism, destruction, copying, reproducing, forgery, theft, censorship, and purchasing as falling under the general rubric of art-critical practices.

The image of art criticism as a unilateral discourse perpetually moving between art object and critic is common to most conventional art histories, which traditionally pay very little attention to critical reception. Inscribed in a conception of the history of art as the history of works of art, this notion of criticism fuses the object of art-critical discourse with that of the discipline of art history itself, and consigns criticism to one of three principal functions. On the one hand, brief citations extracted from the press and other sources are routinely juxtaposed as evidence of *la fortune critique* that an individual artist or artwork acquired. These decontextualized fragments of text are meant to confirm an artist's agency, originality, or intent, or affirm a work's innovation, its prominence within a movement, or its claim to disrupting the established paradigms of the artistic field. On the other hand, a body of texts written by an individual critic is isolated in order to identify the critic's aesthetic principles or personal predilections, or to situate his criticism within the larger sphere of his literary production or in a still more general history of taste. This corpus of criticism, usually selected on the basis of its "literary quality," is limited to those "eminent" figures—Charles Baudelaire, Théophile Gautier, Émile Zola, Joris-Karl Huysmans—who engaged with the work of equally "eminent" artists. The mass of critical texts produced at a given historical moment, of which these accounts are only a small part, is presumed to be homogeneous, and represented as an undifferentiated monologue against which these few brilliant voices emerged. Finally, a growing number of historians employ art criticism in an attempt to trace particular themes, either synchronically or diachronically, across a range of visual imagery and critical texts. Focusing on specific terminology, these investigations have tended to limit themselves to

charting the polysemantic nature of artistic vocabulary and its transformations, or mapping the critics' language as it referred to a particular group of images (women, peasants, the body, Orientalism, etc.).

The work of T. J. Clark (1982) and Nicos Hadjinicolaou (1977, 1979) singularly challenged these conventions. Arguing that the content and form of particular paintings operated to unsettle—and undermine—prevailing ideologies of class and gender at specific moments of social and political crisis in France, they turned to art criticism in order to unpack multiple and contradictory responses to visual culture. Locating the critics' references not simply within the aesthetic but in a much broader and deeper network of social and political concerns, they revealed how the critics' language was itself imbricated in other discourses whose aim, among others, was to negotiate class identity, represent social cohesion, or regulate feminine sexuality. Their studies centered on the complex ideological interests that ultimately underpinned and inflected the critics' readings of art. Here, the language of criticism was constituted as a site that made manifest the intricate layering of a multiplicity of discourses—at once social *and* sexual, political *and* aesthetic—to which art could, often obliquely and always in particular historical circumstances, give rise.

Following their examples, as well as the generalized trend toward greater contextualization of art's histories that has recently permeated the discipline, art criticism has now become a de rigueur category of evidence in social, and often pointedly critical, interpretations of visual representation. Initially springing from Marxist and feminist interrogations of the social and political functions of art, and more recently inflected by poststructuralist and psychoanalytic theories of representation, revisionist art criticism has concentrated on mapping the role of the visual as an instance in broader regimes of knowledge and ultimately power, whether social, political, sexual, or racial. Here, art criticism acquires the status of a sign, illuminating or reflecting a body of deeper social concerns that are considered to be revealed through critical reception. This deeper order of knowledge is drawn not only from the explicit language of the critics' enunciations, but also from what criticism did not say; its refusals, absences, and silences that are interpreted as indicating the critics' anxieties, uneasiness, or confusion with the visual image, which ultimately remains at the core of the revisionist historians' concern. Considered as a reflection of social issues, the knowledge that criticism is seen to produce is immediately corroborated by correlating its terminology with that of a range of discourses and practices from other fields (moral, medical, judicial, economic, etc.). Here, although art criticism no longer performs the role of a simple response to art, it functions as little more than an effect of other cultural and social processes. Because its own objects are fused with those of other discourses, its historical specificity goes uninvestigated, and the particular relationships that criticism maintains with those other fields of knowledge remain entirely unquestioned.

Significant as this revisionist trend has become, it is nevertheless fraught with many of the assumptions that underpin conventional approaches. In neither case is critical discourse presumed to have a history or a materiality of its own. Isolated from their historical context and their immediate conditions of production and circulation, the critics' enunciations are assumed to share the same signifying code, and address a unified and coherent public in more or less the same ways. Thus, critical texts produced under very different circumstances and across a diverse range of sources—literary, journalistic, scholarly, and scientific—are invariably brought together without assessing how their origins, objectives, or sites of publication might in fact implicate incompatible discursive conventions, or whether their readers' "horizon of expectation" (McWilliam, 1993) are at all comparable. For both approaches, the language of criticism is presumed to be transparent. The meanings of words are considered self-evident, and their use straightforward, directly communicative and nonstrategic in function or value. In the case of social and revisionist histories, language itself is deemed remarkably stable and entirely interchangeable across disparate discursive fields, each of which is, in fact, characterized by its own distinct significations, its particular rhetorical codes and conventions, and its asymmetrical development in relation to other domains of knowledge.

Recent cultural and art-historical studies that take art criticism as their focus have addressed some of these issues and seriously reconceptualized the field. Anchored in various theories of discourse, and concerned with the particular historical conditions in which criticism was produced and functioned, these scholars interpret art criticism as a historically determined social and linguistic practice, organized according to a complex of changing social and material conditions—linguistic rules, literary codes, gendered cultural, political and institutional formations—that in different ways mediated the content, the form, and the very objects of critical debate. Conceived in this way, art criticism belongs to the broader history of the consumption and use of artistic products. Yet, it also forms part of the cultural sphere that, along with institutions such as the salon, the academy, state cultural policies, art education, private exhibitions, galleries, museums, collectors, publications, and art history, plays an active and determining role in the production of art. Criticism is seen, therefore, as having a distinct historical development, diverse modes of operation, and a relative autonomy that prohibit its relegation to either a simple "context" for art or just another literary genre. Indeed, because the art object is often little more than the starting point for the unfolding of numerous discursive strategies, the very status of art in art-critical debate is highly ambiguous—historically shifting and always subject to the multiple interests that underpin the critic's enunciations at a given historical moment.

Central to this conception of art criticism is a notion of discourse that interprets criticism as a literary/textual practice on the one hand, and that operates both within—and as—a particular social/institutional process on the other. Taken as discourse, criticism is, like art, a process of representation mediated by the historical limits and possibilities of its modes and spheres of operation. As a corpus, art-critical texts are distinguished by their heterogeneity, by the multiplicity of their historically changing forms and sites of publication, which renders any notion of art criticism as a unified or coherent genre illusory. Salon reviews in mid- to late nineteenth-century France, for example, could take the form of vaudeville, verse, caricatures, schematic diagrams, feuilletons, essays, books, albums, and pamphlets (McWilliam, 1993). Their content ranged from simple lists of artists and titles, or short commentaries on a group of works, to longer descriptions, polemics, diatribes, or erudite dissertations on contemporary aesthetic principles or questions of cultural value, for which art and artist functioned as a mere alibi. Besides appearing in specialized artistic and literary journals, and mass-circulation daily newspapers of various political and social tendencies, salon criticism was published in a host of metropolitan, regional, and local publications that included satirical journals as well as those with specializations as diverse as gastronomy, medicine, dentistry, hunting, military affairs, phrenology, agriculture, anarchism, and feminist politics. Characterized by such heterogeneity, criticism was far from being a codified language, with a normalized body of rhetorical conventions, an internal coherence, and a common set of objectives. It was equally far from addressing a unified and seamless public. Recent attempts to formulate categories for this mass of art-critical discourse have resulted in contrasting approaches. In one approach, texts grouped according to the aesthetic ideologies that their critics are perceived to reveal are correlated with the political opinions of their respective journals (Hadjinicolaou, 1979). This approach, whose merit is to consider aesthetics as a key element of the broader ideological formations of particular social classes, nevertheless tends to collapse the politics of aesthetic and cultural debate into a reflection of politics *tout court*. The other approach is a broadly empirical one that seeks to construct a "typology" of criticism—for example, scholarly, literary, journalistic—by examining the careers of particular authors, their spheres of activity, and their types of journals (Gamboni, 1991). Here, the forms of politics that underwrite art criticism are entirely minimized, reduced merely to the internal machinations and interpersonal strategies of the cultural sphere.

Considered synchronically, the relationship between art-critical texts can equally be characterized by its heterogeneity, that is, by the multiplicity of objects and purposes toward which critical enunciations are directed. When confronting the totality of critical texts produced at a given historical moment, there is little evidence of a consensus dominating this vast dispersion of enunciations. Yet, local patterns do emerge. Since the late 1820s, for instance, criticism in the Parisian press frequently took the form of a debate among a constituency of critics with various and often competing cultural, political, and ideological interests that inflected their use of critical language. Structured in a dialogical fashion, and operating as a terrain of discursive conflict, affiliation, or negotiation, the language of criticism was strategic in function and value, and art often a pretext for polemic. Thus, although the same terms consistently appear across the range of critical enunciations, their meanings vary, shift, and change as the critics' language takes various rhetorical forms, and becomes appropriated, transformed, or negated from one discursive position to another (Orwicz, 1989). It remains to be seen how useful this dialogical model of intertextuality will be to subsequent analyses of the intratextual nature of art-critical strategies, to its diachronic development, and to the broader range of both metropolitan and regional publications in which criticism appeared.

If heterogeneity, multiplicity, and dispersion are symptomatic of the art-critical text, they are equally appropriate in defining the art critic as a social and professional category. Since its inception, writing art criticism was predominantly a literary and, in the vast majority of cases, a journalistic pursuit. Emerging with the gradual diversification of artistic production, and bound up with the increasing commodification of art, criticism as a genre performed what Theodor Adorno (1967) observed (in a somewhat different context) was the mediating function of orienting a public in the market of intellectual products. As the producer of a specialized knowledge that interceded between artist and amateur, the critic's judgments generated, in effect, a range of values that were pertinent within both the artistic and the literary fields, and certainly within the economic. It is precisely the critic's location *between* the literary/journalistic fields on the one hand, and the artistic field on the other, that provides him a strategic role in producing a cultural capital that directly benefits the artist in the artistic sphere, while at the same time affirming the critic's own singularity across both fields. For such well-known literary figures as Denis Diderot, Charles-Augustin Sainte-Beuve, Théophile Gautier, Guy de Maupassant, or Emile Zola, writing art criticism in the mass-circulation press consolidated a reputation already gained in other domains of intellectual production, while providing them with authority and legitimacy as recognized arbiters of cultural value.

The majority of commentators on art were, however, neither eminent literary figures nor professional critics in the contemporary sense. Nearly two thirds of the 440 writers

active under the July Monarchy, for example, published only one art review throughout the entire sixteen-year period; fewer than 9 percent wrote more than four (McWilliam, 1993). Corresponding figures for the Second Empire indicate that even at the height of its production, writing art criticism was an extremely sporadic and fragmented activity, dispersed across diverse professional fields and social formations. Throughout the eighteenth and well into the nineteenth century, the epithet "art critic" comprised a predominantly masculine and bourgeois constituency of politicians, cabinet members, government administrators and functionaries, cultural administrators and entrepreneurs, lawyers, businessmen, educators and academics, writers of all genres, occasionally artists, and most often journalists who routinely furnished articles on social and political, as well as a variety of other cultural issues. As a journalistic genre, writing criticism was usually an ancillary activity, embarked on by columnists out of economic constraint (McWilliam, 1991). For those with aspirations to a serious political or administrative career in official circles, it functioned as an obligatory passage that secured cultural capital as one moved from provincial center to the metropolis and up established social hierarchies. Linked intimately to the organization of the press, the form and content of journalistic art criticism was directly subject to its expansions and contractions, to multiple forms of political censorship, to the vicissitudes of state legislation, and to the increasing rationalization of journalism under industrial capitalism.

With the expansion of the press during the latter half of the nineteenth century, and the accelerated extension of art into the free-market economy, art criticism gradually developed into a professional activity. The increased power and determining influence that the new "dealer-critic" system conferred on critics made the question of their authority, their legitimacy to publicly exercise critical judgments, and the "semblance of competence" (Adorno, 1967) with which those judgments were invested, entirely decisive. Although the criteria of competence were, then as now, relatively arbitrary, they were increasingly located in the critics' intimacy with the artistic sphere on the one hand—for example, an access to artists, dealers, and collectors, a familiarity with technical issues, connoisseurship, art-historical knowledge, and contemporary aesthetic debates—and in a certain literary style on the other (Gamboni, 1991). With a plurality of artistic tendencies characterizing art production in the late nineteenth and the twentieth centuries, art criticism quickly transmuted into a form of direct advocacy, initiating a new genre of critical text: the essay in an artist's exhibition or sales catalog. It is perhaps worth recalling that the language of aesthetic autonomy that developed alongside the critic's evolution from expert to judge, and finally to promoter, has its own dialectic. By guaranteeing the critic the semblance of objectivity that secures the theoretical disinterestedness of art-critical judgment, it provides the appearance of disentangling him from those very economic imperatives that ultimately underwrite his social and historical function.

[*See also* Baudelaire, *article on* Baudelaire and Art; *and* Diderot, *article on* Diderot and the Salon.]

BIBLIOGRAPHY

Adorno, Theodor W. "Cultural Criticism and Society." In *Prisms* (1967), translated by Samuel Weber and Shierry Weber, pp. 17–35. Cambridge, Mass., 1981.

Clark, T. J. *Image of the People: Gustave Courbet and the 1848 Revolution* (1973). Princeton, N.J., 1982.

Desdner, Albert. *Die Entstehung der Kunstkritik (Die Kunstkritik. Ihre Geschichte und Theorie).* Munich, 1915.

Dümchen, Sybil, and Michael Nerlich, eds. *Text-Image/Bild-Text.* Berlin, 1990.

Foucault, Michel. *The Archaeology of Knowledge and the Discourse on Language.* Translated by A. M. Sheridan Smith. New York, 1972.

Gamboni, Dario. *La plume et le pinceau: Odilon Redon et la littérature.* Paris, 1989.

Gamboni, Dario. "Propositions pour l'étude de la critique d'art au XIXᵉ siècle." *Romantisme* 71 (1991): 9–17.

Hadjinicolaou, Nicos. "La 'fortune critique' et son sort en histoire de l'art." *Histoire et critique des arts* 3 (November 1977): 7–25.

Hadjinicolaou, Nicos. "'La Liberté guidant le peuple' de Delacroix devant son premier public." *Actes de la Recherche en Sciences Sociales* 28 (June 1979): 3–26.

McWilliam, Neil. "Opinions professionnelles: critique d'art et économie de la culture sous la Monarchie de Juillet." *Romantisme* 71 (1991): 19–30.

McWilliam, Neil. "Press, journalistes et critiques d'art à Paris de 1849 à 1860." *Quarante-huite/Quatorze* 5 (1993): 53–62.

Orwicz, Michael R. "Confrontations et clivages dans les discours des critiques du salon, 1885–1889." In *La Critique d'Art en France, 1850–1900,* edited by Jean-Paul Bouillon et al., pp. 177–192. Saint-Étienne, 1989.

Orwicz, Michael R., ed. *Art Criticism and Its Institutions in Nineteenth-Century France.* Manchester, 1994.

Schlosser, Julius von. *Die Kunstliteratur: Ein Handbuch zur Quellenkunde der neueren Kunstgeschichte.* Vienna, 1924.

Wrigley, Richard. *The Origins of French Art Criticism: From the Ancien Régime to the Restoration.* Oxford, 1993.

MICHAEL ORWICZ

Cultural Criticism

The first cultural criticism was probably embedded in the drawings found on rocks and caves in many parts of the prehistoric world. The messages there said something about how the world worked and encouraged people to work in specific ways in relationship to it. These are the basic motivations of cultural criticism: analysis of society and moral or, at least, ethical or communal engagement for both the producer and the audience. But few people would consider cave drawings to be real cultural criticism, and they would probably be correct. Painting, sculpture, and other nonverbal or performance art continue to enact the constitutive functions of cultural criticism. But cultural criticism is basically a written art, with the word *writing* understood in the

Western sense of script or typescript directed toward an audience.

Written and circulated cultural criticism can be found among the Greeks and Romans. There, it is usually found as the by-product of other kinds of writing, such as drama or philosophy. Cultural criticism was a common art during the Renaissance, when the genre of the utopia was born. Comic narratives such as Miguel de Cervantes's *Don Quixote* and François Rabelais's *Gargantua* and *Pentagruel* contain rich elements of cultural criticism. Sometimes, as in Cervantes's case, the comedic, narrative elements helped authors to disguise cultural criticism and to avoid persecution by the Inquisition or by tyrannical governments.

The eighteenth century, a great age of satire, was simultaneously a great age of cultural criticism. Jonathan Swift, Alexander Pope, Samuel Johnson, Joseph Addison, and Sir Richard Steele all leap to mind. Nineteenth-century novelists such as Jane Austen, Charlotte Brontë, Charles Dickens, and George Eliot were also masters of cultural criticism, though most of their work, generically, would be classified as novels. One tends to think of cultural criticism as nonfiction, but it has always found resources in narrative or poetic forms, such as the novel, satire, or drama.

Today, essays are a natural—might one almost say *the* natural—form for cultural criticism. They are topic-specific, time-bound "takes" on a particular subject. When "collected" or written on related topics, they can be the building blocks of books and begin to transcend their specific temporal context: collections by Lionel Trilling, Arthur C. Danto, Edmund White, and others show this nicely. Cultural criticism has flourished in connection with essays, often written in the strong authorial voice of the personal essay, a form associated with Michel de Montaigne.

Great eras of prose also tend to be great eras of cultural criticism. Victorian England, for example, produced work fundamental to later cultural criticism: John Stuart Mills's *On Liberty* and *On the Subjection of Women,* Matthew Arnold's *Culture and Anarchy.* It is no accident that Victorian England was also a watershed period for novels. Historically, cultural criticism tends to emerge alongside the novel. This makes sense. Both have an affinity for realism and make a claim to portraying social or cultural realities. Both are made possible by, and react to, the definitive emergence and development of technology and capitalism. In fact, many writers who are closely identified with cultural criticism also had connections, sometimes in different parts of their writerly lives, to the novel. This tendency for great critics of the novel also to be great cultural critics crosses national boundaries, and it crisscrosses the twentieth century. György Lukács, Walter Benjamin, George Orwell, Edmund Wilson, and Trilling are names that come immediately to mind as outstanding cultural critics who were also important critics or theorists of the novel.

In the twentieth century, cultural criticism has enacted strong dramas with fascism, Marxism, and other important political movements. But, as one might expect from the word *criticism,* cultural critics do not usually speak, in an unqualified way, for the values of the state. Typically, they have an adversarial, or at least a gadfly, relationship to officialdom, so that cultural criticism has encountered both opportunities and hard times when confronted with the rupturing events of what Eric Hobsbawm has called "the age of extremes."

One of the great centers of cultural criticism in the twentieth century illustrates just such ambiguous relations: central Europe from World War I through 1960. Many important cultural critics of this time and place wrote in German, though they were not German citizens. Many took up questions from nineteenth-century German philosophy and social theory: for example, the master-slave dialectic in human history; the organicism of communities in the past versus the alienated quality of modern life. A rich collection of minds and temperaments worked on these topics, among them Hannah Arendt in Germany; Martin Buber in Poland; Sigmund Freud in Austria; Georg Lukács in Hungary; and Walter Benjamin in Germany.

All the writers just named were Jews and hence born into a group deemed "outsider." Some, like Benjamin, did not survive the disaster of World War II. Freud tragically found himself persecuted by the Germanic culture he had long defended: with his family, he left Austria for England, where he died in 1939. Others, such as Arendt, emigrated to the United States and forged brilliant careers as commentators on the formative events of their time. Buber emigrated to what is now Israel, where he became an active spokesman for a joint Jewish-Palestinian state, based on his philosophy of mutuality and interdependence. Lukács, a committed Marxist, was a member of various Hungarian governments; he was imprisoned in the wake of the failed revolution of 1956 (and later "rehabilitated").

Cultural criticism cannot buffer itself from historical change. In fact, some have faulted critics of the 1930s for not intervening in more effective ways. But cultural criticism cannot command, or halt, history. All it can do is be where the action is, speak out, and galvanize opinion. Cultural criticism can and should gravitate to areas of controversy or heat in the culture. The places it thrives tend to be exciting, but not always comfortable ("May you be born in interesting times," the Chinese curse says). In a sense, exile is the worst fate that can befall a cultural critic: cast out of the action, he or she becomes a prophetic voice in the wilderness. But, paradoxically, exile is also a necessary fate, at least metaphorically. The cultural critic has to write with some distance, and with self-awareness about the affiliations chosen and endorsed.

The relationship between cultural criticism and difficult times is tricky and controversial. Does cultural criticism require adversity and victimization? Do too much middle-class comfort and a stable social order dull its edge? That is a common accusation made today against critics in the United States. The Mexican writer, Carlos Fuentes, for example, has said several times that Latin American intellectuals do not have the luxury to pursue the kinds of language games associated with postmodernism in the United States. Václav Havel, president of the Czech Republic, has made similar statements about the need for writers to be politically engaged in countries without long traditions of democracy. In a comparable way, in Kenya, Ngugi wa Thiong'o stopped writing in English and begin writing in Gikuyu: his act simultaneously claimed his heritage and asserted that the West will invariably take as its own whatever is marked by a colonial language.

It is highly doubtful, however, that the United States is too comfortable to need or produce good cultural criticism. Just the opposite may be the case. A certain level of social and economic stability can foster cultural criticism. Universities, publishing houses, a large educated public, and a plethora of magazines provide, for example, authors and audiences for cultural criticism. What is more, the sense of residual injustices—in gender and race relations, to give two salient instances—have fostered lively social criticism. In the United States, debate unfolds in periodicals, on Op-Ed pages, and in traditional essay and book form. Public intellectuals such as Henry Louis Gates, Jr., Cornel West, and Edward Said appear in both kinds of venues.

One of the most vital strands in cultural criticism today is postcolonial studies. It is likely to be increasingly important as western Europe confronts the colonial past and assimilates diverse ethnic groups. It very much illuminates continuing debates about race and ethnicity in the United States. Postcolonial criticism includes voices from the third world: writers such as Octavio Paz in Mexico, Frantz Fanon in Algeria, and Wole Soyinka in Nigeria. Said, Palestinian by birth but Western by education and residence, helped launch postcolonial criticism in books such as *Orientalism* (1978). Yet, by 1993, when Said published *Culture and Imperialism,* many Western writers and thinkers had taken up and enriched postcolonial criticism too: Fredric Jameson, James Clifford, Patrick Brantlinger, Eric Hobsbawm, Philip Curtin, Mary Louise Pratt, Ann McClintock, and others.

Feminist criticism is a second vital force in cultural criticism. Women such as Zora Neale Hurston, Ruth Benedict, and Margaret Mead, formative figures in anthropology, should "count" in this context, especially since their work so often gendered political subtexts. Betty Friedan, Adrienne Rich, Eva Figes, Angela Davis, Catherine Stimpson, Elaine Showalter, and many others exemplify how feminism has characteristically probed many areas with feminist goals in mind. In fact, the integration of political approaches within many disciplines is one of the unsung achievements of the women's movement and the birth of women's studies.

So too is the cultivation of personal voice within analytic writing. One motto of early 1970s' feminism in the United States was that "the personal is the political." It is a lesson that many cultural critics outside of feminism have learned too. Said, for example, wrote *After the Last Sky* (part memoir), Gates wrote *Colored People,* and Anthony Appiah includes elements of memoir in *In My Father's House.* Male cultural critics such as Lukács and Trilling were notoriously reluctant to use the personal voice, notorious for writing in the cultural *we.* But female critics such as Nancy Miller in *Getting Personal: Feminist Occasions and Other Autobiographical Acts,* Alice Kaplan in *French Lessons,* Cathy N. Davidson in *36 Views of Mount Fuji,* and Jane Tompkins in *West of Everything* have injected the *I* into cultural criticism as a resource with renewed value.

Cultural criticism today exists in a twinned relationship with cultural studies. The term *cultural studies* originated in Great Britain in the 1970s; in many ways, it named a British New Left version of cultural criticism. Cultural studies was, and often still is, political; its signature topics remain race, gender, and class. A distinguishing trait of cultural studies was its willingness to pay serious attention to mass or popular culture, and to define "texts" as trends or phenomena, such as television shows or wrestling. Well-known cultural critics of the 1950s and 1960s, such as Trilling and Dwight McDonald, tended to write from vantage points imagined as outside of mass culture; sometimes they spoke as advocates for high culture only.

One of the inspirational figures in cultural studies is the legendary critic Raymond Williams, who wrote about literature too. Others include Kenneth Burke, Roland Barthes, and Michel Foucault, whose work crosses over into aesthetics and into the kind of philosophical, meditative intellectual history typical of the French tradition. In practice, therefore, *cultural studies* is no more stable a term than *cultural criticism.* In fact, cultural criticism and cultural studies have moved together.

Today, race, gender, and class are fundamental categories for any form of thinking about culture. Increasingly, cultural criticism addresses these categories, and popular culture too. Writing about culture requires an array of styles, themes, and angles: Andrew Ross, Eve Kosofsky Sedgwick, and Jan Radway provide good examples of work that tends to follow imperatives of its own. Cultural criticism and cultural studies have benefited from the many crossings between them.

In fact, *crossing* is a key term and a key metaphor. Cultural criticism gravitates toward issues that turn up in many parts of a culture. Such issues require thinking from many disciplinary vantage points, so that cultural criticism nurtures, and is in turn nurtured by, interdisciplinary studies. The "disciplines," as we know them, are the invention of universities: many date from the turn of the century. Today, interdisciplinary studies are changing the way universities

are organized and the way many people write. These are two important effects of cultural criticism today.

In *Middlemarch,* George Eliot proposed the image of the web as a way of thinking about social life. The web is interconnected at many points; it hangs together. A tug in one place affects the disposition of the whole. One has the illusion of a center only when holding light up at one particular point. As an image, "the web" has acquired new associations in the 1990s. Computer technologies such as E-mail and bulletin boards offer new sites for cultural criticism: a whole new kind of "worldwide web." More technologies are sure to come. Already, it is clear that many graduate students and scholars use "the net" for research tasks and, increasingly, to disseminate their writing in ways alternative to print media. Participation on "the net" remains an uneven phenomenon but is sure to grow and perhaps to become mandatory, even for scholars currently unfamiliar with electronic media. Routine use of "the net" will quicken the pace of cultural criticism, making responses broader and more instantaneous. But the value of Eliot's image still holds.

Cultural criticism today has many centers. It can be illuminated at many different points or nodes: parts of the world, disciplines, critical approaches, genres, and styles of writing. It can have different accents, emphases, and methods—depending on the task being done, and the critic's own temperament and choices. But a tug at one point of the web should still produce a ripple elsewhere.

Like the drawings in prehistoric caves, cultural criticism should and does have the ability to make things happen. In our time, it has fostered, among other things, women's rights, gay rights, greater awareness of other cultures, communication from and between different racial and ethnic groups, growing awareness of ecological danger, and debate on economic trends and policies. But the jobs that need doing are by no means done.

[*See also* Postcolonialism.]

BIBLIOGRAPHY

Arendt, Hannah. *The Origins of Totalitarianism.* New York, 1951.
Arendt, Hannah. *Eichmann in Jerusalem: A Report on the Banality of Evil.* Rev. enl. ed. New York, 1964.
Barthes, Roland. *Mythologies.* Paris, 1957. Translated and edited by Annette Lavers. New York, 1972.
Benedict, Ruth. *Patterns of Culture.* 2d ed. Boston, 1959.
Danto, Arthur. "The End of Art." In *The Death of Art,* edited by Berel Lang. New York, 1984.
Foucault, Michel. *Histoire de la sexualité,* vol. 1, *La volonté de savoir.* Paris, 1976. Translated by Robert Hurley as *The History of Sexuality* vol. 1. New York, 1982.
Friedan, Betty. *The Feminine Mystique.* New York, 1963.
Grossberg, Lawrence, Cary Nelson, and Paula A. Treichler, eds. *Cultural Studies.* New York and London, 1992.
Jacoby, Russell. *The Last Intellectuals: American Culture in the Age of Academe.* New York, 1987.
Mead, Margaret. *Male and Female: A Study of the Sexes in a Changing World.* New York, 1949.

Paz, Octavio. *The Labyrinth of Solitude: Life and Thought in Mexico.* Translated by Lysander Kemp. New York, 1961.

Said, Edward W. *Orientalism.* New York, 1978.

Said, Edward W. *The World, the Text, and the Critic.* Cambridge, Mass., 1983.

Showalter, Elaine. *Hystories: Hysterical Epidemics and Modern Culture.* New York, 1997.

Torgovnick, Marianna. *Crossing Ocean Parkway: Readings by an Italian American Daughter.* Chicago, 1994.

Torgovnick, Marianna, ed. *Eloquent Obsessions: Writing Cultural Criticism.* Durham, N.C., 1994.

Trilling, Lionel. *The Liberal Imagination: Essays on Literature and Society.* Garden City, N.Y., 1950.

Williams, Raymond. *Culture and Society, 1780–1950.* London, 1961.

MARIANNA DEMARCO TORGOVNICK

Dance Criticism

The province of dance criticism is those dances that are artworks: as Richard Wollheim (1993, p. 133) puts the general point: "the aim of criticism in the arts is . . . to *understand,* or to grasp the *meaning* of, the work of art." The interest in grace, line, and the like appropriate to such works acknowledges them as constructed under the concept "art" (and perhaps more specific subconcepts too); in this way, it treats the dance works as meaning bearing. Acknowledging the dance as so constructed is seeing it as part of the complex traditions and conventions of art making and art understanding. A fuller picture of dance criticism requires an understanding of art criticism, also necessary to understand the point of reading dance criticism. The meaning referred to relates to a specific dance work (*Swan Lake*) rather than to a generic dance ("the meaning of the tango"), and is understood as a property of the dance as art rather than, say, as the dance's social significance (Williams, 1991, pp. 5–14). Furthermore, all dance works that are art are meaning bearing in this sense, because meaning bearing connects with their art status. Yet, critical judgments should be seen as historically specific, such that critical categories can be transformed by the passage of time.

Dance criticism as it occurs in, say, articles in newspapers or magazines typically has a wide variety of purposes that, while part of the practice of criticism, are not all central to the critical enterprise. In addition, these articles relate to particular performances as much as to the dance works themselves. Characteristically, they might include a presentation of the history and background to the piece, and of the performance in question (as well as some general remarks about the company performing); a description of the dance in relation to a recommendation (or the opposite) to go to see it; and some remarks about how the dance is to be understood. These aspects may not be readily separable in the text itself, but only the last of these is the task of criticism proper.

As with criticism in the other arts, the term *dance criticism* should be applied to the activities both of the formal or professional dance critic and of the "informal critic"—that is, the spectator of dance. Informal criticism occurs whenever dances are discussed with a view to understanding them better. Formal dance criticism typically occurs in articles in newspapers and magazines, and these pieces sometimes are collected into a book (for example, Banes, 1994; Croce, 1987; Siegel, 1977) or "written through" to form a book (Acocella, 1993; Banes, 1987; Jordan, 1992). Only occasionally is dance criticism presented in extended studies, at book length (for instance, Siegel, 1979).

The Nature of Criticism. A general account of criticism for the arts must respect the idea that critical judgment is not a matter of inference (Ground, 1989, pp. 90–95); it must reject the thought that critics must come to works with a set of criteria for value (or a checklist of valuable characteristics); and it must treat critical judgment as objective, in the sense of being answerable to the features of the work, rather than what is "read into" the work.

With these constraints in mind, criticism can usefully be modeled as a kind of *noticing;* the noticing of critically relevant features (McFee, 1994, pp. 89–92). Then, first, noticing, like any perceptual mode, is concept-mediated: what one can notice depends on the concepts one has. But noticing is not just looking at. Second, noticing is always the noticing of features, in this case features of the dance. One cannot notice what is not there but, as with the multiple figures beloved of psychologists (such as the duck-rabbit), noticing involves taking the features of the dance in one way: then one can be determinately wrong if the basis for one's claims about a dance are not as one takes them. Third, criticism is a matter of noticing critically relevant features. This idea of critical relevance will rule out, as playing a part in criticism, remarks that, though true of particular dances, do not contribute to our understanding of them. For example, some facts of the dancers' biographies will have no bearing on how the dance works are understood. What will be critically relevant will depend on the particular works, the traditions of art understanding for that art form, the traditional categories of art in which works in that form enter. Fourth, nothing is critically relevant merely because it allows some change in understanding (although that is required): in addition, it must lead to a correct or acceptable interpretation of the dance. Thus, the requirement for relevance sets limits on the acceptability of any interpretation of a dance (McFee, 1992a, pp. 139–145).

Applied to dance, this conception of criticism means, for example, that one *sees* relationships in dance (that is, one notices them if one has the appropriate concepts, training, etc.), and that dances have perceptual properties in virtue of their art status (properties that might conflict with other properties ascribable to them). Further, this conception clarifies the point of reading dance criticism: the reader can learn to employ (in perception of dance works) the concepts that permit him or her to find those works meaning bearing.

Criticism and Understanding. Reading criticism of dance works (and discussing those dances) offers alternative ways of making sense of whole dances, or of aspects of them. In this way, the spectator (or "informal" critic) can begin to enter the world of dance making and dance understanding. Indeed, formal dance critics have been "shapers of taste," revising not only how dances were understood but also how their makers came to conceptualize them—for example, through the work of nineteenth-century dance critic XXX (Chapman, 1984). Thus, dance criticism allows the sharing of understanding of dances. One can learn to appreciate dances through reading criticism because the concepts under which the noticing takes place can be acquired in this way.

The activities of the dance critic can be modeled as having two aspects. The first concerns what is sometimes called the critic's "cognitive stock": the critic's knowledge of the history, traditions, and techniques of the dance form, the concepts through which dance making is appropriately understood. The second aspect, possession of certain concepts, is not sufficient, however; a dance critic must be able to "mobilize" (Wollheim, 1986, p. 48) those concepts in his or her experience. Giving substance in this way to the term of art ("mobilize in one's experience") is also accommodating the sensuous dimension of appreciation of dance, and hence of the sensuousness of the understanding entailed by it. It is locating, as well as recognizing, that "sensitivity" that the dance critic needs. (An "informal" critic might judge himself or herself as inferior to the formal critic in one or other of these dimensions.)

Although critics' interpretations of dances typically consist of words, they need not be in words only but can readily include, say, photographs. In particular, the interpretations of "informal" critics will often include gesture, but understanding here, too, will require appeal to past understandings, to traditions of dance making and dance understanding.

Such an account of the activity of the dance critic is therefore less "rationalistic" than it may appear, for it acknowledges that the appreciation of dance is not a cognitive activity only, although it is a cognitive activity.

Art Status and Meaning/Understanding. What of dance works that "explicitly" lack meaning—works asserted by their choreographers (for example, Merce Cunningham) to lack meaning, or to not express anything? Are they not amenable to dance criticism? The stance of such choreographers is essentially polemical: they are attempting to make fundamental points about the nature of the art forms. But their works can therefore be modeled, like any other explicit revolutionary, as only intelligible against the background provided by more traditional works, hence understood in explicit contrast to the idea of the meaning bearing (Carroll in Fancher and Myers, 1981, p. 102). Moreover,

the expressive potentials of the movement materials of the dance—in particular, those key to a particular dance technique, such as Martha Graham technique—make it difficult to imagine a dance that is both uncontentiously art and yet not meaning-bearing.

Any dance that was definitely not meaning bearing at all would, for that reason, not be art: any human intentions recognized as "behind" it would not be those characteristic of art making. (For a parallel argument for music, see Kivy, 1993, pp. 360–373). In this way, the possibility of informed dance criticism acquires a special importance: it connects with the art status of dance works.

Such an argument might be thought to give conceptual priority to dance criticism, rather than to dance (Sparshott, 1995, p. 337). Instead, it recognizes that the possibility of dance as art and the possibility of dance criticism amount to just one possibility.

Historical Character of Criticism. No general account of the critically relevant features of dance works is possible, because what is and what is not relevant depends on the appropriate category of art, or dance form, into which the work enters. It may also (and relatedly) be historically specific, in at least two ways. First, dance criticism may be part of a narrative that situates a particular dance, or a particular choreographer, at some precise place in some tradition of art making or art understanding (Carroll, 1994, pp. 25–27): and that discussion will emphasize which of the dance's features are the crucial ones for locating it within that narrative. Such a narrative will characteristically turn on the values to be ascribed to the dance in question. Second, dances share in the general historical character of art (McFee, 1992b). Hence, understanding dances at a particular time may change with changes in the tradition of dance understanding within which the dance work is situated. For instance, theatricality was seen as absent from characteristic dances of the 1970s, (Banes, 1987, p. xxix) but increasingly became a useful concept for analysis of dances of the 1980s (Jordan, 1992, p. 189; Mackrell, 1992, p. 123). In part, this was a response to changes in the concerns of choreographers, but in part an outcome of revised ways of conceptualizing both the activities of those choreographers and their place in the tradition of dance making (Carroll, 1992).

Conclusion. Its connection with the meaning of dances (and, perhaps, their art status) ensures that dance criticism will be important to the academic study of dance both as a practice and as an object of investigation. Inquiries into its nature involve comparison and contrast with criticism of the other arts, highlighting what is shared as well as what is distinctive. In part, any account must rely on an account of the purpose and structure of art criticism generally, of the kind exemplified here.

[*See also* Dance, *historical and conceptual overview article.*]

BIBLIOGRAPHY

Acocella, Joan. *Mark Morris.* New York, 1993.

Banes, Sally. *Terpsichore in Sneakers: Post-Modern Dance.* 2d ed. Middletown, Conn., 1987.

Banes, Sally. *Writing Dancing in the Age of Postmodernism.* Middletown, Conn., 1994.

Carroll, Noel. "Theatre, Dance and Theory: A Philosophical Narrative." *Dance Chronicle: Studies in Dance and the Related Arts* 15.3 (1992): 317–331.

Carroll, Noel. "Identifying Art." In *Institutions of Art: Reconsiderations of George Dickie's Philosophy,* edited by Robert J. Yanal, pp. 3–38. University Park, Pa., 1994.

Chapman, John. "XXX and the Changing Ballet Aesthetic, 1828–1832." *Dance Research* 2.1 (Spring 1984): 35–47.

Copeland, Roger, and Marshall Cohen, eds. *What Is Dance? Readings in Theory and Criticism.* New York and Oxford, 1983.

Croce, Arlene. *Afterimages.* London, 1978.

Croce, Arlene. *Sight Lines.* New York, 1987.

Fancher, Gordon, and Gerald Myers, eds. *Philosophical Essays on Dance.* Brooklyn, N.Y., 1981.

Ground, Ian. *Art or Bunk?* Bristol, 1989.

Jordan, Stephanie. *Striding Out: Aspects of Contemporary and New Dance in Britain.* London, 1992.

Mackrell, Judith. *Out of Line: The Story of British New Dance.* London, 1992.

McFee, Graham. "The Historical Character of Art: A Re-Appraisal." *British Journal of Aesthetics* 32 (October 1992): 307–319.

McFee, Graham. *Understanding Dance.* London and New York, 1992.

McFee, Graham. *The Concept of Dance Education.* London and New York, 1994.

Siegel, Marcia B. *At the Vanishing Point: A Critic Looks at Dance.* New York, 1972.

Siegel, Marcia B. *Watching the Dance Go By.* Boston, 1977.

Siegel, Marcia B. *The Shapes of Change: Images of American Dance.* Boston, 1979.

Sparshott, Francis. *Off the Ground: First Steps to a Philosophical Consideration of the Dance.* Princeton, N.J., 1988.

Sparshott, Francis. *A Measured Pace: Toward a Philosophical Understanding of the Arts of Dance.* Toronto, 1995.

Williams, Drid. *Ten Lectures on Theories of the Dance.* London, 1991.

Wollheim, Richard. "Imagination and Pictorial Understanding." *Proceedings of the Aristotelian Society,* suppl. vol. 40 (1986): 45–60.

Wollheim, Richard. *The Mind and Its Depths.* Cambridge, Mass., 1993.

GRAHAM MCFEE

Music Criticism

The criticism of music has a long and complex history in which the question of value (the significance of music) is closely allied with questions of ontology (what music is), theory (how music works), semantics (what music means), and influence (how music evolves). This essay will focus the question of value, defining "music criticism" as the attempt to say what it is about music that *matters.*

Music criticism goes as far back as Plato and Aristotle (fifth to fourth centuries BCE), who were primarily concerned to criticize music's educative effect: the ennobling or corrupting influence of the various modes, melodies, rhythms, and instruments on the soul. Music served other purposes (for Aristotle, music was cathartic and recreational as well as educational), but the critical touchstone, not only in ancient Greece but in Roman times, the Middle Ages, and throughout the Renaissance, was the impact of music on the formation of character. Coincident with and closely related to this ethical conception of music was a metaphysical one stemming from Pythagoras (sixth century BCE). The discovery of mathematical proportion in the musical scale (generally attributed to Pythagoras) contributed significantly to an understanding of reality at every level—the body, the soul, society, the cosmos. Music—"good" music, that is—conduced to virtue because in music as in the well-ordered soul there was *harmonia* (a joining of variously proportioned elements).

In the modern period, usually thought to begin with the *cogito, ergo sum* of René Descartes (1596–1650), criticism shifted from an appeal to tradition (particularly the Ancients) to a grounding in reason, the senses, or both; it shifted, that is, to the authority of taste. Questions of old versus new (the Quarrel of the Ancients and the Moderns, Ars Antigua versus Ars Nova, Prima versus Seconda Pratica) gave way to questions of liking and disliking, to praise and censure by those whose judgment ultimately rested on a spontaneous sympathy with and appreciation of beauty, whether in art or in nature. The value of music was now felt to lie primarily in its capacity to arouse pleasure and delight rather than with its conducing to virtue (although the moral dimension was by no means absent).

One of the earliest and most important documents in the modern history of music criticism is the *Parallèle des Italiens et des Français en ce qui regarde la musique et les opéras* (1702), written by Abbé François Raguenet (1660–c.1722). Raguenet praises the Italians at the expense of the French (the composer Jean-Baptiste Lully, in particular) for a boldness and an inventiveness that break the rules while transporting imagination, senses, soul, and body with their insouciant charms:

> [Although] the French wou'd think themselves undone, if they offended in the least against the Rules . . . and are still doubtful of Success, tho' ev'ry thing be done with an exact Regularity. . . . The Italians venture at ev'ry thing that is harsh, and out of the way, but then they do it like People that have right to venture, and are sure of Success.   (Abbé François Raguenet, 1702)

Although not unrelated to the long-standing Quarrel of the Ancients and the Moderns, the *Parallèle des Italiens et des Français* is strikingly modern in its appeal to Raguenet himself as the ultimate source of authority. A century earlier, advocates of musical invention, such as Vincenzo Galilei (1533–1591) and Claudio Monteverdi (1567–1643), who championed the new monodic style, ground their arguments not in their own preferences (though appeal to the senses was not entirely absent here either) but in the pronouncements of the Ancients, and especially Plato, for whom harmony was subordinate to melody. (The dispute over the superiority of harmony versus melody is continued in the eighteenth century by Jean-Philippe Rameau and Jean-Jacques Rousseau, although no longer on grounds of traditional authority.)

In the words of Rousseau (1712–1778), taste is that which is most felt and least explained. The idea of taste as a sentiment or feeling of delight occasioned by beauty—whether moral, natural, or artistic—was prevalent throughout the eighteenth century, and philosophical debate tended to focus on the question not of rules, either passed down by tradition or evident to the light of reason (neoclassicism), but of the state of mind (e.g., an attitude of disinterested contemplation) in which the right kind of sentiment or feeling was evoked.

The aesthetics of taste did not prevail without a fight, however. Jean Laurent le Cerf de La Viéville, Seigneur of Freneuse (1647–1710) responded to the *Parallèle des Italiens et des Français* with a spirited defense of Lully and the French, the *Comparison de la musique italienne et de la musique française* (1704–1705). Viéville's counterattack, to which Raguenet replied and Viéville responded in turn, contended that what mattered about music was not solely feeling (Raguenet's preferences) but feeling "corrected or confirmed by the best rules."

A central figure in the modern history of criticism is Joseph Addison (1672–1719), whose contribution to the London periodicals *The Tatler* and *The Spectator* played a key role in shaping and giving voice to the emerging "bourgeois public sphere" of the early eighteenth century. Like Raguenet, Addison speaks of likes and dislikes, his authority resting on nothing more than the observations and reactions of a generally cultivated person. Of equal importance for the modern history of criticism is the poet and journalist John Gay (1685–1732), whose libretto for *The Beggar's Opera* (first performed in 1728) satirized Italian *opera seria* and the English gentry with one brilliant stroke by substituting for the usual mythological heroes and historical figures all manner of beggars, prostitutes, and thieves.

In the eighteenth century, one finds the first music histories, the most well known of which is Charles Burney's (1726–1814) *General History of Music* (1789). Burney traveled extensively throughout Great Britain and Europe in search of material, filling his *History* and other works with detailed observations and criticism of contemporary musical events. Although a musician by profession, Burney addressed himself not to the expert but to the amateur, for whom, he lamented, nothing had so far been written (1789): "There have been many treatises published on the art of musical composition and performance but none to instruct ignorant lovers of music how to listen or to judge for themselves." Burney was not the only one concerned with the state of music criticism in his native England. In *An Essay on Musical Expression* (1753) Charles Avison (1709–1770) wrote: "In reflecting on the State of Music in

England, I have often thought, that it might not be altogether foreign to the Design of some periodical Memoir of Literature, to have an Article sometimes, giving an account and character of the best musical, compositions."

It was in Germany and not England that the criticism envisioned by Burney and Avison first appeared—ironically, because of the influence of the London periodicals. Johann Mattheson (1681–1764), composer, theorist, singer, Kapellmeister, and man of letters, published two magazines in Hamburg, *Der Vernünftler* (1713–1714), after *The Spectator*, and *Critica Musica* (1722–1725), in which the leading ideas in music and art were spread throughout Europe. Mattheson's extraordinary impact on the musical life of his time extended from the general reader all the way to Georg Philipp Telemann and George Frideric Handel. Another Hamburg critic, Johann Adolph Scheibe (1708–1776), used the platform of his influential journal, *Der critische Musikus* (1737–1740), to wage war against a composer whose "bombastic and confused style suffocate[d] naturalness" and "obscure[d] . . . beauty through excessive artifice." The composer was Johann Sebastian Bach.

Journals geared to experts and amateurs (*Kenner und Liebhaber*) and devoted entirely to music appeared in cities throughout Germany well before they appeared in England or elsewhere on the Continent. Most of them were owned by music publishing houses—a fact unfortunately reflected by the dullness and superficiality of much of their criticism. The most influential of these journals was the *Allgemeine musikalische Zeitung*, published in Leipzig by Breitkopf and Härtel, and edited initially by J. F. Rochlitz (1798–1819). Composers of no less stature than Franz Joseph Haydn and Ludwig van Beethoven complained bitterly at times about their ill-treatment at the hands of its "ignorant and injudicious" critics.

The year 1810 marks a watershed in music criticism with the publication in the *Allgemeine musikalische Zeitung* of an anonymous review of Beethoven's Fifth Symphony by the Romantic literary figure and composer E. T. A. Hoffmann (1776–1822). Hoffmann's essay was important for two reasons: first, it elevated purely instrumental or "absolute" music, as Richard Wagner was later to call it, to the highest rank in art; second, the essay, too was art. In the words of Friedrich Schlegel, one of the founders of the Romantic movement: "The work of criticism is . . . superfluous unless it is itself a work of art as independent of the work it criticizes as that work is independent of the material that went into it" (as quoted in *Lucinde and the Fragments*, 1971). What mattered to the Romantic critic was music's capacity to connect with a reality (God, emotion, the will) that lay beyond the reach of ordinary experience and the language that communicated it. Hoffmann praised Beethoven for the "inexpressible feelings" and "infinite longing" of his music.

The greatest music critic of the Romantic age was the composer Robert Schumann (1810–1856). Schumann founded the *Neue Zeitschrift für Musik* in Leipzig (1834–1944) with the express aim of improving the quality of criticism by making it independent of publishers' interests and therefore more incisive. Journals such as the *Allgemeine musikalische Zeitung* were faulted by Schumann not for their harshness, as had been the case with Haydn and Beethoven, but for their blandness: "Must this damnable German politeness last for centuries? . . . Why don't the composers write their own journal against the critics, and demand harsher judgments on their works?" (Schumann, *Neue Zeitschrift für Musik*, 1934).

Schumann's idea that composers should become critics was a timely one. The founding of the *Gazette musicale de Paris*, which appeared in 1834, the same year as the *Neue Zeitschrift für Musik*, was urged on its publisher by no less than Frédéric Chopin, Franz Liszt, and Hector Berlioz (Berlioz actually earned his living, and a meager one at that, as music critic for the *Journal des débats*). These composers wanted to express their own critical opinions.

The Romantic composer/critics of the nineteenth century (Carl Maria von Weber and Wagner must also be mentioned here) spoke neither *for* the public, as was the case with Addison and Gay, nor *to* the public, as with Burney and Avison, but for and to *art* itself. They were artists living in an age when art was spiritually exalted and the greatest of artists worshiped as gods, an age in which music's importance was akin to that of religion.

Romanticism did not go unchallenged, however. Its most notable opponent was Eduard Hanslick (1825–1904), the first critic of importance to write for the daily press. For a period of forty years, from 1864 until the time of his death, Hanslick's feuilleton regularly appeared on the front page of the Vienna *Neue Freie Presse*. His influence on the musical life of the city was felt everywhere, because of the circulation of the *Presse* and because he reflected the taste of Viennese society. Hanslick may well have been the most powerful music critic of all time. Anton Bruckner openly feared him and Wagner famously ridiculed him in the character of Beckmesser from *Die Meistersinger von Nürnberg*. In his philosophical treatise *Vom Musikalisch-Schönen* (On the Musically Beautiful), Hanslick championed a formalist aesthetic (which attributed music's significance to its own, tonally moving forms) that was to dominate musical aesthetics well into the twentieth century.

The nineteenth century saw an increasing rift between artist and society, with critic suspended uneasily between the two. Commercialized art, consumer audiences, and alienated artists created a cultural vacuum in which all but the most forceful personalities were left to flounder. There is room here to mention only some of these personalities: Henry Chorley (1808–1872), George Bernard Shaw (1856–1950), and Ernest Newman (1868–1959) in England, Claude Debussy (1862–1918) and Romain Rolland (1866–1944) in France, Vladimir Stassov (1824–1906),

Alexander Serov (1820–1871) and César Cui (1835–1918) in Russia, John Dwight (1813–1893), Philip Hale (1854–1934), James Huneker (1860–1921), Olin Downes (1886–1957), and Virgil Thomson (1896–1989) in the United States.

The vast proliferation of dailies, weeklies, and their obligatory "morning after" reviews turned criticism into the profession it is today. Who were all these critics? What were their credentials? Whose interests did they serve? These are vexing questions, then as now. "The immoral profession of musical criticism must be abolished," wrote Wagner nearly 150 years ago. Wagner's statement is characteristically bombastic and hyperbolic; nevertheless, it reflects the quite prevalent view among musicians and their public that criticism is not always practiced with high-minded purpose.

The twentieth century has been an extremely challenging one for music criticism. Modern music (atonal, twelve-tone, aleatoric) is neither liked nor understood by the vast majority of classical music lovers. In what sense, then, does it matter? One answer is simply that it does not (thus Henry Pleasants in *The Agony of Modern Music* [1955]). Another is that listeners themselves do not matter (music obeys its own formal/historical laws without regard to taste). Yet another is that all art is (like Friedrich Nietzsche's god) dead. According to one important critic, Theodor Adorno (1903–1969), music has *negative* value: it reflects the fragmentation and arbitrariness of human existence in post-Enlightenment society.

Among the more scholarly types, music criticism in this century has shifted primarily from appraisal to analysis, from the humanities (with an emphasis on meaning, purpose, and value) to science (with an emphasis on underlying structure). Recently, however, and in reaction to the scientific approach, a "new musicology" has appeared and the scope of criticism has broadened to include all of cultural practice. Nothing that human beings have ever done or thought now seems to be alien to the criticism of music.

[*See also* Music, *historical overview article; and* Taste.]

BIBLIOGRAPHY

Amis, John, and Michael Rose, eds. *Words about Music*. New York, 1989.

Fubini, Enrico, ed. *Music and Culture in Eighteenth-Century Europe: A Source Book*. Chicago, 1994.

Haskell, Harry, ed. *The Attentive Listener: Three Centuries of Music Criticism*. Princeton, N.J., 1996.

le Huray, Peter, and James Day, eds., *Music and Aesthetics in the Eighteenth and Early Nineteenth Centuries*. Abr. ed. Cambridge and New York, 1988.

Schlegel, Friedrich von. *Lucinde and the Fragments*. Translated by Peter Firchow. Minneapolis, 1971.

Slonimsky, Nicolas, *Lexicon of Musical Invective: Critical Assaults on Composers since Beethoven's Time*. New York, 1953.

Strunk, Oliver, ed. *Source Readings in Music History: From Classical Antiquity through the Romantic Era*. New York, 1950.

Strunk, Oliver, ed., and Leo Treitler, gen. ed. *Source Readings in Music History*. 2d ed. New York, 1995.

Sullivan, Jack, ed. *Words on Music: From Addison to Barzun.* Athens, Ohio, 1990.

Weiss, Piero, and Richard Taruskin, eds. *Music in the Western World: A History in Documents.* New York, 1984.

PATRICIA HERZOG

CROCE, BENEDETTO (1866–1952), Italian philosopher, historian, and critic. Although Croce is now often thought of, outside Italy, as primarily of interest as an aesthetician, and one who, by his influence on R. G. Collingwood, had a considerable impact on English-speaking aestheticians, this is entirely to underestimate both the generality and influence of his neo-idealist philosophy and the basis that that philosophical thinking gave to his extensive practical criticism and to his remarkable contributions to the practical affairs of Italy in the first half of the twentieth century as a senator, minister, and, during the Fascist years, leading liberal dissident. Indeed, the history of Italian thought for the first fifty years of this century is deeply permeated by debate between the differing neo-idealisms of Croce and Giovanni Gentile and by debates about the views of those philosophers. Given that in Italy discussions about the philosophical and the practical are never easy to distinguish, and given the regenerative powers of any major philosophical theory, there is no reason to believe that debates about the Hegelian legacy of neo-idealism, and about its legitimacy as a motivation of both practical politics and applied aesthetics, will become things of the past.

Following the tragic deaths of his family in an earthquake in his late adolescence, and after a brief flirtation with legal studies in Rome, Croce returned to Naples where he built his first reputation as a distinguished and indefatigable historian of that city. His historical studies left him dissatisfied, however, and he became involved with questions about the nature of history, and in particular the question whether history is an art or a science. That naturally presupposed an answer to the question what art is, a question that led Croce to his first ruminations in aesthetics, ruminations that, after various trial runs, issued in 1902 in what is still, for all that few give evidence of having read it, probably his best-known work: *The Aesthetic as the Science of Expression and of the Linguistic in General.* Here, following Vico, among others, he distinguishes between the intuitive knowledge of *things in their particularity* and the logical knowledge of *general concepts.* On his view, and here the connection with idealism is obvious, we are bombarded with stimuli of which, using the faculty of intuition, we make representations that give these otherwise inchoate stimuli a particular form. Thus, a painter, using this faculty, gives the otherwise chaotic welter of stimuli produced by, say, a sunset the form of a particular and unique representational painting of a sunset. But what the painter does is only a striking instance of what we all do all the time. Art, therefore, has its roots in something common to us all and is not, as Croce put it, a club only for aristocrats.

Intuition, then, gives articulated expression to what is otherwise a jumble of stimuli. Hence, expression and intuition are said to be identical with each other, and moreover, identical with art. For Croce, no less than for Nelson Goodman at a much later date, art is a form of world making.

After these assertions about intuition and expression, which occur at the very beginning of *The Aesthetic,* two things happen. The first, confusingly for those who think that that book is concerned solely with art, is the development of a comprehensive picture of the mind (what Croce was to call the "philosophy of the spirit"). According to this picture, aesthetic activity, or intuition, as he also referred to it, is the fundamental capacity of the mind. It is that foundational activity in which we construct and grasp the particular things that constitute our worlds. Once we have done this, and *only* then, we can, using our conceptual or logical powers, extract general concepts from these particulars. By intuition we grasp this or that particular stretch of water. By conceptualization we form the concept of water in general. (This is why, for Croce, art is concerned not with the representations of the general [say, of people like Don Quixote] but with the representations of particulars [namely, of *this* man, Don Quixote]).

The two activities, the intuitive (aesthetic) and the conceptual (logic), constitute our *theoretical* powers. On them are based our practical powers, which Croce refers to as the "economic" and the "ethical"; for until we have theoretically constructed the concepts of things (say, water), by abstraction from the particulars we have intuited (say, Lake Windemere and the Atlantic), we can neither want instances of things falling under these concepts nor decide whether we ought to want them. This is why, for Croce, as we shall see, the making (though not the dissemination) of art is independent of morality.

The second thing that happens in *The Aesthetic* is the deduction of a series of corollaries from the claim that art is simply to be identified with the activity of intuitive expression by which each of us gives particular form or expression to the stimuli that bombard us. The corollaries include the claims that each work of art is a unique expression and that to experience it properly is simply to grasp its uniqueness as an expression. We can, of course, *after* grasping a work of art as a unique expression, classify it conceptually by noting its similarities with other unique works. Thus, we can form the concepts of tragedy or the mock-heroic. But Croce argues that the classification of works of art as belonging to this or that genre must come after and not before their identification as art. Otherwise we have nothing to classify. Hence, the notion of genres is not essential to our judgments of things as art. There is also a ringing declaration in *The Aesthetic* that art is independent of morality, where this means that successful expression is morally innocent; for morality presupposes a choice between particular already-existing alternatives, whereas, on Croce's neo-idealist account, until aesthetic intuition has done its work and expressively constructed the objects of understanding, there are no concrete alternatives between which to choose. At most, we can choose whether to publish our expressive visions. This *is* a moral matter. If expression cannot be a matter of choosing to have this vision rather than that, however, not only is creative expression not a moral matter, but a further corollary is that there are no general rules for the creation of works of art.

Some other corollaries may be mentioned. First, if art essentially involves freely creative human expression, then the beauties of art are not the beauties of nature. Whatever beauty nature has is not artistic beauty. Second, if art is expression, what makes a physical object a work of art is not its physicality but the expression with which that physicality is imbued. No mere facts about the physical properties of an object, nor facts about its techniques, will tell us whether it *is* imbued with that expression. Croce somewhat misleadingly expressed this as the thesis that a work of art is not a physical thing and has been roundly criticized for that claim. But it is clear that his underlying thought is that what makes something art must be something more than what makes it a physical object. With that goes what was to become the extraordinarily influential view that a work of art is an organic unity. It must be grasped as an expression that fuses and forms disparate stimuli into a unity. We can, of course, take this unity apart to see how it works, as when we do musical analysis, but that activity is always secondary to, and is at best a handmaiden to, the attempt to grasp the way in which a work of art functions as an organic whole. Finally, there is the claim that to judge a work of art is to see it from the point of view of its maker, a view that, although initially implausible, may be helped by comparing it with Richard Wollheim's view, first expressed in *Art and Its Objects* (1968), that criticism is "retrieval."

Croce remarks in one of the prefaces to a later edition of *The Aesthetic* that after it was published in 1902 he never ceased to investigate the aesthetic. Indeed, another forty years of aesthetic investigation were to come, so that to think of *The Aesthetic* as definitive of Croce would be as bizarre as to think that Ludwig Wittgenstein did nothing after the *Tractatus*. Croce's further work in aesthetics divides into two parts. First was a very substantial volume of practical criticism, always carried out in accordance with the kinds of theory advocated in his theoretical writings. This practical criticism often appeared in the pages of *La critica*, the journal cofounded with Giovanni Gentile, and which was to have a dominant effect on Italian thought in the first half of the twentieth century. There were also major works on such figures as Dante, Johann Wolfgang von Goethe, and William Shakespeare.

The second major part of Croce's aesthetic work after *The Aesthetic* consisted in developments of the account given in that early text. Here there is some controversy about Croce's view that these developments did not materially change the thrust of the views expressed in his first major work but rather were, as he put it, "enlargements" or "developments" of them. Thus, *The Aesthetic* was emphatic that the art is expression and expression art, a view that apparently commits Croce to the view that any expression, including "Pass the salt" is art. In this earlier work, Croce says that there are no species or gradations of expressions. But it appears not to have been long before he himself qualified this view, arguing first that art is *lyrical* expression, and then that art is *cosmic* expression. That there is something right about the former is suggested by our propensity to say of a poem, for example, as Frank Raymond Leavis did of *Paradise Lost*, that only at a certain points does prosaic quality catch fire and take on the quality of poetry. As for the latter, Croce may have meant to draw attention to the way in which, particularly in the work of the greatest of artists, we feel every detail of a work and of the corpus of which they are part to be permeated by a comprehensive and distinctive view of life. Although Croce asserted these developments merely to be clarifications of his first statement that art is expression, both of those clarifications appeared to others to differentiate the kinds of expressions to be found in art from the kinds of expressions to be found elsewhere, and so to introduce the very notion of distinctions within types of expressions that the earlier work so categorically denied.

Criticisms of Croce's aesthetics can be divided into three broad categories. The most radical would be a proof of the incoherence of any idealist philosophy that would, a fortiori, undermine any aesthetics, such as that found in Croce and Gentile, that rested on an idealist foundation.

A second kind of criticism would be to argue that even granted the coherence of idealism, Croce is not coherent and consistent in developing an aesthetic that is built on that foundation. That, indeed, is the criticism offered by Gentile in his *Philosophy of Art*, a remarkable book on idealism and its implication for our understanding of art. Gentile and Croce, initially friends and coworkers in the idealist tradition, were to become bitterly divided by political and intellectual differences. Gentile never made any secret of his view that Croce's idealism and the aesthetics developed on that basis were incoherent (as, indeed, were the idealisms of Immanuel Kant and G. W. F. Hegel), and that view is caustically expressed in *The Philosophy of Art*, which derides Croce's philosophy of the spirit as the "philosophy of the four words," the four words corresponding to the four parts of the spirit in *The Aesthetic*. Essential to idealism, for Gentile, is, first, the thought that nothing must lie outside the mind's conceiving, for how, then, would it be known? Croce certainly put something outside the mind's conceiving. His account, as we have seen, speaks of the mind as opposing an order on an *antecedently existing* matter. Second, it was,

Gentile claimed, an essential thought of idealism that differences must be overcome in the unity of the mind, whereas, as we have seen, Croce vigorously asserts that the mind is divided into four different capacities. That, to Gentile, was an absurd view for an idealist to take.

The third category of criticisms of Croce's aesthetics is by far the most familiar. This is to snipe at particular claims by Croce, often torn from their context—for example, the claims, certainly entailed by idealism, that works of art are internal rather than external, that art is independent of morality, or that art talk of genres is of dubious utility.

Croce's thinking has, in many, often unacknowledged, ways, been a seminal influence on aesthetic theory and practice in this century. To him we owe the notion of organic unity (still to be fully explored). As to his account of art as expression, some, most notably Wollheim in *The Mind and Its Depths* (1993), have seen ways in which an account of art as expression not unlike that espoused by Croce allows us to give some explanation of the extraordinary power of art to engage and move us.

[*See also* Collingwood; *and* Expression Theory of Art.]

BIBLIOGRAPHY

Works by Croce

"Aesthetics." In *Encyclopaedia Britannica*, 14th ed. London, 1929.
The Aesthetic as the Science of Expression and of the Linguistic in General. Translated by Colin Lyas. Cambridge and New York, 1992.
Benedetto Croce: Essays on Literature and Literary Criticism. Translated by M. E. Moss. Albany, N.Y., 1990.
Benedetto Croce's Poetry and Literature: An Introduction to Its Criticism and History. Translated by Giovanni Gullace. Carbondale, Ill., 1981.
Guide to Aesthetics. Translated by Patrick Romanell. Indianapolis, 1965.
Philosophy, Poetry, History. Translated by Cecil Sprigge. New York and Oxford, 1966.

Other Sources

Brown, M. E. *Neo-Idealistic Aesthetics.* Detroit, 1966.
Gullace, Giovanni. Introduction to the translation of *The Philosophy of Art,* by Giovanni Gentile, Ithaca, N.Y., 1972.
Gullace, Giovanni. Introduction to *Benedetto Croce's Poetry and Literature.* Carbondale, Ill., 1981.
Moss, M. E. *Benedetto Croce Reconsidered: Truth and Error in Theories of Art, Literature, and History.* London, 1987.
Orsini, Gian N. G. *Benedetto Croce: Philosopher of Art and Literary Critic.* Carbondale, Ill., 1961.

COLIN A. LYAS

CROUSAZ, JEAN-PIERRE DE. *See* Origins of Aesthetics.

CUBISM. Cubism is the name given to one of the major developments in the art of the early twentieth century. Applied initially in 1908, by a hostile critic, to a group of paintings by Georges Braque in which the buildings and elements of the landscape were treated as predominantly rectilinear shapes and masses, the term came to designate—in painting and sculpture, and by extension in architecture and the applied arts—a way of thinking about the rendering of three-dimensional objects, or forms, on a two-dimensional or planar surface, and certain procedures of simplification, flattening, and contouring that followed from this. More commonly, and narrowly, the term refers to the work of Pablo Picasso and Braque, twin pioneers of an avant-garde movement in Paris that grew steadily in strength, and the attention it received between 1909 and 1914, attracting associates and followers both there and in other countries as far afield as Czechoslovakia and Russia. The importance of Cubism for later art, and for twentieth-century aesthetics, rests on the effect of its innovations and successes on all of those fronts.

Cubism is most often explained today—especially for those who are not well acquainted with the works themselves, or find their character difficult to decipher and respond to—in accordance with what was written about it by its early expositors: intellectuals and literary figures on the scene at the time, supporters and followers of the artists. Those writers linked Cubism to a wide variety of developments that were seen as marking out a new era in the arts, in modern thought, and in the patterns of modern life more generally. The truth that Cubism sought was, so it was claimed, opposed to the semblance of truth that is offered by objects in their external appearance, marked as this is with a transitory, fugitive, and relative character—such as could be associated with Impressionism, a major prior development in late nineteenth-century art that still held authority as the new century opened and could be seen now, by its detractors, as leading merely to optical illusionism of a banal sort. Cubism could equally be related to the "new" reality being revealed by mathematics and physics. Advanced or speculative thinking in those fields was taken as feeding directly into what Cubist artists did with spatial perspective, and the dissemination among scientists of the principles of non-Euclidean geometry led to a preoccupation with those "new dimensions" of space that were being designated by the term *Fourth Dimension.* That term was not being used in its Einsteinian sense (not yet known about outside a narrow band of specialists), but to illuminate the concept of planes being viewed from different angles (as in Henri Poincaré's popularization of non-Euclidean geometry *La science et l'hypothese* [Science and Hypothesis] published in 1902), or more mystically (as in an article that the American artist Max Weber published in *Camera Work* in July 1910) to represent the "grandeur of the universe," as it bore on the operation of vision in the field of the applied arts.

The way in which Cubist canvases were composed was seen as reflecting the changed conditions of modern experience, born of such developments as the coming of the automobile and the airplane, and their effect on consciousness. A key term used to describe that active, and at the same time disturbing, effect as it impacted on the most vital art forms of the period was *dynamism*. Closely linked was the concept of "duration," referring—in direct descent from the popular and widely commented upon writings of the philosopher Henri Bergson—to sensations and reflections experienced with the passage of time, which could be synthesized visually by the artist, in their density and rhythms, by means of a fusion of elements within a limited space. The concept of "simultaneity," which has had the most long-standing afterlife of all in its supposed application to Cubism, combined "dynamism" and the "Fourth Dimension," as broadly popularized, with relativism of viewpoint. The basic claim was that movement around the object permitted the painter to abstract from it successive "aspects" or "appearances," which could then be fused together into a single image that reconstituted the experience in question in time.

The key figures in the advancement of this body of theory in respect to Cubism were the poet, critic, and artistic impresario Guillaume Apollinaire and the painters Albert Gleizes and Jean Metzinger, who, for a short time, led their own wing of the original Cubist movement—largely distinct from Picasso's and Braque's terms of engagement with it. Apollinaire's direct involvement with the movement, in all of its variations, led to a succession of promotional articles from 1910 on, culminating in a book, *Les peintres cubistes*, which he cobbled together in 1912. Gleizes and Metzinger, baptized in the public eye with the label of "Cubist" as a result of their appearance—along with Henri Le Fauconnier, Fernand Léger, and Robert Delaunay—in a single room at the Salon des Indépendants in the Spring of 1911, were the authors from 1910 on of a series of articles that culminated in an explanatory book, *Du cubisme*, which they brought out late in 1911. Besides linking Cubism to science and to the tenor of modern life, they also affirmed that its stress on principles of color and surface organization formed part of an ongoing tradition in French painting.

The basic problem with these explanatory claims is that they have little or no intrinsic connection with the work that was being done by Picasso and Braque at the time. Their particular version of Cubism—which carries today, along with the authority attaching to their names, a distinctly riddling and perplexing aspect for the unversed viewer—developed in the form of a close partnership between lasting from the end of 1909 until 1913, one that was largely sealed off from the remainder of the avant-garde art world and was not backed up by any conceptual framework that they were prepared to enunciate in those years (though they let others do so for them, without dissociating themselves from what resulted). Their approach was basically more empirical, and oriented to particular technical or structural explorations, from one short-term phase to the next. In the background, by 1909, lay an assimilation on the part of both

men of principles of handling and structure to be found in the work of Paul Cézanne, especially simplifying and geometrizing tendencies that stressed solidity and construction. To this would be added, after they came to know Cézanne's late watercolors closely, a concentration on the major axes of the composition, together with a bleeding away of detail further out and toward the edges; an overall effect of fluctuation, based on the use of transparency and overlap; and a limitation of coloring to predominantly monochrome tones of brown, gray, and ocher, so that the eye would not be distracted from registering the overall structure by any more sensual response.

Picasso especially was drawn to the example of African tribal art, as he became acquainted with it from about 1906 on, from examples that he was exposed to in the hands of fellow artists, curio dealers (from whom he and Braque acquired examples), and the ethnographic display cases of the Musée du Trocadéro. He responded to what he saw as its vi-

CUBISM. Georges Braque, *Le Portugais* (1911), oil on canvas; Kunsthalle, Basel. (Copyright 1998 by the Artists Rights Society, New York/ADAGP, Paris; photograph courtesy of Giraudon/Art Resource, New York; used by permission.)

talism, and to the adaptability of its contouring and rhythms to his own purposes, and, as a result, generating, in 1907–1908 especially, his own form of "primitivism." But the frequently made claim that his large experimental painting of late 1906–1907, *Les Demoiselles d'Avignon* (Museum of Modern Art, New York), leads directly into Cubism represents a misreading of the direction taken there, which was fundamentally Expressionist in cast. A more important stimulus, leading toward Cubism, was provided by the bare, ascetic Spanish landscape of Horta de Ebro, a mountain village where Picasso stayed and which he painted (bringing back his own photographs of the site) in the Summer of 1909. For Braque, a similar role was played in 1908 by the hilly landscape of L'Estaque in the south of France, where Cézanne had worked, and that of La Roche-Guyon the following summer.

In the so-called analytic phase of Cubism, lasting from late 1909 to the winter of 1911–1912, Picasso and Braque concentrated on subjects belonging to the café and studio worlds in which they spent most of their time: mainly table-top still lifes and half- and three-quarter-length figures based on models posing. During this phase, they broke with all of the traditional cues made available in Western art since the Renaissance to facilitate the reading of a painting. Instead of modeled shapes, separated from their background in terms of placement and spatial extension, they created a network of broken lines and planes, jostling and fading into one another in a flattened and compressed formation. Instead of a consistently finished look to the application of paint, they set up effects of flicker and shimmer based on transparency and beaded brushwork. What they did here with their chosen subjects was evidently improvised for the most part, rather than directly transcribed. At the same time, they introduced occasional elements (such as a curtain pull or parts of a musical instrument) that recall or refer to expected features of those subjects and settings. A similar role is played by fragments of words and letters, designating elliptically the presence of common objects identified by such lettering, such as newspapers, song sheets, and posters, and also punning associatively on the sounds, or the physical shapes, of the words in question.

The next phase of Cubism, lasting from the Spring of 1912 to the outbreak of war in 1914, is distinguished from the "analytic" one, with its breaking down of components, by the use—following Kantian terminology, here applied to the creative process—of the term *synthetic*. More integrally recognizable forms and objects are now made present; a sense of mass and tactile surface is reconstituted, particularly in the use of superimposed planes that mount up toward the eye; and consistencies of coloration and arrangement are imaginatively imposed, again by purely pictorial means, such as texturing and decorative patterning. Following the introduction of *collage* in 1912–designating (from the French word *coller,* to glue) the pasting down onto the picture surface of materials alien to the traditional media of the artist, such as oilcloth, scraps of colored paper, or wallpaper imitating wood graining—cutout pieces of text, from newspapers especially, and also complete words and phrases that are drawn or stenciled on, are used to incorporate into the work personal, cultural, and on occasion political or social allusions. They aid further in identifying concretely the context of studio or café in which the subject locates itself. By all of these means, enhanced clarity of presentation and structural integration are progressively built back into serving as equivalents to the traditional cues for the reading of the painting, which had been eliminated during the preceding phase. But there is also a continuity of free invention, based on the detachment of individual "aspects" or "attributes" belonging to an object—especially its familiar contour, color, or texturing—in such a way that they can be redeployed in relation to one another in other parts of the composition.

The analytic and synthetic phases, taken as central to Cubism, contributed between them to the idea of a radically modernist venture, undertaken jointly by Picasso and Braque, with the other figures of the movement as their satellites. Formal invention and purity of means were together to be prized in this connection, as contributing to the advancement of a specifically twentieth-century artistic language. The New York critic Clement Greenberg and Alfred H. Barr, Jr., as curator of exhibitions at New York's Museum of Modern Art, in their accounts of Cubism, stressed above all devices and formal concerns—for example, the flatness of the canvas surface—that Picasso and Braque had in common. They thereby brought into being an excessively linear conception of the unfolding logic of what took place in 1911–1914, and one that was detached, in Kantian fashion, from practical or motivational considerations breaching the containing frame that, in this perspective, had the effect of cutting the art off from sociocultural engagement with the larger outside world.

Attention has shifted correspondingly, in the 1980s and 1990s away from that kind of a reading of Cubism, so as to foreground the ways in which Picasso and Braque, even when closest, chose to differentiate their practices from one another—for example, by the introduction of particular choices of lettering, and a diversity of *collage* materials. In this revisionist pattern of study, emphasis has also moved increasingly away from supporting theory of the time (summarized earlier in its philosophical contributions), to considering a variety of external or circumstantial frameworks, from which explanation along new lines can proceed.

Particularly prominent, in regard to the artists' choices and procedures, has been the argument for an analogy with the structuring of verbal language and the operation of "signs," both there and in modern culture more generally. Claims to this effect, transposed from experimental literature to visual images, had been put forward earlier by the dealer and writer on aesthetics Daniel-Henry Kahnweiler, who was a leading champion of Cubism from his Paris gallery, and by the Russian linguist Roman Jakobson, who as a leading figure of the Moscow, and later the Prague schools, interested himself directly in contemporary developments in the visual arts. In Ferdinand de Saussure's *Course in General Linguistics* of 1906–1911, diffused through students of his prior to its posthumous publication in 1916, one of the central theoretical premises was that the twin components of a linguistic sign, which Saussure termed the *signifier* and the *signified,* stood in an arbitrary relationship to one another.

How this can be seen as pertaining to Cubism remains a much-contested question. It raises particularly the question of what kind of meaning is conveyed by the images, and for whom in the way of a posited audience. At the least, it can be said that there are distinct groups of works of Picasso's and Braque's in which a consistency of reference and connotation is maintained, that stands in some fashion, in the responsive processing that an alert viewer is invited to enter into, for the special interests and creative bent of the personality in question. At the same time, when one adverts critically to the conditions of representation and reception on the part of viewers in general that are entailed, both at that time and subsequently, it is to find that the "language" that is being deployed is more open in its possible meanings than the term *code,* carried over from structural linguistics, would imply. The same applies to the Saussurean notion of a "system of differences," governing the relationship of spoken sounds, or scriptual marks in the case of writing, to what is thereby signified. The kind of play with both visual and verbal cues that takes place within Cubism seems impervious, in key respects, to being governed by any such "system."

As the work of Picasso and Braque came to be shown in foreign capitals and included in group exhibitions outside of France from 1912 on, Cubism took hold and acquired devotees and allied practitioners. The use of flattening and angled shapes, the suggestion of fluctuation and merger between contiguously placed components, and the introduction of *collage* and imported lettering were all features that could be fitted or adapted to other, intrinsically different kinds of subject, to create a modern-looking syntax of arrangement. In France, Léger did this for industrial forms, especially of a cylindrical or circular kind (so that he was christened accordingly a "tubist"). For the Salon d'Automne of 1912, Raymond Duchamp-Villon designed a *maison cubiste* with angular decoration on its facade. He and Alexander Archipenko went on to create stylized and rhythmic sculptural versions of Cubism, mainly in relief.

The themes that interested those artists, involving speed, kinetic effects, and the beauty of the machine, appear also in the work of the Italian Futurists, who took over some Cubist devices (Gino Severini was particularly responsive to them), as did the Vorticists on the British scene, led by Wyndham Lewis, David Bomberg, and the sculptor Henri Gaudier-Brzeska. Their interest in geometric and constructive tendencies—shared by the philosopher and aesthetician T. E. Hulme—is paralleled in the avant-garde group of Czech artists that emerged in Prague in 1912–1914, led by Emil Filla and Bohumil Kubista; in the work of some of the Munich artists, such as Franz Marc, who belonged to the loose alliance calling itself Der Blaue Reiter; and also in the work of the so-called Cubo-Futurists in Russia. But in all of those cases, nationalistic forms of awareness, and a concern with conveying in a suggestive manner deep inner feelings of a spiritually charged kind, imposed themselves on the basic formal discipline of fragmentation and reconstitution along cubistic lines.

During and after World War I, the desire in France to see order and tradition reaffirmed—in the wake of destruction and carnage on an unprecedented scale—asserted itself in Cubism, as it did in all of the arts. Experimentation consequently took on a less radical cast, or had less of a dynamic verve to it. The work of Juan Gris, another Spaniard who settled in Paris early in the century and who moved into Cubism from 1911 onward, illustrates this shift with particular clarity, because of its precise sense of calculation and generally "classical" features. A more purified viewpoint toward the Cubist endeavor is also found in Picasso's and Braque's postwar work, with enhanced restraint and containment coming to the fore and an evident concern for stabilization at work.

After 1920, what Greenberg would call "canonical" Cubism became increasingly adopted, as a mode of composition that served to bond together broadly geometric and starkly contoured shapes, and aligned these elements with the rectilinear format of the canvas itself. Picasso's two versions of the *Three Musicians* from the summer of 1921 (Museum of Modern Art, New York, and Philadelphia Museum of Art) exhibit this principle of organization on a large scale, with strong, contained colors and a shallow but concrete sense of depth throughout. It was a principle that could be combined later and by others with the lessons of Piet Mondrian (who had assimilated Cubism in 1912–1913) and of Constructivism (which was particularly stimulated by the metal and cardboard constructions of Picasso) to produce the kind of subdivision into distinct areas, and play with tensile interconnection between separated planes, that one finds in the early work of the Abstract Expressionists.

In the United States prior to 1940, Cubism tended to be a distinct offshoot of European developments. Even where the American artists had spent time in France and had had a direct opportunity to study and embrace the innovations that they saw in progress there—which had been dramatically brought to public attention on the American scene by the traveling Armory Show of 1913—they came up with their own variegations. In the case of Max Weber, the underlying character and dynamic of the New York scene was interpreted in distinctly metaphysical terms, focusing on the discharge of conflicting energies and the intermixing of harsh discordances. Charles Sheeler and Charles Demuth, a little later, chose to work with their own vernacular imagery of regional and rural architecture, which provided them with constructions, to serve as starting points for their geometric treatment, that were already pure and simplified. In the 1920s and 1930s, Stuart Davis used dancing and floating shapes, drawn from city streets and from more countrified settings, in combination with color schemes that were harsh or boldly gay, and put them into arrangements that, in their tilting and generally screenlike appearance, were suggestive of elaborate stage sets. In none of these cases, however, was the viewer's attention directed to the making of the work and the creative processes underlying it, to the degree that was true reflexively of French Cubism.

In literature, and especially in French poetry, already in the pre-1914 period what Kahnweiler would term a "Cubist spirit" was at work. Its operation, involving effects of syncopation and juxtaposition that opposed themselves to any expectable or logical unfolding, can conveniently be broken down into three main areas of practice. First, there was a circle of writer-friends surrounding Picasso that, in addition to Apollinaire, included, from 1903 on, Max Jacob and André Salmon. Second, from 1915 onward, Pierre Reverdy and the periodicals *Nord-Sud* and *SIC* with which he was associated advocated purity and a stripped-down quality as leading poetic concerns, thereby creating a sense of immediate affiliation to Cubist painting of that time. Third, there was the experimental writing of Gertrude Stein, fueled by her own sense of parallelism to what Picasso was doing, in the years 1907-1912, when she collected his work intensively.

The aesthetic importance of Cubism is inseparable, in today's perspective, from its impact on the arts in general: not just poetry—where Ezra Pound, T. S. Eliot, and William Carlos Williams are prominent names that have been invoked, or prose writing, where the same applies to James Joyce, William Faulkner, and the early Ernest Hemingway—but also in the development of fashion and interior decoration, and in theater and music as well. Film and photography have been importantly touched by it. The role of Cubism with respect to high culture in this century, and the ideology surrounding it, was in fact commonly recognized early on, by a larger audience than existed for the art itself—particularly in the form of humorous and satirical references to it incited not just by its seeming oddity and quirkiness, but by the in-built difficulties of comprehension that it posed (typifying those of modern art more generally). Yet, one might also say that Cubism has no need of aesthetic theorizing to explain and justify what is done to familiar appearances by its practitioners. It established its own princi-

ples of organization and free improvisation as it went along: first experimentally, and then in such a way that, from one set or group of works to another, the image both acts as a source of intense visual stimulation, and—like any developing language—stretches the mind in response to its novel and fructifying idioms.

[*See also* Avant-Garde; Collage; Modernism, *overview article;* Picasso; *and* Primitivism.]

BIBLIOGRAPHY

Cooper, Douglas. *The Cubist Epoch.* New York and London, 1970. Exhibition catalog, Los Angeles County Museum of Art and Metropolitan Museum, New York.

Cooper, Douglas, and Gary Tinterow. *The Essential Cubism, 1907-1920: Picasso, Braque and Their Friends.* London, 1983. Exhibition catalog, Tate Gallery, London.

Daix, Pierre, and Joan Rosselet. *Picasso: The Cubist Years, 1907-1916: A Catalogue Raisonné of the Paintings and Related Works.* London and New York, 1979.

Frascina, Francis. "Realism and Ideology: An Introduction to Semiotics and Cubism." In *Primitivism, Cubism, Abstraction: The Early Twentieth Century,* edited by Charles Harrison, Francis Frascina, and Gill Perry, chap. 2. New Haven, 1993.

Fry, Edward F. *Cubism.* London and New York, 1966.

Golding, John. *Cubism: A History and an Analysis, 1907-1914* (1959). 3d ed. Cambridge, Mass., 1988.

Green, Christopher. *Léger and the Avant-Garde.* New Haven, 1976.

Poincaré, Henri. *La science et l'hypothese.* Paris, 1902. Translated by George Halsted into *Science and Hypothesis.* New York, 1905.

Rosenblum, Robert. *Cubism and Twentieth-Century Art.* New York and London, 1960; rev. eds., 1966 and 1977.

Roskill, Mark. *The Interpretation of Cubism.* Philadelphia, 1985.

Rubin, William. *Picasso and Braque: Pioneering Cubism.* New York, 1989. Exhibition catalog, Museum of Modern Art, New York.

Schwartz, Paul Waldo. *Cubism.* London and New York, 1971.

Stein, Donna, ed. *Cubist Prints, Cubist Books.* New York, 1983. Exhibition catalog.

MARK ROSKILL

CULTURAL PROPERTY. *See* Law and Art.

CULTURAL STUDIES. The first task for any discussion of the relation between aesthetics and the emergent discipline of cultural studies is to clarify the sense of the paired terms, or at least to set parameters within which this will be allowed to vary. Today, aesthetics names two distinct but overlapping domains. On one side, it refers to the more or less technical discussion of styles and genres in the literary, visual, and musical arts that, when it moves to the concept of art or the beautiful, mutates into the philosophy and history of art (Kristeller, 1992). On the other side, the aesthetic names what can only be described as a socioethical doctrine centered on an ideal mode of life and order of society (Gleissner, 1988).

This latter sense, which is central to our discussion, crystallized in Germany toward the end of the eighteenth century. At this time it was possible to draw on the etymological meaning of aesthesis as sensuous knowledge, while simultaneously loading the term with the fruits of German metaphysics, pruned according the dictates of early Romanticism (Barnouw, 1993). The resulting delineation of a privileged or "highest" mode of human knowledge and being, concentrated in the wholeness and immediacy of contemplative perception, is captured in a long footnote by Friedrich von Schiller (1967), explaining the confusing term *aesthetic*. Depending on which faculties are activated, things can appear to us via the senses ("physical character"), the intellect ("logical character"), or the will ("moral character"). But, says Schiller (1967, p. 143), a thing can also "relate to the totality of our various functions without being a definite object for any single one of them: that is its aesthetic character." Schiller then illustrates and elaborates the aesthetic modality as follows:

A man can please us through his readiness to oblige; he can, through his discourse, give us food for thought; he can, through his character, fill us with respect; but finally he can also, independently of all this, and without taking into consideration in judging him any law or any purpose, please us simply as we contemplate him and by the sheer manner of his being. Under this last-named quality of being we are judging him aesthetically. Thus there is an education to health, an education to understanding, an education to morality, an education to taste and beauty. This last has as its aim the development of the whole complex of our sensual and spiritual powers in the greatest possible harmony.   (Ibid.)

Despite its contemplative yearning, this conception of the aesthetic was able to embrace a moral anthropology, a philosophy of history, and a theory of society—all based on the problematic of the fragmentation of human capacities and the promise of their dialectical reconciliation—and in these forms to play a dominant role in the formation of the modern humanities academy.

Cultural studies seems, at least at first glance, to refer to an academic discipline, rather than an ideal mode of life. But this term, no less than the aesthetic, requires careful handling. Commentators have long since given up attempting to construe cultural studies in terms of its object domain. A discipline that includes among its objects of commentary rhetorical structures and labor practices, literary texts and crowd behavior, educational institutions and ethnic lifestyles, the state and the fashion industry, film stars and capitalism—to name just a few—is in little danger of being defined in terms of its empirical field. As a result, there has been a tendency to construe the discipline in terms of its of its locality and history. According to an influential telling of the story (Hall, 1980, 1992), cultural studies emerged in Britain during the 1950s and 1960s, with seminal works being written by Richard Hoggart (1958), E. P. Thompson (1963) and, especially, Raymond Williams

(1958, 1961). It took institutional form in the Birmingham Centre for Contemporary Cultural Studies, was partially transformed by its interaction with Althusserian "structuralist" Marxism during the 1970s, and then underwent a transatlantic boom with its migration to American humanities departments in the 1980s (Grossberg, Nelson, and Treichler, 1992).

Although this account has the advantage of reminding us of the national specifics of cultural studies, it suffers from the lack of a clear account of the form of the discipline and in overestimating the latter's historical novelty. In fact, there has been little innovation on Williams's initial attempt to delineate the discipline in terms of a transition from the "aesthetic" to the "anthropological" conception of culture. Aesthetic culture, according to Williams, embraced only the domain of art and the refinement of sensibility. In order to avoid this narrowness, cultural studies would have to adopt the anthropological conception of culture, which he summed up in the phrase "the whole way of life"—not just the artistic and intellectual, but the economic and political forms of social life (Williams, 1958, pp. 17–18). Still, despite its frequent repetition, this formula does little to clarify the nature of the discipline.

In the first place, the appeal to anthropology did not signify that cultural studies was emerging from aesthetics by aligning itself with the sociology and anthropology of culture, as practiced, for example, by Max Weber or Émile Durkheim, Norbert Elias or Marcel Mauss. In fact, despite his ostensible critique of it, the aesthetic conception of culture continued to play a central role in Williams's delineation of the discipline. It provided the ideal of life that, once suitably "materialized" and democratized, would orient the development of "the whole way of life" toward the goal of human self-realization. Or, as Williams put it:

The positive consequence of the idea of art as a superior reality was that it offered an immediate basis for an important criticism of industrialism. The negative consequence was that it tended . . . to isolate art, to specialise the imaginative faculty to this one kind of activity, and thus to weaken the dynamic function which Shelley proposed for it.   (Ibid., p. 60)

Under Williams's tutelage, cultural studies would invent itself as the means of overcoming the isolation of art—of reinvesting art's promise of human completion in the economic and political fabric of society—thereby providing itself with a mission that was both ethical and scientific, engaged and academic.

Given our initial discrimination of two conceptions of the aesthetic, however, Williams's construction of cultural studies as a critique and transcendence of aesthetics remains quite unstable. It is clear that Williams's project involves a critique of aesthetics in the sense of the discussion of works of art. But what about the aesthetic in Schiller's sense, as an ideal mode of life characterized by the overcoming of the fragmentation of the faculties and the achievement of human completion? Is cultural studies a critique of aesthetics in this sense too? Or is there something about the discipline's own pursuit of human wholeness that makes it appropriate to describe it as an aesthetic critique?

Critique of Aesthetics. Accepting for the moment cultural studies' own view of itself, one can follow conventional wisdom in identifying two different but overlapping modes in which it has pursued the critique of aesthetics. The first, already noted, arose from Williams's project to outflank the aesthetic with the anthropological conception of culture, while simultaneously investing the latter with the promise of aesthetic fulfillment or human completion. This mode, usually called "culturalist," is exemplified, in different ways, in such works associated with the Birmingham school as Paul Willis's *Learning to Labour* (1981) and Dick Hebdige's *Subculture* (1979). The former comes as close perhaps as any work in cultural studies to the methodology of anthropology and sociology. It employs ethnographic techniques in order to follow working-class youths through the transition from rebellion in school to conformity at work. For its part, Hebdige's work carries out Williams's mandate in shifting the focus from high to popular culture, where, in the fashions, music, and lifestyle of teenage subcultures, one glimpses an aesthetic embedded in the materiality of "lived experience."

The second form of the critique of aesthetics, which also emerged in the 1970s, was derived from French structuralist theorizing, and from the work of Louis Althusser and Jacques Lacan in particular. In retrospect, this theorizing looks like a neo-Kantian reworking of Marxian and Freudian themes. Above all, it transmuted such key concepts as the mode of production and the unconscious into Kantian "conditions of the possibility of experience." Cultural studies took from this tradition the notion that knowledge had hidden formal conditions, which—whether in the guise of the "problematic," of "grammar," of the "chain of signifiers," or of an unconscious "structured like a language"—lay behind the apparent immediacy of experience and brought it into being for its own ends. Applied to realist and expressivist conceptions of the work of art, as it was by Roland Barthes (1972) and Christian Metz (1974), structuralist theorizing issued in a critique of aesthetics primarily by rejecting realism and by replacing the author with what Jean Bernard Leon Foucault (1977, p. 120) later called "a transcendental anonymity." In Britain, such work was concentrated in the journal *Screen* (SEFT, 1977), where, at a vast distance from its ostensible forms and uses, the visible film was shown to be little more than the projection of underlying formal codes or linguistically organized libidos, the latter typically serving the needs of society by delivering up suitably class- and gender-differentiated subjectivities.

It was, of course, possible for the culturalist and structuralist critiques of aesthetics to conflict, and they did, sometimes immoderately, especially over the "culturalist"

appeal to culture as an organic totality, to "lived experience," and to the category of the unified person. But a reconciliation was never far away; and its celebration in Stuart Hall's "Cultural Studies: Two Paradigms" (1980) does little more than reveal how remorselessly dialectical the discipline had become. If structuralism had correctly stressed the underlying abstract conditions of social reality, said Hall, then culturalism had correctly insisted on lived experience as a spur to political action. If the former had demonstrated the structural conditions of subjectivity, then the latter had shown that social agency depended on the category of the subject. In short, cultural studies celebrated the union of its two critiques of aesthetics through a dialectical ceremony in which all could affirm the necessary partnership of structure and agency, signification and social causation, theoretical analysis and cultural critique. It is precisely this ceremony, however, that reminds us of Schiller's conception of the aesthetic mode as a unification of the person achieved through the dialectical reconciliation of a series of anthropological and historical oppositions.

Aesthetic Critique. It is, therefore, cultural studies' attachment to the model of a complete realization of the person, to be achieved through a dialectical totalization of the faculties, that qualifies it as a species of aesthetic critique in the Schillerian sense. No doubt it will be objected that Schiller and the Romantics, for all the value of their conception of personal development, lacked a sense of its relation to the economic and political development of society. But this commonplace objection, which reiterates one of the leading themes of Williams's *Culture and Society,* is misplaced. Of course, Schiller was no Marxist but, in the letters *On the Aesthetic Education of Man,* he in fact ascribes the fragmentation of the faculties to the division of labor and makes their reintegration conditional on the overcoming of class differences and political hierarchy (Schiller, 1967, pp. 31–43).

In short, far from demonstrating cultural studies' transcendence of its aesthetic precursor (literary criticism), the discipline's insistence on integrating artistic and intellectual phenomena in the totality of society ("the whole way of life") is the first and leading feature of its aesthetic character. Hence, if cultural studies has seen the importation of sociological themes into aesthetic commentary, it has also been characterized by the exporting of aesthetic themes into the domains of anthropology, sociology, and history. The hallmarks of this latter development are to be seen in the framing of social phenomena against a backdrop of dialectical oppositions and reconciliations, promising human completion. Hebdige's *Subculture* is typical of many studies in this regard. It establishes a core opposition between the emancipatory aspirations of youth subcultures and their economic "commodification," and then reconciles this opposition through the concept of style, construed as a perpetual play between liberation and containment, the ideal and the real, and so on. Hence, it is not Marxism or "materialism" that characterizes the discipline but a specific dialectical discipline common to both the Marxist (Lukács, 1962; Marcuse, 1978) and the non-Marxist (Wolff, 1963; Gleissner, 1988) commentary employing the dialectical-historicist schema.

From here it is a short step to the second aesthetic feature of cultural studies: the oppositional and Romantic character of its social and political critique. By making its goal the complete development of the person—to be achieved through the historical integration of the human fragments or the theoretical recovery of their rational foundation—cultural studies is constitutionally disappointed in the actual machinery of social and political life, which, of course, perpetually fails to deliver "true" human emancipation and self-realization. The differences between Schiller's *On the Aesthetic Education of Man* (where, despite the title, school systems are never mentioned) and Williams's vision of *The Long Revolution* (1961) (where the apparatus of the welfare state is acknowledged, but only as the flawed expression of a future self-governing "common culture") are thus less significant than their similarities. This is because, like its aesthetic archetype, modern cultural studies invests the development of the person in a series of forces—history, the people, oppressed minorities, the common culture, the nation—that relate to the mundane machinery of the welfare state only as its principles of critique and transcendence. Cultural studies thus engages in a type of social critique that Schmitt (1986) had already diagnosed as "political romanticism." There seems little doubt that the posture of a transcendent critique of social institutions in the name of self-realizing personhood smoothed cultural studies' way into the libertarian American humanities academy.

The third and final feature of cultural studies that identifies it as a species of aesthetic critique is the type of relation it establishes between the personality of the critic and the truth of criticism. We have already noted that cultural studies distinguishes itself from the empirical social sciences by subordinating their positive phenomena to the dynamic oppositions of moral anthropology or the philosophy of history. Because the privileged model for these "contradictions" is the fragmentation of the human person, it is always possible for critics to find such contradictions microcosmically present in themselves, thereby making the work of social critique reflexive to a practice of personal ethical integration. From here arises the imperative that critics must not draw up a blueprint for society without first overcoming in themselves the oppositions that have disfigured it. The truth of cultural critique is thus dependent on its practitioners performing the kind of "harmonizing" ethical work on themselves that produces the persona of the cultural critic as a moral exemplar and secular prophet. Schiller is explicit about this:

> The edifice of error and caprice will fall . . . from the moment you are certain that it is on the point of giving way. But it is in man's inner being that it must give way, not just in the externals he presents to the world. It is in the modest sanctuary of your heart that you must rear victorious truth, and project it out of yourself in the form of beauty, so that not only thought can pay it homage, but sense, too, lay loving hold on its appearance.
>
> (1967, pp. 59–61)

The exemplar role of the cultural critic is no less pronounced in modern cultural studies. After all, Williams's *Culture and Society* consists of a series of descriptions of the nineteenth-century cultural prophets, from Samuel Taylor Coleridge to William Morris, arranged in a hierarchy depending on the degree to which each succeeded in integrating the ideal and the material aspects of culture in their life and work. Similarly, Stuart Hall (1992, p. 280) has described the integration of the Althusserian and culturalist tendencies of cultural studies as a personal battle—a "wrestling with angels"—that had to be waged within himself. The "organic intellectual" that emerges from this practice of the self is thus a special moral type—the fully integrated personality—and the truth of cultural studies is inseparable from the social prestige of this moral persona.

While engaging in a limited critique of aesthetics, cultural studies can thus itself be understood as a special kind of aesthetic critique. In its dialectical organization, in its ideal of complete human development, and in its transcendental critique of society, cultural studies is the direct inheritor of the conception and discipline of aesthetic self-realization first elaborated by Schiller.

[*See also* Arnold; Caribbean Aesthetics; Comics; Criticism, *article on* Cultural Criticism; Fashion; Film; Law and Art, *article on* Cultural Property; Marxism; Museums; Popular Culture; Postcolonialism; Sociology of Art; Television; *and* Williams.]

BIBLIOGRAPHY

Barnouw, J. "The Beginnings of 'Aesthetics' and the Leibnizian Conception of Sensation." In *Eighteenth-Century Aesthetics and the Reconstruction of Art,* edited by Paul Mattick, Jr., pp. 52–95. Cambridge and New York, 1993.

Barthes, Roland. *Mythologies.* Translated by Annette Lavers. New York, 1972.

Foucault, Michel. "What Is an Author?" In *Language, Counter-Memory, Practice: Selected Essays and Interviews,* edited by Donald F. Bouchard, translated by Donald F. Bouchard and Sherry Simon, pp. 113–38. Ithaca, N.Y., 1977.

Gleissner, Roman. *Die Entstehung der ästhetischen Humanitätsidee in Deutschland.* Stuttgart, 1988.

Grossberg, Lawrence, Cary Nelson, and Paula A. Treichler, eds. *Cultural Studies.* New York and London, 1992.

Hall, Stuart. "Cultural Studies: Two Paradigms." *Media, Culture, and Society* 2 (1980): 57–62.

Hall, Stuart. "Cultural Studies and Its Theoretical Legacies." In *Cultural Studies,* edited by Lawrence Grossberg, Cary Nelson, and Paula A. Treichler, pp. 277–286. New York and London, 1992.

Hebdige, Dick. *Subculture: The Meaning of Style.* London, 1979.

Hoggart, Richard. *The Uses of Literacy.* Harmondsworth, England, 1958.

Hunter, Ian. "Aesthetics and Cultural Studies." In *Cultural Studies,* edited by Lawrence Grossberg, Cary Nelson, and Paula A. Treichler, pp. 347–367. New York and London, 1992.

Kristeller, Paul Oskar. "The Modern System of the Arts: A Study in the History of Aesthetics." In *Essays on the History of Aesthetics,* edited by Peter Kivy, pp. 3–64. Rochester, N.Y., 1992.

Lukács, György. *The Historical Novel.* Translated by Hannah Mitchell and Stanley Mitchell. London, 1962.

Marcuse, Herbert. *The Aesthetic Dimension: Toward a Critique of Marxist Aesthetics.* London, 1978.

Metz, Christian. *Language and Cinema.* Translated by Donna Jean Umiker-Sebeok. The Hague, 1974.

von Schiller, Friedrich. *On the Aesthetic Education of Man in a Series of Letters.* Translated by Elizabeth M. Wilkinson and L. A. Willoughby. Oxford, 1967.

Schmitt, Carl. *Political Romanticism.* Translated by Guy Oakes. Cambridge, Mass., 1986.

SEFT (Society for Education in Film and Television). *Screen Reader 1: Cinema/Ideology/Politics.* London, 1977.

Thompson, E. P. *The Making of the English Working Class.* London, 1963.

Williams Raymond. *Culture and Society, 1780–1950.* London, 1958.

Williams, Raymond. *The Long Revolution.* London, 1961.

Willis, Paul E. *Learning to Labour: How Working Class Kids Get Working Class Jobs* (1977). New York, 1981.

Wolff, Hans Matthias. *Die Weltanschauung der deutschen Aufklärung in geschichtlicher Entwicklung.* 2d ed. Bern, 1963.

IAN HUNTER

CULTURE. *See* Criticism, *article on* Cultural Criticism; Cultural Studies; Law and Art, *article on* Cultural Property; Politics and Aesthetics; *and* Sociology of Art.

CULTURE, POPULAR. *See* Popular Culture.

CULTURE INDUSTRY. *See* Adorno; Marcuse; *and* Popular Culture.

CYBERSPACE. Cyberspace arises where human perception meets the network of digital data. In the literal Greek sense of aesthetics (*aisthesis* = perception), cyberspace is electronic information configured for the human senses. It is the "matrix" of civilization where banks electronically exchange money (credit) and where information seekers navigate vast amounts of audio, video, and text stored on computers. Cyberspace first emerged in the 1980s from electronic networks in education and national defense (the Internet), and from commercial information services. A system for accessing vast amounts of computerized data demanded new ways to visualize and interpret information, and cyberspace answered the phenomenological needs of users. Cyberspace is the experiential topography of electronic data, the architecture of networked information as it appears to human users. Like any new cultural terrain, cyberspace breeds a batch of thorny issues related to traditional aesthetics, ethics, and law. Architects debate over fluidity versus stability in cyberspace structures. Many observers see in cyberspace a new stage in human evolution where the sheer quantity of accessible information forces a qualitative leap in the relationship to knowledge. Others see in cyberspace a dangerous neglect of the public spaces that have traditionally nourished human cultures.

Definition in Historical Context. Most people know the funny but true definition of cyberspace: "Cyberspace is where your credit card money exists even when your pockets are empty." People today move in and out of the cyberspace of electronic computer networks, electronic banking, televised satellite links, and global phone connections. They enter electronic space whenever they watch international news, speak to long-distance friends, or stare at computer monitors for airline destinations. Communication is no longer the simple transmittal of a message from point A to point B but has become a blip of telepresence on a vast network of electronic systems. Cyberspace refers to that independent realm of shared electronic space. But because electronic space contains no inherent aesthetic shape, the way that data gets its shape and configuration for the human senses becomes a conscious matter of artistic information design.

Cyberspace begins with the set of orientation points by which humans find their way around a huge amount of data. Like the *ars memoriae* of classical rhetoric, cyberspace is a phenomenological entity, an elaborate mnemonic structure for bridging human awareness with raw data. What distinguishes cyberspace from previous structures is its marriage of memory with the computer configuration. Magnetic data storage gives no three-dimensional cues for physical orientation, so users must develop an internally imaged sense of the data topology. Network users must additionally work with orientation points that correspond to the conscious design decisions of computer software and hardware. The widely used graphical user interface (GUI) of Apple or Microsoft Windows software is just one example of such an image-laden, iconic representation on personal computers. An iconic interface, along with the mental expectations that correspond to the hardware/software configuration, constitutes the first elements of cyberspace. Added to this are the network links with high-speed satellite or fiber-optic connection, which then offer the true cyberspace of global data representation. The way that links are made and shaped on arrival constitutes another moment of aesthetic design.

The term *cyberspace* first appeared in the science fiction of William Gibson, who in 1984 described it as "a consensual hallucination. . . . A graphic representation of data abstracted from the banks of every computer in the human system" (Gibson, 1984). What science fiction depicted in

1984 soon appeared in the actual operations of industry, defense, and academia. Access to vast amounts of information on computer networks required users to imagine their way around the data in spatial and architectural terms. By the late 1980s, everything from daily banking to National Aeronautics and Space Administration (NASA) space walks depended on the electronic network. At the First Conference on Cyberspace in Austin, Texas, in 1989, the term *cyberspace* served as an umbrella concept to unify the concerns of technicians, artists, computer scientists, architects, social scientists, and philosophers who were addressing the question of how to design the global electronic dataspace. In the 1990s, cyberspace became more manifest in the coalescence of telephone, data, and television services. By 1994, the U.S. federal government—under the Department of Transportation, the National Institute of Standards, and the National Coordination Office for High Performance Computing and Communications—was developing a plan for widening the data superhighway. Since 1993, the hypertext protocol of the World Wide Web determined the quality of data links and the mosaic texture of visual and auditory content streaming through the Internet.

Relation to Tradition. Software systems and hardware interfaces can support a large variety of imaginary structures, leaving cyberspace an open field for architects and designers. Unlike the memory palaces of classical rhetoric, the structures of cyberspace must comply with actual hardware and software configurations while they model an imagined mental architecture. Nor is cyberspace as simple as the Renaissance rhetoricians' memory palace. Instead of a single building with one interior and one exterior, cyberspace represents a universe of relatively independent data systems, resembling much more galaxies or planetary systems. Architects consider cyberspace a sprawling metropolis like Los Angeles rather than a unified city that fans out from a central cathedral. The complexity of cyberspace requires special designs for gateways, links, and security passages. The Internet's ubiquitous "home pages" show only the beginnings of the vast cultural structure that still awaits major aesthetic decisions. From the viewpoint of phenomenology, cyberspace can mimic or resemble actual physical buildings, or it can support more dimensions than any actual physical topography. With a sufficient bandwidth of sensory stimuli, cyberspace can also generate virtual realities or fully immersive environments. As dataspace, however, cyberspace is not a universal simulator but a vast space for high-speed travel. Cyberspace is not itself a virtual reality, but it is the void in which virtual entities can appear. The image of the data highway through cyberspace has captured widespread attention, because electronic space has its own phenomenological remoteness and proximity, its own corners and main streets. Like a highway, the prime purpose of cyberspace is to move and manipulate data at high speeds. More than distant metaphors, the various aesthetic models invoked by designers actually shape cyberspace because raw data cannot itself appear to human senses without the insertion of spatial perception.

Traditional aesthetics emphasizes the shaping of materials, the process of forming earth, stone, paint, and sounds. By its nature—or rather, by its severance from nature—cyberspace undercuts traditional models of the design process. Traditional design imposes form on matter. Even when emphasizing the process of formation, traditional design distinguishes the concept from the product, the idea from the execution in materials. Traditional art allows the final product to manifest the artist's individual signature, a signature inscribed in resistant materials. Because cyberspace is wholly electronic, it eliminates the formation of resistant, earth-based materials. Hardware, such as the phosphorescent picture elements of computer screens, impose some practical limits, but these limits change rapidly as hardware develops. The electronic data remain open for transmutation into any aesthetic shape. Designing anything in cyberspace is tantamount to building it. The artistic hand signature, consequently, diminishes. Just as the notion of the original manuscript fades in importance for word-processing authors, so too cyberspace designers must emphasize the functionality of their craft over the signature of their individual identities.

Cyberspace calls for the artist to become a "space maker," a void developer, because the artist forms an electronic space devoid of materials. Still, an element of resistance remains for the space shaper. The restrictions on cyberspace reside in its hardware and software configurations. The designer must master enough of the technical details to control the actual platform on which the space making happens. The designer also has to overcome technical resistance by injecting the imaginative power of traditional art. Through the imaginative use of metaphors, the cyberspace artist can overcome hardware and software limitations, because the reality of cyberspace rests neither wholly in its objective conditions nor in the subjective feelings of its users. Metaphors can also engage instinctive archetypal images that release human energy and facilitate the mind's melding with the machine. Again, the simplest example of this appeal to archetypes is the "home page" and "Web site" that localize and personalize data in cyberspace.

Special Problems. The advent of cyberspace has caused a profound shift in the discussion of computing. Previously, the debate centered on the computer as a locus of artificial intelligence. The artificial intelligence debate focused on the computer as a potential rival to human intelligence, as an opponent. The paradigm of artificial intelligence was the chess match where the human vies with a computer rival. The rise of cyberspace, however, shifts the debate to intelligence augmentation. The computer appears not so much as an opponent to human intelligence but as a component of human activity. Computerized devices augment memory and visualization skills. Computing now plays a role in most activities, whether automobile repair or word processing or exploring the moons of Saturn. Cyberspace represents this shift of focus inasmuch as it manifests the field in which human perception meets computer data. To understand computers, we no longer use the paradigm of the chess match but instead understand computers more like contact lenses that augment our vision and that become attached to us so intimately that we hardly notice them. With this shift, the issues of aesthetics take equal place in computing alongside the issues of cognition.

As a component of human activity, the computer must then accommodate its input and output to the human sensory capacity. Our senses are essential for learning about the world, and human imagination must flesh out mental/software abstractions by imposing on them sensory schemata (Immanuel Kant's term), such as spatial and temporal characteristics. The symbiosis of intelligence augmentation, then, implies the spatialization of data as a built-in feature of human intuition. Consequently, the important questions now revolve around the symbiosis of human and machine, of mind and computer, and the task is to discover the various ways in which cyberspace can accommodate the human sensory imagination. Instead of primarily cognitive values, computing now equally explores aesthetic values.

What features should cyberspace have? How should cyberspace designers approach their task? So far the debate has revolved around the tension between either organizing cyberspace or enjoying its free fluidity. Architects disagree on the relative importance of establishing prior rules for building cyberspace. Electronic structures need not follow the physics of the primary world, but basic laws of stability, identity, and commensurability seem requisite for intelligent navigation. Even though electronic territory can display different dimensions than physical territory, human users may benefit from analogies based on the primary world outside cyberspace. Certain formal rules can guide cyberspace development so cyberspace more closely mirrors the ontology of the primary world. On the other hand, some space makers celebrate the fluidity of electronic architecture. They see beauty precisely in the freedom from ontological constraints. Forms can follow the builder's stipulations, and without real-world reference, users will feel less

restriction in the ways they perceive data. Some have suggested that nonreal-world, fantasy references, such as magic or medieval spiritualism, might better serve as analogues for constructing cyberspace. Current Internet experiments, such as Apple Computer's Project-X (Hotsauce), invite users to "fly through" rather than "browse" through data as they currently do in Web browsers such as Netscape or Microsoft Internet Explorer. Cyberspace at present resembles the open frontier of the American continent. Territorial and proprietary rights throughout cyberspace remain unclear. In early days when the U.S. Department of Defense and the National Science Foundation created the first giant backbones of the Internet, the government showed no interest in regulating cyberspace, but since the expansion of the commerce on the network and since the growth of visualization software such as the World Wide Web, legislators have sought to control the Internet. The Internet was originally constructed out of independent computer modules connected in such a way that even if some nodes were destroyed, the exchange of data would continue; parts of the network could be physically damaged, while the whole process of data exchange would continue unabated. Consequently, the Internet has never had a central computer, a central node, or a central governing body. As more users migrate to electronic space, efforts will probably be made to provide a legal framework for adjudicating disputes and resolving proprietary claims. Several organizations have already begun a legislative battle to restrain the movement of legislators to regulate cyberspace. To date, it is unclear to what extent government legislation can or will affect the aesthetic decisions made by cyberspace designers.

[*See also* Artificial Intelligence; Computer Art; Digital Media; Hypertext; Multimedia; *and* Virtual Reality.]

BIBLIOGRAPHY

Benedikt, Michael, ed. *Cyberspace: First Steps.* Cambridge, Mass., 1991.
Gibson, William. *Neuromancer.* New York, 1984.
Heim, Michael. *The Metaphysics of Virtual Reality.* New York and Oxford, 1994.
Mitchell, William J. *City of Bits: Space, Place, and the Infobahn.* Cambridge, Mass., 1995.
Vinge, Vernor. *True Names.* New York, 1984.
Yates, Frances Amelia. *The Art of Memory.* Chicago, 1966.

MICHAEL HEIM

D

DADAISM. Apart from its anecdotal place as a colorful moment in the history of art and aesthetics, Dada, for better or worse, significantly changed the concepts and practices of art in the twentieth century. The noisy debates and wild theatrics of the Dadaists across Europe, and the work and writings of Marcel Duchamp, Man Ray, and Francis Picabia, among others, raised profound conceptual challenges that altered the course of art and aesthetics in the twentieth century. The shift from the idea of art as a selection of attractive visual objects to art as a vehicle for ideas forced artists and aestheticians to reexamine and modify their thinking about the very concept of art, as well as its practice. The upheaval fostered by the Dadaists has called into question all essentialist definitions of art (such as Plato's mimetic theory of representation), as well as the formalist and Expressionist theories that were advanced during the seventeenth to the nineteenth centuries. Modern theories espousing the purity of art media such as painting also would have found no favor with the Dadaists. In contrast to modernist purity, their practices fostered the dissolution of the boundaries of the separate art media. The combined assault of wild, irreverent Dadaist experiments with the cool but deadly wit of the likes of Duchamp and Man Ray called into question all assumptions about art.

Dada represents an aesthetic of action grounded in conflicting anarchist sentiments extending from idealism to nihilism. It exhibits a nonconformist human spirit with respect to societal and artistic conventions and traditions. Dada first established its presence in Europe, and was ultimately more successful there, perhaps owing in part to its incompatibility with the progressive and pragmatic sentiments of American culture. It refers to the artistic practices and ideas of gifted émigré writers and artists in Zurich who founded Cabaret Voltaire in 1916 and launched a movement that appeared more or less coincidentally with related happenings in New York and Paris. The German poet-philosopher Hugo Ball, the Romanian poet Tristan Tzara, the German writer Richard Huelsenbeck, and artists Jean (Hans) Arp and Marcel Janco were the principal activists in Zurich. In New York, the main Dadaists were the artists Marcel Duchamp, Man Ray, and Francis Picabia, who also engaged in Dada activities in Barcelona. In Paris the dominant figures were literary: Tzara, the poet Paul Eluard, and André Breton (who later was active with Surrealism), aided by Duchamp, Man Ray, Picabia, and others. Huelsenbeck took Dada ideas to Berlin, where he attracted the support of such artists as John Heartfield and George Grosz. Artist Max Ernst was active in Dada circles in Cologne, and artist Kurt Schwitters was the leading proponent of Dada in Hanover. Officially, Dada was a short-lived enterprise lasting from 1916 to 1924, when it more or less dissolved over differences among the principals active in Paris. Dada action in New York virtually ceased when Man Ray and Duchamp left for Paris around 1920. While relatively brief in duration, the Dadaist spirit and ideas still dominate within the avant-garde forces of contemporary art.

Although identified with this particular movement in the arts, the term *Dada* exemplifies a prevailing anarchistic element that has existed in some form throughout human history. Both its idealist longings for change in oppressive social and political systems (as espoused by Ball), and its abhorrence of the stifling bourgeois art and life (as expressed in the Dadaist manifestos of Tzara and others), are rooted in the intellectual ferment of the nineteenth century. In general, the Dadaists invoked Arthur Schopenhauer's antirational views that rejected the primacy of reason in favor of unconscious mental processes, although not his Platonist views on aesthetic objects. Both Ball and Huelsenbeck were inspired by Friedrich Nietzsche's critique of bourgeois life and aesthetics. Their belief that reason is the enemy of new and vital forms of experience echoed Henri Bergson's views in *Creative Evolution*.

For the most part Dada's advocates were against Futurist, Expressionist, and Cubist art movements. They did, however, owe some debt to these movements, as well as to Wassily Kandinsky and the *Blaue Reiter*. From the Futurists, they inherited the manifesto as a means of expression, *bruitisme* or noise music, and the practice of altered typesetting in the design of their publications. The use of art as social protest was shared with the Expressionists in Germany, and the radical break with the past found in Cubist art was carried further in Dada art. In Munich, Ball had studied with Kandinsky, who experimented with sound poems lacking semantic elements. Such practices were adapted by Ball and others in the Dada performances at Cabaret Voltaire.

The young Dadaists had every reason to be restless. The world around them was undergoing monumental political, technological, and artistic changes. Political upheaval in

Germany and throughout Europe led to World War I. Down the street from the Cabaret Voltaire in Zurich, Nikolai Lenin was plotting the Russian Revolution. Technological innovations required clearing the way for the changes leading to modern life. Among the remarkable happenings of 1913 to 1920 were the establishing of telephone service between New York and Berlin, the opening of an electrified Grand Central Station in New York City, a constitutional amendment to provide for the graduated income tax in the United States, assembly line production at Ford Motors, the opening of IBM's office in New York, women marching for the right to vote in the United States, and the opening of the first American radio broadcasting station (in Pittsburgh), to mention a few.

Other major intellectual and artistic changes were happening concurrent with Dada. Sigmund Freud published *Totem and Taboo* (1913), and Albert Einstein published his *General Theory of Relativity* (1916). Respectively, these works demanded the rethinking of the psychological and the physical worlds. The arts were rampant with changes: The 1913 Armory Show in New York introduced many Americans to modern visual arts. Vaslav Nijinsky's ballets, D. H. Lawrence's novels, James Joyce's writings, Charlie Chaplin's films, the musical compositions of Erik Satie and Igor Stravinsky, and the emergence of jazz as an art form all happened during the Dada era. Compared to these monumental changes, the voices of the Dadaists might have produced only a small if irritating echo. Nevertheless, Dada added considerable spice to the art of its time and cleared the way for future developments in the arts, initially abstract art and Surrealism.

Differing views among the Dadaist writers and artists and their geographic diversity made agreement on a definitive program for all Dadaists virtually impossible. The very essence of Dada is controversy. This controversy begins with respect to the term *dada* itself, which first appeared in the sole issue of *Cabaret Voltaire* in June 1916. Dada literally refers to a child's hobbyhorse, and was chosen randomly by Huelsenbeck and Ball from a French-German dictionary while they searched for a name for the chanteuse at Cabaret Voltaire. Tzara also claimed credit for the discovery of the name. Dada thus came to symbolize this anarchic social and artistic outlook born in Zurich, and was referred to variously as "a farce of nothingness in which all higher questions are involved," "having a good time," and "life without carpet slippers." A recent exhibit at the Whitney Museum of American Art described Dada simply as "Making Mischief." Both the seriousness and the farce that Dada embraced are suggested in these references.

Dada represented for Ball, Janco, and their colleagues a way to express their profound sense of rage and grief over the suffering and humiliation of humankind as exemplified in the evolving world war. Through their outrageous actions and writings they hoped, however naively, to clear away the debris of an overly rational world and establish a new social order. They attacked art based on the aesthetics of beauty and art for art's sake, as well as Futurism, Expressionism, and Cubism, representing modern art. Despite their assault on art, some of the Dadaists (Ball, Janco, Arp, and Schwitters) believed passionately in art as a meaningful instrument of life, and viewed their efforts as a means of social criticism and as a positive search for meaning and substance. Huelsenbeck placed a lesser value on art, as being only one expression of human creativity.

Apart from these differences, the efforts of the early Dadaists were grounded in a collective social outlook, which fostered collaborative performances and literary efforts. Their chief weapons were an entire arsenal of tactics grounded in deep social concern, as well as satire and laughter. They drew upon elements of irrationality, the unconscious, and a determination to confront the established ways of thinking about art and life itself. Fearless and at times foolhardy, they used their literary and artistic skills to shake the complacency of their fellow citizens with respect to social codes, language, and the practices of the arts. By freeing themselves from established conventions, they in fact invented new forms of expression and opened the way for subsequent generations to follow. Underlying their actions were references to radical philosophical ideas found especially in the works of Nietzsche.

Concrete manifestations of this artillery can be found in their performances and individual art endeavors. An evening at a Dada soirée in Zurich at the Cabaret Voltaire, or later at the Galerie Dada, would have included music, dance, poems, theory, manifestos, masks, and costumes, as well as pictures. These elements were accompanied by jangling keys, gymnastic exercises called *noir cacadou,* and often screaming renditions of poetry or other texts. All of these activities took place in a tight space with audiences jammed together up to the stage, and with minimal technical expertise at stage performance. The audiences included the bourgeois as well as international artists such as choreographers Mary Wigman and Rudolf Laban, as well as the Dadaists. As often as not, the music and dance incorporated African forms, and the costumes designed by Janco featured bizarre body masks made of painted cardboard, also inspired by a mix of African themes and other images based on the machine aesthetics of the times. The paintings shown by Arp in Zurich became increasingly abstract. Ball's innovative sound poem, *Labada's Song to the Cloud,* features indecipherable utterances such as "gadji beri bimba . . ." In New York, Picabia repudiated the conventions of art portraits in his *Portrait of a Young American Girl in a State of Nudity* (1915), which took the form of a spark plug. In Paris, the soirées continued as Breton, Tzara, Eluard, and others proceeded to outrage the bourgeois audiences with assaults on their art, intellectual beliefs, and the conventions of an ordered society. Audiences retaliated, or perhaps merely participated actively, by pelting those on the stage with tomatoes, eggs, and beefsteaks from a local butcher's shop.

From this account of Dadaist actions, it is evident that they differed significantly from the Bolsheviks, whose program for social change focused on political action and violence. Although there were limited attempts to mobilize Dada as a political force, particularly in Germany, the anarchistic nature of Dada was not suited to serious political action. Nor was political action the main interest of its reformist intent. Rather, the Dadaists, like the Surrealists who followed, hoped to challenge the dominance of the rational over social and artistic life and to encourage the population to examine societal conditions from the perspective of the alternative human resources to be found in the irrational unconscious aspects of human creativity. Dadaists also differed from the Surrealists, who turned inward to escape the world that the Dadaists hoped to reform.

Apart from its underlying message of aesthetic anarchy, Dada warrants serious attention for highlighting certain concepts that have further enriched the field of aesthetics, such as the social role of art, the principle of contradiction, and the principle of chance. At the center of Dada action is contradiction. As Duchamp once remarked, anything that seems wrong is right for a true Dadaist. "It is destructive, does not produce, and yet in just that way it is constructive." Contradiction extends to the Dadaists' views on art. Hence, Dada embraces both anti-art and art. Anti-art, when applied to Dada, refers to the revolutionary art intended to debunk existing concepts and practices of making art. It represents a reaction to these concepts and practices, although it may incorporate them to achieve a different end. By its nature it entails an element of protest. The principal target of this anti-art was the "noble" and "beautiful" art derived from an aesthetic of "art for art's sake" that was being used in bourgeois society to mask social ills. While aspects of the Dada performances and exhibitions in Cabaret Voltaire and elsewhere were considered anti-art, as were Duchamp's shovel and urinal, they were at the same time experiments in advancing the future of art forms such as conceptual and abstract art. In addition to an anti-art component, the events at Cabaret Voltaire regularly included a wide range of art made by the Dadaists and others. African carved sculptures, drawings, and chance collages by Jean Arp; paintings by Paul Klee, Pablo Picasso, Henri Matisse, and others; the sound poems by Ball, a sequence of syllables without rhyme or meaning; *bruitisme* or noise music borrowed from the Futurists; dance, skits, storytelling, and the reading of texts, including poetry and manifestos—all were integrated into the evening soirées. At the Galerie Dada in Zurich, the works of Heinrich Campendonk, Kandinsky, Klee, and others were shown in March 1917. In the same year, Duchamp attempted unsuccessfully to exhibit his *Fountain*, signed R. Mutt, in New York at the first annual exhibition of the Society of Independent Artists. In a Paris Dadaist soirée, paintings by Alberto Giacometti, Juan Gris, and Fernand Léger coexisted with poetry readings by Eluard, Jean Cocteau, and Tzara. On the same program, Breton "performed" the erasing of a Picabia drawing as it was produced on a chalkboard. All of these events suggest that the contradictory elements of art and anti-art remained unresolved in Dada circles.

Chance represents another concept advanced into aesthetics through Dada. Chance functioned as a principle of dissolution well suited to the production of anti-art and to the Dadaist's anarchic aims with respect to the practice of art itself. It represented the voice of the unconscious in art and served as a protest against the rigidity of rational elements of art and life. Additionally, Dadaists held that chance helped restore to works of art their primeval magic power and recovered the immediacy that art had lost through the overly rational influences of classicism in prior centuries, reflected, for instance, in the writings of Wolfgang von Goethe and Gotthold Lessing. The chance-based improvisations in the performances and exhibitions of the Dadaists at Cabaret Voltaire included experiments in "accidental" poetry, music, and skits, as well as storytelling and manifestos. Through these means, the Dadaists sought to liberate art from established assumptions and practices intended to represent the world through rational means (such as the laws of geometric perspective) or in accordance with the formalist notion of art for art's sake. Their experiments with chance and improvisation were subsequently incorporated into the work of late-twentieth-century artists, led by John Cage in music, and extended to dance, theater, and other modes of performance.

Other changes in the perception of artists and art were implicit in the Dadaists' activities. By emphasizing the communal character of artistic practice, they helped to demystify the romantic notion of the isolated artist as the center of creativity, and thereby refocused attention away from artists and to their works and the function of art in society. Their assault on art required changes in the public as well as the art-world perception of art. An emphasis on the connections between art and life required that art function in relation to other value-related societal practices, including social criticism. From another perspective, Duchamp's introduction into the art world of commercially produced utilitarian ready-mades such as bottle racks, urinals, and shovels called into question a time-honored presumption that artworks differed from other aspects of the man-made environment, either by their function or by a distinctive set of features. Picabia's incorporation of machine images and Schwitters's practice of using found objects such as theater tickets or other discarded scraps of paper in his constructions raised further doubt about artificial efforts to separate art from other essential activities of life.

Dadaist art also requires rethinking of the canon of art. In order to admit ready-mades into the world of art, it was necessary to disassociate them from their familiar roles and also to expand the canon to include anti-art. Similarly, it was necessary to rethink the identification of aesthetic properties with art. Although attempts have been made to argue that the urinal presented by Duchamp for exhibition as *Fountain* had aesthetic features, these features were incidental to the challenge he posed to the canon of art. He tested the canon in another way in his *L.H.O.O.Q.*, made of an altered reproduction of Leonardo da Vinci's *Mona Lisa* with a mustache and beard. Through these efforts, Duchamp challenged aesthetics in a far more lethal way by questioning the boundaries of the concept of art. In doing so, he and the other Dadaists opened the way to a much wider practice of art in the twentieth century.

What remains as the legacy of Dada? In the arts and literature there is a considerable legacy of artworks by Duchamp, Man Ray, Picabia, Ernst, Arp, and others that has expanded the canon of visual and conceptual art. A repertory of books and poems by Eluard, Huelsenbeck, Tzara, and others has enriched the literature of the twentieth century. These works are of interest for their experiments with language and graphic design as well as for their content. Equally important are the Dada spirit and ideas that helped keep art alive and continue to inspire bold experimentation. Chance and improvisation have extended from their Dada roots to an important place in contemporary Fluxus art in the United States and Germany, especially through the work of composer John Cage and choreographer Merce Cunningham, and the video art of Nam June Paik. Contemporary Fluxus performances such as Cage's silent "performance" at the piano and the videocello performances of Paik and cellist Charlotte Moorman would have been quite at home in the era of Dada. Joseph Beuys enacted similar performances in Germany. The Dada spirit survives even today in the works of the contemporary Belgian artist Jan Fabre, whose theater pieces such as *The Power of Theatrical Madness* continue Dada's assault on traditional art forms and the institutions responsible for their perpetuation. Postmodern art practices of the late twentieth century also benefited from the legacy of Dada, adopting art practices previously introduced by Dada. Looking at art in its cultural context and linking art practices to political and economic issues, disregarding stringent boundaries among art media, and displacing the artist from the center of attention are common themes in Dada and postmodern art.

Finally, through its irreverent attempts to subvert conventional theories and practices of art, and a concerted effort to reunite art and life, Dada enticed public art audiences to expand their understanding of art and challenged aestheti-

cians to rethink traditional aesthetic theories and generate new ones to accommodate conceptual changes and artistic practices in the ever developing world of art.

[*See also* Aleatoric Processes; Anti-Art; Avant-Garde; Cage; Collage; Duchamp; Modernism; Performance Art; *and* Play.]

BIBLIOGRAPHY

Ades, Dawn. *Dada and Surrealism Reviewed.* London, 1978.

Arp, Jean (Hans). *On My Way: Poetry and Essays, 1912–1947.* New York, 1948.

Ball, Hugo. *Flight Out of Time: A Dada Diary.* Edited by John Elderfield, translated by Ann Raimes. New York, 1974.

Barr, Alfred H., Jr. "Abstract Dadaism." In *Cubism and Abstract Art,* pp. 172–178. New York, 1936.

Bigsby, C. W. E. *Dada and Surrealism.* London, 1972.

Cabanne, Pierre. *Dialogues with Marcel Duchamp.* Translated by Ron Padgett. New York, 1971.

Camfield, William A. *Francis Picabia: His Art, Life and Times.* Princeton, N.J., 1979.

Dachy, Marc. *The Dada Movement, 1915–1923.* New York, 1990.

Dada (Zurich and Paris). 1–7. (July 1917–March 1920). Edited by Tristan Tzara; *Dada* 4–5 cover title is *Anthologie Dada; Dada* 6 cover title is *Bulletin Dada; Dada* 7 cover title is *Dadaphone.*

Dada Surrealism (New York) 1–2 (1971–1972). Edited by Mary Ann Caws.

de Duve, Thierry, ed. *The Definitively Unfinished Marcel Duchamp.* Cambridge, Mass., 1991.

Foster, Stephen C., ed. *Crisis and the Arts: The History of Dada,* vol. 1. New York, 1996.

Huelsenbeck, Richard. *Memoirs of a Dada Drummer.* Edited by Hans J. Kleinschmidt, translated by Joachim Neugroschel. New York, 1974.

Huelsenbeck, Richard, ed. *Dada, eine literarische Dokumentation.* Hamburg, 1964.

Last, Rex W. *German Dadaist Literature: Kurt Schwitters, Hugo Ball, Hans Arp.* New York, 1973.

Meyer, Reinhardt, et al. *Dada in Zurich and Berlin, 1916–1920: Literatur zwischen Revolution und Reaktion.* Kronberg Ts., 1973.

Motherwell, Robert, ed. *The Dada Painters and Poets: An Anthology.* New York, 1951; 2d ed., Boston, 1981; reprint, Cambridge, Mass., 1989.

Naumann, Francis M. *New York Dada, 1915–1923.* New York, 1994.

Naumann, Francis M., and Beth Venn. *Making Mischief: Dada Invades New York.* New York, 1996.

Ribemont-Dessaignes, Georges. *Dada manifestes, poèmes, articles, projects, 1915–1930.* Paris, 1974.

Richter, Hans. *Dada: Art and Anti-Art.* New York, 1965; reprint, New York and Oxford, 1978.

Rubin, William S. *Dada and Surrealist Art.* New York, 1968.

Sanouillet, Michel. *Dada à Paris.* Paris, 1965.

Schwarz, Arturo. *New York Dada: Duchamp, Man Ray, Picabia.* Munich, 1973.

Schwarz, Arturo, ed. *Documenti e periodici dada.* Milan, 1970.

Tzara, Tristan. *Approximate Man and Other Writings.* Translated by Mary Ann Caws. Detroit, Mich., 1973.

Tzara, Tristan. *Seven Dada Manifestos and Lampisteries.* Translated by Barbara Wright. London, 1977.

Verkauf, Willy, ed. *Dada: Monograph of a Movement.* New York, 1957; reprint, London, 1975.

Watts, Harriett Ann. *Chance: A Perspective on Dada.* Ann Arbor, Mich., 1979.

CURTIS L. CARTER

DAGUERREOTYPE. *See* Photography.

D'ALEMBERT, JEAN. *See* Alembert.

DANCE. [*This entry comprises just two of many essays on the aesthetics of dance included in this encyclopedia:*
Historical and Conceptual Overview
Contemporary Thought
The first essay is an overview of the history of dance aesthetics, while the second essay covers contemporary aesthetic issues in dance. These two essays together serve as an introduction to five other essays on dance located elsewhere in this work: Criticism, *article on* Dance Criticism; Modernism, *article on* Modern Dance; Notation, *article on* Dance Notation; Ontology of Art, *article on* Ontology of Dance; *and* Postmodernism, *article on* Postmodern Dance. *For further discussion, see* Authenticity *and* Performance.]

Historical and Conceptual Overview

In general, two things make dance distinctive as an object for inquiry in aesthetics. One is the complete human presence of the dancer in the dance; the other is the relation of artistic dance to rituals and ceremonies of direct social significance. Whether they affirm or deny these distinctive features, theorists of the fine arts have not always found it easy to include dance in the scope of their generalizations.

Topics actually discussed in dance aesthetics have arisen from specific cultural concerns at different historical epochs, but have remained available for general discussion. The following account traces some of these continuities.

Aristotle's *Poetics* included dance among the mimetic arts, as the use of movement forms *(schemata)* to convey human action and feeling. When the concept of the "fine arts" was eventually formulated, Jean-Georges Noverre (1760) followed Aristotle's lead in arguing that dance deserved a place among these prestigious "arts of imitation." G. W. F. Hegel, however, excluded dance from his influential canon of the fine arts, because its "imitations" had no distinctive cognitive function. Attempts to specify and vindicate such a function remain basic in dance aesthetics.

Among the relics of classical antiquity, from which Western civilization long sought cultural authorization, is a history of dance ascribed to Lucian of Samosata (second century CE). This history assigned unique cultural significance to the Roman pantomime, a form of dance alleged to dispose of a precultural "language" of gesture capable of fine conceptual discriminations as well as expressive power. The possibility of such a language, its importance relative to that of dance conceived as the formal art of bodies in beautiful motion, and the relation between the two, remain a perennial topic. Lucian's denigration of nonmimetic dance as

meaningless has been countered in the present century by proponents of a purely aesthetic view of "classical" ballet.

Another theme from antiquity, extensively discussed in Plato's *Laws*, is the significance of danced ceremonies as symbolizing civic order. Dance as thus conceived became a powerful instrument of state propaganda at the French court in the sixteenth century. Reflection on this history gives rise to an aesthetic politics of dance, in which oppressive choreography is pitted against subversive execution, the pattern making of the planner against the inarticulate wisdom of the body. Debate in this tradition, reinforced by feminist arguments, flourishes to this day.

Italian precursors of the French court ballet promoted the idea of an erudite, mathematically based dance that would be analogous to the highbrow music of the day and thus win for dance a place among the liberal arts. The convoluted libretti of some French court ballets, with the convoluted geometries they prescribed, took up this idea, but to little effect. Today's less intellectualistic notions about the human mind may lead to a revival of such ambitions, but have not yet done so.

French court ballets were multimedia events. The general aesthetics of such processions and pageants were essayed by Claude-François Ménéstrier (1631–1705), but abortively. The idea of dance as component in a generalized theater art was, however, proposed by Charles Batteux in *Les Beaux arts reduits à un même principe* (1746), who argued that what was "dance" and what was "music" or "drama" depended on which component in a collaborative design was dominant. This suggestion proved more fruitful, and today's use of film and video suggests a dance art in which the moving body either assimilates a whole visual environment to its rhythms or is itself dissolved in electronically generated space.

What aborted Ménéstrier's demarche was Louis XIV's establishment of a Royal Academy of Dance to replace the ballets put on by royalty and nobility. The effect of this professionalization was twofold: to depoliticize and aestheticize the most prestigious dance practice, and (explicitly) to establish a dance-based art of dance institutionally independent of music. The relation between dance forms and music remains a hotly debated issue (enriched by reference to Indian and African theories and practices), as does the legitimacy of politicizing or depoliticizing dance criticism.

The preceding discussion concentrates on the official high culture of Western civilization. There was, however, a continual interchange of performers between ballet and itinerant groups who mounted acrobatic displays for popular audiences, and an exchange of forms and styles between court dancing and social dance. The way art dance is rooted in more general dance practices gives rise to a more general aesthetic of human movement. Thus, Adam Smith (1795) differentiated two excellences of dance movement, grace and athletic elegance. This dichotomy reflects the ambiguity of Edmund Burke's version of the old distinction between the beautiful and the sublime, values that are both general in scope and related to the stereotypical aesthetic excellences of female and male comportment.

The aesthetics of grace, freed from gender connotations and identified with a fusion of the perfection admired in animal movement with human self-control and tact, was much discussed from the eighteenth century to the middle of the twentieth. Debates centered on the moral and social significance of such qualities, especially as exemplified by the work of that perennial agent of social mobility and stability, the dancing master. The aesthetics of grace, as a manifestation of perfected vitality, offers a perennial counterpoise in aesthetics to the influence of Immanuel Kant, who has no place for dance.

The emphasis on grace as the typical excellence of the dancing body has largely been superseded by the application to dance of phenomenological approaches to human experience as essentially corporeal. Such approaches open up for dance, as the art of the embodied human in position and motion, what Hegel had denied it: an important range of meaning to which it has privileged access. In principle, this grounds a fundamental revaluation of the art of dance, but the principle has proved hard to put into practice.

Eighteenth-century speculation on the origins of language and the arts thought of them as specialized developments from a precultural phase of human development in which all behavior was vaguely meaningful. Dance was thought of as a manifestation of this phase. This idea survived, or was revived, in American progressive education that purported to build on a child's "natural" instincts and feelings. For many educational theorists, dance has accordingly been the paradigm of self-expression, and dance purporting to be based on spontaneous movement patterns is an important educational instrument. The phase of aesthetic theory that held all art to be essentially "expression of emotion" did not, however, assign dance a central place in its concerns.

Attempts to base an aesthetics of dance on the conviction that dance must be the most primitive, and hence fundamental, art of humanity flourished in the post-Darwinian period when human behavior was explained by its supposed prehuman animal origins. Courting behavior of mating couples and patterned movements among groups of social animals were cited as revealing the true meaning of dance. This line of thought is now unfashionable, but the genuineness and significance of such connections are still under discussion.

Meanwhile, unrelated to dance practice, a pervasive literary trope has taken dance to be a metaphor, not only for discipline and exuberance in the human microcosm, but for the order of the heavens and for vital processes generally. A sophisticated version of the latter approach was basic to the

theory of biological process in Susanne K. Langer's *Mind* (1967). [*See* Langer.]

Dance aesthetics also finds a rich field for inquiry in the relationship that must obtain between the sophisticated arts of dance and the basic skills that enable the human animal to move successfully through the natural world and to develop cultures involving specialized skills of movement. The somewhat analogous relationship between dances of spontaneous self-expression and learned dance styles, in which the body is trained as a specialized instrument and movement is formally codified, is another perennial theme. Along the same lines, dancemakers have sought to incorporate in their compositions the dynamics discovered or postulated by the various schools of depth psychology, and critics have ferreted out such meanings in other dances. The semiotics and hermeneutics of such interpretations call for explication in all the arts, but it is dance in which the eloquently unspeaking agency of individual presence offers theorists the most direct challenge.

In opposition to all approaches that relate dance dynamically to the dancer's body and personality, some influential thinkers have interpreted dance as a purely aesthetic art. Paul Valéry argued that a dance should be seen as a pure play of energies, of which the dancer's body and individuality are merely the vehicle. In the same vein, Langer's earlier work (1953), treating the fine arts as forms of presentational symbolism, assigned to dance the function of making imaginatively available (and hence aesthetically rewarding) the interplay of vital powers.

The aesthetics of elegant and virtuosic movement and the aesthetics of dance as free expression merged and bore fruit at the end of the nineteenth century, when a new art of dance was developed in the United States as a paradigm of individual liberation. This way of dancing, known as "modern dance," was the first dance movement outside the ballet tradition to claim serious attention from the art world. Conceived in the context of serious thought about the semiotics of human movement, it was ideological from the start, bound up with feminism and the development of women's education. Controversies about the specificity of dance movement, and the significance of dance generally, have accompanied successive revolutions in dance practice throughout the present century.

In the United Kingdom, where these developments arrived late, recent philosophizing about dance has been influenced by the Education Reform Act of 1988 and the proposal to introduce dance into the national curriculum as an examinable subject at the secondary school level. (In the United States, it was at the postsecondary level that dance entered the educational mainstream.) This requires that dance study become an academically viable discipline, with standards that can be formulated, imposed, systematically applied, and defended. Work in this area (Adshead, McFee) has built on Best's work in the philosophy of movement and has drawn largely on the logic of criticism as developed in the British "ordinary language" style of philosophy. The deeper implications of this approach have yet to be worked out.

Independently of the British school, work has begun on the general semiotics of dance as a performing art (Foster). The work in this field best known among philosophers is that of Nelson Goodman, who poses the question whether the development of a satisfactory notation may not effect radical changes in the art of dance. [*See* Goodman.] The existence of rival schemes of dance notation, based on different principles, makes this an intriguing area for philosophers, though technical difficulties make it inaccessible to most.

Institutional theories of art, recently ubiquitous, have special applicability to dance because of the conceptual dissonance between the traditional monopoly enjoyed by the stylized art of ballet and the equally traditional tendency to find "dance" in any expressive movement. Experimental dance of the 1960s and 1970s raised deep questions about the concepts of dance and of art generally. Some of the most sophisticated work on the aesthetics of dance has been in this area (e.g., Sheets-Johnstone, 1984).

Dance aesthetics has much to discuss and presents striking material for general aesthetics, but is little studied. Despite the recent accessibility of videotapes, there is no familiar and available corpus of works to which precise and pointed allusion can be made, and no ongoing debates in the academic world into which fledgling aestheticians can easily enter. An international encyclopedia of dance, expected to appear shortly, may provide a useful reference point. A substantial anthology of writings on dance theory has been produced (Copeland and Cohen). Such journals as *Dance Research Journal* (U.S.A.) and *Dance Research* (U.K.) are receptive to work on dance aesthetics. Journals of general aesthetics are also receptive, but receive few submissions. Graduate departments of dance in which theory is a subject are a relatively recent development; one's view of the subject may change as graduates of these departments publish their dissertations.

The foregoing account confines itself to Western civilization, within whose practices and preoccupations aesthetics took its distinctive forms. The richest source of dance aesthetics, however, is the practice and theory of classical dance in Indian civilization. The *Nāṭyaśāstra*, dating probably from the second century CE, expounds a theory of aesthetic practice and perception in the performing arts. It clearly formulates the idea of a pure art of dance based on the visual beauty of the body in motion, without equating that with any art form actually practiced. But the sheer extent of Indian civilization, the subtlety and intricacy of the practices enshrined in its arts and its methods of cultural

transmission, and the relative unavailability of the relevant literature in the West combine to present a formidable barrier to outsiders.

Other non-Western dance traditions have been influential through their practice and the thought-worlds they exemplify rather than by any aesthetic theories they may have. Recent Japanese dance comes from modern American influences working on the stylized forms of Japanese theater (the Japanese language had no general word corresponding to "dance"). But the new dance practice introduces what seems to be a wholly new range of expressive symbolism for which Western aesthetic theory has yet to find a place.

Similarly, dance forms originating in Africa have spread throughout the world and represent important forms of self-regard and corporate civility, which should expand and deepen aesthetic understanding of the possible scope of dance meaning. But the future of dance aesthetics may lie in mutual appreciation of traditions imperfectly comprehended and accepted as culturally diverse, rather than in mutual reduction or synthesis.

BIBLIOGRAPHY

Adshead, Janet, ed. *Dance Analysis: Theory and Practice.* London, 1988.

Aristotle. *Poetics* (c.350 BCE). Edited and translated by W. Hamilton Fyfe. Loeb Classical Library. Cambridge, Mass., 1927.

Armelagos, Adina, and Mary Sirridge. "The Identity Crisis in Dance." *Journal of Aesthetics and Art Criticism* 37.2 (Winter 1978): 128–139.

Bayer, Raymond. *L'Esthétique de la grâce.* 2 vols. Paris, 1933.

Beardsley, Monroe C. "What Is Going On in a Dance?" In *Illuminating Dance: Philosophical Explorations,* edited by Maxine Sheets-Johnstone, pp. 35–47. Lewisburg, Pa., 1984.

Best, David. *Expression in Movement and the Arts: A Philosophical Enquiry.* London, 1974.

Bharata-Muni. *The Nāṭyaśāstra: A Treatise on Hindu Dramaturgy and Histrionics Ascribed to Bharata-Muni.* 2 vols. 2d rev. ed. Edited and translated by Manomohan Ghosh. Calcutta, 1961–1967.

Carroll, Noël, and Sally Banes. "Working and Dancing: A Response to Monroe Beardsley's 'What Is Going On in a Dance?'" In *Aesthetics: A Critical Anthology,* 2d ed., edited by George Dickie, Richard J. Sclafani, and Ronald Roblin, pp. 644–650. New York, 1989.

Copeland, Roger, and Marshall Cohen, eds. *What Is Dance? Readings in Theory and Criticism.* New York and Oxford, 1983.

Foster, Susan Leigh. *Reading Dancing: Bodies and Subjects in Contemporary American Dance.* Berkeley, 1986.

Guglielmo Ebreo of Pesara. *On the Practice and Art of Dancing* (1463). Edited and translated by Barbara Sparti. Oxford, 1993.

Hegel, Georg Wilhelm Friedrich. *Aesthetics: Lectures on Fine Art* (1835). 2 vols. Translated by T. M. Knox. Oxford, 1975.

Langer, Susanne K. *Feeling and Form.* New York, 1953.

Langer, Susanne K. *Mind: An Essay on Human Feeling* (1967). Abr. ed. Edited by Gary Van Den Heuvel. Baltimore, 1988.

Lucian of Samosata. *The Dance* (c.165 CE). In *Lucian,* vol. 5, edited and translated by A. M. Harmon. Loeb Classical Library. Cambridge, Mass., 1936.

McFee, Graham. *Understanding Dance.* New York and London, 1992.

Margolis, Joseph. "The Autographic Nature of the Dance." In *Illuminating Dance: Philosophical Explorations,* edited by Maxine Sheets-Johnstone, pp. 70–84. Lewisburg, Pa., 1984.

Ménéstrier, Claude-François. *Traité des tournois, joustes, carrousels et autres spectacles publics.* Lyons, 1669.

Noverre, Jean-Georges. *Letters on Dancing and Ballets* (1760). Translated by Cyril W. Beaumont from the 1803 ed. London, 1930.

Plato. *The Laws* (c.360 BCE). Translated by Trevor J. Saunders. New York, 1970.

Sheets, Maxine. *The Phenomenology of Dance* (1966). New York, 1980.

Sheets-Johnstone, Maxine, ed. *Illuminating Dance: Philosophical Explorations.* Lewisburg, Pa., 1984.

Smith, Adam. "Of the Nature of that Imitation which takes place in what are called the Imitative Arts." In *Aesthetic Theories*, edited by Karl Aschenbrenner and Arnold Isenberg, pp. 227–252. Englewood Cliffs, N.J., 1965. First published 1795 in his *Essays on Philosophical Subjects.*

Sparshott, Francis. *A Measured Pace: Toward a Philosophical Understanding of the Arts of Dance.* Toronto, 1995.

Valéry, Paul. "Philosophy of the Dance." In *Collected Works*, vol. 13, translated by Ralph Mannheim, pp. 197–211. Princeton, N.J., 1964.

FRANCIS SPARSHOTT

Contemporary Thought

The aesthetics of contemporary dance is concerned with the interest humans take in the beauty, grace, unity, line, and so on (and their opposites) of objects and events in dance, and especially in dance as an art form. Since judgments concerning beauty, grace, line, and so on (and their opposites) are aesthetic judgments, the aesthetics of dance treats aesthetic judgments of dance. Once the idea of aesthetic interest is grasped—in contrast to such purposive interest as, say, the economic interest one might take in a dance production for which one provided financial backing—we can ask how, if it all, it applies to dance. Dance has not been as widely discussed by contemporary philosophy as have some other art forms, both because aestheticians have focused on problems from literature, music, or painting, and because dance is viewed (correctly) as having few problems of its own.

Overview. Consider the claim: "dance is a performing art." Discussion of the truth of such a claim, or of the senses in which it is true, clarifies some of the dance aesthetician's characteristic concerns. A framework here is provided by elaboration of some of the major issues that grow from such a claim, once each element is interrogated.

First, begin with the relationship between dance and art. Some dances are clearly neither art in themselves nor parts of artworks: for example, "social dance"—the waltz, the tango, or disco. Are these of interest to the aesthetics of dance? What are the boundaries of the concept dance? Do dancelike ritual activities fall within its ambit? For instance, suppose the North American Indian ghost dances to have had a specific purpose (namely, to rid the continent of the white man): should we conclude that they are dance? They seem not to be art: are they even dance? (For philosophical purposes, this issue may be little different from questions potentially asked about, say, the Lascaux cave paintings.) Here, general questions about what is relevant shade into specific questions about one's concerns. Since only some dances are candidate artworks—just as only some paintings are artworks—aestheticians must ask whether or not appreciation of artworks is just a species of some generalized "aesthetic appreciation." Suppose the aesthetic interest appropriate to artworks (or artforms) is importantly different from the aesthetic interest appropriate elsewhere (an artistic/aesthetic contrast is drawn). Then legitimate concern exclusively with those dances that are artworks is justified, not because the others might not be aesthetically interesting, but because one's focus is on art, with such a view typically reflecting a commitment throughout one's aesthetics. Equally, concern could encompass all candidate dances, although now care would be needed to distinguish dances from, say, mating rituals of birds or dolphins—these, too, might be objects of aesthetic interest.

Second, turn to the question of art: what is the nature of our interest in art (and hence in dance as art)? Issues from general philosophical aesthetics appear here, plausibly treated in whatever way is appropriate elsewhere: for example, discussion of the relevance of the choreographer's intention for criticism or understanding of his or her work will largely reproduce similar discussions for other artists, with theorists taking similar positions in both cases. Equally, when interest is in the art form, how is dance criticism related to the understanding of dance? More generally, what relevance have the history and traditions of dance forms to the understanding of those forms? Here, too, familiar questions will concern borderline cases: how can such and such be dance? (As with other art forms, this question seems raised at almost every stage where a dominant image of the art form is being contested.)

Third, consider performing: what follows from the performing status of dance? Here, typically following issues explored for other performing arts (especially music), a number of separate themes may be distinguished.

- The performing/visual art contrast: how is it to be made out? How sustainable is it?
- Performing arts as multiples (at least in principle): what are the identity conditions, if any, for multiples—such that a particular dance (like a particular piece of music) can be performed in London at the same time as it is performed in New York? What flows from any conclusion here? Of course, questioning of the appropriateness of a particular analytical tool for the relationship between the work itself and performances of it—say, a type-token analysis—will be shared with the aesthetics of music. (These might even be thought to be questions of dance's ontological standing.)
- The fact of performing: what roles are appropriately ascribed to dancer as opposed to choreographer?

• What role if any can be ascribed to notated scores of dances? As above, many issues resulting from the recording of dance through notation will be shared with music.

Fourth, since dances are essentially "composed" of movements of human bodies (at least), some discussion appropriately concerns the nature of action (of a kind often associated with the issue of the freedom of the will). Its essential physicality distinguishes the art form of dance from music, literature, and visual art. Music and visual art require human action for their creation and existence, but the art objects are not human action in quite the same sense. Participating in these arts is not, of itself, physical training (although it may require physical training). Fifth, and relatedly, there are at least two different kinds of questions flowing from the (apparent) meaningfulness of (some) dance movement. For such movement both resembles and yet differs from other nonverbal communication: in what ways and with what outcome? Further, what (if any) meaningful character does the fact of embodiment itself entail?

Sixth, and finally, a part of the distinctive interest of (most) dance lies—in contrast to music—in its "mixed" character: a typical dance performance involves not merely the movement but also the costume, music, staging, and so on. (In this respect, the typical art-type dance resembles the

DANCE: Contemporary Thought. Andy Warhol, *Martha Graham: Satyric Festival Song* (1986), from a portfolio of three screenprints, 36 × 36 in. (91.5 × 91.5 cm), printed on Lenox Museum Board. (Copyright by the Andy Warhol Foundation for the Visual Arts/Artists Rights Society, New York; photograph courtesy of the Andy Warhol Foundation, Inc./Art Resource, New York; used by permission.)

typical opera.) What exactly are the roles of these other elements, some already having art status?

Key issues to be addressed by the aesthetics of dance have been mapped out, drawing attention to their connections with similar issues in other areas of aesthetics, and suggesting that many (perhaps most) philosophical issues concerning dance result from considering, with regard to dance, philosophical questions about some other area: sometimes another art form (e.g., music) or art in general or human actions—sometimes singly, and sometimes as a combination of issues from other areas. Often, one's response on such issues gives a possible direction for one's remarks about dance. Also, there is a fine line between aesthetic matters concerning dance and more general philosophical concerns.

Some Themes for an Aesthetics of Dance. The following brief remarks on five topics drawn from the considerations introduced above, focusing on issues for dance as an art, illustrate the diversity of such issues as well as comment on their recurrence in other arts. As such, they provided examples of some debates in the contemporary aesthetics of dance.

The first issue is what narrative is relevant to writing dance history. A developed aesthetics of dance would explore both the history of dance (at least dance as an art form) and the history of dance criticism, because dance, like other art forms, must be understood as part of a complex tradition of art making and art understanding. The point is best explained by means of some examples, illustrative of its complexity.

One question might ask about the beginning of dance: should we, on a parallel with Paul Oskar Kristeller's work on the concept art, think of the art-type dance coming into being with the Baroque ballet in, say, the court of Louis XIV? Or should we conclude that, since the Greeks had a muse for dance (Terpsichore), there must have been the art-type dance in classical Greece? Resolving such questions is partly a matter for history but also calls for philosophical reflection on the implications of calling the activity dance rather than something else.

Or suppose, with Noël Carroll, that we address the relation of the dances of Isadora Duncan to those of the ballet tradition contemporary with her activity, imagining a confrontation with someone who denies that Isadora's "barefoot prancing and posing" (Carroll, 1994, p. 26) is art. In reply, Carroll sketches a narrative to show that "Duncan was able to solve the problem of the stagnation of theatrical dance by repudiating the central features of the dominant ballet and by reimagining an earlier ideal of dance" (ibid.). But, as Carroll illustrates, that narrative also shows the advantages Duncan saw in (and hence the values she brought to) this revitalized dance: both her pronouncements and her actions constitute an "argument" for a modification of practices of art making and art understanding. That this argument succeeded in changing taste (to the degree that it did) is also a reflection on the state of the art-minded community at the time: in that art world, Isadora's strategies were appropriate—we know this because we know that they worked. We also can infer, however, that other strategies would not have been successful, although, typically, we cannot readily give examples here, since the net effect would be the disappearance of the work in question from the tradition of art making and art understanding. So accounting for the artist's activities (rendering them intelligible) is in part looking at the values challenged, in part considering what Carroll has called "the lay of the artworld" (p. 25).

To take another example, consider the term *postmodern dance:* what precisely does it identify? This question has a particular resonance because (1) the term *postmodern dance* acquired a distinct usage in dance theory/criticism, but (2) this occurred prior to the upsurge of interest in the postmodernism of Jean-François Lyotard and others. So what does calling a dance "postmodern" (Banes, 1987, p. xv; see also Banes, 1994) commit us to? In particular, in what sense do dance works urged as postmodern need to be understood by means of notions from, say, Lyotard or Jean Baudrillard? Regardless of our conclusions, that issue is not merely terminological: rather, it is an issue about the values that are embodied in or presupposed by these (different) dances. That is a way of asking about the narratives under which particular works are accommodated within practices of dance making and dance understanding. and hence the elements that must be central to any narrative affirming their art status or artistic value.

A second issue here is the critic's interpretation as distinct from the performer's interpretation. Major aesthetic questions cluster around the claims of artworks to be meaningful or meaning bearing: How is such meaning to be understood (or, better, identified)? Is there just one meaning? Drawing on work in other art forms, one plausible strategy sees the meaning of an artwork as, roughly, its "collected criticism," the sum of things true about it. Such a view (if sustainable) clearly acknowledges a multiplicity of meaning; there need be no suggestion that all the remarks could be simultaneously asserted of the work. Rather, the concern is with what is arguable by reference to the (observable) features of that work. Remarks of this kind about dance works might be called "interpretations" of the works in question.

For performing arts, however, the term *interpretation* has two distinct uses. The first, the critic's interpretation, is characteristically composed of words, strings of sentences discussing the structure and value of the work in question. Such interpretations play a similar role with respect to all art forms. Any problems with understanding the idea of the critic's interpretation—or for seeing the basis or relevance of such interpretation—are equally problems for all the arts, as much for painting or sculpture as for dance or music.

But a dancer's performance of a solo (like a pianist's rendering of a piano piece) is also an interpretation, typically consisting in some set of actions performed in producing that object in which the witnessable work consists. For dance, this involves performing (at least) movements of the body. This second sort—the performer's interpretation—is unique to the performing arts. For dance, the choreographer is the artist. But, even when dancers have not been specifically involved in the initial creation of the particular dance, they should not be considered mere puppets of the choreographer, although any account must acknowledge the possibility of dancers performing previously choreographed pieces. So, for example, concerns about what makes a particular interpretation an interpretation of that particular work of art, and no other, and how to rule out inappropriate interpretations, have two dimensions for the performing arts, applying both to the critic's interpretation (a difficulty shared with other art forms) and also to the performer's interpretation.

Any satisfactory account of meaning for artworks must offer insight into (at least) the role (if any) of criticism in our understanding of artworks, the relation of our (genuine) understanding of artworks to their meaning. For dance, in addition, it must locate the performer's interpretation in the framework.

A third issue, or set of issues, concerns dance, dance notation, and understanding. There are three well-developed notation systems (Labanotation, Benesh, Eshkol-Wachman) in use for dance. Does the possibility (or actuality) of such notation pose philosophical questions?

Any notation system for any art form must meet criteria of adequacy of kinds sketched by Nelson Goodman in his *Languages of Art:* for example, the symbols must be clearly differentiated from one another, picking out different states of affairs. One practical matter therefore will be to determine the degree to which any of these notation systems fulfills Goodmanesque criteria.

But a philosophical issue arises if we question the uses to which notated scores might be put: might they, for instance, play a role in the solution of (numerical) identity questions, such that any performance satisfying a notated score for *Swan Lake* was thereby bound to be an instance of that artwork? Suppose changes made by Rudolf Nureyev (as stager) mean that his production no longer satisfies a particular notated score for *Swan Lake.* One might conclude that the performance was therefore not *Swan Lake:* another alternative would be to doubt the appropriateness of that notation. In the end, is it a dance-critical matter as to whether a performance is genuinely of *Swan Lake?*

Further, both the completeness and the neutrality of dance notations must be properly understood. Such notations describe only movement patterns; they tell us nothing about costume, staging, music, and the like, and they do not fully determine the movements to be performed. Rather, by involving a choice of key characteristics of a particular pattern of movement, notated scores embody perceptions of the movements in question—they are objects that have been analyzed. So notation systems offer interpretive descriptions rather than neutrally documenting movements.

A fourth issue here is the underdetermination of the performer's interpretation. The dance one witnesses is already a performer's interpretation: dances are only brought to determinacy by performance—they are underdetermined at their creation (just as they are underdetermined by their notations). For many features of the dance in a performance will typically not have been explicitly specified in the choreography. In this sense, works in the performing arts should typically be thought of as recipes, embodying an instruction to perform them—an instruction to produce a performer's interpretation. So one way in which the dancer is important is as the creator of the performer's interpretation. The virtue of one dancer as opposed to another can then be understood in terms of their respective abilities to produce interesting and sustainable performers' interpretations.

Once a performer's interpretation is completed, the dance in that performance is determinate. It has a physical instantiation that is then available to a critic's interpretation (and such critical interpretation will draw on the traditions and conventions of the art form). At this point, then, dance works are in the same position (as objects of interpretation) as works of the particular object sort (say, paintings), or nonperforming works of the multiple sort, such as works of literature.

A fifth issue raises the prospect of a philosophy of the dancing body. Some philosophical writing has concerned itself, not straightforwardly with aesthetic (or, better, artistic) issues in respect of dance, but with issues arising from the fact of dances being comprised of bodies in motion. In part, such a concern has been theoretically motivated: Jean-Paul Sartre and Maurice Merleau-Ponty, among others, have been seen as addressing such issues. For example, Merleau-Ponty's account of the "lived present," where—through a peculiarity of self-awareness or self-consciousness—one's history bears on one's immediate experience, might seem revealing with respect to accounts of the dancer, since it reflects our nature as active beings in a human world essentially "ready for action" (Merleau-Ponty, 1993).

There are sizable dangers of unclarity here, especially given both the contentious character of some of the theses and the lack of a clear model for this kind of writing. Of course, this is not a criticism of Sartre or Merleau-Ponty, but only of some of the uses to which their ideas have been put. The best example of successful writing on this topic is Francis Sparshott (1988).

The upshot of such ideas for the aesthetics of dance is far from clear. One thought seems to depend simply on the thought that the "same body" is used in dance and in other action. For example, Judith Hanna tells us that "dancing motion attracts attention," and does so because "the instrument of dance and of sexuality is one—the human body" (*Dance, Sex and Gender,* Chicago, 1988, p. 13). This is no argument, however: the same body is used for walking and for other activities. Because our subject is not simply the human body, but the dancing body, we still need to locate more clearly the impact of dance.

Moreover, a philosophically motivated concern with the body (perhaps even with the dancing body) is not clearly a part of the aesthetics of dance: there are many philosophically revealing concerns that might not have artistic impact. But an account of the dancing body that does justice to the distinctiveness of dance is likely to conclude that the grace of bodily movement is distinctive only insofar as the dance is art. We might therefore conclude, as Sparshott seems to have done, that concern with the dancing body is at best a prolegomenon to aesthetic questions.

BIBLIOGRAPHY

Banes, Sally. *Terpsichore in Sneakers: Post-Modern Dance.* 2d ed. Middletown, Conn., 1987.

Banes, Sally. *Writing Dancing in the Age of Postmodernism.* Middletown, Conn., 1994.

Carroll, Noël. "Identifying Art." In *Institutions of Art: Reconsiderations of George Dickie's Philosophy,* edited by Robert J. Yanal, pp. 3–38. University Park, Pa., 1994.

Copeland, Roger, and Marshall Cohen, eds. *What Is Dance? Readings in Theory and Criticism.* New York and Oxford, 1983.

Fancher, Gordon, and Gerald Myers, eds. *Philosophical Essays on Dance.* Brooklyn, N.Y., 1981.

Goodman, Nelson. *Languages of Art: An Approach to a Theory of Symbols.* 2d ed. Indianapolis, 1976.

Kristeller, Paul Oskar. "The Modern System of the Arts: A Study in the History of Aesthetics, I and II." *Journal of the History of Ideas* 12.4 (October 1951): 495–527; 13.1 (January 1952): 17–46.

McFee, Graham. *Understanding Dance.* London and New York, 1992.

McFee, Graham. *The Concept of Dance Education.* London and New York, 1994.

Merleau-Ponty, Maurice. *The Merleau-Ponty Aesthetics Reader: Philosophy and Painting.* Edited by Galen A. Johnson, translation edited by Michael B. Smith. Evanston, Ill., 1993.

Sheets-Johnstone, Maxine, ed. *Illuminating Dance: Philosophical Explorations.* Lewisburg, Pa., 1984.

Sparshott, Francis. *Off the Ground: First Steps to a Philosophical Consideration of the Dance.* Princeton, N.J., 1988.

Sparshott, Francis. *A Measured Pace: Toward a Philosophical Understanding of the Arts of Dance.* Toronto, 1995.

Williams, Drid. *Ten Lectures on Theories of the Dance.* London, 1991.

GRAHAM McFEE

DANTO, ARTHUR COLEMAN. [*To treat the thought of contemporary American philosopher and art critic Arthur C. Danto, this entry comprises two essays:*

Survey of Thought

Danto's End of Art Thesis

The first essay explains Danto's general aesthetic theory, and the second essay analyzes his thesis of the "end of art," meaning the end of its history as a progressive unfolding of its essence. For related discussion, see Pop Art, *article on* Aesthetics of Andy Warhol; *and* Theories of Art.]

Survey of Thought

The philosophical and art-critical oeuvre of Arthur Danto (b. 1924) is among the most significant in the latter half of the twentieth century. Danto has staked his intellectual adventure on a commitment to thinking through the new, and his work is unfailingly contemporary to the art and philosophy of its time. Philosophers and aestheticians have been stimulated by the systematic—yet also imaginative—character of his philosophical positions on art and art history, while artists have found in his philosophy of art a mirror of their own artistic visions, and in his audacious philosophy of art history a representation of their own genesis. Both have also benefited from his art criticism, a form of criticism as free of the systematic as his philosophy is indebted to it.

Working in the terrain of twentieth-century art where art and philosophy converge, Danto has taken his cue from the theoretical and philosophical character of avant-garde art. Following on the highly theoretical art of this century as its philosopher/interpreter, Danto has attributed to that art a philosophical mission: to discover the essence of art. He believes that while this has been the central concern of avant-garde art from its inception, it is a task that was completed in 1964 by the most unlikely of artists, Andy Warhol. Danto furthermore believes that his own philosophical articulation of what Warhol accomplished in an implicit way—namely, a demonstration of what the essence of art is—has served to complete art history, thus ushering in the postmodern age of art. We shall articulate the substance of these claims in what follows.

The essentialist goal of producing a definition of art has been present in aesthetics since its inception in the eighteenth century. It is given a twentieth-century twist by Danto, who aims to circumvent the difficulties with prior definitions of the art object that the history of aesthetics has offered. Former definitions have typically sought to define art in terms of its manifest (sensual) properties—in terms of what the viewer sees, hears, or feels in the art object (Formalism and the expression theory of art being the most prominent of such theories). Starting from the conviction that what generates philosophical problems in their purest form are thought experiments about perceptually indiscernible objects (or events or conditions), and that these irrevocably demonstrate the failure of all definitions in terms of manifest properties, Danto reasons to a definition of the art object in terms of its nonmanifest (nonsensual, abstract) properties.

Danto's philosophical maneuver is facilitated (if not stimulated) by his reflection on what he believes the work of Andy Warhol and the avant-garde has accomplished (Warhol being in Danto's reconstruction the avant-garde's apex). For Warhol's *Brillo Box,* exhibited in the Stable Gallery in 1964, was on Danto's interpretation a thought experiment relying on perceptually indistinguishable objects. What Warhol did was this: Starting from the assumption that *Brillo Box* is a work of art while its "perceptually indiscernible" cousin—the ordinary Brillo box that one could find on the supermarket shelf—is not, Warhol demonstrated that since there is nothing in *Brillo Box* that is meant to distinguish it from its ordinary cousin, what makes *Brillo Box* a work of art rather than its cousin must depend on its nonmanifest properties, or on a property residing "outside" the art object itself. This "abstract" property residing "outside" *Brillo Box* that makes it art and not merely another supermarket cleanser, Danto identifies as a historically evolving theory of art held by the art world. Note the philosophical scope Danto claims to derive from Warhol's demonstration. Warhol is a philosopher in gel because his artwork is not simply about what defines *it;* it is about what defines *all* art.

In a dramatic reversal of the eighteenth century, matters of taste, beauty, and expression are rendered marginal to the definition of art (as marginal as these former definitions had rendered the factor of theory). (This reversal of traditional values again links Danto with the mentality of the avant-garde, for the avant-garde aimed for a similar reversal of past artistic values.) Thus the expressive gestures, formal virtuosity, and sensuous application of paint that the viewer sees and feels in Titian's *Venus and Mars* are not by themselves central to what makes this object an artwork. It is the theory supervenient on the object as seen and felt that brands it as art. In Danto's philosophical idealism, what turns ordinary objects (real things) into artworks is a theoretical interpretation added to the object. Artworks, unlike real things, have their being from their being theorized into existence.

In pinpointing theory as a factor, Danto is motivated by his desire to produce an essentialist definition of art, a desire that requires him to single out some small number of properties—which will be branded the essential ones—over all others. But we may ask why theory should be chosen as the property of choice as opposed to a variety of other nonmanifest, contextual factors like history, society, the art market, and the history of taste, all of which would appear to be as important as theory in enfranchising objects as art. Danto is led by two interests to single out the property of theory: his interest in the avant-garde and in the work of the philosopher W. V. O. Quine on language. What the avant-garde impressed on Danto is the thought that (all) art "makes a statement" to the world. For the avant-garde has been in the business of speaking to the world about art, life, and the future through its acidic objects, its manifestos, and its conceptual gestures, and Danto takes this conceptual and rhetorical goal—a goal others would consider unique to the avant-garde—to be generally true of art. His basic idea is that what differentiates artworks from ordinary things is that artworks, like language, have semantic values. Art, like language, speaks of the world—and from a point of view. Warhol's *Brillo Box,* in Danto's phrase, "makes a statement" about art and the world in a way that the ordinary Brillo box one purchases in the supermarket does not. Warhol's box speaks to the art world, to art history, to the relation between art and commodities, and, if Danto is right, to the philosophy of art. The Brillo box in the supermarket does none of this; it simply *is* a commodity (albeit perhaps a pleasingly designed one).

It is this view that artworks have semantic properties that leads Danto to take influence from the work of Quine on language. Quine believes that the semantics of a language are given through a web of theory. It is only in virtue of this theory that sentences have meaning and can be about the world. Quine argues that to know a language is to have in mind or to provide an interpretation of it that assigns a theory to its web of sentences. Since, according to Danto, art is like language in having the robust property of "aboutness," it too must be about the world in virtue of a web of theory that lies behind it. Indeed, Quine's famous remarks about radical interpretation are, Danto thinks, perfectly applicable to Warhol and the avant-garde.

Quine argued that the case of radical interpretation, in which a distant language must be interpreted more or less from scratch, is paradigmatic of all interpretation. In the radical case one finds that one is presented with the physical concomitants of language, specifically, the sound utterances that speakers make in empirical circumstances, and one must impose a theoretical interpretation on these physical sounds in order to take them as language. Similarly, according to Danto, the radical character of avant-garde art has required from the viewer or critic an interpretation "from scratch" to make its bold, new gestures comprehensible (hence the need for artists themselves to become theorists whose manifestos will supposedly "explain" what the art is "about"). Thus the avant-garde has demonstrated that what turns scratches on canvas and used auto parts into paintings and sculptures is an interpretive theory of art. So for language and for art, the position of radical interpretation exhibits the essential determinants of all interpretation: in radical interpretation, we discern that manifest properties of the real event (the speaker uttering vocables in an empirical context) radically underdetermine meaning. An interpretation must be assigned to these properties in order for the object or event to be fully enfranchised as a linguistic, or an artistic one, an interpretation simultaneously assigning meaning to the object or event and beliefs to the speaker or artist. Thus it is a theory that turns a real object into a work of art just as it is a theory that turns the physical event of utterance into a linguistic one.

Danto never says very much about what this interpretation is, other than to claim that it is historically evolving and must situate the artwork with other artworks into an art-historical pattern. This art-historical pattern is therefore a basic overall determinant of art interpretation, bringing us immediately to Danto's philosophy of art history. However, before turning to it, note that one may raise a number of questions about Danto's view of theory. First, one might ask whether all artworks really are at basis about something in the way that avant-garde art supposedly is, or whether some are in large part established through their sensual and psychological properties, through, that is, the very properties of form, vision, and expression that Danto marginalizes. Second, one might ask what the role of the artist's intentions is in Danto's account. Are these intentions typically "theoretical"? Third, what then tends to be the relation between the artist's own theories (especially in cases such as avant-garde art where the artist has written at great length about his or her work) and the theory that turns these objects into artworks? And fourth, how accurate is the picture of art that sets up a clear distinction between the art object's manifest (i.e., visual and empathic) properties and its nonmanifest (i.e., theoretical) properties. Why should it not rather be true that the art object's manifest properties are themselves sufficiently permeated by theory, and theory by them, as to challenge a pinpointing of theory that leaves them out? Finally, why should the institutions of art and the history of its technical properties not play as central a role in defining the art object as the history of theory? Indeed, how distinct is the history of theory from these other histories? It begins to look as if art, in being defined by theory, is defined by everything else with which theory is intertwined: vision, feeling, society, technology, and so on. In short, it begins to look as if the picture of art supposedly derived from Warhol's thought experiment is radically deficient as a general picture of the way in which the various factors all intertwine to define art.

Danto's philosophy of art history flows from his notion that central to art interpretation is the assignment to the artwork of a place in art history. His idea is that avant-garde art has striven to attain philosophical knowledge of itself: of its semantic/theoretical character and its place in a history. In the manner of a Hegel reborn in Manhattan's Upper West Side, Danto claims that Warhol's discovery of this essence of art served magnificently to end art history—to "complete" it. Since art history has in its course exhibited a variety of beginnings, middles, and endings (stylistic, iconographic, technological), Danto is not simply claiming that it has ended yet again; his claim is that it has ended in a unique sense. It has *essentially* ended, since its metaphysical task has been completed. This does not imply the absurd thought that no one can make art anymore, that there can be no more artists; it implies the opposite. Art is now liberated from the task of historical correctness, it is free from the modernist headache of having to discover its own essence. No more need a Piet Mondrian or a Clement Greenberg fret about what the true essence of painting is. Artists are now free, like Marx's postrevolutionary man, to inhabit the free space of creation, juxtaposition, and service that will allow art to continue. What now defines art is its condition of having realized itself. This is Danto's conception of the postmodern, a utopian conception worthy of the best of the avant-gardists. Even if postmodern times have (as Danto the critic has himself astutely argued) deflected art from its potential liberty through the forces of contemporary capitalism and political correctness, Danto's theory of the end of art might still be correct. What would challenge that theory would be (1) the argument that art is not yet over with its business of self-discovery, indeed, that such a business is perpetual, because (2) there is no essence to art for art to discover once and for all; art rather exhibits a family of interlinked but historically changing and globally varied features (in a manner pictured by a Ludwig Wittgenstein or a Michel de Montaigne) that require ongoing acknowledgment. Indeed, it might further be argued that the claim to find in the world (even of the West) a single, overarching, art-historical shape is a Hegelian and modernist anachronism, art history being a field of interwoven histories that can be parsed in a variety of different ways with different interpretive results ("the history of women," "the histories of non-Western modernisms and their relations to the west and to each other," "Russian avant-garde history," "French neoclassicism in twentieth-century art," "the history of Marx in modern art," "Cubism and the twentieth century," and so forth).

Danto's maverick, subtle, and fun-loving art criticism exemplifies the postmodern space of the philosopher who, having ended art history by announcing the essence of art, is similarly freed to inhabit the free space of postmodern criticism without philosophic obsession. Like John Ruskin, Danto wanders across the fields of art without the burden of systematic philosophy and with a fine-tuned eye for the telling detail, the significant image, the whiff of the theoretical as it manifests itself in a given case. For those who are skeptical of systematic aesthetics as such, it is Danto the critic who is attuned to the richness and plasticity of what makes art art, rather than Danto the philosopher. For those with a flair for the systematic, Danto's is far-reaching. All agree that there have been few philosophers who have occupied the complex and vertiginous terrain of art and philosophy with his ease and graciousness. Friend to philosopher and artist alike, Danto has stimulated all who wish to respond to what is new in the world, rather than what is sedimented in it.

[See also Art World; Definition of Art; and Interpretation.]

BIBLIOGRAPHY

Works by Danto

"The Artworld." *The Journal of Philosophy* 61.19 (October 15, 1964): 571–584.
The Transfiguration of the Commonplace. Cambridge, Mass., 1981.
The Philosophical Disenfranchisement of Art. New York, 1986.
The State of the Art. New York, 1987.
Encounters and Reflections: Art in the Historical Present. New York, 1990.
Beyond the Brillo Box: The Visual Arts in Post-Historical Perspective. New York, 1992.
Embodied Meanings: Critical Essays and Aesthetic Meditations. New York, 1994.
After the End of Art: Contemporary Art and the Pale of History. Princeton, 1997.

Other Sources

Herwitz, Daniel. *Making Theory/Constructing Art: On the Authority of the Avant-Garde*. Chicago, 1993.
Rollins, Mark, ed. *Danto and His Critics*. Oxford and Cambridge, Mass., 1993.

DANIEL HERWITZ

Danto's End of Art Thesis

For as long as art has been written about as having a history, that history has been said to reach an end. In the first properly historical treatment of art, Pliny the Elder's *Natural History*, there is the claim that bronze art after the 121st Olympiad ceased; Giorgio Vasari describes in the 1550 edition of his *Lives* the work of Michelangelo as embodying the "end and the perfection of art"; Nicolas Poussin complained that Caravaggio had come into the world to destroy painting; Paul Delaroche announced upon seeing a daguerreotype in 1839 that "from today painting is dead"; Kazimir Malevich proclaimed that in Suprematism "there can be no question of painting . . .; painting was done for long ago, and the artist himself is a prejudice of the past"; and, finally, Walter Benjamin famously claimed a distinction between works of art possessed of an aura, because unique, and those that lend themselves to mechanical reproduction, and hence a more integrated place in collective experience—a claim focused by Douglas Crimp on contemporary art to proclaim, along with the museum's existence it defines, "painting's terminal condition."

But whereas these individuals assert that art of a certain sort has *stopped* (Pliny), was no longer *possible* or *required* (Poussin, Delaroche), or was in its continuing existence *politically illegitimate* (Malevich, Crimp), Arthur Danto understands art as having ended because its historical development has reached a kind of internal ending—an ending derived not from forces externally applied or withheld, but from the nature of art itself. Danto's view is unabashedly Hegelian, but unlike Hegel's historical vision, in which the end of art is a thesis drawn from and supported by a teleological metaphysics, Danto's approach is an empirical one. His thesis of the end of art follows from his view of what kinds of developments the history of art has exhibited, and how those developments are explained.

In a recent formulation of his view Danto describes the historical development of art in the West as characterized by two distinct episodes, which he calls the "Vasari episode" and the "Greenberg episode":

> Both are progressive. Vasari, construing art as representational, sees it getting better and better over time at the "conquest of visual appearance." That narrative ended for painting when moving pictures proved far better able to depict reality than painting could. Modernism began by asking what painting should do in the light of that. And it began to probe its own identity. Greenberg defined a new narrative in terms of an ascent to the identifying conditions of the art. And he found this in the material conditions of the medium. Greenberg's narrative . . . comes to an end with Pop. . . . It came to an end when art came to an end, when art, as it were, recognized there was no special way a work of art had to be.   (1997, p. 125)

So the first period of development stretching from around Giotto de Bondone through the Impressionists comes to an end when the theory of art informing it, that art was essentially mimetic—the theory behind Delaroche's lament—can no longer be sustained. Modernism begins after this naturalistic development is over, through artists and theorists looking to forms of art from other traditions not founded on optical realism, such as the Post-Impressionists' exploration of Chinese and Japanese painting. What characterizes the development of art from this time until as late as the work of Andy Warhol is, for Danto, the progressive attempts to offer, in place of the then nullified mandate toward naturalism, a new theory of what art is. Clement Greenberg's narrative of the period from Impressionism through post-painterly Abstraction is that art was progressively realizing its "purity" through shedding itself of whatever was not specific to its medium. Greenberg's theory is important for Danto, not because of whatever truth it may have had, but because it exemplifies and describes the kind of practice of self-definition the visual arts engaged in during Modernism. There is a development in this period of reflexive, self-defining era of art, but that development's ending is not the reaching of an answer to the question of art's essence, but rather the moment at which the limits to the ability of artworks to engage in such self-definition are reached.

Although the limit to art's self-theorizing is marked by many different works in the art world, it is most vividly expressed for Danto in Warhol's *Brillo Box*. There the question of "what is art?" is placed—according to Danto's metaphilosophical views about the nature of philosophical problems—in its proper form, through being posed in such a way as to ask what distinguishes a work of art from an ordinary object when the two are, to the senses, indiscernible.

Henceforward, there can be no more development of art history, because, now that the question of art is put in its proper form, art is not the proper sort of practice typified by theoretical and abstract reasoning suited to provide an answer. But, for Danto, philosophical reflection is, hence the impression that in his theory art becomes philosophy. Art made after the development of art reaches its limit, and thus its ending, is what Danto calls "posthistorical," for there cannot be any art-historical development of the same order as that exhibited by naturalistic and self-reflexive art that art after that ending could press forward. We have entered, in Danto's view, a period of art unstructured by any sort of narrative-like development, and hence a period of pluralism in the kind of art that the art world sanctions. There is no development of art in general against which the legitimacy of any particular art, as succeeding or failing to carry the development further, can be judged.

Commentators on Danto's theory have offered criticisms that fit roughly into three categories. One kind of criticism argues that the beginning/end structure of historical narratives is only in some sense a formal device through which historical exposition is achieved, and thus the claim that art has reached an end mistakes a feature of historical representation for a feature of the actual history to which such representations refer. David Carrier writes: "You can tell a story ending wherever you choose about whatever you wish . . . there are endings in texts, but not in history as such; and so whether we see the history of art continuing or ending depends upon our goals" (1994, p. 33). The problem with this form of criticism is that it does not really meet Danto's thesis head-on. Without a better sense of just what kinds of endings such a theory of historical narrative denies the existence of, it is not clear whether the theory is right and thus Danto's claim is false, or Danto's claim is true and thus undermines, by providing a counterexample to, that theory.

A more persuasive interrogation of Danto's theory would try to show the falsity of the factual claims he makes or the explanations he offers. One might, for example, deny the adequacy of his characterization of modernist art as engaged in self-definition. Certainly, artists who create works indiscernible from their material, nonart, counterparts provoke the question of what is art in the minds of philosophers and others, but one might question how central to the motivation of these works is the desire to assert a particular theory of art. It is one thing to claim that, for example, in extruding a form of mathematically organized perspectival space from their images, Cubist paintings certainly showed—to anyone who thought otherwise—that painting need not be mimetic, even while still suggesting it had to be figurative, but it is a further claim that in providing a demonstration or refutation of a theory of art (that art is essentially mimetic), it was articulating or putting forward a theory of art. One can thus accept that the history of art exemplifies different theories of art—and even that Warhol's work offers the best way of posing the question of what is art that a theory of art tries to answer—without accepting that the art or its development is *explained* by such a drive toward self-definition.

A more straightforward criticism of Danto's thesis would be to accept the characterization he offers of the nature of art within its history, and the developmental shape of that history, but deny that the limit to art history under such a characterization has been reached. One might suggest that Danto has failed to notice some feature about contemporary art that is evidence of there being further development in just the same terms in which that art had developed before its alleged end. Certainly, one who held a different view from Danto about how to ask the question of what is art could see that question as still to be put in its proper form. A criticism, however, that would *fail* to gain any purchase on Danto's theory is that he claims art has ended, yet interesting, novel, moving, and otherwise great works of art, in apparent contradiction to his view, continue to be made. Such a criticism would confuse Danto's view with a wholly different one, that of the "death of art." No doubt *painting*, the art form for which a postmortem is often offered, no longer occupies the central arena of contemporary art, but it would be wholly consistent with Danto's thesis that painting should enjoy a resurgence, or never have been subordinated to the appeal of ordinary objects, writing, photography, video, performance, installation, and performances and installations incorporating all these media, that shape art today.

A third category of criticism appreciates the difference between a stopping and an ending but uses Danto's own philosophy of history in an effort to refute him. Danto argues against the possibility of writing "substantive philosophy of history," characterized by speculative philosophers of history trying "to see events as having meaning in the context of an historical whole which resembles an artistic whole, but, in this case, the whole in question is the whole of history, compassing past, present, and future." For, unlike the way a person can see the significance of one event within a fictional story when he has the whole novel at hand, "the philosopher of history does not have before him the whole of history. He has at best a fragment—the whole past" (Danto, 1985, pp. 8–9).

The charge made by critics attuned to Danto's philosophy of history is that he seems, like those speculative philosophers of history he criticizes, to make a claim about the significance of certain near contemporary events, when all he has before him is the past, not the future through which those events may be rendered significant in as-yet-unknown ways. Noël Carroll thus asserts that we cannot pronounce the end of the self-theorizing of art "until we have a better sense of its consequences." Specifically, we

cannot know whether the end of art as Danto identifies it will result in generating a "new project for art." (See Herwitz [1993] for a critique of the assumption that such projects have existed independent of the theoretical treatment of art.)

It is right to suggest that, from the vantage point of only a few decades after the exhibition of Warhol's *Brillo Box* that may have brought theorizing about the essence of art to as far as art could take it, we cannot know whether that event will have a significance yet to be imagined for later art; that the end of art, in other words, might be revealed in the future as, perhaps, a beginning of something else. But we should not confuse the claim that art history has ended with the kind of claims about endings found in the ordinary narrative redescription historians employ. For in a typical historical description an event acquires a significance through being described with reference to later events it makes possible, where that significance is something to which contemporaries of the earlier event are blind. Identifying Petrarch's ascent of Mont Ventoux as "the opening of the Renaissance," or Edouard Manet's painting as "the origin of Impressionism," redescribes those events as beginnings of what no contemporary of the events could know. Likewise, identifying Martin Luther's posting of his ninety-five theses as "the end to a unified church in the West" or the failed putsch against Mikhail Gorbachev as "the end of Communism," describes those events in terms that only retrospectively could be applied.

Identifying an event in a historical development as an *internal* ending, by contrast, describes that event—that ending—not in terms of what is made possible by it, but in terms of *what made it possible*. To claim that an event is an internal ending is, implicitly, to describe it with reference not to a later event but to an earlier one, its internal beginning. For what makes the event an internal ending is not whatever effect it may or may not have in the future, but, rather, how it is explained by something already having existed in the past. If Danto's claim about the end of art is true, it is because that event is part of an internal development whose beginning requires that manner of ending, to the extent that an internal ending is reached at all. We might not, as is often the case, recognize the ending until well after it has occurred, but whether or not it is an ending is not a question of what in the future it causes, but what in the past caused it.

A final concern that can be raised regarding the thesis of the end of art has to do with precisely what historical development it is an end to. Danto recently described his essay "The End of Art" as intending "to proclaim that a certain kind of closure had occurred in the historical development of art, that an era of astonishing creativity lasting perhaps six centuries in the West had come to an end." He sees this time span as encompassing two narrative structures embedded in history, one defining naturalistic art from Giotto through the Impressionists and the other defining Modernist art from Post-Impressionism to Pop. But Danto also writes that "the end of art consists in the coming to awareness of the true philosophical nature of art" (1994, pp. 21, 30), which suggests that the ending is internal only to the development composed of Modernist art, in which the impulse to define art was a motivating force. Or is it that Danto means for us to understand the tradition of naturalistic art as just one sort of very long lived movement that proposed a certain definition of art, analogous to the way, for example, Post-Impressionism, Cubism, and Abstract Expressionism proposed their definitions of art? The question is whether the end of art is the end internal to the development that includes the discrete developments of mimetic and self-defining art, or is only internal to the latter development's ending. For an end to be internal to the whole of the history of art, that end must be explained by the nature of what subsists, not just through the last episode of art history, but throughout the whole of that history and is there in the beginning.

So for the end of art Danto speaks of to be the end of art history as a whole, it is not enough for there to be first an ending to the naturalistic tradition and then an ending to the Modernist one. There must be an ending to the development of something that existed through both of those periods, and whose nature explains that end. In one formulation of his thesis Danto offers such a description of art in terms of which we can understand its different periods and movements belonging to a single development. That is where he sees art of the past as exhibiting a certain general style, a style that is formed sometime around Giotto, defines the art of the West through Warhol, and explains the parameters through which art's development unfolds. The end to this development occurs when the style's limits are reached in such a way that we can say the style has, in the work of artists in the West, come into perspicuity. Here the development along naturalistic lines was one direction in which the limits to the style were probed and exposed, and the development toward self-definition reached another limit to the style. At this point the shape of the style can be discerned both through these limits having been reached, and, just as important, through an essential feature of the style being exposed: that it demanded art be part of a historical development, one defined by the notions of progress, breaking down barriers, carrying history forward—in short, the style incorporated a certain narrative of what art history was. Art reaches an ending, not because it reaches the limits to the naturalistic or Modernist developments, but because the style of art that mandated those developments has been exposed:

> The end and fulfillment of the history of art is the philosophical understanding of what art is, an understanding that is achieved in the way that understanding in each of our lives is achieved,

namely, from the mistakes we make . . . the first false path was the close identification of art with picturing. The second false path was the materialist aesthetics of Greenberg.

(Danto, 1994, p. 107)

If contemporary art really is not part of the Modernist paradigm, this is reflected in there no longer being a mandate in the style or styles of this art that it enact a narratively structured development.

[*See also* Hegel, *article on* Hegel's Conception of the End of Art.]

BIBLIOGRAPHY

Works by Danto

Narration and Knowledge. New York: 1985.
"The End of Art." In *The Philosophical Disenfranchisement of Art.* New York, 1986.
"Approaching the End of Art." In *The State of the Art.* New York, 1987.
"Narratives and the End of Art." In *Encounters and Reflections: Art in the Historical Present.* New York, 1990.
"Narrative and Style." In *Beyond the Brillo Box: The Visual Arts in Post-Historical Perspective.* New York, 1992.
"Responses and Replies." In *Danto and His Critics,* edited by Mark Rollins. Oxford and Cambridge, Mass., 1993.
"The Shape of Artistic Pasts: East and West" and "Art After the End of Art." In *Embodied Meanings: Critical Essays and Aesthetic Meditations.* New York, 1994.
After the End of Art: Contemporary Art and the Pale of History. Princeton, N.J., 1997.

Other Sources

Belting, Hans. *The End of the History of Art?* Translated by Christopher S. Wood. Chicago, 1987.
Carrier, David. *Artwriting.* Amherst, Mass., 1987.
Carrier, David. *The Aesthete in the City: The Philosophy and Practice of American Abstract Painting in the 1980s.* University Park, Pa., 1994.
Carroll, Noël. "Danto, Art, and History." In *The End of Art and Beyond: Essays after Danto,* edited by Arto Haapala, Jerrold Levinson, and Veikko Rantala. Atlantic Highlands, N.J., 1997.
Greenberg, Clement. "Towards a Newer Laocoön." *Partisan Review* 7 (July–August 1970): 296–310.
Herwitz, Daniel. *Making Theory/Constructing Art: On the Authority of the Avant-Garde.* Chicago, 1993.

JONATHAN GILMORE

DAOIST AESTHETICS. The perceptual modes and expressive strategies of Daoist aesthetics developed from the highly suggestive writings of Laozi (the *Dao De jing*) and Zhuangzi (the *Zhuangzi*), produced between 6 and 3 BCE. These writings began, originally, not as treatises on aesthetics as such, but as a critique of the framing functions of language in the feudalistic Zhou dynasty's (12–6 BCE) construction of names or norms (the Naming System) to legitimize and consolidate its power hierarchies. The Daoists felt that under the Naming System (such as calling the emperor the "Son of Heaven," investing lords, fathers, and husbands with unchallenged power over subjects, sons, and wives, and giving special privileges to firstborn males over other males), the birthrights of humans as natural beings were restricted and distorted.

Politically, when Laozi said, "The speaking Dao (Way) is not the Constant Dao. The nameable Name is not the Constant Name" (chap. 1), and proposed to return to the *Su Pu* (Uncarved Block) (chap. 28), he intended to implode the so-called Kingly Dao, the Heavenly Dao, and the Naming System so that memories of the repressed, exiled, and alienated natural self could be fully reawakened, thus leading to recovery of full humanity. The Daoist project is a counter-discourse to deframe the tyranny of language.

This critique opens up larger philosophical and aesthetic dimensions. From the very beginning, the Daoists believed that the totalizing compositional activity of all phenomena, changing and ongoing, is beyond human conceptions and linguistic formulations. We impose conceptions—by definition partial and incomplete—on total phenomena, but at the peril of losing touch with their concrete appeal. Meanwhile, the real world, quite without human supervision and explanation, is totally alive, self-generating, self-conditioning, self-transforming, and self-complete *(wuyan-duhua)*. Inherent in this recognition is the acceptance of humans as limited, and the rejection of the idea of the human being as preeminently the controller or orderer of things. To represent the original condition in which things and humans freely emerge, first and foremost, humans must understand this position. Humans, as only one form of being among a million others, have no prerogative to classify the cosmic scheme. "Ducks' legs are short; lengthening them means pain. Cranes' legs are long; shortening them means suffering" (Zhuangzi, p. 317). We must leave them as they are in nature. Each form of being has its own nature, its own place; how can we take *this* as *subject* (principal) and *that* as *object* (subordinate)? How can we impose "our" viewpoint upon others as the right viewpoint, the only right viewpoint? "Not to discriminate *this* and *that* as opposites is the essence of Dao . . . There you attain the Central Ring to respond to the endless. . . . [To] obliterate the distinctions and view things from both *this* and *that* (*liangxing*, to travel on two paths)" (Zhuangzi, p. 66) is called the Balance of Dao (Zhuangzi, p. 70).

It is not hard to realize that what is called *this* (the so-called subject, determining and dominating agent) is really also *that* (the so-called object, dominated and determined), for when I say *this,* is it not also *that* from your point of view? Thus, only when the subject retreats from its dominating position—taking "I" from the primary position for aesthetic contemplation—can we allow the Free Flow of Nature to reassume itself. Phenomena do not need "I" to have their existences; they all have their own inner lives, activities, and rhythms to affirm their authenticity as things. Authenticity or truth does not come from "I"; things possess their existences and their forms of beauty and truth be-

fore we name them. Subject and object, principal and subordinate, are categories of superficial demarcation. Subject and object, consciousness and phenomena interpenetrate, intercomplement, interdefine, and interilluminate, appearing simultaneously, with humans corresponding to things, things corresponding to humans, things corresponding to things extending throughout the million phenomena. Thus, each of our perceptual acts, each of our makings of meaning, is provisional and it has to wait for the presence of, and modification by, other angles, other perceptions, in order to be free from the fetters of naming, while using them.

To eschew the domination of things by human subjectivity now also means that we must view things as things view themselves. When Laozi said, "to view the Universe through the Universe" (chap. 54), or when Zhuangzi said, "to hide the Universe in the Universe" (p. 243), this is to reach out to the Whole instead of breaking it into units. One way of achieving this is to view phenomena from the perspective of infinite space. "To see and see not . . . / continuous, it cannot be named, / and returns to nothingness . . . / the condition of no shape, / the form of no things . . . Dao as such / is seen, unseen / Seen, unseen / there is, in it, something forming / Forming, unforming / there are, in it, things" (Laozi, chap. 14, 21). It is no accident that Zhuangzi began his "Free and Easy Wandering" with the skyreaching flight of the great Peng bird, beating the water and rising ninety thousand miles (p. 4). It is no accident that most Chinese landscape paintings use aerial, midair, and ground perspectives simultaneously and freely. Front mountains, back mountains, front villages, back villages, bays in front of mountains, and bays behind mountains are seen simultaneously. This is because the viewers are not locked into only one viewing position. Instead, they are allowed to change positions constantly to undo viewing restrictions, allowing several variations of knowledge to converge upon their consciousness. Consider Fan Kuan's (eleventh century) "Travelers in the Valley." In this large vertical hanging scroll, several travelers, appearing very small, emerge from the lower right corner with large trees behind them. This means that we are viewing them from a distance. But behind the trees a very distant mountain now springs before our eyes, huge, majestic and immediate as if pressing upon our eyes. We are given to view the scene simultaneously from two distances and from several altitudes. Between the foreground and the background lies a diffusing mist, creating an emptiness out of its whiteness, an emptiness that has physicality in the real world. It is this whiteness, this void that helps to dissolve our otherwise locked-in sense of distances, engendering a free-floating registering activity.

A similar free-floating activity is reinvented in the poetic language in classical Chinese poetry. Language now can be used to avoid being locked into one restrictive, subjectively dominating, position; this is achieved by adjusting syntactical structures to allow objects and events to maintain their multiple spatial and temporal extensions, and by providing a gap between objects, events, or frames of meanings, an emptiness, a subversive space, so to speak, whereby one can move back and forth between or among them to evoke a larger sense of the given so as to constantly remodify, and at the same time, deframe and reframe anything that gets stuck.

For example, although classical Chinese also has articles and personal pronouns, these are often dispensed with in poetry, opening up an indeterminate space for the reader to enter and reenter for double to multiple perceptions. The following poem by Li Bai (Li Po) provides an example:

玉	階	生	白	露
yü	*jie*	*sheng*	*bai*	*lu*
jade	step(s)	grow	white	dew(s)

夜	久	侵	羅	襪
ye	*jiu*	*qin*	*luo*	*wa*
night	late	soak/attack	gauze	stocking(s)

卻	下	水	晶	簾
quexia		*shuijing—*		*lian*
let-down		crystal		—blind(s)

玲	瓏	望	秋	月
linglong		*wang*	*qiu*	*yue*
glass-clear		watch	autumn	moon

If we supply "she" as the subject for "let down," then we are standing outside looking in *objectively*, so to speak, at an object (the court lady). But we can also supply "I," in which case we are *subjectively* looking out, being identified with the protagonist. The absence of a personal pronoun allows us to approach reality at once objectively and subjectively, simultaneously moving back and forth between two positions.

There is also the absence of connective elements (prepositions, conjunctions), and this, aided by the indeterminacy of parts of speech and no-tense declensions in verbs, affords us a unique freedom to consort with the real-life world. The degree of syntactical freedom can be illustrated by a palindrome poem of eight lines by Su Dongpo (1036–1101) that can be read forward and backward naturally. One line from this poem should suffice.

潮	隨	暗	浪	雪	山	傾
chao	*sui*	*an*	*lang*	*xue*	*shan*	*qing*
tides	follow	dark	waves	snow	mountains	pour-fall

傾	山	雪	浪	暗	隨	潮
qing	*shan*	*xue*	*lang*	*an*	*sui*	*chao*
pour-fall	mountains	snow	waves	dark	follow	tides

Although not all Chinese lines can be as syntactically free as this palindrome poem, a great percentage of Chinese

poems echo the Daoist position by capitalizing on this flexibility to phase out the interference of the poet's subjectivity. The words in such a poem quite often have a loosely committed relationship with the reader, who remains in a sort of middle ground between engaging with and disengaging from them. The asyntactical and paratactical structures promote a kind of prepredicative condition wherein words, like objects (often in coextensive and multiple montage layout) in the real-life world, are free from predetermined closures of relationship and meaning and offer themselves to us in an open space. Within this space around them, and with the poet stepping aside, so to speak, we can move freely and approach them from various vantage points to achieve different shades of the same moment. We are given to witness the acting out of objects and events in cinematic visuality, and stand at the threshold of various possible meanings.

A comparison of (a) word-for-word with (b) minimum translations with intrusive English syntactical elements inserted in brackets will illustrate this point:

1. a.

雞	聲	茅	店	月
ji	*sheng*	*mao*	*dian*	*yue*
cock/n.	crow/n.	thatch(ed)/n.	inn/n.	moon/n.

  b. (At) cockcrow, (the) moon (is seen above?/ by?) thatch(ed) inn

  a.

人	跡	板	橋	霜
ren	*ji*	*ban*	*qiao*	*shuang*
man/n.	trace/n.	plank/n.	bridge/n.	frost/n.

  b. footprint(s) (are seen upon the) frost (covering the) wooden bridge

2. a.

澗	戶	寂	無	人
jian	*hu*	*ji*	*wu*	*ren*
stream	hut	silent	no	one

  b. (a) hut (by? above? overlooking?) stream (is) silent: (there is) no one

3. a.

星	臨	萬	戶	動
xing	*lin*	*wan*	*hu*	*dong*
Star(s)	come	ten-thousand	house(s)	move.

  b1. (While the) stars (are twinkling above the) ten-thousand households. . . .

  b2. When the stars come, ten-thousand houses move

4. a.

月	落	烏	啼	霜	滿	天
yue	*luo*	*wu*	*ti*	*shuang*	*man*	*tian*
Moon	set(s)	crow(s)	caw	frost	full	sky

  b. (As the) moon set(s), crow(s) caw (against a) full sky (of) frost

5. a. 國　破　山　河　在
   guo　po　shan　he　zai
   country　broken　mountain　river　be (exist)

   b. (Though the) country (is) sunder(ed), mountain(s) (and) river(s) endure

It is not difficult to see how all the b-lines depart from the original mode of perception, changing fluid-viewing mobility (1 and 2) to restrictive, guided directives; changing visual events to *statements* about the events, resulting in an important loss of all the dramatic co-presence, spatial tensions, and counterpoints and interplay between them (3 and 4); and changing the montage format that retains multiple suggestiveness into a mere commentary dominated and guided by the poet's subjectivity (5).

It must be clear by now that the Daoist noninterference with Nature is also an affirmation of the immanence of things in Nature. In the words of one Daoist-inspired Chan (Zen) Buddhist, "Mountains are mountains, rivers rivers." The whole art of landscape poetry in China aims, therefore, to release the objects in Nature from their seeming irrelevance and bring forth their original freshness and thingness—to return them to their first innocence—thus making them relevant as "self-so-complete" objects in their coextensive existence. The poet focuses attention on them in such a way as to allow them to leap out directly and spontaneously before us, unhindered:

> Man (at) leisure. Cassia flower(s) fall.
> Quiet night. Spring mountain (is) empty.
> Moon rise(s). Startle(s)—(a) mountain bird.
> (It) sing(s) at times in (the) spring stream.
>   Wang Wei (701–761), "Bird-Singing Stream"

> (High on the) tree tips, (the) hibiscus
> Set(s) forth red calyces in (the) mountain.
> (A) stream hut, quiet. No man.
> (It) bloom(s) and fall(s), bloom(s) and fall(s).
>   Wang Wei, "Hsin-i Village"

The scenery *speaks* and *acts*. There is little or no subjective emotion or intellectuality to disturb the inner growth and change of the objects. The poet does not step in, or rather, the poet, having opened up the scene, has stepped aside. The objects spontaneously emerge before the reader-viewer's eyes, whereas in most nature poems in the West, the concreteness of the objects often gives way to abstraction through the poet's analytical intervention, or his symbolic, transcendental impulse where an apple cannot be viewed purely as an apple. In both of these poems, Nature rules as an ongoing entity unrestricted by human makeover. "No man. / It blooms and falls, blooms and falls."

It is no accident that the Daoists stress the Fast of the Mind or Sitting-in-Forgetfulness (Zhuangzi, pp. 14, 384), and the Loss of Self. It is only by emptying out all traces of intellectual interference that one can fully respond to things in their concreteness, to their spontaneous, simultaneous, and harmonious presences. A state of stillness, emptiness, silence, or quiescence is prevalent in most Chinese landscape poems.

But the complexity of the Daoist aesthetic is not fully shown until we confront the subtle interplay of the built-in contradictions throughout the Daoist texts, and until we see in what way the decreative process leads to or becomes the creative. This decreative-creative dialectic appears on the surface in the form of negation or renunciation: The Dao (Way of Nature) is ineffable; language is inadequate; we should take no action *(wuwei)*, have no mind *(wuxin)*, no knowledge, no self *(wuwo)*; we should not speak about Dao; Dao is void and there is nothing in it. Paradoxically, in this seeming renunciation is the affirmation of the concrete total world, a world free from and unrestricted by concepts. The renunciation then is not negation, but a new way of repossessing this original concrete world by dispossessing the partial and reduced forms the process of abstract thinking has thus far heaped on us. Thus, without taking actions as those defined by a closed system of abstract thinking, everything is done in accordance with our instinctive nature. Without exercising our conscious mind, we can respond fully to things that come into our ken. With conceptual boundaries removed, our consciousness is thus open, unblocked, a center of no circumference into which and across which a million things will regain their free flow and activity.

It is no accident that Chinese critics and aestheticians, Daoist and Confucian alike, from Lu Ji (261–303), Liu Xie (c.465–520), and the art critic Zhang Yanyuan (fl. 847), to Sikong Tu (837–908), Yan Yü (fl. 1180–1235), and Wang Guowei (1977–1927), have made this no-mind stillness and silence the pivot of their theoretical formulations.

But the ideal Daoist poet, when pushed to the logical end, should be silent and seek no expression, for the affirmation of the nonverbal world cancels out such a possibility. Both Laozi and Zhuangzi were fully aware of this. Dao cannot be told and yet Laozi and Zhuangzi cannot help but use the word *Dao* to circumscribe it. While using it, they remind us that it should immediately be forgotten so that we can be one with Nature again. The word *Dao* is used as though it were merely a pointer, a spark toward the original real world. Thus, the Daoist artist stresses also the emptiness of language. What is written is fixed and solid; what is unwritten is fluid and empty. The empty and fluid wordlessness is the indispensable cooperator with the fixed and solid word. The full activity of language should be like the co-presence of the solid and the void in Chinese paintings, allowing the reader to receive not only the words (the written) but also the wordlessness (the unwritten). The negative space, such as the emptiness in a painting and the condition of silence with meanings trembling at the edge of words in a poem, is made into something vastly more significant and positive, and indeed, has become a horizon toward which our aesthetic attention is constantly directed. By continually de-creasing discursive and explanatory elements and proce-dures in the poetic line, by promoting the coextensive pres-encing of objects, the Chinese poets help bring forth a type of nonmediating mediation, by way of deframing as fram-ing, leading to an art of noninterference akin to the work-ings of Nature, and a use of language as a pointer toward the finer interweaving of the unspeaking, concrete, chang-ing Nature (ziran), like the word *Dao,* which we are to forget once it is pronounced, like the fish trap that can be forgot-ten once the fish is caught (Zhuangzi, p. 944). The words become a spotlight that illuminates, in full brilliance, objects emerging from the real world.

[*See also* Aleatoric Processes; *and* Chinese Aesthetics, *historical overview article.*]

BIBLIOGRAPHY

Primary Sources

Laozi. *Dao De jing.*
Zhuangzi. *Zhuangzi jishi.* Edited by Guo Qingfan. Beijing, 1961.
    All translations of Laozi are the author's, those of Zhuangzi are basi-cally Watson's. (See Other Sources, below.)

Other Sources

Graham, A. C. *Disputers of the Tao: Philosophical Arguments in Ancient China.* La Salle, Ill., 1989. See pp. 215–234.
Graham, A. C., ed. *Chuang-tzu: The Seven Inner Chapters and Other Writings from the Book "Chuang-tzu."* London and Boston, 1981.
Lau, D. C., ed. *Lao-tzu:Tao te Ching.* Hong Kong, 1982.
Watson, Burton, ed. *The Complete Works of Chuang Tzu.* New York, 1968.
Yip, Wai-lim. "The Daoist Theory of Knowledge." In *Poetics East and West.* Toronto Semiotic Monograph Series, N.4.
Yip, Wai-lim. *Diffusion of Distances: Dialogues between Chinese and West-ern Poetics.* Berkeley, 1993. See chs. 2–4.

WAI-LIM YIP

DEATH AND AESTHETICS.

[*This essay explores the difficulties artists have had, historically and in principle, repre-senting in their work issues or emotions related to death.*]

Dying is a solitary, highly individual, and incommunica-ble event, perhaps the most private and most intimate mo-ment in the life cycle of the human subject. Whether it marks, in religious terms, an exchange whereby the dissolu-tion of the body is coterminous with an entry into a new spiritual existence and thus the return to divinity, or whether, in the more secular encoding of what Sigmund Freud calls the death drive, it merely initiates the return to that tensionless, undifferentiated state of the inanimate that is beyond, grounding and prefiguring biological and social human existence, the finitude of death is generally acknowl-edged as the one certainty in any given life. At the same time it is impossible to know in advance what the experi-ence of dying will be like, as it is also impossible to transmit any precise and definitive knowledge of this event to those surviving it.

Yet dying, burial, and commemoration are always also public matters. As cultural anthropology has shown, death, in that it removes a social being from society, is conceived as a wound to the community at large and a threatening signal of its own impermanence. The dying person and then the corpse of the deceased occupy a liminal place, no longer fully present in the world of the living and about to pass into a state inaccessible to them. Rituals of mourning, falling into two phases, serve to redress the disempowering cut that the loss of a member entails, creating a new identity for the de-ceased and reintegrating her or him back into the commu-nity of the survivors. On the one hand, a phase of disaggrega-tion marks the dangerous period of temporal disposal of the corpse and the mourners' separation from everyday life, cel-ebrating loss, vulnerability, and fallibility. On the other hand, a phase of reinstallation or second burial reasserts society, because it emerges triumphant over death. Thus, rituals of mourning, acknowledging the wound to the living that death entails, always also work with the assumption that death is a regeneration of life. Especially once death can conceptually be translated into sacrifice, it serves as a cultural ruse that works against death. The sacrificial victim, representing the community at large but placed in the position of liminality between the living and the dead, draws all the evil or pollu-tion of death onto its body. Its expulsion is then in turn coter-minous with purifying the community of the living from death. While the loss of a cherished member evokes grief and the pain of loss for the survivors, viewing and commemorat-ing the death of another is also a moment of power and tri-umph. Horror and distress at the sight of death turn into sat-isfaction, since the survivors are not themselves dead. Visual or narrative representations of death, meant to comfort and reassure the bereaved survivors as is the case in tragic drama and elegiac poetry, ultimately serve to negotiate a given cul-ture's attitudes toward survival. Signaling such a gesture of recuperation after the disempowering impact of loss, a given society will perpetrate stories about sacrifice, execution, martyrdom, and commemoration, so as to affirm its belief in retribution, resurrection, or salvation, much as an individual family will generate stories about its deceased ancestors to express its coherence after the loss of one of its members.

In discussing the more personal psychic aspects of griev-ing the loss of a beloved person, Freud has suggested that the normal affect of mourning bears resemblances to melancholia. In both cases the response to the loss of a loved one is a turning away from all worldly activity such that the mourner instead clings almost exclusively to the de-ceased love object. However, while melancholia describes a pathological condition because the afflicted person is un-willing to give up his or her libidinal investment in the lost love object, in the case of mourning, the lost love object is ultimately decathected, but only after an extended period during which the survivor works through the memories, expectations, and affects attached to the dead. With worldly reality once more gaining the upper hand, the process of mourning comes to an end and the afflicted subject is again liberated of the painful unpleasure it had been cultivating during the mourning process. Cultural rituals such as attending wakes and seances were designed to assist such a working-through process, for they allow the mourning to enter into a dialogue with the deceased, but under the condition that this exchange will ultimately find closure, in the first case when the body is buried or in the latter when the spirit is once again released. Visits to cemeteries, or in the case of those who died as a result of wars and other political catastrophes, to memorial sites of collective commemoration, furthermore, work with the presupposition that the living no longer harbor a libidinal investment in the lost objects, even while they are meant to assist the survivors in preserving their memory of the dead.

Any discussion of the aesthetic rendition of death is thus fraught with contradictions. On the one hand, it must account for the fact that dying is always a solitary act, a highly ambivalent event of fissure both for the person dying and for the survivors. It can elicit both psychic distress and serenity, induce a sense of burden and relief, fulfill both a desire for and an anxiety about finitude, so that any images or narratives of mortality inevitably touch emotional registers in relation to an event of loss that enmesh the terrifying with the uplifting as well as with the inevitable. What emerges is a highly complex interplay of grief, anger, despair, acceptance, and commemoration of the deceased, an interplay so highly personal, individual, and specific that it is seemingly performed outside historical and social codes. Indeed, because the transitory nature of human existence and the possibility of an afterlife have always preoccupied the living, because all earthly life is directed toward death and one's conduct is fashioned in view of death and the possibility of salvation, representations of death seem to be an anthropological constant that defies periodization.

On the other hand, precisely because burial rites are used to reinforce social and political ideas, with tombs and funerary sculptures endorsing concepts of continuity, legitimacy, and status, historians have also been eager to demonstrate that different periods are characterized by different cultural images of death and attitudes to it. The most prominent, Philippe Ariès, offers a linear development that begins with an early European acceptance of death as an inevitable fact of life, as an organic and integral part of a harmonious reciprocity between living and death. With the emergence of individualism, however, the destiny of each individual or family takes precedence over that of the community and a new emphasis is placed on the funeral as a sign of social status and material wealth. At the same time the focus on the self provokes a passionate attachment to an existence in the material world and hence a resentment of death. By the mid-

eighteenth century an attitude of denial, conjoining the fear of with a fascination for death, becomes the norm. While cemeteries are symbolically removed to the outskirts of the city, the dying person and the corpse become objects of erotic, mystic, and aesthetic interest. Ariès calls this the "period of beautiful death," and in a sense that has permeated well into the late twentieth century, aestheticization hides the physical signs of mortality and decay, so as to mitigate the wound death inflicts on the survivors.

Whether through spiritualism, which offers an androcentric domestication of heaven as a continuation or repetition of earthly existence, or through a cultivation of burial and mourning insignia—consolatory literature, elaborate tombstones, and pompous cemetery monuments—aesthetic beautification renders the terror and ugliness of death's reality palatable by placing it within the realm of the familiar as well as the imaginary. By the mid-nineteenth century, visits to morgues, houses of mourning, and wax museums had become comparable to visiting a picture gallery. This death so lavishly represented was, however, no longer death, but rather an illusion of art. Yet a seminal contradiction came to be inscribed in this so-called modern attitude toward death, persisting today in our visual, narrative, cinematic, and cyber-representations of violence, war, and destruction as well as in the sentimental stories about victims our cultural discourses engender so as to idealize and make into heroes those smitten by death. The more Western culture refuses death, the more it imagines and speaks of it. Aestheticization, meant to hide death, always also articulates mortality, affirming the ineluctability of death in the very act of its denial. With death's presence relegated to the margins of the social world, representations of death also turn away from any reference to social reality, only to implant themselves firmly in the register of the imaginary. Self-reflexivity comes to be inscribed in images of death in that, because their objects of reference are indeterminate, they signify "as well," "besides," "other."

Locating at the end of the eighteenth century the epistemic shift that reinstalls a discourse of mortality, which insists that all knowledge is possible only on the basis of death, Michel Foucault has highlighted the contradiction at issue. Death, which is the absolute measure of life and opens onto the truth of human existence, is also that event which life, in daily practice, must resist. The metaphor Foucault has recourse to, so as to illustrate how death is the limit and center toward and against which all strategies of self-representation are directed, is that of a mirror to infinity erected vertically against death: "Headed toward death, language turns back upon itself. To stop this death which would stop it, it possesses but a single power: that of giving birth to its own image in a play of mirrors that has no limit" (1977, p. 54). As death becomes the privileged cipher for heroic, sentimental, erotic, and horrific stories about the survival and continuity of a culture, about the possibility and limits of its knowledge, it self-consciously implements the affinity between mortality and the endless reduplication of language. What is called forth is a literature, where aesthetic language is self-consciously made into a trope referring to itself, seeking to transgress the limit posed by death even as it is nourished by the radical impossibility of fully encompassing this alterity. In a similar manner Martin Heidegger has argued that all life is a "being toward death" with all existence forcing the human subject into a recognition of this abyss. Such an encounter with the nothingness of the veiledness *(Verhülltheit)* of death, although it initially calls forth anxiety, ultimately leads to the recognition of the truth of being, namely, an experience of the ontological difference between being *(Sein)* and beingness *(Seiendes),* with the former overcoming the latter. Representation for Heidegger is authentic when it bows into the silence evoked by the measurelessness of death, while any language that avoids death is for him mere idle chatter.

Speaking of the aesthetic rendition of death thus ultimately brings into play the issue of misrepresentation, for the paradox inherent in representations of death is that this "death" is always culturally constructed and performed within a given historically specific philosophical and anthropological discourse on mortality, resurrection, and immortality. Since death lies outside any living subject's personal or collective realm of experience, this "death" can only be rendered as an idea, not something known as a bodily sensation. This idea, furthermore, involves imagery not directly belonging to it, so that it is always figural, the privileged trope for other values. Placed beyond the register of what the living subject can know, "death" can only be read as a signifier with an incessantly receding, ungraspable signified, invariably always pointing back self-reflexively to other signifiers. Death remains outside clear categories. It is nowhere, because it is only a gap, a cut, a transition between the living body and the corpse, a before (the painful fear, the serene joy of the dying person) and an after (the mourning of the survivor), an ungraspable point, lacking any empirical object. At the same time, it is everywhere, because death begins with birth and remains present on all levels of daily existence, each moment of mortal existence insisting that its measure is the finitude toward which it is directed.

Put apodictically, death is the one privileged moment of the absolutely real, of true, nonsemiotic materiality and facticity as these appear in the shape of the mutability and vulnerability of the material body. On the one hand, then, it demarcates figural language by forcing us to recognize that even though language, when faced with death, is never referentially reliable, it also cannot avoid referentiality. Nonnegotiable and nonalterable, death is the limit of language, disrupting our system of language as well as our image repertoire, even as it is its ineluctable ground and vanishing point. On the other hand, signifying nothing, it silently points to the indetermination of meaning so that one can speak of death only by speaking other. The aporia at issue can be formulated in the following manner: As the point where all language fails, it is also the source of all allegorical speaking. But precisely because death is excessively tropic, it also points to a reality beyond, evoking the referent that representational texts may point to but not touch. Death, then, is both most referential and most self-referential, a reality for the experiencing subject but nonverifiable for the speculating and spectating survivor.

Yet the numerable literary depictions of deathbed scenes also illustrate that representations of death not only attest to the fallibility of aesthetic language and the impermanence of human existence, but also confirm social stability in the face of mortality precisely by virtue of a language of death. The force of these narratives resides in the fact that in their last moments, the dying have a vision of afterlife, while at the same time, the aesthetic rendition of the deathbed ritual includes the farewell greetings from kin and friends and the redistribution of social roles and property that serve to negotiate kinship succession. Thus a sense of human continuity, so fundamentally questioned in the face of death, is also assured both in relation to ancestors as well as to survivors. Indeed, as Walter Benjamin argues, death is the sanction for any advice a storyteller might seek to transmit. Speaking in the shadow of one's own demise, as well as against this finitude, is precisely what endows these stories with supreme authority.

Representations of death, therefore, ground the way a culture stabilizes and fashions itself as an invincible and omnipotent, eternal, intact symbolic order, but can do so only by incessantly addressing the opposition between death and life. As the sociologist Jean Baudrillard argues, the phenomenon of survival must be seen in contingency with a prohibition of death and the establishment of social surveillance of this prohibition. Power is first and foremost grounded in legislating death, by manipulating and controlling the exchange between life and death, by severing the one from the other and by imposing a taboo on the dead. Power is thus installed precisely by drawing this first boundary, and all supplementary aspects of division—between soul and body, masculinity and femininity, good and bad—feed off this initial and initiating separation that partitions life from death. Any aesthetic rendition of death can be seen in light of such ambivalent boundary drawing. Referring to the basic fact of mortal existence, these representations fascinate because they allow us indirectly to confront our own death, even though on the manifest level, they appear to revolve around the death of the other. Death is on the other side of the boundary. We experience death by proxy, for it occurs in someone else's body and at another site, as a narrative or visual image. The ambivalent reassurance these representations seem to offer is that, although they insist on the need to acknowledge the ubiquitous presence of death in life, our belief in our own immortality is nevertheless also confirmed. We are the survivors of the tale, entertained and educated by virtue of the death inflicted on others. Yet while representations of death may allow us to feel assured, because the disturbance played through in the narrative ultimately finds closure, the reader or spectator is nevertheless also drawn into the liminal realm between life and death so that partaking of the fantasy scenario often means hesitating between an assurance of a recuperated mastery over and submission before the irrevocable law of death.

Any representation of death, therefore, also involves the disturbing return of the repressed knowledge of death, the excess beyond the text, which the latter aims at stabilizing by having signs and images represent it. As these representations oscillate between the excessively tropic and a non-semiotic materiality, their real referent always eludes the effort at recuperation that representations seek to afford. It disrupts the system at its very center. Thus many narratives involving death work with a tripartite structure. Death causes a disorder to the stability of a given fictional world and engenders moments of ambivalence, disruption, or vulnerability. This phase of liminality is followed by narrative closure, where the threat that the event of death poses is again recuperated by a renewed return to stability. Yet the regained order encompasses a shift, because it will never again be entirely devoid of traces of difference. Ultimately these narratives broadcast the message that recuperation from death is imperfect, the regained stability is not safe, and the urge for order is inhabited by a fascination with disruption and split. The certainty of survival emerges over and out of the certainty of dissolution.

Ultimately, the seminal ambivalence subtending all representations of death resides in the fact that, while they are morally educating and emotionally elevating, they also touch on the knowledge of our mortality, which for most is so disconcerting that we would prefer to disavow it. They fascinate with dangerous knowledge. In the aesthetic enactment, however, we have a situation that is impossible in life, namely, that we share death vicariously and return to the living. Even as we are forced to acknowledge the ubiquitous presence of death in life, our belief in our own immortality is confirmed. The aesthetic representation of death lets us repress our knowledge of the reality of death precisely because here death occurs in someone else's body and as an image or a narrative. Representations of death, one could say, articulate an anxiety about and a desire for death, functioning like a symptom, which psychoanalysis defines as a repression that, because it fails, gives to the subject, in the guise of a ciphered message, the truth about his or her desire that he or she could not otherwise confront. In a gesture of compromise, concealing what they also disclose, these fundamentally duplicitous representations try to maintain a balance of sorts. They point obliquely to that which threatens to disturb the order, but articulate this disturbing

knowledge of mortality in a displaced, recoded, and translated manner, and by virtue of the substitution render the dangerous knowledge as something beautiful, fascinating, and ultimately reassuring. Visualizing even as they conceal what is too dangerous to articulate openly, but too fascinating to repress successfully, they place death away from the self at the same time that they ineluctably return the desire for and the knowledge of finitude and dissolution, upon and against which all individual and cultural systems of coherence and continuation rest.

[*See also* Blanchot; *and* Ineffability.]

BIBLIOGRAPHY

Ariès, Philippe. *The Hour of Our Death.* Translated by Helen Weaver. New York, 1981.

Barthes, Roland. *Camera Lucida.* Translated by Richard Howard. New York, 1981.

Bataille, Georges. *L'Érotisme.* Paris, 1957.

Baudrillard, Jean. *L'Échange symbolique et la mort.* Paris, 1976.

Bauman, Zygmunt. *Mortality, Immortality, and Other Life Strategies.* Stanford, Calif., 1992.

Benjamin, Walter. "Der Erzähler." In *Gesammelte Schriften,* vol. 2.2, edited by Rolf Tiedemann and Hermann Schweppenhäuser, pp. 438–465. Frankfurt am Main, 1977.

Blanchot, Maurice. *The Gaze of Orpheus and Other Literary Essays.* Edited by P. Adams Sitney, translated by Lydia Davis. Barrytown, N.Y., 1981.

Bloch, Maurice, and Jonathan Parry, eds. *Death and the Regeneration of Life.* Cambridge and New York, 1982.

Choron, Jacques. *Death and Modern Man.* New York, 1964.

Derrida, Jacques. *The Gift of Death.* Translated by David Wills. Chicago, 1995.

Foucault, Michel. *Language, Counter-Memory, Practice: Selected Essays and Interviews.* Translated and edited by Donald F. Bouchard and Sherry Simon. Ithaca, N.Y., 1977.

Freud, Sigmund. "Mourning and Melancholia" (1917). In *Standard Edition of the Complete Psychological Works of Sigmund Freud,* vol. 14, edited by James Strachey, pp. 237–258. London, 1957.

Freud, Sigmund. *Beyond the Pleasure Principle* (1920). In *Standard Edition of the Complete Psychological Works of Sigmund Freud,* vol. 18, edited by James Strachey. London, 1955.

Goodwin, Sarah Webster, and Elisabeth Bronfen. *Death and Representation.* Baltimore, 1993.

Guiomar, Michel. *Principles d'une esthétique de la mort.* Paris, 1967.

Heidegger, Martin. *Sein und Zeit.* 15th ed. Tübingen, 1979.

Kofman, Sarah. *Mélancolie de l'art.* Paris, 1985.

Kristeva, Julia. *Powers of Horror: An Essay on Abjection.* Translated by Leon S. Roudiez. New York, 1982.

Morin, Edgar. *L'homme et la mort.* Nouv. ed. Paris, 1970.

Romanyshyn, Robert D. *Technology as Symptom and Dream.* London and New York, 1989.

Vernant, Jean-Pierre. *Mortals and Immortals: Collected Essays.* Edited by Froma I. Zeitlin. Princeton, N.J., 1991.

ELISABETH BRONFEN

DEATH OF ART. *See* Anti-Art; Danto, *article on* Danto's End of Art Thesis; Hegel, *article on* Hegel's Conception of the End of Art.

DEBORD, GUY. *See* Situationist Aesthetics.

DECADENCE. *See* Aestheticism; Baudelaire; Camp; Kitsch; Pater; Wilde.

DECONSTRUCTION. *See* Derrida; Heidegger.

DECORATIVE ARTS. *See* Bloomsbury Group; Craft; Morris.

DEFINITION OF ART. It is not atypical for the question "What is art?" to arise when an object or event purporting to be art seems significantly unlike paradigmatic instances of art. In such a context the question "What is art?" is not infrequently a request for a definition of art. Dissatisfaction with the fact that certain works are counted as art has also occasioned the request for a definition.

There have been two major kinds of response to this request. Either a definition has been given, frequently accompanied by a critique of previous definitions, or an attempt has been made to show why a definition cannot be given.

The definitions have themselves been of distinct kinds. One kind singles out some perceptible feature or features that all, and only, artworks have. Dissatisfaction with a particular definition of this kind has led to alternative definitions. Some, however, came to believe that the search for a definition was a futile one, that the concept of art was an open one and, hence, not susceptible to definition. Others replied that while one kind of definition was inadequate, another kind was not. All, and only, artworks have a common property, but it is not an exhibited property of the artwork. Rather, it is a nonexhibited social property, a status. A perusal of a work's perceptual features would not be sufficient for establishing whether it had that status.

A definition of art (of either the activity or the object) was to provide necessary and sufficient conditions; it was to enable one to distinguish art from other things. Early definitions focused on art's mimetic property: its ability to mirror or imitate nature. [*See* Mimesis.] In Aristotle's version, the imitation could have as its purpose the purgation and purification of people's emotions. Art, in imitating nature, put it at a distance and by so doing could allow its audience to experience, indulge in, and get relief from certain "negative" emotions in a way that was nonthreatening to society. The audience of art was to be everyone, and art could have a therapeutic effect; it could ensure the health of a society.

If a definition of art were to specify what property any artwork or any artistic activity must have, then, from a current perspective, imitating nature is not that property. Most musical works, for example, do not have this property, nor do abstract representations, yet some examples of these are art. Imitation, moreover, cannot be sufficient for art; snapshots and home videos attest to that. Nor can imitation aimed at purifying people's emotions be sufficient. Imitation with just this aim governs the kind of representations that are shown to drivers convicted of speeding or driving while drunk.

Historically, imitation was superseded by expression. [*See* Expression Theory of Art.] Expression, not representation, was held to be an essential feature of art. What was expressed was the artist's personal emotion. This expression, and, hence, the art that embodied it, was worthwhile in itself. The audience of this art was not everyone but only those sensitive enough to understand it. Percy Bysshe Shelley, for example, imagines the poet to be "a nightingale, who sits in darkness and sings to cheer its own solitude with sweet sounds."

Not any expression of emotion, however, counted as the right kind of expression. A child having a temper tantrum, while expressing him- or herself, was not engaged in artistic activity. The expression of emotions had to take a certain external form. A composer, for example, might write a requiem and thus express his or her sorrow in the piece of music; an artist might paint a battle scene and express in the painting a horror of war.

From a current perspective, however, expression fares no better as the property all and only artworks are to have. Conceptual Art and some Minimalist Art do not express. Nor is all expression of emotion in external form art. The paintings of mental patients may express emotions without being artworks.

The definition of art in terms of expression did not require the artist to be socially responsible; the audience of art was a select one. Leo Tolstoy's definition makes art once again a social force; the artist is given a social responsibility and the audience of art is everyone. [*See* Tolstoy.]

Although Tolstoy believed that the expression of emotion in external form was necessary for art, it was not sufficient. The emotions had to be communicated and it was the artist's responsibility to do this. Communication through art was a species of infection. The audience of art was to feel the artist's emotion and to feel at one with the artist and whoever else felt the emotion. Works of art would thus contribute to human solidarity; they would enable people to feel together rather than separate and isolated. The greatest art would transmit feelings that brought people together in a spiritual fellowship, but any art would unite people.

Tolstoy's definition was, like the previous definitions, subject to attack. Difficult works often failed to infect, yet arguably these works were art. Infectiousness was also not sufficient for art. Entertainment movies communicate emotions without being artworks.

Some, like Morris Weitz, argued that not only were these definitions of art inadequate, any definition would be, since art was an open concept for which no real definition was possible. It was not that no one had yet been clever enough to find the right definition; there was no right definition to be found. If artworks did not all share some property or properties, any attempt to give necessary and sufficient conditions for art would be doomed to fail. Whatever property a definition specified as necessary, one could always find an acknowledged artwork that lacked that property. Whatever property a definition specified as sufficient, one could find an object that had that property but was not an artwork. Artworks had characteristic features; there was a family resemblance between them, but no one feature or set of features was shared by all artworks.

Many aestheticians, however, were not persuaded that no real definition of art could be given. What was required, they said, was a new sort of definition. They agreed that there was no perceptual property or properties that all artworks had. In the twentieth century some artworks, like Marcel Duchamp's bottle rack, were not perceptually different from objects, ordinary bottle racks, which were not artworks. But aestheticians claimed that all artworks did have something in common. That something was a status.

One definition of this kind developed by George Dickie proposed that an artwork was an artifact on which someone acting on behalf of an informal sort of institution called the artworld had conferred the status of candidate for appreciation. [*See* Dickie]. This definition provoked controversy, for example, about whether a nonviciously circular account of the art world could be given, about what made something a possible candidate for appreciation, about whether potentially anything could be such a candidate and could, therefore, be an artwork.

Another definition of this kind developed by Arthur C. Danto emphasized the role of art theory. [*See* Danto.] Arthood was a status acquired when the appropriate art-historical theory was in place. An object became art when it was related to acknowledged artworks by means of a theoretical claim about the nature and value of art. Art theories came out of the contextual background called the art world. At different times there were different theories, making it possible for objects that lacked the status of artwork at one time or place to attain that status at another time or place. Although the objects in question, say, masks in an anthropological museum, did not change their observable features when they went into art museums and became artworks, the art theory did change. An object could become an artwork only if the art world was ready for it, and such art-world readiness depended on there being a theory within which, for example, the object could make a statement; could be a subject for interpretation, an interpretation limited by the constraints of historical possibility; had a title; was an original, not a fake; and was by an artist.

Questions about this definition were raised as well. For example, what, it was asked, makes something a theory, and in the art world does one have full-blown theories or only fragments of theoretical principles or commitments or slo-

gans? Others questioned whether recognizing an object, such as a Greek vase, as an artwork was necessary for its being an artwork. Why, if Greek vases are artworks, were they not always artworks?

If artworks had characteristic features, and all seemed to agree that they had, even if none of these features was necessary, might not these characteristic features be disjunctively necessary? If, that is, not all artworks perform the same function, if not all either represent or describe or express might not it be necessary that an artwork either represents or describes or expresses or, as Nelson Goodman suggested, exemplifies or complexly refers? [*See* Goodman.] Doing any of these things would not, however, be sufficient for making that which does it art, since snapshots and road maps represent, letters to friends describe, horror movies express, tailors' swatches exemplify, and political caricatures complexly refer. There may, however be characteristics typical of these functions when they are art functions. For example, in the representing done by artworks, many more features of the representation matter than matter, say, in the representing done by diagrams in a science textbook. The slightest difference in a representation in art makes a difference while it does not typically make such a difference in non-art areas.

It has been argued, however, that an ordinary non-art object, a stone from one's driveway, can in suitable circumstances function as an artwork, performing one or more of the functions characteristically performed by artworks in the way artworks perform them without strictly becoming an artwork, and a work that is not performing any art function (a painting is being used as a blanket) can nonetheless be an artwork. While one can specify what may be necessary for functioning as an artwork, functioning as an artwork does not guarantee that the object strictly is an artwork. In light of the difficulties attending the question "What is art?" when it is understood to be a request for a definition of art, Goodman suggested that aestheticians should redirect their attention away from this question and should focus, instead, on the question "When is art?" This redirection, however, has not yet taken place, and efforts to define art continue.

[*See also* Artifact; Essentialism; Historicism, *article on* Historicism and Philosophy; Institutional Theory of Art; Ontology of Art; *and* Theories of Art.]

BIBLIOGRAPHY

Aristotle. *The Poetics*. Translated by Ingram Bywater. In *The Basic Works of Aristotle,* edited by Richard McKeon, pp. 1455–1487. New York, 1941.

Danto, Arthur C. "Artworks and Real Things." *Theoria* 39.1–3 (1973): 1–17.

Danto, Arthur C. *The Transfiguration of the Commonplace.* Cambridge, Mass., 1981.

Dickie, George. "Defining Art." *American Philosophical Quarterly* 6.3 (July 1969): 253–256.

Dickie, George. *The Art Circle: A Theory of Art.* New York, 1984.

Goodman, Nelson. "When Is Art?" In *Ways of Worldmaking,* chap. 4. Indianapolis, 1978.

Shelley, Percy Bysshe. *A Defence of Poetry.* Indianapolis, 1965.

Tolstoy, Leo. *What Is Art?* Translated by Almer Maude. Indianapolis, 1960.

Weitz, Morris. "The Role of Theory in Aesthetics." *Journal of Aesthetics and Art Criticism* 15.1 (September 1956): 27–35.

ANNETTE BARNES

DELACROIX, FERDINAND-VICTOR-EUGÈNE.

[*This essay concerns the French nineteenth-century painter's writings on art and aesthetics rather than his art.*]

The *Journal* of Eugène Delacroix (1798–1863) is one of the most important works in the literature of art history: a masterpiece of art criticism of the stature of the *Salons* of Denis Diderot and Charles Baudelaire, and one of a highly select group of artists' writings including the poems of Michelangelo, the notebooks of Leonardo da Vinci, and the *Discourses* of Joshua Reynolds. The record of a life at once public and private, it documents Delacroix's daily activities and thoughts for a brief period of his youth (1822–1824), and then from 1847 to his death, uniting within its pages all the major artists of his time—composers like Gioacchino Rossini, Frédéric Chopin, and Hector Berlioz, writers such as Baudelaire, Alexandre Dumas, and George Sand, the painters Théodore Géricault, Camille Corot, and Gustave Courbet—and all the major figures of French cultural and political life from the Restoration through the Second Empire, including the historian and politician Adolphe Thiers, the prefect of Paris, Baron Georges Haussmann, and the emperor Napoleon III.

But the *Journal* also constitutes one of the richest and most fascinating aesthetic documents of the nineteenth century. Delacroix copies out passages from his abundant reading and comments on them at length, discusses performances, plays, and concerts he has attended, and reviews his conversations with musicians, actors, poets, scientists, and philosophers. He reflects on artists and techniques past and present, notes ideas for future paintings of his own, and surveys his work in progress. Moreover, from the mid-1850s he uses the diary to draft his long projected, but never completed, treatise on the fine arts, the *Dictionnaire des beaux-arts,* with entries running from "academy" to "varnish," on topics such as "translation," "the sublime," the ancient art of fresco, and the new invention of photography.

In this context, the *Journal* is especially concerned with a major issue of Romantic art theory, the relations between literature and painting. As a painter who wrote extensively and theorized his own writing as he did so, who had a passion for literature and a powerful literary imagination, a narrative painter whose work is rooted in literature and the literary, Delacroix would produce a more penetrating analysis of this question than any other painter in history,

Leonardo and Reynolds notwithstanding. But here we encounter one of the *Journal's* most compelling paradoxes, for Delacroix insists throughout on the *differences* between the two arts. This painter who sought his subjects repeatedly in literature (in Dante, Ludovico Ariosto, Torquato Tasso, and William Shakespeare, Lord Byron, Johann Wolfgang von Goethe, and Walter Scott, this brilliant creator of narrative mural paintings, this most "poetic" of painters, as Baudelaire called him, who "wrote his thoughts on a canvas" and "painted" them, in his many writings, on paper, everywhere claims the superiority of painting *over* literature. Thus the theoretical and practical relations between writing and painting, literary and pictorial, narrative and the image, lie at the heart of Delacroix's aesthetic; and in this, the innovative writing of the *Journal* itself plays a central role.

For Delacroix, a work of literature is indiscreet, importunate, demanding one's undivided attention from first page to last for perhaps only a few outstanding ideas, unable to sustain the same degree of pleasure and interest throughout; a painting is more reserved, more honest, presenting itself all at once, keeping one's attention through its immediate charm and not through a promise—often unfulfilled—of producing it. The writer's materials, words, are abstract, but overwhelming in their abundance; painting is more material but leaves more unsaid, thus reaching further into the mind and soul of the viewer. Narrative literature obscures the whole in a mass of detail and consequently weakens its effect; more limited in time and space, painting privileges the *ensemble,* preserves its force, concentrates the effect, and thus ensures the aesthetic emotion that art is meant to provoke. Delacroix compares the act of reading to a visit to a picture gallery (30 December 1853): the viewer of such a succession of individual paintings cannot sustain the same level of attention, and perceives only a fraction of the total possible beauty. Delacroix thus counterpoises the duration of narrative and the instantaneity of the image; the temporal succession of words and the all-of-a-piece quality of a picture; the ongoing delay, or deferral, of pleasure and understanding in reading, and the sensation of presence, the reality, of viewing; the restrictive linear order of discourse and the infinitely more suggestive possibilities of color.

Delacroix sees narrative as particularly exclusive, presenting only a single point of view, and inadequate to the fullness, variability, and contradiction that characterize human experience. By its instantaneity, concentration, and totality of effect, the visual image, in contrast, offers a multiple and varied perspective. In Delacroix's analogy, it affords the panoramic vision of a climber on a hilltop, who surveys in one glance a vast expanse of landscape. By its linearity, writing sends the climber on a single path, to encounter only one or another of the many natural beauties available; it may even bypass the most important or interesting sights. The distinction had been made before, notably in Gotthold Ephraim Lessing's *Laocoön* of 1766, but to different ends:

for Lessing, whom Delacroix read, the singleness of narrative had been a virtue, providing unity and clarity as against the unavoidable—and unfortunate—ambiguity of painting. A poem, Lessing argued, can concentrate exclusively on the power of Hercules over the lion, but a painting must show the lion's power as well—in its claws, its jaws, its formidable body. [*See* Lessing.] For Delacroix, such inclusiveness is a benefit, closer to the truth of experience. A painting should not present a single point of view, but rather call this into question, confronting the viewer with the "other side," the alternative possibilities, the multiple perspective that he considered a moral, spiritual, and aesthetic ideal: "It is remarkable how the for and against can be found in a single brain. . . . A man of healthy mind conceives of all possibilities, he can put himself at all points of view" (23 February 1858); "subtle minds . . . see easily all the different sides of things" (23 September 1854).

Behind Delacroix's stated theoretical preference for painting stands the *Journal* itself, an effort to explore his own impressions and thoughts through the allegedly inferior medium of words. For if the *Journal* poses the problem of the relations between painting and literature, it also provides a certain solution, as Delacroix seeks to develop a "painter's" writing, having the qualities of painting, adequate to a pictorial vision of the world. It theorizes a kind of writing marked by ambiguity and many-sidedness, which would convey the variety and complexity of the subject: "A man of goodwill should only write a book as a case is pleaded in court: once one theme is set out, he should have another person within him, as it were, to play the role of the other lawyer charged with contradicting him" (23 February 1858); "In reading this preface, I ask myself, why this point of view and not another, or why not both, or why not everything that can be said about the subject?" (Supplement); "Writers of novels do not understand . . . that there are ten men in a single man, and that sometimes they show themselves all at the same time" (7 December 1853). The *Journal* reflects this ideal at every stage, as Delacroix rereads, revises, and recomments on earlier entries, juxtaposes and cross-references disparate and far-flung ones, interweaves and attaches "external" paraphernalia with no explanation of their relation to the text, and employs a complex temporal order in which chronology and narrativity are contravened at every turn. These approaches are crucial to his conception of his enterprise as nonnarrative, noncumulative, varied and inclusive, capable of accommodating multiple points of view and even, as he specifies, outright contradiction. The *Journal*'s writing allows the posing and counterposing, the contrasting positions, the "for and against" of his juridical metaphor noted above—a writing that, in his other analogy, does not follow a single discursive route, but has the panoramic fullness of painting.

These same issues dominate his plans for an aesthetic treatise. The conventional art-critical problem of verbalizing the visual, accounting for the workings and effects of one medium through another and, in Delacroix's view, radically different one, is treated in a way unique in the history of nineteenth-century art writing. The many pages devoted to this project in the *Journal* reveal his foremost concern for an experimental and original kind of writing, which would avoid the progression, singleness, and false consistency of narrative, and instead approach the essayistic freedom, inclusiveness, and variety of his model, Michel de Montaigne. As with the *Journal,* Delacroix theorizes and puts into practice a writing that incorporates the benefits of the image within the domain of time—a writing about the image, which is not based on the superiority of writing over the image, as discursive criticism implies. For this purpose, he considered structuring the treatise as a dialogue, or a correspondence, to allow for maximum variety, contrast, and contradiction. Ultimately, he settled on the dictionary, which, like a diary, consists of separate entries joined by no narrative chain and no transition from one to the next; it follows the purely conventional order of the alphabet; it constitutes a tissue of interconnected and cross-referenced themes and ideas; it allows for the full complexity of the subject and does not attempt to suppress whatever contradictions may arise from this; its entries may be compared and contrasted at will, reordered and reshuffled, as he says, like a deck of cards, for as many points of view.

As far as his paintings are concerned, this aesthetic may account for the striking phenomenon, in his choice of subjects, of transitional moments, scenes of uncertainty, tension, and indecision, posing a struggle or conflict, rather than a resolution—moments when the action could go either way. This relates to his concern for dramatic interest, his conception of the action of history painting; yet it is also significant for his idea of the story itself. Delacroix breaks one of the primary rules of narrative: its status as a self-fulfilling prophecy, with its conclusion always foregone, prepared by what "precedes" elsewhere in the picture—the tradition dominating the theory and practice of pictorial narrative in France from the seventeenth century onward. Instead, he points up the uncertainty of the outcome, and the alternatives to it. He does not abandon a guiding pictorial syntax, however; intelligibility and simplicity had positive aesthetic value for him. Rather, he multiplies the syntax, calling attention to the different ways in which the subject may, indeed should, be interpreted, highlighting the complexities and contradictions within the subject itself. For this was, in his view, the special value of painting among the arts of representation.

Such painting refuses the desire for uncomplicated meanings and neat explanations, the simplistic vision that he harshly criticizes in his comments on politics and society. Instead, it imposes a more extensive, expansive vision: different perceptions of one same object or different conceptions of a single event, alternative possibilities to the single

DELACROIX. Eugène Delacroix, *Page from His Moroccan Notebook, 22 March 1832;* Musée du Louvre, Paris. (Courtesy of Michelle Hannoosh.)

message a painting might be taken to convey. A quotation copied into his diary affirms this function of art to jolt us out of our habits of thought, "confound our judgment," "thwart our traditions," throw the anticipated narrative off course: "It is the property of true masterpieces to cause these sorts of surprises. They catch us unawares, disturb us in our routine admirations, . . . they make us see in a new way." Like the *Journal,* art, for Delacroix, is a response to the difficulty of living with ourselves, an attempt to wrest ourselves from uncritical self-absorption, to free the imagination from the limits of its own perspective (9 November 1857).

Writing was a crucial element in the versatility by which Delacroix defined genius, that "vast imagination" that embraced a plurality of domains. He notes that Michelangelo was a painter, architect, sculptor, poet; Benvenuto Cellini, a goldsmith, architect, and writer; that Leonardo's notebooks prove the extent to which he "discovered everything," "foresaw everything." Amid the tumultuous changes of the modern world, such universality was more difficult, even impossible, as the *Journal* repeatedly suggests. Yet the impossibility of "encyclopedic" knowledge did not stop Delacroix the painter from writing: the thousand pages of the *Journal,* a dozen published essays, a dictionary of the fine arts. For, faced with a world of increasing specialization and abstraction, as he considered it, a world of exclusive

ideologies dangerously distant from truth, an artist writing affirmed what seemed increasingly remote, and increasingly urgent as well: the compatibility of action and meditation, material and abstract, painting and philosophy.

[*See also* Narrative.]

BIBLIOGRAPHY

Works by Delacroix

Journal. 3 vols. Edited by André Joubin, Paris, 1931–1932.
Journal. 3 vols. Edited by Michèle Hannoosh. Paris, 1997.
Oeuvres littéraires. 2 vols. Edited by Elie Faure. Paris, 1923.

Other Sources

Baudelaire, Charles. *Salon de 1846; Exposition universelle de 1855; Salon de 1859; L'Oeuvre et la vie d'Eugène Delacroix.* In *Oeuvres complètes,* edited by Claude Pichois, vol. 2. Paris, 1976.
Berthier, Philippe. "Des images sur les mots, des mots sur les images: À propos de Baudelaire et Delacroix." *Revue d'histoire littéraire de la France* 80. 6 (1980): 900–915.
Damisch, Hubert. "Reading Delacroix's Journal." Translated by Richard Miller. *October* 15 (Winter 1980): 17–39.
Guillerm, Jean-Pierre. *Couleurs du noir: Le Journal de Delacroix.* Lilles, 1990.
Hannoosh, Michèle. *Painting and the Journal of Eugène Delacroix.* Princeton, N.J., 1995.
Horner, Lucy. *Baudelaire, critique de Delacroix.* Geneva, 1956.
Johnson, Lee. *The Paintings of Eugène Delacroix: A Critical Catalogue.* 6 vols. Oxford, 1981–1989.

Larue, Anne. "Fragments ou pensées détachées? Étude de quelques romantiques." *La Licorne* 21 (1991): 239–253.

Mras, George P. *Eugène Delacroix's Theory of Art.* Princeton, N.J., 1966.

Sieber-Meier, Christine. *Untersuchungen zum "Oeuvre littéraire" von Eugène Delacroix.* Bern, 1963.

MICHELE HANNOOSH

DELEUZE, GILLES (1925–1994), French philosopher who taught at the Université de Paris VIII, Vincennes. Deleuze's work covers three areas of philosophy: (1) the interpretation of major thinkers from the history of philosophy; (2) the development of poststructuralist philosophy (Deleuze entered into fruitful debates with many of his poststructuralist contemporaries, most notably Michel Foucault and Jean-François Lyotard); and (3) with Félix Guattari, the creation of a post-Freudian materialism. All three play a part in and influence Deleuze's aesthetics.

The main concept of Deleuze's aesthetics is expression. He emphasizes the aesthetic value of the expression of underlying movements associated with perceptions and ideas; for example, a work of art must express the changes that occur when something is perceived. Art captures these movements and in so doing makes the perception permanent, in the sense that it can be reactivated in a spectator or an audience. The spectator and audience perceive the work of art, but more than that, they are moved by the changes captured in the work such as an emotion or a mood, where these are understood as changes rather than fixed entities. Similarly, a philosophical aesthetics will be concerned with the movements and changes that underlie apparently fixed states. Deleuze thus puts forward a critique of intuition, perception, and experience in order to draw a distinction between static and mobile ways of understanding them. For him, real intuition, perception, and experience are absolute changes in state as opposed to states that can be considered as fixed in some way. Expression is then the activation of those changes in situations that may have become hidden or forgotten, and Deleuzian expressionism is the philosophical aesthetics that seeks to defend and encourage expression against ideas of identity and sameness. Deleuze's most radical claim for aesthetics and art is that they express a truth that is the concealed condition for another, apparently more solid, reality. This does not imply that he is interested in the expression of inner states or meaning in art. On the contrary, expression runs counter to the identity of a subject and to the representation of states. It is to exhibit a changing state in which a fixed identity is lost as the result of an encounter with something external to it. The leading principle of Deleuze's work is therefore that expression is about movement and becoming as opposed to identity and being.

A paradoxical effect of this principle is to render Deleuze's critical and constructive thought particularly difficult and revolutionary, since he must eschew definitions of key concepts in terms of identity. In response to the question regarding what is expressed, Deleuze cannot give a fixed, well-defined answer, for this would bring his philosophy back to a reflection on being and identity. Thus, in order to avoid a contradiction in the definition of expression, Deleuze develops the concept in terms of intensities. Intensity is first defined in terms of the passage from one state to another; it is what occurs when something takes on less or more of a given attribute (less or more red, for instance). Expression captures changes in intensity, and, in effect, expression is to show the change in terms of intensity, as opposed to a comparison of two fixed states. For example, if a landscape is suffused by red light the task of art and philosophy is not to express the relation between two states of the landscape; instead, it is to seek to capture the change in the intensity of the color. Deleuze cannot stop at intensities defined in terms of red, however, or, at a further level of regress, in terms of brightness (the difference between two intensities of red would then be thought of in terms of brightness) and so on. This would be to reintroduce a basis for an aesthetics of identity that would supplant expression through the analysis and classification of colors or light. Instead, even though Deleuze describes specific *intensities,* he defines *intensity* in itself in terms of infinite series of intensities where each specific intensity is only a concentration of infinitely many divergent series (so reddening is a concentration of brightness, but also other colors, other emotions, anger, for example, and so on). Inspired by Gottfried Wilhelm Leibniz's use of infinitessimal calculus, Deleuze conceptualizes this view through an appeal to differential calculus. Yet, consistent with his own theory, he also uses Friedrich Nietzsche's doctrine of eternal return and an original philosophy of repetition.

Deleuze associates expression with a search for difference in itself or difference defined independently of identity; difference is not between two things but rather is a positive perception of an intensity. Deleuze then explains difference in terms of repetition: difference is the perception of change in a series of repeated instances, where a variation in the series cannot be accounted for by reference to individual members of the series. Instead, difference is the perception of a variation in the series, a variation in intensity. The concept of expression, defined in terms of intensity and difference in itself, is the basis for Deleuze's definitions of art and creativity as nonrepresentational and nonconceptual exercises. It is also the basis for his studies of art and literature, insofar as he is interested in the expression of intensity, often through the repetition of series, in works of art. In turn, this consideration of the artwork in terms of series leads to an opposition to the idea of the original and the copy in art. Instead, the artwork is a simulacrum, a coming together of different series of repetitions where no absolute origin can be detected.

According to Deleuze, the artist must express pure perceptions and sensations independent of the conceptual identity of a given thing and, indeed, the identity of the artist as subject. These perceptions and sensations draw us out of ourselves by expressing a world, or more properly a plane, of potential movements and changes that associate our actual existence with something external to it (see *Qu'est-ce que la philosophie* [What Is Philosophy?]). In this sense, Deleuze is Nietzschean: the artist expresses the world as becoming insofar as it has thoroughgoing effects on our identity. For example, an artist may express the animal in human beings, by capturing those typically animal perceptions and sensations that can also overcome humans—Deleuze is particularly fascinated by animal disquiet, the way in which they sense danger prior to perceiving a specific threat (*Le pli: Leibniz et le Baroque* [The Fold: Leibniz and the Baroque]), and by animal alertness, the way in which an animal can be set into an active state from almost complete inertia (the tick in *Mille plateaux* [A Thousand Plateaus]). It is not true, however, that those perceptions and sensations exist only in the animal, and the human as animal; rather, Deleuze wants to suggest that they are freestanding potential becomings that can initiate change in any being. Thus, there is a world characterized by potential movements described by verbs such as *fearing, hungering, greening, smiling.* The artist can express these verbs by capturing them in actual materials, in an actual work of art. By expressing a perception or sensation such as fearing or greening, the artist also expresses the affect, the change that occurs with them. So art is the form of creation associated with affects or becomings and the perceptions that trigger them.

This association leads to a key criterion within Deleuze's aesthetics as well as to a critical function in art. For him, art cannot be defined in terms of representation, since representation depends on identification in resemblance or analogy. These are guaranteed by conceptual identity; that is, there is an identity drawn between the concepts of two analogous or similar things. But, since art creates in order to express change and processes that are intrinsically in movement, such as becoming fearful, creation in art cannot be defined according to representation. The artwork exists because it has the potential to set us in movement, to create affects, by transferring movement in the form of perceptions and sensations. Great art does not lie in the representation of an object, landscape, act, meaning, or, indeed, feeling. It lies in capturing the movements that bring about these things and that also lead to their destruction. This explains the critical and creative functions of art. The artwork reveals the falsity of representation and identity. It shows their illusory nature by expressing the underlying changes that give strength, but also fragility, to any particular identity. Indeed, Deleuze also defines pure potential movements as intensities because they cannot be identified with any given state

or difference between given states; instead, intensities such as becoming brighter exist prior to well-defined states. In creating becoming as opposed to supporting being, the artwork therefore contributes to the intensity of life and militates against its inhibition in identification.

Deleuze's early works were highly original studies of the great philosophers: David Hume, Henri Bergson, Nietzsche, Baruch Spinoza, Immanuel Kant. His own aesthetics owes much to them: in particular to Kant, for the idea of the transcendental; to Nietzsche, for the idea of eternal return; to Spinoza, for the ideas of immanence and expression. These influences are then combined, however, into a properly Deleuzian philosophy in his masterwork, *Différence et répétition* (Difference and Repetition). In this book, the primordial function of art is made clear as is Deleuze's position as to what constitutes great art. The two main concepts of the book are related to aesthetics, because difference is expressed in the artwork through repetition and with the failure of representation: ". . . when the modern work of art develops its permutating series and its circular structures, it indicates to philosophy a path leading to the abandonment of representation" (*Difference and Repetition*, p. 69). Deleuze is heavily influenced by modern works that literally involve repetitions of series of themes, topics, plots, for example, the novels by his friend Michel Butor, or texts by Joe Bousquet. What he notes is that this literal repetition allows for intricate variations that, first of all, undermine our sense of identity. The sense of each object in a series becomes linked to the others to the point where it is impossible to determine which variation is the original. Second, the variations sharpen our sensibility to the minute differences within series, that is, to the processes that bring about differentiation: ". . . repetition interiorises and therefore repeats itself: as Péguy says, it is not Federation Day which commemorates or represents the fall of the Bastille, but the fall of the Bastille which celebrates and repeats in advance all the Federation Days; or Claude Monet's first water lily which repeats all the others" (*Difference and Repetition*, p. 1).

The artwork, then, is neither an original nor a copy nor a representation. It is a simulacrum: a work that forms part of a series that cannot be referred to an original beginning or to a guiding ideal or model. It is a work that testifies as to its accidental and simulated nature. But, in so doing it expresses an underlying "real" world of potential becomings: "If it is true that representation has identity as its element and similarity as its unit of measure, then pure presence such as it appears in the simulacrum has the 'disparate' as its unit of measure—in other words, always a difference of difference as its immediate element" (*Difference and Repetition*, p. 69). In Deleuze's work, the definition of the artwork as a simulacrum within a series of repetitions and variations has ramifications that extend beyond art into the epistemological and the ethical. Thus, he is interested in the way in which linear time and well-ordered Cartesian space are unable to account for his definitions of difference and repetition. Works of art such as Marcel Proust's *Remembrance of Things Past* demand different views where time is subordinate to processes that explain "the apprenticeship to signs" (see *Proust et les signes* [Proust and Signs]). For Deleuze, the sign allows us to learn about our relation to change and becoming and to the processes that come to give us our identity and take it away. Signs are then not about the communication of meaning but rather about the learning of the affects, perceptions, and sensations to which we can be subject. In the case of Proust's involuntary memory, Deleuze is concerned with what we can learn from its possibility, that is, that time returns in such a way as to bring the past and the present into play in the future: "We see, then, that in this final synthesis of time, the present and the past are in turn no more than dimensions of the future: the past as condition, the present as agent."

For Deleuze, literature is not about meaning but about the expression of underlying processes, where learning is not about sense but about coming to feel what we can and do express. This means that the function of literature is, paradoxically, to undermine the constitution of meaning in language in favor of the creation of extralinguistic affects, perceptions, and sensations. In order to achieve this, literature must be modern in the sense of constantly disturbing language, creating new linguistic forms that force us to go beyond established techniques of interpretation. He has always had a fascination with Anglo-American literature—T. E. Lawrence, Herman Melville, F. Scott Fitzgerald, William Burroughs—because of its emphasis on travel and the exploration of the unknown. This is true not only of the effect of these writers, to drive us into the unknown, but also in how they achieve it, by distorting the established structure of language. This view of literature is given its most extensive treatment in Deleuze's study of Franz Kafka cowritten with his longtime friend and collaborator, the psychologist Félix Guattari: *Kafka: Vers une literature mineure* (Toward a Minor Literature). Deleuze's final collection of essays also covered this theme with an added emphasis on the curative function of literature *(Critique et clinique)*, although there the senses of curing, sickness, and health are counterintuitive. In Deleuze's account, to cure is often to release from a comfortable identity and state and to set the cured one off on violent and damaging paths. The point is that the settled existence offers merely an illusion of health that hides great pain and repression. This explains Deleuze's passion for self-destructive authors such as Fitzgerald. What is interpreted as self-destructiveness is a release and, in fact, the beginning of a cure, because a settled state and meaning merely inhibit the potential we have for change and becoming. The point of literature is to invent "minor" becomings that undermine the illusion of states and meanings of the majority: "Health as literature, as writing, consists in the invention of a missing people" (*Critique*

et clinique, p. 14). Writers are involved in delirium, insofar as they seek to make a meaningful language collapse, but that delirium is a cure and a release for what has been downtrodden: "The ultimate goal for literature is to release the creation of health from within delirium, or to create a people, that is, a possibility of life" (*Critique et clinique,* p. 15).

This social and political function of art comes out most clearly in the two volumes of Deleuze and Guattari's *Capitalisme et schizophrenie* (Capitalism and Schizophrenia), *L'anti-Oedipe* (Anti-Oedipus) and *Mille plateaux* (A Thousand Plateaus). In the latter, the definition of art as expression is extended to animals by the claim that the formation of any identity or territory depends on expression. When a boundary to a territory or to an organism becomes apparent there has been an expression of two processes that define the territory, not in terms of a limit, but in terms of a passage into something and a passage away from it. These two processes are called territorialization and deterritorialization—how a living thing associates something with its identity and how that identity is taken over and deformed by changes and becomings. Whenever an animal makes its territory or home it expresses those processes in a form of creation that Deleuze and Guattari call art. So when a bird makes a nest using a pattern of leaves, that pattern expresses the way in which the bird draws a distinction between itself and its environment, but it also expresses the bird's dependence on that hostile environment. In the section on the ritornello in *A Thousand Plateaus,* Deleuze and Guattari study these processes in the context of the musical refrain or tune; the repetition of a tune leads to the recognition of the singularity of a particular being, it marks it out from others, and makes it recognizable to them: "Can we call art this becoming, this emergence? The territory would be the effect of art. The artist, the first man to draw up a boundary or to make a mark . . . Property, whether of the individual or a group, comes from this, even if it is for war or oppression" (*A Thousand Plateaus,* p. 189). The tune is always dependent on components taken from other tunes, however, and from wider patterns of song. So, although any identity can be constructed using the repetition of a pattern, a walk through a territory, for example, that pattern is a sign of the other destructive connections that can be made between an identity and other possible life-forms. This connectedness through the definition of identity as aesthetic expression leads to the most important principle of Deleuze and Guattari's philosophy: Aesthetic expression must open up onto all its possible connections, all possible becomings. Art must be of a cosmic order.

In their last work, *What Is Philosophy?*, Deleuze and Guattari seek to define art, science, and philosophy in such a way as to determine their independence as well as their relatedness. Art, as the expression of perceptions and sensations, complements philosophy as the creation of concepts. This means that art could never be fully conceptualized, since the concept would never express the same sensual affects as the artwork. Instead, philosophy and art must work together to draw up related but independent planes; the conceptual is incomplete without the sensual, and vice versa. This complementarity of art and philosophy is a distinctive aspect of Deleuze's philosophical style and his critical work on art. He does not apply his aesthetics to artworks; rather, when the world of becomings has to be expressed through perceptions, Deleuze turns to art to complement the philosophical concepts of expression, time, and space, for instance. This "patchwork" of philosophy and art is a distinctive aspect of his work on cinema, literature, painting, and architecture. Thus, in Deleuze's groundbreaking work on Francis Bacon (*Francis Bacon: Logique de la sensation* [Logic and Sense]), the painter expresses the sensual aspect of the animal in man and the physical aspect of the expression of movement and becoming in any creation. Deleuze is particularly interested in Bacon's use of flesh and bone to destroy the human image and to set off perceptions of "nonhuman becomings" such as the disembodied scream and flesh cleaved as meat repeated through Bacon's work. Similarly, the tension between the ground (which Deleuze calls the "Diagram") and figure of Bacon's work gives us a sense of the underlying chaotic state that is the condition for any identity. Deleuze can conceptualize that state, while Bacon and the physical aspect of his preparation of the ground express it as a sensual affect as opposed to an intellectual one. Indeed, this leads to a further definition of the role of art and philosophy as expression. They must concentrate certain becomings in the creation of concepts or perceptions in order to draw up a consistent plane out of chaos: "The Diagram must not devour the whole painting, it must be limited in space and time. It must remain operational and controlled. The violent means must not be unleashed and catastrophe must not submerge everything" (*Francis Bacon: Logic and Sense*, p. 71).

The complementarity of art and philosophy comes out most strongly in Deleuze's two volumes on film, *Cinéma 1: L'image-mouvement* (Cinema 1: The Movement Image) and *Cinéma 2: L'image-temps* (Cinema 2: The Time-Image). There, Deleuze combines a careful and comprehensive classification of cinematic techniques with regard to time and movement, inspired by Charles Peirce's semiotics, with a radical reading of Bergson's theses on time and space. He uses Bergson's intuitions to generate the initial classes of movement-image and time-image, that is, a cinematic image that involves a change in spatial relations brought on by acts and a cinematic image that communicates deeper characteristics of what we perceive. For example, Charlie Chaplin's early comedy depends on unexpected links between different movement-images; we may expect a particular action from a particular movement-image—a punch, for instance—but the action that links to the next movement-image confounds those expectations—the punch is answered

by a kiss and a flutter of the eyelids. Or, in Orson Welles's use of mirrors, the time-image and the complex and deep nature of images come to the fore; the reflection of a scene in a mirror creates a double reality in which we begin to realize that the simple idea of a single real image can be broken by the use of the mirror. Although Deleuze gives priority to perception in both classes of image, since we must perceive something in order to be affected or in order to expect an action, the movement-image gives priority to action and hence to movement, while the time-image leads us to a contemplative passivity where we learn about the nature of time and its effect on reality.

The first volume of Deleuze's work on cinema concentrates on movement, and the latter focuses on time. Yet they are linked, not only through a thesis on the history of cinema, but also in terms of an argument that wishes to give priority to the time-image, or the way in which cinema reveals the primordial role of time in reality. Toward the end of the first volume, Deleuze considers paradoxical limit-cases of the movement-image in the films of Robert Altman, John Cassavetes, and Sydney Lumet. He is interested in cases where situations are no longer linked by actions according to the structures Situation-Action-Situation (where an action offers a response to a situation and instigates a new situation) or Action-Situation-Action. Instead, the shift from one image to another takes on a random property, at least from the point of view of conscious acts; an action may lead to no situation, or a situation may lack a corresponding action. The wandering road movie or, more accurately, the image of travel without end is a case of this disintegration of the movement-image (in the films of Wim Wenders, for example). Here, the synthesizing role of action is self-defeating. Although each movement-image is linked to the next by a wander through a landscape, the act of wandering is itself purposeless. Action has begun to give way to the unfolding of the images in terms of deeper perception of the space through which the film is moving, and the film is not so much about movement as it is about time in its relation to different ways of perceiving a landscape. More important, that perception is seen as a negation of action and of the movement-image; the landscape enters those who wander through it and negates their will to act purposively. Deleuze goes on to associate this crisis of the cinema of movement-image, where cinema "loses the plot," with the emergence of *nouvelle vague* French and Italian cinema. Indeed, his work on cinema is of great interest because of this thesis on the new wave. The new wave of cinema is defined in terms of a priority given to the time-image over the movement-image: acts defined in terms of the properties of movement give way to ideas defined in terms of the properties of time.

The study of film allows Deleuze to apply the concept of expression to time and space. This is a radical enterprise that exploits Bergson's intuitions, while also arguing against his critical view of film as the creation, on an industrial scale, of traditional illusions about movement. Deleuze seeks to extend and hence undermine objective, common-sense views of time and space by noting how filmmakers express more varied and effective views—for example, in the way Buster Keaton (one of his favorite directors) creates comic situations by reducing the world to an extension of the counterintuitive actions of a comic hero. Keaton's films ignore conventions of time and space: the hero covers great distances in no time at all and turns complex machinery into simple private mechanisms, thereby making a large world into a reflection of a small mind. The point is that, if the film works in this way, then there must be a corresponding experience of time and space, one that adds to commonsense views. Deleuze classifies great directors according to the way in which they express different views of time and space. Each discovery in terms of that expression is taken as a challenge for the theory; that is, an argument about time and space is developed in parallel to the discovery of forms that have not yet been accounted for. For example, Deleuze tests Bergson's work on time and memory through different uses of flashbacks. He asks how it is possible for Joseph Mankiewicz to use flashbacks, not as records of past events, which can be remembered in the future, but as records of the creation of memory itself. Sometimes a flashback does not show what happened; as an act of remembrance, it shows the creation of a future memory by one of the characters: In the flashback, they decide to remember something, to record it for the future, and this explains their acts. So Bergson has to explain memory not only as an act that looks back but also as a creative act that looks forward. In turn, this leads to a definition of the present in terms of the past and the future; the present is, at the same time, an act of remembrance and a projection into the future.

It is not the case, however, that Deleuze develops his philosophy merely as a response to developments in filmmaking. On the contrary, his theses on film follow from the application of his theories on expression, time, and space to film. In the first chapter of *Cinema 1*, movement is defined as the expression of an intensity as opposed to a simple displacement from one point to another. For example, movement does not lie in the displacement of a character from the chair to the bed, but in the way that displacement expresses the intensity that gave rise to the displacement, a rise in lust, for instance. Thus, movement is not defined in relation to instants, that is, immobile cuts in time (chair position, bed position); it is defined in terms of qualitative changes or intensities (lusting). This definition is then applied to film in order to counter its definition as the succession of images given as static cuts; instead, film is a structure of moving images in the sense of images associated with qualitative changes. In the movement-image, an act is called for by a set of perceptions and affections; in the time-image, ideas are called for—again, by a set of perceptions

and affections. The task of the great filmmaker is to add to the different ways in which these images can make us act and think about space and time. Once again, Deleuze's belief in the revolutionary task of art comes to the fore—great directors disturb established senses of space and time—as does his belief in the primary role of sensations and ideas with respect to the secondary role of narrative and communication: "Cinema brings an intelligible matter to light, like something presupposed, or a condition, a necessary correlate through which language constructs its own 'objects' (signifying units and operations)" (*Cinema 2*, p. 342). It must be stressed, however, that Deleuze sees this great cinema as a rare and endangered thing. Most cinema is neither revolutionary nor creative, in the sense that he wishes to defend ("the enormous proportion of incompetence in cinematic production is not an objection").

Finally, beyond the association of philosophy with the work of particular artists and art forms, Deleuze also developed a parallel between his work and the style of the baroque *(The Fold: Leibniz and the Baroque)*. This is an important study of the baroque because it seals the relation between the baroque aesthetic and seventeenth-century rationalist philosophy, and Leibniz in particular. Deleuze develops a reading of Leibniz in which the concept of the fold takes on a central role within the monadology by providing an explanation for a series of problems in rationalism and Leibniz's system. For instance, the individuality and yet universality of each monad is explained in terms of singular inflections on a mathematical curve; that is, there is a fold on a curve that defines a singular neighborhood but that also defines a property of the curve as a whole: the curve is folded into that neighborhood in the same way as the world is folded into each monad. This conjunction of differential mathematics, philosophy, and aesthetics is typical of Deleuze's work and can be traced back to *Différence et répétition*. Similarly, the problem of the relation of soul and body is explained as an unfolding of the soul into the body and a folding of the body into the soul. The art of the baroque implies an aesthetics that runs parallel to Leibniz's work on the fold. Contradictions between different substances and different realms are resolved through folds; thus, the celestial and the earthbound are related through the folds in the ground plan and facade of the baroque church. Matter is then captured in art as the multiplication of folds to infinity, as in baroque painting of fabric.

Deleuze's most accessible works on aesthetics, *What Is Philosophy?* and *The Fold: Leibniz and the Baroque*, are as yet too recent to have had a great impact, though that is beginning to change (Boundas, 1994). His work with Guattari, in *Capitalism and Schizophrenia*, had a certain *succès de scandale* and was taken as an example of the extremism of post-1968 French philosophy—to the point of being banned in Italy for its alleged influence over extremist politics and terrorism. Again, it is only recently that good commentaries on this work have begun to appear. However, the richness and originality of Deleuze's aesthetics, allied to its rigorous and historically sensitive philosophical concepts, promise an influential future. This is summed up by Foucault's infamous ironic statement, "One day this century will be Deleuzian."

[*See also* Artificial Intelligence and Aesthetics; Expression Theory of Art; Film, *article on* Film Theory; Foucault; Lacan, *article on* Visual and Literary Arts; Metonymy; *and* Perception, *article on* Aesthetics of Perception.]

BIBLIOGRAPHY

Works by Deleuze

Empirisme et subjectivité: Essai sur la nature humaine selon Hume. Paris, 1953. Translated by Constantin V. Boundas as *Empiricism and Subjectivity: An Essay on Hume's Theory of Human Nature* (New York, 1991).

Nietzsche et la philosophie. Paris, 1962. Translated by Hugh Tomlinson as *Nietzsche and Philosophy* (New York, 1983).

La Philosophie critique de Kant: Doctrine des facultés. Paris, 1963. Translated by Hugh Tomlinson and Barbara Habberjam as *Kant's Critical Philosophy: The Doctrine of the Faculties* (Minneapolis, 1984).

Proust et les signes. Paris, 1964. Translated by Richard Howard as *Proust and Signs* (New York, 1972).

Différence et répétition. Paris, 1968. Translated by Paul Patton as *Difference and Repetition* (New York, 1994).

Spinoza et le problème de l'expression. Paris, 1968. Translated by Martin Joughin as *Expressionism in Philosophy: Spinoza* (New York, 1990).

Logique du sens. Paris, 1969. Translated by Mark Lester and Charles Stivale as *The Logic of Sense,* edited by Constantin V. Boundas (New York, 1990).

Francis Bacon: Logique de la sensation. Paris, 1981.

Cinéma 1: L'image-mouvement. Paris, 1983. Translated by Hugh Tomlinson and Barbara Habberjam as *Cinema 1: The Movement-Image* (Minneapolis, 1986).

Cinéma 2: L'image-temps. Paris, 1985. Translated by Hugh Tomlinson and Robert Galeta as *Cinema 2: The Time-Image* (Minneapolis, 1989).

Foucault. Paris, 1986. Translated and edited by Seán Hand as *Foucault* (Minneapolis, 1988).

Le pli: Leibniz et le Baroque. Paris, 1988. Translated by Tom Conley as *The Fold: Leibniz and the Baroque* (Minneapolis, 1993).

Critique et clinique. Paris, 1993.

Works by Deleuze and Guattari

Capitalisme et schizophrenie: L'Anti-Oedipe. Paris, 1972. Translated by Robert Hurley, Mark Seem, and Helen R. Lane as *Anti-Oedipus: Capitalism and Schizophrenia* (New York, 1977; reprint, Minneapolis, 1983).

Kafka: Pour une littérature mineure. Paris, 1975. Translated by Dana Polan as *Kafka: Toward a Minor Literature* (Minneapolis, 1986).

Capitalisme et schizophrenie: Mille Plateaux. Paris, 1980. Translated by Brian Massumi as *A Thousand Plateaus: Capitalism and Schizophrenia* (Minneapolis, 1987).

Qu'est-ce que la philosophie? Paris, 1991. Translated by Hugh Tomlinson and Graham Burchell as *What Is Philosophy?* (New York, 1994).

Other Sources

Boundas, Constantin, and Dorothea Olkowski, eds. *Gilles Deleuze and the Theater of Philosophy.* New York and London, 1994.

Hardt, Michael. *Gilles Deleuze: An Apprenticeship in Philosophy.* Minneapolis, 1993.

Paton, Paul. *Gilles Deleuze: A Critical Reader.* Oxford and Cambridge, Mass., 1997.

JAMES WILLIAMS

DEPICTION. *See* Representation.

DE PILES, ROGER. *See* Piles, Roger de.